THE OXFORD HANDBOOK OF

POLITICAL
LEADERSHIP

Political leadership has made a comeback. It was studied intensively not only by political scientists but also by political sociologists and psychologists, Sovietologists, political anthropologists, and by scholars in comparative and development studies from the 1940s to the 1970s. Thereafter, the field lost its way with the rise of structuralism, neo-institutionalism, and rational choice approaches to the study of politics, government, and governance. Recently, however, students of politics have returned to studying the role of individual leaders and the exercise of leadership to explain political outcomes. The list of topics is nigh endless: elections, conflict management, public policy, government popularity, development, governance networks, and regional integration. In the media age, leaders are presented and stage-managed—spun—as the solution to almost every social problem. Through the mass media and the Internet, citizens and professional observers follow the rise, impact, and fall of senior political officeholders at closer quarters than ever before.

This *Handbook* encapsulates the resurgence by asking, where are we today? It orders the multidisciplinary field by identifying the distinct and distinctive contributions of the disciplines. It brings together scholars from around the world, encouraging a comparative perspective, to provide a comprehensive coverage of all the major disciplines, methods, and regions. It showcases both the normative and empirical traditions in political leadership studies, and juxtaposes behavioural, institutional, and interpretive approaches. It covers formal, office-based as well as informal, emergent political leadership, and in both democratic and undemocratic polities.

THE OXFORD HANDBOOK OF

POLITICAL

LEADERSHIP

Edited by

R. A. W. RHODES

and

PAUL 't HART

OXFORD

UNIVERSITY PRESS

OXFORD
UNIVERSITY PRESS

Great Clarendon Street, Oxford, OX2 6DP,
United Kingdom

Oxford University Press is a department of the University of Oxford.
It furthers the University's objective of excellence in research, scholarship,
and education by publishing worldwide. Oxford is a registered trade mark of
Oxford University Press in the UK and in certain other countries

Published in the United States of America by Oxford University Press
198 Madison Avenue, New York, NY 10016, United States of America

British Library Cataloguing in Publication Data
Data available

Library of Congress Cataloging in Publication Data
Data available

ISBN 978-0-19-965388-1 (Hbk.)
ISBN 978-0-19-877851-6 (Pbk.)

CONTENTS

PART II STUDYING POLITICAL LEADERSHIP: ANALYTICAL AND METHODOLOGICAL PERSPECTIVES

PART III POLITICAL LEADERSHIP AT WORK

PART IV EXECUTIVE LEADERSHIP IN THE WEST

Presidential Leadership: The United States and Beyond

Prime Ministerial Leadership: Westminster and Beyond

PART V POLITICAL LEADERSHIP BELOW AND BEYOND THE NATIONAL LEVEL

PART VI POLITICAL LEADERSHIP BEYOND THE WEST

PART VII DEBATING POLITICAL LEADERSHIP

List of Contributors

Rudy B. Andeweg is Professor of Political Science at Leiden University. He studied law and government at Leiden University and Political Science at the University of Michigan. He has published on personalization in voting behaviour, birth order and political leadership, legislative roles, political representation, and cabinet decision-making. He recently co-edited *Puzzles of Government Formation: Coalition Theory and Deviant Cases* (Routledge, 2011).

Chris Ansell is Professor of Political Science at the University of California, Berkeley. His fields of interest include organization theory, political sociology, public administration, and Western Europe. His current research focuses on risk regulation, collaborative governance, social network analysis, and crisis management.

David S. Bell is Professor of French Government at the University of Leeds and has published extensively about political parties in Europe and on political leadership in France and on leadership theory. Publications (authored or co-authored): two books on the *French Socialist Party* (OUP 1984, OUP 1988); a book on the French Communist Party (OUP 1994); *French Fifth Republic* (Palgrave 2013), with Professor J. Gaffney; articles on French politics, most recently on the presidential elections of 2002 and 2007 in *Parliamentary Affairs*. On leaders and leadership these include: *François Mitterrand* (Polity, 2006), and an edited volume, *Political Leadership* published in 2012 in the SAGE Library of Political Science series (Sage, 2012).

Andrew Blick is Lecturer in Politics and Contemporary History at King's College London. His works include *People Who Live in the Dark: The History of the Special Adviser in British Politics* (2004); and, with Peter Hennessy, *The Hidden Wiring Emerges: The Cabinet Manual and the Working of the British Constitution* (2011). He is writing *Beyond Magna Carta: A Constitution for the United Kingdom*, which will commemorate the 800th anniversary of Magna Carta.

Jean Blondel, born in France in 1929, was educated in Paris and Oxford. He was the first Professor of Government at the University of Essex in 1964, and Professor of Political Science at the European University Institute, 1985–94. He is now Professorial Fellow at the European University Institute and Visiting Professor at the University of Siena. He was awarded the Johan Skytte Prize in Political Science for Lifetime Achievement in political science in 2004. His publications are in comparative government, world-wide, with special reference to parties, governments, and leadership. Apart from a general text on *Comparative Government*, second edition, 1995, his recent books include *Political Cultures in Asia and Europe*, with T. Inoguchi (Routledge, 2006); *Governing New Democracies*, with F. Mueller-Rommel and D. Malova (Palgrave Macmillan, 2007); *Citizens and the State*, with T. Inoguchi (Routledge, 2008); and *Political Leadership, Parties and Citizens*, with J. L. Thiebault (Routledge, 2010).

Arjen Boin is Professor of Public Governance and Crisis Management at the Utrecht School of Governance, Utrecht University, and an adjunct professor at the Public Administration Institute, Louisiana State University. He has published widely on topics of crisis and disaster management, leadership, institutional design, and correctional administration. He is the editor of *Public Administration*, a major journal in the field.

Maryke Botha is a former Masters student in International Studies in the Department of Political Science, University of Stellenbosch.

Geoffrey Brennan was trained as an economist but works now broadly across economics, political science, and philosophy. He has worked extensively with Noble Laureate James Buchanan (famous for his pioneering work in 'public choice'). Brennan's own work in rational actor political theory has emphasized the 'expressive account' of voter behaviour. He is currently Professor in the Research School of Social Sciences at the Australian National University and holds a regular visiting position jointly in the Political Science department at Duke University and the Philosophy Department at UNC-Chapel Hill. He is currently working on a book on *Philosophy and Economics* for Princeton University Press.

Michael Brooks is Associate Professor in the Tasmanian School of Business and Economics, at the University of Tasmania, Australia. Michael completed a Masters of Economics and Diploma of Education at Monash University and a PhD at Virginia Polytechnic Institute and State University. He has lectured at the University of Tasmania for over 30 years. In recent years he has written on taxation, expressive voting, and the economics of esteem. One of Michael's more recent publications is with Geoffrey Brennan on the 'cashing out' hypothesis and 'soft' and 'hard' policies, in the *European Journal of Political Economy*, 2011, 27 (4): 601–10.

David Brulé is an assistant professor of political science at Purdue University, Indiana. David's research interests lie at the intersection of domestic politics and international relations. Specifically, he examines the effects of public opinion, economic conditions, and political institutions on national leaders' conflict decisions.

Elton Chan is currently a doctoral candidate in the Department of Politics and Public Administration at the University of Hong Kong, where he received his undergraduate degree in political theory and history. His research focuses on Confucianism and political philosophy.

Joseph Chan is Professor at the Department of Politics and Public Administration, the University of Hong Kong. He is the author of *Confucian Perfectionism: A Political*

Philosophy for Modern Times (Princeton, 2014). He obtained his undergraduate degree in political science from the Chinese University of Hong Kong, his MSc from the London School of Economics and Political Science, and his DPhil from Oxford University. He teaches political theory and researches in the areas of contemporary liberalism and perfectionism, Confucian political philosophy, human rights, and civil society.

Jeffrey E. Cohen (PhD, University of Michigan, 1979) is Professor of Political Science at Fordham University specializing in the American presidency. He is the author of a dozen books and numerous articles that have appeared in leading journals. His recent book, *Going Local Presidential Leadership in the Post-Broadcast Age* (Cambridge, 2010) won both the 2011 Richard E. Neustadt Award and the 2012 Goldsmith Award.

Colin Copus is Professor of Local Politics and Director of the Local Governance Research Unit in the Department of Politics and Public Policy, De Montfort University. His main research interests are local political leadership, local party politics, local governance, and the changing role of the councillor, and he has published widely on these subjects in academic journals. He has carried out research work for government departments and worked with ministers and MPs on policy issues. He has worked closely with practitioners in local government on a range of consultancy and research projects. Colin has been the editor *Local Government Studies* since 2001. He has also served as a councillor on a London Borough council, a county and a district council, and three parish councils.

Marina Costa Lobo is a researcher at the Institute of Social Sciences at the University of Lisbon, and Guest Lecturer at the Lisbon University Institute (IUL) in political science. She obtained her DPhil at Oxford University in 2001. Her research interests include the role of leaders in electoral behaviour, political parties, and institutions. She is a co-director of the Portuguese Election Study. She has published articles in *Electoral Studies, European Journal of Political Research*, and *Political Research Quarterly*, as well as books on the topic in English and Portuguese.

Richard A. Couto is with Union Institute and University and a founding faculty member of the Antioch University PhD Program in Leadership and Change. Prior to that he was a founding faculty member of the Jepson School at the University of Richmond where he held the George M. and Virginia B. Modlin Chair in Leadership Studies, 1991–2002. His recent books include: *Political and Civic Leadership: A Reference Handbook* (Sage 2010); and (with James MacGregor Burns) *Reflections on Leadership* (University of America Press 2007). His work has won numerous national awards, including best book in transformational politics from the American Political Science Association, and the Virginia A. Hodgkinson Research Prize of the Independent Sector.

Karl DeRouen, Jr., is Professor of Political Science, Director of the International Studies Program, and was College of Arts and Science Faculty Fellow (2008–11) at the University of Alabama. His research interests lie within the field of International Relations, specifically conflict analysis and foreign policy analysis. He is the co-author of *Understanding Foreign Policy Decision Making* (with Alex Mintz; Cambridge University Press, 2010).

Chris Eichbaum is Reader in Government and Deputy Head of School in the School of Government at Victoria University of Wellington in New Zealand. His research interests include the role of political staff in executive government, governance, and public administration reform, and the politics of central banking. He and Richard Shaw have collaborated on an edited volume, *Partisan Appointees and Public Servants: An International Analysis of the Role of the Political Adviser*. In 2008 he was appointed as a non-executive Director to the Board of the Reserve Bank of New Zealand.

Robert Elgie's research career has centred on the systematic study of institutions on political outcomes. Recently, his work has concentrated on whether semi-presidentialism helps or hinders the process of democratization in young democracies. He is the author of *Semi-presidentialism: Sub-types and Democratic Performance* (Oxford University Press, 2011). He is also a very active blogger at presidential-power.com. In addition, he has considerable expertise in the study of contemporary French politics; he is the editor of the journal *French Politics*, published by Palgrave Macmillan; and he is the lead co-editor of the forthcoming *Oxford Handbook of French Politics* (Oxford University Press).

John Gaffney is Professor of Politics at Aston University, UK. He is also a political commentator and author. He specializes in UK and French politics and the discourse and rhetoric of leadership. He regularly contributes to TV and print media. In July 2012, he was awarded £77,000 by the Leverhulme Trust for a two-year study of UK political leadership. His latest book is *Political Leadership in France: From Charles de Gaulle to Nicolas Sarkozy* (Palgrave, 2012). He is the author of three other monographs on UK and French Politics. He has written 50 journal articles and chapters, and has edited a dozen books, his two most recent being *Stardom in Postwar France* (Berghahn, 2011, with Diana Holmes), and *The Presidents of the French Fifth Republic* (Palgrave, 2013, with David Bell).

Francesca Gains is Professor of Public Policy at the University of Manchester and researches political management arrangements and their impact on policy outcomes. She won the 2008 Herbert Kaufman award for the best paper in public administration at the 2007 American Political Science Association Meeting in Chicago and the 2012 best paper in Comparative Policy at the 2011 APSA meeting in Seattle. She has published work on political leadership in *Public Administration, Political Studies, Parliamentary Affairs, Policy and Politics*, and *Public Administration Review*.

Keith Grint is Professor of Public Leadership at Warwick University Business School. He has held chairs at Lancaster and Cranfield Universities and before that taught at Brunel University and Oxford University. He is a founding co-editor of the journal *Leadership* published by Sage, and founding co-organizer of the International Conference in Researching Leadership. His books include *The Sociology of Work*, 3rd edition (2005); *Management: A Sociological Introduction* (1995); *Leadership* (ed.) (1997); *Fuzzy Management* (1997); *The Machine at Work: Technology, Work and Society* (with Steve Woolgar) (1997); *The Arts of Leadership* (2000); *Organizational Leadership* (with John Bratton and Debra Nelson); *Leadership: Limits and Possibilities* (2005); *Leadership,*

Management and Command: Rethinking D-Day (2008); *The Public Leadership Challenge* (ed. with Stephen Brookes) (2010); *Leadership: A Very Short Introduction* (2010); *Sage Handbook of Leadership* (ed. with Alan Bryman, David Collinson, Brad Jackson and Mary Uhl-Bien, Sage, 2010). *Sage Major Works of Leadership* (ed. with David Collinson and Brad Jackson) (2011).

Jean Hartley is an organizational psychologist by background, who is Professor of Public Leadership at The Open University Business School in the UK. Her research centres on two main themes: public leadership (political, managerial, professional, and community leadership) and also innovation and improvement in public services. Her book with John Benington, *Leadership for Healthcare*, provides a framework for theory and practice in relation to leadership and its development. She has researched and created, based on research, instruments for the development of both national and local political leaders. She is also engaged in cross-national research about leadership with political astuteness for public managers. Jean is the author of six books, and numerous journal articles, book chapters and reports on leadership, leadership development, and innovation and organizational change and improvement, mainly in public services.

S. Alexander Haslam, Professor of Social Psychology, University of Queensland. Alex has been influential in developing the social identity approach to group processes, which has become the dominant paradigm in the field. *The New Psychology of Leadership*, with Alex Haslam and Michael Platow, was published by Psychology Press in 2011 and was awarded the best book prize at the International Leadership Association conference in 2012.

Ludger Helms is Professor of Political Science and Chair of Comparative Politics at the University of Innsbruck, Austria. His research focuses on political institutions and democratic governance in liberal democracies, and his recent publications in the field of leadership studies include *Comparative Political Leadership* (ed., 2012) and *Poor Leadership and Bad Governance: Reassessing Presidents and Prime Ministers in North America, Europe and Japan* (ed., 2012).

Frank Hendriks is Professor of Comparative Governance and Research Director at the Tilburg School of Politics and Public Administration, and Co-director of Demos-Center for Better Governance and Citizenship at Tilburg University. His research and teaching is focused on the design and quality of democratic governance, more particularly on the quality of political leadership and democratic citizenship, on the reform and innovation in democratic institutions—at the level of the city and the state at large. He is the author of *Vital Democracy* (Oxford University Press, 2010) and the co-editor of the *Oxford Handbook of Local and Regional Democracy in Europe* (Oxford University Press, 2011).

Margaret G. Hermann is Gerald B. and Daphna Cramer Professor of Global Affairs and Director of the Moynihan Institute of Global Affairs at the Maxwell School of Syracuse University. Her research focuses on political leadership, decision making, and crisis management. Hermann has worked to develop techniques for assessing the leadership styles of heads of government at a distance and has such data on over 450 leaders from around the world. She has been president of the International Society of Political Psychology and the International Studies Association as well as editor of the journals *Political Psychology* and the *International Studies Review*.

Leslie Holmes is Professor of Political Science at the University of Melbourne, and a recurrent visiting professor at the University of Bologna, the Graduate School of Social Research in Warsaw, and the People's University in Beijing. His principal research specializations are post-communism and corruption. Among his numerous publications are *Post-Communism* (Oxford University Press, 1997); *Rotten States? Corruption, Post-Communism and Neoliberalism* (Duke University Press, 2006); and *Communism: A Very Short Introduction* (Oxford University Press, 2009). He was President of the International Council for Central and East European Studies (ICCEES) 2000–5, and has been Fellow of the Academy of the Social Sciences in Australia since 1995.

George Jones has from 2003 been Emeritus Professor of Government at LSE where he was Professor of Government between 1976 and 2003. He authored, co-authored, and edited a number of books, chapters, and articles on British central and local government, including the biography of Herbert Morrison: B. Donoughue and G. W. Jones, Herbert Morrison: *Portrait of a Politician* (1973) and (2001). He has written about advising the Prime Minister and Cabinet in J. M. Lee, G. W. Jones and J. Burnham, *At the Centre of Whitehall* (1998); and a study of prime ministers in G. W. Jones (ed.), *West European Prime Ministers* (1991). He wrote the first study of the private secretaries of prime ministers in G. W. Jones, "The Prime Ministers' Secretaries: Politicians or Administrators?" in J. G. Griffith (ed.), *From Politics to Administration* (1975). He reflected on "Cabinet Government since Bagehot" in R. Blackburn (ed.) *Constitutional Studies* (1992). He was a member of the National Consumer Council (1991–9), and Chairman of its Public Services Committee (1992–8). He was a member of the Layfield Committee on Local Government Finance (1974–6) and of the Department of the Environment's Joint Working Party on the Internal Management of Local Authorities (1992–3).

Christer Karlsson is Associate Professor of Political Science and Lecturer at the Department of Government, Uppsala University in Sweden. He has published books, articles, and book chapters in his principal research areas: climate change politics, European Union studies, constitutional politics, and democratic theory. His work has appeared in journals such as *Acta Politica, Ambio, European Law Journal, Global Environmental Politics*, and *Journal of Common Market Studies*. His latest publication is 'Fragmented Climate Change Leadership: Making Sense of the Ambiguous Outcome of COP-15', *Environmental Politics*, 21 (2): 268–86.

Niels Karsten is Assistant Professor at the Demos-Centre for Better Governance and Citizenship, Tilburg University. He specializes in local political-executive leadership. His PhD thesis, entitled 'Decide and Defend' (2013) investigates public leadership accountability in consensual democracies, with an international comparative case study of how local executives regain authority when making controversial decisions. He has published in journals such as *Administration & Society, Lex Localis,* and *Local Government Studies.*

Nannerl O. Keohane writes and teaches in political philosophy, leadership, and feminist theory. She has served as president and professor at Wellesley College (1981–1993) and then at Duke University (1993–2004). She is the author of *Thinking about Leadership* (Princeton University Press, 2010), *Higher Ground: Ethics and Leadership in the Modern University* (Duke University Press, 2006), *Philosophy and the State in France* (1980) and co-edited *Feminist Theory: A Critique of Ideology* (1981). Keohane has also taught at Swarthmore College, the University of Pennsylvania, Stanford University, and Princeton University. She is a member of the Harvard Corporation, on the board of directors of the American Academy of Arts and Sciences, and on the Board of Trustees of the Doris Duke Charitable Foundation. Her current research interests concern leadership and inequality, including gender issues. B.A. Wellesley College; M.A. St Anne's College, Oxford University; Ph.D. Yale University.

Erik-Hans Klijn is Professor at the Department of Public Administration at Erasmus University Rotterdam. His research and teaching activities focus on complex decision-making, network management, public private and branding, and the impact of media on complex decision-making. He published extensively in international journals and is the author, together with Joop Koppenjan, of the book *Managing Uncertainty in Networks* (2004, Routledge) and of *Branding in Governance and Public Management* (Routledge, 2012) together with Jasper Eshuis.

Harvey F. Kline is Professor Emeritus of Political Science at the University of Alabama. He has studied Colombia since 1964 and has written eight books about Colombian politics, most recently *Historical Dictionary of Colombia, Showing Teeth to the Dragons: State-Building by Colombian President Álvaro Uribe Vélez, 2002–2006,* and *Chronicle of a Failure Foretold: The Peace Process of Colombian President Andrés Pastrana.* In addition he was contributing co-editor of *Latin American Politics and Development,* which has been published in eight editions, and co-author of *Introduction to Latin American Politics and Development.* Currently he is researching the second term of Colombian President Álvaro Uribe.

Steve Leach is Emeritus Professor of Local Government at the Local Governance Research Unit at De Montfort University. He has a long and respected record of research and consultancy in the politics, management, and reorganization of local government. He has researched and published widely on local political leadership and has worked closely with a range of local political leaders on political and policy matters. Steve has also researched, studied and written about the development of overview and scrutiny in local government and has supported many councils in revising and strengthening their scrutiny function by which political leaders are held to account.

Steve is a former editor of *Local Government Studies* and is still a member of the editorial board of the journal.

Rose McDermott is Professor of Political Science at Brown University and President of the International Society of Political Psychology. McDermott received her PhD (Political Science) and MA (Experimental Social Psychology) from Stanford. McDermott has taught at Cornell, UCSB, and Harvard, and has held fellowships at Harvard's Olin Institute for Strategic Studies and Harvard's Women and Public Policy Program. She was 2008–9 Fellow at the Center for Advanced Studies in the Behavioral Sciences at Stanford University and a 2010–11 Fellow at the Radcliffe Institute for Advanced Study at Harvard University. She is the author of three books, a co-editor of two additional volumes, and author of over 90 academic articles across a wide variety of academic disciplines encompassing topics such as experimentation, identity, emotion, intelligence, decision-making, and the biological and genetic bases of political behaviour.

David McKay is Professor of Government at the University of Essex. He is the author of numerous books and articles on American and comparative politics including *Designing Europe: Lessons from the Comparative Experience* (2001) and *American Politics and Society* (Eighth Edition, 2013).

Alex Mintz is Dean of the Lauder School of Government, Diplomacy and Strategy at IDC-Herzliya, and Director of its Program in Political Psychology and Decision Making (POPDM). An expert on foreign policy analysis, he has published ten books and many articles in this area, including *Understanding Foreign Policy Decision Making* (with Karl DeRouen), Cambridge University Press, 2010.

Cas Mudde holds a PhD from Leiden University and is Associate Professor in the Department of International Affairs of the University of Georgia. His book *Populist Radical Right Parties in Europe* (Cambridge University Press, 2007) won the Stein Rokkan Prize and was named a *Choice* Outstanding Academic Title in 2008. His most recent publications include the readers *Political Extremism* (Sage, 2014; 4 volumes) and *Youth and the Extreme Right* (Idebate, 2014)."

Charles F. Parker is Associate Professor of Political Science at the Department of Government and serves as a primary investigator in the Centre for Natural Disaster Science at Uppsala University. His research has focused on climate change politics, the origins and consequences of the warning–response problem, and post-crisis accountability procedures. His work has appeared in the *Journal of Common Market Studies*, *Political Psychology*, *Global Environmental Politics*, *Foreign Policy Analysis*, *Public Administration*, and the *Journal of Contingencies and Crisis Management*. His most recent publication, 'Fragmented climate change leadership: making sense of the ambiguous outcome of COP-15', appears in the journal *Environmental Politics*.

Michael J. Platow, Professor of Social Psychology, Australian National University. Michael has been influential in developing the social identity approach to group processes, which has become the dominant paradigm in the field. His book, with Alex Haslam and Michael Platow, *The New Psychology of Leadership* was published by Psychology Press in 2011 and was awarded the best book prize at the International Leadership Association conference in 2012.

Jerrold M. Post is Professor of Psychiatry, Political Psychology and International Affairs and Director of the Political Psychology Program at the George Washington University. He has published widely on crisis decision-making, leadership, and on the psychology of political violence and terrorism, His other books include *The Psychological Evaluation of Political Leaders, With profiles of Saddam Hussein and Bill Clinton* (University of Michigan Press, 2003) and *Leaders and Their Followers in a Dangerous World: The Psychology of Political Behavior* (Cornell University Press, 2004).

Stephen D. Reicher is Professor of Social Psychology, University of St. Andrews (Scotland). He has been influential in developing the social identity approach to group processes, which has become the dominant paradigm in the field. His book, with Alex Haslam and Michael Platow, *The New Psychology of Leadership* was published by Psychology Press in 2011 and was awarded the best book prize at the International Leadership Association conference in 2012.

Bob Reinalda is Senior Researcher at the Department of Political Science and Public Administration at Radboud University Nijmegen, The Netherlands. He has co-edited studies about autonomous policy-making by, decision-making within, and implementation by international organizations (with Bertjan Verbeek and Jutta Joachim). He has published the *Routledge History of International Organizations: From 1815 to the Present Day* (2009) and has edited the *Ashgate Research Companion to Non-State Actors* (2011) and the *Routledge Handbook of International Organization* (2013). Together with Kent Kille, the College of Wooster, he is editor of IO BIO, the *Biographical Dictionary of Secretaries-General of International Organizations*.

Stanley A. Renshon is Professor of Political Science at the City University of New York, and a certified psychoanalyst. He has published author of over 100 professional articles and 16 books in the areas of presidential leadership, American foreign policy and immigration, and American national identity. His most recent book is entitled *Barack Obama and the Politics of Redemption* (Routledge, 2012). His psychological analysis of the Clinton presidency *High Hopes: The Clinton Presidency and the Politics of Ambition* (Routledge, 1998) won the American Political Science Association's Richard E. Neustadt Award for the best book published on the presidency and the National Association for the Advancement of Psychoanalysis' Gradiva Award for the best published work in the category of biography.

R. A. W. Rhodes is Professor of Government (Research) at the University of Southampton (UK); Professor of Government at Griffith University (Brisbane, Australia); and Emeritus Professor of Politics at the University of Newcastle (UK). He is the author or editor of some thirty books including most recently: *Everyday Life in British Government* (Oxford

University Press 2011). He is life Vice-President of the Political Studies Association of the United Kingdom; a Fellow of the Academy of the Social Sciences in Australia; and Fellow of the Academy of Social Sciences (UK).

Cristóbal Rovira Kaltwasser holds a PhD from the Humboldt University of Berlin and is Associate Professor at the School of Political Science at the Universidad Diego Portales in Santiago de Chile. His coedited volume (with Cas Mudde) *Populism in Europe and the Americas: Threat or Corrective for Democracy?* has just been published by Cambridge University Press and his publications have appeared in *Democratization, Government & Opposition,* the *Latin American Research Review,* and *Political Studies,* among others.

Mark Schafer is a Professor of Political Science at the University of Central Florida. His primary research interests include groupthink, the operational code, and psychological correlates of foreign policy behaviour. His two most recent book projects are *Groupthink vs. High Quality Decision Making in International Relations* (Columbia University Press, 2010; co-authored with Scott Crichlow), and *Rethinking Foreign Policy Analysis* (Routledge, 2011; co-edited with Stephen G. Walker and Akan Malici).

Richard Shaw is Associate Professor in Politics at Massey University in Palmerston North, New Zealand. With Chris Eichbaum he has published widely on the various consequences of the growth in the numbers of political advisers in Westminster executives. His most recent publication, concerning the institutional consequences of the public value approach to public management, will appear in a forthcoming edition of *Public Management Review* (http://www.tandfonline.com/doi/full/10.1080/14719037.2012.664017).

Cris Shore is Professor of Social Anthropology at the University of Auckland. His research focuses on political anthropology and organizational cultures in a contemporary European and global context. He has published on the politics of the European Union, the anthropology of public policy, and higher education reform. He is author of eleven books including *Building Europe: The Cultural Politics of European Integration* (Routledge 2000), *Corruption: Anthropological Perspectives* (with Dieter Haller, Pluto, 2005), and *Policy Worlds: Anthropology and the Analysis of Contemporary Power* (with Susan Wright and Davide Pero, Berghahn 2011). He has held research fellowships at the European University Institute, Harvard, Aarhus and Bristol Universities. He currently leads an EU-funded project entitled University Reform, Globalization and Europeanization and another project examining the impact of commercialization on universities.

Laura Sjoberg is Associate Professor of Political Science at the University of Florida. Her teaching and research focuses on the area of gender and international security, where she has written or edited eight books and dozens of journal articles, including, most recently, *Gendering Global Conflict: Towards a Feminist Theory of War* (Columbia University Press, 2013). Her current research on gender and leadership looks to combine the insights of feminist work in leadership theory and feminist work in International

Relations to build a more comprehensive understanding of the role of gender in diplomatic politics.

Gerrie Swart lectures in African Politics and Political Conflict at the University of Stellenbosch, situated in the Western Cape, South Africa. He has published extensively on a wide array of topics related to the study of African affairs, including peace, conflict, and security matters, with specific emphasis on the African Union. His publications include *A Vanquished Peace? Prospects for the Successful Reconstruction of the Democratic Republic of the Congo* (Adonis and Abbey Publishers, 2010). 'Conflict Resolution Counselling' in *Counselling People of African Ancestry* edited by Elias Mpofu (Cambridge University Press, 2011). He is also the Founding Editor of the newly established *Journal of African Union Studies* published by Adonis and Abbey in London.

Patricia Lee Sykes is Associate Professor of Government in the School of Public Affairs at American University in Washington, DC. She is the author of two books: *Presidents and Prime Ministers: Conviction Politics in the Anglo-American Tradition* and *Losing from the Inside: The Cost of Conflict in the British Social Democratic Party* and numerous articles in scholarly journals such as *Studies in American Political Development*, and *Presidential Studies Quarterly*. She is currently writing a book on female executives in six Anglo-American systems.

Paul 't Hart is Professor of Public Administration at the Utrecht School of Governance and Associate Dean at The Netherlands School of Government in The Hague. Between 2005 and 2010 his main appointment was Professor of Political Science at the Australian National University, and he is a core faculty member at the Australia New Zealand School of Government (ANZSOG). His main books on leadership include: *Groupthink in Government: A Study of Small Groups and Policy Failure* (Johns Hopkins University Press, 1994); *The Politics of Crisis Management* (co-authored with Arjen Boin, Eric Stern and Bengt Sundelius, Cambridge University Press, 2005); *Dispersed Democratic Leadership* (co-edited with John Kane and Haig Patapan, Oxford University Press, 2009); *The Real World of EU Accountability* (co-edited with Mark Bovens and Deirdre Curtin, Oxford University Press 2010); *Understanding Prime-ministerial Performance* (Oxford University Press, 2013; co-edited with Paul Strangio and James Walter); and *Understanding Public Leadership* (Palgrave Macmillan, 2014).

John Uhr is an Australian who completed his graduate research at the University of Toronto, Canada. He is the Inaugural Head of the Centre for the Study of Australian Politics at the Australian National University, Canberra, Australia. He contributed to and co-edited the 2011 Palgrave book, *How Power Changes Hands: Transition and Succession in Government*, with former ANU colleague Professor Paul 't Hart. He has directed the ANU's master of public policy program and now teaches political theory and Australian politics. His recent publications cover leadership, parliament, and government ethics.

Jo-Ansie van Wyk is Associate Professor at the Department of Political Sciences, University of South Africa, Pretoria, South Africa. She has obtained an MA (Political

Science) from the University of Stellenbosch, Stellenbosch (South Africa) and a D Phil (International Relations) from the University of Pretoria, Pretoria. She is Fulbright Alumna and a member of the Suid-Afrikaanse Akademie vir Wetenskap en Kuns (South African Academy for Science and Art). Her publications on leadership in Africa include: 'Cadres, Capitalists, Elites and Coalitions: The ANC and Development in South Africa', Nordiska Afrikainstitutet (Nordic Africa Institute (NAI)) Discussion Paper No. 46, Nordiska Afrikainstitutet: Uppsala, 2009, 61pp; 'Political Leaders in Africa: Presidents, Patrons or Profiteers?', African Centre for the Constructive Resolution of Disputes (ACCORD) Occasional Paper Series, 2/1, 2007, 38pp. Her forthcoming publication (co-edited with Chris Landsberg) is *South African Foreign Policy Review*, Vol. 1 (Institute for Global Dialogue (IGD) and African Institute of South Africa (AISA), 2012).

Bertjan Verbeek is Professor of International Relations at the Department of Political Science and Public Administration of Radboud University Nijmegen, The Netherlands, and Visiting Fellow of Crismart at the Swedish National Defence College, Stockholm, Sweden. He has co-edited studies about autonomous policy making by, decision making within, and implementation by international organizations (with Bob Reinalda and Jutta Joachim). He has published *Decision-Making in Great Britain during the Suez Crisis* (2003) and *Italy's Foreign Policy in the Twenty-First Century: The New Assertiveness of an Aspiring Middle Power* (2011, edited with Giampiero Giacomello). His major research projects are When the Cavalry Comes In: A Comparative Analysis of Foreign Policy Crises, and International Organizations in Contemporary Global Politics.

James Walter is Professor of Political Science at Monash University, Melbourne, and previously held chairs at the University of London and at Griffith University, Brisbane. Fellow of the Academy of Social Sciences in Australia, and former President of the Australian Political Studies Association, he has published widely on Australian politics, political history, the history of ideas, leadership, and political biography. His most recent books are *What Were They Thinking? The Politics of Ideas in Australia* (2010, winner of the APSA/Mayer prize for Australian Politics, 2011) and *Understanding Prime Ministerial Performance* (2013, with Paul Strangio and Paul 't Hart).

John Wanna is the Sir John Bunting Chair in Public Administration at the Australian National University. His research interests include Australian politics and public policy, budgetary systems and reforms, policy implementation, and comparative government. His many books include *The Reality of Budgetary Reform in OECD Nations: Trajectories and Consequences* (Edward Elgar Publishing 2009), and *Policy in Action: the Challenges of Service Delivery* (UNSW Press 2009).

Patrick Weller is a professor in the School of Government and International relations at Griffith University in Australia. Recent publications include *Cabinet Government in Australia* (2007), *Westminster Compared* (with R. A. W. Rhodes and John Wanna) (2009) and *Inside the World Bank* (with Xu Yi-chong) (2009).

Bo Zhiyue is Visiting Distinguished Professor at the School of International and Public Affairs of Shanghai Jiaotong University and Senior Research Fellow at the East Asian Institute of the National University of Singapore. He obtained his Bachelor of Law and Masters of Law in International Politics from Peking University and Ph.D. in Political Science from the University of Chicago. He is the author of a trilogy on China's political leadership, including *Chinese Provincial Leaders: Economic Performance and Political Mobility since 1949* (2002), *China's Elite Politics: Political Transition and Power Balancing* (2007), and *China's Elite Politics: Governance and Democratization* (2010).

CHAPTER 1

···

PUZZLES OF POLITICAL LEADERSHIP*

···

R. A. W. RHODES AND PAUL 't HART

Leaders...can conceive and articulate goals that lift people out of their petty preoccupations carry them above the conflicts that tear a society apart, and unite them in pursuit of objectives worthy of their best efforts.

(Gardner 1968: 5)

Most disasters in organizational life can be attributed to leaders, and being a leader has corrupted more people into leading unattractive lives and becoming unattractive selves than it has ennobled.

(March and Weil 2005: 11)

1 WHY BOTHER?

···

THE contradiction between the epigrams is typical of the puzzling nature of political leadership. Is it a force for good or bad? Is it a pivotal or a marginal influence on public life? If leadership matters, how does it do so? Are leaders born or made? Political leadership is a tricky subject to understand, let alone master. Puzzles abound, and contradictory answers multiply, without clear evidence of a growing consensus about any of them. What we do know is that in democratic societies leadership has always been treated with

* We owe a massive 'thank you' to our contributors. The study of political leadership may be a slightly bewildering enterprise but we learned along the way that it is populated by many exemplary colleagues. Prospective authors overwhelmingly responded enthusiastically to our request to add yet another item to their already long to-do list, delivered the goods we sought promptly, and merrily put up with our editorial 'suggestions'. We also would like to thank Dominic Byatt at Oxford University Press for urging us to 'think big' in devising this Handbook, and thus signing away a year or so of our lives. Finally, we thank our desk editors, Eleanor Rivers and Jennifer Mohan, for their assistance in preparing the final manuscript. Any remaining errors are the responsibility of the editors and authors.

mixed feelings. Pleas for 'strong', 'transformational', 'authentic', 'visionary', or other alleg-edly benign forms of public leadership are not hard to find in public debate in most modern democracies, challenged as they are by a debilitating economic crisis. Yet not long ago, after the horrors of the Second World War, the opposite pleas were voiced with equal vigour. We must protect societies so that they are not at the mercy of all-too ambi-tious, ruthless, cunning, and above all dominant rulers. Democracy needs good leaders, but has no clear theory of leadership to counter its inherent suspicions of strong leaders (Korosenyi et al. 2009; Hendriks 2010; Kane and Patapan 2012). Democratic leaders are caught in the cross fire between the hopes placed in them and the challenges to, and con-straints on, their authority.

Through the ages, theorists and practitioners of government have wondered how to promote 'leadership' while constraining 'leaders', especially in democracies (Keane 2009; Kane and Patapan 2012). The sheer number and variety of offices and platforms for exercising political leadership in liberal democracies has produced political struc-tures that are both complex and opaque. The many spheres of political leadership—party, government, civic, and networks among many—coexist, interact, reinforce, and neutralize one another. Moreover, in open societies, many people who are ostensibly 'non-leaders' inside and outside government also perform leadership roles; for example, 'advisers', 'administrators', and civic entrepreneurs.

Promoters of good governance wonder how much scope can be granted to individ-ual officeholders and to leadership when designing democratic institutions (see also Helms, Chapter 13, this volume). They argue that, in governance systems, multiple lead-ership roles exist in parallel (distributed leadership), with inducements to act in con-cert (collaborative leadership) as well as going in to bat against one another (adversarial leadership). Such systems look messy to other commentators who prefer the clarity of hierarchy, and leadership as command and control from the centre. But, so the argu-ment goes, like any resilient sociocultural or sociotechnical system, governance systems thrive on variety, overlap, and competition among loci of initiative, voice, authority, and accountability (Bendor 1985). Admittedly, these systems have their transaction costs. Aligning enough people and organizations behind any particular set of ideas or pol-icy proposals can be a time-consuming and convoluted process. As many have argued, however, such institutional pluralism produces smart, robust public policies as well as keeping the arrogance of power at bay (Kane, Patapan, and 't Hart 2009).

In contrast, governance systems built around top-down, great-man leadership are said to be inherently unstable and deemed normatively objectionable. They also lack the institutional capacity for effective social problem-solving (Lipman-Blumen 2004). They are governed well only when the supreme leader and her clique are smart, wise, and honest. They are, however, quick to slide into the abyss of tyranny, stupid-ity, and corruption when the ruling elite becomes addicted to its own power, or when enlightened leaders are replaced by less capable and morally upright characters. In this Handbook, Kline's (Chapter 41) and Swart, van Wyk, and Botha's (Chapter 43) accounts of Latin American and African political leadership refer to many studies documenting such abuses.

Before we can get around to (re)designing the institutions that both empower political leaders and hold them to account, however, we must first understand the nature of the beast. How do we know 'political leadership' when we see it? How do we describe, explain, evaluate, and improve it? The study of leadership became both a field and a fad during the late twentieth century (Kellerman 2012). This period left us with a bewildering array of concepts, frameworks, propositions, stories, assessments, prescriptions, and clichés about leadership across many academic disciplines and professional domains. Inspirational books by leadership 'gurus' and biographies of celebrity Chief Executive Officers (CEOs) litter main street and airport bookstores around the world. There is an entire industry of leadership training and consulting. It began in the corporate sector but spilled inexorably into the government and third sectors. Because the study of leadership studies is such a complex and disjointed interdisciplinary enterprise, it is important to locate this Handbook in this vast domain. What are the key characteristics and debates of 'leadership studies' in and beyond the realm of politics? To answer this question, we survey how the field has addressed the key puzzles of political leadership by discussing several key dichotomies that have been the focal point of scholarly inquiry and debate past and present: leaders and leadership; democrats and dictators; causes and consequences; actors and context; personal qualities and luck; success and failure; and art and science.

2 Leaders and Leadership

The first issue concerns what it is we want to understand: is it the people we commonly call leaders, or the process we call leadership? For many scholars and practitioners understanding political leaders comes down to studying the characteristics, beliefs, and deeds of people formally occupying the top roles in political life. Foremost, there are senior politicians: heads of government, cabinet ministers, senior legislators, and key party officials. In this category, we should also include key advisers to these senior politicians, who stay behind the scenes but are often said to be influential (see also Eichbaum and Shaw, Chapter 34, this volume).

Less obvious to outside observers, but all too obvious to those who know how executive government works, senior public officials are influential actors. This category includes top officials in the departments that advise ministers and prepare and administer policies and programmes. It also includes the heads and senior ranks of administrative organizations with the task of implementing policy and delivering public services. Although their institutional role and professional ethos is to be public *servants*, there is little dispute that the upper echelons of the bureaucracy are important in shaping what governments do, when, how, and how well (Rhodes, Chapter 7).

Finally, many political leaders do not hold any formal public office at all. The penumbra of non-government organizations is vast, varied, and vigorous. Democracies nurture a big and active civil society. They value its contributions to the political process even when its leaders are critical of the government of the day. The individuals at the helm of trade unions, churches, social movements, mass media, community organizations, and even business corporations are widely thought of as important public leaders. They do not have the power of office. They do have the power of numbers, supporters, and money. They also have the ideas, access, and moral authority, to shape public problem-solving in important ways (see also Couto, Chapter 23, this volume; see also Rucht 2012).

Understanding political leader*ship* through the lens of lead*ers* takes one to the province of psychology. It rests on the idea that it matters who governs us. It entails an agent-centred view of politics and government. In other words, public debates and decisions are shaped by the views, drives, skills, and styles of individuals who occupy formal office. Comparisons of different leaders in similar circumstances show how their beliefs and practices have an impact on the lives of citizens. Think of Helmut Kohl seizing the historical moment and forging a German reunification that almost no one in Germany, Kohl included, even deemed possible before November 1989. He was in the right position at the right time to make a difference. Counterfactual questions about the roles of leaders at such critical historical junctures may be unanswerable, but they pose interesting conundrums. What if James Callaghan not Margaret Thatcher had still been the British prime minister when the Argentinean junta invaded the Falklands Isles? What would have happened to the course of the Vietnam War or to American–Chinese relations if Robert Kennedy, not Richard Nixon, had won the 1968 US presidential election? Would America have waged war in Afghanistan and Iraq following the September 11 attacks if Al Gore had won the Florida recount during the 2000 presidential election? Would gay marriage be a much more widely accepted practice in the US today if Hillary Clinton and not Barack Obama had become president in 2009?

Once we allow the thought that leaders matter, a whole range of questions about 'leaders' arise (see also Hermann, Chapter 8, this volume). Why do people aspire to hold high public office? What keeps them going in the face of unmanageable workloads, relentless public criticism, and an often-toxic public opinion and irate stakeholders? Why do some leaders take huge gambles with history? Why do they act in sometimes blatantly self-defeating manner? For example, US President Woodrow Wilson undermined his own burning desire to create a League of Nations after the First World War by treating anyone expressing reservations about American accession to the new body with hostility and contempt. In effect, he organized his own opposition, and eventual Congressional defeat (George and George, 1956). Why do some successful, long-serving heads of government, such as Konrad Adenauer or Tony Blair, cling to office long past their political sell-by date, dragging down their party, their government, their successor, and their reputation in the process ('t Hart and Uhr, 2011)?

To answer such questions, leadership scholars have delved into the personalities of leaders, and their underlying motives. They explore the ends or purposes for which they mobilize their personal skills and resources. Some have turned to psychoanalysis and biographical methods (see also Post, Chapter 22; Walter, Chapter 21, this volume). Others have turned to experimental methods, psychometrics, and other modernist-empiricist modes of 'measuring' personalities, motives and behaviour (McDermott, Chapter 18; Schafer, Chapter 20).

The behaviour of people holding high public office has been and will be observed incessantly by leadership scholars. 'Reading' leaders' behaviour is seen as the key to understanding what makes them tick, and a predictor of what impacts they might have. Peers, advisers, subordinates, opponents, and other stakeholders all watch how they allocate their attention, make decisions, interact with people, deal with pressure, conflict and criticism, and perform in public. They do so for good reasons. Like all of us, leaders are creatures of habit. During their personal and professional lives, they develop distinctive styles of thought and action. Such habits allow others to make educated guesses about what they may feel and how they will act when a new situation comes along. The more intimate one's knowledge about a leader's personal style, the more accurate those educated guesses are likely to be.

Questions about the individual leaders' psychological make-up abound. Many scholars display boundless enthusiasm for trying to answer them. Why do individuals holding the same or similar leadership roles display such widely different behavioural styles? The answer almost *has* to be: because of who they are. What is it, however, about leaders that drive them to the top? Are leaders smarter than ordinary people? Are successful leaders smarter than unsuccessful ones? Do they have greater self-confidence? Are they morally superior? In present-day democratic societies, few will answer these questions with a simple, 'Yes' (Winter 2005). Not only are we reluctant to concede their superiority, but there is much casual evidence to the contrary. Wherever and whenever we look, we see a minister who can only be described as 'thick'. A few American presidents suffered from low self-esteem rather than the reverse (Greenstein 2009: 8). Some presidents, like Coolidge, were clinically depressed (McDermott 2007: 34).

Easy answers don't exist. Ronald Reagan is an interesting case. He had no great desire for information before he acted. Many dismissed him as a second-rate mind. In his second term, the effects of his advanced age and the onset of Alzheimer's disease became more obvious (McDermott 2007: 28, 31). Nevertheless, he is one of the most highly-rated American presidents of the twentieth century, mainly because his robust and high emotional intelligence (EQ) compensated for what may have been a modest intellect (IQ). By contrast, intellectually gifted but emotionally impaired individuals such as Richard Nixon and Bill Clinton consistently rank much lower than Reagan, mainly because they failed to control their darker impulses while in office. Jimmy Carter and Gerald Ford were widely seen as both bright and morally upright. Both were consigned to the dustbin of presidential history, the former because of a glaring lack of political skills, the latter mainly because of sheer misfortune (Greenstein 2009). Two of the America's most revered presidents—Franklin D. Roosevelt and John F. Kennedy—were effectively cripples. The latter, holding office in the television and not the radio age, took irresponsibly high doses of strong medication to hide his condition from the public (McDermott 2007; Owen 2008).

Leader-centred analysis has proved hugely popular in the United States despite its failure to deliver definitive answers. Writing in 1978, political scientist James MacGregor

Burns (1978: 1–2) was scathing about the bias created by this emphasis: 'If we know all too much about our leaders, we know far too little about *leadership*. We fail to grasp the essence of leadership that is relevant to the modern age and hence we cannot even agree on the standards by which to measure, recruit, and reject it.'

Over the past 35 years, the balance has been redressed. There is now a growing body of thought and research that understands leadership as an interactive process between leaders and followers; institutions and their rules of the game; and the broader historical context (e.g. Elgie 1995; Goethals, Sorenson, and Burns 2004; Messick and Kramer 2005; Masciulli, Mochanov, and Knight 2009; Couto 2010; Keohane 2010; Ahlquist and Levi 2011; Bryman et al. 2011; Helms 2012; and Strangio, 't Hart and Walter 2013; 't Hart 2014). Once we escape the preoccupation with the individual, a new agenda for the study of political leadership emerges. The focus on interactions leads inexorably to the question, 'Who are being led?' The focus switches to followers. Social psychologists and political communication scholars ask when, how, and why particular groups of people come to accept some people as their leaders. It considers leadership a two-way street. It explores the process by which certain individuals come to be given the authority or support they need to lead others effectively. It also explores how leaders seek to persuade others to think and act in certain ways. In its most radical form, the follower perspective views leadership processes as primarily a product of the identities, needs, desires, and fears of followers and constituencies. More commonly, leadership is viewed as an interactive process between leaders and led, revolving in no small measure around the degree to which leaders succeed in appealing to, embodying or modifying the social identities of their followers (see also Reicher, Haslam and Platow, Chapter 10; Uhr, Chapter 17; Gaffney, Chapter 26; Cohen, Chapter 30, this volume).

Interactionist approaches also accord a significant role to institutional and contextual factors (Elgie 1995; Bennister 2012). In democracies, for instance, many 'event-making' decisions and policies have a whole host of fingerprints on them because power and responsibility are institutionally dispersed across many actors and institutions (Korosenyi, Slomp, and Femia 2009; Kane, Patapan, and 't Hart 2009). Institutions provide the rules of the political game. Organizational cultures provide actors with sets of beliefs about the nature and role of leadership. The historical context and present-day dilemmas and crises offer opportunities to some leaders while constraining others (see also Helms, Chapter 13; 't Hart, Chapter 14; Ansell, Boin and 't Hart, Chapter 28, this volume).

All these factors come into play when, say, a cabinet meets. When, how, and to what extent a prime minister 'leads' that cabinet, is variable (Rhodes, Wanna, and Weller 2009; Strangio, 't Hart, and Walter, 2013). Few heads of government in democracies get their way all of the time, even within the executive. They know that if pushed too far for too long their cabinet members and parliamentary colleagues have ways of undermining their leadership (see also McKay, Chapter 29; Weller, Chapter 32; Blick and Jones, Chapter 33, this volume). Ministers can be powerful leaders in their own right, offsetting prime-ministerial predominance, even if only in some policy domains and only some of the time (see also Andeweg, Chapter 35, this volume). Party rules for leadership selection and removal can limit the job security of leaders even if they are prime ministers. Thus, Margaret Thatcher in the UK and Kevin Rudd as well as Julia Gillard, both Australian Prime Ministers, were ousted from office by their erstwhile supporters in their parties ('t Hart and Uhr 2011; Cross and Blais 2012).

For many students of political leadership, Greenstein's (1975) heuristic for the study of leadership holds as true today as it did on its publication almost 45 years ago. He suggested that it only makes sense for a student of politics or policy to delve into personal characteristics and leadership styles of individual political actors if there was appreciable scope for choice and action for individual actors. The individuals in question must not only have the intention but also the formal roles, and/or the informal power resources (including personal strength and skills) to make a potentially decisive contribution to the handling of the issue at stake. The extent to which these conditions are met varies from issue to issue, leader to leader, and context to context. Often, it will simply not make sense to pay much attention to the personal characteristics of a particular leader because the leader is either not motivated or not powerful enough to make a difference; in short, not indispensable (Greenstein 1975). Leader-centred explanations of public events are most likely to be powerful where leaders have a reputation for holding and wielding much power and influence. They will wield that influence on issues that are of strong personal interest or strategic importance to them; and that cannot easily be handled by routine, institutionalized procedures. Such windows of opportunity arise with unprecedented, acute, risky, and contentious issues, in particular issues seen as 'crises'.

3 Democrats and Dictators

Is political leadership inherently desirable in democratic polities? Following Burns (1978, 2003: 15–16) can we distinguish between 'interactive leaders' and 'power-wielders'? The former rely on bargaining, persuasion, and genuine engagement with followers, and accept the constraints of democracy and the rule of law. The latter are ruthless Machiavellians and cold-hearted narcissists who do not shy away from manipulation and force to prevail on the led. If we adopt this explicitly normative, even moral, distinction, people like Napoleon, Hitler, Stalin, and Mao disappear off the leadership map. Each authorized the use of brutal force against millions they thought unworthy or dangerous. Still, to brand them mere power-wielders would be to overlook their ability to communicate a political vision and persuade millions to comply and even share it. Indeed, followers acted on the leader's vision at great risk to their own lives and limbs. Their values and purposes are morally repugnant to our present-day democratic sensibilities but that must not blind us to their exercise of leadership. Conversely, democratically elected leaders such as George W. Bush and Tony Blair were widely criticized for using deception to launch the war in Iraq and for condoning torture. Does that disqualify them from leadership analysis, or is it more productive to see them as examples of 'bad' leadership (Kellerman 2004)?

Political leaders holding office in democratic societies live in a complex moral universe. Democracy requires good leadership if it is to work effectively. Yet the idea of leadership potentially conflicts with democracy's egalitarian ethos (see also Hendriks and Karsten, Chapter 3, this volume). The more democratic leaders lead from the front, the less democratic they appear; the more they act like good democrats, the less they seem like true leaders. Confronted with this dilemma, the general tendency among scholars has been to accept the need for leadership in practice while overlooking it in theory. As a result, they fail to offer a yardstick for assessing leadership in democracy. Leadership cannot be dispensed with without jeopardizing the conduct of public affairs. In practice, democracy's tendency is not to manage without leadership, but to multiply leadership offices and opportunities, and keep office-holding leaders in check by a web of accountabilities (Geer 1996; Bovens 1998; Ruscio 2004; Wren 2007; Kane, Patapan, and 't Hart 2009; Korosenyi, Slomp, and Femia 2009).

Yet at times democratic leaders have to make tricky trade-offs such as using debatable means to achieve inherently respectable (if politically contested) ends. Some succumb to the fallacy of thinking that the power of their office alone provides them with moral authority to lead. Indira Gandhi was an authoritarian, even repressive, yet elected, prime minister of India (Steinberg 2008). The same applies to all too many post-colonial leaders of the Latin-American 'caudillo' or African 'big man' ilk (see also Kline, Chapter 41; Swart, van Wyk, and Botha, Chapter 43, this volume). 'If the President orders it, it cannot be illegal', Richard Nixon famously claimed, in his attempt to justify to interviewer David Frost his authorization of the Watergate break-in and cover up. Going too far is a grave error for which many—including the leaders themselves—may pay a serious price. The story does not end there, however. The same Richard Nixon is credited with several bold, historic policy initiatives that have met with broad and lasting acclaim. It is unhelpful to ignore the full complexity of this man and his period in office by refusing to consider him a political leader.

Similarly, heads of government who have gained power by non-democratic means and occasionally govern by fear, intimidation, and blackmail may also aim for widely shared and morally acceptable goals (see also Zihuye, Chapter 40; Holmes, Chapter 42, this volume). They may even pursue those goals with respectable means and with the consent of a majority of the population. Mikhail Gorbachev's reforms and eventual dissolution of the Soviet Union and Mustafa Kemal Atatürk's efforts to create and modernize the Turkish state are cases in point. Neither came to power through democratic election. Are such leaders not exercising leadership? Understanding leadership requires us to take in all its shades of grey: leading and following, heroes and villains, the capable and the inept, winners and losers.

4 CAUSE AND CONSEQUENCE

There are two fundamentally different points of departure in understanding political leadership. One is to see it as a shaping force of political life, and explore how, when, and why it works and to what effect. Leadership is commonly portrayed as a source of dynamism in the polity, breathing life into parties and institutions as they strug-gle with major changes. In this view, leadership is about injecting ideas and ambitions into the public arena. It is about grasping existing realities and recognizing that they can affect transformations. Leadership produces collective meaning and harnesses collective energy for a common cause. Great leaders are thus often conceived of as being 'event-making' (Hook 1943). They have the ability to garner momentum for the hopes and ambitions of their followers. Their presence affects the course of history. They have many names: Pied Pipers, visionaries, entrepreneurs, and reformers. Leaders are seen to both read and change their followers' minds, causing them collectively to go on journeys which they would otherwise never have contemplated.

Many accounts of leadership focus on leaders as the supreme decision makers. When an organization or a nation faces high-stakes' decisions that no one else is willing or able to make, somebody has to take responsibility. The buck stops here, read a sign on Harry Truman's Oval Office desk. He practised what he preached, committing the United States to using two atomic bombs in one week and proudly claiming never to have lost any sleep over so doing. Some leaders revel in that position. They do what they can to make sure that every big decision crosses their desk. They feel confident in analysing complex problems. They work through the risks and uncertainties, probing the vested interests and unstated assumptions of the experts, advisers, and colleagues pushing them into (or away from) specific courses of action.

Others leaders may loath deciding. They avoid risk. Some may feel overwhelmed by the complexity of the issues and by the policy-making process itself. George (1974) quotes US President Warren Harding confiding to a friend on how stressful he found his job.

> John, I can't make a thing out of this tax problem. I listen to one side and they seem right, and then God! I talk to the other side and they seem just as right, and there I am where I started....I know somewhere there is an economist who knows the truth, but hell, I don't know where to find him and haven't got the sense to know him and trust him when I find him. God, what a job.
>
> (George 1974: 187)

The point is whether they enjoy it, and whether they display sound judgement. The notion of leaders as strategic decision makers portrays them as being at the helm, in control, reshaping the world around them.

Trying to understand leadership as a cause is important. Although much of social life is governed by shared traditions, rules, and practices, there are always public prob-lems that defy routine solutions. Identifying the novel, understanding it, and making a persuasive case for adapting or abandoning routines is a leadership task. Study the his-tory of every great reform and you will find leadership at work. Commonly, it will be a form of collective or distributed leadership rather than the single 'heroic' activist who gets all the public credit for it. Understanding political leadership as a cause raises many important analytical and practical questions about the impact of different leadership styles and discourses in different contexts. What 'works', and when? Can it be copied and transplanted? How do particular people or groups matter? What characteristics and skills make them matter?

The other main point of departure for understanding political leadership is to look at leadership as a consequence. In modernist-empiricist jargon, leadership is the dependent variable, and we seek to explain variations in it by looking at the other variables that have an impact on it. So we ask who becomes a leader. How do they consolidate their hold on office? When, how, and by whom are they removed? How do people make it to the top in political parties, social movements, and public bureaucracies? How are they selected? What happens to leadership aspirants along their path to the top? How are they socialized? What debts do they incur, and how do these debts affect their ability to exercise leadership? What are the consequences if access to leadership roles is biased towards people of certain social or professional backgrounds (Borchert and Zeiss 2003; Bovens and Wille 2009)? We may also want to know about the offices. What responsibilities, expectations, and resources are attached to them? What are the implications of varying responsibilities, expectations, and resources for the occupant's authority and support among the led? How have they changed?

Finding out who gets to lead can teach us much not just about those leaders but about the societies in which they work. The elevation of Mary Robinson, Nicolas Sarkozy, Evo Morales, Luiz Inácio Lula da Silva, and, most conspicuously, Barack Obama to the presidency of their respective countries would not have been possible only a few decades ago. Making it all the way to the top is evidence of upward social mobility and of the political influence of women, peasants, workers, immigrants, and ethnic minorities. In turn, these changes influence the policy agendas of leaders, and change the structure of incentives for hopefuls to the top job.

Knowledge about the ebb and flow of leadership careers is a source of lessons for future leaders. Leadership becomes possible because the populace select individuals with whom they identify, or whom they trust, or whose claims to authority they respect. Each of these levers for leadership, however, is conditional and temporary in all but the most spellbinding cases of charismatic leadership (see also Gaffney, Chapter 26, this volume). Leaders have to build carefully and maintain their leadership capital. On this view political capital is a resource of the leader who accumulates to spend. The focus of the analysis is the leader, her narrative skills, and personal qualities. Alternatively, political capital can be seen as an attribute of followers who cede reputation, trust, and so on to the leader. It is a loan that cannot be banked but must be spent, and inevitably the borrower ends up in debt and the lender forecloses. It matters whether the focus of analysis is the leader's or the lender's characteristics because the latter switches attention away from the leader's personal qualities to such key influences as the media and the *zeitgeist*. On both views, political capital is contingent and uncertain. Leaders cannot and will not please everyone always. They sometimes teach unpleasant realities, make trade-off choices, and embrace some values and interests while disowning others. Moreover, leaders hardly ever succeed in doing all that they promise. Seldom do they meet all of their followers' hopes. In fact, some scholars argue that reducing followers' expectations at a rate they can absorb is an essential leadership quality (Heifetz, Grashow, and Linsky 2009).

5 Actors and Contexts

Our discussion of leadership as cause makes assumptions about the importance of human agency in any explanation. Does their ability to influence people and events stem from their personal characteristics and behaviour? If so, studying their personalities and actions in depth is essential; or, do we see them as frail humans afloat on a sea of storms larger than themselves that sets the stage for their rise, performance, and fall? In that case, it is as essential to study the context they work in (see also 't Hart 2014; and Chapter 14, this volume).

Of course, the study of political leadership is no different from that of any other social phenomenon. The so-called agency–structure duality lies at the heart of the social sciences, as does the closely related duality between ideas and realities. Is human action shaped by objective physical and social realities, or by socially constructed, contingent, and contestable interpretations of those realities? Academics have debated this topic for over a century, and we cannot review it in full here or offer any resolution. We can note the implications for the study of leadership.

Who governs matters, but not always or all the time. Economic and political context may constrain the range of policies leaders can pursue, but that context is variously understood, as are its effects. Leaders can and do go against the prevailing tide. They may be written off as quixotic. They may have been sent to jail. But they do take a gamble on history:

> Men make their own history, but they do not make it as they please; they do not make it under self-selected circumstances, but under circumstances existing already, given and transmitted from the past. The tradition of all dead generations weighs like a nightmare on the brains of the living. (Marx 1934: 10)

Despite this weight of tradition, sometimes leaders win against all odds. It pays therefore to explore political leadership as a fundamentally disruptive force, and examine how some leaders challenge existing beliefs, practices, and traditions (Skowronek 1993; Bevir and Rhodes 2003; Heifetz, Grashow, and Linsky 2009). An interpretive approach will argue that traditions are not immutable. Traditions are a set of understandings, a set of inherited beliefs and practices, which someone receives during socialization. They are mainly a first influence on people. Social contexts do not determine the actions of individuals. Rather traditions are products of individual agency. When people confront unfamiliar circumstances or ideas, it poses a dilemma to their existing beliefs and practices. Consequently, they have to extend or change their heritage to encompass it, so developing that heritage. Every time they try to apply a tradition, they have to reflect on it, they have to try to understand it afresh in today's circumstances. By reflecting on it, they open it to change. Thus, human agency can produce change even when people think that they are sticking fast to a tradition which they regard as sacrosanct.

Leaders similarly are heirs to traditions. They inherit beliefs and practices: about their office in particular and the polity in general. As they confront the dilemmas of office, they modify that heritage, even when they choose not to openly challenge it. Such an ability to 'smuggle in' change incrementally, indeed almost inadvertently, means that they can survive at the helm when few thought that possible. They achieve policy reforms and social changes against the odds, and the inherited wisdom perishes.

6 PERSONAL QUALITIES AND LUCK

Are political leaders relatively autonomous actors able to make their own luck? The temptation is always to attribute their success to their special qualities or traits—the 'great man' (sic) theory of leadership. Trait theories have had a chequered and largely unsuccessful history (see also Reicher, Haslam, and Platow, Chapter 10, this volume). On close inspection, explanations based on the leader's personal qualities are not persuasive. No public leader achieves all her objectives always, yet presumably she had the same personal qualities throughout. Even heroes of history like Catherine II, Empress of Russia, Winston Churchill, Mahatma Gandhi, Abraham Lincoln, and Margaret Thatcher experienced many vicissitudes and made many discernible errors of judgement before their finest hour arrived and they achieved greatness. No public leader ever worked alone. They are embedded in webs of beliefs and dependence. Behind every 'great' leader are indispensable collaborators, advisers, mentors, and coalitions: the building blocks of the leader's achievements.

We also have to entertain the possibility that these allegedly 'great' leaders might have been just plain lucky; that is they get what they want without trying. They are 'systematically lucky'; that is, although they have resources which they can use if they want to, often they do not have to use them because they occupy an advantageous position. They get their own way by doing nothing (see Dowding 1996, 2008). Leadership and luck are often a matter of perceptions and reputations. Leaders and their reputations can be made or broken by events over which the leader in question exercised little or no control; but we have to understand how reputations are formed. They are not given, objective facts. Rather, they are narratives constructed by the leaders and her followers. They hinge on myths and symbols (Edelman 1985). The most pervasive and pernicious are the myths and symbols of nationalism, but race and religion are rarely far away. We concede that leaders may attend football games because they like the game. Indeed, few would have the sheer disdain for sports of New South Wales Premier, Bob Carr, who was caught reading Dostoyevsky's *Crime and Punishment* while attending one of the Sydney Olympics finals. More likely, political leaders attend expecting the national side to win, thus bolstering the association between leader and country. They are constructing their image and their reputation, trying to ensure that their narrative of events prevails. Opponents have their preferred narrative. Both will draw on deep-seated traditions in telling their stories and to legitimize their view of the world.

All seek to manage meanings and influence followers. Successful leaders are skilled storytellers (see also Rhodes, Chapter 7; Grint, Chapter 16, this volume).

7 SUCCESS AND FAILURE

How do we know when a political leader has been successful? Again, there are no easy answers, or even agreement on the best way to seek an answer. The simplest criterion of all is longevity in office: getting re-elected, maintaining the support of party barons and keeping potential rivals at bay. The literature on leadership succession in both democracies and non-democracies is based at least implicitly on the premise that success equals political survival (Bueno de Mesquita et al. 2004; 't Hart and Uhr 2011). Why do some leaders succeed, that is, survive, so spectacularly? Swedish Prime Minister Tage Erlander's 23 years in office, Helmut Kohl's 16 years as German Chancellor, or Robert Menzies' 17 years as Australian Prime Minister are a few examples. We can also mention the even longer reigns of dictators such as Robert Mugabe in Zimbabwe or Cuba's Fidel Castro. Are they smarter, more persuasive, more persistent, more opportunistic, more ruthless, or just luckier than less 'successful' leaders? Did Kim Campbell, party leader and Prime Minister of Canada for a mere four months, fail to hold on to office because she lacked such skills? Or is it not personal qualities at all, but rather institutional rules of, for example, leadership selection and ejection, and circumstances that determine leaders' fates?

However, many would agree that office-holding is not a sufficient and perhaps not even a necessary condition for success (Heifetz 1994). We need more criteria. The traditional way of assessing leadership success is, of course, the tombstone biography with its measured tone and, usually, an author of forbearing even forgiving disposition (Marquand 2009). British Prime Minister, Harold Wilson, was seen as devious, vacillating, pragmatic to the point of unprincipled, and prone to conspiracy theories. His reputation was rescued by his biographer Ben Pimlott (1992) and much greater credence is now given to his tactical skill in managing divisive issues. Likewise, Fred Greenstein's careful archival research led to a complete overhaul of the predominant image of Dwight Eisenhower as a hands-off, do-nothing president, revealing his 'hidden-hand' style that was far more engaged and activist than contemporary media coverage had revealed (Greenstein 1982).

The problem with biographies is that, when compared, there are no clear criteria of success or failure (see also Walter, Chapter 21, this volume). They are specific to the individual and his or her times. Undeterred, there is a mini-industry in, among others, the United Kingdom and the USA surveying the views of academics and other experts about the relative standing of prime ministers and presidents (for an overview, see Strangio, 't Hart, and Walter 2013). Belying the scientific trappings of a survey and quantitative analysis, the method is inter-subjective. It sums experts' judgement allowing much latitude on the criteria for those judgements. In effect, it fuels debate not only about relative standing, but also the criteria for judging. Such reputational techniques have been widely criticized; for example, they are skewed towards recent political figures. Also, the rankings make some big assumptions; that leaders are 'in charge', 'in control' and, therefore, 'responsible' for their records (see, for example, Bose and Landis 2011). Yet at least they provide a platform for debate and reflection about what values, styles, and accomplishments 'we' seek in leaders past and present.

Of course, there are efforts to identify systematic criteria for measuring success or failure. Hennessy (2000: 528–9) identifies five sets of criteria: backdrop to the premiership; management capacity; insight and perception; change and innovation; and constitutional and procedural. These five categories are further sub-divided into seventeen criteria. However, this 'celestial chief justice', remains unhappy with the exercise, calling his rankings 'crude'. 't Hart (2011, 2014) proposes the much simpler 'assessment triangle' composed of three families of criteria. First, there is impact or smart leadership, which requires the leader to deliver effective policies that solve problems. Second, there is support or accepted leadership, which requires the leader to win and keep the support not only of the electorates, but also of other key actors in governing. Finally, there is trustworthiness or accountable leadership, which requires leaders to be responsive to multiple overlapping accountabilities. Despite obvious limitations, these approaches have two marked advantages. First, they are explicit about the criteria for judging political leaders. If you disagree, then you need to suggest alternative criteria and the discussion is consequently on a much sounder footing. Second, they highlight the ways in which the criteria conflict. There are trade-offs between, for example, smart leadership introducing new policies and preserving support among key actors and from the electorate. Such trade-offs underline the besetting problem of this area; the criteria are not only subjective but change with people and circumstances. All compete for standing in Congress or parliament, in the party, and in the country. Gossip is a key but unreliable currency for all. The media are fickle. Standing and performance are contingent as is the dominance of the president or the prime minister, or the standing of any of his or her colleagues. Command and control is always a possibility. Rivals rise and are vanquished, but, equally, regicide happens.

8 ART AND PROFESSION

From the West to East, many observers of political leadership have chosen to portray leadership as an art (see also Keohane, Chapter 2, Chan and Chan, Chapter 4, this volume). They claim leadership cannot be captured in law-like generalizations based on neutral data and analytical detachment. By inference, it cannot be taught in the cerebral environment of an academic classroom or executive seminar. As so often, Max Weber (1991: 115) was on the mark when he suggested that the challenge of leadership is to forge warm passion and cool judgement together in one and the same soul. In practice, this maxim condemns aspiring leaders to a life of tough judgement calls between the passion that fires them up, the feeling of personal responsibility that drives them on, and a sense of proportion that is necessary to exercise good judgement.

Leadership is conceived by some of its most authoritative scholars as involving a large measure of practical wisdom; of insight that can be gained only through direct personal experience and sustained reflection. The core intangibles of leadership—empathy, intuition, creativity, courage, morality, judgement—are largely beyond the grasp of 'scientific' inquiry, let alone comprehensive explanation and evidence-based prescription. Understanding leadership comes from living it: being led, living with and advising leaders, doing one's own leading. Some understanding of leadership may be gained from vicarious learning: digesting the experiences of other leaders: hence the old and steady appetite for the biographies and memoirs of politicians, and the contemporary market for 'live encounters' with former leaders who strut their stuff at seminars and conferences. When we cannot get the real thing, we are still willing to pay for the next best thing: books and seminars by the exclusive circle of leadership 'gurus' who observe and interrogate the great and the good. Even academia is not immune. Academics, too, seek to get up close and personal in ethnographic fieldwork (see also Gains, Chapter 19, this volume; Rhodes 2011).

In sharp contrast to this long-standing view, a 'science of leadership' has sprung up in the latter half of the twentieth century. Thousands of academics now make a living treating leadership as they would any other topic in the social sciences. They treat it as an object of study, which can be picked apart and put together by forms of inquiry that seek to emulate the natural sciences (see also Blondel, Chapter 46, this volume). Their papers fill journals, handbooks, conference programmes, and lecture theatres. Many among them make in-roads into the real world of political leadership as consultants and advisers, often well paid. Much of this activity prompts a bemused response. It is of little help to know that 45 variables completely explain three cases. It would not persist, however, if such knowledge did not help in grasping at least some of the puzzles that leaders face and leadership poses. Alternatively, it could meet the insatiable need of leaders to understand their world and talk to outsiders 'because they are so worried about whether it makes sense or, indeed, whether they make sense' (Rawnsley 2001: xi).

It is this 'scientific' understanding of leadership that we now see echoed in widespread attempts to erect a leadership profession (see also Hartley, Chapter 44, this volume). The language of leadership has pervaded the job descriptions, training, and performance management of public servants at even junior management levels. Many public service commissions or equivalent bodies have embarked on developing integrated leadership frameworks. These frameworks stipulate bundles of leadership skills, which are linked to performance indicators for each different leadership role. People wanting to move up must meet these criteria of successful performance. They must also attend set courses, accept a set of shared values, and subject themselves to standardized tests. When they manage to get all the boxes ticked, they get ushered into a fraternity rather like a Masonic Lodge. Uniformity is nurtured and celebrated through lucrative rewards packages. Leadership education is ubiquitous. Everyone regularly attends meetings where leadership gurus perform. The aim is not to impart knowledge, but to solidify a shared notion of professionalism. The means for such sharing are the latest nostrums, models, and metaphors. The audience is captive, and willingly so, though one might—like leadership 'guru', Barbara Kellerman (2012)—wonder for how much longer.

9 TRANSCENDING THE DICHOTOMIES?

Clearly, when taken to extremes both the art and the science assumptions about 'understanding leadership' lead to absurd results. The mystifications of wisdom and judgement untainted by evidence confront the quasi-scientific 'one size fits all' generalizations that sustain allegedly evidence-based leadership training and reform. Both privilege one form of knowledge over all others. Both generate their own quacks and true believers. Both do well out of their trade. Sadly, both pay too little attention to what we know and how we know it. Their certainties defy the limits to knowledge and the resulting failures, big and little, do a disservice to practitioners and academics alike. The best we can offer is not prediction but informed conjecture. So *caveat emptor* for those seeking solutions from the study of political leadership. There is much on offer: insight, careful analysis, and lessons for the wary. As Greenleaf (1983) suggests, however:

> The concept of a genuine social science has had its ups and downs, and it still survives, though we are as far from its achievement as we were when Spencer (or Bacon for that matter) first put pen to paper. Indeed it is all the more likely that the continuous attempts made in this direction serve only to demonstrate … the inherent futility of the enterprise.
>
> (Greenleaf 1983: 286)

So, leadership studies have no 'solutions;' nor do leaders. They acquire office by promising to solve problems, but more often than not end up presiding over problem succession as another problem emerges from the one they thought they had just solved. There is no unified theory of leadership. There are too many definitions, and too many theories in too many disciplines. We do not agree on what leadership is, how to study it, or even why we study it. The subject is not just beset by dichotomies; it is also multifaceted, and essentially contested.

Such is the world of leadership, and its contingency and complexity are why so many leaders' careers end in disappointment. In the study and teaching of heroic and transformative leadership, hubris is all too common, so perhaps the final lesson should be: 'A leader is best when people barely know that he exists, not so good when people obey and acclaim him, worst when they despise him. Fail to honour people. They fail to honour you' (Lao Tzu, *The Tao Te Ching*).

10 SUMMARY

As this Handbook demonstrates, political leadership has made a comeback. It was studied intensively not only by political scientists, but also by political sociologists and psychologists, Sovietologists, political anthropologists, comparative and development studies by scholars from the 1940s to the 1970s. Thereafter, the field lost its way with the rise of structuralism, neo-institutionalism, and rational choice approaches to the study of politics, government, and governance. Recently, however, students of politics have returned to studying the role of individual leaders and the exercise of leadership to explain political outcomes. The list of topics is nigh endless: elections, conflict management, public policy, government popularity, development, governance networks, and regional integration. In the media age, leaders are presented and stage-managed—spun—as the solution to almost every social problem. Through the mass media and the Internet, citizens and professional observers follow the rise, impact, and fall of senior political office-holders at closer quarters than ever before.

This Handbook encapsulates the resurgence by asking, where are we today? It orders the multidisciplinary field by identifying the distinct and distinctive contributions of the disciplines. It meets the urgent need to take stock. Our objectives are straightforward:

- to provide comprehensive coverage of all the major disciplines, methods, and regions;
- to showcase both the normative and empirical traditions in political leadership studies;
- to juxtapose behavioural, institutional, and interpretive approaches;
- to cover formal, office-based as well as informal, emergent political leadership;
- to cover leadership in democratic as well as undemocratic polities;
- to draw on scholars from around the world and encourage a comparative perspective.

There was no fixed template for every chapter, but we encouraged contributors to take stock of their topic by covering most, if not all, of the following:

- the historical, intellectual and practical context of political leadership;
- key ideas, questions, and debates;
- landmark contributions—the classics, the mavericks, and the avant-garde;
- the state of the art in each field and its practical import;
- future areas of research.

In our view, a Handbook chapter should not be a cataloguing exercise. Nor is it an advertisement for the contribution of the author and like-minded scholars. Authors were encouraged to air their own views, and not be shy about their own work, *but* they also had to do justice to the breadth and variety of scholarship in the area.

In Part I, we provide a discipline by discipline survey of the field. Although it is a Handbook of *political* leadership, our survey cannot be limited to political science, which is not even the major contributor to the subject. We cover leadership in Western and Eastern political thought, democratic theory, feminism, public administration, psychology, psychoanalysis, social psychology, economics, and anthropology. This section demonstrates the range of insights available and the vast amount of careful analysis. As important, it highlights that there are incommensurable perspectives not only between the several disciplines but also in each one. We believe it supports the case for 'genre blurring' (Geertz 1983): that is, for the several disciplines to draw on one another's theories and methods.

In Part II, we focus on analytical perspectives and methods. We cover institutional analysis, contextual analysis, decision-making analysis, social constructivism, rhetorical analysis, experimental analysis, observational analysis, at-a-distance analysis, biographical analysis, and political personality profiling. Given the persistent desire to emulate the natural sciences in much political science, we believe that this section demonstrates the value of a broad toolkit with which to explore the diverse phenomenon that is political leadership.

In Part III, we turn from theory and methods to look at leadership in several contexts. We examine political leadership at work in civic leadership, political parties, populist movements, the public sphere, policy networks, and during crisis situations. This section demonstrates that a key trend in the present-day study of political leadership is its broader compass. Moving well beyond classic preoccupation with executive government elites, political leadership elides into the broader notion of public leadership. A positional approach has given way to a functional approach (see 't Hart and Uhr 2008). For some, this trend courts the danger of leadership becoming every action that influences others. As a result, leadership loses its distinctive character. For others, it highlights the ubiquity and complexity of leadership.

In Part IV, we look at executive leadership in the West. We begin with varieties of presidential leadership in the USA and then examine presidential communication. Then, we turn to semi-presidential polities, followed by an examination of the varieties of prime ministerial leadership in Westminster and related forms of parliamentary government. Finally, we look at the contingencies of prime ministerial power in the UK, prime ministers and their advisers, and ministers. The aspiration to a comparative science of political leadership confronts the diversity and contingency revealed by these chapters. Not only has any comparative study to encompass the differences between presidential, semi-presidential, and parliamentary polities, but it must also cover the daunting diversity within each category. Idiographic studies offering plausible conjectures seem at least as plausible as nomothetic studies claiming to explain the variations and even to predict.

While the attractions of examining national leaders and leadership are obvious, political leadership below and beyond the national level is also important. So, in Part V, we examine local political leadership, regional political leadership, and international leadership. Then, in Part VI, we look at political leadership in China, Latin America, Russia and the Caucasus, and Africa.

We end in Part VII with three reflective pieces on training political leaders, leadership and gender and a review of what we have learned about political leadership over the past 50 years. We end where we started our overview—with the questions of whether leadership is good or bad and how in democratic societies we contain its worst excesses. The present-day abuses of power in Latin America and Africa should not blind us to the less than auspicious histories of Western democracies which have supported and suffered from some of the worst despots in human history. As the populace of Northern England would phrase it, 'when push comes to shove' the study of political leadership is about the constitutional and political role of leaders in a democratic polity; about how we want to be governed, not about methods, training, and leadership skills.

Even this barest of bare summaries should indicate the scope of this Handbook, whether we are talking about major disciplines, methods, or regions. For those readers who want abstracts for each chapter, they are available at Oxford Handbooks Online (OHO), soon to be renamed Oxford Research Reviews (ORR). Please visit: <www.oxfordhandbooks.com/> and search under 'Political Science'. You will also be able to carry out a keyword search on the volume to identify those chapters most closely aligned with your interests. Finally, and an exciting innovation, the site has changed from an e-book database to an article delivery service and you will be able to download individual chapters through the university library just as you now download articles from journals.

REFERENCES

Ahlquist, J. and Levi, M. (2011). 'Leadership: What it Means, What it Does, and What We Want to Know About It', *Annual Review of Political Science*, 14: 1–24.

Bendor, J. M. (1985). *Parallel Systems: Redundancy in Government*. Berkeley, CA: University of California Press.

Bennister, M. (2012). *Prime Ministers in Power*. Basingstoke: Palgrave.

Bevir, M. and Rhodes, R. A. W. (2003). *Interpreting British Governance*. London: Routledge.

Borchert, J. and Zeiss, J., eds. (2003). *The Political Class in Advanced Democracies*. Oxford: Oxford University Press.

Bose, M. and Landis, M., eds. (2011). *The Uses and Abuses of Presidential Ratings*. New York: Nova Science Publishers.

Bovens, M. (1998). *The Quest for Responsibility: Accountability and Citizenship in Complex Organizations*. Cambridge: Cambridge University Press.

Bovens, M. and Wille, A. (2009). *Diploma Democracy: On the Tension between Meritocracy and Democracy*. Utrecht: Netherlands Organization for Scientific Reasearch (NWO).

Bryman, A., Collinson, D., Grint, K., Jackson, D., and Uhl-Bien, M., eds. (2011). *The SAGE Handbook of Leadership*. Thousand Oaks: SAGE.

Bueno de Mesquita, B., Smith, A., Siverson, R., and Morrow, J. (2004). *The Logic of Political Survival*. Cambridge, MA: MIT Press.

Burns, J. M. (1978). *Leadership*. New York: Harper and Row.

Burns, J. M. (2003). *Transforming Leadership*. New York: Grove.

Couto, R. A. (2010). *Political and Civic Leadership: A Reference Handbook*. Thousand Oaks, CA: SAGE.

Cross, W. and Blais, A. (2012). 'Who Selects Party Leaders?' *Party Politics*, 18 (2): 127–50.

Dowding, K. M. (1996). *Power*. Minneapolis, MN: University of Minnesota Press.

Dowding, K. M. (2008). 'Perceptions of Leadership', in P. 't Hart and J. Uhr (eds), *Public Leadership: Perspectives and Practices*. Canberra: ANU ePress, 93–102.

Edelman, M. (1985) [1964]. *The Symbolic Uses of Politics*. Paperback edition with a new afterword. Urbana, IL: University of Illinois Press.

Elgie, R. (1995). *Political Leadership in Liberal Democracies*. London: Macmillan.

Gardner, J. W. (1968). *No Easy Victories*. New York: Joanna Cotler Books.

Geer, J. G. (1996). *From Tea Leaves to Opinion Polls: A Theory of Democratic Leadership*. New York: Columbia University Press.

Geertz, C. (1983). *Local Knowledge: Further Essays in Interpretive Anthropology*. New York: Basic Books.

George, A. L. (1974). 'Adaptation to Stress in Political Decision Making: The Individual, Small Group, and Organizational Contexts', in G. V. Coelho, D. A. Hamburg and J. B. Adams (eds), *Coping and Adaptation*. New York: Basic Books, 176–248.

George, A. L. and George, J. L. (1964) [1956]. *Woodrow Wilson and Colonel House: A Personality Study*. Mineola, NY: Dover Publications.

Goethals, G. R., Sorenson, G. J., and Burns, J. M., eds. (2004). *Encyclopedia of Leadership*, Vol. 1–4. Thousand Oaks, CA: SAGE.

Greenleaf, W. H. (1983). *The British Political Tradition. Volume 1: The Rise of Collectivism*. London: Methuen.

Greenstein, F. I. (1975) [1969]. *Personality and Politics*. New York: Norton.

Greenstein, F. I. (1982). *The Hidden-Hand Presidency: Eisenhower as Leader*. New York: Basic Books.

Greenstein, F. I. (2009). *The Presidential Difference: Leadership Style from FDR to George W. Bush*. Princeton, NJ: Princeton University Press.

Heifetz, R. (1994). *Leadership Without Easy Answers*. Cambridge, MA: Harvard University Press.

Heifetz, R., Grashow, A., and Linsky, M. (2009). *The Practice of Adaptive Leadership*. Cambridge, MA: Harvard Business.

Helms, L., ed. (2012). *Comparative Political Leadership*. Basingstoke: Palgrave Macmillan.

Hendriks, F. (2010). *Vital Democracy: A Theory of Democracy in Action*. Oxford: Oxford University Press.

Hennessy, P. (2000). *The Prime Minister*. London: Penguin.

Hook, S. (1943). *The Hero in History: A Study in Limitation and Possibility*. New York: John Day.

Kane, J. and Patapan, H. (2012). *The Democratic Leader: How Democracy Defines, Empowers and Limits its Leaders*. Oxford: Oxford University Press.

Kane, J., Patapan, H. and 't Hart, P. (2009). 'Dispersed Democratic Leadership', in J. Kane, H. Patapan and P. 't Hart (eds), *Dispersed Democratic Leadership: Origins, Dynamics, and Implications*. Oxford: Oxford University Press, 1–12.

Keane, J. (2009). *The Life and Death of Democracy*. London: Simon and Schuster.

Kellerman, B. (2004). *Bad Leadership: What it Is, How it Happens, Why it Matters*. Cambridge, MA: Harvard Business School Press.

Kellerman, B. (2012). *The End of Leadership*. New York: Harper Business.

Keohane, N. (2010). *Thinking about Leadership*. Princeton, NJ: Princeton University Press.

Korosenyi, A., Slomp, A., and Femia, J., eds. (2009). *Political Leadership in Liberal and Democratic Theory*. London: Imprint Academic.

Lipman-Blumen, J. (2004). *The Allure of Toxic Leaders*. Oxford: Oxford University Press.

McDermott, R. (2007). *Presidential Illness, Leadership and Decision Making*. Cambridge: Cambridge University Press.

March, J. G. and Weil, T. (2005). *On Leadership*. Oxford: Wiley-Blackwell.

Marquand, D. (2009). 'Biography', in M. Flinders, A. Gamble, C. Hay, and M. Kenny (eds), *The Oxford Handbook of British Politics*. Oxford: Oxford University Press, 187–200.

Marx, K. (1934) [1852]. *The Eighteenth Brumaire of Louis Bonaparte*. Moscow: Progress Publishers.

Masciulli, J. A., Mochanov, M., and Knight, W. A. (2009). 'Political Leadership in Context', in *The Ashgate Research Companion to Political Leadership*. Aldershot: Ashgate, 3–27.

Messick, D. M. and Kramer, R. M., eds. (2005). *The Psychology of Leadership: New Perspectives and Research*. Mahwah, NJ: Erlbaum.

Owen, D. (2008). *In Sickness and Power: Illness in Heads of Government During the Last 100 Years*. London: Methuen.

Pimlott, B. (1992). *Harold Wilson*. London: HarperCollins.

Rawnsley, A. (2001). *Servants of the People: The Inside Story of New Labour*. London: Penguin Books; revised edition.

Rhodes, R. A. W. (2011). *Everyday Life in British Government*. Oxford: Oxford University Press.

Rhodes, R. A. W., Wanna, J., and Weller, P. (2009). *Comparing Westminster*. Oxford: Oxford University Press.

Rucht, D. (2012). 'Leadership in Social and Political Movements: A Comparative Exploration', in L. Helms (ed.), *Comparative Political Leadership*. Basingstoke: Palgrave, 99–118.

Ruscio, K. W. (2004). *The Leadership Dilemma in Modern Democracy*. Cheltenham: Edward Elgar.

Skowronek, S. (1993). *The Politics Presidents Make: Leadership from John Adams to George Bush*. Cambridge, MA: Harvard Belknap University Press.

Steinberg, B. (2008). *Women in Power: The Personalities and Leadership Styles of Indira Gandhi, Golda Meir, and Margaret Thatcher*. Montreal: McGill-Queen's University Press.

Strangio, P., 't Hart, P., and Walter, J., eds. (2013). *Understanding Prime Ministerial Performance: Comparative Perspectives*. Oxford: Oxford University Press.

't Hart, P. (2011). 'Evaluating Public Leadership: Towards an Assessment Framework', *Public Money and Management*, 31 (5): 323–330.

't Hart, P. and Uhr, J. (2008). *Public Leadership: Perspectives and Practices*. Canberra: ANU E Press.

't Hart, P. and Uhr, J., eds. (2011). *How Power Changes Hands: Transition and Succession in Government*. Basingstoke: Palgrave Macmillan.

't Hart, P. (2014). *Understanding Public Leadership*. Basingstoke: Palgrave Macmillan.

Weber, M. (1991) [1948]. 'Politics as a Vocation', in H. Gerth and C. Wright Mills (eds), *From Max Weber: Essays in Sociology*. London: Routledge, 77–128.

Winter, D. G. (2005). 'Things I've Learned about Personality from Studying Political Leaders at a Distance', *Journal of Personality*, 73 (3): 557–84.

Wren, J. T. (2007). *Inventing Leadership: The Challenge of Democracy*. Cheltenham: Edward Elgar.

PART I

THINKING ABOUT POLITICAL LEADERSHIP: TRADITIONS AND DISCIPLINES

CHAPTER 2

··

WESTERN POLITICAL
THOUGHT

··

NANNERL O. KEOHANE

1 INTRODUCTION

'LEADERSHIP' is not a word that often appears in the canonical works of Western political thought. It was first included in English dictionaries in the nineteenth century (Rost 1991: 18). Yet concepts closely connected with leadership are fundamental to many texts of political philosophy. Leadership pervades the familiar concepts of sovereignty, ruling, and representation.

In its broadest sense, leadership is central to all human social activity: 'Leaders determine or clarify goals for a group of individuals and bring together the energies of members of that group to accomplish those goals' (Keohane 2010: 23). Political leadership is an especially prominent example of this behaviour, the type that springs to mind when most of us think about leadership. The history of Western political thought is full of reflections on leadership in this sense, how it originates and what its proper purposes should be, how it can be legitimated and how it can be lost.

Authority, conferred by office or attained by performance, is often linked with leadership. Yet not all political leaders have formal positions of authority, and not all persons who hold official authority provide leadership. As John Gardner puts it: 'We have all occasionally encountered top persons who couldn't lead a squad of seven-year olds to the ice cream counter' (Gardner 2010: 2). Power is also closely connected with leadership; leaders generally exercise power; but not all powerful persons are leaders. Think of a playground bully or a mugger with a gun.

Political leaders, then, are often but not always in positions of official authority. Defining goals and mobilizing energies involve the exercise of power in some form; but leadership cannot be reduced to power per se.

In conversations about political philosophy in ancient Greece and Rome, most discussions of leadership focused on how statesmen or rulers should be educated and how they should use their power. From the Renaissance until the present day, primary attention was shifted to two other questions: the connections between leaders and citizens, and how the scope of appropriate political activity should be defined and settled.

Throughout these eras a defining tension has marked the discussion of leadership in Western political thought. This tension is between the expertise and creative possibilities of leadership, on the one hand, and the dangers of leadership, the need to control the exercise of power, on the other. This tension is also expressed in the stark contrast between a ruler doing whatever he thinks he needs to do to retain his power and accomplish his goals, and the duties and obligations of political leaders. Some political theorists highlight the work of individual leaders; others emphasize the constitutional framework that circumscribes their authority. Both perspectives emphasize important dimensions of leadership, but they are not easily compatible.

This raises a fundamental question: in what circumstances should citizens or subjects support and enable the visionary capacities of a strong leader, and when should they instead institute or bolster confining structures that will make it less likely that leaders can misuse their power? This dilemma has been central in the history of political theory in the West, was very much present in the founding discussions of the Constitution of the United States, and continues to occupy social scientists, journalists, leaders, and citizens today. Contemporary political events indicate the timeless relevance of this question.

I will juxtapose five pairs of theorists in whose work the tensions I have just described can be discerned. These writers all expound complex theories and resist pigeonholing; in broad terms, however, each pair includes theorists who take opposed positions in this debate: Plato and Aristotle, Cicero and Machiavelli, Montesquieu and Rousseau, Michels and Arendt, Lenin and Weber. Readers may question the omission of their favourite theorists from this array. The criterion for inclusion was specific attention to the problems and possibilities of political leadership. Hobbes and Locke, for instance, provide incomparable insights on a number of aspects of political life; but, in my view, they have little to say about leadership. However, if readers are moved to extend the discussion to include other theorists, this chapter will have achieved one of its major purposes.

2   PLATO AND ARISTOTLE

Plato (428–347 BC) provided one of the earliest and most influential statements of the initial perspective in the tension described above. In the *Gorgias, Republic,* and *Statesman,* the statesman or philosopher–guardian's distinctive art and knowledge set him apart from ordinary citizens, and both legitimate and determine the content of his rule. External constraints on this leadership would be counterproductive for all concerned.

In *Gorgias,* Socrates argues that the political art is concerned with the health of the soul, as gymnastics and medicine address the health of the body. He distinguishes those competent to practise this art from orators or tyrants who may sway the people or control them but cannot bring about what is best for the city. Socrates counsels his young interlocutors to consider statesmanship, not as a means of self-advancement or doing what they personally desire, but to 'take in hand the tending of the city and its citizens with the aim of making the citizens themselves as good as possible' (Plato 1961: 513ᵉ).

In the *Republic*, Socrates and his friends engage in constructing a 'city in speech'. Each citizen produces a needed good or service which he is best equipped to provide; in the earliest stages of the story, none of them is charged with governing. Leadership arises only when the city is enlarged, which means going to war. Since fighting is itself an art and a profession, a new class of citizens must be created, the guardians. The remainder of the dialogue is devoted to the talents, education, and lifestyle of these philosopher–guardians.

Thus for Plato, as for Machiavelli and Weber, violence is at the root of political leadership. The philosopher–guardians' duty of readiness for war initially determines the talents they need and how they should be educated. They live in dormitories, exercise together, and take their meals in mess-halls. Yet much of their time is spent preparing to appreciate philosophy as the source of the true knowledge to direct the city. Even though the figure of the political leader in these dialogues was paradigmatically male, in the *Republic* Plato was willing to consider the possibility that women can also be appropriate practitioners of political leadership. Women in the guardian class are educated along with men and have the same pattern of life.

As is also true for Machiavelli and Weber, Plato's political leaders routinely engage in the deception of other citizens, including the younger guardians. Plato says specifically that the rulers (and only the rulers) may appropriately lie for the benefit of the state (389ᵇ).

The philosopher–guardians share all things in common to prevent any private loves or desires from causing strife within the ruling group or interfering with their basic commitment to tend the city and protect its citizens. Plato thus addresses the familiar problem of the inequality between rulers and ruled by dictating a radically different lifestyle for his rulers. Men and women in the producing classes enjoy material possessions, family life, and conventional luxuries, while the guardians have a superior education, the pleasures of comradeship and philosophizing, and the status of rulers of the city. The implication is that no one will want to exchange his pattern of life for the alternative, so envy—a major source of political discontent—is avoided from the outset.

One of the major themes of the *Republic* is the *expertise* of the philosopher–guardians, the hard-won knowledge that sets them apart from ordinary citizens. In book VI (488ᵇ⁻ᵉ), Plato offers an analogy between the political leader and a pilot who has studied the stars and currents and properties of his ship. In the *Statesman*, Plato uses other analogies from pastoral life and cybernetics. He specifies that many of the tasks we normally associate with leadership can be delegated to others, including making speeches, generalship, judging. The king's role is to oversee and guide the work of others, relying on the broad perceptions and understandings that are part of the true kingly art. This art 'weaves all into its unified fabric with perfect skill. It is a universal art and so we call it by a name of universal scope ... statesmanship' (305^{d-e}).

In all these dialogues Plato describes an art of political leadership (that is, states-manship or ruling) that emphasizes natural talent, rigorous training, the possession of arcane expertise, and responsibility for providing directive guidance to human communities. The conception of leadership expressed here is exceptionally lofty, almost godlike in its scope. The abuse of power is avoided, not by external constitutional restraints on the leader's authority, but by internal restraints of character, education, and a profound sense of duty.

Could any human being ever achieve such a lofty level of expertise and commitment, avoiding all temptations to abuse power, truly understanding what is best for all members of a community? Would other men and women be well served where so much authority and power are given to a few individuals, so that most have no role in directing their own lives? One of Plato's earliest and most acute critics was Aristotle, who devoted a large portion of his *Politics* to showing why the answer to both questions is clearly 'No'.

Aristotle (384–322 BC) endorses the principle that those best equipped to rule should do so, but denies that this entails a designated ruling group. Those best equipped to rule are the members of the political association who know the city and have a direct interest in its flourishing. The basic equality of all citizens and the requirement dictated by justice that all participate in office yield the conclusion that citizens should take turns providing political leadership. 'This means that some rule and others are ruled in turn, as if they had become, for the time being, different people' (Aristotle 1995: 1261^a).

Aristotle considers the possibility that one man could be so superior in capacity and virtue that he should be acknowledged as king (1284^b, 1288^a). He regards this, however, as an unlikely situation, and almost surely an unstable one. Like Plato, he was well aware of the tendency for monarchy to degenerate into tyranny. In addition, he was not persuaded by Plato's elaborate plans for preventing his guardians from abusing their power over other citizens. Instead, Aristotle concentrated on constructing a framework for the use of power.

Aristotle describes a constitution as 'an organization of offices in the city, by which the method of their distribution is fixed, the sovereign authority is determined, and the nature of the end to be pursued by the association and all its members should be prescribed' (1289^a). He distinguishes three major types of constitutions, depending on the locus of sovereign authority, the goals of the leaders and the size of the ruling group: kingship, aristocracy, and a constitutional government or polity; and their perversions: tyranny, oligarchy, and democracy. He gives the name of constitutional government to a city in which the citizens as a whole govern with a view to the common interest (1279^a).

On the political capacity of ordinary citizens, Aristotle has a view very different from Plato's; he asserts that 'it is possible that they may surpass—collectively and as a body, although not individually—the quality of the few best ... Each has his share of goodness and practical wisdom; and when all meet together, the people may thus become something like a single person [with] many qualities of character and intelligence' (1281^{a-b}).

The political art is one of a class of skills whose excellence can best be appreciated by the beneficiary rather than the practitioner, just as the diner, not the cook, is the best judge of the quality of the meal. The people as a whole generally own more property than any individual rich citizen and thus have a larger interest to protect. For all these reasons, it is rare to find any particular individual who has more expertise in governing than a group of citizens working together.

Aristotle defines the statesman as one who 'exercises his authority in conformity with the rules imposed by the art of statesmanship and as one who rules and is ruled in turn' (1252^a). In his capacity as ruler, the citizen/statesman shows a distinctive art or skill. This skill, according to Aristotle, must be learned in part by being ruled; men (in this case, only men are included) learn to lead by having been good followers. The distinctive form of skill or excellence that sets the citizen as statesman or leader apart from the same citizen in his capacity as follower is practical wisdom—prudence, or good judgement (1277^b). This shared prudential leadership, exercised only within a constitutional framework, is distinctly different from the godlike vision and extraordinary powers of Plato's statesman.

3 Cicero and Machiavelli

In a Platonic vein, Marcus Tullius Cicero (106–43 BC) gives his highest praise to 'a ruler who is good and wise and versed in all that contributes to the advantage and prestige of the state; who is, as it were, the guardian and steward of the commonwealth, for so we should call anyone who directs and pilots the state' (Cicero 1929: ii, p. xxix). Yet he favours a mixed form of government combining elements of kingship, aristocracy, and democracy (i, pp. xxxv, xlv). In such a framework, the leader's political skill, the merits of the nobler classes, and the rights of the many are all accommodated. In this way he echoes the balanced approach advanced by Aristotle.

Like Plato and Aristotle, Cicero argues that, if a single man could govern the state well by reason of his superior wisdom and prudence, nothing else would be needed (i, p. xxxiv). However, he notes that, even in the best monarchy, everyone except the king is effectively disbarred from the protection of the law and from participating in deliberation about public functions. In Cicero's view, these are rights that should extend to all citizens (i, p. xxvii). Thus the ideal system is one in which the people are wise enough to *choose* superior men for public office, rather than deferring to those best qualified to govern them (as Plato would have it) or sharing equally in the ruling (Aristotle's preferred arrangement).

Political leadership, however, does not depend only on one's qualifications for office; Cicero acknowledges the role of luck in obtaining and maintaining power (Cicero 1991: i. 115). He asks: 'Can anyone be unaware of the great power of fortune, which impels one in either direction, towards success or towards adversity? Whenever we enjoy her prospering breezes we are carried to the haven for which we long; when she blows in our face we are shipwrecked' (ii. 19).

Cicero reserves his sharpest condemnation for the view that a human act can be honourable but not beneficial, or beneficial but not honourable. He says specifically that cruelty can never be beneficial, since this vice is so deeply hostile to the nature of man (iii. 46). When he considers the motivations that lead some men to follow others, he insists that 'there is nothing at all more suited to protecting and retaining influence than to be loved, and nothing less suited than to be feared . . . Fear is a poor guardian over any length of time; but goodwill keeps faithful guard for ever' (ii. 23). With this in mind, he catalogues the virtues that elicit the love of the people, including liberality, beneficence, and keeping faith (ii. 32).

Theorists for more than a millennium built on Cicero's ideas as counsel for rulers. In *Il Principe*, Niccolò Machiavelli (1469–1527) was clearly in dialogue with Cicero and the subsequent 'Mirror of Princes' literature. But he inverted Cicero's message in a bold and shocking fashion. *The Prince* provides the paradigmatic statement in the Western political tradition of the view that effective leadership is personal, powerful, and, to a large degree, unconstrained. The theme of the treatise is not guardianship or statesmanship, but the success of the individual prince in obtaining and retaining power.

Machiavelli notes that rulers succeed primarily because of their innate abilities (*virtú*)—qualities such as courage, decisiveness, good judgement, and ruthlessness— but also by luck (*fortuna*) (Machiavelli 1988: ch. I). Like Cicero, he uses metaphors from nature to describe the power of *fortuna*, comparing it to a dangerous river that destroys everything in its path when it is in flood. A wise man takes precautions to protect against the ravages of fortune, building dikes or dams to control its flow. Princes succeed when their actions are in line with the circumstances they confront, and fail when these two things are not in harmony (ch. XXV).

New princes should imitate great predecessors and learn from their examples. From the lives of men of exceptional ability—Moses, Cyrus, Romulus, and Theseus— Machiavelli draws the insight that leaders are most likely to succeed if they do not have to rely greatly on luck. He notes also that these men were warriors, asserting that 'all armed prophets succeed whereas unarmed ones fail' (ch. VI). In the light of the success of unarmed prophets such as Gandhi or Martin Luther King, Jr, we might question this bold generalization. For Machiavelli, however, it was clear that armed men are feared and respected, whereas unarmed princes are despised by all and distrusted by the military, whose loyalty is crucial to their success. Therefore, a wise prince should study the art of war and be continually prepared to practise it (ch. XIV).

More generally, Machiavelli asserts that 'a ruler who wishes to maintain his power must be prepared to act immorally when this becomes necessary' (ch. XV). It is advantageous to have the *reputation* of being virtuous (generous, merciful, honest, trustworthy), but that does not mean a ruler should always *be* generous or merciful; and he has no obligation to keep his promises when doing so would undermine his power. Quite the opposite: a successful prince must be 'a great feigner and dissembler' (ch. XVIII). The prudent prince should also recognize that 'doing some things that seem virtuous may result in one's ruin, whereas doing other things that seem vicious may strengthen one's position and cause one to flourish' and provide more effective government (chs XV, XVII).

A prince may seek the support either of the populace or of the nobles, since these two classes are found in all cities. The nobles are ambitious for power, whereas the people can be satisfied if they are protected from oppression. Also, it is more difficult to protect yourself from the people because there are so many of them, whereas the ruler can replace hostile nobles if necessary (ch. IX). A wise prince makes sure that the people recognize their dependence on him, and never takes their support for granted.

Machiavelli notes specifically Cicero's question about whether it is better for the prince to be loved than feared (ch. XVII). In his view, 'it is desirable to be both loved and feared; but it is difficult to achieve both, and if one of them has to be lacking, it is much safer to be feared than loved'. No one can count on the love of his people, particularly in hard times, and a wise ruler should always depend on something he can control, not factors that are controlled by others. If the people fear him, they will be less likely to harm or resist him. Above all, the ruler should avoid being hated; a leader who is despised is always vulnerable to being overthrown or assassinated.

Referring to the prince's relationships with his closest followers, the members of his cabinet, or inner staff, Machiavelli says that choosing ministers is a particularly important decision for a ruler (ch. XXII). A prince's intelligence and capacity will be judged by the 'quality of the men around him. If they are capable and loyal, he should always be taken to be shrewd, because he was able to recognize their ability and retain their loyalty.' Even a man with a second-rate mind can appear intelligent and shrewd if he is well counselled; but a prince must always be on guard against flattery, taking counsel wisely (ch. XXIII).

Such direct, practical advice, rooted in Machiavelli's own experience and observation of many leaders, explains the durable influence and fascination of *The Prince*, even for readers put off by its more 'Machiavellian' sections. The text has also served as a perennial handbook for princes interested above all in maintaining power and willing to use any measures to achieve this goal.

4 MONTESQUIEU AND ROUSSEAU

In a passage from *The Spirit of the Laws* that sheds a rather different light on the maxims of *The Prince*, Montesquieu (1689–1755) notes that 'the principle of despotic government is fear', and in such situations, 'the preservation of the state is only the preservation of the prince' (Montesquieu 1949: iii. 14). Against the stark simplicity of despotism he juxtaposes a moderate government akin to that proposed by Aristotle and Cicero, which requires that the lawgiver 'combine the several powers: to regulate, temper and set them in motion; to give, as it were, ballast to one, in order to enable it to counterpoise the other. This is a masterpiece of legislation, rarely produced by hazard, and seldom attained by prudence' (ii. 1).

Explaining how this masterpiece might be assembled, Montesquieu notes that in a country of free citizens everyone should essentially govern himself, and the whole people together should exercise the legislative power. However, such a formula cannot be achieved in large states, and faces significant inconveniences in smaller ones. Therefore, in practice, the best system is one in which representatives of the people undertake what they cannot do for themselves (xi. 6). Unlike Aristotle, Montesquieu regards the people collectively as incapable of dealing with public affairs. He asserts that a monarch should hold executive power because of the need for rapid and expeditious action; this power should not be in the same hands as the legislative power exercised by the people's representatives.

Montesquieu specified that the legislative body should be made up of two parts, which can 'check one another by the mutual privilege of rejecting', and are in turn 'both restrained by the executive power, as the executive is by the legislative'. In a passage that Machiavelli would have scorned, but that holds no surprises for observers of American democracy, Montesquieu notes that 'these three powers should naturally form a state of repose or inaction'. Since, in order to govern, they sometimes have to bestir themselves, 'they are forced to move, but still in concert'. What 'forces' them to move, however, is left unclear.

In his most profound political treatise, *The Social Contract*, Montesquieu's iconoclastic contemporary Jean-Jacques Rousseau (1712–78) identifies with unusual precision the 'forces' that can move a political body. Unlike many later theorists of democratic participation, Rousseau is quite clear that, without leadership, a body of people cannot act, beyond voting yes or no on straightforward questions that are put to them. The people should be the author of the laws, but how will they produce these laws? 'Will it be by common agreement, by a sudden inspiration? Has the body politic an organ to state its wills? Who will give it the foresight necessary to form its acts…?' A 'blind multitude' cannot undertake an action as complex as writing a set of laws, and thus the first requirement for a good political order, in Rousseau's book, is a gifted and inspired Lawgiver (Rousseau 1997: ii. 6).

Rousseau insists that this extraordinary founder is not a prince; he should have no power to command other men. Anticipating recent discussions of charismatic authority, he says that 'the great soul of the Lawgiver is the true miracle which must prove his mission' (ii. 7). Anyone can feign contact with some divinity, bribe an oracle, delude a gullible populace; but Rousseau's Lawgiver is an inspired genius, a leader whose mission ends when the legal system he designs has been accepted by the people. From that point forward, laws must be passed by the whole people assembled as the sovereign (iii. 12). Whenever that happens, the government that has been formed to execute the popular will is temporarily dissolved, because where those who are the principals are assembled, there is no place for representation (iii. 14).

Like Plato, Cicero, and Montesquieu, Rousseau was convinced that the best system is one in which 'the wisest govern the multitude, so long as it is certain that they will govern for its advantage and not for their own' (iii. 5). He was referring here to rule by a small number of wise men rather than a monarch, believing that monarchs will inevitably abuse their power. Kings are told that their true interest lies in having their people flourish, 'but they know perfectly well that this is not true. Their personal interest is first of all that the people be weak, wretched, and never able to resist them' (iii. 6). To prevent such an outcome, instead of Montesquieu's system of elaborate institutional checks and balances, Rousseau preserves the legislative sovereignty of the community assembled as a whole.

Rousseau was insistent that the people are the only appropriate sovereign in any state. Like Montesquieu, however, he believed that ordinary people are not good at making complex political decisions. Moreover, requiring them to do so undermines their effective sovereignty (iii. 15). The implementation of the laws consists in decisions that affect individuals or some portion of the state, not the body of citizens as a whole. If the people had such a power, this would violate their collective wholeness, the foundation of the political system. 'The public force therefore has to have its own agent which unites and puts it to work in accordance with the directives of the general will', and this agent is the government, or the executive (iii. 1). Describing the character and duties of those who hold this executive power is a key purpose of the rest of the treatise.

The Social Contract endeavours to 'combine what right permits with what interest prescribes, so that justice and utility may not be disjointed' (i. 1). In this Rousseau departs both from Cicero, who asserted that what is honest will always be beneficial, and from Machiavelli, who argued that the prince must sometimes be prepared to behave immorally in order to do his job. Rousseau recognizes that justice and utility can sometimes dictate different outcomes; his goal is to find a way to bring them together in a form of leadership that will provide both effectiveness and accountability.

Notwithstanding his normative purposes and commitment to popular sovereignty, Rousseau was an acute realist in thinking about power. Among several different political bodies, he argues that power will gravitate to the one with the smallest number of members (iii. 4). He also asserts that the government (the executive) will strive to gain power from the sovereign (the *demos*), so that the basic political forces will inevitably be in tension (iii. 1, 18). In these generalizations, he anticipates some of the most heated debates about governance and leadership in the next two centuries, as republican and democratic governments were for the first time widely instituted in the West.

5 MICHELS AND ARENDT

Like Rousseau, Roberto Michels (1876–1936) was convinced that broadly shared executive power and a 'leaderless organization' are impossibilities. 'In all times, in all phases of development, in all branches of human activity, there have been leaders' (Michels 1962: 72). Beyond this, however, Michels claims that democracy, in the sense of equal political participation, inevitably encounters obstacles 'not merely imposed from without, but spontaneously surgent from within'. This powerful tendency toward oligarchy rests '(1) upon the nature of the human individual; (2) upon the nature of the political struggle; and (3) upon the nature of organization' (p. 6).

Michels points to several features of human nature that explain the 'inevitability of oligarchy'. One is the ubiquitous desire to transmit good things to your children, including political privilege and status. Like Montesquieu, Michels also had little faith in the political competence of ordinary people or their potential for sustained political involvement. 'Man as individual is by nature predestined to be guided,' he says, and 'the apathy of the masses and their need for guidance has as its counterpart in the leaders a natural greed for power' (p. 367). Some individuals desire power and are willing to expend considerable effort to obtain it; once they have done this, they are often reluctant to return to ordinary life. For their part, followers may be quite content to let others do the hard work of politics while they get on with their own lives. In this way, Michels implicitly rejects Aristotle's system of ruling and being ruled in turn as unrealistic in terms of both human psychology and the dynamics of organizations.

Certain individuals in any society have particular advantages in becoming leaders. These include 'money and its equivalents (economic superiority), tradition and heredi-tary transmission (historical superiority)', and, most important, 'the formal instruction of the leaders (so-called intellectual superiority)'. For Michels, even when roughly equal individuals create an organization such as a political party, the experience and knowl-edge that some obtain through holding positions of leadership soon sets them apart from their fellows (pp. 107–10). It is hard to sacrifice such expertise in favour of enforced rotation in office-holding when the success of the organization may depend on the skills the leaders have acquired through their experience.

'The nature of organization' also promotes oligarchy. Michels says it is impossible for all members of an organization to determine together a course of action, even if they agree on policy directions. Nor can the group as a whole implement decisions. In the same spirit as Rousseau, Michels notes that, 'even in groups sincerely animated with the demo-cratic spirit, current business, the preparation and the carrying out of the most important actions, is necessarily left in the hands of individuals'. In the end, Michels asserts, 'the principal cause of oligarchy in the democratic parties is to be found in the *technical indis-pensability of leadership*' (pp. 111–14, 364; emphasis added). Leadership, in this sense, is about making and implementing decisions for large numbers of other people.

The approach of Hannah Arendt (1906–75) to the exercise of political power was very different from that of Michels. She defines power as a resource available only to a plural-ity of persons. In this, power differs from force or strength.

> While strength is the natural quality of an individual seen in isolation, power springs up between men when they act together and vanishes the moment they dis-perse...What keeps people together after the fleeting moment of action has passed (and what we today call 'organization') and what at the same time they keep alive through remaining together is power.
>
> (Arendt 1958: 200–1)

The citizens of classical Athens experienced this distinctive form of human activity to the fullest; few other peoples have reached this height.

Arendt asserts that most political philosophy from Plato onwards has been dedicated to finding ways to avoid the onerous and exhilarating burdens of direct political engagement. 'The hallmark of all such escapes is the concept of rule, that is, the notion that men can lawfully and politically live together only when some are entitled to command and the others forced to obey' (p. 222). Leadership and initiative become the prerogative of one individual or a few rather than the community of citizens.

In Arendt's view, political freedom means not being subject to 'the command of another *and* not to be in command oneself', neither ruling nor being ruled (p. 32). To this idealized Greek conception of political equality and political involvement, she contrasted the medieval view that 'private individuals have interests in common, material and spiritual, and that they can retain their privacy and attend to their own business only if one of them takes it upon himself to look out for this common interest' (p. 35). This illusion that one individual can initiate political action and perform on behalf of others to achieve the common good is a profound misconception, Arendt argues. It blurs the distinction between the unequal relations characteristic of the Aristotelian household and the true space of political action. This division-of-labour approach to politics has unfortunately become a hallmark of the modern era.

For Arendt, all varieties of one-man rule, including Plato's philosopher-king, are deformations of the essential nature of political life (p. 221). The leaders may be benevolent and well disposed, but such regimes 'all have in common the banishment of citizens from the public realm and the insistence that they mind their private business' and leave the public business to the ruler. Like Aristotle, Cicero, and Rousseau, Arendt was convinced that political participation in governing is the distinctive feature of a truly human life.

For Arendt, 'the reality of the public realm relies on the simultaneous presence of innumerable perspectives and aspects in which the common world presents itself' (p. 57). The *polis* is defined, not by the city walls, but as 'the organization of the people as it arises out of acting and speaking together, and its true space lies between people living together for this purpose, no matter where they happen to be' (p. 198). No one can live in this rarefied space all the time: citizens also need the counterpart world of privacy, the home, and civil society, to which they can retreat. When they are engaged together in this common space, however, they create a political world and a form of plural leadership in which they make provisions for the common good and shape their shared life.

Arendt's theory can be read as describing a 'leaderless' form of political activity. She can also be interpreted, however, as presenting an alternative theory of leadership. Instead of identifying 'ruling' over others as the distinctive activity of political leadership, Arendt describes a situation in which citizens *collectively* craft solutions to common problems, define and clarify their common goals, and mobilize the energies of their community to act in concert. No one is ruling and no one is being ruled: instead, Rousseau's vision of a truly democratic decision-making process is developed in a direction that proved very fruitful for later theorists of deliberative democracy.

6 LENIN AND WEBER

Vladimir Ilyich Lenin (1870–1924) would surely have regarded Arendt's theories as naive abstractions and agreed with Michels on the 'technical indispensability of leadership'. Lenin had no use for broad political participation or vague assemblies producing the general will of the people. It was precisely such sentiments in the socialist parties with which he was familiar that led him to tackle the question 'What is to be Done?' This essay addressed a major lacuna in Marxist theory: the absence of any reference to leadership or practical political strategies in the struggle to overthrow capitalist domination and establish the dictatorship of the proletariat.

Lenin wrote specifically to 'combat spontaneity', a proclivity that he found wasteful and counterproductive (Lenin 1929: 41). He envisioned his party as a vanguard within the proletariat, disciplined, ruthless, and determined to succeed. His rhetoric left no doubt about the embattled nature of the effort: 'We are marching in a compact group along a precipitous and difficult path, firmly holding each other by the hand. We are surrounded on all sides by enemies and are under their almost constant fire.' Lenin's purpose was to overrule those who proposed to try conciliation, who wanted to bring everyone along with them or even 'retreat into the adjacent marsh' (p. 15).

The political consciousness necessary to make a revolution would never emerge spontaneously among the working class; it must be brought to them 'from without', by a small group of enlightened, battle-tested leaders (p. 32). Lenin asserted firmly that 'professional revolutionists' are essential to making a successful revolution, a 'stable organization of leaders to maintain continuity' (p. 116). 'Without the "dozen" of tried and talented leaders... professionally trained, schooled by long experience and working in perfect harmony, no class in modern society is capable of conducting a determined struggle' (p. 114).

This elite cadre of leaders must be thoughtfully chosen, carefully trained, and maintain secrecy among themselves. Lenin was convinced that this would lead to 'complete, comradely mutual confidence among revolutionists'. Members of a revolutionary organization do not have time 'to think about the toy forms of democracy'. However, 'they have a lively sense of their *responsibility*, because they know from experience that an organization of real revolutionists will stop at nothing to rid itself of an undesirable member' (p. 131).

Lenin's chilling conception of the 'responsibility' of leaders as designed to avoid unpleasant retribution by colleagues was very different from the meaning of this term for his contemporary Max Weber (1864–1920). In his lecture entitled 'Politics as a Vocation', Weber asserted that anyone who holds political power needs three qualities: 'passion, a feeling of responsibility, and a sense of proportion'.

Passion in this sense means serving a cause, having a goal larger than your own advancement as a leader. A good leader, however, does not just pursue such a passion single-mindedly. The leader must also be aware of his responsibility for those he leads and for the state, and show a sense of proportion in pursuing the chosen purpose. This detached sense of proportion or perspective is rarely found in conjunction with passionate devotion to a cause, which helps explain why truly exemplary leaders are so rare. For Weber, proportion is 'the decisive psychological quality of a politician: his ability to let realities work upon him with inner concentration and calmness. Hence his *distance* to things and men', and even distance towards himself (Weber 1958: 115). The leader must be able to step back and look coolly at his own behaviour.

One of the reasons this sense of responsibility is so crucial to leadership is that for Weber, as for several of his predecessors in political theory, politics is ultimately about violence. Plato had depicted leadership as rooted in the military duty of the guardians to protect the state. Machiavelli asserted that the first business of the prince should always be preparation for war, and Lenin saw his vanguard party as an embattled group of revolutionary leaders. Weber finds the common thread in such observations when he concludes that the distinctive feature of politics is the legitimate monopoly of violence. This is what makes the politician's task so fraught with difficult ethical choices (p. 125).

Weber noted that the leader's distinctive 'ethic of responsibility' that he distinguishes from the 'ethic of ultimate ends' may sometimes involve behaving 'immorally' by conventional ethical standards. Truth-telling, for example, is morally obligatory for the saintly man, but not always the right course for the politician—if deception is necessary to save the state from enemies, for example. Such assertions recall the arguments of Machiavelli; but, unlike his Florentine predecessor, Weber recognized the agonizing impact that such choices can have on a sensitive leader, who may have to send fellow citizens to their death to defend the state. As he puts it, 'whoever contracts with violent means for whatever ends—and every politician does—is exposed to its specific consequences'.

There is no easy way out from the dilemmas such responsibilities present, no way to avoid their impact on the leader. 'No ethics in the world can dodge the fact that one must be willing to pay the price of using morally dubious means or at least dangerous ones—and facing the possibility or even the probability of evil ramifications' (p. 121). A leader cannot just step away and refuse to decide; he is responsible for the society he leads and has to take one course or another, even when every alternative is fraught with moral ambiguity. A leader is also 'responsible for what may become of himself under the impact of these paradoxes', once he 'lets himself in for the diabolic forces lurking in all violence' (p. 125).

To minimize the negative consequences of leaders being overwhelmed by such diabolic forces, many political theorists since Aristotle have concentrated their attention on devising a framework to institute alternative power centres to prevent the most heinous forms of abuse. Michels believes that all such frameworks are ultimately irrelevant. Lenin spurns them as irritating obstructions on the path towards revolution. Weber, like Plato, appears to assume that in the end these structures are less likely to be effective than the internal character and motivations of a political actor dedicated to providing responsible leadership for his community.

7 CONCLUSION

In this brief sojourn through several millennia, we have noted both the consistencies of attention to certain themes in the writings of ten political theorists, and also how the discussions have evolved over time. The legitimate control of violence; the role of fortune in leadership; the advantages of being loved or feared; what is useful and what is honourable; the implications of ruling and being ruled in turn—all these themes appear with regularity. Developing the tension described at the outset of this chapter, theories that propound the value of political expertise, such as those of Plato, Machiavelli, Michels, and Lenin, are balanced by the constitutional focus of Aristotle, Cicero, and Montesquieu. Other theorists take the tension between expert personal authority and limitations on the abuse of power in alternative directions. Rousseau combines absolute popular sovereignty with effective political leadership provided by a few. Arendt asserts that political power can only be a pluralistic gathering of perspectives and wills. Weber emphasizes the lonely initiative of the leader constrained by his own internal judgement and sense of responsibility.

The most significant new factor in this conversation is the advent of democracy on a large scale, sometimes called representative or republican government. The characteristic feature of such a system is the sovereignty of a large number of self-governing citizens. Self-government in such a system usually consists in collectively choosing those persons who will provide leadership for the community. Political 'leadership' takes on a new meaning: the responsibility for governing citizens who have ultimate authority over the governors (Pettit 2000: 106). The leader as ruler, statesman, or prince is replaced by the elected representative temporarily holding office in the state.

In this representative system the emphasis shifts from the character and internal qualities of the leader towards the rule of law and accountability to those who are governed. The single 'ruler' has been replaced by multiple types of leaders—elected executives and legislators, leaders of political parties and social movements—alongside more traditional leaders of smaller political units—municipal officials, bureaucrats, tribal chieftains, warlords. The 'legitimate control of violence' has surely not disappeared, but it is diffused in situations where persuasion, negotiation, conciliation, and bargaining are the most visible political activities.

It remains crucial to a healthy polity and a satisfying common life that our leaders be persons with good judgement and integrity, seriously dedicated to pursuing the common good, rather than demagogic, narcissistic individuals concerned only with advancing their own power. Both the Platonic emphasis on the beneficial expertise brought to political leadership by those who are gifted, well trained, and dedicated to the common good, and the Aristotelian concern with delimiting the scope of power available to any leader to make abuse less likely, are honoured in our understanding of what makes for good government. The tension between these two remains a vivid source of political dynamics, as it always had been.

Beyond these continuities, however, the novel challenges and opportunities of leadership in a *democracy on a large scale* are still being explored. The heavy demands and deep benefits of participation in decisions that affect your life were well understood by classical Athenians; but they assumed that these benefits were necessarily limited to a small number of free-born male citizens living in a *polis* defined by neighbourhood and proximity. Many people now believe that such rights and benefits should be available to everyone, and that they can be adapted through the devices of representation and accountability to very large political associations incorporating millions of citizens.

However, we have not yet figured out how to design a constitution in which leadership can be broadly shared. How do we conceive of a system where sustained and vigorous political participation can be widely practised by very large numbers of engaged citizens, individuals who are also deeply involved in their own personal lives in the economy and civil society? Even if we could somehow design such a framework, it remains unclear how such a system could yield effective governance for a large and extraordinarily complex organization like a nation state. Dimensions of leadership that depend upon expertise, talent, discretion, and flexibility have been identified by theorists from Plato through Lenin and modern advocates of more authoritarian regimes. It is not easy to see how these factors can be made compatible with broad popular participation.

Despite the beliefs of theorists from Aristotle and Cicero through Rousseau and Arendt to contemporary democratic theorists that a fundamentally human political association is one in which we all actively participate—not just occasionally vote for our representatives and then retreat to private life—such a political system on a large scale has eluded our best efforts. This remains true even for those among us—not everyone, to be sure—who are convinced that such political engagement is indeed essential to a truly human life, and therefore a fundamental right that should be available to all.

Thus, even as we develop new forms of popular participation through social media technologies and other instruments still unknown to us, governance by a small number of representatives will, realistically, continue to be the defining characteristic of the political associations in which most of us will live our lives. The chapters in this volume are dedicated to helping us understand the various forms such leadership can take, and how we can make it more effective and more responsive to those who are governed.

RECOMMENDED READING

These books are thoughtful explorations of the theme of leadership by contemporary political observers, building on the insights of the classical theorists discussed in this chapter.

Burns, James MacGregor (1979). *Leadership*. New York: Harper & Row.
Gardner, John (1990). *On Leadership*. New York: Free Press.
Keohane, Nannerl (2010). *Thinking about Leadership*. Princeton: Princeton University Press.

REFERENCES

Note: In references to the earlier authors, chapter or paragraph numbers are generally used rather than pages, to facilitate finding citations in whatever edition of the work the reader may be using.

Arendt, Hannah (1958). *The Human Condition*. Chicago: University of Chicago Press.

Aristotle (1995). *Politics*, ed. Ernest Barker. Oxford: Oxford University Press.

Cicero, Marcus Tullius (1929). *On the Commonwealth*, ed. George H. Sabine and Stanley B. Smith. Indianapolis, IN: Bobbs-Merrill Co.

Cicero, Marcus Tullius (1991). *On Duties*, ed. M. T. Griffin and E. M. Atkins. Cambridge: Cambridge University Press.

Gardner, John (2010). *On Leadership*. New York: Free Press.

Keohane, Nannerl O. (2010). *Thinking about Leadership*. Princeton: Princeton University Press.

Lenin, Vladimir Ilyich (1929) [1902]. *What is to be Done?* New York: International Publishers.

Machiavelli, Niccolò (1988). *The Prince*, ed. Quentin Skinner and Russell Price. Cambridge: Cambridge University Press.

Michels, Roberto (1962). *Political Parties: A Sociological Study of the Oligarchical Tendencies of Modern Democracy*. New York: Collier.

Montesquieu, Charles Louis de Secondat, Baron de (1949). *The Spirit of the Laws*, ed. Thomas Nugent and Franz Neumann. New York: Hafner.

Pettit, Philip (2000). 'Democracy, Electoral and Contestatory', in Ian Shapiro and Stephen Macedo (eds), *Designing Democratic Institutions*. New York: New York University Press.

Plato (1961). *The Collected Dialogues*, ed. Edith Hamilton and Huntingdon Cairns. New York: Pantheon, Bollingen Series.

Rost, Joseph (1991). *Leadership for the Twenty-First Century*. Westport, CT: Praeger.

Rousseau, Jean-Jacques (1997). *The Social Contract and Other Later Political Writings*, ed. Victor Gourevich. Cambridge: Cambridge University Press.

Weber, Max (1958). 'Politics as a Vocation', in *From Max Weber: Essays in Sociology*, ed. H. H. Gerth and C. Wright Mills. New York: Oxford University Press.

CHAPTER 3

....

THEORY OF DEMOCRATIC LEADERSHIP*

....

FRANK HENDRIKS AND NIELS KARSTEN

1 INTRODUCTION

....

THE idea of democratic leadership is inherently paradoxical. Whereas the concept of democracy rests on the idea of popular sovereignty—that is, self-government by an autonomous citizenry—and is based on an essentially egalitarian ethos, the concept of leadership necessarily encompasses hierarchy and hence inequality (Wren et al. 2005; Hernandez et al. 2011). In a truly democratic society, the leader is the odd one out. This paradox of democratic leadership is broadly recognized, both theoretically and empirically (e.g. Kellerman and Webster 2001; Ruscio 2008; Kane and Patapan 2012). Several scholars have provided insightful studies that have shaped our understanding of the leadership–democracy nexus (e.g. Weber 1992; Brooker 2005; Kane, Patapan, and Wong 2008; Ruscio 2008). However, most of these have not yet incorporated the theoretical diversity of understandings of democracy and its consequences for leadership.

Therefore, this chapter, in the tradition of Wildavsky (1984), aims to elaborate on the theoretical and empirical kinship between different styles of leadership and different models of democracy. The focal question is: what does democratic leadership amount to in different types of democracy? It finds a point of departure in Keane's three-stage model (2009) of democratic transformation (from classic 'assembly democracy', to modern 'representative democracy', to present-day 'post-parliamentary' or 'monitory democracy'), and in Hendriks's four ideal-typical models (2010) of democracy (pendulum, consensus, voter, and participatory democracy). We argue that political leaders increasingly operate in more hybrid forms of democracy—that is, democratic regimes in which characteristics of different forms of democracy are combined, and for that reason are required to develop varying political repertoires.

* The authors would like to thank Dr Krist of Steyvers for his constructive comments on earlier versions of this chapter.

In Section 2, we elaborate on the paradox of democratic leadership. Section 3 presents the typology of democracies that we use in the discussion of political leadership types, the results of which are presented in Section 4. Section 5 provides an outlook for the future of democratic leadership studies.

2   The Paradox of Democratic Leadership

Many scholars have observed the tensions that are embedded in the term 'democratic leadership'. Democracy is, literally, rule by the people, the contraction of *demos* and *kratia*. In classic categorizations, by, for example, Aristotle, Plato, Polybios, and Spinoza, this mode of government is contrasted with autocracy and aristocracy. 'Rule by one' and 'rule by a few' are seen to be fundamentally different from 'rule by many', the latter of which rests on the ideal of self-government (Kane, Patapan, and 't Hart 2009a: 2). Democracy is about an autonomous *demos* governing itself as a collective, which entails that rulers who control the coercive power of the state need to be constrained. As Ruscio notes, 'the theory of democracy does not treat leaders kindly' (2008: p. ix). In a democratic context political leaders face a serious dilemma: 'the more democratic leaders lead from the front, the less democratic they appear; the more they act like good democrats, the less they seem like true leaders' (Kane, Patapan, and 't Hart 2009b: 299).

Yet, many have signalled that democratic practice cannot do without leadership. Although not all may agree with Ruscio's statement (2008: 5) that 'a rejection of leadership is implicitly a rejection of democracy', most will be inclined to recognize the empirical adequacy of such a claim. Modern democracies depend on at least some kind of political leadership (Blondel 1987). All the same, leaders are looked at with Argus' eyes; they are not always trusted, and checks and balances are institutionalized throughout democratic systems to keep them in check. In contemporary democratic regimes, in which political leadership has become vested in the executive branch of government in particular, power is subjected to a series of limits and constraints. Democratic leadership is embedded in an institutional context that aims to prevent corruption and the abuse of power and to ensure that leaders are responsive to their followers, through a variety of accountability mechanisms.

The paradox of democratic leadership is, thus, not just a conceptual ambiguity; it also carries substantial practical relevance. Political leaders in democracies face a multitude of demands, which are hard to reconcile. For that reason, several scholars have asked what being a democratic leader amounts to; and how can those involved manage the unique challenges posed on them (e.g. Ankersmit 1996; Hajer 2009; 't Hart 2011; Kane and Patapan 2012).

Many studies start from the core sense of democracy in its purest form—that is, popular sovereignty, which presents leaders with an inherent dilemma to which there is no real resolution (Kane and Patapan 2012). The picture changes when we look at the various democratic institutions that exist and in which different, equally legitimate conceptions of democracy have materialized. Then, it transpires that leadership and democracy can work together, since some forms of democracy thrive under the guidance of certain types of leaders (see also McAllister 2011: 53–4). For this reason, we introduce a typology of democracy into the debate on democratic leadership. The main thesis is that the relationship between democracy and leadership is strongly influenced by intermediate variables, such as the type of democracy a leader operates in and the variety of accountability mechanisms that have been installed to keep leaders in check.

3 Different Understandings Of Democracy

In his bold attempt to write a new history of democracy, entitled *The Life and Death of Democracy*, Keane (2009) traces back the origins of the democratic mode of government to the 'juvenile' popular assemblies of Mesopotamia that existed up to 4 500 years ago. These are considerably older than the Athenian institutions that are traditionally seen as the first forms of democratic rule. Because of the crucial role of assemblies in the democratic process in these early days, he dubs this era as 'assembly democracy'.

Over time, and as democracy moves westwards, the idea of democracy becomes ever more strongly associated with the notion of representation. In the era of 'representative democracy', the democratic process is characterized by popular elections, political parties, and parliamentary representation. These mechanisms rest on the idea that the popular will is socially constructed in the sense that is has to be 'represented' in decision-making—that is, made present by representatives of 'the people' (see Pitkin 1967; Ankersmit 1996).

Representative democracy faced a recurring crisis in the twentieth century, Keane postulates, providing an impetus for the development of what he calls 'post-representative' or 'monitory democracy', which is characterized by a multitude of checks and balances that have been established in addition to and sometimes outside of the representative regime. Elected bodies and political executives, in the view of Keane, have become subject to extensive scrutiny by other actors, both institutional and social-political. These not only monitor the power, but also share power.

Whereas Keane suggests that post-representative, monitory democracy is a new and separate type of democracy that is essentially different from its predecessors, classic assembly democracy and modern representative democracy, we posit that it is more accurately viewed as a mixture of different and longer-existing types of democracies. The checks that have been placed on the representative regime—public referendums, for example, or citizen forums—stem from essentially diverse, but well-known normative convictions of what democracy should look like.

For our analysis we, therefore, also use Hendriks's theoretically informed typology of models of democracy. Inspired by Douglas (1996), and in the research tradition of Lijphart (1999), Hendriks distinguishes four models: pendulum democracy, consensus democracy, voter democracy, and participatory democracy. These are ideal types, in the Weberian sense, which can be used as conceptual coordinates with which once can assess empirical expressions of democracy. No 'real' democracy is as pure as the ideal types; real-existing democracies tend to a certain model and combine it with others. Switzerland, for example, is a prime example of consensus democracy (Lijphart 1999), which is combined with a relatively strong voter democracy and also participatory overtones (Kriesi 2005).

The typology first distinguishes direct democracy from indirect democracy. This distinction 'concerns the question of who makes the decisions in democracy: the citizens themselves, through self-determination (direct democracy), or caretakers, delegates or trustees, through representation (indirect democracy)' (Hendriks 2011: 48). When we combine this distinction with a second one between aggregative and integrative democracy—that is, between 'a 'counting-heads' process of aggregation in which a simple majority is decisive' and 'an integrative, 'talkative' process of conferring, seeking for the widest possible consensus and voting down minorities as little as possible' (Hendriks 2011: 48)—we arrive at the typology that is presented in Figure 3.1.

Pendulum democracy hinges on electoral competition between two predominant political parties or candidates. After each election, the winning party or candidate dominates the executive branch and makes the decisions. Citizen participation in the political process is mainly limited to casting votes. In voter democracy, however, the aggregative logic is combined with unmediated popular rule, rather than with representative delegation. Citizens take part in democratic decision-making directly by casting their votes in plebiscites. Widespread, direct involvement can also be found in participatory democracy, although here citizens' involvement means taking part in consensus-seeking deliberations, rather than casting votes. An integrative process of democratic decision-making is also characteristic for consensus democracies; yet there agreement is sought by representatives that citizens have designated, by popular election or otherwise, to act on their behalf. These models of democracy assume different types of leadership.

	Aggregative (majoritarian)	Integrative (non-majoritarian)
Indirect (representation)	**Pendulum democracy** *winner-takes-all leadership*	**Consensus democracy** *bridging-and-bonding leadership*
Direct (self-determination)	**Voter democracy** *heuristic leadership*	**Participatory democracy** *(dem)agogic leadership*

FIGURE 3.1 Hendriks's four models of democracy (2010) and corresponding leadership roles

4 THE AFFINITY BETWEEN TYPES OF POLITICAL LEADERSHIP AND FORMS OF DEMOCRACY

Leadership in Assembly Democracy

The early days in the history of democracy were dominated by 'assembly democracy', in essence self-government through public gatherings, assembling often out in the open (Dahl 2000: 12). Keane (2009) argues that this form of democracy goes back some 2000 years before Athens, although the latter is still the strongest and best-documented example of assembly democracy.

We have a relatively good picture of how the *demos*, the free citizens of Athens, have dealt with its *kratia*, its government through the People's Assembly, the Council of 500, the Magistrates, the Law Courts, and the many rotating offices of the Athenian *polis* (Hornblower 1992; Finer 1997). This chapter is not the place to go into its details, but it should be noted that the democratic reforms of Cleisthenes (round about 500 BC) strongly encouraged the 'rule by many', while discouraging the 'rule by a few' (oligarchy), let alone 'the rule by one' (monarchy). Offices with power rotated routinely and were in most cases staffed by lot, a major exception being the military *strategoi*, who could in fact be elected year after year. Such election was how, for example, Pericles developed a strong and long-time leading position (Jones 2008: 126).

In many other ways, however, political leadership could flourish in assembly democracy, which at first sight seems to have been anathema to leadership. Athenian assembly democracy presented a context in which *demagogues* (literally 'people-leaders' or 'teachers of the *demos*') could flourish (Finer 1997: 361). Plato's negative assessment of 'mob orators' in Athenian 'theatrocracy' gave demagoguery a bad name. Finley (1977: 21) argues, however, that these people-leaders were actually 'structural to the system', in the sense that it could not function without them. On the same grounds, Keane (2009: 41 ff) suggests that Athenian democracy was not really 'direct democracy'. Yet, this claim is true only if direct democracy is defined as a political system in which *all* functions are performed by the *demos* as a whole, which is truly impossible.

Here we see direct democracy more conventionally as a system in which not representatives of the citizenry, but the amassed citizenry itself, has the 'political primacy', the mandate, and the tools to make decisions for the *polis* (Dahl 2000: 103; Kriesi 2005: 2; Held 2006: 4). In such a system 'symbolic' or 'aesthetic' representation (Pitkin 1967; Ankersmit 1996) is indeed highly important, but such representation in itself does not bring representative democracy, as is illustrated by the two types of direct democracy that we distinguish—that is, voter and participatory democracy.

Leadership in Voter Democracy

The general logic and some of the crucial institutions of Athenian assembly democracy are clearly evident in the Swiss version of democracy, which has in its turn influenced the Swiss version of referendum democracy—both highly 'direct' in the sense of the conventional definition. At the kantonal level of Switzerland, only two small *Landsgemeinde* still decide on the most important public matters through a communal show of hands, but at the local level no less than 80 per cent of the Swiss municipalities continue to make decisions in this manner. They do so without representative institutions, but not without symbolic representation or political leadership, of sorts (Ladner and Bühlmann 2007).

The Swiss system of referendums and initiatives, which has grown strongly since the nineteenth century, can be seen as a continuation of a tradition of direct democracy with new and additional means—the small-scale, low-tech show of hands of assembly democracy being turned into the large-scale, more refined way of aggregating votes in plebiscites. Referendums and initiatives are truly direct in the sense that the amassed voter, and no one else, ultimately decides about substantial issues. The decision is not delegated to politicians or parties. As Kriesi (2005) has convincingly shown, however, members of the political elite are nevertheless crucial in providing the heuristic cues (who is for/against?) and arguments (what is for/against?) that form the basis for the collective decision. This finding suggests that, in voter democracy, leadership studies must focus less on formal positions and competences and more on heuristic and definitional powers of elites. With its New England Town Meetings (a version of assembly democracy not at all confined to the American East coast) and its initiatives and referendums in many states, the United States has been called Switzerland's 'Twin Republic'—much bigger now, but impressionable earlier on (Arx 2002). There are, however, differences, many of which have to do with the fact that voter democracy is combined with a dominant consensus democracy in Switzerland, and a dominant pendulum democracy in the USA. In the Swiss context, leadership roles are more often assumed by ordinary citizens, committed journalists, alarmed scientists, retired civil engineers, or anyone else with an aptitude for political organizing. In the American context private money plays a much bigger role. The (Californian) referendum democracy is even said to be led by an 'initiative–industrial complex' (Broder 2002; Zakaria 2003), in which direct legislation is written under the auspices of private interests, paying for the collection of individual votes.

Whether they act in a more 'commercial' context (California) or in a more 'public' context (Switzerland), leading actors in voter democracy are expected to be effective and responsive brokers of political movement in settings that are fundamentally horizontal and individualistic. The Californian organization that initiated the recall that was to bring the downfall of Governor Davis and was to usher in former movie actor Schwarzenegger went by the name of 'People's Advocate'—and that is perhaps the best job description of a political leader in voter democracy.

Leadership roles that would suit consensus democracy or pendulum democracy will not be accepted 'just like that' in voter democracy. People who act patronizingly or high-handedly ('just listen to me') will meet with resistance here. Voter democracy, in contrast to participatory democracy, does not cultivate aversion to people who take the lead per se, if only they lead in a way deemed appropriate by assertive individuals who define voter democracy.

Leadership in Participatory Democracy

There is a line that runs from ancient Athens and assembly democracy more in general, to the more aggregative forms of voter democracy that we dealt with in the previous subsection. But there is also a line that—via Rousseau, Marx, and others on the Old and New Left—runs to more transformative or developmental forms of participatory democracy (see Pateman 1970; Held 2006: 187 ff). Traces thereof can be found in many times and places: in the Paris commune, in the Israeli kibbutzim, in the New Social and Political Movements that have grown since the 1960s, in the experiments with communicative and deliberative democracy, with participatory planning and budgeting, with mini publics, and with citizen committees that have developed later on (Barber 1984; Dryzek 2002; Fung 2004; Goodin 2008; Hendriks 2010: 109 ff).

One of the most powerful reproaches that Schumpeter (1934; see also Brooker 2005) made to participation thinkers like Rousseau is that they lack a proper understanding of the leadership function in democracy; present-day discourse on deliberative, discursive, or communicative democracy is also notably silent on leadership. In all strong versions of participatory democracy, authority does not descend from the top down, from competing leadership, but rises up from the bottom, from an in essence undivided base (Gutmann and Thompson 2004; Gastil and Levine 2011). In the practice of participatory democracy, less strict than the theory, leadership roles appear to be feasible but tend to be modelled not on the role of the prominent and decisive leader who makes decisions on behalf of others, but rather on the role of the inspirational coach or guide who teaches others but is also aware that these others—the ones at the base—have to walk their own walk. One could think of the way in which inspirational leaders such as Ghandi and Mandela from a distance coached and guided the movements, which saw them as their leaders, but which also had to lead themselves for lots of the time.

Participatory democracy is, more than any of the other models of democracy, averse to executive leaders who get disengaged from the base. All sorts of constructions have been devised to prevent such disengagement from happening in organizations and movements that are sympathetic to participatory democracy. Decision-making rules in New Social Movements often demand virtual unanimity, or at least massive majorities, before going along with those who try to take a lead. The German *Grünen* like to work with rotating chairpersons, and their political leaders often come in two (not one in the lead, please!). Michels (1925), however, has shown that oligarchy is almost inevitable in large organizations, even in those on the Left that adhere to a participatory ideology, much to their own dismay. Freeman (1980) has revealed that in movements like the American women's movement the oligarchization may be hidden, but nevertheless discernible. To prevent an 'Animal Farm' ('all pigs are equal, but some pigs are more equal than others') from developing, counterweight is often sought in hyper-accountability: a permanent state of being accountable to those at the bottom (Hood 1998).

An exceptional leadership role may develop in the more radical political movements inspired by Rousseau, Marx, or Mao. As an exception to the rule, thus also a demarcation of it, one extraordinary person may be singled out as the shining example, the personification of the lesson that is yet to be learned by all other pupils progressing on the road towards advanced understanding; the one radiant sun shining its light on a cloud of equal stars orbiting around it. An extreme example would be Mao Zedong, the great helmsman inspiring the cultural revolution in the communist 'People's Democracy' of China (Chang and Halliday 2005); or Robespierre, champion of democracy and participation à la Rousseau as well as instigator of the 'Great Terror' following the French Revolution (Scurr 2006).

The latter examples testify that leadership in the more extreme expressions of participatory democracy can become highly problematic. This risk might be less apparent in more moderate forms of participatory democracy, but there the role of leadership tends to be underestimated and understudied.

Leadership in Representative Democracy

Other than the idea of direct democracy, the concept of representative democracy explicitly assumes leadership, since it rests on the principle of collective political representation of citizens' interests in the decision-making process. This, however, does not mean that all representative democracies digest leadership equally well, or that democratic leadership amounts to the same thing in different representative democracies. In this respect, there are substantial differences between leadership in pendulum democracies and leadership in consensus democracies.

Leadership in Pendulum Democracy

Of the four models of democracy that we outlined above, pendulum democracy arguably provides the best breeding ground for strong political leadership. The 'winner-takes-all' electoral system fosters competition between a limited number of political parties, which provides a strong impetus for high-profile political leadership. It necessitates having a recognizable 'face' for one's political party, especially in a mediatized society (Langer 2007; McAllister 2011; see also Karvonen 2010), not only during election times, but also in between elections.

In pendulum democracy power, executive power in particular is concentrated in the hands of a few; it has a strong elitist ethos. Decision-making in this type of democracy necessarily means deciding for all the others, including those who have lost the electoral battle. In pendulum democracy 'power to' closely corresponds to 'power over' (see Stone 1989). Leadership is vested in the institutional make-up of this type of democracy, which places research into constitutional powers and competences at the forefront of leadership studies in this field (e.g. Lijphart 1999; Mouritzen and Svara 2002; McAllister 2011).

The mayors of those cities in the United States that operate under the strong-mayor form of government—such as Rudolph W. L. Giuliani, former mayor of New York City, or Richard J. Daley, former mayor of Chicago—provide examples of how prominently leaders are positioned in pendulum democracies. Having won highly competitive, 'winner-takes-all' elections, they are the prime political leaders of their local governments, possessing a considerable amount of statutory, executive powers; they tend to dominate the local political–administrative system in what Mouritzen and Svara (2002) would label a strong-mayor system. At the same time, Ferman's comparative study (1985) shows that leadership styles that US mayors adopt may vary within some 'feasible space'. For example, while the then San Francisco mayor, Joseph Alioto, struggled to gain indirect influence through bargaining and persuasion, the then Boston mayor, Kevin White, managed to accumulate considerable direct power and to 'take charge'.

Foley (2000) provides a provocative account of what leadership in a pendulum democracy amounts to, arguing that Prime Minister Blair's leadership was of an almost presidential nature. This claim should be qualified, though. Heffernan (2005), among others, reveals how institutional factors significantly constrain the prime minister's power. Although pendulum democracy provides considerable room for strong leadership, political offices like that of the British prime minister, or like that of the American president (Miroff 1993), still operate in complex environments characterized by various checks and balances. Leaders' control over decision-making and over resources is not unlimited (see Yates 1977; Greasley and Stoker 2008). Further, over the last decades the interdependencies between public actors, and also between public and private actors, have increased considerably (Kickert, Klijn, and Koppenjan 1997).

One of the main risks of political leadership in pendulum democracies, therefore, is that of a discrepancy between the public desire for strong public leadership and political leaders' actual abilities to make a difference in free-market economies-*cum*-democracies.

Leadership in Consensus Democracy

Consensus democracy—versions of which can be found in countries such as Austria, Belgium, Germany, the Netherlands, and Switzerland—provides an 'unfavourable biotope' for strong political leadership. Even the vocabulary of leadership—'showing leadership', 'being a leader', 'leading the way', and so on—is approached here with a type of hesitancy that is not encountered so much in, for instance, Anglo-American discourse (Lijphart 1999: 31–47; Andeweg 2000; 't Hart 2005: 234).

Consensus democracy is characterized by the dispersal and sharing of power, by institutionalized interdependencies between different public actors, and by practices of consultation and coalition building (Lijphart 1999, 2001; Andeweg 2000; Hendriks 2010). These leave relatively little room for 'acting boss'. The President of the Swiss Confederation is a case in point. Although the President chairs the Federal Council, he or she is a typical *primus inter pares*, not possessing any special powers that the other six councillors do not have. The presidency is vested in the collective of the Federal Council, rather than in a single actor, and is also kept in check by a system of rotation. As such, the President of the Swiss Confederation has a rather weak position (see Kriesi and Trechsel 2008: 69–80).

Consensus democracy may be inhospitable to the very idea of strong, individualized leadership (see Kellerman and Webster 2001: 487) as its institutional make-up of checks and balances, power dispersal, and power-sharing encages leadership (Lijphart

1999). It does, however, not rule out leadership altogether, especially not in the collegial sense, for which reason leadership studies in consensus democracy must focus less on the leadership behaviour of individuals and more on the leadership function of collective entities. Consensus democracy's leaders tie interests together in umbrella organizations; they represent particular socio-political groupings in the integrative process of decision-making; they bond and build bridges, both within and between interest groups (see Bryson and Crosby 1992; Putnam 2000). Thus, although 'leaders' in consensus democracies are traditionally approached with caution, democratic leadership in the form of 'keeping things together' is rather strongly developed. Former Dutch Prime Minister Wim Kok was renowned for his ability to do this (Velde 2002). Likewise, former mayor of Amsterdam Job Cohen was highly respected for being able to build bridges between different communities in the difficult times that followed the murder of filmmaker Theo van Gogh (see Hajer 2009: 76–96).

A classic criticism of leadership in consensual settings is that it lacks decisiveness. An extreme example is the 1699 *liberum veto* in the *Sjem*, the representative body of Polish nobles. This principle of unanimity rendered the *Sjem* practically unable to pass any legislation (Keane 2009: 257–63). The presumed lack of decisiveness, resulting from power-sharing and dispersal, has legitimized the call for stronger leadership that can be heard throughout Western Europe, both at the national and local level (Leach and Wilson 2002; Borraz and John 2004; Larsen 2005: 208; Bäck, Heinelt, and Magnier 2006).

An interesting development is the rise of quasi-presidential leadership in previously rather consensual settings (see Steyvers et al. 2008). An example is presented by the Belgian city of Antwerp, and its former mayor Patrick Janssens. In a context that is riddled with (institutional) checks and balances, Janssens managed to position himself as the prime leader of his party and also of the governing coalition (Van Aelst and Nuytemans 2007). A leaning to stronger, more expressive, and competitive leadership is also evident in countries such as the Netherlands (particularly post-Fortuyn) and Switzerland (under the influence of Blocher's SVP), where consensus democracy has become mixed with competing (and competitive) notions of democracy.

Developments like these illustrate the hybridization of democracy and the implications thereof for democratic leadership. As contemporary democracy combines characteristics of different forms of democracy, the nature of leadership is also bound to change.

5 HYBRID DEMOCRACY AND THE STUDY OF LEADERSHIP

The advent of monitory democracy, according to Keane (2009), means that public leaders are under constant and intense scrutiny by a variety of public and private actors, which makes it ever more difficult to generate, and especially maintain, authority. Authorities are constantly monitored by a diverse set of forums that can become very active and inquisitive. 't Hart (2001) speaks of an 'inquisition democracy', which evokes images of a ferocious pursuit of public leaders. Keane (2009: 857) uses a more gentle metaphor for the 'chastening of power'—namely that of Gulliver trapped by the Lilliputians, strapped down by a large quantity of little ropes.

Although the metaphor is forceful, it could easily misrepresent important aspects of contemporary democratic governance. Boundary-defying, Houdini-like, leadership is far from absent in modern-day society. Former Italian Prime Minister Berlusconi provides just one example. Moreover, recent structural reforms such as the introduction of elected mayors have strengthened the position of executive leaders throughout Europe. Neither have authoritative ways of working been eliminated, even from consensus democracies (e.g. Karsten 2012). The universal applicability of Keane's metaphor—the political leader as a trapped Gulliver—can thus be questioned.

What is more important is that we question the validity of Keane's claim that 'democracy is morphing into a type of democracy radically different to that our grandparents may have been lucky to know' (Keane 2009: p. xxvii). Conversely, we argue that modern democracy presents a mixture of long-standing models of democracy, rather than a new type of democracy on its own. The checks and balances that indeed are being installed, in the form of recall procedures, watchdog institutions, participatory arrangements, and the like, find their origin in longer-existing alternatives to representative democracy.

While consensus democracy is being spiced up with ingredients of majoritarian democracy of the Anglo-American sort, Westminster democracy is being supplemented with consensual elements of continental-style representative democracy; while self-governance is on the rise on both sides (Hendriks and Michels 2011). More generally, there appears to be an empirical trend towards hybridization of democracies throughout Europe (Loughlin, Hendriks and Lidström 2011). Democratic innovations are introduced into established democratic systems that 'stretch' these systems in directions that may be new to the individual countries, but not to the wider democratic repertoire. Modern democracy thus mixes ingredients that are not really new, although the cocktail they compose might taste quite differently.

We posit that this hybridization of democratic models requires a hybridization of leadership styles, and a study of democratic leadership that is sensitive to both. The expectations and demands regarding political leadership are highly diverse nowadays. Leadership has to show a common face on one stage, and superior qualities on a next. Leadership has to be tough in one arena, and empathic in another. However, different leadership roles cannot be easily 'employed' by a single leader at the same moment. A strong, decisive, authoritative leader can hardly be a power-sharing team-player at the same time. Leadership that finds the lowest common denominator of different leadership styles provides no real solution, since, as we have shown, every type of democracy requires a particular type of leadership. The paradox of hybrid democracies is that they require contradictory ways of governance and leadership. There seem to be two pathways along which this problem can be resolved, both variants of what can be called 'kaleidoscopic leadership' ('t Hart and Hooven 2004).

First, leadership constellations may arise in which several leaders provide counteracting checks and balances for each other's positions and leadership roles. In the institutional make-up of the European Union, for example, different bodies (the European Parliament, the European Commission, the European Council, the President of the European Council, the High Representative of the Union for Foreign Affairs and Security Policy) perform different leadership roles and often compete with each other. Constellations like these, be they leadership tandems, troikas, quintets, and so on, diverge from consensus democracy in the sense that they do not strive for mutual agreement, but, more like pendulum democracy, are characterized by contestation. At the same time they diverge from pendulum democracy in the sense that leadership becomes multilateral instead of unilateral.

Alternatively, the mixed character of democratic leadership may be embedded in single offices. The Dutch mayoral office provides an insightful example. Dutch mayors are expected to play a wide variety of roles (Karsten, Schaap and Verheul 2010; Sackers 2010), varying from being a neutral—that is, non-partisan and non-political—*burgervader* ('father of the citizens'), to being the individual, political leader of the municipal government in socially and politically salient fields such as public safety, which means that Dutch mayors are required successively to adapt their leadership style to varying social and political circumstances. In Dutch discourse this skill is called *schakelen*—that is, 'alternating' between different leadership styles. The hybridization of democracy heightens the need for such alternation.

The study of democratic leadership has to follow and evaluate developments critically along the two pathways just mentioned. To what extent and in which way is the hybridization of democracy connected to the development of variants of kaleidoscopic leadership? How is this connected to notions of good democratic governance? Questions like these need to be posed and answered. The study of democratic leadership is necessarily contextual (Hernandez et al. 2011). The modelling of democracy matters for the expression of leadership. At the same time, however, individual agency does make a difference for what leaders are able to achieve in the leader–follower relationship. The interaction between the modelling of democracy and the expressions of leadership must therefore always be central to research in this field.

Recommended Reading

Keane, J. (2009). *The Life and Death of Democracy*. London: Simon and Schuster.

Kane, J., and Patapan, H. (2012). *How Democracy Defines, Empowers and Limits its Leaders*. Oxford: Oxford University Press.

Ruscio, K. P. (2008). *The Leadership Dilemma in Modern Democracy*. Cheltenham: Edward Elgar.

References

Andeweg, R. B. (2000). 'Consociational Democracy', *Annual Review of Political Science*, 3/1: 509–36.

Ankersmit, F. R. (1996). *Aesthetic Politics: Political Philosophy beyond Fact and Value*. Stanford: Stanford University Press.

Arx, N. von (2002). *Ähnlich, aber anders. Die Volksinitiative in Kalifornien und in der Schweiz*. Basle: Helbing und Lichtenhahn.

Bäck, H., Heinelt, H., and Magnier, A. (2006) (eds). *The European Mayor: Political Leaders in the Changing Context of Local Democracy*. Wiesbaden: VS Verlag.

Barber, B. R. (1984). *Strong Democracy: Participatory Politics for a New Age*. Berkeley and Lose Angeles: University of California Press.

Blondel, J. (1987). *Political Leadership: Towards a General Analysis*. London: SAGE Publications.

Borraz, O. and John, P. (2004). 'The Transformation of Urban Executive Leadership in Western Europe', *Urban and Regional Research*, 28/1: 107–20.

Broder, D. S. (2002). *Democracy Derailed: Initiative, Campaigns and the Power of Money*. New York: Harcourt.

Brooker, P. (2005). *Leadership in Democracy: From Adaptive Response to Entrepreneurial Initiative*. Houndsmill: Palgrave Macmillan.

Bryson, J. M., and Crosby, B. C. (1992). *Leadership for the Common Good: Tackling Public Problems in a Shared-power World*. San Francisco: Jossey-Bas.

Chang, J., and Halliday, J. (2005). *Mao: The Untold Story*. London: Jonathan Cape.

Dahl, R. A. (2000). *On Democracy*. New Haven: Yale University Press.

Douglas, M. (1996). *Thought Styles: Critical Essays on Good Taste*. New York: Sage Publications.

Dryzek, J. J. (2002). *Foundations and Frontiers of Deliberative Governance*. Oxford: Oxford University Press.

Ferman, B. (1985). *Governing the Ungovernable City Political Skill, Leadership, and the Modern Mayor*. Philadelphia: Temple University Press.

Finer, S. E. (1997). *The History of Government from the Earliest Times*. Oxford: Oxford University Press.

Finley, M. I. (1977) (ed.). *The Portable Greek Historians: The Essence of Herodotus, Thucydides, Xenophon, Polybius*. New York: Viking.

Foley, M. (2000). *The British Presidency: Tony Blair and the Politics of Public Leadership*. Manchester: Manchester University Press.

Freeman, J. (1980). *The Tryranny of Structurelessness*. Hull: Anarchist Workers Association Kingston.

Fung, A. (2004). *Empowered Participation: Reinventing Urban Democracy*. Princeton: Princeton University Press.

Gastil, J., and Levine, P. (2011). *The Deliberative Democracy Handbook: Strategies for Effective Civic Engagement in the Twenty-First Century*. Aldershot: Edward Elgar.

Goodin, R. E. (2008). *Innovating Democracy: Democratic Theory and Practice after the Deliberative Turn*. Oxford: Oxford University Press.

Greasley, S., and Stoker, G. (2008). 'Mayors and Urban Governance: Developing A Facilitative Leadership Style', *Public Administration Review*, 68/4: 722–30.

Gutmann, A., and Thompson, D. (2004). *Why Deliberative Democracy?* Princeton: Princeton University Press.

Hajer, M. A. (2009). *Authoritative Governance*. Oxford: Oxford University Press.

Heffernan, R. (2005). 'Why the Prime Minister cannot be a President: Comparing Institutional Imperatives in Britain and America', *Parliamentary Affairs*, 58/1: 53–70.

Held, D. (2006). *Models of Democracy*. Cambridge: Polity Press.

Hendriks, F. (2010). *Vital Democracy: A Theory of Democracy in Action*. Oxford: Oxford University Press.

Hendriks, F. (2011). 'Purity and Democracy: Beauty Ideals and Pollution Reduction in Democratic Reform', *Administative Theory and Praxis*, 33/1: 44–61.

Hendriks, F., and Michels, A. (2011). 'Democracy Transformed? Reforms in Britain and The Netherlands (1990–2010)', *International Journal of Public Administration*, 34/5: 307–17.

Hernandez, M., Eberly, M. B., Avolio, B. J., and Johnson, M. D. (2011). 'The Loci and Mechanisms of Leadership: Exploring a More Comprehensive View of Leadership theory', *Leadership Quarterly*, 22/6: 1165–85.

Hood, C. (1998). *The Art of the State: Culture, Rhetoric, and Public Management*. Oxford: Clarendon Press.

Hornblower, S. (1992). 'Creation and Development of Democratic Institutions in Ancient Greece', in J. Dunn (ed.), *Democracy: The Unfinished Journey 508 BC to AD 1993*. Oxford: Oxford University Press, 1–13.

Jones, P. (2008). *Vote for Caesar: How the Ancient Greeks and Romans Solved the Problems of Today*. London: Orion.

Kane, J., and Patapan, H. (2012). *How Democracy Defines, Empowers and Limits its Leaders*. Oxford: Oxford University Press.

Kane, J., Patapan, H., and 't Hart, P. (2009a). 'Dispersed Democratic Leadership', in J. Kane, H. Patapan, and P. 't Hart (eds), *Dispersed Democratic Leadership: Origins, Dynamics, and Implications*. Oxford: Oxford University Press, 1–13.

Kane, J., Patapan, H., and 't Hart, P. (2009b). 'Dispersed Democratic Leadership Revisited', in J. Kane, H. Patapan, and P. 't Hart (eds), *Dispersed Democratic Leadership: Origins, Dynamics, and Implications*. Oxford: Oxford University Press, 299–321.

Kane, J., Patapan, H., and Wong, B. (2008) (eds). *Dissident Democrats: The Challenge of Democratic Leadership in Asia*. Basingstoke: Palgrave MacMillan.

Karsten, N., Schaap, L., and Verheul, W. J. (2010). 'Stijlen van lokaal leiderschap. Over burgemeesters, rolopvattingen en –verwachtingen', *Justitiële Verkenningen*, 36/3: 31–44.

Karsten, N. (2012). 'Explaining and Justifying Authoritative Decisions: The Case of Controversial Facilities for the Homeless in Rotterdam', *Local Government Studies*, 38/2: 143–60.

Karvonen, L. (2010). *The Personalisation of Politics: A Study of Parliamentary Democracies*. Colchester: European Consortium for Political Research Press.

Keane, J. (2009). *The Life and Death of Democracy*. London: Simon and Schuster.

Kellerman, B., and Webster, S. W. (2001). 'The Recent Literature on Public Leadership Reviewed and Considered', *Leadership Quarterly*, 12/4: 485–514.

Kickert, W. J. M., Klijn, E. H., and Koppenjan, J. (1997) (eds). *Managing Complex Networks: Strategies for the Public Sector*. London: Sage Publications.

Kriesi, H. (2005). *Direct Democratic Choice: The Swiss Experience*. Lanham: Lexington Books.

Kriesi, H., and Trechsel, A. H. (2008). *The Politics of Switzerland: Continuity and Change in a Consensus Democracy*. Cambridge: Cambridge University Press.

Ladner, A., and Bühlmann, M. (2007). *Demokratie in den Gemeinden*. Zurich: Rüegger Verlag.

Langer, A. I. (2007). 'A Historical Exploration of the Personalisation of Politics in the Print Media: The British Prime Ministers (1945–1999)', *Parliamentary Affairs*, 60/3: 371–87.

Larsen, H. O. (2005). 'Transforming Political Leadership: Models, Trends and Reforms', in R. Berg and N. Rao (eds), *Transforming Political Leadership in Local Government*. Basingstoke: Palgrave Macmillan, 195–211.

Leach, S., and Wilson, D. (2002). 'Rethinking Local Political Leadership', *Public Administration*, 80/4: 655–690.

Lijphart, A. (1999). *Patterns of Democracy: Government Forms and Performance in Thirty-Six Countries*. New Haven: Yale University Press.

Lijphart, A. (2001). 'The Pros and Cons—but Mainly Pros—of Consensus Democracy', *Acta Politica*, 36/2: 129–39.

Loughlin, J., Hendriks, F., and Lidström, A. (2011) (eds). *The Oxford Handbook of Local and Regional Democracy in Europe*. Oxford: Oxford University Press.

McAllister, I. (2011). 'Political Leaders in Westminster Systems', in K. Aarts, A. Blais and H. Schmitt (eds), *Political Leaders and Democratic Elections*. Oxford: Oxford University Press, 52–75.

Michels, R. (1925). *Zur Soziologie des Parteiwesens in der modernen Demokratie. Untersuchungen über die oligarchischen Tendenzen des Gruppenlebens*. Leipzig: Kröner.

Miroff, B. (1993). *Icons of Democracy: American Presidents as Heroes, Aristocrats, Dissenters, and Democrats*. New York: Basic Books.

Mouritzen, P. E., and Svara, J. H. (2002). *Leadership at the Apex: Politicians and Administrators in Western Local Governments*. Pittsburgh: University of Pittsburgh.

Pateman, C. (1970). *Participation and Democratic Theory*. Cambridge: Cambridge University Press.

Pitkin, H. F. (1967). *The Concept of Representation*. Berkeley and Los Angeles: University of California Press.

Putnam, R. D. (2000). *Bowling Alone: The Collapse and Revival of American Community*. New York: Simon and Schuster.

Ruscio, K. P. (2008). *The Leadership Dilemma in Modern Democracy*. Cheltenham: Edward Elgar.

Sackers, H. J. B. (2010). *Herder, hoeder en handhaver. De burgemeester en het bestuurlijk sanctierecht* [inaugural address]. Nijmegen: Radboud Universiteit Nijmegen.

Schumpeter, J. A. (1934). *The Theory of Economic Development: An Inquiry into Profits, Capital, Credit, Interest and the Business Cycle*. Cambridge, MA: Harvard University Press.

Scurr, R. (2006). *Fatal Purity: Robespierre and the French Revolution*. London: Chatto and Windus.

Steyvers, K., Bergström, T., Bäck, H., Boogers, M., Ruano de la Fuente, J. M., and Schaap, L. (2008). 'From Princeps to President? Comparing Local Executive Leadership Transformation', *Local Government Studies*, 34/2: 131–46.

Stone, C. N. (1989). *Regime Politics: Governing Atlanta, 1946–1988*. Lawrence, KS: University Press of Kansas.

't Hart, P. (2001). *Verbroken verbindingen. Over de politisering van het verleden en de dreiging van een inquisitiedemocratie*. Amsterdam: De Balie.

't Hart, P. (2005). 'Doing Better, Feeling Worse: Over de erosie van het overheidsgezag', *Beleid en Maatschappij*, 32/4: 226–38.

't Hart, P. (2011). 'Evaluating Public Leadership: Towards an Assessment Framework', *Public Money and Management*, 31/5: 323–30.

't Hart, P., and Hooven, M. ten. (2004). *Op zoek naar leiderschap. Regeren na de revolte*. Amsterdam: De Balie.

Van Aelst, P., and Nuytemans, M. (2007). 'The Electoral Success of 'Patrick': In Search of Evidence and Explanations of the Janssens-Effect in Antwerp', *Res Publica*, 49/1: 150–71.

Velde, H. te (2002). *Stijlen van leidershap. Persoon en politiek van Thorbecke tot Den Uyl.* Amsterdam: Wereldbibliotheek.

Weber, M. (1992) [1919]. *Politik als Beruf.* Ditzingen: Reclam.

Wildavsky, A. (1984). *The Nursing Father: Moses as a Political Leader.* Alabama: University of Alabama Press.

Wren, J. T., Douglas, A., Hicks, A., and Price, T. L. (2005). *Traditional Classics on Leadership.* Aldershot: Edward Elgar.

Yates, D. (1977). *The Ungovernable City: The Politics of Urban Problems and Policy Making.* Cambridge, MA: MIT Press.

Zakaria, F. (2003). *The Future of Freedom: Illiberal Democracy at Home and Abroad.* New York: Norton.

CHAPTER 4

CONFUCIANISM

JOSEPH CHAN AND ELTON CHAN

1 INTRODUCTION

CONFUCIANISM began life more than 2,500 years ago. What preoccupied Confucius (551–479 BCE) and other classical thinkers such as Mencius (379–289 BCE) and Xunzi (340–245 BCE) was the decay of social norms and disintegration of order in their times. These thinkers believed that, although the norms, rituals, and institutions that had developed during the Western Zhou Dynasty (eleventh to eighth centuries BCE) had been fundamentally sound, the problem arose because these norms, rituals, and the virtues began to lose their influence on the corrupt elites who lacked ethical cultivation and discipline. In response, the Confucian thinkers developed a set of ethical ideas such as *ren* (commonly translated as benevolence) and *yi* (righteousness), which they hoped would bring fresh insight and appeal to a social vision that had already been developed, perfected, and settled in ancient times. Over the next two millennia, Confucian scholars and politicians have actively drawn on these fundamental ideas to guide and justify their thinking about society and politics. Like other time-honoured traditions of thought, Confucianism has developed into different schools that conflict as often as they overlap. Nevertheless, one common thread runs through practically all schools of Confucianism—namely, that good leadership is central to good politics.

Leadership is deemed important in many traditions of political thought, but few traditions place such unreserved confidence in leadership as Confucianism. For the ancient Greeks, the key to a good *polis*, or city state, was the constitution; the Romans found their strength in a mixed regime and Roman Law; political thinking in the Middle Ages was deeply intertwined with theology; political thinking after Montesquieu was occupied with the separation of power and institutional design; and since the modern era (especially after the Second World War), although leadership has remained a concern in political thinking, the most invoked concepts for good politics—such as democracy, human rights, and rule of law—have been related to institutions rather than leaders.

To Confucianism, however, good leadership is both the originating and sustaining force behind good politics. Such a position is famously captured by Confucius: 'Let there be the [proper] men and their good political order will flourish; but without such men, their political order decays and ceases' (Confucius 1879a). Therefore the flourishing of political order depends on the appointment of the proper men. Confucians see good leadership, rather than well-designed institutions, as the pivot of good political order.

What does Confucianism view as good political order? Other than being the means of securing the material well-being of the people, good political order is a kind of ideal relationship between the ruler and the ruled. In this sense leadership is very much part of the good order. This chapter will first explicate this understanding of good political order, and then discuss the relative importance of leadership vis-à-vis institutions, the characteristic features of good leaders, the roles and styles of leadership, and the general views of how the politically talented are to be selected.

2 THE IDEAL RULER–RULED RELATIONSHIP

The Confucian conception of the ideal political relationship is one of mutual trust and commitment. Political authority is a kind of *relationship* or *bond* between the ruler and the ruled. What makes political leadership truly authoritative is not just the ruler's ability to protect and promote the people's well-being, but the willing acceptance of his rule by the people. That is to say, authority to lead is not merely externally justified but also internally constituted by a mutual commitment from both sides—the ruler's commitment to care for the people and the people's willing acceptance. Early Confucian masters used words such as *min fu* (that is, the people sincerely follow) (Confucius 1979:bk 2, sect. 19; hereafter Confucius 1979: bk 2.19), and *min yue* (that is, the people delight) (Mencius 1970: bk 1B.10) to describe the idea of people's willing and glad acceptance of political rule. These ideas can often be found in passages from *The Analects* and *Mencius*. The authority of political leaders ultimately resides in the 'hearts of the people'—true authority can only be accepted, recognized, and willingly complied with by the people. External forces such as sheer power will not give a ruler true authority. Even an institutional office of authority cannot guarantee the office-holder true authority.

Precisely because authority is constituted by the attitudes and commitment of the ruler and ruled, early Chinese thinkers thought that political authority is a precarious and fragile relationship. Any one side of this relationship can easily harm or undermine it by withdrawing the attitudes that constitute authoritativeness. These thinkers believed that the ruler rather than the subjects should play an active role in forging and maintaining this relationship—he should care for the people, gain their trust, and win their hearts. Only leaders who have proper virtues and abilities can command the voluntary submission of the people, and only they can develop and sustain the ideal ruler–ruled relationship. In other words, leadership is an important foundation for political order and authority.

3 THE FLOURISHING OF POLITICAL ORDER DEPENDS ON THE PROPER MEN

The significance of leadership in generating good political order can also be appreciated by considering the relative importance of leadership to political institutions. Confucians believe that the effectiveness of institutions depends on the quality of the leaders, not the other way round; some even suggest that empowering statesmen with wide powers of discretion can bring about better governance than establishing complicated institutions (Gu 1929: bk 11.9, 10). This inclination towards relying on leaders above all else is perhaps best articulated by Xunzi: 'There are men who can bring about order, but there is no model that will produce order' (Xunzi 1988: bk 12.1).

Why does Confucianism give priority of place to good leaders? There are two reasons that are complementary to each other. The first reason, as argued by Xunzi, is that leadership has a comparative advantage over the laws and methods of governance that sage kings (or any great leaders in the past) have established over time. The gist of this argument is that the 'model' of governance (*fa*) established by sage kings, however perfect, is only 'the first manifestation of order', and cannot be applied rigidly without noticing the proper sequence of application and making appropriate adjustments in response to changing circumstances. Only a morally exemplary person *cum* ruler with a deep understanding of the moral principles underlying the model knows best how to put it to use. In another place, Xunzi makes a similar point that it is the morally exemplary person, rather than a good model, who is the guarantee for order and stability. He says: 'Although there have been cases in which a good legal model nonetheless produced disorder', he has never heard of a case 'where there was a morally exemplary person in charge of the government and chaos ensued... Order is born of the morally exemplary person, chaos is produced by the small man' (Xunzi 1988: bk 9.2).

What Xunxi argues is not that the ruler should not be bound by law or institutions, but that moral and political judgement is essential in politics. Moral principles and rituals, laws and policies, are only general rules; in the face of changing circumstances they require interpretation, adaptation, revision, or extension, which in turn requires judgement. On some occasions, principles may also conflict, necessitating further judgement. Principles and rules can guide us only to a certain point—beyond which lies the realm of judgement. For this reason, the ability to make sound judgements is essential to leadership. This ability does not come naturally—judgement has to be nourished and guided by experience, learning, and virtue. Thus we need people with moral and intellectual calibre to assume political leadership.

The second reason Confucianism gives for preferring leaders to institutions has to do with the limited effectiveness of institutions in restraining the not-so-virtuous leaders. Confucians understand that institutions are formed by rules that, in themselves, are nothing but words. Without the faithful compliance of incumbents, and adequate enforcement, the rules imposed by institutions may be easily circumvented or manipulated. This is the case no matter whether the rules are simple or elaborate. If the rules are simple, they will provide much discretion for abuse. Thus, a reliance on rules to curb corrupt behaviour naturally leads to the development of increasingly complicated rules. Yet, as rules and procedures become more complex, it becomes more difficult and costly for players to know them and follow them correctly. In such situations, incumbents who have stayed in the system long enough become expert players; and, should they become corrupt, are thus able to find enough loopholes in the rules to exploit for their own gain without fear of recourse. Moreover, even if the acts of the incumbents are ethically wrong, there may be no effective remedy, as their ethical wrongdoing technically does not violate any rules. Gu Yanwu (1613–82), widely regarded as one of the three greatest Confucian scholars of the late Ming Dynasty, states: 'When the institution is complicated, those who are crafty and cunning will be able to manipulate the rules like traders in the market; even if there are virtuous people, they will find themselves unable to help the situation' (Gu 1929: bk 11.10). Consequently, even though Confucians would agree that not all people are virtuous, they still find institutions secondary in importance to leaders who may not be sages but are nonetheless virtuous. Thus, the key to good governance is not to focus on refining and perfecting institutions, something Confucians deem impossible, but to identify, select, and promote virtuous people as leaders and equip them with a wide range of discretional powers to correct matters as they see fit.

Confucians may be unduly pessimistic about the virtue of institutions and too optimistic about the power of virtuous leaders. As history demonstrates, misuse of discretion can do far greater harm than institutional loopholes; and constitutional safeguards have constrained many a tyrant. Nevertheless, Confucians do have a point. After all, the daily news provides plenty of stories about big corporations that get away with acts of gross irresponsibility with the help of legions of lawyers; or corrupt politicians and lobby groups that stay technically or legally 'clean' despite behaving in a way that appears morally outrageous. In other words, while Confucians may have underestimated the role of institutions, they see clearly enough that institutions can never be the full solution. The answer to good governance is likely to rest with good leadership *working with* institutions, not *in spite of* them.

4   THE ORDINARY GREATNESS OF CONFUCIAN LEADERS

What kind of leaders do Confucians want if institutions are not the full answer? It is commonly known that Confucians advocate as leaders those elites who are cultivated in practical capabilities, trained in various arts, and virtuous in both private and public life. These elites are usually referred to as *junzi* or 'superior persons'. Historically, there has been an unambiguously chauvinistic character to Confucianism that believes that man and woman excel in virtues differently—that is, according to one influential view on the cosmic order, as articulated in the *Book of Changes*, man manifests virtues through leadership while woman through submission (Legge 2003). This specific understanding of gender hierarchy, however, seems to have little purchase even among the Confucians in modern society (for detail, see Chan 2000). Thus it is possible for contemporary Confucians to set aside this gender-based distinction and focus on leadership qualities that can be universally acquired and manifested by both sexes. Considering the substantive content of leadership qualities proposed by Confucianism, this superior person does seem to be the most extraordinary; he is expected to be kind (*ci*), benevolent (*ren*), strong (*qiang*), diligent (*qin*), reverent (*jing*), agile (*min*), bright (*ming*), wise (*zhi*), sincere (*zheng*), polished (*wen*), responsive (*neng ying*), reflective (*si*), gentle (*wen*), careful (*shen*), faithful (*zhong*), humble (*qian*), flexible (*bian*), righteous (*zheng*), generous (*wei*), courteous (*gong*), courageous (*yong*), observing (*cha*), forgiving (*shu*), consistent (*heng*), persistent (*yi*), appropriate (*dong*), moderate (*jie*), magnanimous (*kuan*), equanimous (*jing*), impartial (*gong*), public-spirited (*gong*), trustworthy (*xin*), filial (*xiao*), and so on (Confucius 1879a; see also Confucius 1879b, 1979).

Despite this long (yet still incomplete) list of qualities, Confucians repeatedly emphasize that the path to great leadership is open to anyone who has the willpower and persistence to cultivate these qualities. Thus Mencius explains to the Duke of Wei that the reason why he is not a great leader is 'due to [his] refusal to act, not to [his] inability to act' (Mencius 1970: bk 1A.7). Xunzi also believes that even an unintelligent man, if he begins to learn, will, within a short time, 'find the wellspring of humanity and justice and so be able to judge right from wrong, to turn the world round in the palm of [his] hand' (Xunzi 1988: bk 8.5). To Confucians, the ability to acquire leadership qualities is above all else a matter of willpower and persistent self-improvement; it is irrespective of family background, status, or natural talent, barring the most severely mentally compromised ones. This confidence in the improvability of people is derived from the everyday experience that human beings can learn or be trained. It is also directly linked to the core feature of Confucian leadership: that a great leader is someone who is excellent at the most ordinary aspects of being human.

This notion of ordinary greatness is best captured by the *Doctrine of Mean*, which states that

> The way of the superior person is at once great and refined. Common men and women, however ignorant, may have knowledge of it; yet in its full-fledged form, there is something that even the sage does not know. Common men and women, however unworthy, can practise it; yet in its full-fledged form, there is something that even the sage cannot practice.
>
> (Confucius 1879a)

Since the qualities of a *junzi* overlap in kind with those of the commoner, a *junzi* is in fact only a more developed commoner. Therefore, a man need not be a genius like Napoleon or Alexander the Great to become a great leader; he needs only to recognize his virtuous nature, and act upon it with persistence. After all, if we look more closely at the leadership qualities listed above, they are but adjectives of daily usage, and are qualities of which almost anyone will have a little bit. The difference between a leader and a commoner is simply that the former insists on living out these virtues, while the latter does not; and the difference between a leader and a virtuous commoner is merely that the former assumes public office, while the latter does not. As Ye Shi (1150–1223), a Sung Dynasty Confucian scholar famous for his practical political perspective, suggests:

> As recorded, when the ancient kings gave rise to their enterprise...their intellect was not above others, nor did their behaviour stand out from others. They saw only that the cosmic order should not be disrespected, the people should not be treated without fear; they dare not be obstinate, they dare not reject good advice, they dare not flinch when dangers come, they dare not take credit when deeds are done. All that they do was to consider carefully the 'heart of the people' so as to treat them appropriately...The sages are those who kept their *heart of ordinariness* without ever losing it; this is why they are great.
>
> (Ye 1961: 698)

In search of this 'heart of ordinariness', leaders must develop qualities that are commonly valued, though may not always be practised. For instance, qualities such as trustworthiness or faithfulness are generally thought to be positive; a coward may see courage as a virtue, and even a cruel person may recognize the value of benevolence. Although, in modern pluralistic societies, people appear to be sceptical about the notion of 'common virtues', Confucianism invites us to revisit this notion. For Confucians, no matter how different people are in terms of customs, cultural background, or priority of values, there seem to be virtues that no one will seriously challenge; in other words, there are virtues that are fundamentally human. No matter who you are or, as Confucians put it, no matter whether you are 'civilized or barbaric' (Xunzi 1988: bk 2.6),[1] love is welcome; caution is advisable; self-sacrifice for the greater good will be honoured; and humility is the basis for wisdom. People who recognize and manifest these universal virtues in their daily lives are deemed agreeable to others and worthy of being entrusted with responsibilities. In this sense, then, leaders are those who win 'the hearts of the people'.

5 INSPIRATIONAL LEADERSHIP

Confucians' faith in the existence of common virtues deeply affects its conception of leadership style. Confucians not only believe that good leaders will be found agreeable

---

[1] Xunzi argues that, even if someone is trapped in the 'barbaric tribes', as long as he lives by virtues such as respectfulness, reverence, loyalty, faithfulness, ritual proprieties, and love, he will still be considered an honorable person (*Xunzi* 2.6).

by the people; they also claim that, once leaders set themselves as moral exemplars, the people will follow their example. At first glance, the Confucian description of the role-model effect can appear almost magical. Confucius says that the people are like the grass that bends in whatever direction the wind of leadership blows (Confucius 1979: bk 12.19); the *Book of Changes* even claims that, when the sages 'touch and move' the hearts of the people, there will be 'harmony and peace all under the sky' (Legge 2003). This description, however exaggerated it may appear, is nevertheless not nonsensical. From a Confucian perspective, when the people follow their leaders, they are not merely taking orders from them but also deferring to their judgement; and they do so because they believe that the leaders are more virtuous than they are themselves. The leaders, therefore, exercise not only an institutional authority over their followers, but also a moral one. This ethically superior position allows the leaders to influence their followers not only through administrative command or incentive structures, but also through inspirational demonstrations of virtue. This notion is not entirely unfamiliar to Western political traditions: the inspiration brought by Henry V in the 'Saint Crispin's Day Speech' in Shakespeare's *Henry V* (IV. iii) was echoed by Churchill's oration in the Cabinet War Room, while the air of aspiration stirred by the words of JFK was replicated, however short lived, by that of Barack Obama. Political leaders often exercise tremendous moral authority over their followers, and are hence capable of inspiring them to act voluntarily for the greater good.

Confucians hold no patent on the notion of inspirational leadership, but they certainly take this notion most seriously, arguing that, if leaders fail to lead by example, they will lose their followers' respect and loyalty. In time, no matter how many institutional arrangements are in place, their political authority will dissipate into thin air. As Confucius aptly says: 'When a political leader's personal conduct is correct, his government is effective without the issuing of orders. If his personal conduct is not correct, he may issue orders, but they will not be followed' (Confucius 1960: bk 13.6).

Once a leader's moral authority has been established, it can be put to two kinds of use. First, leaders may utilize their followers' trust to enable the efficient execution of policies. Second, they may use their moral authority to inspire their followers to improve their own moral character. However, regarding the first use, although efficiency is important, if it is brought about by coercive measures such as reward and punishment mechanisms, it may be found to be undesirable and to conflict with a more important concern of politics, which is to improve the people's moral well-being. For this reason Confucius finds reward and punishment to be undesirable, because they serve only as external measures of control. Leaders who lead by example, however, can inspire the people to develop their inner qualities and virtues. Thus, in the *Record of Rituals*, Confucians advise political leaders to abide by standards of personal conduct that are much stricter than those expected of commoners, so that the commoners can be encouraged to be 'cordial with each other [*mu*]', 'self-restrained [*bu yin*]', 'reverent [*jing*]', 'loyal [*zuo zhong*]', 'filial [*zuo xiao*]', 'humble [*rang shan*]', 'non-confrontational [*bu zheng*]', and so on (Confucius 1879b).

To summarize, a Confucian leader enjoys both political and ethical authority, with the former grounded on the latter; this dual but interdependent character of Confucian leadership is best captured by Confucius's words:

> If a superior person loves propriety, the people will not dare not to be reverent. If he loves righteousness, the people will not dare not to submit to his example. If he loves good faith, the people will not dare not to be sincere. Now, when these things obtain, the people from all quarters will come to him.
>
> (Confucius 1960: bk 13.4)

Being an ethical leader is essential to being a good political leader.

6 Leadership as Delegation

So far this chapter has emphasized the moral aspect of Confucian leadership qualities; the following discusses the practical aspects of Confucian politics.

Throughout China's long history, Confucians have proposed various institutions, governing strategies, and leadership techniques and styles that are aimed at improving politics in the real world. Many of these recommendations have been made obsolete by modernity. What remains interesting for modern politics, however, is the insight of these recommendations into what constitutes effective leadership.

To begin with, Confucians believe that the most fundamental condition for effective leadership is for government officials to possess practical knowledge of their own policy portfolios. No matter how important inspirational leadership is, it is no replacement for technical know-how about policy-making and policy-execution. Confucians are aware that the difference between policy and fantasy lies in the leader's knowledge and information about economics, administrative design, and judicial practice. Only when leaders are practically capable can they devise policies that are effective and easy to implement. Leaders need not be well-rounded sages in order to count as capable as *The Analects* suggests, 'a [*junzi*] does not seek in one man talents for every employment' (Confucius 1960: bk 18.10). Rather, leaders must possess the necessary qualities for the particular positions they are in. The key to effective leadership, therefore, is to recognize the talents of different individuals and offer them positions that befit their strengths.

Once offices have been filled, however, Confucians believe that leaders should fall back on the role of monitoring and give their subordinates the necessary freedom to discharge their duties—the rationale being that sound judgement must be based not only on knowledge but also on timely and accurate information, which, however, is almost impossible to gather centrally. Consequently, Confucians believe that, for leadership to be effective, authority must be diversified, as no one person can ever possess sufficient information to make sound, highly centralized decisions. Wang Fuzhi (1619–92), regarded as one of the three greatest Confucian scholars of the Ming Dynasty, makes this point clearly:

> For in this world, there are things which are common in general, but also which are diversely different. Hence, since long ago, this world cannot be accounted for by any single perspective…Within the cosmic order, there are different climates and timings; upon the land, there are places with different geographical advantages; among the people, there are talents with different specialties; as for materials, there are resources for different utilities…What is regarded as hazardous here is exactly what others rely upon for survival. What is regarded as good here is exactly the reason for others' failure…If one can understand this, then let the institutions be left to the previous kings' establishment, let daily running of government be left to the hundred corresponding officials, let discretional authority be left to senior local civil servants, and let decisions be left to the liking and disliking of the commoners. In this case, all things under heaven shall move into the positions where they belong.
>
> (Wang 2008: 218)

One of the most important aspects of Confucian leadership, therefore, is delegation; but this delegation is effective only if people who are capable and virtuous are selected to official positions that correspond to their strengths.

7 THE CONFUCIAN LEADER AS VISIONARY STRATEGIST

Although the emphasis on delegation implies that leaders are decreasingly involved in practical matters as they are promoted to higher ranks, the importance of leadership is undiminished because top leaders are constantly required to make critical strategic judgements. In any hierarchical structure, although the lower-ranking officials have access to timely and accurate information, their power and the scope of their information remain significantly limited. Additionally, as China developed from a confederation of small but essentially independent feudal states into a united empire, overall strategic planning and coordination were unavoidable. No matter how much discretion is delegated to local governments, the central government remains irreplaceable in matters of legislation, national defense, empire-wide taxation, standardization of ritual norms for cultural development, selection of civil service officials by competitive examinations, planning of national transportation infrastructures, and any issues that involve empire-wide coordination. These policy issues have one common feature: instead of focusing on micro-managing the day-to-day operations of different governmental offices, these issues are concerned with formulating principles, creating institutional infrastructure, and giving strategic directions at the highest level in support of the empire's long-term development.

Since tackling such issues usually involves a prolonged period of time and considera-tion of a number of diverse factors, the top leaders' decisions are likely to be more about judgement than mechanical execution. For this reason, Confucianism expects top lead-ers to have strong character and strategic vision. The formulation of this strategic vision requires a statecraft that can support the long-term development of the state and its society. Confucians have given many names to this kind of vision: it has been called the 'great plan [*da-you*]' in the *Book of Poetry* (Ma 1987: 590), the 'grand design [*hong-fan*]' in the *Book of History* (Wu 1980: 134–52), 'models of the ancient kings [*xian-wang-zhi-fa*]' in Mencius and Xunzi (Mencius 1970: bk 4A.1; see also Xunzi 1988: bk 5.6). These names usually refer to strategic visions that can be roughly divided into two components: (i) strategic judgements concerning different fields with corresponding policy arrangements, and (ii) the strate-gic mentality required for making these judgements. For the first part, Confucians have proposed measures involving administrative structure, economic planning, adjustments to the agricultural calendar, educational policies, civil-service examinations, and many other fields. As many of these arrangements have been made obsolete by modernity, we will therefore focus on the strategic mentality of leaders as championed by Confucianism.

Various versions of this strategic mentality have been depicted in many different essays and books, and even in government memorandums by Confucian scholars and officials. In all of these versions, however, there are a number of common and repre-sentative features[2] that deserve to be highlighted: (i) the strategic mentality is grounded on (but not identical to) the virtues and capabilities that individuals acquire through self-cultivation; (ii) leaders love the people by putting the long-term interests of the people above private interests (and, if required, by being willing to give their lives for the sake of public interests); (iii) leaders should prioritize principle over benefits in decision-making, unless faced with overriding concerns such as impending catastro-phe; (iv) leaders should be principled but not rigid; thus they need to be flexible by act-ing in the spirit of the principle rather than by following it to the letter; (v) leaders should be able to foresee major dangers and avoid them by altering the present course of action; (vi) leaders should be eager to find people with talents that exceed their own and enlist them to work for the public interest; (vii) leaders should be well balanced in various vir-tues (for example, determined but willing to listen, disciplined but not harsh, generous but not indulgent, analytical but not argumentative, tough but not rough, and so on);

---

[2] These features are drawn from a range of classical texts by early Confucian scholars, including *The Book of Poetry, The Book of History, The Record of Rituals, The Book of Changes, The Zuo Commentary on Spring and Autumn Annals, The Analects, Mencius, Xunzi*, along with some other works of later Confucians such as Qiu Jun (1421–95), *Da xue yan yi bu* (that is, *Completing the Elaboration on the Great Learning*), Huang Zongxi (1610–95), *Waiting for the Dawn*, Gu Yanwu, *Ru zhi lu* (that is, *The Record of Daily Recognition*), Wang Fuzhi's major works (that is, historical commentaries, elaborations on *The Book of Changes*, commentaries on *The Book of History* and *The Book of Poetry*), Yu, *Xin yi Zuo zhuan du ben* (2002), Qiu, *Da xue yan yi bu* (political interpretation of the *Great Learning* in *The Record of Rituals*) (1999), Huang and de Bary, *Waiting for the Dawn: A Plan for the Prince* (1993), and Wang, *Chuanshan yi shu* (the complete works of Wang Fuzhi) (1933).

and, finally, (viii) leaders must be well versed in the skills and macro-vision needed to organize social, economic, and political order.

Although such great leaders are rare, they have existed. In the West, there were, for example, Alexander the Great and the founding fathers of the USA; in China, the emperors who founded their dynasties. When such visionary leaders appear, they are usually able to prolong the peace and prosperity of a society. If they appear in chaotic times, they may start a new age, or, in Confucian terms, construct 'the framework for an epoch' (Wang 2008: 290). The most interesting part of Confucianism's claim, however, is that such great leaders need not be geniuses or demi-gods; they need only be ordinary individuals who are willing continuously to improve themselves.

8 Selecting the Leaders

Given Confucianism's emphasis on the importance of virtuous political leadership, the next question, naturally, is how the politically talented are to be selected. It should be emphasized, however, that theorizing institutional design has never been the focus of Confucianism. Nonetheless, deriving from the most frequently adopted institutions for selecting those with political talents, one may still identify two major competing Confucian views about how these talented individuals can best be found. Given the limitation of space, this section can offer only a brief outline of these views.

First, one popular view is that the selection of those with political talents must rely on local knowledge. In this view, if political leaders should be virtuous people, then the government should seek to identify people who are already virtuous in their private conduct. This kind of information, however, cannot be gathered centrally. Therefore, the initial selection process must be put in the hands of the local elites, such as local officials or local gentry who may screen and recommend those politically talented people who should be promoted[3] (Qiu 1999: bk 11.1).

A competing view among Confucians is that the process of selecting the politically talented should be centralized for the purpose of fairness and quality control. In this view the recommendations from local gentry and officials are not reliable, because they leave too many loopholes for abuse and corruption[4] (Qiu 1999: bk 11.1). That which

---

[3] In its institutional manifestation, it is generally referred to as 'local selection'. The exact arrangement of this mechanism varies from time to time, but the most typical form was proposed by Dong Zongshu in Han Dynasty: 'I humbly suggests that: the local aristocrat, province governors and local officials should each select the virtuous ones among the civil servants and the commoners so as to recommend two persons each year as tribute to the central government ... if the recommended persons are truly virtuous, the referees should be rewarded, and vice versa. In this way, these local officials will wholeheartedly seek the virtuous one, and the virtuous ones under heaven can be offered political positions to govern' (Ban 2004: bk 4.26).

[4] As suggested by Qiu Jun: 'The method of "selection by local recommendation" can no longer be adopted in later ages; this is because the people have been becoming more hypocritical every day. They dare deceiving each other for private interests, publicly forming cliques so as to cover up for each other.

counts as virtuous is also too subjective. Therefore, these Confucians advocate that the selection process should be centralized through periodically holding competitive civil-service examinations in which anyone may participate. The candidates must demonstrate superior understanding of Confucian classics; this supposedly can indicate how virtuous they are. They will also be tested about current affairs so as to guarantee their practical capability.

Critics of these two views, however, believe that neither way can effectively identify the politically talented. After all, the examination candidates may simply toe the official line without actually being virtuous. These critics believe that any selection mechanism can provide only prima facie results; that is, any selection mechanism essentially can screen out only the obviously vicious and incapable candidates, but it cannot identify the truly virtuous ones. They, therefore, suggest that those with appropriate political talents can be identified only through long-term observation and assessment of a person's behaviour and contribution in his or her political career. Hence selecting the politically talented requires a two-step process; first, the seemingly capable ones should be identified through either of the two ways mentioned above, and, second, the truly talented ones will be promoted in time.[5] In fact, these critics are merely pointing out an obvious phenomenon of the daily running of politics; nonetheless, this perspective also illustrates how Confucians in general hold many reservations about relying on institutions to identify those with appropriate political talents.

Despite these disagreements among Confucians, there is, nonetheless, a view that is shared by all: they agree that deliberate intensive grooming is necessary for generating political talents. This is especially pertinent to the monarchical political reality facing Confucianism; since the senior political leaders (that is, the emperor and the aristocracy) are always born into power, the only peaceful way to ensure the quality of the leaders is to educate them as early as possible. Hence, state education endorsed by Confucianism has been initially set up to cultivate the governing aristocracy (Confucius 1879d). Yet, as the effectiveness of education has been widely recognized by all Confucians, promotion of education through setting up schools at both central and local level has also been

Should there be no standards for vetting, policy for scrutinizing, and methods for reporting abuses, employing people only on the basis of trust and believing their words without suspicion will only lead to a situation in which hierocracy grows daily while whether one is truly virtuous can no longer be found out' (Qiu 1999: bk 9.1).

[5] On this point, Wang Fuzhi has given an excellent discussion: 'If using private conduct as standard to screen in the virtuous ones does not work, then would adopting knowledge as the basis be successful in getting the virtuous talents? This is not what I am saying. The purpose of setting up civil service examination is limited to distinguishing the educated ones from the uneducated commoners. Even if one has the wisdom of knowing the quality of a person, he still will not be able to distinguish for sure the vicious ones from the virtuous ones in the beginning of their political career . . . Taking these ritual norms as standard, in nine out of ten cases the educated ones can be distinguished from the uneducated ones. Beyond this distinction, they can only be evaluated by observing what proposals they say and what contributions they make after they have begun their political career. Only then can one identify the vicious one and the virtuous ones so as to decide on the matter of promotion and demotion' (Wang 1933: 879).

endorsed by many Confucians as an important measure of generating political talents (Confucius 1879c). Nevertheless, except for the selection of the emperor or other hereditary leaders, grooming alone is insufficient, because it does not entail any mechanism for selecting the politically talented. Therefore, although it is treated as the foundation for generating political talents, it still requires the supplementation of selection mechanisms such as those already outlined.

Since theorizing institutional designs (including the ones for selecting those with political talents) has never been the focus Confucianism, it is difficult to discuss the issue of identifying virtuous leaders in ways more concrete than the general views laid out above. Beyond these general views, selecting the politically talented, on the whole, has been treated as a pragmatic matter of which the focus is on arranging the mundane institutional details. Historically, these institutional arrangements have indeed played an important role in filling the government positions with the politically talented; but they have mostly been made obsolete by the conditions of modernity.

9   CONCLUSION

This chapter has sought to demonstrate that Confucianism views leadership as the central factor for good politics and remains sceptical of the effectiveness of even well-designed institutions. This distrust of institutions, of course, need not be exaggerated (institutional reforms are after all proposed by Confucians all the time), but there is little doubt that, in politics, leadership is viewed as being far more important. This emphasis on political leadership is proportional to Confucianism's demands on the requisite qualities of a leader: namely, that, for a leader to hold greater power, he must himself be greater in virtue.

At first glance, this Confucian demand may seem too ideal, almost naive—the rareness of such leaders must surely mean that institutions are the better safeguard. Nevertheless, in modern times, our world is full of stories about failed democracies and corrupted rule of law. Institutions that lack proper leaders appear to be empty words on thin paper. Even for well-entrenched democracies, politics sometimes remain plagued with character assassination, fear-mongering, and sensational sound bites uttered by political leaders for personal gain. Since the end of the Second World War, the remarkable success of institutional safeguards such as constitutional democracies in warding off political catastrophe seems to be marred by an equally weighty failure to generate a political order that can resolve problems satisfactorily.

Even when social and economic progress takes place, it still seems to be brought about by visionary leadership as much as by institutions. After all, there were democratically elected leaders who turned a blind eye to grave social injustices such as disenfranchisement of black people, which was redressed only by courageous and visionary leaders who pushed for the Civil Rights Act. In a sense, therefore, Confucianism seems correct to suggest that 'there are men who can bring about order, but there is no model that will produce order' (Xunzi 1988: bk 12.1). Although institutions play a certain role in the improvement of political order, the importance of leadership should not be underestimated.

Confucianism believes that the role of leaders is to gain trust from the people so as to 'win their hearts'; to inspire the people towards self-improvement; to select the right talents and delegate power for effective governance; and to provide strategic vision and judgement to guide the state's long-term development. What is most important, however, is that Confucians believe that such leadership is rooted in the moral qualities shared by all human beings. Historically the ranks of such leadership endorsed by Confucianism were mostly filled with the economically well-off; this phenomenon, however, should be deemed only as historical contingency. Considering the theoretical perspective of Confucianism, anyone can become a great leader if she recognizes her own moral nature and is willing to develop herself into a morally exemplary person.

Recommended Reading

De Bary, W. T. (2004). *Nobility and Civility: Asian Ideals of Leadership and the Common Good*. Cambridge, MA: Harvard University Press.

De Bary, W. T. (1991). *The Trouble with Confucianism*. Cambridge, MA: Harvard University Press.

Pines, Y. (2002). *Foundations of Confucian Thought: Intellectual Life in the Chunqiu Period (722–453 BCE)*. Honolulu: Hawai'i University Press.

References

Ban, G., An, P., and Zhang, C. (2004). *Han shu (History of Han)*. Shanghai: Han yu da ci dian chu ban she.

Chan, S. Y. (2000). 'Gender and Relationship Roles in The Analects and the Mencius', *Asian Philosophy*, 10/2: 115–32.

Confucius (1879a). 'Record of Rituals: The Doctrine of Mean', in *The Sacred Books of China: The Texts of Confucianism*, ed. James Legge, CADAL. Oxford: Clarendon Press <http://ctext.org/pre-qin-and-han/zh?searchu=%E7%82%BA%E6%94%BF%E5%9C%A8%E4%BA%BA anden=on>. Accessed 15 September 2012.

Confucius (1879b). 'The Record of Rituals: Record of Dykes', in *The Sacred Books of China: The Texts of Confucianism*, ed. James Legge, CADAL. Oxford: Clarendon Press <http://ctext.org/liji/fang-ji>. Accessed 15 September 2012.

Confucius (1879c). 'The Record of Rituals: Record of Learning', in *The Sacred Books of China: The Texts of Confucianism*, ed. James Legge, CADAL. Oxford: Clarendon Press <http://ctext.org/liji/fang-ji>. Accessed 15 September 2012.

Confucius (1879d). 'The Record of Rituals: Royal Regulations', in *The Sacred Books of China: The Texts of Confucianism*, ed. James Legge, CADAL. Oxford: Clarendon Press <http://ctext.org/liji/fang-ji>. Accessed 15 September 2012.

Confucius (1960). *The Chinese Classics: With a Translation, Critical and Exegetical Notes, Prolegomena, Copious Indexes*, ed. James Legge. Hong Kong: Hong Kong University Press <http://ctext.org/analects/zi-lu/zh?en=on>. Accessed 15 September 2012.

Confucius (1979). *The Analects (Lun yü)*, ed. D. C. Lau. Harmondsworth: Penguin Books.

Gu, Y. W. (1929). *Ri Zhi Lu [32 juan]*. Shanghai: Shang wu yin shu guan.

Huang, Z. (1993). *Waiting for the Dawn: A Plan for the Prince*, ed. William de Bary. New York: Columbia University Press.

Legge, J. (2003). *I Ching or Book of Changes*. Kessinger Publishing <http://ctext.org/book-of-changes/xian/zh?en=on>. Accessed 15 September 2012.

Ma, C. (1987). 'Xiao Min', in *Shi jing jin zhu jin yi* (*The Book of Poetry*). Taibei Shi: Taiwan shang wu ying shu guan.

Mencius (1970). *Mencius*, ed. D. C. Lau. Harmondsworth: Penguin.

Qiu, J. (1999). *Da xue yan yi bu* (political interpretation of the *Great Learning* in *The Record of Rituals*), ed. G. Lin, J. Zhou, and D. Zhen. Beijing Shi: Jing hua chu ban she.

Wang, F. J. (1933). *Chuanshan yi shu* (the complete works of Wang Fuzhi). Shanghai: Taiping yang shu ju.

Wang, F. J. (2008). *Song Lun* (historical commentary on the Song Dynasty). *[15 juan]*. Beijing Shi: Zhonghua shu zhu.

Wu, Y. (1980). *Xin yi Shang shu du ben* (*The Book of History*). Taibei Shi: San min shu ju.

Xunzi (1988). *Xunzi: A Translation and Study of the Complete Works*, ed. John Knoblock. Stanford, CA: Stanford University Press.

Ye, S. (1961). *Ye Shi ji* (collected essays of Ye Shi)., ed. G. Liu, X. Wang, and Z. Li. Beijing: Zhonghua shu ju.

Yu, X. (2002). *Xin yi Zuo zhuan du ben* (the Zuo commentary on *Spring and Autumn Annals*). Taibei Shi: San min shu ju.

CHAPTER 5

....

FEMINISM

....

LAURA SJOBERG

1 INTRODUCTION

....

THERE is a growing body of scholarship critiquing both theoretical approaches to and practices of political leadership from a feminist perspective. This scholarship is inspired by the under-representation not only of women but of femininity in political leadership, and the under-theorization of gender in leadership studies generally and work on political leadership more specifically.

Women are under-represented in political leadership. In 2011, women were, for the first time, approaching 20 per cent of the world's parliamentarians. Women at that time constituted a full 20 per cent of single-house or lower-house representatives, and 18.5 per cent of upper-house representatives. Regionally, women are best represented in the Americas (falling at 22.7 per cent, just above the world's average), and worst represented in Asia (falling at 18.0 per cent, just below the world's average). There is one woman-majority parliamentary chamber in the world, in Rwanda. Other countries with more than 40 per cent representation of women come from all over the world: Andorra, Sweden, South Africa, Seychelles, Cuba, Iceland, Finland, Nicaragua, and Norway. Some countries that perhaps one would not expect (Afghanistan, Iraq, South Sudan, Ethiopia) have representation of women well above the world's average. The United States of America falls below the world's average, with 16.8 per cent representation of women. Several countries in the world (Belize, Micronesia, Nauru, Palau, Qatar, Saudi Arabia, and the Solomon Islands) still do not have a single woman representative in their parliamentary bodies (IPU 2011).

Of 193 United Nations member states, women are currently the heads of government of 22 of them, or 11.4 per cent. Women's representation in cabinets is about the same as parliaments—averaging about 18.3 per cent. There are two woman-majority cabinets in the world at the time of writing: Finland's cabinet is 58 per cent women, and Norway's is 56 per cent women (IPU 2011). While data are available for less than half of the world's justice systems, women represent around 27 per cent of the judges and prosecutors in the world, and about 9 per cent of its police forces (UN Women 2011).

In fact, women's under-representation in political leadership remains stark in most countries that would be classified as progressive on other gender issues. Not only women but also femininity are under-represented in leadership. The under-representation of femininity is evidenced by the fact that even women who do hold positions of political leadership are often either neglected in discussions of leadership, or treated differently from the men who hold similar positions. Studies of female political leaders show that, as compared to male leaders, their personal lives receive significantly greater attention both in campaigns and as they govern (Tickner 2001). If a female political leader and a male political leader make a similar decision, the woman's leadership capacity is more likely to be questioned as a result (Duerst-Lahti and Kelley 1995). Leadership is not only *sex-specific* but also *gender-specific*, where the ideal-typical leader is 'male in appearance and gender, and masculine in character traits' (Sjoberg 2009). Feminists have argued that this is related to particular gendered ideas that we (as political communities and as scholars) hold of leaders and leadership.

While women remain under-represented in actual leadership positions, both females and femininity remain neglected in our concepts of what it means to be a political leader. Our gendered narratives about political leadership 'reinforce the belief, widely held…by both men and women, that military and foreign policy-making are arenas of policy-making least appropriate for women' and limit both women's access and the influence of femininity in politics (Tickner 1992). Both news coverage of, and scholarship on, political leadership often contain gender-biased notions of the processes of leadership and the traits of leaders.

After laying out some key concepts, this chapter begins by providing evidence of the sex (male) of most people who hold political leadership positions and the gender (masculine) of ideal-typical understandings of leadership in global politics. Despite these sex and gender disparities in actual leadership, this chapter does not focus on how to add more women to the ranks of the world's leadership. Instead, it critiques traditional interpretations of who counts as a leader, what counts as leadership, and how leaders make decisions. It makes the case, with feminist scholars on political leadership, that the characteristics that we value in leaders in global politics privilege masculine characteristics and devalue feminine ones, rendering women unqualified by default because they are associated with those devalued feminine characteristics. In addition to making the case that current conceptions of good leadership are gendered, this chapter critiques the idea of leadership itself through feminist lenses, arguing that it assumes a reactively autonomous concept of human decision-making. The chapter concludes with a discussion of feminist alternative frameworks for thinking about and studying leaders and leadership, based on relational autonomy.

2 Women, Gender, and Leadership

The idea that 'sex' and 'gender' mean different things may not be intuitive, as we read them used interchangeably all the time, especially on government documents and other data-collection tools. When this chapter uses the word 'sex', it refers to the (perceived) biological sexes of 'women' and 'men'.[1] Gender is used to discuss the social expectations of those we see as 'women' and as 'men'. Simply put, 'sex' is used as a rough signifier for biology, and 'gender' for the social world we build around those biologies.

In politics, gender is manifested in the highlighting of certain characteristics of women politicians that conform to gender expectations, like Queen Elizabeth's 'virginity' (see Moss 2006), as well as the punishing of certain characteristics of women politicians that defy gender expectations, like Hillary Clinton's 'anger' (see Dowd 2006, who classified media treatment of her as 'a she-monster melding images of Medea, the Furies, harpies, and a knife-wielding Glenn Close in "Fatal Attraction"'). There are certain traits that we *see women as* (passive, sympathetic, pure, dependent, emotional, caring, and soft) as opposed to the traits that we *see men as* (strong, powerful, autonomous, authoritative, rational, and aggressive). There are also places where *we see women* (in homes, in schools) and places where *we see men* (in militaries, in governments). The exact content of what is expect of men *as men* and women *as women* changes, but gender expectations are salient across widely variant social and political organizations around the world (Hartmann 2006).

Social gender is often talked about in terms of femininities and masculinities, where femininities are associated with 'being a woman' and masculinities are associated with 'being a man'. They include behaviour expectations, stereotypes, and social rules that apply to people on the basis of sex (Enloe 2004). Most of these gender expectations are subordinating to women and femininities (Rissman 2004; Hey 2006). Feminists have pointed out two subordinating moves: first, gender itself is a social construction (e.g. Prügl 1999). Biological sex does not make people into particular sorts of people—'men' are not *naturally* rational compared to 'women's' *natural* propensity for emotion. Instead, gender is 'a set of discourses which can set, change, enforce, and represent meaning on the basis of perceived membership in or relation to sex categories' (Sjoberg 2007, citing Connell 1995; see also Gibson-Graham 1994). Second, the social construction of masculinities and femininities subordinate women and femininity.

That means that, while gender is not *natural*, it is experienced. Social constructions *construct* the organization of social and political life. People live, and live with, gender stereotypes. There is not one experience that 'men' have with gender and one experience that 'women' have with gender, but gender is a lens (see Peterson and Runyan 1999: 21) through which we read *men as men* and *women as women*. 'Gender hierarchies' are socially constructed hierarchies based on gendered expectations of people (or states). This chapter is interested in unpacking what that means for the theory and practice of political leadership from a feminist perspective.

A few words about what 'a feminist perspective' means might be useful before going forward. Some people (erroneously) assume that a feminist perspective is necessarily

---

[1] Perceived, because there are actually a number of different biological sexes (see Fausto-Sterling 2005), but we usually collapse them into two.

about promoting women over men, or about assuming that women need help to be men's equals. This is not accurate generally, and not how it is used in feminist scholarship broadly interpreted or in this chapter specifically. Instead, feminism has its roots in a political movement primarily interested in women's rights and gender emancipation, but those interests have led feminist scholars to look through gender lenses to understand both gender and how gender helps us learn more about the world more broadly. As such, 'a feminist perspective' is 'neither just about women, nor the addition of women to male-stream constructions' (Peterson 1992: 205). Instead, 'it is about what we see in global politics by looking at and for [both] women and gender, and what those things tell us about how the world works' generally and how leadership works specifically (Tickner and Sjoberg 2011). This is not to say that there is just one feminist perspective. Instead, there are many feminisms, both generally and in my field of international relations. This chapter focuses on combining a variety of feminist insights to 'focus on gender as a particular kind of power relation, [and] trace out the ways in which gender is central to understanding international processes', particularly leadership (Steans 1998: 5).

Feminist work on political leadership across academic disciplines has asked important questions about gendered ideas of leadership as well as gendered expectations of political leaders. Gendered lenses have been used to examine how women are under-represented in positions of political leadership and to encourage consideration of 'how the epistemological and ontological bases of conceptual frameworks may misrepresent the experiences of women as leaders, thereby distorting our specific knowledge of such experiences and our general knowledge of the phenomena of leadership as gender-encompassing' (Bensimon 1989: 149). The remainder of this chapter explores some of those contributions.

3 Gendered Expectations of Leaders and Leadership

Feminist scholarship has identified two places in our understandings of leadership where gendered expectations are significant: in gendered ideas of what constitutes good leadership, and in gendered stereotypes that dominate theories of leadership in scholarly settings.

Harry Truman once characterized leadership as 'the ability to get men to do what they don't like to do and like it' (Kets de Vries 1994). In Truman's account, both the leader and his subject are male. In fact, in most accounts of the qualities leadership requires, the leader is described as a 'him' even in contemporary analysis. For example, Sadler describes voters' idea of a good leader as 'capable of making decisions of his own, strong-willed, ambitious, energetic, and motivated by power' (Sadler 2003). In addition to being male-sexed, Sadler's 'good' leader is typified by characteristics associated with masculinity. Other descriptions of voters' ideas of good leadership focus on stereotypically masculine traits as well, emphasizing 'a facility for abstract or strategic thought' (Bennis 1999), 'abstraction' and 'result-oriented behaviour' (Best and Williams 1990), 'assertiveness, coarseness, toughness, aggressiveness, sternness, masculinity, activeness, rationality, and confidence' (Huddy and Terkildsen 1993: 508), and 'courage, ambition...[and] decision-making' (Hogan and Warrenfeltz 2003). These traits have been consistently associated with not just masculinity (see Connell 1995) but militarized masculinity (see Enloe 2000). In fact, scholars of leadership have noted that voters often value these traits associated with masculinity over 'traits representing *warmth and expressiveness* (warmth, gentleness, sensitivity, emotionalness, talkativeness, and cautiousness)' (Huddy and Terkildsen 1993: 508).

The association of 'good' leadership with traits associated with masculinity means that the *definition of what it means to be a good leader* overlaps significantly with what it means *to be a good man (as a man)*, while there is very little overlap between leadership and what we expect of women *as women*. Still, to say that these are characteristics traditionally associated with masculinity is not to say either that they are characteristics women cannot have or that they are necessarily negative characteristics. Women can be (and have been) masculine leaders, and men can be (and have been) feminine. Gendered understandings of what it means to be a good leader, however, still affect the sex composition of leadership. This is because men are associated with masculinity, and therefore assumed to have a number of the positive characteristics we associate with good leadership. Women are associated with many traits that are opposites, or foils, of those traits we associate with men. Therefore, 'the burden of proof to demonstrate masculine capacity is higher on a woman (who is assumed to be incapable until proven differently, while a man is assumed to be masculine until his masculinity is questioned' (Sjoberg 2009: 164).

As a result, many women who seek political office emphasize their masculine characteristics, attempting 'to portray themselves as women who do not conform to traditional gender stereotypes' in their political decision-making, even while living up to expectations of femininity in their appearance and personal lives. Therefore, even when women are integrated into the ranks of political leadership (which remains statistically rare), their integration is (for now, at least) maintaining masculine understandings of what it means to be a good leader. Political leadership is not an area where traditional gender expectations and ideal-types of femininity have disappeared, but one where women are (sometimes) successfully navigating gendered expectations.

The gendered stereotypes that voters have of their leaders are often replicated in scholarly accounts of leadership. Briefly, five different kinds of accounts of leadership can be found in the broad scholarly literature on how leaders come to be and how people select them: trait-based, rational actor, situational, psychodynamic, and (explicitly) gender-based. The remainder of this section will address them in turn.

Trait-based theories of leadership, 'also known as 'great-man' theories, postulate common qualities and characteristics of effective leaders', much like the results of popular surveys already discussed. Trait-based theories have identified psychological characteristics (technical ability, strategy, capacity for abstraction, strength, intelligence, and courage) as well as sociological properties (social class; education; gender; and religious, ethnic, and kinship networks) that make good leaders (Whittington 1993; Dingfelder 2004). These trait-based approaches both favour masculinities over femininities (Alexander and Andersen 1993: 536) and amplify pre-existing social exclusions based on (race and class and) gender. Charlotte Hooper described this as masculinism that 'justifies and naturalizes gender hierarchy by not questioning the elevation of ways of being and knowing associated with men and masculinity over those associated with women and femininity' (Hooper 1998: 31). Trait-based theories of leadership are also, in feminist terms, primarily agential (a product of the person leading) to the neglect of the structural (a product of those being led) and the intersubjective (the co-constitution of the leader and the led).

Recent growth in trait-based theories of leadership that builds on the 'Big Five' framework of personality traits as those effective in political leadership might at first appear to have transcended the feminist critique of the masculinism of trait-based theories, if not the critique of the agent-centred nature of the work. This is especially true insomuch as these 'Big Five' leadership studies find that there is a difference between leaders (and voters' preferences) on different sides of the political spectrum (Caprara, et al. 1993). While the 'Big Five' traits preserve some of the traditional gender dichotomies (inventive/cautious, efficient/careless, outgoing/reserved, compassionate/cold, and sensitive/secure), there is some evidence that some constituencies value one of the traditionally 'feminine' traits (compassion) in their leaders, and that leaders then act on compassion. That said, even this analysis both preserves the gendered dichotomies of traits in earlier work and fails to analyse the gendered nature both of those dichotomies and of leadership traits more generally.

A number of international relations theorists impute and assume rather than study leadership, and those theorists most often think about leadership in terms of the 'rational-actor' model. Rational-actor theories of leadership see leadership and followership as 'the product of rational calculations based on objective or subjective considerations of self-interest' (Edinger 1990: 514). This sort of leadership is strategic, and based on cost–benefit analysis—the rational leader chooses on the basis of his followers' interests, and the followers choose him because he does so. The rational-actor model also understands leadership as 'highly individualistic, competitive behaviour' (Tickner 2001). Feminists have argued that, for the rational-actor model to be representative of how and why people choose leaders, people would have to be fully autonomous decision-makers, rather than the 'relationally autonomous' decision-makers that they are (Hirschmann 1989). This disrupts a purely cost–benefit analysis model of leader selection and leader behaviour. As such, such a model is only possible if we assume that men's experiences are a prototype for human behaviour (Tickner 2001). Feminists have also been critical of rational-actor approaches to leadership because their logic 'gives normative privilege to self-interest: it argues that selfishness is necessary and successful' (Sjoberg 2009, citing Zalewski 1996). This is at odds with feminisms' fundamental commitment to see the world from the point of view of the marginalized (Brown 1988). Even were feminist scholars normatively to embrace selfishness, the rational subject model assumes a homogeneity of those being led that is misleading (Peterson 1992: 197). Finally, the very idea that rational cost–benefit analysis is possible has been questioned in feminist theory, where the idea of objective cost–benefit analysis has been framed as partial, impersonalized, and gendered (e.g. Seidler 1994: 109; Connell 1995: 73).

Unlike trait-based and rational-actor theoretical approaches to leadership, situational approaches to leadership look more at the political context than at the leader. Situational theories of leadership 'postulate that leaders may emerge who have the characteristics and skills to meet the needs to their group, organization, or society at a given time' (Gill 2006: 36). While situational theories of leadership pay attention to the 'structure' part of the agent–structure divide, feminists have still raised the criticism that they do not pay attention to intersubjectivity, or the interdependence of agent and structure. Instead, 'feminist alternatives...do not promote more universal abstractions, but demand greater context in order to map more adequately the complexity and indeterminacy of agent and structure' especially since situational analysis still often 'assumes interpretations of power, rationality, security, and sovereignty which are gendered' (True 1996: 229, 233). Also, situational theories of leadership recognize many of the traits associated with masculinity as being 'called for' in a variety of situations (strength in times of war, rationality in times of peace, and so on), while many characteristics associated with femininity (emotion, interdependence) are rarely if ever called for. Feminists have also expressed concern that, in addition to the leadership traits that are needed situationally being gendered, many political situations are themselves influenced by gender stereotypes and subordinations. In other words, the 'situations' that choose leaders do so with race, gender, and other biases that reflect political subordination in the world(s) where they rise (Sjoberg 2009).

A fourth approach to political leadership common in the literature is psychodynamic in nature. According to Gill, 'psychodynamic theory, or leader–member exchange theory, explains the effectiveness of leaders as a function of the psychodynamic exchange that occurs between leaders and group members' where 'leaders provide direction and guidance through influence permitted them by members' (Gill 2006: 26, 36). While psychodynamic approaches to leadership break out of the agent/structure dichotomy, feminists have critiqued the power-neutral position of these approaches. In psychodynamic theories, citizens are represented as having equal influence on their leader and equal standing among their peers, while leaders are held in equal esteem with followers. In this view, the difference between leaders and followers is in role rather than constitution. A simple look at the information on the sex composition of the world's political leadership at the beginning of this chapter shows that such a model is oversimplified—the people that leaders lead are not equal in esteem, power, or material resources, and leaders are not representative of the populations that they lead.

The fifth and final category of theoretical approaches to leadership that this section addresses is those that treat gender as a dependent variable. For example, Ole Holsti and James Rosenau studied 'the foreign policy beliefs of women in leadership positions' with the expectation that 'women will tend to have a more benign and optimistic view of the international system, to give priority to social-economic-humanitarian issues rather than political-strategic concerns, and to be less inclined toward the use of military capacities' (Holsti and Rosenau 1981: 328). They found that 'whatever the differences between women and men among the entire population, their views converge at the leadership level' (Holsti and Rosenau 1981: 329). Still, a number of other studies have been launched with the goal of figuring out who women leaders are and what they do differently from men. Feminists have identified two major problems with such an approach. First, 'the discussion of women qua women implies that all women hold the same views and that it is possible to view women as a single force in politics' (Palley 2001: 247). Second, as Bensimon explains, women are still being compared to a masculine concept of leadership in these studies, 'because organization frames are based on the experience of men' (Bensimon 1989: 148–9). The question 'do women and men approach politics differently?' is, in the view of many feminists, the wrong place to start a study of gender and leadership, given the heterogeneity of women and men and the social construction of gender. Instead, feminists have suggested that it is important to question the gendered expectations of leaders, the gendered tools that we use to construct our ideas of what a leader is, and the extent to which leadership is a gendered concept. These ideas are explored in the next section of this chapter.

4 A FEMINIST PERSPECTIVE ON LEADERSHIP

Feminist readings of leadership have looked to correct a number of the flaws that feminists have critiqued in both (purportedly) gender-neutral and sex-specific theoretical approaches to leadership. In this section, I will discuss three of them specifically: the assumption of representativeness, the assumption of leader autonomy, and the assumption of leader power as power-over.

Representation

As already mentioned, feminists have problematized traditional approaches to the study of leadership for assuming that leaders are representative of, or randomly selected from, the citizenry of states or other political organizations, solely on the basis of situational needs, traits, or exchange agreements between leader and followers. Instead, for example, men are over-represented among political leaders, more so than would be expected by traits, situational needs, or exchange agreements between leaders and followers. This is because, feminist theorists might suggest, rather than being randomly selected from among the population or from among a portion of the population with particular traits, leaders are chosen based on preconceived notions of what makes a good leader and in line with pre-existing organizations of privilege in that society on the basis of race, class, gender, religion, or other social group.

The very existence of those pre-existing privileges throws into question the assumption of several models (including the rational-actor and situational models) that rely on the needs or interests of the governed to understand how leaders are selected and how they behave once they are selected. Feminists have consistently argued that the idea of a population having homogenous needs is not only flawed, but insidious (Tickner 1992). This is because, often, the interests of an elite, exclusive portion of the population is made synonymous with the interests of the population as a whole, when, in reality, it is not only unrepresentative of the interest of the marginalized citizens of a state but often harmful to the state's weakest citizens (Peterson and Runyan 1999).

In line with these critiques, feminist studying global politics generally and political leadership specifically have suggested that it is important to look past the appearance of population unity and leaders as representative. One important way to do this is to improve the scope of our knowledge about leadership. To accomplish this, gender theorists might encourage scholars of leadership to use a method that Sandra Harding and Uma Narayan (1998) call 'strong objectivity' and Evelyn Fox Keller (1985) calls 'dynamic objectivity'. Instead of looking for 'objective' knowledge in privileged perspectives about what 'good' leadership is and always has been, this perspective would look to approximate universality of knowledge by collecting as many perspectives about what leaders are or ought to be and assimilate them without valuing interpretations more because they are uttered by the powerful or fit neatly in inherited models.

Another tool gender theorists might suggest is a method feminists have called 'searching for silences', where it is important to seek and point out 'the gendered silences inherent in dominant stories' (Gibson-Graham 1994: 216). Hilary Charlesworth pointed out that 'all systems of knowledge depend on deeming certain issues irrelevant, therefore silences are as important as positive rules' (Charlesworth 1999: 381). Therefore, statements on leadership that ignore gender dynamics are making a statement about gender as clearly as those that are focused on gender. Feminist research has long looked for meaningful silences about gender as a way to understand gendered power in global politics (e.g. Kronsell 2006). Such a method is no less important in the study of political leadership, where silences about gender as an influence in the selection and behaviour of political leaders is as loud as criticisms of women politicians' hair, wardrobe, and body type.

Autonomy

Another area of scholarship on leadership that feminists have problematized is the tendency for theoretical approaches to leadership to separate 'agent' and 'structure' and privilege either one or the other. Instead, feminists have argued that agent and structure are interdependent, both in terms of identity and in terms of decision-making, which has important implications for both the selection of leaders and the process of leadership. To understand this, a little bit of background on the argument is necessary. Several feminists have critiqued the political science reading of the agent/structure dichotomy as based on liberal understandings of obligation as voluntaristic. In trait-based and rational-actor approaches to leadership, the 'leader' makes autonomous choices without constraints. In situational models, the 'situation' chooses the 'leader' as if the leader is not embedded in the situation. In psychodynamic models, the citizens and the leader interact iteratively and autonomously.

Feminist theorists have suggested that all of these theoretical approaches rely on a flawed notion of human relationships, which, relying on social contract theory, define obligation as voluntary. Yet feminist approaches to politics and political theory have time and time again shown gendered situations in which women incur involuntary obligations (such as dealing with a pregnancy resulting from rape) (Hirschmann 1989: 1233). Often, in social relationships, women are obligated by male obligers, an 'oppressive socialization' that limits individuals' available choices (Hirschmann 2004: 204). This work shows people do not make their decisions in a vacuum, and the lines between inside and outside of the agent are not impenetrable, but fluid, because 'factors "outside" the self may inhibit or enhance one's ability to pursue one's preferences, including the kind and number of choices available, the obstacles to making the preferred choice, and the variable power that different people have to make choice' (Hirschmann 2004: p. ix). If not all choices are made fully freely and not all obligations are assumed voluntarily, then decision-making is relationally autonomous, rather than fully autonomous. As Caron Gentry and I once explained, 'in a world of relational autonomy, decisions can be made within constraints or with fellow constrainees, but are never entirely unavailable and never without any constraint… given this interdependence, actors can choose to use their limited autonomy to act against, around, or with others' (Sjoberg and Gentry 2007: 194).

As a result, feminists have thought of 'responsibility in the sense of response' (Hirschmann 1989: 1241), where 'relational autonomy establishes identity independence for oneself in and while maintaining relationships with difficult others' (Sylvester 2002: 119). This suggests that leaders do not 'lead' followers who simply 'follow', nor do 'situations' dictate 'leaders' who lack agency. Leaders do not act and then await a reaction to act again, nor do followers simply react to leaders' actions. Instead, relational autonomy suggests that leaders are interdependent with followers, both in terms of identity and in terms of decision-making. Seeing leaders personally and leadership specifically as relationally autonomous suggests that it is important to begin to study and understand intersubjectivity, interdependence, communication, and perhaps affective characteristics of leaders and leadership as well as social inequalities among citizens (and between citizens and leaders) that produce inequalities in terms of the number and variety of choices available to those actors.

Power

In order fully to understand the inequalities that exist in terms of the number and variety of choices that leaders and followers have, it is important to explore the relationship between power and the selection of leaders as well as the practice of leadership. Feminist work has suggested that it is a key part of the study of leadership to think about what power is and how it operates. Leaders have varying, though usually substantial, power vis-à-vis followers, whether that power is bestowed by followers (as in the rational-choice and psychodynamic models) or not (in the trait and situational models). Existing work on leadership often pays attention to only a part of this power, the 'power-over' a group of followers perceived to be functionally equal.

Feminist theorist Amy Allen has characterized 'power-over' as the ability to wield coercive force and 'constrain the choices available to another actor or set of actors in a non-trivial way' (Allen 1998: 33). Feminists have argued that this view of power is both incomplete and gendered. According to Spike Peterson and Anne Runyan, 'to ungender power...we must alter the gendered division of power that established and had continued to reproduce masculinist politics. The latter privileges an androcentric definition of power—as power-over—and discriminates against women as political actors' (Peterson and Runyan 1999: 213).

As a result of this critique, feminists have been more interested in other sorts of power. In addition to power-as-domination, feminist work has looked at power-as-empowerment and power-as-the-ability to work in concert, or power-to and power-with (Allen 1998: 32). In other words, they are looking for power as the ability to work together or fight against oppression, rather than just to dominate or oppress (Dahl 2000). This sort of power can be seen as deconstructive of top-down, coercive forms of leadership, and provide direction towards cooperative, empathetic, bottom-up forms of leadership.

5 IS LEADERSHIP ITSELF GENDERED?

These feminist contributions to the study of leadership demonstrate several contributions of gender analysis. First, feminists have established that our concepts of good leaders are masculinized, and that those masculinized conceptions of leadership have been naturalized in our understanding of leadership. Second, feminist work suggests that the ways that we traditionally study leadership need to be seriously rethought, including gendered assumptions about representation, autonomy, and power. Feminist approaches demonstrate the importance of inclusive analysis, searching for silences, understanding interdependence, and holding a broad view of power.

These contributions, taken together, suggest that it is not only that our understandings of what a leader is and how to study leadership that are gendered, but the concept of leadership itself. After all, in practice, the concept of political leadership entrenches gender (and other) hierarchies among participants in global politics, and is exclusive of women (and other minorities). These issues may just be in practice, but they may also be theoretical shortcomings in the idea of leadership and the attraction of studying it. Most feminist work on global politics has taken a different direction, studying the private sphere and the margins of global politics in order to understand where politics happens and why. In Cynthia Enloe's words:

> Read forward, 'the personal is international' insofar as ideas about what it means to be a 'respectable' woman or an 'honorable' man have been shaped by colonizing policies, trading strategies, and military doctrines…the implications of a feminist understanding of international politics are thrown into sharper relief when one reads 'the personal is international' the other way round: *the international is personal.*

(Enloe 1990: 196)

Enloe suggests that this calls for a 'radical reimagining' of how we think about politics, such that we recognize the role that gender tropes play in the selection and behaviour of our 'leaders' but also that we recognize the complex interdependence between gendered politics and gendered leadership.

6 Conclusion: Looking Forward in the Study of Leadership From a Feminist Perspective

I suggest that such a 'radical reimagining' is a good direction forwards for feminist perspectives on political leadership. It is important to study not just the gendered characteristics we expect of and are assigned to leaders and the gendered assumptions made in traditional approaches to studying leadership, but also the gendered nature of political leadership as an institution. Particularly, as R. W. Connell contends, the fact that most people who are in power are men is a result, or at least a path-dependent tendency, of expectations of leader masculinity, rather than a cause. Connell argues that most leaders 'are men because there is a gender configuring of recruitment and promotion, a gender configuring of the internal divisions of labor and systems of control, a gender configuring of policy making, of practice routines, and ways of mobilizing pleasure and consent' (Connell 1995: 73).

These observations, with Cynthia Enloe's about the relationship between the personal and the political, suggest that feminist research on political leadership looking forwards should try to understand the gendered configurations of recruitment, promotion, and behaviour of political leaders as well as the gendered production of the concept of political leadership. Asking 'where are the women?' (Enloe 1990) in political leadership leads feminist theorists to explore the gender-based expectations that we have of leaders, the gendered ways in which we study political leadership, how gendered politics interacts with gendered leadership, and (potentially and hopefully in the future) the gendered implications of conceptualizing politics in terms of leaders and leadership.

Recommended Reading

Alexander, D., and Andersen, K. (1993). 'Gender as a Factor in the Attribution of Leadership Traits', *Political Research Quarterly*, 46/3: 527–45.

Hartmann, H. (1993) (ed.) *Gendering Politics and Policy: Recent Developments in Europe, Latin America, and the United States.* New York: Haworth Press.

Tickner, J. Ann (2001). *Gendering World Politics.* New York: Columbia University Press.

References

Alexander, D., and Andersen, K. (1993). 'Gender as a Factor in the Attribution of Leadership Traits', *Political Research Quarterly*, 46/3: 527–45.

Allen, A. (1998). 'Rethinking Power', *Hypatia*, 13/1: 21–40.

Arendt, H. (1970). *On Violence.* New York: Harvest Books.

Bennis, W. (1999). 'The Leadership Advantage', *Leader to Leader*, 12 (Spring 1999): 18–23.

Bensimon, E. M. (1991). (1989). 'A Feminist Reinterpretation of Presidents' Definition of Leadership', *Peabody Journal of Education*, 66(3), 143–56.

Best, D. L., and Williams, J. E. (1990). *Sex and the Psyche: Gender and Self Viewed Cross-Culturally.* London: Sage.

Brown, S. (1988). 'Feminism, International Theory, and International Relations of Gender Inequality', *Millennium: Journal of International Studies*, 17/3: 461–75.

Caprara, G. V., Barbaranelli, C., Borgogni, L., and Perugini, M. (1993). 'The "Big Five Questionnaire": A New Questionnaire to Assess the Five Factor Model', *Personality and Individual Differences*, 15/3: 281–8.

Charlesworth, H. (1999). 'Feminist Methods in International Law', *American Journal of International Law*, 93: 379–94.

Connell, R. W. (1995). *Masculinities.* Berkeley and Los Angeles: University of California Press.

Dahl, H. M. (2000). 'A Perceptive or Reflective State?', *European Journal of Women's Studies*, 7/4: 475–94.

Dingfelder, S. F. (2004). 'A Presidential Personality', *Monitor on Psychology*, 35/10: 26–9.

Dowd, M. (2006). 'Who's Hormonal, Hillary or Dick?', *New York Times*, 8 February.

Duerst-Lahti, G., and Kelley, R. M. (1995). *Gender, Power, Leadership, and Governance.* Ann Arbor: University of Michigan Press.

Edinger, L. J. (1990). 'Approaches to the Comparative Analysis of Political Leadership', *Review of Politics*, 52/4: 509–23.

Enloe, C. (1990). *Bananas, Beaches, and Bases.* Berkeley and Los Angeles: University of California Press.

Enloe, C. (2000). *Maneuvers: The International Politics of Militarizing Women's Lives.* Berkeley and Los Angeles: University of California Press.

Enloe, C. (2004). *The Curious Feminist: Searching for Women in a New Age of Empire.* Berkeley and Los Angeles: University of California Press.

Fausto-Sterling, A. (2005). 'The Bare Bones of Sex: Part I, Sex and Gender', *Signs: Journal of Women in Culture and Society*, 30/2: 1491–528.

Gibson-Graham, J. K. (1994). ' "Stuffed if I know!": Reflections on Post-Modern Feminist Social Research', *Gender, Place, and Culture: A Journal of Feminist Geography*, 1/2: 205–24.

Gill, R. (2006). *Theory and Practice of Leadership*. London: Sage.

Harding, S., and Narayan, U. (1998). 'Border Crossings: Multicultural and Postcolonial Feminist Challenges to Philosophy', *Hypatia*, 13/3: 1–5.

Hartmann, H. ed. (2006) (ed.). *Gendering Politics and Policy: Recent Developments in Europe, Latin America, and the United States*. New York: Haworth Press.

Hey, V. (2006). 'The Politics of Performative Resignification', *British Journal of the Sociology of Education*, 27/4: 439–57.

Hirschmann, N. (1989). 'Freedom, Recognition, and Obligations: A Feminist Approach to Political Theory', *American Political Science Review*, 83/4: 1217–44.

Hirschmann, N. (2004). *The Subject of Liberty: Towards a Feminist Theory of Freedom*. Princeton: Princeton University Press.

Hogan, R., and Warrenfeltz, R. (2003). 'Educating the Modern Manager', *Academy of Management Learning and Education*, 2: 74–84.

Holsti, O. R., and Rosenau, J. N. (1981). 'The Foreign Policy Beliefs of Women in Leadership Positions', *Journal of Politics*, 43/2: 326–47.

Hooper, C. (1998). 'Masculinist Practices and Gender Politics: The Operation of Multiple Masculinities in International Relations', in M. Zalewski and J. Parpart (eds), *The Man Question in International Relations*. Boulder, CO: Westview Press, 28–53.

Huddy, L., and Terkildsen, N. (1993). 'The Consequences of Gender Stereotypes for Women Candidates at Different Levels and Types of Office', *Political Research Quarterly*, 46/3: 503–25.

IPU (2011). Inter-Parliamentary Union, *Women in National Parliaments* <www.ipu.org/wmn-e/world.htm> (accessed 1 January 2012).

Keller, E. F. (1985). *Reflections on Gender and Science*. New Haven: Yale University Press.

Kets de Vries, M. F. R. (1994). 'The Leadership Mystique', *Academy of Management Executive*, 8/3: 73–92.

Kronsell, A. (2006). 'Methods for Studying Silences: Gender Analysis in Institutions of Hegemonic Masculinity' in B. Ackerly, M. Stern, and J. True (eds), *Feminist Methodologies for International Relations*. Cambridge: Cambridge University Press, 108–28.

Moss, D. G. (2006). 'A Queen for whose Time? Elizabeth I as Icon for the Twentieth Century', *Journal of Popular Culture*, 39/5: 796–816.

Palley, M. L. (2001). 'Women's Policy Leadership in the United States', *PS: Political Science and Politics*, 34/2: 247–50.

Peterson, V. S. (1992). 'Security and Sovereign States: What is at Stake in Taking Feminism Seriously?', in V. S. Peterson (ed.), *Gendered States: Feminist (Re)visions of International Relations Theory*. Boulder, CO: Lynne Rienner, 31–64.

Peterson, V. S., and Runyan, A. S. (1999). *Global Gender Issues* (Boulder, CO, Westview Press).

Prügl, E. (1999). *The Global Construction of Gender: Home-Based Work in the Political Economy of the 20th Century* (New York: Columbia University Press).

Rissman, B. (2004). 'Gender as a Social Structure: Theory Wrestling with Activism', *Gender and Society*, 18/4, 429–50.

Sadler, P. (2003). *Leadership*. London: Kogan Page.

Seidler, V. (1994). *Recovering the Self: Morality and Social Theory*. London and New York: Routledge.

Sjoberg, L. (2007). 'Agency, Militarized Femininity, and Enemy Others', *International Feminist Journal of Politics*, 9/1: 82–101.

Sjoberg, L. (2009). 'Feminism and Styles of Political Leadership', in J. Mascuiulli, M. A. Mochanov, and W. A. Knight (eds), *The Ashgate Research Companion to Political Leadership*. Aldershot: Ashgate, 149–76.

Sjoberg, L., and Gentry, C. (2007). *Women's Violence in Global Politics: Images of Mothers, Monsters, and Whores*. London: Zed Books.

Steans, J. (1998). *Gender and International Relations: An Introduction*. New Brunswick: Rutgers University Press.

Sylvester, C. (2002). *Feminist International Relations: An Unfinished Journey*. Cambridge: Cambridge University Press.

Tickner, J. A. (1992). *Gender in International Relations*. New York: Columbia University Press.

Tickner, J. A. (2001). *Gendering World Politics*. New York: Columbia University Press.

Tickner, J. A., and Sjoberg, L. (2011). 'Introduction: International Relations through Feminist Lenses', in J. A. Tickner and L. Sjoberg (eds), *Feminism and International Relations: Conversations about the Past, Present, and Future*. London and New York: Routledge, 1–21.

True, J. (1996). 'Feminism', in Scott Burchill and Andrew Linklater (eds), *Theories of International Relations*. London: MacMillan, 179–209.

UNIFEM (2010). 'Ending Violence against Women and Girls: UNIFEM Strategy and Information Kit' <www.unifem.org/attachments/products/EVAWkit_01_InvestingInGender Equality_en.pdf> (accessed 1 January 2012).

UNWomen (2011). 'Women's Representation in the Justice System' <http://progress.unwomen. org/2011/06/womens-representation-in-the-justice-system/> (accessed 1 January 2012).

Whittington, R. (1993). *What is Strategy, and Does it Matter?* London: Routledge.

Zalewski, M. (1996). 'All these Theories yet the Bodies keep Piling up': Theorists, Theories, and Theorizing', in S. Smith, K. Booth, and M. Zalewski (eds), *International Relations: Positivism and Beyond*. Cambridge: Cambridge University Press, 1–17.

CHAPTER 6

POLITICAL SCIENCE

DAVID S. BELL

1 INTRODUCTION

IN Western political studies, political leadership has been under continuous investigation, although not always in the same terms. In the early years of political philosophy there was a concentration on aspects of character and morality. In the twentieth century the modern theoretical focus became mainstream only with the so-called Behavioural Revolution in political study in the United States. This wave of research in 'political science' (to use the American term) is systematic and empirical and shifts the focus onto the way in which the world works rather than on the morality of leadership. What, in other words, is the 'leadership factor'; can the 'leadership variable' be isolated and what form does it take; and what role does political leadership play? These are the questions that inform political research into leadership after the 1940s, although other, older questions (moral, psychological, and structural) have not been neglected.

It must also be added that the 'political science' community has drawn from, and embraced, many researchers from other disciplines and eclectically incorporated concepts and findings into the mainstream of political enquiry. However, political leadership is not the same as management or military efficiency. In open societies the command relationship is substantially absent, and political leadership requires a different set of skills and relationships. There is also a difference in objectives, so that, whereas management leadership can be measured in monetary terms, there is no simple yardstick for the judgement of political leaders. Thus the main developments in political research have been in model-building and in extending the factual basis for the study of leadership.

2 HISTORICAL TEMPLATES

In this branch of the discipline, as in others, the starting point, and the framing of the debate, is the classical world (Plato 1941; see also Keohane, Chapter 2, this volume).

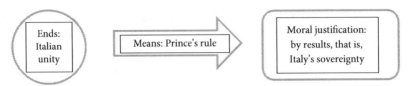

FIGURE **6.1** The ends justifying the means

Plato, of course, begins the search for the right kind of leader and discusses how leaders can be identified; Aristotle, in keeping with the modern mind, classifies and links up the regime type and the form of leadership that can be identified with each (Aristotle 1984). Aristotle separates democracies from the monarchies and dictatorships, which, in this schema, have different properties.

It is with Machiavelli (1469–1527) that the political theory of leadership comes to maturity. If philosophy is a footnote on Plato, leadership study is a footnote on Machiavelli. Machiavelli starts lines of research that continue to inform politics and, in fact, many other disciplines, and it is no surprise to find Machiavelli cropping up in management and in organization theory. But there are caveats. Machiavelli is subject to varying interpretations and to disputed readings. There is a sense in which Machiavelli is a modern empiricist and a modern objective and amoral reader of the political world (perhaps by accident), and Renaissance Italy was a brutal and callous milieu with little room for the institutions of the open society now regarded as basic.

One reading of Machiavelli is as an ends–means moralist. That is to say, Machiavelli sets aside the 'common good' and argues in terms of basic state functions. In particular, there is the *sine qua non* of security. Machiavelli's direction of vision away from the moral considerations, and towards the questions of how political ends are to be accomplished, however, is crucial to subsequent studies of leadership in politics. Machiavelli is the theorist of means and of the object, although the moral implications are (perhaps) assumed and not made explicit enough. It was left to subsequent theorists to consider these problems. Thus, Machiavelli sets up a debate, provides a racy commentary, and turns leadership theory in a distinctly modern direction. But there is also Machiavelli's under-explained notion of 'respect' that could separate the leadership of *The Prince* from mere gangsterism (see Figure 6.1).

The 'Great Man' Thesis

Before the establishment of 'political science' as a discipline, there were numerous thinkers whose contributions to leadership studies have to be acknowledged. Most notable among these is Carlyle, whose (Hegelian) *On Heroes*... sees history as the history of the Great Leaders, as stated on page 1 (Carlyle 1927). Ultimately this view stands or falls by the identification of the undefined 'Divine Idea' and Carlyle's notion that leaders appear as the conditions of the political era demand. Carlyle brings to attention the contrary Tolstoyan view that, whatever individuals do, the course of history is unaltered by particular leaders. But there is also the view that, although the tide of events moves in its own way, if it is taken at the flood it may, for the individual who rides it, lead on to fortune. Carlyle is at one end of the range, describing politics as leadership, and the social theorists (Marxists at the fore) are at the other. In this discussion, most modern researchers have been at the opposite pole to Carlyle (Tucker, 1995). A satisfactory synthesis between these poles has not been agreed, but the trend was towards political leadership as the dependent variable, and this was the thrust of Marxist analysis. However, this field is now burgeoning and as a subset includes the projection of personality and other political arts (King 2002; Aarts 2011). Yet neither the varied Marxisms, in their more mature theorizing, nor the wider social sciences have developed a consensus view about whether or not leadership is the cork bobbing on the water.

Bringing Social Context in

Max Weber provides the groundwork for future developments with 'charisma'—a small corner of his sociology (Weber 1958). Typologies are one of the objects of contemporary leadership study, developing classifications that in turn can become containers of data and make comparison between individuals meaningful.

Weber's understanding of 'charisma' is something attributed to a leader in times of crisis and is radical leadership that sweeps away old restraints and makes new systems. Because it makes predictions about the likely developments of this type of leader, it is attractive to researchers. 'Charisma' depends on the perception of the leader and requires a more than normal devotion from followers. It has been difficult to study empirically for this reason and it has had to be adapted to be usable. In the 1960s and 1970s there was a good deal of interest in the concept, as it appeared to provide a key to the emergence of the striking leadership of post-colonial societies. 'Charisma' as an operational concept of leadership has never fallen into disfavor, and the development of the study has continued. Most recently in Europe the emergence of 'populist leadership' has been evident, and the typologies engendered from 'charismatic' leadership are far from exhausted.

As part of the argument with Marxism, the American philosopher Sidney Hook distinguished in *The Hero in History* between 'eventful' and 'event-making' leaders (Hook 1943). An 'eventful' leader is one to whom things happen, but an 'event-making' leader changes the course of events. In the last category are the leaders who create a new route in a social crisis. Conditions provide opportunities for leadership—Sidney Hook details these—and the imaginative politicians find creative ways to move and shape political life. H. D. Lasswell, realizing the importance of leadership study, issued a call for the development of this field and for recognition of its importance (Lasswell 1962).

3 CONTEMPORARY RESEARCH

In the present condition of 'political science' there are several streams that feed into the study of political leadership. In leadership studies the scene is more a limestone plateau than a river system making its way to the sea in well-defined channels. Thus the various streams run with apparent force only to disappear and re-emerge in unexpected places and with renewed vigour, and then disappear again.

This relationship can be set out in schematic form (see Figure 6.2). Political leadership falls within the general matrix of comparative politics. There are biographies and individual case studies, but, with rare exceptions, they are not comparative studies. Comparative research is the principal means of building up transferrable generalizations in the social sciences. This is, therefore, a conspectus of comparative propositions developed and tested in empirical studies and based on the widely discussed issues of political leadership in open societies. Thus there is continuity, but also, on all fronts, progress.

In the middle and late twentieth century the American 'science of politics' became the predominant academic mode, and with that the search for the empirical and verifiable in political research became imperative. One product of the new lines of research, and somewhat subsequent to the 'behaviouralist revolution', is G. D. Paige's *The Scientific Study of Political Leadership*. Paige establishes one framework for the systematic and empirical study of political leadership that (Paige 1977a) provides a research strategy. *The Korean Decision: June 24–30, 1950* analysed the leadership decision-making and (using the approach of Richard C. Snyder) detailed the process and leadership, but it is more concerned with decision-making than leadership *per se* (Paige 1977b). Behaviouralism moves from the identification of the features of leadership to the way in which political leaders react to events and situations, and that appreciation remains pertinent.

It was J. MacGregor Burns, working on this problem area, who provided the conceptual tools for advancing the study of political leadership (Burns 1978). Burns's compendious *summa* is an overview of leadership as a political phenomenon. However, Burns weaves into the consideration of political leadership the ethical and psychological aspects that are usually thought essential but that are rarely part of the political analysis. Burns was influenced by Abraham Maslow's *Theory of Human Needs*, which was then used to provide the psychological foundations for the view that there were different levels of values on which

Theory	Ethics	Psychology	Social	Anthropology	Methodology	Models/Skills	Rhetoric
Aristotle	Aquinas	Freud	Weber	Goldberg	Lasswell	Hargrove	Atkinson
Plato	Hampshire	Erikson	Burns	Bailey	Blondel/ Bunce	Skowronek	Edelman
Machiavelli	Wolfers	Owen	Tucker	Goldberg	Berrington	Greenstein	Gaffney

Figure 6.2 The streams that feed into the study of political leadership

leadership drew. There is a very big agenda in Burns's work, but the *distinguo*: 'transactional' and 'transformational' leadership is crucial for subsequent research and pervades the current work on leaders. For Burns, political leadership is based in the competing interests of society and in their transformation through a political resolution. Burns directs attention to the relationship between the political leader and their followers, and the balance (or otherwise) of this relationship (Burns 2003). Transactional leadership is utilitarian, needs based, and provides goods depending on the bargain between the leader and the follower. By contrast, transformational leadership is more demanding and requires a higher purpose, with, in most cases, a strong moral component. Transformational leadership, particularly given the problems in moving mass societies, has attracted great attention and is a widely used category (Burns 2003). As Burns defines it, 'transactional leadership' is when 'one person takes the initiative in making contact with others for the purpose of an exchange of valued things' (Burns 2003: 19). This is political leadership typified in the exchanging of demands for votes and is based on self-interest and basic needs. It also moves into the territory of power which 'is the probability that one actor within a social relationship will be in a position to carry out his own will despite resistance' (Burns 2003: 12).

'Transforming leadership', however, is when one or more persons engage with others in such a way as to raise one another to higher levels of motivation and morality (Burns 2003: 20). As a concept this has affinities with 'charisma', but the problems with that concept have led Burns to seek a new formula. This concept is carefully separated from the idea of a dictatorial leader, and this need for consent is also a Weberian theme. Transformational leadership is a type of political leadership that moves society and achieves collective goals that are long term, and works through the leader's understanding with the followers. Thus Burns' point is that: 'Essentially the leader's task is consciousness-raising on a wide plane…The leader's fundamental act is to induce people to be aware or conscious of what they feel—to feel their true needs so strongly, to define their values so meaningfully, that they can be moved to purposeful action' (Burns 2003: 43–4). This is a formulation of a type of leadership that has its origins in political action but that has become a widely used category in management and other disciplines (Bernard Bass, for example). Transformational leadership points in the direction of contemporary concern. Leaders who inspire are the leaders who catch the imagination, but how this is done and how the inspiration relates to the values, needs, and goals of the followers has been researched by a variety of works in different fields—not just politics. 'Transactional leadership' has also been fleshed out in further studies (Bass 1990). These categories are important, and their development and testing make the comparative enterprise possible, as does the increasing sophistication of typologies.

4 Models of Leadership Action

As is well known, the late nineteenth century also saw the revolution in the study of the human psyche in the development of modern psychology. There was a postulated irrationality in behaviour that could, it was asserted, be traced only to the psyche, but at this time there was little study of the psyche with respect to political leadership. In the study of leadership Freud identifies leadership as key to political activity; however, political leaders are, in Freud's analysis, able to stand apart: they do not need the psychological support of the crowd and they are self-sufficient (Freud 1921).

Freud's ideas and concepts have been imported into political studies as they have into other branches of study. Freudianism starts the exploration of the psychological springs of leadership and is continued by mainstream political analysts. Lasswell takes this Freudian postulate and identifies a desire both for power and for deference in leaders, but in political leadership this is transformed into a social involvement in their society (Lasswell 1962: 38). But the upheavals of the twentieth century and the emergence of murderous dictators placed the less flamboyant and rational leaders in a research siding while the century's monsters were investigated. Karen Horney and others have shown that much can be said about political leadership in Western societies, and clearly research is needed, although mainstream political analysis has been tardy in this line of investigation ('t Hart 2010). By the same token, Erikson has used Freudian concepts to look at phases of human development as well as at the place of leadership in the psychological make-up of top politicians (Roazen 1976; see also Renshon, Chapter 9, this volume). Particular psychological aptitudes might make someone suited to some particular circumstances, but not to others, and a psychology that might be seen as incapacitating in some circumstances might be fitting in another. Thus W. S. Churchill was a crisis leader who, in wartime, imparted a sense of optimism and resolution that was at odds with the objective situation and that depended on unknowable future developments. One study of British prime ministers reveals not a calm, rational, unflappable, and gregarious political leader but a general tendency to a personality of a rather different type (Iremonger 1970; Berrington 1971). Studies on more psychological or medically structured lines 'have also raised doubts over whether the abilities required to take the helm, and those required to steer in a rational direction, are in many cases actually at odds with one another' (Weinberg 2012). There is also the well-worn problem of how illness impinges on leadership and on leadership decision-making (Owen 2007). This attempts to answer the central question of the link between the character of a leader and his or her subsequent actions. F. I. Greenstein's research on personality and politics has been pioneering and has extended to political leadership in three leadership styles: crusaders, strategists, and pragmatists (Greenstein 2009).

5   RHETORIC

There is for political leaders the need to win over and to enthuse (not to say enrapture) an audience (Edelman 1988; Jamieson 1990; Gaffney 1991). This branch of the study of political leadership takes research into the methods of linguistics, communication, and, most importantly, discourse analysis (see also Uhr, Chapter 17, this volume). More recently the world economic crisis has brought the problem of leadership to the fore, and the rhetorical reaction to uncertainty has been studied in comparative research, showing that there were clear stages to the collective reaction to economic meltdown ('t Hart and Tindall 2009).

Political leadership depends on the ability to persuade, much as did the lawyers of the classical world, and there are textbook primers on how to make presentations. Atkinson's *Our Masters' Voices* is not free standing and is accompanied by a large literature on the use of discourse and the analysis of symbolism in political leadership. Much of this is American-oriented, given the importance of the presidency in the United States (unlike Europe, where the party organization has predominated), but it is not American-centred and has insights, typologies, and concepts of universal applicability. In the view of many the political world is one of non-rational or subrational symbols (both language and images or signs) that are manipulated by political leaders.

In the social sciences, the investigation of these symbols is an important aspect of political leadership, in particular, where the unconscious and non-rational impulses in the politics of mass society are recognized or, more pointedly, where the rational actor of the political/economic model is not accepted as a sound generalization. This is a useful corrective to the view that the politics of leadership is a straightforward calculation of advantage and disadvantage and the automatic translation of public opinion into acts (these public forces in turn are assumed to transmit underlying political/economic interests). These findings are controversial (especially Edelman's framework of interpretation), but the concern about the subliminal aspects of political leadership—and manipulation—is enduring (Edelman 1988).

6 New Methods

Some of the work on leadership pushes the factual material into the field where statistical data can be gathered. However, studies of political leadership are primarily qualitative, and this has been a problem with leadership research, although there are attempts to make this a more mathematically manipulable configuration. In the first place there are works by Blondel and Thiebault that try to find statistical regularities in the patterns of political leadership worldwide (e.g. Blondel and Thiebault 2010). These put the study of leadership in a frame so that it can be compared with the other social researches, even though leadership is a very discrete set of roles and not easily comparable. Bunce, in another statistical study, takes the problem of leadership transition to show that new leaders do have a measurable impact—in other words, that there is a leadership variable in politics (Bunce 1981). In more recent studies the impact of leadership in elections has been examined with reference to the European party competitions (King 2002). This is an under-exploited field, perhaps because of the need for conceptual clarification before categorization can be developed, but it is one area where modern techniques in research and categorization can be exploited.

In contemporary debate, one of the key questions is why leaders are men (see also Sykes, Chapter 45, this volume). This generalization holds across societies, systems, and time. In this branch of the study of political leadership the facts are less disputed than the reasons behind them and, following from that, the implications for policy. This question has led to research into the content and creation of 'gender stereotypes' in political systems and in political communication in several countries. Comparative work has looked at the construction of social expectations and the barriers to advance that they make for potential political leaders (Murray 2010).

The idea of the rational self-interested actor in politics has been imported from the study of economics. Many studies of leadership involve an element of rational-choice analysis, but the study of political leadership includes a number of research works explicitly using the rational-choice analysis approach: that is, viewing the political leaders as the 'rational actor' maximizing power, and the followers maximizing self-interest (Frohlich, Oppenheimer, and Young 1971). In this view political leadership is the essential part of a Namierite paradise—with no Burke to interrupt the free flow of self-interest. Leaders can be seen in this theory as 'entrepreneurs' providing public goods that are indivisible and provided to everybody (Schneider and Teske 1995). Competition between political leaders results, and hence the construct becomes amenable to the mathematical models of behaviour that are the central feature of economics (Jones 1989). It has to be said that these have become rather arid and theoretical and the models somewhat detached from political life as it is experienced, despite the elegance of the mathematics.

Riker's work on political manipulation, although not a study of leadership itself, is a handbook for the modern political leader and has proved impressively fruitful (Riker 1986). Riker sees politics at the top—or leadership—level as the domain of manipulation where no outcomes are predetermined. This so-called heresthetic (manipulation) is intrinsic to the art of political leadership, and its moral value depends on the end that it is intended to achieve Thus Lincoln's famous question to Stephen Douglas—a sort of Morton's fork—on the issue of slavery manœuvred the Senator into pleasing or displeasing one sector of his support. Leaving aside the contention over this example, the 'heresthetic' enabled Lincoln to divide the Democratic Party and to prepare a winning ground for the Republicans. It has been argued by some commentators on political leadership that misleading—or lying—is inevitably part of the armory of the leader and is an inescapable part of politics. Riker does not take that view and sees the 'heresthetic' as a form of political action that is universal in an open society and is a legitimate ordering of needs and values in a bargaining situation.

In the field of legislative research there have been notable advances in leadership studies. Thus Barber's study of the lawmakers and the presidential personnel is at odds with Lasswell and others in their assumptions about the personalities that are at the top of the leadership scale (Barber 1965). Barber's division of the presidents into active doers and inactive bystanders, and into those who liked the job and those who hated it, is revealing. Most presidents are assumed to be like F. D. Roosevelt in their relish for the job of leading the world's one superpower, but this appears to be far from the case

(Barber 2009). Barber provides an observation that the leadership position is not often relished and frequently is disliked, but does not provide an explanation, although the suggestion is that an emotional deprivation in childhood is the motivating force for certain US presidents, as perhaps Berrington (based on e.g. Iremonger's work) elaborates. Psychologists of the political like Renshon have taken this study further and have looked at the nature of ambition and background personality in political leaders (Renshon 1996 and Chapter 9, this volume; 't Hart 2010). In some ways, Renshon returns to the idea of the political leader with reliable judgement and the contrast with leaders who have conflicted personalities and consequently erratic or troubled personalities. Lipman-Blumen, meanwhile, investigates and develops the category of the leader who leads to disaster—the 'toxic leader'—and why he or she is followed (Lipman-Blumen 2004).

There is an under-investigated aspect here to political leadership—more commonplace in popular studies and in biographical studies—and that is the close associates of the leader or the informal entourage. However, the motivation and control of these close followers is an important—not to say essential—part of the art of political leadership and a necessary part of the process of leadership at the top level. How a leader manages and motivates this group is under-researched, and yet it is an essential part of political leadership. Some of the study of the followers of political leaders (and others) has drawn on psychological work to explain relationships between leaders and close associates, and there is substantial doubt about how these small 'sofa groups' are controlled (Bailey 1988).

As would be expected, much of the work on leadership is conducted in or derived from the United States. Richard Neustadt, through the study *Presidential Power*, is one of the most influential of political leadership theorists in the post-war world. There are a series of profound insights in Neustadt's work on the American presidency that are highly relevant to today's political studies. To start with, the theory puts to one side the idea of leadership in what is apparently the most commanding of institutions— the US presidency—as one of giving orders to be carried out. Presidential leadership depends on the ability to persuade and to bargain, and, where the presidency falls back on the use of power—like the heavy-handed intervention in the steel mills crisis by President Truman in 1952—then this is a sign that leadership authority has failed and not a sign of strength. This is more evident in the US situation, where the separation of powers demands a continuous negotiation with different institutions, each with its own remit, competence, and constituency, than in the European fused legislature/ executive parliaments. However, the central postulate remains powerful: that political leadership is not a command relationship but one of persuasion and influence rather than an isolated site of decision-making. Neustadt places the emphasis on the skill of political leaders in this bargaining process of government, and this is a firmly political emphasis.

One point, made by Skowronek, is that the Neustadt depiction of the presidency is of the mid-twentieth-century position and confined to a particular era in history. Leadership, like political power, is situational and that has to be taken into account in any general theory of political leadership. Skowronek's conceptual framework in *The Politics Presidents Make* is intricate and dense. His book is a study of the US presidency, but it provides a basis for comparative research on a number of different fronts. Skowronek makes the point that the approach delimited in *The Politics Presidents Make* enables a comparison across time and through different political eras without assumption of a linear or sawtooth development of the presidency. Thus particular presidents can be put in specific categories for assessment, and the theory deals elegantly with the problem of the political situation that leaders find themselves in. It has always been difficult to abstract the situational element from the political leadership type: what would have happened had Hoover been elected after Woodrow Wilson, rather than after Coolidge, and what would Eisenhower have done in another Great Depression? Skowronek's theory enables advances in the understanding of the situational aspects of leadership in modern societies.

Skowronek's theory depends on the idea of 'political time'—that is, of the political situation as the leader finds it—but the book develops a somewhat abstruse vocabulary that is often difficult to disentangle. There is the use of the term 'regime', for example, that in this work has to be carefully handled, and other aspects of the conceptualization need careful exposition. There is also a problem of the categorization that Skowronek uses, and there is the problem of the residual category, which intrudes into the pattern and in the depiction of the various stages. It is also unclear whether Skowronek's pattern is detected in hindsight or whether the political actors in leadership positions are aware of their place in the cycle—they would seem to need this awareness (though not in Skowronek's terms) if the theory is soundly based.

Another development that draws together threads of mid-century ideas in political research is Greenstein's *The Presidential Difference: From FDR to Barack Obama*. This sets out another of the research agendas on the US presidency, but has a comparative dimension that makes it important as a set of general postulates. Greenstein enables the researcher to walk around political leadership, as with a Henry Moore sculpture, noting its cadences and distortions, but also its solidity and substance. Greenstein's conceptual framework is a sound basis for the evaluation of leadership, and leads to the consideration of a range of ethical implications.

7   ETHICS IN A TURBULENT WORLD

Ethical and moral studies are also crucial in politics, because they are inseparable from the study of leadership, and in the investigation of political leadership they are a core concern. These moral considerations are also something that the general public looks for when judging leaders, but the judgement of political leadership is also an academic study. Leaders, whether of organizations or of states, have ethical outlooks and are judged by moral yardsticks, and these are illuminated by academic research (Hampshire 1991; Gane 1997).

Political morality is the part of the study that depends on the philosophical tradition of Western societies (Uhr 2005). In discussion about what political leaders ought to do and how they should be judged, the discipline has no fixed answers, although this is—as would be expected—a public concern, and judgements made are based on existing traditions. There have been surges of moral theorizing about leadership in response to major conflicts from the Vietnam War and subsequently until the invasion of Iraq. It is impossible to encapsulate these intricate arguments in a narrow compass (Garrett 1994; Ciulla 2002).

Stuart Hampshire's (1978) work and the case of the Iraq War have made urgent the problems of the status of international law and of international organizations. Leaving aside the argument that there is no way of ethically judging political leaders, there are proponents of diverging views. In the first place is the Kantian argument that the moral law applies across the board to all people—leaders included—and in the second is the view advanced by Wolfers. This is the difficulty that any action by a leader will be morally ambiguous—the so-called clean and dirty hands problem. In Wolfers's view, this dilemma can be resolved, because the art of political leadership is one of finding moral solutions to weighty problems in a substantially different setting from the domestic (Wolfers 1967).

8 Paradigm Regained

Model-building is one of the more recent developments, and here appreciable advances have been made. Although models of leadership are frequently the constructs of disciplines such as management studies, the political leadership models have needed to bring together the circumstances of political life and the skills of the leaders. In *The President as Leader*, E. C. Hargrove develops a model of presidential leadership, synthesizing research on political leadership and providing a dynamic set of relations (Hargrove 1998). This model integrates the skills that are required of a leader in Western societies with the situation within which they have to work. It is an ambitious formulation, but it is one that can be transferred from the American presidency to other societies. However, political leadership also requires an appreciation of the cultural resources upon which a society can draw, and how these can be put to use in different situations from the dramatic (war) to the domestic (sometimes quotidian). Although the emphasis is on skills such as manœuvre and personality, the model uses the social background to enable the development of a leadership style and to judge its effectiveness, so that the discussion is in part at least an extended contribution to the idea of transformative leadership (though transactional leadership is given its due).

There is a central moral core evident in the 'teaching of reality' that depicts the task of a leader as being to understand and communicate to their followers the realities of the world as they experience them, not just 'develop a vision' some desire future state of the world (Hargrove 1998). However, the anti-social side is not explored, and self-serving

Machiavellian politics are rejected in Hargrove's formulation, although the components of the model and its articulation are used in the discussion of the American presidency, and the model has been applied elsewhere to other countries' political leaders.

9 CONCLUSION

In the social sciences, the disciplinary boundaries are porous. Although the challenge of finding a route to the understanding of political leadership has been fraught, the research itself remains a work in progress. However, the study of political leadership has moved away from the speculative, the biographical, and the impressionistic, and has gained a solid grounding in research and theoretical understanding (Masciulli et al. 2009). There remains a danger in the social sciences of reductionism in the models of political leadership that are constructed to deal with an intractable reality, but they have evolved to include the many intricacies of political action and environment. In the discussion about the very weighty bag of political leadership, it is tempting to grab it by the handle; it is tempting, and easier, to write about the handle, because that is what you have the best grip on. This reduction to a single factor or force is not a trap that the models of political leadership have fallen into. By contrast, the study of political leadership has retained its eclectic outlook and has depended on many insights from disparate sources. This, however, has led to corners of the subject being lit by the light of research, while the whole picture has still to be uncovered in its entirety (Elcock 2001; Derfler 2012).

For this branch to grow there needs to be both an expansion of the partial theories that have enabled the understanding of particular leaders and situations, and more of the model-building theoretical groundwork on which the social sciences rely. In the flourishing state of political leadership studies, both of these routes are likely to be followed to the benefit of the subdiscipline.

RECOMMENDED READING

Burns, J. M. (2003). *Transforming Leadership: A New Persuit of Happiness*. New York: Atlantic Monthly Press.
Ciulla J. (2002). *The Ethics of Leadership*. New York: Wadsworth.
Hargrove, E. C. (1998) *The President as Leader*. Lawrence, KS: University Press of Kansas.

REFERENCES

Aarts, K. Blais, A., and Schmitt, H. (2011) (eds). *Political Leaders and Democratic Elections*. Oxford: Oxford University Press.
Aristotle (1984). *Politics*. Harmondsworth: Penguin.

Atkinson, M. (1984). *Our Masters' Voices*. London: Methuen.

Bailey, F. G. (1988). *Humbuggery and Manipulation*. New York: Cornell University Press.

Barber, J. D. (1965). *The Lawmakers*. New Haven: Yale University Press.

Barber, J. D. (2009). *The Presidential Character: Predicting Performance in the White House*. Harlow: Longman Classics in Political Science.

Bass, B. M. (1990). 'From Transactional to Transformational Leadership: Learning to Share the Vision', *Organizational Dynamics* (Winter), 19–31.

Berman, L. (2006). *The Art of Political Leadership*. New York: Rowman.

Berrington, H. (1971). 'The Fiery Chariot: British Prime Ministers and the Search for Love', *British Journal of Political* Science, 4: 345–69.

Blondel, J., and Thiebault, J.-L. (2010). *Political Leadership, Parties and Citizens*. London: Routledge.

Bunce, V. (1981). *Do New Leaders Make a Difference?* Princeton: Princeton University Press.

Burns, J. M. (1978). *Leadership*. New York: Harper Colophon.

Burns, J. M. (2003). *Transformational Leadership*. Oxford: Oxford University Press.

Carlyle, T. (1927). *On Heroes, Hero-Worship and the Heroic in History*. London: Macmillan.

Ciulla, J. (2002). *The Ethics of Leadership*. New York: Wadsworth.

Derfler, L. (2012). *The Fall and Rise of Political Leaders*. Harmondsworth: Palgrave.

Edelman, M. (1988). *Constructing the Political Spectacle*. Chicago: Chicago University Press.

Elcock, H. (2001). *Political Leadership*. Cheltenham: Edward Elgar.

Freud, S. (1921). *Group Psychology and the Analysis of the Ego*. New York: Bantam.

Frohlich, N., Oppenheimer, J., and Young, O. C. (1971). *Political Leadership and Collective Goods*. Princeton: Princeton University Press.

Gaffney, J. (1991). *The Language of Political Leadership in Britain*. London: St Martin's Press.

Gane, N. (1997). 'Max Weber and the Ethical Irrationality of Political Leadership', Sociology, 31 August: 549–84.

Garrett, S. A. (1994). 'Political Leadership and the Problem of Dirty Hands', *Ethics and International Affairs*, 8: 159–75.

Greenstein, F. I. (1992). 'Can Politics and Personality be Studied Systematically?', *Political Psychology*, 13: 105–28.

Greenstein, F. I. (2009). *The Presidential Difference: From FDR to Barack Obama*. Princeton: Princeton University Press.

Hargrove, E. C. (1998). *The President as Leader*. Lawrence, KS: University Press of Kansas.

Hampshire, S. (1978). *Public and Private Morality*. Cambridge: Cambridge University Press.

Holloway, C. (2008). *Magnanimity and Statesmanship*. Boulder, CO: Lexington Books.

Hook, S. (1943). *The Hero in History*. Boston: Beacon Press.

Iremonger, L. (1970). *The Fiery Chariot*. London: Secker and Warburg.

Jamieson, K. H. (1990). *Deeds Done in Words: Presidential Rhetoric and the Genres of Governance*. London: University of Chicago Press.

Jones, B. D. (1989) (ed.). *Leadership and Politics*. Lawrence, KS: Kansas University Press.

King, A. (2002) (ed.). *Leaders' Personalities and the Outcome of Democratic Elections*. Oxford: Oxford University Press.

Lasswell, H. D. (1962). *Power and Personality*. New York: Free Press.

Lipman-Blumen, J. (2004). *The Allure of Toxic Leaders*. Oxford: Oxford University Press.

Machiavelli, N. (1961). *The* Prince, trans. G. Bull. Harmondsworth: Penguin.

Masciulli, J., Molchanov, M. A., and Knight, W. A. (2009) (eds). *The Ashgate Research Companion to Political Leadership*. Aldershot: Ashgate.

Murray, R. (2010). *Cracking the Highest Glass Ceiling: A Global Comparison of Women's Campaigns for Executive Office*. London: Praeger.

Neustadt, R. E. (1990). *Presidential Power and the Modern Presidents*. New York: Free Press.

Owen, D. (2007). *The Hubris Syndrome*. London: Politico.

Paige, G. D. (1977a). *The Scientific Study of Political Leadership*. New York: Free Press.

Paige, G. D. (1977b). 'On Values and Science: The Korean Decision Reconsidered', *American Political Science Review*, 71: 1603–9.

Plato (1941). *The* Republic, trans. C. M. Cornford. Oxford: Oxford University Press.

Renshon, S. A. (1996). *The Psychological Assessment of Presidential Candidates*. New York: New York University Press.

Roazen, P. (1976). *Erik H. Erikson*. New York: Free Press.

Riker, W. (1986). *The Art of Political Manipulation*. New Haven: Yale University Press.

Schneider, M., and Teske, P. (1995). *Public Enterpreneurs*. Princeton: Princeton University Press.

Skowronek, S. (1993). *The Politics Presidents Make: Leadership from John Adams to Bill Clinton*. Cambridge, MA: Belknap.

Skowronek, S. (2011). *Political Leadership in Political Time*. Lawrence, KS: University Press of Kansas.

't Hart, P. (2010). 'Political Psychology', in David Marsh and Gerry Stoker (eds), *Theory and Methods in Political Science*. Basingstoke: Palgrave, 99–113.

't Hart, P., and Tindall, K. (2009) (eds). *Framing the Global Economic Downturn*. Canberra: ANU Press.

't Hart, P., and Uhr, J. (2008) (eds). *Public Leadership: Perspectives and Practices*. Canberra: ANU E Press.

Tucker, R. C. (1995). *Politics as Leadership*. Columbia, MO: University of Missouri Press.

Uhr, John (2005). *Terms of Trust: Arguments over Ethics in Australian Government*. Sydney: UNSW Press.

Weber, M. (1958). *From Max Weber: Essays in Sociology*. Oxford: Oxford University Press.

Weinberg, A. (2012). *The Psychology of Politicians*. New York: CUNY.

Wolfers, A. (1967). *Discord and Collaboration*. Baltimore, MD: Johns Hopkins.

CHAPTER 7

···

PUBLIC ADMINISTRATION*

···

R. A. W. RHODES

1 INTRODUCTION

PUBLIC administration is an irredeemably multidisciplinary field, which draws on theories, models, and methods from a wide range of disciplines. Much work in public administration on leadership is derivative, drawn mainly from political science and organization theory. I do not cover the literature on leadership in the private sector or the generic leadership literature that claims to cover all organizations. This chapter focuses on the distinctive work about administrative leadership from individuals recognized as scholars of public administration and political science writing mainly for and about public organizations and practitioners.

The term 'administrative leader' covers 'the front-line supervisor...to the non-political head of the organization' (Van Wart 2003: 216). This positional definition of a leader is narrower than the increasingly popular term 'public leadership', which encompasses not only the holders of formal leadership positions in public organizations but also elected political leaders and civic leadership (Morse and Buss 2007: 4–5). Morse and Buss (2007: 4) see leadership as 'a process of influence where a person or group influences others to work towards a common goal'. Cleveland (2002: p. xv) prefers 'bringing people together to make something different happen'. After that, we are in the land of developing vision, mission statements, and 'challenges' to everyone. Leadership eludes a short, simple definition.

In the study of public administration, not only was leadership hard to define but studies of administrative leadership were also hard to find. The dominant view was that the task of senior bureaucrats was to apply top-down authority; they were cogs in the machine, not leaders (Weber 1947). Times changed as recognition grew that senior

* I would like to thank Arjen Boin, Jenny Fleming, Paul 't Hart, Anne Tiernan, and Pat Weller for their helpful comments on earlier drafts.

bureaucrats also manage conflict, power, values, and change (Burns 1978: 298). So, the question of whether public servants should be leaders is at the heart of the public administration literature on reinventing government, the new public management, the entrepreneurial public servant, and public value. All confront recurring dilemmas between discretion and accountability, and responsiveness and efficiency.

I begin with a brief historical survey before turning to the distinctive contributions to the study of administrative leadership by students of public administration. I focus on: leadership theory, the study of bureaucratic elites, ethnographic studies of bureaucrats, life histories of administrative leaders, and network governance and collaborative leadership. For each topic, I identify and discuss key texts. Finally, I argue for a broader analysis than the instrumental view of leadership, suggesting that we encompass fiscal retrenchment, the 'dark side' of administrative leadership, and interpretive approaches.

2 Two Traditions in the Study of Administrative Leadership

There are two distinct traditions in the study of administrative leadership: the mainstream account of instrumental leadership, which draws its inspiration from the literature on organizational leadership; and the institutional leadership school inspired by the work of Philip Selznick.

The Mainstream: Instrumental Leadership

The textbook account of the history of leadership theory in public administration parallels mainstream histories (see, e.g., Henry 2009: ch. 5).

The history of leadership studies begins with the 'great man' theory of history followed by the study of leadership traits. When it became clear there was no one set of leadership traits, the study of leadership switched to the relationship between leaders and followers in small groups (see the articles in Gibb 1969 for several examples). Such situational theories evolved into contingency theory (Fiedler 1967) and transactional approaches (Blake and Mouton 1985), which stressed the variety of leadership styles and the need for style to 'fit' the managerial context. However, the field became mired in inconclusive micro-studies, and doubts grew about the suitability of these theories for the study of large organizations and political institutions. The 'New Leadership' approach (Bryman 1986: 280) came not from mainstream leadership studies but from political science. Interest shifted from small groups and transactional approaches to transformational leadership (Burns 1978). The debate about the relative efficacy of transactional and transformational leadership dominated the literature for two decades. It was still lingering in the literature in the 2000s, although there was by then a much greater concern with integrated leadership approaches (see, e.g., Bass 1985; Van Wart 2005, 2013).

Students of public administration contributed little to this story. They 'translated' private-sector theories of leadership to the public sector. Overall, mainstream studies 'have failed to create a critical mass of scholarly work on public sector leadership' (Kellerman and Webster 2001: 487).

Van Wart (2005) provides the best public administration example of work in this idiom. He seeks a model of leadership that integrates previous approaches. It is said 'to be useful in training and applied settings', treating leadership as 'competency based', with his concepts forming a 'scientific causal chain' determining the leadership style or mix of styles (Van Wart 2005: 392; see also Van Wart 2013). Like all the work in this idiom, it retrofits private-sector theories to the public sector. It is instrumental in seeking to improve managerial practice and modernist in that it is 'imbued with the rational model of organizational thinking' (Bryman 1996: 289). This instrumental idiom constitutes the mainstream in the study of leadership in public administration.

Philip Selznick: Institutional Leadership

Doig and Hargrove (1987: 2 and n. 9) note that Selznick's work, although seminal, was ignored in public administration for many years (see Selznick 1984a and 1984b). Selznick was not a scholar of public administration nor of political science, but he exercises a pervasive influence in this subfield. There are too many case studies drawing on his work to cite here (see Boin and Christensen 2008 for a review). The key texts include Lewis (1980), Doig and Hargrove (1987), Wilson (1989), Hargrove (1994), Moore (1995), Boin (2001); the best commentaries are by Heclo (2002) and Krygier (2012).

Philip Selznick's work on leadership builds on his distinction between an *organization*, which is 'a rational instrument engineered to do a job', and an *institution*, which is 'a responsive, adaptive organism'. An organization becomes an institution over time; 'to institutionalize is *to infuse with value* beyond the technical requirements at hand'; and '*the executive becomes a statesman as he makes the transition from administrative management to institutional leadership*'. The role of a leader as statesman is to 'define the mission of the enterprise'; 'the institutional leader...is primarily an expert in the protection and promotion of values'; and 'the problem is always *to choose key values and to create a social structure that embodies them*'. Institutionalization also involves 'organizational character formation', which 'aids the organization to adapt itself to its internal and external social environment'. Leaders not only define the mission but they also protect its distinctive character, defend institutional integrity, and manage internal and external conflict. In sum, leadership is seen as a set of tasks, and an institutional leader is a statesman presiding over a polity, seeking to win consent for the institution from internal and external interest groups (all quotations from Selznick 1984b: chs 1 and

2; all emphases in original). Thus, in his study of the Tennessee Valley Authority (TVA), Selznick (1984a argues that the agency used the myth of decentralization to grass-roots partnerships to co-opt local interests into its decision-making in an effort to win over a suspicious and conservative community. Unfortunately, he argues, this strategy back-fired because it led to the larger agricultural interests capturing the agency's goals (and see Hargrove 1994 for an account of how the TVA leaders became prisoners of their grass-roots myth). This focus on the tasks of leadership, statesmanship, values, and managing internal and external conflicts underpins subsequent analyses of administrative entrepreneurs.

3 The Contribution from Public Administration

What has public administration contributed to the study of leadership? The short answer is not a lot (Terry 1995: 2); although Van Wart (2011: 89) claims that 'public sector leadership is slowly becoming its own specialized area of leadership study'. In this section, I suggest that public administration has made a distinct contribution on administrative leadership in five areas: leadership theory, the study of bureaucratic elites, ethnographic studies of bureaucrats, life history, and network theory and collaborative leadership. Admittedly each had limited impact outside the study of public administration.

Leadership Theory

The defining debate in public administration's contribution to leadership theory is between proponents of the public servant as entrepreneur and the supporters of the administrative conservator. The debate has its roots in the work of Selznick, and its most recent incarnation can be found in the contributions of Terry (1995) and Frederickson and Matkin (2007).

Terry is critical of public administration scholars (e.g. Doig and Hargrove 1987; Moore 1995) for borrowing from the private-sector leadership literature. He sees that heroic model of leadership with the great man radically changing the organization and disdaining its existing traditions as a threat to 'institutional integrity'. An institution has integrity when 'it is faithful to the functions, values, and distinctive set of unifying principles that define its special competence and character' (Terry 1995: 44). The task of administrative leaders is to preserve this institutional integrity—that is, to conserve the institution's mission, values, and support. They must balance the autonomy necessary to maintain integrity with responsibility to elected politicians. Administrative leaders practise 'administrative conservatorship'. Like Selznick's leader, the conservator practises 'a form of statesmanship', which 'requires professional expertise, political skill, and a sophisticated understanding of what it means to be an active participant in governance'. Such skills are deployed to 'maintain commitment among the executive cadre to core agency values and sustain support among key external constituents and internal interest groups' (Terry 1995: 172).

For Terry (1995: 172; 1998: 197), advocates of the public entrepreneur are on a 'misguided quest', and he mounts a vigorous attack on the twin evils of public entrepreneurs and neo-managerialism. Together, they encourage self-promotion, rule-breaking, power politics, and risk-taking. They undermine democratic accountability and are 'oblivious' to such values as fairness, justice, and the public interest (see Lewis 1980 for examples). Behn (1998: 220) seeks a middle ground that envisages a leadership role for public officials on issues 'for which the elected chiefs lack either the inclination or the time'. Moreover, their task is also 'to help the agency not only [to] achieve its purpose today but also to create new capacity to achieve its objectives tomorrow'. So, they should exercise initiative, but be subject to checks and balances. Once again, the ever-present elephant in the room is the exercise of discretion and the problem of its regulation.

A decade later, the debate will not die. Frederickson and Matkin (2007: 36–8) are critical of the change agent or transformative view of leadership. They concede leadership as vision may be appropriate for the private sector but it is just plain 'wrong' for the public sector. Citing Szanton (1981: 24), they compare public leadership to 'gardening', requiring time, patience, experience, and political awareness. Public leaders work with available resources, understand and work with administrative culture, recognizing that change is incremental. They are realists who know that problems are complex, admitting of no easy solutions. Public leaders are 'quiet leaders' who are in 'for the long haul', and their craft is compromise. Much government is about coping, the appearance of rule and keeping things going (Rhodes 2011). The contrast with the transformative or change agent leader is as sharp as the parallels with the administrative conservatorship are obvious. Throughout, the debt to Selznick is marked.

The arguments for administrative leadership as gardening are dismissed as 'the ghosts of PA orthodoxy'. The ghosts include leadership infringing on politics; unwarranted degrees of administrative discretion; and leadership without checks and balances (Getha-Taylor et al. 2011: 185). The ghosts, however, are all too real and not figments of excitable imaginations. It is not axiomatic that 'public leadership is leadership for the common good, for the purpose of creating public value' (Getha-Taylor et al. 2011: 184). This assertion is a value statement, not a given. It is more plausible to suggest that 'the tension between bureaucracy and democracy, between efficiency and responsiveness, will always be there' (Getha-Taylor et al. 2011: 187). What is indisputable, however, is that the debate about public entrepreneurs versus administrative conservators is not limited to leadership theory. It is also about the role of public administration in the polity; about public accountability and the public interest. Under the label 'administrative ethics', students of Public Administration have a long-standing interest in the ethical standards governing bureaucratic behaviour (see, e.g., Rohr 1989; Cooper 2000).

The Study of Bureaucratic Elites

Elite studies have a long and distinguished history, and the study of bureaucratic elites is a small subset of this larger enterprise. It is considered rarely in reviews of leadership, but most countries have research on the origins, education, social networks, and behaviour of their top public officials—too many to cite here. There are even a few genuinely comparative studies as distinct from compendia of individual country studies. For example, Aberbach, Putnam, and Rockman (1981) conducted a survey of politicians and bureaucrats in seven countries. They explored their social origins, their roles and styles in policy-making, their ideology, their commitment to democratic principles, and the interactions between politicians and bureaucrats. They use their findings to evaluate elite strengths and weaknesses as policymakers. One of the significant findings among many is American exceptionalism. They conclude that 'bureaucrats and politicians are less distinct in the United States than in Europe', with American bureaucrats acting as advocates, policy entrepreneurs, and even partisans (Aberbach, Putnam, and Rockman 1981: 244).

Although the socio-demographic features of elites might seem a dry, even sterile, topic, it throws up some interesting debates. First, it raises questions about the representative nature of bureaucracy; for example, about the representation of women in the senior post in the public service (see, e.g., Ferguson 1984; Savage and Witz 1992). Second, it raises questions about the changing role of top officials—especially whether they are still 'frank and fearless' in giving advice after decades of administrative reform (see, e.g., Weller 2001). In their study of six parliamentary democracies, Rhodes and Weller (2001: ch. 9) show that there has been a demand for officials to be more responsive to political direction, with corresponding fears that advice has been compromised. The verdict on whether officials still offer frank and fearless advice is, at best, non-proven. There have always been tenured officials who prevaricated and procrastinated and contract appointees who acted in the great tradition and 'told it as it was'. There is no substitute for spine.

Ethnographic Studies of Bureaucrats

Few students of public administration use observation as a research tool. Of course, there are exceptions. There are a handful of studies of central or federal bureaucrats (see, e.g., Rhodes, 't Hart, and Noordegraaf 2007; Rhodes 2011), and a growing number of studies of street-level bureaucrats (see, e.g., Lipsky 1980; Maynard-Moody and Musheno 2003). In the ethnographic study of both, Herbert Kaufman (1960, 1981) is the pioneer, even doyen, of empirical studies of administrative leadership.

In his analysis of central bureaux chiefs, Kaufman (1981) studied six federal bureaux for fourteen months, including thirty-one full days when he observed the bureaux chiefs sitting in their offices and at meetings. The conventional wisdom is that bureaux chiefs have much power and independence. Kaufman (1981: ch. 3) highlights the 'confines of leadership'. He compares it to 'stepping into a large fast-flowing river' and contending with 'an array of forces not of his own making that carried him and his organization along—sometimes at an unwanted rate and in an unwanted direction' (Kaufman 1981: 134). So, 'they make their marks in inches, not miles'. He suggests that, 'for all the power and influence attributed to their office and for all their striving, [bureau chiefs] *could not make a big difference in what their organizations did* during the period in which they served' (Kaufman 1981: 174, 139; emphasis added). Getting up close and personal changes the angle of vision and leads, as Kaufman freely admits, to surprises, especially about the confines of administrative leadership.

Although the term 'street-level bureaucrat' was not in common currency, Kaufman's *The Forest Ranger* (1960) pioneered the topic. He studied forest rangers and their supervisors in five districts. He visited the first district for seven weeks and the other districts for one week each; all the rangers' time was set aside for his 'conversations' and observations. There were also social visits to their families in the evening. He diagnoses a tendency to fragmentation created by hierarchy and specialization in the ways in which, for example, forest supervisors and district rangers in the field apply policies to concrete situations. Anyone who tries 'to direct activities on a Ranger district without going through the Ranger can be sure of swift and vehement objection by the field officer' (Kaufman 1960: 210). He calls them 'switchboards', adapting general directives to specific conditions and areas. It is a pivotal position. It is a classic example of the street-level bureaucrat, only they patrol trails, not streets. However, local discretion did not fuel conflict with the centre. Rather, the rangers were 'principled agents' using their discretion to further organizational goals (Boin 2001: 9).

The term 'street-level bureaucrat' was coined by Michael Lipsky (1980: p. xii) and refers to teachers, police officers, and social workers and any other semi-professionals in face-to-face contact with clients of state services. It draws attention to 'the decisions of street-level bureaucrats, the routines they establish, and the devices they invent to cope with uncertainties and work pressures', which 'effectively become the public policies they carry out' (Lipsky 1980: p. xii). Lipsky's main concern is that street-level bureaucrats are increasingly rule bound and are at risk of losing professional discretion. Maynard-Moody and Musheno (2003: ch. 12) disagree, claiming street-level bureaucrats 'actually make policy choices rather than simply implement the decisions of elected officials'. They fix client identities, often stereotyping them, which, in turn, fixes the occupational identity of the street-level bureaucrat as, for example, bleeding heart or hardnosed, which, in turn, sets the decision premises for the street-level bureaucrat's judgements. They use their everyday routines for managing time, client demands, and the pressure on resources. They even evade decisions by rubber-stamping decisions made by other authoritative individuals, or by referring cases to such individuals. They have to manage the 'irreconcilable' dilemmas posed by clients' needs, administrative supervision (of rules and resources), and the exercise of state power. They are not heroes, but they are an example of bottom-up leadership.

The key issue running through this literature concerns the extent of professional discretion and the effectiveness of managers in reasserting control, mainly through rules. Evans and Harris (2004) suggest that multiplying rules can create opportunities for more discretionary action, not less. Riccucci (2005: ch. 5) suggests that managing street-level bureaucrats should rely less on rules and reporting and more on open management with the participation of professionals, better education, and, on occasion, more micro-management. The exercise of discretion by street-level bureaucrats is an example of bottom-up leadership and, at its heart, is the same dilemma that stokes the debate about entrepreneurs and conservators—that is, discretion versus accountability.

Life History

As Lambright and Quinn (2011: 782) observe, the American literature on life history is 'relatively small' (but see the occasional series in *Public Administration Review*). It is seen as old-fashioned narrative, which is not theoretical or methodologically rigorous, or explanatory (Roberts 2002: 6–13). The key question is what is the use of life history in public administration? Is it the traditional biographer's aim of a chronological history with narrative drive that uncovers the character of its subject? Or is it the historian's aim of a better understanding of evolving public institutions and processes? Or is it the public administration scholar's aim of answering some broader disciplinary question about public leadership? Harold Lasswell (1986: 1) suggested that 'political science without biography is a form of taxidermy'. Equally, life history without an explicit use or theoretical stance is mere reportage.

In public administration, there are some fine examples of chronological life histories (see, e.g., Caro 1974; O'Halpin 1989). There are also single life histories that develop a larger argument. For example, Richard Chapman's study of Sir Edward Bridges, Head of the British Civil Service in 1945–56, seeks to show that professional conduct depends on ethical leadership by 'outstanding' civil servants (Chapman 1988: 307; see also Cooper and Wright 1992). Comparative life histories organized around a single theme have more to offer. A good example of this approach is Doig and Hargrove (1987). In the introduction, they explain that they want to contest Kaufman's pessimistic view that senior officials can introduce only limited incremental change. They want to reclaim individual leadership. So, they chose twelve individuals who held high-level executive positions in American federal, state, and local governments. They looked for 'individuals whose careers at managerial levels were linked to innovative ideas and to efforts to carry those ideas into effect'. The authors of the individual biographies were asked to focus on a checklist of activities, including: crafting new missions or programmes, developing external constituencies, motivating new organizational members, and enhancing technical expertise. They then identify the several variables that sustained innovative leadership. There are three personal characteristics: capacity for rational analysis, the ability to see the political logic and new opportunities, and a desire to 'make a difference'. There are also four external factors: governmental fragmentation and overlap, public support, new technologies, and political support from elected officials. The innovative leaders also had significant rhetorical and coalition-building skills. So, it is possible to conduct comparative life history around a common set of themes and illuminate such questions as what conditions favour innovative leadership—no mean feat for an approach too often dismissed as not academic, subjective, and partial.

Network Governance and Collaborative Leadership

Morse and Buss (2007: 9) describe leadership in networks as 'the most dramatic trend' in public leadership. They argue leadership 'across organizations within government as well as across sectors' is 'superseding the traditional image of government as top-down bureaucracy'. This interest in network governance (see Rhodes 2006) mutated to embrace working in partnerships and collaboration, and it is this strand that has the most to say about leadership.

Ansell and Gash (2007: 544) define collaborative governance as a collective decision-making process 'where one or more public agencies directly engages non-state stakeholders' in the 'formal, consensus oriented, and deliberative' implementation of public policy or management of public programmes. The key question is whether opposing stakeholders can work together in a collaborative way. The answer is a 'cautious yes', and a key part of that answer is leadership, which is 'crucial for setting and maintaining clear ground rules, building trust, facilitating dialogue, and exploring mutual gains' (Ansell and Gash 2008: 547). Such leadership is variously described as hands-off, soft, integrative, facilitative or diplomatic. The shared feature is that it is not directive, hands-on, or command and control.

Much of this work draws lessons for practitioners (see, e.g., Huxham and Vangen 2005; Agranoff 2007). It focuses on steering, on instrumental knowledge. There is little acknowledgement of the problem of accountability. Bovens (1998: 46) identifies the 'problem of many hands', where responsibility for policy in complex organizations is shared, and it is correspondingly difficult to find out who is responsible. He also notes that fragmentation, marketization, and the resulting networks create 'new forms of the problem of many hands' (Bovens 1998: 229). Even more troublesome is the frequency with which networks are closed to public scrutiny. The brute fact is that multiple accountabilities weaken central control (Mulgan 2003: 211–14, 225). The extreme examples of such private governments are the 'dark networks' of arms-trading and drug-smuggling (Raab and Brinton Milward 2003).

4 FUTURE DIRECTIONS

In the mainstream literature, there is a set of 'perennial debates' in the study of public leadership. Van Wart (2005: 14–20) itemizes four. 'What do leaders do? Does leadership make a difference? Are leaders born or made? What is the best leadership style?' These debates reflect the mainstream's ambition for cumulative, generalized, instrumental knowledge and are not the most germane in the study of administrative leadership. I prefer to expand the research agenda by considering: the changing context of public administration, the 'dark side' of administrative leadership, and interpretive approaches.

Fiscal Retrenchment and the Changing Context of Public Administration

The context of leadership has changed dramatically since 2008. Previously, most discussions of public leadership focused on the issues posed by: globalization; the 'triumph' of neo-liberal ideas; the rise of managerialism in its guises of performance measurement, marketization, and, most recently, service delivery and consumer choice; and the IT revolution. The 2010s have turned into an age of austerity, with massive public-sector retrenchment, which will have many specific consequences for public administration. In the 'hard times' of the late 1970s and 1980s, we debated whether governments could go bankrupt and whether administrative practice favoured decrementalism over quantum cuts (Dunsire and Hood 2010). This time around, we know the new austerity will change leaders' understanding of their organizational context. It is plausible to suggest that these understandings will support centralization, 'head kicking' (or the use of threats and inducements rather than persuasion), and financial retrenchment. Specific examples of such leadership include compulsory and voluntary redundancies, shorter working weeks, shedding female employees, and unilateral pension cuts. It can also provoke union militancy and a demoralized workforce. In particular, the European banking and debt crisis will have repercussions for administrative leaders for years, probably decades, to come. We need to trace the intended and unintended consequences.

The Dark Side of Leadership

The leader as hero is a common image in the public administration literature. They are presented as unsung heroes (Doig and Hargrove 1987), innovators (Moore 1995), and bastions of integrity (Cooper and Wright 1992). There is an unthinking equation of administrative leadership with good leaders, no doubt as an antidote to the incessant criticisms of bureaucracy. There are far too many examples of corruption, maladministration, and incompetence for anyone to be comfortable with this equation. Leaders are 'villains', adept at 'humbuggery and manipulation' (Bailey 1988), who commit bad, sometimes evil, acts. Lipman-Blumen (2004: 19–22) provides a scary portrait of 'toxic' leaders. They leave their followers and possibly everyone else worse off. At one end of the spectrum, they undermine, demean, seduce, marginalize, intimidate, and demoralize employees. At the extreme end, they disenfranchise, incapacitate, imprison, torture, terrorize, and kill (Lipman-Blumen 2004: 19–20; see also Adams and Balfour 2004; Nye 2008: ch. 5).

Some of these characteristics and behaviours may seem unlikely for your everyday bureaucrat. The examples of bad leadership in our newspapers headlines describe venal corporate executives, fanatical religious leaders, and corrupt political leaders. It would be a mistake, however, to ignore the extent of administrative evil, whether the example is 'big' (J. Edgar Hoover's 'inappropriate' uses of the FBI) or 'small' (the cynical 'outing' of British defence official David Kelly for an unauthorized conversation with a journalist, which led to his suicide). If we turn our attention to common, everyday actions, there are many examples of management practices such as head kicking and bullying fuelling low morale. Employees are demeaned, marginalized, and intimidated. Unethical behaviour can lower public confidence and trust in public authority and encourage whistle-blowing.

The analysis of bad public leadership is rare. If we are serious about holding administrative leaders to account, then we need to know why they failed, why and in what ways they were 'bad', why we supported them, and how they evaded accountability. There is a dearth of studies of the effects of ineffective and unethical administrative leadership on other bureaucrats, and on citizens.

Interpretive Approaches

The idea of 'meaning' lies at the heart of the interpretive approach. An interpretive approach seeks to understand the webs of significance that people spin for themselves. The researcher's task is to write 'our own constructions of other people's constructions of what they and their compatriots are up to' (Geertz 1973: 9). Any organization 'hinges on the creation of shared meaning and shared understandings' (Morgan 1993: 11, see also 276–80). Stories spell out the shared meaning and shared understandings. All organizations have a storehouse of many stories. This storehouse provides the everyday theory and shared languages for storytelling. As Boje (1991: 106) suggests, 'stories are to the storytelling system what precedent cases are to the judicial system'. Leaders use stories not only to gain and pass on information and to inspire involvement but also as the repository of the organization's institutional memory (see also Gabriel 2000; Rhodes 2011).

The focus on meaning and on telling stories may seem far removed from the concerns of practitioners; that is not the case. Leadership is about 'the management of meaning' and a way of leaders 'exerting their influence on followers'; they 'educate, inspire, indoctrinate and convince' (Shamir, Dayan-Horesh, and Adler 2005, 14 and 15). It is 'socially constructed through interaction', and effective leadership 'rests heavily on the framing of the experience of others' in which 'language, ritual, drama, stories, myths and symbolic construction...play an important role' (Smircich and Morgan 1982: 258, 262). Rhodes (2011) reports that most, if not all, British civil servants accept that the art of storytelling is an integral part of their work. Such phrases as: 'Have we got our story straight?' 'Are we telling a consistent story?', and 'What is our story?' abound. Civil servants and ministers learn and filter current events through the stories they hear and tell one another.

Storytelling is not an example of academic whimsy, but an integral part of the everyday practices of civil servants. Stories explain past practice and events and justify recommendations for the future. So, research on leadership should also explore the ways in which leaders construct their own life stories as part of an organization's storehouse of myths and legends.

5 Conclusions

For mainstream leadership studies, its proponents concede that there is limited cumulative knowledge. Rather, we have competing theories and eclectic methods. The study of administrative leadership mirrors the general state of public administration. There is no single way to study administrative leadership.

Although there may be a plurality of approaches, nonetheless there are also shared concerns, most notably around the recurring dilemmas between discretion and accountability, and responsiveness and efficiency. These dilemmas lie at the heart of the debate about entrepreneurs versus administrative conservators; the professional discretion of street-level bureaucrats, the responsiveness of bureaucratic elites to their political masters, controlling bad leaders, and the problem of many hands in networks. The distinct and distinctive contribution of public administration lies in its analysis and debates around public accountability and the public interest. Social science's leadership theory does not answer such questions of political theory.

The most obvious trend is for studies of administrative leadership to have a broader and broader compass. What are the merits of increasing the scope of administrative leadership studies? The defining characteristic of administrative leadership is its basis in the authority of the state. Any action by a person in the administrative hierarchy that influences another person inside or outside the bureaucracy to work together becomes an example of administrative leadership. So, street-level bureaucrats are seen as leaders. Local-level, social entrepreneurs in a collaborative project may be emergent *civic* leaders, but they cannot be *administrative* leaders because they are not bearers of state authority. Leadership is not a given, but socially constructed. A formal organization such as a public bureaucracy 'is premised upon shared meanings that define roles and authority relationships' (Smircich and Morgan 1982: 259). Civic leaders do not share those meanings. So, studies of administrative leadership seek to answer questions about leadership in hierarchical organization, even when they are teasing out the contests over meaning and resistance to the top-down views of leadership.

The study of administrative leadership has a clear core: holders of formal leadership positions in public organizations. It also has a classic question: how do we hold such office-holders to account? As the boundaries of the state become more opaque, then roles become blurred and the old certainties are challenged. We must follow where we are led but heedful of the danger that, if leadership is everything, maybe it is nothing. We must not forget where we have come from, because administrative leadership is about the constitutional and political role of public administration in the polity; it is not just about better management.

RECOMMENDED READING

Kaufman, H. (1981). *The Administrative Behavior of Federal Bureau Chiefs*. Washington, DC: Brookings Institution.
Selznick, P. (1984) [1957]. *Leadership in Administration: A Sociological Interpretation*. Berkeley and Los Angeles: University of California Press.
Terry, Larry D. (1995). *Leadership in Public Bureaucracies*. Thousand Oaks, CA: SAGE.

REFERENCES

Aberbach, J., Putnam, R. D., and Rockman, B. A. (1981). *Bureaucrats and Politicians in Western Democracies*. Cambridge, MA: Harvard University Press.
Adams, G. B., and Balfour, D. L. (2004). *Unmasking Administrative Evil*. Rev. edn. Armonk, NY: M. E. Sharpe.
Agranoff, R. (2007). *Managing within Networks: Adding Value to Public Organizations*. Washington: Georgetown University Press.
Ansell, C., and Gash, A. (2008). 'Collaborative Governance in Theory and Practice', *Journal of Public Administration Theory and Practice*, 18/4: 543–71.
Bailey, F. G. (1988). *Humbuggery and Manipulation: The Art of Leadership*. Ithaca, NY: Cornell University Press.
Bass, B. M. (1985). *Leadership and Performance beyond Expectations*. New York: Free Press.
Behn, R. (1998). 'What Right Do Public Managers Have to Lead?', *Public Administration Review*, 58/3: 209–24.
Blake, R. R., and Mouton, J. S. (1985) [1964]. *The Managerial Grid*. 3rd edn. Houston, TX: Gulf.
Boin, R. A. (2001). *Public Institutions: Leadership in Two Prison Systems*. Boulder, CO: Lynne Rienner Publishers.
Boin, A., and Christensen, T. (2008). 'The Development of Public Institutions: Reconsidering the Role of Leadership', *Administration and Society*, 40/3: 271–97.
Boje, D. (1991). 'The Storytelling Organization: A Story of Story Performance in an Office-Supply Firm', *Administrative Science Quarterly*, 36/1: 106–26.
Bovens, M. (1998). *The Quest for Responsibility: Accountability and Citizenship in Complex Organizations*. Cambridge: Cambridge University Press.
Bryman, A. (1996). 'Leadership in Organizations', in Stewart R. Clegg, Cynthia Hardy, and Walter R. Nord (eds), *Handbook of Organization Studies*. London: Sage, 276–92.
Burns, J. M. (1978). *Leadership*. New York: Harper and Row; paperback edn, 1979.
Caro, R. A. (1974). *The Power Broker: Robert Moses and the Fall of New York*. New York: Vintage Books.
Chapman, R. A. (1988). *Ethics in the British Civil Service*. London: Routledge.
Cleveland, H. (2002). *Nobody in Charge: Essays on the Future of Leadership*. San Francisco: Jossey-Bass.

Cooper, T. L. (2000) (ed.). *Handbook of Administrative Ethics*. 2nd edn. Boca Raton, FL: CRC Press.

Cooper, T. L., and Wright, N. D. (1992) (eds). *Exemplary Public Administrators: Character and Leadership in Government*. San Francisco CA: Jossey-Bass.

Doig, J.W., and Hargrove, E.C. (1987) (eds). *Leadership and Innovation: A Biographical Perspective on Entrepreneurs in Government*. Baltimore, MA: Johns Hopkins University Press.

Dunsire, A., and Hood, C. (2010) [1989]. *Cutback Management in Public Bureaucracies: Popular Theories and Observed Outcomes in Whitehall*. Cambridge: Cambridge University Press.

Evans, T., and Harris, J. (2004). 'Street-Level Bureaucracy, Social Work and the (Exaggerated) Death of Discretion'. *British Journal of Social Work*, 34/6: 871–95.

Ferguson, K. (1984). *The Feminist Case against Bureaucracy*. Philadelphia: Temple University Press.

Fiedler, F. E. (1967). *A Theory of Leadership Effectiveness*. New York: McGraw-Hill.

Frederickson, H. G., and Matkin, D. S. T. (2007). 'Public Leadership as Gardening', in R. S. Morse, T. F. Buss, and C. M. Kinghorn (eds), *Transforming Public Leadership for the 21st Century*. Armonk, NY: M. E. Sharpe, 34–45.

Gabriel, Y. (2000). *Storytelling in Organizations: Facts, Fictions and Fantasies*. Oxford: Oxford University Press.

Geertz, C. (1973). 'Thick Descriptions: Towards an Interpretive Theory of Culture', in C. Geertz, *The Interpretation of Cultures*. London: Fontana, 3–30.

Getha-Taylor, H., Holmes, M. H., Jacobson, W. S., Morse, R. S., and Sowa, J. E. (2011). 'Focusing the Public Leadership Lens: Research Propositions and Questions in the Minnowbrook Tradition', *Journal of Public Administration Research and Theory*, 21 (Supp. 1), 183–197. Doi:10.1093/jopart/muq069

Gibb, C. A. (1969) (ed.). *Leadership*. Harmondsworth: Penguin Books.

Hargrove, E. C. (1994). *Prisoners of Myth: The Leadership of the Tennessee Valley Authority, 1933–1990*. Princeton: Princeton University Press.

Heclo, H. (2002). 'The Statesman: Revisiting *Leadership in Administration*', in Robert Kagan, Martin Krygier, and Kenneth Winston (eds), *Legality and Community: The Legacy of Philip Selznick*. Lanham, MD: Rowman and Littlefield, 295–310.

Henry, N. (2009). *Public Administration and Public Affairs*. 11th edn. London: Pearson Longman.

Huxham, C., and Vangen, C. (2005). *Managing to Collaborate: The Theory and Practice of Collaborative Advantage*. London: Routledge.

Kaufman, H. (1960). *The Forest Ranger: A Study in Administrative Behavior*. Baltimore, MD: Johns Hopkins Press.

Kaufman, H. (1981). *The Administrative Behavior of Federal Bureau Chiefs*. Washington, DC: The Brookings Institution.

Kellerman, B., and Webster, S. (2001). 'The Recent Literature On Public Leadership: Reviewed and Considered', *Leadership Quarterly*, 12/4: 485–514.

Krygier, M. (2012). *Philip Selznick: Ideals in the World*. Stanford, CA: Stanford University Press.

Lambright, W. H., and Quinn, M. M. (2011). 'Understanding Leadership in Public Administration: The Biographical Approach', *Public Administration Review*, 71/5: 782–90.

Lasswell, H. D. (1986) [1930]. *Psychopathology and Politics*. Chicago: Chicago University Press.

Lewis, E. (1980). *Public Entrepreneurship*. Bloomington, IN: Indiana University Press.

Lipman-Blumen, J. (2004). *The Allure of Toxic Leaders: Why We Follow Destructive Bosses and Corrupt Politicians—and How We Can Survive Them*. New York: Oxford University Press.

Lipsky, M. (1980). *Street-Level Bureaucracy: Dilemmas of the Individual in Public Services.* New York: Russell Sage Foundation.

Maynard-Moody, S., and Musheno, M. (2003). *Cops, Teachers, Counsellors: Stories from the Front Lines of Public Service.* Ann Arbor, MI: University of Michigan Press.

Moore, M. H. (1995). *Creating Public Value: Strategic Management in Government,* Cambridge, MA: Harvard University Press.

Morgan, G. (1993). *Imaginization.* London: SAGE.

Morse, R., and Buss, T. F. (2007). 'Transformation of Public Leadership', in R. Morse, T. F. Buss, and C. M. Kinghorn (eds), *Transforming Public Leadership for the 21st Century.* Armonk, NY: M. E. Sharpe, 3–19.

Mulgan, R. (2003). *Holding Power to Account: Accountability in Modern Democracies.* Houndmills, Basingstoke: Palgrave Macmillan.

Nye, J. S. (2008). *The Powers to Lead.* New York: Oxford University Press.

O'Halpin, E. (1989). *Head of the Civil Service: A Study of Sir Warren Fisher.* London: Routledge.

Raab, J., and Brinton Milward, H. (2003). 'Dark Networks as Problems', *Journal of Public Administration Research and Theory,* 13/4: 413–39.

Rhodes, R. A. W. (2006). 'Policy Network Analysis', in M. Moran, M. Rein, and R. E. Goodin (eds), *The Oxford Handbook of Public Policy.* Oxford: Oxford University Press, 423–45.

Rhodes, R. A. W. (2011). *Everyday Life in British Government.* Oxford: Oxford University Press.

Rhodes, R. A. W., 't Hart, P., and Noordegraaf, M. (2007) (eds). *Observing Government Elites: Up Close and Personal.* Houndmills, Basingstoke: Palgrave-Macmillan.

Rhodes, R. A. W., and Weller, P. (2001) (eds). *The Changing World of Top Officials: Mandarins or Valets?* Buckingham: Open University Press.

Riccucci, N. M. (2005). *How Management Matters: Street-Level Bureaucrats and Welfare Reform.* Washington: Georgetown University Press.

Roberts, B. (2002). *Biographical Research.* Buckingham: Open University Press.

Rohr, J. A. (1989). *Ethics for Bureaucrats: An Essay on Law and Values.* New York: Marcel Dekker.

Savage, M. and Witz, A., (1992)(eds). *Gender and Bureaucracy.* Oxford: Blackwell.

Selznick, P. (1984a) [1949]. *TVA and the Grass Roots: A Study of Politics and Organization.* Berkeley and Los Angeles: University of California Press.

Selznick, P. (1984b) [1957]. *Leadership in Administration: A Sociological Interpretation.* Berkeley and Los Angeles: University of California Press.

Shamir, B., Dayan-Horesh, H., and Adler, D. (2005). 'Leading by Biography: Towards a Life-Story Approach to the Study of Leadership', *Leadership,* 1/1: 13–29.

Smircich, L., and Morgan, G. (1982). 'Leadership: The Management of Meaning', *Journal of Applied Behavioral Science,* 18/3: 257–73.

Szanton, P. (1981). 'So you Want to Reorganize the Government?' in Peter Szanton (ed.), *Federal Reorganization: What Have We Learned?* London: Chatham House, 1–24.

Terry, L. D. (1995). *Leadership in Public Bureaucracies.* Thousand Oaks, CA: Sage.

Terry, L. D. (1998). 'Administrative leadership, Neo-Managerialism and the Public Management Movement', *Public Administration Review,* 58/3: 194–200.

Van Wart, M. (2003). 'Public Leadership Theory: An Assessment', *Public Administration Review,* 63/2: 214–28.

Van Wart, M. (2005). *The Dynamics of Leadership in the Public Service: Theory and Practice.* Armonk, New York: M. E. Sharpe.

Van Wart, M. (2011). 'Changing Dynamics of Administrative Leadership', in D. C. Menzel and H. L. White (eds), *The State of Public Administration: Issues, Challenges, and Opportunities*. Armonk, NY: M. E. Sharpe, 89–107.

Weber, M. (1947). *The Theory of Social and Economic Organization*. Translated by A. M. Henderson and Talcott Parsons. London: Collier-Macmillan Publishers.

Weller, P. (2001). *Australia's Mandarins: The Frank and the Fearless*. Sydney: Allen and Unwin.

Wilson, J. Q. (1989). *Bureaucracy: What Government Agencies Do and Why They Do It*. New York: Basic Books.

CHAPTER 8

....

POLITICAL PSYCHOLOGY

....

MARGARET G. HERMANN

1 INTRODUCTION

SCHOLARS taking a political psychology perspective on the study of political leadership are generally focused on establishing the linkages between what political leaders are like and the actions and policies of the institutions they run. They seek (1) to understand the factors that influence who becomes a political leader, (2) to explore what characteristics of leaders are likely to affect what they do politically, and (3) to examine the conditions under which political leaders' personalities and experiences are likely to shape what their political units do. It is the purpose of this chapter to overview what has been learned in each of these three areas.

2 WHO BECOMES A POLITICAL LEADER?

What kinds of people choose to run, or work to get themselves selected, as political leaders? How are the decisions of those with the potential to assume such leadership positions shaped by the nature of the political system, the recruitment process, current demographic trends, and the zeitgeist of the time? Roughly sixty years ago, members of the scholarly and intelligence communities began wrestling with these questions, intrigued by some work that argued people become interested in political power and, in turn, positions of political leadership to compensate for low self-esteem (a lack of self-confidence) (Lasswell 1948). Like the authors of so many of the guides to becoming a successful leader found in bookstores today, these researchers sought to learn whether there was a set of traits that distinguished political leaders from their non-political counterparts. Or, if that was not the case, could they distinguish one group of political leaders from another—for example, those in legislatures and parliaments from those aiming to be cabinet secretaries or presidents. Armed with such information, these students of political leadership believed that we would be able to identify people who were born to lead and foster their careers as well as weed out those without the appropriate characteristics. In the late 1970s, this line of research was fuelled by Burns's (1978) description of the leadership traits that characterize transformational leadership and by Barber's (1977) description of the traits that define being an effective and not so effective president.

In general, however, the results of these types of studies proved contradictory and unsatisfactory. There was little homogeneity among leaders. Even those who explored the social backgrounds of various political elites (e.g. Quandt 1970; Rejai and Phillips 1983) were frustrated by the difficulties in finding consistent patterns allowing them to relate biographical data to accession to positions of leadership. In the process, however, these same researchers began to discover that who becomes a political leader appears to involve the interaction between what the leader is like and the context in which the leadership is exercised. For example, they found that individuals chose to run for offices that facilitated their particular leadership style (Browning and Jacob 1964); crisis and non-crisis situations catapulted different types of leaders into positions of power (Stewart 1977); and the nature of the recruitment process appeared differentially to include and exclude certain kinds of leaders (DiRenzo 1977).

At about the same time, students of both political and organizational leadership were coming to terms with the idea that leadership is a more complicated concept than had previously been thought. Indeed, there are no leaders without some kinds of followers; candidates are *potential leaders*. Even terrorist leaders must muster a group of followers to merit the title. So part of the answer to who becomes a political leader rests with learning more about those making the choices of who should lead. Moreover, leadership involves the relationship between those chosen and their followers. It is an interaction or exchange between the leader and those constituents (be they special interests, the military, party members, or the voting public) to whom he or she is accountable. Moreover, leadership is exercised in a particular context—point in time, institutional setting, culture. The interrelationships among these various facets of leadership were studied in different kinds of organizational environments and evolved into what is called the contingency theory of leadership (e.g. Fiedler and Garcia 1987; Winter 1987; Hargrove 1989). This theoretical framework emphasizes the importance of the 'match' between what the potential leader is like, what relevant followers or constituents want, and what the setting calls for in understanding who is likely to become a political leader. Let us consider several examples of what we have learned about this matching process.

Correlations between type of political system (indicators of how democratic a government is) and national leaders' scores on responsiveness to the political context over the last three decades are, on average, 0.56 (Hermann and Kegley 1995; Hermann and Gerard 2009). The data suggest that there is a bias in the selection processes in these two types of political systems favouring leaders with particular types of predispositions. There appears to be a push in democratic cultures and institutions for voters to elect leaders who respect and respond to democratic values, who are not only attuned to public opinion but also inclined to empower people to help shape policy, and who concentrate their attention on building coalitions through bargaining and compromise. Electoral politics and the institutional constraints that define democracy reward leaders who pay close attention to what their various constituencies want and who work to win approval by representing these interests. In more autocratic and hierarchically organized settings, leaders are more likely to be selected if they espouse and are guided by a set of ideas, a particular cause, a problem to be solved, or an ideology. Challenging constraints or successfully tackling a task others deem impossible becomes one way of gaining an audience with potential patrons or those who count, as well as facilitating the mobilization of followers dissatisfied with their current lives. Political leadership involves leaders persuading or coercing others to accept their positions and facilitates them in shaping norms and institutions to achieve their goals.

There is also the question of who can hold a particular leadership position. In other words, what are the formal requirements for the role (for example, age, training needed, party affiliation, political experience, time involved, relevant networking) and what are the informal expectations about the position (for example, the amount of influence the position affords, its flexibility, its usefulness as a stepping stone to higher office). The answers to these questions begin to narrow the field of potential candidates (e.g. Whitney 2001; Li 2002; Bank and Shlumberger 2004). Then there is the nature of the selection process itself. Who does the selecting (for example, party, leader or group of leaders, electorate)? How is selection generally made (for example, cooptation, conscription, self-nomination)? How complex is the selection process—how many steps or stages are there? What happens in the selection process indicates the level of control that others have over who can run for the position. If control is tight, the candidates are likely to be mirror images of those doing the selection. Loyalty, conformity, and agreement with the political attitudes and motivations of the sponsor become important. With less control and an emphasis on self-nomination, a wider range of points of view and leadership styles are likely to be represented among those who choose to run; unless there are particular beliefs among those doing the electing or selecting about the kind of leader that is sought (Taber and Lodge 2006).

Demographics and the political zeitgeist of the moment also affect who is recruited as a political leader. For example, consider what will happen in European countries as the median age of their populations goes from 40.6—in 2012—to the predicted 52.7 by 2050 and the percentage of their population over 60 goes from 24 per cent to 40 per cent (Economist Intelligence Unit 2011)? If this older group participates in elections in numbers even roughly proportional to their size, they will increasingly influence not only the nature of issues given priority in party platforms but also the types of candidates who will be viewed as viable. Large demographic groups, if they can be mobilized, have the ability not only to set the issue agenda but also to define who can become a political leader (Kotkin 2010).

Furthermore, research has indicated that, as we move from times of peace to those of crisis, from periods of relative stability to those of rapid change, and from times where resources are plentiful to those when they are scarce, different types of leaders are required of those involved in both the recruitment and the selection processes (e.g. Hargrove 1989; Strategic Assessment Group 2003; Hermann and Gerard 2009). In more turbulent times, constituencies as well as those playing the gatekeeper role in the recruitment process seek leaders who have the skills needed to keep the political unit afloat—to take charge and provide the public with some sense of security if not optimism. When the situation is less turbulent, we find both constituents and gatekeepers wanting to be part of the process and quick to complain when their interests are not taken into account. Leaders who are good at day-to-day politics, at listening and building consensus, become more in demand. The elections and defeats of Winston Churchill and Charles de Gaulle are often used as examples of the relevance of the nature of the situation for who is chosen to lead. Both men were elected to positions of power during periods of turmoil and 'unelected' during times of relative peace. Both were 'take-charge' kinds of people who were less comfortable with the politics of consensus and compromise.

3 What Personal Characteristics of Leaders Matter?

A second question of interest to political psychologists studying political leaders focuses on which characteristics of leaders are likely to affect what they do politically. Here we are interested in what political leaders are like. A search of journalistic and scholarly writings on political leaders suggests five pieces of information that are important to learn about leaders. We want to know: (1) their basic political beliefs and views on politics, (2) their leadership style, (3) their motivation for seeking a political leadership position, (4) their reactions to stress and pressure, and (5) certain background factors (for example, their previous political experience). In effect, leaders' rationality is bounded by their beliefs, what they want, the ways in which they process information and define problems, and their experiences (Simon 1985).

Beliefs

One of the most direct means of understanding the relationship between what political leaders are like and what they are likely to urge on their followers comes through learning about their basic political beliefs—in other words, how they view political reality. Beliefs indicate how leaders are likely to interpret their political environment and help them chart and map the political terrain in which they are operating. Indeed, as Abelson (1986) has observed, beliefs are like possessions and have implications for the goals and strategies that leaders will adopt as well as what in the political environment is likely to capture their interest. Furthermore, their beliefs can become embodied in the norms guiding the political institutions they are leading, framing what is 'right' and 'wrong' behaviour and difficult to change (e.g. Hagan 2001; Feng 2006).

In 1969, George proposed that leaders are generally guided by an 'operational code'—a set of philosophical and instrumental beliefs that set their parameters for action. These beliefs help to define what is viewed as a problem and which options are seen as viable within that particular political orientation. For instance, consider what might be the differences in the proposals of leaders who believe that conflict is endemic to politics and those that view conflict as generally temporary and the result of misunderstanding. For the first type, the world is full of threats, vigilance is necessary as control and predictability are limited, and all other actors are potential rivals; whereas with a misunderstanding, there is an opportunity to change the other's view and, thus, to control any escalation as well as to establish a climate that can foster negotiation (Walker 2004). In effect, 'instead of passively reflecting reality', beliefs 'shape leaders' perceptions of reality, acting as mechanisms...that [can] distort, block, and recast incoming information from the environment' (Schafer and Walker 2006: 5). Translating what George (1969) proposed into an assessment-at-a-distance tool has allowed those studying political leaders to learn more about the impact of a leader's general view of political reality on leadership behaviour as well as the effects of beliefs focused on a particular issue or target and those involved in the interaction between leaders and followers during a crisis.

In addition to learning about what leaders believe, we need to learn how strongly they hold such beliefs. Are the leaders so persuaded of a particular belief or world view that it becomes a dominant force in their lives, acting as a lens through which all external events are interpreted, or are they more responsive to the environment, letting events shape and change certain beliefs? Leaders' beliefs have more direct impact on the leadership setting the more resistant they are to outside influences (Thies 2006). Like the crusader of old, the leader with a strong belief or world view seeks to convince others of his position and is likely to view much of what is happening as relevant to the cause. Leaders whose beliefs or world views are less firmly entrenched are likely to be more pragmatic. The nature of the situation will generally determine how firmly—and whether—such leaders press their case.

Leadership Style

Leadership style can also influence what political leaders do. The influence, however, is more indirect than that of beliefs. Whereas political beliefs can directly impact policy, leadership style sets the tone and pattern of leadership: how the leader interacts with those he or she is leading and how he or she acts when representing those being led. For example, does the leader emphasize personal diplomacy and face-to-face meetings or does he or she prefer to work through intermediaries? Does the leader tend to work with other people or does he or she prefer to 'go it alone'? Is there an emphasis on political rhetoric and propaganda? Does the leader have a flair for the dramatic? Is the leader interested in studying problems in detail or satisfied with general information? Is secrecy essential during the policy-making process? Each of these questions focuses on an element of leadership style.

Since the beginning of the twentieth century, there is growing evidence that there are differences among leaders in whether they respect (work within) or challenge (go around) the constraints in their environments (e.g. Keller 2005; Kille 2006). Two recent presidents in Iran represent this difference: Khatami, president until 2005, though charismatic, was concerned with working for change within the constraints of the political system in which he found himself; Ahmadinejad, president from 2005 to 2013, tackled the constraints that he had to work within head-on, willing to challenge the outside world and his own people. Data suggest that leaders willing to challenge constraints often come to their positions with an agenda and seek 'true believers' as advisers to help them implement that agenda. They are interested in controlling the flow of information; issues and events are not perceived as important or relevant unless they pertain to or affect the implementation of their agenda. On the other hand, leaders who focus on respecting constraints often seek out others' perspectives, are interested in diverse opinions, work well in a team, and focus on building consensus and working towards compromise. In effect, leaders who focus on working within the constraints that are found in their positions of leadership are sensitive to the context and define as well as respond to problems on a case-by-case basis, while those who challenge constraints do so based on what they want or need—their personal predispositions.

Leadership style can have limiting effects on those working with the leader in at least two ways. First, those around the leaders tend to cater to their stylistic preferences in order to keep open access to them. Second, there is the doppelgänger effect: that is, political leaders tend to surround themselves with people who are their doubles—people with similar stylistic preferences or complementary styles. They select advisers and staff with whom they feel 'comfortable' and 'compatible' (Preston and Hermann 2004). It may mean that at times they look for a 'team of rivals' while at other times a group that is loyal—all depending on their own leadership style (Greenstein 2009).

Motivation

What are a leader's reasons for seeking a leadership position? Among the motives attributed to political leaders are the need for power, a cause (a problem they want to fix, a philosophy they want adopted, a crisis), a sense of obligation, the need for approval and esteem from others, the challenge of the position, the need for status and recognition, and the need to compensate for personal shortcomings (Winter 2002). These motives have implications for what political leaders will do. In studying Connecticut legislators, Barber (1965) found that different motives for becoming a member of the state legislature were associated with different kinds of legislative behaviour. Some legislators were interested in status and recognition and used the legislature as a forum for self-advancement; others were motivated by the need for approval and were essentially submissive in the legislative process; still others were in the legislature out of a sense of obligation and became the moral compass for what happened in that arena; and some were challenged by the position and became actively involved in initiating legislation and in committee work. Studies have found similar relationships between motivation for leadership and political behaviour in revolutionaries (Winter 2011).

In addition to influencing what they will do, leaders' motives can drive them to seek political leadership positions that provide them with the opportunity for satisfying their needs. Indeed, several studies have reported a match between leaders' motivation and the demands of the leadership role they occupy; moreover, those with the strongest motivation tend to seek out leadership positions with the greatest likelihood of satisfying their needs (e.g. Hermann and Gerard 2009; Winter 2010). In effect, there often appears to be a fit between what the leadership position will enable a leader to do and what the leader wants to do.

It is tempting at this point to suggest that political leaders fail or leave their positions at least partly because their motives are no longer compatible with the leadership position. The needs and interests of important constituents may have changed; the leader may have misperceived an opportunity; the situation may have changed with time; or the leader's own needs may be different. Winter (1987) found that American presidents were more likely to be elected if their needs matched those of the public's at that point in time as assessed through the mass media. Moreover, others have found that those in leadership positions are often forced out of these positions when their motivations and those demanded by the situation differ (e.g. Hermann and Gerard 2009; Hermann, Sakiev, and Smith 2010).

Reactions to Stress

Leadership positions are often stressful because the situations leaders face generally involve uncertainty and high stakes, depend on the cooperation of multiple groups and organizations, and force value trade-offs. To achieve such positions, political leaders have had to learn to deal with stress. What happens when stress becomes higher than usual or in situations when leaders become particularly vulnerable to stress?

A large literature has developed on political leaders' reactions to stress (e.g. Boin et al. 2005; Hermann 2008). As stress increases, leaders tend to reach conclusions more quickly, to focus less on the consequences of their actions, to see the present in terms of the past, to rely only on close associates whose opinions and support can be counted on, and to want to take direct control of the decision-making process. These reactions result in a reduction in the number of options as well as the amount and kinds of information that are considered and enable leaders to focus more on searching for support than on dealing with the situation—that is, they permit leaders to deal with the stress by avoiding facing all the ramifications of the problem.

Not all leaders react in this fashion, however. As Robert Kennedy (1968: 81) observed about the group that composed the ExCom during the Cuban Missile Crisis, the quality of the performances of these advisers and cabinet members was quite varied. Some were highly creative and resourceful while others were erratic and 'even appeared to lose their judgment and stability'. As Kennedy's comment suggests, some leaders find stressful situations motivating and rise to the challenge, others experience some distress in such situations and respond as the literature indicates, while a few become debilitated and unable to act. These various types of responses have implications for the leadership that the individual leader will provide. Thus, it is important to ascertain how a leader usually responds to stress.

Learning how leaders are likely to respond to stress becomes particularly relevant in situations where the stress is no longer something threatening only the group, organization, or government but is also threatening the leaders personally—that is, they internalize the threat and their own self-esteem becomes involved. Internalization can occur in situations that pose a threat to the leader's position as leader, to a policy in which the leader has invested time and political capital, to those immediately around him or to issues over which the leader has little control but for which he will be held accountable. The Iranian hostage crisis, 9/11, and the meltdown of Wall Street in 2008 have posed such situations for American presidents, the Arab spring to political leaders in the Middle East, and the tsunami in the spring of 2011 to the leadership of Japan. When internalized, these situations and problems can become all-consuming for the leaders and those they lead. Other issues are forgotten or set aside and attention becomes riveted on dealing with the 'life-or-death' issue. All resources are directed towards coping with the problem. Political leadership becomes focused, drawing the attention of all in the political unit to what is now the leader's problem. By studying how leaders have handled other potentially stressful situations, we gain some idea about which threats they are likely to internalize and how they will deal with the resulting stress once the threat is internalized.

Background Factors

Information about leaders' backgrounds can also provide insights into the kind of leadership they are likely to exercise. In particular, information on their first political positions, on the nature of their political experiences, and on the political climate into which they were socialized can help us in understanding what they will do.

Barber (1977) has argued that knowledge about a political leader's first political position provides clues about later leadership behaviour. The nature of the position, the means by which it was acquired, and the ways in which the leader behaved while in the position have implications for future leadership activities. In effect, in future situations leaders fall back on the rhetoric and practices that helped them succeed the first time. Because it is the first, this experience is often given added significance in memory and remains especially vivid. In talking over the initial political experiences of women members of the US Senate, Whitney (2001) learned how their first political interactions shaped not only how they considered politics but also the ways they chose to act in exercising leadership. 'Don't get mad, get elected' became their motto.

What kind of experiences have political leaders had in the kinds of positions they now hold? How similar is the present position to others they have held? How long a tenure have the leaders had in their present positions? The answers to these questions provide us with some ideas about the repertoire of behaviours the leaders are likely to have as well as how concerned they will need to be with consolidating and legitimating their power as opposed to getting on with the task at hand, how much influence the leaders will have over policy, and how much they will have to learn on the job. With experience, leaders gain a sense of what will work and not work and also which cues in the environment need to be taken into account and which are superfluous in specific situations (Beer, Healy, and Bourne 2004; Preston and Hermann 2006).

Just how did the leaders acquire their present positions and why? Did they work their way through the system; were they advanced by a patron; were they co-opted because of certain expertise or a particular set of beliefs? This information tells us how much the leaders know about the individuals, groups, and organizations with which they must work; how likely they are to be imbued with the organization's norms and goals; how dependent they will be on certain other individuals and groups; and how broad a mandate they will have to institute change. Consider the difference between being an elected versus an appointed official.

In addition to their experiences, leaders are also products of their times. What was going on when the leader was growing up, seeking that first job, and assuming responsibility? What were the events and ideas shaping young people during the time that the leader was moving from adolescence through early adulthood, often the time when political socialization is occurring most rapidly? What were the problems and issues with which people were having to cope? As Schlesinger (2007: A23) has observed, leaders, like historians, 'are prisoners of their own experience'; they bring with them 'preconceptions' of how politics works that are characteristic of their age. In effect, common generational experiences have an effect on those who become leaders, helping to shape the norms and beliefs of both leaders and their constituents about the nature of the political environment. If not completely imbued themselves with the ideas that have shaped their generation, leaders have to deal with these ideas in their constituents to retain their positions of leadership (e.g. Strategic Assessment Group 2003; Jennings 2004).

4 WHEN DO LEADERS MATTER?

The third question that political psychologists have explored with regard to political leadership focuses on the conditions under which the characteristics of political leaders just described are likely to shape what their political units do. In effect, are there certain times when it becomes critical to know something about what leaders are like to understand what is happening in the governing process? Several conditions that have received attention in the literature revolve around (1) the ill-structured nature of most political problems, (2) the tendency for authority to contract to leaders during crises, (3) turn-over in government, and (4) the experience of the leader.

Most political problems are ill-structured and invite interpretation. As ill-structured problems, they have no 'correct' answer, often are laced with uncertainty regarding the nature and salience of the problem, provoke in the policymaker a need to provide some structure or frame to what is happening, and usually involve value trade-offs (Sylvan and Voss 1998). How policymakers define and represent the problem may or may not match how an outside observer might view it. In fact, research (Beasley et al. 2001) has shown that, on average, around 70 per cent of the time policymakers involved in dealing with such ill-structured problems disagree about the nature of the problem, the options that are feasible, or what should happen. Note how the same event—11 September 2001—was framed by leaders differently in Britain and in the United States. Tony Blair announced at the Labor Party Conference just hours after the Twin Towers had collapsed that we had just experienced a crime against civilization—the police and the courts were the instruments for dealing with what had happened with justice as the goal; George W. Bush framed the event as an attack on America and pronounced a war on terror engaging the military and calling forth nationalism. Here is where lead-ers' beliefs can become like possessions, as noted earlier; the stronger said beliefs, the more likely they are to shape any interpretation (Taber and Lodge 2006). Moreover, how policymakers view the problem—as being a loss or a gain (things are going poorly ver-sus well)—can shape how risk prone or averse they are likely to be in the options and solutions they pursue (McDermott 2001). Rationality becomes bounded by the leaders' perceptions of reality and problems become structured in a particular way (Chollet and Goldgeier 2002).

Research has also shown that there is a contraction of authority to those most accountable for policy in crisis situations—to the leadership (Boin et al. 2005). Such a contraction appears to happen in decentralized as well as centralized political organiza-tions (Hermann and Kegley 1995). Crises are considered to involve a serious threat to the values and interests of the political unit, provide little time for making a response, and come as a surprise (Stern 2003). Leaders and their interpretations of what is happening become important in these situations. Indeed, in a study of eighty-one crises that were identified as such by journalists, historians, and those involved, how leaders viewed the amount of time available to them and the degree of surprise in the situation led to dif-ferent decision-making processes (Hermann and Dayton 2009). When they viewed themselves as having little time and were surprised (an 11 September 2001 type of event), leaders pushed to frame the event quickly; to reach consensus rapidly on what to do; and to implement their decision with little interest in, or reaction to, feedback regard-ing what they were doing—either positive or negative. They engaged in path-dependent behaviour. However, when leaders perceived themselves to have a little more time in which to respond to what was happening, even if they were caught by surprise (the US reaction to the Iraqi invasion of Kuwait, for example), they became more innovative—searching for information and expertise that could help them ascertain what was hap-pening and trying to think outside the box. Leaders' general reactions to stress and how likely they are to internalize the crisis situation and make it their own suggest which of these two types of decision-making processes they will pursue. Moreover, leadership style often shapes how fast contraction of authority occurs and who becomes involved with the leaders in dealing with the crisis (Preston 2001).

Leaders of governments often change, and with each change can come a difference in perspective regarding politics that has the ability to influence what governments do. Consider the change from a George W. Bush to a Barack Obama, a Sarkozy to a Hollande, a Kim Jong Il to a Kim Jong Un, a Tony Blair to a Gordon Brown. At the least, leadership style and level of experience are different between these leaders (e.g. Kaarbo and Hermann 1998; Dyson 2006). Now note the fact that, between 1998 and 2008, the 29 Asian countries bordering the Pacific Rim had 133 governments—on average each had 4.6 governments during this time period (Dayton et al. 2009). Examining the leadership styles of those who came to positions of power as a result of these changes in govern- ment, we learn that 60 per cent of those who came to their positions with a specific agenda and the intention to control the policy-making process—they were prepared to challenge constraints—lost their positions after a short period of time through votes of no confidence, calls for early elections, parties withdrawing from a coalition, or coups. Interestingly, only 21 per cent of leaders who believed in the use of informal power and preferred to work behind the scenes to make policy experienced such an irregular loss of power—when regime change occurred for these leaders, it was through a regular and planned process. Furthermore, the first leadership style was associated with the use of repression and diversion in dealing with opposition to government policies, while the second leadership style was associated with bargaining and accommodation (Hermann, Sakiev and Smith 2010). In effect, leadership style and strategy affected longevity in office as well as how influential the leaders' views were on what was considered a prob- lem and who was involved in making policy.

Experience also appears to count as an important influence on how political lead- ers interpret and respond to events (e.g. Preston 2001; Beer, Healy, and Bourne 2004; Dyson and Preston 2006). With some expertise, they are more likely to rely on their knowledge and background and to engage in situations on a case-by-case basis. Indeed, such leaders are increasingly willing to assert, and actively advocate for, their positions in the policy-making process, even as they quickly integrate new information into their previous knowledge base, differentiate between relevant and irrelevant information, and make decisions using analogies based on past events. Without expertise, leaders are more affected by their personal predispositions such as their beliefs, motivations, or leadership style as well as led to depend on those whom they trust who have such experience. Moreover, policymakers feel more comfortable and confident dealing with domains in which they have some expertise and often drift towards these arenas. Consider, for example, the effects that Dick Cheney had on American foreign policy under the two Bush presidents. President George H. W. Bush had extensive experi- ence in the foreign policy-making process and could differentiate between relevant and irrelevant information as well as recognize inconsistencies in the information pro- vided to him and exceptions to the rules—he could say 'no' to Cheney based on his own knowledge and expertise. His son, President George W. Bush, came to office with little foreign-policy experience and very little international travel. By necessity, he viewed Cheney as an expert and relied on his advice as well as on his own beliefs regarding the importance of the United States and democracy in the world in making policy (Preston and Hermann 2006).

5 In Conclusion

To understand leadership, political psychologists have argued that it is important to learn not only what the leaders involved are like but also what those they lead want and the nature of the context in which they are operating. Leadership can change as these factors change, with consequences for who is likely to become a political leader and for when gaining knowledge about what leaders are like will matter. From a political psychology perspective, leadership is an umbrella concept that can be understood only be examining these ingredients in combination. As this chapter suggests, we are currently more involved in exploring what leaders are like and are just in the initial stages of examining the effects such characteristics can have on who becomes a political leader as well as their impact on what the political organizations, institutions, or governments they lead do. Our challenge is to tackle the interaction among the ingredients of leadership. The studies overviewed here suggest the payoffs that may result from accepting this challenge.

References

Abelson, R. P. (1986). 'Beliefs are Like Possessions', *Journal of the Theory of Social Behaviour*, 16: 223–250.

Bank, A., and Shlumberger, O. (2004). 'Jordan: Between Regime Survival and Economic Reform', in V. Perthes (ed.), *Arab Elites: Negotiating the Politics of Change*. Boulder, CO: Lynne Rienner, 35–60.

Barber, J. D. (1965). *The Lawmakers*. New Haven: Yale University Press.

Barber, J. D. (1977). *The Presidential Character: Predicting Performance in the White House*. Englewood Cliffs, NJ: Prentice-Hall.

Beasley, R., Kaarbo, J., Hermann, C. F., and Hermann, M. G. (2001). 'People and Processes in Foreign Policymaking', *International Studies Review*, 3: 217–50.

Beer, F. A., Healy, A. F., and Bourne, L. E., Jr (2004). 'Dynamic Decisions: Experimental Reactions to War, Peace, and Terrorism', in M. G. Hermann (ed.), *Advances in Political Psychology*. London: Elsevier, 139–68.

Boin, A., 't Hart, P., Stern, E. K., and Sundelius, B. (2005). *The Politics of Crisis Management: Public Leadership under Pressure*. Cambridge: Cambridge University Press.

Browning, R. P., and Jacob, H. (1964). 'Power Motivation and the Political Personality', *Public Opinion Quarterly*, 28: 75–90.

Burns, J. M. (1978). *Leadership*. New York: Harper & Row.

Chollet, D. H., and Goldgeier, M. M. (2002). 'The Scholarship of Decision Making: Do We Know How We Decide?', in R. C. Snyder, H. W. Bruck, B. Sapin, V. M. Hudson, D. H. Chollet, and J. M. Goldgeier (eds), *Foreign Policy Decision Making (Revisited)*. New York: Palgrave Macmillan, 153–80.

Dayton, B. W., Hermann, M. G., Sakiev, A., Karakas-Keles, H., Smith, M. and Derksen, H. (2009). *Crisis-Prone Governments: A Study of 29 Pacific Rim Countries*. Syracuse, NY: Moynihan Institute of Global Affairs.

DiRenzo, G. J. (1977). 'Politicians and Personality: A Cross-Cultural Perspective', in M. G. Hermann (ed.), *A Psychological Examination of Political Leaders*. New York: Free Press, 147–73.

Dyson, S. B. (2006). 'Personality and Foreign Policy: Tony Blair's Iraq Decisions', *Foreign Policy Analysis*, 2: 289–306.

Dyson, S. B., and Preston, T. (2006). 'Individual Characteristics of Leaders and the Use of Analogy in Foreign Policy Decision Making', *Political Psychology*, 27: 265–88.

Economist Intelligence Unit (2011). *The World in 2011*. London: The Economist.

Feng, H. (2006). 'Crisis Deferred: An Operational Code Analysis of Chinese Leaders across the Strait', in M. Schafer and S. G. Walker (eds), *Beliefs and Leadership in World Politics: Methods and Applications of Operational Code Analysis*. New York: Palgrave Macmillan, 151–70.

Fiedler, F. E., and Garcia, J. E. (1987). *New Approaches to Leadership, Cognitive Resources and Organizational Performance*. New York: Wiley.

George, A. L. (1969). ' "Operational Code": A Neglected Approach to the Study of Political Leaders and Decision Making', *International Studies Quarterly*, 23: 190–222.

Greenstein, F. I. (2009). *The Presidential Difference: Leadership Style from FDR to Barack Obama*. 3rd edn. Princeton: Princeton University Press.

Hagan, J. D. (2001). 'Does Decision Making Matter? Systemic Assumptions vs Historical Reality in International Relations Theory', *International Studies Review*, 3/2: 5–46.

Hargrove, E. C. (1989). 'Two Conceptions of Institutional Leadership', in B. D. Jones (ed.), *Leadership and Politics: New Perspectives in Political Science*. Lawrence, KS: University Press of Kansas, 57–85.

Hermann, M. G. (2008). 'Indicators of Stress in Policymakers during Foreign Policy Crises', in R. A. Boin (ed.), *Crisis Management*, Vol. 2. Beverly Hills, CA: SAGE Publications.

Hermann, M. G., and Dayton, B. W. (2009). 'Transboundary Crises through the Eyes of Policymakers: Sense Making and Crisis Management', *Journal of Contingencies and Crisis Management*, 17: 233–41.

Hermann, M. G., and Gerard, C. (2009). 'Leaders and their Effects', in B. W. Dayton and L. Kriesberg (eds), *Conflict Transformation and Peacebuilding*. New York: Routledge, 30–44.

Hermann, M. G., and Kegley, C. W. (1995). 'Rethinking Democracy and International Peace: Perspectives from Political Psychology', *International Studies Quarterly*, 39: 511–33.

Hermann, M. G., Sakiev, A., and Smith, M. (2010). 'Governance in Context: Understanding the Ingredients of Political Leadership'. Paper presented at the annual meeting of the American Political Science Association, Washington, DC, 4 September.

Jennings, M. K. (2004). 'American Political Participation as Viewed through the Political Socialization Project', in M. G. Hermann (ed.), *Advances in Political Psychology*. London: Elsevier, 1–15.

Kaarbo, J., and Hermann, M. G. (1998). 'Leadership Styles of Prime Ministers: How Individual Differences Affect the Foreign Policymaking Process', *Leadership Quarterly*, 9: 243–63.

Keller, J. 2005. 'Leadership Style, Regime Type, and Foreign Policy Crisis Behavior: A Contingent Monadic Peace', *International Studies Quarterly*, 49: 205–31.

Kennedy, R. (1968). *Thirteen Days: A Memoir of the Cuban Missile Crisis*. New York: Norton.

Kille, K. J. (2006). *From Manager to Visionary: The Secretary-General of the United Nations*. New York: Palgrave Macmillan.

Kotkin, J. (2010). *The Next Hundred Million: America in 2050*. New York: Penguin.

Lasswell, H. D. (1948). *Power and Personality*. New York: Viking Penguin.

Li, C. (2002). *China's Leaders: The New Generation*. New York: Rowman & Littlefield.

McDermott, R. (2001). *Risk-Taking in International Politics: Prospect Theory in American Foreign Policy*. Ann Arbor, MI: University of Michigan Press.

Preston, T. (2001). *The President and his Inner Circle: Leadership Style and the Advisory Process in Foreign Affairs*. New York: Columbia University Press.

Preston, T., and Hermann, M. G. (2004). 'Presidential Leadership Style and the Foreign Policy Advisory Process', in E. R. Wittkopf and J. McCormick (eds), *The Domestic Sources of American Foreign Policy*. 4th edn. New York: Rowman & Littlefield, 363–80.

Preston, T., and Hermann, M. G. (2006). 'Exploring Leader Policy Expertise, Experience, and Interest: Developing and Evaluating Assessment-at-a-Distance Measures for World Leaders'. Paper presented at the annual meeting of the International Studies Association, San Diego, CA, 22–25 March.

Quandt, W. B. (1970). 'The Comparative Study of Political Elites', *SAGE Professional Papers in Comparative Politics*, No. 01–004. Beverly Hills, CA: SAGE Publications.

Rejai, M., and Phillips, K. (1983). *World Revolutionary Leaders*. New Brunswick, NJ: Rutgers University Press.

Schafer, M., and Walker, S. G. (2006) (eds). *Beliefs and Leadership in World Politics: Methods and Applications of Operational Code Analysis*. New York: Palgrave Macmillan.

Schlesinger, A. M., Jr (2007). 'Folly's Antidote'. *New York Times*, 1 January: A23.

Simon, H. A. (1985). 'Human Nature in Politics: The Dialogue of Psychology with Political Science', *American Political Science Review*, 79: 293–304.

Stern, E. K. (2003). 'Crisis Studies and Foreign Policy Analysis: Insights, Synergies, and Challenges', *International Studies Review*, 5: 183–205.

Stewart, L. H. (1977). 'Birth Order and Political Leadership', in M. G. Hermann (ed.), *A Psychological Examination of Political Leaders*. New York: Free Press, 206–36.

Strategic Assessment Group (2003). *The Next Generation of World Leaders*. Washington: Central Intelligence Agency.

Sylvan, D. A., and Voss, J. F. (1998) (eds). *Problem Representation in Foreign Policy Decision Making*. Cambridge: Cambridge University Press.

Taber, C. S., and Lodge, M. (2006). 'Motivated Skepticism in the Evaluation of Political Beliefs', *American Journal of Political Science*, 50: 755–69.

Thies, C. G. (2006). 'Brokers and Beliefs: The Political Psychology of the Asian Financial Crisis', in M. Schafer and S. G. Walker (eds), *Beliefs and Leadership in World Politics: Methods and Applications of Operational Code Analysis*. New York: Palgrave Macmillan, 219–32.

Walker, S. G. (2004). 'Role Identities and the Operational Code of Political Leaders', in M. G. Hermann (ed.), *Advances in Political Psychology*. London: Elsevier, 71–106.

Whitney, C. (2001). *Nine and Counting*. New York: HarperCollins.

Winter, D. G. (1987). 'Leader Appeal, Leader Performance, and the Motive Profiles of Leaders and Followers: A Study of American Presidents and Elections', *Journal of Personality and Social Psychology*, 52: 196–202.

Winter, D. G. (2002). 'Motivation and Political Leadership', in L. Valenty and O. Feldman (eds), *Political Leadership for the New Century*. Westport, CT: Praeger, 25–47.

Winter, D. G. (2010). 'Why Achievement Motivation Produces Success in Business but Failure in Politics: The Importance of Personal Control', *Journal of Personality*, 78: 1637–67.

Winter, D. G. (2011). 'Scoring Motive Imagery in Documents from Four Middle Eastern Opposition Groups', *Dynamics of Asymmetric Conflict*, 4: 144–54.

CHAPTER 9

··

PSYCHOANALYTIC THEORIES

··

STANLEY A. RENSHON

PSYCHOANALYTIC theory is unalterably associated with the seminal work of Sigmund Freud, as it should be. It was Freud, after all, whose decades of work, spanning the years 1886–1938 and embodied in the 24 volume *Standard Edition*, conceptualized, defined, refined, and applied psychoanalytic theory. Freud saw his theory as providing an understanding of the nature of individuals' emotional lives and the impact of these experiences on the development of their characters and psychologies.

Freud also came to believe that his theories could provide a set of theoretical tools by which some parts of social and political life might be better understood. He himself explored these links with papers on the use of psychoanalytic theory in legal proceedings (Freud 1906), Social Anthropology and the nature of group emotional ties (Freud 1913), war and peace (Freud 1915, 1919, 1933), leadership and group emotional dynamics (Freud 1921), the psychological costs and benefits of civilization (Freud 1930), and presidential and political leadership (Freud 1939; Freud and Bullitt 1966).

Given this history and the debates that have accompanied the theory, it is not surprising that the lineage of psychoanalytic studies of political leaders and leadership has had a long and controversial history. That history began in 1912 when Freud himself criticized one of his followers for using his theories to 'psychoanalyze' an American presidential candidate (Prince 1912; McGuire 1978: 500), characterizing that effort as 'absolutely inadmissible, an infringement on privacy'. Yet, Freud himself later co-authored a controversial book on Woodrow Wilson (Freud and Bullitt 1996) that was published after his death. Those who followed Freud and used his theory to study leaders have sometimes descended into the abyss of absurd reductionism (deMause 1977: 28) while others' efforts have provided illuminating insight (Lasswell 1930, 1948; George and George 1956).

Controversy some of it well deserved, notwithstanding, the premise of this chapter is that psychoanalytic theory, generally and including a number of its variants, has a critical role to play in understanding political leaders and leadership. Paradoxically, however, that role is limited. Not every aspect of political leadership is advanced by the application of psychoanalytic theory. Indeed, one can say quite bluntly that there are some elements of leadership analysis that are not amenable to it at all.

Therefore, this chapter contains no clarion calls for the automatic or obligatory application of psychoanalytic theories to studies of political leaders and leadership. Indeed, it contains quite the opposite, a suggestion that psychoanalytic theory be used only sparingly and in the areas in which it is theoretically and substantively suited.

As it happens, however, these areas are central to understanding individual political leaders and how they carry out key aspects of their leadership responsibilities. They are, as well, central to understanding the nature of political leadership, the relationship between those who aspire to lead and those toward whom leaders' efforts are directed.

The psychoanalytic study of political leaders and leadership, therefore, is in the paradoxical position of having limited utility and being absolutely essential.

1 THE PSYCHOANALYTIC ANALYSIS OF POLITICAL LEADERSHIP: STRUCTURAL BARRIERS

Any essay focused on the relationships between psychoanalytic theory and the study of political leaders and leadership must begin by acknowledging two complicating, but nonetheless true, facts. First, the term 'psychoanalytic theory' is a bit of a misnomer. In reality, there are a number of quite different psychoanalytically based theories, some of which are more useful in the analysis of political leaders than others.

Even while Freud was alive his followers expanded his theory, and that continued at a rapid pace after his death. A partial listing of theories that qualify under this rubric would include: attachment theory (Bowlby 1969, 1973); 'borderline' personality organization (Kernberg 1984); culturally framed psychoanalytic theories (Fromm 1941; see also Horney 1939); ego psychology (Hartmann 1975); identity and adulthood (Erikson 1986); interpersonal relations (Sullivan 1953); object relations (Greenberg and Mitchell 1983; Klein 2002), narcissism (Kohut 1971, 1977); and the psychology of emotional environments (Winnicott 1986) to name but a few (Makari 2008).

Fred Greenstein's (1969) early, prudent warning to political scientists seeking to borrow from psychology more generally still applies more specifically to psychoanalytic theory and political leadership. Those looking for answers to their questions about the psychological sources of a leader's behaviour, as well as those who support him or her, will find rival theories and unanswered questions rather than easily borrowed solutions.

Second, real training in psychoanalytic theory is time and effort intensive as George and George (1956: viii) noted early on and is, in my view, best accompanied by personal experience with the operation of the theory in practice. Early pioneers, and those who followed, did get first-hand training—Harold Lasswell in Vienna, Alexander George as a fellow in Stanford's Department of Psychiatry, Arnold Rogow as a training candidate at the New York Psychoanalytic Institute, and Graham Little both at the Yale Political Psychology postdoctoral programme and as a student at Chicago's Institute for Psychoanalysis. The field has drawn, and continues to draw historians (Loewenberg 1971a, 1971b), psychiatrists

(Volkan and Fowler 2009; see also, Post 2005), and psychologists from a number of areas within their larger fields (see Runyan 1984; Schultz 2005), yet their numbers remain small. In its early days the small number who used psychoanalytic theory to study leaders and leadership had had some training and/or had the familiarity that comes with having been psychoanalysed. Most of those who made use of psychoanalytic theories, however, did not themselves receive training nor have therapeutic first-hand experience. They were, rather, consumers and translators of Freud's theories—with mixed results.

Training in political psychology is now much more widely available than it was even two decades ago. There are several full-fledged programmes providing training and an international summer institute in political psychology. Yet almost every single political psychology programme, including the summer institute, stresses social and cognitive psychology to the near exclusion of psychoanalytic theory. Therefore, given what is required to be really conversant with those theories, users are more likely to borrow disparate undigested parts of psychoanalytic theory than to be actually trained in it. These circumstances mitigate against psychoanalytic theory aspiring to anything more in the foreseeable future than a critically important, but nonetheless niche framework to analyse some core psychological aspects of political leaders and leadership.

Myths and Misconceptions

Since psychoanalytic theory has always held a minority position within political science, the familiarity that most political scientists did acquire was framed though larger cultural views of it and the small number of trained colleagues whose work they read or were aware of. This did not result in either indepth or sophisticated knowledge of the theory, its development, or its usefulness for leadership analysis.

As a result, some of what is said about psychoanalytic theory is more caricature than fact. Perhaps the three most common misconceptions about Freud's theories are that they were and remain mostly about sex (but see Adler 1927; Horney 1937; and even Freud 1914), that they are only about unconscious motivation, and that the only important causes of adult behaviour are to be found in childhood. These mistaken assumptions often function as 'conventional wisdom' and are the theoretical equivalent of intact prehistoric mammoths that are excavated periodically from the frozen tundra of Siberia. They are perfect specimens of a theoretical past that no longer exists, and hasn't for some time.

2 PSYCHOANALYTIC THEORY AND POLITICAL LEADERSHIP: THE BASIC MODEL REVISITED

As refined as psychoanalytic theory became during Freud's lifetime and as refined as it subsequently became, there are certain basic tenets that are accepted by almost all who are conversant with the theory. All psychoanalysts accept the existence of unconscious motivation. All accept the importance of early experience as a *foundation* of an individual's psychology, but not its sole determinant. And all psychoanalysts accept the view that individuals develop stable and understandable patterns of adult functioning which reflect how they have been able to integrate into their psychologies and identities their experiences, skills, and circumstances beginning in childhood but extending across adolescence into early and later adulthood.

The Character Patterns of Political Leaders: Ambition Observed

The development of psychological patterns is a particularly important core tenet in psychoanalytic theories. It is the basis for being able to observe patterns in a political leader's behaviour that are accessible to direct observation and that have their origin in basic elements of character. Character, as I have noted (Renshon 2008b), is a vertical psychological concept, not solely a horizontal one. That is, the effects of character are evident throughout an individual's individual's psychological functioning.

Character is not only found in the deepest recesses of an individual's psyche, but in the everyday world of accessible and observable behaviour. An individual's values and ideals that help provide a guide through life and the capacity to sustain fidelity to them (the domain of character integrity), the level and means by which persons pursue their life purposes (the domain of ambition), and how individuals organize their interpersonal relationships (the domain of relatedness) are often manifestly evident, even to untrained observers, although theory and training helps us to make sense of what we might see.

Consider the character element of ambition. In ordinary life, ambition is the fuel that powers self-realization and that in turn is a key building block of self-regard and self-confidence. It is also the life's blood of leadership performance, providing the motivational foundation of the purpose and direction that underlie a political leader's policy choices. That much seems obvious regarding leadership ambition, but that said, just what, exactly, can psychoanalytic theory contribute?

Its major contributions here lie in providing the theoretical tools for mapping and understanding the ways in which leaders exercise political power, the nature and especially the purpose of their policy and political initiatives, and the relation of their ambitions to their core political identities.

Why Do Political Leaders Seek Power?

Why leaders seek power, and what they do with it once they get it, are among the oldest and most important questions that can be asked of political leaders. Harold Lasswell's early answer (1930; see also Lasswell 1948) drawing on work by Alfred Adler (1927) was that the relentless pursuit of political power reflected an effort to overcome a leader's low estimates of self. Such leaders became specialists in accumulating power, though not necessarily successful in exercising it. George and George's detailed study of Woodrow Wilson (George and George 1956) suggested that when such leaders invested heavily in particular policies and were thwarted by opposition, they tended to take it very personally and become rigid and ultimately politically self-destructive.

Yet, while political power can provide some compensation for low or labile self-esteem, the demanding rigours of reaching the top tiers of political life would seem to make this enormous effort problematic. After all, at this level, opponents are legion, major victories rare, and easier more rewarding pursuits readily available. These caveats raise the question of whether most, or even many political leaders fit Lasswell's 'political man' type and formulation. Research is accumulating that they do not.

It is increasingly clear for example, that some political leaders to seek power to *validate* high estimates of self rather than compensate for feelings of low self-esteem. Presidents in this category, like Bill Clinton (Renshon 2008a) and Barack Obama (Renshon 2012) grew up and accumulated a record of achievement, whether earlier (Clinton) or later (Obama) in their developmental histories, in which their skills were mostly equal to, or even outmatched, their circumstances and they gained the legitimate expectation of success. In these cases, the attainment and exercise of political power is viewed as a natural and legitimate consequence of their talents.

Yet, even those who gain and feel they deserve their political power must figure out what to do with it. Bill Clinton for all his intelligence, policy knowledge, and political skills had no driving ambition to bend the country's domestic and foreign policy premises (paradigms) to his singular ambitions. Indeed his whole governing strategy, triangulation, was a method for preserving left-centre policies in the context of public fatigue with 'big government' solutions. His famous characterization of his stance towards affirmative action ('mend it don't end it'), abortion ('safe, legal, and rare') and large-scale government programmes ('the era of big government is over') make this abundantly clear.

President Obama on the other hand, whose ambition blossomed late, made repeatedly clear during his campaign and his first four years of office that he wanted to 'transform' America, and he meant it (Renshon 2012: 75–98).

At the start of the Obama Presidency, the country's economic circumstances had improved a little from dire to extremely difficult. The public uniformly wanted the president to focus on the economy and specifically on creating jobs. However, Mr Obama had other plans including passing an historic healthcare plan, putting into place far-reaching environmental legislation (cap and trade), regulating the financial sector, reforming education policy, and passing comprehensive immigration reform.

Some of the president's closest advisors, among them Secretary of the Treasury Timothy Geithner, urged him to delay his transformative initiatives and focus on the economy to which the president replied: '*That's not enough for me*' (Calmes 2011, emphasis added).

The president's pursuit of his ambitions resulted in a calamitous set of Democratic Party losses during the 2010 midterm elections. Having won reelection, the major question of his second term is whether he will still see transformation as the key to his historical legacy and standing, or whether he will chose to find common ground with a still powerful Republican House majority that will result in more bipartisan, incremental deal making.

Leadership's Real Ambitions: Hidden in Plain Sight?

The psychoanalytically inspired search for leaders' conflicted power motivations (compensation or validation) may well have obscured a far more common one—the desire to simply do a good job (Renshon 2014). Such leaders are not primarily motivated by the effort to overcome any personal inadequacies. They are not motivated primarily by the desire to demonstrate their unique, and superior, qualifications for office. They are instead motivated by a combined desire for public service, a wish to leave their mark, and a sincere, but not grandiose set of convictions about why *their* leadership would matter. In the United States, their names are found among the modal ranks of presidential leadership: Dwight D. Eisenhower, John F. Kennedy, Lyndon B. Johnson, Richard M. Nixon, Gerald Ford, George H. W. Bush, Jimmy Carter, Bill Clinton, and George W. Bush.

Some of these leaders were more successful politically than others, taking into account the basic metric of reelection. Some might even be considered transformational in one specific arena, domestic (LBJ) or foreign policy (GWB), but even these two presidents did not begin their quest for the presidency with the ambition to be transforming. They became transformative in responding to unusual political circumstances. In Johnson's case, the political opportunity that arose after the tragic death of John F. Kennedy and in Bush's case America's dire circumstances after the 9/11 terrorists attacks.

Some scholars, like Burns (1966), deride presidents and leaders like those in the larger list above as transactional, comparing them unfavourably with transformative leaders. However, having a keen eye for political common ground while retaining personal principles and a capacity for building specific and perhaps shifting policy coalitions has the virtue of allowing mature capitalist/democratic societies to bridge the many elements—cultural, economic, ethno/racial, and political, of which they consist in the search for balanced and effective progress on the issues leaders now face.

Psychoanalytic approaches to political leadership, while being concerned with compensatory and validating ambition, may well have overlooked the more usual and perhaps equally important core contributions of leaders with a preference for getting things done rather than building grand policy monuments to their ambition. Furthermore, psychoanalytic approaches may also have underestimated how changes in political circumstances, for example, a more diverse citizenry, provide one illustration of the ways in which the times set the psychological stage for the kinds of leaders who can be successful—in this case those who can find common ground with those they seek to lead.

Psychoanalytic Theory and the Adulthood of Political Leaders

Sceptics may legitimately ask: if psychoanalytic theory offers a paradigm that extols the crucial importance of childhood, how is it useful for the study of political leadership which, after all, takes place almost exclusively in adulthood? The answer to that question lies in the post-Freudian development of psychoanalytic theory, and more specifically the work of Eric H. Erikson. Erikson's major contribution was to develop a theory of the eight stages of man, which stretches from early childhood though the very last stages of adult life. Important for our purposes here is that he illustrated the power and importance of adult life with two major biographies of important political leaders—one of Martin Luther (1958) and the other of Mahatma Gandhi (1969).

Erikson's study of Luther is entitled *Young Man* Luther (1958) (emphasis added) that immediately propels the analysis into early adulthood. Luther's historical stature came about not because of his intra-psychic conflicts, of which he had many, but rather because his emotional and religious doubts reflected 'a political and psychological vacuum which history had created in a significant portion of Western Christendom' (Erikson 1958: 15). In short, some of his conflicts were in part an embodiment of the larger conflicts surging through the culture in which he was born. The solution to his identity crisis came in the form of a new and paradigm-breaking theology and led to a transformative moment in Western history, The Reformation. It is thus that psychological conflict, historical moments and the possibility of transformation, and the determined, resilient, and creative response of singular individuals can become a recipe for 'greatness'.

Erikson's (1969) *Gandhi* focuses on The Event, a local labor dispute in Ahmedabad in 1918 when Gandhi was forty-nine years old. That strike marks the beginning of Gandhi's use of fasting and non-violent resistance as tools of moral leadership. In using this event as a springboard to explore Gandhi's past and his future as an iconic leader of historical stature, Erikson pushes psychoanalytic theory directly into mid-life adulthood. He also demonstrates again the ways in which intra-psychic conflicts, though very real, are not crippling impediments to creative leadership solutions that bridge a historical gap between status quo politics and major unresolved political problems like decolonization.

However, we see the importance of adulthood not only in the lives of transformational political leaders like Luther and Gandhi, but also in more 'ordinary' political leaders as well. That is because every successful political leader must forge a personal and political identity to help them navigate the swirling currents of public life and to help the public know where they stand. Of necessity, this critical leadership element is the work of adulthood.

James David Barber (1992: 7–8) called our attention to the importance of a future president's 'first independent political success'. Barber defined this term somewhat broadly as the period when a future president 'found himself' and 'moved beyond the detailed guidance of his family, then his self-esteem was dramatically boosted; then he came forth to be reckoned with by other people.'

However, a leader's political style can sometimes take a long period to develop and consolidate. This is in part a function of career choices. President Obama did not run for and win political office until 1997 by which time he was 34 years old. Moreover, based on the evidence, Obama's political style did not really develop and consolidate until he had served several terms as a state legislator.

In any event, the fusion of a leader's ambition with a style that reflects a core personal and political identity is at one and the same time a character element occupying a central place within a leader's core psychology and one that is inescapably tied to adulthood. And of course, that style has implications for the kinds of political leadership that a person does and can provide, and its fit with the views and needs of those who will help him gain office or power.

Political Leaders: Psychoanalytic Theory and Embedded Patterns

There is one more element needed to complete our analysis of the basic psychoanalytic model. That is the understanding that psychological traits and characteristics are *layered* and also *embedded* within a leader's overall psychology. The concept of 'layered' refers to the fact that psychological characteristics have an origin and then develop over time. They often mature with the addition of developing skills and learning experience. Political leaders, and their psychologies, therefore are *not* essentially children dressed up in adult clothes.

The concept of embedded *patterns* is a critical but often missed aspect of psychoanalytic theory. No psychological characteristic stands alone. Trait theorists subscribe to a form of binary psychology. They write as if a leader's characteristics are either there or not, causally important or not, always consistent in their operation and effects or not. As a result, trait theorists often treat specific personality elements of political leaders as if they exist apart from and unconnected to other psychological characteristics. They do not.

Consider the leadership skill of intelligence. It is a well-founded view that some level of 'intelligence', the capacity to assemble, understand, and have the good judgement to choose fitting courses of action, is a desirable characteristic for political leaders. There is even empirical research (Simonton 2006) supporting the idea that intelligence in presidents is correlated with other desirable political characteristics.

Let us leave aside the substantial measurement issues that affect such studies. Let us also assume that independent data and verification are available to confirm the lists that many make of our 'most intelligent presidents', and also those who have been seen as 'dim bulbs'. If we took as examples two presidents frequently ranked as highly intelligent, Bill Clinton and Barack Obama, what would we discover?

Our first obvious discovery would be that intelligence is a trait in the service of ambitions, ideals, and the willingness to take risks to reach one's political goals. Bill Clinton knew a great deal about policy and politics but had a great deal of difficulty coming to a conclusion and sticking with it (Renshon 2008a). Nor is intellectual capacity synonymous with good judgement. Clinton's putative intelligence did not keep him from taking up a presidency-altering dalliance with a young vulnerable White House intern.

The same mismatch between reputed intelligence and good political or policy judgement can be found in President Obama (Remnick 2010). His intelligence did not keep him from pursuing his transformative policy ambitions in the face of widespread public opposition to them and the public insistence that he concentrate instead on the economy. Indeed, a case could be made that it was exactly Obama's own confidence in his intellectual abilities and judgement that led him to disregard public sentiment and plunge full speed ahead.

In short, leadership traits and characteristics do not exist in a psychological or political vacuum. And it is psychoanalytic theory that is uniquely positioned to help make sense of their relationships.

3 Unconscious Motivation and the Analysis of Political Leadership

The role of unconscious motivation is central to Freud's theory and certainly to the therapy that bears his name. This puts those who wish to use psychoanalytic theory to study political leaders in an odd position. On one hand unconscious motivation is a key element of the theory. On the other hand, the search for unconscious motivation in the behaviour of political leaders has more than occasionally led to rampant and, as I will argue below, unnecessary speculation. The unconscious motivation of political leaders therefore occupies a paradoxical and ironic position. It obviously exists. Political leaders are not exempt from the general consequences of developmental psychological experiences. On the other hand political analysts, even if they are trained in Freud's theories, have no psychotherapeutic access to a leader's unconscious. If they are untrained it is even less legitimate to attempt uniformed speculations. What then to do?

The answer begins with uncovering the patterns of a leader's *choices*, over time and across circumstances. Each significant choice reflects a distillation of a leader's ambitions, understanding of the circumstances, risk assessment and comfort with risk, and the patterns of successful strategies that they have developed for use in similar circumstances in the past. There is nothing mysterious about the development of observable behavioural patterns in political leaders. They develop because they are consistent with the leader's skills, aspirations, and experiences. And in politics, as in other walks of life, these must reflect some assessment of circumstances' requirements for success.

Leadership style is related to personal and political identity and they too develop out of individual ideals and past successes. They too become consolidated and stable over time, even if that includes the capacity for a certain amount of situational expediency. And patterns of policy understanding and conviction also develop in political leaders over time.

It is likely that all these leadership elements are influenced to some degree by unconscious motivations. Certainly the sources, development, and meaning of ambition owe some portion of their nature to emotion-laden experiences and choices in a person's past, of which he or she may not be aware. The same might well be said of the style that a leader develops to reflect the personal and political identity he or she prefers and which has proved successful. It is also likely that a leader's policy outlook owes something to the emotionally-based assumptions or attachments that have become fused with a leader's basic worldview, identity, and style. These too are likely to have deeper emotional roots than the immediate requirements of political circumstance.

How then should one inquire about the 'deeper' sources of these leadership elements? The answer is with extreme caution. Those who use the theory should be amply conversant with it as they assemble a hopefully wide array of documentable facts with which to support their inferences and interpretations.

Political Success Among the Ruins: A Cautionary Tale

The need for extreme caution when inquiring into the possible unconscious motivation of a political leader is necessary for several obvious reasons. Among them is the fact that in real life, that kind of material becomes evident in the interplay between an analyst and his or her patient only over a long period of time, as they both grapple with the nature and causes of the patterns that have led the patient into treatment in the first place. The origin and nature of these issues are often very complex because they are intertwined with other emotional and motivational issues, and of course with other important parts of a patient's character elements or the psychological traits associated with them.

Unconscious motivation per se, in and of itself, is not necessarily detrimental to overall well-being or capacity. It depends on what those conflicts are, how central they are to the person's psychology and what other 'balancing' factors have been developed. This means that a political leader's inner emotional conflicts and maladaptations, whatever their nature and origin, often exist side by side with enormous skills and accomplishments. After all, these leaders would hardly be in a political position to merit our attention if that weren't the case.

Of course political leaders can and do make motivated mistakes, sometimes very large ones. And these often reflect patterns that can be directly traced to aspects of their psychology and the developmental experiences that helped to consolidate it. Even so, scrupulous care must be taken in such analyses to take account of motivational complexity, to develop carefully the observational basis for patterns across time while being sensitive to circumstance, and while doing so to build a solid evidentiary case.

There is probably no better example of the virtues of this kind of analysis than the Georges' book on Woodrow Wilson (1956). In that meticulously-researched analysis, the Georges detailed Wilson's prodigious ambition, intelligence, and skills that led him to become, in short order, president of Princeton University, Governor of New Jersey, and President of the United States. They are equally painstaking in detailing how, in each of those positions, for all that Wilson accomplished, he became enmeshed in a fight to the finish, which he lost, over his insistence that each and every aspect of his plans be accepted as is, without qualification.

The Georges link this pattern of Wilson's demands for absolute and complete compliance to his proposals with his difficult relationship with his father, who demanded no less of young Woodrow Wilson. There is ample evidence presented regarding the nature of that relationship and the ways in which the principal setbacks in each of the three stages of Wilson's illustrious career featured men at the head of the opposition to his plans who resembled his father in important ways. This apparently triggered in Wilson an insistence to have it done his way, or else. And in the case of the Graduate School design and location at Princeton, and the ill-fated League of Nations initiative this insistence led to the political defeat of these plans.

Yet Wilson was no psychological automaton helplessly acting out his inner compulsions. He was a smart, skilled, and accomplished person who held major intellectual and political positions before becoming president. And he accomplished much of significance in each of those positions, along with his self-generated major setbacks. As George and George note:

> While burdened with serious, at times crippling temperamental defects, Wilson was capable in many types of situations of behaving expediently in pursuit of his political objectives and of acting creatively and constructively in political life. The impressive success that Wilson was able to achieve as President of Princeton, Governor of New Jersey, and President of the United States, it emerged, were due in no small measure to the fact that he was able to adapt the driving ambition and energy engendered by personal maladjustment into an effective pattern of leadership.
>
> (George and George 1956: 318)

Wilson's success, like his failures, were related to the nature of the political time and circumstances in which he operated, an important point. For example, the Georges note that his 'hard driving, essentially autocratic leadership' seemed suitable for a period 'which favored political reforms and strong leadership'. That formula worked better for Wilson as Governor of New Jersey than it did for him as president, and in fact his expectation that he would be able to replicate his political successes with the same authoritarian style may have been part of the problem.

Is the Analysis of Unconscious Motivation in Political Leaders Necessary?

It is always possible to attribute an unconscious motivation to a political leader, but is it necessary? Consider the earlier analysis on Barack Obama's transformational ambitions and his clear choice to focus on grand policies consistent with them at the expense of a more prosaic focus on a stumbling economy and jobs. It is certainly the case that Obama willfully disregarded repeated warnings from his advisers and public opinion data that the broad American electorate did not share his ambitions, but he went ahead anyway.

Obama was certainly aware that in pursuing transformational ambitions in political circumstances that were not hospitable to them was the cause of his father's similar failure in Kenya. Indeed, Obama had said of his father that he 'had returned to his native

Kenya bursting with intellect and ambition, only to devolve into an embittered *bureaucrat because he couldn't find a way to reconcile his ideals with political realities*' (quoted in Secter and McCormick 2007, emphasis added; see also Obama 2004: 39, 344).

Based on this evidence, one could speculate that the president had an identification with his father and his failed transformation efforts and sought, unconsciously, to replicate it. That's one way to understand what Obama chose to do during his first two years in office, but a moment's thought leads to the conclusion that while that idea may be possible, it is not particularly plausible.

First, there is no evidence of this pattern when Obama served in the Illinois House of Representative and the United States Senate. That may be because the presidency was the first executive office that Obama occupied, but still the lack of some indication of this dynamic earlier in Obama's life is inconsistent with its supposed unconscious power.

Second, there is a formulation that better fits the facts as they have been developed and which has a great deal more evidence to support it. That is the hypothesis that part of Obama's transformative ambition was an effort to *redeem* his father's failed legacy. Among the evidence for this is Obama's (2004) moving narrative of his relationship and graveside reconciliation with his real father and the myth he had been fed while growing up, the many conversations he had with those close to him about the weight of his father's failed legacy on him (NPR 2004; see also Mendell 2007: 40), and Obama's view repeated over many years with different people that, 'Every man is either trying to live up to his father's expectations or making up for his mistakes' (Obama 2006: 11).

In reality, the trajectories of Obama and his father do resemble each other. They do so, however, because of some very basic psychological similarities and not because of unconscious motivation. Both men were extremely smart and accomplished and had extraordinary confidence in their own abilities. Both men strongly desired, and believed they were destined, to leave their mark on their respective countries. Both undertook transformative initiatives without building the necessary public or political support for them. In consequence, both suffered politically because they had done so.

The above analysis is an illustration of using a political psychology theory that relies on observable, not unconscious, character elements embedded in visible political circumstances. It does not rely on unconscious motivation; it does rely on accumulating patterns of available facts.

4 THE INTERNATIONALIZATION OF THE PSYCHOANALYTIC ANALYSIS OF POLITICAL LEADERSHIP: THE AUSTRALIAN DIMENSION

We live in a globalized age, and it is fortunate for the psychoanalytic study of political leaders and leadership that we do. In this age of globalization it is not surprising that scholarship, as well as people and capital, migrate. Ironically that may just be one of the modern developments that help rescue a venerable, threatened, but essential intellectual tradition.

The ease of global travel, the instantaneous transmission of papers and commentary, and the increasing ease and global range of scholarly collaborations have all widened the playing field for a variety of subjects and the psychoanalytic study of leaders is one of them. Small groups of scholars can now more easily develop their own networks both within their own countries and worldwide. The United States, which was the home of many psychoanalytic theorists of political leadership, no longer needs to be or is the sole incubator or centre of such work.

We can see this in the career and leadership theories of Australian Graham Little. His mentor, Alan F. Davies (1966, 1981), introduced him to 'political psychology', and this then led to a trip to the United States to gain more training and undertake his own psychoanalysis (Brett 2009). Once home he was sustained in his interests, throughout, by the Melbourne Psychosocial Group and the support of his own academic department, Political Science, at the University of Melbourne.

His formulations on leaders and leadership (Little 1970, 1973, 1985, 1988) are unique in taking quite seriously the relationship between the two terms. His formulation of leadership begins with his three leadership types—strong leaders, group leaders, and inspiring leaders. The first and third correspond roughly to their general meaning—decisiveness in the service of 'getting things done' is the hallmark of the first (1985: 3), while communication, 'of his own gifts and ideas', 'energy and hopefulness' is the essence of third (1985: 4). Between inspiration and accomplishment lies the group leader whose raison d'être is 'establishing or deepening solidarity' (1985: 3), presumably in societies whose common ground is fraying or otherwise in danger.

Two of these three types have long intellectual pedigrees. However, the more novel formulation and appearance of the 'group leader' may well reflect a new development in large multi-racial, multi-ethnic Western liberal democracies in which finding common ground for civic and political solutions to pressing problems is becoming increasingly difficult regardless of the inspiration or determination of political leaders.

One important contribution of Little's theory of leadership is that it shifts the focus to the psychological underpinnings of leaders' support. The basic connection is a similarity of purpose. In Little's words, 'like finds like…the leader attracts followers and is drawn to a following because their projects are the same' (1985: 10). Little's theory makes leaders and their supporters (my preferred term) partners, not exactly equal, but not wholly hierarchical either. Moreover, supporters themselves are aware of this common enterprise, both with regard to the leader and to like-minded supporters. This represents a useful advance beyond Freud's hierarchical view (1921) that followers were individually connected to the leader, but not with each other.

Although Little relies extensively on Wilfred Bion's (1961) classic work on groups, another way of understanding his formulation is that every successful leader, of whatever type, is in Kohut's (1971) terms, a *selfobject* for his or her supporters. That is, the leader's essential purpose and his or her capacity to achieve it provides a possible answer to as yet unfulfilled aspects of the supporter's psychology, hopes, or fears.

Little's innovative theoretical efforts lead us to a new and more useful understanding of the emotional compact that exists between leaders and their supporters. That compact, based on supporter's hopes and the leader's capacity to successfully engage them, is the often unseen foundation of what we are accustomed to thinking of as the normal give and take of political life—parties, issues, demographic groups, and so on. Implicit in this formation is that those more familiar themes have, in their underlying origin, a powerful emotional foundation.

5 CONCLUSION

The future of psychoanalytic theories of leaders and leadership seems destined to occupy an important but indirect role. Mastering the theories requires no less training than before, limiting the number of scholars who are likely to undertake it. Still, as the examples cited herein suggest, theoretical entrepreneurs with an interest in what lies beneath the easily observable and measureable behaviour of leaders and their supporters can gain the necessary theoretical and practical experience to develop our understanding of the patterns that shape both.

The core insights of psychoanalytic theory—the importance of experience in developing consolidated patterns of behavioural choice, and individual psychology as a reflection of dynamically interrelated elements are now firmly embedded in most political and social scientists' understanding, even if they themselves are not trained or conversant in detail with psychoanalysis' particular theories.

However, the importance of these theories does not lie solely in the acceptance of their basic premises as part of legitimate conventional wisdom. The power and importance of political leaders means that it is legitimate on the part of those who are affected by their actions to wish to understand just who, really, these people are, and not just to be satisfied with accepting who they claim to be.

What kinds of leadership are they are likely or able to provide? Can they live up to public wishes for strong, principled leadership? Do they have the skills to get things done? Do citizens and leaders share common purposes?

These important questions are difficult to answer without analysis that looks to a leader's psychological patterns, their development, and the ways in which they manifest themselves in the context of actual political leadership. Nor can these core questions be answered without closely attending to what citizens, be they supporters or opponents of a leader, hope that their country's politics and policies will reflect.

Certainly, the use of psychoanalytic theories for such analyses is no guarantee of success. On the other hand, asking such large and central questions and not making use of the variety of theories that might well provide important substantive traction on them is likely to be a recipe for failure.

Analysing political leadership without psychoanalytic theory is tantamount to deciding to build a house on quicksand. The superstructure may look good when it is finished, and its specifications may appear exacting, but its usefulness is likely to rapidly sink.

RECOMMENDED READING

Greenstein, F. I. (1969). *Personality and Politics: Problems of Conceptualization, Evidence, and Inference*. Chicago: Markham.

Renshon, S. (2008b). *The Psychological Assessment of Presidential Candidates*. New York: Routledge.

Runyan, W. Mc., ed. (1988). *Psychology and Historical Interpretation*. New York. Oxford University Press.

REFERENCES

Adler, A. (1927). *Understanding Human Nature*. New York: Greenberg; reprint edition.

Barber, J. D. (1992). *The Presidential Character: Predicting Performance in the White House*. Englewood Cliffs, NJ: Prentice Hall.

Bion, W. (1961). *Experiences in Groups*. London: Tavistock.

Bowlby, J. (1969). *Attachment and Loss Vol. I*. New York: Basic Books.

Bowlby, J. (1973). *Attachment and Loss Vol. II: Separation: Anger and Anxiety*. New York: Basic Books.

Brett, J. (2009). 'Graham Little's Theory of Political Leadership', *International Journal of Applied Psychoanalytic Studies*, 6 (2): 103–10.

Burns, J. M. (1966). *Presidential Government: The Crucible of Leadership*. Boston: Houghton Mifflin.

Calmes, J. (2011). 'Spotlight Fixed on Geithner, a Man Obama Fought to Keep', *New York Times*, 12 November.

Davies, A. F. (1966). *Private Politics: Study of Five Political Outlooks*. Melbourne: Melbourne University Press.

Davies, A. F. (1981). *Skills, Outlooks, and Passions: A Psychoanalytic Contribution to the Study of Politics*. London: Cambridge University Press.

deMause, L. (1977). 'Jimmy Carter and the American Fantasy', in L. deMause and H. Edel (eds), *Jimmy Carter and the American Fantasy*. New York: Two Continents/Psychohistory Press, 9–31.

Erikson, E. H. (1969). *Gandhi's Truth: On the Origins of Militant Nonviolence*. New York: Norton.

Erikson, E. H. (1958). *Young Man Luther*. New York: Norton.

Erikson, E. H. (1986). *Childhood and Society*. New York: Norton.

Freud, S. (1999) [1906]. 'Psycho-analysis and the Establishment of the Facts in Legal Proceedings', in J. Strachey (ed.), *The Standard Edition of the Complete Psychological works of Sigmund Freud*. London: Vintage, 97–115.

Freud, S. (1913). 'Totem and Taboo', in: J. Strachey (ed.), *The Standard Edition of the Complete Psychological Works of Sigmund Freud*. London: Vintage, 13: 1–162.

Freud, S. (1914). 'On Narcissism: An Introduction', *Standard Edition*, 14: 67–104.

Freud, S. (1915). 'Thoughts for the Times on War and Death', *Standard Edition*, 14: 273–300.

Freud, S. (1919). 'Psycho-analysis and the War Neuroses', *Standard Edition*, 17: 205–16.

Freud, S. (1921). 'Group Dynamics and the Psychology of the Ego', *Standard Edition*, 18: 65–144.

Freud, S. (1930). 'Civilization and its Discontents', *Standard Edition*, 21: 57–146.

Freud, S. (1933). 'Why war?' *Standard Edition*, 22: 195–218.

Freud, S. (1939). 'Moses and Monotheism: Three Essays', *Standard Edition*, 23: 1–138.

Freud, S. and Bullitt, W. (1966). *Thomas Woodrow Wilson: A Psychological Study*. New York: Avon.

Fromm, E. (1941). *Escape from Freedom*. New York: Farrar and Rinehart.

George, A. L. and George, J. (1956). *Woodrow Wilson and Colonel House: A Personality Study*. New York: John Day.

Greenberg, R. J. and Mitchell, S. (1983). *Object Relations in Psychoanalytic Theory*. Cambridge, MA: Harvard University Press.

Greenstein, F. I. (1969). *Personality and Politics: Problems of Conceptualization, Evidence, and Inference*. Chicago, IL: Markham.

Hartmann, H. (1975). *Ego Psychology and the Problem of Adaptation*. New York: International Universities Press.

Horney, K. (1937). *The Neurotic Personality of Our Time*. London: Kegen, Paul Trench and Co.

Horney, K. (1939). *New Ways in Psychoanalysis*. New York: Norton.

Kernberg, O. F. (1984). *Severe Personality Disorders: Psychotherapeutic Strategies*. New Haven: Yale University Press.

Klein, M. (2002). *Love, Guilt and Reparation: and Other Works 1921–1945*. New York: Free Press.

Kohut, H. (1971). *The Analysis of the Self: A Systematic Approach to the Psychoanalytic Treatment of Narcissistic Personality Disorders*. New York: International Universities Press.

Kohut, H. (1977). *The Restoration of the Self*. New York: Universities Press.

Lasswell, H. D. (1930). *Psychopathology and Politics*. Chicago: University of Chicago Press.

Lasswell, H. D. (1948). *Power and Personality*. New York: Norton.

Little, G. (1970). *The University Experience: An Australian Study*. Melbourne: Melbourne University Press.

Little, G. (1973). *Politics and Personal Style*. Melbourne: Thomas Nelson.

Little, G. (1985). *Political Ensembles: A Psychosocial Approach to Politics and Political Leadership*. Melbourne: Oxford University Press.

Little, G. (1988). *Strong Leadership: Thatcher, Reagan and an Eminent Person*. Melbourne: Oxford University Press.

Loewenberg, P. (1971a.) 'The Unsuccessful Adolescence of Heinrich Himmler', *The American Historical* Review, 76/3: 612–41.

Loewenberg, P. (1971b). 'The Psychohistorical Origins of the Nazi Youth Cohort', *The American Historical* Review, 76/3: 1457–502.

McGuire, W., ed. (1978). *The Freud–Jung Letters (translated by Ralph Manheim and R. F. C. Hull)*. Princeton, NJ: Princeton University Press.

Makari, G. (2008). *Revolution in Mind: The Creation of Psychoanalysis*. New York: Harper.

Mendell, D. (2007). *Obama: From Promise to Power*. New York: Harper Collins.

National Public Radio. (2004). 'Interview: Barack Obama Discusses his Background', National Public Radio, 27 July.

Obama, B. (2004). *Dreams from My Father*. New York: Crown.

Obama, B. (2006). *The Audacity of Hope*. New York: Three Rivers Press.

Post, J. Md., ed. (2005). *The Psychological Assessment of Political Leaders: With Profiles of Saddam Hussein and Bill Clinton*. Ann Arbor, MI: University of Michigan Press.

Prince, M. (1912). 'Roosevelt as Analyzed by the New Psychology', *The New York Times Sunday Magazine Section*, Part IV: 1.

Remnick. D. (2010). *The Bridge: The Life and Rise of Barack Obama*. New York: Knopf.

Renshon, S. (2008a). *High Hopes: The Clinton Presidency and the Politics of Ambition*. New York: Routledge.

Renshon, S. (2008b). *The Psychological Assessment of Presidential Candidates*. New York: Routledge.

Renshon, S. (2012). *Barack Obama and the Politics of Redemption*. New York: Routledge.

Renshon, S. (2014). 'The Decline of the Obama Presidency: A Political Psychology Perspective', *Journal of Comparative Government and European Policy* (Zeitschrift für Staats- und Europawissenschaften, ZSE), 2.

Runyan, W. Mc. (1984). *Life Histories and Psychobiography: Explorations in Theory and Method*. New York: Oxford.

Schultz, T. (2005). *Handbook of Psychobiography*. New York: Oxford University Press.

Secter, B. and McCormick, J. (2007). 'Portrait of a Pragmatist', *Chicago Tribune*, 30 March.

Simonton, D. K. (2006). 'Presidential IQ, Openness, Intellectual Brilliance and Leadership: Estimates and Correlations for 42 US Chief Executives', *Political Psychology*, 27/4: 511–26.

Sullivan, H. S. (1953). *The Interpersonal Theory of Psychiatry*. New York: Norton.

Volkan, V. D. and Fowler, J. C. (2009). 'Large-group Narcissism and Political Leaders with Narcissistic Personality Organization', *Psychiatric Annals*, 39/4: 214–22.

Winnicott, D. W. (1986). *Home is Where We Start From*. New York: Norton.

CHAPTER 10

SOCIAL PSYCHOLOGY

STEPHEN D. REICHER, S. ALEXANDER HASLAM,
AND MICHAEL J. PLATOW

1 INTRODUCTION

THROUGHOUT history, leaders and leadership have been viewed with both fascination and revulsion. On the one hand, as Freud wrote, leaders seem to have 'a mysterious and irresistible power' sometimes called 'prestige'. He continues: '[p]restige is a sort of domination exercised over us by an individual, a work or an idea. It entirely paralyses our critical faculty, and fills us with astonishment and respect' (1949: 21). He further notes '[p]ersonal prestige is attached to a few people, who become leaders by means of it, and it has the effect of making everything obey them as though by the operation of some magnetic magic' (1949: 22). In this period, Freud was but one of many—the great German sociologist, Max Weber, amongst them—who looked to such strong dominant leaders as heroes who would save society from a dull, mechanical lifeless future.

One should be careful about what one wishes for, however. In the middle of the last century the strong leaders came and, far from saving us, dragged us into the abyss. Fascination gave way to revulsion. Strong leaders began to be seen in terms of psychopathy rather than heroism—as individuals whose desire to dominate and subjugate others must reflect some psychological disturbance (see, for instance, Pick (2012) on allied speculations about Hitler's psyche). As so often happens, however, a dramatic shift on the surface concealed important continuities beneath.

On the one hand, even if leaders were pathologized rather than glorified, the relationship between the leader and the led was still viewed as one of domination. Indeed, one of the signs of pathology was precisely the desire to dominate over others. This leaves us with the question of whether strong and effective leadership is necessarily at odds with democracy. Is 'will' necessarily a zero-sum game such that the more a leader exerts his or her will, the less say the masses have? Or is it possible for each to facilitate the other? This question, one of profound psychological and political significance, of course, is one to which we will return once we have discussed the various social psychological approaches to the study of leadership.

Leadership, on the other hand, whether for good or for evil, continued to be conflated with the leader. That is, the ability to sway the masses—in more mundane terms, to exert influence—was seen as deriving entirely from the nature of the source. This led to a quest to isolate the (remarkable) qualities which allow some (remarkable) people to move other more ordinary people. There may be differences as to what those qualities are. There may be a difference in the value set on those qualities, but there is agreement as to where to look for these qualities. So, for a very long time the study of leadership remained restricted to the study of eminent men (and the occasional woman or two).

Indeed this is an approach that goes back millennia, to Plato and beyond, and to the idea that society should be run by that tiny minority of exceptional individuals who excel in intellectual, moral, and even physical qualities (Plato 1993). Originally such notions were illustrated by biographical and historical anecdotes. The psychometric techniques of the twentieth century allowed for more systematic investigations of the quality of leaders, and this led to an explosion in the amount of research. An influential review by Ralph Stogdill in 1948 examined 148 studies. Another review by Richard Mann in 1959 encompassed over 500 studies. Both came to a similar conclusion. There is precious little evidence that there are any qualities which mark out leaders. Overall, the highest proportion of leadership performance explained by any characteristic (that being intelligence) was 5 per cent—and recent research suggests that even this may be a generous estimate (Judge, Colbert, and Ilies 2004).

This impasse led to a relative decline in the quest for general leadership characteristics, although in recent years the field has been reinvigorated by two developments. The first is a shift away from intellectual and moral to emotional qualities. Although the issue remains fiercely contested, there is some evidence that the ability to understand, to care about, and to empathize with others—to demonstrate 'emotional intelligence'—is an important quality of leaders (Antonakis 2003; Rosete and Ciarrochi 2005). The second is a shift from measuring the qualities of leaders to measuring perceptions of leadership qualities. Thus, for instance, a leader may not need to be intelligent, but it helps to be seen as intelligent (Lord, Foti, and De Vader 1984; Rubin, Bartels, and Bommer 2002).

Even as this work revives personality approaches to leadership, however, it marks a subtle but critical shift away from them. It begins, at least implicitly, to broaden the focus of leadership research beyond the leader alone. Thus, empathy may well be a quality, but it is about the ability to form relationships with others and hence necessarily brings these others into the analysis. These others move even more to centre-stage when one deals with perceptions, for here the focus shifts from how the leader relates to his constituency to how the constituency relates to the leader. At this point, if any quality is essential to leadership, it is the ability to shape the way others see you—or, as the British comedian, Bob Monkhouse, quipped, '[T]he secret of success is sincerity. Once you can fake that, you've got it made.'

Nonetheless, despite both the empirical problems and the conceptual problems, there was still a great reluctance to give up on the search for those qualities which make for great leaders. If it proved hard to find any quality (or qualities) which make for effective leadership in any situation, the obvious fallback position was to argue that the qualities which make for effective leadership differ from situation to situation. The search then became modified and researchers began to ask what qualities are demanded in which situations. Such so-called 'contingency models' dominated the field for some three decades from the 1950s. There were many such models, the best known of which was Fielder's (1964, 1978) 'least preferred co-worker' (LPC) theory. The model is rather complex, and the exact meaning of some of its constructs is open to debate. Its essence, however, is that unambiguous situations (where everything is good or everything is bad) demand leaders who are focused on the task, whereas ambiguous situations (in which some elements are good and some bad) demand leaders who are focused on people. Again, however, evidence for this model (and indeed contingency models more generally) proved elusive. Although Fiedler himself produced data that are consistent with his model, others were less successful. A meta-analysis which included studies of over a thousand groups provided only limited support (Schriesheim, Tepper, and Tetrault 1994). Evidence from real world (as opposed to laboratory) studies was particularly weak.

In brief, contingency theory, like 'great men' theories proved to be a cul-de-sac. Only once that became apparent did it become possible to argue for a new direction of research. Only then was it possible to discard entirely the notion that leadership is the study of leaders. Only then could the focus widen so as consistently to encompass followers as well as leaders. Only then could leadership studies be understood clearly as the study of a social relationship. This was the true starting point for a social psychology of leadership.

2 THE LEADER–FOLLOWER RELATIONSHIP: TRANSACTIONAL AND TRANSFORMATIONAL MODELS

Theories of leader–follower relationships come in a wide range of varieties, but can be grouped into two broad strands. The first consists of transactional models which essentially conceptualize leadership in market terms—as an exchange in which each party provides something that is valued and needed by the other.

Some transactional approaches focus on the equity of this exchange, showing how problems arise when one side is seen to benefit far more than the other (Hollander 1985). This has strong contemporary relevance insofar as a host of studies in different domains (academia, sports, politics, industry) show that when the highest paid members of an organization get disproportionately more than the lowest paid, then a sense of *in*equity will arise which undermines the influence of those at the top and the commitment of those at the bottom (e.g. Cowherd and Levine 1992; Hollander 1995).

Other transactional approaches, notably leader–member-exchange (LMX) theory, focus on issues of quality. Thus, the more each party believes that the other is genuinely concerned with their interests—as opposed to simply being part of a contractual relationship—the more effective that leadership will be (Graen and Uhl-Bien 1995).

Yet other approaches focus upon on the different forms of power which allow leaders to satisfy the needs of their followers (Kerr and Jermier 1978; Bailey 1980) and the conditions under which leaders are able to use some forms of power (for example, the ability to provide rewards) as opposed to others (for example, providing respect). The key premise is that the more a leader is able to amass resources and to deploy them appropriately, the more effective he or she will be.

At root, though, the strength of these approaches is also their weakness. An analysis of leadership in terms of a set of cost–benefit analyses by the various parties involved clearly chimes with a much more general attempt across the human sciences to explain behaviour in terms of economic rationality. As with all such approaches, however, the problem lies in the ability to define a priori what constitutes a cost and what constitutes a reward, especially as the different parties may have very different perceptions of these things. Without being able to define these terms, any explanation is in danger of becoming tautological.

This problem becomes all the more acute if one acknowledges that the things that people value or else fear (and hence what constitutes a benefit or else a cost) may not be static but actually evolve through the interaction between leader and follower. This takes us back to an argument we have encountered before: leadership is not simply about providing what people already want and desire. It is about creating new needs and desires and hence creating new motivations. Leadership is not locked into the status quo, it is fundamentally about change. To ignore this, is to explain the phenomenon at the cost of paring it down to something barely worth studying.

One of the originators of transactional theory, Ervin Hollander, was well aware of this issue and sought to address it. Hollander (1958) suggested a temporal process whereby leaders need to start off by doing what their followers already want. In so doing they build up a stock of 'idiosyncrasy credit' which then allows them to innovate. Change is possible, but only through conservatism. Over time, however, innovation has been rather overlooked by transactional theories. This explains the rise of a second strand of leader–follower analysis: transformational theory.

In his original outline of the transformational approach, Burns (1978) mounts a sharp critique of the contractual approach. Along the lines outlined above, he argues that leadership is about much more than satisfying wants and needs in exchange for support. Indeed it is not only about changing wants and needs. Using hierarchical concepts derived from theorists such as Kohlberg (1963) and Maslow (1963), Burns sees leadership in terms of encouraging a progression from lower-level needs (for example, fulfilling bodily urges) to higher-level needs (for example, for self-actualization and sociality).

More fundamentally, though, Burns notes that the very notion of a contract sets leaders apart from followers and sees them as bound together through constraint. People follow a leader because they have accepted an obligation to do so whether they like it or not. Yet, he argues, an effective relationship depends upon people following because they actively *want* to and because they believe in what they are doing.

So how do leaders transform the desires of their followers? Transformational theory has little to say about this and focuses more on the 'who' than on the 'how.' What is more, when it comes to identifying leaders, the assumption is that certain people have the gift and others do not and that, using the right measurement technique (specifically, Bass and Avolio's 1997 *Multifactor Leadership Questionnaire*, or MLQ), it will be possible to pick out those with the capacities (for example, charisma, inspiration, intellect, and consideration for others) to transform anybody and everybody.

This, however, sounds dangerously like a reintroduction of 'great man' theories through the back door and it brings us back to an old impasse. That is, how can we accord some autonomy to the leader in terms of being able to shape the ideas and visions of followers without suggesting that leaders are able to mould followers at will? How can we theorize the active nature of leadership without rendering followers entirely passive? The problem is, that as long as we limit our analysis to the leader–follower relationship, then necessarily the two parties are set against each other in a zero-sum game. There is nothing else to regulate or constrain leaders but followers. There is no possibility of the two coming together to facilitate each other in advancing a common cause. It is time to broaden the focus once more.

3 Leaders and Followers in Social Groups: Social Identity Models

Leaders are never just leaders. To describe them as such is always a shorthand, an abstraction from the particular context in which they lead. Leaders are always the leaders of a particular social group: a nation, of a political party, of a religion or sect or organization. Correspondingly, the relationship between leaders and followers is always a relationship within a particular social group. It is a 'we' relationship. Leaders gain influence precisely to the extent that they are not speaking for themselves or telling followers what to do, but rather speaking for the group and clarifying what forms of action best accord with shared collective understandings and interests.

These insights are at the core of social identity models of leadership which, in recent years, have reignited interest in the topic within social psychology (Hogg 2001; Reicher and Hopkins 2001; Haslam, Reicher, and Platow 2011). These models develop one of the core premises of the social identity approach and, more specifically, of self-categorization theory (SCT) (Turner et al. 1987). Rather than regarding the group as coming together through an aggregation of inter-personal relationships, SCT asserts that the psychological underpinning of collectivity lies in acts of self-definition. It is when a set of people come to see themselves as members of the same social category ('we are all Americans', 'Catholics', 'socialists', or whatever) that they begin to act together as group members. This happens through a process of *self*-stereotyping. Upon identifying with a particular group, people seek to elucidate the position of the group and to conform to it. This means that anyone who is in a position to provide information about the group position will be able to exert influence over his or her fellow group members. This will be true in particular of those who are seen to exemplify what makes the group special and distinctive from other groups—in the jargon of SCT, *prototypical* group members who are then in a privileged position to exert leadership.

Over the years, there has been a substantial amount of research to support this premise. Prototypical group members exert more influence. They inspire group members to invest more thought and more effort in advancing their projects. They are seen as more charismatic (see Haslam and Reicher 2012; Hogg 2001; Platow, Mills, and Morrison 2000).

What is more, there are no set qualities which lead people to be seen as prototypical and as having leadership potential. The qualities which are associated with what makes 'us' special will be different for different groups and for the same group in different contexts. For instance, when confronted by an unintelligent outgroup we may well favour intelligence in our own group and its leaders. However, when confronted with a highly intelligent antagonist, we may prefer a leader with warmth and dedication over one with intellect (Reicher, Haslam, and Platow 2007).

These findings are highly relevant and may help explain why Bush beat Gore in 2000 despite the fact that most Americans thought Gore to be the more intelligent and that even a good proportion of Bush supporters (28 per cent) accepted this to be the case. The fact was that far less of the Bush constituency valued intelligence in a president compared to those supporting Gore. They valued the fact that he was (or at least, that he presented himself as) a regular guy—an image he carefully nurtured through his cowboy hats, his leather jackets, and perhaps even his 'mis-speaking'. Those who condemned him could then be dismissed as sneering intellectuals at odds with ordinary Americans. As Weisberg (2004) put it: 'elitist condescension, however merited, helps cement Bush's bond to the masses'. In this group context, then, stupidity not only trumped intelligence, but intelligence—insofar as it distanced people from the group prototype—was a positive impediment to influence and leadership.

The social identity approach to leadership is not limited to an analysis of prototypicality, however (see Haslam, Reicher, and Platow 2011). First of all, as the above examples suggest, leaders do not simply wait around until they happen to be seen as prototypical of the group. Rather, they actively define the nature of the context, the character of the group and their own selves in order to render themselves representative of ingroup identity. Leaders, that is, are 'entrepreneurs of identity' (Reicher and Hopkins 2001). Bush was, of course, the privileged son of an East Coast dynasty, and his populist all-American image was a skillful portrait devised by the President and his advisers. Without seeking to draw broader parallels, just as Goebbels admitted to creating a wholly fabricated picture of Hitler's personality as symbolizing 'the indestructible life-force of the German nation' (Kershaw 1987: 72) and also claimed that the 'Hitler myth' was his greatest propaganda creation, so it might be argued that the Bush myth was the greatest contribution of Karl Rove, the President's long-term adviser and sometimes dubbed 'Bush's brain' (Moore and Slater 2004). It is important, though, to note that while the self of the leader need not be a fabrication, nonetheless it is always a construction in the sense of being a selection amongst many possible elements designed to link the leader to the group. Augoustinos and de Garis (2012), for instance, analyse the way in which Obama used the very complexity of his background to position himself as someone who embodied the very diversity of American society—and hence with the ability to overcome the destructive divisions of previous years.

This takes us to a second extension: leaders do not simply have to promote themselves as prototypical of the group, but also need to promote their policies and practices as the practical realization of the group interest. In slightly different terms, leaders must be seen to be acting in furtherance of shared norms and values. To continue with the Bush example, his all-American performances are designed to persuade his electorate that he understands and will act on the priorities of ordinary Americans.

Putting these various elements together, it follows that skilled leadership involves creating a consonance between self, policy, and nation. This is exemplified in the campaigns of Franklin Roosevelt, regularly designated as the most charismatic of all US Presidents (Simonton 1988). In 1921 Roosevelt was diagnosed with polio or 'infantile paralysis'. This was seen as the end of his political ambitions at a time when masculine potency was seen as a necessary attribute of political leadership. During the election campaign of 1932 he was strongly advised not to display his physical afflictions to the nation and certainly not to undertake a 'whistlestop' train tour across the country. Yet the tour proved remarkably successful (Rosenman 1952). The image of Roosevelt painfully struggling from train to rostrum in order to deliver his speeches chimed with his narrative of a nation struggling to overcome paralysis—most famously expressed in his 4 March 1933 inaugural address: 'This nation will endure as it has endured, will revive and will prosper. So first of all, let me assert my firm belief that the only thing we have to fear is fear itself—nameless, unreasoning, unjustified terror which paralyzes needed efforts to convert retreat into advance' (cited in Haslam, Reicher, and Platow 2011: 150). What is more, in eliding his personal narrative and political programme with the national narrative, Roosevelt was seen to connect with the experiences and needs of ordinary Americans—even if their hardships were of a very different sort to the President's. Famously, after he died, a reporter asked one mourner if he had come because he knew Roosevelt. ' "No" the mourner is said to have replied, "but he knew me" ' (cited in Haslam and Reicher 2012: 43). In sum, Roosevelt's skilled entrepreneurship of identity allowed him to turn a seemingly fatal impediment into the pivot around which he could articulate his relationship with fellow Americans within the nation, and hence proved to be the source of his success. It was as someone who could endure, revive and overcome paralysis that he was able to speak for America.

There is one further and final element to the social identity analysis. In the longer term it is not sufficient for leaders to represent themselves as prototypical of the group or indeed to represent their policies as the instantiation of group values. In the longer term it is necessary for leaders to succeed in transforming the world in the image of group identity. This clearly involves a number of institutional and organizational factors that are beyond the scope of a social psychological analysis. It also involves no small measure of luck. Harold Macmillan, the Conservative British Prime Minister, allegedly once remarked to a journalist that the greatest source of political failure was 'events, dear boy, events'—but he might equally have said the same of the sources of political success. Nonetheless, the ability to control events, as opposed to being controlled by them, is increased to the extent that one has the power of a mobilized population on one's side. Social identity models describe the process of mobilization, the creation of this social power whereby leaders can act through their followers to shape the world (see Turner 2005), but it remains to direct that energy in the most effective way to achieve results. Social identity processes, then, are a necessary but certainly not a sufficient account of successful leadership. It is important to acknowledge the limits of any disciplinary approach to the study of this phenomenon.

4 CONCLUSION: LEADERS, IDENTITIES, AND DEMOCRACY

To conclude, let us now reconsider a question which has formed a constant thread through this review. Is it possible to have strong and effective leadership without rendering followers weak and passive? In other words, is democratic leadership possible? We suggested that the answer to this question depends upon the breadth of one's analytic focus. In particular, we argued that it can only be resolved by viewing leadership as not just about leaders, not just about leaders and followers, but about leaders and followers in situated social groups.

From the social identity perspective, then, leadership is a process of social identity management oriented to the creation of a powerful relationship between person, policy, and group. In this relationship, authority derives from the ability to define group identity and the relationship of phenomena to that identity. In this regard, the leader does not have completely free rein. The meaning of any given identity may always be open to debate and to situated interpretation—that is, 'what does it actually mean to be "us" in this specific context' (Reicher and Hopkins 2001). At the same time, the interpretative process is constrained by what people have learned about their identities in school books, how it is tied to certain cultural and historical phenomena, and how these points of reference have become part of the material environment (for example, in the form of statues, monuments, street names).

The critical issue, however, is not simply about how the interpretation of identity is constrained by the weight of past histories, but how leaders and followers work together in actively elaborating identity in order to shape social action and hence social reality. Who gets to interpret group identity? This could be said to be the core question not only of political leadership but, indeed, of political life. It is particularly evident where there is a canonical text which is accepted by all as foundational for the group—a holy book, a constitution, and so on. Indeed, religious wars have been fought over who should have access to the Bible, many have been killed for interpreting the holy book into the vernacular and hence giving ordinary people a say in its interpretation, riots have erupted over the slightest change in the balance between clergy and congregation in making sense of the text (McGrath 2002; MacCulloch 2010).

The different ways in which leaders relate to followers in the interpretation of identity underpin different forms of politics. Schematically, we can apply a threefold typology. Democratic leadership involves the leader guiding followers in a conversation about who we are, what we value, and where our priorities lie. It may involve drawing on accepted cultural and historical figures, but, equally, it involves questioning which figures should be chosen and how their significance should be interpreted.

Hierarchical leadership involves the attempt to impose a monologue whereby leaders claim special knowledge over group identity (often by virtue of their prototypical status), and in which they take certain historical and cultural references for granted and essentialize their meanings, and whereby they seek to obscure or else delegitimize any alternative interpretations of identity (see Reicher and Hopkins 2001, for an account of such techniques).

Finally, autocratic leadership involves eliding the leader with the group such that he or she becomes the living incarnation of the group identity. At this point, what the leader says is, by its very nature, what group members should do and to stand against the leader is to stand outside of and against the group. This, most often, then legitimizes severe repression. Here we return to the characterization of Hitler as 'the purest embodiment of the German character, the purest embodiment of a National Socialist Germany' (cited in Kershaw 1987: 30), or else, in the climactic words with which Hess concluded the 1934 Nuremburg Rally: 'The Party is Hitler. But Hitler is Germany, just as Germany is Hitler. Hitler! Sieg Heil!' (Kershaw 1987: 69). Woe betide anyone who criticized Hitler, then, for they became 'community aliens' with all the terrible consequences that flowed from that (Peukert 1987).

As a final word, then, social psychological analyses show that leadership *can* be democratic. Leaders can involve people in determining the bases for joint action. They can facilitate rather than substitute for the agency of their followers. Indeed, it is only as group members acting together, particularly when coordinated and directed by skillful leadership, that most ordinary people are in a position to shape their own world rather than live in a world shaped by others (Haslam and Reicher 2007). Equally, however, leadership is not inherently democratic. Leaders can exclude people from determining the bases of joint action. They can marginalize or even crush their followers. So when will leadership facilitate and when will it destroy democracy? The answer to this question depends upon understanding the social identity processes through which leaders claim and assert authority. By the same token, such an understanding can give us greater choice and control over our political fate.

RECOMMENDED READING

Haslam, S. A., Reicher, S. D., and Platow, M. J. (2011). *The New Psychology of Leadership: Identity, Influence and Power*. London and New York: Psychology Press.

Hogg, M. A. (2001). 'A social identity theory of leadership', *Personality and Social Psychology Review*, 5: 184–200.

Hollander, E. P. (1985). 'Leadership and power', in G. Lindzey and E. Aronson (eds), *The Handbook of Social Psychology*, 3rd edn. New York: Random House, 485–537.

REFERENCES

Antonakis, J. (2003). 'Why "Emotional Intelligence" Does Not Predict Leadership Effectiveness', *International Journal of Organizational Analysis*, 11: 353–9.

Augoustinos, M. and De Garis, S. (2012). '"Too Black or Not Black Enough": Social Identity Complexity in the Political Rhetoric of Barack Obama', *European Journal of Social Psychology*, 42: 564–77.

Bailey, F. G. (1980). *Stratagems and Spoils: A Social Anthropology of Politics*. Oxford: Blackwell.

Bass, B. M. and Avolio, B. J. (1997). *Full Range Leadership Development: Manual for the Multifactor Leadership Questionnaire*. Redwood City, CA: Mind Garden.

Burns, J. M. (1978). *Leadership*. New York: Harper and Row.

Cowherd, D. M. and Levine, D. I. (1992). 'Product Quality and Pay Equity between Lower-level Employees and Top Management: An Investigation of Distributive Justice Theory', *Administrative Science Quarterly*, 37: 302–20.

Fiedler, F. E. (1964). 'A Contingency Model of Leader Effectiveness', in L. Berkowitz (ed.), *Advances in Experimental Social Psychology*, Vol. 1. New York: Academic Press, 149–90.

Fiedler, F. E. (1978). 'The Contingency Model and the Dynamics of the Leadership Process', in L. Berkowitz (ed.), *Advances in Experimental Social Psychology*, Vol. 11. Academic Press: New York, 59–112.

Freud, S. (1949) [1922]. *Group Psychology and the Analysis of the Ego*. London: International Psychoanalytic Library.

Graen, G. B. and Uhl-Bien, M. (1995). 'Relationship-based Approach to Leadership: Development of Leader-member Exchange (LMX) Theory of Leadership over 25 Years. Applying a Multi-Level Multi-domain Perspective', *Leadership Quarterly*, 6: 219–47.

Haslam, S. A. and Reicher, S. D. (2007). 'Social Identity and the Dynamics of Organizational Life: Insights from the BBC Prison Study', in C. Bartel, S. Blader and A. Wrzesniewski (eds), *Identity and the Modern Organization*. New York: Erlbaum, 135–66.

Haslam, S. A. and Reicher, S. D. (2012). 'In Search of Charisma', *Scientific American Mind*, 22 (4): 42–9.

Haslam, S. A., Reicher, S. D., and Platow, M. J. (2011). *The New Psychology of Leadership: Identity, Influence and Power*. London and New York: Psychology Press.

Hogg, M. A. (2001). 'A Social Identity Theory of Leadership', *Personality and Social Psychology Review*, 5 (3): 184–200.

Hollander, E. P. (1958). 'Conformity, Status and Idiosyncrasy Credit', *Psychological Review*, 65 (2): 117–27.

Hollander, E. P. (1985). 'Leadership and Power', in G. Lindzey and E. Aronson (eds), *The Handbook of Social Psychology*, 3rd edn. New York: Random House, 485–537.

Hollander, E. P. (1995). 'Organizational Leadership and Followership', in P. Collett and A. Furnham (eds), *Social Psychology at Work: Essays in Honour of Michael Argyle*. London: Routledge, 69–87.

Judge, T. A., Colbert, A. E., and Ilies, R. (2004). 'Intelligence and Leadership: A Quantitative Review and Test of Theoretical Propositions', *Journal of Applied Psychology*, 89 (3): 542–52.

Kerr, S. and Jermier, J. M. (1978). 'Substitutes for Leadership: Their Meaning and Measurement', *Organizational Behaviour and Human Performance*, 22 (3): 375–403.

Kershaw, I. (1987). *The Hitler Myth*. Oxford: Clarendon Press.

Kohlberg, L. (1963). 'Moral Development and Identification', in H. W. Stevenson (ed.), *Child Psychology*. Chicago: University of Chicago Press, 277–332.

Lord, R. G., Foti, R. J., and De Vader, C. L. (1984). 'A Test of Leadership Categorization Theory: Internal Structure, Information Processing, and Leadership Perceptions', *Organizational Behavior and Human Performance*, 34: 343–78.

MacCulloch, D. (2010). *A History of Christianity*. London: Penguin.

McGrath, A. (2002). *In the Beginning: The Story of the King James Bible*. London: Hodder and Stoughton.

Mann, R. D. (1959). 'A Review of the Relationship between Personality and Performance in Small Groups', *Psychological Bulletin*, 56: 241–70.

Maslow, A. H. (1963). 'A Theory of Motivation', *Psychological Review*, 50 (4): 370–96.

Moore, J. and Slater, W. (2004). *Bush's Brain: How Karl Rove Made George W. Bush Presidential*. New York: John Wiley and Sons.

Peukert, D. (1987). *Inside Nazi Germany: Conformity, Opposition and Racism in Everyday Life*. London: Batsford.

Pick, D. (2012). *The Pursuit of the Nazi Mind: Hitler, Hess and the Analysts*. Oxford: Oxford University Press.

Plato (1993). *The Republic*. Oxford: Oxford University Press.

Platow, M. J., Mills, D., and Morrison, D. (2000). 'The Effects of Social Context, Source Fairness, and Perceived Self-source Similarity on Social Influence: A Self-categorisation Analysis', *European Journal of Social Psychology*, 30: 69–81.

Reicher, S. D. (2011). 'Mass Action and Mundane Reality: An Argument for Putting Crowd Analysis at the Centre of the Social Sciences', *Contemporary Social Science*, 6: 433–50.

Reicher, S. D. and Hopkins, N. (2001). *Self and Nation: Categorization, Contestation and Mobilisation*. London: SAGE.

Reicher, S. D., Haslam, S. A., and Platow, M. J. (2007). 'The New Psychology of Leadership', *Scientific American Mind*, 17 (3): 22–9.

Rosenman, S. (1952). *Working with Roosevelt*. New York: Harper and Brothers.

Rosete, D. and Ciarrochi, J. (2005). 'EI and its Relationship to Workplace Performance Outcomes of Leadership Effectiveness', *Leadership Organizational Development*, 26 (5): 388–99.

Rubin, R. S., Bartels, L. K., and Bommer, W. H. (2002). 'Are Leaders Smarter or do They Just Seem that Way? Exploring Perceived Intellectual Competence and Leadership Emergence', *Social Behavior and Personality*, 30 (2): 105–18.

Schriesheim, C. A., Tepper, B. J., and Tetrault, L. A. (1994). 'Least Preferred Co-worker Score, Situational Control, and Leadership Effectiveness: A Meta-analysis of Contingency Model Performance Predictions', *Journal of Applied Psychology*, 79: 561–73.

Simonton, D. K. (1988). 'Presidential Style: Personality, Biography and Performance', *Journal of Personality and Social Psychology*, 55 (6): 928–36.

Stogdill, R. M. (1948). 'Personality Factors Associated with Leadership: A Survey of the Literature', *Journal of Psychology*, 25 (1): 35–71.

Turner, J. C. (2005). 'Examining the Nature of Power: A Three-process Theory', *European Journal of Social Psychology*, 35 (1): 1–22.

Turner, J. C., Hogg, M. A., Oakes, P. J., Reicher, S. D. and Wetherell, M. S. (1987). *Rediscovering the Social Group: A Self-Categorization Theory*. Oxford: Blackwell.

Weisburg, J. (2004). *The Misunderestimated Man*. Available at <www.slate.com/id/2100064/>.

CHAPTER 11

RATIONAL CHOICE APPROACHES TO LEADERSHIP*

GEOFFREY BRENNAN AND MICHAEL BROOKS

1 THE DOG THAT DOES NOT BARK?

In Dennis Mueller's encyclopedic survey (2003) of the field of 'public choice' (or more generally rational choice theory of politics[1]) (RCT in what follows) there is no chapter on leadership and no such category mentioned in the index. There is a section of one chapter dealing with the relations between President and Congress, a brief mention of 'political entrepreneurship', and a chapter on 'dictatorship' largely following Wintrobe (2000).[2] Writers in the tradition of 'rational choice institutionalism' (see Shepsle 2006) suggest that leadership may be an important theme in that tradition (see, specifically, Fiorina and Shepsle 1989); but the associated literature is small. Taking a bird's-eye view of rational choice literature, 'leadership' is, if not a dog that does not bark, at least one that does not bark very loudly![3]

In some ways, the silence is surprising. A primary focus of RCT is democratic electoral competition; and casual observation suggests that features of rival *leaders* are significant elements in electoral races. It might be observed that RCT sets itself

---

* We are grateful to the editors for detailed and incisive comments on earlier drafts of this chapter.

[1] The 'rational-choice theory' (RCT) enterprise goes by a number of names and the various titles have their own nuances. For a discussion of some of the nuances and commonalities, see Mitchell (1988) and Diermeier and Krehbiel (2003).

[2] Arguably, the analysis of dictatorship, emphasizing the role of loyalty and repression, does involve leadership issues. Our interest here, however, is with leadership in democratic systems and with political institutions that meet some broad contractarian test.

[3] Public choice does not stand alone in its failure to address the leadership feature of economic landscape. In mainstream economics, leadership is hardly a major analytic category either—though see Hermalin (2013) for a survey of the small set of technical papers in the field.

to explain the *systematic* features of political processes—and so the idiosyncracies of particular leaders (though no doubt of considerable 'human interest') do not fit this bill.[4] In explaining the 'actions' of governments (policy outcomes in the broadest sense), 'biographical politics' and RCT stand as rival approaches.

Nevertheless, virtually all democratic systems exhibit a 'representative' structure, with political parties, majority coalitions, and government 'leaders', and this structural feature does demand some explanation and justification. These institutional features *are* systematic and structural, so they would seem to fall naturally within the RCT explanatory domain.

There is a further notable feature of the RCT approach to leadership. Within the RCT tradition, and in contrast to most other traditions in political theory, 'leadership' is an (often implicitly) negative category. In Section 2, we seek to explain and expose this negative attitude.

The explanation/justification of leadership involves two questions: one is the issue of delegation (that is, why democracy is representative rather than direct); the other is the issue of hierarchy (that is, why representative institutions are organized with 'leaders' at the top). In what follows, we shall investigate what the RCT tradition has to say on both these aspects of leadership–delegation in Section 3; and hierarchy in Section 4.

Much of RCT literature on leadership involves reference to the 'principal/agent' problem and the incentives that systems of delegation imply. In Section 5 we explore 'selection' as another dimension of the 'agency' issue. In Section 6, we offer an alternative view of leadership based on 'expressive voting' (the account of voting that we regard as the uniquely best account of voting within RCT logic). Section 7 offers a brief conclusion.

2 LEADERSHIP AND THE BENEVOLENT DESPOT

Public choice theory—that variant of RCT associated with Nobel Laureate James Buchanan and his disciples—began life as an attack on what Buchanan (following Wicksell 1896) termed the 'benevolent-despot' model of government. In standard public economics, the object of analysis was to determine among a set of policy options that which is best, given certain normative criteria. The public-choice critique of this approach involved two elements. The first involved insisting that policies should be treated, not as directly *chosen*, but rather as emerging from political processes. So the working properties of those political processes must be a core piece of proper analysis. The second strand involved a rejection of differences in the motivational assumptions used to characterize policy-*makers* and policy-*takers*: individuals should not

---

[4] One significant result in RCT is the median voter theorem—and the thrust of that theorem is that candidates are forced by the process of electoral competition to adopt more or less identical policy positions. Hence, in explaining policy positions, any distinctive characteristics of parties and their leaders become essentially epiphenomenal.

be assumed to behave differently in their political and market roles. In particular, if policy-makers *were* 'despots', in the sense that they could make unilateral decisions about policy unencumbered by electoral (and other 'political') constraints, then methodological principles of consistency required that such 'despots' should be modelled in self-interest terms (exactly as their market counterparts are modelled).

Put another way, RCT regards the appropriate framework for treating 'leadership' as involving a broad principal/agent approach, in which it is assumed that 'political power will be abused to promote the particular purposes of the holder', as J. S. Mill (1861: 505) put it, or as Hume remarked, 'every man ought to be supposed a knave and have no other end in all his actions than private interest' (Hume 1985: 117). Simply put, 'leadership' implies some discretion on the part of political agents. Given the methodological strictures on which the public-choice approach insists, such discretion is a presumptively bad thing!

This negative presumption colours much of the public choice literature on leadership, sometimes more so than is evident. So consider, for example, the various points in the RCT corpus outlined below where 'leadership' enters.

Non-Dictatorship

When Arrow (1951) develops his well-known 'impossibility' theorem, he stipulates several apparently simple and compelling desiderata that any 'aggregation' process of individual preferences should meet. Non-dictatorship is one of those desiderata. Other desiderata, under various descriptions, include: completeness; transitivity; Pareto postulate; independence of irrelevant alternatives. Arrow's theorem shows that not all of these desiderata can be satisfied simultaneously, but that a subset of any four can be (that aspect of his theorem is the 'possibility' dimension). The conclusion is that (at least) one of the desiderata (possibly non-dictatorship) has to be jettisoned: this is what gives the theorem its tragic bite.

Agenda-Setting

A related RCT result is that, when the policy space has two or more dimensions, there is in general no political outcome that cannot be defeated under majority rule (or indeed under any decision rule short of unanimity). McKelvey's classic 1976 formulation begins by showing that, for any two points in policy space, there will be a finite sequence of majority approved moves that can take the polity from one to the other (so *no* policy outcome under majority rule can be entirely ruled out); and hence that a strategic agenda-setter can secure any outcome she wants by putting the items on the agenda in an appropriate order.

Of course, the particular sequence of issues on the agenda required for manipulation will be influenced by voters' preferences. In that sense the citizenry's preferences represent a structural constraint on the agenda-setter's behaviour. This structural constraint is, however, a shadow tiger, because the agenda-setter/ruler is able to achieve any outcome she desires.

This is bad news—both for democracy's credentials as a means of directing political power to citizens' ends; and for analytical political science, because where there is no political equilibrium, there can be no robust predictions as to how changes in underlying parameters will affect political outcomes.[5]

Principal-Agent Models

As Fiorina and Shepsle (1989) rightly emphasize, leadership is typically modelled in RCT circles as a principal-agent problem. The 'problem' at issue here is how the 'principal' (in this case the citizens) can constrain the agent (political 'leaders') to act as far as possible in the principal's interests. In economic applications, such constraint is secured by a contract that embodies the relevant set of incentives. In the political case, constraint is usually secured by some institutional arrangement—but again the focus is on structuring incentives so as to bring agents' interests into line with those of principals. As Hamilton put it, 'the best security for the fidelity of mankind is to make their interest coincide with their duty' (Hamilton 2012: 210). Strictly speaking, principal-agent theory purports to *explain* the type of contract that principals will rationally seek to impose: the 'problem' of agent discretion is a problem *for the principal*, not necessarily a 'problem' in any wider normative sense.

Note that the principal-agent formulation *presupposes* agency. It is just taken as given that agents can do things that principals cannot do for themselves.

Political Entrepreneurship

The notion of political entrepreneurship entered the public choice literature at the hands of Richard Wagner (1966) in a review of Mancur Olson's (1965) *The Logic of Collective Action*. Olson's 'logic' emphasizes the role that apparently 'incidental' private interest must play in any provision of public goods: public goods for a group are more likely to be provided if they come with incidental 'selective' private benefits available for contributors. Wagner conceives of the political entrepreneur as the broker—the one who conceives and delivers the peculiar package of selective private (and general public) benefits. Wagner emphasizes (in the Olsonian spirit) that such entrepreneurs are more likely to be forthcoming if they themselves will receive 'selective benefits'—either electoral advantage or rents from office.

---

[5] Many empirical applications of RCT seem simply to ignore this fact and employ the one-dimensional median voter model, even when there appear to be multi-dimensions in policy space.

Political entrepreneurship tends to interpret 'leadership' in a somewhat more favourable light than elsewhere in the RCT corpus.[6] Certainly, entrepreneurship in its market setting receives quite a favourable gloss, but that is because there is a presumption that market discipline will channel agent discretion into desirable activities. In the political setting, whether an analogous presumption is in place is precisely what is at issue.

Political entrepreneurs will broker deals involving provision of public goods to the extent that activity is profitable to them. Entrepreneurial behaviour will track the incentives prevailing under the existing arrangements. Unless those incentives favour the provision of public goods specifically, then political entrepreneurship in itself offers no solution to public goods problems. The chief implication of political entrepreneurship for leadership, then, is, as Shepsle remarks, that 'it invites us to scrutinize some of the less obvious motives of those who assume the mantle of leadership' (Shepsle 2006: 31).

The general point we seek to underline in this section is that, wherever themes in RCT intersect with issues of 'leadership', there is a negative connotation. In that sense, on the few occasions in RCT where 'leadership' 'barks', it remains pretty clearly a 'mongrel'!

3   WHY AGENCY? THE LOGIC(S) OF DELEGATION

Standard principal-agent literature presumes that there is a *reason* for agency: that the agent has some skill, knowledge, or locational advantage that the principal does not.[7] Within the marketplace, such a division of labour will be a routine feature of economic organization. In the case of political delegation, however, the grounds for specialization are not so self-evident. Defenders of direct democracy, for example, have long insisted that 'representative' institutions involve a level of agency lacking a clear explanation/justification. Any capacity to exploit the citizenry that political agents possess is a self-inflicted wound on the part of the citizenry: direct democracy allows the citizens to avoid the agency problem. Under direct democracy, there will remain a need to contract out the provision of public services: principal-agent problems will arise between the decision-making and 'bureaucratic'/executive functions of government. The decision-making itself, however, does not necessarily require representative assemblies; or 'leaders' within them. Any such delegation needs to be argued for.

We canvass five possibilities in this regard: a 'transactions cost' possibility; a vulnerability possibility; an epistemic possibility; a 'strategic' possibility; and a 'leadership habit' argument. We examine these in turn.

---

[6] See Buchanan and Vanberg (1989) for a rare paper, at least in public choice, that sees leadership in a positive light.

[7] See Jensen and Meckling (1995) for an account of why business organizations should be designed so that specific knowledge and decision-making power go hand in hand.

Transactions Costs Possibility

The transactions cost line begins with the claim that collective decision-making is a matter of perpetual problem-solving. New situations are constantly arising that require collective decisions, and organizing plebiscites at short notice is too costly. Governments must act and often act quickly; and, so the claim goes, they must therefore be assigned the power to do so.[8]

Perhaps there is something to this argument in modern democracies, though both the demand-side and the supply-side elements are questionable. To be sure, natural disasters occur and various social conflicts arise; quick decisions are occasionally required. In such settings, however, the decisions are not typically taken by representative assemblies: they are delegated to agents closer to the locus of action—to the executive branch, or within it to 'fire chiefs' or 'emergency teams' or generals. Such cases seem the exception rather than the rule. Lots of collective decisions can be, and are, taken over an extended period, allowing sufficient time for plebiscites to be mounted.[9] Modern technology is such that collective decisions can be made very quickly and quite cheaply—as coordination of the 'Arab Spring' demonstrations suggests. The least we can say is that, aside from emergency situations, the 'transactions cost' argument alone does not seem persuasive in explaining representative institutions.

Vulnerability Possibility

A second argument takes off from the principal-agent problem between legislature and executive with an eye to the specific case of the military. The idea is that political power is always vulnerable to military takeover; and that an institutionalized representative body serves to keep the military in its place in a manner that the citizenry directly cannot do effectively. Call this the 'vulnerability' argument (VA). We think this argument carries some weight. It is, after all, one of the non-negligible accomplishments of most Western democracies that the political influence of the military is minimal.[10] However, the argument is vague on the source of the comparative advantage that smaller political bodies are supposed to have in exercising oversight.[11] There is an obvious question, moreover, as to why, if VA constitutes the primary rationale for representative government, the 'representative' bodies are elected rather than appointed by lot. We note these questions but do not attempt here to answer them.

---

[8]   It is, for example, not surprising that Leeson (2009) finds that sixteenth- and seventeenth-century pirate-ship captains, a position that was routinely elected by the entire crew, held absolute decision power—though only when engaged with the 'enemy'.

[9]   To continue the pirate example, Leeson reports that, except in conflict situations, the crew on pirate ships took unanimous decisions on a range of issues and the captain as leader had no privileged position in their resolution.

[10]   See Finer (1962) for an account of the role of the military in the democratic state.

[11]   An interesting incidental question in the present setting is why military institutions themselves are so rigidly hierarchical.

Epistemic Possibility

The third argument for representation revolves around the idea of a division of labour in politics. One version of the argument of the division of labour argument is that there is some kind of talent in the business of exercising political power over others: some people are, so the argument goes, just 'better rulers'. This version has a dubious history, since it has long been used as a justification for the retention of political power by the aristocratic classes.[12] An alternative version focuses on epistemic considerations.[13] The cost of every voter acquiring all the information necessary to deal with the complicated issues of public policy would be exorbitant. In that sense, it is, we think, self-evident that a representative assembly will be more efficient in dealing with relevant policy information than the entire citizenry. It was one of the central claims in Downs's seminal work (1957) in RCT that voters will be predictably under-informed about policy issues: the point we would underline is that, within a representative system, it is not just rational but also *efficient* that voters be so!

Of course, to see representation as grounded in an epistemic division of labour presupposes that information about political decisions and/or participation in the decision-making process are not ends in themselves. There is a long-standing tradition in political theory that citizens ought to be engaged in political processes (and presumably informed about them) either in itself or for the sake of the intrinsic virtue that such participation instils in them. RCT has never expressed much sympathy with such claims—but if anything the argument would seem to support direct rather than representative procedures.

As noted above in relation to VA, if the primary rationale for representative institution lies in the informational aspect, the principles that govern selection of 'representatives' could well be statistical[14] rather than elective.[15]

Strategic Possibility

A fourth possibility invokes the idea of 'strategic' representation. The idea here is akin to that of an abandoned spouse employing a divorce lawyer, precisely because the lawyer will inflict greater losses on the sued partner than the abandoned spouse would herself be able to inflict. She knows that, if she pursues mediation, she will find herself 'having to be reasonable'—that her better nature will intervene and prevent her from inflicting the full fury the louse deserves! Divorce lawyers, so the thought goes, are skilled in suppressing any 'better nature': and so the vindictive party uses court procedures and the most aggressive lawyer she can find to inflict losses on her former partner of a severity that she herself would not inflict.

---

[12] See Levy (2002) for an examination of one such argument when economists first earned their label of being from the 'dismal science' when they fought against slavery.

[13] See Baurmann and Brennan (2009) for an extended discussion.

[14] See Burgers (2012) for an examination of the use of a lottery to appoint political representatives.

[15] In the manner of Fishkin's 'deliberative polls' (1991).

The political analogue is that when policy is determined directly by voting procedures the ideal of the median voter will tend to emerge as equilibrium. All voters may, however, prefer an agent who will deliver an outcome different from that. In a close analogue to the divorce lawyer case, Hamlin and Jennings (2007) suggest why, in situations of conflict, a group may select a leader who is more bellicose than the group itself: such a leader is expected to be more successful in negotiating with the opposition than the group itself would be.[16]

Leadership-as-Habit Possibility

The final consideration makes appeal not to directly justificatory arguments but more to matters of historical fact. Begin with the observation that, in our immediate non-democratic past, political power was exercised by a small number of persons highly hierarchically organized. In the process of institutional evolution from that past, some of these hierarchical features remained—either because of a purely 'political need' to buy off the existing power elite, or because of the social capital tied up in familiarity with existing ways of doing things. In a detailed study, redolent, at times, of Tsebelis's work (2002) on the role of players in determining the size of the set that can defeat all other proposals, Congleton (2011) explains how non-democratic rulers could attempt to retain effective veto power over the final outcome, even when they had traded off some elements of their decision-making domain in return for access to additional finance or favour. Over the centuries, hereditary monarchs gave way to popularly elected ones, with much of the rest of the prevailing institutional structure remaining in place. On this view, we more or less inherited a 'leadership habit': at any point, leadership structures now operate as a *fact*—even though the discretionary power possessed by the holders of political power is being gradually whittled away. The normative issue, on this view, is less 'what justifies leadership?' and more the question: 'how much reduction in the discretionary power of leaders (and representative assemblies) would be "optimal" given the factors that give rise to the historical stickiness?' This conception of the issue is doubtless attractive to 'direct democrats': they become the vanguard in casting off the remaining shackles of a non-democratic past.

4 WHY HIERARCHY?

Agency is one thing; hierarchy another.[17] It is perfectly possible to imagine the representative assembly, whether selected on statistical grounds or via popular election,

---

[16] For treatments in the same spirit, see Persson and Tabellini (1992) and Chari, Jones and Marimon (1997).

[17] Laver and Shepsle (1990) offer an account of how coalitions and cabinet structures limit the set of outcomes that can emerge when there is more than one dimension. The analysis is primarily concerned

making collective decisions as if by committee, without any office of 'leader' as such at all. What then makes for hierarchy in the structure of that assembly?[18] Perhaps there is a person who manages the discussion—orders the speakers, ensures that they do not speak beyond their allotted time, and so on—but that person (the 'Speaker' in Australian/British parlance) is not a 'leader' in the conventional sense.[19] To make a case for leadership in that common-sense version requires something else.

It is useful here to distinguish between those considerations that arise from the nature of the problems concerning which collective decision-making is required; and those that reflect features of voter psychology. In this section, we focus on the former supply-side aspects. The demand-side aspects are postponed to the next section.

One important supply-side argument is the argument from 'coordination'. On a certain view, the central problem of social order revolves around the need for individuals to coordinate their activities so that each can know what others will do. The classic example of such predicaments is choice of which side of the road to drive on: in this case, everyone is assumed to be indifferent between 'all drive on the left' and 'all drive on the right', but there is a need for a clear rule (one that everyone believes all others will follow) in order to minimize risk of accidents. Assigning determination of that choice to a single person is an apparently efficient solution to this problem (not quite[20]): alternatively put, if there is someone already designated as leader, we can justify her role in terms of her delivering determinations on the many such coordination problems that arise in social life. Typically, different equilibria will be differentially beneficial to different players—as in an n-person version of the 'battle of the sexes'.[21] A collectively preferred solution to such coordination games may evolve spontaneously.[22] This cannot be guaranteed, however; and then, despite the inherent element of conflict of interest, it may be better for all players that one of them be 'dictator' (and choose her own preferred equilibrium) than for individuals to squabble over who will be the chooser. This predicament is redolent of Hobbes's picture of the state of nature and has the same presumptive solution.

Hobbes's point seems to be that whoever (by whatever means) emerges as the 'dictator' should be endowed with presumptive authority—essentially because of the superior

---

with how political hierarchies structured along different policy dimensions actually work. Strøm (2003: 70) claims without any attempt at justification that one of the justifications for delegation is to avoid McKelvey's chaos theorem.

[18] Proponents of deliberative democracy do not address the question, though it seems clear that, though deliberative democrats support delegation (as conducive to 'ideal speech conditions'), they will not support hierarchy within the deliberative process itself.

[19] Cox (1987) argues the rise of cabinet was an institutional response to controlling the open-acess problem that had emerged when individual members started to use the floor to make speeches that might receive an airing in the emergent press.

[20] If no such leader exists, then there is a prior coordination problem as to whom to appoint—with as many contenders in principle as persons. There is then a radical asymmetry between cases in which there is a leader and those where the collectivity enquires as to whether to retain her/select a leader.

[21] On the 'battle of the sexes' see Luce and Raiffa (1957: ch. 5).

[22] See Sugden (1986) for an account of how coordination may evolve.

efficiency of hierarchical decision-making.[23] Although Hobbes's discussion allows that his 'dictator' could be a collective body of some kind, the problem with any such solution is that the coordination problems seem likely to resurface within the collective body: Hobbes's logic is in that sense especially hospitable to specifically *individual* leadership. An elegant recent treatment of 'leadership' grounded in the coordination game approach can be found in Dewan and Myatt (2007, 2008).

An alternative source for insights into hierarchy might be thought to lie in the economics literature, but again the papers are sparse and not very helpful. As Radner states in his survey on the economics of hierarchy:

> I... have to admit that research to date has not provided an adequate explanation on economic grounds alone of the conditions under which one expects to see a hierarchical organization of business firms. In fact, the explanation of hierarchy may in many cases be more sociological and psychological than purely 'economic' in the mainstream sense.
>
> (Radner 1992: 1384)

Radner may have had in mind predispositions such as servility and authoritarianism (redolent perhaps of Adorno et al. (1950) that lie somewhat outside the RCT lexicon.[24]

One strand in economics that may be relevant is the 'tournament' literature. The idea is that one may solicit greater effort from a group of agents by structuring rewards in a manner that assigns very high rewards to the 'best' performer and low rewards to all others. Each then strives to be the tournament winner because of the disproportionate rewards; and each thereby expends more effort than she would if rewards were distributed more equally. This reward structure will, of course, be defensible only if the criteria for determining the winner track closely enough the features that it is desirable to promote. So, if the most public-spirited, trustworthy, and competent person is the one who wins the tournament, then incentives to develop and exhibit those characteristics will be encouraged by the competition. Here, however, the primary function of the 'hierarchical structure' is to provide incentives to contenders all the way down the chain rather than to provide for 'leadership' as such.

5 SELECTION VERSUS INCENTIVES

In standard principal-agent theory, principals respond to the fact of agency by devising appropriate incentives for the agent. There is another way of thinking about principal–agent problems—less in terms of incentives and more in terms of selection effects.

---

[23] For an elegant non-technical discussion of the Hobbes problem, see Don Ross's (2010) entry on game theory in the *Stanford Encyclopedia of Philosophy*.

[24] For a more recent treatment that explains leadership-by-example as a way of credibly communicating to subordinates the special knowledge held by individuals at the top of a hierarchy, see Hermalin (1998, 2013).

Suppose that agents are not routinely self-interested. Suppose they are heterogeneous in just the features in which principals are interested: their trustworthiness; their competence; and their 'public-interestedness' (TCP features). Then citizen–voters will select for these things. On this basis, the right way to think of electoral competition is in terms less of the incentives it creates for agents to do what voters want, and more of the capacity of voters to select agents with higher TCP. If voters are reasonably good at discerning TCP, then not only will agents exhibit more of such features than the average citizen, but aspiring candidates will tend to self-select for possession of the features and indeed will have incentives to cultivate TCP in themselves. To be sure, candidates will have an incentive to *pretend* to have the relevant features whether they possess them or not, but this may have the effect of their behaving *as if* they possessed those features. Besley (e.g. 2006) is the RCT scholar who has developed this set of thoughts most formally.[25] As he puts it, his account offers a defence of the idea of 'principled agents'. Principled agents are worthy of greater delegation than unprincipled ones![26] More to the point perhaps, the possibility of selection allows an independent argument for 'representative' institutions—namely, that it allows the citizenry to select the best from among themselves for 'leadership' roles. Unlike some other arguments for delegation, this argument relies on electoral processes specifically to select representatives—not mere random selection.

One noteworthy aspect of this selection story relates to its epistemic demands. We said earlier that voters' assessments of alternative policies are likely to be ill-informed. Arguably, the cost of acquiring information about *policies* is more complicated and less engaging than information about candidates. After all, people have to make judgements of the qualities of others in ordinary arenas of life; and have been doing just this throughout their evolutionary history. Of course, the capacity to dissemble has also evolved, but our evolutionary legacy is likely to help us assess the character of other persons. Little in that evolutionary legacy is likely to equip us, however, to make the fine judgements of policy issues demanded by direct collective decision-making.

6 LEADERSHIP AND EXPRESSIVE VOTING

A remark finally about the 'demand' side of delegation and leadership. A standard part of (most) RCT is an account of electoral demand in which voter behaviour is extrapolated directly from market settings. Hence, the ultimate object of voter concern is the policy outcome and the effect of that outcome on the individual voter's material interests. So

[25] Though for an attempt by one of the present authors in a different collaboration, see Brennan and Hamlin (2000).

[26] Several questions arise (which we will not pursue here). First, to what extent does the widespread inclination to engage in 'politician bashing' undermine the force of social esteem and with it the nurture of principled political leadership? Second, can we devise institutional arrangements that augment esteem effects and, if so, would these be desirable?

RCT models of political process typically treat candidates and parties simply as ciphers for policy platforms. Electoral options are often referred to as 'party/candidate/policy', as if the three were coterminous.

We believe that the appropriate account of voter behaviour involves seeing voting much more as an expressive act than an instrumental one. Because each individual vote is highly unlikely to be decisive, it is not appropriate to treat electoral and market choice identically.[27] Voting is rather more like cheering at a football match than choosing an assets portfolio.

Accordingly, electoral candidates will maximize their 'cheerability'—and this may include an array of features independent of policy platform (such as candidate charisma and party identification). The expressive underpinning has implications specifically for leadership—both for the fact of it and the sorts of features that successful 'leaders' will tend to exhibit. Suppose party *A* has a charismatic 'leader' while party *B* has none (and simply stands as a collection of individuals); and suppose (plausibly) that the leader's charisma garners (some) additional votes. Then *A* will do better against *B* than otherwise. Hence, competitive parties will tend to *have* leaders and to seek, for these leadership roles, those individuals with the most vote-catching features.

In this sense, we think the (true) expressive account of voting is extremely hospitable to a highly personality-based account of electoral competition; and hence to an account of leadership that is grounded in vote-maximizing party strategy. Rather than leaders' personal characteristics being epiphenomal features of the electoral process, they can be crucial for at least some voters and influential for almost all. 'Leadership' exploits the human interest dimension of electoral competition—and casual observation suggests that this dimension is quite significant. RCT tends to background such features because of its reliance on a particular view of electoral behaviour that, we think, is itself faulty on RCT grounds.

7 Leadership: Unfinished Agenda

RCT, in its emphasis on the systematic features of political processes, has tended to set aside the personal features of leaders in explaining policy outcomes. In that sense, leadership as an explanatory category receives little attention in the RCT literature. However,

---

[27] The logic is that of the 'rational ignorance' argument originally advanced by Downs (1957). The argument, however, goes further. In the Downsian model, voters vote their interests, but those interests are (rationally) dimly perceived. In the expressive account, voters (rationally) attend to the intrinsically attractive features of parties and candidates quite independently of expected instrumental benefits— which are very low when weighted by the probability of being decisive. Brennan and Lomasky (1993) provide a detailed account of expressive voting theory (which does not canvass implications for the phenomenon of leadership).

at a more institutional level, leadership is a structural feature of virtually every Western democratic system, and, as such, calls for explanation/justification in itself.

There are two basic facts to be explained here: delegation (that is, representative as against direct democracy); and hierarchy *within* delegated bodies. In this chapter, we have canvassed the kinds of considerations that RCT addresses to see what light can be thrown on each element.

The 'principal-agent' approach, characteristic of RCT treatment of leadership, has tended to emphasize the scope for all delegated power to be directed to the purposes of the agent. In that sense, leadership has tended to be regarded disparagingly in the RCT literature: leadership implies delegation; and delegation is presumptively costly. We might ask, however, what positive features of delegation can be put on the other side of the ledger to justify this cost or explain why it might be worth bearing.

The RCT literature engaging this issue explicitly is sparse. Accordingly, we see ourselves here sketching out a landscape for future research and pointing to some possible resources, rather than reporting on well-established findings. One relevant element with a distinctively RCT flavour is the phenomenon of Downsian 'rational ignorance'; but this phenomenon in itself does not justify delegation unless it is the case that 'rationally ignorant' voters are better at selecting competent and trustworthy agents than at selecting appropriate policies. We think there are reasons why this might be so; but, given its centrality in the analysis of delegation, it is surprising that the issue has not received more explicit attention among RCT scholars.

Even if voters are no better at evaluating persons than they are at evaluating policies directly, they may find the exercise of evaluating persons more 'interesting' and 'engaging'—in which case representative institutions may emerge even where they offer no normatively relevant advantage. The 'expressive' account of voting behaviour, which we favour, is hospitable to this possibility.

RECOMMENDED READING

Besley, T. (2006). *Principled Agents? The Political Economy of Good Government*. Oxford: Oxford University Press.

Brennan, G., and Hamlin, A. (2000). *Democratic Devices and Desires*. Cambridge: Cambridge University Press.

Congleton, R. (2011). *Perfecting Parliament: Constitutional Reform, Liberalism, and the Rise of Western Democracy*. Cambridge: Cambridge University Press.

REFERENCES

Adorno, T., Frenkel-Brunswik. E., Levinson, D., and Sanford, N. (1950). *The Authoritarian Personality: Studies in Prejudice Series*, i. New York: Harper and Row.

Arrow, K. (1951). *Social Choice and Individual Values*. Cowles Foundation Monograph 12. New Haven, CT: Yale University Press.

Baurmann, M., and Brennan, G. (2009). 'What Should the Voter Know? Epistemic Trust in Democracy', *Grazer Philosophische Studien*, 79/1: 159–186.

Besley, T. (2006). *Principled Agents? The Political Economy of Good Government*. Oxford: Oxford University Press.

Brennan, G., and Lomasky, L. (1993). *Democracy and Decision: The Pure Theory of Electoral Preference*. Cambridge: Cambridge University Press.

Brennan, G., and Hamlin, A. (2000). *Democratic Devices and Desires*. Cambridge: Cambridge University Press.

Buchanan, J. M., and Vanberg, V. (1989). 'A Theory of Leadership and Deference in Constitutional Construction', *Public Choice*, 61/1: 15–27.

Burgers, J.-W. (2012). 'The Virtues of Using Lotteries in Public Decision-Making and Institutional Design'. Unpublished Ph.D. thesis. Canberra: Australian National University.

Chari, V. V., Jones, L. E., and Marimon, R. (1997). 'The Economics of Split-Ticket Voting in Representative Democracies', *American Economic Review*, 87/5: 957–76.

Congleton, R. (2011). *Perfecting Parliament: Constitutional Reform, Liberalism, and the Rise of Western Democracy*. Cambridge: Cambridge University Press.

Cox, G. W. (1987). *The Efficient Secret: The Cabinet and the Development of Political Parties in Victorian England*. Cambridge: Cambridge University Press.

Dewan, T., and Myatt, D. (2007). 'Leading the Party: Coordination, Direction and Communication', *American Political Science Review*, 101/4: 827–45.

Dewan, T., and Myatt, D. (2008). 'The Qualities of Leadership: Direction, Communication and Obfuscation', *American Political Science Review*, 102/3: 351–68.

Diermeier, D., and Krehbiel, K. (2003). 'Institutionalism as a Methodology', *Journal of Theoretical Politics*, 15/2: 123–44.

Downs, A. (1957). *An Economic Theory of Democracy*. New York: Harper and Row.

Finer, S. E. (1962). *The Man on Horseback: The Role of the Military in Politics*. London: Pall Mall.

Fiorina, M., and Shepsle, K. (1989). 'Formal Theories of Leadership: Agents, Agenda-Setters, and Entrepreneurs', in Bryan D. Jones (ed.), *Leadership and Politics*. Lawrence, KS: University Press of Kansas, 17–40.

Fishkin, J. S. (1991). *Democracy and Deliberation*. New Haven, CT: Yale University Press.

Hamilton, A. (2012). 'Federalist No. 72 The Same Subject Continued, and Re-Eligibility of the Executive Considered from the Independent Journal. Wednesday, 19 March 1788', in *The Federalist Papers*, ed. A. Hamilton, J. Madison and J. Jay. New York: Tribeca Books, 209–12.

Hamlin, A. and Jennings, C. (2007). 'Leadership and Conflict', *Journal of Economic Behavior and Organization*, 64/1: 49–68.

Hermalin, B. (1998). 'Toward an Economic Theory of Leadership: Leading by Example', *American Economic Review*, 88/5: 1188–206.

Hermalin, B. (2013). 'Leadership and Corporate Culture', in R. Gibbons and J. Roberts (eds), *The Handbook of Organizational Economics*. Princeton: Princeton University Press, 432–78.

Hume, D. (1985) [1758]. 'Of the Independency of Parliament', in *Essays Moral, Political and Literary*. Vol. 1, ed. E. Miller. Indianapolis, IN: Liberty Classics, 42–6.

Jensen, M., and Meckling, W. (1995). 'Specific and General Knowledge, and Organizational Structure', *Journal of Applied Corporate Finance*, 8/2: 4–18.

Laver, M., and Shepsle, K. (1990). 'Coalitions and Cabinet Government', *American Political Science Review*, 84/3: 873–90.

Leeson, P. (2009). *The Invisible Hook: The Hidden Economics of Pirates*. Princeton: Princeton University Press.

Levy, D. (2002). *How the Dismal Science Got Its Name: Classical Economics and the Ur-Text of Racial Politics*. Ann Arbor, MI: University of Michigan Press.

Luce, R. D., and Raiffa, H. (1957). *Games and Decisions: Introduction and Critical Survey*. New York: Wiley.

McKelvey, R. (1976). 'Intransitivies in Multidimensional Voting Models and Some Implications for Agenda Control', *Journal of Economic Theory*, 12/3: 472–82.

Mill, J. S. (1861). *Considerations on Representative Government*. London: Parker, Son and Bourn, West Strand.

Mitchell, W. (1988). 'Virginia, Rochester, and Bloomington: Twenty-Five Years of Public Choice and Political Science', *Public Choice*, 56: 101–19.

Mueller, D. (2003). *Public Choice III*. Cambridge: Cambridge University Press.

Olson, M. (1965). *The Logic of Collective Action: Public Goods and the Theory of Groups*. Cambridge, MA: Harvard University Press.

Persson, T., and Tabellini, G. (1992). 'The Politics of 1992: Fiscal Policy and European Integration', *Review of Economic Studies*, 59/4: 689–701.

Radner, R. (1992). 'Hierarchy: The Economics of Managing', *Journal of Economic Literature*, 30/3: 1382–415.

Ross, D. (2010). 'Game Theory', in *Stanford Encyclopedia of Philosophy* <http://plato.stanford.edu/entries/game-theory> accessed 2 December 2011.

Shepsle, K. (2006). 'Rational Choice Institutionalism', in R. A. W. Rhodes, S. A. Binder and B. A. Rockman (eds), *The Oxford Handbook of Political Institutions*. Oxford: Oxford University Press, 23–38.

Strøm, K. (2003). 'Parliamentary Democracy and Delegation', in K. Strøm, W. C. Müller, and T. Bergman (eds), *Delegation and Accountability in Parliamentary Democracies*. Oxford: Oxford University Press, 55–106.

Sugden, R. (1986). *The Economics of Rights, Co-operation and Welfare*. Oxford: Basil Blackwell.

Tsebelis, G. (2002). *Veto Players: How Political Institutions Work*. Princeton: Princeton University Press.

Wagner, R. (1966). 'Pressure Groups and Political Entrepreneurs: A Review Article', *Public Choice*, 1/1: 161–70.

Wicksell, K. (1896). *Finanztheoretische Untersuchungen*. Jena: Gustav Fischer; in R. Musgrave and A. T. Peacock (eds), *English Classics in The Theory of Public Finance: A New Principle of Just Taxation*. 1958. London: Macmillan, 1958, 72–118.

Wintrobe, R. (2000). *The Political Economy of Dictatorship*. Cambridge: Cambridge University Press.

CHAPTER 12

··

ANTHROPOLOGY*

··

CRIS SHORE

1 INTRODUCTION

··

ONE of the paradoxes about political leadership is that, while the subject has been extensively studied, the concept itself remains poorly understood, and studies have produced
no unified theory or even an agreed definition (Elgie 2001). One reason for this, as
anthropologists have noted, is because the meaning of leadership varies cross-culturally
and temporally, as do the qualities expected of a leader. Social anthropology, as the study
of social relations and human cultures, begins from the premiss that how people perceive
and engage with the world—the categories they use to construct and interpret it—are
profoundly shaped by the social milieu they inhabit, and what Bourdieu (1977) termed
habitus: those enduring sets of socially learned dispositions and taken-for-granted ways
of acting. From a theoretical perspective, this takes us beyond the argument that the
meaning of political leadership is socially constructed: it also destabilizes the category
of the 'political' itself by highlighting the fluid, contingent, contested, and socially constructed nature of what different societies understand as the political field (Gallie 1964).
As John Davis (1977: 146) argued, these social processes constitute 'the bedrock of political life' in most of those communities that anthropologists and political scientists study.

Within anthropology, political leadership is generally understood as a system of social
relationships involving authority, charisma, and other forms of personal or institutional
power, whose rules are specific to, and embedded within, particular cultural contexts.
Early anthropological studies of leadership focused on power relations in small-scale
tribal societies and the evolution of the state. As the focus of anthropology shifted to
include more complex societies, traditional concerns with authority, kinship, informal

* I would like to thank my colleagues at the University of Auckland—particularly Christine Dureau,
Susanna Trnka, Julie Park, and Charlotte Joy—for their constructive feedback on an earlier version of
this chapter.

mechanisms of social control, and dispute resolution gave way to more nuanced ethnographic studies of political behaviour, including the micro-politics of reputation management, political brokerage, and an interest in the dynamics of followers and factions. Since the 1980s, anthropology has devoted relatively little attention to political leadership *per se*. However, that does not mean a lack of anthropological interest in the topic. Rather, anthropologists have addressed questions of leadership through other debates from the politics of race, ethnicity, and nationalism, to the anthropology of organizations, elites, post-colonial governance, and the state. In short, anthropological studies of political leadership have been subsumed within wider debates over power, ideology and gender relations, hegemony and resistance, and political ritual and symbolism.

This chapter reviews anthropological contributions to the study of political leadership since the 1960s. The argument is set out in four sections. The first explores what the concept of political leadership *is* and why it matters anthropologically. The second examines anthropology's pioneering contributions to debates about leadership from the 1960s to 1980s. The third outlines directions that anthropological work has taken since the 1980s, particularly regarding the ritual and symbolic underpinnings of leadership. Finally, I conclude by reviewing some potential new avenues for research that highlight anthropology's relevance for understanding how political leadership works, how it is performed, and the meanings it holds in different societies.

2 POLITICAL LEADERSHIP: WHAT IT IS, AND WHY IT MATTERS

While its protean character and cross-cultural variations in meaning renders 'leadership' problematic as an analytical concept, it nevertheless remains important as an empirical and anthropological term for the simple reason that most societies (but by no means all) have elements of leadership and recognize categories of leaders. Prime ministers and presidents—be they Barack Obama, Vladimir Putin, Nickolas Sarkozy, Nelson Mandela or Fidel Castro, Ghandi, and Kim Il Jong—not only speak for their countries; they often symbolize them too. When institutions fail to work properly, it is often put it down to a 'problem of leadership'—yet people still look to leadership to solve the problems. Political leaders are expected to be adept performers in that social field called the 'political stage', or 'public life'; as an old British Labour Party maxim goes, 'if you can't ride two horses at the same time, you shouldn't be in the circus'. Yet, despite the rise of leadership consultants and experts and the transformation of leadership itself into a field of study, understanding the qualities, abilities, and behaviour that make for effective leadership still seems more like a search for the Holy Grail than science.

Why political leadership matters also lies in the implications of its absence. For example, despite the aspirations for 'good governance' and enlightened leadership set out in the 2004 'Mombasa Declaration' and 'Code of African Leadership', the succession of ineffective and selfish leaders in Africa's developing countries has produced a legacy of 'bad governance' and all its associated problems of political instability, social malaise, corruption, lack of accountability and transparency, and lack of respect for the rule of law (Udogu 2008: 13–14).

What, therefore, is the secret of good leadership? Ever since Max Weber, social scientists have sought to identity the personal traits that might make someone an effective leader. This focus on individual qualities, however, tended to locate leadership studies in the realm of Thomas Carlyle's 'Great Man Theory'. While that androcentric bias has been critiqued and corrected in later analyses, much of the literature on leadership still tends to focus on individual personality traits or psychological characteristics and motives. For example, Jean Blondel (1987: 3) defined leadership as 'the power exercised by one or a few individuals to direct members of the nation towards actions', while Joseph Rost (1991: 2) calls it 'an influence relationship among leaders and followers who intend real changes that reflect their purpose', and Burns describes it in terms of the mobilization of 'institutional, political, psychological and other resources' in order 'to arouse, engage, and satisfy the motives of followers' (Burns 1978: 18). Political leaders themselves often reinforce this methodological individualist approach. 'Leadership is personal,' declares Tony Blair (2010: 1) in his autobiography—although he later acknowledges that the 'awe' great leaders inspire in people derives more from the office they occupy than their personal characters. According to the *Oxford English Dictionary* (2010), a leader is variously 'a person who commands a group, organization, or country: a member of the government officially responsible for initiating business in Parliament', or 'the person or team that is winning a sporting competition at a particular time'.

These definitions with their emphasis on action verbs ('command', 'initiative', 'win') suggest that leadership can be understood in at least two different ways. The first is in the sense of institutional office-holding. Here leadership becomes shorthand for occupying a senior position in an organization such as President or Chief of Police. The second refers to leadership as a category of behaviour and type of relationship between members of a particular group. Here, a leader is someone who is able to convince a group to follow a particular course of action. Leadership in this more anthropological sense concerns the interaction between leader and followers, which Elgie (2001: 8578) describes as 'a reciprocal and essentially noncoercive relationship'. What constitutes 'reciprocity' and 'coercion' in political relationships are themes we will consider later; but, as Elgie notes, this distinction is important for recognizing that leadership does not necessarily have to be exercised by leaders, in the same way that not all leaders actually lead.

3   ANTHROPOLOGY'S CONTRIBUTION TO THE STUDY OF POLITICAL LEADERSHIP

Anthropologists also tend to highlight the dynamic, relational, and contextual nature of leadership and to understand political leadership as something processual and performative rather than simply a matter of institutional position-holding or a mode of domination. Anthropology's contribution to the study of political leadership in the early decades of the twentieth century lay in its examination of power relations in small-scale tribal societies. Of particular concern were questions about the evolution of the state, dispute resolution, and how political order is maintained in 'primitive societies' lacking institutionalized forms of rule: that is, 'tribes without rulers', or 'acephalous' polities (Evans-Pritchard 1940; Fortes and Evans-Pritchard 1940). Later works of political anthropology during the 1940s–50s concerned themselves more with issues of dispute settlement and informal mechanisms of social control such as reciprocity, kinship obligations, and informal sanctions, or with how leadership functions in tribal societies tend to be distributed across various roles, including clan elders and village headmen.

As anthropology became more interested in complex societies, the concerns of political anthropologists also changed. Traditional preoccupations with law and the maintenance of order gave way during the 1960s–70s to a concern with conflict, resulting in action-based and individually oriented studies of political behaviour. Since the 1980s and 1990s, political anthropology's interest in leadership has developed in several important new directions, including studies of hegemony and resistance (Comaroff and Comaroff 1991), political oratory, language, and power (Parkin 1984), political symbolism and ritual (Kertzer 1988; Abélès 2005), and the analysis of the state, elites, and policy assemblages (Grillo 1980; Steinmetz 1999; Greenhalgh 2008; Wedel 2009; Feldman 2011).

Within anthropology, political leadership is generally understood as a system of social relationships involving authority, charisma, or other forms of personal or institutional power, but whose rules are specific to, and embedded within, a particular cultural context. Anthropologists have long recognized that leadership as an institution hinges on culturally specific and relational understanding of authority, or, as Sahlins (1963: 290) put it, 'leadership is a creation of followership' acquired by demonstrating that the leader 'possesses the kind of skills that demand respect'. Max Weber's classical distinction between 'legal rational', 'traditional', and 'charismatic' ideal-typical forms of authority continues to inform most anthropological analyses of leadership. Legitimate authority in every society constitutes a type of power in which leaders (as rulers) successfully uphold the claim that they govern in accord with law or tradition and in which people willingly obey commands because they perceive the exercise of power to be legitimate.

4 BIG MEN VERSUS CHIEFS: THE MAKING OF POLITICAL LEADERS

Most anthropologists working in small-scale societies encounter actors and leaders who mediate between the local community and the larger world and observe how local politics involves competition between different leaders, factions, and followers. As Gledhill (1994: 123) remarks, 'conflict is partly about parochial issues, and understanding what sometimes seems byzantine maneuvers over little of significance demands local knowledge, of who the actors are, what their background is, and what the issues represent in the eyes of those involved'. That contextualization and attention to local detail are perhaps anthropology's main contribution to understanding leadership in practice, as the work of early political anthropologists such as Barth (1959), Sahlins (1963), and Bailey (1969) illustrates.

A key figure in the anthropology of leadership is the 'Big Man', the prototypical Melanesian political leader who stands at the centre of a complex of economic and political structures found throughout Melanesia, and, in particular, Papua New Guinea (PNG) and the Solomon Islands. The term Big Man derives from the Anglicized phase *bikpela man*, meaning 'prominent man', but 'was widely adopted in Melanesian ethnography to refer to male leaders whose political influence is achieved by means of public oratory, informal persuasion, and the skillful conduct of both private and public wealth exchange' (Lederman 2001: 1162; see also Godelier 1986). The study of Melanesian Big Men has intrigued anthropologists. It provided both a marker of delineation (albeit much contested) between Melanesian and Polynesian societies (where political leadership was vested in the figure of the chief) and a 'vantage point for understanding how economic intensification might be possible in the absence of institutionalized political structures' (Lederman 2001: 1162).

According to Sahlins, Big Men are exemplary charismatic leaders. Drawing on studies of Bougainville and Papua New Guinean political systems, Sahlins describes the Big Man as

> reminiscent of the free-enterprising rugged individual of our own heritage. He combines with an ostensible interest in the general welfare a more profound measure of self-interested cunning and economic calculation.
>
> (Sahlins 1963: 289)

Sahlins argued that Melanesia and Polynesia represent different points on an evolutionary continuum: whereas Melanesia political systems are 'segmental' and characterized by small autonomous kinship groups living in small villages or hamlets, each a copy of the others and each economically self-governing, Polynesian political structures are pyramidal, larger scale, based on genealogical ranking, and capped by a paramount chief. Melanesian Big Men and Polynesian chiefs reflect two fundamentally different sociological types and historically particular forms of leadership. According to Sahlins, Big Men epitomize many of the qualities of Western capitalists, their authority being based on personal powers and entrepreneurship. To attain Big Man status they must rely on skills of oratory, leading by example, haranguing, or through sheer force of personality. Polynesian chiefs, by contrast, are more feudal; their authority comes from their office and their ascribed status or pedigree upon which they claim their right of rule.

And, whereas Melanesian leaders have to master compelling oratorical style, 'Polynesian paramount chiefs often had trained "talking chiefs" whose voice was the chiefly command' (Sahlins 1963: 295)—a tradition that has continued in many parts of the Pacific (White and Lindstrom 1997).

What is striking about these comments, albeit typical of the scholarship on political leadership, is the continuing androcentrism (not to mention Eurocentrism) that underpins assumptions about the relationship between leadership and masculinity. Sahlins makes three further interesting points about Big Man political systems:

1. They are inherently unstable. The 'shifting disposition and magnetisms of ambitious men in a region may induce fluctuations in factions', while the death of a Big Man can result in the dissolution of the entire group.
2. Because Big Men acquire influence through economic production and exchange, political ambition results in the production of surpluses within Melanesian horticultural and cash economies. Competitive politicking encourages people to produce goods beyond local needs and to participate in trade networks that circulate these goods throughout extensive regions. In parts of Melanesia, this has inflated customary brideprice payments; young women in Vanuatu, for example, are sometimes called 'Toyotas' after the sort of good their families demand (Lindstrom 1996: 65).
3. They act as a brake on development. By pursuing status, Big Men must encourage followers to produce more pigs, yams, taro, etc., but that in turn encourages defection. A Big Man who underperforms risks being pushed out by his competitors and abandoned by his following.

By contrast, Polynesian chiefdoms unified much larger populations, producing wealthier and more complex political systems that resulted in 'subsidized craft production and a division of labor unparalleled in extent and expertise in most of the Pacific' (Sahlins 1963: 296). But Polynesian chieftainship also generated internal contradictions, including a tendency to over-tax and too much wealth being diverted to the chiefly establishment, which provoked periodic rebellions.

Although the Big Man as a Melanesian prototype unravelled with further studies—and as the 'evolutionary narrative of progression from traditional to legal-bureaucratic authority…proved only a romantic political fable' (White and Lindstrom 1997: 17)—the concept was usefully extended beyond Melanesia as a label for leaders who achieve status by astutely engaging in imbalanced reciprocal exchanges—and who use wealth to place others in their debt. As Lindstrom (1996: 66) observes, Big Men have also been spotted by anthropologists 'in the halls of the United States congress as well as within a number of other political organizations worldwide'. Lindstrom's work (1984) extended Sahlins's argument to show how some Big Man political systems are based not on economic wealth but on control of particular kinds of knowledge—what Bourdieu (1977) has termed 'symbolic capital'.

5 POLITICAL SYSTEMS AND POLITICAL LEADERSHIP: ACTION APPROACHES

The 1960s saw other attempts to move beyond the typologizing accounts of functionalist anthropology towards more dynamic approaches that viewed behaviour in terms of purposeful action rather than simply enactment of fixed norms. An important contribution to political theory and studies of political leadership that emerged from this was Frederik Barth's so-called transactionalist approach. His 1959 book *Political Leadership among Swat Pathans* examined the political organization of the segmentary and faction-ridden Pahktun tribes of north-west Pakistan. Following Edmund Leach's study (1954) of the political systems of highland Burma, Barth challenged many of anthropology's core assumptions about social order and cultural change, rejecting the Durkheimian conception of society as a system of morals that exist independently of behaviour, and focusing instead on the choices that individuals make in pursuit of their interests.

Barth argued that, although individuals are born into particular structural positions, in Swat society people can choose where they wish to place their loyalties among different office-holders, and these decisions may be temporary and revocable, which explains why alliances are so volatile and unstable. The result is a political system 'built up and maintained through the exercise of a continual series of individual choices' (Barth 1959: 2). Political allegiance is not something given automatically but is something 'bartered between individuals against a return in other advantages': that is, local *khans* provide protection in return for services and loyalty from followers who effectively 'sell' their allegiance to whichever landlord offers the best charity. What are exchanged are loyalty and protection for honour and prestige. Individuals build up their own positions of power and authority by systematically manipulating these relations. Barth concluded that analyses of leadership must be processual rather than normative, and must explain how various social forms are generated, not simply how order is maintained. This requires a focus on transactional behaviour, which Barth (1959: 4) defines as 'sequences of interaction systematically governed by reciprocity'. Transactions themselves are seen as subject to the same kind of rules of strategy advanced in game theory models, according to which the value gained is greater than or equivalent to the value lost (Kapferer 1976: 3).

Barth pioneered a new way of explaining political organization in terms of the strategizing behaviour of individuals interacting with each other. This entailed a theoretical shift away from norms and social structure towards a Weberian 'social action' approach. However, Barth was heavily criticized by other scholars, notably Talal Asad (1972), a Marxist anthropologist, and Akbar Ahmed (1976), a Muslim and former Pakistani government official. Both rejected his interpretation as partial and ethnocentric. For Asad, Barth's individualistic, contractual market model of transactional relations between Pakhtuns overlooked the fact that land is controlled by a small number of men who dominate those without land. It is not free choice but 'the presence of a sovereign land-owning class that was the key to political leadership in Swat' (Edwards 1998: 714). Asad's complaint was that Barth failed take into account history, or acknowledge the role of the state. Both highlighted the fact that Swat society is not as segmentary and acephalous as Barth assumed. In a more recent essay, Edwards (1998) has shown how these early anthropological studies of the Pakhtuns provide valuable insight into ethnic politics in contemporary Afghanistan and how they help us to understand the relative success of the Taliban in unifying a country where other regimes have signally failed.

6 Political Leaders as Cultural Brokers

During the 1970s, transactionalist approaches were pioneered by numerous anthropologists and proved particularly useful for studying local-level politics and conflicts over resources. Anthropologists developed a raft of new theoretical concepts to analyse the political forms generated by individuals in these situations of leadership and conflict.

> Among these were quasi-group, action-set, clique, gang, faction, coalition, interest group, and party. Others related to modes of political behaviour: choosing, maximising, decision-making, strategising, interacting, transacting, manipulating, career-building, spiralling, recruiting, excluding, manoeuvring, competing, fighting, dominating, encapsulating.
>
> (Vincent 1978: 176)

Others focused on specific kinds of power relationship, including 'friendship', 'godparenthood', and 'patron–client linkages' (Waterbury and Gellner 1977) or the contexts in which political action occurs (that is, field, arena, situation, political system, environment, and power structure). This new methodology produced some pioneering studies of local politics, power brokerage and issues such as the politics of honour, reputation management, and the rise of the mafia (Blok 1974; Arlacchi 1986).

A key focus of interest was the role played by gatekeepers or 'middlemen' in face-to-face rural societies;—that is, individuals whose structural position enables them to mediate between the relative isolation of peripheral communities and the institutions of the modern state. These positions create the social and economic space for a different kind of political leader: the community mediator or 'broker'. An important anthropological contribution was in analysing the character and quality of these relationships to show how most contain both moral and reciprocal elements (Silverman 1965: 176). Patron–client relations were a fundamental aspect of the social organization of rural societies throughout Latin America, the Mediterranean, and other developing countries (Gilmore 1982).

This provoked heated debate over how to theorize the patron–client relationship; was it a dyadic, interpersonal, and moral bond, or a disguised form of class domination? (See Silverman 1965; Davis 1977). Earlier studies had claimed that these brokers played a vital role in 'bridging the gap' between the peasantry and urban elites, linking rural hinterlands to the resources of the state. Later studies, often inspired by Marxist analysis, questioned this assumption and argued that these cultural brokers constituted a class of leaders whose political and economic interests lay more in maintaining rather than closing these gaps. Elizabeth Rata's work (2011) on Maori leadership strategies in New Zealand and the rise of what she terms 'neotribal capitalism' suggests similar processes are at work in other contexts (see also Comaroff and Comaroff 2009; Levine 2010).

Other anthropologists, including Boissevain, Cohen, and Bailey also contributed to the methodological tool-kit for studying competitive political action and leadership. Boissevain (1974) developed a theoretical taxonomy for analysing political 'action-sets' and networks, and the way individuals—seen as 'social entrepreneurs'—manipulate relations to attain goals and solve problems. The subject matter of his so-called transactionalist approach, he wrote, includes

> the network of friends, relatives and work mates; the visiting, bargaining, gossiping and manoeuvring that goes on between them; the impact of these on promotion, ideology, and conflict; the steps an ambitious man [*sic*] takes to build up his fund of credit among useful relations; and the operation of neighbourhood and workplace cliques and factions. These are processes and situations with which we are all involved and they are the basic stuff of social life.
>
> (Boissevain 1974: 4)

Cohen (1974) showed how effective political leadership rests on the manipulation of symbols, insights that he later applied to the study of complex Western societies. And Bailey (1969, 1988, 2001) produced numerous books that sought to theorize leadership as a type of economic transaction and disruption of conventional morality. Like capitalist entrepreneurs, political leaders, as cultural brokers, seek to maximize returns on their expertise, take a cut from their interventions to help clients, and create 'vote banks' of potential voters and favours owed (Bailey 1969: 41).

7 Political Leadership: Ritual and Symbolic Aspects

Since the mid-1980s political leadership has received far less critical attention within anthropology, largely because the rich lines of research stimulated by earlier debates over 'Big Men' political brokerage and the politics of reputation management were absorbed into other projects. Explicit concern with the individual qualities of leaders shifted towards wider considerations of the contexts in which leadership takes place, including issues of power, performance, gender, ideology, and political economy. Political anthropology developed new lines of research, including studies of language, discourse, oratory, symbolism, and political rituals. Whereas political scientists often dismiss ritual and symbols as secondary to the 'real stuff of politics'—namely, interest groups, economic forces, and power relations—anthropologists and historians have long recognized that the symbolic and ceremonial dimensions of political life are not simply window dressing. The notion of individuals as rational actors who base their decisions and actions on instrumental calculations of self-interest tends to ignore most of what makes people human. As David Cannadine (1992: 3) wrote: 'the rituals of rulers, the "symbolics of power", are not mere incidental ephemera, but are central to the structure and working of any society'. They are also central to understanding political leadership.

The work of Marc Abélès and David Kertzer exemplifies this point. Both authors show how effective political leadership depends upon a leader's ability to harness ritual in ways that mobilize followers, and how symbols can be powerful vehicles for shaping emotion and cognition—or 'snares for thought', as Abélès (1988) puts it. One reason for the political potency of symbols is because a crucial facet of modern power is the ability to define what constitutes reality. As Kenneth Burke (1945) noted long ago, all social and political life is constructed around symbols. For example, people are mobilized to fight wars in defence of concepts such as 'freedom', 'democracy', 'our nation', or 'our way of life'—abstract notions that are rendered meaningful or knowable only through symbols. Mass industrial societies are increasingly ruled by powerful office-holders whom people rarely encounter except in highly symbolic representations. We encounter our government or state only when it is represented in symbolic form (such as a flag and anthem) or personified in the figure of our president. Kertzer (1988: 6) quotes one shrewd observer who remarked: 'In electing a president, we elect "the chief symbol-maker of the land"'—a point cogently illustrated by James McLeod (1999) in his study of US presidential election campaigns.

Abélès (1988, 2005) illustrates this brilliantly in his study of former French President François Mitterrand's use of political rituals: from the inauguration of new railway stations (with the ritual redcarpet, ribbon-cutting, wreath-laying, and choreographed speeches and handshakes) to the annual Pentecost Day 'pilgrimage' to the ancient hill-top of Soutré—the rural village where Mitterrand, as a young partisan during the war, hid from the Nazis. Abélès concludes that modern French society is far less 'secular' than is popularly assumed. He shows that truly successful leaders can even invent their own personal rituals that blend the political and the sacred. All the key elements of ritual power work here to confirm the legitimacy of the President: dramatization is combined with the suspension of ordinary time and 'focalizing elements' presuppose rather than demand solidarity in such a way that even the most cynical spectators become ensnared in the emotion of the performance. Participants may recognize the facile elements involved, but seem unable to escape 'a sentimentality which, in more discursive contexts, they would probably despise' (Abélès 1988: 399).

8 POLITICAL LEADERSHIP, ORATORY, AND POWER

This idea of political rituals as 'snares for thought' was also developed in Bloch's study (1975) of political oratory among the Merina of Madagascar. Bloch noted how, in Merina society, political leaders imbue their speeches with a repertoire of allusions, allegories, images, and metaphors that are typically confined to 'a body of suitable illustrations, often proverbs or scriptures, which tend to be fixed, eternal and orthodox' (Bloch 1975: 15). As political authority depends on oratorical skill, Merina political speeches are highly formalized and follow predetermined codes that Bloch (1975: 11) calls 'linguistic rituals'. By adopting such formalized codes, Merina political leaders endow their oratory with the authority of those scriptures. The effect of shifting political discussion into this formalized register is to endow the speaker's arguments with a sacrosanct quality. A speaker who can claim to speak with the authority of the 'ancestors'—or 'tradition'— can thus claim to be the mouthpiece for a higher authority (like speaking as a prophet). As Bloch (1975: 15) writes: 'The most important social effect of this merging of the specific into the eternal and fixed is that it moves the communication to a level where disagreement is ruled out—since one cannot disagree with the right order.' By adopting this formalized code, both speaker and listener are subjugated to their respective roles and the protocols demanded by that code and the 'being, doing and saying' that is appropriate to a particular setting (Rancière 1998).

Despite being criticized as overly deterministic (Parkin 1984), Bloch's (1975) notion of 'linguistic ritual' has been successfully used to examine the relationship between discourse and power in contemporary Western societies, including the rise of the far right, neo-liberalism, and the politics of nationalism in Europe (Gal 1991; Shore and Wright 1997, 1999; Holmes 2000). This analytical concern with oratory and power has continued in the work of Susanna Trnka (2011), who has examined the rhetorical tropes and discourses used by the political leaders of Fiji's different military coups since the 1990s.

These studies suggest that political leadership can be seen as a type of performance; a ritualized 'socio-drama' in which both leader and followers enter into a choreographed and often highly prescriptive social field. This approach recalls Gramsci's work (1971) on hegemony and Pierre Bourdieu's concept (1977) of *doxa*, or the way an established political order establishes itself by becoming so naturalized that it ceases to be questioned. As Bourdieu (1977: 166) wrote, 'it goes without saying because it comes without saying'. These themes have been developed extensively in political anthropology and the anthropology of policy, an emerging disciplinary sub-field that studies policies as political technologies and 'techniques of the self' (Rose 1999) that work to construct new kinds of subjects and regimes of governance (Wedel et al. 2005; Shore, Wright and Però 2011).

There is also an extensive body of anthropological literature on the themes of colonialism, hegemony, resistance, and nationalism—beyond the scope of this short chapter—that raises debates of importance to the study of how leadership is enacted (or resisted) in different cultural contexts (Comaroff and Comaroff 1991; Gledhill 1994; Gupta and Ferguson 1997).

9 CURRENT AND FUTURE DIRECTIONS

The anthropology of political leadership typically emphasizes the wider contexts and social relations in which both leadership and followership are embedded and performed. Successful leadership entails mastering those conditions. As Bailey (1988: 5) states, 'leadership is the art of controlling followers'. Being an art, it necessarily requires 'cultural capital'—or talent. In developing this idea, Stanley Renshon (2000: 200) uses the term 'leadership capital' to highlight the way the competences and capacities for the performance of leadership are 'deeply embedded in and reflective of the cultures in which they operate'. However, 'successful' leadership is a term that needs qualifying, as these capacities for domination and manipulation do not always produce positive accomplishments, as twentieth-century history shows. In this vein, several recent anthropological studies stand out as particularly interesting examples of how anthropological research on political leadership might develop in future.

The first is Katherine Verdery's book *Political Lives of Dead Bodies* (1999), which explores one of the most fascinating aspects of post-socialist change in Eastern Europe: the politics of dead bodies. As she observes with irony, corpses have played a powerful role in 'animating' the study of politics in post-socialist societies. Starting with an analysis of tearing down and erection of statues (including those of Lenin, Marx, and Bishop Micu), Verdery proceeds to analyse the way political leadership is expressed and contested through monuments and rituals, and how aspects of history are remembered or effaced from the social memory of nations struggling to reinvent their past after decades of Communist rule. Drawing on vivid examples of the politics of reburial in the former Yugoslavia, she reminds us that politics is 'a realm of continual struggles over meaning, or signification' (Verdery 1999: 14) and that political transformation includes 'meanings, feelings, the sacred, ideas of morality, the nonrational—all ingredients of "legitimacy" or "regime consolidation" (that dry phrase) yet far broader than what analyses employing these terms usually provide' (Verdery 1999: 25).

This calls for a much wider conception of 'the political' than is normally provided by rational choice theory. As she cogently demonstrates (Verdery 1999: 26), nationalism is not simply about borders, resource competition, state-making, or 'constructionism'; it is also part of 'kinship, spirits, ancestor worship and the circulation of cultural treasures' and the reconfiguring of time and space. She also shows us that the 'political lives' of some leaders continue long after their death.

The second study is Janine Wedel's book *Shadow Elite* (2009). Drawing on insights from post-socialist Eastern Europe, Wedel reveals how a similar confluence of factors (which include neo-liberal policies of deregulation and outsourcing, the end of the cold

war, the growth of information technologies, and the 'embrace of "truthiness"') enabled certain well-connected entrepreneurial individuals to shift between their public-
and private-sector roles in order to exploit the new financial opportunities available to
them. Labelling this new breed of players 'flexians', she shows how one particular group
of neo-conservative cold warriors (including Donald Rumsfeld and Richard Pearl) rose
to power under the Bush administration. By operating 'at the nexus of official and private power' (Wedel 2009: 7) and shifting between their various roles as lobbyists, 'independent' experts, think-tank pundits, retired military or government officials, and
corporate representatives), these individuals were able to craft public policy in pursuit
of personal interests, flouting the rules designed to prevent conflicts of interest and subverting the democratic process by hiding their industry connections and consultancy
projects. Wedel shows how this shadow elite gained an extraordinary position of influence, co-opting public policy agendas to serve the private purposes of their benefactors.

If malfeasance and criminality can shed light on the darker and less conventional
dimensions of leadership, then Jane and Peter Schneider's (2003) study of the Italian
mafia should also be included among the list of 'must-reads'. Following earlier studies by
Blok (1974) and Arlacchi (1986), their work illustrates the value of combining detailed
ethnography with a wider political economy perspective in order to understand the
curious cultural codes and social dynamics that have both given rise to the modern
Mafia and transformed its leadership. In a similar vein, Bailey's later books also merit
consideration. Bailey (1988: 174) argues that 'malefaction' and 'villainy' are the essentials
of political leadership, as politics is inherently 'polluting', and political leaders everywhere are obliged to transcend the morality they recommend to others. However, in his
2001 book *Treasons, Stratagems and Spoils: How Leaders Make Practical Use of Beliefs
and Values*, he seems optimistically surprised to find that the 'politics of conscience' is
'at war with a politics of advantage' rather more often than he expected, as iconic leaders
such as Mahatma Gandhi, Nelson Mandela, and Aung San Suu Kyi illustrate.

Finally, anthropological studies of institutions, particularly those of the European
Union by Abélès (2000a, 2005b), Holmes (2000), Shore (2000), and others have pioneered new approaches to the analysis of power and leadership in international—or
rather 'supranational'—organizations. These authors have made valuable contributions
to opening up for scrutiny the 'black box' of the European Commission and European
Parliament. They have also shed light on the complex political dynamics and webs of
relations that constitute the EU's organizational culture. Like that of Bailey, their work
illustrates the tensions and contradictions that exist between the formal and informal
aspects of these institutions and their *modus operandi*. The EU institutions, as Shore
(2000, 2011) has argued, have become crucibles for the formation of a new kind of political leadership: a transnational European political elite that is having a transformative
effect on political leadership throughout Europe.

The value of studies like those cited above is that they remind us that political leadership is a process of continuous contestation and negotiation fought over what are
largely symbolic grounds. Political leadership is the art of winning and controlling followers, which, as anthropologists remind us, requires the strategic uses of morality and

successful mobilization of rituals and symbols. If cultural forms are the bedrock of political life, they are equally the foundation upon which political leadership is constructed and performed. Anthropology's main contribution to the study of political leadership, beyond the 'thick description' of its ethnographic studies, lies in its sensitivity to context, its concern with understanding politics both from the local perspective of leaders and that of the led, and the complex, shifting contexts in which leadership occurs. Anthropology is particularly well placed to explore the *meaning(s)* of leadership rather than simply its form. It can also provide a useful corrective to the ethnocentric—and androcentric—assumptions that tend to characterize academic studies of political leadership in the West.

RECOMMENDED READING

Bailey, F. G. (2001). *Treasons, Stratagems, and Spoils: How Leaders Make Practical Use of Beliefs and Values*. Boulder, CO: Westview Press.

Verdery, K. (1999). *The political Lives of Dead Bodies: Reburial and Postsocialist Change*. New York: Columbia University Press.

Wedel, J. (2009). *Shadow Elite: How the World's New Power Brokers Undermine Democracy, Government, and the Free Market*. New York: Perseus Books.

REFERENCES

Abélès, M. (1988). 'Modern Political Ritual: Ethnography of an Inauguration and a Pilgrimage by President Mitterrand', *Current Anthropology*, 23/3: 391–404.

Abélès, M. (2000a). *Un ethnologue à l'Assemblée*. Paris: Odile Jacob.

Abélès, M. (2000b). 'Virtual Europe', in I. Bellier and T. Wilson (eds), *An Anthropology of the European Union*. Oxford: Berg, 31–52.

Abélès, M. (2005). *Anthropologie de l'État*. Paris: Payot.

Ahmed, A. (1976). *Millennium and Charisma among Pathans*. London: Routledge and Kegan Paul.

Arlacchi, P. (1986). *Mafia Business: The Mafia Ethic and the Spirit of Capitalism*. London: Verso.

Asad, T. (1972). 'Market Model, Class Structure and Consent: A Reconsideration of Swat Political Organization', *Man, New Series*, 7: 74–94.

Bailey, F. G. (1969). *Stratagems and Spoils: A Social Anthropology of Politics*. Oxford: Blackwell.

Bailey, F. G. (1988). *Humbuggery and Manipulation: The Art of Leadership*. Ithaca, NY: Cornell University Press.

Bailey, F. G. (2001). *Treasons, Stratagems, and Spoils: How Leaders Make Practical Use of Beliefs and Values*. Boulder, CO: Westview Press.

Barth, F. (1959). *Political Leadership among Swat Pathans*. London: Athlone Press.

Blair, T. (2010). *A Journey*. London: Hutchison.

Bloch, M. (ed.)(1975). *Political Language, Oratory and Traditional Society*. London: Academic Press.

Blok, A. (1974). *The Mafia in a Sicilian Village, 1860–1960: A Study of Violent Peasant Entrepreneurs*. Oxford: Blackwell.

Blondel, J. (1987). *Political Leadership: Towards a General Analysis*. London: SAGE.

Boissevain, J. (1974). *Friends of Friends: Networks, Manipulators and Coalitions*. Oxford: Blackwell.

Bourdieu, P. (1977). *Outline of a Theory of Practice*. Cambridge: Cambridge University Press.

Burke, K. (1945). *A Grammar of Motives*. New York: Prentice-Hall.

Burns, J. M. (1978). *Leadership*. New York: Harper and Row.

Cannadine, D. (1992). *Rituals of Royalty: Power and Ceremonial in Traditional Societies*. Cambridge: Cambridge University Press.

Cohen, A. (1974). *Two Dimensional Man: An Essay on Power and Symbolism in Complex Society*. London: Routledge and Kegan Paul.

Comaroff, J., and Comaroff, J. (1991). *Of Revelation and Revolution: Christianity, Colonialism and Consciousness in South Africa*. Chicago: University of Chicago Press.

Comaroff, J., and Comaroff, J. (2009). *Ethnicity, Inc*. Chicago: University of Chicago Press.

Davis, J. (1977). *The People of the Mediterranean: An Essay in Comparative Social Anthropology*. London: Routledge and Kegan Paul.

Edwards, D. B. (1998). 'Learning from the Swat Pathans: Political Leadership in Afghanistan, 1978–97', *American Ethnologist*, 25(4): 712–28.

Elgie, R. (2001). 'Political Leadership', *International Encyclopedia of the Social and Behavioral Sciences*. Amsterdam: Elsevier, 8578–90.

Evans-Pritchard, E. E. (1940). *The Nuer*. Oxford: Clarendon Press.

Feldman, G. (2011). *The Migration Apparatus: Security, Labor, and Policymaking in the European Union*: Stanford, CA: Stanford University Press.

Fortes, M., and Evans-Pritchard, E. E. (1940) (eds). *African Political Systems*, London: Oxford University Press.

Gal, S. (1991). 'Bartók's Funeral: Representations of Europe in Hungarian Political Rhetoric', *American Ethnologist*, 18/3: 440–58.

Gallie, W. B. (1964). 'Essentially Contested Concepts', in W. B. Gallie (ed.), *Philosophy and the Historical Understanding*. London: Chatto and Windus, 157–91.

Gilmore, D. (1982). 'Anthropology of the Mediterranean Area', *Annual Review of Anthropology*, 11: 175–205.

Gledhill, J. (1994). *Power and its Disguises: Anthropological Perspectives on Politics*. London: Pluto.

Godelier, M. (1986). *The Making of Great Men*. Cambridge: Cambridge University Press.

Gramsci, A. (1971). *Selections from The Prison Notebooks of Antonio Gramsci*, trans. Q. Hoare and G. Nowell Smith. New York: Columbia University Press.

Greenhalgh, S. (2008). *Just One Child: Science and Policy in Deng's China*. Berkeley and Los Angeles, CA: University of California Press.

Grillo, R. D. (1980). *'Nation' and 'State' in Europe: Anthropological Perspectives*. London: Academic Press.

Gupta, A., and Ferguson J. (1997) (eds). *Culture, Power, Place: Explorations in Critical Anthropology*. Durham, NC: Duke University Press Books.

Holmes, D. (2000). *Integral Europe: Fast-Capitalism, Multiculturalism, Neofascism*. Princeton: Princeton University Press.

Kapferer, B. (1976) (ed.). *Transaction and Meaning: Directions in the Anthropology of Exchange and Symbolic Behavior*. Philadelphia, PA: Institute for the Study of Human Issues.

Kertzer, D. (1988). *Ritual, Politics, and Power*. New Haven, CT: Yale University Press.

Leach, E. R. (1954). *Political Systems of Highland Burma*. London: Athlone.

Lederman, R. (2001). 'Big Man, Anthropology of', in *International Encyclopedia of the Social and Behavioral Sciences*. Amsterdam: Elsevier, 1162–5.

Levine, H. (2010). 'Claiming Indigenous Rights to Culture, Flora and Fauna: A Contemporary Case from New Zealand', *PoLAR: Political and Legal Anthropology Review*, 33/1: 36–56.

Lindstrom, L. (1984). 'Doctor, Lawyer, Wise Man, Priest: Big-Men and Knowledge in Melanesia', *Man* (ns), 19/2: 291–309.

Lindstrom, L. (1996). 'Big Man', in A. Barnard and J. Spencer (eds), *Encyclopedia of Social and cultural Anthropology*. London and New York: Routledge, 65–6.

McLeod, J. (1999). 'The Sociodrama of Presidential Politics: Rhetoric, Ritual, and Power in the Era of Teledemocracy', *American Anthropologist*, 101/2: 359–73.

Parkin, D. (1984). 'Political Language', *Annual Review of Anthropology*, 13: 345–65.

Oxford Dictionary of English (2010), Oxford and New York: Oxford University Press.

Rancière, J. (1998). *Disagreement: Politics and Philosophy*. Minneapolis, MN: University of Minnesota Press.

Rata, E. (2011). 'Discursive Strategies of the Maori Tribal Elite', *Critique of Anthropology*, 31: 359–80.

Renshon, S. A. (2000). 'Political Leadership as Social Capital: Governing in a Divided National Culture', *Political Psychology*, 21/1: 199–226.

Rose, N. (1999). *Powers of Freedom: Reframing Political Thought*. Cambridge: Cambridge University Press.

Rost, J. (1991). *Leadership for the Twenty-First Century*. New York: Praeger.

Sahlins, M. (1963). 'Poor Man, Rich Man, Big-Man, Chief: Political Types in Melanesia and Polynesia', *Comparative Studies in Society and History*, 5/3: 285–303.

Schneider, J., and Schneider, P. (2003). *Reversible Destiny: Mafia, Antimafia, and the Struggle in Palermo*. Berkeley and Los Angeles: University of California Press.

Shore, C. (2000). *Building Europe: The Cultural Politics of European Integration*. London: Routledge.

Shore, C. (2011). ' "Governance" or "Governmentality?" The European Commission and the Future of Democratic Government', *European Law Journal*, 17/3: 287–302.

Shore C., and Wright, S. (1997) (eds). *Anthropology of Policy: Critical Perspectives on Governance and Power*. New York: Routledge.

Shore C., and Wright, S. (1999). 'Audit Culture and Anthropology: Neo-Liberalism in British Higher Education', *Journal of the Royal Anthropological Institute*, 5/4: 557–75.

Shore C., Wright S., and Però D. (2011) (eds). *Policy Worlds: Anthropology and Analysis of Contemporary Power*. New York: Berghahn Books.

Silverman, S. (1965). 'Patronage and Community–Nation relationships in Central Italy', *Ethnology*, 4/2: 172–89.

Steinmetz, G. (1999) (ed.). *State/Culture: State-Formation after the Cultural Turn*. Ithaca, NY: Cornell University Press.

Trnka, S. (2011). 'Re-Mythologizing the State: Public Security, "the Jesus Strategy" and the Fiji Police', *Oceania*, 81: 72–87.

Udogu, E. (2008). 'The Issue of Political Leadership in the Third World: What Is to Be Done?', *Journal of Third World Studies*, 25/1 Spring), 13–24.

Verdery, K. (1999). *The Political Lives of Dead Bodies: Reburial and Postsocialist Change*. New York: Columbia University Press.

Vincent, J. (1978). 'Political Anthropology: Manipulative Strategies', *Annual Review of Anthropology*, 7: 175–94.

Waterbury, J., and Gellner, E. (1977) (eds). *Patrons and Clients in Mediterranean Societies*. London: Duckworth.

Wedel, J., Shore, C., Feldman, G., and Lathrop, S. (2005). 'Towards an Anthropology of Public Policy', *Annals of the American Academy of Political and Social Sciences*, 600 (July), 30–51.

Wedel, J. (2009). *Shadow Elite: How the World's New Power Brokers Undermine Democracy, Government, and the Free Market*. New York: Perseus Books.

White, G., and Lindstrom, L. (1997) (eds). *Chiefs Today: Traditional Pacific Leadership and the Postcolonial State*. Stanford, CA: Stanford University Press.

PART II

STUDYING POLITICAL LEADERSHIP: ANALYTICAL AND METHODOLOGICAL PERSPECTIVES

CHAPTER 13

INSTITUTIONAL ANALYSIS

LUDGER HELMS

1 INTRODUCTION

To some extent, institutional analysis of political leadership is somewhat of a contradiction in itself. Indeed, even the most abstract institutionalist conceptions of leadership accept that leadership is a behavioural concept, and that leadership is exercised by people, individuals, or groups of individuals, rather than by the institutions themselves. Thus, many institutionalist perspectives in political leadership research could be said to focus more on the institutional context in which leaders operate and less on the phenomenon of leadership itself (Hargrove 1989: 80). Obviously, the belief behind such endeavours is that institutions shape the behaviour of individual and collective actors, and that a reasonable knowledge of the institutions provides a fair share of information about what forms of leadership are likely to develop and prevail within a given institutional setting. As Robert Elgie notes, 'institutionalists identify similarities and differences in the general patterns of political leadership across countries' (Elgie 2012: 274), or, as should be added, across other political systems at the sub- or transnational level.

However, this is not the only way to look at institutions in leadership research. Alternatively, institutions may be studied as dependent variables. In this latter case, leadership is defined in terms of the willingness and ability of individuals to shape and change their institutional and organizational environments, or to create new institutions. Such a perspective was prominently developed by Philip Selznick in his classic essay *Leadership in Administration*, where 'institutional leadership' is understood to be mainly about the promotion and the protection of values within and for the benefit of a particular institution or organization (Selznick 1957: 28, 62–3). About two decades later James MacGregor Burns hailed 'the creation of an institution…that continues to exert moral leadership and foster needed social change long after the creative leaders are gone' as 'the most tangible act of leadership' (Burns 1978: 454). Such assessments do, of course, raise the perennial question as to how to define institutions, which for Burns do not only include, for example, political parties or bureaucracies but also social movements and nations

(Burns 1978: 454). When institutions are conceptualized to include even public policies, as has been suggested more recently by Paul Pierson (2004: 165), this second direction of research on leadership and institutions, which treats institutions as dependent variables, encompasses the whole area of public policy-making and policy leadership.

The brief overview of institutional leadership analysis offered in this chapter will mainly focus on the first set of approaches that centres on institutions as a key independent variable shaping the performance of political leaders. Also, the main focus will be on executive leadership and political 'chief executives' (that is, presidents and prime ministers), although several other areas of leadership will also be addressed briefly. Even this somewhat constrained remit offers ample room for highlighting the rather different understandings of institutions, and the evolutionary dynamics of institutional leadership analysis that have sprung from it.

2 THE HISTORICAL CONTEXT AND EVOLUTIONARY PATTERNS OF INSTITUTIONAL LEADERSHIP ANALYSIS

The overall direction of the evolutionary dynamics in political leadership research has been characterized as a turn 'from institutions to behaviour back to institutions' (Rockman 2008: 320). This formula captures the basic developments fairly well but leaves in particular the major differences between traditional and more recently devised institutionalist approaches, commonly referred to as old and new institutionalism, to be sorted out.

Generally, old institutionalism, which dominated the early chapters of political science as an academic discipline in most of continental Europe and even played a role in the United States, with its less state-centred tradition, focused on the formal institutions of government. It included both a legalistic and a strong normative element, and tended to develop holistic perspectives on whole polities rather than particular aspects or sectors. Where the holders of formal leadership offices were studied, their power was often defined largely in terms of their respective powers of office.

However, a careful rereading of some of the contributions that have been identified by many as primary examples of 'old institutionalism' suggests that matters are easily oversimplified. Take, for example, Woodrow Wilson's *Congressional Government*, originally published in 1885. The focus of this study is on analysing the relationship between the president and Congress, and their respective leadership capacities, in the light of the Constitution. Yet Wilson is in no doubt that 'institutions constantly undergo essential alterations of character, whilst retaining the names conferred upon them in their first estate' and that 'the leading inquiry in the examination of any system of government must, of course, concern primarily the real depositaries and the essential machinery of power' (Wilson 2006: 28, 30). Indeed, the study not only offers a substantive analysis of the leadership capacities of presidents and legislatures under the living constitution; it culminates in a passionate plea for establishing a new system of responsible parliamentary and prime ministerial government. All this is duly reflected in the perception of this study by several other early scholars of the presidency whose work has been considered to represent a classic example of 'old institutionalism' as well. Edward S. Corwin, author of *The President*, first published in 1940, refers to Wilson's work as a 'pioneer attempt to give a *nonlegalistic*, factual description of the reciprocal roles of Congress and the President' (Corwin 1957: 26; emphasis added), and it is this tradition in which Corwin seeks to place his own analysis.

While the holders of high political office kept a prominent position on the agenda of many behaviouralist leadership studies, which came to challenge old institutionalism in the middle of the twentieth century, its proponents argued that it was the personal resources and strategic capacities of individual office-holders that really mattered, and mattered more than any institutional resources. However, even in Richard Neustadt's *Presidential Power*, published in 1960, which came to represent to many one of the primary examples of behaviourialist studies on the American presidency, the relevance of institutions is by no means denied. Indeed, it was Neustadt who coined one of the most-cited phrases on the inherent logic of the American separation-of-powers system, which he described as a 'government of separated institutions *sharing* power' (Neustadt 1990: 29; emphasis in original). In his work, institutional aspects also matter more explicitly in terms of presidential leadership. 'Presidential power is the power to persuade,' as Neustadt famously contended, and, 'the power to persuade is the power to bargain'; however, he did not fail to acknowledge that 'status and authority yield bargaining advantages' (Neustadt 1990: 11, 32).

What is now commonly being referred to as 'new institutionalism' in institutional theory emerged in the mid-1980s. Pressed to name one particular study that launched the new paradigm in political science, most scholars would arguably opt for *Rediscovering Institutions* by James G. March and Johan P. Olsen (1989), a book-length study that was foreshadowed by a major journal article, published in the *American Political Science Review* five years earlier (March and Olsen 1984). In making their case of 'new institutionalism', the authors had to rely on what comes close to a caricature of earlier approaches in political science. Yet, as Adcock, Bevir, and Stimson rightly contend, 'without this caricature, the appearance of commonalities, as well as the supposed novelty of some of this scholarship, dissipates, leaving no grand paradigm shift to promote' (Adcock, Bevir, and Stimson 2007: 273).

In contemporary international political science, 'new institutionalism' stands for an exceptionally broad and heterogeneous body of conceptions of institutions that is considered to comprise at least three fundamentally different directions of institutional theory and research: rational-choice institutionalism, historical institutionalism, and sociological institutionalism (Hall and Taylor 1996). While some scholars have distinguished a significantly larger number of different 'new institutionalisms' (see Peters 2012), it is still possible to identify some shared features of the different approaches gathering under the general label.

The shared basic features of different new institutionalisms that separate them from older institutionalism have been considered to include: a considerably broader notion of institutions that reaches beyond legalistic conceptions of purely formal institutions, a dismissal of deterministic assumptions about the role of institutions, a greater interest in studying particular aspects of institutional arrangements rather than whole polities, and a strong commitment to combining institutional research with sophisticated theories and methods. Indeed, for many neo-institutionalists, the glaring 'lack of theory' would appear to mark the most characteristic feature of 'old institutionalism' to be overcome. However, it would be misleading to argue that old institutionalists simply do not care for theory. As R. A. W. Rhodes has argued, 'from a constructivist standpoint, the absence of the conventional battery of social science theories is…not a problem because…proponents [of old institutionalism]…emphasize the meanings of rules for actors seeking the explanations of their practices in the reasons they give' (Rhodes 2006: 103).

A more specific shared feature of the three traditionally recognized new institutionalisms (rational choice, historical, and sociological) is that they tend to consider institutions primarily as constraints to actors. A closer look at how these constraints are conceived of brings into focus some of the fundamental differences between rational-choice, historical, and sociological institutionalism. From the perspective of rational-choice institutionalism, institutions, understood in terms of structures and incentives, effectively constrain the behaviour of rational actors by establishing a 'logic of calculation'. Historical institutionalism, which conceives of institutions as regularized patterns and routinized practices, emphasizes the 'path dependence' of institutional evolutions and developments. Finally, by contrast, sociological institutionalism, which thinks of institutions as socially constituted and culturally framed rules and norms, sees social agents acting within political institutions effectively constrained by a 'logic of appropriateness' (see Schmidt 2010: 2).

Overall, there seems to be a growing consensus in recent leadership research that 'understanding the office and the strategic situation is perhaps more important than the occupant of the office at a particular moment' (Ahlquist and Levi 2011: 7). As in other areas of political science, the 'institutional turn' in the study of political leadership has been facilitated by the pluralism of institutional approaches. Frustrating any attempts at a strictly chronological systematization, including claims of an orderly replacement of old institutionalism by new institutionalism, both sets of approaches continue to play a role in contemporary political leadership research. Older notions of institutions and forms of institutional analysis of political leadership have remained prominent, especially in parts of continental European political science, and some eminent scholars even make the case for an *increasing* relevance of old institutionalism that is earned by its 'focus on texts *and* custom and its commitment to historical and philosophical analysis' (Rhodes 2006: 104; emphasis in original).

While reconstructing the evolutionary dynamics of different approaches and schools in political science is useful and necessary in order to secure the conditions for systematically advancing our knowledge, many leadership scholars evince a limited willingness to engage in discussing theoretical issues. As much as Richard Neustadt was once surprised to learn that his book was hailed by many for bringing the behaviouralist revolution to the study of the presidency, even though he had not consciously sought to make any particular theoretical contribution (Jones 2003: 10), many contemporary leadership scholars using institutional approaches to studying political leadership would appear happy to leave the meta-theoretical categorization and critique of their work to others.

3 Key Ideas, Concepts, and Findings

One of the key ideas in contemporary leadership research applying institutionalist approaches is that the formal institutional features of the governmental system have a decisive influence on the nature of leadership in various areas. 'Individuals play institutional roles' (Hargrove 2001: 68), and thus the performance of leaders may best be understood in terms of 'structured agency' (Jacobs and King 2010: 794). The effects of the major formal institutions have been considered to be tangible in particular at the level of executive and legislative leadership.

The most basic, and single most important, institutional distinction at regime level remains that between parliamentary and presidential government (see Lijphart 1992). Among the numerous distinguishing criteria that have been put forward, the existence or absence of parliamentary responsibility of the prime minister and the cabinet has been widely accepted as the key discriminating factor for distinguishing parliamentary and presidential democracies or, in the terminology of most American scholars, fusion-of-powers and separation-of-powers systems.

A recent comparative study drawing on this distinction is that by Ludger Helms (2005), which analyses the leadership performance of American presidents, British prime ministers, and German chancellors since 1945. This study can be considered exemplary for many recent contributions that seek to combine different strains of institutionalist theory and analysis. Whereas the organization of the case selection on the basis of the constitutional architecture of different regimes places this work in a tradition of 'old institutionalism', it incorporates many elements of new institutionalist thinking, such as and in particular the ideas of rational-choice-inspired 'actor-centred institutionalism', which distinguishes between institutions (understood as formal rules and social norms that create both constraints and options without determining choices and outcomes) and actors (Scharpf 1997). The study also acknowledges that leaders are not determined by the institutional context in which they operate and that they may actively shape their institutional environment, even though there are strong path dependencies, as historical institutional analysis suggests. Individual political leaders may produce specific institutional legacies that effectively constrain the choices of their successors and that are not normally confined to issues of how to organize the office but may include particular public expectations of the office and its holders.

Many findings of this study provide support for, and refine, earlier assessments of comparative leadership analysis that point to the huge difference between the conditions and manifestations of executive leadership under presidentialism and parliamentarianism (see, e.g., Rose 1980, 2005; Rockman 2003). Parliamentary and presidential government do not only create very different patterns of political responsibility and accountability, which tend to be marked by both more collectivity and more collegiality in parliamentary regimes with their established structures and cultures of cabinet and party government; they also set very different time cycles for executive leaders: whereas, at the time a bill enters parliament, much of the job of a prime minister in a parliamentary democracy is done, the launching of a bill in presidential systems usually marks just the beginning of the president's efforts to leave his mark on a measure. Even where there is some convergence between presidential and prime ministerial leadership in both types of regime, such as, in particular, at the level of public leadership, the overall institutional conditions for political leadership under presidential and prime ministerial government remain fundamentally different, letting many claims of a 'presidentialization' of politics and leadership in different institutional contexts appear somewhat ill-conceived (Peters and Helms 2012: 29–30).

Arguably the single most important development in theorizing the patterns of horizontal separation of powers in liberal democracies (and beyond) concerns the 'discovery' of semi-presidential systems (see also Elgie, Chapter 31, this volume). Semi-presidential systems combine the institutional features of parliamentary responsibility of the prime minister and the cabinet, and a directly elected presidential head of state. A more specific distinction within the family of semi-presidential systems has been that between president–parliamentary and premier–presidential systems: in president–parliamentary systems the prime minister and the cabinet are responsible to both the legislature and the president, and the president has the power to dissolve parliament or possesses legislative powers; in premier–presidential systems the prime minister and cabinet are responsible solely to the legislature and the president's powers are more circumscribed.

While such distinctions have been developed and used primarily in democratization research with a focus on regime stability and democratic performance (see, e.g., Shugart and Carey 1992; Samuels and Shugart 2010; Elgie 2011a; Elgie, Moestrup, and Wu 2011), semi-presidential systems do also have a particular institutional leadership profile. This is bound to change, however, with the prevailing pattern of power distribution between the presidency and parliament. Whereas during phases of divided government (or *cohabitation*, as the French call it) presidents tend to be only modestly more powerful than their counterparts in parliamentary democracies, presidential power during phases of broad political majorities encompassing the presidency, the government, and parliament can be tremendous. Somewhat paradoxically, under certain circumstances—if prime ministers are willing to perform an institutionalized role of political scapegoats, as has been typical for most of the political history of the French Fifth Republic—the existence of a dual executive including a president and a prime minister may enhance the power of the former, making him or her considerably more powerful than presidents in presidential democracies.

The distinction of various forms of semi-presidentialism has proven particularly fruitful in assessing patterns of executive leadership in old and new democracies. Whereas most of the older democracies are parliamentary democracies, many of the younger democracies have adopted semi-presidential constitutions (and a majority of them operate premier–presidential systems). The redistribution of regime types means that, generally, political leadership is less parliamentarized in new democracies than in old democracies, and heads of state in new democracies have greater powers than their counterparts in old democracies. The combination of constitutional architectures with other structural features of political systems, such as and in particular the structure of the party system, have made prime ministers in new democracies less secure in office and less powerful than many of their counterparts in older democracies (Elgie 2012).

Comparisons across time and space suggest, however, that institutional features beyond the basic distinction between parliamentary, presidential, and semi-presidential government—such as the territorial dimension of different polities, or the institutional strength of judicial review—may be of similar, or even greater, relevance to what presidents and prime ministers can and cannot do. Indeed, in terms of coalition-building and political communication, institutionally complex parliamentary democracies seem to have more in common with compound presidential democracies than with institutionally simple Westminster-type parliamentary democracies (Rockman 1997, 2003; Helms 2005).

Some recent approaches to studying the institutional complexity of political regimes and the nature of political decision-making therein go well beyond such simplifying distinctions as between majoritarian and consensus democracies (Lijphart 1984, 2012) or simple and compound polities (Schmidt 2005). The most radical attempt at overcoming the classical differentiation between parliamentary and presidential government has been the veto players theorem by George Tsebelis (2002). The key dependent variable in Tsebelis's work is not exactly leadership but the policy status quo, or, more specifically, a regime's capacity for policy change. Veto players are conceptualized as individual or collective actors whose agreement is required for a change in policy. For Tsebelis, the chances for the policy status quo to be altered depend, however, not exclusively on the number of veto players (which include institutional veto players such as second chambers as well as partisan veto players such as a coalition party), but also on their internal cohesion, and their position within a given configuration (that is, the degree of incongruence between different veto players). The theoretical value and analytical potential of the veto-players theorem for comparative political research, including executive leadership studies (O'Malley 2010), is very substantive indeed. However, the *ceteris paribus* assumption underlying Tsebelis's model is quite sizeable. Veto players are conceptualized as strictly rational actors who use their veto power whenever they can, unless their veto power is effectively being absorbed by a strong congruence between different players. Further, only those actors are considered veto players who possess formal veto power, which excludes many powerful actors, such as interest groups or the mass media. Also systematically excluded are all those irrational elements that form part of the leadership process in political reality.

As in executive leadership research, there is a strong consensus among scholars of *legislative leadership* as to which institutional aspects are of particular relevance in shaping the performance of legislative leaders. As many executive scholars start with looking at the constitutional powers of chief executives to hire and fire personnel, their institutional capacities to organize the executive branch, or the administrative support available to them, scholars studying legislative leadership from an institutional perspective usually pay particular attention to the institutional opportunity structure of individual MPs, the formal and informal rules for legislative agenda-setting, the institutional features of the committee system, and the written and unwritten rules for establishing and upholding party discipline (Döring 1995; Döring and Hallerberg 2004).

Again, the conditions and manifestations of legislative leadership differ starkly in particular between parliamentary and presidential regimes (Norton 2012). Despite the more recent development towards strong polarization and coherence of congressional parties, party discipline in the USA has remained moderate by West European standards. Members of Congress continue to see themselves primarily as representing their constituencies, and the obvious limits to party government are much to do with the basic formal institutional arrangements of the presidential system, which make strong party discipline dispensable in terms of government stability. This creates fundamentally different conditions for legislative leadership—be it by members or groups from the legislative assembly themselves, or by executive leaders acting in the legislative arena.

More specifically, executive–legislative relations in both types of regime generate patterns notably different. Even during periods of unified government, there is no equivalent in presidential systems of stable majority governments in parliamentary democracies. Under split party government, which prevailed for more than two-thirds of the post-war period, congressional majority leaders have the potential to become serious competitors of the president in the fight for public attention and as public agenda-setters, which is largely inconceivable in parliamentary democracies. At the same time, American constitutional practice suggests that—some spectacular examples, such as that of Newt Gingrich in the 1990s, notwithstanding—any attempt at challenging the structurally superior position of the president from Capitol Hill cannot be sustained successfully for very long, which has precluded a deeper institutionalization of this role (Helms 2005: 250).

Even though in most parliamentary democracies the room for manoeuvre for independent legislative leadership by parliaments or parliamentary actors is effectively circumscribed by the institutionalized pre-eminence of the executive, the idea of parliament-bound actors providing genuine leadership is an old one that dates back to the writings of Walter Bagehot (1826–77) and has more recently been rediscovered by scholars of political representation. Rather than just representing the interests and preferences of the voters, the parties represented in parliament actively seek to garner electoral support for their respective manifestos and thereby exercise leadership—a phenomenon that has been labelled 'representation from above' (Esaiasson and Holmberg 1996).

A more specific form of legislative leadership in parliamentary regimes is *oppositional leadership* within the legislative arena. Oppositional leadership by an official 'opposition leader', as to be found in the UK and other Westminster systems (Heppell 2012), marks, no doubt, the most famous type of opposition leadership. There are many others, though, that may involve 'legislative and policy leadership from non-government legislators who have no formal status as "Opposition Leaders"' (Uhr 2009: 61). Even within the family of Westminster democracies with their traditionally strong emphasis on a clear-cut binary divide between government and opposition, institutional and political variations are reflected in significantly different patterns of parliamentary oppositional leadership (Kaiser 2009). There are at least two other fundamentally different forms of parliamentary oppositional leadership that can be distinguished: opposition leadership by the leader of a political party that operates as junior partner in either a formal or an informal coalition, and by the leader of an opposition party who stays outside the government but seeks to extract legislative concessions from the government in exchange for parliamentary support (Uhr 2009: 62).

Party leadership is another subject that has been studied from an institutional perspective (see Costa Lobo, Chapter 24, this volume). It is widely acknowledged that institutional configurations (in terms of rules) at both the micro- and the macro-level can have a major impact on party organizations and party leadership. In the early history of political parties the gradual extension of mass suffrage transformed elite parties into mass parties with a complex party organization and mass party membership. Later generic transformations of party organizations, from mass parties into catch-all parties and cartel parties (Katz and Mair 1995), were less obviously shaped by developments at the regime level of institutions. There is, however, a certain impact of the basic type of electoral system, PR or plurality, on the dominant forms of party organizations in different regimes. Plurality electoral systems tend to favour the emergence of fewer and larger parties, though PR does by no means preclude the emergence and persistence of truly major party organizations. Even more direct and far-reaching effects of a system's constitutional framework on the internal balance of power within political parties can be observed in territorially complex regimes. Parties at the national level of federal systems tend to have complex power-sharing organizations designed to accommodate the interests of the different regions and single-member states that they represent, and that require more integrative forms of party leadership.

In line with the presidentialization thesis in party leadership research, several recent studies suggest, though, that there are certain developmental dynamics in terms of party leadership, and in particular with regard to the dominance of party leaders, that cut across institutionally different regimes. As Paul Webb, Thomas Poguntke, and Robin Kolodny have concluded, 'the direction of travel in favour of (even) greater leadership autonomy has been broadly similar in many major parties within all types of institutional regime' (Webb, Poguntke and Kolodny 2012: 89). In many countries, the structurally enhanced autonomy of party leaders from party bodies and party activists has been accompanied by a more direct linkage between the party leaders and the electorate.

There is an impressive body of institutional analysis in recent research on social movements (Schneiberg and Lounsbury 2008) but at the same time a notable scarcity of institutionalist research on *leadership of and within social movements*. This is true in particular of the role of institutions in terms of rules for leadership *within* social movements, which can to some extent be explained by the exceptionally volatile character, and the relatively moderate degree of institutionalization, of many movements (Ganz 2010; Rucht 2012). Again, however, the relevance of institutions in a given sub-field of leadership studies depends largely on how they are conceptualized. Important insights into the nature of leadership in social movements are to be expected from more recently devised approaches of new institutionalism, such as discursive institutionalism, which conceptualizes institutions as ideas. 'Actors can gain power from their ideas', as Vivian Schmidt argues,

> even where they may lack the power of position—as in the case of social movements...Power itself, moreover, derives not only from position, meaning actors' ability to wield power, but also purpose, since actors' ideas and discourse about how they can and should yield that power (i.e., not just in their own strategic interest but in the general interest) may reinforce or undermine the power they derive from their position, depending upon the responses of their audience to their stated purposes. This is the essence of political leadership.
>
> (Schmidt 2010: 18)

4 FUTURE AGENDAS AND PRACTICAL RELEVANCE

In addition to the approaches presented in the sections above, several other forms of institutional analysis have been introduced more recently that are waiting to be used more broadly in the field of leadership studies, and may well shape the future of institutional leadership analysis. This is true, in particular, for anthropologic and ethnographic approaches to studying institutions, which form part of the larger family of interpretative approaches (see also Grint, Chapter 16, and Gains Chapter 19, this volume). As the advocates of interpretative institutional analysis argue, institutions cannot be understood without taking into account the beliefs and constructions of actors in an institution. Challenging popular notions of institutions as rules with objective features, interpretative approaches focus on 'what institutions mean to the people who work in them', and more specifically on 'how beliefs and actions are created, recreated, and changed in ways that constantly reproduce and modify institutions' (Rhodes 2011: 3). Conceptually, interpretative institutional analysis seeks to 'decentre institutions'—that is, 'to focus on the social construction of a practice through the ability of individuals to create, and act on, meaning' (Rhodes 2011: 299).

Applying interpretative approaches to empirical research requires the use of appropriate methods, which include in particular close-up observation of actors in leadership processes (Rhodes, 't Hart, and Noordegraaf 2007)—a methodological tool that has been conspicuous for its absence in mainstream leadership research, if perhaps not only for conceptual qualms but also for the exceptional problems in getting access to the relevant actors.

Other facets of future institution-centred leadership research relate to the choice of subjects rather than any particular theoretical or methodological approaches. One such aspect concerns the role of informal institutions (Helmke and Levitsky 2004), whose major relevance has been readily acknowledged by many leadership scholars but whose exact effects on leaders and followers remain largely to be discovered and explained, especially from a comparative perspective. On a more general level, there is a strong bias in contemporary institutional leadership analysis towards focusing on the established liberal democracies, which is backed by prominent notions of leadership that explicitly exclude mere power-wielding by authoritarian leaders. Much research on leaders and leadership in non-democratic regimes, for its part, tends to focus on the personal traits of leaders at the expense of institutional analysis. This notwithstanding, it is precisely recent research on political leadership in authoritarian regimes that offers some of the most impressive examples of how institutional and non-institutional factors can be combined into fruitful concepts and empirical analysis of leadership (see, e.g., Svolik 2009; Ezrow and Frantz 2011). More of this kind of research is needed in order to overcome the unsatisfactory regime-related bias in the study of political leadership.

In theoretical and methodological terms, future agendas of institutionalist leadership research are likely to remain exceptionally rich, complex, and difficult to reconstruct. Any attempt by over-zealous reviewers at bringing order to the field faces the danger of producing untenable oversimplifications. Even well-established assessments, such as that continental European political science is the natural heartland of old institutionalism, and is inherently more averse to adopting conceptual innovations, require some qualification. For example, the core executive concept, put forward by British scholars committed to overcoming the dominance of structural approaches in executive leadership research (Dunleavy and Rhodes 1990), has been eagerly adopted by many leadership scholars in continental Europe, but has conspicuously failed to travel to the USA (Elgie 2011b: 64).

The exceptional complexity that marks the theoretical and conceptual debate about the nature of institutions is at times criticized even by scholars firmly affiliated with the institutionalist paradigm, as it dramatically increases the transaction costs even between closely related areas of research. However, there is no denying that the seemingly chaotic pluralism of theories and conceptions of institutions, and of institutional analysis, has produced a unique richness of complementary insights and findings—a genuinely collaborative achievement whose future prosperity would be endangered by any successful attempt at establishing increased conceptual conformity in institutional analysis. Therefore, notwithstanding the considerable costs of dealing with complexity, any more streamlined agendas of institutional analysis, in leadership studies and beyond, cannot really be wished for.

What, eventually, can be said about the practical relevance of institutional analysis of political leadership? Again, much depends on how institutions are understood. If institutions are conceptualized as rules and structures, institutional leadership analysis does have a strong practical value, if only because 'institutions are...the manipulable feature in a sea of largely nonmanipulable ones' (Rockman 1997: 64). Even though constitutional engineering is bound to fall short of its own ambitions, institutional leadership analysis provides constitution-makers with important insights as they seek to anticipate the possible effects of constitutional rules and institutional arrangements on political leadership in nascent regimes.

Political leaders themselves may feel to have less to learn from institutional leadership analysis than students and scholars of political leadership. Compared to studies that focus on leadership skills, tactics, and strategies, many subjects and issues of institutionalist leadership analysis may appear rather abstract and, perhaps, far-fetched. However, as there can be no successful leadership strategy without considering the particular context, including its institutional features, the practical relevance of institutionalist perspectives on, and insights into, the opportunities and constraints of leaders operating in different contexts is too obvious to be seriously disputed. Thus, it is no wonder that even leadership studies with an explicit practical focus, such as Carnes Lord's *The Modern Prince: What Leaders Need to Know Now* (2003), carefully take into account the particular institutional circumstances. If institutional analysis is understood and exercised in Selznick's terms— that is, analysing how leaders manage to build special values and a distinctive competence into an organization (Selznick 1957: 27)—leaders, and those being affected by their actions, would appear to have even more to gain from institutional leadership analysis.

Recommended Reading

Helms, L. (2005). *Presidents, Prime Ministers and Chancellors: Executive Leadership in Western Democracies*. London: Palgrave Macmillan.

Helms, L. (2012) (ed.). *Comparative Political Leadership*. London: Palgrave Macmillan.

Peters, B. G. (2012). *Institutional Theory in Political Science: The New Institutionalism*. 3rd edn. London: Continuum.

References

Adcock, R., Bevir, M., and Stimson, S. C. (2007). 'Historicizing the New Institutionalism(s)', in R. Adcock, M. Bevir, and S. C. Stimson (eds), *Modern Political Science: Anglo-American Exchanges since 1880*. Princeton: Princeton University Press, 259–89.

Ahlquist, J. S., and Levi, M. (2011). 'Leadership: What it Means, What it Does, and What We Want to Know about it', *Annual Review of Political Science*, 14: 1–24.

Burns, J. M. (1978). *Leadership*. New York: Harper and Row.

Corwin, E. S. (1957). *The President: Office and Powers 1787–1957*. 4th edn. New York: New York University Press.

Döring, H. (1995). *Parliaments and Majority-Rule in Western Europe*. Frankfurt and New York: Campus.

Döring, H., and Hallerberg, M. (2004) (eds). *Patterns of Parliamentary Behaviour*. Aldershot: Ashgate.

Dunleavy, P., and Rhodes, R. A. W. (1990). 'Core Executive Studies in Britain', *Public Administration*, 68: 3–28.

Elgie, R. (2011a). *Semi-Presidentialism: Sub-Types and Democratic Performance*. Oxford: Oxford University Press.

Elgie, R. (2011b). 'Core Executive Studies Two Decades on', *Public Administration*, 89: 64–77.

Elgie, R. (2012). 'Political Leadership in Old and New Democracies', in L. Helms (ed.), *Comparative Political Leadership*. London: Palgrave Macmillan, 272–91.

Elgie, R., Moestrup, S., and Wu, Y. (2011) (eds). *Semi-Presidentialism and Democracy*. London: Palgrave Macmillan.

Esaiasson, P., and Holmberg, S. (1996). *Representation from Above: Members of Parliament and Representative Democracy in Sweden*. Aldershot: Dartmouth.

Ezrow, N. M., and Frantz, E. (2011). *Dictators and Dictatorships: Understanding Authoritarian Regimes and their Leaders*. New York: Continuum.

Ganz, M. (2010). 'Leading Change: Leadership, Organization and Social Movements', in N. Nohria and R. Khurana (eds), *The Handbook of Leadership Theory and Practice*. Boston: Harvard Business School Press, 527–68.

Hall, P., and Taylor, R. C. R. (1996). 'Political Science and the three New Institutionalisms', *Political Studies*, 44: 936–57.

Hargrove, E. C. (1989). 'Two Conceptions of Institutional Leadership', in B. D. Jones (ed.), *Leadership and Politics*. Lawrence, KA: University Press of Kansas, 57–83.

Hargrove, E. C. (2001). 'The Presidency and the Premiership as Institutions: An American Perspective', *British Journal of Politics and International Relations*, 3: 49–70.

Helmke, G., and Levitsky, S. (2004). 'Informal Institutions and Comparative Politics: A Research Agenda', *Perspectives on Politics*, 2: 725–39.

Helms, L. (2005). *Presidents, Prime Ministers and Chancellors: Executive Leadership in Western Democracies*. London: Palgrave Macmillan.

Helms, L. (2012) (ed.). *Comparative Political Leadership*. London: Palgrave Macmillan.

Heppell, T. (2012) (ed.). *Leaders of the Opposition: From Churchill to Cameron*. London: Palgrave Macmillan.

Jacobs, L. R., and King, D. (2010). 'Varieties of Obamaism: Structure, Agency, and the Obama Presidency', *Perspectives on Politics*, 8: 793–802.

Jones, C. O. (2003). 'Richard S. Neustadt: Public Servant as Scholar', *Annual Review of Political Science*, 6: 1–22.

Kaiser, A. (2009). 'Parliamentary Opposition in Westminster Democracies: Britain, Canada, Australia and New Zealand', in L. Helms (ed.), *Parliamentary Opposition in Old and New Democracies*. London and New York: Routledge, 1–26.

Katz, R. S., and Mair, P. (1995). 'Changing Models of Party Organization and Party Democracy: The Emergence of the Cartel Party', *Party Politics*, 1: 5–28.

Lijphart, A. (1984). *Democracies: Patterns of Majoritarian and Consensus Government in Twenty-One Countries*. New Haven and London: Yale University Press.

Lijphart, A. (1992). *Parliamentary versus Presidential Government*. Oxford: Oxford University Press.

Lijphart, A. (2012). *Patterns of Democracy: Government Forms and Performance in Thirty-Six Countries*. 2nd edn. New Haven and London: Yale University Press.

Lord, C. (2003). *The Modern Prince: What Leaders Need to Know Now*. New Haven: Yale University Press.

March, J. G., and Olsen, J. P. (1984). 'The New Institutionalism: Organizational Factors in Political Life', *American Political Science Review*, 78: 734–49.

March, J. G., and Olsen, J. P. (1989). *Rediscovering Institutions: The Organizational Basis of Politics*. New York: Free Press.

Neustadt, R. (1990). *Presidential Power and the Modern Presidents: The Politics of Leadership from Roosevelt to Reagan*. New York: Free Press.

Norton, P. (2012). 'Comparing Leadership Patterns and Dynamics in the Legislative Arena', in L. Helms (ed.), *Comparative Political Leadership*, London: Palgrave Macmillan 56–76.

O'Malley, E. (2010). 'Veto Players, Party Government and Policy-Making Power', *Comparative European Politics*, 8: 202–19.

Peters, B. G. (2012). *Institutional Theory in Political Science: The New Institutionalism*. 3rd edn. London: Continuum.

Peters, B. G., and Helms, L. (2012). 'Executive Leadership in Comparative Perspective: Politicians, Bureaucrats and Public Governance', in L. Helms (ed.), *Comparative Political Leadership*. London: Palgrave Macmillan, 25–55.

Pierson, P. (2004). *Politics in Time: History, Institutions and Social Analysis*. Princeton: Princeton University Press.

Rhodes, R. A. W. (2006). 'Old Institutionalisms', in R. A. W. Rhodes, S. A. Binder and Bert A. Rockman (eds), *The Oxford Handbook of Political Institutions*. Oxford: Oxford University Press, 90–108.

Rhodes, R. A. W., 't Hart, P., and Noordegraaf, M. (2007) (eds). *Observing Government Elites: Up Close and Personal*. London: Palgrave Macmillan.

Rhodes, R. A. W. (2011). *Everyday Life in British Government*. Oxford: Oxford University Press.

Rockman, B. A. (1997). 'The Performance of Presidents and Prime Ministers and of Presidential and Parliamentary Systems', in K. von Mettenheim (ed.), *Presidential Institutions and Democratic Politics*. Baltimore, MD, and London: Johns Hopkins University Press, 45–64.

Rockman, B. A. (2003). 'The American Presidency in Comparative Perspective: Systems, Situations, and Leaders', in M. Nelson (ed.), *The Presidency and the Political System*. 7th edn. Washington: Congressional Quarterly Press, 48–75.

Rockman, B. A. (2008). 'When it Comes to Presidential Leadership, Accentuate the Positive, but Don't Forget the Normative', in B. A. Rockman and R. W. Waterman (eds), *Presidential Leadership: The Vortex of Power*. New York: Oxford University Press, 311–29.

Rose, R. (1980). 'Governments against Sub-Governments: A European Perspective on Washington', in R. Rose and E. N. Suleiman (eds), *Presidents and Prime Ministers*. Washington: American Enterprise Institute for Public Policy Research, 284–47.

Rose, R. (2005). 'Giving Direction to Government in Comparative Perspective', in J. Aberbach and M. Peterson (eds), *The Executive Branch*. New York: Oxford University Press, 72–99.

Rucht, D. (2012). 'Leadership in Social and Political Movements: A Comparative Exploration', in L. Helms (ed.), *Comparative Political Leadership*. London: Palgrave Macmillan, 99–118.

Samuels, D. and Shugart, M. (2010). *Presidents, Parties, and Prime Ministers: A Framework for Analysis*. Cambridge: Cambridge University Press.

Scharpf, F. W. (1997). *Games Real Actors Play: Actor-Centered Institutionalism in Policy Research*. Boulder, CO: Westview.

Schmidt, V. A. (2005). 'Democracy in Europe: The Impact of European Integration', *Perspectives on Politics*, 3: 761–79.

Schmidt, V. A. (2010). 'Taking Ideas and Discourse Seriously: Explaining Change through Discursive Institutionalism as the Fourth "New Institutionalism"', *European Political Science Review*, 2: 1–25.

Schneiberg, M., and Lounsbury, M. (2008). 'Social Movements and Institutional Analysis', in R. Greenwood, C. Oliver, K. Sahlin-Andersson, and R. Suddaby (eds), *The Handbook of Organizational Institutionalism*. London: Sage, 650–72.

Selznick, P. (1957). *Leadership in Administration: A Sociological Interpretation*. Berkeley and Los Angeles: University of California Press.

Shugart, M. S., and Carey, J. M. (1992). *Presidents and Assemblies: Constitutional Design and Electoral Dynamics*. Cambridge: Cambridge University Press.

Svolik, M. (2009). 'Power-Sharing and Leadership Dynamics in Authoritarian Regimes', *American Journal of Political Science*, 53: 477–94.

Tsebelis, G. (2002). *Veto-Players: How Political Institutions Work*. Princeton: Princeton University Press.

Uhr, J. (2009). 'Parliamentary Oppositional Leadership', in J. Kane, H. Patapan, and P. 't Hart (eds), *Dispersed Democratic Leadership: Origins, Dynamics, and Implications*. Oxford: Oxford University Press, 59–81.

Webb, P., Poguntke, T., and Kolodny, R. (2012). 'The Presidentialization of Party Leadership? Evaluating Party Leadership and Party Government in the Democratic World', in L. Helms (ed.), *Comparative Political Leadership*. London: Palgrave Macmillan, 77–98.

Wilson, W. (2006). *Congressional Government: A Study in American Politics*. Mineola, NY: Dover.

CHAPTER 14

....

CONTEXTUAL ANALYSIS

....

PAUL 't HART

1 INTRODUCTION: CONTEXT MATTERS, BUT HOW?

....

READING their historical moment and their contemporary political context surely is one of the chief arts of political leaders need to master. It shapes their abilities to consummate the authority associated with these roles. When to push which ideas, wage which battles, confront or ignore which social problems: considerations of political opportunity, timing, and momentum are crucial to leadership. In political life, temporal dynamics such as the daily news cycle, the three- or four-year electoral cycle, and the more opaque and disputed recurrent 'tides' of public opinion and 'party realignment' are pivotal in shaping the considerations and behaviours of most actors. Given their importance in structuring public life, anticipating, utilizing, and perhaps even modifying the parameters of such cycles, and the 'windows of opportunity' they present, constitute important avenues for exercising leadership (Kingdon 1984).

Some leaders are arguably simply better at grasping and utilizing this importance of context than others. That is not the end of the story. Every political system has had its share of politicians who were highly successful in one leadership role and failed in another. Think of Jimmy Carter as a successful governor of Georgia, then as a struggling and ultimately largely ineffective president, and then as a widely respected post-presidential peacemaker, or of Barack Obama, the highly charismatic campaigner of 2008 and the hemmed-in president whose pragmatism disappointed his erstwhile followers and failed to placate his Republican opponents.

There are also plenty of political leaders whose effectiveness varied even within one and the same role, depending upon the issue area or moment in which they intervened. German Chancellor Helmut Kohl is a prime example of this: in autumn 1989, after seven years in the job, he seemed destined for a quiet life after two terms of domestic policy stasis; but after the collapse of the Berlin Wall in November, he displayed hitherto unsuspected international statesmanship to secure the unification of Germany while simultaneously binding it closely to the European Union and in the process prolonging his hold on the office for another two terms (Zelikow with Rice 1995).

There is an entire cohort of government leaders who had the bad luck of being in office when the second oil shock and stagflation of the late 1970s happened, and who ended up being booted out of office ignominiously None of them—whether from the Left or the Right—was quick enough on his or her feet to abandon the Keynesian paradigm of economic management they had all been socialized into accepting as the policy orthodoxy. It took their predicament of policy paralysis and deep fiscal crisis to bring to power an alternative set of leaders who were not bound to these conventions, and who ended up as event-making reformers (for example, Thatcher and Reagan, as well as Hawke and Keating in Australia, and Lange and Douglas in New Zealand).

These examples clearly suggest that context is important for leadership. They also suggest that even astute leaders are able to act in tune with their context only to some extent and only some of the time. What students of political leadership therefore need to know is *when and how* contexts shape leadership possibilities, and, conversely, when and how leaders are able to mould the contexts in which they operate. This chapter reviews scholarship that has taken the importance of context as the basic premiss of its approaches to the study of (political) leadership. I first cobble together a disparate body of research from different social science disciplines as constituting the field. I then signal some key analytical and methodological issues facing the studies of this kind. I conclude by suggesting priority areas for future research on the nexus between context and political leadership.

2 An Overview of the Field

If we go back as far as Plato's Philosopher-King and Plutarch's *Lives of the Noble Greeks and Romans*, political leaders have long been portrayed as 'heroes in history' (Hook 1943). The hero, however, has two faces: the wise, resourceful, and tenacious individual who overcomes great odds to put his stamp on history (dubbed the 'event-making' leader by Hook), but also the tragic figure facing overwhelming forces stacked against him, which at best limit him to a role as 'trend follower' and at worst condemn him to the dustbin of history ('eventful' leaders, according to Hook). The 'event-making' hero type has been the subject of centuries of biography and hagiography, a robust and lucrative—people like to read about 'heroes'—tradition that continues to this day. Its traditional preoccupation with the drives, character, skills, and deeds of the leaders in question, however, all too often seduces scholars of the genre into person-centric, reductionist accounts of complex historical processes.

Even early Greek writers were aware of this, and in their tragedies explored the opposite end of the spectrum, depicting would-be heroic leaders either prospering or perishing at the whim of the gods in the Pantheon. This emphasis on external factors—natural and metaphysical forces—prevailing over human volition was echoed in Christian historiography and political theory. In Augustine's theology, for example, the outcome of the central, history-shaping conflict between the City of Man (dominated by earthly politics) and the City of God (based on submission to the will of God) is preordained: the latter is bound to win.

Eventually, Machiavelli found a formula for folding the two opposing perspectives into one neat formula. He saw all of human life and history as determined by only two forces: *virtù* (competent statecraft, or, in today's parlance, 'good leadership') and *fortuna* (chance, or, in other words, contextual influences). If leaders lacked the will or the competence to display *virtù*, human affairs would be fully controlled by *fortuna*. Truly competent leaders should be able considerably to tame *fortuna* through effective foresight and robust pre-emptive action. He ends *The Prince* with a now notorious analogy: 'Fortune is a woman, and if she is to be submissive it is necessary to beat and coerce her' (*The Prince*, book XXV). Yet even Machiavelli conceded that even the most competent rulers could perhaps control only half of their fate and that of their subjects. So, even the most competent rulers still need a degree of 'luck' to go down in history as successful leaders. Likewise, the potential impact of malevolent and incompetent leaders is partly shaped by circumstances (Lipman-Blumen 2006), or, in today's parlance, 'it depends' (Goodin and Tilly 2006).

Contingency Models

Moving into twentieth-century scholarship, the person–context nexus was tackled most explicitly in organizational theory, which has seen various classic 'situational' and 'contingency' approaches become part of its staple diet of theories reviewed in all its textbooks (e.g. Northouse 2009). Classic situational and contingency theories within the field of leadership studies all grapple with the issue of *which* matters most *when*. Most tend to come out on the deterministic end: situations shape leadership opportunities more than leaders are able to improve the odds of their success. Fiedler's classic model (1967) of leadership effectiveness, for example, surmises that a leader's orientation towards task accomplishment versus maintaining positive relationships with co-workers is more or less fixed. Therefore, particular types of situations—defined by low–high scores on their position power over others, structure of the task at hand, and the prevailing climate of leader–subordinate relationships—favour or disfavour leaders. The best prospects exist when leaders are 'in control', the task at hand is straightforward, and they enjoy positive relationships with their team members; and the worst prospects when the reverse conditions apply. If one leader's orientation profile does not 'fit' the characteristics of the situation, failure is all but inevitable—unless, of course, the leader manages to change one more of the three context parameters in a game-changing way. Fiedler was never really able to explain why he observed these correlations in the many studies he conducted, but this did not stop him from coming out with a strong prescriptive approach.

House (1996) sought to improve upon Fiedler by adopting a more flexible approach. He allowed for the possibility that, despite each person having a preferred style type, individuals are actually able to display a range of different leadership behaviours, which they can vary according to their perceptions of the requirements of the situation. He also added follower characteristics (for example, their ability level, their attitude towards authority, their need for affiliation, as well as for structure, and their locus of control) to the variables soup. Leaders in House's path–goal theory thus have to be masterful readers of multiple layers of context (task, authority, relationships, follower characteristics), and have the ability to rise above their own personality make-up in order continuously to adjust their leadership style to fit the exigencies of the context as they interpret it. That is a very big ask, well beyond the grasp of most ordinary mortals (and robustly testing such a complex, multivariate construct has—not surprisingly—proven elusive).

The elegance of contingency models of leadership bears the promise of clarity and of clear-cut 'if…then…' analytical linkages and behavioural imperatives—stated with some provisos but nevertheless often worded strongly enough to be easily mistaken for contextual determinism. Such a stance is methodologically deeply problematic, and encourages a rush towards prescription that is likely to set itself up for disappointment. For contemporary students of organizations, management, and leadership, their neat efforts at 'if…then…' matching of types of contexts to leadership styles feels somewhat quaint and too good to be true. This has not stopped dozens of self-help books on leadership propagating their own idiosyncratic versions of contingency models, many of which stake their mostly prescriptive claims on limited empirical evidence; virtually none explicitly addresses political leadership.

Adopting a largely similar analytical strategy, a wide range of studies across a range of disciplines emphasize variability in the properties of 'problems at hand' facing a particular government, policy sector, or organization. This literature offers typologies based on, for example, the degree of complexity, ambiguity, controversiality, volatility, and 'wickedness' of the issues and circumstances facing policymakers and managers (Thompson and Tuden 1959; Lowi 1972; Hickson et al. 1986; Aldrich 2003; Pfeffer and Salancik 2003; Grint 2010; Hoppe 2010) and argues that they set different types of challenges for leaders and policymakers. Much of this literature is quite prescriptive, either explicitly or in its implications: if leaders do not grasp the kind of problem with which they are struggling—and adjust their modes of problem-solving accordingly—things do not get done, and they risk compromising their effectiveness and their positions.

Notwithstanding its determinism, an extraordinarily helpful specimen of such a problem-centred typological approach to leadership analysis is Ronald Heifetz's work (1994) on adaptive leadership. It is premised on the contrast between 'technical' and 'adaptive' challenges facing a group. Technical challenges are those where the nature of the problem is agreed upon, and potential solutions to it are well honed and uncontroversial, if still difficult to achieve in a practical sense. Think of dealing with an imminent risk of flooding after heavy rainfall, or of tackling growing demand for public transport in a particular region. Adaptive challenges, in contrast, exist in contexts where there is fundamental uncertainty and lack of agreement about the nature of the problems as well as about ways to address the problems. In his 1994 book Heifetz uses micro-settings, such as patients for whom it is discovered that their illness is going to be fatal, as well as macro-settings, such as race relations in the United States in the 1960s. Today's adaptive challenges would include the debt crisis, climate change, ageing populations, and mass migration.

In dealing with a technical challenge, Heifetz argues, leaders can basically do what is expected of them—namely, to provide the protection, direction, and order needed to mobilize people to take up and implement the optimal approach of dealing with the challenge at hand. Leaders lead from the front, develop the vision, sketch a roadmap, and persuade others to follow. The same approach will go nowhere when applied to an adaptive challenge. It would only reinforce what Heifetz calls 'inappropriate dependencies' from the community vis-à-vis the leader, which will turn ugly when it becomes clear that the leader does not really know either, or advocates a particular definition of the issue disputed by others. Adaptive leadership therefore amounts to giving the work of change back to the group, instead of falling into the trap of prescription from on high. It amounts to training people's attention onto the conditions at hand, closing off all the escape routes, and providing an environment that conduces people to engage with the real issues and underlying differences.

Institutionalist Approaches

In a parallel universe, the so-called old institutionalism in political science (Finer 1970; Rhodes, Binder, and Rockman 2006) has long focused on describing and interpreting the formal architecture of party systems, electoral systems, executive government, executive–legislative relations, and judicial review. This has, *inter alia*, yielded an interest in penetrating how these institutional parameters in various jurisdictions shape, and are being interpreted by, individual office-holders. This has resulted in a wealth of studies on party leaders, presidents, prime ministers, legislators, public servants, and constitutional courts as political actors, exercising leadership under different institutional conditions by navigating and renegotiating the institutionalized expectations of their roles (Cooper and Brady 1981; Weller 1985, 2007; Blondel 1987; Peters 1990; Elgie 1995; Helms 2005; Bevir and Rhodes 2003; Rhodes, Weller and Wanna 2009; Rhodes 2011; Heppell 2012).

One strand of research in this vein examines the role of political party rules for selecting and ejecting leaders. Given the key role of party leaders in an era of growing 'personalization' of politics and voting, a range of scholars have started to study the manner in which leaders are selected. Since the 1990s, parties have begun to change their rules, with the ostensible aim of increasing the influence attributed to rank-and-file party members at the expense of party elites and particularly the parliamentary party. The question is: do such rules and rule changes matter at all in who get to be leaders and how those leaders are able to operate?

The resulting body of studies examining the consequences of these rule changes comprised a range of in-depth case studies of individual parties over time as well as comparative and cross-national case studies covering a wide range of parties and large numbers of succession episodes (Heppell 2008, 2010; Laing and 't Hart 2011; Cross and Blais 2012; Quinn 2012; Strangio et al. 2013). Its conclusions show that the longevity of party leaders as well as their relative autonomy in shaping their party's policy and strategy vary significantly depending upon the kind of selection and removal regime they happen to encounter. As one recent study covering twenty-two parties in five Westminster countries notes:

> Different rules for party leader (de-)selection do produce significant differences in the vulnerability of leaders to removal attempts…We suggest that the key variables in this regard are: whether a removal mechanism exists; whether the extra parliamentary party must in some way act to remove the leader; and when the parliamentary party has this authority, whether it is in any significant way encumbered in its use. The most secure leaders are those who cannot be formally removed. While pressure may be brought to try and force them from the leadership, at the end of the day, the decision and timing are ultimately theirs alone. These are closely followed by those whose removal requires the participation of the extra parliamentary party. We find that this authority is almost never formally used. While the threat of removal by the extra parliamentary party has resulted in leaders leaving office, the difficulty in organizing this large and dispersed group, and the time involved in doing so, provides leaders with significantly more security than when the parliamentary caucus can depose them. Those removable by their parliamentary colleagues are the most vulnerable.
>
> (Cross and Blais 2011: 146–7)

On balance, therefore, the research on the effects of changes in party rules on leadership authority ends up underpinning Mair's hunch (1994) that paradoxically widening the selectorate has tended to strengthen the hand of party leaders, made them less accountable to their colleagues in the party room and the party hierarchy, and made them better placed to hold onto the top spot for a long time—as long as they nurture the mandate given to them directly by the rank-and-file members of the party.

The arrival on the scene of the so-called new institutionalism in the 1980s sparked a resurgence of attention for the rules of the political game—not just formal–legal but also normative–cultural and rational–tactical ones (March and Olsen 1989; Scharpf 1997; Peters 2005). Thus understood, such rules of the game are contextual in that they act as incentive structures constraining some and enabling other policy preferences and behaviours on the part of political actors. Studies in this mould find that contexts can be quite overbearing, limiting the scope for ambitious leadership. They tend to stress the prevalence of policy continuity because of 'path dependence' and 'inheritance' (e.g. Rose and Davies 1994; Pierson 2004), and suggest that change occurs incrementally (Kay 2006; Mahoney and Thelen 2010). Others engage in a more culture-focused form of contextual determinism, arguing that the shared mindsets of the communities induce political leaders towards particular styles of leadership (Wildavsky 1984, 1989).

In its valiant attempts to capture the dynamic interplay between structure and agency, neo-institutionalism has, however, also sparked investigations of how and why certain leaders are capable of forging and sustaining non-incremental policy change, instigating institutional reforms (Moon 1995; Goldfinch and 't Hart 2003). To firm believers in the power of context and structure, findings such as these may appear somewhat startling, highlighting as they do the 'exogenous interventions of imaginative individuals' (Aldrich and Shepsle 2000: 41). To others, they are the very essence of political agency, in proud Machiavellian fashion: 'structuring the world so you can win' (Riker 1986: p. ix). Yet others sensibly return to the middle ground, asserting that leadership in politics matters but that it inevitably occurs 'in context' and that students of leadership therefore need to encompass both contextual and individual factors in their research designs without a priori according more weight to one or the other (Hargrove and Owens 2003).

Macro-Approaches

More macro-conceptions of context are understandably dominant in the subfield of international relations: the structure of the international system (Waltz 1979), the dynamics of ecosystems (Sprout and Sprout 1965; Chasek, Downie, and Brown 2010), globalization (Gilpin 2001), legalization (Abbott et al. 2000), and, more generally, the rate of change in a range of parameters facing actors in the international system (Rosenau 1990). Studies in this vein tend to focus on how such macro-trends are game-changers in the relations between states, the role and position of international organizations, the relations between public and non-governmental including multinational corporations, the governance of regions as well as transnational issues. However, they rarely explicitly touch upon how macro-contexts affect the incentive and opportunity structures of political leaders (see also Dahlberg 1983).

Breaking New Ground: Skowronek

The single most important contingency study of political leadership is Stephen Skowronek's *The Politics Presidents Make*, published in 1993. Skowronek sought to explain why some American presidents transformed US politics while others became prisoners of it. He argues that presidents are the primary agent of change in US politics, but that their success or failure hinges much more on their 'fit' into the political context in which they find themselves than on their personal competencies and style (as opposed, for example, to Simonton 1987; Greenstein 2010). The most significant factor is the relationship between the president and the central policy ideas and institutional arrangements that constitute the governing orthodoxy of the day (which he terms the 'regime'). Presidents are either opposed to or affiliated with the prevailing regime and its ideas. In a sweep encompassing all presidents from Washington to Clinton, Skowronek plausibly demonstrates that all incumbents of the presidency can be usefully classified into these positions. Opposed presidents seek warrants to shatter the regime and create a new order based on new ideas, while affiliated leaders seek warrants to defend and strengthen the status quo.

Yet the strength of these warrants varies. When a regime is resilient, the political order is ideologically, organizationally, and institutionally well supported, diminishing the opportunity space for opposed presidents. When the regime is vulnerable, it represents an orthodoxy that has lost public credibility and is beset by problems that its policy ideas and routines cannot solve. Presidents who gain power in opposition to a weak and discredited regime have the greatest opportunity to act and change politics. In contrast, those who gain power affiliated with and defend a weak regime have difficulty gaining traction and usually find themselves with limited political capital.

Despite inevitable criticism directed at its schematic approach and potentially deterministic implications (see Skowronek 2010; Laing 2012), Skowronek's theory has been widely acclaimed for providing broad explanatory narratives for the course of the presidential leadership throughout US history, inviting scholars to compare like with like among presidencies in terms of the political context faced by various office-holders rather than by roughly dividing US political history into two or three periods and assuming that no meaningful comparison is possible between presidents from these different eras. Recently, students of political leadership in parliamentary democracies have begun to explore the potential of his contextual theory of executive leadership for understanding the dynamics of prime-ministerial leadership (Laing and McCaffrie 2013; see also 't Hart 2014).

3 Assessing Contextual Approaches

As noted, the face value plausibility of contextual approaches to leadership is high. Methodologically and analytically, however, the genre has its challenges.

Proximate or Distal Contexts?

How should one deal with the tremendous range and differential aggregation levels of 'context factors'? Macro-level context phenomena such as demography, and economic and climatic conditions, might be pervasive and to some extent 'non-negotiable' in their agenda-setting and attention-focusing impact, but they are also non-specific. They encompass entire polities, not just one leader or set of leaders, and might therefore be treated as 'background noise'. So, the operating conditions of *all* contemporary political elites include trends such as increased transparency through Internet and social media, the rise of new economic giants in Asia, the juridification of governance, and global population growth. How, therefore, can one tell that any or all of these exert a significant influence on particular leaders and not on others? What if the interest lies with local political leadership, or with leadership in macro-economic policy? Does the analyst simply assume or does she try empirically to verify that different types and levels of context factors are the most salient in each of these two instances? Perhaps the mayor of London cannot but pay a great deal of attention to global economic conditions, but can the mayor of Strasbourg afford to ignore them and concentrate on the economic situation in and around his immediate region and yet be successful in his role?

Reversely, micro-level context phenomena right on the border of the leader's life world, such as the longevity, mode of exit, and level of popularity at exit of the predecessor of a new leader, are highly person-specific. Although in-depth case studies may reveal that their impact on the individuals in question has been quite considerable, it is hard reliably to grasp and interpret them in the context of large-N comparative studies aimed at explaining longevity variations across whole populations of leaders (see Horiuchi, Laing, and 't Hart forthcoming).

'Out There' or 'Constructed'?

The ontological status of 'context' is a second challenging issue. Do we take contexts as given? Do we assume, for example, that the leaders whose behaviours we study treat things such as population numbers, unemployment figures, poll ratings, weather statistics, treaties, and contracts as akin to physical realities—as things that exist in the world 'out there' and that cannot be willed away or enhanced by human sense-making capabilities? Or do we take the subjectivist position that even the most material, directly observable of phenomena—the condition of the polar ice caps, the size of tropical rain forests, streets of boarded-up houses, 2001 terrorist attacks on the twin towers—assume meaning in the world of political leaders only through the stories that they choose to tell or believe about them. As Hajer (1993: 44) famously argued: 'large groups of dead trees as such are not a social construct; the point is how one makes sense of dead trees. In this respect there are many possible realities. One may see dead trees as the product of natural stress caused by drought, cold, or wind, or one may see them as victims of pollution.'

Just assuming contexts are what they are is, therefore, frankly implausible. For example, across three major books and numerous articles on the subject, Heifetz provides little if any empirical evidence for the central typology of 'challenges' that underpins the entire edifice. Where does the 'technical' end and the 'adaptive' begin when different group members interpret the catalogue of issues facing them at any given time? What levels of (dis)agreement are needed to make them fall into one box rather than the other? Contingency scholars should explicitly address those issues rather than obfuscate them.

Looming large in the background of this problem are, of course, philosophical challenges. Depending on one's ontological point of view, contextual analysis of leadership assumes different methodological guises. In what Bevir and Rhodes (2003) call the modernist–empiricist tradition, the analyst would strive to establish correlation and preferably causality between certain 'states' of context variables and certain types of leadership behaviour (rhetoric, decisions, actions) and/or assessment of that behaviour by other actors (media, opinion polls, voters). She would accordingly formulate and test generalizations such as 'no prime minister can get reelected when unemployment levels are in the double digits', or 'the higher the level or rate of population ageing in a country, the higher the number of healthcare reform proposals put forward by its policy elites and the more importance voters attach to government performance on healthcare policy in choosing to support or reject heads of government'.

This approach has a number of key problems. The first goes to the heart of the ontological issue: the modernist–empiricist approach requires a big leap of faith that the context actually is as the analyst says it is. For example, Skowronek's key notion of the vulnerability of regimes is not particularly well operationalized. He simply dishes out a panoply of historical sources and decides to accord a particular presidency a particular place in his two-by-two regime typology. So George H. W. Bush is said to have taken office at a time when the Reagan-induced neo-liberal regime was well entrenched, while Herbert Hoover (1929–33) was fated for tragedy, as the regime he adhered to was about to become obsolete. It is plausible, but it remains a sweeping judgement call: the square peg of an entire presidency has to be fitted through the round hole of an ideal-typical fourfold regime context classification. Not surprisingly, some of Skowronek's calls have been roundly criticized (Laing 2012). The second problem is that the step from observing correlations in large-N designs not only to firmly establishing causality but also to providing a credible account of the causal mechanisms at work proves to be a large one (see Laing and 't Hart 2011). Third, and perhaps most difficult to remedy: who decides on what grounds which of the many potentially relevant context factors are selected into the analysis? Analysts follow their instincts—economists will look for economic factors as determinants of leader stances; historical institutionalists will look for policy legacies, path dependencies for collective memory, and historical analogies; and rational choice institutionalists will look at rule-based strategic incentive structures for leaders assumed to be utility-maximizing cue-takers (rather than as 'constraint challengers', see Keller 2005). All of these are potentially worthy endeavours. All of them, however, involve the analyst deciding for us which bits of context we are going to explore and which not.

In contrast, an interpretivist approach to contextual leadership analysis seeks to penetrate, as Hajer did in his work on acid rain policy in the UK, how policy elites 'make sense' of contextual data and the stories that are being told about them. It requires penetrating how leaders develop their private understandings of those data: whether they pay any attention to them at all, whose advice they seek and take on assessing their significance, on which bits of 'evidence' they focus, and which bits they ignore or distort. It also requires analysing how they then use those data in their leadership work of crafting their own persuasive narratives designed to build or consolidate coalitions around their political projects and policy platforms. The big advantage of the interpretive approach is that it allows the analyst to go a long way towards avoiding the problem of a priori selection of context factors or clusters. By means of intensive tracking of a leader's or leadership group's private sense-making and public utterances at various points in time, an interpretive analysis can demonstrate rather than postulate which dimensions of context were deemed salient by leaders at which time. The big drawback is that doing so is a labour-intensive business hardly devoid of its own analytical judgement calls (see also Gains, Chapter 19, this volume).

Determinism or Probabilism?

For those on the modernist–empiricist side of leadership analysis, a closely related issue is that of the strength that is to be expected of the causal nexus between contexts and leaders. Can context factors make or break the careers of leaders, or merely provide a more or less better 'fit' for leaders with certain policy preferences or operating styles? Many leaders of note appear to rise to become great influencers because of a strong, innate belief that circumstances conspire to make them destined for greatness—even if their contemporaries do not regard them as natural born leaders. 'The times will suit me', Australian politician John Howard put it at a time when he was still a deposed former leader of his party, to general ridicule. In the end, however, they did: he clawed back the leadership of his party, and served nearly eleven years as prime minister. Was that because—as he predicted—by 1996 the times themselves had changed, or because he had learned from his early leadership failure better to fit the requirements of leadership within the context of Australian federal politics, as his biographers claim (Van Onselen and Errington 2008)? Likewise, were those leaders of Western governments in the late 1970s condemned to preside over protracted policy failures and their own political oblivion, or were they simply not sufficiently smart and agile to change tack when they still could?

4 A FUTURE FOR CONTEXTUAL ANALYSIS

What then lies ahead? Clearly, there is a need for improving upon the now disparate attempts to understand the nexus between leaders, leadership, and context in the world of politics. Students of political leadership need to start talking to one another about the ways in which they can usefully study this nexus in ways that are more purposeful, coherent, and methodologically self-conscious.

One promising direction is to provide a more robust counterweight to the historically dominant objectivist-deterministic modes of contextual analysis, particularly to their overly schematic and deterministic trappings. Context is never just 'out there'. It can also never be fully caught in analysts' elegant two-by-two tables. Things happening 'out there' are perceived differently by political actors with different beliefs, roles, loyalties, and vantage points. Factors such as 'the economy', 'the zeitgeist', or 'the geostrategic situation' are not simply given. They are assigned meaning in stories that are framed in particular ways—often with strategic intent—and that are challenged by other stories propagated by other actors. It is the course and outcomes of the ensuing meaning-making contests that are going on around them, and in which they often actively participate, that are pivotal in motivating political leaders to take notice of and act upon contextual changes.

A key challenge for future studies of the leadership–context nexus is, therefore, to examine much more rigorously than it has done to date the constructed nature of this nexus. For example, under which macro-economic and political conditions can political leaders successfully 'talk up' or 'talk down' the national economy, and when do they lose the ability to do so (Wood 2007)? How do constraint-accepting versus constraint-challenging leaders respond to changes in their geo-strategic environment (Keller 2005)? To whose stories about context do leaders listen? Which individuals and institutions are considered to be authoritative interpreters of economic, sociocultural, historical, ecological, and geo-political context by different political leaders and their inner circles, and how does this affect their policy agendas? How do broader governance traditions and cultural practices shape elite beliefs about the capacity of existing institutions to absorb demographic and sociocultural changes in the population (Bevir and Rhodes 2010)? How do we get a solid grip on the possibility of mutual influence between context and leadership, whether operating in a modernist-empiricist or an interpretive epistemology? How can we reliably ascertain when the nature of influence is entirely unidirectional?

These questions should be at the forefront of any serious effort to remove the contextual analysis of leadership from the outdated shackles of contingency theory, avoid the false clarity of deductive typological reasoning, and provide us with more firmly empirically grounded insight into how political leaders notice, interpret, use, and leave their mark upon the various contexts in which they operate.

RECOMMENDED READING

Heifetz, R. (1994). *Leadership without Easy Answers*. Cambridge, MA: Harvard University Press.
Skowronek, S. (2010). *Presidential Leadership in Political Time*. Lawrence, KS: University Press of Kansas.
Wildavsky, A. (1989). 'A Cultural Theory of Leadership', in B. D. Jones (ed.), *Leadership and Politics*. Lawrence, KS: University Press of Kansas, 87–113.

REFERENCES

Abbott, Kenneth, Keohane, Robert, Moravscik, Andrew, Slaughter, Anne-Marie, and Snidal, Duncan (2000). 'The Concept of Legalization', *International Organization*, 54/3: 401–19.
Aldrich, H. (2003). *Organizations and Environments*. Stanford, CA: Stanford University Press.
Aldrich, J. H., and Shepsle, K. A. (2000). 'Explaining Institutional Change: Soaking, Poking and Modeling in the US Congress', in W. A. Bianco (ed.), *Congress on Display, Congress at Work*. Ann Arbor, MI: University of Michigan Press, 23–46.
Bevir, M., and Rhodes, R. A. W. (2003). *Interpreting British Governance*. London: Routledge.

Bevir, M., and Rhodes, R. A. W. (2010). *The State as Cultural Practice*. Oxford: Oxford University Press.

Blondel, J. (1987). *Political Leadership: A General Analysis*. London: Sage.

Chasek, P. S., Downie, D., and Brown, J. (2010). *Global Environmental Politics*. Boulder, CO: Westview.

Cooper, J., and Brady, D. W. (1981). 'Institutional Context and Leadership Style: The House from Cannon to Rayburn', *American Political Science Review*, 75/3: 423–4.

Cross, W., and Blais, A. (2011). 'Holding Party Leaders to Account: The Westminster Cases', in J. Uhr and P. 't Hart (eds), *How Power Changes Hands*. Basingstoke: Palgrave, 135–56.

Cross, W., and Blais, A. (2012). *Politics at the Centre: The Selection and Removal of Party Leaders in the Anglo Parliamentary Democracies*. Oxford: Oxford University Press.

Dahlberg, K. A. (1983). 'Contextual Analysis: Taking Space, Time, and Place Seriously', *International Studies Quarterly*, 27/3: 257–66.

Elgie, R. (1995). *Political Leadership in Liberal Democracies*. Basingstoke: Macmillan.

Fiedler, F. (1967). *A Theory of Leadership Effectiveness*. New York: McGraw Hill.

Finer, S. E. (1970). *Comparative Government: An Introduction to the Study of Politics*. Harmondsworth: Penguin.

Gilpin, R. (2001). *Global Political Economy*. Princeton: Princeton University Press.

Goldfinch, S. and 't Hart, P. (2003). 'Leadership and Institutional Reform', *Governance*, 16/2: 235–70.

Goodin, R. E., and Tilly, C. (2006) (eds). *The Oxford Handbook of Contextual Political Analysis*. Oxford: Oxford University Press.

Greenstein, F. G. (2010). *The Presidential Difference*. Princeton: Princeton University Press.

Grint, K. (2010). 'Leadership: An Enemy of the People?', *International Journal of Leadership in Public Services*, 6/4: 22–5.

Hajer, M. (1993). 'Discourse Coalitions and the Institutionalization of Practice', in F. Fischer and J. Forester (eds), *The Argumentative Turn in Policy Analysis and Planning*. Durham, NC: Duke University Press, 43–77.

Hargrove, E. D., and Owens, J. E. (2003) (eds). *Leadership in Context*. Lanham, MD: Rowman and Littlefield.

Heifetz, R. (1994). *Leadership without Easy Answers*. Cambridge, MA: Harvard University Press.

Helms, L. (2005). *Presidents, Prime Ministers and Chancellors*. Basingstoke: Palgrave.

Heppell, T. (2008). *Choosing the Tory Leader: Conservative Party Leadership Elections from Heath to Cameron*. London: Taurus.

Heppell, T. (2010). *Chosing the Labour Leader: Labour Party Leadership Elections from WIlson to Brown*. London: Taurus.

Heppell, T. (2012). *Leaders of the Opposition: From Winston Churchill to David Cameron*. Basingstoke: Palgrave.

Hickson, D. J., Butler, R. J., Cray, D., Mallory, G. R., and Wilson, D. C. (1986). *Top Decisions: Strategic Decision-Making in Organizations*. Oxford: Basil Blackwell.

Hook, S. (1943). *The Hero in History*. New York: John Day.

Hoppe, R. J. (2010). *The Governance of Problems*. Bristol: Policy Press.

Horiuchi, Y., Laing, M., and 't Hart, P. (forthcoming). 'Hard Acts to Follow', *Party Politics*.

House, R. J. (1996). 'Path–Goal Theory of Leadership: Lessons, Legacy, and a Reformulated Theory', *Leadership Quarterly*, 7/3: 323–52.

Kay, A. (2006). *The Dynamics of Public Policy: Theory and Evidence*. Cheltenham: Edward Elgar.

Keller, J. W. (2005). 'Constraint Respecters, Constraint Challengers, and Crisis Decision Making in Democracies', *Political Psychology*, 26/6: 835–67.

Kingdon, J. W. (1984). *Agendas, Alternatives and Public Policies*. Boston: Little, Brown.

Laing, M. (2012). 'Towards a Pragmatic Presidency: Exploring the Waning of Political Time', *Polity*, 44/3: 234–59.

Laing, M., and 't Hart, P. (2011). 'Seeking and Keeping the Hot Seat', in J. Uhr and P. 't Hart (eds), *How Power Changes Hands*. Basingstoke: Palgrave, 111–32.

Laing, M., and McCaffrie, B. (forthcoming). 'The Politics Prime Ministers Make: Political Time and Executive Leadership in Westminster Systems', in P. Strangio, P. 't Hart, and J. Walter (eds), *Understanding Prime Ministerial Performance*. Oxford: Oxford University Press.

Lipman-Blumen, J. (2006). *The Allure of Toxic Leadership*. Oxford: Oxford University Press.

Lowi, T. J. (1972). 'Four Systems of Policy, Politics and Choice', *Public Administration Review*, 33/4: 298–310.

Mahoney, J. P., and Thelen, K. D. (2010) (eds). *Explaining Institutional Change*. Cambridge: Cambridge University Press.

Mair, P. (1994). 'Party Organizations: From Civil Society to the State', in R. S. Katz and P. Mair (eds), *How Parties Organize*. London: Sage, 1–22.

March, J. G., and Olsen, J. P. (1989). *Rediscovering Institutions: The Organizational Basis of Politics*. New York: Free Press.

Moon, J. (1995). 'Innovative Leadership and Policy Change', *Governance*, 8/1: 1–25.

Northouse, P. G. (2009). *Leadership*. London: Sage.

Peters, B. G. (2005). *Institutional Theory in Political Science: The New Institutionalism*. London: Continuum.

Peters, R. M. (1990). *The American Speakership: The Office in Historical Perspective*. Baltimore, MD: Johns Hopkins University Press.

Pfeffer, J., and Salancik, G. (2003). *The External Control of Organizations: A Resource Dependence Perspective*. Stanford, CA: Stanford University Press.

Pierson, P. (2004). *Politics in Time: History, Institutions, and Social Analysis*. Princeton: Princeton University Press.

Quinn, T. (2012). *Electing and Ejecting Party Leaders in Britain*. Basingstoke: Palgrave.

Rhodes, R. A. W. (2011). *Everyday Life in British Government*. Oxford: Oxford University Press.

Rhodes, R. A. W., Binder, S. A., and Rockman, B. W. (2006) (eds). *The Oxford Handbook of Political Institutions*. Oxford: Oxford University Press.

Rhodes, R. A. W., Weller, P., and Wanna, J. (2009). *Comparing Westminster*. Oxford: Oxford University Press.

Riker, W. (1986). *The Art of Political Manipulation*. New Haven, CT: Yale University Press.

Rose, R., and Davies, J. (1994). *Inheritance in Public Policy*. Oxford: Oxford University Press.

Rosenau, J. (1990). *Turbulence in World Politics*. Princeton: Princeton University Press.

Scharpf, F. (1997). *Games Real Actors Play: Actor-Centered Institutionalism in Policy Research*. Boulder, CO: Westview Press.

Simonton, D. (1987). *Why Presidents Succeed*. New Haven, CT: Yale University Press.

Skowronek, S. (1993). *The Politics Presidents Make*. New Haven, CT: Yale University Press.

Skowronek, S. (2010). *Presidential Leadership in Political Time*. Lawrence, KS: University Press of Kansas.

Sprout, H., and Sprout, M. (1965). *The Ecological Perspective on Human Affairs*. Princeton: Princeton University Press.

't Hart, P. (2011). 'Reading the Signs of the Times: Regime Dynamics and Leadership Possibilities', *Journal of Political Philosophy*, 19/4: 419–39.

't Hart, P. (2014). *Understanding Public Leadership*. Basingstoke: Palgrave Macmillan.

Thompson, J. D., and Tuden, A. (1959). 'Strategies, Structures, and Processes of Organizational Decision', in J. D. Thompson, P. B. Hammond, R. W. Hawkes, B. H. Junker, and A. Tuden (eds), *Comparative Studies in Administration*. Pittsburgh: University of Pittsburgh Press, 195–216.

Van Onselen, P., and Errington, W. (2008). *John Winston Howard: The Definitive Biography*. Melbourne: Melbourne University Press.

Waltz, K. W. (1979). *Theory of International Politics*. New York: McGraw Hill.

Weller, P. (1985). *First among Equals*. Oxford: Oxford University Press.

Weller, P. (2007). *Cabinet Government in Australia, 1901–2006*. Sydney: UNSW Press.

Wildavsky, A. (1984). *The Nursing Father: Mozes as a Political Leader*. Tuscaloosa, AL: Alabama University Press.

Wildavsky, A. (1989). 'A Cultural Theory of Leadership'. in B. D. Jones (ed.), *Leadership and Politics*. Lawrence, KS: University Press of Kansas, 87–113.

Wood, B. D. (2007). *The Politics of Economic Leadership*. Princeton: Princeton University Press.

Zelikow, P., with Rice, C. (1995). *Germany Unified and Europe Transformed: A Study in Statecraft*. Cambridge, MA: Harvard University Press.

··

CHAPTER 15

DECISION ANALYSIS

··

DAVID BRULÉ, ALEX MINTZ, AND
KARL DEROUEN, JR.

1 INTRODUCTION

ELITE decision-making analysis focuses on the choices made by the leadership, whether conceived as individuals, groups, or coalitions representing nation states. There are various directions for approaching this rather broad topic. This chapter will focus on the decision-making models and biases used to explain the decisions of political leaders with a particular focus on foreign-policy decisions. The approaches covered here are applicable to many domestic decisions as well—for example, on public policy reforms, budgetary decisions, elite decisions concerning political appointments, personnel decisions, and so on (see, e.g., Jones and Baumgartner 2005). In the area of political behaviour most decisions focus on candidate evaluation and voters' response. Consequently, we highlight in this chapter the topic of leadership as it pertains to foreign policy. Throughout, we summarize some of the key debates and criticisms of the various approaches. We conclude with a detailed discussion of the rational–cognitive debate as well as some thoughts for future progress in decision-making analysis.

2 DECISION MODELS

Models of decision-making typically specify processing characteristics by describing how individuals acquire and assess information, as well as how a final choice is selected among alternatives under consideration. These information-processing characteristics and decision rules may lead to biases and deviations from an ideal rational choice. Consequently, we consider the rational choice model first.

Rational Choice Model

Rooted in economics (see von Neumann and Morgenstern 1947; Friedman 1953), rational choice conceives of decisions as means–ends calculations (Zagare 1990; Morrow 1997). Decision-makers choose among a variety of options on the basis of their expectation that the choice selected will serve some goal better than the alternatives. This is frequently framed in terms of a simple cost–benefit analysis; decision-makers are expected to select the choice that has greater expected net benefits (that is, benefits minus the costs) than those of other alternatives under consideration. However, many rational theories may simply posit a preference-ordering over outcomes (see Morrow 1997). For example, if alternative X is expected to yield A and A is preferred to B, a decision-maker should prefer alternative X to an alternative that is expected to yield B. The primary claim of rational choice is that choices are consistent with preferences. But, in practice, rational decisions are likely to require a good deal of time, careful and exhaustive deliberation, as well as some familiarity with the type of problem the decision aims to address. Greg Cashman (1993: 77–8) provides a useful set of steps in the rational model:

1. identify problem;
2. identify and rank goals;
3. gather information (this can be ongoing);
4. Identify alternatives for reaching goals;
5. analyse alternatives by considering consequences and effectiveness (costs
6. and benefits) of each alternative and probabilities associated with success
7. select alternative that maximizes chances of selecting best alternative (as
8. determined in step 5);
9. implement decision;
10. monitor and evaluate.

According to the rational choice model, the decision-maker is assumed to be able to rank preferences 'according to the degree of satisfaction of achieving these goals and objectives' (Sage 1990: 233). The rational actor is also expected to be able to identify alternatives and their consequences and to select from these alternatives in an effort to maximize satisfaction. In this setting, the rational economic decision-maker is expected to be able to access a set of objectives and goals. Graham Allison defines rationality as a 'consistent, value-maximizing choice within specified constraints' (Allison 1971: 30). According to Allison (1971: 29), the rational decision-maker chooses the alternative that provides the consequence that is most preferred. The brevity of this definition belies the strength of the model. The rational model is parsimonious. This means that a few rather straightforward assumptions, taken together, are thought to explain a wide range of foreign-policy decisions and actions (Schelling 1966; Bueno de Mesquita et al. 2003).

MacDonald (2003: 552) summarizes the three parts of the rationality assumption. First, actors are assumed to employ purposive action motivated by goal-oriented behaviour and not simply by habit or social expectations. The decision-maker must be able to identify an a priori goal and move with the intention of reaching that objective: for example, an unemployed person looking for a job is behaving purposively if he or she actively searches for work. Second, actors display consistent preferences as manifested in the ability to rank the preferences in transitive order. Transitivity means that, if alternative 1 is preferred over alternative 2, and 2 is preferred to 3, then 1 is preferred to 3. For example, if diplomacy is preferred to sanctions and sanctions are preferred to use of force, then diplomacy is preferred over the use of force. Invariance means that a decision-maker's preference holds steady in the face of various means of information presentation (McDermott 2004b: 52–7). For example, sometimes information can be framed in a particularly leading manner. William Riker (1995: 24) observes that preference ordering is a hallmark of purposive behaviour so that, taken together, these first two assumptions mean that actors must know what they want and be able to rank outcomes in relation to the goal. In other words, you need to know your destination if you hope to get there. Finally, and as noted by Allison (1971), utility maximization means that actors will select the alternative that provides the greatest net benefit.

Bounded Rationality/Cybernetic Models

Simon (1957) proposed a model of bounded rationality. According to the model, individuals are thought to possess cognitive constraints on their information-processing capacities such that it is impossible for a decision-maker to identify all potential alternatives and adequately assess their implications. If a dynamic model of sequential decision-making is considered, the problem is further complicated. Thus, in order to overcome the cognitive and organizational costs associated with choice search and analysis, individuals frequently make suboptimal decisions. Simon suggests that a decision made today may yield satisfactory results for one problem, but actually work against an optimal outcome in subsequent decision problems. For example, US efforts to arm the mujahedeen in Afghanistan against Soviet forces promoted US goals during the 1980s, but helped establish the rise of al-Qaeda.

The model of bounded rationality/cybernetic decision-making (Steinbruner 1974) assumes an order-sensitive search process by which the sequence in which alternatives are considered will influence the selection of a choice. Rather than maximize with respect to a goal, decision-makers are thought to employ a satisficing selection rule—the first alternative that is deemed satisfactory is adopted. In terms of information-processing, the model assumes that decision-makers limit the amount of information considered at any given time to that deemed relevant to the single alternative under consideration, eliminating the complexity associated with pair-wise comparisons of all available alternatives (Steinbruner 1974: 66). Empirical research evaluating the bounded rationality/cybernetic model with respect to foreign-policy decision-making offers qualified support (see Ostrom and Job 1986). Perhaps the most prominent example is Ostrom and Job (1986); they apply a cybernetic model of decision-making to presidential decisions to use force, finding that presidents tend to dispatch military forces when faced with difficult political circumstances at home.

Organizational Process Model

An outgrowth of Simon's work (1957) on bounded rationality is the organizational process model. The seminal work here is Cyert and March (1963); they argue that the alternatives available for addressing a given problem are typically determined ex ante by organizational routines and standard operating procedures. The organizational role of a decision-maker is likely to influence foreign-policy decisions via predetermined routines and areas of responsibility. A problem cannot be addressed with resources or processes that do not exist; the choice is likely to be one that is organizationally feasible and promises adequate success with respect to implementation.

Although the organizational process model had existed for some time, and bedrock studies of foreign-policy decision-making (Snyder, Bruck and Sapin 1954, 1962) posited the importance of organizational roles, Allison (1969, 1971: ch. 3) was perhaps the first to apply the model to a foreign-policy decision in his analysis of the Cuban Missile Crisis. He argues that the decision to blockade Cuba can be understood as an available option—that is, such options as a 'surgical' air strike were not said to be available as a routine option—with a pre-existing plan for implementation. Since Allison's 1971 work, however, relatively little effort has been made to apply the organizational process model to foreign-policy decisions. Welch (1992) suggests that this may be the case because there has been some conflation of the organizational process model with the bureaucratic politics model.

Bureaucratic Politics Model

The bureaucratic politics model has its roots in research on bureaucracies and foreign policy (e.g. Huntington 1960; Hilsman 1967). According to Allison's formulation (1971) of the model, foreign-policy decisions are made by a collective executive (a cabinet), with each member of the group possessing his or her own bureaucratic interests. The position/choice advocated by any group member is likely to be one that serves his or her bureaucratic interests. Specifically, they seek to 'promote the positions their organizations have taken in the past' that 'are consistent with the interests their organization represents' (Feldman 1989: 13). The process by which decisions are made can be characterized by the 'pulling and hauling' of group bargaining (Allison and Halperin 1972: 43). The choice selected by the group is likely to reflect the preferences of the group member(s) who is best able to garner 'bargaining advantages, skill and will in using bargaining advantages, and other players' perceptions of the first two ingredients' (Allison and Halperin 1972: 50). Much of the empirical support for the bureaucratic politics approach was produced through the analysis of defence policy decisions (Allison and Halperin 1972; Halperin 1974), finding that US decisions concerning arms production and limitations were consistent with the bureaucratic approach.

Prospect Theory

Unlike the rational choice approach, prospect theory assumes that preferences over alternatives are not transitive, but depend on net asset levels vis-à-vis a reference point—gains and losses from a frame of reference (Kahneman and Tversky 1979: 277). Decision-makers treat gains and losses asymmetrically, overvaluing losses relative to commensurate gains. This asymmetry produces a non-linear utility function characterized by greater steepness on the loss side than on the gain side. Consequently, decision-makers pursue a strategy of loss aversion, which has been corroborated in a number of studies (Kahneman and Tversky 1979). The central implication of framing and loss aversion is that decision-makers will pursue riskier strategies to reverse losses, but eschew risk when gains have been accumulated. In foreign-policy decision-making, risk-taking in order to avoid (or reverse) losses has been shown to be associated with decisions involving crisis situations (see, e.g., McDermott 1992; Berejikian 2002).

Poliheuristic Theory

An effort to integrate cognitive and rational approaches to decision-making is poliheuristic theory (e.g. Mintz and Geva 1997; Mintz et al. 1997). Poliheuristic theory postulates a two-stage decision-making process in which leaders utilize a dimension-based search of the alternatives, ruling out those that fail to satisfy requirements on a key, non-compensatory dimension in the first stage of the process. In the second stage, a final choice is made through the analytic (that is, rational) comparison of the remaining alternatives (see, e.g., Payne, Bettman, and Johnson 1993; Mintz et al. 1997; Mintz 2004). The non-compensatory heuristic (cognitive short cut) employed in the first stage reduces the menu of alternatives to a manageable set, reducing the mental effort required in the search for a choice. This procedure is thought to mirror the process by which individuals make decisions (Payne, Bettman, and Johnson 1993). However, for political *leaders* the political dimension is often the non-compensatory dimension.

The use of the non-compensatory principle for the elimination of unsatisfactory/ unlikely alternatives is also useful for scholars in analyses of leaders' foreign policy and national security decisions—in both theory-testing and forecasting projects. Poliheuristic theory is thought to account for a variety of phenomena, including crisis decision-making (e.g. Mintz 1993; DeRouen and Sprecher 2004), international bargaining (Astorino-Courtois and Trusty 2000), and the influence of political advisers in foreign-policy decision-making (e.g. Mintz 2005a).

3 Decisional Biases

Psychological approaches to foreign policy and/or national security decision-making also point to how attributes of leaders and their information-processing behaviour in various settings influence decisions. Such features are thought to produce decisional biases, which result when decision-makers overlook or intentionally disregard relevant information.

Personality and Beliefs

Research on leaders' personalities suggested that means employed for achieving the specified ends of a decision problem may serve other purposes altogether, producing biased decisions. For instance, decision-makers may possess ethnocentric or nationalistic attitudes learned from their own socialization, which may influence their choices if they seek to satisfy a need to affirm national/ethnic superiority rather than the ends of policy (Levinson 1957). A set of studies by Margaret Hermann (1974, 1980) identified a set of personality traits—nationalism, control over events, dogmatism, and cognitive complexity—that corresponded to overall foreign-policy orientation and behaviour of leaders.

Research on personality has evolved into two additional research agendas. The first explores the impact of leadership styles on foreign-policy decision-making (Kissinger 1966; Hermann et al. 2001). This approach argues that leadership style influences decisions via delegation–management arrangements. Leaders who tend to delegate and take advice seriously can be expected to have less of an impact on the decision than micro-managers. The second research agenda is the operational code approach. Operational code analysis argues that decision-makers' beliefs, as 'subjective representations of reality' in political life, critically influence (that is, distort, block, and recast) incoming information (Leites 1951; Walker and Schafer 2006: 4–6). Given a stimulus from the external environment, beliefs may steer decision-makers towards some courses of action and away from others (George 1979).

One's beliefs about international objects (that is, actors, events, and the decision environment) may be referred to as the decision-maker's cognitive structure. For example, operational codes, schemas, and cognitive maps all refer to naive theories held by policy-makers (see, e.g., Axelrod 1973). Such cognitive structures drive decision-makers' perceptions and responses to international events, aiding the organization and interpretation of data. Information that appears to contradict a decision-maker's preconceived beliefs may initially be ruled out (e.g. Axelrod 1973; Jervis 1976), resulting in biased decisions. But when the bulk of information contradicts the initial beliefs, decision-makers may become increasingly vigilant and seek additional information in the evaluation of available options (Pruitt 1965: 411–14).[1]

---

[1] See also Staw and Ross (1989) and Brockner (1992) summarizing the escalation of commitment perspective.

Group Decision-Making

Because leaders must contend with a variety of issues, policy-making tends to be largely an organizational endeavour. Research on the organizational roles of decision-makers suggests that alternatives advocated by a given group member are likely to be dictated by his or her own organizational routines or organizational interests (Allison 1971). But group dynamics can influence how information is processed and decisions are ultimately made. For example, group features such as size, role of the leader, and decision rules have an impact on the outcome of deliberations (Hermann and Hermann 1989). Perhaps the most detrimental consequence of group decision-making arises when members of the group seeks consensus at the expense of thoroughly exploring other alternatives—groupthink.

Groupthink, which was introduced by Janis (1982), occurs when members of the group come to disregard information that does not conform to the majority position. Indeed, the overarching goal for each group member is to achieve conformity, resulting in self-censorship and the stifling of dissent. Groupthink situations are more likely if the group is isolated from outside input. It is also more likely if the group lacks an impartial leader who can tolerate dissent. A lack of norms or procedures for decision-making also leaves the group vulnerable to a groupthink dynamic. Groupthink provides safety and security for decision-makers, and these qualities can be inviting if the situation at hand is a crisis or has moral overtones, or if there was a recent policy failure. Consequently, it is not surprising to find that decision-making during major crises are susceptible to groupthink, because members rely on each other for support and validation. Janis notes several reasons why groupthink is normally expected to be deleterious to decision-making. The most obvious problem is that the search for information and alternatives is inadequately carried out. Outside experts are not solicited and thinking is conformist. After a decision has been made, it is not likely to be vetted for possible problems and undesired outcomes. Because the group often has an unrealistically high opinion of itself and its ability to succeed, it is less likely to have a back-up plan in case of failure or the ability to monitor past decisions.

More recent work on group decision-making has refined and expanded the groupthink model to include additional group processes and pathologies. In *Beyond Groupthink*, Paul 't Hart, Eric Stern, and Bengt Sundelius (1997a) point out that small groups working in an advisory process are varied in composition and role, and that there are political and institutional factors that operate above the level of the group and that define and shape its role. The authors raise additional questions ('t Hart, Stern, and Sundelius 1997b) regarding the groupthink model. First, it is unclear how applicable the model is. Most of the extant research on the model is confined to the USA, raising the question of the model's applicability outside the presidential system and its rather unique presidential advisory system.

't Hart and colleagues (1997b: 11) caution that the groupthink bias is not the only possible result of group decision-making. Indeed, George's multiple-advocacy model (1980) points to conditions under which the quality of a decision may be enhanced in a group setting. The model posits a loose decision structure in which the leader moderates a diversity of views within the group of advisers. The leader advocates competition between agencies or individuals (Dougherty and Pfaltzgraff 1990: 472–3) and chooses from the several policy options that have been openly debated. George and Stern (2002) argue that the multiple-advocacy model is likely to produce desirable decisions when an advisory group represents a diversity of opinions, advisers have equal access to resources, the leader actively monitors the debate, and there is little time pressure.

Another alternative to groupthink is polythink (Mintz, Mishal, and Morag 2005; Mintz and DeRouen 2010: ch. 3), which is characterized by varied and multiple views, opinions, and perceptions of the same goals and alternatives among group members. In contrast to the homogenous, uniform, monolithic world view of group members that characterizes groupthink, polythink reflects group heterogeneity. Some of the distinguishing features of polythink are independence of thought and the existence of contradictory interests among group members. These may create a situation in which it becomes virtually impossible for group members to reach a common interpretation of reality and common policy goals.

Summary Approaches

Recent research (see Thaler and Sunstein 2009; Kahneman 2011) presents an integrated view of cognitive psychological approaches as they influence everyday decision-making. Such research begins with the distinction between two separate 'operating systems' within each decision-maker: an automatic/fast system and a reflective/slow system. When a decision-maker is in the automatic/fast mode, he or she tends to reason 'from the gut'—make choices consistent with easily retrieved information. When operating in the reflective/slow mode, decision makers are more deliberative and logical.[2] Thaler and Sunstein (2009) explain that many choices made by individuals are not in their best interests. Indeed, individuals operating in the automatic/fast mode tend to be myopic, self-indulgent, and subject to peer pressure. Consequently, the quality of decision-making can be improved by manipulating the presentation of choices such that decision-makers can choose desirable courses of action.[3]

4 THE RATIONAL–COGNITIVE DEBATE

Perhaps the most prominent debate within the subfield of foreign-policy decision-making is between advocates of rational choice and those advancing cognitive

---

[2] Note that the two-stage process is not unlike that postulated by poliheuristic theory described above.

[3] Thaler and Sunstein's work (2009) reportedly influenced leaders and officials at the 2012 London Olympics. For example, rather than employ command-and-control policies such as those used at the 2008 Olympics in Beijing, Londoners and spectators were 'nudged' into public transport by receiving travel passes with event tickets (*The Economist* 2012).

psychological approaches. The debate has tended towards three issues: (1) the importance of process relative to outcome; (2) the large variety of cognitive models; and (3) deductive versus inductive theory construction. Regarding the first issue, cognitive psychological approaches to foreign-policy decision-making tend to privilege the role of process over outcome, focusing on how framing, beliefs, schemata, and (among other things) information-processing influence decision-making. Rational choice approaches tend to focus on preferences and outcomes (Hudson and Vore 1995; Rosati 2000). Initially, the cognitive critique of rational choice involved the characterization of a decision-maker as a cool-headed 'superhuman' capable of identifying all possible goals and alternatives and carrying out precise expected utility calculations in order to arrive at the 'best' choice (see, e.g., Simon 1957). According to critics, such a characterization of decision-makers was patently unrealistic, providing an erroneous account of the decision-making process. In response to these claims, rationalists argue that the account of rationality typically set forth by critics refers to procedural rationality rather than instrumental rationality (see, e.g., Zagare 1990). While the former refers to an ideal type developed to avoid errors in judgement, the latter type of rationality relies on fewer assumptions and allows for miscalculations, which are thought to occur commonly in foreign policy.

Despite the forceful restatement of instrumental rationality's assumptions, cognitivists renewed their calls for greater process validity. Following the discoveries of Kahneman and Tversky (1979) in particular, cognitivists argued against the utility of a theory whose assumptions appeared to be largely disconfirmed in experimental psychology and economics. In response, rationalists point to the long-standing tradition that the usefulness of the rational choice assumptions lies in the accuracy of the predictions deduced by the assumptions. If the predictions are accurate and the model outperforms its competitors, decision-makers can be treated 'as if' they are rational (see Friedman 1953).

A related defence of the rational model concerns parsimony. From only a few simple assumptions, the rational choice model is capable of explaining a variety of political decisions. The capacity for abstraction is regarded as a virtue. Simplifying assumptions are not intended to recreate actual behaviour, but to generate accurate and robust predictions. Consequently, the rational choice model is devoid of psychological factors. Indeed, rationalists point out that the consideration of psychological variables tends to contribute little to the explanatory power of the rational model, reducing parsimony (Danilovic 2003).

As a result of the relative emphases on process or outcome validity, the rational and cognitive approaches have developed largely in mutual isolation, each dominant in its own realm (see Kaufmann 1994; Hudson and Vore 1995; Rosati 2000). Such mutual isolation, however, does not bode well for scientific progress. In order to evaluate theories relative to their competitors, one must be able to draw direct comparisons between them (Lakatos 1970). If one approach focuses primarily on one type of phenomenon (for example, process) while a competing approach focuses on another (such as outcomes), they may be incommensurable (see Kuhn 1970), complicating useful comparisons and progress in theory development and testing (see Kaufmann 1994).

The second issue concerns the large variety of cognitive models. Some argue that the cognitive approach is fragmented and consists of islands of theory with 'no dominant decision rule' (Stein and Welch 1997: 53). In contrast, the rational choice model seems to have attained the status of a unified framework for understanding decision-making (see, e.g., MacDonald 2003). While the former claim can be supported by the myriad mechanisms identified by cognitivists (that is, schemata, heuristics, and so on), the latter is difficult to defend. There is no single rational choice theory. Recent advances in non-cooperative game theory highlight the variety of models employing the basic rational choice assumptions. For instance, rational choice models vary according to the number and preferences of the actors, the number and type of alternatives, the number of moves each player makes, the completeness of information, and so on. Each model is implicitly embedded in a particular situation with a variety of psychological factors assumed: 'actors do what they believe is in their best interest at the time' (Morrow 1997: 12). Rather than account for the origins of beliefs and interests, these concepts are treated as exogenous. Moreover, rationalists continue to be at odds with each other over appropriate solution concepts for identifying predictions in game theory models. Most political scientists are familiar with the Nash equilibrium as a solution concept. However, this solution concept—and, indeed, other refinements—do not always provide a unique solution for a game. Consequently, scholars have developed new solution concepts to narrow down the number of equilibrium outcomes in a given model (see, e.g., Danilovic 2003). Overall, the rational choice approach is no more coherent or unified than the cognitive approach.

The third issue in the debate concerns the merits of deduction relative to the pitfalls of induction—a practice ascribed to cognitivists. Simply put, induction relies on the incorporation of observed relationships and phenomena into a theory, while deduction involves the construction of a theory from abstract and frequently unobserved assumptions that are used to develop hypotheses. Deduction is thought to be the superior technique for theory construction because it avoids problems associated with selection and sample bias, avoiding erroneous conclusions. Rationalists point out cognitive theories incorporate assumptions that were obtained through experiments, surveys, or archival materials (Morrow 1997). As a consequence, such cognitive models are merely descriptions of observed phenomena. In contrast, rational models begin from first principles and formulate assumptions before examining the phenomena of interest. Cognitivists defend their practice on the basis of added scientific realism. But the differences between these methods for theory construction are rather narrow in practice. When developing a model, rationalists typically attempt to explain as many known phenomena as possible (see Bueno de Mesquita et al. 1999). Indeed, much of the formal rational literature during the 1970s and 1980s consisted of analyses of single cases in which the outcome was known and the purpose of the analysis was to induce the preferences of the decision-makers. Even models that attempt to explain a large number of cases must be constructed such that they account for known phenomena. Alternatively, cognitivists identify (that is, deduce) implications of their theories and test them in research settings external to the cases(s) in which the theory was developed. Thus, theory is not constructed in a vacuum for either school, and deduction leads to novel hypotheses that are then tested.

Despite these seemingly insurmountable issues, the rational–cognitive debate has spawned some cross-fertilization between the approaches. For instance, with poliheuristic theory, Mintz and colleagues have fruitfully incorporated expected utility into a cognitive model of decision-making, enhancing the precision of predictions (that is, outcome validity). Similarly, scholars working within the operational code research programme have integrated the theory with game theory. Specifically, operational code analysis has made explicit the strategic nature of the theory through the use of subjective games rooted in the rules of play developed by Brams (1993)—the theory of moves (TOM). For example, Walker (1977) argued that Kissinger's belief system led to preferences akin to the logic of the prisoner's dilemma game. Recent operational code research has relied extensively on formal modelling using 2×2 games and simulations (see, e.g., Walker and Schafer 2006). Rationalists have also incorporated psychological factors in their models such as perceptions and beliefs (see, e.g., Kim and Bueno de Mesquita 1995).

5 Conclusion and New Directions

As this chapter has demonstrated, there are a number of decision approaches and biases that are applicable to leadership decision-making. Most of the models and theories discussed in this chapter are applicable to both domestic policy-making and to foreign-policy decision-making. Scholars often disagree on an overarching theory of political decision-making, however. These controversies provide fertile areas for future study. For example, the poliheuristic decision model is posited as a hybrid approach involving elements of both the rational and cognitive schools. While much work on political decision-making has been done from experimental approaches, there is much more that can be done using statistical methods. In order to do this, more empirical data are needed.

Wilkenfeld and colleagues (Wolak, Jonas, and Wilkenfeld 2012) have created the International Crisis Behavior (ICB) dataset, which is built around international crises since 1918. The dataset includes several interesting decision-making variables such as size and structure of decision unit that can be looked at alongside crisis variables such as duration, intensity, and outcome. A study of decision-making during mediation would make a strong contribution to the literature. For example, one could study the decision by rebels and government to accept mediation. Similarly, studies of political reform, civil-war onset, war termination, peace marketing, and peace agreement implementation could each benefit from decision-making approaches.

Three areas are particularly promising for future research:

1. Effective elite decision-making. Academic research can contribute not only to explaining and forecasting decisions by political elites (e.g. Bueno de Mesquita 1984; Mintz 2005b), but also to producing high-quality decisions of leaders.

2. Elite decision-making and neuroscience—for example, understanding how the brain affects decisions on war and peace and how certain decisions affect the mind (see, e.g., McDermott 2004a).

3. Genetic influences on decision-making—understanding the role of genetic variables in decision-making (see, e.g., Fowler and Schreiber 2008).

Recommended Reading

Allison, G. (1971). *Essence of Decision: Explaining the Cuban Missile Crisis*. New York: Little Brown.

Mintz, A., and DeRouen, K. (2010). *Understanding Foreign Policy Decision Making*. Cambridge: Cambridge University Press.

Steinbruner, J. D. (2002) [1974]. *The Cybernetic Theory of Decision*. Princeton: Princeton University Press.

References

Allison, G. (1969). 'Conceptual Models and the Cuban Missile Crisis', *American Political Science Review*, 63/3: 689–718.

Allison, G. (1971). *Essence of Decision: Explaining the Cuban Missile Crisis*. New York: Little Brown.

Allison, G., and Halperin, M. (1972). 'Bureaucratic Politics: A Paradigm and Some Implications', in R. Tanter and R. Ullman (eds), *Theory and Policy in International Relations*. Princeton: Princeton University Press, 40–79.

Astorino-Courtois, A., and Trusty, B. (2000). 'Degrees of Difficulty: The Effect of Israeli Policy Shifts on Syrian Peace Decisions', *Journal of Conflict Resolution*, 44/3: 359–77.

Axelrod, R. (1973). 'Schema Theory: An Information Processing Model of Perception and Cognition', *American Political Science Review*, 67/4: 1248–66.

Berejikian, J. D. (2002). 'A Cognitive Theory of Deterrence', *Journal of Peace Research*, 39/2: 165–84.

Brams, Steven J. (1993). *Theory of Moves*. Cambridge: Cambridge University Press.

Brockner, J. (1992). 'The Escalation of Commitment to a Failing Course of Action: Toward Theoretical Progress', *Academy of Management Review*, 17/1: 39–61.

Bueno de Mesquita, B. (1984). 'Forecasting Policy Decisions: An Expected Utility Approach to Post-Khomeini Iran', *Political Science*, 17/2: 226–36.

Bueno de Mesquita, B., Smith, A., Siverson, R., and Morrow, J. (1999). 'An Institutional Explanation for the Democratic Peace', *American Political Science Review*, 93/4: 791–807.

Bueno de Mesquita, B., Smith, A., Siverson, R., and Morrow, J. (2003). *The Logic of Political Survival*. Cambridge, MA: MIT Press.

Cashman, G. (1993). *What Causes War? An Introduction to Theories of International Conflict*. New York: Lexington Books.

Cyert, R. M., and March, J. G. (1963). *A Behavioral Theory of the Firm*. Englewood Cliffs, NJ: Prentice Hall.

Danilovic, V. (2003). 'The Rational–Cognitive Debate and Poliheuristic Theory', in A. Mintz (ed.), *Integrating Cognitive and Rational Theories of Foreign Policy Decision Making*. New York: Palgrave Macmillan, 127–37.

DeRouen, K., and Sprecher, C. (2004). 'Initial Crisis Reaction and Poliheuristic Theory', *Journal of Conflict Resolution*, 48/1: 56–68.

Dougherty, J., and Pfaltzgraff, R. (1990). *Contending Theories of International Relations*. New York: Harper and Row.

The Economist (2012). 'The Joy of the Nudge Olympics', *The Economist*, 12 August.

Feldman, M. S. (1989). *Order without Design: Information Production and Policy Making*. Stanford, CA: Stanford University Press.

Fowler, J. H., and Schreiber, D. (2008). 'Biology, Politics, and the Emerging Science of Human Nature', *Science*, 322/5903: 912–14.

Friedman, M. (1953). *Essays in Positive Economics*. Chicago: University of Chicago Press.

George, A. (1979). 'The Causal Nexus between Cognitive Beliefs and Decision-Making Behavior: The Operational Code Belief System', in L. Falkowski (ed.), *Psychological Models in International Politics*. Boulder, CO: Westview.

George, A. (1980). *Presidential Decision-Making in Foreign Policy: The Effective Use of Information and Advice*. Boulder, CO: Westview Press, 95–121.

George, A. L. and Stern, E. K. (2002). 'Harnessing Conflict in Foreign Policy Making: From Devil's to Multiple Advocacy'. *Presidential Studies Quarterly*, 32 (3): 484–505.

Halperin, M. (1974). *Bureaucratic Politics and Foreign Policy*. Washington: Brookings Institution.

Hermann, M. G. (1974). 'Effects of Leader Personality on National Foreign Policy Behavior', in J. N. Rosenau (ed.), *Comparing Foreign Policies: Theories, Findings, and Methods*. Beverly Hills, CA: Sage, 201–34.

Hermann, M. G. (1980). 'Explaining Foreign Policy Behavior Using Personal Characteristics of Political Leaders', *International Studies Quarterly*, 24/1: 7–46.

Hermann, M. G., and Hermann, C. F. (1989). 'Who Makes Foreign Policy Decisions and how: An Empirical Inquiry', *International Studies Quarterly*, 33/3: 361–87.

Hermann, M. G., Preston, T., Korany, B., and Shaw, T. M. (2001). 'Who Leads Matters: The Effects of Powerful Individuals', *International Studies Review*, 3/2: 83–132.

Hilsman, R. (1967). *To Move a Nation*. New York: Doubleday.

Hudson, V., and Vore, C. S. (1995). 'Foreign Policy Analysis Yesterday, Today, and Tomorrow', *Mershon International Studies Review*, 39/2: 209–38.

Huntington, S. P. (1960). 'Strategic Planning and the Political Process', *Foreign Affairs*, 38/2: 285–99.

Janis, I. L. (1982). *Groupthink*. 2nd edn. Boston: Houghton Mifflin.

Jervis, R. (1976). *Perception and Misperception in International Politics*. Princeton: Princeton University Press.

Jones, B. D., and Baumgartner, F. R. (2005). *The Politics of Attention: How Government Prioritizes Problems*. Chicago: University of Chicago Press.

Kahneman, D. (2011). *Thinking, Fast and Slow*. New York: Farrar, Straus and Giroux.

Kahneman, D., and Tversky, A. (1979). 'Prospect Theory: An Analysis of Decision under Risk', *Econometrica*, 47/2: 263–92.

Kaufmann, C. (1994). 'Out of the Lab and into the Archives: A Method for Testing Psychological Explanations of Political Decision Making', *International Studies Quarterly*, 38/4: 557–86.

Kim, W., and Bueno de Mesquita, B. (1995). 'How Perceptions Influence the Risk of War', *International Studies Quarterly*, 39/1: 51–65.

Kissinger, H. (1966). 'Domestic Structure and Foreign Policy', *Daedalus*, 95/2: 503–29.

Kuhn, T. S. (1970). *The Structure of Scientific Revolutions*. Chicago: University of Chicago Press.

Lakatos, I. (1970). 'The Methodology of Scientific Research Programmes', in I. Lakatos and A. Musgrave (eds), *Criticism and the Growth of Knowledge*. Cambridge: Cambridge University Press, 91–195.

Leites, N. (1951). *The Operational Code of the Politburo*. New York: McGraw-Hill.

Levinson, D. J. (1957). 'Authoritarian Personality and Foreign Policy', *Journal of Conflict Resolution*, 1/1: 37–47.

McDermott, R. (1992). 'Prospect Theory in International Relations: The Iranian Hostage Rescue Mission', *Political Psychology*, 13/2: 237–63.

McDermott, R. (2004a). 'The Feeling of Rationality: The Meaning of Neuroscientific Advances for Political Science', *Perspectives on Politics*, 2/4 691–706.

McDermott, R. (2004b). *Political Psychology in International Relations*. Ann Arbor, MI: University of Michigan Press.

MacDonald, P. (2003). 'Useful Fiction or Miracle Maker: The Competing Epistemological Foundations of Rational Choice Theory', *American Political Science Review*, 97/4: 551–65.

Mintz, A. (1993). 'The Decision to Attack Iraq: A Noncompensatory Theory of Decision Making', *Journal of Conflict Resolution*, 37/4: 595–618.

Mintz, A. (2004). 'How Do Leaders Make Decisions? A Poliheuristic Perspective', *Journal of Conflict Resolution*, 48/1: 3–13.

Mintz, A. (2005a). 'Are Leaders Susceptible to Negative Political Advice? An Experimental Study of High-Ranking Military Officers', in A. Mintz and B. M. Russett (eds), *New Directions for International Relations: Confronting the Method of Analysis Problem*. Lahman, MD: Lexington Books, 223–38.

Mintz, A. (2005b). 'Applied Decision Analysis: Utilizing Poliheuristic Theory to Explain and Predict Foreign Policy and National Security Decisions', *International Studies Perspectives*, 6/1: 94–8.

Mintz, A. and DeRouen, K. (2010). *Understanding Foreign Policy Decision Making*. Cambridge: Cambridge University Press.

Mintz, A., and Geva, N. (1997). 'The Poliheuristic Theory of Foreign Policy Decision Making', in N. Geva and A. Mintz (eds), *Decision Making on War and Peace: The Cognitive-Rational Debate*. Boulder, CO: Lynne Rienner Publishers, 81–101.

Mintz, A., Mishal, S., and Morag, N. (2005). 'Victims of Polythink? The Israeli Delegation to Camp David 2000'. Unpublished manuscript, UN Studies, Yale University.

Mintz, A., Geva, N., Redd, S., and Carnes, A. (1997). 'The Effect of Dynamic and Static Choice Sets on Political Decision Making: An Analysis Using the Decision Board Platform', *American Political Science Review*, 91/3: 533–66.

Morrow, J. (1997). 'A Rational Choice Approach to International Conflict', in N. Geva and A. Mintz (eds), *Decision Making on War and Peace: The Cognitive-Rational Debate*. Boulder, CO: Lynne Rienner Publishers, 11–31.

Ostrom, C., and Job, B. (1986). 'The President and the Political Use of Force', *American Political Science Review*, 80/2: 541–66.

Payne, J., Bettman, J., and Johnson, E. (1993). *The Adaptive Decision Maker*. Cambridge: Cambridge University Press.

Pruitt, D. G. (1965). 'Definition of the Situation as a Determinant of International Action', in H. C. Kelman (ed.), *International Behavior: A Social-Psychological Analysis*. New York: Holt, Reinhart and Winston, 391–432.

Riker, W. (1995). 'The Political Psychology of Rational Choice Theory', *Political Psychology*, 16/1: 23–44.

Rosati, J. A. (2000). 'The Power of Human Cognition in the Study of World Politics', *International Studies Review*, 2/1: 45–75.

Sage, A. (1990). *Concise Encyclopedia of Information Processing in Systems and Organizations.* New York: Pergamon Press.

Schelling, T. (1966). *Arms and Influence.* New Haven, CT: Yale University Press.

Simon, Herbert (1957). 'A Behavioral Model of Rational Choice', in H. Simon (ed.), *Models of Man: Social and Rational.* New York: John Wiley and Sons, 24–60.

Snyder, R. C., Bruck, H., and Sapin, B. (1954). *Decision-Making as an Approach to the Study of International Politics.* Foreign Policy Analysis Project Series No. 3. Princeton, NJ: Princeton University Press.

Snyder, R. C., Bruck, H., and Sapin, B. (1962). *Foreign Policy Decision Making.* New York: Free Press.

Staw, B., and Ross, J. (1989). 'Understanding Behavior in Escalation Situations', *Science*, 246/4927: 216–20.

Stein, J. G., and Welch, D. A. (1997). 'Rational and Psychological Approaches to the Study of International Conflict: Comparative Strengths and Weaknesses', in N. Geva, and A. Mintz (eds.), *Decision-making on war and peace: The cognitive-rational debate.* Boulder, CO: Lynne Rienner Publishers: 51–80.

Steinbruner, J. D. (2002) [1974]. *The Cybernetic Theory of Decision.* Princeton: Princeton University Press.

Thaler, R., and Sunstein, C. (2009). *Nudge: Improving Decisions about Health, Wealth and Happiness.* New York: Penguin.

't Hart, P., Stern, E., and Sundelius, B. (1997a). *Beyond Groupthink: Political Group Dynamics and Foreign Policy-Making.* Ann Arbor, MI: University of Michigan Press.

't Hart, P., Stern, E., and Sundelius, B. (1997b). 'Foreign Policy-Making at the Top: Political Groups Dynamics', in P. 't Hart, E. Stern, and B. Sundelius (eds), *Beyond Groupthink: Political Group Dynamics and Foreign Policy-Making.* Ann Arbor, MI: University of Michigan Press, 1–33.

Tversky, A. and Kahneman, D. (1981). 'The Framing of Decisions and the Psychology of Choice', *Science*, 211/4481: 453–8.

von Neumann, J., and Morgenstern, O. (1947). *Theory of Games and Economic Behavior.* Princeton: Princeton University Press.

Walker, S. G. (1977). 'The Interface between Beliefs and Behavior: Henry A. Kissinger's Operational Code and the Vietnam War', *Journal of Conflict Resolution*, 21/1: 129–68.

Walker, S., and Schafer, M. (2006). 'Belief Systems as Causal Mechanisms in World Politics: An Overview of Operational Code Analysis', in M. Schafer and S. Walker (eds), *Beliefs and Leadership in World Politics.* New York: Palgrave Macmillan, 3–22.

Welch, D. (1992). 'The Organizational Process and Bureaucratic Politics Paradigms: Retrospect and Prospect', *International Security*, 17/2: 112–46.

Wolak, P. E., Jonas, A., and Wilkenfeld, J. (2012). 'International Crisis Behavior Dataset' <www.cidcm.umd.edu/icb/data/>, accessed 1 October 2013.

Zagare, F. C. (1990). 'Rationality and Deterrence', *World Politics*, 42/3: 238–60.

CHAPTER 16

......

SOCIAL-CONSTRUCTIONIST ANALYSIS

......

KEITH GRINT

1 ORIGINS AND 'ESSENCE'

CONSTRUCTIVISM has roots in psychology, and especially social psychology, but the origins of constructionism also lie more generally in the discipline of sociology (Wright-Mills 1959; Berger and Luckmann 1966) and the postmodern world of Derrida (2001) and Foucault (2003). Burr (2003) provides an excellent introduction, but its most significant writer in social psychology is probably Kenneth J. Gergen (1999, 2001). Gergen argued that the approach embodied four separate elements: the role of language, the social nature of knowledge, the political aspects of knowledge, and the centrality of the relational aspects of life. Social constructionism has a parallel history in the social studies of science and technology (Grint and Woolgar 1997), but its roots in the field of politics are probably best represented by the work of Edelman, whose 1964 work, *The Symbolic Use of Politics*, began to draw a line in the academic sand against the overwhelming traditions of rational choice political analysis. While the latter insisted (and still does) that political life is rooted in the rational decision-making capacities of individuals, Edelman insisted in his early work that political life was open to rational analysis but was primarily a symbolic art, so that elections, for example, were as much about *persuading* voters that they actually had a choice to make as actually providing the infrastructure and legitimacy for elected leaders to do anything. Towards the end of his life, however, Edelmen had shifted away from the rational methodology altogether and adopted what became known as a constructionist approach (DeCanio 2005).

Social constructionism is an approach that eschews looking for 'the truth' about political leadership and focuses instead upon the persuasive mechanisms that are used to persuade us that something is 'true', 'right', 'appropriate', 'evil', or whatever the writers and readers are concerned with. In other words, it insists that—in this context— political leadership is a *social* construct that is wrought from the interactions of people.

Constructivism—as opposed to constructionism, though these terms are often used interchangeably in many writings—tends to have a more cognitivist approach, which is locked into an individual's perspectives, rather than the social or interactive or relational line adopted by constructionists (Cunliffe 2008). Constructionists, despite their variable approaches, tend not to concern themselves with the alleged 'essential' nature of political leaders such as Mandela, Stalin, or Angela Merkel or more generally with 'leadership', and instead try to understand why these individuals are considered to be more successful instantiations of political leadership and what the role of their relatedness is. What makes us think that Stalin was responsible for what happened in the USSR during his lifetime? Why do we assume that Merkel should have the answer to the Euro crisis? What persuades us that Mandela was a great political leader and the rest of the ANC were mere bit players in the displacement of apartheid? Why do we need to imagine that 'we' are different from, and better than, 'them'? Constructionists are interested in these kinds of process questions rather than 'What individual leadership competencies can guarantee success?' or 'What is the objective effect of a leader on the performance of his or her organization?'

These latter questions are 'senseless': we cannot assess leadership without assessing the relationship between leaders and followers (Collinson 2005) or their opponents, so it makes no sense to follow either just the leaders or just the followers; what we should be following is the mobilization or demobilization of the group through the relationship of the former to the latter. This, of course, also means that the phrase 'we get the leaders we deserve' has more than an element of relevance; as does the apparent opposite, 'we get the followers we deserve'. If leadership is necessarily relational, then blaming the paucity of good leaders on your own organization, or complaining about the quality of your followers, is something of a self-reflected admission of failure.

It might be that the questions are 'pointless': we cannot isolate the independent effects of an individual on collective enterprises in any objective way. In short, the questions depend upon assumptions about the objectivity of social life and our ability to measure it, and the constructionist challenge lies in the flexibility and indeterminacy of language in particular and social life more generally. For constructionists, life is irredeemably social and socially negotiated, so the real question is how political leadership is brought off, achieved, and performed (Grint 2010).

2 NARRATIVE, LANGUAGE, AND PERFORMANCE

In sum, the world is socially shaped by the language we use, by the conversations, the books, the blogs, the tweets, and so on, through which we make sense of the world (Calas and Smircich 1988; Fairclough and Grant 2010). This means not that there is a linear relationship between the world and the subsequent word that we use to make sense of the world but that the word constructs the world differently—we do not see 'a tree' and then label it 'a tree', thus using the word to categorize the world—but rather that the 'thing' becomes 'a tree' only when we constitute it through the word. In effect, the word makes the world different. It is, then, through language that we frame the 'reality' and that implies that we can reframe it through language (Fairhurst and Sarr 1996).

For instance, 'waterboarding' was introduced as an interrogation technique by the USA by arguing that it involved the use of a wet towel and dripping water which induced the misperception of drowning. The consequence of the word 'misperception' is that it transfers responsibility from the interrogator to the detainee: if the latter thinks he or she is being drowned, then he or she has 'misperceived' what is happening and what the former intends. Of course, the detainee *cannot* know this, and from his or her per- spective it may very well seem like 'torture'; but the reframing of the term facilitates a changed perception from torture to misperception: it constitutes the world differently.

Likewise, the whole debate around 'terrorism' is shot through with disputes that are 'fixed' by language. As Fisk (2001: 438–41) suggests:

> when Israeli soldiers were captured by Lebanese guerrillas they were reported to have been 'kidnapped', as if the Israeli presence in Lebanon was in some way legiti- mate. Suspected resistance men in southern Lebanon, however, were 'captured' by Israeli troops... By the mid-1980s, the AP [Associated Press] used 'terrorists' about Arabs but rarely about the IRA in Northern Ireland, where the agreed word was 'guerrillas', presumably because AP serves a number of news outlets in the United States with a large Irish–American audience. The BBC, which increasingly referred to Arab 'terrorists', *always* referred to the IRA as 'terrorists' but scarcely ever called ANC bombers in South Africa 'terrorists'... *Tass* and *Prada*, of course, referred to Afghan rebels as 'terrorists'... In September 1985 a British newspaper reported that a [Soviet] airliner carrying civilian passengers [over Afghanistan] had been 'downed by rebels'. 'Terrorists' are those who use violence against the side that is using the word. The only terrorists whom Israel acknowledges are those opposed to Israel. The only terrorists that the United States acknowledges are those that oppose the United States or their allies. The only terrorists Palestinians acknowledge—for they too use the word—are those opposed to the Palestinians.

This also implies that leadership in general and political leadership in particular are a performance, and a performance that includes scripts, extemporizations, props, stages, icons, symbols, and bodies. Put another way, language is performative: it does not reflect the world; it constitutes the world (Austin 1962). Thus, while more conventional approaches to political leadership might concern themselves with the social class of the supporters, their material well-being, the unemployment rate, and so on, construc- tionists remain sceptical that success or failure can be predicted (determined) by such 'structural' features of the political landscape and more interested in the way the sym- bolic aspects of political life can be used to promote or undermine political ambitions, policies, and identities. To put it another way, political leadership is about the leadership of meaning as well as the meaning of leadership.

As a consequence of this approach, narratives become critically important to politi- cal analysis. Narratives involve a series of events that are linked in causal terms rather than just randomly associated (Gabriel 2004). The most famous original example of this is from Forster (1962) (cited in Gabriel 2008: 195): 'the king died then the queen died'—which is not a narrative, because there is no apparent causal connection; versus 'the king died then the queen died of grief'—which is a narrative. Narratives, then, are sense-making devices, and, in the absence of a narrative, we literally 'lose the plot' (Gabriel 2008: 196). Hence, if we lock this back into Lakoff's argument (2004), it becomes clear that political leadership is deeply rooted in the construction of a narrative that embodies the identity of the group (Sims 2003) or political 'tribe' (see also Reicher, Haslam, and Platow, Chapter 10, this volume). It is this context that, in January 2012, Ed Miliband, the leader of the British Labour Party, was accused by Lord Glasman (a former supporter) of having 'no strategy, no narrative and little energy' (quoted in Wintour 2012: 1). In fact, the absence of strategy rather than the absence of a narrative became the focus of the subsequent debate—as if the most important aspect was the strategy for acquiring and retaining power rather than the narrative that might explain the *purpose* of acquiring power. As Oborne (2008) has suggested, the rise of the 'political class' in the UK seems to have ensured (in a remarkable refraction of Michels's prediction of 1915 (1949): 'who says organization says oligarchy') that a political elite now dominates British politics; not an elite formed from the same social class or the small group of private schools and the same universities, but one whose only concern is the acquisition and retention of political power—in and for itself. This might also help explain the increasing importance of narrative and the decreasing importance of demography as an explanation for contemporary British politics.

Storytelling and stories have formed the basis of many constructionist accounts of leadership, but even here disputes persist in terms of whether stories are relatively coherent accounts of events (Gabriel 1997; Czarniawska 2004) mythical or 'true', or relatively incoherent accounts without the conventional structure of beginning, middle, and end (BME): something that Boje (1991, 2001) calls 'antenarrative'. For Boje, myths provide a means for confused and contradictory organizational issues to be melded into some kind of coherent story; in effect, the myth facilitates collective sense-making. One might see this in the way countries refer to their original founding in ways that frequently obscure or elide their contested nature. In contrast, Czarniawska's work (e.g. 1997) is often locked in a theatrical frame where leaders enact positive roles to achieve organizational success and narratives are 'emplotted' to construct meaning retrospectively. In other words, narratives operate as sense-making stories providing the metaphorical scaffolding to support management in its contested attempt to control the organization.

Despite the concerns of Iyengar (2005), it remains the case that the narrative element of leadership does appear critical to explaining its success and failure. In other words, part of the differentiator between successful and unsuccessful political leadership is the ability to weave a story that induces or seduces the voter or follower into following the storyteller. Social constructionist approaches often adopt narrative approaches in their methodologies, focusing upon the stories that participants construct, though the narrative approach is not necessarily constructionist; the same holds for ethnography: many ethnographers adopt constructionist philosophies (Grint 2005), but the former are not coexistent with the latter. Let us consider a lodestone of leadership studies to explore the constructionist approach to political leadership in a little more detail: charisma.

3 The Social Construction of Charisma

Traditional positivist approaches (Bryman 1992: Bass 1997; Wofford 1999) assume that charisma is objective—that is, it can be measured—and therefore perhaps that it can even be 'taught'. However, this assumes that charisma is the possession of an individual—that is, that it exists in the absence of a particular group of followers. According to this approach, we can take an alleged 'charismatic' and assess him or her in some kind of scientific laboratory—and hopefully reduce his or her charisma to its 'essence' that can then be reassembled and taught. Who counts as charismatic, however, depends upon the audience, not the 'charismatic'. Some people regard all members of the British royal family as necessarily charismatic because of their origins—but others dispute whether any of them are, irrespective of their origins, and it is this essentially contested nature on which the constructionists focus (Billig 1995). Thus, while charisma is often linked to crisis—'come the moment, come the leader'—constructionists ask not just why we think some leaders are charismatic, but what counts as crisis, and why. For instance, a run on a currency or a fall in profits does not in itself generate an objective financial crisis; a crisis occurs when influential individuals and groups persuade a sufficient number of others that, indeed, it is now time to dump the currency or the shares. Others will deny this moment and seek to persuade us otherwise. In effect, the 'truth' lies not in the numbers, the exchange rates, or 'the market', but in the persuasive facility of influential people ('t Hart and Tindall 2009). This is the equivalent of endless disputes in soccer about whether the action of one player on another can be deemed 'a penalty'. The point is that it is the referee who determines 'reality' here, not the allegedly 'objective truth' and certainly not the opinions of the spectators.

A second element of charisma is the meaning of the term. The original work undertaken by Max Weber (1978) considered charisma to be restricted to a very small number of humans who exhibited superhuman qualities that were enacted during times of crisis and provided a solution to the perennial problems facing a group of people. In Weber's work, charismatics were usually religious individuals who appeared destined or who prophesied in some way, but their influence over their followers persisted only as long as their ability to undertake apparent miracles continued; I shall call this the 'strong' version of charisma: it is essentially irrational, emotional, rare, and fleeting. Some management scholars (Bass 1960; House 1977, 1999; Hughes, Ginnett, and Curphy 1999) who despaired of operationalizing Weber's concept argued, in contrast, that charisma was the equivalent of a strong, forceful, and focused character, what I shall call 'weak' charisma. Two aspects of this are worthy of note: first the assumption that the difficulty of measuring a concept implies that it should be 'tamed' until it can be measured implies something about the positivist essence of much management theory; second, that it still does not resolve the relational problem: if an individual measures 9 out of 10 of some putative score for 'charisma', this implies that all followers will agree with both the label and the evaluation—but there are never any robust empirical data to support this kind of assertion (Van Dooren 1994).

The same is 'true' for opinions about political leaders: whether Churchill was a great leader, or just in the right place at the right time, or merely the irrelevant pawn of greater structural forces is not settled by any publication, let alone 'the truth'. How could we know what 'the truth' actually was? Constructionists, then, argue that what we usually have are contested accounts of 'the truth' that vie for dominance by seeking to secure networks of supporters and undermining opponents. This is not to claim that any account is as good as any other; that some kind of value-free relativism prevails or that there is no objective reality or that everything exists only in the heads of the observers. Rather it is to insist that the problem is one of knowledge: that we cannot get to a level of objectivity that would allow us to conclude that, without Churchill, Britain would have lost the Second World War or that we can predict leadership success based on objective leadership competencies. That the Second World War would have been different if Churchill had not become the British Prime Minister is almost certainly the case— but quite how it would have been different, how we would measure this, or whether the answer would last across all time is highly debateable.

What, for example, is the reality of the 'charismatic' Cuban revolutionary Che Guevara? Was he a revolutionary driven by a burning desire to right the world's wrongs or a tyrannical terrorist or both or neither? If we were to examine all the writings by and about Che, I doubt that we would be in a better position to answer these questions because the reality is what Gallie (1955–6) referred to (talking about power not leadership) as 'essentially contested', and no amount of 'balanced analysis' is likely to avail us of the truth. What we can say is that Korda's iconic photograph of Che, taken in March 1960, was then used by Feltrini some seven years later in 1967—just before Guevara's death—on a series of posters, and by 1968—the year of students' and leftist protests around the world—Che's image had become associated with international protests against oppression, capitalism, racism, imperialism, the Vietnam War, and just about any other of the celebrated political 'causes' of the time. In effect, Che's image captured the collective desires of the political left in a way that nothing else did. Of course, Guevara himself may not have supported these causes, and the diversity of the causes was both astonishing and full of tensions and self-contradictions; but that is the point: a single icon embodied the zeitgeist, because the movements could not be captured in any other way. It is the very flexibility of the social construction that allows this performance to occur; no dry academic tome, no detailed analysis of the class or ethnic background of Che, no evaluation of his speeches compared to his achievements of himself or those of the Cuban revolutionaries could have possibly mobilized such a diverse group of people (Seidman and Buhle 2008). Note that the mobilization is usually more effective when the mobilization is against the symbolic 'other'.

It is precisely this form of social construction that enabled Joe Rosenthal's iconic flag raisers on Mount Suribachi on Iwo Jima in 1945 to be portrayed as the symbolic identity of the USA: a land where diversity, democracy, and freedom could overcome the ferocity of the Japanese fascist military machine (Bradley 2000). That helps explain how important the ownership of the Red Flag was to the Bolsheviks in the Russian Revolution: because the Red Flag became the charismatic symbol of resistance to the old regime, whoever owned the flag owned the revolution (Figes and Kolonitskii 1999).

4 SYMBOLISM, ICONS, AND BINARIES

The consequences of a constructionist approach to political leadership are intriguing, for, while the theory insists on the constitutive but flexible nature of language, the practice of political leadership shifts us from the fuzzy world of indeterminacy to the binary world of hostile camps (Grint 1997). Lilla (2012) is right to suggest that lumping all political views into left or right, conservative or revolutionary, as he suggests Robin (2011) does, is lazy, generalizing, and ultimately dangerous: the apocalypticism of the current American right is radically different from previous incarnations and significantly more of a threat to civil society. In effect, political views of all kinds are extraordinarily complex and should not be reduced to any binary divisions between us and them. This is the equivalent of attributing negative or positive characteristics to all members of a particular gender or ethnic group or age category irrespective of the evidential diversity. Yet this is precisely how political leadership tends to operate, particularly in a political system such as the USA, where the two-party system is virtually the only game in town; it coerces voters into one of two channels.

For example, Lakoff (2004) suggests that the American political system is riven by two competing world views: the 'strict parent' of the Republicans, which bears echoes of Thomas Hobbes's *Leviathan* and the necessity to maintain discipline to hold chaos at bay, and the 'nurturing parent' of the Democrats, which echoes more of Rousseau's *Social Contract* where existing social, political, and institutional barriers inhibit the ability of individuals to realize their true potential. For Lakoff the role of moral identity supersedes self-interest in explaining voting patterns, and this is manifest by—and mobilized through—the politics of language. Thus, while Republicans display moral soaked messages (freedom, choice), their Democratic opponents tend to eschew these in favour of material interests (tax benefits, levels of economic growth, and so on). The trick for Democrat supporters would, for example, be to switch the language frame of taxation from legal demand to patriotic duty—in other words, to imbue the strategy of the Democrats with a moral purpose that political liberals have always found more difficult than the more traditional parties of the political left (social equality) or right (individual freedom). Yet Iyengar (2005) points out that this is to assume an unmediated communication channel between political candidate and voter, when the role of the news media is paramount for how such messages are interpreted and transmitted; this can be critical when 'likeability' seems to be such an influential determinant of voting behaviour for the centrist floating or uncommitted voter.

To summarize so far, social constructionism implies that what counts as 'true', as 'objective', and as 'fact' are the results of contending accounts of 'reality'. That implies that 'reality' is constructed through language, and, in turn, since language is a social phenomenon, that the account of reality that prevails is often both a temporary and a collective phenomenon.

When we apply this to the Iraq War, it becomes clear that the 'truth'—for example, about Saddam's weapons of mass destruction (WMD)—is not a direct reflection of some objective facts that are undeniable; just because none were found does not mean that there were none. This is the equivalent of Karl Popper's falsification approach (1977) to science: we cannot prove science true; we can just make its suggestions more robust by subjecting it to tests of falsification. For constructionists 'the truth' about WMD—and what is more important, what this truth allowed political leaders to do—is not derived from scientific experiment or empirical proof, but neither is it merely a figment of some fetid imagination. Rather, it is the consequence of the temporary ability of particular groups to persuade themselves and others that WMD did (or did not) exist. In contrast, the failed attempt by different groups to deny the existence of WMD rendered their account subordinate and facilitated the invasion of Iraq. The failure of the post-war searchers to discover WMD does not, however, simply mean that the WMD account was false and therefore should have failed: despite the falsehoods, the result was an invasion, and hence the temporary nature of the persuasive account is all that matters in any pragmatic sense. It also implies that we will probably never know whether there ever were WMD, or what amount of chemicals or biological elements actually counts as WMD. In short, the book is never closed but is permanently open to contestation, just as reviews of, say, Winston Churchill, are never finally agreed but are always open to different renderings and potential inversions.

In order to understand the role of leadership in this we need to consider what kind of story was provided by political leaders as to the nature of the terrorist threat, and then what kind of power was constituted through that account as necessary to try and resolve that problem. As should become clear, the temptation of leaders is to define the problem in such a way that it becomes more aligned to their own predisposition to act: just as hammers see everything as a nail, so 'Commanders' see Critical Problems all around them, Managers see Tame Problems, and 'Leaders' see Wicked Problems (Grint 2005, 2008).

The quagmire that Iraq became for the Americans played some part in the election of Barack Obama to the White House, but it was only one element in many. Rather more important seems to have been the story that Obama managed to weave (Alexander 2010). If the power of storytelling remains dubious, then the resurgence of the American Right within a year of Obama's presidential victory has to be a good case to silence the sceptics. As Franks (2012) explains, when the Western world is brought to the brink of financial disaster by the failure of Western governments to regulate their own financial institutions and the same governments then rescue the same financial institutions from bankruptcy because they are 'too big to fail', one might have thought the political Left would gain credit from the shambles. Instead, however, and not just in the USA, the response has been the resurgence of market-driven 'solutions' either manifest in the Tea Party and the associate deregulation movement within the Republican Party or in the encroachment of 'free' schools and private health providers in England. Thus, while the apparent 'evidence' points to the absence of regulation as the problem, the consequence is a call for greater deregulation. How did this occur? For Franks the answer lies in the skill with which the Republican Right concocted a new narrative: that the market had never been free enough to work properly and the real cause was the overbearing presence of the government, not its negligent absence. Even the bail-out was construed through this same laissez-faire prism: look what the government did—first it oversees a financial catastrophe, then in the subsequent massive bail-out it gives all our money away to save the banks that it undermined in the first place! Obviously the solution is to remove the government altogether. The success of the Republicans can be explained only through the associated failure of the Democrats: the absence of any definitive story that put the blame for the financial crisis squarely in the laps of big business and their supporters allowed the contrary story to prevail. It was never about 'evidence' or 'responsibility for failure'; it was about contending narratives that best translated the past into a version of the present that foretold the future. The Democrats, as Lakoff (2004) had already implied, just did not get it: numbers do not persuade, stories do. Even Clinton's famous election winning strategy 'It's the economy stupid!' is itself a symbol; it was not an academic analysis of the economic numbers that persuaded people to vote; it was the collectively symbolic 'feel good' factor.

Alexander's account (2011) of the then-ongoing Egyptian revolution nicely captures the constructionist focus upon the collective symbolic representations over which the antagonists fought and also the way in which the plurality of debate is filtered by the media and gradually channelled into a binary system: us versus them. To traditional realist writers, the revolution can be understood through the macro lenses of social and economic forces of mass unemployment, demographic changes, political corruption, rising literacy, and increasing disenchantment. In contrast, Alexander argues that the symbolic aspects of the revolution are far more significant, but that these are channelled through binary linguistic codes: black becomes understood only through its contrast to white; good through bad, and so on. Thus the revolution became understood, not through the numbers of unemployed or the proportion of the population in absolute poverty, but through the hopes and dreams of the Egyptian population for a different and better future. This indeterminacy at the heart of the revolution also explains why such events can literally explode onto the streets—because they are only indirectly related to conventional assumptions of material 'facts' and more related to the emotional and cultural elements of social life, identities, and the vagaries of political consciousness. The latter implies that the actions of participants cannot be directly 'read-off' from their 'position' in society. As Soueif (2011: 1, quoted in Alexander 2011: 10–11) suggested:

> Young people of every background and social class marched and sang together. Older, respected figures went round with food and blankets. Cigarette-smoking women in jeans sat next to their niqab-wearing sisters on the pavement. Old comrades from the

students' movement of the 1970s met for the first time in decades. Young people went round collecting litter. People who stayed at home phoned nearby restaurants with orders to deliver food to protesters. Not one religious or sectarian slogan was heard. The solidarity was palpable. And if this sounds romantic, then it was, and is.

5   FUTURE RESEARCH

The implications of this kind of approach to political leadership is that we should pay more attention to the narratives, the stories, and the symbols that participants adopt and be wary of assuming that 'the facts' speak for themselves. Critics insist that 'facts', especially 'material' or economic facts, speak for themselves, but social constructionists tend to be deaf to the dulcet tones of mute numbers. Facts do not seem to say anything; they have to be interpreted, and this ensures that little is predictable in political life. Critics suggest that social constructionist approaches imply that the political world is open to all kinds of emotional and symbolic—that is, non-rational—aspects of life, and the implication of that is that political life might not be so easily explained, predicted, or controlled. Perhaps you, dear reader, should watch a news channel for an hour and work out whether what you see is the product of entirely rational minds in action—or that an entirely rational analysis could account for what you see.

Future research in this approach might eschew methods such as quantitative surveys or analysis of social class or mobility or ethnic composition of the voters or supporters and concentrate instead on the precise nature of the mobilization of the support: what exactly is the story, the narrative, the identity that the contestants develop in their quest for power and why does it resonate—if it does—with the supporters? Is the Euro crisis of 2012 simply the result of financial distress (and if so how is this 'measured?') or are there competing narratives of value and identity that are just as critical? Why do people vote against their allegedly objective material interests? How do political leaders and their advisers devise successful strategies for the acquisition of power, given the apparently objective nature of the context? In what ways do political narratives perform different versions of the present, the past, and the future? How significant are the cultural conditions within which politics is performed and to what extent are the cultural conditions themselves socially constructed? Is the Syrian conflict just a contest between rival interests that will be settled by the side with the greatest material resources, or do the narratives of cruelty, struggle, and freedom play a crucial role in mobilizing and demobilizing supporters and enemies?

6   CONCLUSION

Social constructionism is implacably opposed to 'essentialist' accounts of social life in general and political leadership in particular. It insists that what we know about either remains rooted in language, in contested accounts of 'reality', and in the (con)temporary nature of 'truth'. This implies that we cannot predict the outcomes of political contests based upon the material conditions that exist at the time; that what counts as 'the truth' is dependent upon which social group has (temporary) control, and that political narratives and stories matter—in other words, that through politics the world is made and therefore can be remade. This does not mean that 'reality' is simply constituted in people's heads and bears no relationship to what realist approaches count as 'reality'. It does not imply that the Iraq War may not have happened or that any one account of President Bush's and Prime Minister Blair's decisions are as good as any other. Instead it insists that we subject these accounts to scrutiny and try to explain why we take some accounts to be more persuasive than others. Part of that persuasiveness appears to be rooted in the power of the narrative account—that a call to arms because of a direct threat by terrorists to the security of the people is often a better mobilizer than claims about GNP or a percentage decrease in personal taxation. In short, political leadership is constructed through narrative and the most successful political leaders are often the greatest storytellers: Raconteurs Rule OK!

Recommended Reading

Alexander, J. C. (2010). *The Performance of Politics*. Oxford: Oxford University Press.
Gergen, K. J. (2001). *Social Construction in Context*. London: SAGE.
Grint, K. (2005). 'Problems, Problems, Problems: The Social Construction of Leadership', *Human Relations*, 58/11: 1467–94.

References

Alexander, J. C. (2010). *The Performance of Politics*. Oxford: Oxford University Press.
Alexander, J. C. (2011). *Performative Revolution in Egypt: An Essay in Cultural Power*. London: Bloomsbury.
Alvesson, M. (1996). 'Leadership Studies: From Procedure and Abstraction to Reflexivity and Situation', *Leadership Quarterly*, 7/4: 469–85.
Austin, L. J. (1962). *How to do Things with Words*. Cambridge, MA: Harvard University Press.
Bass, B. M. (1960). *Leadership, Psychology and Organizational Behaviour*. New York: Harper and Row.
Bass, B. M. (1997). 'Does the Transactional–Transformational Leadership Paradigm Transcend Organizational and National Boundaries?', *American Psychologist*, 52/3: 130–9.
Berger, P. L., and Luckmann, T. (1966). *The Social Construction of Reality: A Treatise in the Sociology of Knowledge*. Garden City, NY: Anchor Books.
Billig, M. (1995). *Banal Nationalism*. London: Sage.
Boje, D. (1991). 'The Storytelling Organization', *Administrative Science Quarterly*, 36: 106–26.
Boje, D. (2001). *Narrative Methods for Organizational and Communication Research*. London: Sage.

Bradley, J. (2000). *Flags of our Fathers*. New York: Bantam Press.

Bryman, A. (1992). *Charisma and Leadership in Organizations*. London: Sage.

Burr, V. (2003). *Social Constructionism*. 2nd edn. London: Routledge.

Calas, M. B., and Smircich, L. (1988). 'Reading Leadership as a Form of Cultural Analysis', in J. G. Hunt, J. R. Baliga, P. Dachler and C. A. Schriesheim (eds), *Emerging Leadership Vistas*. Lexington, MA: Lexington Books, 201–26.

Collinson, D. (2005). 'Dialectics of leadership', *Human Relations*, 58/11: 1419–42.

Cunliffe, A. (2008). 'Orientations to Social Constructivism: Relationally Responsive Social Constructionism and its Implications for Knowledge and Learning', *Management Learning*, 39/2: 123–39.

Czarniawska, B. (1997). *Narrating the Organization: Dramas of Institutional Identity*. Chicago: University of Chicago Press.

Czarniawska, B. (2004). *Narratives in Social Science Research*. London: Sage.

DeCanio, S. (2005). 'Murray Edelman on Symbols and Ideology in Democratic Politics', *Critical Review*, 17/3–4: 339–50.

Derrida, J. (2001). *Writing and Difference*. London: Routledge.

Edelman, M. (1964). *The Symbolic Uses of Politics*. Champaign, IL: University of Illinois Press.

Fairclough, G., and Grant, D. (2010). 'The Social Construction of Leadership: A Sailing Guide', *Management Communication Quarterly*, 24/2: 171–210.

Fairhurst, G. T., and Sarr, R. A. (1996). *The Art of Framing: Managing the Language of Leadership*. San Francisco: Jossey-Bass.

Figes, O., and Kolonitskii, B. (1999). *Interpreting the Russian Revolution: The Language and Symbols of 1917*. New Haven: Yale University Press.

Fisk, R. (2001). *Pity the Nation*. Oxford: Oxford University Press.

Forster, E. M. (1962). *Aspects of the Novel*. Harmondsworth: Penguin.

Foucault, M. (2003). *Society Must be Defended*. London: Allen Lane.

Franks, T. (2012). *Pity the Billionaire*. London: Harvill Secker.

Gabriel, Y. (1997). Meeting God. *Human Relations*, 50/4: 315–42.

Gabriel, Y. (2004). 'Narratives, Stories and Texts', in D. Grant, C. Hardy, C. Oswick, and L. Putnam (eds), *The Sage Handbook of Organizational Discourse*. London: Sage, 61–78.

Gabriel, Y. (2008). *Organizing Words*. London: Sage.

Gallie, W. B. (1955–6). 'Essentially Contested Concepts', *Proceedings of the Aristotelian Society*, 56: 167–198.

Gergen, K. J. (1999). *An Invitation to Social Construction*. London: Sage.

Gergen, K. J. (2001). *Social Construction in Context*. London: Sage.

Grint, K. (1997). *Fuzzy Management*. Oxford: Oxford University Press.

Grint, K. (2005). 'Problems, Problems, Problems: The Social Construction of Leadership', *Human Relations*, 58/11: 1467–94.

Grint, K. (2008). 'Wicked Problems and Clumsy Solutions', *Clinical Leader*, 1/2: 54–68.

Grint, K. (2010). *Leadership: A Very Short Introduction*. Oxford: Oxford University Press.

Grint, K., and Woolgar, S. (1997). *The Machine at Work*. Cambridge: Polity Press.

House, R. J. (1977). 'A Theory of Charismatic Leadership', in J. G. Hunt and L. L. Larson (eds), *Leadership: The Cutting Edge*. Carbondale, IL: Southern Illinois University Press, 189–207.

House, R. A. (1999). 'Weber and the Neo-charismatic Paradigm', *Leadership Quarterly*, 10/4: 563–74.

Hughes, R. L., Ginnett, R. C., and Curphy, G. J. (1999). *Leadership: Enhancing the Lessons of Leadership*. Singapore: Irwin-McGraw-Hill.

Iyengar, S. (2005). 'Speaking of Values: The Framing of American Politics', *The Forum*, 3/3: 7.

Lakoff, G. (2004). *Don't Think of an Elephant: Know Your Values and Frame the Debate*. White River Junction, VT: Chelsea Green Publishing.

Lilla, M. (2012). 'Republicans for Revolution', *New York Review of Books*, 6 January.

Michels, R. (1949) [1915]. *Political Parties: A Sociological Study of the Oligarchical Tendencies of Modern Democracy*. New York: Free Press.

Oborne, P. (2008). *The Triumph of the Political Class*. Bury St Edmunds: Pocket Books.

Popper, K. (1977). *The Logic of Scientific Discovery*. London: Routledge.

Robin, C. (2011). *The Reactionary Mind: Conservatism from Edmund Burke to Sarah Palin*. Oxford: Oxford University Press.

Seidman, S., and Buhle, P. (2008). 'Che Guevara, Image and Reality: Postscript to S. Rodriguez', in *Che: A Graphic Biography*. London: Verso.

Sims, D. (2003). 'Between the Millstones: A Narrative Account of the Vulnerability of Middle Managers' Storytelling', *Human Relations*, 56/10: 1195–211.

Sorenson, G., Goethals, G., and Haber, P. (2011). 'The Enduring and Elusive Quest for a General Theory of Leadership: Initial Efforts and New Horizons', in A. Bryman, D. Collinson, K. Grint, and M. Uhl-Bien (eds). *The SAGE Handbook of Leadership*. London: Sage, 29–36.

Soueif, A. (2011). 'Fittingly, it's the Young of the Country who are Leading us', *Guardian*, 28 January.

't Hart, P., and Tindall, K. (2009) (eds). *Framing the Global Economic Downturn: Crisis Rhetoric and the Politics of Recessions*. Sydney: Australian National University/ANZSOG.

Van Dooren, R. (1994). *Messengers from the Promised Land: An Interactive Theory of Political Charisma*. Leiden: DSWO Press, Leiden University.

Weber, M. (1978). *Economy and Society: An Outline of Interpretive Sociology*, Vol. 2, ed. G. Roth and C. Wittich, trans. E. Fischoff, H. Gerth, A. M. Henderson et al. Berkeley and Los Angeles: University of California Press.

Wintour, P. (2012). 'Miliband's Former Guru Says He Has No Strategy', *Guardian*, 5 January.

Wofford, J. C. (1999). 'Laboratory Research on Charismatic Leadership: Fruitful or Futile? *Leadership Quarterly*, 10/4: 523–9.

Wright-Mills, C. (1959). *The Sociological Imagination*. Oxford: Oxford University Press.

CHAPTER 17

....

RHETORICAL AND PERFORMATIVE ANALYSIS

....

JOHN UHR

1 INTRODUCTION

THIS chapter explores political leadership through rhetorical and performative analysis. My aim is to highlight the classical intellectual foundations of rhetorical analysis. Rhetorical analysis generally examines the scripts or *wordcraft* used by leaders; performative analysis examines their actions or *stagecraft*. Generally, political rhetoric is a *persuasive* performance using plausible but non-scientific evidence to persuade and convince audiences of the benefits of proposed action. This chapter argues that a primary ingredient of studies of leadership rhetoric has been the sustained use of Aristotle's classic *Rhetoric* with its elaborate defence of *deliberative* political rhetoric about what a community regards as politically expedient, rather than simply just or ideal (Aristotle 2005). Versions adopting or adapting classical deliberative schemes are valued because of their potential to deepen deliberation among citizens as well as strengthen elite leadership in contemporary policy communities (Garver 1994; Garsten 2006).

2 THE RHETORIC OF RHETORIC

The rhetoric of rhetoric is itself an academic study (Booth 2004). Performance analysis of politics places 'the text' of rhetoric into 'contexts' of audience mobilization. One link between classical rhetoric and modern schools of performative analysis is 'discourse', a term that bridges old and new forms of rhetorical analysis (Wilson 1990; Cohen 1994; Gottweis 2006). Various forms of discourse analysis are important to those examining what leaders say, in and out of government, and what audiences really hear. All approaches deal with the presentational and communicative side of political leadership, investigating the many demands leadership makes on *personal* as well as *official* communicative competency. My approach here is to treat the many types of analysis as parts of a larger whole dealing with the broad language of leadership (Nye 2008: 72–4; Keohane 2010: 97–1). Each form of analysis captures something important about leadership communication, including what is *not* said and what *is* said through gesture and body language. Generally, rhetoric is initially 'thought out' and then 'acted out', which helps explain why so many political leaders are experienced, if not always gifted, public actors. Accordingly, recent approaches to leadership performance have revived the rich study of 'role' in theatrics and dramaturgy (Charteris-Black 2005; Tourish and Jackson 2008; Cassin and Goffey 2009; Hackman and Johnson 2009; Biehl-Missal 2010; Sharma and Grant 2011).

Although leadership has its own language, which can be identified and translated through rhetorical and performative analysis, the study of rhetoric is not always flattering to performers of rhetoric (O'Keefe 2001; Garsten 2006). Governance scholars have been criticized for abuse of 'the theatre metaphor' to explain public leaders as rare and heroic figures with inspiring social visions (Terry 1997; Biehl-Missal 2010). So, too, the phrase 'just rhetoric' can suggest that rhetoric is make-believe: constructed stories hiding the truth. Rhetoric is a very real communicative power performed by leaders to persuade or influence others. In some cases, rhetoric is manipulative, with leaders using clever skills to mislead opponents or sometimes even their own supporters. Yet, in other cases, rhetoric can be used freely and fairly, when competing leaders openly participate in a public contest to determine who deserves the higher public trust. Leadership provided by independent brokers can help interested communities test the claims of competing political leaders. Trust is usually ranked according to the leaders' credibility, which is judged in terms of *who* they are ('are they really so representative?') as well as *what* they say ('does she really believe that?'). Measuring political actors' capacity to move constructively 'from beliefs to arguments' implies measuring their *non-populist* leadership performance, pioneered in significant ways by UK scholar Finlayson (2007). Evaluating the merits of competing rhetoric is never easy: rhetorical contests often reward clever winners, with public credibility reduced to simply gaining public support, however poorly informed. Just rhetoric can achieve unjust results, especially when supporters are unaware of the injustice (Oakeshott 1991; Uhr 2001).

The performative power of rhetoric to shape politics encouraged classical Western thinkers like Aristotle to warn citizens of the dangerous capacity of unjust rhetoric and to teach them about the rare but beneficial practices of fair deliberation. Aristotle anchors the study of leadership by promoting a very wide variety of rhetorical and performative practices as politically valuable. He appreciated that 'the whole business of rhetoric [is] concerned with appearances', so that *form* ('manner, rhythm, tone and style of delivery...metaphor and simile', as Rorty (2011: 724) puts it) is as important as the *content* of speech (Aristotle 2005: 399; see also Peck et al. 2009: 25–40).

Aristotle's analysis holds up today because it is remarkably empirical, particularly in the way it unpacks big things like 'rhetoric' into component parts, like the menu of multiple choice available from the three common modes of 'rhetoric' (*deliberative, ceremonial, forensic*: each with its distinctive strength and limitation) and the three common types of 'evidence' or 'proof' used in rhetoric (*ethos, logos, pathos*: each with its distinctive appeal and limitation) (Aristotle 2005: 105–7). How citizens respond to leadership rhetoric depends in large part on leaders' choices over mode of rhetoric and type of evidence. Not all modes of leadership rhetoric are the same and not all modes are equally appropriate to all circumstances: for example, a forensically acute speech about 'who is to blame' will rarely be rhetorically effective (that is, will win a majority of supporters) in deliberative debate over gridlock in, say, health policy. So too a deliberatively incisive speech about 'our real foreign policy interests' will rarely be rhetorically effective at a veterans' day commemoration.

Ethos, logos, and *pathos* are Aristotle's three terms to define the common proofs of rhetorical power. The persuasive power of rhetoric comes from whatever evidence leaders can provide that is credible: acceptable to their audience. Audiences differ in what they are prepared to *consent* to, *believe* in, *accept* as credible or trustworthy. Leaders who look to audiences for potential followers have no alternative but to work within the limits of the audience. Leadership rhetoric varies according to the proofs likely to be accepted by the relevant audience. For this reason, rhetoric is very much audience reactive: leaders persuade by using whatever evidence generates acceptance by their targeted audience. What is effective with one audience is not necessarily likely to prove effective with another audience, or the same audience under different circumstances (Arnhart 1981: 40–3; Carey 1994: 26–45). Since Aristotle's time, rhetoric analysts have considered some combination of these three sources of evidence as the secret of effective persuasion: the *ethos* or character of the advocate as it is presented to the audience by the advocate and chosen witnesses; the *logos* or chain of reasoning provided by the advocate and witnesses; and the *pathos* or sympathetic bond constructed by advocates with their audience (Arnhart 1981: 35–8; Rorty 1996: 8–11).

3 LEADING OR MISLEADING?

The message depends on what the audience makes of the behaviour of the messenger, and that in turn depends on the rhetorical skill and indeed goodwill of the messenger. Rhetoric is exactly that art from which the ancient but cynical sophists made their money, offering to teach students the secrets of political power and influence by revealing how to make the weaker argument appear the stronger. In Rorty's clinical analysis: 'A brilliant Persuader can offer sophistical argument, one that makes the worse seem the better course. Less culpably, he can also judge that it is sometimes best to offer attractive but shoddy and questionable considerations for a good cause' (Rorty 2011: 722). Some political leaders will be accomplished rhetors; others will lack these influential gifts. Some with the rhetorical touch will be committed to the public interest; others with similar gifts will use it to cloak their driving self-interest. Some who lack persuasive power will still be public spirited; others driven by self-interest will find other means to advance those interests.

The capacity to wield leadership rhetoric and to attract a sustained following is a necessary but insufficient requirement of sound political leadership. Those political leaders who gain or retain power solely by talking their way into public affection can weaken a society's political health. Their popularity reflects their credibility but not their credentials. Here again the Greeks had names for this problematic popularity: *demagogues* practising *demagogy*. These terms of disrepute bring us to an important theme in leadership rhetoric, which is the place of leaders using rhetoric to *mislead* rather than lead political affairs. Rhetoric gets the poor reputation is does precisely because so many political leaders are clever enough to trick voters and followers with false and misleading promises designed to buy cheap support.

How seriously misleading this might be depends on what leaders do with their newly won power once the initial rhetoric begins to fade. Contemporary political science retains a keen critical interest in one prominent form of demagogy that involves *pandering* or appeasing voters or supporters (Cohen 2001: 540–3; Canes-Wrone 2005; Zarefsky 2008). This current interest reflects much older classical interests in the very real problem of pandering where leaders unduly *flatter* and mislead those whose support they need. The implication is that pandering falls short of genuine leadership when leaders seek support for public office by claiming to reflect whatever interests prevail among their target audience. Two forms of misleading conduct emerge. First, leaders say whatever it is their audience wants to hear, simply in order to win the confidence of that audience, resembling a hired agent who faithfully carries out the instructions of the master. Second, leaders disguise their real intentions beneath soothing rhetoric, tricking their target audience into thinking that their leadership will faithfully follow audience interests when in fact the leaders are secretly intent on alternative plans. Either way, misleading politicians can, in Finley's terms, be seen as 'playing on the ignorance and emotions' of those they target. Those who lack 'genuine leadership' tend to 'mislead by failing to lead' (Finley 1962: 4).

For Aristotle, the outstanding example of the genuine leader more than capable of leadership rhetoric was *Pericles*, the Athenian general and author of the famous 'Funeral Oration' so celebrated by the pioneering political historian Thucydides. The standard example of the demagogue was *Cleon*, also immortalized by Thucydides as the dangerously ambitious provider of misleadingly harsh advice in the Mytilene debate over how best to deal with rebellious allies (Thucydides 1972: 143–51, 212–17). According to Finley: 'the crucial distinction is between the man who gives leadership with nothing else in mind but the good of the state, and the man whose self-interest makes his own position paramount and urges him to pander to the people' (Finley 1962: 5; see also Hannah and Avolio 2011a and 2011b).

4 LIBERALISM AND LEADERSHIP

Contemporary studies of political leadership owe much to the pioneering political sociology of Max Weber (1864–1920). In particular, studies of leadership rhetoric remain indebted to Weber's theory that modern representative government is informed by a spirit of *plebiscitary democracy*: a form of democracy where the primary political role of the people is formally to endorse their preferred political elite as legitimate rulers. Weber wrote much about political leadership, most of which examines the organizational sources of formal authority in modern society, especially the place of bureaucracy as one of the primary building blocks of modern political organization (Peck et al. 2009: 35–6). Many will be aware of Weber's recognition of the place of *charisma* as a source of publicly venerated political power among outstanding political leaders relying more on personalized popular legitimacy than organized party support (Hackman and Johnson 2009: 102–33). The Indian nationalist and political founder Mahatma Gandhi is a good example of the charismatic type, complete with his own distinctive leadership rhetoric (Bligh and Robinson 2010). Related to this charismatic version of rare political leadership is Weber's sketchy and somewhat impressionistic account of the rise of modern plebiscitarian leadership (leadership legitimated through popular endorsement), which we can think of as a routinized and less extraordinary version of charismatic leadership, typically exercised by successful leaders of modern political parties (Weber 1994: 341–2; Uhr 2001).

Weber identifies the nineteenth-century British prime minister William Gladstone (and not his conservative opponent Disraeli, another fascinatingly rhetorical prime minister) as the exemplar of this modernizing progressive leader. Gladstone is an early master of mass-democratic politics who, in the formative period of adult male suffrage, eagerly takes the political contest 'out of doors', beyond the inner sanctum of parliament, competing publicly for electoral support as head of a political party with ambitions for mass membership. For Weber, Gladstone pioneers the leadership rhetoric characteristic of heads of modern political parties in the transition towards plebiscitarian democracy, which replaces the former period of oligarchical democracy managed 'within-doors' by the parliamentary club. Weber argues that 'democratization of suffrage' provided the basis for the rise of a new form of political leadership, which is illustrated by 'Gladstone's "grand" demagogy', with its pronounced 'Caesarist plebiscitary element', elevating the successful party leader to a place of prominence as 'the dictator of the electoral battlefield'. The 'charismatic appeal of the leader's personality' drives the political machine, fuelled by the energetic popular support for 'the leader' whose public credibility begins to dwarf the policy details of the party platform. Put simply, this is 'leadership democracy', which is the stable core of all modern variations of democracy (Weber 1994: 351; see also Pakulski and Higley 2008).

Weber uses the Greek terms 'demagogy' and 'demagogue' to identify the Gladstone model of progressive public leadership. The original Greek terms are neutral in their ethical connotations, and Weber is very much a realist intent on classifying rather than evaluating: for him, modern leadership rhetoric necessarily conforms to 'demagogy' or what we might now call *populism*. To get a richer picture of demagogic leadership rhetoric, it helps to go deeper into the Gladstone example in search of an inner account to match Weber's richly suggestive external account. Gladstone was 'without question the dominant orator in the House of Commons' in late-nineteenth-century Britain, and the innovator who showed how to 'govern by speaking' (Meisel 2001: 83). It was Gladstone who pioneered the practice of leader-led Question Time in parliament. He also pioneered the practice of leader-led electoral campaigning, to such an extent that his 'greatest oratorical legacy was outside the House of Commons' (Meisel 2001: 88).

What is important for our purposes is Gladstone's studious attention to classical Greek leadership rhetoric. Weber's chosen model just happens to be the author of the three-volume *Studies on Homer and the Homeric Age* (Gladstone 1858). In addition to his close literary study of Homer, Gladstone also examines 'the polities of the Homeric age' with extensive investigation of the importance of 'publicity and persuasion' in classical politics generally (Gladstone 1858: vol. 3). Gladstone uncovers in Homer the origins of a more systemic Western interest in 'speech as an instrument of government' in the literary remains of that remarkable ancient 'culture of the art of persuasion' and 'rhetorical address'. He drills deep into classical sources to retrieve 'the faculty of what in England is called debate', where the orator becomes 'a wrestler' competing for victory with all 'the processes of a rhetorician'. Gladstone claims to see in the political scenes depicted by Homer 'a near resemblance to that of a political leader under free European and, perhaps it may be said, especially under British, institutions... worked in part by accommodation, and in part by influence' (Gladstone 1858, vol. 3, 102–3, 111–13, 138).

5 RHETORICAL PRESIDENCIES

Gladstone's remarkably astute analysis of leadership rhetoric crossed the Atlantic and was picked up by Woodrow Wilson, later to be president of the United States (Kraig 2004: 40–1, 71–4, 103–4). Wilson is now regarded as one the pioneers of 'the rhetorical presidency': a chief political executive exercising what Gladstone called 'the action of the tongue' to appeal directly to citizens and so consolidate publicity and prestige around the central office of the presidency (Tulis 1987: 117–37; see also Andrews 2002; Crockett 2009; Laracey 2009). The rhetorical strategy was very much a power ploy, designed to subordinate public regard for competing political offices in Congress. There was only one elected official holding executive power, compared to hundreds of elected legislators and a handful of appointed holders of judicial power. Thus the comparative advantage of 'the rhetor in chief' reflects the importance of executive power (the core power of government) resting in one person, ideally selected by the people at large. Wilson appreciated that the one political leader who can speak directly *to* the people is also the one political leader who can claim to speak *for* the people. The term 'rhetorical presidency' acknowledges that the head of national government can exercise unusual public leverage by appealing over the heads of other office-holders directly to citizens, speaking to them as their sole nationally elected representative. This role is consistent with Gladstone's view of a chief minister's national responsibilities but reinforces the rhetorical role by relating to the citizen audience as the source of the political executive's special electoral *legitimacy* or public honour. Wilson was an influential reform figure who assisted with the transition from the original constitutional formalities of a presidency determined by the Electoral College to the twentieth-century innovation of a presidency determined in substance by popular vote based on an ever-widening franchise.

Why Wilson committed himself to such reforms is made clear from his extensive prior commitment to a model of leadership rhetoric that anticipates the 'rhetorical presidency' (Eden 1983: 2–33; Bimes and Skowronek 1998). The best illustration is Wilson's 1890s 'Leaders of Men' lectures, which put into practice his theories about leadership rhetoric by providing something of a self-portrait of those who hold that people 'are clay in the hands of the consummate leader' (W. Wilson 2000). The secret of persuasion is determining ways of 'creeping into the confidence of those you would lead' by using rhetoric shaped by audience interests. Wilson acknowledges that his own academic rhetoric will be misunderstood as flattering 'the delicate arts of the demagogue': arts that empower a leader to take selfish advantage of 'the momentary and whimsical popular mood, the transitory or mistaken popular passion'. The genuine leader differs from the demagogue, however, through his *interpretative* style of leadership, which reformulates rather than reinforces popular interests. The 'leader-as-interpreter' model differs from that of the demagogue by looking further ahead to determine how people can be prepared for political progress. The demagogue uses leadership rhetoric to take advantage of popular power by becoming a mouthpiece for the people, reflecting their resentments but without any strong commitment to improve the situation of the people. The alternative 'leader as interpreter' is a very different type of representative, who *refracts* rather than *reflects* popular sentiment. Although the two modes of leadership might converge in their leadership rhetoric, the two modes derive from quite different strategies of popular support. Wilson's model leader is prepared to forsake passing popularity because his eyes are on a larger prize, which is sustained popularity open only to those who discern what Wilson grandly terms 'the permanent purposes of the public mind' (W. Wilson 2000; see also Tulis 1987: 130–2).

Wilson restarts the story of the rhetorical presidency. Three influential presidential followers include F. D. Roosevelt, Ronald Reagan, and Barack Obama, all gifted public speakers who used the power of speech to help them perform, or try to perform, miracles in public policy. FDR was the last president to serve four elected terms, with the constitutional scheme since limited to two four-year terms. One of Roosevelt's most effective public performances were his famous 'radio chats' in the 1930s, using then-new technology to speak directly to American citizens before the emergence of television. Never before had a US president attempted to form such a public contract with ordinary citizens, which helps explain his remarkable electoral success over four terms. President Reagan was an experienced film actor before his governorship of California and his presidency of the United States. Yet there was something special about his very best presidential speaking performances, such as the famous 1982 address to the British Parliament, which has attracted serious research as an important weapon of the cold war (Rowland and Jones 2010). Obama replaced President G. W. Bush through a surprising strategy of extra-party political mobilization that captured the support of many lost or neglected voters who heard reassuring themes in Obama's professional grass-roots rally for new trust in the head of government. In practice, Obama's presidency has been less reformist than many supporters had hoped, in part because of the renewed political opposition to Obama's ambitious reform rhetoric, which promised more than the circumstances of fiscal restraint or reawakened opposition could deliver (Jacobson 2011).

6 DEMOCRACY AND DRAMATURGY

The main focus of many contemporary studies is 'crisis rhetoric' performed by political executives who use their powers of public leadership as 'meaning-makers': crafting public understanding of the deliberative value of the hard choices of crisis management made by responsible leaders (Masters and 't Hart 2012). Our task now is to unpack three influential schools of performance analysis that test the boundaries of 'crisis rhetoric'. Each school includes a small number of exemplary works that students of leadership rhetoric should consider very closely as exemplars of thoughtful alternatives.

Restoring Republican Rhetoric

First, we can locate a cautious exploration of leadership rhetoric from what we can call the first wave of deliberative researchers: those closest to the original meaning of the concept of deliberative democracy, with an explicit foot in Aristotle's camp, which overlaps with the US 'rhetorical presidency' school. This first-wave school can be thought of as contriving to use deliberation as a republican ballast to democracy to make democracy *more* rather than *less* deliberative, with a focus on the role of leadership rhetoric in managing debate over law and policy in what should be genuinely 'deliberative assemblies'. Republicanism here refers to the model of constitutional government of checks and balances articulated with such campaigning flair in the *Federalist Papers* at the time of the ratification of the US Constitution. The empirical side here investigates actual deliberative debate over law and policy; the normative side constructs a benchmark about norms of due deliberation in representative democracy.

The exemplary theorist of first-wave deliberative democracy is American political scientist Joseph Bessette, who appears to have coined the term, which entered the world as the title to a contribution to a conservative US think-tank publication investigating the political theory of the US Constitution (Bessette 1980; Uhr 1998). The standard approach was to ask how *democratic* was the Constitution. Bessette's contribution asked instead how *republican* was the Constitution. His argument was that the evidence adduced by others to show signs of institutionalized anti-democracy was really evidence of a different set of institutional norms around republicanism. Where democratic critics of the Constitution saw checks and balances thwarting majority rule, Bessette discerned a design for what he termed 'deliberative democracy': a republican version of majority rule that consciously spread the risk of dispersed government in order to avoid the even bigger problem of 'majoritarianism'. Bessette's later book, *The Mild Voice of Reason*, continued the project of republican recovery and included a subtitle about 'deliberative democracy'. The argument was an articulation of liberal constitutional theory: good politics requires good political deliberation managed through the constitutional medium of an effective deliberative assembly. The book provided a demonstration of how political deliberation could be evaluated, matching examples of US congressional decision-making with the constitutional norms of due institutional deliberation and with associated republican political theory from such sources as *The Federalist Papers* (Bessette 1994; Ceaser 2009).

Negotiating Authoritative Rhetoric

Second, we note steadily increasing attention to deliberative dramaturgy among researchers interested in the political sociology of 'reflexive' rhetoric that frames the policy process by 'hiding and highlighting' public space (Vogel 2012). Reflexivity here refers to the matching mechanisms required in leadership, as competitors negotiate shared pathways for 'authoritative' public decision-making. Authority is the political end and reflexivity is the appropriate means of governance relationships used by creatively networking negotiators in fluid systems of governance. There are no simple 'off-the-shelf' models of leadership rhetoric, which instead has to be crafted freshly from the 'give-and-take' of flexible political relationships. The project here is to map out the many ways that political communities can bring life back to deliberative practices, particularly through what we can call *deliberative dramaturgy*: the staging of political contestation and public argument outside the walls of formal deliberative assemblies, analysing but also promoting increased public participation in democratic politics. Here the empirical side charts the theatrics of governance, including political protest, aligned to norms of participatory democracy.

A good illustration of the second school of deliberative dramaturgy is the reflective rhetoric of Dutch scholar Maarten Hajer (2006, 2009). The focus on dramaturgy comes across in many studies of the stagecraft of political activists using various forms of political theatre to reflect on and influence law and policy. The focus on deliberation is quite different from the liberal-constitutionalism of the first school, tending to examine unconventional policy activists intent on bypassing the exclusion zones constructed by the state when regulating public access to the constitutionally protected forms of political deliberation. Hajer in particular is a fine exponent of performative analysis examining the era of 'mediatization' we now occupy, with 'authority' being demonstrated as a public or observed spectacle of improvised or negotiated leadership, with potentially different scripts for different audiences (Hajer 2007; see also Gottweis 2006). The larger theme is that even such a core concept as political authority has its distinctive performative dimensions: authority is what authority does, typically through an applied form of leadership rhetoric that uses the power of spectacle to secure public attention. Authority typically rests with those who rule, but Hajer shows that in the twenty-first century authority also rests in the hands of those who can perform authority by making a spectacle of their relationships with the state. Julian Assange and his wikileaks activities are good examples of performative authority using the power of spectacle to influence the behaviour of major nation states. Hajer's concept of 'mediatization' spells out the powers of mediated discourse relationships, with competing 'stages' erected by government and non-government interests as intermediary performance platforms. Traditional formal government becomes the informal governance of networks across state and society, with 'the state' increasingly vulnerable to rhetorical ambush and newly accountable through the scrutiny of spectacle (Hajer 2005; see also Edelman 1988).

Democratizing Discursive Rhetoric

Third, we highlight critical rather than conservative or republican forms of deliberative democracy. Here the task is to make political deliberation more democratic by protecting practices of self-representation by disadvantaged or marginalized citizens usually thought of as 'the represented' in systems of representative democracy. The empirical side here collects varieties of deliberation across different political cultures, related to norms of global democracy across state boundaries.

An outstanding example of the third school is Australian deliberative theorist John Dryzek, who has made explicit investigation of leadership rhetoric (Dryzek 2010). Dryzek's approach reflects his preference for the label of 'discursive' democracy over the often-precious label 'deliberative' democracy, which leads to his championing the 'communicatively competent': political activists with leadership rhetoric that can generate a hearing among the disaffected about ways in which they can be heard by political elites. Dryzek's explicit theory of rhetoric relates to general or 'systemic' properties of democracy, abstracting from the particulars of effective rhetoric used by influential democrats. Dryzek asks us to recognize those rare but valuable instances when 'categorically ugly rhetoric produces good systemic results' by confronting established power in ways that generate a stronger deliberative infrastructure (Dryzek 2010: 333–4).

Dryzek openly acknowledges the 'well-known hazards' of political rhetoric and sceptically searches for 'new tests for evaluating rhetoric' as a general political strategy: 'tests that distinguish between desirable and undesirable rhetorical invocation and suppression of particular discourses' (Dryzek 2010: 320, 327). Dryzek's 'key test' of systemic health is whether leadership rhetoric promotes 'an effective deliberative system joining competent and reflective actors' (Dryzek 2010: 320). The test sifts out leadership rhetoric that internally 'bonds' particularized political interests and communities, in favour of rhetoric that 'bridges' otherwise opposed interest and communities. Dryzek's bridging strategies have often been used as forms of leadership rhetoric to forge 'a coalition—but not a deliberative relationship', as was the case at the time of Gladstone's electoral struggle with Disraeli over harvesting votes of the poor (Dryzek 2010: 331, 333). In practice, leadership rhetoric does not match what Dryzek calls the 'configuration of discourses' likely to found in contemporary democratic audiences. Deliberative systems need 'to be constructed and performed' through political rhetoric, including 'dramaturgy before multiple audiences' (Dryzek 2010: 332).

7 CONCLUSION

Politics is often defined as a war of words, with each leadership team using its own rhetoric to undermine its opponent's rhetoric (Oakeshott 1991; Nye 2008: 72–4). Many sources of political commentary, like so many media and press outlets, also engage in their own carefully constructed rhetoric to tilt our view of politics in one direction or another. Established academic journals like *Rhetoric and Public Affairs* regularly examine the routines of rhetoric deployed by political leaders, so that students now have rich archives of analysis of many of the competing forms of political rhetoric dominating current societies.

One of the sources of renewed interest in leadership rhetoric has been the debates over the style and substance of political orator Barack Obama, who in 2008 became the first African-American US president, sparking new interest in 'the revitalization of public reason' (Rowland 2011; see also Jacobson 2011). The growth of interest in leadership rhetoric, however, is also driven by emerging research on unelected public officials such as 'rhetorical secretaries' (for example, administrative heads of central government agencies) who perform new public roles through regimes of carefully scripted public address (Grube 2012). The current revival of academic interest in 'public address' might suggest that new forms of analysis of individual leadership rhetoric are emerging, filling gaps between traditional studies of 'great speeches' and contemporary studies of shared rhetorical performances. The dedication to David Zarefsky in one recent collection honours this outstanding analyst of political communication whose work deserves very close examination by leadership students (Parry-Giles and Hogan 2010). In fact, Zarefsky's own chapter in that collection provides a state-of-the-art review of the emerging world of US leadership rhetoric (Zarefsky 2010). The field is becoming broader and deeper each year, so that students need to look around for unusual contributions, which, to our surprise, continue to draw on Aristotle, albeit in fresh and rewarding ways.

Contemporary social science has many alternative approaches to the study of rhetoric, many of which have turned away from political science in the hope that recent developments in the behavioural social sciences will teach us more about the pathology of persuasion (Wilson 1990; Dillard and Pfau 2002; Finlayson 2007; Nye 2008; Benoit and Benoit 2008). Many developments in social psychology have cut through traditional barriers by revealing the power of leaders to manipulate frameworks of social identity with group-based rhetoric that, in Dryzek's language, 'bond' followers to leaders as members of an 'in-group'. These studies have generated compelling insights into the fervour of followership through graphic case studies highlighting the enduring power of leadership rhetoric in the hands of influential 'identity entrepreneurs' (Turner, Reynolds, and Subasic 2008). Yet these themes of social influence and political power also remind us of the merits of retaining something like Aristotle's interest in *moral* as well as *social* psychology, so that questions of justice remain central to our assessment of leadership rhetoric. It is not enough to know that certain types of leadership rhetoric establish trust. At the end of the day, it pays to remember Rorty's advice that many influential performers of leadership rhetoric are 'thoroughly untrustworthy' (Rorty 2011: 717; see also Kane and Patapan 2010). Such summary judgements tell us that many of the standards, if not all of the practices, of political ethics retain more than we might suspect of Aristotle's study of deliberative rhetoric (Keohane 2010: 186–7).

Recommended Reading

Dryzek, J. (2010). 'Rhetoric in Democracy', *Political Theory*, 38/3: 319–39.
Garsten, B. (2006). *Saving Persuasion*. Cambridge, MA: Harvard University Press.
Zarefsky, D. (2007). 'Making the Case for War: Colin Powell at the UN', *Rhetoric and Public Affairs*, 10/1: 275–302.

References

Andrews, J. R. (2002). 'Presidential Leadership and National Identity', in L. G. Dorsey (ed.), *The Presidency and Rhetorical Leadership*. College Station, TX: Texas A&M University Press, 129–44.
Aristotle (2005). *The Rhetoric*, in Poetics *and* Rhetoric, ed. E. Garver. New York: Barnes and Noble Classics.
Arnhart, L. (1981). *Aristotle on Political Reasoning*. DeKalb, IL: Northern Illinois University Press, 21–4.
Benoit, W. L., and Benoit, P. J. (2008). *Persuasive Messages: The Process of Influence*. Oxford: Basil Blackwell.
Bessette, J. M. (1980). 'Deliberative Democracy', in R. A. Goldwin and W. A. Schambra (eds), *How Democratic is the Constitution?* Washington, DC: American Enterprise Institute Press, 102–16.
Bessette, J. M. (1994). *The Mild Voice of Reason*. Chicago: University of Chicago Press.
Biehl-Missal, B. (2010). 'Hero takes a Fall: A Lesson from Theatre for Leadership', *Leadership*, 6/3: 279–97.
Bimes, T., and Skowronek, S. (1998). 'Woodrow Wilson's Critique of Popular Leadership', in R. J. Ellis (ed.), *Speaking to the People*. Amherst, MA: University of Massachusetts Press, 134–61.
Bligh, M. C., and Robinson, J. L. (2010). 'Was Gandhi "Charismatic"?', *Leadership Quarterly*, 21/5: 844–55.
Booth, W. C. (2004). *The Rhetoric of Rhetoric*. Oxford: Basil Blackwell.
Canes-Wrone, B. (2005). *Who Leads Whom?* Chicago: University of Chicago Press.
Carey, C. (1994). 'Rhetorical Means of Persuasion', in I. Worthington (ed.), *Persuasion: Greek Rhetoric in Action*. London: Routledge, ch. 2, pp. 26–45.
Cassin, B., and Goffey, A. (2009). 'Sophistics, Rhetorics, and Performance: Or How To Really Do Things with Words', *Philosophy and Rhetoric*, 42/4: 349–72.

Ceaser, J. (2009). 'Demagoguery, Statesmanship and Presidential Politics', in J. M. Bessette and J. K. Tulis (eds), *The Constitutional Presidency*. Baltimore, MD: John Hopkins University Press, 265–74.

Charteris-Black, J. (2005). *Politicians and Rhetoric*. Basingstoke: Palgrave.

Cohen, D. (1994). 'Classical Rhetoric and Modern Theories of Discourse', in I. Worthington (ed.), *Persuasion: Greek Rhetoric in Action*. London: Routledge, ch. 4, pp. 69–82.

Cohen, D. (2001). 'Oratory', in T. O. Sloane (ed.), *Encyclopaedia of Rhetoric*. Oxford: Oxford University Press, 538–47.

Crockett, D. A. (2009). 'The Rhetorical Presidency', *Presidential Studies Quarterly*, 39/4: 932–40.

Dillard, J. P., and Pfau, M. (2002) (eds). *The Persuasion Handbook*. London: Sage.

Dryzek, J. (2010). 'Rhetoric in Democracy', *Political Theory*, 38/3: 319–39.

Edelman, M. (1988). *Constructing the Political Spectacle*. Chicago: University of Chicago Press.

Eden, R. (1983). *Political Nihilism and Leadership*. Gainesville, FL: University Press of Florida.

Finlayson, A. (2007). 'From Beliefs to Arguments', *British Journal of Politics and International Relations*, 9 (4 November), 545–63.

Finley, M. I. (1962). 'Athenian Demagogues'. *Past and Present*, 21/1: 3–21.

Garsten, B. (2006). *Saving Persuasion*. Cambridge, MA: Harvard University Press.

Garver, E. (1994). *Aristotle's Rhetoric: An Art of Character*. Chicago, IL: University of Chicago Press.

Gladstone, W. E. (1858). *Studies on Homer and the Homeric Age*. Oxford: Oxford University Press; 3 volumes.

Gottweis, H. (2006). 'Argumentative Policy Analysis', in B. Peters and J. Pierre (eds), *Handbook of Public Policy*. London: Sage, 461–79.

Grube, D. (2012). 'A Very Public Search for Public Value: "Rhetorical Secretaries" in Westminster Jurisdictions', *Public Administration*, 90 (2): 445–65.

Hackman, M. Z., and Johnson, G. E. (2009). *Leadership: A Communication Perspective*. 5th edn. Long Grove, IL: Waveland Press.

Hajer, M. (2005). 'Setting the Stage', *Administration and Society*, 36/6: 624–47.

Hajer, M. (2006). 'Doing Discourse Analysis', in M. van den Brink and T. Metze (eds), *Words Matter in Policy and Planning*. Utrecht: Graduate School of Urban and Regional Research, 65–74.

Hajer, M. (2007). 'Performing Authority', *Public Administration*, 86/1: 5–19.

Hajer, M. (2009) (ed.). *Authoritative Governance*. Oxford: Oxford University Press.

Hannah, S. T., and Avolio, B. J. (2011a). 'The Locus of Leader Character', *Leadership Quarterly*, 22/5: 979–83.

Hannah, S. T., and Avolio, B. J. (2011b). 'Leader Character, Ethos and Virtue', *Leadership Quarterly*, 22/5: 984–88.

Jacobson, G. C. (2011). 'Legislative Success and Political Failure', *Presidential Studies Quarterly*, 41 (2 June), 220–43.

Kane, J., and Patapan, H. (2010). 'The Artless Art', *Australian Journal of Political Science*, 45 (3 September), 371–89.

Keohane, N. O. (2010). *Thinking about Leadership*. Princeton: Princeton University Press.

Kraig, R. A. (2004). *Woodrow Wilson and the Lost World of the Oratorical Statesman*. College Station, TX: Texas A&M University Press.

Laracey, M. (2009). 'The Rhetorical Presidency Today', *Presidential Studies Quarterly*, 39/4 (December), 908–31.

Masters, A., and 't Hart, P. (2012). 'Prime Ministerial Rhetoric and Recession Politics', *Public Administration*, 90/3: 759–80.

Meisel, J. S. (2001). *Public Speech and the Culture of Public Life in the Age of Gladstone*. New York: Columbia University Press.

Nye, J. S. (2008). *The Powers to Lead*. Oxford: Oxford University Press.

Oakeshott, M. (1991). 'Political Discourse', in T. Fuller (ed.), *Rationalism in Politics and Other Essays*. Indianapolis: Liberty Press, 70–95.

O'Keefe, D. J. (2001). 'Persuasion', in T. O. Sloane (ed.), *Encyclopedia of Rhetoric*. Oxford: Oxford University Press, 547–83.

Pakulski, J., and Higley, J. (2008). 'Towards leader democracy?', in P. 't Hart and J. Uhr (eds), *Public Leadership*. Canberra: Australian National University E Press, 45–54.

Parry-Giles, S. J., and Hogan, J. M. (2010) (eds). *The Handbook of Rhetoric and Public Address*. Oxford: Wiley-Blackwell.

Peck, E., Freeman, T., Perri 6, and Dickinson, H. (2009). 'Performing Leadership', *Leadership*, 5/1: 25–40.

Rorty, A. (1996). 'Structuring *Rhetoric*', in A. Rorty (ed.), *Essays on Aristotle's Rhetoric*. Berkeley and Los Angeles: University of California Press, 1–33.

Rorty, A. (2011). 'Aristotle on the Virtues of Rhetoric', *Review of Metaphysics*, 64 (June), 715–34.

Rowland, R. C. (2011). 'Barack Obama and the Revitalization of Public Reason', *Rhetoric and Public Affairs*, 14/4: 693–726.

Rowland, R. C., and Jones, J. M. (2010). *Reagan at Westminster*. College Station, TX: Texas A&M University Press.

Sharma, A., and Grant, D. (2011). 'Narrative, Drama and Charismatic Leadership', *Leadership*, 7/1: 3–26.

Terry, L. D. (1997). 'Public Administration and the Theater Metaphor', *Public Administration Review*, 57/1: 53–61.

Thucydides (1972). *History of the Peloponnesian War*. London: Penguin Classics.

Tourish, D., and Jackson, B. (2008). 'Guest Editorial: Communication and Leadership', *Leadership*, 4/3: 219–25.

Tulis, J. K. (1987). *The Rhetorical Presidency*. Princeton: Princeton University Press.

Turner, J. C., Reynolds, K. J., and Subasic, E. (2008). 'Identify Confers Power: The New View of Leadership in Social Psychology', in P. 't Hart and J. Uhr (eds), *Public Leadership: Perspectives and Practices*. Canberra: Australian National University E Press, 57–72.

Uhr, J. (1998). *Deliberative Democracy in Australia*. Cambridge: Cambridge University Press.

Uhr, J. (2001). 'Political Leadership and Democracy', in G. Brennan and F. G. Castles (eds), *Australia Reshaped*. Cambridge: Cambridge University Press, 261–94.

Vogel, R. (2012). 'Framing and Counter-Framing New Public Management', *Public Administration*, 90/2: 370–92.

Weber, M. (1994). 'The Profession and Vocation of Politics', in P. Lassman and R. Speirs (eds), *Political Writings*. Cambridge: Cambridge University Press.

Wilson, J. (1990). *Politically Speaking*. Oxford: Basil Blackwell.

Wilson, W. (2000). 'Leaders of Men (1890)', in T. Fuller (ed.), *Leading and Leadership*. Notre Dame, IN: University of Notre Dame Press, 191–7.

Zarefsky, D. (2007). 'Making the Case for War: Colin Powell at the UN', *Rhetoric and Public Affairs*, 10/1: 275–302.

Zarefsky, D. (2008). 'Strategic Maneuvering in Political Argumentation', *Argumentation*, 22/3: 317–30.

Zarefsky, D. (2010). 'Public Address Scholarship in the New Century: Achievements and Challenges', in S. J. Parry-Giles and J. M. Hogan (ed.), *Handbook of Rhetoric and Public Address*. Oxford: Wiley-Blackwell, 67–85.

CHAPTER 18

....

EXPERIMENTAL ANALYSIS

....

ROSE MCDERMOTT

1 INTRODUCTION

....

As other chapters in this handbook admirably demonstrate, there has been a major resurgence of interest and investigation into the phenomenon of political leadership. Perhaps it is not accidental that the study of leadership fell into abeyance during the cold war, when the actions of states seemed to dominate international interactions, and rose once again when the role and influence of non-state actors in general, and individuals such as Osama bin Laden and Saddam Hussein in particular, re-emerged as consequential in the wake of the 9/11 terrorist attacks on America. Political pundits and citizens alike seem to acknowledge and recognize the critical role of leadership in shaping political outcomes, and decry its absence in the current political environment, but few seem explicitly to define or to delineate its meaning or proper role. Part of the reason for this lack of clarity derives from the reality that the ideal representation of leadership may change not only across time and culture, but also in the wake of different kinds of challenges. In addition, there may be different types of leadership. For example, effective political and military leadership may vary in their optimal characteristics, and each category may dominate in a particular kind of environmental context. Therefore, one type of leader may excel in some situations, but might utterly fail in other environments, or facing different kinds of challenges.

Just as there may be different types of leadership, there are various methodological ways to go about studying the phenomena and its various manifestations. One of the most promising, if under-utilized, ways of investigating leadership involves the use of an experimental paradigm. Not surprisingly, experiments involving political and social forms of leadership tend to be conducted by psychologists, while those related to business and financial leadership are largely conducted by economists. I will therefore focus on the former.

This chapter seeks to provide an overview of the experimental study of leadership historically, describing a few seminal studies that outline the central concepts and debates in the field in detail. Very little work has been done in this area involving real political leaders, but some relevant experimental work has been conducted on leadership in business contexts, and within legislative bodies, which may help to share some light on the larger phenomenon. Specific studies are described because they highlight particularly important aspects of the experimental study of leaders. Following this discussion, some experimental work on the public perception of leaders is provided, for there can be no leaders without followers, and their perception often determines who becomes elevated to such positions and whose power might be terminated. The chapter then describes some critical challenges and opportunities confronting the use of experiments to investigate political leadership, and ends with a discussion of promising future directions in this area.

2   HISTORICAL OVERVIEW

Experiments offer unique purchase on the study of any given phenomenon, not only because they allow observers to manipulate the characteristics of central interest, but also because they allow unparalleled inferential analysis (Aronson et al. 1989). Experiments let scholars make causal arguments about the processes by which one variable affects another. In typical experiments, a researcher can randomly assign subjects to various conditions wherein one or more variables is systematically manipulated and the effect of that change on the dependent variable of interest is measured and categorized to analyse the effect of the independent variable on the dependent variable. For example, in a study of leadership, some variable, such as degree of public opinion support, might be manipulated in order to see how that factor might affect a dependent variable, such as the leader's choice of policies.

This very manipulation makes it easy to see why experiments have not provided a common way to examine leaders. For one thing, most leaders are busy, and they do not want private information to get into the wrong hands. The costs loom large and the benefits small, particularly if they see no reason or no clear benefit that they would derive from participating in research.

As a result of these logistical and ethical concerns, most investigations of political leadership have not employed an experimental methodology. Rather, they have tended to use historical case-study analyses, which often involve archival or interview work (Lasswell 1930, 1936; George and George 1956) or other forms of analysis of leaders from a distance (Hermann 1980; Post 1991). One of the most famous of these kinds of studies was conducted by James David Barber (1972), in his book *The Presidential Character*. Arguing that a president's personality shapes his behaviour, Barber examined leaders' character, world view, and style in order to categorize American presidents along two dimensions: energy (passive/active); and affect (positive/negative). By classifying leaders into one of the four categories that emerge from the intersection of these categories, Barber argued that it was possible to explain and predict presidential performance.

In reality, however, very little genuine experimental work has been conducted using real-world political leaders as subjects. A few studies have examined military leaders, but these have been scarce in number as well.

Some work has involved research with actual leaders, but this research has not tended to be experimental in nature. One of the most impressive examples of survey work with real-world leaders involved an examination of State Department officials undertaken by Etheredge (1978). In his study, Etheredge administered personality batteries to thirty-six State Department officials and then correlated their responses with their tendency to use force in forty-nine crises in American foreign policy between 1898 and 1968. He found that he was able to predict their responses to the crises with greater than 75 per cent accuracy based on the answers they supplied in the personality inventories. Most tellingly, he reported that those who advocated the greatest use of military force in response to foreign-policy challenges were those most likely to show high dominance displays towards their underlings at work, revealing a systematic pattern of belligerent response styles across personal and professional domains.

Although some survey work with actual real-world leaders has proved illuminating, remarkably little experimental work with leaders has occurred. The earliest work noted, and tried to tackle, this problem. Verba's seminal *Small Groups and Political Behavior* (1961) was perhaps the first to attempt to apply the methods and findings of small group research and experiments from social psychology and sociology to political topics. In this work, he explicitly addressed the challenging issue of leadership, and suggested that political scientists might learn a great deal from small group research methods and findings. In particular, he remained interested in the differences between the affective (keeping the group together) and instrumental (getting the task done) aspects of leadership, and how advancing these goals might often work in opposition to one another. He appeared sensitive to the problems associated with translating work from the laboratory to real-world politics, and noted critical differences in the meaning of such phenomena between the two contexts. For example, power in a laboratory—immediately imposed or generated among participants who have not known each other previously—actually represents a quite different phenomenon from established, long-standing, legitimate forms of political authority and needs to be explored in different ways.

In his early and comprehensive overview of the literature on small group behaviour, Golembiewski (1962) found that there was a lack of empirical support, which would otherwise allow for broader applications to political science research. Examining three types of 'panel' variables in this literature—the structural, involving such things as power and roles, and the stylistic, encompassing such factors as norms and processes and populations—he argued that all such work remained highly limited and that experimental attempts to examine factors across panels had been problematic.

In 1966 James David Barber argued that, 'rather than lifting findings from small group research, political scientists might consider imitating some of the methods of small group research' (Barber 1966: 3). In his *Power in Committees*, he did just that, noting that 'we should be most cautious in transferring findings directly from the small, artificial laboratory group to the governmental committee' (Barber 1966: 11). In this work,

Barber undertook a careful examination of leadership within a legislative context using real-world leaders, using twelve local government committees from the Connecticut Board of Finance. These leaders agreed to come to the Yale Interaction Library, where Barber studied six aspects of decision-making during tasks that he administered. These dimensions included calculation (or how leaders treated uncertainty); cultural; personality; roles; integration; and interpersonal power. These fascinating studies are not experiments in the true sense of manipulating variables across actors, so much as explorations of how actors go about making decisions along theoretically informed dimensions.

Perhaps one of the most influential and truly experimental studies of political leadership, and the influence of leadership style on outcomes of interest, was also one of the first. Kurt Lewin and his colleagues (Lewin, Lippett, and White 1939), motivated to understand how Hitler could have exerted such decisive control over the German population, sought to investigate the influence of leadership style on levels of aggression and group dynamics. In this study, they randomly assigned groups of boys to one of three conditions that varied in leadership style. The leader of each group was a confederate of the experimenters. In one group, the leader was an autocrat. He made all the decisions himself, he assigned individuals to tasks, and he did not participate in any of the work of the group. The second leader took a democratic approach, having boys participate in group decision-making and planning. Participants decided for themselves who would take on what job and the leader participated in the work of the group. The third leader was a laissez-faire leader, who let everyone in the group do pretty much what he wanted to do with little oversight, surveillance, or involvement.

Lewin's results proved provocative and fascinating. In the autocratic group, the boys worked hardest, but only when they were under the surveillance of the leader. In the democratic group, the boys emerged as the most efficient overall, mostly because they tended to work regardless of whether the leader was observing them or not. In addition, these boys produced the most original and creative work. The laissez-faire group was characterized by laziness, not surprisingly, and the boys in this group essentially got nothing done.

The most intriguing aspect of the study, however, related to the primary dependent variable of aggression. The boys in the authoritarian group proved to be thirty times more aggressive than the boys in either of the other groups. In particular, members of this group were much more likely to scapegoat others, expressing their anger and frustration against weaker members. In addition, they were also more likely to destroy their own property. By contrast, boys in the democratic group showed more friendliness and loyalty towards other members of the group, and offered much more praise to one another than members of either of the other groups.

A later experiment that similarly manipulated the effect of leadership training on followers' performance in a real-world sample administered either transformative or eclectic leadership training to a group of 54 military leaders, 90 of their direct followers, and 724 indirect followers. In a longitudinal field experiment design, these authors found that transformative leadership training exerted a more positive effect on followers' performance (Dvir et al. 2002). Another study that used military leaders as subjects examined the officers' responses to a counter-terrorism scenario (Mintz, Redd, and Vedlitz 2006). Interestingly, in this study, Mintz and colleagues found that their student sample displayed dramatically different responses compared to the military population. While a third of students advocated doing nothing, more than 90 per cent of military leaders preferred to take action in the face of threat. Military leaders also appeared more prone to satisficing than students. This discrepancy suggests that using student samples to imply leader responses may not provide a very accurate indicator of leaders' preferences. Thus, the ability to generalize from accessible populations to leaders' behaviour may not be as straightforward as scholars might hope, indicating that accurate samples would need to rely on leaders themselves, and not proxies drawn from populations who may differ in either their disposition, background, or experience in critical ways from other populations.

Note that these experiments investigate the influence of leadership on followers, and do not actually interrogate or manipulate leaders themselves, or seek to understand the nature of leadership independent of followership. In fact, many studies of leadership in fact actually constitute studies regarding the nature of followership. In many cases, these studies involve public perceptions of political leaders. Some of the most interesting early experimental work in this area involved the examination of public support of leaders based on their facial expressions (Sullivan and Masters 1988). Subjects viewed videotapes of leaders displaying either neutral or happy expressions; participants' attitudes were more influenced by facial expression, even without sound, than by such standard predictors as party identification or issue position. Subsequent work comparing viewer reaction to facial expressions in the United States and France showed some cultural differences, with the French responding more positively to angry expressions than Americans (Masters and Sullivan 1989).

One of the most evocative methods exploring public perception of political actors involves Q-sort techniques, whereby observers report their impressions about various traits and characteristics of particular leaders. Participants are typically presented with a list of descriptive adjectives and then asked to rank them according to some scale, like from most to least characteristic, for some particular leader. These words night include traits such as 'friendly' or 'strong'. The responses of many individuals are then aggregated. Many studies of public opinion and mass political behaviour, including experiments regarding voting behaviour, are designed to examine public perceptions of political leaders in a more systematic light.

There are, of course, additional studies that examine the public perception of leaders and leadership. Strictly speaking, these studies concentrate more on the influence of followers on leaders than the reverse, and so do not constitute the primary concern of this chapter. However, some of this work is worth noting for the insight it provides into the use of experimental methods to examine these dynamic relationships. One line of research in this regard revolves around explorations of poliheuristic theory. Such work includes experiments to examine the threshold at which leaders may reject particular alternatives as politically unacceptable as well as how constituents' views affect such choices (Keller and Yang 2008), as well as studies examining the influence of advisers on foreign-policy decision-making showing that leaders are sensitive to the political consequences of their choices (Redd 2002).

A more nuanced experimental examination of the subtle dynamics that drive the relationships between leaders and followers is provided by Smith et al. (2007). Employing evolutionary theory, they find that individuals remain sensitive to the potential for leaders to exploit them, but that some individuals appear much more attentive to such risks than others. However, as with most of this work, the experimental manipulations are designed not to test how various characteristics of leadership affect its quality, but rather to examine the effect of various kinds of public response to leader action.

3   KEY CONCERNS

One of the reasons that experimental work with leaders has been so rare does not derive merely from logistical and ethical concerns. Important key definitional and other questions have limited the ability of scholars to examine leaders experimentally. Critically, many of the key conceptual and theoretical issues in the broader study of political leadership remain unresolved, and so it can prove challenging to design careful and sophisticated experiments to explore largely amorphous concepts and ideas. In addition, many of the central debates revolve around issues that also appear to be difficult to investigate experimentally. Are leaders born or are they made? What defines a leader? How can leadership be defined so as to allow for experimental manipulation without risking ethical or practical concerns, which often prevent or limit leader participation? The stakes in some of these issues can be very high in both political and scholarly domains. Yet relying on memoirs or reports from a distance may misrepresent some of the real dynamics underlying the nature of leadership. Extrapolating from student populations poses obvious disadvantages. Similarly, attempting to generalize from other domains, such as business, where the stakes may be high, but also tend to lie largely in the financial domain, may not properly inform our understanding of the nature of risk-taking in life and death domains, such as are involved in decisions to go to war.

One of the real challenges in terms of operational development of the central variables involved in leadership studies results from the fact that the very phenomenon can take many forms, and this makes it quite difficult to know how best to measure and quantify various aspects of it. Everyone can agree that leadership matters and that effective leadership can exert an enormous impact on many downstream variables such as motivation and performance, and yet it often appears ineffable, like an ephemeral or amorphous quality that itself can come and go depending on the individual, the context, and the specific situation. As US Supreme Court Justice Potter Stewart opined about pornography, leadership may be impossible to define, but everyone knows it when they see it. This observation is not flip, but implies that some aspects of leadership may derive from physical, biological, or other neurochemical processes that can be immediately and universally recognized, if not easily or accurately described in words. Would warriors follow a slight academic into combat, despite his obvious strategic brilliance? Unlikely. Similarly, do politicians follow warriors' suggestions about when to go into battle? If so, we would have many fewer wars. This insight suggests not only that leadership itself is domain specific, but also that different kinds of leadership may be most effectively communicated through different types of mediums as well. Such dynamics appear amenable to experimental exploration.

Part of the conceptual difficulty in figuring out how to define and measure leadership may revolve around the likelihood that leadership, like intelligence, has various forms. Just as musical intelligence differs in kind from athletic intelligence, and social and emotional intelligence may not correlate all that well with cognitive intellectual intelligence, leadership skills may take different forms. Successful business leaders may differ in important and systematic ways from effective military leaders, and these individuals may not be easily interchangeable, even within the same cultural and political contexts. Indeed, effective leadership may vary with time as well, so that the same person is more effective under certain challenges than others; one need look no further than Churchill's unceremoniously abrupt removal from office as British prime minister at the end of the Second World War to find evidence of the process whereby the same person loses relevance as the threat shifts. A person who becomes a powerful political leader may not prove similarly dominant in a military context and vice versa. Part of this may be a function of inherent skills, abilities, and predilections, but part of it may also have to do with the kinds of connections particular people are able to establish with real and potential followers. The kind of people who have no difficulty following a bureaucrat's instructions may differ in important and predictable ways from those who would follow someone into battle; similarly, the characteristics that constitute an efficient and effective bureaucrat may also diverge in significant and noticeable ways from the kind of person who would lead others into combat. Yet, similar to the argument that Verba (1961) raised about the import of political legitimacy on perceptions of leadership, it does not appear simple or obvious how such factors might be either identified or manipulated experimentally.

Further to complicate this already convoluted methodological conundrum, there may be biological and genetic aspects of individual variance that also influence a person's propensity and ability to manifest effective leadership. This proclivity could take several different forms. For example, it may be that certain types of individuals are simply more predisposed to self-select into particular high-risk or high-reward situations and environments. Or it could be that certain individuals possess specific innate biological, perhaps hormonal, traits that make them either more likely to want dominance over others, or to garner loyalty and followership among others. Such a possibility might help explain both why some individuals become more effective leaders than others, as well as why some individuals can more easily garner support, including seemingly mindless adherence, than others.

Such a perspective would suggest that leadership skills and abilities are domain specific as well as context specific. While some characteristics may generalize across domains in leadership, others may remain quite specific to particular domains (e.g. military, political, or financial) and may not easily translate across them. Scholars and observers might be well served to strive to distinguish more effectively between types of leadership, and seek to determine which traits generalize, which do not, and how each might relate to performance, and follower recruitment.

4 Recent Developments

As noted, very little experimental work has been done in the past to examine the nature of political leadership itself and its effect on followers, as distinct from the effect of followers on leaders—where some work, has been undertaken. However, more recent work indicates some potential new insights, drawn largely from evolutionary models, which might help increase the ability of scholars experimentally to study some aspects of leadership, followership, or their interaction, from a distance. The following provides some very brief examples, ideas, and models from the psychological study of leadership, which suggests potential experimental avenues by which future related experimental work designed to test such theories might proceed.

Many of these leadership processes, including those that undergird the sex differences reported, appear potentiated by biological factors and precipitants. One of the most innovative new studies exploring this phenomenon involved the use of eye-tracking technology to examine how the gaze of political leaders affects the gaze of ingroup and outgroup followers (Liuzza et al. 2011). Ingroup members in this case included those who supported the political part of the leader while outgroup members were those who endorsed the political opposition. Of course, in broader political contexts, ingroup members can be those who support a given coalition whether or not it is a political party, just as outgroup members are those perceived to oppose the interests of one's own group. The authors hypothesized these relationships based on primate literature, which suggested that the automatic tendency to follow the gaze of other group members can be affected by relative social status. In this study, researchers examined the directional gaze of right-wing Italian leader Silvio Berlusconi. They found that ingroup members followed his gaze whereas outgroup members tended not to look where he was looking. In this way, a leader's gaze proved predictive of seemingly reflexive shifts in perceptual attention based on affiliation with that person. In other words, behaviour that may feel automatic and unconscious can nonetheless systematically reflect, and be driven by, higher-order social processes such as social rank and leader status. This work highlights one example of the way in which theories drawing upon evolutionary models can illuminate novel forms of association in seemingly unexpected areas, including the inherently interactive nature of leadership and followership.

Just as the example of eye gaze with Berlusconi suggests, facial expressions carry important information about leadership as well. As Spisak et al. (2011) suggest, different group coordination problems may expect and elicit different leadership preferences.

They show, for example, that followers expect masculine faces to behave competitively in intergroup conflicts and feminine faces to behave cooperatively in intragroup contexts. Further, individuals prefer the face that best matches the adaptive challenges, desiring the masculine face in intergroup competition, for example. This may explain, in part, why men tend to be chosen as secretaries of defence, while women are more likely to be put in charge of domestic departments such as health and human services. Thus, biological factors, such as human facial expression, may provide reliable and dependable signals regarding the emergence and appropriateness of particular leaders under specific kinds of group threat.

5 Inherent Limitations?

The logistical challenges of conducting experiments with real-world political leaders pose tremendous hurdles for any researchers who hope to examine real-world leaders in context, or to generalize their findings beyond easily studied student populations. The problems may be surmountable, but are not trivial. Problems with generalizing from such a rare and extreme sample population remain challenging. Like suicide, genuine leadership potential and ability may be hard to predict, but it is very important to do so. Certain tendencies may appear correlated with leadership, but discerning causal connections within complex environments and interactions will be daunting.

As noted, the real limitation confronting past experimental work on leadership revolves around the logistical and ethical problems confronting scholars who wish to study real-world leaders, as their would-be subjects often prove reluctant to participate in such research for fear of negative exposure or indiscreet release of confidential information. As a result, most of the experimental work has either focused on the reaction of followers to particular kinds of leadership styles, as exemplified by the classic Lewin, Lippett and White (1939) study, or manipulated normal individuals into various kinds of leadership roles. This research, while critically illuminating the dynamics undergirding the phenomenon of leadership, still remains limited in its ability to generalize unless and until the posited causal mechanisms and dynamics can be replicated in actual leader samples.

Of course, the criticism that research into leadership needs to include real-world leaders in order to generalize begs the prior question of what constitutes a leader. As noted, leaders may represent domain-specific actors whose skills and abilities do not easily translate across areas of expertise and action. So even knowing something meaningful about political leaders may not easily translate into generalizable knowledge about military leaders, for example.

Thus, while evolutionary models and insights have helped generate many productive and novel hypotheses for investigating the role of leadership and the function of followership, knowledge accumulation has proceeded most successfully in those areas that study leadership styles and their effects among followers, rather than among leaders themselves, for all the primarily logistical reasons enunciated above. While this work often constitutes elegant and experimentally robust findings, it remains limited by the populations available for investigation and the uncertainly regarding how well non-leader populations can generalize to actual leader perceptions and behaviour. Until such work can include real-world leaders, even in a domain-specific way, it may prove especially challenging for real-world leaders and other policy-makers to take this research seriously or to have it inform public understanding of the nature and role of leadership more broadly. This seems unfortunate at least partly because greater understanding and appreciation for the role of leadership in overcoming collective action problems not only offer important insights into the purpose of leadership and the influence of followership, but also offer critical cautions concerning the potential for leaders to manipulate the public for personal political gains as well.

6 Promising Ways Forward

One methodological and one theoretical line of enquiry appear most promising for the future study of leadership. Specifically, theoretical work that engages evolutionary models has offered fecund and novel predictions regarding the emergence, function, nature, and manifestations of leadership. Such models clearly provide useful hypotheses further to investigate the phenomenon of leadership and also followership, and are amenable to experimental investigation.

Such work also provides unique insight into common real-world occurrences, such as how many powerful male leaders seemingly self-destruct their professional and political lives in the wake of sex scandals. While many political pundits marvel over the number of powerful men who risk their careers for seemingly casual sex, with Dominic Strauss Kahn providing only the most recent high-profile example, and observers marvel about the perversity of some of these occurrences, with Anthony Weiner's case offering a salient example, evolutionary analysis offers a simple and straightforward explanation. If the unconscious but driving force motivating men towards achieving high-status positions in the first place lies in increased reproductive opportunities, such individuals can be understood as seeking power in order to get sex. Sex, not power, becomes the ultimate goal. In this case, such individuals are not only taking advantage of what they can, but may actually be motivated to achieve high positions of power for just such a reason. Without saying anything about respective substantive leadership competence, this can also explain why powerful females seem less likely to become embroiled in such scandals.

The methodological innovation that goes hand in hand with an evolutionary perspective lies in the use of hormonal, genetic, and physiological measures to study leadership behaviour. Some possibilities, including the use of eye-tracking technology or hormonal analysis, offers one potential technique by which to bridge the gap between the desire to study real-world leaders and their desire to avoid such interrogation. Videos and pictures of leaders can provide one mechanism by which real-world leaders, and their biology and physiology, might be studied, if not always manipulated by researchers. If leaders might prove willing to participate anonymously in some studies, by providing biological samples in return for information about their relative status on such measures, such findings might further our understanding of how biology may interact with environmental precipitants. Such work might examine how hormones track with incipient threats or opportunities involving cherished ingroup values, precipitating leadership behaviour from those whose proclivities may incline them towards such action, but only under certain conditions. Real-time studies of soldiers may provide the best model of such an experimental design; smartphones might ping participants to answer a survey and supply a saliva sample at particular intervals, for example, reporting activities and responses as well as biological markers.

Such an evolutionary model assumes that leaders are as portrayed as they emerge in Van Vugt's theoretically informed work (Van Vugt 2006; Van Vugt and Spisak 2008; Van Vugt, Hogan, and Kaiser 2008): social individuals aware of the individual costs but also wishing to serve their community to overcome important challenges to collective action. It may be that such leaders exist and emerge under particular conditions, such as those of great threat, and are valued by followers at such times. However, following intergroup competition, fickle followers concerned with potential exploitation may shift their loyalties to different kinds of leaders who appear differentially to excel at intragroup cohesion during times of relative peace. Such a perspective offers a novel explanation for why constituents often throw victorious wartime leaders out of elected office once the threat is past, with Winston Churchill losing to Clement Attlee following Allied victory in the Second World War providing only the most iconic example.

7 Conclusions

Remarkably little experimental work with real-world leaders has been conducted, owing largely to the inherent challenge in obtaining their consent to participate in such research. However, some important experimental work has taken place that examines the effect of leadership style on followers' behaviour as well as experimental work on how various leadership roles may affect individual behaviour, and how followers may affect leaders.

In this vein, three experimental studies on leadership constitute seminal studies. First, the classic experimental study by Lewin, Lippett, and White (1939) provides the iconic study of the effect of leadership style on follower performance. This work, demonstrating the effect of autocratic style on increased levels of ingroup aggression, provides a model of how real-world problems inspired creative scholars to design a clever experiment to try to understand an important phenomenon. Van Vugt, Hogan, and Kaiser's important theoretical analysis and overview of their experimental work (2008) showing the contingent role of both instrumental and relational forms of leadership in overcoming the collective action problem offers a sophisticated example of how a hard-working theory can generate a wide variety of testable hypotheses that can demonstrate counterintuitive effects. Josephs et al.'s study (2006) examining the contingent interaction of testosterone, cortisol, and social status impressively demonstrates how meticulous attention to the ways in which contingent circumstances can influence observable effects can illuminate conditional phenomena that might otherwise remain hidden, and provides a superb example of how future work on the biological basis of leadership might progress.

Leadership represents an omnipresent phenomenon that influences all our lives for both good and ill. We can bemoan the ways in which it fails us, even though each individual may have a different notion of what constitutes leadership success or failure, and one person's success can easily constitute another's failure. We can be inspired to follow those leaders among us who offer the possibility of joining with others to achieve something that would be impossible to accomplish alone. We can even be moved when leaders offer the possibility of subsuming our individual identities to values and forces greater than our own, giving our own transitory life meaning in service of greater goals and missions. In retrospect, some of those actions may appear foolish; in other cases, they result in the greatest scientific, social, and military achievements humanity has ever achieved. Each follower may have a different notion of what constitutes an ideal leader, just as each leader may hold a different vision for the kind of followers he wishes to direct. These notions probably differ across domains, cultures, times, and contexts. Some characteristics may appear universal, while others may remain quite specific to a particular time and place. Understanding the nature of their origin, defining their meaning conceptually, and measuring their manifestation biologically and behaviourally, however, offer a unique opportunity for researchers to examine their foundation, function, and expression experimentally. Opportunities abound, and, while challenges to studying real-world leaders remain, the rewards allow the possibility of finding and creating more effective leaders. Furthermore, such ability also allows for the possibility of differentiating between leaders who wish to represent and serve their constituencies effectively and responsibly, and those who wish to exploit their followers in service of some grand ideology or for personal gain. Since the latter have so obviously contributed to the wide range of human suffering, recognizing those who wish to take advantage of individuals willing to participate fully in collective action that benefits all can only serve the greater goals of humanity.

RECOMMENDED READING

Josephs, R. A., Sellers, J. G., Newman, M. L., and Mehta, P. H. (2006). 'The Mismatch Effect: When Testosterone and Status are at Odds', *Journal of Personality and Social Psychology*, 90/6: 999–1013.

Lewin, K., Lippett, R., and White, R. (1939). 'Patterns pf Aggressive Behavior in Experimentally Created "Social Climates"', *Journal of Social Psychology*, 10: 271–99.

Van Vugt, M. (2006). 'Evolutionary Origins of Leadership and Followership', *Personality and Social Psychology Review*, 10/4: 354–71.

REFERENCES

Aronson, E., Ellsworth, P., Carlsmith, J. M., and Gonzalez, M. H. (1989). *Methods of Research in Social Psychology*. New York: McGraw-Hill.

Barber, J. D. (1966). *Power in Committees: An Experiment in the Governmental Process*. Chicago: Rand McNally.

Barber, J. D. (1972). *The Presidential Character: Predicting Performance in the White House*. Englewood Cliffs, NJ: Prentice-Hall.

Dvir, T., Dov, E., Bruce, J. A., and Boas, S. (2002). 'Impact of Transformational Leadership on Follower Development and Performance: A Field Experiment', *Academy of Management Journal*, 45/4: 735–44.

Etheredge, L. (1978). 'Personality Effects on American Foreign Policy, 1989–1968', *American Political Science Review*, 72/2: 434–51.

George, A., and George, J. (1956). *Woodrow Wilson and Colonel House: A Personality Study*. New York: Dover.

Golembiewski, R. T. (1962). *The Small Group: An Analysis of Research Concepts and Operations*. Chicago: University of Chicago Press.

Hermann, M. (1980). 'Explaining Foreign Policy Behavior using the Personal Characteristics of Political Leaders', *International Studies Quarterly*, 24/1: 7–46.

Josephs, R. A., Sellers, J. G., Newman, M. L., and Mehta, P. H. (2006). 'The Mismatch Effect: When Testosterone and Status are at Odds', *Journal of Personality and Social Psychology*, 90/6: 999–1013.

Keller, Jonathan, W., and Yang, Y. E. (2008). 'Leadership Style, Decision Context, and the Poliheuristic Theory of Decision Making: An Experimental Analysis', *Journal of Conflict Resolution*, 52/5: 687–712.

Lasswell, H. (1930). *Psychopathology and Politics*. Chicago: University of Chicago Press.

Lasswell, H. (1936). *Power and Personality*. New Brunswick, NJ: Transaction Books.

Lewin, K., Lippett, R. and White, R. (1939). 'Patterns of Aggressive Behavior in Experimentally Created "Social Climates"', *Journal of Social Psychology*, 10: 271–99.

Liuzza M. T., Cazzato V., Vecchione M., Crostella F., Caprara G. V., and Aglioti, S. (2011). 'Follow my Eyes: The Gaze of Politicians Reflexively Captures the Gaze of Ingroup Voters', *PLoS ONE*, 6/9: e25117.

Masters, R., and Sullivan, D. G. (1989). 'Nonverbal Displays and Political Leadership in France and the United States', *Political Behavior*, 11/2: 123–56.

Mintz, A., Redd, S. B., and Vedlitz, A. (2006). 'Can we Generalize from Student Experiments to the Real World in Political Science, Military Affairs, and International Relations?', *Journal of Conflict Resolution*, 50/5: 757–76.

Post, J. (1991). 'Saddam Hussein of Iraq: A Political Psychology Profile', *Political Psychology*, 12/2: 279–89.

Redd, S. (2002). 'The Influence of Advisers on Foreign Policy Decision Making: An Experimental Study', *Journal of Conflict Resolution*, 46/3: 335–64.

Smith, K. B., Larimer, C. W., Littvay, L. and Hibbing, J. R. (2007). 'Evolutionary Theory and Political Leadership: Why Certain People do not Trust Decision Makers', *Journal of Politics*, 69/2: 285–99.

Spisak, B., Homan, A. C., Grabo, A., and van Vugt, M. (2011). 'Facing the Situation: Testing a Biosocial Contingency Model of Leadership in Intergroup Relations Using Masculine and Feminine Faces', *Leadership Quarterly*, 23/2: 273–80.

Sullivan, D., and Masters, R. D. (1988). ' "Happy Warriors": Leaders' Facial Displays, Viewers' Emotions, and Political Support', *American Journal of Political Science*, 32/2: 345–68.

Van Vugt, M. (2006). 'Evolutionary Origins of Leadership and Followership', *Personality and Social Psychology Review*, 10/4: 354–71.

Van Vugt, M., and Spisak, B. R. (2008). 'Sex Differences in the Emergence of Leadership during Competitions within and between Groups', *Psychological Science*, 19/9: 854–8.

Van Vugt, M., Hogan, R., and Kaiser, R. B. (2008). 'Leadership, Followership, and Evolution: Some Lessons from the Past', *American Psychologist*, 63/3: 182–96.

Verba, S. (1961). *Small Groups and Political Behavior*. Princeton: Princeton University Press.

CHAPTER 19

....

OBSERVATIONAL ANALYSIS

....

FRANCESCA GAINS

1 INTRODUCTION

....

THE observation of a political leadership is associated with ethnographic investigation and interpretation. This chapter argues that the observation of political leadership practices, alongside extended conversations and the analysis of artefacts and documents, allows the researcher to provide a rich 'thick description' of the inner world of powerful elites, their decision-making, and their interactions. The use of observational analysis to research political leadership is relatively rare, as achieving access is difficult for researchers without official sanction or personal connections. Nevertheless, many observational studies of national and local, elected and non-elected political and administrative leadership have been undertaken. These studies provide insights that temper more deterministic rational choice, institutional, and constitutional theories of political leadership. In settings where political agency and individual judgement both are interesting and can have an impact, observational research can provide insights on political leadership unavailable through other means. Observing political leaders not only serves to triangulate other data but can uncover the important informal 'rules of the game' and remind us that the interpretation of the 'organization of political life' makes a difference, as well as reminding us of the opportunities for powerful, resource-rich actors to exercise agency even in circumstances of constraint.

This chapter begins by setting out the aims of observation and what a researcher interested in political leadership could hope to achieve through the use of this method. It reviews the literature on observational methods in anthropology, sociology, public administration, and political science. Next, it discusses three key methodological issues that arise in these disciplines before turning to broader questions around the use of ethnographic methods. The chapter focuses on the issues of: access; the ability of observers to provide an objective detached account, and, finally, the extent to which the findings can be generalized. The different approaches taken by observers of political leadership to resolve these methodological considerations illustrate this section. In concluding, a role for observational analysis of political leadership is advocated. For, although it is likely to be difficult to negotiate access for all but the well connected, the insights described by those able to observe the inner worlds of political leaders, on the making and remaking of politics, are important for understanding the exercise of creativity in the practice of political leadership.

2 WHY OBSERVE POLITICAL ELITES?

Observation is a key method of data generation in ethnographic and in-depth case-study research (Waddington 2004; Angrosino and Rosenberg 2011: 467; see also Rhodes, Chapter 7, Grint, Chapter 16, Shore, Chapter 12, and Walter, Chapter 21, this volume), and observational studies are found in anthropological, sociological (and the related field of public administration, organizational, and management studies), and political literatures. Associated with constructivist and interpretive approaches to data generation, and inductive theorizing, the observer/researcher hopes to uncover the inner world of those being observed, their beliefs and practices (Hammersley and Atkinson 2007). Observational notes can be triangulated with interview material and the study of artefacts and documentary analysis to research the everyday practices of people, communities, or organizations of interest. In a process that often involves lengthy immersion in a social setting, the observer hopes 'to study first-hand the day to day experiences and behaviours of subjects in particular situations, and if necessary, to talk to them about their feelings and interpretations' (Waddington 2004). The aim of the researcher is to provide a 'thick description' of meaningful social practices, the formal and informal rules, and how they are interpreted and operationalized by participants (Geertz 1973). The research approach is usually naturalistic—observing practices as they occur in the settings where they occur and not re-created in laboratory or other artificial settings (Brewer 2004: 313; Angrosino and Rosenberg 2011: 467).

Observational analysis, drawing from both anthropological and sociological ethnographic traditions, has uncovered thick descriptions of political actors in various settings (for a review of the development of political ethnography in general, and the differences between traditions of ethnography, see Gains 2011). However, ethnographic and observational studies of political *leadership* are comparatively rare. That observational studies of political leadership are rare is really not surprising. Access is a critical issue for ethnographic research in general. Accessing the highly sensitive, closely guarded, and secretive inner worlds of political elites is particularly difficult. This is not a method of researching political leadership that is accessible, transparent, or easy to replicate.

The potential rewards of such observational analysis, however, are rich (Fenno 1990). Not only do political leaders, more than any other political actors, or other organizational leaders, have the legitimacy, resources, capacity, and power to influence their own immediate world; through their interpretations and their decision-making, they can then create the parameters within which others must exercise their agency. The exercise of political leadership is, in Hay's terms (2002), both conduct- and context-shaping. As Rhodes, 't Hart, and Noordegraaf note in the introduction to their collection of observational studies of political elites, an ethnographically informed approach to researching political leadership opens up these 'black boxes of elite behaviour' (Rhodes, 't Hart, and Noordegraaf 2007: 2–3), and this kind of knowledge is an essential complement to what is known about elite traits and characteristics, studies of elite attitudes, and studies of elite decision-making in context (Rhodes, 't Hart, and Noordegraaf 2007: 5).

3 A GUIDE TO OBSERVATIONAL STUDIES OF POLITICAL LEADERS

What follows is a guide to the key works and more recent research from across anthropological, sociological, and political literatures that have used observation as a key method in studying political leadership (see also Rhodes, Chapter 7, Grint, Chapter 16, Shore, Chapter 12; and Walter, Chapter 21, this volume). Lengthy observation in the field is most strongly associated with anthropological work. One of the earliest examples of an anthropological observational account of political leadership was produced by Bailey in *Political Stratagems and Spoils: A Social Anthropology of Politics* (1969), which depicted the universal strategies undertaken by those striving for power. Adopting an anthropological approach in the UK, Heclo and Wildavsky's 1974 study *The Private Government of Public Money* undertook a ground-breaking study of the UK's public expenditure community, the elite politicians and officials who coordinated the budgeting process operating in the Whitehall 'village' in close networks of mutual trust. In Europe, anthropological insights also informed Marc Abeles's fascinating study of local political leadership in France, *Quiet Days in Burgundy* (1989). Abeles, like other anthropologists, turned his attention to communities in far distant places, and utilized the insights developed from studying them to the analysis of communities of interest nearer to home. Abeles notes:

> Having just spent many long months trying to understand the concept of politics held by the people of Ethiopia, I could not be content with the level of knowledge which had hitherto informed my life as a citizen of my own country ... I felt the desire to cast an anthropologist's eye over political life in France.
>
> (Abeles 1989: p. xvii)

More recently, anthropological work in this tradition has used observation to study political leadership in the House of Lords (Crewe 2005) and party conferences (Faucher-King 2005), while Rhodes's study *Everyday Life in British Government* (2011) is an extensive political ethnography of ministers and permanent secretaries in three departments of state in the UK Government.

The work of US sociologists, such as Kaufman's seminal study of US forest rangers (1960) and Lipsky's study of street-level bureaucrats (2010) first published in 1980, has informed a rich vein of sociologically inspired studies of administrative leadership. In the USA, Kaufman went on to examine how federal bureau chiefs went about their work (1981; and see also Rhodes, Chapter 7, this volume). In the UK, observational studies examined political leadership in national institutions such as the BBC (Burns 1977), the UK's telecommunications regulatory body (Hall, Scott, and Hood 2000), ministers and senior civil servants in the core executive (Richards and Smith 2004), and the Department of the Environment, Farming and Rural Affairs (Wilkinson 2011). In local political settings, Maynard-Moody and Musheno updated Lipsky in their work *Cops, Teachers, Counsellors* (2003); Noordegraaf (2000) examines the work of middle managers in public organizations, and Durose (2011) observed the activities of front-line workers. Observation as part of in-depth case studies formed a central part of the examination of new leadership structures and decision-making in English local government in evaluative studies (Stoker et al. 2004, 2007; Gains 2009), and local political decision-making was also the subject of an ethnographically informed study of local government in the Netherlands (van Hulst 2008).

In the related fields of organizational studies and management, observational studies of 'leadership' in different organizations are well established; for example, in Canada, Mintzberg and Bourgault (2000) examine the working practices of Canadian public managers. This management literature is associated with the study of career paths, the exercise of management control, and decision-making (Brewer 2004: 313). Contemporary management observational studies of leadership in organizations have moved away from seeing leadership as a set of 'trait' characteristics and view leadership more as a set of practices and meaning-making in organizational settings (Kelly 2008).

In the political science literature, Fenno (1986, 1990) was an early advocate of the need to observe political actors to appreciate the importance of context and timing in political decision-making. There is also a strong tradition of political insiders who draw on observational methodologies and insights from the anthropological and sociological academic literature to inform their biographies and studies of political leadership. Crossman explicitly drew on the methods of observational analysis in gathering material for his *Diaries of a Cabinet Minister*, which opened with the words: 'I was not only a politician. I was an observer as well as a doer, a political scientist as well as a journalist MP' (Crossman 1976: 11) and described his diary entries as akin to the classic field notes produced by anthropologists, 'a day to day account as seen by one participant' (Crossman 1976: 13). Like Crossman's, Watson's fascinating insider account of Australian Prime Minister Paul Keating's political leadership also explicitly acknowledges the methodologies and conventions of observational analysis. Watson explains: 'This book essentially records events as I saw and reacted to them from within the Prime Minister's Office' (Watson 2002: p. x). In the UK, Minkin's mighty *The Contentious Alliance*, a study of the alliance between the leadership of the Labour Party and the trade union movement, also drew on an insider's extended observations of the decision-making and deliberations of the most senior Labour politicians and trade-union officials (Minkin 1991; see also 1997).

4 KEY METHODOLOGICAL CONSIDERATIONS FOR ASPIRING OBSERVERS

Three related issues face all researchers wishing to undertake observational analysis: getting access to the phenomena they wish to observe, how to make sense of what they see, and then a consideration of the general relevance of their findings in other settings. The considerations and choices made by individual researchers on these matters partly depend upon the methodological approach and stance of the researcher and also reflect special considerations associated with the phenomena of observing political elites.

Negotiating Access

One of the first issues a researcher wishing to undertake observation of political leadership will confront is gaining access. This is a key task for any observational research—and one that is repeated many times during the course of a period of immersion, in different settings and situations in the field (Fenno 1990; Fielding 2003). The quality of data is related to the quality of access, and textbook advice suggests utilizing existing contacts or making use of key informants (Myers 2010: 144). Early anthropological work assumed that a year was the minimum period to witness the full range of the annual calendar of events. Observational work conducted closer to home associated with more recent ethnographic conventions is more likely to be conducted as 'yo-yo fieldwork', with the researcher making repeated visits over an extended period of time rather than spending a lengthy period of observation on one visit (Rhodes 2011: 9).

For those wishing to observe the secretive and sensitive world of political elites, negotiating access is even harder. Heclo and Wildavsky convincingly set out the difficulty,

> Ministers and officials need to be reassured that they are talking to fellow insiders who will understand what is being said. They also want a return on their investment of time in the form of an exchange of information.... Hence the researchers dilemma: to learn more he must already know much; he cannot get information without at least a small fund to begin with and he has trouble obtaining that without prior knowledge. No loan with good credit—no job without experience.
>
> (Heclo and Wildavsky 1974: p. xviii)

In the key works cited above, gaining access has sometimes been made easier by the 'insider' status of the researcher.

'Observant Participants' or 'Participant Observers'?

Observers can have different status depending upon the extent of their involvement in the setting. A *full participant* may be entirely involved in the normal routines under scrutiny, and the observer is therefore acting as an 'observant participant'. Both Watson's study of Paul Keating's office and Crossman's diaries would fall into this category. Minkin's observations of the UK's Labour leadership were undertaken in part in circumstances where he played a role in the decision-making in question. He writes that his research of such events followed 'a lifetime of being a participant within it' (Minkin 1997: 20).

At the other extreme in the field of observation analysis it is also possible for the observer to play the role of *complete observer* and to play no role at all in the proceedings—indeed, even to attempt to go unnoticed by those under observation. This kind of observation analysis is more associated with the observation of behaviour in social settings (especially perhaps in the observation of new work routines in organizational studies) and less concerned with uncovering meaning. Researchers adopting this kind of observer role may seek to avoid unduly influencing the situation under observation. However, this detachment means 'complete observer' studies of political leadership are unlikely to provide a meaningful analysis of political leadership beyond journalistic-type preoccupation with who stands next to whom at staged photograph events, for example.

More likely is the case where a researcher acts to varying degrees as 'participant observer', watching the day-to-day routines and decision-making but interspersing this with a dialogue with those involved about the meaning of events, of the significance of routines, decisions, and actions. The participant observer seeks to understand and appreciate the viewpoint of those under observation, to see the world as they see it. Their aim is to navigate the balance between their insider and outsider status, gradually becoming acclimatized and developing an understanding of the routines and norms of interaction while retaining a sense of objectivity and the ability to take an analytical perspective on what is observed (Waddington 2004: 155). Abeles, in his account of local political leadership in France, wrote: 'I was now observing a society which I understood intimately', and he expressed the hope that he would 'glimpse some truths about our way of practising and talking about politics' (Abeles 1989: p. xviii). Heclo and Wildavsky, in writing of the community of senior elite bureaucrats, wrote: 'we must begin by seeing the world through their eyes... the participant is the expert on what he does; the observer's task is to make himself expert on why he does it' (Heclo and Wildavsky 1974: p. xvii). That this is a difficult balance to achieve is discussed by Fenno (1990) in his account of observing Dan Quayle prior to Quayle's elevation to Vice President.

Making Sense of Observations

In anthropological studies, ethnography associated with early 'realist' work endeavoured to understand whole communities and belief systems, with observers striving for objectivity and seeking findings that could be generalized (Angrosino and Rosenberg 2011: 467). For traditional anthropological approaches and sociologically informed research (including some organizational studies) the essential requirement of seeking to capture events and interactions while simultaneously developing the researcher's understanding of the meaning of events begins with the production of full field notes (Burns 1977). The aim is to capture initially a detailed record of impressions written as soon as possible after the occasion, and written without attempt to analyse. This presents challenges to the observer, who has to make decisions about how to make notes and record significant events without disrupting the flow of proceedings. Subsequently, reflections on these field notes are used to seek patterning and themes, turning 'the flow of experiences into descriptions of the actors, settings, events and practices' (van Hulst 2008: 147), and for Waddington this can lead to 'analytical induction' (Waddington 2004: 156). For most researchers, the sheer volume of data generated is enormous and requires organizational and data-processing techniques as well as a critical perspective.

Seeking to manage the balance between seeing the world through the eyes of the observed, and maintaining a critical detached or objective analysis, is recognized as difficult in most of the methodological guides to observational work; Waddington suggests that it requires a 'critical self reflection' (Waddington 2004: 157). Striving to achieve objectivity is also mentioned by many of the observational researchers cited above. Heclo and Wildavsky expressed the hope of getting inside the situation without being captured: 'like good Treasury men, we have listened carefully to each viewpoint but remained presumptuous enough to think that we see the larger picture' (Heclo and Wildavsky 1974: p. xxii). Crossman writes: 'Of course the picture this diary provides is neither objective nor fair—although as a lifelong political scientist I have tried to discipline myself to objectivity' (Crossman 1976: 13). Minkin writes of making 'a conscious effort to gain an appropriate mood of critical self awareness and detachment in the role of observer' (Minkin 1997: 21).

In more recent approaches to observation analysis, however, the expectation for an observer to attempt a neutral or even critical analysis while seeking to understand a group or culture is problematized, particularly in contemporary anthropological approaches. Angrosino and Rosenberg (2011) suggest that the 'classic' anthropological traditions became challenged by the colonialist critique of the power relations involved in early anthropological work. In responding to the interpretive turn and postmodernism, contemporary anthropology problematizes traditional anthropology, with its standardized procedures, seeking to minimize researcher bias with the goal of achieving an objective account. Rather, contemporary anthropology seeks a more collaborative approach to the generation of knowledge, so that the observed and the observer are seen as partners who share an understanding of the goals of the research and a responsibility for its production. Here observation is seen less as a method of data collection and more as an opportunity for an 'extended conversation'. Researcher bias is accepted (Crang and Cook 2007), and the subjectivity of the researcher is seen as intrinsic to the processing of data and a degree of reflexivity in making sense of the sense-making of others is expected (van Hulst 2008: 148). Rhodes acknowledges that 'I accept that the department's story is my construction of how my interviewees see their world' (Rhodes 2005: 20).

For most ethnographers, however, an acknowledgement of the subjectivity of the researcher does not undermine the search for 'credibility' of the account (Fielding 2003: 155). Ethnographic researchers are encouraged to provide openness in their accounts of their data generation, to be explicit about how they formed their explanation. Techniques, such as triangulating data from different sources, assist in establishing the veracity and reliability of an account (Rhodes 2005: 22). Ultimately the researcher must seek to produce a narrative that is recognizable to others. For Rhodes, 't Hart, and Noordegraaf, 'a fact is a statement, typically about a piece of evidence, which nearly everyone in a given community would accept as true', and whether an account can be considered 'objective' reflects the extent to which there is agreement about the sense made of agreed facts (Rhodes, 't Hart, and Noordegraaf 2007: 11)—what Hay describes as an 'inter-subjective consensus' on empirical matters (Hay 2011: 178). For Angrosino and Rosenberg, 'observation based research nowadays must certainly consider the attributes and activities of ethnographers themselves', but they add that it 'cannot become so utterly subjective that it loses the rigor of carefully conducted, clearly recorded and intelligently interpreted observations' (Angrosino and Rosenberg 2011: 468). Navigating the extent to which the observer includes his or her own voice is one of the key contemporary considerations of observational researchers.

Are the Insights of Observations Generalizable?

A third dilemma for would-be observers is in addressing what Rhodes describes as the 'So what?' question (Rhodes 2011: 280). What does an in-depth, 'thick description' of political leadership in action in one setting add to knowledge about political leadership in general? Here again methodological approach is key. Kubik maps three contemporary approaches to ethnographic epistemologies. First, a 'realist perspective' seeks to capture insights that can be generalized (some sociological and organizational research approaches would share this aim). Second, an 'interpretivist perspective' problematizes the meaning-making of the researcher and therefore makes the co-production of knowledge a more situated experience. Finally, Kubik identifies a 'postmodern perspective', which problematizes the whole idea of generalizability (Kubik 2009: 37). These different methodological stances reflect different ontological understanding about the degree to which is it possible to think of and therefore research an external reality beyond that constructed by situated shared meanings (Schatz 2009: 4).

Some of the observational research cited above begins with the expressed aim of capturing generalizable insights on the practice of political leadership—for example,

Bailey (1969), Abeles (1989), and Gains (2009). Some accounts seek to provide insight into the particular leadership in question (Minkin 1991; Watson 2002; Rhodes 2011), though they may differ in the extent to which the observers' puzzlements and presence is foregrounded. For those contemplating observational research, these methodological stances need to be considered and appropriate research aims adopted to generate the insights required. In the next section the potential for observational research of different kinds to offer insight into political leadership is discussed.

5 The Insights of Observational Studies of Political Leadership

What can the identification of the meaningful social practices of political leaders tell us? What insights flow from this method of generating and making sense of observational data? Four separate but related generic insights from observational studies of political leadership are highlighted here. They are presented in ascending order of the degree of ethnographic 'sensibility' associated with the insights identified.

Observation for Triangulation

Myers sees a key difference between true ethnographic fieldwork and case-study work, suggesting case studies 'study people' whereas ethnography 'learns from people' (Myers 2010: 95). The first example of how observations can inform research into political leadership is drawn from in-depth case-study work, undertaken by the author, of changing leadership practices in local government. This work was part of a formal evaluation of new legislation designed to introduce streamlined executive decision-making practices to the pre-existing 'committee style' local government decision-making. The research aim was to use the logic of multiple case studies, mixed methods, and triangulation to produce generalizable insights into how new constitutional arrangements were influencing leadership practices (for a full account of the research design, see Stoker et al. 2004, 2007). The authors' experience of extensive observations of decision-making forums over a period of five years was that observational analysis contributed in a very meaningful way to gathering a full appreciation of the exercise of leadership in practice and how it varied. One example from this research will illustrate that potential.

The aim of the reforms was to encourage a single executive (elected) councillor to take policy decisions on his or her own, replacing time-consuming and costly committee-style decision-making. A review of constitutional arrangements across all authorities, and interviews with the local leaders, both elected and bureaucratic, revealed that yes—many authorities were complying with this. They had changed their constitutions and had identified leading elected executive councillors who were policy leads with the constitutional responsibility to make decisions. This decision-making had to be recorded and publicized in order to ensure transparency and accountability requirements, and therefore key decisions were made at set times, with an official present to record the outcome.

Having arranged to sit in on such a 'key decision' session, the author was amazed to walk into the appointed room to find it filled with more than fifty people. Also present at this meeting were a large number of the non-executive (or 'backbench') councilors, whose job was to scrutinize the work of the key decision-makers. Also in attendance were many of the bureaucrats, policy officers, whose role was to provide briefing advice. Finally, also present were members of the public with an interest in the key decision under consideration, and the local press. In fact, to all intents and purposes the streamlined 'key decision meeting' replicated almost exactly, in terms of the participants and style of decision-making, the previous and allegedly replaced committee for the policy area. This observation of the practice of political leadership demonstrated that, although constitutional reforms had been made, actual leadership practices and the understanding of how political leadership should be enacted were virtually unaffected in some local government areas (see Gains 2009). This example also illustrates a second insight that observational analysis can identify—that the informal 'rules of the game' are often more meaningful than the formal.

The Importance of the Informal

March and Olsen drew attention to the importance of informal conventions and understandings in providing powerful guides to action for organizational actors, often more so than the formal 'rules of the game' (March and Olsen 1984). Observational research can reveal these informal norms and conventions and their meaning for political actors, and, in so doing, can provide a helpful corrective to accounts of political leadership that place an over-reliance on normative, calculus, or prescriptive models of leadership behaviour (Crewe 2005).

Minkin (1991) described the relationship between the Labour Party and the trade unions as being analogous to a family relationship where bonds of trust and dependency underpinned their otherwise conflicting goals. Heclo and Wildavsky, in their anthropology of UK Treasury elite actors, identified a culture of civility, of community, and of how that commitment to maintaining the vital personal relationships that sustained the community of senior officials involved in negotiating expenditure over-rode base calculations on what would be most advantageous in each particular situation.

> Community refers to the personal relationships between major political and administrative actors—sometimes in conflict, often in agreement, but always in touch and operating within a shared framework. Community is the cohesive and orienting bond underlying any particular issue. Policy is government action directed toward

and affecting some end outside itself. There is no escaping the tension between policy and community, between adapting actions and maintaining relationships, between decision and cohesion, between governing now and preserving the possibility of governing later. This is the underlying dilemma facing the community of political administrators.

(Heclo and Wildavsky 1974: p. xv)

Thirty years later, back in Whitehall examining the workings of ministers' private offices at the apex of the UK government, Rhodes (2011: 300) also observed the same culture of civility and how the tradition of the tea trolley served to punctuate and soothe the pressured working schedule of senior political and bureaucratic actors.

The Organization of Political Life Makes a Difference

Observational studies can also provide a window into how 'the organization of political life makes a difference' (March and Olsen 1984). Both the formal and informal 'rules of the game' have the effect of guiding the flow of demands for attention, for resources, for action. Observation can capture how the rules of the game guide action and provide the cues for behaviour. Observation can, therefore, sometimes highlight how these structuring logics—Rhodes describes them as 'traditions'—can lead to substantive policy consequences, such as in regulatory decision-making (Hall, Scott, and Hood 2000). Questions such as 'Who is on the circulation list?', chance and not-so-chance informal meetings, previous protocols remembered and used to deal with dilemmas—these features of organizational life in politics have an impact. Abeles (1989) describes the nested political geography of local French politics and how the conflicting and competing demands of different tiers of government are resolved. Rhodes (2011) describes how the relentless pressure of policy-making under the scrutiny of twenty-four-hour media attention can result in crisis, sometimes with serious consequences for those in high office. Rhodes also describes how shared traditions of political conduct get challenged by governing dilemmas, and how the solution to these dilemmas leads to changing traditions. Since Rhodes's immersion in Whitehall, the establishment of a new coalition government in the UK will have created many such dilemmas, requiring political leaders both to adapt and to develop forgotten protocols and creatively negotiate new governing arrangements. Finally, the way in which observational analysis, particularly that conducted by 'observant participants', can uncover the creativity of political leaders is highlighted next.

Creativity and Leadership

The strongest claim for the insights offered through observation are made by Westbrook, who suggests that politics, 'however and by whoever conducted, is done in accordance with some set of beliefs held by the powerful, an imagination of what can and should be done' (Westbrook 2008: 129). The imagination of actors who make the rules for citizens, and their ideas of how to act, create the parameters of the possible, and Westbrook argues that it is ethnographic observation that can 'clarify and make explicit ways in which such social connections are formed, channels through which info flows and decisions are made' (2008: 135).

It is in the 'observant participant' accounts by Crossman (1976), Minkin (1991), and Watson (2002), with their focus on both process and politics, that the rich and nuanced account of the governing dilemmas of political elites and their creative responses is best depicted. Watson, writing about Paul Keating, states:

> Keating was governed by an idea for Australia, or rather many ideas which over time cohered as one expanding vision. He practiced politics precisely for the purpose of mastering events because politics was the only means by which he could turn this thing of his imagination into something real. Politics was power, it was the hunt, the game, a way to the unrivalled pleasure of destroying his enemies—but it was, as well, always an act of creation.
>
> (Watson 2002: p. xi)

6 Conclusion: Observing Elites

In concluding, observational analysis of political leadership presents some key methodological challenges. Gaining access is unlikely and difficult. Those most likely to be in a position to observe the inner worlds of political elites are almost certainly going to be in positions of trust and engagement already. This raises questions about the objectivity of any account, even where the researcher makes strenuous attempts to maintain an objective stance. Of course, for some, objectivity is an unrealizable goal, and the meaning-making of the researcher is part of the finished account. Whatever the perspective taken on the reliability of the observation, researchers may also question how much the findings can be generalized. Does the observation of political decision-making in one setting provide any insights that can be applied or utilized elsewhere? Access, objectivity, generalizability—all these key research issues can be problematic for this method of analysis.

Depending upon the stance of the researcher, these problems may be addressed through research protocols, strenuous self-analysis, and research design. Observing the exercise of political leadership can inform other research approaches and be used in a mixed method or a standalone approach; or—for postmodern observers—they may simply be ignored, because, for them, that is not the point of the exercise anyway.

This survey of how the methods of observational analysis have been used to research the exercise of political leadership demonstrates the potential for deep immersion in the inner worlds of political leaders to triangulate leadership practices against other indicators of leadership, to illustrate the importance of the informal, and to show how the organization of political life makes a difference. The potential of observational analysis, it is argued here, is to capture and describe how political problems are perceived and understood; how the search for solutions to political problems is resolved and the trade-offs and judgements made; how these decisions themselves create new 'webs of belief', and the how the ideational becomes institutionalized. A key overriding value of good observational studies of political leadership is found in the capacity for this method to capture the *creativity* of political leadership: to challenge accounts that see only calculations based on the maximization of advantage, votes, or influence—although these may occur. As Heclo and Wildavsky argue, 'politics proceeds not only by powerful men bargaining but also by puzzled men learning to adapt their minds and operations to emerging problems' (Heclo and Wildavsky 1974: p. xix). Where access is obtained, trust gained, and observation possible, such analysis is a rare but welcome contribution to the understanding of the exercise of power.

RECOMMENDED READING

Abeles, M. (1989). *Quiet Days in Burgundy: A Study of Local Politics*. Cambridge: Cambridge University Press.

Rhodes, R. A. W., 't Hart, P., and Noordegraaf, M. (2007). *Observing Elites: Up Close and Personal*. Basingstoke: Palgrave.

Watson, D. (2002). *Recollections of a Bleeding Heart: A Portrait of Paul Keating PM*. New York: Knopf.

REFERENCES

Abeles, M. (1989). *Quiet Days in Burgundy: A Study of Local Politics*. Cambridge: Cambridge University Press.

Angrosino, M., and Rosenberg, J. (2011). 'Observations on Observations', in N. Denzin and Y. Lincoln (eds), *Sage Handbook of Qualitative Research*. London: Sage Publications, 468–78.

Bailey, F. (1969). *Political Strategems and Spoils: A Social Anthropology of Politics*. Oxford: Blackwell.

Brewer, J. (2004). 'Ethnography', in C. Cassell and G. Symon (eds), *Essential Guide to Qualitative Methods in Organizational Research*. London: SAGE, 312–322.

Burns, T. (1977). *The BBC: Public Institution and Private World*. Houndmills: Macmillan.

Cassell, C., and Symon, G. (2004) (eds). *Essential Guide to Qualitative Methods in Organizational Research*. London: Sage.

Crang, M., and Cook, I. (2007). *Doing Ethnography*. London: Sage.

Crewe, E. (2005). *Lords of Parliament: Manners, Rituals and Politics*. Manchester: Manchester University Press.

Crossman, R. (1976). *The Diaries of a Cabinet Minister*. Vol. 1: 1964–1966. Worcester: Trinity Press.

Denzin, N., and Lincoln, Y. (2011) (eds). *Sage Handbook of Qualitative Research*. London: Sage Publications.

Durose, C. (2011). 'Revisiting Lipsky: Front-Line Work in UK Local Governance', *Political Studies*, 59/4: 978–95.

Faucher-King, F. (2005). *Changing Parties: An Anthropology of British Political Conferences*. Houndmills: Palgrave Macmillan.

Fenno, R. E. (1986). 'Observation, Context and Sequence in the Study of Politics', *American Political Science Review*, 80/1: 3–15.

Fenno, R. E. (1990). *Watching Politicians: Essays on Participant Observation*. Berkeley and Los Angeles: Institute of Governmental Studies, University of California.

Fielding, N. (2003). 'Ethnography', in N. Fielding (ed.), *Researching Social Life*. London: Sage, 145–63.

Gains, F. (2009). 'Narratives and Dilemmas of Local Bureaucratic Elites: Whitehall at the Coalface?', *Public Administration*, 87/1: 50–65.

Gains, F. (2011). 'Elite Ethnographies: Potential, Pitfalls and Prospects for "Getting Up Close and Personal"', *Public Administration*, 89/1: 156–66.

Geertz, C. (1973). *The Interpretation of Cultures*. New York: Basic Books.

Hall, C., Scott, C., and Hood, C. (2000). *Telecommunications Regulation: Culture, Chaos and Interdependence inside the Regulatory Process*. London: Routledge.

Hammersley, M., and Atkinson, P. (2007). *Ethnography: Principles in Practice*. London: Routledge.

Hay, C. (2002). *Political Analysis*. Houndmills: Palgrave Macmillan.

Hay, C. (2011). 'Interpreting Interpretivism Interpreting Interpretations: The New Hermeneutics of Public Administration', *Public Administration*, 89/1: 167–82.

Heclo, H., and Wildavsky, A. (1974). *The Private Government of Public Money: Community and Policy inside British Politics*. Houndmills: Macmillan.

Kaufman, H. (1960). *The Forest Ranger: A Study in Administrative Behavior*. Baltimore, MD: Johns Hopkins University Press.

Kaufman, H. (1981). *The Administrative Behavior of Federal Bureau Chiefs*. Washington: Brookings Institution.

Kelly, S. (2008). 'Leadership: A Categorical Mistake?', *Human Relations*, 61/6: 763–82.

Kubik, J. (2009). 'Ethnography of Politics: Foundations, Applications, Prospects', in E. Schatz (ed.), *Political Ethnography: What Immersion Contributes to the Study of Power*. Chicago: University of Chicago Press, 25–52.

Lipsky, M. (2010) [1980]. *Street-Level Bureaucracy: Dilemmas of the Individual in Public Service*. New York: Russell Sage Foundation.

March, J., and Olsen. J. (1984). 'The New Institutionalism: Organisational Factors in Political Life', *American Political Science Review*, 73/3: 734–49.

Maynard-Moody, S., and Musheno, M. (2003). *Cops, Teachers, Counsellors: Stories from the Front Lines of Public Service*. Ann Arbor, MI: University of Michigan Press.

Minkin, L. (1991). *The Contentious Alliance*. Edinburgh: Edinburgh University Press.

Minkin, L. (1997). *Exits and Entrances: Political Research as a Creative Art*. Sheffield: Sheffield Hallam University Press.

Mintzberg, H., and Bourgault, J. (2000). *Managing Publicly*. Toronto: Institute of Public Administration of Canada.

Myers, M. D. (2010). *Qualitative Research in Business and Management*. London: Sage Publications.

Noordegraaf, M. (2000). *Attention! Work and Behaviour of Public Managers amidst Ambiguity.* Delft: Eburon.

Rhodes, R. A. W. (2005). 'Everyday Life in a Ministry: Public Administration as Anthropology', *American Review of Public Administration*, 35/1: 3–25.

Rhodes, R. A. W., 't Hart, P., and Noordegraaf, M. (2007). *Observing Elites: Up Close and Personal.* Basingstoke: Palgrave.

Rhodes. R. A. W. (2011). *Everyday Life in British Government.* Oxford: Oxford University Press.

Richards, D., and Smith, M. J. (2004). 'Interpreting the World of Political Elites', *Public Administration*, 82/4: 777–800.

Schatz, E. (2009). *Political Ethnography: What Immersion Contributes to the Study of Power.* Chicago: University of Chicago Press.

Stoker, G., Gains, F., Greasley, S., John, P., Rao, N., and Harding, A. (2004). *Operating the New Council Constitutions in English Local Authorities: A Process Report.* London: Office of the Deputy Prime Minister (ODPM).

Stoker, G., Gains, F., Greasley, S., John, P., and Rao, N. (2007). *The Outcomes and Impacts of the New Council Constitutions.* London: Communities and Local Government (CLG).

Van Hulst, M. (2008). 'Quite an Experience: Using Ethnography to Study Local Governance', *Critical Policy Studies*, 2/2: 143–59.

Waddington, D. (2004). 'Participant Observation', in C. Cassell and G. Symon (eds), *Essential Guide to Qualitative Methods in Organizational Research.* London: Sage, 154–64.

Watson, D. (2002). *Recollections of a Bleeding Heart: A Portrait of Paul Keating PM.* New York: Knopf.

Westbrook, D. (2008). *Navigators of the Contemporary: Why Ethnography Matters.* Chicago: University of Chicago Press.

Wilkinson, K. (2011). 'Organised Chaos: An Interpretive Approach to Evidence Based Policy Making in DEFRA', *Political Studies*, 59/4: 959–77.

CHAPTER 20

....

AT-A-DISTANCE ANALYSIS*

....

MARK SCHAFER

1 INTRODUCTION AND OVERVIEW

....

AT-A-DISTANCE psychological methods were born of pragmatic necessity, but they have quickly become critically important in the field of political psychology and leadership studies. Throughout virtually all written history about politics, thinkers have considered the role of idiosyncratic factors in leaders and their effects on public policy. Yet, for obvious reasons, analysts are unable to study the psychology of leaders using direct experimental or clinical methods. If we assume individual psychology matters, how then can we assess psychological characteristics of political leaders? The answer is that we must do so 'at-a-distance'—that is, by careful observation and analysis of the things we can see in a leader's present and past.

Careful observation and analysis are hardly novel ideas. Indeed, traditional experimental and clinical methods rely on these same techniques: they observe behaviour in carefully controlled settings and draw inferences about the meaning of the behaviour and its connection to other behavioural patterns found in the subjects. Our at-a-distance analyses of political leaders, if theoretically grounded and well executed, should hardly be considered less valid than experimental and clinical research. Indeed, one could easily argue that they might be more valid: after all, at-a-distance analyses are generally based upon observations taken in natural settings rather than in the artificial setting of an experiment or under the watchful eye of the clinical psychologist.

What should we observe about political leaders to enable us to make inferences about their psychology? That depends upon our research question and the theoretical development of appropriate indicators, but we can sum up in one word the basis for most of our observations: *behaviour*. We see, from a distance, how a subject behaves, perhaps in

* Many thanks to the editors of this volume for the constructive feedback on an earlier draft. Thanks also to Austin Geraghty, who helped with construction of the manuscript.

a variety of ways, draw psychological inferences from the patterns of observed behaviour, and use those inferences as independent or causal variables to help explain political choices.

It is not surprising that there are both qualitative and quantitative approaches to at-a-distance analysis, and there are advantages associated with each. Qualitative approaches typically look at the psychology of one or a small number of individuals at a time. This allows for extensive, in-depth analysis of each subject. Researchers using qualitative approaches can investigate many different psychological components, look for causes of psychological characteristics, provide examples of behavioural manifestations of the individual's psychology, and generally tell a comprehensive, in-depth psychological story for the subject under investigation. On the other hand, quantitative approaches generally determine measurements of a few specific psychological characteristics for many individuals. As a result, these studies provide a limited number of insights on any one individual, but allow for statistical analyses of patterns found across a sample of individuals. Quantitative measurements can be used for such things as numerical comparisons of two or more individuals (for example, Actor A is more mistrustful than Actor B), comparisons across time for one or more actors (for example, Actor A became more distrusting over time), quantitative comparisons of two or more groups of individuals (for example, leaders from political party A are more distrusting than leaders from political party B), and statistical models of the effect of psychological characteristics on leadership behaviour (for example, leaders who score higher levels on distrust tend to have poorer-quality decision-making processes and quicker tendencies to escalate conflict situations). Neither qualitative nor quantitative approaches are better or worse; they each simply provide different kinds of information and insights regarding leadership.

Most of this chapter will focus on quantitative approaches, but I will say a few words here on qualitative ones (for additional insights and methods regarding qualitative approaches, see also Post, Chapter 22, this volume). Qualitative approaches may look at the subject's behaviour on several different fronts, such as behaviour that occurred earlier in the subject's political career, or the formative years of late adolescence and early adulthood, or even childhood. Sometimes the psychology of a subject and its effect on *public* policy choices is inferred from *private*, personal, or interpersonal behaviour (see, e.g., the work on interpersonal generalization theory, Etheredge 1978).

Greenstein (1969) provides a classic formula for conducting qualitative psychobiographies. He suggests that a psychobiography ought to include three parts. The first, called the phenomenology, is the public policy or process-based actions taken by the leader. Most psychobiographies focus on *puzzling* actions by the leader—a policy or behaviour that others in the same situation might not have taken. The general hypothesis is that the psychology of the leader might solve the puzzle of the unusual behaviour. The second part of the psychobiography is called the dynamic. Here the researcher analyses the adult-manifest psychology of the leader to discern patterns and posit the psychological mechanisms that contributed to the unusual behaviour by the leader. The final part of a classic psychobiography is the genesis. In this part, the researcher investigates the origins of the dynamic by looking at the leader's childhood and formative years (for additional information and insights, see Greenstein 1969; Barenbaum and Winter 2003; Winter 2003b, c; see also Personality Profiling Analysis by Post, and Psychoanalysis byRenshon). Some very good examples of qualitative at-a-distance analyses include Erik Erikson (1958) on Martin Luther, Betty Glad (1980) on Jimmy Carter, and Stanley Renshon (1996) on Bill Clinton.

Turning to quantitative at-a-distance methods, the vast majority of current research uses the *verbal behaviour* of subjects to make inferences about psychological character-istics. The basic assumption is that what a leader says and how she or he says it will indi-cate at least some components of the leader's psychology. There are a number of reasons why researchers have developed programmes using this approach. First, verbal behav-iour is behaviour, and as such it has all the advantages of using almost any behaviour for psychological assessment, as discussed above: it is done by the subject; it is observable; it differs from the behaviour of others; and it tells something about the psychology of the subject. Take, for instance, an individual who tells us a glass is half full; we infer that the individual is more of an optimist than a pessimist. Second, verbal behaviour is a type of behaviour that is readily available for political psychology research: virtually all political actors engage in various forms of public speaking. Third, verbal behaviour is analysable: it is possible to analyse patterns of words, and, as a result, systematic content analysis can produce highly reliable measurements of specific psychological character-istics. It is certainly possible to imagine other types of observable behaviour that may also be available and produce reliable measurements of psychological characteristics, such as analysis of eye movements, body language, tone in rhetoric, or breathing pat-terns (indeed, good poker players use various combinations of these to infer 'tells' in their opponents). However, the theoretical and methodological advancements neces-sary for these are still down the road, whereas there are already available today excellent theoretical and methodological foundations for systematic content analysis of verbal behaviour as quantitative indicators of subjects' psychological characteristics.

In the following sections, we shall see examples of this kind of research and make note of some classics in the field. For now, let us look briefly at the early development and basic descriptions of four major, yet very different, research programmes using ver-bal at-a-distance methods: Peter Suedfeld's work on integrative complexity; Margaret Hermann's work on several different psychological traits in a research programme called 'Leadership Trait Analysis' (LTA); David Winter's work on motives; and Stephen Walker's work on operational code analysis (OCA).

Peter Suedfeld began publishing work on complexity in the mid-1960s (Suedfeld 1966; Suedfeld and Hagen 1966; Suedfeld and Streufert 1966) and specifically became interested in the verbal indicators of complexity a few years later (Suedfeld 1968). Later, Suedfeld, working in conjunction with Phillip Tetlock, developed the research pro-gramme on integrative complexity (Suedfeld and Tetlock 1976; see also Suedfeld and Tetlock 1977; Suedfeld, Tetlock, and Ramirez 1977; Tetlock and Suedfeld 1987; Suedfeld, Guttieri, and Tetlock 2003). Integrative complexity methods analyse paragraphs in a leader's verbal material and code each paragraph on a scale of 1 to 7, with higher scores representing higher levels of complexity. Integrative complexity consists of two underlying dimensions that come in different, escalating stages of complexity. Scores increase from one to three as subjects show more *differentiation* in assessing a topic area—that is, higher scores indicate more facets or dimensions pertaining to the topic. Scores five through seven show increasing levels of *integration* by the speaker—that is, more connections and relationships across the already differentiated facets and dimensions (four serve as a transition score, very high level of differentiation, but very little integration). Siece then, Phillip Tetlock has also become quite prolific in this research programme (see, e.g., Tetlock 1983a, 1983b, 1985).

In the 1970s, Margaret Hermann began conducting research on the psychological characteristics of subjects and their effect on foreign-policy matters (Hermann, Hermann, and Cantor 1974), with one publication discussing methods (Hermann 1974) and two others investigating the effects of characteristics on foreign-policy patterns (Hermann 1977, 1978). By 1980, her LTA system had taken clear shape, with a well-cited publication in *International Studies Quarterly*, 'Explaining foreign policy behaviour using personal characteristics of political leaders'. Hermann's method focuses on counts of specific words and phrases as indications of seven different psychological characteristics. An example is the variable conceptual complexity, which differentiates between those who see the world in simple, black-or-white terms and those who see the world in much more complex terms, with many shades of grey. To operationalize this variable, Hermann developed large dictionaries of words and phrases that mark high and low complexity: low complexity is marked by such words and phrases as *always, never, must be, for ever*; high complexity is marked with such words as: *possibly, perhaps, maybe, sometimes*. The trait indicator is a ratio between these two kinds of words. Hermann's system includes seven different traits: conceptual complexity, need for power, distrust, self-confidence, in-group bias, task focus, and belief in ability to control events, each of which has two dictionaries of words, one marking the positive and one marking the negative manifestations of the trait. Each individual trait may have explanatory power in its own right, but Hermann's theoretical work also anticipates effects associated with various combinations of the traits (Hermann and Preston 1994; Hermann 1999).

David Winter's research programme has focused on motive imagery in the verbal behaviour of political actors. Motives are the psychological needs that move individuals towards goal-directed behaviours. Motive analysis has intellectual origins going back to Freud, and different researchers have identified many different possible categories of motives. Winter first focused on the power motive (Winter 1973), but later developed a three-component conception of motives that is particularly salient for leadership studies, and this has become the basis for his quite prolific research programme (see, e.g., Winter 1980, 1987, 1993, 1998). The three motives (often referred to as 'needs') that are the focus of Winter's research are: power (need to be in charge), affiliation (need for belonging and involvement), and achievement (need for accomplishment or mastery). Working with Abigail Stewart, Winter began developing the methods for at-a-distance analysis in the 1970s (Winter and Stewart 1977), and he has published several pieces that explain the theory and methods involved in at-a-distance motive analysis (see,

e. g., Winter 1992, 1994, 2003a). The general method is to look for specific imagery (such as stories, representations, images, or interactions) that demonstrate the motive being investigated. For example, power imagery would be seen in a subject who advocates strong or forceful action or who talks about the importance of control and influence.

Stephen Walker's work on the operational code is unique because he has made significant contributions to the research programme in terms of both qualitative and quantitative research (e.g. Walker 1977, 1995; Walker, Schafer and Young 1998; Schafer and Walker 2006). Nathaniel Leites (1951, 1953) coined the term 'operational code' with his psychoanalytic assessment of leaders in the Soviet Politburo. Alexander George (1969) converted the operational code into a cognitive research programme. George posited ten questions regarding the beliefs of leaders. He argued that the qualitative answers to those questions represented a belief system that, once determined, would provide insights regarding leader behaviour.

Though these key theoretical and empirical contributions preceded Walker's own work on the operational code, he has since become the most prolific researcher in this area, and he pioneered the conversion of George's qualitative construct to a quantitative, at-a-distance research programme. The core of quantitative OCA is its focus on the cooperative and conflictual beliefs of leaders along two different dimensions: beliefs about others and beliefs about self's strategy and tactics, coined by George (1969) as 'philosophical' and 'instrumental' beliefs, respectively. Building on event-data methods in international relations, Walker constructed the Verbs in Context System, which codes for two important elements in verbal source material: the verb, which indicates direction and magnitude of conflict versus cooperative actions; and the grammatical subject of the sentence, which indicates who the actor sees as taking the action. Aggregations of verbs with others as the subject provide information about how the leader sees others in the world, while those with self as the subject provide information about the leader's beliefs about his own side's strategies and tactics (for additional information on OCA methods and theory, see Walker, Schafer, and Young 1998; Schafer and Walker 2006). Since Walker developed the quantitative version of the operational code, it has become perhaps the most prolific research programme in leadership political psychology (see examples of quantitative OCA research discussed later in this chapter). However, as already discussed, there remain advantages to conducting qualitative OCA—namely, the depth and thoroughness associated with descriptive analysis.

2   DEVELOPMENTS, ISSUES, AND DEBATES

Though some of these at-a-distance research programmes have been around since the 1960s, perhaps the most important breakthrough for them has happened only in the 2000s: the development of computer-based coding systems. Prior to this, all four of the programmes discussed in the previous section relied on hand coding of verbal material, something that was highly labour intensive and also introduced human coding problems such as errors, biases, and fatigue—now, all four have automated coding systems available for computers.[1] While it used to take a human several hours or more to hand code a speech, a computer can code hundreds of speech acts in that same time. While computer-based programs are not a panacea, they have significantly opened the coding bottleneck, allowing for much more substantive and methodological analysis.

Automated coding of verbal behaviour means other major developments relative to leadership studies are likely to be forthcoming. Much more data create the possibility of developing extensive datasets of psychological correlates, much as the conflict field in international relations has developed a number of major datasets about international conflict (such as the Correlates of War, Militarized Interstate Disputes, and International Crisis Behaviour projects). Furthermore, once larger datasets of psychological characteristics are developed, researchers will be able to use those data in combination with other large datasets, meaning that major advancements will be forthcoming in terms of the science of political psychology. Indeed, the early 2000s have seen exactly this kind of research being presented at major professional conferences (see, e.g., Beieler 2011; Foster and Keller 2011; Schafer, Butler and Hartmann 2011; Butler 2012; Robison 2012).

There remain many questions, concerns, and issues regarding at-a-distance methods. These include such things as speech-writer effects, impression management by political actors, prepared versus spontaneous verbal material, public versus private verbal behaviour, and aggregation issues. Though these are valid concerns, they have already been at least partially investigated and addressed extensively in the literature elsewhere,[2] and space prohibits an extensive discussion of each of them here. Nonetheless, a few words regarding general concerns about at-a-distance methods are in order. The main concern we hear with regularity is simply that one cannot accurately assess psychological characteristics in political actors using verbal material -it is laden with insurmountable problems.

This argument is unconvincing for a number of reasons. First, as noted above, linguistic behaviour is simply another form of behaviour, and behaviour, broadly construed, is the basis of many forms of psychological analysis. Second, over the years there has been enough research conducted using these methods that a simple review indicates we have very extensive, broad-based validity for these methods, particularly construct validity; this research has shown many times that it is producing indicators very much as hypothesized. Third, these methods are not intended to get every dimension of psychology: each research programme specifies certain psychological characteristics that

[1] All four systems are available using the same full-language parser software program called Profiler Plus from Social Science Automation. For more information, see <http://socialscience.net>.

[2] For a general discussion of these issues and others, see Schafer (2000). Regarding speech-writer effects, see Hermann (1980); Crichlow (1998). Regarding impression management in verbal behaviour of political actors, see Tetlock and Manstead (1985). On the topic of appropriate source material, see Suedfeld and Wallace (1995); Walker, Schafer, and Young (1998); Marfleet (2000); Schafer and Crichlow (2000). Regarding aggregation issues, see Hermann (1985); Walker and Schafer (2000).

are likely to have some effect on political behaviour. They measure specific psychological characteristics that are, well, measurable using these methods. We have no doubt that other research programmes will come along in the future that measure additional psychological characteristics, just as virtually all scientific fields expand and develop over time. Finally, while the concerns and issues noted above are questions about the method's appropriateness, they are not rejections of it; they are empirical questions that—existing research notwithstanding—warrant continued investigation. Some may wish to argue that a speech act that is (at least partially) written by someone other than the political actor cannot be a valid indicator of that actor's psychology, but this is actually an empirical question. There is actually plenty of evidence that supports the effectiveness of using prepared speech acts as psychological indicators (see, e.g., Winter 1987; Schafer and Crichlow 2000; Schafer and Walker 2006; Walker and Schafer 2007).

Another broad and valid concern is that these methods are reductionist—that is, they reduce the complex set of a subject's psychology to just a few measurable characteristics. To a great extent, this refers back to the qualitative–quantitative distinction discussed above. It is true that each individual is a unique and complex story, and there is much to be gained by comprehensive, in-depth qualitative analysis. Quantitative methods simply do not do that, and much is lost or overlooked as a result. The trade-off, of course, is that quantitative approaches gather numerical data that are directly comparable and can be used in statistical models.

The point is not that these methods are perfect or without their limitations, but rather that they are already well proven to be effective for their intended use. We certainly should continue to investigate these and other empirical questions as the research programmes continue to develop; today's computer-based methods allow us to do so quickly and efficiently. Meanwhile, the contributions associated with these methods are very exciting as they allow us effectively to demonstrate the importance of psychology in explaining conflict behaviour in international relations. Because these methods allow for statistical models, their contributions to leadership studies are essential. It is true that each individual human is unique and a story unto herself or himself; but it is equally true that there are discernible patterns across samples of humans. Applying this logic to leadership studies means that using these quantitative at-a-distance methods allows us to ascertain measurements of psychological characteristics of leaders and then model the effect of those characteristics across various samples of leaders on many different kinds of leadership behaviour.

3 SOME IMPORTANT CONTRIBUTIONS USING AT-A-DISTANCE METHODS

Though at-a-distance methods have been around for many years now, they are still very much in development. However, with the breakthroughs associated with automated coding, the possibilities for new research questions using these methods are almost unlimited. In the field of international relations alone, there is already an abundance of quantitative indicators on the dependent variable side of the equation, but very little work has been done using psychological indicators on the independent side. The result is that the field is very wide open in terms of potential research projects. Furthermore, we know enough from existing research that the psychological characteristics of leaders can have very powerful explanatory power. In this section, we shall consider a handful of important contributions that have been made to the literature using at-a-distance methods in political psychology. Some of these are classics in the field, and some are more modern.

The most basic conceptual dependent variable in the field of international relations is conflict behaviour by a state. Indeed, over the years many different studies have used at-a-distance methods to distil psychological characteristics of leaders and demonstrate their effects on conflict behaviour. For example: lower levels of integrative complexity correlate with more conflict behaviour (Suedfeld and Tetlock 1977; Suedfeld, Tetlock and Ramirez 1977); higher levels of mistrustfulness correlate with higher propensities towards conflict behaviour (Schafer and Crichlow 2010; Foster and Keller 2011); high need for power also predicts increased conflict behaviour, while high need for affiliation results in less conflict behaviour (Winter 1993); and, conflict-oriented operational codes of state and group leaders correlate with conflict actions taken by the leaders' organizations (Schafer and Walker 2006; Schafer, Robison and Aldrich 2006; Walker and Schafer 2007). These are only a few examples of research demonstrating, quite convincingly, that the psychological characteristics of a leader play an important role in a state's conflict behaviour. While explaining state conflict behaviour remains central in International Relations research, at-a-distance methods have been used to explain a large range of other kinds of dependent variables. Indeed, in the rest of this section, I highlight several articles that have used very interesting dependent variables; these show some of the range and some of the potential for at-a-distance research.

Sometimes political behaviour can be anticipated by looking at changes in psychological characteristics over time. Suedfeld and his colleagues provide two such examples of this kind of research. Suedfeld and Tetlock (1977), using a sample of crises that ended either peacefully or in war, found that diplomatic communication became less complex in those cases ending in war and became more complex in those cases that ended peacefully. Suedfeld and Bluck (1988) found—looking at a set of international crises involving a significant surprise attack—that the attacker showed a notable decline in integrative complexity in the three months prior to the attack.

Turning to a very different research question, Suedfeld and Rank (1976) wondered if changes in integrative complexity are related to success in governing for individuals who were previously revolutionary leaders. They hypothesize that successful leaders of revolutionary movements need low complexity associated with single-mindedness, whereas success in governing requires more 'graduated, flexible, and integrated' views (Suedfeld and Rank (1976: 169)), which means higher levels of complexity. That is exactly what they found: former revolutionary leaders who are successful in government show significant increases in their integrative complexity, whereas those revolutionaries who were unsuccessful with governing showed no changes in their integrative complexity.

In LTA research, we shall look at three different contributions, each of which uses quite different dependent variables. Hermann's article (1980) explaining the foreign-policy behaviour of states using the leaders' psychological characteristics remains a classic in the field. It was the first major presentation of what later came to be called her LTA research programme, and it did so in a project that included a large number of cases (forty-five different leaders), something that had not been done in the literature until recent times. Hermann also used many different and unique dependent variables in the study. For instance, she found that a leader's high level of distrust and need for power explained more independent action (rather than interdependent action) by the state, whereas high levels of conceptual complexity and need for affiliation had the opposite effect. High levels of control orientation and distrust resulted in lower levels of state commitment in various situations, while the leader's participatory orientation correlated with more state commitment.

A more recent contribution comes from the work of Foster and Keller (2011). Using two different, large-n conflict datasets, these researchers investigate the extent to which the psychological characteristics of leaders have an effect on diversionary behaviour by states. Diversionary theory—the idea that a leader might decide to escalate an external conflict as a way to divert attention from poor domestic political and economic conditions—is a major research area in the field of international relations, and this article demonstrates how good research using psychological at-a-distance methods can make critically important contributions to such areas. Using the automated coding system (Profiler Plus) for LTA, they find that two psychological characteristics, distrust and conceptual complexity, have significant independent and interactive effects on whether leaders attempt diversionary actions. Whereas earlier research thought of diversionary behaviour in strictly structural terms (if the structure of the economy or political situation is poor, diversion is more likely to happen), Foster and Keller demonstrate that the psychology of the leader is a critically important intervening variable: not all leaders act in the same way, and much more variance in diversionary behaviour can be explained by knowing these psychological characteristics of the leader. Schafer and Crichlow (2010) turn the focus of LTA variables in a very different explanatory direction. They investigate whether the psychological characteristics of leaders have an effect on the *quality* of the decision-making process. This is another example where at-a-distance research directly engages other important research programmes in the field of international relations, such as foreign policy analysis. Using a combination of case-study methods, for which they develop a quantitative coding system, and automated LTA coding, Schafer and Crichlow find that several psychological characteristics of leaders have a direct effect on the quality of decision-making in their administrations. The most important of these traits is distrust, which resulted in significant increases in group-structural faults and decision-processing faults in those administrations where the leaders were more distrusting (see also Hermann, Chapter 8, this volume).

Turning to OCA, we see some studies that use at-a-distance methods creatively to solve some puzzles in international relations, provide insight on learning, and engage other major research programmes in both psychology and international relations. In another research project looking for changes in psychology prior to significant behavioural change, Schafer, Robison, and Aldrich (2006) provide insight on an interesting historical puzzle regarding Irish independence in the twentieth century: why did the Irish Volunteers (a previously non-violent organization) suddenly join with the Irish Citizens Army (a quite militant organization), which led to the violent (and failed) Easter Rising in 1916? The researchers linked two operational code variables to form a proxy for *frustration*, thus testing the well-known frustration–aggression hypothesis. They found specifically that the leader of the Volunteers, Padraig Pearse, grew increasingly frustrated in the months immediately preceding the Easter Rising, which created the psychological imperative for aggression against the British. Of course, there were historical and political reasons contributing to the situation as well, such as the refusal of the United Kingdom to grant Home Rule status to Ireland, and the possibility of forced Irish military conscription in service to the UK's First World War effort. Indeed, these seem likely to have contributed to Pearse's rising frustration. However, had Pearse's frustration level not risen so quickly and dramatically, Irish history might be quite different today.

We generally think of psychological characteristics as independent variables having a causal effect on state behaviour, but it is also possible to consider them as dependent variables. This is particularly the case with cognitive variables, such as those in the operational code, which, when they change over time, demonstrate learning effects. Sam Robison (2006) does this kind of work with his analysis of US President George W. Bush and several of his advisers. Using at-a-distance methods in a simple design, Robison tests for changes in the operational code beliefs of the president and his advisers before and after the events of 11 September 2011. Bush's philosophical and instrumental beliefs changed dramatically after 9/11: he went from seeing the world in moderately positive terms and having a generally cooperative orientation to strategy and tactics, to seeing the world in fairly hostile terms and preferring more conflict-driven policy choices. His advisers, on the other hand, showed only small shifts in their operational code (and, surprisingly, not always in the same direction). Of course, Bush had very little international experience prior to being elected president, while his advisers were well seasoned in global politics, leading Robison to conclude that psychological characteristics may change more quickly and dramatically for neophyte leaders.

The 'democratic peace' is another one of the most important research areas in international relations. It is a structural theory, based upon a variety of empirical investigations, that suggests that democracies are more peaceful than non-democracies (the monadic version) or that democracies are just as prone to conflict as non-democracies but that they never go to war with other democracies (dyadic version). Using OCA, Schafer and Walker (2006) engage this major research programme and posit a theory that individual-level psychology is likely to affect behaviour in democracies, rather than just the structures of the political systems on the other side. Using event data regarding the behaviour of the USA and the UK during the Kosovo conflict, they found that each state behaved in patterned ways better predicted by their leaders' operational codes than by political structures and cultural constructions in each state. Structures may provide some broad brushstrokes in helping us understand state behaviour, but, without accounting for individual-level psychology, the models will always be underspecified.

4 CRITICAL ASSESSMENT OF THE STATE OF THE ART

In this section we shall consider the 'state of the art' in at-a-distance methods. Specifically, I shall discuss three different areas: the practical benefits of the methods; the normative implications of the methods; and the limitations of existing research.

At-a-distance methods have been fifty years in the making, so it is fair now to ask if they have given us the goods—if they have been productive and helpful in contributing to academic research and our knowledge about leadership. In my view, the answer is a definitive yes. What probably started as something like an intuitive hunch—that systematic analysis of verbal material might provide some indications regarding the psychology of individuals—has developed into a burgeoning science. From a perusal of the literature using these methods, one can see two important points: (1) there is support for the validity of the measures—that is, they appear to be measuring psychological characteristics largely as expected; and (2), once measured, these psychological characteristics provide important insights regarding leadership behaviour. Put somewhat differently: the science of these methods is supported and the substantive contributions being made are valuable. Make no mistake, however: the methods are not yet widely used, some people still have a number of questions about the mechanisms and their value, and there is still much room for increasing the quality, scope, and effectiveness of the science. We shall return to some of those themes shortly. For now, however, we are left with the following: at-a-distance methods are good science, providing us with good insights.

In addition, these methods may be used for many different kinds of normative applications. The science of the psychology of leaders has implications for such fields as security studies, terrorist research, peace and conflict resolution, revolutionary movements, rogue states, old and new cultures, partisan politics, the process of policy-making, legislative studies, and many other areas. Indeed, any place in politics where individuals are generating some form of verbal material presents opportunities for significant research using at-a-distance methods.

Now let us take note of some limitations of current at-a-distance research. In my view, the most significant limitation is the dearth of data. Perhaps the best science in the field of international relations is associated with large datasets, such as Correlates of War and International Crisis Behaviour; such datasets allow for sophisticated analyses of many different research questions. Yet there is no comparable dataset for psychological characteristics. It is possible, of course, using today's technology, to develop such a data-set, but the lack of one right now limits the number of people working in these areas and limits the kinds of questions we can investigate.

The limitation on available data has also resulted in limitations on the kind of meth-odological enquiries that help a young field advance as a science. Here I refer to some of the questions and concerns we often get from individuals who have not seen the validity checks and empirical contributions, questions and concerns about such things as pri-vate versus public verbal behaviour; prepared versus spontaneous comments, audience and impression-management effects. While I have argued that current methods have had quite good validity checks, this does not mean we have resolved all these methodo-logical concerns. Indeed, these standard concerns are valid in their own right, and there are certainly many other methodological questions to be investigated. At-a-distance methods have come a long way and made valuable contributions and advancements, but this is still a very young science.

There is also room for additional constructs. Here we have primarily considered just four major research programmes using at-a-distance methods: integrative complexity, LTA, motive analysis, and OCA. These are major research programmes and cover some important parts of psychology, including cognitive structure, traits, motives, and cog-nitive content. Others have used different at-a-distance constructs (such as Weintraub 1989; Gottschalk 1995; Smith 2008), but their impact has not yet been as far reaching. Yet, when one thinks about psychology, and the potential number of characteristics that might affect political behaviour, there are certainly many opportunities to develop new constructs, indicators, and research programmes. It is also possible to imagine the development of additional at-a-distance methods using non-verbal indicators (such as body language or eye movements). The research to date leaves little doubt that ver-bal behaviour provides insight into subjects' psychological characteristics, but it seems equally clear that there are other, perhaps quite significant, components of psychology that are not being captured by verbal behaviour, but could be captured by other types of at-a-distance analysis.

As the science of at-a-distance methods moves forward, researchers working in this area must be more conscientious about tying at-a-distance indicators to political dependent variables. For instance, those of us working in the field of international rela-tions most often want to explain state behaviour—though, of course, there are many other dependent variables of interest as well, such as terrorist behaviour, alliance behav-iour, behaviour of international organizations, corporations, or other transnational organizations—and yet many of our studies using psychological at-a-distance methods spend more time explaining psychology than international behaviour. In other words, it is common to see psychology as the dependent variable, such as Walker, Schafer, and Young's study (1988) of Jimmy Carter, the first publication using the new quantitative OCA. They demonstrated significant changes in Carter's belief system during his fourth year in office, when such things occurred as the Soviet invasion of Afghanistan, the tak-ing of American hostages in Iran, and the conflict in the Horn of Africa. The article is valuable, as it demonstrates the validity of the new OCA and introduces the method to the field, but the dependent variable is Jimmy Carter's belief system, whereas most of the time in the field of international relations we are interested in explaining behaviour between actors in global politics.

Finally, and related, those working in these areas need to move beyond simple case studies. Many projects we see using these methods focus on one actor, or just a couple of actors, perhaps as they change over time. While there is certainly value in case studies, and I am quite a proponent of the value of qualitative in-depth case studies such as those mentioned earlier, the real value of at-a-distance quantitative research is that it lets us look for larger patterns of effects across larger numbers of cases. This is what makes quantitative psychological indicators so valuable. It is not only possible but imperative that this science increases its scope and begins to engage other large data projects, several of which have been mentioned already. The logic is simple: we believe that individuals matter, that there is something about their psychological characteristics that affect political behaviour. To support that simple assertion, and to make specific contributions to our understanding of the effect of individuals on politics, we must put our theories and constructs to the most significant tests possible, including in the area of prediction, which is woefully under-addressed throughout many areas in the social sciences.

5 For the Future

All the areas identified in the previous section as limitations can be summed up as follows: the science of at-a-distance methods must continue to improve: more data, more constructs, more approaches, more answers to methodological questions; more engagement of large-n research. While the previous section also offered some specific ideas for future work, here we turn to a few other areas that offer possibilities.

One area of opportunity in at-a-distance studies continues to be progress in automated content analysis. Right now, one software program, Profiler Plus, has applications for all four of the major research programmes discussed above, but that same software program also has many other applications that may be of interest to researchers for future projects, such as anger words, efficacy, victimization, optimism, helplessness, and many others.[3] In addition, at least two other software programs are available, at reasonable costs, which conduct content analysis of verbal material: Diction (for more information, see <www.dictionsoftware.com>) and Linguistic Inquiry and Word Count (information available at <www.liwc.net>). Both programs have their own sets of constructs, and both allow for researchers to operationalize and develop their own constructs. If we have already learned many things with existing constructs, certainly we can and should expand in other directions, and the procedures may be as simple as learning a new software program.

---

[3] Information on Profiler Plus can be found at <http://socialscience.net>.

Another possibility for future research relevant to leadership studies is connecting at-a-distance leadership studies with other major research programmes. As already discussed briefly, a natural fit is to use these methods in conjunction with large-n conflict datasets pertaining to wars, crises, or event data streams. Using existing datasets will give researchers access to validated dependent variables of interest, and an opportunity to add psychological variables to cases for statistical analyses. Similarly, it is possible to use at-a-distance methods in conjunction with rational and game-theoretic models. Game theorists often make broad, generalized assumptions about preferences, but at-a-distance methods might provide much better, individual-based data in that regard.

Likewise, at-a-distance methods may provide new insights and new data on old psychological questions, such as the trait–state debate, temporal stability of personality and cognitive constructs, and the connections (causal or correlative) of a wide variety of psychological indicators. Of course, much of this research is being done using more traditional psychological methods, but at-a-distance methods can contribute in several ways. First, as discussed, these methods capture psychological indicators in real-world, real-time settings, which may provide many different insights from those gathered under experimental or clinical settings. Second, at-a-distance methods are particularly intended for leadership studies, and leaders may be a very different population of actors from those available for more traditional studies. Third, at-a-distance methods offer potential for much more data over much longer time periods of analysis than can be done cheaply using other methods. For example, it would be quite simple in a single afternoon to get longitudinal data, broken down by year, half year, quarter year, or even month for a subject like Franklin Delano Roosevelt.

These methods, and the results associated with them, have come a long way since their early years. Yet at-a-distance methods are still a young science. Much has been accomplished; there is much left to do. As recently as the late 1990s the price of entry for this kind of research was quite high: there were only a handful of studies off which to build; validity of constructs was still being established; there were plenty of critics and sceptics; there were new theories and methods to learn; and, perhaps most importantly, the cost associated with hand coding was exorbitant. Not all those concerns have gone completely, of course. There are still sceptics; there is room for more theory development; validity assessments will continue—but today the science of at-a-distance methods is significantly advanced in terms of existing studies, validity checks, and automated coding systems. This science, young though it may be, has an extremely bright future indeed.

RECOMMENDED READING

Hermann, M. G. (1999). *Assessing Leadership Style: A Trait Analysis*. Columbus, OH: Social Science Automation.

Post, J. (2003) (ed.). *The Psychological Assessment of Political Leaders*. Ann Arbor, MI: University of Michigan Press.

Schafer, M., and Crichlow, S. (2010). *Groupthink vs High-Quality Decision-Making in International Relations*. New York: Columbia University Press.

REFERENCES

Barenbaum, N. B., and Winter, D. G. (2003). 'Personality', in D. K. Freedheim (ed.), *Handbook of Psychology*, vol. 1. *History of Psychology*. New York: Wiley, 147–72.

Beieler, J. (2011). 'Effects of Presidential Psychology on Militarized Interstate Disputes from 1945–2001', Presented at International Studies Association 2011 Annual Conference, 16 March, Montreal, Quebec.

Butler, J. R. (2012). 'The Effect of Terrorist Leader Psychology on Operational Tactics', Presented at International Studies Association 2012 Annual Conference, 22 March, San Diego, California.

Crichlow, S. (1998). 'Idealism or Pragmatism? An Operational Code Analysis of Yitzhak Rabin and Shimon Peres', *Political Psychology*, 19/4: 683–706.

Erikson, E. (1958). *Young Man Luther: A Study in Psychoanalysis and History*. New York: W. W. Norton and Company.

Etheredge, L. S. (1978). 'Personality Effects on American Foreign Policy, 1898–1968: A Test of Interpersonal Generalization Theory', *American Political Science Review*, 72/2: 434–51.

Foster, D. M., and Keller, J. (2011). 'Leader's Cognitive Complexity, Distrust and the Diversionary Use of Force', Presented at International Studies Association 2011 Annual Conference, 16 March, Montreal, Quebec.

George, A. L. (1969). 'The "Operational Code": A Neglected Approach to the Study of Political Leaders and Decision-Making', *International Studies Quarterly*, 13/2: 190–222.

Glad, B. (1980). *Jimmy Carter: In Search of the Great White House*. New York: W. W. Norton and Company.

Gottschalk, L. A. (1995). *Content Analysis of Verbal Behavior*. Hillsdale, NJ: Lawrence Erlbaum Associates.

Greenstein, F. (1969). *Personality and Politics; Problems of Evidence, Inference, and Conceptualization*. Chicago: Markham.

Hermann, C. F., Hermann, M. G., and Cantor, R. A. (1974). 'Counterattack of Delay: Characteristics Influencing Decision Makers' Responses to the Simulation of an Unidentified Attack', *Journal of Conflict Resolution*, 18/1: 75–106.

Hermann, M. G. (1974). 'Leader Personality and Foreign Policy Behavior', in J. N. Rosenau (ed.), *Comparing Foreign Policies: Theories, Findings, and Methods*. New York: Free Press, 201–34.

Hermann, M. G. (1977). 'Some Personal Characteristics Relations to Foreign Aid Voting of Congressmen', in M. G. Hermann (ed.), *A Psychological Examination of Political Leaders*. New York: Free Press, 313–34.

Hermann, M. G. (1978). 'Effects of Personal Characteristics of Political Leaders on Foreign Policy', in M. A. East, S. A. Salmore, and C. F. Hermann (eds), *Why Nations Act*. Beverly Hills, CA: SAGE, 49–68.

Hermann, M. G. (1980). 'Explaining Foreign Policy Behavior Using the Personal Characteristics of Political Leaders', *International Studies Quarterly*, 24/1: 7–46.

Hermann, M. G. (1985). 'Validating a Technique for Assessing Personalities of Political Leaders at a Distance: A Test Using Three Heads of State', Report prepared for Defense Systems, Inc., as part of Contract DSI-84-1240.

Hermann, M. G. (1999). *Assessing Leadership Style: A Trait Analysis*. Columbus, OH: Social Science Automation.

Hermann, M. G., and Preston, T. (1994). 'Presidents, Advisers, and Foreign Policy: The Effect of Leadership Style on Executive Arrangements', *Political Psychology*, 15/1: 75–96.

Leites, N. (1951). *The Operational Code of the Politburo*. New York: McGraw-Hill.

Leites, N. (1953). *A Study of Bolshevism*. New York: Free Press.

Marfleet, B. (2000). 'The Operational Code of John. F. Kennedy during the Cuban Missile Crisis', *Political Psychology*, 23/3: 545–58.

Renshon, S. (1996). *High Hopes: The Clinton Presidency*. New York: New York University Press.

Robison, S. (2006). 'George W. Bush and the Vulcans', in M. Schafer and S. Walker (eds), *Beliefs and Leadership in World Politics*. New York: Palgrave Macmillan, 101–24.

Robison, S. (2012). 'The Influence of Presidential Beliefs on US Foreign Policy Behavior', Presented at International Studies Association 2012 Annual Conference, 22 March, San Diego, California.

Schafer, M. (2000). 'Issues in Assessing Psychological Characteristics at a Distance: An Introduction to the Symposium', *Political Psychology*, 23/3: 511–28.

Schafer, M., and Crichlow, S. (2000). 'Bill Clinton's Operational Code', *Political Psychology*, 21/3: 559–71.

Schafer, M., and Crichlow, S. (2010). *Groupthink vs High-Quality Decision-Making in International Relations*. New York: Columbia University Press.

Schafer, M., and Walker S. G. (2006). 'Democratic Leaders and the Democratic Peace: The Operational Codes of Tony Blair and Bill Clinton', *International Studies Quarterly*, 50/3: 561–83.

Schafer, M., Butler, J. R., and Hartmann, S. (2011). 'Leader Psychology and State Behavior in Crisis Situations', Presented at International Studies Association 2011 Annual Convention, 16 March, Montreal, Quebec.

Schafer, M., Robison, S., and Aldrich, B. (2006). 'Operational Codes and the 1916 Easter Rising in Ireland', *Foreign Policy Analysis*, 2/1: 63–82.

Smith, S. S. (2008). 'Risk Assessment of Threatening Communications from FBI Case Files Using Gottschalk–Gleser Content Analysis Scales', in L. Gottschalk and R. J. Bechtel (eds), *Computerized Content Analysis of Speech and Verbal Texts and its Many Applications*. Hauppauge, NY: Nova Science Publishers, 111–21.

Suedfeld, P. (1966). 'Information Processing: The Effects of Differential Pattern Complexity and Input Rate', *Psychodynamic Science*, 6: 249–50.

Suedfeld, P. (1968). 'Verbal Indices of Conceptual Complexity: Manipulation by Instructions', *Psychodynamic Science*, 12: 377.

Suedfeld, P., and Bluck, S. (1988). 'Changes in Integrative Complexity Prior to Surprise Attacks', *Journal of Conflict Resolution*, 32/4: 626–35.

Suedfeld, P., and Hagen, R. L. (1966). 'The Measurement of Information Complexity: I. Conceptual Structure and Information Pattern as Factors in Information Processing', *Journal of Personality and Social Psychology*, 4: 233–6.

Suedfeld, P., and Rank, A. D. (1976). 'Revolutionary Leaders: Long-Term Success as a Function of Changes in Conceptual Complexity', *Journal of Personality and Social Psychology*, 34/2: 169–78.

Suedfeld, P., and Streufert, S. (1966). 'Information Search as a Function of Conceptual and Environmental Complexity', *Psychodynamic Science*, 4: 351–2.

Suedfeld, P., and Tetlock, P. (1976). 'Inducing Belief Instability without a Persuasive Message: The Roles of Attitude Centrality, Individual Cognitive Differences, and Sensory Deprivation', *Canadian Journal of Behavioural Science*, 8: 324–33.

Suedfeld, P., and Tetlock, P. (1977). 'Integrative Complexity of Communications in International Crises', *Journal of Conflict Resolution*, 21/1: 169–284.

Suedfeld, P., and Wallace, M. (1995). 'President Clinton as a Cognitive Manager', in S. A. Renshon (ed.), *The Clinton Presidency*. Oxford: Westview Press, 215–33.

Suedfeld, P., Guttieri, K. and Tetlock, P. (2003). 'Assessing Integrative Complexity at a Distance', in J. M. Post (ed.), *The Psychological Assessment of Political Leaders: With Profiles of Saddam Hussein and Bill Clinton*. Ann Arbor, MI: University of Michigan Press, 246–72.

Suedfeld, P., Tetlock, P., and Ramirez, C. (1977). 'War, Peace, and Integrative Complexity', *Journal of Conflict Resolution*, 21/3: 427–42.

Tetlock, P. E. (1983a). 'Accountability and Complexity of Thought', *Journal of Personality and Social Psychology*, 41: 74–83.

Tetlock, P. E. (1983b). 'Cognitive Style and Political Ideology', *Journal of Personality and Social Psychology*, 41: 18–126.

Tetlock, P. E. (1985). 'Integrative Complexity of American and Soviet Foreign Policy Rhetoric: A Time-Series Analysis', *Journal of Personality and Social Psychology*, 49/6: 1565–85.

Tetlock, P. E., and Manstead, A. S. R. (1985). 'Impression Management versus Intrapsychic Explanations in Social Psychology: A Useful Dichotomy?', *Psychological Review*, 92: 59–77.

Tetlock, P. E., and Suedfeld, P. (1987). 'Integrative Complexity Coding of Verbal Behavior', in C. Antaki (ed.), *Analyzing Lay Explanation: A Casebook of Method*. Beverly Hills, CA: SAGE, 114–139.

Walker, S. G. (1977). 'The Interface between Beliefs and Behavior: Henry Kissinger's Operational Code and the Vietnam War', *Journal of Conflict Resolution*, 21: 129–68.

Walker, S. G. (1995). Psychodynamic processes and framing effects in foreign policy decision-making: Woodrow Wilson's operational code. *Political Psychology*, 16 (4): 697–717.

Walker, S. G., and Schafer, M. (2000). 'The Political Universe of Lyndon B. Johnson and his Advisors: Diagnostic and Strategic Propensities in their Operational Codes', *Political Psychology*, 21/3: 529–43.

Walker, S. G., and Schafer, M. (2007). 'Theodore Roosevelt and Woodrow Wilson: Realist and Idealist Archetypes'?, *Political Psychology*, 28: 747–76.

Walker, S. G., Schafer, M., and Young, M. D. (1998). 'Systematic Procedures for Operational Code Analysis: Measuring and Modeling Jimmy Carter's Operational Code', *International Studies Quarterly*, 42: 175–90.

Weintraub, W. (1989). *Verbal Behavior in Everyday Life*. New York: Springer Publishing Company.

Winter, D. G. (1973). *The Power Motive*. New York: Free Press.

Winter, D. G. (1980). 'An Exploratory Study of the Motives of Southern African Political Leaders Measured at a Distance', *Political Psychology*, 2/2: 75–85.

Winter, D. G. (1987). 'Leader Appeal, Leader Performance, and the Motive Profiles of Leaders and Followers: A Study of American Presidents and Elections', *Journal of Personality and Social Psychology*, 52: 196–202.

Winter, D. G. (1992). 'Content Analysis of Archival Data, Personal Documents, and Everyday Verbal Productions', in C. P. Smith (ed.), *Motivation and Personality: Handbook of Thematic Content Analysis*. New York: Cambridge University Press, 110–25.

Winter, D. G. (1993). 'Power, Affiliation and War: Three Tests of a Motivational Model', *Journal of Personality and Social Psychology*, 65: 532–45.

Winter, D. G. (1994). *Manual for Scoring Motive Imagery in Running Text*. Ann Arbor, MI: University of Michigan Department of Psychology.

Winter, D. G. (1998). 'A Motivational Analysis of the Clinton First Term and the 1996 Presidential Campaign', *Leadership Quarterly*, 9: 253–62.

Winter, D. G. (2003a). 'Assessing Leaders' Personality: A Historical Survey of Academic Research Studies', in J. M. Post (ed.), *The Psychological Assessment of Political Leaders: With Profiles of Saddam Hussein and Bill Clinton*. Ann Arbor, MI: University of Michigan Press, 11–38.

Winter, D. G. (2003b). 'Measuring the Motives of Political Actors at a Distance', in J. M. Post (ed.), *The Psychological Assessment of Political Leaders: With Profiles of Saddam Hussein and Bill Clinton*. Ann Arbor, MI: University of Michigan Press, 153–77.

Winter, D. G. (2003c). 'Personality and Political Behavior', in D. O. Sears, L. Huddy, and R. Jervis (eds), *Handbook of Political Psychology*. New York: Oxford University Press, 110–45.

Winter, D. G., and Stewart, A. J. (1977). 'Content Analysis as a Technique for Assessing Political Leaders', in M. G. Hermann (ed.), *A Psychological Examination of Political Leaders*. New York: Free Press, 28–61.

CHAPTER 21

BIOGRAPHICAL ANALYSIS

JAMES WALTER

1 INTRODUCTION

STUDYING political leadership should encompass many elements: models of governance, opportunity structures within elites, institutional history and requirements, group activity, social expectations, and executive dynamics. Nonetheless, at one level it is inherently about the performance of an individual in a role. Biography was one of the earliest modes of leadership study. However, as the social sciences developed in the twentieth century, emphasizing broad, law-like generalizations, there was increasing scepticism about the fundamental indeterminacy of biography, diverting attention to approaches that gave limited credence to individual influence in politics and society. Yet biography cannot be ignored: it remains a dominant form in published discussion of leaders outside the academy, and it offers insights that must be taken seriously.

2 HISTORICAL CONTEXT

The forerunner of Western biography, Plutarch's *Lives of the Noble Greeks and Romans* (*c.* AD 98–120), can equally be regarded as an early disquisition on leadership. Plutarch's parallel lives of great Greeks and Romans were intended to illustrate the character of the leaders of empires. A moralist rather than a historian, Plutarch's analysis was nonetheless much influenced by then current political theory: the Aristotelian ethic of leadership virtue, and Platonic ideals of a successful polity as being shaped by the quality of its ruler, a philosopher-king. Revived early in the sixteenth century, and gaining wider influence through utilization in Shakespeare's 'Roman' plays and a seventeenth-century translation by John Dryden and others, Plutarch's *Lives* (Plutarch 1932) suited the individualist historiography of emergent capitalism, seeding modern interpretations of history as shaped by 'great men'.

The interest in personality is a defining feature of modernity. As industrial, urban, and capitalist development eroded traditional social forms, which defined roles and status and expected patterns of hierarchy and deference, individual decisions and personal life choices gained valency. The narrative of the personal journey was the catalyst for the modern novel as well as for the emerging genres of memoir and biography—including political biography—and individualism was the premiss of liberal democratic politics. A popular means of interpreting the political was via biography; it was Thomas Carlyle who insisted that history was the story of the achievements of 'great men' (Carlyle 1840), and biographies of modern statesmen proliferated in the nineteenth century. An interpretation of history entailing continual economic and social development prevailed. The biographies of leaders exemplified such assumptions. These stories sometimes drew on intuitive interpretations of personality, but such insights were idiosyncratic and usually subsidiary to the celebration of greatness: the mode was what Marquand (2009: 189) calls 'tombstone' biography (see also Rhodes 2012), more akin to the 'lives of the saints' (hagiography) than to the systematic study of political life. These are familiar points, but worth recalling, since their traces persist even in contemporary approaches to the political life I explain later. What is more, they persist alongside quite different approaches to the study of personality, driven by the collapse of the conditions that sustained the 'great-man' thesis, and that generated much more complex interpretations of modernity, and of personality.

Three factors influenced contemporary life writing. First, the failure of bourgeois liberalism to deliver individual benefit to all led to oppositional identities and class division, giving rise to the great novels of social/economic dysfunction (such as those of Charles Dickens), to systematic social analysis (like that of Tonnies and Durkheim), and to the swingeing critique of capitalist excess (by Karl Marx): the 'progressive' theory of history was undermined. The sons of the Victorian age began to question the verities of their fathers, leading to a more critical vein in biography (Gosse 1907), including a forensic evaluation of Carlyle himself (Froude 1882, 1884). Second, rapid social change posited individualism itself as insecurely grounded, a reflexive and provisional enterprise, and generated more systematic attempts to understand the ways in which personality was rooted in psychological needs and social relationships: Freud was to be the harbinger of twentieth-century personality studies (and of a new variant, psychobiography—see Freud 1910; Freud and Bullitt 1967). Third, the First World War signalled not only the end of empire and the start of the age of extremes (Hobsbawm 1994), but demolished the pretensions of 'great men' whose foolishness had led to the catastrophes of the age. Lytton Strachey's influential exposé of 'Eminent Victorians' (Strachey 1989 [1918]) captured the zeitgeist of that time, abjured failed leadership, and also foreshadowed the 'modernist "interpretive" turn in biography:' his work (Strachey 1989 [1918], 1928, 1933) was much influenced by Freud.

The grounds for a more systematic biography were laid, but social scientists faced a dilemma. Having demolished the assumptions of the Victorian age, and embraced a more 'scientific' mode, they established disciplinary credibility by adopting a strong positivist orientation to data, depending, for example, upon social surveys and the statistical analysis of mass behaviour. The favoured methods could be adapted to life writing to a limited extent, for instance, by the collective often statistically grounded analysis of elites known as prosopography (e.g. Namier 1957 [1929]). However, areas that were not easily amenable to testable propositions, such as leadership, were not favoured by the new approach. The incipient theoretical division was between recognizing that complex modern societies demanded high levels of organization and bureaucratic management (promoting the sociological analysis of emergent structures, for example, Weber), on the one hand, and the reflexive achievement of individual identity (promoting individualistic theories of psychology, for example, Freud), on the other—with the latter always subject to suspicion. The dominant approach, then, was to take the empirical and positivist path: sceptical of the psychological turn, focused on institutional development, public administration, and policy studies. Political biography continued to flourish, but was regarded as a not-quite-respectable subsidiary (Skidelsky 1988): much of it was descriptive, under-theorized, limited for purposes of systematic comparison, and useful at best for showing politicians at work or illustrating social history (Rhodes 2012). However, a more rigorous biographical subfield was to emerge, promising a productive means of leadership analysis.

3   KEY DEBATES IN LEADERSHIP BIOGRAPHY

There were three trends in twentieth-century biography that generated questions for leadership research. The first was a general debate about methodologies appropriate to the genre, not specific to social science applications of biography, but nonetheless having implications for leadership research. The second was a much more focused approach to leadership as such. Both of these were essentially modernist—in the sense that they assumed unified narratives and progressive elaboration of methodology as their objectives—and together, from about the 1980s on, they were challenged by a third trend, a resistance to grand theories that reinstated the interpretive approach, but now in a postmodern sense.

With reference to the first trend, for much of the twentieth century, it was commonplace to identify Freud's elucidation of the unconscious, and the iconoclasm of Lytton Strachey, as profoundly effecting the questions biographers asked of themselves, and their materials. Freud's was an argument not only for systematic psychology, but also for interpretation—as behaviour and events were plumbed for motives and meanings beyond their surface manifestations. Strachey's was an argument for selection and discrimination, for brevity, and—above all—for a point of view: a book without a point of view, he said, 'resemb[les] nothing so much as a very large heap of sawdust', and 'uninterpreted truth [is] like buried gold' (quoted in Edel 1984: 183). The 'new biography', with its concessions to interpretation, promoted ongoing dialogue about the weight to be accorded to research (or craft) versus art.

Modernist biographers confronted the philosophical problem of 'other minds:' 'that I can have direct knowledge of my own experiences and that I cannot have direct knowledge of anyone else's' (Ayer 1967: 348). However, psychoanalysis raised questions even about unmediated knowledge of personal experience. Indeterminacy, then, has long been recognized as the characteristic feature of modern biography, and the fact that biographical truth can never finally be settled, that biography is always tendentious, has inflected every other methodological strategy. To acknowledge the problem of 'other minds' is to accept that biography works by analogy and inference rather than empiricism alone. Methods of interpretation are as important as factual precision. Allowing interpretation brings in its wake open resort to various bodies of theory as providing tools for interpretation.

Leon Edel, a distinguished biographer, attempted to annunciate the modern *Principia Biographia* in a series of books and essays between the mid-1950s and the mid-1980s (Edel 1984). He sought to bring together theory and method, and to show how the 'art' demanded by interpretation could be reinforced by 'the science of man' (Edel 1981: 8–11). Psychological awareness solved the problem of getting inside another skin to understand the story ('life myth') a subject tells him or herself as the means of coping with the psychological tasks that confront us all. That story illuminates how and why a subject acted as he or she did: theory unlocks the dynamic of the life myth, and the meaning of a life's work.

A second trend was manifest among social scientists that shared similar concerns to those above, but translated them more specifically to leadership studies. A small group of American political scientists, using case studies essentially biographical in nature, resisted their discipline's scepticism about the idiographic to develop this more considered approach to leadership. Rather than asking only about how one might make 'scientific' sense of the individual life (*pace* Edel), they pursued broader questions about how patterns of action by incumbents of leadership roles might illuminate the whole domain of leadership: its possibilities, dangers, significance in the public sphere, and typologies. They fostered a thriving subdiscipline of presidential studies, and pioneering studies of personality and politics. Harold Lasswell, a founding figure in both political psychology and leadership studies, exemplified the trend (see Lasswell 1930). He laid the groundwork taken up in 'the scientific study of leadership' after the war. Lasswell's message was that personality was integral to particular skill sets (agitating, administering, theorizing) that are crucial in politics: biographers would later utilize his typologies in works on particular leaders (e.g. Walter 1980: 177–84). Further impetus came from historical studies of the way that the psychological dispositions of particular leaders meshed with contingent circumstances to allow some leaders to speak for 'the historical moment' (e.g. Erikson 1958). This entailed recognition not only that leadership success depended on a resonance with followers' needs, but also that those needs in turn were shaped by a specific temporal and cultural context.

One outcome of these approaches was the turn to psychobiographies of political leaders. Despite the influence of psychoanalysis on some of Strachey's essays, this was less favoured in England than in the United States. A pioneering—but trenchantly

criticized—instance was a study of Woodrow Wilson to which Freud himself allegedly contributed (Freud and Bullitt 1967); a serious analysis of Wilson by Alexander
and Juliette George (George and George 1956) was to have more lasting impact. It was
argued that theoretically informed research demanded a more rigorous approach
to the foundational questions to be addressed by political biography (e.g. Edinger
1964a, b; Davies 1972): what is the catalyst for political ambition? How do personal
traits and formative experiences generate the skills and passions that foster political
success or seed failure? What variants of the 'power motive' flourish in specific historical circumstances?

Another influential direction was the sustained comparative study of presidential
leadership, aiming to develop typologies, with regard to identifiable patterns of skills
and qualities that enhance or diminish performance in particular aspects of the role,
and addressing sociological and historical features of the context in which particular
'types' flourish. These were exercises in collective biography, but driven by questions
about performance within institutional contexts rather than by questions purely about
the individual life histories. Landmark studies include James D. Barber's *The Presidential
Character* (1972) and James M. Burns's *Leadership* (1978).

The rigour advocated by such analysts was to be complicated by a third twist, the
'deconstructive' approach of postmodernism from roughly the 1980s onwards. In
the humanities and social sciences, this encouraged scepticism about the progressive
assumptions of twentieth-century modernism and the demise of 'grand narratives'. The
heuristic models of biographically based leadership typology came under question as
some biography became more radical (was there a single life, or many lives—see, e.g.,
Manso 1985) and fictional elements were (controversially) incorporated in political
analysis (as in Edmund Morris's biography of Ronald Reagan (1999)). Theoretical contestation provoked outrage among those who saw any resort to theory as an incursion
into the 'commonsensical, humane and empirical' domain of biography (Homberger
and Charmley 1988: pp. ix–xv). In parallel, an even more acute questioning of the structure–agency relationship emerged in the 1980s with 'new institutionalism', which 'tries
to avoid unfeasible assumptions that require too much of political actors…The rules,
routines, norms, and identities of an "institution", rather than micro rational individuals or macro social forces, are the basic units of analysis' (March and Olsen 2005: 20).
The question, then, for contemporary biography and leadership analysis has been: can it
meet the challenge Fred Greenstein once formulated as the test of 'actor dispensability'
(Greenstein 1975: 46–61)?

4   EXAMPLES

A preliminary to assessing the state of the art is to consider leading examples, the patterns they illuminate, and what they achieve in relation to analysing leadership (and
actor dispensability). The 'commonsensical, humane and empirical tradition' remains

well represented. One might consider as instances Robert Skidelsky's biography of *John Maynard Keynes* (1983, 1992, 2000), Ben Pimlott's *Harold Wilson* (1992), John Keane's *Tom Paine* (1995), A. W. Martin's *Robert Menzies* (1993, 1999), or Anthony Seldon's *Blair* (2004; see also Seldon with Snowden and Collings 2007). A feature of these latter two is that both direct us to consider the importance of individuals who produce influential ideas in shaping the character of an age. All immensely comprehensive, these works all have in common a commitment not only to recovering a life, but to placing it securely in its cultural, historical, and institutional contexts, exercising judicious judgement about the achievements and limitations of their subjects in the process.

Somewhat more maverick examples are Bernard Crick's *George Orwell* (1980) and Robert Caro's four volume biography of Lyndon Johnson (1982, 1990, 2002, 2012, with another volume projected). Crick goes to great lengths to provide detail, but to avoid the 'empathetic fallacy' that he argues besets political biography. He directs us towards relationships rather than inner life, and some questions, he implies, cannot be resolved, so multiple interpretations must be acknowledged as feasible. Caro's multiple volumes on Johnson over many years challenge Strachey's insistence that the complete life can never be told: the implication is that if you watch someone long and closely enough all will be revealed. He avoids the empathetic fallacy, becoming increasingly splenetic as his story unfolds, but his fascination (and ours) never flags.

While cautious about overt reference to psychology, all these authors show us the circumstances that produced their subjects, the skill sets they developed, how these applied within the institutions they inhabited, and the extent to which they met the needs of their times. Clearly much has been learned from contemporaneous scholarly studies of social and institutional history, relationships and networks, temporal context, and authorial perspective, and this sets these works apart from their 'tombstone' predecessors: these are astute analyses of political actors at work.

These biographies have an evident engagement with politics as work (cf. Davies 1980: chs 1–4), so they resonate with other recent developments—on the one hand, case studies that start from the question of *how* leaders work (e.g. Pat Weller's study of *Malcolm Fraser* (1989)); or collective instantiation of the working lives of political elites that borrow from both prosopography and ethnography (Rhodes and Weller 2001; Rhodes, 't Hart, and Noordegraaf 2007). On the other hand, they have had a formative impact on the best of those political journalists who have made a speciality of studying politics from the perspective of addressing questions about leadership rather than pandering to celebrity, often producing finely calibrated studies not only of government but also of individuals: for instance, Hugo Young on Margaret Thatcher (1989), Andrew Rawnsley on Tony Blair (2000, 2010); or Paul Kelly (2009) on a series of Australian prime ministers.

There has been a recurrence of parallel lives, like Plutarch, trying to draw a lesson from comparison, although not now informed by Aristotelian or Platonic ideals. Indeed, a notable example, Allan Bullock's *Hitler and Stalin: Parallel Lives* (1991) instead aimed to explore the links between cultural crisis and the sorts of messianic personalities that can seize on such circumstances for perverse purposes, with catastrophic results. Having exhaustively canvassed the empirical evidence, the nature of those who supported these dictators, and the dynamics of their regimes in cultural context, Bullock reached a conclusion that directly addresses both Greenstein's question about actor dispensability, and the rationale for biographical analysis of leaders:

> I do not believe that circumstances by themselves in some mysterious way produce the man; I am not convinced that, if Hitler and Stalin had failed to seize the opportunity, someone else would have done and the result would have been much the same. (Bullock 1997: 81–2)

Collective biography has long been a mode of leadership study, as was noted in those typological analyses of the US presidency by Barber and Burns referred to earlier. A more contemporary instance is Fred Greenstein's *The Presidential Difference* (2009). While methodologically similar to those earlier works, Greenstein's adds an additional dimension—emotional intelligence—to the list of capacities usually explored, and it is this (emotional stability, ability to connect with others—in contrast with perturbation, inability to empathize, or scarcely governable passions) that often makes the difference between success and failure. Another contemporary development has been attention to the intersecting lives of those who work together within a leadership collective. A compelling example is Walter Isaacson's and Evan Thomas's *The Wise Men*, examining six friends whose development of cold war foreign policy decisively influenced America's role in the world (Isaacson and Thomas 1986). Another stimulating instance is Doris Kearns Goodwin's *Team of Rivals* (2005). Focusing on the 'political genius' of Abraham Lincoln. Goodwin deals initially with Lincoln's path to the presidency and his rivals along the way. Then she concentrates on his skill in drawing some of those rivals into his administration, and how their joint capacities explain the nature of his leadership: Lincoln's ability to win rivals to his cause and his mastery of the evolving group dynamic were the core of his 'political genius'. An innovative collective biography of intellectual rather than institutional leadership, brilliant in its interweaving of successive cohorts of thinkers with historical and cultural contingency, is Stephan Collini's *Absent Minds* (2006).

Alongside the recent skillful augmentation of the empirical tradition, there has been a flourishing of more overtly theoretical biography, often in dialogue with it. Psychobiography, often drawing on psychoanalysis, provides the best instances. Freud's own controversial efforts (Freud 1910; Freud and Bullitt 1967) and path-breaking examples such as the Georges' *Woodrow Wilson and Colonel House* (George and George 1956) have been referred to earlier. They paved the way for others, such as Greenstein's influential revisionist interpretation of Dwight Eisenhower (1982), Mitzman's study (1970) of Max Weber, and Erikson's works on Luther (1958) and Ghandi (1969). The Georges' analysis of the meshing of Wilson's and House's idiosyncratic personalities alerted us to the complementary relationships frequently at the heart of leadership; Greenstein showed us a president at work behind the scenes, providing an astute analysis of his mastery of group dynamics in policy-making; Mitzman illuminated the links between personal needs, intellectual formation, and the generation of ideas; and Erikson interpreted the intersection of individual psychodynamics and the historical moment to show how particular drives, contingent on personal circumstances, enabled specific leaders to translate their own problems into a message that followers 'heard' as appropriate to the time and as responding to their own needs.

The nature of the dialogue between conventional biography and psychobiography is most evident when one compares works on the same subject from both genres. There is conflict. There has, for example, been a cottage industry in biography of one of the most controversial US presidents, Richard Nixon, with 'conventional' biographers (e.g. Ambrose 1987, 1990, 1991) inclined to challenge the interpretations of psychobiographers (e.g. Brodie 1981). However, the fame-gaining prediction about how Nixon would respond to crisis in Barber's *Presidential Character* (1972)—before Watergate—affirmed the credibility of psychologically informed approaches. On the other hand, there is more measured exchange. Fred Greenstein (1982), as already mentioned, effected an influential recalibration of Eisenhower's standing by showing that the bland public man on whom earlier biographers had concentrated was in effect a screen for the much more effective operator behind the scenes, who could determine outcomes because of his skill in group processes. Leo Abse (1996), although intensely antipathetic to his subject, nonetheless provided an accurate pointer to the extraordinary narcissism that drove Blair, and the likely outcomes for his leadership, before he became prime minister and well before Rawnsley, Seldon, and others came to grips with it. Judith Brett's study (1992) of Robert Menzies uncovered dimensions that Martin's fine scholarly biography (1993, 1999) had not penetrated. Brett avoided the constraints of historical institutionalism and the life-course approach with an unusual concentration on discourse and public life. Her contention was that the man lives on through his language: it is there that the career is immediately accessible. She linked Menzies's public discourse to instances of his private language and analysed the psychological dynamics underpinning the whole (what it meant to the man) and the messages it conveyed (what it meant to an audience). Brett's approach illustrated one of the emerging features of political psychobiography: the practice of bringing to the fore the subtextual assumptions concealed in conventional biography, by making explicit the theoretical tenets on which judgements are based, and relating these to the questions about leadership that the biographer seeks to address (for another pointed instance, see Walter's analysis (1980) of Gough Whitlam).

The reflexive and theoretically informed approach has encouraged more questioning, provisional, and exploratory tactics in what might be deemed 'insider' biography, such as Don Watson's revelatory reflections (2002) on life inside the Australian prime minister Paul Keating's office, *Recollections of a Bleeding Heart*. Standard biographies of Keating (Carew 1992; Gordon 1993) found his transitions from brilliance to despondency, intensity to disengagement, difficult to explain. Watson offered an account of a leader at work, of group dynamics, and of psychological interpretation (reflecting on Keating's depressive traits), but one in which the narrator is part of the story, actively reflecting on his own perceptions.

The postmodern element in biography has been met with caution by social scientists. The refusal to resolve all questions, however, and the denial of narrative closure in Crick's *Orwell* (1980) were indicative of the transition. Feminist biographers have been at the forefront in exploring new techniques, interrogating the construction of identity, and the culturally- and gender-specific situatedness of their subjects (e.g. Lake 2002), but the dominance of 'masculinist' political leadership (see Sykes 2009) has meant that feminist leadership biographies have been few and far between. Biographers of outstanding female politicians have often treated them as successfully exercising the masculinist elements of 'strong leadership' (see Little 1988: 3–116, on Thatcher). Those who 'led' in more indirect ways have been more amenable to unconventional approaches. Carolyn Steedman's (1990) study of the socialist theorist of education Margaret McMillan is an example. Steedman challenged 'the dead weight of interiority that hangs about the neck of women's biography', focused on McMillan as 'a public woman who lived in a public space', and explained: 'I want to make the implied meaning of McMillan's own life and writing some kind of denial of interiority—which denial may be a pretense or a fiction, but one which might do some political or public good' (Steedman 1990: 250–1). The lesson was that women's public 'self-fashioning' was a means to power (see Riall 2010: 381), in this case the power to shape policy and opinion.

5   THE STATE OF THE ART

Despite the continuing critique by proponents of alternative methodologies, such as new institutionalism, and repeated assertions that biography is not a proper mode of analysis (O'Brien 1998), the books discussed above indicate both that field is thriving, and that—with respect to leadership—it has long been oriented to the sorts of questions any serious analysis would need to address. Such limitations as persist derive from social scientists' own failure of 'sociological imagination'—that is, an inability to 'range from the most impersonal and remote transformations to the most intimate features of the human self—and to see the relations between the two' (Mills 1959).

In relation to leadership, what do books such as those discussed here have to teach us? Perhaps, most importantly, they raise the question prompted by Greenstein: would any actor, placed in like circumstances, behave in the same way and/or produce the same outcomes? The answer, as Bullock argues above, is that, in the case of his subjects, almost certainly not. Others, who have dealt with, say, Stalin, both before (Tucker 1973) and after (Montefiore 2003) Bullock add compelling detail to his assertion. Then we find that such biographical studies provide the empirical base for more broadly based analyses of 'toxic' leadership (see Padilla, Hogan, and Kaiser 2007). In fact, with close reading of almost any of the books discussed above, it becomes difficult to imagine any other agent achieving just the same outcomes: institutions do not, then, simply provide the scripts for leadership (or, if they do, individual actors have considerable capacities to interpret those scripts on their own terms). Nonetheless, that reading also reveals patterns suggestive of predictable types of behaviour—adding rich detail to the sorts of typological characterizations pioneered in presidential studies, but with increasing nuance as the number and detail of cases is augmented.

The practical implications for leadership analysis can be captured by considering a series of more specific questions prompted by the examples discussed above. What triggers political engagement and the drive to lead (Lasswell 1930, and most of the psychobiographies)? How do leaders gain salience within a particular historical moment (Erikson 1958, 1969)? What might explain the intersection between a specific leader's personal projection and the response of others within the same historical and cultural frame (Bullock 1991; Brett 1992; Montefiore 2003)? What is the conjunction of personal character and historical contingency that produces toxic leadership (Tucker 1973; Bullock 1991; Montefiore 2003)? What explains the connection between leaders and followers (Brett 1992)? How are particular skill sets, or elite patterns of work, related to effective leadership (Weller 1989; Rhodes, 't Hart, and Noordegraaf 2007; but also Rawnsley 2000; Seldon 2004)? Where do political ideas come from and how might leaders mobilize them to create a public following (Mitzman 1970; Brett 1992; Keane 1995; Collini 2006)? Do leaders fall into particular types (Barber 1972; Greenstein 2009)? Do parallel lives illuminate universals that transcend cultural contingencies (Plutarch 1932; Bullock 1991)? How important are relationships compared to the interior life (Crick 1980 Steedman 1990)? How can we explore the group dynamics within core executive groups; to what extent should leadership be understood as a collective enterprise (Greenstein 1982; Goodwin 2005)? Should we reconsider the nature of 'public life' in our exploration of leadership (Steedman 1990; and note the manner in which feminist biographies have augmented our sense of what constitutes the political, our understanding of activism, and 'self-fashioning' as a means to power, for which see Riall (2010: 381))?

6 FUTURE DIRECTIONS

It is clear that conventional biography will survive, both because of its popularity with the 'common reader' and because the traditional narrative arc of a life retains an intrinsic appeal in what remains an individualist age. Furthermore, as Caro illustrates, a leader watched for long and closely cannot but reveal a great deal about his or her nature, institutional setting, social context, era, and above all the exercise of power. It is still argued that, 'even if Great Men and their deeds can no longer take center stage in history as they once did, the lives and reputations of extraordinary people can still express something of the ideas and meanings of a previous age' (Riall 2010: 397). Yet the extraordinary leader does not act alone: there is likely now to be more attention to collective biography and intersecting lives, given the pioneering exercises in analysis of leadership as a group enterprise.

It is also clear, however, that biography has become more experimental, more fragmentary, and more reflexive—none of which is of concern as long as its purpose in leadership studies is to address key questions, attending to 'the tasks of biography' (Davies 1972). The imperative of remaining focused not on the individual journey (which can be left to the likes of Tony Blair (2010)) but rather on key questions has led to an argument for much more truncated political lives: essays that, disciplined by brevity, must bring an argument to the fore and come clean about why a particular life deserves consideration, and what it tells us about leadership (Walter 2006; Backhouse 2007). The foregrounding of analytical questions also encourages attention to theory: explicit attention, that is, to shared, contestable modes of interpretation with a defined relation to empirics rather than the inchoate assumptions of 'common sense'. This is bound to remain an important aspect of contemporary biography. Some have described this as 'biography with the utility services on the outside...like Richard Rogers Centre Pompidou' (McKillop 1998: 328), but it is a productive means of incorporating dialogue with other leadership analysts about authorial judgement and intention within biography.

Another approach has been to argue that political analysts need to attend more closely to the interpretive insights of ethnography and anthropology, 'focusing on "situated agency": that is, on the webs of significance that people spin for themselves, on their inherited beliefs and practices, and on the ways they adapt, develop, and reject their inherited traditions' (Rhodes 2012). This posits the task of analysis as being to explain how meaning is constructed by leaders and interpreted by followers: politics as meaning making. It of course reminds us that life histories have had quite another use in disciplines like anthropology (see Frank 1995), which also reinforces the point that there can be no single model, and that biography will remain interdisciplinary and multifaceted.

RECOMMENDED READING

Edel, L. (1981). 'Biography and the Science of Man', in A. M. Friedson (ed.), *New Directions in Biography*. Honolulu, HI: University Press of Hawaii, 1–11.

Pimlott, B. (1994). 'The Future of Political Biography', in his *Frustrate their Knavish Tricks: Writings on Biography, History and Politics*. London: HarperCollins, 149–61.

Walter, J. (2002). 'The solace of doubt? Biographical methodology after the short twentieth century', in P. France and W. St Clair (eds), *Mapping Lives: The Uses of Biography*. Oxford: Oxford University Press, 321–35.

REFERENCES

Abse, L. (1996). *The Man behind the Smile: Tony Blair and the Politics of Perversion*. London: Robson Books.

Ambrose, S. (1987). *Nixon: The Education of a Politician, 1913–1962*. New York: Simon and Schuster.

Ambrose, S. (1990). *Nixon: The Triumph of a Politician, 1962–1972*. New York: Simon and Schuster.

Ambrose, S. (1991). *Nixon: Ruin and Recovery, 1973–1990*. New York: Simon and Schuster.

Ayer, A. J. (1967). 'One's Knowledge of Other Minds', in D. F. Gustafson (ed.), *Essays in Philosophical Psychology*. London: Macmillan, 346–64.

Backhouse, R. (2007). 'Lives in Synopsis: The Production and Use of Short Biographies by Historians of Economics', *History of Political Economy*, 39 (annual suppl.), 51–75.

Barber, J. D. (1972). *The Presidential Character: Predicting Performance in the Whitehouse.* Englewood Cliffs, NJ: Prentice Hall.

Blair, T. (2010). *A Journey.* London: Hutchinson.

Brett, J. (1992). *Robert Menzies' Forgotten People.* Chippendale, NSW: Pan Macmillan.

Brodie, F. (1981). *Richard Nixon: The Shaping of his Character.* New York: W.W. Norton.

Bullock, A.(1991). *Hitler and Stalin: Parallel Lives.* New York: Knopf.

Bullock, A. (1997). 'Have the Roles of Hitler and Stalin been Exaggerated?' *Government and Opposition*, 32/1: 65–83.

Burns, J. M. (1978). *Leadership.* New York: Harper and Row.

Carew, E. (1992). *Paul Keating: Prime Minister.* Sydney: Allen and Unwin.

Carlyle, T. (1840). *On Heroes, Hero-Worship and the Heroic in History.* London: Chapman and Hall.

Caro, R. (1982). *The Years of Lyndon Johnson, Vol. 1. The Path to Power.* New York: Knopf.

Caro, R. (1990). *The Years of Lyndon Johnson, ii. Means of Ascent.* New York: Knopf.

Caro, R. (2002). *The Years of Lyndon Johnson, iii. Master of the Senate.* New York: Knopf.

Caro, R. (2012). *The Years of Lyndon Johnson, iv. The Passage of Power.* New York: Knopf.

Collini, S. (2006). *Absent Minds: Intellectuals in Britain.* Oxford: Oxford University Press.

Crick, B. (1980). *George Orwell.* London: Secker and Warburg.

Davies, A. F. (1972). 'The Tasks of Biography', in his *Essays in Political Sociology.* Melbourne: Cheshire, 109–72.

Davies, A. F. (1980). *Skills, Outlooks and Passions: A Psychoanalytic Contribution to the Study of Politics.* Cambridge: Cambridge University Press.

Edel, L. (1981). 'Biography and the Science of Man', in A. M. Friedson (ed.), *New Directions in Biography.* Honolulu, HI: University Press of Hawaii, 1–11.

Edel, L. (1984). *Writing Lives. Principia Biographica.* New York: Norton.

Edinger, L. J. (1964a). 'Political Science and Political Biography', *Journal of Politics*, 26/2: 423–39

Edinger, L. J. (1964b). 'Political Science and Political Biography', *Journal of Politics*, 26/3: 648–76.

Erikson, E. (1958). *Young Man Luther: A Study in Psychoanalysis and History.* London: Faber and Faber.

Erikson, E. (1969). *Ghandi's Truth: On the Origins of Nonviolence.* New York: Norton.

Frank, G. (1995). 'Anthropology and Individual Lives: The Story of the Life History and the History of the Life Story', *American Anthropologist*, NS 97/1: 145–8.

Freud, S. (1910). 'The Origin and Development of Psychoanalysis', *The American Journal of Psychology*, 21 (2): 181–218.

Freud, S. (1964). *Leonardo Da Vinci and a Memory of his Childhood.* New York: Norton.

Freud, S., and Bullitt, W. (1967). *Thomas Woodrow Wilson, Twenty-Eighth President of the United States: A Psychological Study.* London: Weidenfeld and Nicolson.

Froude, J. A. (1882). *Thomas Carlyle: A History of the First Forty Years of his Life, 1795–1835.* London: Longmans, Green.

Froude, J. A. (1884). *Thomas Carlyle: A History of his Life in London, 1834–1881.* London: Longmans, Green.

George, A. L., and George, J. L. (1956). *Woodrow Wilson and Colonel House: A Personality Study.* New York: Day and Co.

Goodwin, D. K. (2005). *Team of Rivals: The Political Genius of Abraham Lincoln.* New York: Simon and Schuster.

Gordon. M. (1993). *A Question of Leadership: Paul Keating, Political Fighter*. Brisbane: University of Queensland Press.

Gosse, E. (1907). *Father and Son: A Study of Two Temperaments*. London: Heinemann.

Greenstein, F. I. (1975). 'When does Personal Variability Affect Behaviour ("Actor Dispensability"'?', in his *Personality and Politics: Problems of Evidence, Inference and Conceptualization*. New York: W.W. Norton, 46–61.

Greenstein, F. I. (1982). *The Hidden Hand Presidency: Eisenhower as Leader*. New York: Basic Books.

Greenstein. F. I. (2009). *The Presidential Difference: Leadership Style from FDR to Barack Obama*. Princeton: Princeton University Press; third edition.

Hobsbawm, E. J. (1994). *Age of Extremes: The Short Twentieth Century, 1914–1991*. London: Michael Joseph.

Homberger, E., and Charmley, J. (1988) (eds). *The Troubled Face of Biography*. Houndmills, Basingstoke: Macmillan.

Isaacson, W., and Thomas, E. (1986). *The Wise Men: Six Friends and the World they Made*. New York: Simon and Schuster.

Keane, J. (1995). *Tom Paine: A Political Life*. London: Bloomsbury.

Kelly, P. (2009). *The March of Patriots*. Melbourne: Melbourne University Press.

Lake, M. (2002). *Faith Bandler: Gentle Activist*. Sydney: Allen and Unwin.

Lasswell, H. (1930). *Psychopathology and Politics*. Chicago: University of Chicago Press.

Little, G. (1988). *Strong Leadership: Thatcher, Reagan and an Eminent Person*. Melbourne: Oxford University Press.

McKillop, I. (1998). 'Vignettes: Leavis, Biography and the Body', in W. Gould and T. Staley (eds), *Writing the Lives of Writers*. New York: St Martin's Press, 293–301.

Manso, P. (1985). *Mailer, his Life and Times*. New York: Simon and Schuster.

March, J. G., and Olsen, J. P. (2005). 'Elaborating the "New Institutionalism"'. Oslo: Centre for European Studies, Working Paper No. 11 <www.arena.uio.no> (accessed 5 December 2009).

Marquand, D. (2009). 'Biography', in M. Flinders, A. Gamble, C. Hay and M. Kenny (eds), *The Oxford Handbook of British Politics*. Oxford: Oxford University Press, 187–200.

Martin, A. W. (1993). *Robert Menzies: A Life, i. 1894–1943*. Melbourne: Melbourne University Press.

Martin, A. W. (1999). *Robert Menzies: A Life, ii. 1944–1978*. Melbourne: Melbourne University Press.

Mills, C. W. (1959). *The Sociological Imagination*. New York: Oxford University Press.

Mitzman, A. (1970). *The Iron Cage: An Historical Interpretation of Max Weber*. New York: Knopf.

Montefiore, S. (2003). *Stalin: the Court of the Red Tsar*. London: Weidenfeld and Nicolson.

Morris, E. (1999). *Dutch: A Memoir of Ronald Reagan*. New York: Random House.

Namier 1957 [1929]. *The Structure of Politics at the Accession of George III*. London: Macmillan; first published in 1929.

O'Brien, P. (1998). 'A Polemical Review of Political Biography', *Biography: An Interdisciplinary Quarterly*, 21/1: 50–7.

Padilla, A., Hogan, R., and Kaiser, R. (2007). 'The Toxic Triangle: Destructive Leaders, Susceptible Followers, and Conducive Environments', *Leadership Quarterly*, 18/3: 176–94.

Pimlott, B. (1992). *Harold Wilson*. London: HarperCollins.

Pimlott, B. (1994). 'The Future of Political Biography', in his *Frustrate their Knavish Tricks: Writings on Biography, History and Politics*. London: HarperCollins, 149–61.

Plutarch (1932). *Lives of the Noble Greeks and Romans*, ed. A. H. Clough. New York: Modern Library.

Rawnsley, A. (2000). *Servants of the People: The Inside Story of New Labour*. London: Hamish Hamilton.

Rawnsley, A. (2010). *The End of the Party: The Rise and Fall of New Labour*. London: Viking/Penguin.

Rhodes, R. A. W. (2012). 'Theory, Method and British Political "Life History"'. *Political Studies Review*, *10* (2): 161–176.

Rhodes, R. A. W., and Weller, P. (2001). *The Changing World of Top Officials: Mandarins or Valets?* Buckingham and Philadelphia, PA: Open University Press.

Rhodes, R. A. W., 't Hart, P., and Noordegraaf, M. (2007) (eds). *Observing Government Elites: Up Close and Personal*. London: Palgrave Macmillan.

Riall, L. (2010). 'The Shallow End of History? The Substance and Future of Political Biography', *Journal of Interdisciplinary History*, 40/3: 375–97.

Seldon, A. (2004). *Blair*. London: Simon and Schuster.

Seldon, A., with Snowden, P., and Collings, D. (2007). *Blair Unbound*. London: Simon and Schuster.

Skidelsky, R. (1983). *John Maynard Keynes*, i. *Hopes Betrayed, 1883–1920*. London: Macmillan.

Skidelsky, R. (1988). 'Only Connect: Biography and Truth', in E. Homberger and J. Charmley (eds), *The Troubled Face of Biography*. Houndmills, Basingstoke: Macmillan, 1–16.

Skidelsky, R. (1992). *John Maynard Keynes*, ii. *The Economist as Saviour, 1920–1937*. London: Macmillan.

Skidelsky, R. (2000). *John Maynard Keynes*, iii. *Fighting for Britain, 1937–1946*. London: Macmillan.

Steedman, C. (1990). *Childhood, Culture, and Class in Britain: Margaret McMillan, 1860–1931*. New Brunswick, NJ: Rutgers University Press.

Strachey, L. (1928). *Elizabeth and Essex: A Tragic History*. London: Chatto and Windus.

Strachey, L. (1933). *Queen Victoria*. London: Chatto and Windus.

Strachey (1989) [1918]. *Eminent Victorians*. Harmondsworth: Penguin Classics.

Sykes, P. (2009). 'The Gendered Nature of Leadership Analysis: Lessons from Women Leaders as Executives in Anglo-American Systems', in J. Masciulli, M. A. Molchanov, and W. A. Knight (eds), *The Ashgate Research Companion to Political Leadership*. London: Ashgate, 210–40.

Tucker, R. (1973). *Stalin as Revolutionary, 1879–1929: A Study in History and Personality*. London: Chatto and Windus.

Walter, J. (1980). *The Leader: A Political Biography of Gough Whitlam*. Brisbane: University of Queensland Press.

Walter, J. (2002). 'The Solace of Doubt? Biographical Methodology after the Short Twentieth Century', in P. France and W. St Clair (eds), *Mapping Lives: The Uses of Biography*. Oxford: Oxford University Press, 321–35.

Walter, J. (2006). 'The Utility of Short Lives', *Biography*, 29/2: 329–37.

Watson, D. (2002). *Recollections of a Bleeding Heart: A Portrait of Paul Keating PM*. Sydney: Knopf.

Weller, P. (1989). *Malcolm Fraser, PM: A Study in Prime Ministerial Power*. Ringwood, Victoria: Penguin.

Young, H. (1989). *One of Us: A Biography of Margaret Thatcher*. London: Macmillan.

CHAPTER 22

....

PERSONALITY PROFILING ANALYSIS

....

JERROLD M. POST

1 INTRODUCTION

....

WITH the end of the cold war,[1] the relative balance in the international system, characterized by the superpower rivalry, had been replaced by an international arena populated by rogue leaders with widely differing individual agendas and psychologies. The Carnegie Commission on Preventing Deadly Conflict was convened in the late 1990s, with its report entitled 'Preventing Deadly Conflict: The Critical Role of Leadership' published in 1999. In the report, co-author Alexander George emphasized the importance of what he called *actor-specific behavioural models* in undergirding coercive diplomacy as well as in managing crisis situations. Given the variability of such leaders as Saddam Hussein of Iraq, President Mahmoud Ahmadinejad of Iran, Kim Jong-il of North Korea, and Mu'ammar Qaddafi of Libya, deterrence had to be tailored and based on nuanced actor-specific behavioural models. That these leaders are often reputed to be seeking weapons of mass destruction makes it all the more important to understand what 'makes them tick.' And how their behaviour can be influenced.

In the balance of this chapter, the method for developing such profiles will be described in detail. After a detailed discussion of the elements of psychobiography, there will be a discussion of the personality study, including characterizations of three important political personality types—the narcissistic personality, the obsessive–compulsive personality, and the paranoid personality, with examples of each, emphasizing political implications. The outline for the political personality profile is depicted in Figure 22.1.

[1] This chapter draws significantly on Post (2003a).

Part I Psychobiographic discussion: the development of the individual in the context of his nation's history

Use parallel time lines

1. Cultural and historical background. Describe constraints of the political culture on the role of leader.
2. Family origins and early years
   a. Family constellation—grandparents, parents, siblings, relationships—politics of family
   b. Heroes and models
3. Education-Socialization
   a. Climate in country,
   b. Student years, Leadership
4. Professional career
   a. Mentors
   b. Early career
   c. Successes and failures
5. The subject as leader
   a. Key events
   b. Crises
   c. Key political relationships, influences
6. Family and friends

Part II Personality

1. General personal description
   a. Appearance and personal characteristics (include description of life style, include work/personal life balance, working hours, hobbies, recreation
   b. Health (include energy level, drinking, drug use
2. Intellectual capacity and style
   a. Intelligence
   b. Judgment
   c. Knowledge
   d. Cognitive complexity
3. Emotional reactions
   a. Moods, mood variability
   b. Impulses and impulse control
4. Drives and character structure
   a. Identify personality type (if possible)
   b. Psychodynamics
      i. Self-concept/self-esteem
      ii. Basic identification
      iii. Neurotic conflicts
   c. Reality (sense of/testing/adaptation to)
   d. Ego defense mechanisms
   e. Conscience and scruples
   f. Psychological drives, needs, motives:
      Discriminate to degree possible among drive for power, drive for achievement, drive for affiliation.

     g. Motivation for seeking leadership role:
        To wield power, to occupy seat of power, to achieve place in history
  5. Interpersonal relationships
     a. Identify key relationships and characterize nature of relationships
        i. Inner circle, including unofficial advisors, "kitchen cabinet"
        ii. Superiors
        iii. Political subordinates
        iv. Political allies, domestic and international
        v. Political rivalries, international adversaries

Part III World View

1. Perceptions of political reality (include cultural influences/biases)
2. Core beliefs (include concept of leadership, power)
3. Political philosophy, ideology, goals, and policy views (domestic, foreign, and economic policy views and view of US. Include discussion of which issues most interest the leader, in which issue areas his experience lies, and which issues are particularly salient for his political psychology.) N.B. Not all leaders have a core political philosophy or body of governing political ideas.
4. Nationalism and identification with country

Part IV Leadership Style

1. General characteristics (include discussion of the role expectations—both general public and elite—placed on the individual emphasizing their political and cultural determinants and leader's skill in fulfilling them)
     a. How does subject define his role?
     b. Relationship with public
     c. Oratorical skill and rhetoric
2. Strategy and tactics-goal directed behaviour
3. Decision making and decision implementation style
     a. Strategic decision making
     b. Crisis decision making
     c. How does he use his staff/inner circle? Does he vet decisions or use them only for information? How collegial? Does he surround himself with sycophants or choose strong self-confident subordinates?
     d. Dealing with-formal and informal negotiating style

Part V Outlook

1. Note particularly political behaviour closely related to personality issues. Relate personality to key issues emphasizing in which direction the psychological factors point. Estimate drives, values, and characteristics that are the most influential.
2. Attempt to predict how the individual will interact with other political figures, including opposition leaders and other key foreign leaders.

FIGURE 22.1 Conceptual framework and organization design for an integrated political personality profile

2 THE METHODOLOGY OF PERSONALITY PROFILING

The political personality profile was developed in order to provide policymakers with understanding concerning the psychological issues that affect a leader's political leadership, decision-making, and negotiations. Thus, it embodies not only the conventional aspects of psychological assessment, but also such leadership considerations as strategic decision style, crisis decision style, negotiating style, and management style, as well as core attitudes. It typically consists of two major parts: first, a longitudinal section, the psychobiography, and, second, a personality study, which is more cross-sectional and characterizes the predominant defence mechanisms and the basic personality structure.[2] In addition, there are sections on world view and leadership style, with implications contained in a final outlook section.

In creating a political personality profile of a political leader, the psychobiography is designed to understand the key life experiences that shaped the individual developmentally, and how they contributed to his[3] becoming a leader, and to what kind of leader he became. It rests on the principle so eloquently summarized in William Wordsworth's epigram 'The child is father of the man'. This longitudinal psychobiography is a central feature of the political personality profile.[4]

It is essential accurately to locate the subject in his historical/political/cultural context in order to understand the manner in which the history, politics, and culture shape and constrain the leader. It is useful to develop parallel times to begin the psychobiographic discussion that graphically depicts where the individual was in his life course when key events in the nation's history were unfolding.

As an example, consider the Soviet adolescent who heard of Khrushchev's de-Stalinization speech at the 20th Congress of the Communist Party in 1956 decrying the cult of personality surrounding Stalin's rule at the very time when developmentally that adolescent was psychologically required to dethrone paternal authority. He would react very differently to it from a 50-year-old who had long been conditioned to revere the Soviet dictator.

One simply cannot understand the power of Menachem Begin's vow 'Never again!', with reference to the requirement for Israel to defend itself against aggression and always to be strong and on alert, never again yielding to nations out to destroy the Jewish

---

[2] The noted presidential scholar Stanley Renshon, who was educated as a political scientist and trained in psychoanalysis, has also developed a method for analysing political leadership, which draws on psychodynamic psychology and considers the formative influences of life experiences. See further Renshon, Psychoanalysis.

[3] I will use the masculine pronouns to refer to both male and female leaders in this discussion.

[4] See further Post (forthcoming).

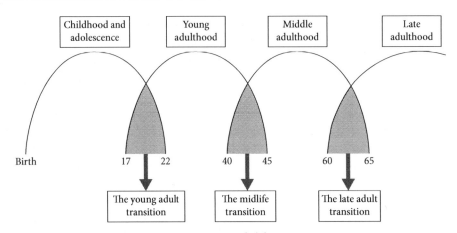

FIGURE 22.2 Levinson's life transitions

people, without understanding that most of his family had been killed in the Holocaust (Post 2003b).

These two examples emphasize the crystallization of political identity in youth. Erik Erikson, noted for his delineation of the stages of psychosocial development (Erikson 1950), gave important emphasis to the manner in which individual psychological development always occurs within a context, well summed up later in his pithy observation 'We cannot lift a case history out of history' (Erikson 1958: 15–16). Drawing on Erikson, Dan Levinson (1978) has emphasized three major life transitions: the young adult transition, between childhood/adolescence and young adulthood; the midlife transition, between young adulthood and middle adulthood; and the late adult transition, between middle adulthood and late adulthood. This is illustrated in Figure 22.2.[5]

These life transitions have important implications for political psychology and the study of political leadership (Post 1980). The establishment of identity, including political identity, already discussed, occurs during the young adult transition. This is the period of the so-called identity crisis. Establishment of mentor relationships can be quite influential during these formative years, and identifying mentors and heroes is an important task in developing the psychobiography. For example, the importance of Lenin as mentor to Stalin cannot be overemphasized. As a teenager in a harsh Orthodox religious seminary in Tbilisi, which forbade any books other than religious texts, young Iosif Dzugashvili (who was not to assume the pseudonym Stalin until twenty years later) rebelled by smuggling in the works of Marx and Lenin. He came to idealize and admire Lenin from a distance, and left the seminary to become his acolyte, loyally pursuing the revolutionary cause of his mentor. At the age of 41, however, in the midlife transition, desiring power for himself, Stalin confronted Lenin, who shortly thereafter suffered a debilitating stroke, and Stalin went on to consolidate power in his own right.

[5] This schematic is drawn from Post (2004: 23).

Another issue that comes into focus in studying the formative years of the leader is the formation of 'the dream', which for many can be traced back to childhood. When dreams of glory are formed, and are not modified during subsequent development, they can lead to precipitous acts during the midlife transition, during the so-called midlife crisis.

Especially for narcissistic leaders, there can never be enough glory, and we often see a reluctance by ageing leaders to let go of the reins of power. The pressures of the late adult transition and reluctance to yield to the next generation would seem to have contributed to the so-called Arab spring of 2011. International attention focused on the political decisions and actions of ageing Middle Eastern autocrats. First was the 74-year-old Zine al Abidine Ben Ali, leader of Tunisia for thirty years. Then it was 82-year-old Hosni Mubarak, the autocratic leader of Egypt, who had been at its helm for thirty-two years, from 1979 to 2011. Both left office after facing mammoth political demonstrations. Mubarak showed a very paternalistic attitude to his people, initially characterizing the protestors as thugs. He related to Egypt and its people as if he were their king, their pharoah. The overthrow of Ben Ali and Mubarak, in turn, stimulated the uprising in Libya, led for forty-two years by Mu'ammar Qaddafi, 68 years old, who was killed by the rebels after being forced from power; and to demonstrations in Yemen against the leadership of 65-year-old President Ali Abdullah Saleh, in power since 1994, who under duress agreed to a transfer of power in November 2011. Ageing dictators may increasingly come to see themselves as synonymous with their countries, and, protected by sycophantic subordinates, may be late in recognizing how much discontent has been brewing in response to their repressive policies.

The second part of the political personality profile, the personality study, represents a cross-sectional cut through the leader who has emerged from this formative process. To the degree possible, it seeks to identify a political personality type that characterizes the leader. Three personality types of importance to the study of leadership are: the narcissistic personality, the obsessive–compulsive personality, and the paranoid personality. A summary description of each of these personality types follows (see also Post 2004).

3 The Narcissist in Power

It is probably not an exaggeration[6] to state that, if narcissistic characters were stripped from the ranks of public figures, the ranks would be significantly thinned. The label of narcissism covers a broad range of behaviours. At the healthiest end of the narcissistic spectrum are egotistical individuals with extreme self-confidence. Primitive narcissism, so-called malignant narcissism, represents an extremely severe and dangerous personality disorder. It is characterized by such extreme compensatory messianic dreams of

---

[6] This section draws significantly on Post (1992).

glory and self-absorption that there is a lack of ability to empathize with one's own people; a paranoid outlook, not paranoid psychotic, but always ready to find an external cause for difficulties and consequent scapegoating; an absence of conscience; and a willingness to use whatever aggression is necessary to accomplish his goals. This is a particularly dangerous political personality type, one that is found in many dictatorial leaders.

There are a number of apparent contradictions in the narcissistic personality. This is because, for each of the dimensions, there is both an overt and covert aspect (Akhtar and Thompson 1982). Thus, the overt picture of haughty grandiosity overlies feelings of inferiority, which helps explain the narcissist's continuous search for fame and glory. There is a hunger for acclaim and a tendency to change the interpretation of reality when self-esteem is threatened. The overt picture of zealous morality overlies a corruptible conscience.

A notable aspect of the narcissist in power is the manner in which he seeks to gratify his psychological needs through the exercise of leadership. Despite the apparent sustained devotion of their energies to socially productive endeavours, and the 'selfless' rationales, the primary goal of self-oriented narcissists is actually to gain recognition, fame, and glory. This search for recognition and adulation that drives these individuals springs from their excessive self-absorption, their intense ambition, and their grandiose fantasies. Underlying and impelling this quest are an inner emptiness and uncertainty about identity.

The interpersonal relationships of narcissists are regularly and characteristically disturbed. There is a quality of personal exploitativeness, with a disregard for the feelings and needs of others. The narcissist surrounds himself with admirers, and requires a constant stream of adulation from them. Yet it is a one-way street, and, when the loyal follower is no longer useful to the psychological economy of the narcissist, he can be dropped suddenly without a backwards glance. This precipitous fall from grace will frequently be bewildering to the individual dropped, who mistakenly believed he was highly valued by his hero. Indeed, his provision of psychological supplies, of adulation, was valued, but he had been seen not as a separate individual, with needs of his own, but rather as an extension of the narcissist—in the terminology of Heinz Kohut, a 'self object'. The narcissist is often extremely charming and delightful to be with, contributing to the false spell cast over his intimates. There is, however, a characteristic difficulty in sustaining loyal relationships over time.

The mirror image of the quest for adulation is sensitivity to slight and criticism. The narcissist is vulnerable and easily hurt, and goes through complicated manœuvres to avoid being hurt. He can put on a mask of cold indifference, and can envelop himself in what Volkan (1979) has called a 'glass bubble'. Like the Little Prince, narcissists feel that they live by themselves in splendid isolation, a glorious but lonely existence, enclosed by an impervious but transparent protection.

Because the narcissist is so vulnerable to psychological injury, he cannot afford to acknowledge ignorance. This in turn leads to major difficulties with learning, for the learning process carries with it an implicit assumption of lack of knowledge, and it profoundly inhibits acceptance of constructive criticism. Dogmatic certainty with no foundation of knowledge is a posture frequently struck by the narcissist. This discomfort with learning is related to the sensitivity to constructive criticism noted above. If the narcissist's self-concept of perfection and brilliance is to be sustained, no one can give him new knowledge, and no aspect of his understanding is to be faulted.

Volkan (1979) has emphasized that the narcissist in power has special psychological advantages in terms of sustaining his grandiose self-image. He can actually restructure his reality by devaluing or even eliminating those who threaten his fragile self-esteem. This leads to a tendency for the narcissistic leader increasingly to be surrounded by sycophants who sense their leader's need for uncritical adulation and agreement, and have been sensitized by the abrupt departure of advisers who dared to criticize or bring unpleasant news. Thus, the narcissistic leader can be in touch with reality psychologically, but, by dint of surrounding himself with anxious sycophants, he can be totally out of touch with political reality.

The conscience of the narcissist is dominated by self-interest. Unlike the sociopath, who is without an internal beacon, without an internalized body of scruples and principles, the narcissist does indeed have a conscience, but it is a flexible conscience. He sincerely believes himself to be highly principled, but can change positions and commitments rapidly as 'circumstances change'. The righteous indignation with which he stands in judgement of the moral failure of others often stands in striking contrast to his own self-concerned behaviour, which seems hypocritical to the outside observer. The narcissist's self-image, however, is of himself as someone who is principled and scrupulous, but who has had to change his position. The sincerity of his beliefs is communicated, so that the unwary may be completely persuaded of the sincerity of the narcissist; and indeed, *at that moment*, he is sincere.

It is hard to identify the narcissistic personality with any consistent beliefs about the world, the adversary, and so on, because these beliefs tend to shift. Additionally, more than any other personality type, what the narcissistic personality says should be viewed as 'calculated for effect'. Accordingly, to place great weight on the analysis of core determining beliefs from speeches when dealing with a narcissistic personality is apt to lead the unwary political analyst far astray. Words do not convey deeply held beliefs for the narcissist. Their only use is instrumental, to enhance his personal position and gain admiration and support. *The only central and stable belief of the narcissist is the centrality of the self. What is good for him is good for his country*. The interesting point here is that this attitude goes beyond 'naked' self-interest. In fact, the narcissistic individual comes to believe that the national interest and national security are in fact crucially contingent upon his staying in power.

The centrality of the self has interesting implications for his image of the adversary. For one thing, the narcissistic personality has a profound inability to empathize with, or understand, different points of view, different interests, or different perspectives. For the narcissist, the problems are not 'What are the threats to the USA or Iraq and what can be done to meet these threats?' but 'How can I use this situation either to preserve or to enhance my own reputation?' Information search is undertaken in as public a manner as possible with a view towards making the leader look good.

Because of the narcissist's sensitivity to being slighted and the underlying fragility of his self-esteem, there would be strong pressure to avoid dissension to help meet this person's need for reassurance and to prevent him from looking bad. Moreover, because of his need to be omniscient, to know everything, it is hard to present the consummate narcissist with new information. That would be to indicate his ignorance, and that is unacceptable. The purpose of the group is not to generate new options or to provide additional cognitive capacity for evaluating these options, but to serve as means for reassurance, shoring up the narcissistic leader's self-esteem, and supporting his personal needs for attention. Bright ambitious individuals seeking themselves to shine do not last long in the circle of the narcissist. The narcissist, in subtle fashion, often plays one adviser against another, to ensure that he is the major domo. The narcissist in power is particularly apt to stimulate the collective decision-making malady of 'groupthink' as the circle of advisers contributes to the illusion of false consensus because of a reluctance to disagree with their leader.

Example: Saddam Hussein: 'Saddam is Iraq: Iraq is Saddam'

Saddam Hussein's exaggerated dreams of personal glory[7] rested on a foundation of insecurity, produced by a painfully traumatic background (Post, 1990). Saddam Hussein's traumas can be traced back to the womb. In the fourth month of his mother's pregnancy, his father died of cancer. In the eighth month of the same pregnancy, his mother's first-born son died under the surgeon's knife. Not surprisingly, she became gravely depressed, and first tried to abort herself of the pregnancy, and then to commit suicide. When Saddam was finally born, in a mud hut in Tikrit, his mother turned away from her newborn son, refused to accept him, and gave him to her brother, Kairallah, to raise, which he and his extended family did for the first two-and-a-half years of Saddam's life. When his mother remarried, Saddam went to her for the first time, and the new step-father was abusive to Saddam, both physically and psychologically. This is not a good foundation for this life, and it would have produced what is called a wounded self.

With such a background, most adults would be deeply scarred, insecure, and unable to function well later in life. When Saddam was 8 and his parents refused to send him to school, however, he fled from his home and returned to his uncle, Kairallah. Kairallah filled him with dreams of glory and told his young charge that some day he would be a hero to the Iraqi people, following in the path of Saladin and Nebuchadnezzar, who had rescued Jerusalem from the infidels. When Saddam came to power, he dotted the countryside with magnificent palaces, which represented those grandiose dreams of glory, just as the mud hut was an architectural motif for the economic and psychological

---

[7] This material is drawn from testimony presented to hearings conducted in December 1990 by the House Military Affairs Committee, Les Aspin, Chair, and the House Foreign Affairs Committee, Lee Hamilton, Chair.

poverty of Saddam's origins and the wounded self within. But what was underneath the palaces? Fortified underground bunkers, bristling with weapons and communications equipment, representing Saddam's siege psychology, the default position in his political personality, ready to be attacked, ready to lash out.

The personality that emerged from this traumatic background represents the particularly primitive form of narcissism, malignant narcissism, described earlier. Throughout his career, Saddam believed he should be recognized as one of history's great socialist leaders, along with Mao Zedong, Ho Chi Minh, Josip Tito, and Fidel Castro, but he had never received the recognition he deserved, until the summer of 1990, when he invaded Kuwait. Suddenly his name was in the headlines. When he gave a guttural grunt, oil barrel prices jumped $20 and the Dow Jones stock average plunged 200 points. At last, he was recognized as a powerful world leader, and the Palestinian people saw him as their new hero, who would return Jerusalem to them, fulfilling his uncle's prophecy. It was an explosion of narcissism, dreams of glory fulfilled.

In the past, Saddam had retreated when he had miscalculated in the name of 'revolutionary pragmatism', but only when he could do so and regain face and retain his power base. Inflated with *hubris*, however, Saddam had painted himself into a corner, and, as the conflict played out, this double contingency could not be satisfied. Once he had tasted glory, the notion that he would meekly retreat in the face of the approaching major conflict was inconceivable. He survived, albeit gravely weakened, until the Second Gulf War. He was executed in 2006 by an Iraqi court, displaying a grandiose defiance until the very end.

4 THE OBSESSIVE–COMPULSIVE PERSONALITY IN POWER

The obsessive–compulsive (O–C) personality is frequently encountered in government and business executives, scientists and engineers, academic scholars and military leaders. The strengths of this personality style—organizational ability, attention to detail, emphasis on rational process—can all contribute to significant professional success. Under stress, however, these traits become exaggerated, and can become disabilities.

The O–C personality places heavy reliance on the ego defence of intellectualization, emphasizing rationality, and abhorring emotionality, which implies lack of rational control. The O–C is preoccupied with details, order, and organization. There is an inappropriate preoccupation with trivial details, often losing perspective of 'the big picture'. These characteristics can systematically influence decision-making, and can adversely affect crisis decision-making. Decision-making is avoided, postponed, or protracted. This springs from an inordinate fear of making a mistake, for *the over-weaning goal of the O–C personality is to leave no room for error, to not make mistakes, to be certain and achieve perfection.*

Frequently such individuals are excessively conscientious, moralistic, scrupulous, and judgemental of the self and of others. Location in the interpersonal hierarchy is of great importance to individuals with this character type, who are preoccupied with their relative status in dominant–submissive relationships. Although oppositional when subjected to the will of others, they stubbornly insist on others submitting to their way of doing things, and are unaware of the resentment their behaviour induces in others. It is not that they oppose contrasting views; rather they actively do not attend to them in the service of persevering with their own views. The O–C will have a sharp focus, will indeed get the facts in examining the situation, but in getting the facts he will often 'not see the forest for the trees'.

These individuals have considerable difficulty with warm and tender feelings, and are stingy both with their emotions and with their material possessions. Their everyday relationships tend to be serious, formal, and conventional, lacking charm, grace, spontaneity, and humour. Wilhelm Reich has described these individuals as 'living machines' (Reich 1949: 199). The preoccupation with productivity and concentration imparts a special cast to the cognitive style and lifestyle of these individuals. They are immensely productive and show impressive abilities to concentrate on their work, often cranking out huge volumes of work, especially in technical areas. Everything seems laborious, determined, tense, and deliberate; there is a quality of effortfulness, leading to the frequent characterization of the obsessive–compulsive as 'driven'. The O–C is dominated by 'shoulds' and 'oughts'; he regularly tells himself (and others) what he should do, what he ought to do, and the language of 'wants' is alien. There is a necessity to maintain a rigid and continuous state of purposeful activity.

The O–Cs, then, are not free men. While these directives to which the O–C is subjected are, on the one hand, burdensome, they also provide clear guidelines for behaviour. These individuals do not feel comfortable with any non-purposive activity. To relax for the sake of relaxation is unthinkable, and is indeed anxiety-producing—thus the gravity with which leisure-time activity is planned. This has major consequences for decision-making. The preoccupation with 'doing what is right' places a premium on avoiding mistakes. O–Cs accordingly often have difficulty coming to decisional closure, searching for additional evidence to ensure they are not making a mistake, a particular problem in crisis decision-making, when there is often incomplete or conflicting information. They live in a world of ambivalence and mixed feelings, and their decision-making is like that of the character Tevya from *The Fiddler on the Roof*—'on the one hand, but on the other hand'. To travel through a decision-making process with a thoroughgoing O–C is an exhausting journey. Just as they are apparently coming to a decision, all of the doubts rush up to question, and often undo, the conclusion.

This decisional agony can be forestalled if there is a rule that can be applied. Thus, if the elements of a situation fit a psychological template that is well established for the individual, he can apply the formula without thinking. If there is no formula, however, the O–C will become quite anxious. Thus, new and unanticipated situations are particularly threatening. The O–C is characterized more by rigidity in cognitive processes than rigidity in cognitive beliefs. The O–C individual will want to receive raw data, will want to see the minutiae about almost everything. The strong preference here is to act later rather than sooner, preferring procrastination rather than the dangers of hasty action or 'premature closure'. Because of his lack of certainty, the O–C will have a strong tendency to opt, by default, for the status quo or perhaps make incremental change. He has a strong bias for satisficing rather than optimizing.

The absence of definitive data is extremely anxiety-producing. Because of their strong need for raw data, many O–Cs would not be content with the summaries and general policy analysis of their immediate advisers. Thus, they have a great deal of difficulty delegating and relying upon subordinates, who, after all, might make a mistake. Dominated by a strong conscience, the O–C personality is a man of his word. When he has made a commitment in negotiations, he can be relied upon, in contrast to the narcissist, who can reverse himself as circumstances dictate. Moreover, to the extent that he has committed to writing policy goals and preferences, these can be taken as a reliable map of intentions.

Example: Menachem Begin at Camp David

While Menachem Begin certainly had many narcissistic personality features and saw himself as having a central role in guiding Israel to a safe and secure future, his personality in general had strong obsessive–compulsive personality features. He focused endlessly on the precise meaning of words and was intolerant of ambiguity. This made for great difficulty in sustained negotiations. And he regularly 'lost sight of the forest for the trees'. In his 1977 memoir, *White Nights*, concerning his period of incarceration in Siberia, Begin, educated as a lawyer, describes with pride his arguing with his Soviet captors on details of the Soviet legal code, and proving to be correct. For his troubles, he was rewarded by being placed in solitary confinement.

To assist him in his negotiations at Camp David in 1978, three profiles were prepared for President Jimmy Carter: a profile of Menachem Begin, emphasizing his rigidity, his preoccupation with details, and his difficulties in compromising; a profile of Anwar Sadat, emphasizing his 'big picture' mentality and distaste for details; and a third quite important paper concerning the implications and problems in simultaneous negotiations posed by these differences in their cognitive styles, which recommended that Carter serve as an intermediary, keeping the two protagonists separated as much as possible (Post 1979).

In his 1982 memoir, *Keeping Faith*, Carter describes his study of the three profiles in his preparation for the Camp David summit negotiations, and/ how he employed these understandings in resolving a stalemate. The three men were stuck on a twenty-five-word clause; it was an important clause, concerned with the autonomy of the Palestinian people, but neither participant would budge. Carter described meeting Prime Minister Begin individually, and taking words from the prepared profile and putting them in the mouth of President Sadat, saying something to the effect of 'Your Excellency, President Sadat is concerned that we will get so caught up in details that we will lose sight of the big picture and lose the opportunity of a breakthrough'. As Carter described it, Begin drew himself up proudly and said: 'I too can focus on the big picture. We'll leave the details to our subordinates,' and they got past this impasse. It is a brilliant example of employing insights from profiles to assist in complex negotiations.

5 THE PARANOID PERSONALITY IN POWER

The essential features of the paranoid personality disorder are a pervasive and long-standing suspiciousness and mistrust of people in general. Individuals with this disorder are hyper-sensitive and easily slighted. They continually scan the environment for clues that validate their original prejudicial ideas, attitudes, or biases.

Suspicious thinking is the *sine qua non* of the paranoid personality. A striking quality is the pervasive rigidity; the suspicious person has something on his mind, and searches repetitively, and only, for confirmation of it. Suspicious people do not ignore new data, but examine them extremely carefully. The goal of the examination, however, is to find confirmation of their suppositions of danger, dismissing evidence that disconfirms their fearful views, and seizing upon what apparently confirms them.

In many life circumstances, being suspicious and on guard is both appropriate and adaptive. However, the psychologically healthy individual can abandon his suspicions when he is presented with convincing contradictory evidence. The paranoid, in contrast, has a firm conclusion of danger in search of evidence. Hostile, stubborn, and defensive, he will reject evidence that disproves his suspicions. Indeed, well-meaning attempts to reassure him or reason with him will usually provoke anger, and the 'helpful' one may himself become the object of suspicions as well.

The paranoid is hyper-vigilant, ever alert to a hostile interpersonal environment, always expecting plots and betrayal. He has a readiness to see himself alone, surrounded by enemies. This explains why paranoia is the most political of mental disorders, because of the requirement for enemies (Robins and Post 1997).[8]

Paranoids tend to be rigid and unwilling to compromise. In a new situation, they intensely and narrowly search for confirmation of their bias with a loss of appreciation of the total context. They usually find what they anticipated finding. Theirs is a world of hidden motives and special meanings. They have a readiness to counterattack against a perceived threat, and can become excited over small matters, making mountains out of molehills. Priding themselves on always being objective, unemotional, and rational, they are uncomfortable with passive, soft, sentimental, and tender feelings. They avoid intimacy except with those they absolutely trust, a minute population. They show an

---

[8] See Robins and Post (1997), which offers an extended treatment of the political manifestations of paranoia. A number of the key points expanded at length in Robins and Post (1997) are summarized in a preliminary article by Post with Robins (1987).

exaggerated need to be self-sufficient, relying on no one. They avoid participating in a group setting unless they are in a dominant position. Keenly aware of rank and power, and who is superior or inferior, they are often jealous of and have feelings of rivalry with people in power. Their wary hyper-vigilance and readiness to retaliate often generate fear and uneasiness in others. One treads carefully around a paranoid, 'walking on egg-shells', lest he become upset.

He is always on the alert for danger, his antennae constantly sweeping the horizon for signs of threat. Clearly, insofar as the paranoid intentionally seeks out only data that confirm his premise of external danger, and systematically excludes evidence to the contrary, his evaluation of reality is often skewed. In effect, his views of external reality are distorted by his internal needs.

The primary basis of the paranoid style's characteristic suspiciousness is an over-reliance on the ego defence of projection—the attribution to external figures of internal motivation, drives, or other feelings that are intolerable and hence repudiated in oneself. An important characteristic of the paranoid that has significant implications for his leadership style, but that also affects his cognitive style, is the exaggerated need for autonomy. The paranoid is constantly seeking for evidence that dangerous others are out to control him or betray him. The only defence in such a dangerous world is to rely on no one, exaggeratedly to emphasize independence and autonomy.

The paranoid guards against losing control of his feelings, especially warm, soft, tender, and passive feelings. There can be no humour or playfulness, and, without spontaneity, there is clearly a major inhibition of creative expression. Schafer has characterized this constant state of internal surveillance as 'an internal police state' (Schafer 1954). Like an army, the paranoid is constantly on the alert, mobilized to counterattack against the ever-present danger. Thus, the paranoid is simultaneously defending himself against external danger and against internal impulses, a burdensome and exhausting psychological war on two fronts. As internal tension builds, suspiciousness grows, and through the process of projection an external (and more manageable) threat is constructed. The individual then has a state of heightened alertness, a state of continuous alert guardedness against the now external danger.

It is evident that an individual who views the world through a suspicious lens and is continually seeking to confirm his core premise of external danger, against which he must defend himself, has significant constraints on his interpretation of the political world and his manner of dealing with it. There are many similarities between the obsessive–compulsive and the paranoid. For both, there is a focusing on detail, an emphasis on autonomy, and a guarded rigidity; but, these qualities have significant differences, too. The O–C fixes on details, while the paranoid searches for clues. The O–C is searching for certainty, while the paranoid is searching for confirmation of his fixed conclusion of danger. While the O–C is stubborn and obstinate, the paranoid is touchy and guarded. The O–C is dominated by conscience, by what he should do, whereas the paranoid is dominated by fear and is in a constant state of perceived external danger. The paranoid style is more extreme, more unstable, and more psychologically primitive.

The paranoid personality tends to hold very strong, rigidly entrenched cognitive beliefs. The paranoid personality typically includes a belief system with a vivid and central image of the enemy. As one might suspect, the adversary is seen as inherently and pervasively evil and a major and incorrigible threat to one's own personal/national interest. There is little doubt that the adversary will respond to conciliatory moves by taking advantage of them. The paranoid personality, by definition, sees enemies everywhere. Therefore, he sees the world in polarized terms. His is a Manichean universe, divided into two camps: allies and adversaries. Neutrals are impossible: 'If you are not strongly for me—you must be against me.'

People or nations are never compelled to do things by virtue of circumstances. Rather their actions are always a product of their negative adversarial qualities. For example, there is no such thing as a 'defensive' action by the adversary taken solely to protect his own security—all actions of one's adversary are necessarily aggressive. The world is a conflictual place, and the source of conflict is the evil nature or character of other nations or people. The enemy would never engage in a crisis for inadvertent reasons; war occurs because of the nefarious, aggressive motivations of the adversary.

An important related topic of interest will be information relating to the 'enemy within' or 'fifth column activity'. The adversary is believed to be very creative and devious in this sort of covert subversion, and people of one's own nation who do not fully share the views of the paranoid leader are believed to be either suspect themselves or, at best, naive, unwitting dupes.

Faced with the need to make a decision, the paranoid personality will manifest a strong tendency to act sooner rather than to procrastinate, out of fear that 'he who hesitates is lost'.

Because of his image of the world as very conflictual, and because of the image of the adversary as incorrigibly aggressive and politically devious, the paranoid leader has a strong preference for the use of force over persuasion. In a crisis, there is a strong preference for what is seen as pre-emptive action. The paranoid may even initiate a crisis or a war out of the belief that preventive action against the adversary is necessary and one might as well 'strike while the iron is hot'—that is, since the adversary is preparing to act, it is preferable to act first while the military balance is more in one's favour.

Example: Josef Stalin

There is not space here to present a full profile of Stalin, but suffice it to say that, without being highly suspicious in the conspiracy-ridden Kremlin, one could not survive. The manipulative subordinate can take advantage of the paranoid leader's suspiciousness to plant suspicions concerning bureaucratic rivals, as did Beria with Stalin. A whisper in Stalin's ear by Beria concerning doubts about the loyalty of a subordinate was sufficient to eliminate the individual in question. There is an important dynamic for the paranoid in power that Stalin well exemplifies. As the paranoid leader seeks to unmask and counter plotters against him, seeking out enemies real and imagined, the very actions he takes to eliminate enemies can create enemies. Stalin created a formidable internal police state, based on a wide and pervasive network of informers. Robert Conquest, in *The Great Terror* (1968), estimates that between 23 million and 26 million Soviets were killed in the series of purges between 1933 and 1936. As this widening gyre of terror spiralled in an all-encompassing way, as perfectly innocent individuals got caught up in this internal terrorism, they began to plot and conspire to protect themselves. Thus, there is a self-fulfilling prophetic aspect of the paranoid in power. The enemies that began in his mind can be created in reality. Stalin became increasingly paranoid in his later years, and was probably in a frankly paranoid state when, with the manipulation of Beria, he had become convinced that there was a conspiracy among Jewish doctors, 'The Doctors' Plot', and was about to embark on another major purge when a massive cerebral haemorrhage ended his life.

Having described these character types in detail for illustrative purposes, I must emphasize that most individuals, and most leaders, possess a broad array of characteristics that do not fit one pure type. Rather, it is the predominance of one style over another that affects outcomes, and the analyst is searching for patterns. The healthy leader personality has characteristics that contribute to effective leadership, sound decision-making, the ability accurately to diagnose the environment, and working effectively with a leadership circle chosen for its expertise and wisdom from which the self-confident leader can learn and take wise counsel. Under the stress of crisis, however, the somewhat suspicious leader can become paranoid, the somewhat obsessive leader can become paralysed with indecision. As a narcissistic leader faces the end of his life, his drive to achieve his unfulfilled dreams of glory can produce nightmares for us all.

RECOMMENDED READING

Erikson, E. (1950). *Childhood and Society*. New York: Norton.
Levinson, D. (1978). *The Seasons of a Man's Life*. New York: Knopf.
Post, J. (2004) (ed.). *The Psychological Assessment of Political Leaders*. Ann Arbor, MI: University of Michigan Press.

REFERENCES

Akhtar, S., and Thompson, J. A. (1982). 'Overview: Narcissistic Personality Disorder', *American Journal of Psychiatry*, 139/1: 12–20.
Begin, M. (1977). *White Nights: The Story of a Prisoner in Russia*. New York: Harper and Row.
Carter, J. (1982). *Keeping Faith: Memoirs of a President*. Toronto: Bantam Books.
Conquest, R. (1968). *The Great Terror: Stalin's Purge of the Thirties*. New York: Macmillan.
Erikson, E. (1950). *Childhood and Society*. New York: Norton.
Erikson, E. (1958). *Young Man Luther: A Study in Psychoanalysis and History*. New York: Norton.
Levinson, D. (1978). *The Seasons of a Man's Life*. New York: Knopf.

Post, J. (1979). 'Personality Profiles in Support of the Camp David Summit', *Studies in Intelligence*, Spring: 1–5.

Post, J. (1980). 'The Seasons of a Leader's Life: Influences of the Life Cycle on Political Behavior', *Political Psychology*, 2/3–4: 35–49.

Post, J. (1990). '*Saddam Hussein: A Political Psychology Profile*', Testimony to House Armed Services Committee, Chairman, Les Aspin, November.

Post, J. (1992). 'Current Concepts of Narcissism: Implications for Political Psychology', *Political Psychology*, 13/1: 99–121.

Post, J. (2003a). 'Assessing Leaders at a Distance: The Political Personality Profile', in J. Post (ed.), *The Psychological Assessment of Political Leaders, with Profiles of Saddam Hussein and Bill Clinton*. Ann Arbor, MI: University of Michigan Press, 69–104.

Post, J. (2003b). 'Leader Personality Assessments in Support of Government Policy', in J. Post (ed.), *The Psychological Assessment of Political Leaders, with Profiles of Saddam Hussein and Bill Clinton*. Ann Arbor, MI: University of Michigan Press, 39–61.

Post, J. (2004). *Leaders and their Followers in a Dangerous World: The Psychology of Political Behavior*. Ithaca, NY: Cornell University Press.

Post, J. (forthcoming). 'Psychobiography: The Child Is Father of the Man', in D. O. Sears, L. Huddy, and H. Levy (eds), *The Oxford Handbook of Political Psychology*. New York: Oxford University Press.

Post, J., and Robins, R. (1987). 'The Paranoid Political Actor', *Biography*, 10/1: 1–19.

Reich, W. (1949). *Character Analysis*. New York: Orgone Institute Press.

Renshon, S. (2003). 'Psychoanalytic Assessments of Character and Performance In Presidents and Candidates: Some Observations on Theorand Method', in J. Post (ed.), *The Psychological Assessment of Political Leaders, with Profiles of Saddam Hussein and Bill Clinton*. Ann Arbor, MI: University of Michigan Press, 105–33.

Robins, R., and Post, J. (1997). *Political Paranoia: The Psychopolitics of Hatred*. New Haven, CT: Yale University Press.

Schafer, R. (1954). *Psychoanalytic Interpretation in Rorschach Testing: Theory and Application*. New York: Grune and Stratton.

Volkan, V. (1979). 'The Glass Bubble of a Narcissistic Patient', in J. Le Boit and A. Capponi (eds), *Advances in Psychotherapy of the Borderline Patient*. New York: Jason Aronson, 405–31.

PART III

POLITICAL LEADERSHIP AT WORK

CHAPTER 23

··

CIVIC LEADERSHIP

··

RICHARD A. COUTO

1 INTRODUCTION

CIVIC leadership challenges the conceptual boundaries that we set for politics and leadership. It extends politics beyond the realm of government and leadership beyond positional authority. Civic leadership may also challenge the practice of ordinary politics that often ignores the inconvenient truths of social, economic, and political conditions. To thrive effectively, civic leadership requires civil society to be a space autonomous from the economic and political realms. This chapter examines some of the bedrock assumptions about political leadership; the nature of civil society and civic leadership; and some of the anomalies that civic leadership presents for our paradigms about politics and leadership. The chapter concludes with a discussion of future directions for the study of civic leadership.

2 POLITICS, LEADERSHIP, AND LEADERS

For most of human history, politics and leadership were one and the same subject. Notable thinkers, in different times and contexts, concerned themselves with public purpose and its corollaries of processes and leadership to achieve it (Strauss and Cropsey 1987). Even the myths of oral tradition (Flowers 2010) asked the primary questions of politics: where does the authority of political leaders come from? For what purposes are political leaders entrusted with authority and power? Who may hold them accountable to those purposes? Unfortunately, for most of this time our thoughts about leadership also had a leader-centric focus on the desired or observed characteristics or styles of people with positional authority. From Plato and Confucius to the present day, our notions of political leadership have imbibed the leader-centric tradition of much of political philosophy and the current paradigms of leadership studies. Despite dramatic democratic revolutions over the past several centuries, which have redefined the nature of authority and invested it in new forms of participation and legitimation, the largest part of the study of politics and leadership still identifies leadership with leaders—that is, people in positions of authority and formal power.

To examine civic leadership is to invite a departure from those traditional approaches to political leadership and a shift in attention to leadership as an action, not a position; that is, specifically taking initiative on behalf of shared values and common benefit. We expect our leaders with formal roles of authority to lead—that is, to take that initiative. The frequent call for leadership clearly entails a request for action because leadership is more than a title or position. Moreover, this definition of leadership implies that everyone, regardless of position, can be a leader by taking initiative on behalf of shared values and common benefit. Robert Tucker (1981), a political scientist, makes this distinction as one of constituted and non-constituted leadership. Ronald Heifetz (1994) built on Tucker to distinguish between authority and leadership and measured the latter in terms of the mobilization of a group's resources to meet challenges to its well-being within its environment. Civic leadership involves leadership as an action and not a position. It includes the actions of ordinary people without positions of power and authority, such as the legendary Dutch boy who plugged the leak in the dike that protected his city. To explore civic leadership as leading without formal political authority, we need to explore the realm where we find it—civil society.

3 CIVIL SOCIETY AND CIVIC LEADERSHIP

John Ehrenberg distills civil society's changing forms and conceptualizations over time and finds that 'civil society delineates a sphere that is formally distinct from the body politic and state authority on the one hand, and from the immediate pursuit of self-interest and the imperatives of the market on the other' (Ehrenberg 1999: 235). In the 2000s, civil society is often equated with another space distinct from government and business, appropriately termed the 'third sector' (Salamon et al. 2004). Figure 23.1 presents these three distinct sectors.

Unfortunately, as is often the practice, Figure 23.1 conflates disparate parts of the third sector with civil society. We offer business executives—for example Bill Gates, Microsoft founder and billionaire—accolades for their philanthropy; for their participation on boards of third-sector organizations that address a community problem or need; or for their promotion of the arts, cancer research, or some other worthwhile cause. Voluntary associations within the third sector, also called non-profit organizations or non-governmental organizations, provide civic leadership through the cultural events, human services, and other vital and valuable programmes they conduct for the general benefit of the community. Local public officials may be praised for their

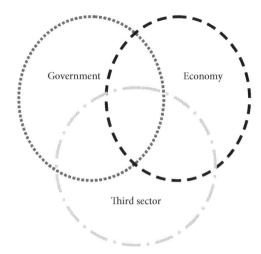

FIGURE 23.1 Civil society as the third sector

civic-mindedness when they support the non-governmental organizations of the third sector in their efforts for some community improvement. These all touch upon the vital centre of civil society but do not express its core.

This conflation of civil society with the third sector ignores the political differences within the third sector and thus obscures a more precise meaning of civil society (Edwards 2011: 83). For example, some environmental groups in the third sector, such as Greenpeace, are more deliberate and intentional in their political purpose than other environmental groups, such as bird-watching clubs. In addition, normative or even utopian aspirations for a world in which more people have greater opportunities for complete human development are part of the space of civil society.

Among ameliorative voluntary associations, some protect and nourish happiness or attempt to extend its opportunities as a matter of charity or voluntary individual and social responsibility and thus reflect the differences of wealth and opportunity within society. Others seek to do so as a matter of justice (Rawls 1971; Freire 1993: 27; Sen 1999; Nussbaum 2000) and thus highlight the differences of wealth and opportunity within society. Saul Alinsky, an iconic US community organizer, is alleged to have said that his role was 'to comfort the afflicted and afflict the comfortable', but, in practice, the voluntary associations within civil society may comfort the afflicted while afflicting the comfortable in varying degrees. Dom Helder Camara, a Brazilian archbishop and pioneer of liberation theology, portrayed a balancing act between running voluntary associations and exercising civil-society leadership, when he observed that when he gave food to the poor, people called him a saint, but when he asked why they were poor, they called him a Communist. Hillel Schmid contrasts an inclusive definition of civil society that embraces all groups of the third sector with a narrower definition that distinguishes service providers from advocacy and watchdog groups (Schmid 2009). Just like the very earliest accounts of advocacy and monitoring groups, Schmid presents them as counterweights

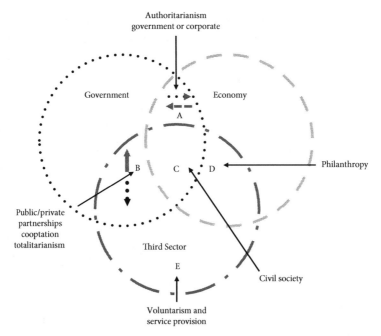

Authoritarianism
government or corporate

Government

Economy

A

B   C   D

Philanthropy

Public/private
partnerships
cooptation
totalitarianism

Third Sector

E

Civil society

Voluntarism and
service provision

FIGURE 23.2 Distinctions within the third sector and within civil society

to government and gives less attention to their role vis-à-vis business and the collusion of business and government. Figure 23.2 portrays one model of civil society as the overlap of the government, business, and third sectors, but distinct from all of them. It suggests that the realm of government may overlap with business and the third sector and that business may overlap with government and the third sector. The model presents a balance among the sectors seldom achieved. Leadership within civil society pushes out and attempts to create or contain the appropriate boundaries of the first and second sectors, especially their overlap—where politics and civil society may be commodified by economics, or economics and civil society folded into the political sector within an authoritarian state.

This chapter takes the more specific view of civil society as the space within which people attempt to redress conditions, such as human needs and rights or environmental degradation, ignored or exacerbated by the ordinary practice of politics and economics. Kumi Naidoo, formerly secretary general of CIVICUS, a global alliance for citizen participation, and executive director of Greenpeace International, and his co-author Siddharth Bannerjee explain that the developing southern hemisphere especially has witnessed the development of more civil-society organizations, nationally and transnationally, as legitimate public actors to participate alongside state and market 'in the making of public policies designed to resolve collective problems and advance the public good' (Naidoo and Bannerjee 2010: 37).

Having distinguished between service and advocacy groups in the third sector, we must now attempt to distinguish between advocacy groups. We are dealing with the form of civil society that provides hope for social transformation for democratic ends and by participatory and inclusive processes (Cohen 2010). We can find one statement of the transforming agenda of civil society in the UN Universal Declaration of Human Rights. Robert Putnam, drawing upon a Toquevillean emphasis on the efficacy and democratic nature of voluntary associations for mutual help (Putnam, Leonardi, and Nanetti 1993; Putnam 2000), stressed only the salutary political nature of associational life, especially in the development of social capital (Wood 2010). He, like Figure 23.2 and our discussion so far, ignores the civic leadership associations committed to upholding caste-like restrictions of inequality—uncivil society groups (Bob 2011). These groups suggest the dark side of social capital that bonds similar groups without bridging them to other groups. In its most ideal forms, such as Martin Luther King's 'beloved community', civil society leadership builds bridging bonds of social capital and explains that the lifting of caste restrictions liberates those upon whom they were applied and those who applied them (Orwell 1936; King 1957; Freire 1993: 27). Clearly, however, King encountered white supremacist groups, formal and informal associations, determined to resist changes in segregation and civil rights that also reside in civil society.

This brings us to one final distinction among advocacy groups. Some of them represent the realm of deliberative democracy in which principles—such as liberty, equality, accountability, and transparency—and decision-making processes—such as deliberation, bargaining, and negotiation among groups—assure that policies and decisions are justified to those who are bound by them. The values of deliberative democracy flow from reciprocal relationships in democratic politics—public spiritedness, mutual respect, and moral understanding (Gutmann and Thompson 2010: 326). The realm of deliberative democracy has an obvious relationship with the perspective of civil society that Naidoo and Bannerjee offered.

Some civil-society groups advocating social justice, however, may have to contend with other groups from all three sectors to achieve reciprocity and the capacity to participate in deliberative democracy. Thus, advocacy groups may employ tactics of contention to halt the ordinary processes of politics to have their claims against another group or sector taken seriously and thus accorded the respect that precedes deliberation. Thus, a labour union may conduct a strike. A racial, ethnic, or religious group may boycott merchants. Recent scholarship has brought these and other tactics such as social movements, protest, and revolution under the umbrella of contentious politics (McAdam, Tarrow, and Tilly 2001; Tilly and Tarrow 2006).

Rather than being distinct realms, contentious politics and deliberative democracy complement each other within civil society—although the former deals explicitly with power and violence, a point to which we will return. For the moment, let us stress the common elements of these realms with advocacy in civil society. Betsy Leondar-Wright and William Gamson suggest that the distinctive leadership of social movements functions similarly to civil-society leadership, especially advocacy groups. It provides a collective action frame of political consciousness that supports participation in collective action. The three components of this frame, listed here in a rough order from less to more similarity between social movement and civil-society leadership, include an identity component that defines a group as *we* and a set of adversaries as *they* who have responsibility for an injustice; an injustice component that is a 'hot cognition', that is laden with emotion; and, particularly significant, an agency component:

> The *agency component* (also known as empowerment or collective efficacy) refers to the belief that it is possible to change conditions or policies through collective action. Collective action frames deny the immutability of some undesirable situation and empower people by defining them as potential agents of their own history. They suggest not merely that something can be done but that *we* can do something.
>
> (Leondar-Wright and Gamson 2010: 350)

The space of civil society, which defines civic leadership, requires some degree of autonomy from government and economic actors; speaks to collective and individual interests and needs; contests the efforts of government or the economy to encroach the space of the other sectors; and brings people together individually and in associations to hidden or taken-for-granted spaces to envision and practise democratic forms of increased equality, representation, and participation in decision-making on public matters.

4 CIVIC LEADERSHIP

Working within this space, civic leadership regularly contends with existing assumptions about politics and leadership. As Dom Helder Camara (1971) pointed out, the question 'Why?', is the anthem of civil society and distinguishes it from other segments of the third sector. Of the ordinary assumptions of the political sector, the authoritative allocation of values or who gets what, when, and how (Lasswell 1936; Easton 1953), it asks: why? This question broadens the definition of politics by raising the possibility that the legitimacy of authoritative political arrangement may itself be a social, political, and economic allocation and subject to examination and political change. The way in which civil leadership challenges the cognitive and cultural forms of power and legitimacy may appear to those in formal positions of authority, and with coercive power, as criminal sabotage. It may be for this reason that the most profound reflections on peaceful social transformation often involve jails (Thoreau 1849; Dostoyevsky 1948; King 1963; Gandhi 1993; Gramsci 1998; Suu Kyi 1999). Similarly, the most iconic images of oppressive violence come from the repression of disruptive, but peaceful, dissent, such as the detention, torture, and execution of thousands of dissidents at the national soccer stadium ordered by Augusto Pinochet in 1973; the military repression of students in Tiananmen Square in 1989; and the hanging of Ken Saro-Wiwi in Nigeria in 1995.

The study of civic leadership may be as contentious to the field of leadership studies as the practice of civic leadership is to politics, because it challenges three premisses of leadership:

- Intentionality: is it leadership if someone's action sets off consequences even if they were not deliberately intended?

- Leadership without position and power: can we separate leadership from people with formal power of position and authority—and link it to the *act of leading* that anyone can undertake?
- Followers: finally, are followers always essential to leadership, as we seem to think they are? Can we have leadership without them?

The examination of these challenges probes the nature of civic leadership and some of the challenges it presents to our assumptions about politics and leadership.

Intention, Causality, and Leadership

On 17 December 2010, Mohamed Bouazizi, a Tunisian street vendor—despondent that police had confiscated the produce he was trying to sell from his wheelbarrow and that his appeals for the return of his scales were ignored—acquired gasoline, poured it on himself, and set himself and much of the Arab world ablaze. In what has become known as the Arab spring, protests in his city started immediately, grew more intense with his death on 4 January 2011, and spilled over into other nations. Ten days after Bouazizi's death, the president of Tunisia fled the country he had ruled for twenty-three years. Little less than a month later, the president of Egypt resigned. Eighteen days of citizen insurrection ended his thirty years in power. Despotic rulers in other countries yielded their power, were forced to do so, or resorted to the violent repression of protesters to fend off demands for their ouster. Bouazizi's actions instigated a series of clearly dramatic events throughout the Arab world, but was it leadership?

James MacGregor Burns suggests that it was not. Burns sets as the litmus test of leadership, especially transforming political leadership, 'the achievement of purpose in the form of real and *intended* social change' (Burns 1978: 251; emphasis added). The real social change that he has in mind brings absolute values such as freedom, liberty, and justice closer to realization by reducing or removing political, economic, and social caste-like restrictions on a group. In a later work, Burns pointed to 'the protection and nourishing of happiness, for extending the opportunity to pursue happiness to all people', as the intentional agenda of transforming leadership (Burns 2003: 3). Although the Arab spring exemplifies this agenda of transforming leadership, there is little reason to believe that Bouazizi intended this consequence of his action.

Bouazizi voiced publicly, albeit tragically, what many others dared not say; his personal troubles were public issues (Mills 1959). He did not so much lead others to make similar protests for similar reasons as much as he signalled their condition and catalysed their decision to find an alternative to despair with autocratic regimes and repressive conditions that stifled ordinary human aspirations and universally recognized human rights.

The same is true of other people who catalysed equally dramatic changes that were mostly unanticipated. For example, it is unlikely that Lech Walesa intended the dissolution of the Soviet Union when, in 1980, he scaled the fence at the Lenin Shipyard in

Gdańsk to join its striking workers. Similarly, in 1955 Rosa Parks may have had something in mind greater than maintaining her seat on the segregated bus in Montgomery, Alabama, when she refused to move further towards the back of the bus. Her intentions, however, probably did not include bringing about a year-long bus boycott and decades of struggles for the civil rights of African-Americans and other Americans that would inspire people around the world to confront forms of subordination and injustice. Clearly, the consequence of their actions exceeded their intentions. Unless we discount their actions for the central role they played in subsequent events, they challenge the assumption that leadership is linked to intended change.

Recent leadership scholarship that borrows from complexity theory also challenges the causality of leadership. Mary Uhl-Bien and Russ Marion assert that no one person, even if he or she is an apparent major figure in making new possibilities apparently necessary, can completely understand or predict the outcome of his or her action. 'Leaders [with and without authority] are *not* really in control' (Uhl-Bien and Marion 2008: pp. xvii–xix).

Despite this disconnect between intentions and causality, intentions remain central to leadership as a source of change. The deliberate efforts of Bouazizi to protest against the caste-like restrictions of his situation and that of other people like him made his actions leadership even if only a catalytic one rather than the causal factor in removing or reducing those restrictions. This interpretation of causation marks a shift from implicit or explicit assumptions about leadership as leader-centric command and control, to more process-centric and purpose-centric approaches to leadership, thus placing emphasis for the success of an initiative on behalf of shared values and common benefits on its context and environment. Leadership emerges as a necessary but not sufficient condition for change with an emphasis on its context, intention, and values rather than causality of events.

Power, Position, and Authority

All three of the people whom we are discussing had no authority for the initiative that they took for shared values and the benefit of others. This violates the assumption that leadership, especially political leadership, goes along with power, position, and authority. This hails from a venerable tradition going back to Max Weber (1946), who discussed politics in terms of the formal authority of the state and its use of physical force. Joseph Nye (2008) 'softens' power to include influence as well as coercion, but still assumes, however, that a leader has the power, position, and authority to choose influence or coercion. Bouazizi, Walesa, and Parks, however, did not have positions of authority with power and thus no choice about how to use that power. Their leadership had to do with the role they played without the ordinary accoutrements of power (Couto 1995). Thus civic leadership requires us to shift our attention from *power over* others to coerce compliance, to non-coercive *power with* others to resist coercion and caste-like restrictions. This power starts with *power within* that rejects the dominant cognitive and cultural forms that legitimize authority (VeneKlasen and Miller 2002; Gaventa 2006).

The conventional view of leadership as positional authority (rather than the act of leading) dates back to and continues the myth of heroes with its emphasis on personal traits, including charisma, and person-centric causation theories about leadership (Hook 1992; Flowers 2010). Ronald A. Heifetz regards the conflation of leadership with position and authority as the 'central source of confusion in the leadership field' (Heifetz 2007: 42). He illustrates this point in recounting the leadership of Lois, a First Nation tribal member of British Colombia, in addressing the epidemic of alcoholism within her band. Lois went out every Tuesday night for several months before her friend and babysitter Maggie got curious and followed her, with children in tow, to the tribal community centre. They saw Lois sitting in a folding chair within a circle of other chairs, all of them empty. When Lois got home, Maggie asked her what she was doing, and Lois explained that she was holding an AA (Alcoholics Anonymous) meeting. It was three years before people began attending those meetings and ten years before the room was full. Lois's example and commitment inspired Maggie, and the two of them achieved remarkable success in their efforts. Heifetz concludes his story with a paean to leadership as the action of ordinary people.

> The world is full of people like Maggie and Lois…who have exercised leadership sometimes only at key moments, and sometimes in sustained efforts, but quietly without notice…So to equate leadership with authority not only ignores a widespread and critically important social phenomenon, but also does injustice to all of these heroic people practicing necessary everyday leadership.
>
> (Heifetz 2007: 36–7)

Robert Tucker (1995) makes an equally powerful critique of another debilitating conflation, that of politics and power. Critiquing Weber, Tucker distinguished between constituted and non-constituted leaders—those with formal authority and those without it—and included both in his definition of a political leader: 'One who gives direction, or meaningfully participates in the giving of direction, to the activities of a political community' (Tucker 1995: 15). He extends the boundaries of politics beyond the state; replaces power as the foci of politics with values, the well-being of the polity; and suggests that non-constituted leadership has a large role in promoting the well-being of a political community.

In practice, non-constituted or unauthorized leadership brings 'creeping crises' (Boin et al. 2005: 16) to the attention of society and to constituted political leaders who have the authority to handle apparent or acute crises. Tucker calls this political function *signalizing*—'appraising leaders of circumstances that appear meaningful enough to merit diagnosis and response' (Tucker 1995: 31). Both non-constituted and constituted leadership have subsequent political roles in defining the attention demanding conditions and mobilizing support for their remedy. The unique authority of constituted leadership entails responsibility to prescribe action and policy and assign responsibility to carry them out. Heifetz refines the power of constituted leadership further when he explains authority as conferred power: a resource provided to a constituted leadership to do the adaptive work of responding to changes or conditions in a group's environment that challenge its well-being (Heifetz 1994: 8, 49, 57, 103).

Civic leadership, such as the examples we have used, may signal that constituted leadership has ignored or denied a creeping crisis long enough and challenge the legitimacy of its conferred power and authority. This happens in elections. When elections are not sufficient, civic leadership may devise new ways, such as advocacy and contentious politics, to express the illegitimacy of authority. These challenges shift our attention away from A's coercive power over B to the far more important cultural and cognitive dimensions of power. These dimensions construct the legitimacy of constituted and non-constituted authority and ordinarily make coercion unnecessary or, if necessary, legitimate (Foucault 1980; Tucker 1995: 79–85; Lukes 2005). Civic leadership with its ubiquitous question 'Why?' confronts the hidden dimensions of power. Steven Lukes called them the second and third dimensions of power, which operate to modify the public's wants, needs, desires, and beliefs, and politicizes culture (Lukes 2005; Calhoun 2011: 315; Gaventa 2011). Michel Foucault, like Lukes, distinguished coercive and non-coercive forms of power, sovereign and non-sovereign, and called the latter the regime of truth where we find the central problem of politics: 'detaching the power of truth from the forms of hegemony, social, economic, and cultural, within which it operates at the present time' (Foucault 1980: 133).

Despite the hegemonic appearances of power and authority as Foucault and Lukes portray them, Paulo Freire maintains another form of power that comes with the possibility of people knowing the political and social ramifications of their knowledge and culture (Freire 1993: 96; see also Horton and Freire 1990). He argues that, since the reality of non-coercive forms of power comes from a cultural process in which we all participate, there is also a possibility for the social reconstruction of reality, a pedagogy of liberation (Freire 1993: 56). The recurrence and ubiquity of civic leadership for social change suggests that Freire's hope is well founded: ordinary people, such as Lois and Maggie, can and do take unauthorized actions of leadership that challenge sovereign as well as non-sovereign forms of power. The practice of civic leadership not only broadens our understanding of the cultural and cognitive dimensions of power, position, and authority, but also suggests the non-coercive power of those without position and authority to confer and withdraw the legitimacy of authority from those with them.

Civic Leadership and Followers

When we take away position, authority, and coercive power from civic leadership, the subordination of 'followers', implied ordinarily in leadership studies, becomes problematic. Heifetz explains the inadequacy of the term 'followership' in those instances where leadership inspires the agency of others and the power within to find power with others.

> The black and white people mobilized by the Civil Rights Movement in the 1960s felt mobilized to exercise leadership themselves; and most became engaged citizens. Few,

if any, had an experience of 'followership'. In short, the term inaccurately describes a leadership that mobilizes responsibility-taking and generates more leadership.

(Heifetz 2007: 41–2).

Although specific to Civil Rights Movement in the 1960s, Heifetz's words describe the engaged people of the Arab spring and the Solidarity Movement in Poland and beyond. Lest we link civic leadership only with social movements, his observation applies to the alcoholics and addicts whom Lois and Maggie assisted to attempt their own recovery.

Burns recognizes the interdependence of leaders and followers and attempts to distinguish among them by a difference in initiative. The first, or proximal, action 'breaks up a static situation and establishes a relationship' (Burns 2003: 172). The efficacy of this first action, though, does depend upon others to take their own initiative on behalf of the values and benefits expressed, however inchoately, in that first action (Tucker 1995: 86). In this sense, civic leadership attracts other leaders, not followers, who act on their own behalf for shared values and for benefits for others like them. If they are followers, it is only because of the sequence of the discovery of their powers enabling them to take efficacious action with others. In this sense, all of leadership follows upon the initiative of others that preceded it, even if only to leave a legacy and strategy of resistance and pride in the group (Walters 2007: 152).

In addition to time as sequence, civic leadership entails space, physical (Evans and Boyte 1992; Evans 2010; Boyte 2011), psychological (VeneKlasen and Miller 2002), and, increasingly, virtual (Shirky 2009), to mobilize responsibility-taking and the initiative of others. The space of the conventional considerations of leadership is organizational with an implied hierarchy; leadership is the space above a subordinate until you get to the top of the pyramid. The spaces of civic leadership begin within people who identify with a narrative that conveys the values of a group and explains the need for action on its behalf. The narratives that legitimate marginalization, human need, and caste-like restrictions, the hidden dimensions of power, find their counter-narrative in the shared spaces of civic leadership. James Scott (1990) argues that oppressed groups, such as Bouazizi's counterparts and those of Walesa and Parks, maintain a set of 'hidden transcripts', their own knowledge of what is right and true, and hence their own power, in spite of an apparent allegiance to mechanisms of domination, the non-sovereign forms of power. 'The process of domination generates a hegemonic public conduct and a backstage discourse consisting of what cannot be spoken in the face of [coercive] power' (Scott 1990: p. xii). When public dissent or even free speech is not permissible in public, it continues in 'free spaces'—semi-public places, such as some faith-based or labour groups, and more private spaces where small groups of like-minded dissidents may gather. Sara Evans, one of the first theorists on free spaces, suggest that free spaces are

key preconditions for democratic insurgencies, and…fundamental requirements for sustaining democratic societies in the face of consolidating power in globalizing corporations and massive state bureaucracies… Free spaces are those spaces of political freedom—even when they are niches in an otherwise totalitarian context—in which people can use the freedom to speak as equals to begin the process of envisioning a democratic future that they can work toward together.

(Evans 2010: 359)

In the words of Jackie Reed, a community organizer in Chicago, leadership may be defined in terms of this provision of space. 'Leadership sets up an opportunity for others to give their gifts, for others to contribute to community' (Reed, in Couto 2002: p. xii).

John Gaventa and his colleagues at the Institute for Development Studies explore the concept of power and empowerment in connection with space. Free spaces are those spaces for political participation that marginalized groups make for themselves: sometimes publicly taken—for example, Tiananmen Square, Tahrir Square, and Plaza de Mayo—and sometimes borrowed for a political purpose—a union hall or theatre such as the Green Lantern in Prague during the Velvet Revolution. In these spaces, people rediscover the human agency that Freire holds dear—the capacity of people to make history as well as being made by it.

5 THE FUTURE OF CIVIC LEADERSHIP

Civic leadership suggests a space for politics and political associations outside the state and with power other than coercion. In its forms of advocacy and contention, civic leadership gives additional meaning to politics as the art of the possible by raising our sights to new possibilities for democratic equality and processes of representation and participation. What would a methodology look like that reflected this subject of study? It would seem to require the sociological imagination (Mills 1959) that finds public issues in personal troubles; the signaling function of civic leadership (Tucker 1995); and normative assumptions about democracy, democratic practice, power, and human agency. The validity and legitimacy of the voices of civic leadership are much more likely to be claimed by researchers employing ethnographic methods grounded in phenomenology and the social construction of meaning than by researchers wedded to modernist-empiricist assumptions of social science research (Guba and Lincoln 2000). This may mean a range of methodologies that explicitly promote democratic ends and means by not only the study *of* or even *for* civic leadership, but through participatory action research *with* and *by* civic leadership (Couto, Hippensteel Hall, and Goetz 2005). The more it reflects its subject, the more the study of civic leadership may have to deal with the authoritative allocation of values, the politics, of research. Civic leadership informs us that, behind politics, there is power.

RECOMMENDED READING

Ehrenberg, J. (1999). *Civil Society: The Critical History of an Idea*. New York: NYU Press.
Freire, P. (1993). *Pedagogy of the Oppressed*, trans. M. B. Ramos. New York: Continuum.

Tucker, R. C. (1995) [1981]. *Politics as Leadership*. Rev. edn. Columbia: University of Missouri Press.

REFERENCES

Bob, C. (2011). 'Civil and Uncivil Society', in M. Edwards (ed.), *The Oxford Handbook of Civil Society*. New York: Oxford University Press, 209–19.

Boin, A., 't Hart, P., Stern, E., and Sundelius, B. (2005). *The Politics of Crisis Management: Public Leadership under Pressure*. Cambridge: Cambridge University Press.

Boyte, H. C. (2011). 'Civil Society and Public Work', in M. Edwards (ed.), *The Oxford Handbook of Civil Society*. New York: Oxford University Press, 325–36.

Burns, J. M. (1978). *Leadership*. New York: Harper and Row.

Burns, J. M. (2003). *Transforming Leadership: A New Pursuit of Happiness*. New York: Atlantic Monthly Press.

Calhoun, C. (2011). 'Civil Society and the Public Sphere', in M. Edwards (ed.), *The Oxford Handbook of Civil Society*. New York: Oxford University Press, 311–23.

Camara, D. H. (1971). *Spiral of Violence* London and Sydney: Sheed and Ward.

Cohen, D. (2010). 'Citizen advocacy and civil society', in R. Couto (ed.), *Political and Civic Leadership: A Reference Handbook*. Thousand Oaks, CA: SAGE, 319–24.

Couto, R. (1995). 'Defining a Citizen Leader', in S. W. Morse (ed.), *Public Leadership Education: The Role of Citizen Leaders. Volume VI*. Dayton, OH: Kettering Foundation, 3–9.

Couto, R. A. (2002). *To Give their Gifts: Health, Community, and Democracy*. Nashville, TN: Vanderbilt University Press.

Couto, R. A., Hippensteel Hall, S., and Goetz, M. (2005). 'Community Change Context', in G. R. Hichman (ed.), *Leading Change in Multiple Contexts*. Thousand Oaks, CA: Sage, 163–95.

Dostoyevsky, F. (1948) [1880]. *The Grand Inquisitor on the Nature of Man*. New York: Macmillan.

Easton, D. (1953). *The Political System: An Inquiry into the State of Political Science*. New York: Knopf.

Edwards, M. (2011) (ed.). *The Oxford Handbook of Civil Society*. New York: Oxford University Press.

Ehrenberg, J. (1999). *Civil Society: The Critical History of an Idea*. New York: NYU Press.

Evans, S. M. (2010). 'Free Spaces', in R. Couto (ed.), *Political and Civic Leadership: A Reference Handbook*. Thousand Oaks, CA: Sage, 359–64.

Evans, S. M., and Boyte, H. C. (1992). *Free Spaces: The Sources of Democratic Change in America*. Chicago: University of Chicago Press.

Flowers, B. S. (2010). 'The Hero Myth', in R. Couto (ed.), *Political and Civic Leadership: A Reference Handbook*. Thousand Oaks, CA: Sage, 56–9.

Foucault, M. (1980). *Power/Knowledge: Selected Interviews and Other Writings 1972–1977*, ed. C. Gordon. New York: Pantheon.

Freire, P. (1993). *Pedagogy of the Oppressed*, trans. M. B. Ramos. New York: Continuum.

Gandhi, M. (1993). *Gandhi: An Autobiography: The Story of my Experiments with Truth*, trans. M. Desai. Boston: Beacon Press.

Gaventa, J. (2006). 'Finding the Spaces for Change: A Power Analysis', in R. Eyben, C. Harris and J. Pettit (eds), *Exploring Power for Change. IDS Bulletin*, 37/6: 23–5.

Gaventa, J. (2011). 'Civil Society and Power', in M. Edwards (ed.), *The Oxford Handbook of Civil Society*. New York: Oxford University Press, 416–27.

Gramsci, A. (1998). *Selections from the Prison Notebook*. London: Lawrence and Wishart.

Guba, E. G., and Lincoln, Y. S. (2000). 'Paradigmatic Controversies, Contradictions, and Emerging Confluences: Competing Paradigms', in N. K. Denzin and Y. S. Lincoln (eds), *Handbook of Qualitative Research*. 3rd edn. Thousand Oaks, CA: Sage, 163–88.

Gutmann, A., and Thompson, D. F. (2010). 'Deliberative Democracy', in R. Couto (ed.), *Political and Civic Leadership: A Reference Handbook*. Thousand Oaks, CA: Sage, 325–32.

Heifetz, R. (1994). *Leadership without Easy Answers*. Cambridge, MA: Belknap Press.

Heifetz, R. A. (2007). 'The Scholarly/Practical Challenge of Leadership', in R. Couto (ed.), *Reflections on Leadership*. Lanham, MD: University Press of America, 31–44.

Hook, S. (1992). *The Hero in History: A Study in Limitation and Possibility*. New Brunswick, NJ: Transaction Publishing.

Horton, M., and Freire, P. (1990). *We Make the Road by Walking: Conversations on Education and Social Change*. Philadelphia: Temple University Press.

King, M. L., Jr (1957). 'Justice without Violence' <http://mlk-kpp01.stanford.edu/>. Last accessed 7 August 2013.

King, M. L. Jr (1963). 'Letter from a Birmingham Jail' <http://www.africa.upenn.edu/Articles_Gen/Letter_Birmingham.html>. Last accessed 7 August 2013.

Lasswell, H. D. (1936). *Politics: Who Gets What, When, How*. New York: P. Smith.

Leondar-Wright, B., and Gamson, W. A. (2010). 'Social Movements', in R. Couto (ed.), *Political and Civic Leadership: A Reference Handbook*. Thousand Oaks, CA: Sage, 349–358.

Lukes, S. (2005). *Power: A Radical View*. 3rd edn. New York: Macmillan.

McAdam, D., Tarrow, S., and Tilly, C. (2001). *Dynamics of Contention*. Cambridge: Cambridge University Press.

Mills, C. W. (1959). *The Sociological Imagination*. New York: Oxford University Press.

Naidoo, K., and Bannerjee, S. (2010). 'Civil Society', in R. Couto (ed.), *Political and Civic Leadership: A Reference Handbook*. Thousand Oaks, CA: Sage, 37–46.

Nussbaum, M. (2000). *Women and Human Development*. Cambridge: Cambridge University Press.

Nye, J. S., Jr (2008). *The Powers to Lead*. New York: Oxford University Press.

Orwell, G. (1936). 'Shooting an Elephant' <orwell.ru/library/articles/elephant/english/e_eleph>. Last accessed 24 January 2012.

Putnam, R. D. (2000). *Bowling Alone: The Collapse and Revival of American Community*. New York: Simon and Schuster.

Putnam, R. D., Leonardi, R., and Nanetti, R. (1993). *Making Democracy Work: Civic Traditions in Modern Italy*. Princeton: Princeton University Press.

Rawls, J. (1971). *A Theory of Justice*. Cambridge, MA: Harvard University Press.

Salamon, L. M., Sokolowski, S. W., et al. (2004). *Global Civil Society: Dimensions of the Nonprofit Sector*. Bloomfield, CT: Kamarian Press.

Schmid, H. (2009). 'The Contingencies of Nonprofit Leadership', in P. 't Hart, J. Kane and H. Patapan (eds), *Dispersed Democratic Leadership: Origins, Dynamics and Implications*. New York: Oxford University Press, 193–210.

Scott, J. C. (1990). *Domination and the Arts of Resistance: Hidden Transcripts*. New Haven, CT: Yale University Press.

Sen, A. (1999). *Development as Freedom*. Oxford: Oxford University Press.

Shirky, C. (2009). *Here Comes Everybody: The Power of Organizing without Organizations*. New York: Penguin.

Strauss, L., and Cropsey, J. (1987). *History of Political Philosophy*. 3rd edn. Chicago: University of Chicago Press.

Suu Kyi, A. S. (1999). *Voice of Hope: Conversations with Alan Clements*. New York: Seven Stories Press.

Thoreau, H. D. (1849). 'On the Duty of Civil Disobedience' <www.gutenberg.org/files/71/71-h/71-h.htm>. Last accessed 18 January 2012.

Tilly, C., and Tarrow, S. (2006). *Contentious Politics*. New York: Paradigm

Tucker, R. C. (1995) [1981]. *Politics as Leadership*. Rev. edn. Columbia, MO: University of Missouri Press.

Uhl-Bien, M., and Marion, R. (2008). *Complexity Leadership: Part 1. Conceptual Foundations*. Charlotte, NC: Information Age.

VeneKlasen, L., and Miller, V. (2002). *A New Weave of Power, People and Politics*. Oklahoma City, OK: World Neighbors.

Walters, R. (2007). 'Leadership from the Bottom up', in R. Couto (ed.), *Reflections on Leadership*. Lanham, MD: University Press of America, 149–62.

Weber, M. (1946). 'Politics as a Vocation', in *From Max Weber: Essays in Sociology*, trans. H. H. Gerth and C. Wright Mills. New York: Oxford University Press, 77–128 [originally published as monograph, 1919].

Wood, C. (2010). 'Social Capital', in R. Couto (ed.), *Political and Civic Leadership: A Reference Handbook*. Thousand Oaks, CA: Sage, 619–628.

CHAPTER 24

PARTY AND ELECTORAL LEADERSHIP*

MARINA COSTA LOBO

1 PARTY LEADERSHIP: A LONG-NEGLECTED TOPIC

THE relationship between parties, society and political institutions has evolved dramatically during the twentieth century, and a large literature has tried to capture that change. This chapter will examine the importance of leaders for political parties in the second decade of the twenty-first century. In so doing, it will focus on two interconnected areas: on the importance of leaders for party organization, and on the electoral arena. Existing studies on party leadership can be divided into two groups. Authors who work on party organization seldom draw on research carried out in the field of electoral research, and vice versa. Without an integrated understanding of the factors, it is not possible fully to explain the way leadership is exercised in parties. Leaders, to an extent, are defined by their followers. Indeed, it would be difficult to understand the nature of leadership in parties without trying to understand the importance that electors attribute to them, since, in any democracy, an important part of a leader's followers are the voters who chose her (or her party) at the ballot box.

Before analysing the state of the art in the discipline, it is important to note that in studies of both party organization and the electoral arena there seems to have been some reticence in recognizing the role of leaders in parties. To a significant extent, democratic arrangements and their study are about limiting the possibility of despotic behaviour, abuses of power, and the concentration of authority around any individual leader. This is not to say that democracy, or democratic theory, does not recognize a role for political

* This chapter was written in the context of the project 'The personalisation of politics in the XXIst century—A Research Project on Democratic Elections—PTDC/CPJ-CPO/120295/2010' funded by Fundação para a Ciência e Tecnologia (FCT).

leaders, but it does so reluctantly (Ruscio 2008). In addition, within the electoral studies literature, it is often implicit that voters should be driven by their social anchors, and/or concern themselves exclusively with issues, rather than use leaders as a cue for voting, presumably because social anchors and issues are seen as political cues, whereas leaders are not. Recognition of leaders is also scant, owing to the fact that leadership is comparatively difficult to define: '[it] is the unidentifiable in pursuit of the indefinable' (Elgie 1995: 2). Yet, the definition of leadership has been dealt with extensively, involving the wielding of political power to influence, direct, or alter the authoritative values within that society. Moreover, leadership typologies also have a rather long tradition in political science, from Weber's definition of charismatic leadership to Burns's distinction between transactional versus transformational leadership (Weber 1968; Burns 1978). A more recent strand of the literature, borrowing from business studies, has explored the concept of 'toxic leadership' (Heppell 2011), seeking to deconstruct the inherent positive light in which the concept of 'leadership', when it is actually studied, is often regarded in political science. However well defined leadership has been, it does seem that its rather abstract qualities make it a difficult topic in a discipline that has been moving fast towards quantification of phenomena.

This reluctance has had negative repercussions on the scholarly attention given to leaders in studies of parties and elections. For example, the recent *Handbook of Party Politics* (Katz and Crotty 2006), a comprehensive volume on political parties, does not include a chapter on party leadership, even though its importance is recognized in the chapters that deal with party organization (Katz and Crotty 2006: pt 3, pp. 249–348). The segmented and rather incipient nature of studies on party and electoral leadership mean that the chapter will necessarily reflect the state of the discipline. Nonetheless, it is the chapter's aim to show that slowly but surely those who study parties and elections within political science are coming to terms with the reality of 'leaders mattering'.

The chapter starts by setting the intellectual background in both areas, and surveying the main developments in the discipline. Next, the concept of personalization and the way it has been discussed by recent literature are examined. The following section presents four volumes published in the early 2000s, which can be considered to be landmark contributions to the field. The chapter ends with a discussion on future areas of research.

2 THE HISTORICAL AND INTELLECTUAL CONTEXT

Most research on party leadership has a marked European and US bias, thus much of what is discussed in this chapter is applicable only to advanced industrial democracies. Within these studies, scholars have not defined party leadership equally. In the field of electoral behaviour, it is mostly equated with the individual party leader, normally the main candidate who leads the party in an election; in studies of party organization, the party leadership is often understood in broader terms: it may include the top organs of the party.

Leaders and Party Organization

The idea that parties as organizations tend towards a concentration of power in the hands of leaders dates back to Michels (1971), who followed in the footsteps of Weber's wider study (1968) of political leadership. Michels proposed an 'iron law of oligarchy' inherent in the functioning of parties, owing to the logic of organizations. Tendentially, leaders would take control of the decision-making processes and the channels of information, instituting a top-down power structure within parties, while invalidating the principle of democratic, bottom-up, decision-making in parties (Farrell 2006). Thus, the idea of personalization is not new at all. What are new are the form and the causes of this phenomenon, which most recent studies have highlighted.

In past research, a substantial number of party typologies have been but forward, but this production has not developed into a more general theory on the transformation of political parties (Krouwel 2006: 150). Maurice Duverger (1954) first characterized the mass party as a response to the emergence of the universal suffrage in Western democracies. The mass party was innovative in that it drew its strength and originated from specific groups in civil society, in direct contrast with the parliamentary, cadre parties of nineteenth-century Europe. Although originally the mass party was essentially a creation of the left of the ideological spectrum, its emphasis on territorially spread organizations seeking to mobilize electors and encapsulate social groups was soon followed on the right—namely among Christian Democratic parties.

Since the decline of the mass or social integration party, the party types put forward (namely, the catch-all, the electoralist, or the movement parties) emphasize this shift of power towards the leaders within the party organization, which is mirrored by a decreased importance of members within the organization (Kirchheimer 1966; Panebianco 1988; Kitschelt 1995).

The electoralist party emerged from key literature in the mid-1960s that tried to account for party transformations—namely, Epstein's 'contagion from the right' (1967); Kirchheimer's characterization (1966) of the catch-all party; and Panebianco's 'electoral–professional party' (1988). Parties belonging to this type are organizationally thin, maintaining a relatively skeletal existence except at election time. They use modern campaign techniques, stressing television and mass-communications media, over mobilization of party members in order to win votes. The electoralist party is characterized also by the large importance that the party leadership acquires for election purposes (Gunther and Diamond 2001: 185).

Even in movement parties, or anti-systemic parties, leaders tend to be fundamental. Within this type, extreme-right-wing parties stand out for their lack of institutionalization, and their dependence on the personality of a charismatic leader (Kitschelt 1995).

Leaders and Electoral Behaviour

As party scholars have tried to characterize the changing importance of leaders for party organization, an equivalent line of enquiry has investigated whether leaders have become more important as explanatory factors in voting choice.

Campbell's funnel of causality is considered a fundamental framework to conceptualize individual decisions on the vote (Campbell et al. 1960) and is the basis for an extensive array of election studies in the world (see Comparative Studies of Election Systems (CSES) at <www.umich.edu/cses>). In that framework, long-term socio-economic conditions structure society broadly into social divisions such as class, race, ethnic group, or religiosity. These social conditions shape individuals' group loyalties—that is, through membership of a class, or religious group, his or her attitudes and consequent political behaviour. Given these, Campbell et al. explain voting decisions in terms of three attitudes: partisanship, issue opinions, and candidate evaluations (Dalton 2002: 173). This model assumes that there is a causal relationship between the various long- and short-term factors. That is, the determinants reinforce each other: belonging to a certain social group will make certain political attitudes more likely. These attitudes then feed into party attachment, appraisal of candidates, and position on issues.

One of the first studies to dispute the stability model (Franklin, Mackie, and Valen 1992: 2) described a 'new political world in which social cleavages no longer condition partisanship as was once the norm'. In consequence, questions arose on whether other factors—particularly issue positions and candidate preferences—had become more important in determining voting choice (Dalton 2002: 212). Thus, both in studies on party organization, as well as in electoral behaviour, leaders have been emerging as an important research topic. Next we will survey the main ideas debated in each of these subfields.

3 Understanding Party Leadership: Mapping The Terrain

Key Concepts about Leaders in Party Organization

New party models put forward since the demise of the mass party tend to emphasize the importance of leadership for the party organization, and a concomitant decline in the importance of membership. Not all studies concur, however, with some studies dismissing the idea that parties function hierarchically (Katz and Mair 1994: 18). Parties have different faces: namely, the party on the ground (membership), the party organization (central staff), and the party in office (incumbents). Thus, the question of which face of the party is becoming more powerful is misleading, since what may be occurring is a growing autonomy of parties (Katz and Mair 1994: 17). For these authors, intra-party relationships have become *stratarchical*—that is, parties include diverse strata, each functioning on its own sphere of influence.

The party type that accompanies this perspective on party change is the cartel party (Katz and Mair 1995). It tries to capture a fundamental distancing of the party from the electorate, and a growing dependence on the state's resources for its survival.

Accordingly, those components of the party that are represented in the state become more important: 'colluding parties become agents of the state and employ the resources of the state to ensure their own survival' (Katz and Mair 1994: 5). Organizationally, the cartel party is very similar to the electoralist party. However, it is even less ideological, less dependent on members, and more reliant on professional campaigning for vote mobilization. On the latter point, there is research on the way leaders exercise a 'permanent campaign', even as incumbents, which highlights the importance of the 'leader brand' for the party's success (Ingram and Lees-Marshment 2002; Needham 2005). It is, however, unclear what the role of leadership in this party type is, since the main attention is given to the party in the state. The cartel party thesis, as well as the idea that parties have become stratarchical, have been widely discussed in subsequent literature (Katz and Mair 2009), even though the extent to which the stratarchy can be maintained in a world of ever-dwindling party membership remains to be seen.

On the subject of leaders' selection, there has been a lot more work on candidates (Katz 2001; Rahat and Hazan 2001) than on leaders themselves, perhaps, as Cross and Blais (2012: 129) argue, owing to the fact that in many parties there have been significant changes to the way in which leaders are elected since the 1990s. The selection of leaders is important, because parties are gatekeepers to the polity's highest executive office. It is also the case that the methods of selection have important consequences for leaders' survival (Bynander and 't Hart 2007; Cross and Blais 2012). Extant research has shown that the emergence of more open methods of leader selection (LeDuc 2001; Kenig 2009) has resulted in several consequences for the health of party organizations. Putative gains in grass-roots participation in leader choice have come at the expense of the capacity of party activists to control the leadership, thus contributing to a hollowing-out of the party organization (Marsh 1993: 230; Mair 1994: 16). Notwithstanding the trend that has been identified, there is still scant comparative research on the topic, with most studies being single case studies (Kenig 2009: 434).

Key Concepts about Leaders in Electoral Behaviour

Within the literature on electoral stability and change described in the previous section, an increasing number of studies have begun to track the importance of leader effects, defined as the increment in variance explained, which can be attributed to the leader of a given party in a comprehensive model of voting behaviour.

One of the problems of this research is that it is often not cumulative. Leader effects have not been calculated in the same way across all studies, sometimes being measured as leader barometers, and at other times as an index of leader traits. The first method is a simple like–dislike 0 to 10 scale for each leader and is all-encompassing. As such, it has been criticized for including a significant amount of party and political predispositions. Even so, there are good strategies to ensure that the scale can be used, provided a multivariate model of analysis is employed. The second method is to measure leader traits, which are purportedly much closer to what is in fact intended to be calculated—that is, what is added by a leader qua leader, in terms of a particular trait, or set of traits to a party choice.

Not only do studies vary in the way that the heuristic for leader effects is chosen, but it is also not clear what exactly counts as leader effects. King notably distinguishes between gross and net leader effects. Gross effects are those that measure leader effects for individual voters of a given party, whereas net effects are the measurement of whether leaders were decisive for a given election's outcome (King 2002: 41). Moreover, the studies of leaders, which deal with magnitude, have seldom been comparative, and rarely longitudinal. Both reasons have made it comparatively difficult either to confirm or to falsify the personalization thesis, which involves a time dimension.

The (non-cumulative) findings have been accumulating in this area of electoral studies, although not consensually. McAllister (1996: 281) argues that 'public perceptions of leaders, if not decisive, have a modest but significant influence on the vote'. Also Dalton (2002: 209), finds evidence from certain elections in the USA, Britain, France, and Germany that point to the *growing* importance of candidate evaluations even in parliamentary systems. Others are not so sure: on the basis of evidence for the importance of leaders in the USA, Britain, Germany, France, and Russia, King (2002: 216) concludes that, 'far from being normal, it is quite unusual for leaders' and candidates' personalities to determine election outcomes—not rare but unusual'. Dalton, McAllister, and King are not necessarily at odds with each other, since they are trying to measure different things: the first two authors are stating that appraisals of leaders matter, while King is measuring the importance of leaders for deciding the outcome of an election.

The evidence on the importance of candidate appeal varies between and within countries. In the USA, a landmark study, *The American Voter* (Campbell et al. 1960), established voters as minimally interested in politics, voting on the basis of partisan predispositions, largely inherited from their parents, or candidate characteristics. An updated version of the volume, *The American Voter Revisited* (Lewis-Beck et al. 2008: 426–7), also seconds the view that candidate characteristics continue to be important vote factors, more than forty years later. Other scholars, however, contend that, in the USA, the importance of candidates is rather limited for the outcome of presidential elections. In particular, Wattenberg found that US presidential candidates mattered little for vote choices and the outcome of elections in the Reagan–Bush era. These presidential contests were determined by performance and perceptions on incumbency rather than perceptions on leader personality (Wattenberg 1991: 134). This minimalist view on the importance of candidates has been also corroborated by Miller and Shanks (1996).

For the UK, the evidence is no more consensual. Some authors contend that supposedly parliamentary elections are now effectively presidential contests (Bean and Mughan 1989; Mughan 2000; Stewart and Clarke 2000; Clarke et al. 2004). However, this claim has been contested (Bartle 2002; Bartle and Crewe 2002; King 2002). In other countries, such as Germany (Brettschneider and Anderson 2006), Spain (Rico 2009), or Portugal (Lobo 2006), evidence has been gathered that points to the importance of leader effects.

More recently, a large comparative study has found that leaders do matter for voter choice (Bittner 2011). Using character traits as independent variables in the large pooled multi-country, multi-election dataset, in a fully comprehensive model of voting behaviour, it is found that leaders are systematically a relevant factor for vote choice. Not only that, but leaders also have a relevant impact on party success and electoral outcomes.

The trend of personalization, however, does not simply state that leaders matter. It implies *the growing importance* of leaders in vote choices. The comparative studies that have actually tried empirically to test this claim reach quite cautious conclusions (Curtice and Holmberg 2005; Aarts, Blais, and Schmitt 2011). The Curtice and Holmberg study analyses the importance of leader effects in the following countries: Britain, Germany, the Netherlands, Denmark, Norway, and Sweden, from the 1960s to the 1990s, and concludes that 'voters' evaluations of party leaders appear to be as important or unimportant now as they were when they were first measured by the series of surveys we have been analysing' (Curtice and Holmberg 2005: 252). It is difficult to test more widely the 'personalization' thesis, given that it hinges on the availability of longitudinal data series, which exist mostly in long-established consolidated democracies.

In the 2000s, there has been a move from the study of magnitude to the study of contexts within which electoral choices are made (Barisione 2009). It is worth distinguishing between micro—that is, individual—and macro—that is, institutional contexts.

At the micro-level, a frequently tested hypothesis proposes that those who rely on leaders as cues for voting would be the less sophisticated voters (Campbell et al. 1960; Nie, Verba, and Petrocik 1976). Those who have little information on the issues at stake in a campaign would be more inclined to vote according to their sympathies towards a given candidate. Conversely, those who have more political information would pay less attention to personal characteristics, and use their knowledge on the political landscape to inform their vote choice. Recent research has begun to show that, on the contrary, it is those with most political knowledge that tend to be more sensitive to leader effects (Kroh 2004; Bittner 2011). An interesting hypothesis was recently put forward by Clarke et al. (2009: 174–6), which nonetheless could not be fully proven: that leader effects might follow a curvilinear pattern, with voters with moderate levels of political expertise experiencing the largest effect. Leader effects would be lowest for voters with low levels of expertise, since we would expect that political cues would not affect them. Effects would also be lower at the high end of voter sophistication voters, since these rely on other sources of information that require higher levels of expertise.

A parallel hypothesis that has been tested involves the degree of exposure to the media by electors, with those most exposed expected to exhibit higher leader effects. The main idea is that the ubiquity of television, which stresses image over content, has served to increase the importance of leaders for voting behaviour. Initial research (Mughan 2000) argued that the increasing use of television for political communication purposes was contributing to the greater leader effects. However, again little consensus has been found, with other authors contesting the importance of the media in enhancing leader effects for voting (Kroh 2004; Curtice and Hunjan 2007).

At the macro-level, leaders matter more in presidential and semi-presidential regimes than in parliamentary ones. In a parliamentary context, however, as might be expected, leadership evaluations appear to be more important where a majoritarian electoral system is in place or where the battle for power is focused on two parties (Curtice and Holmberg 2005; Curtice and Hunjan 2007), or on the type of parties that exist: catch-all versus electoralist (Lobo 2008). Research shows that there are indeed statistically significant differences in the importance of leader effects concerning mass-based parties (class-mass and denominational) and catch-all parties. An enquiry on the importance of leader effects for extreme-right-wing parties found negative results (van der Brug and Mughan 2007). Looking at the relative impact of three populist extreme-right-wing parties in the Netherlands, in three different elections the authors found little evidence of a disproportional effect of leaders for electors choosing these parties.

It seems then that there is no consensus about the importance of leaders in either the party or the electoral studies literature, although greater unanimity seems to exist in the first rather than in the second field. Party organization studies have remained generalist and typological, whereas, in the electoral field, the research has moved decisively into research on the conditionality of leader effects.

4   FOUR KEY CONTRIBUTIONS

The main idea that has been developed and tested in both area of studies is that of *personalization*, which seeks to identify leaders not only as important, but as *increasingly* important for political parties, from the perspective of both party organization as well as electoral effects (Karvonen 2010). A similar term, which is not exactly synonymous, is that of *presidentialization*—that is, the process whereby parliamentary regimes are becoming more presidential in their actual practice without, in most cases, changing their formal structure—that is, their regime type (Mughan 2000; Poguntke and Webb 2005; Blick and Jones, this volume). There are three arenas where leaders may have become more important: in government, in the party, and in elections (Poguntke and Webb 2005). It is possible to say, then, that presidentialization encompasses the two phenomena being surveyed in this chapter.

According to the party organization as well as the electoral studies literature, personalization is a consequence of several factors. First, the documented decline in structures and long-term forces that shape electors' loyalties to political parties has had a large impact in raising the importance of leaders both for party organization and for the way elections are fought. Second, the continuous and growing mediatization of the political process, especially during political campaigns (Swanson and Mancini 1996), is held responsible for the growing attention attributed to leaders. According to Farrell (2006: 123), campaigns in Europe are following an Americanizing trend, which implies an emphasis on the candidate and the candidate's personal campaign organization. The introduction of television, and especially the widespread use of televised debates among the main party candidates, have arguably contributed to the centrality of leaders during campaigns (LeDuc, Niemi, and Norris 1996; Garzia 2011). Third, the overall downsizing of the state since the late 1980s, and globalization, paradoxically, have led to a more central and visible role for leaders, as they perform as states' representatives across the globe in international forums (Poguntke and Webb 2005: 16). Fourth, internal party change has further personalized politics. Parties have responded to exogenous pressures for more visibility to candidates with reforms that reinforce the role of leaders (Webb 2002). Nonetheless, as shown above, the concept of personalization has not commanded a consensus in either subfield.

We now discuss four key books that have been important in advancing knowledge and debates on party and electoral leadership. In the book by Dalton and Wattenberg, *Parties without Partisans* (2000), the recent changes in party organization and their consequences for the political system as a whole are analysed. In it, Scarrow documents the fall in party membership that has occurred across established party systems since the 1960s. Also, Webb and Farrell account for changes in parties as campaign organizations. The huge mediatization of politics in general and campaigns in particular has forced parties' organization to adapt. Since the 1980s, campaigns changed from exercises in mass mobilization toward professionally managed enterprises that sought to project the best possible image.

In the same volume, Scarrow, Webb and Farrell test directly the growth in the importance of leaders for party organization. In an age where political debates are increasingly populist in tone, the degree to which party leaders and their policies can claim that they have a mandate from their membership may be viewed as particularly important (Dalton and Wattenberg 2000: 132). Thus, they expect that leaders 'balance upward power shifts with attentiveness to members' political privileges' (p. 132). They look at three arenas where leaders may have attempted that strategy: candidate selection, leadership selection, and policy-making. In the case of candidate selection, the authors do not find a lot of evidence of centralization of decisions, but that is due to the fact that the procedures have been centralized from the outset. Concerning *leader* selection, the authors expect that more leaders will be directly elected by ordinary members. This trend would purport greater autonomy for the party leadership, while simultaneously enhancing a symbolic greater power to ordinary members (see e.g. Mair 1994). These ordinary members, once they elect the party leader, are unlikely to mount any opposition to the leadership. Scarrow, Webb, and Farrell however, do not find unequivocal evidence that parties are moving in this direction (p. 143). In a more recent study, though more limited in scope, Cross and Blais (2012) find that the decision to broaden the selectorate has been made by most parties in the UK, Canada, and Ireland, while parties in Australia and New Zealand have generally resisted reform. Regarding policy-making, there is some evidence of party leaderships extending inclusiveness over policy formation as a means of stifling internal debate. The authors conclude that overall there is evidence of a growth in the power of party leadership.

A second important contribution has been Poguntke and Webb's *The Presidentialization of Politics* (2005). In this edited volume, the editors and authors test the presidentialization hypothesis in Britain, Germany, Italy, Spain, the Low Countries,

Denmark, Sweden, Canada, France, Finland, Portugal, Israel, and the USA (Poguntke and Webb 2005: 3). They encounter a clear-cut trend in the growth of leaders' power within, and autonomy from, their parties. Leaders of governing parties have enjoyed a growth in intra-party power and autonomy, or these were already high and have remained so (p. 343). On the issue of electoral presidentialization, three components were considered—namely, campaigning trends, media coverage of leaders, and finally the importance of leaders for electoral behaviour. In this respect, leaders have become more important in the first two components with an increase in leadership images in campaigns and media coverage (p. 345).

Thirdly, originating in the electoral behaviour literature, another important comparative contribution to the field was Anthony King's *Leaders' Personalities and the Outcomes of Democratic Elections* (2002). It included chapters on the USA, Britain, France, Germany, Canada, and Russia, and analysed the degree to which leaders are determinant for the outcomes of elections. As stated in the conclusion, 'approximately four dozen elections are covered...of these it is possible to say in the cases of scarcely more than a handful that their outcomes definitely or probably turned on voters' differing perceptions of the personal qualities and traits of the principal party leaders and candidates' (King 2002: 216). The evidence from all countries suggests that issues of performance and issues of policy loom much larger in most voters' minds than do the issues of personality (King 2002: 220). King concludes that leaders matter for the way in which they have an impact on their party's policies and government programmes, more than they matter for being telegenic, media-friendly, or even charismatic figures.

Finally, almost ten years later, Aarts, Blais, and Schmitt (2011) edited *Political Leaders and Democratic Elections*, with a similar goal. The volume uses election surveys over the previous fifty years to assess systematically the impact of political leaders on voting decisions in nine democracies (United States, Britain, Canada, Germany, the Netherlands, Norway, Spain, Sweden, and Australia). It analyses issues such as the changes in political communication (particularly the rise of televised politics), and the relative importance accorded to political leaders in different types of political systems. It demonstrates how electoral systems and other political institutions have a discernible effect on the importance that voters accord to actual political leaders. It is argued that the characteristics of political leaders, parties, and indeed voters themselves are not important for voting patterns. These findings, important as they are, may not have settled the issue. Thus it seems that the scholarly shift to a fully comparative, longitudinal, and contextual analysis of leaders has not reduced the amount of controversy, which should mean greater discussion in the future for this subfield. We turn next to this issue.

5 A Promising Future?

Leaders have not been the focus of a large number of studies, and existing research has not been consensual. Among scholars who investigate party organization, there seem to be differences between those who argue that organization has become increasingly hier-archical and leader-centred as membership has dwindled; and those who put forward a stratarchical view of political parties. In the electoral field, the dominant view of early studies concerning leader effects' magnitudes was that they mattered, but seldom for the outcome of elections. More recently, research has concentrated on both institutional and individual contexts, although once again without much agreement. The challenge remains to combine both the insights of electoral behaviour within the party organiza-tion literature and vice versa. Leaders act in context, and the electoral arena, as well as the type of party to which they belong, are essential components of the context that will determine their leadership.

If we look at both subfields, there seems to be a different discourse: whereas the idea of personalization or presidentialization tends to be common in studies of party organi-zation, it is less so in electoral studies. What does it mean, for example, to know that extreme-right-wing parties organize around a strong leader (Kitschelt 1995), and at the same time that these types of parties do not distinguish themselves in terms of leader effects (van der Brug and Mughan 2007)? Future research should try to encompass both aspects of party change—that is, the way in which organization has an impact on elec-tions, and viceversa.

Finally, in most studies, the significance of leader effects for the quality of the demo-cratic process is seldom addressed. If leaders are found to matter, then it is necessary to understand what that tells us about the democratic process. Is a growing importance of leaders detrimental or beneficial to democracy? That is perhaps the fundamental ques-tion to which political scientists in this field should seek to answer.

ESSENTIAL READING

Aarts, K., Blais, A., and Schmitt, H. (2011) (eds). *Political Leaders and Democratic Elections*. Oxford: Oxford University Press.

Dalton, R., and Wattenberg, M. (2000). *Parties without Partisans*. Oxford: Oxford University Press.

Poguntke, T., and Webb, P. (2005). *The Presidentialization of Politics: A Comparative Study of Modern Democracies*. Oxford: Oxford University Press.

REFERENCES

Aarts, K., Blais, A., and Schmitt, H. (2011) (eds). *Political Leaders and Democratic Elections*. Oxford: Oxford University Press.

Andersen, R., and Evans, G. (2003). 'Who Blairs Wins? Leadership and Voting in the 2001 Election', *British Elections and Parties Review*, 13: 229–47.

Barisione, M. (2009). 'So what Difference do Leaders Make? Candidates' Images and the Conditionality of Leader Effects on Voting', *Journal of Elections, Public Opinion and Parties*, 19/4: 473–500.

Bartle, J. (2002). 'Why Labour Won—Again', in A. King (ed.), *Britain at the Polls 2001*. Chatham, NJ: Chatham House, 164–206.

Bartle, J., and Crewe, I. (2002). 'The Impact of Party Leaders in Britain: Strong Assumptions, Weak Evidence', in A. King (ed.), *Leaders' Personalities and the Outcomes of Democratic Elections*. Oxford: Oxford University Press, 70–95.

Bean, C., and Mughan, A. (1989). 'Leadership Effects in Parliamentary Elections in Australia and Britain', *American Political Science Review*, 83/4: 1659–79.

Bittner, A. (2011). *Platform or Personality? The Role of Party Leaders in Elections*. Oxford: Oxford University Press.

Brettschneider, Neller, and Anderson, C. (2006). 'Candidate Images in the 2005 German National Elections', *German Politics*, 15/4: 481–99.

Burns, J. M. (1978). *Leadership*. New York: Harper and Row Publishers.

Bynander, F., and 't Hart, P. (2007). 'The Politics of Party Leader Survival and Succession: Australia in Comparative Perspective', *Australian Journal of Political Science*, 42/1: 47–72.

Campbell, A., Converse, P., Miller, W., and Stokes, D. (1960). *The American Voter*. Chicago: University of Chicago Press.

Clarke, H. D., Sanders, D., Stewart, M., and Whiteley, P. (2004). *Political Choice in Britain*. Oxford: Oxford University Press.

Clarke, H. D., Sanders, D., Stewart, M., and Whiteley, P. (2009). *Performance Politics and the British Voter*. Cambridge: Cambridge University Press.

Cross, W., and Blais, A. (2012). 'Who Selects the Party Leader', *Party Politics*, 12/2: 127–50.

Curtice, J., and Holmberg, S. (2005). 'Party Leaders and Party Choice', in J. Thomassen (ed.), *The European Voter: A Comparative Study of Modern Democracies*. Oxford: Oxford University Press, 235–54.

Curtice, J., and Hunjan, S. (2007). 'O impacto das avaliações dos lideres no comportamento de voto. Qual a importância das regras?', in A. Freire, M. C. Lobo, and P. Magalhães (eds), *Eleições e Cultura Política*. Lisbon: Imprensa de Ciências Sociais, 227–73.

Dalton, R. J. (2002). *Citizen Politics*. New York: Chatham House.

Dalton, R., and Wattenberg, M. (Eds) (2000). *Parties without Partisans*. Oxford: Oxford University Press.

Duverger, M. (1954). *Political Parties*. New York: Wiley.

Elgie, R. (1995). *Political Leadership in Liberal Democracies*. London: Macmillan.

Epstein, L. (1967). 'Political Parties in Western Democratic Systems', in Roy Macridis (ed.), *Political Parties: Contemporary Trends and Ideas*. New York: Harper and Row.

Evans, G., and Andersen, R. (2005). 'The Impact of Party Leaders: How Blair Lost Labour Votes', *Parliamentary Affairs*, 58: 818–36.

Farrell, D. (2006). 'Political Parties in a Changing Campaign Environment', in R. Katz and W. Crotty (eds), *Handbook of Political Parties*. London: Sage, 122–33.

Franklin, M., Mackie, H., and Valen, H. (1992). *Electoral Change: Responses to Evolving Social and Attitudinal Structures in Western Countries*. Cambridge: Cambridge University Press.

Garzia, D. (2011). 'The Personalisation of Politics in Western Democracies: Causes and Consequences on Leader–Follower Relationships', *Leadership Quarterly*, 22/4: 697–709.

Graetz, B., and McAllister, I. (1987). 'Popular Evaluations of Party Leaders in the Anglo-American Democracies', in H. Clarke and H. Czudnowski (eds), *Political Elites in Anglo American Democracies*. DeKalb, IL: Northern Illinois University Press, 44–64.

Gunther, R., and Diamond, L. (2001). 'Species of Political Parties: A New Typology', *Party Politics*, 9/3: 167–99.

Gunther, R., and Montero, J. R. (2001). 'The Anchors of Partisanship', in N. Diamandouros and R. Gunther (eds), *Parties, Politics and Democracy in the New Europe*. Baltimore, MD: Johns Hopkins University Press, 83–153.

Heppell, T. (2011). 'Toxic Leadership: Applying the Lipman-Blumen Model to Political Leadership', *Representation*, 47/3: 241–9.

Ingram, P., and Lees-Marshment, J. (2002). 'The Anglicisation of Political Marketing: How Blair 'Out-Marketed' Clinton', *Journal of Public Affairs*, 2/2: 44–56.

Karvonen, L. (2010). *The Personalisation of Politics*. London: European Consortium for Political Research (ECPR) Press.

Katz, R. (2001). 'The Problem of Candidate Selection and Models of Party Democracy', *Party Politics*, 7: 277–96.

Katz, R., and Crotty, W. (2006). *Handbook of Party Politics*. London: Sage.

Katz, R., and Mair, P. (1994). *How Parties Organize*. London: Sage.

Katz, R., and Mair, P. (1995). 'Changing Models of Party Organization and Party Democracy: The Emergence of the Cartel Party', *Party Politics*, 1: 5–28.

Katz, R., and Mair, P. (2009). 'The Cartel Party Thesis: A Restatement', *Perspectives on Politics*, 7/4: 752–66.

Kenig, O. (2009). 'Classifying Party Leaders' Selection Methods in Parliamentary Democracies', *Journal of Elections, Public Opinion and Parties*, 19: 433–47.

King, A. (2002). *Leaders' Personalities and the Outcome of Democratic Elections*. Oxford: Oxford University Press.

Kirchheimer, O. (1966). 'The Transformation of the Western European Party Systems', in J. Palombara and M. Weiner (eds), *Political Parties and Political Development*. Princeton: Princeton University Press, 177–200.

Kitschelt, H. (1995). *The Radical Right in Western Europe: A Comparative Analysis*. Ann Arbor, MI: University of Michigan Press.

Kroh, M. (2004). 'Personal Voting: Individual and Contextual Determinants of Political Leadership', Working Paper, Deutsches Institut für Wirtschaftsforschung (DIW) Sozio-oekonomisches Panel (SOEP). Berlin: DIW.

Krouwel, A. (2006). 'Party Models', in R. Katz and W. Crotty (eds), *Handbook of Party Politics*. London: Sage, 249–70.

LeDuc, L. (2001). 'Democratizing Party Leadership Selection', *Party Politics*, 7/3: 323–41.

LeDuc, L., Niemi, P., and Norris, P. (Eds) (1996). *Comparing Democracies: Elections and Voting in Global Perspective*. Thousand Oaks, CA: Sage.

Lewis-Beck, M., Jacoby, W., Norpoth, H., and Weisberg, H. (2008). *The American Voter Revisited*. Ann Arbor, MI: University of Michigan Press.

Lobo, M. C. (2006). 'Short-Term Voting Determinants in a Young Democracy: Leader Effects in Portugal in the 2002 Legislative Elections', *Electoral Studies*, 25/2: 270–86.

Lobo, M. C. (2008). 'Parties and Leader Effects: The Impact of Leaders in Different Types of Parties', *Party Politics*, 14/3: 281–98.

McAllister, I. (1996). 'Leaders', in L. LeDuc, P. Niemi, and P. Norris (eds), *Comparing Democracies: Elections and Voting in Global Perspective*. Thousand Oaks, CA: Sage, 280–96.

Mair, P. (1994). 'Party Organizations: From Civil Society to the State', in R. Katz and P. Mair (eds), *How Parties Organize: Change and Adaptation in Party Organizations in Western Democracies*. London: Sage, 1–22.

Marsh, M. (1993). 'Introduction: Selecting the Party Leader', *European Journal of Political Research*, 24/3: 229–31.

Michels, R. (1971). *Les Partis politiques: Essai sur les tendances oligarchiques des démocraties.* Paris: Flammarion.

Miller, W., and Shanks, J. (1996). *The New American Voter.* Cambridge, MA: Harvard University Press.

Mughan, A. (2000). *Media and the Presidentialization of Parliamentary Elections.* Basingstoke: Palgrave.

Mughan, A. (2009). 'Partisan Dealignment, Party Attachments and Leader Effects', *Journal of Elections, Public Opinion and Parties,* 19/4: 413–31.

Needham, C. (2005). 'Brand Leaders: Clinton, Blair and the Limitations of the Permanent Campaign', *Political Studies,* 53: 343–61.

Nie, N., Verba, S., and Petrocik, J. (1976). *The Changing American Voter.* Cambridge, MA: Harvard University Press.

Panebianco, A. (1988). *Political Powers: Organization and Power.* Cambridge: Cambridge University Press.

Poguntke, T., and Webb, P. (2005). *The Presidentialization of Politics: A Comparative Study of Modern Democracies.* Oxford: Oxford University Press.

Rahat, G. and Hazan, R. (2001). Candidate selection methods: an analytical framework. *Party Politics,* 7: 297–322.

Rico, G. (2009). *Líderes políticos, opinión pública y comportamiento electoral en España.* Madrid: Centro de Investigaciones Sociológicas.

Ruscio, K. (2008). *The Leadership Dilemma in Modern Democracy.* London: Edward Elgar.

Scarrow, S. (2000). 'Parties without members?', in R. Dalton and M. Wattenberg (eds), *Parties without Partisans.* Oxford: Oxford University Press, 79–101.

Stewart, M., and Clarke, H. (2000). 'The (Un)Importance of Party Leaders: Leader Images and Party Choice in the 1987 British Election', *Journal of Politics,* 54/2: 447–70.

Swanson, D., and Mancini, P. (1996). *Politics, Media and Modern Democracy.* Westport, CT: Praeger.

Thomassen, J. (2005) (ed.). *The European Voter: A Comparative Study of Modern Democracies.* Oxford: Oxford University Press.

Van Biezen, I., and Mair, P. (2002). 'Party Membership in Twenty European Democracies 1980–2000', *Party Politics,* 7: 5–21.

Van Biezen, I., Mair, P., and Poguntke, T. (2012). 'Going, Going, Gone…the Decline of Party Membership in Contemporary Europe', *European Journal of Political Research,* 51: 24–56.

Van der Brug, W., and Mughan, A. (2007). 'Charisma, Leader Effects, and Support for Right Wing Populist Parties', *Party Politics,* 13/1: 29–51.

Wattenberg, M. (1991). *The Rise of Candidate-Centred Politics: Presidential Elections of the 1980s.* Cambridge, MA: Harvard University Press.

Webb, P. (2002). 'Conclusion: Political Parties and Democratic Control in Advanced Industrial Societies', in P. Webb, D. Farrell, and I. Holliday (eds), *Political Parties in Advanced Industrial Democracies.* Oxford: Oxford University Press, 438–60.

Webb, P., Farrell, D., and Holliday, I. (2002). *Political Parties in Advanced Industrial Democracies.* Oxford: Oxford University Press.

Weber, M. (1968). *On Charisma and Institution Building,* ed. S. Eisenstadt. Chicago: University of Chicago Press.

CHAPTER 25

POPULISM AND POLITICAL LEADERSHIP

CAS MUDDE AND
CRISTÓBAL ROVIRA KALTWASSER

1 INTRODUCTION

LIKE so many terms commonly used in the social sciences, populism is an essentially contested concept. While many scholars employ the concept of populism to refer (exclusively) to radical right parties in Europe, such as the Northern League in Italy or Austria's Freedom Party, others use the term to allude to radical social movements, such as the Occupy Wall Street and Tea Party movements in the United States. At the same time, populism is widely used in Latin America to draw attention not only to a 'dangerous' type of economic development, characterized by the implementation of an unsustainable type of redistributive policies, but also to the formation of multi-class constituencies by powerful leaders exploiting anti-elitist sentiments. Moreover, populism has become a popular term used in political and public debates to taint political opponents; and sometimes to claim democratic credentials.

This short overview of different ways in which the concept of populism is employed reveals that defining populism is anything but simple. Nevertheless, many scholars argue that, above and beyond its diverse manifestations, a defining attribute of populism is its reliance on leaders able to mobilize the masses and/or conduct their parties with the aim of enacting radical reforms. From Venezuelan President Hugo Chávez to Dutch politician Geert Wilders, populism seems always guided by a strong person. After all, by talking like 'the common people', populist actors have the ability to present themselves as the voice of a (silent) majority, whose ideas and interests are not being addressed by the establishment.

Although most manifestations of populism do give rise to usually flamboyant and strong political leaders, the link between political leadership and populism is not straightforward. In fact, it would be erroneous to equate populism with charismatic or strong leadership. In this chapter we will try to shed light on this complex relationship, arguing, in the main, that neither charismatic nor strong leadership is inherent to populism. While it is true that these elements are relevant in most manifestations of populism, we maintain that populism is first and foremost a Manichean world view or ideology that assumes that society is characterized by a distinction between 'the pure people' and 'the corrupt elite'. While this ideology has often been professed, most successfully, by charismatic or strong political leaders, it is inherently about the belief of different groups in society and not a type of political leadership for society.

This chapter consists of six sections. We begin by offering an overview of the most common conceptual approaches that have been developed in the scholarly debate. Here we examine in particular the place that leadership plays in the definitions of populism, before developing our own conceptual approach. In the following section we present some historical and contemporary examples of the relationship between populism and leadership. We then argue that charismatic leadership is a facilitator rather that a defining feature of populism and analyse the conceptions of democracy that populist actors and constituencies tend to favour. We subsequently deal with the complex relationship between populism, leadership, and gender, focusing in particular on the Latin American phenomenon of *caudillismo*. Finally, we pay attention to the oft-ignored phenomenon of leaderless populism, which is particularly common in the USA. We close the chapter with a short conclusion.

2 DEFINING POPULISM

Before we offer an overview of different concepts of populism, two caveats are in order. First, presenting and discussing all the definitions of populism that have been developed in the scholarly debate would be a titanic endeavour. The problem is not only the multitude of definitions at hand, but also the fact that most scholars tend to employ the notion of populism because of its rhetorical force rather than its analytical leverage. Second, given that almost all concepts of populism have been developed by scholars specializing in a particular case (for example, Peronism) and/or region (for example, Western Europe or North America), the existing definitions usually do not 'travel' well when it comes to studying populism in different places and times. It is only recently that scholarship has paid attention to this problem and tried to develop a concept able to grasp the common core of all manifestations of populism. With these caveats in mind, we will refer to the four most common conceptual approaches, according to which populism is defined as a discourse, a pathology, a style, or a strategy.

When we talk about populism as a discourse, we are dealing with a conceptual approach that emphasizes that populism should be defined as a set of ideas. From this angle, populism is first and foremost a mental map that holds that powerful elites are acting against the interests of the people. Take, for instance, the position of Michael Kazin (1995: 1), a well-known scholar on US populism, who defines the latter as 'a language whose speakers conceive of ordinary people as a noble assemblage not bounded narrowly by class, view their elite opponents as self-serving and undemocratic, and seek to mobilize the former against the latter'. As this quotation shows, the discursive approach conceives of populism as a particular interpretation about the nature of the political world, in which the 'the common people' are being exploited by the establishment.

Another option is to define populism as a pathology, or, to be more specific, as a democratic malformation or disease. Often described in medical and psychological language, populism is seen as a dangerous political force that not only criticizes the existence of an inevitable gap between the governors and the governed, but also proposes irresponsible and even authoritarian solutions to overcome the problems that democracies tend to face. In this vein, Pierre Rosanvallon (2008: 265) argues that populism 'is a perverse inversion of the ideals and procedures of democracy', because it uses the notion of popular sovereignty and the principle of majority rule to attack the ideas, institutions, and practices of political representation. According to this view, the emergence of populism is directly related to the health of the democratic system.

A third conceptual approach, which is widespread in both the social sciences and the media, refers to populism as a particular political style, which helps politicians and parties to stay in tune with their constituencies by appealing to emotional clues, employing spin doctors, and proposing simplistic solutions to complex problems. According to this view, Tony Blair and his New Labour project in the UK are a prime example of contemporary populist leadership, since his government not only relied on plebiscitarian techniques of winning support from the electorate, but also exerted a massive top-down intervention within the Labour Party to avoid criticisms to the policies implemented by the Prime Minister (Mair 2002). Allegedly, this populist style of politics is becoming increasingly widespread in contemporary democracies, because it seems impossible to please the voters and win elections without showing a minimal degree of opportunism and demagogy.

Finally, some have argued that populism alludes not to a particular style of politics, but rather to a deliberated strategy employed by skilful political actors. For example, Kurt Weyland (2001: 14) defines populism as 'a political strategy through which a personalistic leader seeks or exercises government power based on direct, unmediated, uninstitutionalized support from large numbers of mostly unorganized followers'. He developed this concept with the aim of explaining the prevalence of populism in Latin America, a region where many leaders win elections because of their capacity directly to mobilize the people, rather than by obtaining the support of political parties. Seen in this light, populism is a strategy that permits the rise of political entrepreneurs, who are able to form a coalition of a number of very heterogeneous social groups that blame the establishment for the country's social ills.

What do these different definitions tell us about the relationship between populism and leadership? At least the last two conceptual approaches assume that populism is directly linked to flamboyant and strong figures. In fact, those who define populism as a style or strategy are prone to argue that it is impossible to think of populism without strong leaders, in terms of their ability both to catch the attention of the people and to control the political organization behind them. This is particularly evident in the conceptualization of populism as a strategy, because here the idea is that a political actor develops a well-thought-out plan with the aim of seducing the electorate and bypassing the institutions that are at odds with his will. Interestingly, this idea also appears in the definition of populism as a pathology, although in a more indirect manner: the populist disease is usually incarnated by a strong leader, whose rise to power might well lead to the fall of democracy.

The link between populism and leadership is also present in the case of the discursive approach, since many are of the opinion that populism should be considered as an artificially constructed set of ideas, which is employed by political actors and/or organic intellectuals to manipulate society. It is worth noting, however, that not all scholars who adhere to the discursive approach share the idea that populism is an ideology constructed from above by strong and charismatic leaders. As Kirk Hawkins (2010) has pointed out, many people believe in the populist discourse and often have good reasons for doing so. Put in another way, under certain circumstances there is a real demand for populism, so that the leader is not the creator but rather the *vehicle* for the promotion and establishment of the populist set of ideas.

In line with the discursive approach, but in contrast to other definitions within this approach, we propose a *minimal* concept of populism, which fosters cross-regional and cross-temporal studies of populism (Mudde and Rovira Kaltwasser 2012). Populism is defined as 'a thin-centered ideology that considers society to be ultimately separated into two homogenous and antagonistic camps, "the pure people" and "the corrupt elite", and which argues that politics should be an expression of the *volonté générale* (general will) of the people' (Mudde 2004: 543). This definition is capable of avoiding the two main problems in comparative populism studies: conceptual travelling (that is, the application of concepts to new cases) and conceptual stretching (that is, the distortion that occurs when a concept does not fit the new cases). Indeed, most populist leaders and movements identified in the mainstream literature meet our definition.

By conceiving of populism as a 'thin-centered' ideology, we follow Michael Freeden's approach (1996), which is helpful for understanding the oft-alleged malleability of the concept. Indeed, populism should be seen as a Manichean world view that maintains a parasitic relationship with other concepts and ideologies. This is why populism can be both right-wing and left-wing. Populism has three core concepts: the people, the elite, and the general will. While the concepts of 'the people' and 'the elite' function like empty vessels that can be filled in various ways (that is, different manifestations of populism have different views regarding who does belong and does not belong to both the people and the elite), the notion of 'the general will' alludes to the very idea that all individuals *as a whole* unify their wills and are able to identify a common interest (Canovan 2005).

Finally, it is worth indicating that elitism and pluralism are the two direct opposites of this conceptualization of populism. Elitism shares populism's Manichean distinction between 'the elite' and 'the people', but assumes that the elite is intellectually and morally superior to the dangerous and vulgar people. Pluralism takes for granted that societies are composed of different individuals and groups, but is sceptical about the existence of 'a unified will of the people'. These two direct opposites of populism—elitism and pluralism— are helpful to draw clear boundaries and foster empirical research. By way of illustration, although certain scholars have argued that Tony Blair, Bill Clinton, and Gerhard Schröder should be seen as populist actors (e.g. de Beus 2009), the definition advanced here contradicts this statement. After all, these leaders might have behaved opportunistically in certain occasions, but they supported pluralism and did not attack the establishment.

3 POPULISM AND LEADERSHIP IN TIME AND PLACE

Throughout time and space, populism has manifested itself in many different guises, not least in terms of political leadership. The two first populist movements, the Russian *Narodniki* and the US Populists, were very different, but both were characterized by the absence of a dominant leader (e.g. Taggart 2000). The *Narodniki* were essentially a small collective of urban intellectuals who moved to rural areas to be among 'the true people' (that is, the peasants), while the American Populists were a loose collection of mostly peasants who, in part, found political expression in the short-lived People's Party (1891–1908). Tellingly, rather than putting up one of its own leaders, the American Populists endorsed William Jennings Bryan as a 'fusion' candidate of both the People's Party and the Democratic Party for the presidential elections in 1896.

While no major populist leaders or movements have reappeared in Russia since the fall of the *Narodniki*, itself a fairly marginal phenomenon, populism has shown a remarkable capacity to re-emerge and take very different shapes in the USA. As Michael Kazin (1995) has pointed out, populist ideas are an important element of the American political culture, which have been used by many political actors across the twentieth century. However, at least since the mid-twentieth century, conservatives have been much more proactive than progressives in attacking 'the corrupt elite' and mobilizing 'the pure people'. A similar development can be noticed in Canada, where left-wing populism played an important role between the 1930s and 1960s, but since then right-wing populism has become predominant (Laycock 2005).

By contrast, European populism is a relatively new phenomenon, which has appeared only after the fall of the Berlin Wall in many countries. Before the 1980s there were probably only two very clear examples of populism in Europe: on the one hand, the populist peasant movements that appeared in several parts of Eastern Europe and the Balkans in the inter-war years, and, on the other hand, the populist movement leaded by Pierre Poujade in France in the 1950s. Both examples were different with regard to political leadership. While the Eastern European populist peasant movements relied on strong grass-roots networks, Poujade's populist movement was heavily dependent on his own figure.

Compared to the rest of the world, Latin America is probably the region with the richest tradition of populist leaders, movements, and parties. In fact, the scholarship of Latin American politics has identified 'three waves of populism' in the region: classic populism of the 1930s and 1960s (for example, Juan Domingo Perón in Argentina and José María Velasco Ibarra in Ecuador), neo-liberal populism of the 1990s (for example, Alberto Fujimori in Peru and Fernando Collor de Mello in Brazil), and radical leftist populism since the beginning of the new millennium (for example, Hugo Chávez in Venezuela and Evo Morales in Bolivia). Although all these cases have employed the populist ideology, they show important variations concerning who belongs to 'the pure people' and who to 'the corrupt elite'. At the same time, these different populist experiences have supported not only divergent policy proposals, but also leftist and rightist political projects (de la Torre 2010).

In addition to these differences, one commonality among all forms of Latin American populism is the relevance of strong and powerful leaders, often referred to as *caudillos* in the academic and public debate. While populist movements and parties do exist in the region, individual leaders tend to play a key role, monopolizing power and portraying themselves as the incarnation of the 'unified will of the people'. In many cases the official party is nothing more than a shell, completely dependent upon and subjugated to the populist leader. A good example is former Peruvian president, Alberto Fujimori, who won three consecutive presidential elections by building a new party organization for each electoral cycle, showing that 'there could be no Fujimorismo without Fujimori' (Roberts 2006: 93). The few notable exceptions, in which populist parties outlive their original leader, include the Peronist Justicialist Party (PJ) in Argentina and the American Popular Revolutionary Alliance (APRA) of Víctor Raúl Haya de la Torre in Peru.

The predominance of populist leaders with subservient movements also seems prevalent in the new democracies in Africa and Asia (Mizuno and Phongpaichit 2009). A prime example is the former Thai prime minister Thaksin Shinawatra, whose Thais Loves Thais (TRT) party was officially disbanded in 2007, after Shinawatra himself had been ousted and exiled by a military coup. Since then, the unofficial successor, the For Thais Party (PTP), run by his sister Yingluck, has been his personal vehicle for indirect political power in Thailand. Similar successful populist politicians exist in Africa, most notably Ugandan President Yoweri Museveni and Zambian President Michael Sata. In just a few cases, populist leaders have emerged within established (non-populist) political parties, such as South African President Jacob Zuma (ANC), South Korean President Roh Moo-hyun (MDP), and Taiwanese President Chen Sui-Bian (DPP).

In most contemporary Western democracies, with the notable exception of the United States, populism finds its most prominent expressions in political parties, often built around a prominent leader. In many cases these dominant leaders are also (among) the party founders, such as Pauline Hanson and One Nation in Australia, Jean-Marie Le Pen and the National Front (FN) in France, Silvio Berlusconi and Forza Italia in Italy, and Geert Wilders and the Party for Freedom (PVV) in the Netherlands. However, while particularly founding leaders tend to dominate populist parties, many such parties have either outlived their founding leader or never had an overarching leader. For example, the Belgian Flemish Interest (VB) literally outlived its founder Karel Dillen, while the leader of the Danish People's Party (DFP), Pia Kjærsgaard, is certainly important to the party's success, but she is not particularly dominant. In some cases a populist politician will take over an existing political party, changing not only the ideology of the party, but also its style of leadership. For instance, Jörg Haider transformed the Austrian Freedom Party (FPÖ) into a populist radical right party with a dominant leader, as happened with the Swiss People's Party (SVP) under Christoph Blocher (e.g. Mudde 2007).

In summary, an elective affinity between populism and a strong leader seems to exist. However, the former can exist without the latter. Indeed, sometimes populist leaders have been quite successful in terms of winning elections and changing the political agenda, but their very existence will become superfluous, since a new political cleavage comes to the fore: populism versus anti-populism. For instance, the rise of Perón in Argentina gave rise to a new political cleavage, which is orthogonal to the left–right distinction (Ostiguy 2009). Not by coincidence, Argentina has seen the appearance of populist presidents supporting right-wing (Carlos Menem) and left-wing (Néstor and then Christina Kirchner) governments since the return to democracy in 1983. This means that under certain circumstances the rise of populist actors can contribute not only to the breakdown, but also to the realignment and reconfiguration, of the party system.

4 CHARISMATIC LEADERSHIP AND POPULIST DEMOCRACY

Charismatic leadership is a fiercely contested topic in the social sciences in general, and in the study of populism in particular. Many accounts of populism emphasize the importance of charismatic leaders (e.g. Weyland 2001), even within Europe, where populist leaders often function within relatively well-organized political parties (e.g. Taggart 1995). Yet several other scholars of European populism argue that ideology (or discourse) is at least as important as personality, and some even denounce the whole concept of charisma as imprecise or even tautological (e.g. Van der Brug, Fennema, and Tillie 2005).

In a strict Weberian interpretation, charismatic leadership refers to 'the authority of the extraordinary and personal *gift of grace* (charisma), the absolutely personal devotion and personal confidence in revelation, heroism, or other qualities of individual leadership' (Weber 1992: 5). Weber believed that charismatic leadership would thrive particularly in times of crisis, when people would seek refuge in the specific characteristics of certain individuals, often political outsiders, rather than in the traditional sources of authority (that is, custom and statute). Weber's theory of charismatic leadership has strongly influenced scholarship on populism, although this is not often explicitly acknowledged. One of the more developed theoretical accounts in this tradition is

José Pedro Zúquete's study of 'missionary politics', which sees Europe's contemporary populist radical right parties as 'sacred defenders of their communities, driven toward a holy mission and composed of a devoted followership around a charismatic leader' (Zúquete 2007: 233).

Various electoral studies have shown the importance of individual leaders for the electoral success of populist parties, giving way to terms such as 'l'effect Le Pen' (Plenel and Rollat 1984) and the 'Haider Phenomenon' (Sully 1997). The question is whether this is proof for the charismatic leadership thesis, which in the strict Weberian interpretation refers to a personal bond between the leader and his or her followers. In other words, do these voters indeed merely follow the populist leader, or do they support the broader party ideology as well? Given the fact that many of these parties have exceptionally loyal supporters, and both the FN and FPÖ seem to have been able to hang on to most of their supporters despite a change in leadership, classic charismatic leadership seems less important than is often stated.

Some scholars have argued that charismatic leadership can be institutionalized within political parties, leading to 'charismatic parties' rather than mere charismatic leaders (Pedahzur and Brichta 2002). Given the existing diversity in organizational structures within the populist party family, it would go too far to argue that populist parties are by definition charismatic parties, however. Others have focused on the internal rather than the external effects of charismatic leadership, arguing that certain populist leaders have 'coterie charisma', which ties an inner core of activists to a specific leader (Eatwell 2002). This would enable this 'charismatic' leader to overcome internal divisions within a broader movement. Examples of populist leaders with this coterie charisma would be FN-leader Jean-Marie Le Pen and Vladimir Zhirinovsky, leader of the ill-named Liberal Democratic Party of Russia (LDPR).

In addition, scholars have argued that populist leaders promote the formation of a particular political regime, which should be called 'populist democracy' (e.g. Mair 2002). Allegedly, this model of democracy is characterized by a strong and charismatic leader, who is able to represent 'the unified will of the people', and, in consequence, should govern without power restrictions. Otherwise stated, since the leader embodies the interests of the majority, no institution should constrain him. To a certain extent, this type of democracy is quite similar to the model of 'leader democracy' advanced by András Körösényi (2005). After all, both populist and leader democracy share a basic assumption: politics is primarily about the conflict between rival elites, who continuously try to shape and produce the electoral preferences of the people themselves. Hence, *the people* is seen as a passive entity that is activated and mobilized from above.

Not all manifestations of populism, however, show sympathy for 'leader' or 'populist' democracy. By way of illustration, whereas in certain cases populism coexists with grass-roots networks that are quite autonomous and limit the room of manœuvre of the chief executive (for example, Evo Morales in Bolivia), there are other examples in which populism follows a top-down dynamic and the leader can govern almost without constraints (for example, Hugo Chávez in Venezuela). In this sense, rather than supporting a specific model of democracy, those who adhere to populism tend to favour majoritarian and participatory conceptions of democracy, and are prone to disdain deliberative and liberal conceptions of democracy (Rovira Kaltwasser forthcoming). Moreover, most manifestations of populism have a difficult relationship with electoral and egalitarian conceptions of democracy, since populist constituencies and leaders are prone to depict their foes as illegitimate actors, who should not have the right to participate in elections or have access to public resources. After all, populism is above all a *moral* set of ideas.

5 Populism, *Caudillismo*, and Gender

Latin American populism has often been analysed through the lens of *caudillismo*, a generic term with roots in the Latin *caput* (head), which is normally employed to allude to a particular type of politics characterized by a strong leader, who not only exercises a power that is independent of any office and free on any constraint, but who also tends to develop patron–client relationships (Lynch 1992). Factors like deep economic crises or the existence of a political vacuum favour the rise of *caudillos*, who, helped by their charisma, attempt to keep political forces under control by promoting allegiance to the person of the leader. Moreover, the notion of *caudillismo* emphasizes that the leader depicts himself as a masculine and potentially violent figure. Hence, by using sexual symbols and vulgar language, the *caudillo* seeks to idolize the values of 'the common people'.

The notion of *caudillismo* is useful for interpreting the history of Latin America, and, to some extent, also current developments in this world region. However, it should not be equated with populism. While the *caudillismo* refers to a specific type of leadership, which relies on charisma and clientelism, populism denotes an ideology that assumes that society is characterized by a Manichean distinction between 'the pure people' and 'the corrupt elite'. Many studies of Latin American populist leaders and parties take for granted that the development of patron–client relationships is a defining attribute of populism. However, clientelism is a political strategy that has been used by Latin American political parties that both do adhere (for example, the Peronist Justicialist Party in contemporary Argentina) and do not adhere (for example, the Independent Democratic Union in contemporary Chile) to the populist ideology.

At the same time, the notion of *caudillismo* is normally related not only to strong leadership, but also to authoritarianism. In fact, Juan Manuel de Rosas in Argentina (1793–1877), Porfirio Díaz in Mexico (1830–1915), and even Francisco Franco in Spain (1892–1975) are common examples of *caudillos* in the scholarly literature. All these leaders can be considered as absolute rulers exercising personal power, and thus anything but democrats. By contrast, populist leaders in Latin American maintain an ambivalent relationship with democracy: while they tend to promote the incorporation of marginalized sectors into society and defend (the realization of) elections, they are also prone to disregard the rules of public contestation, particularly when it comes to tolerating the forces that oppose populism (Rovira Kaltwasser 2012). Consequently, the authoritarianism characteristic of *caudillismo* is not inherent to populism.

Although it is true that *caudillismo* and populism should not be conflated, there are some interesting parallels between both phenomena, particularly with regard to gender. Indeed, Latin American populist leaders are predominantly male and they are prone to draw upon masculine models, including the vulgar man, the priest, the father, and the military man. Not by coincidence, as Espina and Rakowski (2010) have recently pointed out, President Chávez projected an image of women as self-sacrificing mothers and housewives nurturing their children and giving birth to a new Venezuela. In summary, Latin American populist leaders commonly have an ambivalent discourse with respect to gender: on the one hand, they tend to favour the idea of justice for everyone regardless of race or gender, and, on the other hand, they tend to defend traditional female and masculine roles.

6 LEADERLESS POPULISM

While populism is closely associated with strong political leaders, there is a long tradition of leaderless populism, particularly in the United States. In itself, this makes perfect sense, as populism stresses government by the people, for the people, and is intrinsically suspicious (though not necessarily negative) of political representation. After all, populism is always essentially about getting rid of a corrupt elite that impedes the formation of the general will.

Although the United States has had its share of populist leaders, though often at the state level (such as Governor Huey Long in Louisiana), almost all significant populist *movements* have been largely leaderless (e.g. Kazin 1995). The Populists of the 1880s emerged spontaneously and were mostly loosely and regionally organized. Lacking a single leader with cross-regional appeal, they supported a relative outsider for the presidential elections of 1896.

Similarly, the two key populist movements of today, the right-wing Tea Party and the left-wing Occupy Wall Street, emerged spontaneously and function without a strong leader. While many politicians have tried to become the unofficial leader of the Tea Party, and some factions within the movement have supported certain individual politicians as voices of the Tea Party (most notably former Alaskan governor Sarah Palin), the movement remains leaderless. Similarly, the Occupy Wall Street movement jealously guards its leaderless status, despite criticism that this undermines its political effectiveness.

While leaderless populism is strongest in the United States, it can be found around the world, most notably in more or less spontaneous (and often short-lived) protest movements that attack the (local) elite in the name of the (local) people. Recent examples include the amorphous coalition protesting against the 'stuttgart 21' project in Germany, the so-called White Marches in Belgium, the various anti-austerity-measures protests in

Europe and Israel, and even the spontaneous protest movements that collectively constitute the Arab Spring. In all these cases an important section of the social movement is populist, attacking a corrupt elite in the name of the pure people, but essentially leaderless, in the sense that no one leader (or even group of leaders) speaks for the whole movement. In almost all cases the movements explode on the scene, generate a quick but short-lived buzz, and quickly disappear, giving rise to more organized, and often less populist, organizations.

7 CONCLUSION

Populism has appeared in different times and places. Allegedly, one of the few commonalities between all the different manifestations of populism is the existence of a charismatic and strong leader, who is able to mobilize the masses and control the political organization behind him. In this chapter we have argued instead that this type of leadership is *not* a defining attribute of populism. We defined populism as an ideology or world view that assumes that society is characterized by a Manichean division between 'the pure people' and 'the corrupt elite'. This means that populism is not always constructed from above—that is, by a powerful leader; many societies count a significant number of people who believe in the populist set of ideas, irrespective of the presence of a populist leader.

Accordingly, populism exists with various types of leadership and can even be leaderless. This is particularly evident in social movements that employ the populist ideology, such as the Tea Party or Occupy Wall Street. In this case, populism operates as a 'master frame' through which very different groups develop a common identity, but without a visible leader commanding the movement. But it is also true that there are many examples of populism in which a strong leader is key for mobilizing the people and (re)founding political organizations specialized in fostering a direct and unmediated relationship with the electorate (for example, Fujimori in Peru or Pim Fortuyn in the Netherlands). In addition, there are cases of strong party organizations supporting a populist leader, who does not (yet) have absolute autonomy when it comes to developing policy proposals and implementing political reforms (for example, the Austrian Freedom Party or the Bolivian Movement for Socialism).

In this chapter we have argued that charisma is not a defining attribute of populism. While it is true that the success of many populist parties and movements is related to the existence of charismatic leaders, the latter are also relevant for *non*-populist parties and movements. Hence, charisma facilitates the rise of populist ideas, but it also makes the formation of strong populist organizations more difficult. Moreover, there seems to be an elective affinity between strong male leaders and populism. Indeed, the most famous examples of populism are usually related to masculine figures such as José María Velasco Ibarra in Ecuador, Silvio Berlusconi in Italy, and Hugo Chávez in Venezuela. However, the link between male leadership and populism must not be seen as 'sociological law'.

There are cases of populism in which women play an important role, like Pia Kjærsgaard of the Danish People's Party (DFP), Pauline Hanson of One Nation in Australia, and Sarah Palin in the USA.

In summary, the link between political leadership and populism is much more complicated, as much of the literature suggests. Given that populism is an ideology that has appeared in different times and places, a great variety of concrete manifestations of populism exist. This means that the historical and regional context in which populism arises is key for understanding its specific characteristics, including the type of political leadership. Thus, future studies should examine under which conditions populism fosters or hinders the emergence of strong leadership. At the same time, cross-regional research could help to identify subtypes of populism, which not only defend particular conceptions of 'the pure people' and 'the corrupt elite' but also show different leadership styles and approaches to deal with the presence or absence of strong leaders.

RECOMMENDED READING

Canovan, M. (2005). *The People*. Cambridge: Polity.

De la Torre, C. (2010). *Populist Seduction in Latin America: The Ecuadorian Experience*. 2nd edn. Athens, OH: Ohio University Press; second edition.

Mény, Y., and Surel, Y. (2002) (eds). *Democracies and the Populist Challenge*. Basingstoke: Palgrave.

Taggart, P. (2000). *Populism*. London: Open University Press.

REFERENCES

Canovan, M. (2005). *The People*. Cambridge: Polity.

De Beus, J. (2009). 'Populist Leadership'. in J. Kane, H. Patapan, and P. 't Hart (eds), *Dispersed Democratic Leadership. Origins, Dynamics, and Implications*. Oxford: Oxford University Press, 83–103.

De la Torre, C. (2010). *Populist Seduction in Latin America: The Ecuadorian Experience*. 2nd edn. Athens, OH: Ohio University Press.

Eatwell, R. (2002). 'The Rebirth of Right-Wing Charisma? The Cases of Jean-Marie Le Pen and Vladimir Zhirinovsky', *Totalitarian Movements and Political Religions*, 3/3: 1–23.

Espina, G., and Rakowski, C. A. (2010). 'Waking Women Up? Hugo Chávez, Populism, and Venezuela's "Popular" Women', in K. Kampwirth (ed.), *Gender and Populism in Latin America: Passionate Politics*. University Park, PA: Pennsylvania State Press, 180–201.

Freeden, M. (1996). *Ideologies and Political Theory: A Conceptual Approach*. Oxford: Clarendon.

Hawkins, K. (2010). *Venezuela's Chavismo and Populism in Comparative Perspective*. Cambridge: Cambridge University Press.

Kazin, M. (1995). *The Populist Persuasion: An American History*. Ithaca, NY: Cornell University Press.

Körösényi, A. (2005). 'Political Representation in Leader Democracy', *Government and Opposition*, 36: 559–82.

Laycock, D. (2005). 'Populism and the New Right in English Canada', in F. Panizza (ed.), *Populism and the Mirror of Democracy*. London: Verso, 172–201.

Lynch, J. (1992). *Caudillos in Spanish America, 1800–1850*. Oxford: Clarendon Press.

Mair, P. (2002). 'Populist Democracy vs Party Democracy', in Y. Mény and Y. Surel (eds), *Democracies and the Populist Challenge*. Basingstoke: Palgrave, 81–98.

Mény, Y., and Surel, Y. (2002) (eds). *Democracies and the Populist Challenge*. Basingstoke: Palgrave.

Mizuno, K., and Phongpaichit, P. (2009) (eds). *Populism in Asia*. Singapore: National University of Singapore Press.

Mudde, C. (2004). 'The Populist Zeitgeist', *Government and Opposition*, 39/4: 541–63.

Mudde, C. (2007). *Populist Radical Right Parties in Europe*. Cambridge: Cambridge University Press.

Mudde, C., and Rovira Kaltwasser, C. (2012) (eds). *Populism in Europe and the Americas: Threat or Corrective for Democracy?* Cambridge: Cambridge University Press.

Ostiguy, P. (2009). 'Argentina's Double Political Spectrum: Party System, Political Identities, and Strategies, 1944–2007', *Kellogg Institute Working Paper*, 361.

Pedahzur, A., and Brichta, A. (2002). 'The Institutionalization of Extreme Right-Wing Charismatic Parties: A Paradox?', *Party Politics*, 8/1: 31–49.

Plenel, E., and Rollat, A. (1984). *L'Effet Le Pen*. Paris: La Découverte.

Roberts, K. (2006). 'Do Parties Matter? Lessons from the Fujimori Experience', in J. F. Carrión (ed.), *The Fujimori Legacy: The Rise of Electoral Authoritarianism in Peru*. University Park, PA: Pennsylvania State University Press, 81–101.

Rosanvallon, P. (2008). *Counter-Democracy: Politics in an Age of Distrust*. New York: Cambridge University Press.

Rovira Kaltwasser, C. (2012). 'The Ambivalence of Populism: Threat and Corrective for Democracy', *Democratization*, 19/2: 184–208.

Rovira Kaltwasser, C. (forthcoming). 'Latin American Populism: Some Conceptual and Normative Lessons', *Constellations*.

Sully, M. A. (1997). *The Haider Phenomenon*. Boulder, CO: East European Monographs.

Taggart, P. (1995). 'New Populist Parties in Western Europe', *West European Politics*, 18/1: 34–51.

Taggart, P. (2000). *Populism*. London: Open University Press.

Van der Brug, W., Fennema, M., and Tillie, J. (2005). 'Why Some Anti-Immigrant Parties Fail and Others Succeed: A Two-Step Model of Aggregate Electoral Support', *Comparative Political Studies*, 38/5 537–73.

Weber, M. (1992) [1919]. *Politik als Beruf*. Stuttgart: Reclam.

Weyland, K. (2001). 'Clarifying a Contested Concept: Populism in the Study of Latin American Politics', *Comparative Politics*, 34/1: 1–22.

Zúquete, J. P. (2007). *Missionary Politics in Contemporary Europe*. Syracuse, NY: Syracuse University Press.

CHAPTER 26

....

PERFORMATIVE POLITICAL LEADERSHIP

....

JOHN GAFFNEY

1 INTRODUCTION

....

THE central concern of this chapter is with the nature of the relationship between a speaker/leader and his or her audience. Throughout the history of rhetorical studies, how a speaker effects outcomes—that is, how he or she persuades an audience—of peers, of judges, of the public—to do something or to agree to something, or punish, or exonerate, or pass legislation, or vote, or go on strike, or rise up, or invade, and so on—has been the principal focus of analysis. We are concerned with, not what the audience does after a speech, but how it feels about the speaker, or rather why it feels the way it does. We want to demonstrate how leaders rhetorically construct a privileged relationship with their audience, and what the performative and cultural conditions of this are (Kane 2001).

In the study of leadership and leadership rhetoric, moreover, there is more research on the conditions, determinants, and background, as well as the outcomes of leadership rhetoric, than on the analysis of rhetoric itself. Yet, in many ways, or rather one way, the rhetoric is all there is, the rhetoric as performance (whether spoken or written, or, indeed, sung or expressed visually); all the rest is the conditions of its coming into being or the consequences of its having been.

It is as if, when analysing a Leonard Cohen song, research focused upon his secular Jewish intellectual background in Montreal in the late 1950s rather than upon the performance of 'the minor fall, the major lift',[1] the song itself and the singing of the song.

---

[1] *Hallelujah* (1984). Rhetoric is everywhere. Virtually nothing exists in interpersonal and social interaction without it (Leith 2011). We ourselves do not make a substantive distinction between spoken and written rhetoric, the latter in our view having as much a structure as the former (Booth 1961; Hyman 1962; Williams 1987; Empson 2004; Eagleton 2008; Ramage et al. 2009), but our emphasis will be upon the fundamental role of the author (persona, leader, speaker) of spoken rhetoric.

One cannot overemphasize the crucial importance of trusting the tale rather than the teller. Having said that, in this chapter, we are going to do the opposite; our precise focus will be upon the telling of the tale by the teller; the role of the persona of Leonard Cohen, as it were, in the singing of the song. There is a lacuna in the study of the performed rhetoric of leadership, but a prerequisite to remedying this is an understanding of the persona of the speaker/leader, and the conditions and modalities of persona performance—that is to say, an understanding of the conditions of perception and reception. In order better to analyse leadership rhetoric, we need to revisit and problematize the conditions of performance, and so contribute to leadership theory. In a word, because rhetorical performance is in our view so central, we need to revisit the relational conditions of the performance of leadership. This will be the focus of the chapter.

In order to identify these conditions, we shall examine five issues of leadership persona, or rather one issue from five perspectives: first who the speaker is, or would have him- or herself to be. For this, we shall refer to Aristotle, and his notion of *ethos* (which we shall tweak a little). Second, we shall examine, however real a speaker and an audience might be, how they are 'constructed' and 'imagined' for and by one another, and what this means for the perception or projection of the leader's leadership qualities. This brings us, third, and inevitably, to a critique of Weber's notion of 'charisma' and what needs to be added to it to give the leader–follower relationship what we consider to be its dynamism. Fourth, we shall locate leadership interpolation in its wider institutional framework, and, fifth, examine the cultural context informing rhetoric and performance, which also informs the institutions themselves, the types and styles of leadership, the audience itself, and the way it constructs or imagines itself. Finally, we shall critique the literature as it has treated this area of leadership rhetoric, and identify the prospects and challenges facing us.

2 THEM IMAGINING US IMAGINING THEM: ETHOS AND CHARISMA

Let us update Aristotle's category of *ethos* to contemporary purpose (Aristotle 1991). We can leave *pathos* relatively intact. For us, just as traditionally, *pathos* is the means of persuasion by which a whole range—perhaps *the* whole range—of emotions is evoked and exploited. As regards *logos*, we would tweak that too, but need not go into it here, only say in passing that, for us, *logos*, rather than being the argument of the speech wherein facts and examples are given in order to persuade with supporting evidence and enthymeme, we see more as the architecture, the structure of the whole speech, as it is performed. That is why the musical analogy is apt. *Logos* is the playing of the score, the dynamic shape of the speech, its syntax.

We are concerned here with the rhetorical category of *ethos*, much less addressed in contemporary rhetoric (outside business studies and marketing, where it is synonymous with 'credibility', which explains little, or rather states what needs to be explained). We shall take *ethos* to mean the persona of the speaker, both in and imagined outside the speech. *Ethos* refers to all the aspects of the character and performance of the speaker that contribute to the speech's reception. Character is a composite constructed by both the speaker (which might itself be a composite of him- or herself and speechwriters and advisers) and the audience (which itself is, by definition, composite, but is also composite in its self-construction).

The speaker is real, as is the audience, but the performance involves imagined and constructed notions of these real people. Meryl Streep and Colin Firth are not, though they may appear to be, respectively, Margaret Thatcher and George VI.[2] When not in a state of suspended disbelief, we know this. It is other for the political speaker, for we know that Obama is Obama, Putin, Putin, and so on; but the real person and the 'imagined' interpolated persona are not the same. Few of us know Obama beyond his rhetorical and mediated persona. We 'imagine' the real person. The opposite is also true: he or she invents us, the audience, even though each of us is real (Gaffney 2001; Anderson 2006). This means, moreover, that the scope afforded to the audience and to the speaker in how they depict both themselves and one another will be not limitless but will range well beyond their real 'selves'. It also means that the capacity for emotional (and rational) interaction will also be extensive, making the possibilities of emotional experience (and, of course, the potential for 'deception' and disappointment) also extensive, well beyond any 'real' contractual relationship.

Let us then return to our initial point about the nature of the leader's privileged relationship to the audience. At one level of rhetoric (and for the purposes of its analysis here), the only intention of the speaker is the desire to make a good speech and win allegiance to the 'self' of the speaker. We need to analyse leadership rhetoric, its relation to intention, and to its audience, in terms of that element within it concerned with 'the character' portrayed by the rhetoric, a character who is also 'outside' the rhetoric— that is, is perceived or constructed and imagined as existing outside the rhetoric. Both inside and outside the rhetoric, the persona of the speaker is imagined, yet of course is no less real for that (although El Cid should give us pause for thought!).[3] This raises the question of who the imagined person is whom the audience is imagining (and we are analysing), and what 'qualities' he or she might have. How does this composite character—constructed by itself and others—inform and fashion 'our' (the listeners') reception of the character, and how do the listeners and other influences, in turn, fashion it? We need to examine whether (and if so how) this imagined character precedes as well as is deployed in the rhetoric of leadership. This raises the question of the nature and modalities of our relationship to such 'characters' and the qualities of leadership they possess;

[2] *The Iron Lady* (2011); *The King's Speech* (2010).

[3] In order to maintain the morale of the Christian troops, the dead body of El Cid, killed the day before, was strapped onto his horse. His visor down and sword outstretched, he led his battalions the following morning, putting the Moors to flight, expelling them from the continent of Europe. It is extremely unlikely any of this true, but it illustrates our point.

and this raises the question of charisma. So, before coming back to Aristotle, we need to do a detour via Max Weber.

In spite of a century of theoretical/methodological difficulty[4] with Weber, his notion of 'charisma', elaborated in *The Theory of Social and Economic Organization*, and later in 'Politics as a Vocation' (Weber 1964, 2004) still dominates. Inside academia, it prevails. Outside academia, it is universal. But does it help with our understanding of the interpolation of persona, the privileged nature of the leader–audience relationship, the mutual and consequential invention of the speaker and audience by one another, and the notion of mutual consideration? Let us look at Weber's definition:

> A certain quality of an individual personality by virtue of which he is set apart from ordinary men and treated as endowed with supernatural, superhuman, or at least specifically exceptional powers or qualities. These are such as are not accessible to the ordinary person, but are regarded as of divine origin or as exemplary, and on the basis of them the individual concerned is treated as a leader.
>
> (Weber 1964: 358)[5]

An uncontentious first point that we can make about this definition is that it is long. In part, because it is long, it is also unclear, as well as being both tentative and assertive, and contradictory. It is as if Weber himself is trying to identify charisma rather than tell us what it is. From the definition, it is difficult to pin down *what* charisma is, in part because it is difficult to pin down *where* it is. To begin with, it is based not on one thing but on several things ('qualities ascribed'), as well as upon both qualities (plural) and the act of ascription. Is the charisma in the ascribed or the ascribing? And 'where' is each of these? The latter, in the ascribing, is where the focus of scientific (although not popular) attention has come to be placed, in our postmodern, relativist world. It is in the eye/s of the beholder/s, rather than in the qualities held. This, however, takes us off in the wrong direction, away from the persona we are trying to analyse. The most extreme form of this view, and extremely influential, is Theodore Adorno's development of the idea of the 'authoritarian personality' (Adorno et al. 1950). In a word, Adorno identified Hitler's persuasive power as lying in the psychic dependence of a particular type of audience,

---

[4] Willner (1984) has a very good (and positive) discussion of Weber's term. For sources critical of charisma, see the many articles on Weber over the decades in the *Journal of Classical Sociology* (London: Sage) and the *British Journal of Sociology* (Oxford: Blackwell).

[5] 'Charisma' soll eine als ausseralltäglich (ursprünglich, sowohl bei Propheten wie bei therapeutischen wie bei Rechts-Weisen wie bei Jagdführern wie bei Kriegshelden: als magisch bedingt) geltende Qualität einer Persönlichkeit heissen, um derentwillen sie als mit übernatürlichen oder übermenschlichen oder mindestens spezifisch ausseralltäglichen, nicht jedem andern zugänglichen Kräften oder Eigenschaften oder als gottgesandt oder als vorbildlich und deshalb als 'Führer' gewertet wird. Wie die betreffende Qualität von irgendeinem ethischen, ästhetischen oder sonstigen Standpunkt aus 'objektiv' richtig zu bewerten sein würde, ist natürlich dabei begrifflich völlig gleichgültig: darauf allein, wie sie tatsächlich von charismatisch Beherrschten, den 'Anhängern', bewertet wird, kommt es an (M. Weber, *Wirtschaft und Gesellschaft*, i (Cologne: Kiepenheuer and Witsch, 1964), 179).

and its need for authority and domination. General use of this idea is somewhat more benign than in Adorno, but still maintains that the power of charisma proceeds from those in its thrall, the implication being that it does not really exist.

Perhaps the confusion in Weber's definition is itself telling, and that the entity is relational in some way. This must be so in some sense, but at the Adorno end of the spectrum there is the danger of emptying the relational of its fundamental quality, in that there is nothing for the audience truly to relate to or with. So, the first issue for us is to identify what is happening in the relationship. One thing that is, within a vast range of intensity, depending upon each case is feeling, and, therefore, feelings.

After the war, in radio and television programmes about the 1939–45 period, there was often a fierce allegiance to Winston Churchill expressed by many interviewees, which was highly emotional and 'attached'. The memory, at least, of those interviewed was that they would have done anything for the war effort *because of Churchill's speeches*. The emotion was partly related to them imagining him imagining them as heroes (who would fight on the beaches).[6] What we need is a way of apprehending both this relational allegiance and its emotional intensity (whether real or 'constructed' later is a separate issue), as well as the role of the perceived *ethos* of the persona of Churchill in the affective relationship.

What was being expressed was a willingness to die because of dramatic radio broadcasts in a crisis situation. Charisma as a concept does not really offer very much as a relational concept—leadership qualities ascribed and (perhaps) possessed; nor does it help us see *why* the listener was prepared to die, or what precisely it was they were prepared to die for. What is dramatically missing from Weber's analysis is precisely the drama of the relationship, its emotional character (Willner 1984). It is certainly true that what is provoking the emotion and allegiance is very difficult to grasp (Marcus 2002). Could we say perhaps that there is something in the nature of the, let us call it here, 'charisma' such that we do not know what it is? Is charisma a *Je ne sais quoi*, I know not what? Of course, that is not sufficient for scientific analysis. However, one of the problems with seeing charisma as either qualities or qualities ascribed, or else as just a relational concept (however empty or complex), is that it still leaves us uncertain of the *quoi* of *je ne sais quoi*! The charismatic concept has to be entered into by all concerned, and imagined in some way; and, for this, the leader has to *do* something. But what? Let us first establish the conditions of this imagined relationship.

It is clearly not a one-to-one relationship. There is only one speaker, and it is he, here Churchill, who rhetorically invents 'our island' (which 'we' shall defend).[7] Churchill also creates, or evokes at least, the qualities of the audience too; but there is something emotionally shared by those subscribing to the relationship. It is akin to, or rather an adaptation of, the Sartrian notion of the group-in-fusion (Sartre 1960): that each person, through sharing what is both an ontological and an emotional relationship with

---

[6] Winston Churchill, 'Wars are not won by evacuations', speech 4 June 1940, reprinted in Cannandine (1989: 156–65).

[7] Churchill, in Cannadine (1989: 156–65).

Churchill, shares with one another, and that each is 'held' by the other in their mutual emotion vis-à-vis Churchill, and this is dramatically reinforced by their sharing the same crisis situation. The initial problem, however, remains: if the audience is 'sharing' with each other the perception of a quality ascribed, what is the *quoi* of the quality?

Perhaps leadership in action exhibits the quality of the *ineffable*, or unknowable, a truly *je ne sais quoi*—its ineffable nature being one of its major qualities and functions. This is truly tantalizing. Part of the quality we are trying to grasp is elusive, hence its allure and compelling nature. This may also have a psychological dimension (Haslam, Reicher, and Platow 2011). Our response to leadership has undoubtedly a relationship to our lived experience, perhaps to childhood, even to the pre-verbal (hence the inability to 'put it into words'); or the symbolic, for example, the leader as the (literal) embodiment of desire; and a mythical dimension too, mythical in the sense that the leader or aspirant leader evokes legend (for example, Lancelot undergoing 'trials' in a (mythical) place to which the speaker has taken us); and religious/symbolic interpolations: it is not without significance that many of the aspects informing Western leadership—special grace, the bringing of comfort, justice, succour, deliverance, and so on, evoke the West's Christian tradition (itself 'mythical' and deeply psychological (Edinger 1999, 2004)). Charisma itself (grace), of course, implies a direct divine connection.

Those leaders we call 'charismatic' do seem, at the very least, to enact possession of 'a certain something', a something that we cannot quite 'put our finger on'. No wonder Weber's definition is long; it truly is hard to define. Social science, however, seems here to be little further forward than 'the X factor'—charisma as 'star quality'. We need, therefore, to 'pursue' the *quoi* of *je ne sais quoi*, for, if we accept that leadership is in a relationship to followership, and that 'charismatic' leadership (we shall abandon the term in due course) is a relational term, we still need to say what it is. What it is, is an event.

We have already argued that, however determining, context is not the 'certain something'. In a theory of the rhetoric and image of leadership, leadership as an *act*, an *action*, a *performance*, needs to be integrated; and—at its best—experience of the performance is in a relationship to epiphany. Perhaps this is the certain something. We need, therefore, to understand the act or *enactment* and *voicing* of 'charismatic' leadership—that is, leadership as an act *performed*, an act enacted, but with specific qualities and skill in its deployment.

'Vision' can be enlightening here. We need to remind ourselves that this is in no way an equal partnership between speaker and audience. Indeed, at a certain rhetorical level the audience exists only in the rhetoric of the speaker; and the relationship needs to be hierarchical in order for the leader to be the leader. Speaker 'vision' (inside, interpolated and, outside, imagined) also evokes emotion and a speaker–audience relationship of proximity, empathy, and sharing. Envisioning is crucial to the valorization of the persona of the speaker. It can span a whole range of perceptions from visions to insights, depending upon the nature of the occasion and the community. It can be vision at its 'highest'—for example, de Gaulle contemplating history; or at a lower register, the vision of the new managing director of a company; but there is a constant puzzle in leadership studies, as well as in daily conversation about leaders: that the speaker/leader is 'like us' and yet different. They have to be like us, for us to identify; unlike us, for us to confer or recognize leadership. It is the envisioning that allows for this powerful duality. As well as showing that he or she is in some respects 'like' (at least can empathize with) the audience, leaders also use 'vision' to distinctive purpose. Enough of the content of the leader's vision is offered to the audience for the audience to 'see' the content of the vision ('a nation where they will not be judged by the color of their skin but by the content of their character') (Washington and King 1986). The vision, however, is only partly seen; and, even to see the part, the speaker is needed. It is the speaker's vision, not the audience's. They get a recounted version of another's vision. Belief in achieving, for example, 'the Promised Land' involves acquiescence in the vision of the speaker.[8] Acquiescence is a prerequisite to the fulfilling of desire. So, to a certain but fundamental degree, the speaker, contrary to received opinion, must maintain what he or she knows as somehow unknown. Emotion is partly based upon ineffable vision. The audience, paradoxically, feels an affinity with the speaker because he or she can 'see' something that they cannot see. To return to our notion of leadership as a creative act, and to our dissatisfaction with Weber's characterization, 'vision' is a perfect example of our thesis: the vision is whatever it is; it is the act of envisioning that constitutes the speaker–audience relationship and the speaker's exceptional status.

This dominance of the speaker and interrelationship with the audience is often like a choreographed dance of pronouns. Pronouns are fundamental to the speaker–audience relationship because they define it. They allow for intimacy between the speaker and the audience (often in a dynamically choreographed way) through the structured interplay of I, you, and we (and they); and, because I and you are not the same thing, they are distinct things. Of course, I and you can make we; I and you are prerequisites of 'we'; each is needed for the we to exist. Hence, often, the rhetorical device used by many speakers—in a near-evangelist way—of the (feigned) need for I to draw upon the strength of you in order that I be I (on behalf of and in the name of you, and in order that 'we' fulfil our mission). Let us give a small illustration of this in action.

There is both intimacy and differentiation in de Gaulle's words 'Je vous ai compris' (I have understood you), the opening lines of his speech to the crowd in Algiers on 4 June 1958 at the height of a regime crisis (de Gaulle 1970). 'I have understood you' implies 'they' did not/have not ('they' are often another major element of the choreography). It also implies, however, that you have not understood you, and that, to the extent that you now do, I am central to that understanding, because, in fact, you did not understand you until I understood you. The status of I is enhanced greatly at the moment of intimacy between I and you. The enthusiasm that greeted de Gaulle's speech (in both Algiers and France) masked a national acquiescence not just in de Gaulle's privileged leadership, but in his singular depiction of the world and of leadership in it.

---

[8] One of the best examples of this comes in Martin Luther King's speech in Memphis on 3 April 1968; 'I just want to do God's will. And He's allowed me to go up to the mountain. And I've looked over. And I've seen the Promised Land' (Washington and King 1986: 279–86).

Before the audience is assembled and the leader performs, there will be institutions and a culture that make performance and audience possible (Thompson, Ellis and Wildavsky 1990; Goffman 1990; Berger and Luckmann 1991). Let us look at how these frameworks frame.

3   THE CONTEXT OF LEADERSHIP PERFORMANCE

Institutions

The institutional context of leadership can be understood as a myriad of things, from the conventions of leadership performance, to the nature and conditions of, say, executive office, to political parties, the media, the education system, or, more immediately, the television studio, the convention hall, the Congress, the House, the Agora, and so it could go on: institutions are sites and practices that, over time, become *where* performances take place. For the purposes of analysis here, we can take institutions to mean the conventions and places that pertain to, by framing, leadership 'acts'. A president, for example, will 'perform' in a different configuration of institutions from a prime minister, and this for a set of procedural, conventional, and cultural reasons. The performance will also be different, depending upon the media or medium; but you cannot be a president without a presidency.

The institution itself, moreover, evolves and changes the conditions of performance. Institutions also have a fundamental relationship to culture and to political traditions.

Culture

Culture incorporates both the institutional (March and Olsen 1984; Hay 2008) and wider notions of memory and identity (Geertz 1980; Thompson, Ellis, and Wildavsky 1990). Our emphasis is upon culture's influence upon an institution, such as the presidency (for example, a strong mythology of leadership), but also incorporates often assumed and even unrecognized notions pertaining to identity and memory: traditions, dispositions, secrets even, shared by a community. Let us take an example, and look again at de Gaulle.

The circumstances surrounding de Gaulle's coming to power in France in 1958 (Rémond 1983)—the collapse of a regime, a possible military coup—were *dramatic*, and, as it were, called forth dramatic leadership, his own. In the de Gaulle case, leadership performance and the institutional configuration, or reconfiguration, of institutions in the weeks of May–June 1958 were sharply influenced by drama and dramatic circumstances, and we should interpret the former (performance) while bearing in mind the latter (drama). However, as regards culture, we could take this a stage further, and say that 'drama' is part of the political culture of French politics, hence the recognition when in a dramatic crisis of the (need for) dramatic crisis leadership. Also, in the case of de Gaulle, we see the 'recognition' of the Cassandra figure (who had warned them all, in 1946) and the 'saviour' (who had earlier saved them all, in 1944, the returning 'First Resister' of 1940). Mythically, of course, Cassandra was unheeded. In 1958, she triumphs (for a while). These mythical elements are part of the shared culture in which the institutions (and the leader, and the leader's performance, and the audience) are embedded.

Drama, therefore, is a cultural artefact, as well as constituting the contingent circumstances of leadership performance in this case. This will have, dare we say, dramatic consequences for leadership. If drama is itself not just facilitative of (allows for or gives opportunity to) providential leadership, but is also part of the culture that gives rise to it, it will also inform the nature of the leadership and its opportunities, as well as being a cultural prerequisite to this type of leadership. Some cultures, moreover, have more influence upon leadership because of the intensity of the 'memory' within the community. In France, for example, there is a very active memory of French history (sometimes inaccurate, sometimes partial, but this does not reduce its strength), and of the upheavals within it, and of the individuals who have played a part (and who often 'embody' a tradition—revolutionary, reactionary, adventurous, foolhardy, salutary, and so on). This will throw into relief the perceived relationship of individuals to events. From 1789, France became politically unstable, and the more unstable the more... unstable; and the more unstable, the more responsive to 'individual' solutions, and therefore to 'heroes', and *l'aventure*, a highly charged and pejorative term in French political culture. The more dramatic, and therefore the more romantic and 'providential', the leadership, the more unstable and dramatic the situations become, and so on.

4 Critique of the Field

What do we know about political leadership as 'performance' in the sense described above? In our review of the literature on our topic, let us begin contentiously and say that there is little literature to review. We are concerned with establishing a place for the study of leadership rhetorical performance and its relationship to culturally fashioned audience reaction and participation. We can begin, however, by saying that in Europe the study of contemporary rhetoric barely exists, let alone the subdiscipline study of leadership rhetoric. In Europe, one can posit the decline from almost any time in the last 200 years or so. Ironically, the American and French Revolutions, which rang out the old and rang in the new, and saw the eclipse of rhetorical study, each produced some of the best rhetoricians of all time.

In the twentieth century, rhetoric as a discipline was replaced, in part, because of changes in how language itself was perceived (and, negatively, how rhetoric was perceived). Developing out of Saussurean linguistics (Saussure 1995), the focus of twentieth-century enquiry was upon the system (*langue*), which expressed itself through speech (*parole*). One of the most thorough revisions of the study of language as rhetoric was the arrival, in the 1950s and 1960s (drawing explicitly upon Saussurean linguistics), of structuralism. Structuralism colonized just about everything, but in our field, its essential effect and purpose was—to cut a long story short—to demonstrate that people do not use language, language uses people. The extension of linguistic study in the social sciences saw a radicalization of this approach through the development in the 1970s and 1980s of discourse analysis, and then, from the 1990s onwards, of critical discourse analysis (CDA). There has been a lot of interesting work, sometimes bordering on rhetorical analyses, that demonstrates the how of (the rhetoric of) the interpolation of language (Fairclough 1995; van Dijk 2008; Wodak 2009). The overall Saussurean structure remains, however, and is adapted in order to demonstrate not only how speech (*parole*) mediates language, but how it mediates power relations in society (rather than power relations in the rhetoric). When examining Tony Blair's discourse of New Labour, for example, CDA's preoccupation is less with how Blair persuades than with how his discourse is the giving of voice to an underlying ideology (Fairclough 2001).

The study of leadership rhetoric touches upon a vast set of literatures: linguistics, political theory, democratic theory, biography, communication studies, psychology, cultural studies, performance studies (and cinema studies and literary criticism), gender studies, marketing, business studies, and so on (see also Uhr, Chapter 17, this volume). The irony is that, as we said at the beginning of this section, actual rhetorical studies are like a wasteland surrounded by these mountain ranges of literature. That is how it is in Europe—France, the UK, and elsewhere. Much of what I have said above does not actually apply to the United States.

The United States—in part through active research forums such as the National Communication Association and the Rhetoric Society of America—has a thriving rhetorical studies tradition. Much of it is due to the seminal and consequential (phenomenal, in fact) influence of Kenneth Burke (1897–1993) (Burke 1969), and his approach to rhetoric, which situates it by means of his 'dramatistic pentad' (Act, Scene, Agent, Agency, Purpose). In the more recent period, a range of figures with major academic influence have further shaped rhetoric studies (Brock, Scott, and Chesebro 1990). Perhaps the most prestigious and influential has been, since the 1980s, Kathleen Hall Jamieson, who, along with others, redefined the study of leadership rhetoric as it moved through its classical period (1940–70) into the Reagan and post-Reagan eras, the 'Electronic Age' (Hall Jamieson 1988). As regards presidential rhetoric, much of this scholarship focuses upon 'Presidents creating the Presidency' (Kohrs Campbell and Hall Jamieson 2010). In this way, a lot of its emphasis is 'performative' in the Austinian sense (Austin 1975): by speaking, the president becomes the presidency (and vice versa).

We can, moreover, make three points about the place of this approach. First, US research is overwhelmingly American. This may seem obvious, but it means that it is not only US rhetorical studies that are almost completely national specific; the institutional, cultural, and other frameworks are also national specific. Second, and again overwhelmingly, political leadership research is about the US presidency. There is equally paradigm shifting work on, for example, feminist and African American rhetoric (Jackson

2003; Richardson and Jackson 2007); very good work, for example, on such figures as Elizabeth Cady Stanton and Frederick Douglass (whose rhetoric alone made rhetorical studies inevitable!) (Waggenspack 1989; Kohrs Campbell 1993; Chesebrough 1998), and, of course, Martin Luther King and Malcolm X; but the thrust remains presidential. Third, whether presidential or other, the general thrust of US rhetorical studies is upon individuals. This raises epistemological questions, particularly about the nature of agency and the subject, for in European scholarship a much greater emphasis is placed upon the rhetoric and discourses of institutions and practices than upon individual interpolation.

We should not, however, while identifying the crucial differences, overemphasize what to some degree reflects the divisions of labour in academic institutions. A lot of the best discourse analysis specialists in Europe would be perfectly at home in a rhetorical studies environment (some of Wodak's work is specifically on rhetoric); and journals like *Discourse and Society* are great sources for analysts of rhetoric.

5 The Future: A 'European' Renaissance?

One of the essential features underpinning 'European' discourse studies—and, in part, one of the reasons for its development in contradistinction to rhetoric studies, was and is its preoccupation with social questions wider than rhetoric, even wider than language itself. This is in part, as we have mentioned, because of the Saussurean thrust of discourse studies (*langue* as preceding *parole* ontologically). It is also partly the result of the post-war influence on all European thought of Marxism, particularly upon cultural studies (Hall 1980; Williams 1987; Barker and Galasinski 2001), and for many continental European scholars the influence of the Frankfurt School. One of the essential features of European cultural studies, particularly in its language-related aspects, is that language and culture do not just reflect one another, but constitute one another: culture is constituted in and through language, which in turn is culturally constituted. It follows from this that there will be great emphasis upon the social, historical, and economic, in that relations of power are discursively mediated, both in terms of oppression and in terms of resistance (there is much less research, however, on this latter). This means that a lot of discourse analysis, and especially critical discourse analysis is political, even committed in a Sartrean sense. European feminist research is, like American (Butler 2006), informed, perhaps inevitably, by this political dimension (Baxter 2006; Shepherd 2008). It also means that a lot of the focus is upon meta-narratives (of a Foucauldian type), meta-discourses, and so on, rather than upon rhetoric as understood as the performance of the specific speaker. It also follows that in discourse analysis the distinction between the rhetoric of the spoken and the rhetoric of the written is considered less of a quintessential dividing line (Eagleton 2008).

As well as potential synergies with discourse studies, another sign of the renaissance in rhetorical studies comes from a very practical quarter. In the UK today, as has been the case for many years in the USA, there have been major developments in political speechwriting. The UK Speechwriters' Guild is a recent (2009) and highly successful organization bringing together political practitioners, speechwriting experts and novices, political advisers and academics in the study of contemporary leadership rhetoric (<http://www.ukspeechwritersguild.co.uk/>). Many of today's speechwriters, moreover, write, lecture, and give workshops, and write books and articles, some running very active blogs (Atkinson 1984, 2004; Charteris-Black 2005; Lancaster 2010), the whole carrying the practice of speechwriting and its place in the political process to new levels of enquiry, and reviving and adapting many of the traditional practices of classical rhetoric.

Political leadership studies are minuscule compared to the literature on leadership in business studies. The shelves of the business sections of bookshops, in Europe as in the USA, groan under the weight of them. Much of this literature is frankly bad, prescriptive, and transpierced with the clichés and self-delusions of much self-help literature. Much of it is theoretically bereft. Some of it, however, is excellent, and provides real bridges between organizational theory, education, and politics: Bruce (1992); Bryman (1992); Soder (2001); Adair (2005); Hofstede, Hofstede and Minkov (2010), and the highly entertaining Grint (2010) are just some examples.

New rhetorical studies, therefore, are beginning in Europe to define themselves, and not least through the pioneering work of a range of individuals. We have mentioned such ground-breaking work as that of Atkinson, and Charteris-Black, and, in more popular, yet erudite (and hilarious) mode, Leith. There has also been a small but very high-quality surge of academic scholarship in modern and contemporary political rhetoric in several UK universities (*inter alia*, Finlayson 2002; Street 2004; Drake and Higgins 2012; Gaffney and Lahel 2013a, 2013b; Martin 2013), as well as the creation of rhetoric and politics groups in learned societies such as the UK Political Studies Association. The elements therefore exist for a significant contribution to the discipline and new synergies in research.

Recommended Reading

Hall Jamieson, K. (1988). *Eloquence in an Electronic Age: The Transformation of Political Speechmaking*. Oxford: Oxford University Press.

Kane, J. (2001). *The Politics of Moral Capital*. Cambridge: Cambridge University Press.

Leith, S. (2011). *You Talkin' To Me? Rhetoric from Aristotle to Obama*. London: Profile Books.

References

Adair, J. (2005). *The Inspirational Leader: How to Motivate, Encourage and Achieve Success*. London: Kogan Page.

Adorno, T., Frenkel-Brunswik, E., Levinson, D., and Sanford, N. (1950). *The Authoritarian Personality*. New York: Harper and Rowe.

Anderson, B. (2006). *Imagined Communities*. London: Verso.

Aristotle (1991). *The Art of Rhetoric*. London: Penguin Classics.

Atkinson, M. (1984). *Our Masters' Voices*. London: Methuen.

Atkinson, M. (2004). *Lend Me Your Ears*. London: Random House.

Austin, J. L. (1975). *How To Do Things with Words*. Oxford: Clarendon Press.

Barker, C., and Galasinski, D. (2001). *Cultural Studies and Discourse Analysis: A Dialogue on Language and Identity*. London: Sage.

Baxter, J. (2006) (ed.). *Speaking out: The Female Voice in Public Context*. Basingstoke: Palgrave.

Berger, P., and Luckmann, T. (1991) [1959]. *The Social Construction of Reality*. London: Penguin.

Booth, W. C. (1961). *The Rhetoric of Fiction*. Chicago: Chicago University Press.

Brock, B. L., Scott, R. L., and Chesebro, J. W. (1990) (eds). *Methods of Rhetorical Criticism: A Twentieth-Century Perspective*. Detroit, MI: Wayne State University Press.

Bruce, B. (1992). *Images of Power: How the Image Makers Shape our Leaders*. London: Kogan Page.

Bryman, A. (1992). *Charisma and Leadership in Organizations*. London: SAGE.

Burke, K. (1969) [1945]. *A Grammar of Motives*. Berkeley and Los Angeles: University of California Press.

Butler, J. (2006). *Gender Trouble: Feminism and Subversion of Identity*. London: Routledge.

Cannadine, D. (1989). *Blood, Toil, Tears and Sweat: Winston Churchill's Famous Speeches*. London: Cassell.

Charteris-Black, J. (2005). *Politicians and Rhetoric*. Basingstoke: Palgrave.

Chesebrough, D. (1998). *Frederick Douglass: Oratory from Slavery*. Westport, CT: Greenwood.

De Gaulle, C. (1970). *Discours et Messages*, vol. 2. Paris: Plon.

Drake, P., and Higgins, M. (2012). 'Lights, Camera, Election: Celebrity, Performance, and the 2010 UK General Election Leadership Debates', *British Journal of Politics and International Relations*, 14/3: 375–91.

Eagleton, T. (2008) [1983]. *Literary Theory*. Oxford: Blackwell.

Edinger, E. (1999). *Archetype of the Apocalyse*. Chicago, IL: Open Court.

Edinger, E. (2004). *The Sacred Psyche*. Toronto: Inner City Books.

Empson, W. (2004) [1930]. *Seven Types of Ambiguity*. London: Pimlico.

Fairclough, N. (1995). *Critical Discourse Analysis: The Critical Study of Language*. London: Longman.

Fairclough, N. (2001). *Language and Power*. London: Longman.

Finlayson, A. (2002). 'Elements of the Blairite Image of Leadership', *Parliamentary Affairs*, 55/3: 586–99.

Gaffney, J. (2001). 'Imagined Relationships: Political Leadership in Contemporary Democracies', *Parliamentary Affairs*, 54/1: 120–33.

Gaffney, J. and Lahel, A. (2013a) ' The Morphology of the Labour Party's One Nation Narrative: Story, Plot and Authorship', *The Political Quarterly*, 84/3: 330–41.

Gaffney, J. and Lahel, A. (2013b). ' Political Performance and Leadership Persona: The UK Labour Party Conference of 2012', *Government and Opposition*, 48/3: 1–25.

Geertz, C. (1980). *Negara*. Princeton: Princeton University Press.

Goffman, I. (1990) [1959]. *The Presentation of Self in Everyday Life*. London: Penguin.

Grint, K. (2010). *Leadership: A Very Short Introduction*. Oxford: Oxford University Press.

Hall Jamieson, K. (1988). *Eloquence in an Electronic Age: The Transformation of Political Speechmaking*. Oxford: Oxford University Press.

Hall, S. (1980). *Culture, Media, Language*. London: Routledge.

Haslam, S., Reicher, S., and Platow, M. (2011). *The New Psychology of Leadership*. Hove: Psychology Press.

Hay, C. (2008). 'Constructivist Institutionalism', in R. A. W. Rhodes, S. Binder, and B. A. Rockman (eds), *The Oxford Handbook of Political Institutions*. Oxford: Oxford University Press, 56–74.

Hofstede, G., Hofstede, G. J., and Minkov, M. (2010). *Cultures and Organizations: Software of the Mind*. London: McGraw-Hill.

Hyman, S. E. (1962). *The Tangled Bank*. New York: Atheneum.

Jackson, R. (2003). *Understanding African-American Rhetoric*. Carbondale, IL: Southern Illinois University.

Kane, J. (2001). *The Politics of Moral Capital*. Cambridge: Cambridge University Press.

Kohrs Campbell, K. (1993). *Women Public Speakers in the United States: 1800–1925*. Westport, CT: Greenwood.

Kohrs Campbell, K., and Hall Jamieson, K. (2010). *Presidents Creating the Presidency: Deeds Done in Words*. Chicago: University of Chicago Press.

Lancaster, S. (2010). *Speechwriting: The Expert Guide*. London: Hale.

Leith, S. (2011). *You Talkin' To Me? Rhetoric from Aristotle to Obama*. London: Profile Books.

March, J. G., and Olsen, J. P. (1984). 'The New Institutionalism: Organizational Factors in Political Life', *Americal Political Science Review*, 78/3: 734–49.

Marcus, G. E. (2002). *The Sentimental Citizen: Emotion in Democratic Politics*. University Park, PA: Pennsylvania State University Press.

Martin, J. (2013). *Rhetoric and Politics*. London: Routledge.

Ramage, J., Callaway, M., Clary-Lemon, J., and Waggoner, Z. (2009). *Argument in Composition*. West Lafayette, IN: Parlor Press.

Rémond, R. (1983). *Le Retour du général*. Brussels: Éditions Complexe.

Richardson, E., and Jackson, R. (2007). *African-American Rhetoric(s)*. London: Routledge.

Sartre, J.-P. (1960). *Critique de la raison dialectique*. Paris: Gallimard.

Saussure, F. de (1995) [1916]. *Course in General Linguistics*. New York: Columbia University Press.

Shepherd, L. (2008). *Gender, Violence, and Security*. London: Zed Books.

Soder, R. (2001). *The Language of Leadership*. San Francisco, CA: Jossey-Bass.

Street, J. (2004). 'Celebrity Politicians: Popular Culture and Political Representation', *British Journal of Politics and International Relations*, 6/4: 235–452.

Thompson, M., Ellis, R., and Wildavsky, A. (1990). *Cultural Theory*. Boulder, CO: Westview.

Van Dijk, T. A. (2008). *Discourse and Context: A Sociocognitive Approach*. Cambridge: Cambridge University Press.

Waggenspack, B. M. (1989). *The Search for Self-Sovereignty: The Oratory of Elizabeth Cady Stanton*. Westport, CT: Greenwood.

Washington, J. M., and King, M. L. (1986). *A Testament of Hope: The Essential Writings and Speeches of Martin Luther King, Jr*. San Francisco, CA: HarperCollins.

Weber, M. (1964). *The Theory of Social and Economic Organisation*. New York: Free Press.

Weber, M. (2004). *The Vocation Lectures*. Indianapolis, IN: Hackett Publishing.

Williams, R. (1987). *Culture and Society*. London: Hogarth Press.

Willner, A. R. (1984). *The Spellbinders: Charismatic Political Leadership*. New Haven, CT: Yale University Press.

Wodak, R. (2009). *The Discourse of Politics in Action: Politics as Usual*. Basingstoke: Palgrave.

....

CHAPTER 27

POLITICAL LEADERSHIP IN NETWORKS

....

ERIK-HANS KLIJN

1 INTRODUCTION: POLITICAL LEADERSHIP IN A NETWORKED AND MEDIATIZED WORLD

IN March 2007, the complex process around restructuring the Zuidplas Polder, the area between the cities of Rotterdam, Gouda, and Zoetermeer in the Netherlands, suddenly found itself in the media spotlight. A member of the national parliament voiced strong criticisms against plans to construct 7,500 to 15,000 new dwellings in the area. Building houses at the lowest point of the Netherlands made no sense, according to the MP, and should be reconsidered. In her view, the area should retain its green and agricultural character. The regional and national newspapers immediately picked up the issue, and the project suddenly found itself under full public and media scrutiny. This is illustrated by headlines such as: 'Politics wants to get rid of new neighborhood in the polder' (*de Volkskrant*, 28 March 2007).

This was a serious threat to the complex decision-making process involving twenty-seven different actors that had started in 2001 to create an integrated plan for environmental protection, water storage, building new dwellings, and relocating the greenhouses in the area. However, the project manager and the province deputy effectively disarmed the potential threat by countering the news and staging various stakeholder appearances in the media. For instance, the representative of the environmental organization, part of a large steering board involved in the interactive decision-making process, strongly voiced her discontent with the MP's intervention: 'The past years, everywhere greenhouses and dwellings have been added incrementally. I rather prefer an integral plan than this unnoticed messing up of the area.... The past years, we have been seriously engaged with this polder. Voicing protests now without knowing anything about the project is cheap politics' (*Trouw*, 29 March 2007).

This case shows the difficult life of a modern political leader. At a time when society and governance processes have become considerably more complex, and many authors argue that most service delivery and public decision making take place within networks of interdependent actors that require collaborative leadership (Koppenjan and Klijn 2004; Ansell and Gash 2008), leaders are also very visible in the political arena and media. Leaders are followed and covered by the media at every step they take, as are their personnel characteristics as leaders, and even their private lives are extensively covered (see Bennett 2009). These two trends create a tension for modern political leaders that has to be managed carefully.

The Question: Tension Between Drama Democracy and Network Practice

The current wide variety of literature on governance, collaborative management, and networks stresses that modern policy is made and implemented not by governments alone but in networks of interdependent actors (see Rhodes 1997; Kickert, Klijn, and Koppenjan 1997; Mandell 2001; Meier and O'Toole 2007; O'Leary and Bingham 2009). This literature stresses that political leaders and administrators must engage in interactions with various stakeholders to be successful in these networks to be effective and to actively manage their network (Koppenjan and Klijn 2004; Huxham and Vangen 2005; O'Leary and Bingham 2009). The image that arises from this literature is that being effective as a political leader means extensive negotiations with stakeholders, having the capabilities to bind stakeholders together, and showing long-lasting dedication to the interaction process and the network of actors that has to secure the desired outcomes.

However, these capacities and leadership skills seem to contrast strongly with the skills needed to survive in a mediatized and dramatized political world. Authors stress that politics has become more and more theatrical—largely boosted by the media. In drama democracy (Elchardus 2002), with its focus on individuals and powerful imagery, it is crucial for politicians to direct their performance, but they can also be demonized by media processes. The mediatized world, where politics has become personalized and communicating ideas is more important than implementing them (see Elchardus 2002; Fischer 2003), calls for strong leaders that communicate strong ideas.

This Chapter: Exploring the Front- and the Back-Stage

In this chapter, the tension between what we call the front-stage and the back-stage of political life is explored. We first deal with the backstage world, the world of complex decision making in networks. Drawing on the by now impressive amount of literature on networks, collaborative leadership, and so forth, in the next section we show the challenges and the requirements to solve public policy problems in this context. We then turn to the front-stage of political life and explore the tension between networks and representational democracy, and especially between the leadership style in networks and the demands of mediatized political life. In the following section, we deal with the tensions between the front-stage and the back-stage and discuss some ways in which political leaders try to deal with these. The final section offers some reflections and suggests interesting topics for future research.

2   POLITICAL LEADERSHIP IN A NETWORKED WORLD: THE BACK STAGE

Many authors have pointed to the difficulty of achieving solutions to policy problems in modern (network) society (Hanf and Scharpf 1978; Kickert, Klijn, and Koppenjan 1997; Rhodes 1997; Agranoff and McGuire 2001). Authors stress that many problems have become more complex because of changes in the nature of society (more plurality in values, more active citizens that foster their interest and organize themselves to influence policy-making processes, and more dispersed information). There is, however, also a need for more integration in many policy-making and service delivery processes, and this makes the task more complex (see Osborne 2010); and knowledge is more widespread and thus collaborative efforts are needed to bring knowledge together to solve problems (Bryson and Crosby 1992; Ansell and Gash 2008). Consequently, many problems have a 'wicked' character (Rittel and Webber 1973), that is, there is little agreement among the involved actors on the nature of the problem, many different actors are involved, and these actors do not always agree on the standards by which possible solutions should be judged. We discuss first the condition of leadership in a networked world: networks and interdependencies; then we focus on leadership activities, explore the role of trust, and conclude with the type of leadership required in a networked world.

Networks and Interdependencies as a Setting for Leadership

Political leaders and public managers who want to initiate governance processes or arrange service delivery find themselves in networks of interdependent actors (Hanf and Scharpf 1978; Kaufmann, Majone, and Ostrom 1986; Marsh and Rhodes 1992; Kickert, Klijn, and Koppenjan 1997; Rhodes 1997). Dependency relations between actors are crucial to the emergence and existence of networks (Hanf and Scharpf 1978). The resource dependencies around policy problems or policy programs require actors to interact with one another and create more intensive and enduring interactions (Laumann and Knoke 1987). Networks are, on the one hand, consciously planned in the sense that actors deliberately interact and attempt to structure these interactions with organizations and rules, but, on the other hand, are also unplanned as a result of coincidental interactions and strategies, and previously created rules.

Governance networks can roughly be defined as 'more or less stable patterns of social relations between mutual dependent actors, which form around policy problems and/ or cluster of means and which are formed, maintained and changed through series of games' (Koppenjan and Klijn 2004: 69–70).

Because of the relatively autonomous position of the actors, it is difficult to use more classical hierarchical steering methods (although we also find hierarchical relations in networks). Because actors have their own perceptions on the nature of the problem and the solution, and because each actor acts strategically from his/her own perceptions, networks often manifest complex interaction and decision-making processes; or as Ansell and Gash (2008: 550) state: 'The collaborative process itself is highly iterative and nonlinear.'

This means that it is not easy to achieve socially relevant outcomes in these networks. The literature on networks thus deals extensively with leadership and/or managerial strategies and roles to stimulate and facilitate complex processes in networks. A number of terms have been coined to describe this management activity, including meta governance (Sørensen and Torfing 2007) and collaborative leadership (O'Leary and Bingham 2009), but probably the most popular terminology in use is network management (Gage and Mandell 1990; Kickert, Klijn, and Koppenjan 1997; Agranoff and McGuire 2001; Mandell 2001). The basic argument is usually that without adequate leadership or network management strategies it is very difficult—or even impossible—to achieve appealing outcomes in these complex interaction processes in networks.

Leadership Activities: Collaboration and Network Management

There is certainly broad consensus in the literature that the type of leadership and/or management required in network and collaborative settings differs significantly from the classical leadership image of leaders of organizations. Ansell and Gash (2008) talk about facilitating leadership; by this they mean that the task of a leader is to mediate between actors and empower the process of collaboration. Huxham and Vangen (2005: 203) state: 'This line of argument [about leadership] steers the theory in sharp departure from classical notions of leadership....Not surprisingly, those researchers who have focused on leadership in collaboration have tended to emphasize relational leadership, processes for inspiring, nurturing, supporting and communicating.' Kickert, Klijn, and Koppenjan (1997: 11) state: 'managing networks, however, should not be confused with the "classical management approach"....Network management is, in essence, an inter-organizational activity.' Thus the leadership and management style appropriate in networks and collaborative processes is one of facilitating, activating actors, and enhancing their collaboration (see also Gage and Mandell 1990; Agranoff and McGuire 2001).

If we look at the literature on network management, frequently mentioned management and leadership strategies include: initiating and facilitating interaction processes between actors (Friend, Power, and Yewlett 1974), for instance by activating (or de-activating) actors and resources; creating and changing network arrangements for better coordination (Scharpf 1978; Rogers and Whetten 1982); creating new content and win–win situations (Mandell 2001), for example by exploring new ideas, working with scenarios, organizing joint research (and joint fact finding) (Koppenjan and Klijn 2004), and guiding interactions (Gage and Mandell 1990; Kickert, Klijn, and Koppenjan 1997).

The literature on collaborative governance and collaborative advantages mentions similar activities. Huxham and Vangen (2005) mention activities like mobilizing member organizations, dealing with power relations, empowering actors that can deliver collaborative aims, and trust building. Ansell and Gash (2008) mention elements like committing to the process, creating shared understanding, aiming for participatory inclusiveness.

It is clear, however, that another type of leadership is required in collaborative processes and networks—a type of leadership that requires negotiating skills, skills to bind actors, and skills to forge new solutions that appeal to various actors whose resources are required to implement solutions.

Some Empirical Evidence of Networked Leadership

In the last 10 to 15 years, a lot of empirical research has been undertaken on the importance of network management strategies and collaborative leadership. Although many of these studies have been case studies (Marcussen and Torfing 2007; Ansell and Gash 2008; O'Leary and Bingham 2009) there are also some survey studies (Meier and O'Toole 2007; Provan, Huang, and Milward 2009; O'Leary and Bingham 2009; Klijn, Steijn, and Edelenbos 2010).

Both types of study emphasize that network management and collaborative strategic leadership are required to achieve good results. Thus, activating actors and networking, mentioned as important in collaborative leadership and network management, has been shown to be important in many studies. Huang and Provan (2007) have shown that network involvement, or network embeddedness, is positively related to social outcomes. Meier and O'Toole (2007), in well-known studies on educational districts in Texas, have shown that networking by district managers is positively correlated with the performance of the district; but the deployment of network management strategies also proves to be important. Klijn, Steijn, and Edelenbos (2010) show in a survey of respondents involved in spatial planning projects that networks where more, and more intensive, network management strategies are deployed perform better (measured as perceived by the respondents) than networks where fewer managerial strategies are deployed.

Trust in Collaborative Processes and Networks

Huxham and Vangen (2005: 153) observe that trust is often mentioned as essential but that practitioners actually talk about situations where trust is relatively weak or absent.

This observation is also made in the literature on networks. Many authors observe that trust in networks is relatively rare and that networks are characterized by conflicts of interest and strategic behaviour (Scharpf 1978; Marin and Mayntz 1991; Rhodes 1997; Meier and O'Toole 2007). This stands in sharp contrast to the literature, which considers trust as an inherent coordination mechanism of networks (as compared with hierarchy [control] and markets [price]; see Thompson et al. 1991). Even if one accepts that this is an ideal typology, one can wonder what the value of it is (other than confusing the discussion about networks).

Nevertheless, trust may play an important role in networks according to many scholars (Ansell and Gash 2008; Klijn, Edelenbos, and Steijn 2010). Trust tackles strategic uncertainty because actors take one another's interest into account; it reduces the necessity for complex contracts; and it enhances the possibility of actors sharing information and developing innovative solutions (see Lane and Bachman 1998; Nooteboom 2002). Empirical research shows that the level of trust has a positive influence on network performance (for evidence, see Provan, Huang, and Milward 2009; Klijn, Edelenbos, and Steijn 2010).

Given these findings, it is probably better to reverse the argument about trust and networks: trust is not the sole coordinating mechanism of networks, but trust is an important asset to achieve in networks. One could even further reverse the argument and state that networks are formed to increase the relations between actors to achieve goals that actors cannot achieve alone, and trust building is one of the core mechanisms by which this is achieved. It reduces strategic uncertainty, thus facilitating investments in uncertain collaboration processes among interdependent actors with diverging and sometimes conflicting interests. Thus, trust is a feature to be achieved by management and effective leadership (Ansell and Gash 2008; O'Leary and Bingham 2009), as many authors argue, rather than something that is already present.

Political Leadership in a Networked World

There is evidence, therefore, that network management and collaborative leadership are not only inevitable in a situation of mutual dependency but also that they seem to work or are at least positively related to outcomes and performances of networks. If this is so, however, and politicians and public managers have to deploy such strategies, what does this mean for their role as leaders in a networked world?

First of all, it is clear that a different kind of leadership is required (see also 't Hart 2011): a leadership that is capable of building relations in the network and uses the knowledge and collective strength of the network. Thus, leaders must have connective abilities; but this is not the only characteristic of a (political) leader in a networked world. Since it is essential for leaders in a network context to be able to mobilize actors, they also have to be able to understand the other actors' perceptions and desires about the problems and the solutions. Leaders in networks have to be able to construct policy solutions (or service packages and conditions) that are attractive to the actors involved. Collaborative leadership requires the ability to be flexible with goals and content proposals so that the leader can manœuvre them to create the support that is essential. Last but not least, it requires dedication to the process and the skill to create trust relations between actors. Often, these network processes take a long time to work through, and consequently actors must be willing to exchange information and cooperate over a long time period. Thus, trust building is very important for achieving results in networks.

3 Political Leadership in a Mediatized World: The Front Stage

How, however, do these leadership requirements meet the challenges of elected leaders on the front-stage, that is, the politically elected arena where leaders are very visible and accountable as office-holders to elected bodies and the media?

General Tensions Front-Stage: Networks and Representational Bodies

As the example in the introduction to this chapter shows, tensions can emerge between the horizontal process among actors in interdependent networks—which requires negotiation and give and take—and the political 'handiwork' in which politicians have to be visible to their electorate and the media—which requires them to be associated with clear points of view and decisions.

This matches the empirical findings in the literature and research about networks, interactive decision-making, collaborative governance, and so forth that often reveal strong clashes between representational bodies and collaborative processes (see for instance Klijn and Koppenjan 2000; Edelenbos 2005; Skelcher, Mathur, and Smith 2005). In general, one can observe a tension between the idea of representative democracy, with its more vertical accountability structure, and governance processes, which have more horizontal accountability.

If we look at the relation between networks and collaborative governance on the one hand and representative democracy on the other, we find four main positions concerning this issue (Klijn and Skelcher 2007).

1. Incompatible position: classical representational democracy is incompatible with governance processes because these are a threat to the position of democratic institutions. The authority and accountability of these institutions is 'hollowed out' by the involvement of other stakeholders.

2. Complementary position: governance processes provide for additional links to society and can perfectly co-exist beside classical democratic institutions. Elected officials are provided with more information, political office-holders retain their important place, but accountability is shared.

3. Transition position: governance networks offer greater flexibility and efficiency, and they will gradually replace representative democracy as the dominant model in the network society.

4. Instrumental position: governance networks provide a means for democratic institutions to increase their control in a situation of societal complexity. By setting performance targets or constraints, elected office-holders secure their dominant position.

The various positions are strongly influenced by the view that their proponents take of democracy. Authors who write from a representational view of democracy tend to be more critical about networks than authors who write from a deliberate or participatory view. They tend to emphasize that networks and collaborative processes should be organized to open up decision making to stakeholders and see this as enhancing the democratic legitimacy of decisions (see Innes and Booher 2003; Sørensen and Torfing 2007; Ansell and Gash 2008). Thus, most authors observe empirical tensions, but their normative judgement is correlated to their perspective on democracy.

Front-Stage as a Mediatized World

However, the front-stage is also very much determined by the media landscape. Many authors have argued that the media, because of the growing competition between various media outlets and the growing commercialization of the media (and the need to attract advertising and thus many readers/viewers), have changed the nature of news provision (see Bennett 2009). Bennett identifies four types of informational biases that result from the recent developments in the media business:

1. *Personalization*, or a strong tendency in the news, and certainly in the US news, to emphasize the personal aspect of news and downplay the social economic or political context in which the event takes place. The idea is that, when news is framed in a more personal way, it appeals to more readers and viewers. Personalization tends to down play or ignore the larger complexity of the issue.

2. *Dramatization*, or a strong tendency toward dramatizing news, emphasizing crisis and conflict in stories, rather than continuity or harmony. The recent trend of providing news live at the scene has only reinforced the dramatization bias.

3. *Fragmentation*, or an increasing focus on isolated stories and events, separating these from the larger context and from each other.

4. An *authority–disorder bias*, or a preoccupation with order and whether authorities are capable of maintaining or restoring that order. At the same time, a shift has taken place from an attitude where the media are favourable to politicians and authorities toward an attitude where media are suspicious of authorities.

Patterson's (2000) analysis of 5,000 news stories between 1980 and 1999 confirms many of these biases and shows a sharp increase in stories without policy-related content. It also shows that politicians were treated significantly more negatively as the years progressed (the authority–disorder bias). Research in other countries seems to confirm these trends (Kleinnijenhuis, van Hoof, and Oegema 2006; Reunanen, Kunelis, and Noppari 2010). Most of these studies focus on national political events. Not much is known about media attention on complex decision making in networks. However, recent research undertaken at Erasmus University Rotterdam looking at the media attention on five complex decision-making processes around environmental issues also shows the same biases (except for the personalization bias, see Korthagen 2011). This seems to indicate that many of the findings about media attention on national political issues would also hold for attention to complex decision making in networks.

This view is supported by Baumgartner and Jones' (2009) work looking at dynamics in agendas and policy subsystems in the USA over the longer term. Baumgartner and Jones also emphasized the positive feedback often provided by media attention. This has to do with the tendency among journalists (also labelled as a pack of journalists, see Bennett 2009) to seek out new dramatic stories, publish them, and repeat them (and follow one another in order not to miss a scoop). Baumgartner and Jones (2009: 106), in their research on agenda setting and the role of the media therein, write: 'These features of journalistic homogeneity imply positive feedback: with each success in attracting the attention of new media outlets, still more are likely to become interested.'

Political Leadership in a Mediatized World

The media biases discussed above change not only the nature of the news but also the way we view news and judge our (political) leaders and how they have to operate in the democratic arena. We tend to see the world, authors argue, as a drama and seek out the villains and the heroes, the winners and the losers; but we also tend to use the same criteria to judge our political leaders as we use to judge famous rock stars, soccer players, or movie stars (Richards 2009). Style and emotions have become very important in that judgement (Corner and Pels 2003). We want our leaders to be authentic, and accessible and open, but at the same time we want them to be better than us.

Thus, political and public leaders are operating in a rapidly changing media environment. Many authors argue, however, that they do adapt. Politics and democracy have turned into, as Elchardus, a Belgian sociologist, termed it, a drama democracy; or as Elchardus (2002: 82, current author's translation) states: 'In a drama democracy it is tempting to score by communication and performing. That is easier than taking care of policy dossiers and taking decisions, activities that make not only friends but also enemies. Communication takes the place of ideology, the announcement of policy proposals replaces taking decisions, and catchy words replace policy concepts.' What is crucial in the drama democracy is that the leader stages his/her performance. This also means adapting the performance to the media logic rules. In drama democracy, it is not the strength of the argumentation but the strength of the image that prevails. Fischer (2003) states in his book *Reframing public politics*:

> Politicians and the media...have turned contemporary politics into a political spectacle that is experienced more like a stage drama rather than reality itself. Based on socially constructed stories designed more to capture the interest of the audience than to offer factual portrayal of events, the political spectacle is constituted by a set of political symbols and signifiers that continuously construct and reconstruct self-conceptions, the meaning of past events, expectations for the future, and the significance of prominent social groups.
>
> (Fischer 2003: 58)

This of course echoes Edelman's (1977) observations more than thirty years ago in his book with the subtitle *Words that Succeed and Policies that Fail*.

However, these demands of political leaders in the mediatized world are completely different from those in the networked world. Leaders have to convey strong images, show they can make a difference, and create associations with which the electorate can identify.

4 Front-Stage and Back-Stage: Coping with Network Complexity and Media Attention

In the previous two sections we have sketched two developments—the growing complexity of policy- and decision making in a networked world and the growing mediatization of society—that both have consequences for political and public leadership. These consequences also manifest tensions. We deal with some of the most important ones.

Complex Multi-Valued Problems and Solutions versus Simple Easy Communications

The complex network reality of the back-stage is characterized, as we saw, by value conflicts between actors, by uncertainty about the nature of the problem, and a careful search for inclusive solutions that satisfy many actors. Thus, it is not easy to communicate strong images about solutions that provide easy answers. Political leaders must therefore balance between communicating front-stage in relatively easy sound bites without losing their credibility back-stage with the wide arrange of involved actors.

Personalized Strong Profile versus Connecting Leader

The mediatized world requires the leader not only to communicate strong statements that will be noticed in the media landscape, but also to have a strong profile. The audience, and especially the media, want a leader who is responsible for solving the problem and who takes ownership of the process, but this clashes strongly with the need to be a connective leader who binds various actors together and can communicate on behalf of a wide coalition. In a networked world, it is important to communicate collective ownership to enhance the binding of actors to the process and the outcomes. Front-stage, the (political) leader needs to claim success, whereas, back-stage, success has many fathers.

Long-Term Oriented Dedication versus Short-Term Visibility

This tension is clear. In a mediatized world, the short term is important. There is pressure to achieve and thus pressure to show quick results. This is problematic, however, because we are dealing with complex problems and actors have to be associated with attractive solutions. In a network and collaborative context, it is crucial to bind actors for the longer term and thus avoid quick wins but rather incorporate revenues and results that will be realized later in the process in order to bind actors to the full development and implementation process (see Koppenjan and Klijn 2004). That is not, however, an interesting and appealing story to tell front-stage.

Trust Building versus Conflict Framing

As stated, trust building is important in networks because many unexpected events can happen and trust is the essential glue that holds the network together in difficult times. Media attention, however, is focused on dramatizing events, and constructing conflicts and competition between political parties front-stage will enhance this characteristic. Thus, media attention is probably often a threat to trust since it fuels existing conflicts between actors or creates new ones (for empirical evidence of this see Korthagen and Klijn 2012). Furthermore, if conflicts are framed and reported by the media, there will be pressure on the individual actors to react to them. This in turn will encourage complexity and the possibility of conflicts increasing because actors have to inflate their position vis-à-vis the media. This effect is well-known in research on negotiation processes followed by the media (Sporer-Wagner and Marcinkowski 2010).

   All these tensions require modern leaders to engage in a balancing act—a balancing act that is far from easy since some of the tensions are almost impossible to resolve. Leaders will probably manage these tensions by alternating between emphasizing conflict and emphasizing trust, switching their attention between the dilemmas and the choices within dilemmas.

Reflections: Practical and Research Consequences

In this chapter, we have highlighted the tension between a leader's role in a modern networked world, where he/she has to face complex interdependencies and negotiate policy implementation and service delivery, and a leader's role in a modern mediatized world that expects adaptation to the profiling in the political world and to the media logic that requires drama and strong images. We finish by speculating where this will lead in the future.

5 An Image of the Future: Leaders Co-Creating Brands with the Public...

If we argue that we see tensions and dilemmas between the front-stage and the back-stage, and follow the literature on both—which stresses that the back-stage will become more complex and the front-stage will be more mediatized—then the conclusion must be that these tensions will increase. This will require the almost impossible of leaders: to be able to communicate both back-stage and front-stage. It will require leaders to be able to convey images and emotions that fit in a mediatized world and at the same time communicate back stage. It is likely that we shall see the use of brands and images replacing traditional policy communication vehicles like documents, master plans, and so forth. We can already witness this development in elections where politicians use marketing and brands to position themselves, and it also shows in the growing positioning of policies and projects (see Eshuis and Klijn 2012). Brands will also be used to create shared feelings and possibly to encourage participation. Instead of boring formal meetings where leaders inform the public and receive negative reactions to their master plans, citizens will be asked to contribute to the brand and co-create with stories, associations, and images—a way that far better fits the virtual world of social media. This will be the way to bridge the gap between front- and back-stage, or at least attempt to do so.

6 ...Leadership Research

Leadership research will follow this development and explore how the gap between the front-stage and the back-stage can be bridged. It will pay more attention to emotions (although leadership research is probably an exception to the rule that emotions are neglected in public administration) and involve stakeholders in innovative ways that can also be communicated front-stage. So we will see a merging of collaborative leadership and network theories with theories on marketing, branding, and communications.

This opens new avenues for research such as the effectiveness of public brands and the communicative value of collaborative processes, but also for more attention to be paid to the emotional and associative—rather than the rational—values of communication. This will probably make many public administration scholars uneasy since almost all public administration theories still emphasize the rational, or at least the reasonable, side of policy and politics. However, there is no escape for public administration in relation to coping with the demands of the front-stage. The challenge will be to integrate this with existing theories and move on to a better understanding of the tensions between front- and back- stage.

Recommended Reading

Hanf, K. and Scharpf, F. W., eds. (1978). *Interorganisational Policy Making*. London: Sage.

Kickert, W. J. M., Klijn, E. H., and Koppenjan, J. F. M. (eds) (1997). *Managing Complex Networks: Strategies for the Public Sector*. London: Sage.

Huxham, C. and Vangen, S. (2005). *Managing to Collaborate: The Theory and Practice of Collaborative Advantage*. London: Routledge.

References

Agranoff, R. and McGuire, M. (2001). 'Big Questions in Public Network Management Research', *Journal of Public Administration Research and Theory*, 11/3: 295–326.

Ansell, C. and Gash, A. (2008). 'Collaborative Governance in Theory and Practice', *Journal of Public Administration Research and Theory*, 18/4: 543–71.

Baumgartner, F. R. and Jones, B. (2009). *Agendas and Instability in American Politics*, 2nd edition. Chicago, IL: University of Chicago Press.

Bennett, W. L. (2009). *News: The Politics of Illusion*, 8th edition. New York: Pearson Longman.

Bryson, J. M. and Crosby, B. (1992). *Leadership for the Common Good: Tackling Public Problems in a Shared Power World*. San Francisco, CA: Jossey-Bass.

Corner, J. and Pels, D. (eds) (2003). *Media and the Restyling of Politics. Consumerism, Celebrity and Cynicism*. London: Sage.

Edelenbos, J. (2005). 'Institutional Implications of Interactive Governance: Insights from Dutch Practice', *Governance*, 18/1: 111–34.

Edelman, M. (1977). *Political Language: Words that Succeed and Policies that Fail*. New York: Academic Press.

Elchardus, M. (2002). *De Dramademocratie*. Tielt: Lannoo.

Eshuis, J. and Klijn, E. H. (2012). *Branding in Governance and Public Management*. London: Routledge.

Fischer, F. (2003). *Reframing Public Policy: Discursive Politics and Deliberative Practices*. Oxford: Oxford University Press.

Friend, J. K., Power, J. M. and Yewlett, C. J. L. (1974). *Public Planning: The Inter-corporate Dimension*. London: Tavistock.

Gage, R. W. and Mandell, M. P. (eds) (1990). *Strategies for Managing Intergovernmental Policies and Networks*. New York/London: Preager.

Hanf, K. and Scharpf, F. W. (eds) (1978). *Interorganisational Policy Making*. London: Sage.

't Hart, P. (2011). 'Evaluating Public Leadership: Towards an Assessment Framework', *Public Money and Management*, 31/5: 323–30.

Huang, K. and Provan, K. G. (2007). 'Structural Embeddedness and Organizational Social Outcomes in a Centrally Governed Mental Health Service Network', *Public Management Review*, 9/2: 169–89.

Huxham, C. and Vangen, S. (2005). *Managing to Collaborate: The Theory and Practice of Collaborative Advantage*. London: Routledge.

Innes, J. E. and Booher, D. E. (2003). 'Collaborative Policymaking: Governance through Dialogue', in M. A. Hajer and H. Wagenaar (eds), *Deliberative Policy Analysis: Understanding Governance in the Network Society*. Cambridge: Cambridge University Press, 33–59.

Kaufmann, F. X., Majone, G., and Ostrom, V. (eds) (1986). *Guidance, Control and Evaluation in the Public Sector: The Bielefeld Interdisciplinary Project*. Berlin: Walter de Gruyter.

Kickert, W. J. M., Klijn, E. H., and Koppenjan, J. F. M. (eds) (1997). *Managing Complex Networks: Strategies for the Public Sector*. London: Sage.

Kleinnijenhuis, J., van Hoof, A. M. J., and Oegema, D. (2006). 'Negative News and the Sleeper Effect of Distrust', *The Harvard International Journal of Press/Politics*, 11/2: 86–104.

Klijn, E. H. and Koppenjan, J. F. M. (2000). Politicians and Interactive Decision Making: Institutional Spoilsports or Playmakers. *Public Administration*, 78/2: 365–87.

Klijn, E. H. and Skelcher, C. K. (2007). 'Democracy and Governance Networks: Compatible or Not? Four Conjectures and their Implications', *Public Administration*, 85/3: 1–22.

Klijn, E. H., Edelenbos, J., and Steijn, B. (2010). 'Trust in Governance Networks: Its Impact and Outcomes', *Administration and Society*, 42/2: 193–221.

Klijn, E. H, Steijn, B., and Edelenbos, J. (2010). 'The Impact of Network Management Strategies on the Outcomes in Governance Networks', *Public Administration*, 88/4: 1063–82.

Koppenjan, J. F. M. and Klijn, E. H. (2004). *Managing Uncertainty in Networks*. London: Routledge.

Korthagen, I. (2011). 'The Soft Side of Hard News: The Biased Journalistic Construction of Complex Decision Making'. Paper presented at Netherlands Institute of Government conference, 1–2 December 2011, Rotterdam.

Korthagen, I. and Klijn, E. H. (2012). 'Two Clashing Logics: The Influence of Media Logic and Mediatized Politics on Decision Making Processes in Governance Networks'. Paper presented at the International Society of Public Management conferences, Rome, 11–13 April 2012. Panel: Solving Policy Problems: Expertise, Mind Sets, and Management.

Lane, C. and Bachman, R. (eds) (1998). *Trust Within and Between Organizations: Conceptual Issues and Empirical Applications*. Oxford: Oxford University Press.

Laumann, E. O. and Knoke, D. (1987). *The Organizational State: Societal Choice in National Policy Domains*. Wisconsin, WI: University of Wisconsin Press.

Mandell, M. P. (ed.) (2001). *Getting Results Through Collaboration*. Westport, CT: Quorum Books.

Marcussen, M. and Torfing, J. (eds). (2007). *Democratic Network Governance in Europe*. Cheltenham: Edward Elgar.

Marin, B. and Mayntz, R. (eds) (1991). *Policy Networks: Empirical Evidence and Theoretical Considerations*. Boulder, CO: Westview Press.

Marsh, D. and Rhodes, R. A. W. (eds) (1992). *Policy Networks in British Government*. Oxford: Clarendon Press.

Meier, K. and O'Toole, L. J. (2007). 'Modelling Public Management: Empirical Analysis of the Management–performance Nexus'. *Public Administration Review*, 9/4: 503–27.

Nooteboom, B. (2002). *Trust: Forms, Foundations, Functions, Failures and Figures*. Cheltenham: Edward Elgar.

O'Leary, R. and Bingham, L. B. (2009). *The Collaborative Public Manager: New Ideas for the Twenty-First Century*. Washington, DC: Georgetown University Press.

Osborne, S. P. (2010). *The New Public Governance: Emerging Perspectives on the Theory and Practice of Public Governance*. London: Routledge.

Patterson, T. E. (2000). *Doing Well and Doing Good: How Soft News and Critical Journalism Are Shrinking the News Audience and Weakening Democracy—And What News Outlets Can Do About It*. Faculty Research Working Papers Series. Boston, MA: Joan Shorenstein Center on the Press, Politics and Public Policy, Kennedy School of Government, Harvard University.

Provan, K. G., Huang, K., and Milward, B. H. (2009). 'The Evolution of Structural Embeddedness and Organizational Social Outcomes in a Centrally Governed Health and Human Service Network'. *Journal of Public Administration Research and Theory*, 19/4: 873–93.

Reunanen, E., Kunelis, R., and Noppari, E. (2010). 'Mediatization in Context: Consensus Culture, Media and Decision Making in the 21st Century, the Case of Finland'. *Communications*, 35/3: 287–307.

Rhodes, R. A. W. (1997). *Understanding Governance*. Buckingham: Open University Press.

Richards, B. (2009). 'The Emotional Deficit in Political Communication', in M. Greco and P. Stenner (eds), *Emotions: Social Science Reader*, London: Routledge, 361–67.

Rittel, H. and Webber, M. (1973). 'Dilemmas in a General Theory of Planning', *Policy Sciences*, 4/2: 155–69.

Rogers, D. L. and Whetten, D. A. (eds) (1982). *Interorganizational Coordination: Theory, Research and Implementation*. Iowa, IA: Iowa State University Press.

Scharpf, F. W. (1978). 'Interorganizational Policy Studies: Issues, Concepts and Perspectives', In K. Hanf and F. W. Scharpf (eds), *Interorganisational Policy Making*. London: Sage. 345–70.

Skelcher, C., Mathur, N., and Smith, M. (2005). 'The Public Governance of Collaborative Spaces: Discourse, Design and Democracy', *Public Administration*, 83/3: 573–96.

Sørensen, E. and Torfing, J. (eds) (2007). *Theories of Democratic Network Governance*. London: Palgrave Macmillan.

Sporer-Wagner, D. and Marcinkowski, F. (2010). 'Is Talk Always Silver and Silence Gold: The Mediatisation of Political Bargaining', *Javnost—The Public*, 17/2: 5–26.

Thompson, G., Frances, J., Levacic, R., and Mitchell, J. (eds) (1991). *Markets, Hierarchies and Networks*. London: Sage.

CHAPTER 28

···

POLITICAL LEADERSHIP IN TIMES OF CRISIS

···

CHRIS ANSELL, ARJEN BOIN, AND PAUL 't HART

1 UNDERSTANDING CRISIS LEADERSHIP

···

> 'Today there is no longer such a thing as strategy; there is only crisis management.'

IF this observation by the late US Secretary of Defence, Robert McNamara, was meant to suggest that the nature of foreign policy had changed as a result of the Cuban missile crisis, he was surely wrong. If, however, he meant that in today's world, political leaders may well be defined in terms of their performance under pressure and stress, he was right.[1] Modern societies are besieged by a wide variety of natural and man-made disruptions—ranging from unprecedented natural disasters to new forms of terrorism, from climate change to tectonic shifts in the international order, from financial mayhem to cybercrime.

Citizens worry about their safety and security in the face of these threats (Beck 1999; OECD 2003). They expect their leaders and government to protect them against threats and fears, whether 'real' or 'imagined' (Furedi 2005). When major disruptions do occur, they expect them to provide comprehensive response and recovery operations, embody the collective determination, punish the guilty (or take the blame), and learn the right lessons.

Just as crisis politics differs from politics as usual, crisis leadership differs from leadership in routine times. Its stakes are much higher, the public is much more attentive, its mood more volatile, and institutional constraints on elite decision making are

---

[1] The quote is taken from Bell (1971: 2). See also Lord (1998). Dick Neustadt (1990: 5) wrote in similar vein: 'Cold war is not a crisis; it becomes a way of life.'

considerably looser. Fundamentally ambiguous, crises provide political elites with power chances *and* with acute threats to their legitimacy (Edelman 1977). Likewise crises can be more stressful *and* easier for leaders to master than 'politics as usual'.

This makes political leadership in times of crisis an important topic of study. In this chapter we examine the fruits of the efforts of scholars across a range of disciplines to document and interpret the challenges, behaviour, and impacts of political leaders during crises. First we briefly signal the various sources of crisis leadership research across the social sciences.

2 A BROAD CHURCH

Insight into political crisis leadership comes from many sources. First, in political biography, the crises that happened during the careers of leaders always play a stark role. It seems, in fact, one cannot write about political leaders without mentioning crises (Neustadt 1990). Richard Nixon (1962) grasped this when he entitled his mid-career autobiography, *Six Crises*. George W. Bush's (2010) recent memoirs likewise are entirely organized around a few critical calls he made during his term in office.

In comparative politics studies of political development, elite statecraft during crises played a key role (Binder et al. 1971; Almond, Flanagan, and Mundt 1973; Linz and Stepan 1978). Early scholarship in this area was inspired by the collapse of the Weimar government and similar episodes of 'loss of democratic authenticity'. Constitutional scholars and political theorists debated the merits of crisis government, conceiving of it as a trade-off between the constitutional need to enable state elites to wield extraordinary executive powers in the face of existential threats, and the risk that such provisions could be hijacked by ruthless political leaders seeking to hijack and abuse state power (Friedrich 1963; Bracher 1971). Shades of this debate were visible decades later in critiques of post 9/11 counter terrorism policies and legal reforms (Wolf 2007).

A separate and very productive strand of crisis scholarship developed in the 1960s within International Relations, particularly the subfield of foreign policy analysis. It was triggered academically by intensive studies of the escalation of the Summer 1914 crisis (Holsti 1972), the Korean War (Paige 1968), the Cuban missile crisis (Allison 1971; Bell 1971), and a growing range of comparative and multi-case monographs and collections (Hermann 1972; George and Smoke 1974; Snyder and Diesing 1977; Brecher 1993).

Two strands of theory emerged from it. The first strand offers detailed propositions on elite decision making under conditions of crisis, focusing strongly on the effects which stress and centralized and informal structures of decision making have upon the judgement of political leaders and their advisers. The second strand develops propositions about the dynamics of 'brinkmanship' in international crises, employing game theory, cognitive psychology, and communications analysis to study how the leaders' perceptions, calculi, and signals to their adversaries shaped crisis (de-)

escalation processes and outcomes (Jervis 1976; Lebow 1981; Jervis, Lebow, and Stein 1985).

During the 1980s, scholars in the field of public policy and public administration started to study crises. One strand of this scholarship has focused on how government structures and processes change in response to having to deal with the unexpected, the undesirable, and the uncertainties which crises entail. It has since produced a wide array of case studies and comparative analyses yielding its own set of generalizations about the determinants of public sector resilience in the face of extreme adversity (Rosenthal, Charles, and 't Hart 1989; Rosenthal, Boin, and Comfort 2001; Drennan and McConnell 2007). Another strand has conceptualized crises as 'critical junctures' in politics and public policy. Its proponents have demonstrated that crises are 'focusing events' which 'punctuate' the institutional status quo. This creates possibilities for advocates of change to exercise a form of 'situational leadership': to call publicly into question existing policy paradigms and institutional practices, and use the 'window of opportunity' provided by public outrage and political imperatives to forge coalitions for non-incremental reforms (Kingdon 1984; Keeler 1993; Birkland 2006; Kuipers 2006).

Over time, a genuinely interdisciplinary venture has emerged, held together by a key foundational premise: that conditions of crisis—high threat, urgency, and deep uncertainty—evoke political and psychological mechanisms that change the way in which people, organizations, governments, polities, and media act and interact, yielding both great challenges and great opportunities for the exercise of public leadership. As the study of crisis leadership is fragmented across and beyond the political science field, however, it is helpful to understand how scholars have defined crises and the leadership challenges that they entail.

In structural-functionalist accounts, a crisis is most often defined as an urgent threat to the core values or critical systems of a society (for example, an acute threat of violent conflict and war), that must be addressed under conditions of deep uncertainty and risk (Rosenthal, Charles, and 't Hart 1989; Brecher 1993). From a broader systemic perspective, the term crisis is used to describe a turning point in the evolution, 'life cycle', 'health', and legitimacy of governing elites, policy paradigms, political regimes, or even the political system as a whole. For example, within party politics, acute drops in polls, major electoral losses, political scandals, and overt challenges by competitors all constitute crises from the perspective of incumbent party elites. Likewise, policy fiascos, implementation failures, major economic downturns, and/or fiscal stress, can acutely threaten the political efficacy and legitimacy of the beliefs, values, problem definitions, institutional structures, and coalitions underpinning current policies and programmes ('t Hart 1993; Bovens and 't Hart 1996; Boin and 't Hart 2000).

Crises can pertain to policy issues, sectors, or organizations, but can also threaten the status quo of entire regimes and political systems. Such macro-level crises can be induced by major shifts in the geostrategic (the end of the Cold War) or economic (the 1970s OPEC price hikes and the 2008 financial meltdown) balance of power. They can also emerge through an escalation of domestic socio-economic and ethnopolitical tensions, spill-over effects of regional conflict, or breakdowns in civil–military relations (Linz and Stepan 1978, 1996; Tilly and Tarrow 2006; Boix and Stokes 2007).

As noted, crisis analysis has developed as a broad epistemological and methodological church. Modernist-empiricist approaches abound in international relations and disaster studies. Conversely, many other crisis scholars cite the Thomas theorem ('if men define their situations as real, they are real in their consequences') to argue that it is *perceptions* of crisis—however exaggerated, manufactured, or delusional—that matter most, requiring the analyst to reconstruct actors' beliefs and interpretations of events as much as the events themselves (Thomas and Thomas 1928). On that view, crises exist when actors not only publicly frame (which political leaders are always tempted to do opportunistically) but privately *believe* particular situations to be threatening, urgent, and highly uncertain—no matter what the statistics, experts, or impartial observers say.[2]

3 Dissecting Crisis Leadership

Any approach to crisis leadership must take into account the fact that political leaders (particularly, but not exclusively government leaders) in times of crises are often called upon to juggle at least three distinctive roles: sovereign, facilitator, and symbol. As a sovereign, a crisis leader is called upon to make authoritative decisions about the deployment of state resources to intervene in the crisis; as a facilitator, leaders are meta-governors who mobilize and align the actions of different stakeholders; and as symbol, the leadership role is iconic for both the response effort and the political community at large.

These roles can be complementary. Heads of government, for example, may call upon their sovereign and symbolic powers to strengthen their capacity to effectively facilitate crisis coordination; and yet these roles can also be in tension during a crisis. It is by understanding these tensions that we can more fully understand the challenges of crisis leadership. As sovereigns, crisis leaders must make authoritative decisions. Their authority gives them the power to initiate and direct. The facilitative role, by contrast, often requires crisis leaders to recognize that power is shared and hence that they must operate more by negotiation than by direction (Waugh and Streib 2006). In both their sovereign and facilitative role, crisis leaders may find that they are sending signals that are in conflict with their symbolic task of reassuring the public.

Each of these roles can be complex and can produce unintended consequences. For example, crisis leaders are called upon to make final, authoritative decisions. The price of this authority, however, is a heightened demand for accountability, or at least, intense

---

[2] A corollary of this view holds that anything labelled a crisis by the mass media becomes a crisis for politicians in its consequences through discursive dynamics such as 'scandal amplification'.

public scrutiny. This authority–accountability nexus places crisis leaders at the centre of the 'blame game', which frequently permeates a crisis and its aftermath.

This description of sovereign, facilitative, and symbolic roles reinforces why it is often so difficult to separate crisis leadership from crisis outcomes. As the sovereign, the crisis leader has the 'final' authority and is ultimately given credit or held responsible for good decisions (often judged in hindsight). As the facilitator, the crisis leader is expected to ensure that any barrier to effective action is removed. As a symbol, the crisis leader is an icon of both the response and of the political community in crisis.

Following Selznick's (1957) work on institutional leadership, we conceptualize crisis leadership as a set of functions that—one way or the other—will need to be performed, often repeatedly over the course of an evolving crisis. Who ought to perform these functions is partly a legal but mostly a matter of strategic judgement. How and by whom they actually get performed in any given crisis is a matter of empirical research. How well existing governmental and other political leaders perform them is a matter of evaluation research, which presupposes normative criteria for 'good' crisis management, an analytic leap that very few crisis scholars have dared to make. Following Boin et al. (2005), we highlight five core tasks of political crisis management:

1. *Sense-making.* Political leaders are expected to make authoritative interpretations of the causes, characteristics, dynamics, and consequences of an emerging crisis. They must 'test' emerging realities (Burke and Greenstein 1989). While they are often supported in this task by experts and information systems, the responsibility ultimately falls to political leaders to decide how to cut through the uncertainty, ambiguity, and competing interpretations to authorize a working theory of the situation.

2. *Shaping responses.* Political leaders are expected to provide direction and coordination to the emerging crisis response network. A response may be orchestrated via well-established professional roles and organizational protocols, requiring little direction. However, political leaders are called upon to ensure that these roles and protocols unfold as expected, that exceptional circumstances are handled, and that emerging needs are anticipated in a timely way. Moreover, political leaders are expected to make critical decisions (the 'hard calls') that set priorities and make difficult trade-offs.

3. *Meaning making.* Political leadership pertains to the act of defining a crisis: 'sovereign is he who decides on the exceptional case', as Carl Schmitt (1985: 5) famously remarked. Political leaders face the delicate task of explaining to citizens and stakeholders what the nature of the crisis is and what is being done to minimize the crisis. They are expected to maintain and restore trust in government. They must ensure that the response itself is regarded as legitimate.

4. *Account giving after a crisis.* Political leaders are expected to manage the process of expert, media, legislative, and judicial inquiry and debate in such a way that responsibilities are clarified and accepted, destructive blame games are avoided, and a degree of catharsis is achieved (Boin, McConnell, and 't Hart 2008).

5. *Learning*. Political leaders are expected to organize the process that culls lessons from the crisis, translating these lessons into reform initiatives that will help prevent similar crises (Stern 1997).

This task-based approach allows crisis analysts to make a distinction between the immediate response phase (sense-making, shaping the response, meaning-making) and the crisis aftermath (account-giving and learning). This is purely an analytical distinction, as the tasks typically play out simultaneously, during and after the crisis; and yet they enable us to organize our discussion of the vast literature that deals with the various dimensions of political crisis management.

Making Sense of Crisis

After a crisis, leaders are often asked why they 'did not see it coming'. History is replete with examples of leaders 'sleepwalking' into crisis (think of the First World War, Pearl Harbor, the Yom Kippur War, or the 2008–9 financial crisis). Whereas they may not have received proper warnings before a crisis, leaders can drown in information *during* a crisis. In many crises, leaders struggle with the mountains of raw data (reports, rumours, pictures) that are quickly amassed for them when something extraordinary happens. Turning them into a coherent picture of the situation is a major challenge by itself. All this adds up to the challenge of sense-making (Weick 2001).

Sense-making refers to the capacity of leaders to recognize that an urgent threat is emerging which requires remedial action. In addition, it refers to their capacity to grasp an unfolding crisis process, to understand what can be done to stop it or minimize its impact. Sense-making has at least two dimensions: a social-psychological and a political one.

Scholarship has described in much detail the human capacity to make sense of dynamic and threatening environments. Psychological research demonstrates that most people find it extremely hard to recognize deviating patterns and are masterful at deceiving themselves into thinking that 'it will not happen to them' (Kahneman 2011). They use cognitive short cuts to simplify their information-processing loads, are prone to biases in assessing evidence, and have difficulty acknowledging facts that are inconsistent with their existing view of the world. In a crisis, this problem becomes even harder.

Scholars of foreign policy crises and international conflict management, in particular, have made use of the psychological perspective. They have given us a wealth of in-depth, structure-focused comparative studies of how leaders, their advisers, and their bureaucracies operate when interstate relations are on the brink of war and peace, or have descended into open warfare. These studies show how the personalities, beliefs, emotions, interpersonal styles, information-processing proclivities and communication propensities of political leaders shape crisis management processes (Janis 1972;

Lebow 1981; Vertzberger 1990; Brecher 1993; Schafer and Crichlow 2010).[3] This research strongly suggests that the pre-existing world views or dominant frames of leaders heavily affect how they see the world and understand the causes of crisis (Welch Larson 1994; Boin, 't Hart, and Van Esch 2012). The so-called threat–rigidity thesis holds that under crisis-induced stress leaders rigidly cling to their world view and old behavioural patterns.

The small groups who support leaders during crisis processes might, in theory, compensate for individual shortcomings. Research shows, however, that under stress and duress, and when structured and led in an unhelpful fashion, small groups can become dysfunctional sense-making units ('t Hart, Stern, and Sundelius 1997), as witnessed in the Bush administration's handling of, for example, post-invasion Iraq (Badie 2010) and hurricane Katrina ('t Hart et al. 2009). Tensions between bureaucratic units may further undermine sense-making capacities, especially when units refuse to share information (Rosenthal, 't Hart, and Kouzmin 1991). For example, the tug of war between various agencies in the US intelligence 'community' prevented Presidents Clinton and Bush from grasping the impending threats of suicidal terrorism on American soil (Parker and Stern 2005). Also, intergovernmental or party-political tensions between key players— think of the relations between the mayor of New Orleans and the governor of Louisiana during the immediate aftermath of hurricane Katrina—may undermine the effective communication that is required in order to arrive at a common operational picture.

Shaping Responses

President George W. Bush prided himself on being the 'decision-maker in chief'. He epitomized the common idea that presidents are the ultimate decision makers in times of crisis. The key assumption here is that in times of crisis someone—preferably the political leader—has to make the truly crucial decisions. ('The buck stops here', as a sign read on President Truman's desk.)

Not surprisingly, the first generation of crisis leadership studies trained its focus on crisis decision making (Janis 1989). Scholars asked why political leaders made (or refrained from making) certain decisions (and non-decisions) that in hindsight proved critical to the shaping of crisis responses.

Critical choices that must be resolved at the political level are in fact quite rare during most crises and disasters. Particularly when it concerns large-scale, fast-moving emergencies, crisis responses emerge from the bottom-up at least as much as they are designed, planned for, and directed from the top-down. To try and have it any other way amounts to inviting delay and paralysis, as crisis responses grind to a halt when the

[3] Excellent case studies of, for example, British prime ministers setting their countries on controversial war paths based on diabolic enemy images and exaggerated self-beliefs include Verbeek's (2003) analysis of Anthony Eden and his cabinet during the Suez crisis and Dyson (2009).

centre insists on comprehensive control of operations: it will be overwhelmed by the sheer volume of communications and demands for urgent decisions ('t Hart, Rosenthal, and Kouzmin 1993; Waugh and Streib 2006; Moynihan 2007).

In fact, many of the decisions that shape the course of crises only turn out to be 'critical' in hindsight. The key challenge for political executives is to recognize which decisions should be made at the strategic level. Empirical studies show that an effective response entails more than making critical decisions. It is about coordination: organizing a response in which everybody who should be involved is involved, knows what should be done, and accomplishes set tasks in time. Leaders appear most effective when they facilitate and safeguard effective collaboration between responding organizations.

This challenge of strategic crisis coordination is not an easy one (Boin and 't Hart 2012). In fact, as the doyen of disaster sociology Enrico Quarantelli (1988) once observed, coordination often poses more problems than it helps to solve. To understand how hard it is, we must realize crisis coordination has two dimensions: *vertical* and *horizontal* coordination.

Vertical coordination pertains to the orchestration of activities between subordinate units. It can be politically expedient to be seen in charge of a response network—or not to be seen at all. It is a tool to assume power or to avoid responsibility. Students of presidential disaster declarations have shown the political character of vertical coordination. Issuing a disaster declaration is a symbolically powerful act with few negative side effects (Sylves 2008). Presidential opponents understand that as well. After hurricane Andrew struck Florida in the summer of 1992, and a few months before the presidential election, the (democratic) governor of Florida was reportedly slow to request federal assistance as he did not want to embellish the standing of President Bush (a Republican) in the eyes of Floridians.

Such reports, accurate or not, illustrate the often-made observation that crises are opportunities to demonstrate leadership. They are also potential pitfalls for leaders who do not understand the political nature of crisis management. To their frustration, political leaders tend to discover that it is rather hard to coordinate the actions of various administrative units. A key example, again, is the response to hurricane Katrina: President Bush, Governor Blanco, and Mayor Nagin all discovered that being in charge may not mean much when a leader's chain of command breaks down under the pressures of crisis.

These insights feed into a core debate in the crisis management subfield centring on the tension between bottom-up (emergent) crisis response and top-down organization of response. The emergent perspective suggests that crisis leaders typically have unique skill sets that are in demand during a specific crisis. These leaders are, however, not necessarily those who have been pre-designated to be crisis leaders. The top-down perspective stresses the leadership vacuum that can arise in chaotic situations and hence emphasizes the importance of clearly established authority structures.

Horizontal coordination pertains to the orchestration of units that are not hierarchically related. Political leaders must operate in a 'shared power' world to make things happen (Crosby and Bryson 2005). In large-scale crises, leadership tends to be 'distributed' across different jurisdictions and functional domains (Ansell, Boin, and Keller 2010). In federal countries like the United States, it is often not clear who exactly is in charge when a transboundary crisis (such as a large-scale epidemic) threatens. In the international arena, it is perfectly clear that no country or organization is in charge when a transboundary crisis happens. In both cases, crisis leadership can only be informal. It becomes a matter of persuasion.

An example of effective horizontal coordination is found in President George Bush Senior's crafting of an international coalition in response to Iraq's invasion of Kuwait in the summer of 1990. Bush managed to bring on board all the actors that mattered at the time (including bitter foes) and, what is important, he managed to keep the coalition together during the brief war and its immediate aftermath. This was a show case of international crisis diplomacy and coordinated warfare (see George 1991).

Meaning-Making

Carl Friedrich (1963: 94) observed that 'men's finite minds need the myth for the purpose of mastering their situation'. This is even truer in crisis, marked by deep uncertainty and pervasive confusion with regard to its causes and consequences, and the required actions to deal with this emerging threat (Barton 1969). In normal times, societal institutions provide and maintain what Friedrich referred to as a 'sustaining myth'. A crisis indicates that the key institutions have broken down and have stopped providing meaning (Turner 1978; 't Hart 1993). An important task of political leaders is to fill the vacuum and restore trust in institutions whose effectiveness, reliability, and/or integrity appear to have been severely compromised by crisis.

In a crisis, people expect their leaders to reduce uncertainty and provide an authoritative account of what is going on, why it is happening and what needs to be done. The challenge of *meaning-making* is to communicate an unprecedented and threatening event politically while taking into account the politically charged issue of causation, responsibility, and accountability. It is not enough to offer a story; leaders must get others to accept their definition of the situation.

Public leaders are not the only ones trying to frame the crisis. Their messages coincide and compete with those of other parties, who hold other positions and interests, who are likely to espouse various alternative definitions of the situation and advocate different courses of action. Contestants manipulate, strategize, and fight to have their frame accepted as the dominant narrative ('t Hart 1993; Tarrow 1994; Brändström and Kuipers 2003). If other actors succeed in dominating the meaning-making process, the ability of incumbent leaders to decide and manœuvre is severely constrained.

Crisis communication is thus an important element of political leadership. Political leaders, however, are often constrained in their capacity effectively to communicate, as correct information is rarely available in the early phases of a crisis when the need for meaning is possibly at its peak. Providing the public with accurate, clear, and actionable information can also be hindered by the collective stress pervading crisis-affected communities (Barton 1969). Moreover, they do not necessarily see the government as their ally.

Crises are a mixed-motive game for incumbent governments. They offer executive leaders the opportunity to show that they are caring yet statesmanlike leaders: calm, composed, and committed when under pressure. They also, however, make incumbent leaders a likely target of blame games. Particularly if they have been in office for a while, they may find it difficult to avoid being held to account for alleged regulatory failures, mismanagement of projects and programmes, or failures of interagency coordination that media coverage and inquiry reports suggest have contributed either to the escalation of latent vulnerabilities or to inadequate responses to exogenously triggered crises (Boin et al. 2010). Political leaders may, consequently, lose control over the emerging crisis narrative to their critics and contenders, who push alternative interpretations and seek to exploit the crisis to advocate political and policy change (Primo and Cobb 2003).

Account-Giving

Once the acute phase of a crisis has ended, it is tempting for leaders to return to (a new) normal. Most case studies of crisis show that the aftermath of a crisis typically presents leaders with new and complex challenges, which may threaten their political survival. This has little to do with the role leaders play in shaping the material responses to crises. It has everything to do with the way in which they seek to manage, or fail to manage, political consequences as well as policy implications of the crisis.

While a crisis de-legitimizes power and authority relationships, it often fuels demand for accountability and the allocation of blame, which places the roles and choices of government leaders in stark perspective. Accountability rituals offer opposition leaders and moral entrepeneurs chances of inflicting damage on incumbent office-holders and other bulwarks of the status quo; none of whom, however, are going to take this lying down.

Crisis-induced accountability processes have therefore been conceptualized as 'framing contests' (Boin, McConnell, and 't Hart 2008). Their outcomes are hard to predict (Kuipers and 't Hart, forthcoming). For example, the German Chancellor Gerhard Schröder miraculously emerged as the winner of the national elections following his well-performed role as the nation's symbolic 'crisis manager' during the riverine floods in 2002 (Bytzek 2008). The Spanish reigning party, on the other hand, suffered a stunning electoral loss in the immediate aftermath of the Madrid train bombings of 2004 (Olmeda 2008). President George W. Bush saw his hitherto modest approval ratings soar in the wake of the 9/11 attacks and exploited his political capital to implement structural reforms; but an already unpopular Bush administration further lost prestige in the aftermath of hurricane Katrina (Boin et al. 2010). The emerging literature on blame management has only just begun to address the mechanisms determining the fate of office-holders in the wake of major disturbances and scandals (Brändström, Kuipers, and Daleus 2008; Hood 2011).

Learning

Crises invite self-examination. They create a need to know why it happened and provide a strong impulse to never let it happen again. What lessons are to be drawn by whom, when, and how, is an important political question as much as it is one of institutional design of 'learning capacity'. An important leadership role in crisis is therefore to engage with the felt need for learning, and, normatively, to protect the integrity of the learning process from the heat and harshness of accountability politics. At the same time, learning itself can be an intensely political question, particularly when the crisis experience is invoked by proponents in ongoing struggles about continuity and change in policies and institutions. As noted above, crises can be an important vehicle for driving change in arenas otherwise stabilized by the forces of path dependence, inheritance, and veto-playing (Hay 2002; Kuipers 2006; Klein 2007).

Analysts should not make the mistake of equating 'change' with 'learning', or seeing the former as an indicator that the latter has occurred. Crises give rise not only to symbolic, hasty, and opportunistic policy gestures, but also to regulatory overkill. Both may be initiated by leaders who feel the need to be (seen to be) 'doing something', without bothering to wait for the slow diagnostic and reflective work of learning to be completed.

4 AN AGENDA FOR CRISIS LEADERSHIP STUDIES

We organized our overview of the literature on crisis leadership in terms of five functional tasks that crisis leaders are called upon to perform. In this concluding section, we shift our attention to what we do not yet know and what we would like to know. We see several prominent agenda points for future research on political crisis management.

First, we need to know more about public expectations of political leadership in crisis. The studies discussed in this chapter seem to agree that in a time of crisis the public looks to its political executives to demonstrate leadership. But it is not always clear what, exactly, the public expects from its leaders during a crisis. Moreover, expectations may vary. To understand political behaviour in times of crisis, we must know more about public expectations in those times.

Second, we need more research on the effects of leadership on the process and outcomes of crisis management, starting with crisis prevention and going all the way through to recovery and learning. Assessments of this relation tend to be somewhat impressionistic at best (see Janis 1989). We do not have a really good picture of success and failure factors (but we understand failure better than success). In hindsight, when considering crisis prevention, political leaders are all too often blamed for not recognizing the crisis in time ('they did not see it coming'). To foresee a crisis, or to recognize an emerging crisis before it escalates, however, one needs a theory of crisis causation (Boin and Smith 2011). We may well question if such theories exist.

We know that meaning making is important, both during and after a crisis, but we do not have a firm theory that explains why some leaders manage to impose their definition of the situation whereas others become enslaved to someone else's definition. We do not have a theory that explains why some leaders emerge as statesmen whereas other leaders lose their job over their crisis performance. We certainly don't have an encompassing theory of crisis leadership that connects the performance on all crisis tasks with the personality traits, leadership styles, and previous experience of political leaders.

Finally, we need to have more research on what makes political actors effective in performing crisis leadership tasks. Current research on the nexus between stress and performance gives us a good idea of why leaders break down or fail during a crisis. These same insights, however, cannot explain why some leaders 'rise to the occasion': staying calm, coming to a clear understanding of the situation, making and communicating critical decisions, and combining the need for immediate action with a sound grasp of the longer term. There is such research on operational emergency commanders (Flin 1996; Klein 1999), but not on political office-holders. This requires answering the notoriously tricky question of whether the harsh conditions and dilemmas that leaders face under conditions of crisis warrant some form of relaxation of the criteria of good governance or 'effective and democratic' leadership that we normally apply to evaluate their performance. This is an area that scholars have only just begun to explore (McConnell 2011).

RECOMMENDED READING

Lebow, R. N. (1981). *Between Peace and War: The Nature of International Crisis*. Baltimore, MD: Johns Hopkins University Press.

Janis, I. (1982). *Groupthink*. Boston, MA: Houghton Mifflin.

Boin, A., 't Hart, P., Stern, E., and Sundelius, B. (2005). *The Politics of Crisis Management: Public Leadership Under Pressure*. Cambridge: Cambridge University Press.

REFERENCES

Allison, G. T. (1971). *Essence of Decision: Explaining the Cuban Missile Crisis*. New York: Addison Wesley Longman.

Almond, G. A., Flanagan, S. C., and Mundt, R. J. (1973). *Crisis, Choice and Change: Historical Studies of Political Development*. Boston, MA: Little brown.

Ansell, C., Boin, A., and Keller, A. (2010). 'Managing Transboundary Crises: Identifying Building Blocks of an Effective Response System', *Journal of Contingencies and Crisis Management*, 18/4: 195–207.

Badie, D. (2010). 'Groupthink, Iraq, and the War on Terror: Explaining US Policy Shift toward Iraq', *Foreign Policy Analysis*, 6: 277–96.

Barton, A. H. (1969). *Communities in Disaster*. Garden City, NY: Doubleday.

Beck, U. (1999). *World Risk Society*. Malden: Blackwell Publishers.

Bell, C. (1971). *The Conventions of Crisis: A Study in Diplomatic Management.* Oxford: Oxford University Press.

Binder, L., Pye, L. W., Coleman, J. S., Verba, S., LaPalombara, J., and Weiner, M. (1971). *Crisis and Sequences in Political Development.* Princeton, NJ: Princeton University Press.

Birkland, T. A. (2006). *Lessons of Disaster: Policy Change after Catastrophic Events.* Washington, DC: Georgetown University Press.

Boin, A. and 't Hart, P. (2000). 'Institutional Crises and Reforms in Policy Sectors', in H. Wagenaar (ed.), *Government Institutions: Effects, Changes and Normative Foundations.* Dordrecht: Kluwer, 150–76.

Boin, A. and 't Hart, P. (2012). 'Aligning Executive Action in Times of Adversity: The Politics of Crisis Co-ordination', in M. Lodge and K. Wegrich (eds), *Executive Politics in Times of Crisis.* Basingstoke: Palgrave, 179–96.

Boin, A. and Smith, D. (2011). 'The Importance of Failure Theories in Assessing Crisis Management: The Columbia Space Shuttle Disaster Revisited', *Policy and Society*, 30/2: 77–87.

Boin, A., 't Hart, P., Stern, E., and Sundelius, B. (2005). *The Politics of Crisis Management: Public Leadership under Pressure.* Cambridge: Cambridge University Press.

Boin, A., McConnell, A., and 't Hart, P., eds. (2008) *Governing after Crisis: The Politics of Investigation, Accountability and Learning.* Cambridge: Cambridge University Press.

Boin, A., 't Hart, P., McConnell, A., and Preston, T. (2010). Leadership Style, Crisis Response and Blame Management: The Case of Hurricane Katrina. *Public Administration*, 88/6: 706–23.

Boin, A., 't Hart, P., and Van Esch, F. A. W. J. (2012). 'Political Leadership in Times of Crisis: Comparing Leader Responses to Financial Turbulence', in L. Helms (ed.), *Comparative Political Leadership.* Basingstoke: Palgrave Macmillan, 119–141.

Boix, C. and Stokes, S. (2007). *Oxford Handbook of Comparative Politics.* Oxford: Oxford University Press.

Bovens, M. A. P. and 't Hart, P. (1996). *Understanding Policy Fiascoes.* Piscataway, NJ: Transaction Publishers.

Bracher, K. D. (1971). *The German Dictatorship.* London: Methuen.

Brändström, A. and Kuipers, S. L. (2003). 'From "Normal Incidents" to Political Crises: Understanding the Selective Politicization of Policy Failures', *Government and Opposition*, 38: 279–305.

Brändström, A., Kuipers, S., and Daleus, P. (2008). The Politics of Tsunami Responses: Comparing Patterns of Blame Management in Scandinavia', in A. Boin, A. McConnell, and P. 't Hart (eds), *Governing After Crisis: The Politics of Investigation, Accountability and Learning.* Cambridge: Cambridge University Press, 114–47.

Brecher, M. (1993). *Crisis in World Politics: Theory and Reality.* Oxford: Pergamon Press.

Burke, J. P. and Greenstein, F. J. (1989). *How Presidents Test Reality: Decision on Vietnam, 1954 and 1965.* New York: Russell Sage.

Bush, G. W. (2010). *Decision Points.* New York: Random House.

Bytzek, E. (2008). 'Flood Response and Political Survival: Gerhard Schröder and the 2002 Elbe Flood in Germany', in A. Boin, A. McConnell and P. 't Hart (eds), *Governing After Crisis: The Politics of Investigation, Accountability and Learning,* Cambridge: Cambridge University Press, 85–113.

Crosby, B. C. and Bryson, J. M. (2005). *Leadership for the Common Good: Tackling Public Problems in a Shared-Power World.* San Francisco: John Wiley and Sons.

Drennan, L. and McConnell, A. (2007). *Risk and Crisis Management in the Public Sector.* London: Routledge.

Dyson, S. P. (2009). *The Blair Identity*. Manchester: Manchester University Press

Edelman, M. (1977). *Political Language: Words that Succeed and Policies that Fail*. New York: Academic Press.

Flin, R. (1996). *Sitting in the Hot Seat*. London: Wiley.

Friedrich, C. J. (1963). *Man and His Government: An Empirical Theory of Politics*. New York: McGraw-Hill.

Furedi, F. (2005). *Politics of Fear*. London: Continuum.

George, A. L., ed. (1991). *Avoiding War: Problems of Crisis Management*. Boulder, CO: Westview Press.

George, A. and Smoke, R. (1974). *Deterrence is American Foreign Policy*. New York: Columbia University Press.

't Hart, P. (1993). 'Symbols, Rituals and Power: The Lost Dimension in Crisis Management', *Journal of Contingencies and Crisis Management*, 1/1: 36–50.

't Hart, P., Rosenthal, U., and Kouzmin, A. (1993). 'Crisis Decision Making: The Centralization Thesis Revisited', *Administration and Society*, 25/1: 12–45.

't Hart, P., Stern, E. K., and Sundelius B., eds. (1997). *Beyond Groupthink: Political Group Dynamics and Foreign Policy-making*. Ann Arbor, MI: The University of Michigan Press.

't Hart, P., Tindall, K., Brown, C. (2009), 'Crisis Leadership of the Bush Presidency: Advisory Capacity and Presidential Performance in the Acute Stages of the 9/11 and Katrina Crises, *Presidential Studies Quarterly*, 39/3: 473–93

Hay, C. (2002). *Political Analysis*. Basingstoke: Palgrave.

Hermann, C. F. (1972). *International Crises: Insights from Behavioral Research*. New York: The Free Press.

Holsti, O. R. (1972). *Crisis, Escalation and War*. Montreal: McGill-Queens University Press.

Hood, C. (2011). *The Blame Game: Spin, Bureaucracy and Self Preservation in Government*. Princeton, NJ: Princeton University Press.

Janis, I. L. (1972). *Victims of Groupthink*. Boston, MA: Houghton, Mifflin.

Janis, I. L. (1989). *Crucial Decisions*. New York: Free Press.

Jervis, R. (1976). *Perception and Misperception in International Politics*. Princeton, NJ: Princeton University Press.

Jervis, R., Lebow, R. N., and Stein, J. G. (1985). *Psychology and Deterrence*. Baltimore, MD: Johns Hopkins University Press.

Kahneman, D. (2011). *Thinking Fast and Slow*. New York: Farrar, Straus and Giroux.

Keeler, J. T. S. (1993). 'Opening the Window for Reform: Mandates, Crises and Extraordinary Policy Making', *Comparative Political Studies*, 25/3: 433–86.

Kingdon, J. W. (1984). *Agendas, Alternatives and Public Policies*. Boston, MA: Little, Brown.

Klein, G. (1999). *Sources of Power: How People Make Decisions*. Cambridge, MA: MIT Press

Klein, N. (2007). *The Shock Doctrine: The Rise of Disaster Capitalism*. New York: Metropolitan Books.

Kuipers, S. (2006). *The Crisis Imperative: Crisis Rhetoric and Welfare State Reform in Belgium and the Netherlands in the Early 1990s*. Amsterdam: Amsterdam University Press.

Kuipers, S. and 't Hart, P. (forthcoming). 'Crisis and Accountability', in M. Bovens, R. E. Goodin and T. Schillemans (eds), *Oxford Handbook of Public Accountability*. Oxford: Oxford University Press.

Lebow, R. N. (1981). *Between Peace and War: The Nature of International Crisis*. Baltimore, MD: Johns Hopkins University Press.

Linz, J. J. and Stepan, A. (1978). *Problems of Democratic Transition and Consolidation: Southern Europe, South America, and Post-Communist Europe*. Baltimore, MD: The Johns Hopkins University Press.

Linz, J. J. and Stepan, A. (1996). *Problems of Democratic Transition and Consolidation*. Baltimore, MD: Johns Hopkins University Press.

Lord, C. (1998). 'Crisis Management: A Primer', *IASPS Research Papers in Strategy*. Institute for Advanced Strategic and Political Studies, available at <www.iasps.org/strategic7/crisis.htm>.

McConnell, A. (2011). 'Success? Failure? Something In-between? A Framework for Evaluating Crisis Management', *Policy and Society*, 32/2: 63–76.

Moynihan, D. P. (2007). *From Forest Fires to Hurricane Katrina: Case Studies of Incident Command Systems*. Washington, DC: IBM Center for Business and Government.

Neustadt, R. E. (1990). *Presidential Power and the Modern Presidents: the Politics of Leadership from Roosevelt to Reagan*. New York: Free Press.

Nixon, R. (1962). *Six Crises*. New York: Touchstone.

Olmeda, J. A. (2008). 'A Reversal of Fortune: Blame Games and Framing Contests after the 3/11 Terrorist Attack in Madrid', in A. Boin, A. McConnell, and P. 't Hart (eds), *Governing After Crisis: The Politics of Investigation, Accountability and Learning*. Cambridge: Cambridge University Press, 62–84.

Organisation for Economic Co-operation and Development (OECD). (2003). *Emerging Risks in the 21st Century: An Agenda for Action*. Paris: OECD.

Paige, G. D. (1968). *The Korean Decision*. New York: Free Press.

Parker, C. and Stern, E. (2005). 'Bolt from the blue or avoidable failure? Revisiting September 11 and the origins of strategic surprise', *Foreign Policy Analysis*, 1/3: 301–31.

Primo, D. M. and Cobb, R. W. (2003). *The Plane Truth: Airline Crashes, the Media, and Transportation Policy*. Washington, DC: Brookings Institution Press.

Quarantelli, E. L. (1988). 'Crisis Management: A Summary of Research Findings', *Journal of Management Studies*, 25/3: 373–85.

Rosenthal, U. and 't Hart, P. (1991). 'Experts and Decision-makers in Crisis Situations', *Knowledge*, 12/4: 350–72.

Rosenthal, U., Charles, M. T., and 't Hart, P., eds. (1989). *Coping With Crisis: The Management of Disasters, Riots and Terrorism*. Springfield, IL: Charles C. Thomas.

Rosenthal, U., 't Hart, P., and Kouzmin, A. (1991). 'The Bureau-politics of Crisis Management', *Public Administration*, 69/2: 211–33.

Rosenthal, U., Boin, A., and Comfort, L. C., eds. (2001). *Managing Crises: Threats, Dilemmas, Opportunities*. Springfield, IL: Charles C. Thomas.

Schafer, M. and Crichlow, S. (2010). *Groupthink Versus High-quality Decision Making in International Relations*. New York: Columbia University Press.

Schmitt, C. (1985). *Political Theology*. Chicago, IL: The University of Chicago Press.

Selznick, P. (1957). *Leadership in Administration*. Berkeley, CA: University of California Press.

Snyder, G. H. and Diesing, P. (1977). *Conflict Among Nations*. Princeton, NJ: Princeton University Press.

Stern, E. K. (1997). 'Crisis and Learning: A Balance Sheet', *Journal of Contingencies and Crisis Management*, 5/1: 69–86.

Sylves, R. T. (2008). *Disaster Policy and Politics: Emergency Management and Homeland Security*. Washington, DC: CQ Press.

Tarrow, S. G. (1994). *Power in Movement: Social Movements, Collective Action and Politics.* Cambridge: Cambridge University Press.

Thomas, W. and Thomas, D. S. (1928). *The Child in America: Behavior Problems and Programs.* New York: Alfred A. Knopf.

Tilly, C. and Tarrow, S. (2006). *Contentious Politics.* Boulder, CO: Paradigm Publishers.

Turner, B. A. (1978). *Man-made Disasters.* London: Wykeham.

Verbeek, B. (2003). *Decision Making in Great Britain During the Suez Crisis.* Aldershot: Ashgate.

Vertzberger, Y. Y. I. (1990). *The World in their Minds: Information Processing, Cognition and Perception in Foreign Policy Decisionmaking.* Stanford, CA: Stanford University Press.

Waugh, W., Jr. and Streib, G. (2006). 'Collaboration and Leadership for Effective Emergency Management', *Public Administration Review*, 66/2: 131–40.

Weick, K. (2001). *Making Sense of the Organization.* Oxford: Blackwell.

Welch Larson, D. (1994). 'The Role of Belief Systems and Schemas in Foreign Policy Decision-making', *Political-Psychology*, 15/S1: 17–33.

Wolf, N. (2007). *The End of America.* New York: Chelsea Green.

PART IV

EXECUTIVE LEADERSHIP IN THE WEST

Presidential Leadership: The United States and Beyond

CHAPTER 29

LEADERSHIP AND THE AMERICAN PRESIDENCY

DAVID MCKAY

1 THE CONTEXT OF PRESIDENCY STUDIES

ONE of the most notable characteristics of the presidency is its unitary nature. In most democratic political institutions chief executives are constrained by parties or by their peers within government. Neither applies in the USA. In almost all European polities and in many others throughout the world, for example, premiers can be removed either by coalition partners within ruling governments or by pressures applied through their own party colleagues. Thus in the UK Margaret Thatcher was famously ousted by her own cabinet members in 1990, and in continental Europe and Japan chief executives are frequently replaced when ruling coalitions fail to agree on policy positions. Even in France, where the presidency has most of the features of a unitary institution, the executive role is shared with a prime minister whose power is constrained by the incumbent's parliamentary base. In stark contrast, American presidents cannot be removed either by cabinet members or by party pressures. Indeed, presidents can do as they wish with cabinet members, none of whom has defined constitutional powers. On two occasions in recent history, presidents have asked for the resignations of whole cabinets without imperilling their political positions (Richard Nixon in 1972 and Jimmy Carter in 1979). And the loose, decentralized nature of the party system ensures that presidents can usually ignore party pressures with relative impunity. Only impeachment for 'high crimes and misdemeanors' can remove a president, and this sanction has never been implemented to the point where presidents have been forced to stand down.[1]

---

[1] Andrew Johnson and Bill Clinton were both impeached by the House of Representatives but acquitted by the Senate and thus remained in office. Richard Nixon resigned in 1972 before the House had voted on articles of impeachment.

The unitary nature of presidential power largely explains the vast scholarly literature on the subject. Presidents can and do act alone when exercising their extensive constitutional powers of chief executive and commander in chief. Of course they are subject to political constraints imposed by Congress, public opinion, and numerous other forces, but *constitutionally* they have a large degree of independence within a separated executive branch. It is, therefore, appropriate that scholars should study the office as a separate entity, rather than, as is generally the case in parliamentary systems, concentrate on national governments as the basic unit of analysis.

The uniquely powerful status of the United States as an economic and military power also helps explain the prominence of presidential scholarship. The US president simply has no peer among the world's chief executives. This has been demonstrably true since the end of the cold war, and even in the 1945–91 period it would be difficult to argue the case for some sort of symmetry between American presidents and Soviet leaders. Even if one puts aside the relative strength and influence of the two countries, undertaking academic study of the Soviet system was notoriously difficult, given the cloak of secrecy surrounding executive decision-making.

For all these reasons, presidential 'studies' have become an important subdiscipline within political science, along with attendant journals, research institutes, conferences, and the like. It is hard to imagine anything remotely approaching the sheer size of this research infrastructure supporting the study of (say) the British or Indian prime ministership or the Chinese or Russian leadership. What is the nature of this scholarship and how has it evolved through time?

2 Approaches to the Study of the Presidency: Concepts and Methodology

Although American political scientists have written many millions of words about the office of the presidency, the study of the institution remains a constant source of concern in the profession. There are two related strands to this debate. There is, first, the obvious fact that the presidency is far less amenable to quantitative measurement than almost all other aspects of American politics. For, notwithstanding the pleadings and admonishments of methodologists (see, e.g., King and Ragsdale 1988; King 1993), most presidential scholarship remains firmly rooted in narrative and descriptive, rather than in systematic quantitative approaches. The $n = 1$ problem is, of course, at the heart of this problem. Studies of presidential elections, presidential influences on congressional voting, and presidential popularity can be measured with comparative ease (see, e.g., Polsby, Wildavsky, and Hopkins 2008; Bond and Fleisher 1990; Cohen 1997), but quantifying leadership skills across presidents, let alone within a single presidency, is simply not amenable to the sort of testable causal inferences that are the lifeblood of other specialisms within the profession. There is only one president at any one time, and differences in the personalities, leadership qualities, not to mention the political and economic context vary so much through history, that quantifying differences using the standards that are commonplace in other areas of research presents formidable methodological difficulties (see also Hermann, Chapter 8; Schafter, Chapter 20; Cohn, Chapter 30, this volume).

The second strand to this debate is that, while systematic qualitative studies have grown in number and influence in such areas as international relations and comparative politics (see the discussion in King, Keohane, and Verba 1994), they have been few and far between in the study of the American presidency. Instead, students of the presidency continue with traditional biographical and historical approaches—albeit while often utilizing more theoretical approaches from leadership, personality, and other studies (see, e.g., Nelson 2009).

3 CONCEPTS AND METHODOLOGY: THE MAIN CONTRIBUTIONS

Richard Neustadt

It is generally accepted that the publication of Richard Neustadt's *Presidential Power: The Politics of Leadership* in 1960 represented a watershed in the study of the presidency. Prior to this most studies of the office concentrated on historical evolution or descriptions of the formal powers of the president (see, e.g., Corwin 1957, first published in 1940). By moving beyond analysis of the formal powers of presidents and instead stressing the incumbents' bargaining resources, Neustadt correctly identified the essentially *political* nature of the office. As he put it:

> Effective influence for the man in the White House stems from three related resources: first are the bargaining advantages inherent in his job with which to persuade other men [*sic*] that what he wants of them is what their own responsibilities require them to do. Second are the expectations of those other men regarding his ability and will to use the various advantages they think he has. Third are those men's estimate of how their publics may view him and how their publics may view them if they do what he wants. In short, his power is the product of his vantage points in government, together with his reputation in their Washington community and his prestige outside.
>
> (Neustadt 1960: 150)

So presidential resources consist of much more than constitutional powers such as those inherent in the commander in chief role, or the exercise of the veto over legislation. Indeed, the power to bargain or to persuade was a much better measure of the quality of presidential leadership. This Neustadt demonstrates well with his two examples from the Truman years—his sacking of MacArthur in 1951 and his 1952 decision to seize the steel mills in the face of a crippling strike; and one from the Eisenhower era—the decision to send troops into Little Rock in 1957. In all three instances the use of command power showed the limitation of presidential leadership, for if, instead, Truman and Eisenhower had used their bargaining resources more effectively, the presidents' objectives could have been met without suffering the reputational and political costs inherent in the blunt use of command (see Neustadt 1980: ch. 10). Identifying political *strategy* as central to understanding the office did, of course, reflect intellectual fashions within political science. Systematic observation of political behaviour became the preferred methodology during the 1960s, and when this was later married to rational choice theory, studying the strategic choices of political actors, became one of the most influential, if not the paradigmatic, approach of the discipline.

Note that Neustadt's analysis makes no moral judgements regarding the performance of presidents. He is concerned with the effective use of power, not with the ends to which power is used. So, by implication, in the Little Rock example, had Eisenhower brokered some sort of deal with Governor Faubus that pre-empted the use of force, the outcome might have been a slower transition to integration in Arkansas schools. Presidential power would have been used more effectively, but not necessarily in ways that served the wider public interest (this is a recurring criticism of Neustadt; see, e.g., Kellerman 1984: 52). Notwithstanding this criticism, there is no doubting the influence of Neustadt's approach, and numerous scholars have adapted and refined his perspective (see, e.g., Pfiffner 1996; Cameron 2000; Dickinson and Neustadt 2007; Kernell 2008).

These advances did not, for the most part, prevent scholars from subdividing the office in the traditional manner. So there is a sizeable literature on the presidential secretariat or the institutional presidency (Hess and Pfiffner 2002), on presidential/congressional relations (Jones 1994; Conley 2002; Mayhew 2005), presidents and the public (Canes-Wrone 2006; Kernell 2008), and presidential selection (Crotty and Jackson 1997; Wayne 2010). Some of these studies are discursive in approach, while others involve original research; many are time- and president-specific and thus do not lend themselves to systematic comparison across several presidencies.

There is, however, another body of work that not only focuses on the leadership skills of individual presidents but also attempts to discern patterns of behaviour across several presidents. Very generally, this opus can be divided into two categories: studies that emphasize the personality characteristics of individual presidents and relate this to presidential performance; and studies that attempt to find systematic patterns of presidential behaviour resulting from changes in the political environment over time.

Personality Approaches

Analysing the personality of leaders is, of course, the very stuff of biography, but political scientists have gone far beyond the essentially descriptive approach of individual presidents that is typical even of the very best biographies (see, e.g., Kearns Goodwin

1991; Burns 1996; and chapters in this book by Post, Renshon, Hermann, Cohen, and Schafer). One of the first and most influential of these studies was the Georges' analysis of Woodrow Wilson's response to crises during the First World War and its aftermath (George and George 1964). Much of Wilson's behaviour they attribute to a repressed childhood that obliged him to seek reforms in government and education that accorded with the highest moral standards. Wilson sought power precisely to achieve these goals. Unfortunately, however, his often-unrealistic moral ambitions ended in disaster and most notably in his failure to win Senate acceptance of US membership of the League of Nations in 1919. Wilson's drive for moral perfection also damaged his relations with confidants and advisers. He broke with his trusted White House aide Colonel House when House abandoned his usual flattery of the President in 1919 by insisting that Wilson's uncompromising stand on the League would lead to political failure.

Since it combined careful archival research with psychoanalytical theory, this study was recognized as a breakthrough in presidential studies. It also inspired a vehement debate among Wilson scholars about the impact of Wilson's stroke at the time of Versailles on his bargaining capacity and style (see, e.g., the discussion in Friedman 1994). Since then, numerous personality studies have been published, one of which caught the imagination not only of political scientists and historians but also the wider public. In his *Presidential Character: Predicting Performance in the White House*, James David Barber (1992) creates a four-way personality taxonomy, one dimension measuring energy level in the job (active/passive), and the other measuring emotional attitude to and satisfaction from the job (positive/negative). Barber favours the active positives who invest a great deal in the office and receive great emotional satisfaction from their efforts. These presidents are secure, self-confident individuals. Active/negatives, in contrast, are compulsive, driven men whose search for achievement is a long, lonely struggle. Franklin Roosevelt and John Kennedy are the archetypal active/positives, while Lyndon Johnson and Richard Nixon are active/negatives. Active negatives make 'bad' presidents because their time in office is dominated by a desire to win political battles at all costs. By inference they cannot easily compromise and see themselves as constantly threatened by political enemies. Hence Woodrow Wilson would not compromise over the League of Nations; Herbert Hoover could not adapt his economic agenda during the Great Depression; Lyndon Johnson would not negotiate over Vietnam; and Richard Nixon dug himself into a deeper and deeper hole over Watergate. All four presidencies ended in failure.

By way of contrast, Franklin Roosevelt, Harry Truman, and John Kennedy are 'good' presidents because they enjoyed being in power and were able to compromise with opponents or adapt failed strategies if that was necessary to achieve results. Of Barber's other two categories, one, the passive/negative, is not applicable to modern presidents. Why, after all, would such an individual seek high office? Similarly, few recent presidents have been passive/positives, although Barber classifies Ronald Reagan thus. Reagan famously invested relatively little time and effort in the job, but enjoyed huge satisfaction from it. Like the Georges, Barber traces these psychological impulses to presidents' childhoods and especially their relationships with fathers.

Criticism of Barber's work has focused on its inherent overdependence on simple psychological categories (see George 1974). Why should there be just four discrete categories to accommodate all the subtleties and nuances of presidential behaviour? As serious is the utility of the classification as a predictor of presidential performance. By implication, Jimmy Carter (an active/positive) was a better president than Woodrow Wilson (active/negative), yet historians repeatedly rank Wilson much higher than Carter (see the summary of the leading polls in Wikipedia 2012). Even more problematic is the case of the highest-ranked president, Abraham Lincoln, who was frequently passive and often depressed (Kearns Goodwin 2009).

The fundamental difficulty with Barber's analysis is, of course, the familiar structure and agency problem. Presidents do have some discretion to act as free agents, but they are also greatly constrained by the context or structure within which they have to operate. In retrospect it was easy for Barber to categorize Lyndon Johnson as an active/negative, given his handling of the Vietnam War. But prior to that he executed his job as Senate Majority Leader and later as architect of the Great Society with great success—and with great relish (on his stewardship of the Senate, see Caro 2003). Historical circumstance plays such a vital role that it often moulds presidential performance and thus the reputations of incumbents—witness Lincoln and the Civil War, or Kennedy and the Cuban missile crisis.

A final problem with *Presidential Character* is that, with the exception of Ronald Reagan, all presidents from Gerald Ford up to Barber's death in 2004 were classified as active/positives. Given the very different experiences and records of this sample, the analytical utility of the theory has seriously to be questioned.

Other scholars have utilized psychological theories in a less ambitious but often more careful fashion. Prominent among these is the work of Fred Greenstein. Beginning with his *Hidden Hand Presidency: Eisenhower as Leader* (1982), Greenstein has built up an impressive opus on the interaction of leadership skills and the decision-making environment in the White House. By researching archival material, Greenstein analyses Eisenhower's leadership style in depth and concludes that the president's reputation as a passive, avuncular, golf-playing figurehead is seriously misleading. Instead, Eisenhower is portrayed as a shrewd and manipulative operator who consciously created a media image that was greatly at odds with his real persona. Presidential scholars now broadly accept Greenstein's revisionist view.

The rehabilitation of Eisenhower's reputation was reinforced by Burke and Greenstein's carefully researched book *How Presidents Test Reality: Decisions on Vietnam, 1954 and 1965* (1988). Again Eisenhower is portrayed as an astute and careful decision-maker who used his bureaucratic resources (notably the National Security Council) to support his decision not to intervene in Vietnam in support of the French at Dien Bien Phu in 1954. In contrast, Lyndon Johnson rode roughshod over his advisers when he decided to escalate the war in Vietnam in 1965. Greenstein's conclusions are clear: Eisenhower possessed superior leadership skills, especially in the ways that he used his advisory system to negotiate support for his preferred position (Burke and Greenstein 1988).

In *The Presidential Difference: Leadership Style from FDR to Barack Obama*, Greenstein (2009) refines his thesis further so as to facilitate comparisons across all recent presidents. For each incumbent, six leadership qualities are identified: public communication, organizational capacity, political skills, vision, cognitive style, and emotional intelligence. Greenstein is at pains to emphasize that it is the combination of these talents that makes for successful or unsuccessful presidencies. Moreover, these must, of necessity, be measures of relative leadership ability. Some incumbents may be brilliant on one dimension but clearly deficient on another—for example, Clinton scores highly on public communication but low on emotional intelligence, while Truman had great organizational capacity but limited cognitive intelligence. No president features consistently high on all dimensions, but some—Eisenhower and Roosevelt, for example—score more highly than others such as Nixon and Carter. Greenstein is in no doubt as to the most important of these qualities. As he puts it:

> The importance of cognitive strength in the presidency should be self-evident. Still Presidents Johnson, Nixon, Carter and Clinton had impressive intellects but defective temperaments. Clinton's foibles made him an underachiever and a national embarrassment. Carter's defective temperament contributed to making his time in office a period of lost opportunity. Johnson and Nixon presided over major policy breakthroughs, but also over two of the most unhappy episodes of the twentieth century. All four presidential experiences point to the following moral: Beware the presidential contender who lacks emotional intelligence. In its absence all else may turn to ashes.
>
> (Greenstein 2004)

One obvious deficiency of this approach is that the judgements are non-numerical; no quantitative scale is established. Another limitation is that the assessments are those of the author and based for the most part on his reading of the secondary literature. Having said this, it is always going to be the case that a deficiency of hard data exists in this area. By definition, researchers will have limited access to exactly what goes on in the White House, so that, if they are to make assessments of presidential leadership, they are obliged to fall back on inferences drawn from sometimes quite limited information.

Similar criticism can be levelled at other personality approaches to presidential leadership. For example, in Barbara Kellerman's *The Political Presidency* the first few chapters are devoted to a quite complex analysis of the linkages between personality characteristics and the exercise of presidential power. In the subsequent accounts of specific policy choices made by Presidents Kennedy through Reagan, however, the inferences drawn from the personalities of the incumbent, while interesting, are not sufficiently systemized to allow meaningful application to other policy areas or to other presidents (Kellerman 1984).

Similarly, several psycho-biographical studies of individual presidents have often made for fascinating reading, but have done little to contribute to theory-building across several presidencies. The collection of essays on Bill Clinton edited by Stanley Renshon (2005), for example, examines the Clinton psyche in depth, but none of the contributions anticipates the moral failings that were to become so evident later in his second term. Similarly, Steven Wayne's assessment of Obama's personality written towards the end of his first term borders on the hagiographic and fails to explain the policy- and decision-making lacunae that by 2012 were all too apparent in the Obama presidency (Wayne 2010). Wayne does, however, recognize the main methodological handicap of psychological approaches:

> Character is not directly observable. It is inferred from behavior on the basis of theories proposed by psychiatrists and psychologists. Political scientists do not like to make such inferences. They prefer to study identify and measure data that they can directly observe.
>
> (Wayne 2012: 3)

Historical/Structural Approaches

By far the most theoretically ambitious attempt to establish systematic patterns of presidential behaviour over time is Stephen Skowronek's *The Politics President's Make: Leadership from John Adams to George Bush* (1993). Skowronek's work was path-breaking because he was the first to link the leadership capacities of individual presidents to broader changes in society and economy. Moreover, he did this systematically across a very broad historical span, taking in almost all presidents from the beginning of the Republic through to the time he was writing. Recurring patterns occur in what he calls 'political time', and, because the similarities recur, it is possible to predict the extent to which incumbents re-create political order. So, secular time is ever changing, as are the personalities and capacities of incumbents, but political time recurs in an analytically amenable fashion. Thus, at several times in American history, presidents have been 'transformational', while at other times the political context in which they operate has limited their capacity for change. Whether or not presidents can effectively perform such a role depends not so much on their personal abilities as on their position in relation to the prevailing political environment and in particular the status of the prevailing 'political regime'. Regimes change in accordance with shifts in elite values, which in turn reflect major changes in economy and society. Presidential performance is partly determined by incumbents' congruence or non-congruence with the dominant value system. From this reasoning, Skowronek is able to construct a simple classification identifying presidents' political identities in relation to different regimes (Figure 29.1).

The most fortunate presidents are those in office during the politics of reconstruction, when, because they are opposed to a disintegrating regime, they are afforded the opportunity to transform the political agenda. Jefferson, Jackson, Lincoln, and Franklin Roosevelt were so placed. In contrast, presidents affiliated to a vulnerable regime, such as Pierce, Buchanan, Hoover, and Carter, are constantly battling against a tide of opposition, as values shift against the old order. Polk, Teddy Roosevelt, and Lyndon Johnson were all elected in eras when their own affiliation was congruent with a resilient regime, so were given the opportunity to expand and develop the values and policies of the time.

President's Political Identity		
Previously established commitments	Opposed	Affiliated
Vulnerable	Reconstruction	Disjunction
Resilient	Pre-emption	Articulation

FIGURE 29.1 Presidents' political identities in relation to different regimes

Finally, presidents whose values are opposed to a resilient regime will practise the politics of pre-emption. In terms of the opportunities these contrasting 'political times' offer presidents, reconstructive presidents can achieve a great deal; disjunctive presidents are prone to policy and electoral failure; 'articulative' presidents can do much, but tend to overreach; and pre-emptive presidents will probably take unnecessary risks in order to bypass the prevailing order.

Skowronek is not so naive as to attribute all presidential performance to the nature of the times. He is, rather, concerned to establish that the *potential reach* of presidential power is greatly influenced by of the prevailing regime. As he puts it: 'I would simply point out how *The Politics Presidents Make* uses these recurrent patterns, the cycles if you will, to highlight the impact of individual presidents in bolstering roles, stretching types, and reshaping patterns' (Skowronek 1995: 524).

So Jackson, Lincoln, and Roosevelt were afforded the opportunities to make new politics—often through successful confrontation of political enemies—in ways that Pierce or Carter could not. In effect, reconstructive presidents can bring new groups to power—the New Dealers, for example—that, once in office, can change the values of governing institutions including Congress, the bureaucracy, and the courts.

Three main criticisms have been levelled at Skowronek's work. First that it is a work of historical determinism that leaves little room for presidential leadership, as such. In other words, it is not presidents who 'make politics', as he claims, but rather the recurring cycles of American history. While this is a serious problem for the analysis, Skowronek is at pains to demonstrate that presidents do have considerable leeway within the confines of their regime status to exercise power. Thus the constraints imposed on Franklin Pierce after 1853 were similar to those experienced by Carter after 1976, but the two presidents operated within these constraints in different ways and with different degrees of success. A second criticism dwells on the author's alleged failure to take full account of the dramatic changes in the political and bureaucratic status of the office over time. So is it possible to compare FDR with Jackson, given the vastly different contexts, or even the early FDR with the later FDR, given the internationalization of the office and vast bureaucratic structure that had developed by the 1940s? This point is partly addressed by Skowronek in his claim that, since the 1980s, increasing pluralism in the USA has resulted in the politics of 'permanent pre-emption', or, as time has passed, so 'As the POWER of all presidents to get things done has expanded the

AUTHORITY to reproduce political ORDER has constricted' (Skowronek 1993: 31–2). This is not necessarily a negative development, however, for, as Sydney Milkis notes:

> *The Politics Presidents Make* ends with surprisingly high hopes for a new era that will be dominated by a politics of 'perpetual preemption'. As Skowronek puts it somewhat cryptically, 'A State of perpetual preemption ultimately favors pragmatism, that is, a vigorous assertion of freedom from established dogmas. With presidents more consistently independent of received formulas, the pragmatic stance can become a less episodic feature of our national leadership.' Such a development, Skowronek urges optimistically, 'should prompt recognition that American government and politics must be continually reconstructed and that fashioning a reputable place in history now entails finding solutions to problems collectively'.

(Milkis 1995: 444–5)

But, if permanent pre-emption prevails, what remains of the theory's predictive value? Not much, it would seem—a claim reinforced by the author's most recent reflections on the first two years of the Obama Administration. In a later work Skowronek (2008) asks whether transformational leadership is still possible, but hedges his bets by providing no less than four answers to the question: (*a*) yes Obama could still pull it off; (*b*) yes for a future president but not Obama; (*c*) no, the reconstructive model is now irrelevant; and finally (*d*) yes, reconstruction can happen but only from the political right (see Skowronek 2008: ch. 6). In his last paragraph Skowronek hints that the most likely outcome is a reconstructive politics from the right—a prediction that hardly sits comfortably with the results of the 2012 elections (Skowronek 2008: 194) (for incisive critiques of Skowronek's work, see 't Hart 2011 and Laing 2012).

4 THE RISE OF THE MODERN (AND THE POSTMODERN?) PRESIDENCY?

By the 1980s it had become common practice for presidential scholars to divide the office into the pre-modern and the modern presidency (see Greenstein 1988: ch. 10 and sources cited) and for them to date this transition very precisely with the coming of the first presidency of Franklin Roosevelt in 1933. During the subsequent dozen years the office was, indeed, transformed, both by the rapid expansion of a civilian and military bureaucracy and by the elevation of the United States to an international position that was close to hegemonic in economic and foreign policy affairs. Prior to the 1930s, presidents actually did very little except during periods of war. The federal government was tiny in relation to state and local governments; in the absence of a secretariat, the institutional presidency barely existed, and the USA was signatory to few international treaties or commitments. By the 1950s, however, presidents were recognized as chief legislators, national figureheads, and leaders of the free world.

Because of the ability of the position to command a vast array of resources, the status of the office underwent a fundamental change, and most observers concluded that this gave to presidents a much higher degree of autonomy in the making and implementation of policy. Whole programmes of change came to be associated with particular presidents: FDR's New Deal, Truman's Fair Deal, Kennedy's New Frontier, and Johnson's Great Society. This transformation extended to foreign policy, with the Truman Doctrine of the containment of communism shaping world affairs for more than a generation. Scholars also noted important differences between the extent of presidential autonomy in foreign as opposed to domestic affairs. In 1966 Aaron Wildavsky argued: 'In the realm of foreign policy there has not been a single major issue on which presidents, when they were serious and determined, have failed' (Wildavsky 1966: 7). This was, of course, his famous 'Two Presidencies' thesis, which highlighted the serious constraints exercised by Congress, interest groups, and public opinion in domestic policy (witness civil rights, health-care reform), compared with the comparative freedom enjoyed by presidents in foreign policy.

Unfortunately for Wildavsky he was writing at precisely the point in American history when foreign affairs began seriously to constrain presidents, and he effectively rejected his own thesis as 'time and culture bound and an artifact of the shared values engendered by the cold war' (Wildavsky and Oldfield 1989: 54). Nonetheless, political scientists continue to test the thesis, and there is an emerging consensus that, although presidents are constrained in all policy areas, foreign policy does afford the opportunity for the exercise of great discretion, even if that sometimes carries with it great political costs (witness, Vietnam, Iran Contra, and the 2003 invasion of Iraq; and on the difference that leaders can make in key policy areas, see Hermann et al. 2001). Given these differences, it comes as no surprise that:

> Regardless of who is president, their ability to achieve objectives on issues of foreign and defense policy should contrast strikingly with the progress of their domestic agenda. This disjuncture is likely to be all the more striking if presidents mistakenly believe that they can translate their achievements in foreign affairs to ones in domestic policy.
>
> (Canes-Wrone, Howell, and Lewi 2008: 14)

One important variation on the theme of the modern presidency is the claim that changes in domestic and foreign affairs since the 1970s are such that a new category is required, which Richard Rose entitled the 'postmodern' presidency. Put simply, he argues that, in this new context, public opinion is more divided and fickle, foreign affairs more complex and less amenable to the exercise of 'hard power', and Congress more assertive. Above all, White House resources are insufficient to meet these new demands, especially in foreign affairs (Rose 1991: 25). Increasingly, foreign policy impinges on domestic affairs, whether it be trade policy, military procurement, or increasing interdependence in international finance. What this new context demands above all is a deep understanding by incumbents of the nature of international affairs and of both the opportunities and limitations this imposes on presidential power. As Rose notes:

> A new century has now commenced, based on global interdependence. In this new era the postmodern President is even more important, for the Oval Office is the best place to see the links between the international system and America's domestic concerns. While responsibilities are larger, the White House is palpably subject to checks and balances on every continent. In this new world of interdependence, there is much less latitude for ignorance and luck. The postmodern president depends on power armed by an understanding of how the world works.
>
> (Rose 1991: 304)

While it is difficult to believe that (say) FDR's or Eisenhower's presidencies were deemed successful in spite of some dependence on 'ignorance and luck', it is certainly true that increasing complexity and interdependence have made sweeping transformational change more difficult. These developments also put premium on the intellectual talents of presidents and their ability both to understand and to communicate to others complex policy issues.[2]

Hence, recent presidents have all been obliged to 'go public' in order to win support for their policies (Kernell 2008). This is particularly true of the hothouse world of American domestic politics in the context of divided party government. But appeals for public support are now almost as common when presidents are trying to build support in foreign policy. In both cases, of course, an enormous premium is placed on the ability of presidents to communicate well—in effect to use their powers of persuasion not just inside the beltway but also outside Washington and even outside the United States.

5 RESEARCHING THE PRESIDENCY ASSESSMENT

The idiosyncratic status of the American presidency is evident from the almost complete absence of references in presidency studies to the experiences of chief executives elsewhere. In contrast, other areas of American politics, including public opinion, elections, federalism, and Congress, have been the subject of extensive cross-national comparison (on comparative method covering these areas, see Landman 2008). There are both constitutional and historical reasons for this. Unusually among democracies, the presidency is a unitary institution with incumbents almost totally secure from removal by political opponents outside elections. In addition, since the emergence of the modern presidency in the mid-twentieth century, the United States has held a uniquely powerful position in global economic, diplomatic, and military affairs. And, notwithstanding

---

[2] In the many post-mortems following Mitt Romney's defeat in 2012 this point was recognised by both sides, especially given the Republicans' tendency to oversimplify and obfuscate complex policy questions.

recent setbacks and the rise of a competing power in the guise of China, the USA, and therefore its chief executive, will retain this privileged position for many years to come.

It should come as no surprise, therefore, that the office has attracted inordinate attention from scholars working in a wide variety of intellectual traditions. This essay's brief review has been able to touch on only a few of the more important contributions, from which a number of broad conclusions can be drawn.

1. Comparisons across presidencies have been greatly aided by the fact that the constitutional status of the office has remained virtually unchanged since the beginning of the Republic. Presidents were and remain chief executives, commanders in chief, recruiters to the executive branch, and key actors in the checks and balances that characterize executive/legislative relations. No other chief executive among democracies has retained his or her powers consistently intact over such a long period.

2. Unsurprisingly, therefore, the most influential contributions have come from scholars who compare the capacities and performance of a sample of presidents working within this essentially unchanging constitutional context. Given that the non-constitutional powers of the president have varied quite dramatically with changes in the historical environment, most of these studies have made comparison across presidents incumbent during particular historical periods. Hence Neustadt's opus extends across the post-Second World War period and Greenstein's in the age of the modern presidency. By definition, all of these studies involve some assessment of the leadership capacities of incumbents, including judgements relating to personality. Some of these (Barber) border on psychologism, while others (Greenstein) are less ambitious but more considered. While quantitative studies have enriched our understanding of the office, the $n = 1$ problem means that they have served more to provide background in such areas as executive/legislative relations and public opinion rather than provide definitive judgements of success or failure.

3. Studies that attempt to identify recurring patterns of presidential behaviour over much longer historical periods—and notably Skowronek's contributions—have also enriched our understanding of the office. However, the agency/structure problem looms large in such efforts. The leadership opportunities afforded by contrasting political regimes vary so much that it is all too easy to infer from such work that it is the 'times' that determine presidential performance rather than the capacities of individual office-holders.

6 Researching the Presidency: The Way Forward

One of the more interesting aspects of presidential scholarship is that, in terms of concepts and methodology, the most important contributions were published between

1960 and the mid-1990s. During this period the three seminal works cited (Neustadt, Skowronek, and Greenstein) were published and pioneering methodological work on some aspects of presidential behaviour was undertaken. Since then, presidential studies have been greatly influenced by what most see as the increasing intractability of the office, for, while the job of president has never been easy, it has almost certainly grown more difficult over time. The unitary nature of the office means that presidents can rarely enjoy the support from party and peers that typically apply in parliamentary systems. An ever more open and pluralistic political system has steadily added more pressures, as has the increasing internationalization of the office. To get elected, presidential candidates have to undergo a uniquely gruelling nomination process, and, once elected, they must almost immediately prepare themselves for a re-election campaign.

Above all, public expectations of the office are inordinately high; presidents are subject to constant analysis and criticism; they rarely satisfy the almost impossible demands placed on them. In such an institutional environment, it is small wonder that presidential research has increasingly focused on the capacities and personalities of incumbents, neither of which are amenable to careful measurement. In this sense, the subfield has diverged further from mainstream political science with its preoccupation with causal inference and testable hypotheses.

This suggests that, notwithstanding the problems raised by access to reliable data and the measurement of the data that are available, future research should focus on refining the assessment of personality and its relationship to the capacity for leadership. By definition, this research agenda would place leadership in what is a complex and ever-changing institutional environment. One thing is for sure: no matter what direction future scholarship takes, the study of the American president will continue to generate enormous interest both from professional political scientists and from the broader political community. The power and influence of the office ensure its academic prominence.

Recommended Reading

Greenstein, F. I. (2009). *The Presidential Difference: Leadership Style from FDR to Barack Obama.* 3rd edn. Princeton: Princeton University Press.
Neustadt, R. E. (1991) [1960]. *Presidential Power: The Politics of Leadership.* New York: Wiley.
Skowronek, S. (1993). *The Politics Presidents Make: Leadership from John Adams to George Bush.* Cambridge, MA: Belknap/Harvard.

References

Barber, J. D. (1992). *The Presidential Character: Predicting Performance in the White House.* 4th edn. New York: Pearson.
Bond, J. R., and Fleisher, R. (1990). *The President in the Legislative Process.* Chicago: University of Chicago Press.

Burke, J. J., and Greenstein, F. I. (1988). *How Presidents Test Reality: Decisions on Vietnam, 1954 and 1965*. New York: Russell Sage.

Burns, J. M. (1996). *Roosevelt: The Lion and the Fox*. New York: Smithmark.

Canes-Wrone, B. (2006). *Who Leads Whom?: Presidents, Policy, and the Public Opinion*. Chicago: University of Chicago Press.

Canes-Wrone, B., Howell, W. G., and Lewi, D. E. (2008). 'Toward a Broader Understanding of Presidential Power: A Reevaluation of the Two Presidencies Thesis', *Journal of Politics*, 70/1: 1–16.

Cameron, C. M. (2000). *Veto Bargaining: The Politics of Negative Power*. New York: Cambridge University Press.

Caro, R. A. (2003). *Master of the Senate: The Years of Lyndon Johnson III*. New York: Vintage.

Cohen, J. E. (1997). *Presidential Responsiveness and Public Policy Making: The Publics and the Policies that Presidents Choose*. Ann Arbor, MI: University of Michigan Press.

Conley, R. S. (2002). *The Presidency, Congress and Divided Government: A Postwar Assessment*. College Station, TX: Texas A&M University Press.

Corwin, E. S. (1957) [1940]. *The President: Office and Powers: 1787–1957*. 4th edn. New York: New York University Press.

Crotty, W., and Jackson, J. S. (1997). *The Politics of Presidential Selection*. New York: Pearson.

Dickinson, M. J., and Neustadt, E. A.(2007). *Guardian of the Presidency: The Legacy of Richard A. Neustadt*. Washington, DC: Brookings Institute.

Friedman, W. (1994). 'Woodrow Wilson and Colonel House and Political Psychobiography', *Political Psychology*, 15/1: 35–59.

George, A. L. (1974). 'Assessing Presidential Character', *World Politics*, 26/2: 234–82.

George, A., and George, J. L. (1964). *Woodrow Wilson and Colonel House: A Personality Study*. New York: Dover Publications.

Greenstein, F.I. (1982). *The Hidden Hand President: Eisenhower as Leader*. New York: Basic Books.

Greenstein, F. I. (1988). *Leadership in the Modern Presidency*. Cambridge, MA: Harvard University Press.

Greenstein, F. I. (2004). 'The Qualities that Bear on Presidential Performance' <www.pbs.org/wgbh/pages/frontline/shows/choice2004/leadership/greenstein.html>. Last accessed 11 January 2013.

Greenstein, F.I. (2009). *The Presidential Difference: Leadership Style from FDR to Barack Obama*. 3rd edn. Princeton: Princeton University Press.

Hermann, M. G., Preston, T., Korany, B., and Shaw, T. M. (2001). 'Who Leads Matters: The Effects of Powerful Individuals', *International Studies Review*, 3/1: 83–131.

Hess, S., and Pfiffner, J. C. (2002). *Organizing the Presidency*. 3rd edn. Washington, DC: Brookings Institute.

Jones, C. O. (1994). *The Presidency in a Separated System*. Washington, DC: Brookings Institution.

Kearns Goodwin, D. (1991). *Lyndon Johnson and the American Dream*. New York: St Martin's Press.

Kearns Goodwin, D. (2009). *Team of Rivals: The Political Genius of Abraham Lincoln*. New York: Penguin.

Kellerman, B. (1984). *The Political Presidency: Practice of Leadership from Kennedy Through Reagan*. Oxford: Oxford University Press.

Kernell, S. (2008). *Going Public: New Strategies of Presidential Leadership*. Washington: Congressional Quarterly.

King, G. (1993). 'The Methodology of Presidential Research', in G. Edwards III, B. Rockman, and J. H. Kessel (eds), *Researching the Presidency: Vital Questions, New Approaches*. Pittsburgh, PA: University of Pittsburgh Press, 387–412.

King, G., and Ragsdale, L. (1988). *The Elusive Executive: Discovering Statistical Patterns in the Presidency*. Washington: Congressional Quarterly Press.

King, G., Keohane, R. S., and Verba, S. (1994). *Designing Social Enquiry: Scientific Inference on Qualitative Research*. Princeton: Princeton University Press.

Laing, M. (2012). 'Towards a Pragmatic Presidency? Exploring the Waning of Political Time', *Polity*, 44/2: 234–59.

Landman, T. (2008). *Issues and Methods in Comparative Politics: An Introduction*. 3rd edn. London and New York: Routledge.

Mayhew, D. R. (2005). *Divided We Govern: Party Control, Lawmaking and Investigations, 1946–2002*. New Haven, CT: Yale University Press.

Milkis, S. M. (1995). 'What Politics do Presidents Make? In "Polity Forum on *The Politics Presidents Make*"', *Polity*, 27/3: 485–96.

Nelson, M. (2009) (ed.). *The Presidency in the Political System*. 9th edn. Washington, DC: Congressional Quarterly.

Neustadt, R. E. (1960). *Presidential Power: The Politics of Leadership*. New York: Wiley.

Neustadt, R. E. (1980). *Presidential Power: The Politics of Leadership from FDR to Carter*. New York: Wiley.

Pfiffner, J. P. (1996). *The Strategic Presidency: Hitting the Ground Running*. 2nd edn. Lawrence, KS: University Press of Kansas.

Polsby, N., Wildavsky, A., and Hopkins, D. A. (2008). *Presidential Elections: Strategies and Structures of American Politics*. Foreword by Charles O. Jones. 12th edn. New York: Rowman and Littlefield.

Renshon, S. (1995) (ed.). *The Clinton Presidency: Campaigning, Governing and the Psychology of Leadership*. Boulder, CO: Westview.

Rose, R. (1991). *The Post Modern President: George Bush Meets the World*. New York: Chatham House.

Skowronek, S. (1993). *The Politics Presidents Make: Leadership from John Adams to George Bush*. Cambridge, MA: Belknap/Harvard.

Skowronek, S. (1995). 'Response', in 'Polity Forum on *The Politics Presidents Make*', *Polity*, 27/3: 517–34.

Skowronek, S. (2008). *Presidential Leadership in Political Time: Reprise and Reappraisal*. Lawrence, KS: University Press of Kansas.

Skowronek, S. (2011). *Personality and Politics: Obama for and against Himself*. Washington: Congressional Quarterly and Sage.

't Hart, P. (2011). 'Reading the Signs of the Times: Regime Dynamics and Leadership Possibilities', *Journal of Political Philosophy*, 19/4: 419–439.

Wayne, S. (2010). *Is this any Way to run a Democratic Election?* 4th edn. Washington, DC: Congressional Quarterly.

Wikipedia (2012). 'Historical Rankings of the Presidents of the United States' <http://en.wikipedia.org/wiki/Historical_rankings_of_Presidents_of_the_United_States/>. Last accessed 11 January 2013.

Wildavsky, A. (1966). 'The Two Presidencies', *Trans-Action*, 4/1: 7–14.

Wildavsky, A., and Oldfield, D. M. (1989). 'Reconsidering the Two Presidencies', *Society*, 26/5: 54–9.

CHAPTER 30

PRESIDENTIAL COMMUNICATION FROM HUSTINGS TO TWITTER

JEFFREY E. COHEN

1 INTRODUCTION: PRESIDENTIAL COMMUNICATION STYLES

FROM a relatively restrained institution, the presidency has evolved into a central policy-maker. Presidents now use public communication to further their policy aims; the high volume of communication keeps the president in the public eye. We cannot understand the evolution of the presidency without regard for the co-evolution of presidential communication. The style of presidential communication is defined by its objectives and by how much effort the president puts into communicating with the public. Research on presidential communication has focused on two major questions: e.g. what factors influence the style of presidential communication? How effective are presidential communication efforts?

2 OBJECTIVES OF PRESIDENTIAL COMMUNICATION

George Washington set the tone for presidential communication into the twentieth century. Like most of the founding generation, Washington feared democracy and its potential for demagoguery; thus his public communication were few and rarely aimed directly at the people. When targeting the populace, Washington mainly sought to educate it about republican citizenship; never did he attempt to mobilize the public in support of his policies or presidency (Flexner 1970). This 'republican-schoolmaster' approach remained the model for presidential communication for over a century.

In contrast, modern presidential communication aims to mobilize public opinion in support of the president and his policies. Theodore Roosevelt was the first to rally public opinion behind policy, viewing public opinion as a counterweight to big business (Tulis 1987: 97–116). Roosevelt also used his family to burnish his public image and deflect attention from his sometimes controversial policies. Woodrow Wilson gave a theoretical rationale for presidential communication, which was to educate the public on policies and transform the public into an active participant in the policy-making (Tulis 1987).

The above suggests modern presidential communication emerged at the turn of the twentieth century (Tulis 1987). Kernell (2007), in contrast, argues that 'going public'—direct presidential appeals to the public to apply public pressure on Congress— supplanted bargaining with Congress only in the 1960s: only then did television offer presidents a technology to reach the mass public directly.

One question asks whether presidential communication is aimed more at symbolic enhancement (Waterman, St Clair, and Wright 1999) or policy accomplishment. Image and policy goals may be more intertwined than Waterman, St Clair, and Wright contend. Policy accomplishment may lead the public to view the president as an effective leader; such an image may increase the odds for significant policy accomplishment, as opponents may be less likely to challenge a president reputed to be effective. A third question asks why presidents engage in such a high volume of public communication if they are so ineffective at moving the public and gaining support in Congress (Edwards 2003).

3   Degree and Venues of Communication Efforts

Some presidents invest heavily in public communication, others less so. Figure 30.1 traces the number of presidential public communication from 1901 to 2010. From issuing approximately one statement per week early in the twentieth century, presidents issued three per day a century later, a stunning and transformative increase, reflecting the growing importance of the presidency to the public, to politics, and to governing. External forces in part impelled heightened public communication efforts, but so did the presidential view that public communication offered an opportunity to enhance their policy-making influence (Cornwell 1965; Kernell 2007).

The steady rise in communication suggests that individual presidential preferences and talents are less important in explaining this trend than forces like technological change and public expectations for presidential leadership. Technologies of mass communications offered the potential to reach a national audience and reduced the reliance

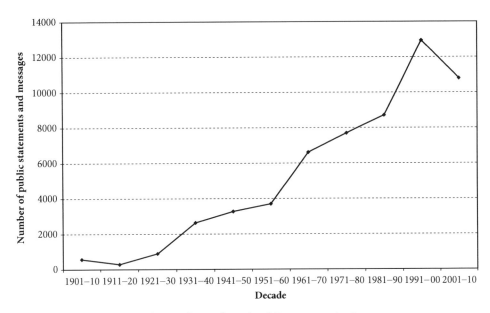

FIGURE 30.1 Volume of presidential public communication, 1901–2010

on journalists to mediate those communication efforts. In the early twentieth century, as the presidential policy-making role expanded, presidents relied most heavily upon press conferences. Even during the mid-century, when presidents could use radio to speak to the nation, such broadcasts, like Franklin Roosevelt's fireside chats, were used sparingly compared to press conferences (Kernell 2007).

The televising of press conferences, first undertaken by John F. Kennedy, led to their waning use, as they in effect became speeches. Journalists were relegated to the roles of spectator or supporting player. The decline of the press conference altered journalists' behaviour, leading them to became more aggressive in questioning presidents, which provided another reason to limit the frequency of press conferences and restrict journalists' participation (Clayman et al. 2010).

The rise of the Internet and social media may further alter presidential public communication. These new media offer presidents a pathway to direct communication with the mass public, but do not necessarily reach as large and heterogeneous an audience as does broadcast television. With these media, presidents can target specific types of individuals, most likely supporters of the president, who may be most easily mobilized to political action on behalf of the president. Such mobilization efforts may come with strings attached, as these more narrow demographic sections expect presidential fealty to their political viewpoints, which may be more extreme than that of the general public. The implications of this new style of presidential communication are not yet evident. An early assessment of the Obama presidency, which pioneered the use of social media like YouTube and Facebook, suggests the limits of these communication portals for the president (Bai 2011).

The political context, especially partisan polarization, may also affect presidential communication. As people's political attitudes harden, it becomes increasingly difficult for presidents to gain their support, and so presidents' communication efforts may boomerang by activating opponents. The mass-based strategy employed during the broadcasting age may become less relevant in an age of polarized attitudes. Consequently, presidents employ a strategy that focuses communication efforts on narrow clusters of voters, such as co-partisans and friendly interest groups (Cohen 2008, 2010).

4 Effectiveness of Communication on Public Opinion

Presidential communication seeks to affect the public's agenda, presidential approval, and public preferences on issues and policies. Presidents utilize both direct communication as well as news coverage towards these ends. Ultimately, presidents want to apply public pressure on other policy-makers, like members of Congress, to enact presidential policies.

The Public's Agenda

The public's agenda consists of those issues of concern to citizens. Commonly, studies use the 'most important problem' question to identify the public agenda. Usually the economy and international affairs emerge as concerns to large numbers of voters. Priming appears to be the causal mechanism for influencing the public agenda (Druckman and Holmes 2004). The emphasis that issues receive from the president or in the news affects their relative importance to the public. Cohen (1995, 1997) demonstrated that presidential emphasis in the State of the Union Address affected the importance of three issues in the mass public: the economy, international affairs, and civil rights. These effects faded quite rapidly, with lasting effects only for international affairs. Young and Perkins (2005) contextualized this research: presidential leadership effects waned in the mid-1980s, as cable television diffusion led to smaller audiences for presidential speeches (Baum and Kernell 1999).

Why do presidential communication effects persist on international affairs but not other issues? The behaviour of other political elites may be crucial. Generally, they support the president on foreign policy and international affairs, but are less likely to follow the president on domestic issues unless they hold the same policy preferences as the president. This means that, whereas the public receives essentially the same message from various leaders on international affairs, in domestic affairs it hears competing messages from competitive elites. This raises the question of presidential manipulation of other elites, the media, and the public on foreign affairs (Entman and Page 1994; Herman and Chomsky 2002; Entman 2007).

Presidential Approval

Presidential approval is among the most studied attributes of public opinion; the bulk of the literature looks at economic influences on approval. Invariably, presidents enjoy higher approval when the economy is healthy as opposed to sick. Several studies have looked at whether presidential communication also affects approval. Unlike the public agenda research, this literature has investigated the effects of different types of presidential communication, from major speeches, to trips around the nation and the globe.

Ragsdale (1984, 1987) investigates the impact of major speeches upon approval. For monthly approval from 1949 to 1980, she finds a 2.9 approval boost following a major speech; she also finds that presidential speech-making activity is responsive to the approval climate, as change in approval stimulates presidential speech-making. It appears that presidents try to capitalize on approval increases, perhaps trying to link their speech to their rising approval. That major speeches also lift approval suggests presidents use them to stem or arrest approval declines.

Brace and Hinckley (1993) compare domestic and foreign travel with major speeches (Simon and Ostrom 1989), finding a positive approval effect from foreign travel. The amount, tone, and glamor of the news concerning foreign travel may account for this effect. Domestic travel appears modestly to dampen approval. Cohen and Powell (2005) and Cohen (2006) critique Brace and Hinckley, arguing that, rather than look at national effects, the focus should be on local opinion. Domestic trips, they argue, rarely attract national attention, but will be covered profusely by local news media. Their findings are equivocal on the effects of domestic trips. They detect small positive effects, but Cohen (2006) fails to unearth a significant association. Limited data on local opinion hamper the ability to address this question definitively.

Given the massive literature on approval, oddly few studies tackle the issue of speech effects. Most studies lump speeches with other events into one variable, obscuring whether speech effects differ from other events. Moreover, most of that research is now over two decades old and in need of updating. Since the 1980s, the gap in approval of partisans has widened spectacularly (Jacobson 2007; Newman and Siegle 2010). In a polarized environment, it is unlikely that opposition party identifiers will respond to presidential speeches, as they appear to have done from the 1950s to the 1980s (Lebo and Cassino 2007).

Second, the emergence of new communications technology, especially cable television and the Internet, has reduced and fragmented the audience for presidential speeches (Baum and Kernell 1999; Cohen 2008). Presidents can no longer count on numerous independents watching their speeches. Independents may be more susceptible to presidential leadership efforts than partisans, whose partisan predisposition filters the messages they receive. In the post-broadcast age (Prior 2007), presidents are speaking mostly to their political allies and supporters.

The decline in the impact of major speeches has altered presidential communication efforts. Now presidents rely less on national strategies and more on specialized speeches to narrower audiences (Cohen 2008, 2010). Further, the polarized climate steers presidents to friendly audiences, and more towards activating them than generating broad-based support. This leadership strategy may feed back into the political system, furthering polarization, at least among partisans.

Policy Preferences

Less research exists on the ability of presidents to alter the public's preferences on policies and issues. Edwards (2003, 2009) argues that presidents have limited ability to move public preferences on issues. His framework to account for the lack of presidential influence incorporates the following factors: the messenger (the president), the message, characteristics of the audience, and the audience response. Subsequent research is not as pessimistic as that of Edwards. Wood (2007) finds that optimism in presidential economic rhetoric affects public optimism about the economy.

Rottinghaus (2009) suggests that, rather than view presidential influence on public preferences as an either/or prospect, we should contextualize the problem: under what conditions will presidential communication efforts move the public? His analysis indicates that presidential leadership of public preferences is most likely when presidents actively and persistently try to lead the public, and that popular presidents can influence the public, especially on salient issues. Further, when presidents inform the public, they are often able to move voters who previously did not have an opinion to the president's side on the issue. The trick is getting anyone to tune into presidential speeches in the post-broadcast age (Baum and Kernell 1999; Prior 2007; Cohen 2008).

The difficulty presidents have in moving public opinion may have implications for presidential leadership. Canes-Wrone (2005) argues that presidents do not move the public; rather they activate public opinion, a priming effect. She attempts to explain why presidents go public on some issues but not others. Her theory assumes that Congress responds to activated public opinion, enacting legislation close to the public's preference. Rational presidents, thus, will go public only when public preferences are closer to the president's than the status quo.

5 EFFECTIVENESS OF COMMUNICATION ON THE NEWS MEDIA

Presidents cannot rely solely on major addresses to lead the public. They must reserve those speeches for special occasions. Using major speeches frequently will turn them into routine events not worthy of public attention. Still, presidents require a consistent presence before the public, which daily news coverage can provide.

Presidents have to be able to affect the quantity, content, and tone of news reports on their activities if they are to influence public opinion through news coverage. If the president receives little or no news coverage, he cannot lead the public through the news. If the news does not emphasize or report on the issue the president wants highlighted, he cannot lead on that issue. Even if presidents receive coverage on issues they deem important, reporting critical of the president may undermine his leadership.

Goal Conflict Between Presidents and Journalists

Presidential influence over news coverage would not be much of a problem if presidents and journalists saw news coverage the same way. This is not the case, of course. They have differing needs and definitions of newsworthiness: presidents need news coverage for policy or popularity goals; journalists want news about the president for profit and professional reasons. Journalists think news about the president will sell newspapers or attract viewers to their broadcasts. They also want to apply their professional judgement, reporting stories they think voters should know about in order to be responsible and informed citizens (Groeling 2010).

Given these two goals, journalists define newsworthiness as events that are novel, contain some conflict, and are about authoritative figures. Their professionalism leads them to present stories in a balanced manner by reporting on both sides of the issue. Although presidents benefit when they are presented as authoritative sources about news events, they do not like conflict or balance in their news coverage. Conflict and balance in news gives voice to critics of the president, which presidents believe undermines their ability to lead the mass public.

Overcoming Goal Conflict: News Management Strategies

Goal conflict between presidents and the news media insures that there will be some news that presidents dislike. Presidents develop a news management strategy to minimize unfavourable news coverage (Althaus 2000; Cohen 2010). News management strategies can involve a range of activities, from offering services to journalists to controlling and regulating the access journalists have to information.

Presidents have offered several services to journalists. The aim of service provision is to make news collection easier and less costly for journalists, resulting in journalist dependence on the White House for news and, consequently, news coverage that serves presidential needs (Cornwell 1965; Grossman and Kumar 1981; Kumar 2007). Presidential administrations have also amassed large staffs to help in news provision and other publicity operations. It is not clear that service provision is effective in producing news to the president's liking. To date no research presents any evidence on the effectiveness of service provision for presidential influence on the news.

News management strategies may involve regulating journalistic access to information. Presidents may time announcements for maximum impact or to limit journalists' ability to gather information from other sources. Presumably, announcements made near reporter deadlines will have such an effect, but this proposition has never been tested empirically. Presidents, too, may limit how much information is fed to reporters, holding back information that may be harmful to presidential aims. Some presidents have tried to present a message of the day or week (for example, the Reagan Treatment) in hopes of restricting journalist reporting to that topic. Since the Reagan administration, several presidents, including both Bush's, have limited journalist access to bureaucrats and White House staffers for interviews. Such central control is aimed at plugging leaks and limiting the ability of those who disagree with the president from being able to voice that opposition to journalists. The list of possible techniques that presidents can use to influence their news coverage is endless.

Studies of president–press interactions present long lists of things presidents can do and have done, and journalist reactions. Anecdotes are offered as evidence. A few studies use interviews with journalists and White House staffers to assess the effectiveness of presidential news management (Rozell 1993, 1995). Rarely are theoretically grounded hypotheses posed or tested. Grossman and Kumar (1981) employ an exchange metaphor to characterize the interactions between the president and the press, while Cook (1998) and Cook and Ragsdale (1998) opt for a 'negotiating the news' metaphor, but offer little guidance on testable hypotheses from these frameworks. Cohen (2009) argues that non-cooperative game theory may better describe the nature of president–press interactions, but he does not develop the point or offer a game suitable for testing.

Only Althaus (2000) and Cohen (2010) generate testable hypotheses from underlying theories. Althaus suggests that such simple devices as emphasizing an issue or an issue frame present a clear signal to journalists. Emphasis may also indicate how important the topic is to the president. Althaus hypothesizes that journalists will follow the president's lead when the president signals that a topic is important and provides some supportive evidence. Cohen's distraction hypothesis (2010) assumes that presidents alter their information presentation to journalists in anticipation of their news reporting. Cohen detects important non-linear relationships with regard to the quantity and tone of news consistent with his hypothesis. The literature on presidential–press interactions is theoretically and empirically underdeveloped.

6 PRESIDENTIAL EFFECTS ON NEWS QUANTITY

The quantity of presidential news measures the importance of the president to the public, and the importance of the public to the president. As the quantity of news about the president grows, the president becomes increasingly important to the public. In turn, public support becomes ever more vital to presidential leadership efforts.

Presidents value a high volume of news to keep competitors, such as congressional leaders, from receiving as much news coverage; if competitors receive less coverage, this makes them look less important than the president and less able to challenge presidential leadership. This suggests 'a more news is better' strategy for the president (Miroff 1982). The raw materials for news on the president are his public activities, including his speeches. If we compare the volume of presidential communication effort—that is, the number of public statements he makes (see Figure 30.1)—with trends on news coverage (e.g. Cohen 2008, 2009), we see that in the 1980s communication effort continued to grow, but the volume of news coverage began to recede, perhaps indicating that presidents are unable to affect the quantity of their news coverage.

Cohen's distraction hypothesis (2010) offers an alternative explanation. He argues that it is costly for journalists to collect news and that presidents do not always have discretion in making newsworthy announcements. Presidents can reduce attention to controversial decisions by making other newsworthy announcements at the same time, which will deflect attention from controversial to less controversial announcements. Cohen (2010) reports evidence in support of his hypothesis.

7 PRESIDENTIAL NEWS MANAGEMENT AND CONTENT

Few studies have gauged the content or subject matter of presidential news or whether presidents can affect the topic of news reports. Does news reporting on the president reflect the activities and aims of the president? If presidents cannot affect the policies or issues discussed in the news, presidents can have little impact on the larger policy agenda. A small empirical literature exists, which emphasizes a discontinuity between what presidents do and their news coverage. Early studies found modest effects of State of the Union Addresses on subsequent news coverage (Gilberg et al. 1980; Wanta et al. 1989), but Barrett (2007) found that only a fraction of presidential announcements regarding legislation receive news attention.

Another strand of research asks whether presidential attention to specific issues affects media attention (Wood and Peake 1998; Edwards and Wood 1999). In general, these authors find that presidents rarely affect the news media agenda, other than for less important issues. On more important issues, presidents are more likely to follow media reporting than to lead it. Clearly, more research needs to be done linking presidential activities with the content of presidential news. We also require basic studies describing the policy content of presidential news.

8 PRESIDENTIAL NEWS MANAGEMENT
AND TONE

Tone refers to the degree of support or criticism (opposition) to the president in news stories. Presidents contend that criticism undermines their leadership and that much criticism is unfair, motivated out of a need for profit by the news organization in question, or out of partisan or ideological concerns. Balanced reporting styles and bias are the foundations for criticism of the president in news. Balanced reporting presents both sides of an issue, implying through balance that not everyone agrees with the president. In biased reporting, criticism of the president grows out of the partisan or ideological preferences of journalists, as well as the news organizations' need for profit.

It is unrealistic for presidents to expect laudatory news in an open, democratic, and heterogeneous society like the United States. The question is whether the news is unfairly critical, whether journalists are biased against the president. To a degree all news reporting is inherently biased. The process of news reporting distils a large amount of raw material, presenting to readers and viewers what journalists deem are the most important facts, hopefully in a coherent manner. Much raw information that journalists possess never reaches news consumers because of this distillation process. As human beings, journalists make decisions on what is important and what is not, and reasonable people may disagree with these journalistic judgements about what to include in the news. The judgements of journalists, however, may not be motivated by partisan or ideological antagonism to the president, or by profit motivations (Groeling and Kernell 1998; D'Alessio and Allen 2000; Kahn and Kenney 2002; Groseclose and Milyo 2005; Gentzkow and Shapiro 2006; Della Vigna and Kaplan 2007; Entman 2007; Groeling 2008).

Contextual factors may affect the degree of criticism in presidential news. Cohen (2008) demonstrates that news reporting became increasingly critical of the president from the 1950s to the mid-1990s, arguing that the restructuring of the news media in the 1980s accounts for some of the increase in criticism. By the 1980s, cable television and talk radio (and later the Internet) displaced the virtual monopoly held by the three major broadcast networks—the ABC, CBS, and NBC—from the 1950s to mid-1980s. During the 'golden age of broadcasting' (1960–80), negativity in presidential news arose because of balance in news reporting. For economic and ideological reasons, the new media of the post-broadcast era did not feel bound by the balanced reporting norm. Talk radio and cable television aimed to tap into market segments not well served by broadcast news fare, offering dramatic and ideologically motivated programming instead, and finding that hefty profits could be generated with relatively small audiences. This collapse of the broadcast monopoly shifted the basis of criticism from balance to bias. Entertainment fare on cable television also led to shrinking broadcast audiences for presidential and other types of hard news. Broadcast news responded by increasing the amount of 'soft news' in place of hard news (Baum and Kernell 1999; Patterson 2000; Baum 2003; Prior 2007; Cohen 2008).

Other research suggests presidents have advantages in foreign over domestic policy. His role as chief executive; the control the president has over information, which allows him to keep some information secret for national security reasons; and the threat implications of international crises all combine to encourage the news media to follow the president's lead (Hallin 1986; Entman and Page 1994; Bennett 1990; Mermin 1999; Herman and Chomsky 2002). Domestic issues lack these characteristics, and journalists have alternative news sources on domestic issues. This suggests some leeway for presidents to manipulate the news media on foreign-policy issues.

Opposition to the war in Iraq raised questions about the media as presidential lapdog in international affairs. Baum and Groeling (2010) isolate conditions under which we can expect more or less favourable news coverage of the president. In early stages of international crises, when presidents monopolize information, and when threat and uncertainty appear most distressing, presidential advantages will be at their highest. This advantage may wane as the crisis becomes an ongoing problem, other information sources become available to journalists, and political leaders begin to question the president's policy. The decline of network broadcasting, the rise of polarized politics, and the breakdown of the cold-war consensus, may have increased the incentive to challenge the president on international issues.

In this environment of greater news hostility, presidents have pursued several strategies to take the sting out of negative news. One strategy has been to 'go local' (Barrett and Peake 2007; Eshbaugh-Soha 2008, 2010; Eshbaugh-Soha and Peake 2008; Cohen 2010), which entails presidential travel around the nation, meeting with local reporters, and reducing or limiting interactions with the Washington-based press. The idea underlying this strategy is that local news media do not possess the resources to investigate presidential statements, actions, and decisions. They will be more likely to report uncritically on the president, basing their report on statements and materials provided to them by the administration. Furthermore, local journalists and residents will be flattered by a presidential visit to them, which will further undermine any impulse towards criticism. Research is mixed on the effectiveness of this approach.

Zaller's product substitution theory (1998) points to the counter-productive impact of some presidential behaviour. He argues that tight control of information access by presidential candidates reduces the role of journalists in the co-production of news. To reconstruct an active role in news production, journalists will criticize tight control in their news reports. Although Zaller applies his theory to presidential campaigns, it may have implications for presidential governing practices too. Still there is little research on the effectiveness of presidential news management on news tonality, despite our gathering understanding of other sources of negativity in presidential news.

9 WHITHER PRESIDENTIAL COMMUNICATION RESEARCH?

The above reviews reveal several limitations of research on presidential communication. First, what are the implications of partisan polarization and the rise of the Internet, especially the social media, on presidential leadership? Presidents have always been faced with opponents, especially from the opposition party. Polarization heightens the intensity and stridency of that opposition, reducing incentives for cross-party cooperation. We know little about the implications of polarization on presidential leadership. Recent reviews of the voluminous literature on polarization barely mention the president (Layman, Carsey, and Horowitz 2006; Hetherington 2009), a nagging oversight considering the importance of the president within the political system. Second, the Internet and new social media, like Facebook, are establishing a larger political presence, especially for fundraising during election campaigns. Barack Obama has been a pioneer in the use of the Internet and social media for governing, with mixed to minimal effects thus far (Bai 2011). Research on the Internet and presidential communication is thin.

Polarization and the new media may feed on each other. Cohen (2008) argues that extreme politicians have greater access to media in the post-broadcast age, especially on talk radio and cable television. This access may enhance their legitimacy and political appeal. The Internet may provide politicians with greater independence from the news media in trying to reach the mass public. Recently, Sarah Palin has made such use of the Internet, keeping her status as a national political figure and allowing her greater control over her public image. We know nearly nothing about the implications of Internet use on polarization, governing, or presidential communication.

Most research finds presidential leadership through public communication to be problematic. Rarely are presidents able to alter public opinion, especially on policy debates (Edwards 2003). This raises the question of why presidents 'go public' so frequently and routinely if there is so little pay off. Cameron and Park (2011) argue that presidents go public when their leadership is contested; thus, presidential public communication is primarily defensive. As presidents have taken on more policy responsibility, they find themselves engaged in more situations where policy competitors will challenge their leadership, which may account for the long-term trend in presidential public activity. The contested leadership hypothesis has been applied only to the case of Supreme Court nominations. This hypothesis should be assessed for other policy activities.

The above research generally utilizes observational data on presidential behaviour and large-scale surveys. Experimentation has become a favoured methodology of public opinion and communication effects scholarship, yet has hardly been employed in presidential communication studies outside of election contexts (Druckman and Holmes 2004). Besides the common issue of generalizability, the fact of sitting presidents contaminates experimental designs. Respondent attitudes towards the incumbent may affect his response to experimental treatments. Overcoming this contextual contamination is necessary for experimentation to become a major methodology for studying presidential communication effects.

Moreover, most research on presidential communication focuses on the American president. Studies have begun to explore the public communication of other chief executives, most notably the UK prime minister (Foley 2008). A comparative approach to executive communication suggests two obvious hypotheses (Weyland 1999). Are presidents more prone to public communication than prime ministers because of the limited legislative policy-making resources of presidents compared to prime ministers? Second, how does economic development, especially in the form of increased public access to electronic communications such as broadcasting and the Internet, affect executive communications? American presidential communication grew with the advent of the electronic media; is there a cross-national relationship between the structure and development of communications systems and executive communication behaviour?

10 SIX LANDMARK CONTRIBUTIONS

Cornwell (1965) initiated the study of presidential relations with the public and the press from the lens of presidential modernization and institutionalization. Research on presidential communication was virtually non-existent thereafter, until Grossman and Kumar (1981), who reoriented scholarship towards presidential–press interactions in the television age. Kernell's *Going Public* of 1997 reacts to Neustadt's bargaining model. Edwards (2003) also reacts to Neustadt, arguing that presidential leadership is problematic. Cohen (2008, 2010) studies presidential communication in the post-broadcast era.

RECOMMENDED READING

Cohen, J. E. (2010). *Going Local: Presidential Leadership in the Post-Broadcast Age.* New York: Cambridge University Press.

Kernell, S. (2007). *Going Public: New Strategies of Presidential Leadership.* 4th edn. Washington: CQ Press.

Groeling, T. (2010). *When Politicians Attack! Party Cohesion in the Media.* New York: Cambridge University Press.

REFERENCES

Althaus, S. (2000). 'Presidential Influence over Evening News Content: Assessing the Effects of Strategic Communication on News Coverage of the Gulf Crisis'. Paper presented at the 2000 American Political Science Association.

Bai, M. (2011). 'For Obama, Getting Message out Online is a Challenge', *New York Times,* 24 January <www.nytimes.com/2011/01/25/us/politics/25bai.html?_r=1&emc=eta1>. Last accessed on 4 August, 2013.

Barrett, A. W. (2007). 'Press Coverage of Legislative Appeals by the President', *Political Research Quarterly,* 60 (December): 655–68.

Barrett, A. W., and Peake, J. S. (2007). 'When the President Comes to Town: Examining Local Newspaper Coverage of Domestic Presidential Travel', *American Politics Research,* 35 (January): 3–31.

Baum, M. A. (2003). *Soft News Goes to War: Public Opinion and American Foreign Policy in the New Media Age*. Princeton: Princeton University Press.

Baum, M. A., and Groeling, T. J. (2010). *War Stories: The Causes and Consequences of Public Views of War*. Princeton: Princeton University Press.

Baum, M. A., and Kernell, S. (1999). 'Has Cable Ended the Golden Age of Presidential Television?', *American Political Science Review*, 93 (March): 99–114.

Bennett, W. L. (1990). 'Toward a Theory of Press–State Relations in the United States', *Journal of Communication*, 40/2: 103–27.

Brace, P., and Hinckley, B. (1993). 'Presidential Activities from Truman through Reagan: Timing and Impact', *Journal of Politics*, 55 (May): 382–98.

Cameron, C., and Park, J. (2011). 'Going Public when Opinion Is Contested: Evidence from Presidents' Campaigns for Supreme Court Nominees, 1930–2009', *Presidential Studies Quarterly*, 41 (September): 442–70.

Canes–Wrone, B. (2005). *Who Leads Whom? Presidents, Policy Making and the Mass Public*. Chicago: University of Chicago Press.

Clayman, S. E., Elliott, M. N., Heritage, J., and Beckett, M. K. (2010). 'A Watershed in White House Journalism: Explaining the Post-1968 Rise of Aggressive Presidential News', *Political Communication*, 27 (July–September): 229–47.

Cohen, J. E. (1995). 'Presidential Rhetoric and the Public Agenda', *American Journal of Political Science*, 39 (February): 87–107.

Cohen, J. E. (1997). *Presidential Responsiveness and Public Policy-Making*. Ann Arbor, MI: University of Michigan Press.

Cohen, J. E. (2006). 'The Polls: The Coalitional Presidency from a Public Opinion Perspective', *Presidential Studies Quarterly*, 36 (September): 541–50.

Cohen, J. E. (2008.) *The Presidency in an Era of Twenty-Four Hour News*. Princeton: Princeton University Press.

Cohen, J. E. (2009). 'The Presidency and the Mass Media', in G. Edwards and W. Howell (eds), *The Oxford Handbook of the American Presidency*. New York: Oxford University Press, 254–87.

Cohen, J. E. (2010). *Going Local: Presidential Leadership in the Post-Broadcast Age*. New York: Cambridge University Press.

Cohen, J. E., and Powell, R. J. (2005). 'Building Public Support from the Grassroots up: The Impact of Presidential Travel on State-Level Approval', *Presidential Studies Quarterly*, 35 (March): 11–27.

Cook, T. E. (1998). *Governing with the News: The News Media as a Political Institution*. Chicago: University of Chicago Press.

Cook, T. E., and Ragsdale, L. (1998). 'The President and the Press: Negotiating Newsworthiness in the White House', in M. Nelson (ed.), *The Presidency and the Political System*. 5th edn. Washington: CQ Press, 323–57.

Cornwell, E. E., Jr (1965). *Presidential Leadership of Public Opinion*. Bloomington, IN: Indiana University Press.

D'Alessio, D., and Allen, M. (2000). 'Media Bias in Presidential Elections', *Journal of Communication*, 50/4: 133–56.

Della Vigna, S., and Kaplan, E. (2007). 'The Fox News Effect: Media Bias and Voting', *Quarterly Journal of Economics*, 122 (August): 1187–234.

Druckman, J. W., and Holmes, J. W. (2004). 'Does Presidential Rhetoric Matter? Priming and Presidential Approval', *Presidential Studies Quarterly*, 34 (December): 755–78.

Edwards, G. C., III (2003). *On Deaf Ears: The Limits of the Bully Pulpit*. New Haven, CT: Yale University Press.

Edwards, G. C., III (2009). *The Strategic President: Persuasion and Opportunity in Presidential Leadership*. Princeton: Princeton University Press.

Edwards, G. C., III., and Wood, B. D. (1999). 'Who Influences Whom? The President, Congress, and the Media', *American Political Science Review*, 93 (June): 327–44.

Entman, R. M. (2007). 'Framing Bias: Media in the Distribution of Power', *Journal of Communication*, 57 (March): 163–73.

Entman, R. M., and Page, B. (1994). 'The Iraq War Debate and the Limits to Media Independence', in W. L. Bennett (ed.), *Taken by Storm: Media, Public Opinion, and US Foreign Policy in the Gulf War*. Chicago: University of Chicago Press, 82–101.

Eshbaugh–Soha, M. (2008). 'Local News Coverage of the Presidency', *Harvard International Journal of Press/Politics*, 13 (April): 103–19.

Eshbaugh–Soha, M. (2010). 'The Tone of Local Presidential News Coverage', *Political Communication*, 27 (April–June): 121–40.

Eshbaugh–Soha, M., and Peake, J. S. (2008). 'The Presidency and Local Media: Local Newspaper Coverage of President George W. Bush', *Presidential Studies Quarterly*, 38 (December): 606–27.

Flexner, J. T. (1970). *George Washington and the New Nation, 1783–1793*. Boston: Little Brown.

Foley, M. (2008). 'The Presidential Dynamics of Leadership Decline in Contemporary British Politics: The Illustrative Case of Tony Blair', *Contemporary Politics*, 14/1: 53–69.

Gentzkow, M., and Shapiro, J. M. (2006). 'Media Bias and Reputation', *Journal of Political Economy*, 114 (April): 280–316.

Gilberg, S., Eyal, C., McCombs, M., and Nicholas, D. (1980). 'The State of the Union Address and the Press Agenda', *Journalism Quarterly*, 57 (Winter): 584–88.

Groeling, T. (2008). 'Who's the Fairest of them all?' An Empirical Test for the Partisan Bias on ABC, CBS, NBC, and Fox News', *Presidential Studies Quarterly*, 38 (December): 631–57.

Groeling, T. (2010). *When Politicians Attack! Party Cohesion in the Media*. New York: Cambridge University Press.

Groeling, T., and Kernell, S. (1998). 'Is Network News Coverage of the President Biased?', *Journal of Politics*, 60 (November): 1063–87.

Groseclose, T., and Milyo, J. (2005). 'A Measure of Media Bias', *Quarterly Journal of Economics*, 120 (November): 1191–237.

Grossman, M. B., and Kumar, M. J. (1981). *Portraying the President: The White House and the News Media*. Baltimore, MD: Johns Hopkins University Press.

Hallin, D. C. (1986). *The 'Uncensored War'*. Berkeley and Los Angeles: University of California Press.

Herman, E. S., and Chomsky, N. (2002). *Manufacturing Consent: The Political Economy of the Mass Media*. New York: Random House.

Hetherington, M. J. (2009). 'Review Article: Putting Polarization in Perspective', *British Journal of Political Science*, 39 (March): 413–48.

Jacobson, G. C. (2007). *A Divider, not a Uniter: George W. Bush and the American People*. New York: Longman.

Kahn, K. F., and Kenney, P. J. (2002). 'The Slant of the News', *American Political Science Review*, 96 (June): 381–94.

Kernell, S. (2007). *Going Public: New Strategies of Presidential Leadership*. 4th edn. Washington: CQ Press.

Kumar, M. J. (2007). *Managing the President's Message: The White House Communications Operation*. Baltimore, MD: Johns Hopkins University Press.

Layman, G. C., Carsey, T. M., and Horowitz, J. M. (2006). 'Party Polarization in American Politics: Characteristics, Causes, and Consequences', *Annual Review of Political Science*, 9/1: 83–110.

Lebo, M. J., and Cassino, D. (2007). 'The Aggregated Consequences of Motivated Reasoning and the Dynamics of Partisan Presidential Approval', *Political Psychology*, 28 (December): 719–46.

Mermin, J. (1999). *Debating War and Peace: Media Coverage of US Intervention in the Post-Vietnam Era*. Princeton: Princeton University Press.

Miroff, B. (1982). 'Monopolizing the Public Space: The President as a Problem for Democratic Politics', in T. Cronin (ed.), *Rethinking the Presidency*. Boston: Little, Brown, 218–32.

Newman, B., and Siegle, E. (2010). 'Polls and Elections: The Polarized Presidency: Depth and Breadth of Public Partisanship', *Presidential Studies Quarterly*, 40 (June): 342–63.

Patterson, T. E. (2000). *Doing Well and Doing Good: How Soft News and Critical Journalism are Shrinking the News Audience and Weakening Democracy—and What News Outlets Can Do About It*. Cambridge, MA: Joan Shorenstein Center for Press, Politics, and Public Policy, John F. Kennedy School of Government, Harvard University.

Peake, J. S. (2007). 'Presidents and Front-Page News: How America's Newspapers Cover the Bush Administration', *Harvard International Journal of Press/Politics*, 12 (October): 52–70.

Peake, J. S., and Parks, A. J. (2008). 'Presidential Pseudo-Events and the Media Coverage they Receive', *American Review of Politics*, 29 (Summer): 85–108.

Prior, M. (2007). *Post–Broadcast Democracy: How Media Choice Increases Inequality in Political Involvement and Polarizes Elections*. New York: Cambridge University Press.

Ragsdale, L. (1984). 'The Politics of Presidential Speechmaking, 1949–1980', *American Political Science Review*, 78 (December): 971–84.

Ragsdale, L. (1987). 'Presidential Speechmaking and the Public Audience: Individual Presidents and Group Attitudes', *Journal of Politics*, 49 (December): 704–36.

Rottinghaus, B. (2009). 'Strategic Leaders: Determining Successful Presidential Opinion Leadership Tactics through Public Appeals', *Political Communication*, 26 (July–September): 296–316.

Rozell, M. J. (1993). 'The Limits of White House Image Control', *Political Science Quarterly*, 108 (Fall): 453–80.

Rozell, M. J. (1995). 'Presidential Image–Makers on the Limits of Spin Control', *Presidential Studies Quarterly*, 25 (Winter): 67–90.

Simon, D. M., and Ostrom, C. W., Jr (1989). 'The Impact of Televised Speeches and Foreign Travel on Presidential Approval', *Public Opinion Quarterly*, 53 (Spring): 58–82.

Tulis, J. K. (1987). *The Rhetorical Presidency*. Princeton: Princeton University Press.

Wanta, W., Stephenson, M. A., Van Slyke Turk, J., and McCombs, M. E. (1989). 'How Presidents State of Union Talk Influenced News Media Agendas', *Journalism Quarterly*, 66 (Autumn): 537–41.

Waterman, R. W., St. Clair, G., and Wright, R. (1999). *The Image–Is–Everything Presidency: Dilemmas in American Leadership*. Boulder, CO: Westview Press.

Weyland, K. (1999). 'Neoliberal Populism in Latin America and Eastern Europe', *Comparative Politics*, 31: 379–401.

Wood, B. D. (2007). *The Politics of Economic Leadership*. Princeton: Princeton University Press.

Wood, B. D., and Peake, J. S. (1998). 'The Dynamics of Foreign Policy Agenda Setting', *American Political Science Review*, 92 (March): 173–84.

Young, G., and Perkins, W. B. (2005). 'Presidential Rhetoric, the Public Agenda, and the End of Presidential Television's "Golden Age"', *Journal of Politics*, 67 (November): 1190–205.

Zaller, J. R. (1998). 'The Rule of Product Substitution in Presidential Campaign News', *Annals of the American Academy of Political and Social Science*, 560 (November): 111–28.

CHAPTER 31

EXECUTIVE LEADERSHIP IN SEMI-PRESIDENTIAL SYSTEMS

ROBERT ELGIE

1 INTRODUCTION

COMPARED with the study of presidentialism and parliamentarism, the study of semi-presidentialism is still in its infancy. While the concept was first operationalized at the beginning of the 1970s, work in this area only became part of the mainstream political science research agenda at the beginning of the 1990s. Since then our understanding of semi-presidentialism has been transformed. The key point to take away from the recent scholarship is that semi-presidentialism is not a unimodal category. Previously, the folk wisdom understood semi-presidentialism as the situation where there was a dual authority structure with a president and prime minister battling for control of the executive. Recent scholarship has demonstrated that there is a tremendous variety of executive politics under semi-presidentialism and has identified some of the effects of this variety. This chapter places the study of executive politics under semi-presidentialism in context, identifies some of the major scholarly developments since the 1990s, and outlines a research agenda for the future.

2 THE STUDY OF SEMI-PRESIDENTIALISM: HISTORICAL AND INTELLECTUAL CONTEXT

The term 'semi-presidential' was used only sporadically until the late 1950s and 1960s. At that time, it came to be used more frequently to describe the Constitution of the Fifth French Republic. In 1970, the study of semi-presidentialism began in earnest when Maurice Duverger became the first person to use the term systematically. In the eleventh edition of his French textbook, he identified a set of 'semi-presidential regimes', including France, Austria, Finland, and the defunct system in Weimar Germany (Duverger 1970: 279). Over the course of the next decade, Duverger refined his definition and extended his examples to include Iceland, Ireland, and Portugal. This work culminated in his book *Échec au roi*, which constitutes the mature statement of Duverger's analysis in French (Duverger 1978). In 1980 he summarized his book in an English-language article that brought his work to a much wider audience (Duverger 1980).

In the 1980s, almost exclusively as a result of Duverger's work, the concept of semi-presidentialism was studied somewhat more widely. The concept was accepted as part of the Portuguese political lexicon (e.g. Pereira 1984). In Spanish, Noguiera Alcalá (1986) helped to popularize the term, arguing that a semi-presidential system should be introduced in Chile. All the same, the study of semi-presidentialism was still confined to a relatively small number of scholars, who applied the concept to a fairly limited number of countries. This situation was transformed in the early 1990s with the wave of democratization and constitutional change at that time. There was an increase in the literature on semi-presidentialism in German (e.g. Bahro and Veser 1995), partly because of the presence of semi-presidentialism in so many countries in Central and Eastern Europe. Debates about the reform of the Italian system generated a considerable literature there (e.g. Ceccanti, Massari and Pasquino 1996). In English, the first edited volume devoted to the topic appeared in 1999 (Elgie 1999). Given the spread of semi-presidential constitutions across the globe, there is now a scholarly interest in the topic almost everywhere.

In the period since 1990, the question of how to define semi-presidentialism has been ever present. At the beginning of the period, Duverger's definition was unquestioningly accepted. In his 1980 article, he defined the concept as follows:

> [a] political regime is considered as semi-presidential if the constitution which established it combines three elements: (1) the president of the republic is elected by universal suffrage; (2) he possesses quite considerable powers; (3) he has opposite him, however, a prime minister and ministers who possess executive and governmental power and can stay in office only if the parliament does not show its opposition to them'.
>
> (Duverger 1980: 166)

On the basis of this definition a country was classed as semi-presidential if it had a fairly powerful president. For some people, it did not even matter whether or not the president was directly elected (O'Neil 1993) as long as the president was more powerful than a standard indirectly elected president but less powerful than a typical directly elected president. In the mid-1990s Giovanni Sartori (1997: 131–2) reformulated the definition, but in a way that was fundamentally consistent with Duverger's version. The problem with Duverger's definition was that it rested on a fundamental ambiguity as to what constituted a president with 'quite considerable powers'. What one writer believed to be quite considerable was not what another person believed it to be. The result was that the list of semi-presidential countries varied from one scholar to the next. This variation did not facilitate reliable cross-national comparisons. Moreover, this way of understanding semi-presidentialism generated a cottage industry of publications by country experts claiming that their country was or, more usually, was not semi-presidential because they considered their president to have either too few or too many powers than could rightly be counted as 'quite considerable'. The solution to this problem and the confusion it generated was to remove any reference to the powers of the president from the definition of the concept. To this end, Elgie (1999: 13) proposed the following definition: 'Semi-presidentialism is the situation where a constitution makes provision for both a directly elected fixed-term president and a prime minister and cabinet who are collectively responsible to the legislature.' One advantage of this definition is that countries can be classed as semi-presidential or otherwise simply by referring to a small number of constitutional criteria that can almost always be identified unambiguously. Therefore, one person's list of semi-presidential countries should be identical to any other person's. According to a recent review of the literature on semi-presidentialism, 'the majority' of scholars have now adopted this definition (Schleiter and Morgan-Jones 2009a: 874).

This post-Duvergerian definition of semi-presidentialism is purely taxonomic. On the basis of a small number of publicly available criteria and without the need for any country-level expertise, it allows countries with semi-presidential constitutions to be reliably distinguished from those with presidential constitutions—where there is a directly elected (or popularly elected) fixed-term president and where cabinet members are not collectively responsible to the legislature—and parliamentary constitutions—where there is either a monarch or an indirectly elected president, and where the prime minister and cabinet are collectively responsible to the legislature. Crucially, the post-Duvergerian definition of semi-presidentialism is not explanatory. While it allows countries with semi-presidential constitutions to be reliably classified, it has the effect of generating a very heterogeneous set of semi-presidential countries. (For a list, see Elgie 2011: 24.) For example, Ireland with its very weak president is just as semi-presidential as Mozambique with its very strong president. Consequently, there is no reason to expect the set of semi-presidential countries to operate in one particular way. This means that semi-presidentialism should not be used as a discrete explanatory variable. This heterogeneity still leads some observers to question the validity of the concept and/or its empirical usefulness (Reestman 2006). It should be appreciated, though, that there is variation within both presidentialism and parliamentarism too. Presidentialism in the USA with its system of separation of powers and checks and balances is very different from presidentialism in Venezuela. Parliamentarism in the UK with its strong prime minister is different from parliamentarism in Japan.

The heterogeneity of the set of semi-presidential regimes has obliged scholars to try to capture the variation within semi-presidentialism in a systematic way. Generally, this exercise leads to either a dichotomous or a continuous subclassification of semi-presidential countries. The standard example of the former is Shugart and Carey's distinction (1992) between president–parliamentary and premier–presidential forms of semi-presidentialism. For Shugart (2005: 333): 'Under premier–presidentialism, the prime minister and cabinet are exclusively accountable to the assembly majority, while under president–parliamentarism, the prime minister and cabinet are dually accountable to the president and the assembly majority.' So this exercise takes the form of an additional classification rule that allows a distinction to be drawn between two subtypes of semi-presidentialism. The advantage of this rule is that, as with the post-Duvergerian definition itself, it is based on a publicly available constitutional criterion and requires no specialist country knowledge, thus generating a reliable classification of the two subtypes. An alternative way of capturing variation within semi-presidentialism is to take a continuous measure of presidential power, such as the ones proposed by either Siaroff (2003) or Metcalf (2000), and to distinguish between semi-presidential countries on the basis of the relative power of the president. The advantage of this approach is that it allows more fine-grained distinctions to be made within semi-presidentialism. A disadvantage is that any measure of presidential power may suffer from a problem of construct validity. Overall, whereas the post-Duvergerian definition of semi-presidentialism is purely taxonomic, these subclassifications are explicitly explanatory. They allow the effect of institutional variation within semi-presidentialism to be studied as well as the outcome of such variation relative to the effects of presidentialism and parliamentarism.

The controversy over how the concept of semi-presidentialism should be understood and operationalized dogged the study of this form of government in the immediate post-1990 period. Nonetheless, substantive empirical work has now been conducted. Much of this work has comprised single-country studies in academic journals (Pugačiauskas 2002; Protsyk 2003) or collections of country studies in edited books (Elgie 1999; Elgie and Moestrup 2007, 2008; Costa Lobo and Amorim Neto 2010; Elgie, Moestrup, and Wu 2011). There is a limited literature in journals that focuses solely on semi-presidentialism but that is explicitly comparative (Shugart 2005; Cheibub and Chernykh 2008), although most of this work tends to compare countries in a particular region of the world (Kirschke 2007), usually Europe and/or the former USSR (Roper 2002; Protsyk 2005a, 2005b, 2006; Schleiter and Morgan-Jones 2010; Sedelius and Ekman 2010). There is a very small number of monographs devoted solely to the comparative study of semi-presidentialism (Frison-Roche 2005; Skach 2005; Elgie 2011). Finally, there is a limited but growing number of comparative studies that includes semi-presidential countries alongside presidential and/or parliamentary countries (Hellwig and Samuels 2008; Cheibub and Chernykh 2009; Samuels and Shugart 2010). Overall, the development of a standard definition and more rigorous empirical work has led Schleiter and Morgan-Jones to conclude that 'scholars have made impressive progress in the study of semi-presidentialism over recent years' (Schleiter and Morgan-Jones 2009a: 891). In the next section, some of the main findings of this work are presented.

3 Semi-Presidentialism and Executive Politics

What do we know about executive politics under semi-presidentialism? We know that on the basis of a post-Duvergerian definition of the concept there is no single answer to the question 'who is in charge?' (Schleiter and Morgan-Jones 2010). The variation in executive leadership within the set of countries with a semi-presidential constitution is so great that the answer to the question depends on the particular circumstances in the country or the set of countries that is being studied. So, contrary to Tavits's interpretation (2009) of the existing work, scholars of semi-presidentialism do not claim that direct election necessarily makes any inherent difference to the functioning of a regime. There are countries with a directly elected president that operate in a manner that is perfectly consistent with countries that have a purely parliamentary system of government with an indirectly elected president. For example, Ireland has a semi-presidential constitution, but the Irish president is so weak that the country operates in a manner that is equivalent to a standard parliamentary regime. Consequently, in Ireland the general answer to the question 'who is in charge?' is very clear: the prime minister. Equally, there are countries with a directly elected president where the answer to the question is equally clear, but different. In these countries, the president is in charge and the prime minister is merely an assistant. This situation characterizes many of the less democratic semi-presidential countries where parties are highly presidentialized and where there are very few checks and balances in the system. There are also countries where to a greater or lesser extent both the president and the prime minister are relevant political actors. In these countries, there is likely to be considerable variation in presidential–prime-ministerial relations over time. For example, periods of presidential predominance may be interspersed with periods of prime-ministerial government. France is the standard case in this regard. Overall, semi-presidentialism is not a unimodal category. There is both variation in presidential and prime-ministerial power across the set of semi-presidential countries as well as variation across time within all countries, but particularly in those where there is a mix of presidential and prime-ministerial/legislative power.

Why are presidents in some semi-presidential countries generally more powerful than others? At least part of the reason is due to variation in the constitutional powers of semi-presidential presidents. So, Siaroff's index (2003) of presidential power shows that—on a scale from 0 to 9—countries with semi-presidential constitutions register scores between 1 and 8. By contrast, the equivalent range for presidential countries, and for parliamentary countries with an indirectly elected president, is 6–8 and 0–5 respectively. Thus, reference to constitutional powers can help to explain both why semi-presidential Mozambique with a Siaroff score of 8 has a highly presidentialized system, and why semi-presidential Slovenia with a Siaroff score of 1 has a president who is almost always merely a figurehead and a prime minister who is in charge of the government's business. A problem, though, is that constitutional powers can sometimes be a poor indicator of presidential power in practice. For example, Samuels and Shugart (2010, 89) exclude Austria from their comparative study because of the 'degree of de facto political deviation from the de jure constitutional form'. Cheibub (2009) makes a similar point about Iceland. Another problem is that measures of constitutional power fail to capture within-country variation. For example, in Russia President Putin moved from the presidency to the prime ministership without any significant decrease in his influence and without any constitutional change. What is more, as Tavits (2009) demonstrates, presidential power can vary over time even within countries where there is a dominant form of executive politics. So, even though the Irish president is almost always a mere figurehead and the prime minister has always been a more consequential political actor, there have been occasions when the presidency has been more active.

Why then does presidential power vary so much within some semi-presidential countries? The answer lies mainly in the variation that can occur in the relationship between the president and the legislature (Duverger 1980: 182–6). For example, without the president's constitutional powers varying, the president may sometimes be the leader of a cohesive single-party legislative majority. This form of unified government is likely to make the president a powerful political actor. Indeed, Lijphart has argued that these conditions 'make it possible for the president to be even more powerful than in most pure presidential systems' (Lijphart 2004: 102). At other times, though, the president may be the representative of one of a more or less heterogeneous coalition of parties with a legislative majority. As a result, the president's party may be represented in the government, but the prime minister may be from a coalition party. This situation is known as a divided executive. Under these conditions, the president and prime minister will have to work together, but they may also be in competition, trying to maximize the influence of their respective parties. Equally, sometimes the legislature may be extremely fragmented, and there may be no majority. This is the situation that Skach (2005) dubs 'divided minority government'. Under these conditions, Skach argues that the president is disempowered. She warns, however, that presidents are likely to react by trying to exercise authority unilaterally, forming technical governments, ruling by decree, and so forth. These actions will bring them into direct competition with the legislature. Indeed, Skach (2005: 17) calls divided minority government semi-presidentialism's 'most conflict-prone sub-type'. Alternatively, there may be a majority in the legislature, but it may be actively opposed to the president. This situation generates what is known as 'cohabitation', where the prime minister is from an opposing party to the president and where the president's party is not represented in the government. All else being equal, presidents are likely to be weaker during periods of cohabitation than under unified government and the level of conflict between the president and the prime minister may increase.

Much of the work on semi-presidentialism has tried to account for the variation in executive politics. For example, Samuels and Shugart (2010) have shown that cohabitation almost never occurs under president–parliamentarism and that when it occurs under premier–presidentialism it leads to a 'parliamentarization' of the system in a manner that is consistent with a diminution of presidential power. Schleiter and Morgan-Jones (2009a, 2009b, 2010) propose a principal-agent framework as a way of explaining variation in presidential power under semi-presidentialism. They argue (Schleiter and Morgan-Jones 2009b: 669–70) that variation in constitutional rules from one semi-presidential country to another creates differences in the bargaining framework between the president and the legislature. These differences mean that presidential power can vary across time within countries as the conditions of the bargaining framework change. Tavits (2009: 35–40) provides an alternative political opportunity framework. She states that 'constitutional powers are the most important aspect of the opportunity structure' (Tavits 2009: 52), but she argues that incentives for presidential activism will be greater when political consensus is low, notably during periods of cohabitation or divided government, and when other political institutions are weak, particularly during periods of coalition and minority government. All three approaches are instructive, because they are all based on comparative studies that examine semi-presidential countries alongside parliamentary countries and, in the case of Samuels and Shugart, alongside presidential countries as well. In other words, even if semi-presidentialism generates scenarios such as cohabitation that are not found in other types of systems, variation in presidential power is a general phenomenon that needs to be explained on the basis of a general approach rather than one that is limited solely to countries with semi-presidential constitutions.

While much of the work on semi-presidentialism has tried to explain the variation in executive politics, there is also now a considerable amount of work that focuses on the effect of such variation. By far the majority of this work has focused on the impact of semi-presidentialism on democratization. Indeed, this is the only area where there has been an ongoing normative debate about the effects of semi-presidentialism. The early work in this area was dominated by Linz's argument (1994) that semi-presidentialism was a poor choice for new democracies and Sartori's counter-claim (1997) that semi-presidentialism had certain advantages. Both studies, however, were based on very thin empirical evidence. Thereafter, much of this work comprised single-country studies. For example, Fish (2001: 331) argued that 'Mongolia's choice of semi-presidentialism has been a boon to democratization'. By contrast, Freeman (2000: 277) argued that coalition building in Poland 'was impeded by the "dual executive" nature' of the system there. On balance, while semi-presidentialism has had its supporters (Pasquino 2007), more people have warned against the adoption of this system than have supported it (Lijphart 2004; Skach 2005).

The problem with this debate is that it has relied almost exclusively on a Duvergerian interpretation of semi-presidentialism. As a result, policy recommendations have been based on the experience of a relatively small number of countries that have exhibited a balance of presidential and prime-ministerial powers. By contrast, the post-Duvergerian interpretation of semi-presidentialism has shown that countries with a semi-presidential constitution can operate in much more varied ways. This way of thinking about semi-presidentialism has yet to be integrated fully into the normative debate. For example, Slovenia operates like a parliamentary system, even though it has a directly elected president. Thus, it would tend to be excluded from a set of semi-presidential countries on the basis of a Duvergerian interpretation of the concept. With the exclusion of cases such as Slovenia from the universe of semi-presidentialism, however, the number of countries with a directly elected president that have successfully transitioned to democracy is underestimated. As a result, the standard wisdom that parliamentarism is a better constitutional choice than semi-presidentialism may be subject to a problem of selection bias. In short, while the standard wisdom may be valid, it would be risky to place too much store by it.

In the context of a post-Duvergerian interpretation of semi-presidentialism, the most reliable conclusion that can now be drawn is that president–parliamentarism is more dangerous for democracy than premier–presidentialism. Shugart and Carey (1992) were the first to present this argument. While they provided only anecdotal empirical support for their argument, recent work (Elgie 2011; Elgie and Schleiter 2011) has subjected the argument about the relative perils of president–parliamentarism to rigorous testing. The results show that, all else being equal, democracy is more likely to collapse in president–parliamentary regimes than in premier–presidential systems and that, even if democracy survives, the quality of democracy is likely to be worse in the former relative to the latter. Obviously, the argument is not deterministic. Democracy in president–parliamentary Taiwan has survived and flourished. Moreover, the empirical work has largely been confined to the relative effect of the two types of semi-presidentialism rather than to the performance of semi-presidentialism relative to presidentialism and parliamentarism. Nonetheless, if a country is thinking about choosing semi-presidentialism, then the recent work has generated a very clear policy recommendation: choose premier–presidentialism above president–parliamentarism. Again, though, the limitations of any such normative recommendation need to be borne in mind.

More recently, the research agenda has shifted somewhat. There is now work that follows the effect of variation under semi-presidentialism through the whole executive cycle, from government formation, through behaviour in office, to government termination. This work has not yet generated a genuine normative debate, even if it has the potential to do so. In terms of the government formation, Protsyk (2005a: 742) demonstrates that cabinet formation in premier–presidential regimes is 'much more predictable' than under president–parliamentarism. Under premier–presidentialism, the choice of prime minister 'more consistently reflect[s] the preferences of the parliamentary majority' (Protsyk 2005a: 742). This finding is particularly interesting, because it is consistent with the work on the effects of the two types of semi-presidentialism and democratization (Elgie 2011; Elgie and Schleiter 2011). Building on work by Strøm and Amorim Neto (2006), Schleiter and Morgan-Jones (2010) demonstrate that variation in the president's constitutional power affects the outcomes of the cabinet formation process. The greater the president's power, the more control the president has over cabinet composition. Equally, the greater the fragmentation of party groups in parliament, the greater the president's control over formation outcomes. If, however, the cabinet formation process immediately follows a parliamentary election, then the president's influence is reduced. Schleiter and Morgan-Jones (2009b) also compare the outcome of cabinet formation under semi-presidentialism with its outcome under parliamentarism. They find that the level of non-partisan ministers is higher under the former relative to the latter. They account for the variation in ministerial non-partisanship by reference to differences in the powers of presidents under semi-presidentialism and to the more complex nature of the government formation process under semi-presidentialism, owing to the president's involvement under this type of regime.

Given the emphasis on the potentially conflictual relations between the president and prime minister under semi-presidentialism, it is perhaps surprising that this aspect of executive politics remains relatively understudied. The early work by Linz (1994: 48–59) outlined various theoretical reasons why intra-executive relations were likely to be problematic under semi-presidentialism. Reiterating many of these points, Linz and Stepan (1996: 279) warned against semi-presidentialism because of the potential for cohabitation, which leads to the 'possibility for deadlock and constitutional conflict' between the president and the prime minister. For the most part, subsequent scholarship has tended to focus on country-specific narratives of presidential–prime-ministerial relations rather than more general comparative studies (Morgan-Jones and Schleiter 2004; Millard 2008). One of the reasons why such studies are somewhat rare is the difficulty in measuring conflict in a way that is susceptible to rigorous enquiry. Whereas presidential activism is increasingly being modelled by way of the percentage of non-partisan ministers in government (Strøm and Amorim Neto 2006; Tavits 2009; Schleiter and Morgan-Jones 2010), the frequency and intensity of intra-executive conflict are much more difficult to capture systematically. Protsyk's work provides an exception to this rule. Focusing on semi-presidential governments in Eastern Europe, Protsyk (2005b, 2006) relies on the examples of intra-executive conflict that were recorded in *East European Constitutional Review*. On that basis, he finds that presidents were more likely to initiate conflict than prime ministers. He also finds that they were particularly quick to do so when the prime minister headed a minority government, suggesting that the presidents sensed potential prime-ministerial weakness and moved to try to capitalize on the situation. By contrast, when there were technocratic cabinets, the level of presidential–prime-ministerial conflict declined.

In this context, it is perhaps not surprising that attention is also starting to be paid to the issue of government termination under semi-presidentialism. Like cabinet formation, this aspect of the political process is easy to observe and, therefore, to model. Sedelius and Ekman (2010) use a mixture of secondary reports and an expert survey to determine whether there is a link between intra-executive conflict in Eastern Europe and cabinet instability. They find that there is an association and that intra-executive conflict is particularly destabilizing in president–parliamentary countries relative to premier–presidential countries. By contrast, in a comparative study of parliamentary and semi-presidential regimes in Europe, Schleiter and Morgan-Jones (2009c) find no relationship between the type of semi-presidential regime and government survival. They do find though that, if the president has the power to dissolve the legislature, then there is a greater likelihood of governments being replaced between elections. By contrast, in their study of semi-presidential and parliamentary countries, Cheibub and

Chernykh (2009) show that variation in government stability is more affected by the electoral system than by whether or not the president is directly elected or by the powers of the president. These somewhat contradictory results suggest that scholarship is only just beginning in this domain.

Overall, the main conclusion to be drawn from the empirical studies of semi-presidentialism is that there is no single model of semi-presidential politics. By distinguishing between different types of semi-presidentialism, such as premier–presidentialism and president–parliamentarism, we can compare the effect of each type relative to the other. We can also compare the effect of each type relative to other forms of government. Recent scholarship has shown that the variation within semi-presidentialism can, however, be operationalized in a more fine-grained way in relation both to specific presidential powers, such as the power to dissolve the legislature, and to relations with the legislature—for example, whether there is majority or minority government. Doing so has helped to push back the boundaries of the research agenda.

4   WHERE TO FROM HERE?

There are three main aspects to the contemporary research agenda on semi-presidentialism. First, and quite simply, more study of semi-presidential countries is needed. Tavits (2009) has criticized those who focus solely on semi-presidentialism. This criticism is unjustified. While, as will be argued, more general comparisons are necessary, there are plenty of studies that focus only on parliamentarism or on presidentialism. Indeed, there is a vibrant literature that confines itself to the study of Latin American presidentialism alone. In this context, focusing solely on semi-presidentialism is no less legitimate. More than that, the extreme variety of political practice within semi-presidentialism raises questions that are not as relevant to other regimes types. Why do countries with the same basic constitutional features operate in such different ways? What is the effect on policy and political outcomes of cohabitation relative to the other types of situations that can occur under semi-presidentialism? Is Skach right to claim that divided minority government is semi-presidentialism's most conflict-prone subtype? These are questions that can legitimately be asked solely within the confines of a study of semi-presidential countries. To answer them, finer ways of capturing the variation within semi-presidentialism are needed, and better ways of understanding the potential effects of such variation are required. Moreover, even though single-country studies can be a vital source of second-hand information for outside observers, to gain better purchase on the explanatory variables more medium-n regional and large-n comparative studies are needed. Ideally, a rich mix of such studies will help to answer at least some of the questions that are now being asked about semi-presidentialism.

Secondly, while studies that focus on semi-presidentialism alone can be methodologically legitimate, more studies that compare semi-presidential, presidential, and parliamentary countries are required. For example, even though there is very robust evidence that president–parliamentarism is more dangerous for democracy than premier–presidentialism, there is no large-*n* systematic study of the effects of these two subtypes of semi-presidentialism relative to their presidential and parliamentary counterparts. Recently, there have been studies that have focused on the variation within semi-presidentialism relative to parliamentarism (Cheibub and Chernykh 2008; Schleiter and Morgan-Jones 2009b, 2009c, 2010). Whereas Cheibub and Chernykh have concluded there is no difference in terms of outcomes between the two, Schleiter and Morgan-Jones have found that it is best not to lump semi-presidentialism in with parliamentarism. These contradictory interpretations suggest that more studies are required. We need to be sure that the results are not dependent upon different case selection, definitions of democracy, years included in the study, and so forth. For their part, Samuels and Shugart (2010) have shown that semi-presidentialism, particularly its president–parliamentary form, is closer to presidentialism than parliamentarism in much of its effects. In so doing, these studies have started to answer a question that has been asked since the concept of semi-presidentialism was first identified. Can this form of government be subsumed into one of the two more established categories of regimes, or is it a stand-alone system? The extreme variation within semi-presidentialism means that it should not be treated as a discrete third type of system except taxonomically. On the other hand, it is entirely plausible to think that, for example, outcomes under premier–presidentialism may more resemble those under parliamentarism, while outcomes under president–parliamentarism may resemble those under presidentialism. Samuels and Shugart's work on political parties suggests that this way of approaching the different types of regime may be useful. As things stand, though, much more comparative work needs to be done before any general conclusions can be drawn about the relative effects of the different types of semi-presidentialism, presidentialism, and parliamentarism.

Finally, whether the analysis focuses purely on semi-presidential countries or comparisons of semi-presidential, presidential, and parliamentary countries, there is a need to deepen and broaden the scope of scholarship. In terms of depth, more data are needed. Previously, it was demonstrated that the study of intra-executive conflict (or cooperation), which is often said to be central to semi-presidentialism, has been hampered by the absence of reliable data about the level and the intensity of such conflict. There is only so much to be learnt from country-specific narratives. To understand the reasons why the level of intra-executive conflict varies across countries and across time, reliable indicators of such conflict need to be identified and mapped on a cross-national basis. A similar point applies to other aspects of political behaviour. For example, even though the rules concerning presidential vetoes differ from one country to the next, there is the potential, all else being equal, to identify the level of presidential intervention by reference to the frequency with which vetoes are used. Such information is often difficult for country experts to gather, however, and is certainly unavailable for comparativists. If basic questions about political life are to be answered, then more data about some of its most basic aspects are needed. In terms of breadth, it must be remembered that scholars of semi-presidentialism are studying topics that scholars elsewhere are also studying but in very different contexts and different ways. For example, the study of semi-presidentialism often focuses on presidential and/or prime-ministerial leadership. There is already a vast literature on this topic broadly understood from a variety of different epistemological and methodological perspectives. Unsurprisingly, the literature on semi-presidentialism often relies on some basic institutionalist assumptions. This approach may be perfectly valid, but it is not the only way in which political leaders and/or leadership can be studied. The study of semi-presidentialism would benefit from the application of a broader set of approaches than have been applied up to this point.

5 CONCLUSION

Relative to the study of presidentialism and parliamentarism, the study of semi-presidentialism is still in its infancy. That said, like all infants, the rate of learning is very quick. Since the 1990s in particular, we have learnt a lot about this constitutional arrangement: how to identify it, why there is so much variation within it, and what effects such variation has on certain political outcomes. There is, though, still much more to learn. The study of semi-presidential countries is likely to remain a focus of academic attention in itself. In the future, however, there are likely to be more comparative studies, with semi-presidential cases being analysed alongside presidential and parliamentary cases. In this sense, whereas just twenty years ago the study of semi-presidentialism was confined to just a small number of scholars looking at an even smaller number of countries, in twenty years' time it is likely that the study of semi-presidentialism will be part of the scholarly mainstream. Such a development would be welcomed, not just for its essential academic interest, but also because semi-presidentialism is likely to remain a tempting choice for constitution-makers. The more that is known about this type of constitutional arrangement, the better the advice that can be provided as to the pros and cons of this form of government and its almost infinite variety.

RECOMMENDED READING

Duverger, M. (1980). 'A New Political System Model: Semi-Presidential Government', *European Journal of Political Research*, 8/2: 165–87.

Elgie, R., Moestrup, S., and Wu, Y-S. (2011) (eds). *Semi-Presidentialism and Democracy*. London: Palgrave.

Samuels, D., and Shugart, M. (2010). *Presidents, Parties, and Prime Ministers: How the Separation of Powers Affects Party Organization and Behavior*. Cambridge: Cambridge University Press.

REFERENCES

Bahro, H., and Veser, E. (1995). 'Das semipräsidentielle System. "Bastard" oder Regierungsform sui generis?', *Zeitschrift für Parlamentsfragen*, 26/3: 471–85.

Ceccanti. S., Massari, O., and Pasquino, G. (1996). *Semipresidenzialismo. Analisi delle esperienze europee*. Bologna: Il Mulino.

Cheibub, J. A. (2009). 'Making Presidential and Semi-Presidential Constitutions Work', *Texas Law Review*, 88/7: 1375–407.

Cheibub, J. A., and Chernykh, S. (2008). 'Constitutions and Democratic Performance in Semi-Presidential Democracies', *Japanese Journal of Political Science*, 9/3: 269–303.

Cheibub, J. A., and Chernykh, S. (2009). 'Are Semi-Presidential Constitutions Bad for Democratic Performance?', *Constitutional Political Economy*, 20/3–4: 202–29.

Costa Lobo, M., and Amorim Neto, O. (2010) (eds). *O semipresidencialismo nos países de língua portuguesa*. Lisbon: Imprensa de Ciências Sociais.

Duverger, M. (1970). *Institutions politiques et droit constitutionnel*. Paris: Presses Universitaires de France.

Duverger, M. (1978). *Échec au roi*. Paris: Albin Michel.

Duverger, M. (1980). 'A New Political System Model: Semi-Presidential Government', *European Journal of Political Research*, 8/2: 165–87.

Elgie, R. (1999) (ed.). *Semi-Presidentialism in Europe*. Oxford: Oxford University Press.

Elgie, R. (2011). *Semi-Presidentialism: Sub-Types and Democratic Performance*. Oxford: Oxford University Press.

Elgie, R., and Moestrup, S. (2007) (eds). *Semi-Presidentialism Outside Europe*. London: Routledge.

Elgie, R., and Moestrup, S. (2008) (eds). *Semi-Presidentialism in Central and Eastern Europe*. Manchester: Manchester University Press.

Elgie, R., and Schleiter, P. (2011). 'Variation in the Durability of Semi-Presidential Democracies', in R. Elgie, S. Moestrup and Y-S Wu (eds), *Semi-Presidentialism and Democracy*. London: Palgrave, 42–60.

Elgie, R., Moestrup, S., and Wu, Y.- S (2011) (eds). *Semi-Presidentialism and Democracy*. London: Palgrave.

Fish, M. S. (2001). 'The Inner Asian Anomaly: Mongolia's Democratization in Comparative Perspective', *Communist and Post-Communist Studies*, 34/3: 323–38.

Freeman, M. (2000). 'Constitutional Frameworks and Fragile Democracies: Choosing between Parliamentarism, Presidentialism and Semi-Presidentialism', *Pace International Law Review*, 12/2: 253–82.

Frison-Roche, F. (2005). *Le 'Modèle semi-présidentiel' comme instrument de la transition en Europe post-communiste*. Brussels: Bruylant.

Hellwig, T., and Samuels, D. (2008). 'Electoral Accountability and the Variety of Democratic Regimes', *British Journal of Political Science*, 38: 65–90.

Kirschke, L. (2007). 'Semipresidentialism and the Perils of Power-Sharing in Neopatrimonial States', *Comparative Political Studies*, 40/11: 1372–94.

Lijphart, A. (2004). 'Constitutional Design for Divided Societies', *Journal of Democracy*, 15/2: 96–109.

Linz, J. J. (1994). 'Presidential or Parliamentary Democracy: Does it Make a Difference?', in J. J. Linz and A. Valenzuela (eds), *The Failure of Presidential Democracy: Comparative Perspectives*. Baltimore: Johns Hopkins University Press, 3–87.

Linz, J. J., and Stepan, A. (1996). *Problems of Democratic Transition and Consolidation. Southern Europe, South America, and Post-Communist Europe*. Baltimore: John Hopkins University Press.

Metcalf, L. K. (2000). 'Measuring Presidential Power', *Comparative Political Studies*, 33/5: 660–85.

Millard, F. (2008). 'Executive–Legislative Relations in Poland, 1991–2005: Institutional Relations in Transition', *Journal of Legislative Studies*, 14/4: 367–93.

Morgan-Jones, E., and Schleiter, P. (2004). 'Governmental Change in a President-Parliamentary Regime: The Case of Russia 1994–2003', *Post-Soviet Affairs*, 20/2: 132–63.

Noguiera Alcalá, H. (1986). *El Regimen Semipresidencial. Una Nueva Forma de Gobierno Democrático*. Santiago: Chile.

O'Neil, P. (1993). 'Presidential Power in Post-Communist Europe: The Hungarian Case in Comparative Perspective', *Journal of Communist Studies*, 9/3: 177–201.

Pasquino, G. (2007). 'The Advantages and Disadvantages of Semi-Presidentialism: A West European perspective', in R. Elgie and S. Moestrup (ed.), *Semi-Presidentialism outside Europe*. London: Routledge, 14–29.

Pereira, A. G. (1984). *O Semipresidencialismo em Portugal*. Lisbon: Ática.

Protsyk, O. (2003). 'Troubled Semi-Presidentialism: Stability of the Constitutional System and Cabinet in Ukraine', *Europe-Asia Studies*, 55/7: 1077–95.

Protsyk, O. (2005a). 'Prime Ministers' Identity in Semi-Presidential Regimes: Constitutional Norms and Cabinet Formation Outcomes', *European Journal of Political Research*, 44/5: 721–48.

Protsyk, O. (2005b). 'Politics of Intraexecutive Conflict in Semipresidential Regimes in Eastern Europe', *East European Politics and Societies*, 19/2: 135–60.

Protsyk, O. (2006). 'Intra-Executive Competition between President and Prime Minister: Patterns of Institutional Conflict and Cooperation under Semi-Presidentialism', *Political Studies*, 54/2: 219–44.

Pugačiauskas, V. (2002). 'Lithuania's Semi-Presidential Model: Prospects for the Stability of the Inter-Institutional Relations', *Lithuanian Political Science Yearbook 2002*, 11–21.

Reestman, J. H. (2006). 'Presidential Elements in Government: Introduction', *European Constitutional Law Review*, 2/1: 54–9.

Roper, S. D. (2002). 'Are All Semipresidential Regimes the Same? A Comparison of Premier-Presidential Regimes', *Comparative Politics*, 34/3: 253–72.

Samuels, D., and Shugart, M. (2010). *Presidents, Parties, and Prime Ministers: How the Separation of Powers Affects Party Organization and Behavior*. Cambridge: Cambridge University Press.

Sartori, G. (1997). *Comparative Constitutional Engineering: An Inquiry into Structures, Incentives and Outcomes*. 2nd edn. London: Macmillan.

Schleiter, P., and Morgan-Jones, E. (2009a). 'Review Article: Citizens, Presidents and Assemblies: The Study of Semi-Presidentialism beyond Duverger and Linz', *British Journal of Political Science*, 39/4: 871–92.

Schleiter, P., and Morgan-Jones, E. (2009b). 'Party Government in Europe? Parliamentary and Semi-Presidential Democracies Compared', *European Journal of Political Research*, 48/5): 665–93.

Schleiter, P., and Morgan-Jones, E. (2009c). 'Constitutional Power and Competing Risks: Monarchs, Presidents, Prime Ministers, and the Termination of East and West European Cabinets', *American Political Science Review*, 103/3: 496–512.

Schleiter, P., and Morgan-Jones, E. (2010). 'Who's in Charge? Presidents, Assemblies, and the Political Control of Semipresidential Cabinets', *Comparative Political Studies*, 43/11: 1415–41.

Sedelius, T., and Ekman, J. (2010). 'Intra-Executive Conflict and Cabinet Instability: Effects of Semi-Presidentialism in Central and Eastern Europe', *Government and Opposition*, 45/4: 505–30.

Shugart, M. S. (2005). 'Semi-Presidential Systems: Dual Executive and Mixed Authority Patterns', *French Politics*, 3/3: 323–51.

Shugart, M. S., and Carey, J. M. (1992). *Presidents and Assemblies. Constitutional Design and Electoral Dynamics*. Cambridge: Cambridge University Press.

Siaroff, A. (2003). 'Comparative Presidencies: The Inadequacy of the Presidential, Semi-Presidential and Parliamentary Distinction', *European Journal of Political Research*, 42/3: 287–312.

Skach, C. (2005). *Borrowing Constitutional Designs: Constitutional Law in Weimar Germany and the French Fifth Republic*. Princeton: Princeton University Press.

Strøm, K., and Amorim Neto, O. (2006). 'Breaking the Parliamentary Chain of Delegation: Presidents and Non-Partisan Cabinet Members in European Democracies', *British Journal of Political Science*, 36/4: 619–43.

Tavits, M. (2009). *Presidents in Parliamentary Systems: Do Direct Elections Matter?* Oxford: Oxford University Press.

Prime Ministerial Leadership: Westminster and Beyond

CHAPTER 32

....

THE VARIABILITY OF PRIME MINISTERS

....

PATRICK WELLER

1 INTRODUCTION

....

IF political leadership is described as both providing ways of solving common problems and mobilizing the energy of others to follow those directions (Keohane 2009: 19; also Burns 1978, 2003; Blondel 1987), then the situations in which prime ministers find themselves provide different opportunities for the exercise of leadership. Obviously all leaders will bring their own personality to the position; consequently the exercise of leadership will differ from person to person *within* any polity and over time. Here I am concerned to show how the opportunities for prime ministers to lead will vary *between* countries. Different traditions and institutional arrangements will shape the terrain over which prime ministers will weave their spells.

Prime ministers share a number of characteristics that make them distinct from presidents and other national leaders. Each characteristic in turn leads to series of debates, both normative and pragmatic, about prime ministers' position, role, powers, and legitimacy (extracted from Weller 1985; Jones 1991; Lijphart 1999; Poguntke and Webb 2005). So here I first identify those characteristics and then turn to the debates that some at least of them have engendered:

- *Prime ministers will usually be party leaders*, selected by their parties to win elections and head governments. Even when politics has reached such a crisis point in some countries that parliaments seek to install non-party technocrats as prime minister (as in Greece and Italy in 2012), they will still have to rely on parties in parliament to pass the legislation needed to implement their plans. How do prime ministers rise to their position and how vulnerable are they to removal?
- *Prime ministers depend for their position on the continuing support of a parliament.* Their time in office has no term limit, but rather relies on their ability to maintain

that parliamentary majority. Since they are not directly elected, their mandate is from the parliament and not from the people. How accountable are they therefore to the parliament and how effective are the lines of control over their actions?

- *In parliaments based on single-member electoral systems, prime ministers will often lead majority government*s and they can be sure their programme will be passed. Minority governments have, however, occurred in recent years in Canada, Australia, and the UK; they may be temporary but they change the political calculus. *Where there is proportional representation, in continental countries, the prime ministers' powers will be circumscribed by the need to coordinate their decision with partners.* Electoral systems thus create parliamentary conditions where prime ministers have to negotiate. How restricted are prime ministers who lead minority or coalition governments?
- *Prime ministers head collective governments* where the statutory authority is vested in ministers, rather than in a single individual. They must govern with the consent, or at least the acquiescence, of their ministers. They will have few fixed powers and will depend on their capacity to exercise authority through the existing traditions and conventions, which they will seek to interpret to their advantage. What is the balance between collective and individual leadership in these circumstance?

These are the traditional determinants of prime ministers opportunities. An additional two can be added that have shaped the role of prime ministers since the 1960s.

- *Prime ministers speak for their governments* in a media environment that becomes ever more demanding, with a twenty-four-hour news cycle and the expectation that they should appear omniscient and ever ready to comment.
- *Prime ministers must attend international summits.* Their schedules require meetings on the G7, the G20, the EU, APEC, and other forums, where only the prime minister can effectively represent his or her country. What were once occasional meetings have now become constant demands.

Prime ministers have these conditions in common; but they have different consequences across countries. I distinguish here between prime ministers and those semi-presidential systems such as Germany, Finland, and France where prime ministers must compete with directly elected presidents.

Prime ministers are often compared with presidents, usually to their disadvantage. Where presidents are directly elected, prime ministers are chosen by parliaments. Where presidents have a personal mandate and individual authority, prime ministers must share authority, always with ministers, often with coalition partners. Where presidents are vested with the executive power, prime ministers must shape their roles as best they can, using convention, inherited practice, and political skills. Not all the comparisons run to the president's advantage, however. Prime ministers can usually be assured of legislative support for their proposals; it is almost a condition of survival. Presidents must negotiate every item through the Congress, even when their own party nominally has a majority. Prime ministers can stay as long as they maintain political and party support. Presidents are term limited and can be recognized as lame ducks. While prime ministers may at times wish they had the presidents' powers, they must be glad that they do not face their structured weaknesses. Prime ministers with dominance over their party and their parliament have much greater capacity to determine and implement policy than any president can dream of having (Rhodes, Wanna, and Weller 2009).

2 DEBATES ON THE POWERS OF PRIME MINISTERS

The title of prime minister has a long provenance that pre-dates the party system. In England Robert Walpole was the first leader who was recognized as, even if not formally titled, prime minister. He was the king's first (but not only) minister from 1722 to 1742. Later the emphasis moved from 'minister' to 'first', as royal power declined and parliament's supremacy was consolidated. Walpole had maintained his position by ensuring that he continued to enjoy the confidence of the House of Commons through the judicious use of patronage and favours. Only as the suffrage widened did it become necessary to develop mass parties to organize the vote outside parliament. It was 120 years after Walpole that party government replaced the shifting alliances that dominated the parliaments. By that time the position of the prime minster was well established; its *parliamentary* origins still shape the way the tasks are fulfilled. PMs depend on tradition, convention, and practice, not on statutes.

That lack of precision has led to continuing debates on the powers of the prime ministers over the past decades. Here I select only a few instances to show how they developed. The first studies were detailed historical accounts of the rules and workings of cabinet (Jennings 1959) as the repository of power. Then the alternative argument proposed that cabinet government had been replaced by prime-ministerial government. It was initiated by John Macintosh (1962), and popularized by Richard Crossman (1963: 51), who epitomized the changed circumstance in the comment that Bagehot's 'buckle' was now not the cabinet but one man. By contrast, George Jones has consistently argued the traditional line: that the right term for British government was still 'ministerial government' (e.g. Jones 1965). The problem with the debate was that it often seemed to contrast prime-ministerial government with cabinet government, as though the two were polar opposites. They never were. Tony King (1975: 232) suggests the debate 'had been conducted at the level of a bar room brawl' because neither side specified what prime-ministerial government was or what its empirical referents might be. Indeed they described the 1960s as 'prime ministerial' in contrast to earlier periods. Later writers in turn thought that the 1960 and 1970s were examples of cabinet government from which recent prime ministers have retreated. Nor, it can be added, was either group specific about what conditions had to be fulfilled to justify the tern 'cabinet government' (Weller

2003). The 'prime minister versus cabinet' debate in the UK then became transferred to discussions of PMs' powers elsewhere (see also Blick and Jones, Chapter 33, this volume).

Comparative work is too often limited to series of chapters surveying individual countries, with a concluding chapter (e.g. Blondel and Muller-Rommel 1997). If tightly organized (see Poguntke and Webb 2005; Strangio et al. 2013), they raise interesting questions but too often cannot entertain specific comparisons. Helms (2005) and Bennister (2012) are much more focused—for example, Bennister looks at just two prime ministers. Weller (1985) and Rhodes, Wanna, and Weller (2009) look at the Westminster systems, with a narrow focus on prime ministers in the former and as part of a broader systemic analysis in the latter. Weller, Bakvis, and Rhodes (1997) look at the role of leaders in different roles across five countries.

Rational-choice institutionalism focuses on the analysis of prime ministers and cabinets. One example must suffice: Kaare Strøm and his colleagues' principal-agent theory of delegation and accountability in parliamentary democracies (Strøm, Müller, and Bergman 2003; see also Cox 1987; Laver and Shepsle 1994, 1996; and Tsebelis 2002). Strøm and his colleagues (2003: chs 3, 23) conceive of parliamentary democracy as a chain of delegation from principals to agents: from voters to their elected representatives, from legislators to the chief executive, from the chief executive to ministerial heads of departments, and from ministers to civil servants. Principals and agents are in a hierarchic relationship; both act rationally to gain exogenously given preferences. This analysis raises general issues of importance but it is often hard to apply in particular circumstances.

Some attempts to quantify the positions of prime ministers are just bizarre. O'Malley (2007) uses a survey of 'experts' to rank the powers of prime ministers across countries. The subjective choice of experts and their scores is then systemically analysed to provide standard deviations and the illusion of precision. It may masquerade as political science, but such analyses are surely political nonsense, relying on the opinions of outsiders selected from websites, without any clear ideas of their comparative or particular knowledge of the leaders concerned. This is saying nothing more than Dogan and Pelassy (1990: 116; cited in Rhodes 2006), when they commented that large 'n' comparative studies disappoint because 'comparability is very low'. Citing Blondel's analysis (1980) of all 'heads of government in the post-war period', they ask what sense there is in comparing the 'regular ministerial career' in the Middle East and in the developed countries.

These discussions often talk past one another. They all raise a key issue for practitioners: is there, or can there be, a job description for a prime minister? More recent constitutions may specify some of the prime minister's powers. Thus the Spanish constitution followed the German model to create a strong executive leader (van Biezen and Hopkin 2005: 109, 112). The Swedish constitution was amended in that direction (Aylott 2005: 179). Where prime ministers are not even recognized in the constitutions, though, critics ask: Are there functions that prime ministers should fulfil and others that they should not? On the one side are those who argue that prime ministers' job descriptions require self-denial (Rose 1980), that constitutionally there are activities that prime ministers should be restrained from pursuing (Walter and Strangio 2007). On the other, there is an acceptance that prime ministers will do what they can to achieve their objectives. The first school has been called the theorists; it adopts normative assumptions about what a prime minister should do, and argues that it is wrong for him or her seek to extend his or her powers (French 1979). The second are the realists, who recognize that, where there can be no rules, prime ministers will seek to extend their influence according to political rather than constitutional criteria. This disposition is all the stronger where the position of prime minister is played out within a set of, often tendentious, conventions that are assumed to apply but that can have no precision or legal force.

Practitioners have to find ways to support prime ministers. The Canadian Privy Council Office (1979) draws a distinction between the prime minister's prerogatives and his or her priorities. The *prerogatives* are the tasks that come with the position: choosing ministers, establishing administrative arrangements, running cabinet, answering to parliament, representing the nation abroad. These functions can be fulfilled only by the head of government and cannot be delegated. The prime minister must always be provided with support to do them. Cabinet handbooks or rules will often illustrate how prime ministers choose to assert their prerogatives by determining the workings of cabinet.

Then there are the prime minister's *priorities*: the areas where he or she wants to spend time and have an influence. Some areas such as international relations and economic management are almost inevitably in this category and have been for decades. Prime ministers cannot avoid either, as they lie at the heart of all governing. Nevertheless, the degree to which prime ministers may choose to be involved in, for instance, the making of a budget may differ, depending on the economic circumstances and their relations with the chancellor/treasurer/finance minister. In coalition governments such as the Netherlands, where the details of the pact have been negotiated in detail, the prime minister may in effect feel more constrained from interfering in the activities of ministers. Elsewhere, prime ministers will make choices about what matters: climate change, education, industrial relations, service delivery, or immigration. Their interest may be continuing, or it may wax and wane. The systems have to be devised so that they support prime ministers where they want to go, not where others think they should (Yeend 1979; Weller, Scott, and Stevens 2011). They may want to take a series of initiatives, and then leave the running of the programmes to the responsible ministers. Or they may become involved because the policy area is in crisis and needs the weight that a prime minster can apply until the moment has passed. There can be no set of rules that determine when and where prime ministers should be involved, only the counsel of prudence that is concerned with outcomes and government cohesion.

3 THE SPECIFIC DEBATES ON PRACTICE

Prime ministers work in a network of dependencies, determined both by formal rules and by traditions. The older the system, the less likely it is that the position of prime minister will be specified in any binding form. Even when the prime minister is given formal constitutional status, as in the Netherlands in 1983 (Fiers and Krouwel 2005: 133), those rules are not the determining factor in delineating the power of the role. If it is assumed that prime ministers have three core dependencies, with the party that elected them, with the executive government they run, and with the community outside, seen in terms of the parliament, the media, the electorate, and the international community, it is possible to track some of the differences from one system to another

Prime Ministers and Their Parties

Prime ministers' standing and legitimacy depend in part on the means by which they win that position (Strangio et al. 2013). The electorate for the leadership varies from the party in parliament to the party membership at large. In Australia, Denmark, and New Zealand it remains the prerogative of the MPs. In the British Conservative Party, the MPs run an exhaustive ballot until the candidates are reduced to two, and then there is a vote of the membership at large. In the Labour Party the leaders are elected by a party conference, with representation from the parliamentary party, the branches, and the affiliated trade unions. In Canada a leadership convention has elected leaders since 1925, although there is now pressure to extend the electorate to all party members. In Belgium the election merely endorses the nomination of the party executive (Fiers and Krouwel 2005: 141).

The means of election, and the breadth of the electorate, affect the standing, security, and accountability of the prime minister. A leader elected by a broad ballot of the party has a personal legitimacy that can be used to advantage. Canadian prime minister John Diefenbaker had little support among his cabinet ministers but would remind them that they did not elect him and could not remove him. Even Belgium's oligarchic selection gives the leader additional standing (Fiers and Krouwel 2005: 141). Yet in Australia a coup to remove the prime minister can be, and has been, launched and completed within twelve hours. In the British Labour Party it requires a vote of the conference, and there is no scope for the parliamentary party to express a lack of confidence in the prime minister.

The larger the electorate, the harder it is to mobilize and the longer it takes if the position is contested. Even when there was a vacancy while British Labour was in opposition, it took six months to fill. The formal process for Brown's unchallenged succession took a month, and that was nine months after Blair had said he would go.

The patronage that assists prime ministers to maintain party support is most apparent in the selection of ministers. Most prime ministers can determine who will be ministers, who will hold which portfolios, and what reshuffles will take place. All ministers are, in that sense, the prime minister's agents (a phrase used initially by Douglas Home, ironically one of the least insistent prime ministers in the last fifty years); their presence and future depend on the support of the leader. In Australia for 100 years Labor ministers were elected by the party caucus (but no more). In Sweden PMs have selected 'policrats,' people who are neither in the party nor formal experts; they rely totally on their relationship with the prime ministers (Aylott 2005: 185)

There are a number of constraints on prime ministers, however. Cabinets will include the principal powerbrokers; to leave them out would be to create a source of instability on the backbench. Indeed, prime ministers will face, around the cabinet table at the weekly meeting, their former rivals and probably their future successors. Ministries are a combination of collaboration and competition.

Then there is a downside: for every minister chosen, many others are bypassed. For each supporter made, an enemy may be created, particularly among those who feel that they will have no ministerial future under the present leader. They will then be looking for other opportunities, perhaps under a different leader.

In coalition governments, prime ministers negotiate, ceding both portfolios to their partners and the right to intervene there. Where the coalition agreement has a detailed programme, often carefully constructed over months, there is less freedom of action. In many of these systems prime ministers have little power to determine ministers who are nominated by, and in effect responsible to, the coalition leaders.

Prime Ministers and the Executive

As leaders of the government, prime ministers exercise a number of prerogative powers (Burch and Holliday 1996; Weller 2007). prime ministers chair cabinet. In Westminster systems they choose who will be members, allocate the responsibilities, settle the agenda, determining what will be discussed and what will not, set the terms of debate in cabinet by establishing what the issues are, identify the speakers, sum up the discussion, and thus determine what the cabinet has decided; the formal minutes are then the currency of government ('Cabinet has decided....'). Prime ministers also determine the existence, membership, terms of reference, and authority of any cabinet committees. Where there are rules of procedure, whether in the guise of handbooks or rules of procedure, they are essentially the prime minister's rules, to be enforced, bypassed, or ignored as the incumbent sees fit. In some coalitions the role of the full cabinet has been reduced, with decisions being taken in committee, often chaired by the prime minister; the rearrangement gives the prime minister great ability to influence, even if not direct, policy directions.

There is a constant debate about the degree to which prime ministers are, or should be, supported by a strong department or a circle of personal political advisers. In Australia and Canada PMs have both a Prime Minister's Office (PMO) and a powerful central agency. Such a proposal is treated with suspicion in the UK, even though the PMO there has grown in influence since the 1990s (House of Lords 2010). In Spain the prime minister's advisers, once called 'plumbers', have grown in importance (van Biezen and Hopkin 2005: 117). In the Netherlands the Department of General Affairs (Fiers and Krouwel 2005: 135) and in Italy the General Secretariat (Calisse 2005: 94–5) respectively have increased the civil-service support for the centre of government. In Sweden prime ministers principally rely on career civil servants, but they can appoint a few 'specific advisers' (Pedersen and Knudsen 2005: 165). Prime ministers have increased the assistance they get, but whether that advice should be political or career civil servants and how it should be organized remains contested.

One consequence is that prime ministers are often accused of ignoring cabinet government, although the critics are seldom clear on what real or effective cabinet government would look like (apart from being different from what exists). Blair was said to run a 'sofa' government, whereby cabinet seldom made decisions but was used as a forum for the exchange of information and discussion of political tactics. Decisions were made in committees and settled by the chair of the committee in discussions with the prime minister. In Canada functional cabinet committees approved programmes, but they were unfunded until the prime minister and minister of finance decided which would be supported and duly informed cabinet. Most prime ministers have inner groups, whether a Blair–Brown duumvirate or a Strategic Priorities and Budget Committee as under Rudd in Australia.

For prime ministers, cabinet has always served two principal functions: to maintain political support and to ensure consistency and coherence in political decision-making (Weller 2003, 2007). Prime ministers will balance those two in a range of ways. There can be no single ideal means of ensuring both.

Parliamentary systems are governed by the principle of collective responsibility. It is a doctrine of political caution as much as constitutional sanctity. If ministers disagree, then the government is in chaos. It has never really meant that every cabinet minister is consulted about, and has agreed to, every decision of government. That would be impossible with the modern pace of business. Edmund Dell (1980) argued that collective responsibility provides myths about the degree to which all ministers are aware, or concerned with everything that cabinet discusses. He argues for a strategy of collective purpose where prime ministers ensure that the government is working consistently in the one direction.

This picture of tight coherence is, however, less marked in those places where the prime minister remains very much the chair of the cabinet, rather than the dominant figure. In places such as the Netherlands and Finland, full cabinet meetings may cede decision-making to ministerial committees and a principle of non-intervention prohibits ministers from interfering whimsically in the detailed policy of another portfolio. Prime ministers must then act as brokers where there are divisions of opinion (Fiers and Krouwel 2005: 134). Coalition governments force a degree of coexistence.

Prime Ministers as Public Figures

Prime ministers in parliament. For all the rhetoric about the decline of parliament, prime ministers will take their performances in question time very seriously. UK prime ministers may appear only once or twice a week for PM's questions, but they will be thoroughly prepared for the follow-up questions that will follow the harmless opening. In

Australia and Canada prime ministers will appear every day that the House is sitting. They will be the principal focus of the Opposition's attack, often in a series of coordinated questions that seek to embarrass the prime minister or to catch him or her in inconsistencies. Prime ministers will often spend some hours on the morning preparing for the ordeal. Parliamentary question times are big occasions, not because the leader is about to lose control but because reputations matter; it is the occasion for showing the backbench that they are in control and that they have the measure of the leader of the Opposition. It is about morale, standing, and confidence.

Indeed the great benefit of prime ministers, in contrast to presidents, is that they can usually guarantee that the parliament will support the government measures. Party members rarely vote against the government in Canada and Australia. There is a quid pro quo, however. In these environments, when parliament is sitting, prime ministers attend weekly party meetings, where the members of the caucus can discuss and approve government legislation and question prime ministers and ministers. The expectation is that any misgivings or opposition can be expressed in private and the party members then accept the decision of the majority in public. Even when discontent is known to exist, it is kept in house. In the UK discontent was often not displayed in the Commons, to Blair's occasional embarrassment.

Prime ministers, technology and the media. While it is possible to identify continuity in the need to manage relations between prime ministers and other parts of the polity, the changes in technology have forced them to alter the way that they do their job. While these changes have increased the pressure under which they work, there are clear benefits. They can exert controls over government processes through mobile technology, email, and other means that they could never do before. It is not that modern prime ministers are more controlling than their predecessors, but that they now can do what their forebears could only dream of. In the past they would be largely out of touch when they travelled overseas; now they are always able to contact ministers. So the change in communications has brought internal benefits. There are obviously external benefits too. Once they could directly reach only a small proportion of the electorate through their speeches; now, radio and television have given them an ability to address the nation.

On the other hand, the speed of communications through the Internet and technology, the need to fill a twenty-four-hour news cycle, and the ubiquity of cameras puts pressure on prime ministers to perform all the time. What was once seen as trivial—a slight difference in wording between a prime minister and ministers, an off-the-cuff comment by a minister—now becomes the story of the hour. Prime ministers always wanted to manage the image of their governments, but now the pressure is constant. As a consequence, media management is derided as spin, as an attempt to get governments' messages across on an hourly basis. The media both attacks spin and condemn governments when they do not react immediately to stories. As Blair has complained, managing the media well is a benefit to government but governments cannot choose to opt out. Technology both assists and hamstrings modern government (Meyer 2002; Seymour-Ure 2003).

Crises and initiatives. Where prime ministers choose to spend their political capital may often be externally determined. Prime ministers will have to choose areas where they want to become deeply involved. In other areas, ministers may be allowed to continue to run their own race. It is inevitable that prime ministers will be involved in economic and foreign affairs. The former is the key to survival, the latter an area where only prime ministers can represent the country. Prime ministers will waft in and out of other policy areas. Where they are strong, with high standing and public support, no one will object. Prime ministers will also be attached to the principal items on the party platform; it is likely that they identified these items as election winners, fought the campaign on promises related to these items, and therefore will want to ensure that what the party promised the party will deliver. It is the prime ministers who will be held accountable for election promises. Many ministers like prime ministers to be interested, as it gives them a greater chance of successfully implementing new policies. As an opening gambit, 'The prime minister wants…' is a powerful weapon in government.

Prime ministers will be involved when an issue has become a national priority, whether because of external pressure or internal demands. Riots, accidents, pandemics, bank collapses, education failures, ministerial misdemeanours: all these may move on and then off the agenda, but, while they are prominent issues catching the attention of the public, it would be impossible to imagine the prime minister telling the media that he or she is not involved. None of these is new or novel. Prime ministers in all countries have a set of issues about which they care, and they have the power, the right, and indeed the responsibility to push their ideas there.

International ambassador. Prime ministers must work in global conditions. Summits proliferate. The G7 and the G20, the EU and APEC, ASEAN and the OAU are all post-Second World War creatures. Globalization has linked national economies; PMs can no longer work in isolation, occasionally travelling overseas to meet their foreign counterparts. Faster air travel has made lightening visits possible and desirable. Chart the modern travel of prime ministers, and they will be far greater than those of their predecessors; visits and summits will come more often and leaders will fly in and out. The annual diary of a prime minister is shaped by a series of international meetings fixed long in advance and for which only leaders bring the gravitas necessary to reflect their national interests. In Belgium one prime minister was surprised that foreign affairs took up half his time (Fiers and Krouwel 2005: 133). In Sweden joining the EU changed the priorities of the prime minister (Aylott 2005: 180). Whereas their predecessors would once go by sea and spend weeks out of the country, but not do it often, now prime ministers travel often but for very short periods.

In part it is because most prime ministers enjoy the international connections, and the longer they stay in power the more they do so. They meet their equals, the only other people who can understand the pressures of national leadership. Leaders from smaller countries enjoy the reflected glory of negotiating with leaders of the great powers.

Personal satisfaction apart, however, only prime ministers can speak for their nation and commit the government to some agreement without the need to refer back to the cabinet. The conclusions of international negotiations might cut across several portfolios; in these cases ministers are essentially the prime-ministerial aides, as prime ministers seek to balance the interests of several portfolios into a whole-of-government perspective. Even in those countries such as the Netherlands and Sweden, where there was traditionally a non-intervention principle that restricted prime ministers, the need to coordinate responses to these summits has added to their authority (Fiers and Krouwel 2005: 133). When heads of government sat down at Copenhagen to redraft the communiqué of climate change, they spoke for their countries in the knowledge that their cabinets would be committed to whatever the outcomes were. In effect, the cabinets must endorse the decisions or reject the prime minister. For international credibility there is little choice.

4 CONCLUSIONS

The art of political management depends, then, on the institutional framework within which prime ministers must operate. Prime ministers depend for their continued tenure on the support, or at least the acquiescence, of ministers and the parliamentary caucus. Parliamentary government retains important elements of collective government; prime ministers ensure that their ministerial colleagues work effectively together.

Prime ministers have always been ambitious; otherwise they would not be national leaders. Within their governments public expectation is that they lead, that they set the tone and direction of their governments. They always tried to. Their activities are determined by decisions about political priorities. Prime ministers are involved where issues are difficult, intractable, or running across the interests of several other ministers. They will move in and out of issues as circumstances demand. Their powers lie in convention and practice. Their position has adjusted to take account of the new pressures on government, whether from the demands of the media, the expectations of the public, or the requirements of international summitry. There is, and can be, no job description outside the core functions described as their prerogatives. Even then there is no particular weight that they have to give to their particular responsibilities. Nor are there binding rules to determine how they will run their governments. They need to chart an effective policy course and maintain a solid political base in the party and in the electorate. They do what they must to lead the government, to achieve their objectives, to implement their dreams—and to survive.

5 FUTURE RESEARCH

First, future comparisons of prime ministers are needed at three levels. First will be the studies of a single country over time, to see whether the circumstances have changed and what effect those changes have on a prime minister's powers. The benefit of such studies is that they can show how small alterations to position and process can lead to substantial effects. Often such studies can be drawn from the extensive political memoirs and biographies. I have not tried to reference them here, but they need to be mined for detail because they tell of crises but rarely about the routines that dominate political activity (Rhodes 2011). A second approach is to take a number of 'most similar' countries (Weller 1985; Rhodes, Wanna, and Weller 2009; Strangio et al. 2013), and to ask how comparatively similar institutions and traditions have led to divergent practices and opportunities. Third, studies can adopt approach of the large 'n' comparative studies that contrast prime ministers across different political systems, although the questions that can be answered will relate more to performance than to the capabilities of prime ministers in different political circumstances and systems.

Second, research will need to show how the task of prime ministers has changed as they struggle to meet new demands on their time: the twenty-four-hour media cycle and international summitry. Accountability to parliament may remain the traditional route, but media demand much more immediate briefing and responses. Often prime ministers need to run harder just to stand still and retain what influence they used to have.

Third, those normative studies that seek to define what prime ministers *should* do need to ask what they *can* do. So studies that complain that the central facilities available to prime ministers illustrate increased authority might also ask what is needed to allow prime ministers to do their job effectively. The questions are what they can do alone, how they can work with ministers and advisers, and what control they can exert. The answers will not only differ from country to country but will probably show how the tasks are becoming harder as the ever-present demands on prime ministers speed up and increase, thanks to modern technological advances.

Recommended Readings

Crossman, R. H. S. (1963). 'Introduction', in W. Bagehot, *The English Constitution*. London: Fontana, 1–57.

Poguntke, T., and Webb, P. (2005) (eds). *The Presidentialization of Politics*. Oxford: Oxford University Press.

Rhodes, R. A. W., Wanna, J., and Weller, P. (2009). *Westminster Compared*. Oxford: Oxford University Press.

References

Aylott, N. (2005). 'President Persson: How did Sweden get him?', in T. Poguntke and P. Webb (eds), *The Presidentialization of Politics*. Oxford: Oxford University Press, 176–98.

Bennister, M. (2012). *Prime Ministers in Power: Political Leadership in Britain and Australia*. Houndmills: Palgrave.

Blondel, J. (1980). *World Leaders*. London: Sage.

Blondel, J. (1985). *Government Ministers in the Contemporary World*. London: Sage.

Blondel, J. (1987). *Political Leadership*. London: Sage.

Blondel, J., and Muller-Rommel, F. (eds) (1997). *Cabinets in Western Europe*. 2nd edn. Houndmills: Macmillan.

Burch, M., and Holliday, I. (1996). *The British Cabinet System*. Hemel Hempstead: Prentice Hall/Wheatsheaf.

Burns, J. M. (1978). *Leadership*. New York: Harper Row.

Burns, J. M. (2003). *Transforming Leadership*. New York: Atlantic Monthly Press.

Calisse, M. (2005). 'Presidentialization, Italian Style', in T. Poguntke and P. Webb (eds), *The Presidentialization of Politics*. Oxford: Oxford University Press, 88–106.

Cox, G. W. (1987). *The Efficient Secret: The Cabinet and the Development of Political Parties in Victorian England*. Cambridge: Cambridge University Press.

Crossman, R. H. S. (1963). 'Introduction', in W. Bagehot, *The English Constitution*. London: Fontana, 1–57.

Dell, E. (1980). 'Collective Responsibility: Fact; Fiction or Façade', in Royal Institute of Public Administration, *Policy and Practice*. London: RIPA, 27–48.

Dogan, M., and Pelassy, D. (1990). *How to Compare Nations*. 2nd edn. Chatham, NJ: Chatham House.

Elgie, R. (1995). *Political Leadership in Liberal Democracies*. Houndmills: Macmillan.

Fiers, S., and Krouwel, A. (2005). 'The Low Countries: From "Prime Minister" to "President-Minister"', in T. Poguntke and P. Webb (eds), *The Presidentialization of Politics*. Oxford: Oxford University Press, 128–58.

French, R. (1979). 'The Privy Council Office: Support for Cabinet Decision Making', in R. Schultz, O. M. Kruhlak and J. Terry (eds), *The Canadian Political Process*, ed. R. Schultz, O. M. Kruhlak and J. Terry. 3rd edn. Toronto: Holt Rhinehart and Winston, 363–94.

Helms, L. (2005). *Presidents, Prime Ministers and Chancellors: Executive Leadership in Western Democracies*. Houndmills: Palgrave.

House of Lords, Select Committee on the Constitution (2010). *The Cabinet Office and the Centre of Government, Report with Evidence*. HL Paper 30. London: HMSO.

Jennings, I. (1959). *Cabinet Government*. 3rd edn. Cambridge: Cambridge University Press; third edition.

Jones, G. (1965). 'The Prime Minister's Powers', *Parliamentary Affairs*, 18/2: 167–85.

Jones, G. (1991) (ed.). 'West European Prime Ministers', *Western European Politics*, 14/2, special edition.

Keohane, N. (2009). *Thinking about Leadership*. Princeton: Princeton University Press.

King, A. (1975). 'Executives', in N. Polsby and F. Greenstein (eds), *A Handbook of Political Science, Volume 5*. Reading, MA: Addison Wesley.

Laver, M., and Shepsle, K. A. (1994). *Cabinet Ministers and Parliamentary Government*. Cambridge: Cambridge University Press.

Laver, M., and Shepsle, K. A. (1996). *Making and Breaking Governments*. Cambridge: Cambridge University Press.

Lijphart, A. (1992) (ed.). *Parliamentary versus Presidential Government*. Oxford: Oxford University Press.

Lijphart A. (1999). *Patterns of Democracy*. 2nd edn. New Haven, CT: Yale University Press.

Macintosh, J. (1962). *The British Cabinet*. London: Stevens and Sons.

Meyer, T. (2002). *Media Democracy: How the Media Colonizes Politics*. Cambridge: Polity Press.

O'Malley, E. (2007). 'The Power of Prime Ministers: Results of an Expert Survey', *International Political Science Review*, 28/1: 7–27.

Pedersen, K., and Knudsen, T. (2005). 'Denmark: Presidentialization in a Consensual Democracy', in T. Poguntke and P. Webb (eds), *The Presidentialization of Politics*. Oxford: Oxford University Press, 159–75.

Privy Council Office (Canada) (1979). Submission to the Royal Commission on Financial management and Accountability, *PCO*. Ottawa.

Poguntke, T., and Webb, P. (2005) (eds). *The Presidentialization of Politics*. Oxford: Oxford University Press.

Rhodes R. A. W. (2006). 'Executive in Parliamentary Governments', in R. A. W. Rhodes, S. A. Binder and B. A. Rockman (eds), *The Oxford Handbook of Political Institutions*. Oxford: Oxford University Press, 323–43.

Rhodes R. A. W. (2011). *The Politics of Everyday Life*. Oxford: Oxford University Press.

Rhodes, R. A. W., Wanna, J., and Weller, P. (2009). *Westminster Compared*. Oxford: Oxford University Press.

Rose, R. (1980). 'British Government: The Job at the Top', in R. Rose and E. Suleiman (eds), *Presidents and Prime Ministers*. Washington: American Enterprise Institute Press, 1–49.

Seymour-Ure, C. (2003). *Prime Ministers and the Media*. Oxford: Blackwell.

Strangio, P., 't Hart, P. and Walter, J. (eds) (2013). *Understanding Prime Ministerial Performance*. Oxford: Oxford University Press.

Strøm, K., Müller, W. C., and Bergman, T. (2003). *Delegation and Accountability in Parliamentary Democracies*. Oxford: Oxford University Press.

Tsebelis, G. (2002). *Veto Players: How Political Institutions Work*. Princeton: Princeton University Press and Russell Sage Foundation.

Van Biezen, I., and Hopkin, J. (2005). 'The Presidentialization of Spanish Democracy', in T. Poguntke and P. Webb (eds), *The Presidentialization of Politics*. Oxford: Oxford University Press, 107–27.

Walter, J., and Strangio, P. (2007). *No Prime Minister: Reclaiming Politics from Leaders*. Sydney: University of New South Wales Press.

Weller, P. (1985). *First among Equals*. Sydney: Allen and Unwin.

Weller, P. (2003). 'Cabinet Government: An Elusive Ideal', *Public Administration*, 81/4: 701–22.

Weller, P. (2007). *Cabinet Government in Australia 1901–2006*. Sydney: University of New South Wales Press.

Weller, P., Bakvis, H., and Rhodes R. A. W. (1997). *The Hollow Crown: Countervailing Trends in Core Executives*. Houndmills: Macmillan.

Weller, P. Scott, J., and Stevens, B. (2011). *From Post Box to Power House: A Centenary History of the Department of the Prime Minister and Cabinet, 1911–2011*. Sydney: Allen and Unwin.

Yeend, G. (1979). 'The Department of the Prime Minister and Cabinet in Perspective', *Australian Journal of Public Administration*, 38/2: 133–50.

CHAPTER 33

··

THE CONTINGENCIES OF PRIME-MINISTERIAL POWER IN THE UK

··

ANDREW BLICK AND GEORGE JONES

1 INTRODUCTION

··

In October 2011 the first edition of the UK *Cabinet Manual* (Cabinet Office 2011) was published. Describing itself as 'a guide to laws, conventions and rules on the operation of government', the manual included within it what was probably the fullest official account of the office of British prime minister ever placed in the public domain. It succeeded in confirming the amorphous nature of the premiership.

In the words of the manual: 'The Prime Minister has few statutory functions but will usually take the lead on significant matters of state.' As this statement suggests, the leadership role of the UK premiership is founded neither in a constitutional text (since the UK has no such entity) nor even to a large extent in parliamentary enactment, but in convention—that is, various constitutional understandings that have developed over time and are by definition difficult both to define and to enforce. While UK constitutional arrangements are notable for their vagueness, even within such a setting the office of prime minister stands out as less formally defined than many institutions of governance.

To overcome their slight official existence, prime ministers in exercising leadership are obliged to obtain the cooperation of those—in particular cabinet ministers—in possession of more precise formal authority than their own. Their ability to do so is dependent to a significant extent upon various personal and political considerations—such as their personal qualities and standing—and upon circumstances within their party and parliament. The need for help from others makes prime ministers partly reliant upon forces beyond their immediate control; and the personal and political bases for their authority are subject to change both from one prime minister to another, and during the course of each premiership. In this sense the office of prime minister is doubly subject to what can be termed 'power contingencies'—the topic of this chapter.

2 The Development and Importance of the Study of Prime-Ministerial Power

Studies of leadership and of power are closely connected. Leadership involves in part seeking to secure the successful pursuance of particular personal and collective objectives (for discussions of the concept of leadership, see MacGregor Burns 1978; Blondel 1987; 't Hart and Uhr 2008). Power can be defined as the ability to achieve desired outcomes (see Beetham 1991; Morriss 2002). Consequently, leaders, including prime ministers, are partly in the business of wielding power.

A constant defining feature of the UK office of prime minister throughout its historical development has been the role of providing public leadership (Blick and Jones 2010). This task has always been more important to the premiership than any other responsibility—a primary duty to which all others are secondary. While imparting public leadership is a function carried out across the whole of Whitehall, nowhere other than in the office of prime minister is it such an overriding duty.

Discussions of the premiership from the time the UK office of prime minister first began to develop have often concentrated on the issue of power, which has frequently been a focus for contention. Sir Robert Walpole is traditionally regarded as the first prime minister (1721–42). A contemporary, John, Lord Hervey, described in his memoirs how 'ciphers of the Cabinet signed everything [Walpole] dictated...without the least share of honour or power'. In the Commons in 1741 Walpole asked rhetorically whether his critics had produced 'one instance of this exorbitant power, of the influence which I extend to all parts of the nation, of the tyranny with which I oppress those I oppose, and the liberality with which I reward those who support me' (Williams 1960). Debate about prime-ministerial power has continued to the present.

Analysis of this discourse shows that a concept often identified as important to understanding prime-ministerial power is that of contingencies. In their recent evidence submission to the House of Commons Political and Constitutional Reform Committee (House of Commons 2011), Professors Martin Smith and David Richards argued, in a section entitled 'The Contingency of Prime Ministerial Power', that 'the power of the Prime Minister is contingent to a large extent on informal powers and authority'. Traditionally British premiers possessed power in as far as they were able to 'persuade their colleagues to undertake specific policy goals'. As a consequence, 'their power relies greatly on their personal authority'. Smith and Richards went on: 'Contingency can also be seen when, for example, they have a high level of authority, allowing them to intervene in policy areas of their choosing.' This process, though, was not 'systematic...The contingent nature of authority means it is both partial and subject to change overtime.' It could not 'be regarded as a consistent and effective mechanism. Prime ministerial activism only lasts as long as [the] prime minister remains focused on a particular issue and ministers are prepared to allow the [premier's] intervention.'

Contingencies appear in this account to be circumstances and tendencies that are variable and/or outside the immediate remit of the office of prime minister. The part played by contingencies (to use Smith's and Richard's term) of a personal and political nature in the functioning of the premiership has long been noted. W. E. Gladstone observed in an article from 1878 that 'The head of the British Government is not a Grand Vizier. He has no powers, properly so called, over his colleagues... The Prime Minister has no title to override any one of his colleagues in any one of the departments. So far as he governs them... he governs them by influence only' (Gladstone 1879). Another former prime minister, Herbert Asquith, wrote 'the office of Prime Minister is what its holder chooses and is able to make of it' (Earl of Oxford and Asquith 1926). One of the present authors, in an essay first published in 1965, wrote of the prime minister that 'his office has great potentialities, but the use made of them depends on many variables, the personality, temperament, and ability of the prime minister, what he wants to achieve and the methods he uses' (Jones 1965). In a more recent historical analysis of the premiership in the twentieth century, Vernon Bogdanor emphasized the 'ebb and flow of power determined by political vicissitudes' as opposed to 'any trend towards increasing prime ministerial power' (Bogdanor 2003).

In contrast to contingencies, however, some of the literature depicts lasting changes in the office of prime minister; and the possession of considerable power by the premiership not dependent to a substantial extent upon outside tendencies. Sidney Low, writing in the early twentieth century, argued that for 'the greater part of the past half century... The office of Premier has become more than ever like that of an elective President' (Low 1904); and 'Much of the authority of the Cabinet has insensibly passed over to that of the Premier' (Low 1914). Harold Laski wrote in 1951: 'if we compare 1850 with 1950, or even 1900 with 1950, the centralization of power in the Prime Minister's hands has proceeded at a swift pace, and... its judicious use is mainly dependent upon his own self-restraint' (Laski 1951). In the 1960s John P. Mackintosh argued that, unlike in earlier, more collegiate eras, 'the position and power of the Prime Minister has been the focal point of modern Cabinets'; and that this development had come about 'not due to the personality of any particular Premier or to the triumph of personal desires to arrogate power' (Mackintosh 1968). Around the same time, Richard Crossman claimed 'the postwar epoch has seen the final transformation of cabinet government into prime ministerial government' (Crossman 1963). More recently the Conservative Democracy Taskforce (Gough 2007) observed 'a rise in the power of the Prime Minister at the expense of the Cabinet' over a number of decades; while Sir Christopher Foster described how 'power has drained from Parliament, Cabinet and Civil Service into the PM and those around him' (Foster 2005).

The apparent lack of agreement over the role of contingencies in prime-ministerial power calls for a clearer focus upon them. Two considerations are important to such an approach. First, in the sense that they involve tendencies beyond the immediate control of the premiership, it is necessary to avoid any temptation to accept contingencies simply as forces impacting upon power interactions from outside any given model. There is a need instead to develop a framework wide enough fully to incorporate contingencies, seeking out theoretical approaches in political science that may help with this task. By this means a better appreciation of their significance can be achieved. Second, in as far as contingencies may seem to take in circumstances that are by their nature fleeting, it is important to see if any patterns can be discerned, rather than to convey the impression of a random succession of events. A combination of the theoretical analysis of political science with a long-term historical approach is useful here.

3 Key Ideas and Debates

One way of approaching the discussion of prime-ministerial power is broadly to group it into one of two schools. Within the first there is often an emphasis on prime-ministerial dominance, which is frequently held to be becoming more marked over time. It is sometimes claimed the premiership is developing the characteristics of a presidency. This approach has a long historical antecedence. It may focus on particular incumbents, or on the institution of the premiership in general (Aspinall 1952; Benn 1979; Foley 1993, 2000; Allen 2002; Dover 2005; Power Inquiry 2006). Criticisms of components of this school include the questioning of the idea often advanced within it that the premiership has somehow become more 'personalized'. Ana Inés Langer has unpacked this concept, distinguishing between the leadership qualities of prime ministers—their competence at governing—and their personal and private lives, and arguing that there is no clear tendency towards more 'personalization' (Langer 2011). Both forms of personalization identified by Langer are often combined to support the notion that 'presidentialization' has elevated the prime minister above collegiate forms of government and their political parties. Keith Dowding has, however, shown that prime ministers have more powers than US presidents, and that it would be more accurate to talk, as if following Heffernan (Heffernan 2003, 2005), of 'prime-ministerialization' rather than of 'presidentialization' (Dowding 2012), reflecting 'the growing centralization of policy and a growing personalization of politics'. Yet Dowding's thesis, though critical of part of the first school, can still be placed within this general category, since it identifies an ongoing process of centralization.

In the second school there is an emphasis on the contingent constraints upon prime-ministerial power: a denial that they are lessening, and sometimes the claim that they are becoming more restrictive (Gladstone 1879; Rosebery 1899; Jones 1965; Kavanagh and Seldon 2000; King 2007; Buller and James 2011). The 'core-executive' approach, which explains power interactions as an exchange of resources, can be seen as an extension of this second school (Rhodes and Dunleavy 1995; Elgie 2011). In 1999 Martin Smith described the 'core executive' as 'the heart of British government' containing 'the key institutions and actors concerned with developing policy, coordinating government activity and providing the necessary resources for delivering public goods'. Within this framework all actors—including the prime minister—possessed various resources that they exchanged with each other to secure their goals. None had a monopoly and they depended on each other to achieve objectives (Smith 1999).

A query has been raised about whether the core executive is anything more than a framework within which power is exercised, omitting to explain how it is wielded (O'Malley 2007). Kevin Theakston found fault with the lack of importance attached to the personality of individual prime ministers within core-executive interpretations (Theakston 2002). The 'core-executive' approach is challenged further by the theory of 'prime-ministerial pre-dominance'. This model seeks to combine an acknowledgement of the importance of resources with an appreciation of the 'locational' advantages of the premiership, placed as it is at the centre of government; and observes the ability of No. 10, subject to certain conditions, to achieve dominance (Heffernan 2003, 2005; see also O'Malley 2007). Mark Bennister has explored the idea of predominance, partly through comparing the tenures of the Australian premier, John Howard, and the UK prime minister, Tony Blair (Bennister 2007, 2008). Bennister argues that Blair and Howard demonstrated 'strong leadership', were 'autonomous agents, reaching beyond the executive, and party to engage directly with the electorate', and were able through 'personality, control and public projection' to be 'predominant forces' outside the executive. While 'agency (and the power to influence)' were important, however, 'prime ministerial power is still contingent on location, relation, environment and events' (Bennister 2008). In a more recent work Bennister emphasizes: 'prime ministers...do make a difference and can shape or stretch existing processes. However, they are constrained actors' (Bennister 2012).

A key difference between the two schools discussed above is that the second tends to place a greater emphasis upon contingencies in determining prime-ministerial power. Often some within the latter school argue that rather than holding a position of structural dominance the premiership possesses power that fluctuates over time and varies with different issues, according to a range of tendencies including the qualities of the particular incumbent prime minister and prevailing political circumstances. This divergence between the two schools can involve varying interpretations not only of the office of prime minister but also of the concept of power (and, by extension, leadership). For example, core-executive accounts argue that 'power cannot be conceived as an object that belongs to the Prime Minister or the cabinet...power is everywhere...Notions of prime-ministerial government, cabinet government or presidentialism are irrelevant, because power within the core executive is based on dependency not command' (Smith 1999). Any attempt to resolve disagreements about prime-ministerial power and the role of contingencies within it requires a re-examination of the concept of power.

The present authors (Blick and Jones 2010) adapt core-executive interpretations of prime-ministerial power, taking into account criticisms that have been made of this approach. They propose certain qualifications and clarifications of the core-executive school. There is a need to differentiate between different kinds of power resources, which can be divided into political, personal, constitutive, and institutional assets. The balance in which these resources are held, or the way in which they are combined when used, is important to the outcome of the interplay between the actors in any power process. Such resources can have different impacts according to the nature and circumstances of their deployment or possession. They can help achieve a desired objective, or they can become toxic and undermine the attainment of a particular goal. No.10, however—having monopolized certain power resources and being able at times to hoard a preponderant proportion of others—can, if the resources are deployed in the correct combination in appropriate circumstances, unilaterally ensure that government pursues courses of action over certain issues at particular times. In this sense the free market of the core executive is like the imperfect market of the real world, in which some players can enjoy structural advantages over others.

4 EMERGING FRAMEWORKS

A number of other recent theoretical discussions offer potential for different perspectives on prime-ministerial power. Jim Buller and Toby S. James have recently considered various possible models that might be imported from the USA and applied to the study of UK political leadership (Buller and James 2011). One such approach is to rate political leaders, for instance through a scoring system, following consultation with a range of experts (see also Theakston and Gill 2006; Strangio, 't Hart, and Walter 2013). Another is the technique used by Fred Greenstein, assessing presidents according to six personal attributes: as public communicator, as organizer, political skill, vision of public policy, cognitive style, and emotional intelligence (Greenstein 2009). These approaches could potentially be adapted to consider the *power* of the premiership more directly, though at present they do so more tangentially.

Buller and James's preferred model is that of 'statecraft', as developed by Jim Bulpitt (1986) in his assessment of Margaret Thatcher. It involved assessing how politicians addressed issues affecting their electoral prospects. Statecraft took into account not only individual leaders, but other individuals around them at elite level. Attention was given to the structural environment within which prime ministers operated, including features such as the electoral system. Finally, the emphasis placed on winning UK-level elections, associated with the relatively centralized political system, was taken into account. Within the statecraft model the ability of prime ministers to win elections and establish a reputation for governmental competence for their parties was regarded as a crucial quality. In applying the statecraft model to Tony Blair, Buller and James draw mixed conclusions. They note Labour's considerable electoral success under Blair's stewardship. They argue, however, that it was partly attributable to favourable prevailing circumstances and the achievements of others around him. In this sense they can be seen as accommodating the importance of contingencies.

Academic interest has focused on a key device available to the premiership in its efforts to exert power: the ability to appoint and remove ministers and to allocate portfolios. Nicholas Allen and Hugh Ward have applied the rational choice model to such activity. They consider the personnel decisions of prime ministers from the perspective of their desire to achieve certain policy goals, while allowing that premiers may vary in the extent to which they have firm policy commitments. The authors note a need to distinguish power from luck—the latter entailing premiers getting their way because colleagues by chance happen to agree with them (Allen and Ward 2009). In this sense contingencies surface once more.

A further analysis of the power of appointment is provided by Keith Dowding and Elizabeth McLeay. In a comparison with arrangements in New Zealand, they note a variety of constraints—or contingencies—serving to limit the UK premiership. Leaders of parties inherit teams they have not chosen; and may be bound to some extent by other external selection criteria of various kinds. Dowding and McLeay apply agency theory to the power of appointment to establish another set of contingencies. In their model, ministers are agents, to whom tasks are delegated by a principal—the prime minister—who lacks particular skills or the time to carry out the tasks allotted to ministers. The constraints that emerge are associated with the phenomena associated with agency theory of 'agency rent'—where agents do not perform as desired—and 'adverse selection', where a problematic appointment is forced upon a principal (Dowding and McLeay 2011).

An important theme in a number of theoretical approaches is the relative importance of, on the one hand, individual prime ministers and, on the other hand, the wider environment within which they operate. David Denver and Mark Garnett have analysed public-opinion research since the 1930s, undermining the idea of a single figure dominating public perception of a government. The research evidence suggests that views on the overall effectiveness of the government are more important than the popularity of the prime minister in determining voter behaviour (Denver and Garnett 2012).

Theakston has developed a framework offering the possibility of connecting the assessment of individual characteristics with the group dynamics that characterize institutions. He refers to the importance of ' "group biography"—the mapping of the networks, connections and career-linkages of an elite group . . . By regarding biographies as case studies, we can attempt to link theory and practice, to generalize, and to test and evaluate theories about leadership in bureaucracies and the development of the civil service' (Theakston 1999). While Theakston was considering particular civil servants, his approach could be extended to take in politicians, including prime ministers, as well as their aides. It could reconcile the importance of individual holders of the premiership with that of other actors beyond their immediate control (for the wider government 'court', see R. A. W. Rhodes in Strangio, 't Hart, and Walter 2013), and the contingencies that are entailed.

Bertjan Verbeek's analysis of the role of Anthony Eden in the Suez crisis offers another means of connecting the individual with the group. While acknowledging the importance of Eden, Verbeek holds that 'Suez was much more a small group's war than Eden's war'. Applying social psychology, Verbeek suggests that a foreign-policy emergency such as the Egyptian nationalization of the Suez Canal tends to prompt centralization of decision-making, which in turn can encourage a tendency known as 'groupthink'. It involves collections of individuals reaching a decision 'too early', otherwise known as 'premature concurrence seeking'. Groupthink 'increases the likelihood of a disastrous policy outcome' (Verbeek 2003). Alongside social psychology, other frameworks from beyond immediate political science might be usefully adapted. For example, in his book *Everyday Life in British Government* (Rhodes 2011), R. A. W. Rhodes employs anthropological methods, applying observation and interviews to show what governmental elites actually do in different contexts.

Verbeek's reference to the heightened possibility of a policy disaster suggests there may be a connection between the leadership styles of prime ministers and the quality of the outcomes they help generate. In his assessment of the foreign policy pursued by Tony Blair, Stephen Dyson argues that Blair was disposed towards 'forward leaning, proactive foreign policies'. He tended to approach circumstances as 'clear cut and not particularly complex'; and did not favour the use of collective mechanisms of government. Sometimes he was 'lucky' in his methods; but at other times he found himself in 'situations that he could not . . . control, and ended up in very bad shape indeed' (Dyson 2009). The implication here could be that, in their efforts to wield power, domineering premiers might help bring about outcomes they do not desire: the opposite of the exercise of power.

5 ASSESSING THE STATE OF THE ART AND ITS IMPACT ON PRACTICE

Through applying historical and theoretical analysis, the present authors (Blick and Jones 2010) identify common errors in the present literature on the UK premiership, including:

- mistaking the exploitation of potential already present within the premiership for material change;
- over-eagerness to identify substantive alteration when not real, and overlooking its genuine occurrence;
- identification of trends that either cannot be verified by the available evidence or, if they can, are unsatisfactorily analysed; and
- reference to the concept of power without adequate exploration of its conceptual and contextual complexity.

These mistakes, the authors argue, have led to the prevalence of flawed interpretations of the premiership. When a historical perspective is used, it is possible to identify defects in both of the two broad schools associated with the assessment of prime-ministerial power, particularly the first, which tends to stress the strength of No. 10. As already shown, arguments that traditional forms of government have been, or are in the process of being, or are about to be, supplanted by a dominant premiership have a long lineage. Because of this repetition across different eras, whatever similarities they may share, such theses inevitably contradict each other. If one period has seen the emergence of a presidential system or the ending of cabinet government, then how can this process take place once again later on? There is a tendency for one participant's time of No. 10 ascendancy to be portrayed later as a golden age for collegiality.

Each individual who advances an interpretation of the tenure of an individual premier, or of the development of the office in general, is not responsible and cannot be condemned for the work of others, but, where two theories disagree, the inescapable conclusion is that one or both must be wrong.

There are to some extent similar problems with the second school of prime-ministerial analysis, which emphasizes the restraints upon No. 10. Periods in which the pressures on prime ministers were already being held to be unbearable have subsequently been depicted as lost eras of a leisured premiership. Once again we are confronted with difficulties in reconciling two theories and may be led to conclude that one or both may be wrong.

Core-executive theory offers an approach that escapes these difficulties revealed by historical analysis. By using this framework it is possible to view prime-ministerial power as in neither longstanding decline nor increase, but as variable, like power wielded by all actors within the core executive, according to circumstance—or 'contingency'.

A broader analysis, however—using ideas advanced by some theorists that power should be considered as possessing different 'faces' or 'dimensions' (see, e.g., Lukes 2005; Gaventa 2006)—throws up problems with the core-executive school. Discussions about the strength of the office of prime minister—including those in core-executive analysis—have tended to concentrate on power as wielded by one actor *over* one or more others, rather than other possible forms of its exercise; and they have focused attention on the taking of particular decisions rather than their outcomes. These outcomes, the present authors argue, comprise the ultimate measure of power. They must be assessed in their widest sense. Such analysis should include the extent to which a policy succeeded on its own terms—that is, whether it achieved the immediate goals towards which it was officially directed. This kind of assessment should take into account as well the broader political consequences of decisions, such as the government becoming more or less divided, and the survival prospects of the government and/or of the prime minister being helped or hindered.

A particular deficiency in core-executive studies is that by definition they focus on activities and tendencies within Whitehall at the expense of a wider perspective. There are many other institutions in the outside world, including parliament, parties, other tiers of governance, and media outlets, each of which could be seen as being in possession of its own 'resources' as defined by exponents of resource dependency within the core executive. Such deficiencies in analysis of the strength of the premiership can be both exposed and corrected by examination of the objectives of the individual people involved and of how far they achieve their objectives—an apt approach, given the definition of power as the ability to achieve desired goals. An improved understanding of prime-ministerial power can be attained through considering specific instances of its exercise, asking questions such as:

- How ambitious was the objective?
- How clear was the objective?
- Was the objective reconcilable with other goals?
- How propitious were circumstances for its attainment?
- Where did a particular desired outcome stand in the hierarchy of objectives for the premiership?
- To what extent was the decision to pursue a particular objective contested?
- To what extent was the objective shared?
- Did the pursuance of an objective have side effects?

Often analysis of prime-ministerial power identifies a pathology in need of cure. Those who observe increasing prime-ministerial strength may claim it to be an undesirable phenomenon, since it undermines such desirable features of the UK constitution as collective government (Gough 2007). At the same time, in studies in which restraints on No.10 are emphasized, it is sometimes claimed that a weak No. 10 is ill-equipped to provide the necessary leadership (Barber 2007).

Such ideas have been influential both upon the substance of No. 10 as an institution; and upon the style pursued by particular incumbent premiers. Ideas of the sort advocated by Sir Kenneth Berrill—who in 1980 proposed the establishment of a 'Prime Minister's Department' to enable the premiership to cope with increased demands upon it—helped encourage various attempts to expand the administrative structures in No. 10 and the Cabinet Office, most notably during the 1997–2007 Tony Blair premiership (Berrill 1980; see also Weller 1985).

The narrative developed by accounts of the premiership such as that provided by the Conservative Democracy Task Force (Gough 2007), in which No. 10 was held to have become excessively powerful, seem to have influenced the initial decision (possibly soon reversed) by David Cameron to approach the role of prime minister in a manner less interventionist than that of Tony Blair and Gordon Brown.

On the one hand, it may appear desirable that decisions about the structure and operation of the office of prime minister should be based on research by academics and others. On the other hand, there is cause for concern if the analysis of the premiership that shaped those decisions is flawed.

6 Prospects for Future Analysis

A clear opportunity for research lies in studying how the UK premiership operates in the circumstances of the first coalition government since 1945, formed in May 2010, for which both historical and international comparisons may be of value. Questions that might be asked include whether the need for cross-party cohesion has strengthened or weakened collective government. Developments that should be assessed include the fact that, as a consequence of the coalition, the premiership has to varying extents lost control over key functions that have in the past been held as central to its exercise of power. The coalition deal specifies a role for the Liberal Democrat Deputy Prime Minister, Nick Clegg, in decisions about ministerial appointments. With the *Fixed-Term Parliaments Act 2011* the ability of the prime minister to determine election dates through requesting dissolutions from the monarch under the Royal Prerogative has been removed. Furthermore the circumstances of the coalition provide ample evidence of the importance to prime ministers of their parties, the compliance of which is not always guaranteed (Jones 1991). For example, late in 2011 David Cameron was forced by pressure from his own backbenchers to refuse to sign a key fiscal proposal for the European Union that, left to his own devices, he might have assented to. The existence of contingencies serving to qualify the power of the premiership has been demonstrated once more.

More broadly, there is scope for combining the disciplines of history and political science to achieve a fuller understanding of the premiership in the UK and elsewhere.

History has many possible values if applied to debates about the premiership (for an important historical account of the premiership since 1945, see Hennessy 2000). It can challenge the selective use of precedent to emphasize or downplay the significance of any particular action: a practice that needs to be supplanted by a fuller historical consideration, enabling identification and assessment of the genuinely new or rare. Another tendency that can be counteracted is that of secular millennialism. The claim that the end is nigh, or upon us, can be correct at most at only one moment. Yet for more than a century the demise of cabinet, with its effective replacement by a hegemonic No. 10, has frequently been identified as imminent, underway, or, even, as having already occurred.

Despite its wide potential as a tool of analysis of the premiership, however, the historical discipline has limitations. It provides a firm empirical basis but not an analytical framework nor a set of theoretical propositions, creating the danger that accounts of the institution become a stream of unconnected occurrences. One means of avoiding this problem is through introducing the historical method into the framework and theoretical setting for the analysis of power provided by political science, which can enhance the value of both disciplines.

Every interaction through which participants seek to achieve particular goals takes place over time. The framework within which it plays out may change while it occurs, with implications for the outcome. A given process both operates in an environment affected by such earlier activities, and has implications for the setting within which subsequent activities take place. For all these reasons history—concerned as it is with events in a temporal trajectory—can combine with political science to produce a better understanding of power.

The emphasis placed by some historians on biographical analysis has uses as well. If power is the ability to achieve desired objectives, including at times political survival, then its assessment requires an understanding of individuals either seeking their own personal goals or pursuing shared agendas in a group. Institutions—though they may be configured in such a way as to encourage certain predilections on the part of those attached to them—do not possess ends in their own right. Consequently the study of power processes necessitates the examination of particular people and their objectives.

More broadly, if political scientists are involved in establishing general laws about concepts such as power, then it is important to test the applicability of their theories across different time periods. History can help identify a spread of case studies from various eras that enable the verification, modification, or refutation of particular models. If there is a point in the past before which a particular idea cannot be seen to apply, an explanation is needed as to why not.

RECOMMENDED READING

Blick, A., and Jones, G. (2010). *Premiership: The Development, Nature and Power of the Office of the British Prime Minister*. Exeter: Imprint Academic.
Foley, M. (1993). *The Rise of the British Presidency*. Manchester: Manchester University Press.
Hennessy, P. (2000). *The Prime Minister: The Office and its Holders since 1945*. London: Allen Lane.

REFERENCES

Allen, G. (2002). *The Last Prime Minister: Being Honest about the UK Presidency*. Exeter: Imprint Academic.
Allen, N., and Ward, H. (2009). ' "Moves on a Chess Board": A Spatial Model of British Prime Ministers' Powers over Cabinet Formation', *British Journal of Politics and International Relations*, 11/2: 238–58.
Aspinall, A. (1952). *The Cabinet Council: 1783–1835, The Raleigh Lecture on History*. London: British Academy.
Barber, M. (2007). *Instruction to Deliver: Tony Blair, Public Service and the Challenge of Achieving Targets*. London: Politico's.
Beetham, D. (1991). *The Legitimation of Power*. Basingstoke: Macmillan.
Benn, T. (1979). *The Case for a Constitutional Premiership*. Nottingham: Institute for Workers' Control.
Bennister, M. (2007). 'Tony Blair and John Howard: Comparative Predominance and "Institution Stretch" in the UK and Australia', *British Journal of Politics and International Relations*, 9/3: 327–45.
Bennister, M. (2008). 'Blair and Howard: Predominant Prime Ministers Compared', *Parliamentary Affairs*, 61/2: 334–55.
Bennister, M. (2012). *Prime Ministers in Power: Political Leadership in Britain and Australia*. Basingstoke: Palgrave/Macmillan.
Berrill, K. (1980). *Strength at the Centre: The Case for a Prime Minister's Department*. London: University of London.
Blick, A., and Jones, G. (2010). *Premiership: The Development, Nature and Power of the Office of the British Prime Minister*. Exeter: Imprint Academic.
Blondel, J. (1987). *Political Leadership*. London: Sage.

Bogdanor, V. (2003) (ed.). *The British Constitution in the Twentieth Century.* Oxford: Oxford University Press.

Buller, J., and James, T. (2011). 'Statecraft and the Assessment of National Political Leaders: The Case of New Labour and Tony Blair', *British Journal of Politics and International Relations*, 14/4: 534–55.

Bulpitt, J. (1986). 'The Discipline of the New Democracy: Mrs Thatcher's Domestic Statecraft', *Political Studies*, 34: 19–39. doi:10. 1111/j. 1467-9248. 1986. tb01870.x

Burns, J. M. (1978). *Leadership.* New York: Harper and Row.

Cabinet Office (2011). *The Cabinet Manual: A Guide to the Laws, Conventions and Rules on the Operation of Government.* London: Cabinet Office.

Crossman, R. H. S. (1963). 'Introduction', in W. Bagehot (ed.), *The English Constitution.* London: Collins/Fontana, 1–57.

Denver, D., and Garnett, M. (2012). 'The Popularity of British Prime Ministers', *British Journal of Politics and International Relations*, 14/1: 57–73.

Dover, R. (2005). 'The Prime Minister and the Core Executive: A Liberal Intergovernmentalist Reading of UK Defence Policy Formulation 1997–2000', *British Journal of Politics and International Relations*, 7/4: 508–25.

Dowding, K. (2012). 'The Prime Ministerialization of the British Prime Minister', *Parliamentary Affairs*, 1–19, doi:10.1093/pa/gss007

Dowding, K., and McLeay, E. (2011). 'The Firing Line: When and Why Do Prime Ministers Fire Ministerial Colleagues?', in P. 't Hart and J. Uhr (eds), *How Power Changes Hands: Transition and Succession in Government.* Basingstoke: Palgrave/Macmillan, 157–73.

Dyson, S. (2009). *The Blair Identity: Leadership and Foreign Policy.* Manchester: Manchester University Press.

Earl of Oxford and Asquith (1926). *Fifty Years in Parliament*, Vol. 2. London: Cassell.

Elgie, R. (2011). 'Core Executive Studies Two Decades on', *Public Administration*, 89/1: 64–77.

Foley, M. (1993). *The Rise of the British Presidency.* Manchester: Manchester University Press.

Foley, M. (2000). *The British Presidency: Tony Blair and the Politics of Public Leadership.* Manchester: Manchester University Press.

Foster, C. (2005). *British Government in Crisis, or the Third English Revolution.* Oxford: Hart.

Gaventa, J. (2006). 'Finding the Space for Change: A Power Analysis', *Institute of Development Studies Bulletin*, 37/6: 22–33.

Gladstone, W. E. (1879). *Gleanings of Past Years*, Vol. I. *The Throne, and the Prince Consort, the Cabinet, and Constitution.* London: John Murray.

Gough, R. (2007). *An End to Sofa Government: Better Working of Prime Minister and Cabinet.* London: Conservative Democracy Task Force.

Greenstein, F. (2009). *The Presidential Difference: Leadership Style from FDR to Barack Obama.* 3rd edn. Princeton and Oxford: Princeton University Press; third edition.

Heffernan, R. (2003). 'Prime Ministerial Predominance? Core Executive Politics in the UK', *British Journal of Politics and International Relations*, 5/3: 347–72.

Heffernan, R. (2005). 'Exploring (and Explaining) the British Prime Minister', *British Journal of Politics and International Relations*, 7/4: 605–20.

Hennessy, P. (2000). *The Prime Minister: The Office and its Holders since 1945.* London: Allen Lane.

House of Commons (2011). *Political and Constitutional Reform Committee. Role and Powers of the Prime Minister: Written Evidence.* London: House of Commons.

Jones, G. W. (1965). 'The Prime Minister's Power', *Parliamentary Affairs*, 18/2: 167–85.

Jones, G. W. (1991) (ed.). *West European Prime Ministers.* London: Frank Cass.

Kavanagh, D., and Seldon, A. (2000). *The Powers behind the Prime Minister: The Hidden Influence of Number Ten*. London: HarperCollins.

King, A. (2007). *The British Constitution*. Oxford: Oxford University Press.

Langer, A. I. (2011). *The Personalization of Politics in the UK: Mediated Leadership from Attlee to Cameron*. Manchester: Manchester University Press.

Laski, H. (1951). *Reflections on the Constitution: The House of Commons, the Cabinet, the Civil Service*. Manchester: Manchester University Press.

Low, S. (1904). *The Governance of England*. London: T. Fisher Unwin.

Low, S. (1914). *The Governance of England*. 2nd edn. London: T. Fisher Unwin.

Lukes, S. (2005). *Power: A Radical View*. Basingstoke: Palgrave Macmillan.

Mackintosh, J. (1968). *The British Cabinet*. London: Methuen.

Morriss, P. (2002). *Power: A Philosophical Analysis*. Manchester: Manchester University Press.

O'Malley, E. (2007). 'Setting Choices, Controlling Outcomes: The Operation of Prime Ministerial Influence and the UK's Decision to Invade Iraq', *British Journal of Politics and International Relations*, 9/1: 1–19.

Power Inquiry (2006). *Power to the People: The Report of Power*. York: Power Inquiry.

Rhodes, R. A. W. (2011). *Everyday Life in British Government*. Oxford: Oxford University Press.

Rhodes, R. A. W., and Dunleavy, P. (1995) (eds). *Prime Minister, Cabinet and Core Executive*. London: Macmillan.

Rosebery, Lord (1899). *Sir Robert Peel*. London: Cassell and Company.

Smith, M. J. (1999). *The Core Executive in Britain*. Basingstoke: Palgrave Macmillan.

Strangio, P., 't Hart, P., and Walter, J. (2013) (eds). *Prime Ministerial Performance*. Oxford: Oxford University Press.

't Hart, P., and Uhr, J. (2008). *Public Leadership: Perspectives and Practices*. Canberra: Australian National University Press.

Theakston, K. (1999). *Leadership in Whitehall*. Basingstoke: Macmillan.

Theakston, K. (2002). 'Political Skills and Context in Prime Ministerial Leadership in Britain', *Politics and Policy*, 30/2: 283–323.

Theakston, K., and Gill, M. (2006). 'Rating 20th-Century British Prime Ministers', *British Journal of Politics and International Relations*, 8/2: 193–213.

Verbeek, B. (2003). *Decision-Making in Great Britain during the Suez Crisis: Small Groups and a Persistent Leader*. Aldershot: Ashgate.

Weller, P. (1985). 'Do Prime Ministers' Departments Really Cause Problems?', *Public Administration*, 61/1: 59–78.

Williams, E. N. (1960). *The Eighteenth Century Constitution: Documents and Commentary*. Cambridge: Cambridge University Press.

CHAPTER 34

PRIME MINISTERS AND THEIR ADVISERS IN PARLIAMENTARY DEMOCRACIES

CHRIS EICHBAUM AND RICHARD SHAW

1 INTRODUCTION

IT is questionable whether Macbeth needed to be advised to 'look like the innocent flower but be the serpent under't' (and even more so whether the advice should have been taken). It is a truism, nonetheless, that 'executives need advice' (Peters, Rhodes, and Wright 2000: 3) and, moreover, sometimes need to be seen to be taking it. Not only do prime ministers require advice; they inherit institutions and traditions that provide it, and they can also be active participants in reshaping those institutions and creating new ones.

This chapter focuses squarely on prime ministers in parliamentary systems, and on the formal and conventional institutional configurations from which advice to prime ministers flows. Prime ministers are characterized in spatial terms as occupying the political and policy centre; as standing astride the summit; or, in Shakespearian terms, as located within the 'hollow crown that rounds the mortal temples of a king'. Unlike presidents, prime ministers are—at least in Westminster systems—creatures of Bagehot's 'efficient secret' (Bagehot 1963: 48). They are likely, therefore, to receive advice from their parliamentary and cabinet colleagues and, in certain circumstances, from the head of state. Advice, some would argue, is inevitably political in nature, and in some contexts is the product of constitutional obligation. It may be respons*ible* advice in this sense, or it may be respons*ive* to some degree. Too much of the former and the accusation—from those to whom advice is directed—may be of unnecessary institutional scepticism (or, more commonly, 'departmentalism'); too much of the latter, and the risk may be represented as anything from 'group think' to opportunistic politicization.

The story told here, then, is of the ways in which advice to prime ministers is institutionally shaped and reshaped, and of the drivers and consequences of these changes. Our core concerns here are:

- to place this aspect of political leadership studies in its historical and intellectual context;
- to differentiate between the principal frameworks and approaches within the sub-field in order to present key ideas, concepts, questions, and debates;
- to identify some of the more significant contributions to the field;
- to provide an assessment of the 'state of the play'; and, finally,
- suggest potential lines of enquiry for future work in this corner of political leadership studies.

2 PRIME-MINISTERIAL ADVISORY STRUCTURES IN CONTEXT

Our focus is on the ways in which advice to prime ministers is organized. The work undertaken on this issue—which became 'an important emerging focus in public administration' in the early 1990s (Castles 1994: 412)—sits within a rich scholarship directed at the institutional and other contexts in which political leaders govern in contemporary parliamentary democracies (most if not all of the dimensions of which are canvassed in other contributions to this volume). Studies of new public management reforms are a case in point (Christensen and Laegreid 2011), as is the wider governance literature (Rhodes 1997, 2007; Kjaer 2004; Marsh 2011), in that both speak to the institutional conditions in which prime ministers function. More particularly, work on the structuring of prime-ministerial power has 'tended to be trapped in the traditional debate of cabinet government against prime ministerial government [which] has given way to a more contemporary academic divide between analyses of presidentialism and core-executive dependency' (Bennister 2007: 327). Following hard on the heels of the articulation of the 'hollow crown', those scholars of core-executive studies have explored the webs of relationships that prime ministers must negotiate in order to exercise influence, and within which good advice is a significant determinant of success (Dunleavy and Rhodes 1990; Peters, Rhodes, and Wright 2000; Smith 2000; Elgie 2011). Some of the most important of these relationships are probed in the extensive scholarship on the interface between political and administrative leaders (Page and Wright 1999; Peters and Pierre 2001; Pollitt and Bouckaert 2004).

On our particular terrain, several approaches are on offer. There are individual country case studies (Savoie 1999; Weller 2000; Tiernan 2007a), most of which concern West

European and Anglo-Westminster nations. There is also a comparative dimension to the work—or, rather, there are collections of individual country case studies (e.g. Eichbaum and Shaw 2010), which are not quite the same thing. Rose and Suleiman (1980) traverse the roles of leaders in Britain, Canada, France, Italy, Norway, Spain, and West Germany; that focus is complemented by Peters and Barker's study (1993) of the institutional production of advice.

One of the seminal contributions concerns the administration of the core executive in twelve developed countries (Peters, Rhodes, and Wright 2000). The authors distinguish between Westminster systems (the United Kingdom, Canada, and Australia), 'other' parliamentary systems (Germany, Italy, Spain, Sweden, Denmark, Greece, and Japan), and presidential/semi-presidential systems (France and the United States). Dahlstrom, Peters, and Pierre (2011), in their review of centring and decentring tendencies in contemporary states, adopt a slightly different classification, based on Westminster, Napoleonic, Germanic (or *Rechstaatt)*, Mediterranean, and Scandinavian administrative traditions (see also Rhodes and Weller 2001: 244–5 on points of divergence and commonality between administrative traditions).

The point of departure for most scholars is that prime ministers' advisory structures have undergone significant changes in recent decades, reflecting the advent of new technologies, the emergence of more sceptical and demanding publics, and the consequences of both globalization outside and devolution within states. It is generally accepted that a central trait of the state restructuring occasioned by this complexity has been 'a gradual accretion of power and responsibility towards the office of the chief executive' (Peters, Rhodes, and Wright 2000: 265). As to the broad menu from which prime ministers draw when structuring their resources, Peters and Barker (1993) provide an early slate of options. Civil servants, especially those in the offices of political leaders, are key actors. Other central elements include trusted ministerial colleagues or 'inner cabinets'; caucus colleagues and members of the wider party; seconded officials; think-tanks and consultancies; political advisers; advisory committees or units; commissions; technical expert advisers; and *les éminences grises* who enjoy no formal status but who have the ear of the prime minister.

Beyond that broad range of sources of support, there are substantial and durable differences between countries in the organization of advisory structures. Diversity concerning the size of the aggregate advisory resource, its internal structure and roles, the bases on which appointments are made, and so on, preclude simple classification either within or across administrative traditions. One example should make the point. Some Westminster nations—Australia, Canada, and New Zealand—have a prime minister's department (albeit variously named). The United Kingdom does not (although the range of resources to which its prime minister has access is such that one exists in all but name). There is, however, in the United Kingdom—as in Australia, but not in either Canada or New Zealand—a Prime Minister's Office. In short, while there are similarities in the sources and types of support on which prime ministers can call, there is considerable variety in the ways in which those resources are arranged.

If there are profound differences in organization, the business of identifying what is done within those arrangements is more straightforward. Peters, Rhodes, and Wright (2000: 11–13) list six core functions of advisory structures: systemic management (maintaining oversight of a nation's international interests); ensuring 'good governance' (overseeing the smooth functioning of government business); managing the state apparatus (from involvement in reform initiatives to appointments of senior bureaucrats); policy coordination (securing consistency across ministers' initiatives); policy advice (speaking 'truth to power'); and political management (of the political, legislative, and other relationships upon which governments rest).

3 KEY IDEAS, CONCEPTS, QUESTIONS, AND DEBATES

Much of the literature on advisory systems eschews overt theorization for rich empirical description (and is no less valuable for doing so). To the extent that studies are explicitly or implicitly located within particular understandings of executive arrangements, four approaches can be discerned, each providing a different way of framing institutional and conventional relationships between prime ministers and their advisers.

Westminster: Location, Bilateral Monopoly, and Hierarchy

Clearly, prime ministers operate in other than Westminster systems, but, given the affinity between role and system, this 'family of nations' is the first approach. The Westminster model, best described as a 'family of ideas' (Rhodes 2006: 325) rather than as a unified model, has historically dominated thinking on the structuring of executive power in jurisdictions with parliamentary government.

Notwithstanding that a formal focus on the prime minister and cabinet generated a somewhat skewed view of matters, the Westminster approach endured for much of the twentieth century. The 'Westminster smokescreen' (Bevir and Rhodes 2006a), however, also obscured the extent to which developments—globalization, marketization, devolution—increasingly gave the lie to Westminster representations of strong central control. To paraphrase Bagehot (1963: 44), dignified representations of Westminster diverged from efficient accounts of empirical arrangements.

The turn to governance has brought other narratives to the fore (see below). But there is one aspect of the Westminster framework worth noting for what it says about the tests of 'good advice' in the context of good governance: the often overlooked adjective 'constitutional' that characterizes both the role of the civil service in a Westminster system and the nature of the advice required. In part, its use reflects the offence Westminster commits against the doctrine of the separation of powers: Bagehot's efficient secret

(1963: 44) can be *too* efficient in the absence of a constitutionally separate legislature. Add the absence of an upper chamber and/or a constitutional court of review and the 'constitutional' role of the public servant is as much one of meeting the duty *pro bono publico* as of meeting a duty of service to the government of the day.

For prime ministers in Westminster systems the constitutional import of the provision of advice that is free, frank, comprehensive, and tendered fearlessly may be clear (in theory if not in practice). The imperative is not, however, confined to prime ministers in parliamentary—much less Westminster—contexts, and is reflected in the Quaker notion of speaking truth to power, which informs notions of responsible policy-advising in other political systems (Wildavsky 1987).

The Core Executive: Function, Pluralization, and Complexity

Core-executive studies emerged as a corrective to the insularity of and limitations associated with the Westminster narrative, and became the dominant means of conceptualizing executive arrangements—and in particular relations between prime ministers and other core xecutive actors—within and beyond Westminster nations (Elgie 2011). First used by Dunleavy and Rhodes (1990), the term 'core executive' denotes an approach to the study of executive power that eschews formalist explanations based on positions within executive hierarchies. Instead, the method is to ask which functions define the core executive, such that 'the key question becomes: "Who does what?"' (Rhodes 2007: 1247). A focus on functions, rather than positions, illuminates a spectrum of actors—prime ministers, ministers, political advisers, senior civil servants, central agencies, and so forth—who play roles in shaping and coordinating policy at the centre.

The resource-dependency variant presently dominates core -xecutive studies (Elgie 2011: 75). The core insight is that 'actors in the core executive depend on other actors to achieve their goals. So, they must exchange resources, for example money, legislative authority or expertise' (Rhodes 1997: 203). To 'Who does what?' is added a second question: 'And with which resources?' For a prime minister, clearly, a well-resourced support structure is critical to interactions with the other core -xecutive actors whose resources are needed to achieve his or her goals (Tiernan 2007a).

Within the resource-dependency camp, however, there are sharp disagreements regarding the bases of executive power Bevir and Rhodes (2006b) and Rhodes (2007) take the view that power 'does not inhere in any institution, position, or structure' (Elgie 2011: 68). Their differentiated polity model proposes that political power is instead relational and decoupled from structural arrangements. (Indeed, Bevir and Rhodes (2008: 730) find the very concept of structure 'unhelpfully vague'.) The asymmetric power model advanced by Marsh, Richards, and Smith (2003) sits across the ontological and epistemological divide. Here, the exercise of executive power is structured and asymmetrically distributed. While partially contingent on personal resources, power is also a function of institutional resources. Therefore, location matters: some actors possess more (and more powerful) resources than others, and exchange relations are asymmetrical.

This distinction has consequences for thinking about prime ministers' advisory systems. For proponents of the differentiated polity model, prime ministers are neither more nor less inherently powerful than other core-executive players. Rather, the possession of power reflects the exchange of the requisite resources and the skill with which the 'court politics' of the executive are negotiated. Conversely, for those who cleave to the asymmetric power approach, 'the key resources in the system lie with the prime minister and the chancellor of the exchequer' (Marsh, Richards, and Smith 2003: 308). Yet prime ministerial power is relative: the predominance of the prime minister enables him or her 'to lead, but not command, the executive; to direct, not control, its policy development; and to manage, but not wholly dominate, the legislature' (Heffernan 2003: 350).

Rational Choice: Asymmetry and Agency

Rational choice institutionalism is also marked by asymmetrical relations, albeit of a different normative stripe. The central insight is that information is asymmetrically distributed among core-executive actors, with agents (and senior civil servants, in particular) enjoying advantages over their political principals. Set alongside the standard rational-choice assumption that political agency is motivated by the desire to maximize utility, this provides a particular understanding of choices made regarding the structuring of advice to prime ministers.

Prime ministers faced with monopoly provision of advice, for example, may seek contestable advice, either from extending and personalizing the civil-service machinery, and/or via recourse to political staff (Eichbaum and Shaw 2007). Other developments have also shaped prime ministers' choices. Public-sector reforms provide a good example: the policy–operations split, marketization, and devolution (themselves predicated upon rational-choice principles), mean that prime ministers require advice on the purchase of outputs, and advisers who will monitor the implementation of policy decisions.

As 'first magistrate' (Crossman 1963: 22–3), prime ministers are also principals in relation to their ministerial colleagues. Thus, their advisory arrangements may embody principal–agent relations—for example, between a prime minister's chief of staff and other ministers' political advisers—intended to align ministers' portfolio activities with the government's collective interests as articulated by the prime minister. Peters and Barker (1993: 12) note that 'government rarely speaks with only one voice or listens with only one ear': advisory arrangements, then, represent an opportunity to increase the number of veto points a prime minister can exploit in seeking to coordinate or control a core executive.

The standard remedy to the dilemma of a political principal faced by a single agent under circumstances of information asymmetry is the classical contract. At the risk of oversimplification, pre-new public management environments were characterized by relational and implicit 'contracts', and post-reform conditions by greater recourse to classical and quasi-legal contracts. In short, there has been a transition from one type of 'bargain' to another.

The notion of the public service bargain (PSB) is useful when thinking through relationships between prime ministers and their advisory agents (Hood and Lodge 2006). To suggest that the literature on PSBs sits comfortably within rational-choice institutionalism understates its subtlety and reach. The notion does, however, illuminate different types of relationships, with the distinction between 'trustee'- and 'agency'-type bargains implying different approaches to the provision (or contracting) of advice (Hood and Lodge 2006: 41–4). In the present context, the competency dimension of PSBs is of most interest, with Hood and Lodge differentiating between four types: (*a*) 'sage' bargains, involving the provision of intellectual or moral insight (approximating the 'constitutional' role of the adviser that speaks truth to power); (*b*) 'wonk' bargains, where advice involves technical knowledge and judgement; (*c*) 'deliverer' bargains, in which what matters is the capacity to get things done; and (*d*) 'go-between' bargains, where the capacity to work across different worlds is what is needed. Advisory arrangements—both sources of advice and their organization—will reflect prime ministers' needs in these four respects.

Managerial Challenges: Complexity, Capacity, and Implementation

The final category is somewhat eclectic and more applied in focus, and concerns cases of institutional shaping informed by the need to deploy prime-ministerial advisory capacity to opportunity and risk. The focus here is on mapping ways in which prime ministers (and those acting on their behalf) seek to increase advisory capacity at the centre.

Forward- and reverse-mapping approaches can be distinguished. The former examines the evolution of advisory systems over time, often by focusing on a particular prime minister and the factors influencing the shaping of advisory structures. It produces detailed accounts of specific arrangements and maps the influence of various actors—political and bureaucratic—in establishing them. It can also clarify which is the dependent and which the independent variable as between prime ministers and the institutions in which they are situated. Tiernan (2007b) provides an example, drawing on Moe (1993) and Walcott and Hult (2004) to articulate the 'deep' structures of advisory systems.

The reverse-mapping approach works back from institutional innovation and identifies causal factors. The literature on the development of implementation capacity under particular prime ministers provides examples (see Lindquist 2006). Evoking the classical 'implementation' literature (Pressman and Wildavsky 1973), this work examines the institutional topographies of different jurisdictions, the capacity (formal or ad hoc) directed at policy implementation, and the drivers behind the development of this capacity. It reflects a recurring point of convergence in the narrative concerning prime ministers and advice: complexity in policy and compression in time, twinned with challenges posed by increasingly wicked issues and (in a post-reform world) fragmented structures.

4 LANDMARK CONTRIBUTIONS

Rose and Suleiman (1980) provide an early systematic study of the arrangements through which advice is provided to the political summit. Peters and Barker (1993) built upon that heritage (albeit in relation to governments rather than prime ministers), but, in proposing a state-centered typology for making sense of the provision of advice, they were among the first to 'map the terrain or cumulate the evidence' (Castles 1994: 413), laying down a marker for subsequent comparative contributions. Their acknowledgement, that states can be other than integrated and rational systems, also foreshadowed the turn to governance and core-executive studies.

Halligan's (1995) contribution on advisory systems remains seminal. Similarly, Peters, Rhodes, and Wright (2000) remains a touchstone in the literature, and its findings continue both to apply and to frame the work of others. The authors establish three major conclusions regarding trends and trajectories in prime ministers' advisory systems:

1. The progressive decentring of government continues to produce pressures for centralization within the core executive. The 'hollowing-out' of the state has been accompanied by institutional in-building at the centre, as prime ministers struggle to maintain control in the face of institutional differentiation and fragmentation.

2. Political leaders' staffs have grown across jurisdictions in response to those pressures, but the precise nature and distribution of the tasks those staffs carry out reflect countries' historical-cultural particulars.

3. As to the arrangement of advisory structures, divergence tends to be the rule. However, the pressures to centralize have led to some convergence. There has been widespread (*a*) growth in the advisory resources available to prime ministers; (*b*) institutionalization—that is, formalization and consolidation—of advice to prime ministers; (*c*) politicization (or, for those who distinguish politicization from a prime-ministerial preference to have around him/her people who are known, the personalization) of those resources; and (*d*) hybridization of advice—that is, the blurring of boundaries between the administrative and political realms—particularly via recourse to political staff.

Hood and Lodge's concept of the PSB provides a means of illuminating executive government 'that combines comparative historical analysis of political systems with a strategic-action perspective on the making, breaking and maintenance of the compacts between bureaucrats and other players in politics' (Hood and Lodge 2006: 14). The construct draws on the 'Schafferian' notion of a bargain in which political principals accept merit (and procedural independence) as the basis for the employment of their advisory agents in exchange for a duty of loyalty and competence on the part of those agents. The distinction between 'trustee' and 'agency' bargains, and the influence of different forms of competency, loyalty, and reward both illuminates the particular and provides heuristics for future enquiry. It also adds an important 'lens' to the study of advisory structures, conventions and cultures, and how these evolve (and multiply) in different political systems.

5 THE STATE OF THE PLAY

Organizing Enquiry

The scholarship on prime-ministerial advisory structures tends to take the form of descriptively rich single-country cases, or is found in collections of country case studies (Rose and Suleiman 1980; Eichbaum and Shaw 2010; Dahlstrom, Peters, and Pierre 2011).

Particularly in Anglo-Westminster contexts, there are a good many studies of dominant prime ministers. In the United Kingdom, Prime Ministers Thatcher and Blair are frequently invoked (Foley 2000; Rose 2001), while, in Australia, John Howard's premiership is the exemplar. As independent variables, these three figures serve contradictory purposes: their records may be interpreted as an empirical case for the 'presidentialization' thesis (which thesis Bevir and Rhodes (2006a: 686) and Dowding (2013) vigorously contest), or as support for the argument that prime ministers' agency is constrained by exogenous factors, including their dependence upon other core-executive actors. Whatever one's views, the methodological question raised by a focus on dominant leaders concerns the extent to which a concern with prime-ministerial exceptionalism might obscure the wider institutional/contextual rule.

Be that as it may, genuinely analytically comparative analyses—as opposed to collections of country studies—are thin on the ground. Rhodes and Weller (2001) is perhaps an exception (although the primary unit of analysis is the departmental secretary rather than the prime minister), as is Bennister (2007). Consequently, while we know an increasing amount about the particulars of different nations' arrangements, and changes therein over time, we know rather less about the consequences—on policy, and on prime ministers' tenures—of different ways of organizing advice to the political chief executive.

The reasons for this extend to the substantial methodological challenges associated with undertaking comparative research, the most challenging of which stem from the fluid nature of executive authority. Other complicating factors include the considerable variety of structural arrangements adopted across jurisdictions, the presence in some countries of roles that do not exist in others, and—as a function of structural reform and of the accretion of individual leaders' choices—the constantly evolving character of summit staff.

What Do We Know?

Nonetheless, the literature has yielded findings of general salience. Those established by Peters, Rhodes, and Wright (2000) have already been noted. To their conclusions regarding convergence we can add that, even where there are indications that particular country clusters are taking a broadly similar trajectory, there can be divergence among countries within those groups. Thus, prime ministers in the Anglo-Saxon, Germanic, and Scandinavian traditions appear to be appointing more political advisers: among Scandinavian countries, however, Sweden is markedly more enthusiastic about political advisers than is Denmark (Dahlstrom, Peters, and Pierre 2011: 15).

Others have confirmed that choices regarding prime-ministerial advisory arrangements are path dependent and reflect prevailing administrative traditions (Dahlstrom, Peters, and Pierre 2011: 19). Rhodes and Weller (2001: 237) begin their comparative analysis of the roles of top officials with the salutary caveat that 'one country is always the exception to any general statement'. While it emerged from a study of presidential support structures, Walcott and Hult's (2004) finding that arrangements inherited from prior administrations constrain leaders' room for manœuvre is also apposite. It explains, for one thing, the tendency for 'deep' advisory structures to bed down and endure across administrations (Tiernan 2007c).

So, institutions and administrative traditions matter, insofar as specific arrangements are 'embedded in each country's mix of constitutional, cultural, political and administrative factors' (Peters, Rhodes, and Wright 2000: 21). Apropos of this, Bevir, Rhodes, and Weller (2003: 6) point out that governmental traditions—the 'inherited beliefs about the institutions and history of government'—provide the context for, and shape sense-making and agency on the part of political actors. Hence, the Westminster tradition of strong core-executive government and an impartial public service shapes choices regarding the provision of advice to prime ministers in those contexts.

The literature also suggests that neither reification nor determinism is advisable when it comes to considering the importance of government traditions. For instance, the narrative of the Napoleonic tradition is of a strong and indivisible republic, but the architecture of the bicephalous French executive, with its ebb and flow of power between the president and the prime minister, can make it difficult to determine the extent to which advisers work to the government as a whole or to a central political actor (Peters, Rhodes, and Wright 2000: 4).

Traditions may well matter, but prime ministers' agency—reflecting their experiences, capacity to learn on the job, personality, leadership style, and the issues in which they take a direct interest—also influences the structuring of support. Prime ministers, especially in constitutional contexts resting substantially upon conventions, can bolster their authority through their 'ability to create new institutions (policy, delivery and media units) and shape existing ones (via patronage)' (Bennister 2007: 340).

6 ENDURING ISSUES

Our consideration of enduring issues is framed by the four areas in which Peters, Rhodes and Wright (2000) found evidence of cross-national convergence. There continues to be *growth* in advisory capacity—in terms of both professional and partisan advisers—at the centre. In particular, the centralization of resources invested in achieving the 'holy grail of coordination' (Rhodes and Weller 2001: 242) has accelerated, partly in response to the institutional fragmentation of the public sector. Contra the fashionable view that governments have ceded any influence over policy they once had, Saward observes that 'core executive actors…continue to reshape the state in order to (*a*) underscore what remains of their distinctive capacities, (*b*) foster new forms of selective and flexible policy intervention, and (*c*) ultimately, to reinforce sources and forms of legitimacy' (Saward 1997: 33).

Political executives are also investing in core civil-service capacity in the search for control over implementation in an era of decentred governance. The irony is that the very reforms giving rise to greater policy complexity (marketization, devolution, and outsourcing)—and therefore to the demands for such capacity—have themselves generated more sources of advice that might feed into a more contestable process.

The *institutionalization* of advice to prime ministers also continues apace. This can take the form of what Lindquist (2006) calls 'unitization': the development of a plethora of units advising prime ministers on various matters. Lindquist represents such units as adhocracies: transient arrays of advisory functions that fracture and relocate, and that emerge from the 'complexity of governance challenges and the expectation that governments need to identify commitments and demonstrate results' (Lindquist 2006: 429). A recent review of arrangements within the United Kingdom Cabinet Office illustrates just how bewildering this can appear:

> In addition to four units that were already present in the Cabinet Office in 1996, and three for which no 'in' date has been listed, a further 18 units have either been established in or entered the Cabinet Office since 1996. Of this total of 25 units, 18 have been transferred out (some of which have since been disbanded) and seven remain. At least two units were transferred out, only to be subsequently transferred back in, while the remnants of other transferred units, subsequently disbanded, have also returned to the Cabinet Office. Other units were transferred in from other departments only to be transferred out again.
>
> (House of Lords 2010: 18)

More important than the bewildering topography of institutional changes at the centre is the lack of correspondence between form and function. Attempts to craft advisory structures around the imperatives of command and control will fail if what is needed is capacity that speaks to negotiation and diplomacy. A key issue, then, is the extent to which the design of advisory structures is informed by the need to accommodate the bargaining uncertainty associated with network governance and variants of society-centric politics and policy-making.

In terms of *politicization*, two of the dimensions of the phenomenon noted by Peters, Rhodes, and Wright (2000)—the subordination of the bureaucracy to partisan interests, and the appointment of officials with identifiable political affiliations—are apposite. The formal recognition of political staff—through legislation, say, or dedicated codes of conduct—merits mention. At one level this has to do with numbers, in which the evidence suggests that there has been steady growth in the presence of political advisers (Eichbaum and Shaw 2010; Dahlstrom, Peters, and Pierre 2011: 14–15). Relative to the number of 'permanent' officials, however, in all jurisdictions the size of this 'third element' is modest. Function (and in popular and academic discourse *dys*function) tends to attract the greatest attention. We have noted that political staff represent one remedy to the asymmetries that position political principals as the political and policy hostages of their administrative agents. In this respect, prime-ministerial recourse to political staff reflects the need to leaven responsibility with heightened responsiveness. Other factors have also been important: not just greater policy complexity, the 24/7 news cycle and the continuous campaign, but also changes to electoral systems and the creation of zones of political and administrative action not suited to 'permanent' officials (Eichbaum and Shaw 2010).

As to ongoing *hybridization*, the evidence is less convincing. In some cases it remains acceptable for individuals to migrate to and fro across the partisan and professional public-service divide, but, if anything, there appears to be a tendency more clearly to demarcate political from non-political advice. The advent of codes of conduct and model employment contracts for political staff in many (but not all) jurisdictions is perhaps an indication that, beyond a certain point, prime ministers will not entertain any blurring of the boundaries between different sources of advice. A key development has been a trend towards self-censorship. Mulgan (2007) notes that the triumph of responsiveness over the provision of responsible advice can result in advice that builds or reinforces a political case, evidence to the contrary, notwithstanding. In such circumstances hybridization takes the form of a diminution in standards that reinforces the need to speak truth to power and to self-censor advice (Mulgan 2007).

7 WHERE TO FROM HERE?

If we look to the future, several matters merit closer attention than they have hitherto attracted. There remains the problem of the dearth of genuinely comparative research on prime ministers' advisory arrangements. The case for the prosecution is most persuasively made by Peters, Rhodes, and Wright (2000), who observe that not the least challenge lies in identifying an appropriate heuristic for facilitating comparative analyses. In this respect, the 'deep' structures framework developed by Walcott and Hult (2004)—and tested in the Australian context by Tiernan (2007c)—recommends itself.

There is also a need for more explicit theorization of the evolving impact of prime ministers' political staff on relations with (a) other members of the core political executive, and (b) the administrative executive. (The latter is a particular issue in Westminster contexts in which the 'third element' is a newer arrival on the executive stage than is the case in other parliamentary jurisdictions.) There are nascent moves in this direction (Maley 2011), but, assuming a slow but steady increase in the numbers of such staff (as do Dahlstrom, Peters, and Pierre 2011), a clearer theoretical and empirical understanding of matters will become more pressing.

Lastly, Elgie's observations on the challenges facing core-executive studies are, in our assessment, also apposite to the field of prime-ministerial advisory systems. Elgie (2011: 75) warns of the possibility that the resource-dependence approach will itself 'become one of the long-running "chestnuts" of political science...In this scenario, the reossification of core executive studies is a genuine risk. The challenge is for new approaches to emerge.'

Elgie looks to a 'resolutely positivist account' (Elgie 2011: 75) as a potential challenger both to the interpretative turn advanced by Bevir and Rhodes (2006b, 2008) and to the asymmetric power-relations model. We also call for greater theoretical and methodological catholicism than is perhaps presently the case in studies of prime ministers' advisory structures. Such pluralism may go some way to building the bridge between country case studies and the genuinely comparative analyses that remain to be written.

RECOMMENDED READING

Hood, C., and Lodge, M. (2006). *The Politics of Public Service Bargains: Reward, Competency, Loyalty—and Blame*. Oxford: Oxford University Press.

Peters, B. G., Rhodes, R., and Wright, V. (2000) (eds). *Administering the Summit: Administration of the Core Executive in Developed Countries*. New York: St Martin's Press.

Rose, R., and Suleiman, E. N. (1980) (eds). *Presidents and Prime Ministers*. Washington: American Enterprise Institute for Public Policy Research.

REFERENCES

Bagehot, W. (1963) [1873]. *The English Constitution*. London: Collins.

Bennister, M. (2007). 'Tony Blair and John Howard: Comparative Predominance and "Institution Stretch" in the UK and Australia', *British Journal of Politics and International Relations*, 9/3: 327–345.

Bevir, M., and Rhodes, R. A. W. (2006a). 'Prime Ministers, Presidentialism and Westminster Smokescreens', *Political Studies*, 54/4: 671–90.

Bevir, M., and Rhodes, R. A. W. (2006b). 'Interpretive Approaches to British Government and Politics', *British Politics*, 1/1: 84–112.

Bevir, M., and Rhodes, R. A. W. (2008). 'The Differentiated Polity as Narrative', *British Journal of Politics and International Relations*, 10/4: 729–34.

Bevir, M., Rhodes, R. A. W., and Weller, P. (2003). 'Traditions of Governance: Interpreting the Changing Role of the Public Sector', *Public Administration*, 81/1: 1–17.

Castles, F. (1994). 'Review of Advising West European Governments: Inquiries, Expertise and Public Policy', ed. B. G. Peters and A. Barker, *Australian Journal of Political Science*, 29/2: 412–13.

Christensen, T., and Laegreid, P. (2011) (eds). *The Ashgate Research Companion to New Public Management*. Farnham: Ashgate.

Crossman, R. (1963). 'Introduction', in *The English Constitution*, ed. W. Bagehot. London: Fontana, 1–57.

Dahlstrom, C., Peters, B. G., and Pierre, J. (2011) (eds). *Steering from the Centre: Political Control in Western Democracies*. Toronto: University of Toronto Press.

Dowding, K. (2013) 'The Prime Ministerialisation of the British Prime Minister', *Parliamentary Affairs* 66 (3), 617–35.

Dunleavy, P., and Rhodes, R. A. W. (1990). 'Core Executive Studies in Britain', *Public Administration*, 68/1: 3–28.

Eichbaum, C., and Shaw, R. (2007). 'Ministerial Advisers and the Politics of Policy-Making', *Australian Journal of Public Administration*, 66/4: 453–67.

Eichbaum, C, and Shaw, R. (2010) (eds). *Partisan Appointees and Public Servants: An International Analysis of the Role of the Political Adviser*. Cheltenham: Edward Elgar.

Elgie, R. (2011). 'Core Executive Studies Two Decades on', *Public Administration*, 89/1: 64–77.

Foley, M. (2000). *The British Presidency*. Manchester: Manchester University Press.

Halligan, J. (1995). 'Policy Advice and the Public Sector', in B. Peters and D. Savoie (eds), *Governance in a Changing Environment*. Montreal: McGill-Queen's University Press, 138–72.

Heffernan, R. (2003). 'Prime Ministerial Predominance? Core Executive Politics in the UK', *British Journal of Politics and International Relations*, 5/3: 347–72.

Hood, C., and Lodge, M. (2006). *The Politics of Public Service Bargains: Reward, Competency, Loyalty—and Blame*. Oxford: Oxford University Press.

House of Lords (2010). *The Cabinet Office and the Centre of Government*. Report with evidence, Select Committee on the Constitution, 4th Report of Session 2009–10. London: The Stationery Office.

Kjaer, A. M. (2004). *Governance*. Cambridge: Polity Press.

Lindquist, E. (2006). 'Organizing for Policy Implementation: Comparisons, Lessons and Prospects for Cabinet Implementation Units', *Journal of Comparative Policy Analysis*, 8/4: 421–35.

Maley, M. (2011). 'Strategic Links in a Cut-Throat World: Rethinking the Role and Relationships of Australian Ministerial Staff', *Public Administration*, 89/4: 1469–88.

Marsh, D. (2011). 'The New Orthodoxy: The Differentiated Polity Model', *Public Administration*, 89/1: 32–48.

Marsh, D., Richards, D., and Smith, M. (2003). 'Unequal Plurality: Towards an Asymmetric Power Model of British Politics', *Government and Opposition*, 38/3: 306–32.

Moe, T. (1993). 'Presidents, Institutions and Theory', in G. Edwards, J. Kessel, and B. Rockman (eds), *Researching the Presidency: Vital Questions, New Approaches*. Pittsburgh, PA: University of Pittsburgh Press, 337–54.

Mulgan, R. (2007). 'Truth in Government and the Politicization of Civil Service Advice', *Public Administration*, 85/3: 569–86.

Page, E., and Wright, V. (1999). *Bureaucratic Elites in Western European States: A Comparative Analysis of Top Officials*. Oxford: Oxford University Press.

Peters, B. G., and Barker, A. (1993) (eds). *Advising West European Governments: Inquiries, Expertise and Public Policy*. Edinburgh: Edinburgh University Press.

Peters, B. G., and Pierre, J. (2001) (eds). *Politicians, Bureaucrats and Administrative Reform*. London: Routledge.

Peters, B. G., Rhodes, R., and Wright, V. (2000) (eds). *Administering the Summit: Administration of the Core Executive in Developed Countries*. New York: St Martin's Press.

Pollitt, C., and Bouckaert, G. (2004). *Public Management Reform: A Comparative Analysis*. 2nd edn. Oxford: Oxford University Press.

Pressman, J. L., and Wildavsky, A. B. (1973). *Implementation*. Berkeley and Los Angeles: University of California Press.

Rhodes, R. A. W. (1997). *Understanding Governance*. Buckingham and Philadelphia: Open University Press.

Rhodes, R. A. W. (2006). 'Executive Government in Parliamentary Systems', in R. A. W. Rhodes, S. Binder, and B. Rockman (eds), *The Oxford Handbook of Political Institutions*. Oxford: Oxford University Press, 324–45.

Rhodes, R. A. W. (2007). 'Understanding Governance: Ten "Years" On', *Organization Studies*, 28/8: 1243–64.

Rhodes, R. A. W., and Weller, P. (2001). 'Conclusions: "Antipodean Exceptionalism, European Traditionalism"', in R. A. W. Rhodes and P. Weller (eds), *The Changing World of Top Officials: Mandarins or Valets?* Buckingham: Open University Press, 229–54.

Rose, R. (2001). *The Prime Minister in a Shrinking World*. Cambridge: Polity Press.

Rose, R., and Suleiman, E. N. (1980) (eds). *Presidents and Prime Ministers*. Washington: American Enterprise Institute for Public Policy Research.

Savoie, D. (1999). *Governing from the Centre*. Toronto: Toronto University Press.

Saward, M. (1997). 'In Search of the Hollow Crown', in P. Weller, H. Bakvis, and R. A. W. Rhodes (eds), *The Hollow Crown: Countervailing Trends in Core Executives*. London: Macmillan, 16–36.

Smith, M. (2000). 'Prime Ministers, Ministers and Civil Servants in the Core Executive', in R. A. W. Rhodes (ed.), *Transforming British Government*. Basingstoke: Macmillan Press, 25–45.

Tiernan, A. (2007a). *Power without Responsibility*. Sydney: University of New South Wales Press.

Tiernan, A. (2007b). 'Advising Howard: Interpreting Changes in Advisory and Support Structures for the Prime Minister of Australia', *Australian Journal of Political Science*, 41/3: 309–32.

Tiernan, A. (2007c). 'The Learner: John Howard's System of National Security Advice', *Australian Journal of International Affairs*, 61/4: 489–505.

Walcott, C., and Hult, K. (2004). *Empowering the White House: Governance under Nixon, Ford and Carter*. Lawrence, KS: University Press of Kansas.

.Weller, P. (2000). 'Administering the Summit: Australia', in B. G. Peters, R. A. W. Rhodes, and V. Wright (ed.), *Administering the Summit: Administration of the Core Executive in Developed Countries*. New York: St Martin's Press, 59–80.

Wildavsky, A. (1987). *Speaking Truth to Power: The Art and Craft of Policy Analysis*. New Brunswick, NJ: Transaction Books.

CHAPTER 35

CABINET MINISTERS

Leaders, Team Players, Followers?

RUDY B. ANDEWEG

1 THE STUDY OF CABINET MINISTERS

'THE most curious point about the Cabinet is that so little is known about it,' Bagehot wrote in 1867 (Bagehot 1963: 68). Published diaries, from Richard Crossman's famous *Diaries of a Cabinet Minister* (e.g. Crossman 1975) to David Blunkett's tapes (2006), or memoirs, from Françoise Giroud's *La Comédie du pouvoir* (1981) to Peter Mandelson's *The Third Man* (2010), still constitute our most important source of knowledge. They provide great reads and priceless insights. They are, however, by their nature subjective accounts, often written with a political agenda in mind or in an attempt to get history on the author's side. Moreover, few former ministers reflect on the nature of the job itself, or on the mechanics of government.

There are at least two reasons for the relative paucity of academic studies of the role of ministers. Access is one. Direct observation itself is virtually impossible: minutes of cabinet meetings remain out of bounds for decades, and transcripts of other meetings involving ministers often do not exist. The social and political backgrounds of ministers escape official secrets acts, and hence systematic studies of the recruitment and tenure of ministers have been conducted (e.g. Blondel and Thiébault 1991; Dowding and Dumont 2009b), but studies of the actual decision-making processes involving ministers still suffer from lack of reliable data. Some studies have sought to fill the gap with expert surveys (e.g. Blondel and Müller-Rommel 1993; Strøm, Müller, and Bergman 2008), but for this subject academic country 'experts' also have little more to go on than journalistic accounts or the memoirs discussed above. Occasionally, ministers agree to cooperate and provide some form of access. Rhodes (2011) provides a rare anthropological account based largely on direct observation of and conversations with a few ministers and their entourage. Others conducted interviews with former or incumbent ministers (e.g. Headey 1974; Andeweg 1990; Searing 1994; Marsh, Richards, and Smith 2000). Both types of studies are still exceptional in this field.

A second problem is cross-country variation. Most studies are still country specific (see Strøm, Müller, and Bergman 2008 for an exception), or limited to a small set of 'most similar systems' (e.g. Rhodes, Wanna, and Weller 2009). In itself, variation offers the opportunity to study the impact of different institutional arrangements, but here the variation extends into the meaning of the term 'minister' itself. Danish governments, for example, contain twenty-odd ministers who are all members of the cabinet, whereas the number of ministers in the UK may exceed a hundred, even when the whips are not counted, with only a quarter having a seat in cabinet. In some countries all cabinet ministers are heads of departments, and all heads of departments are cabinet ministers, but other countries' cabinets include non-departmental ministers, and some or even all departments may not be represented in cabinet. Even the term 'cabinet' can be misleading: occasionally there are so many members that cabinet becomes unwieldy, and an inner cabinet is set up, which then becomes the functional equivalent of another country's full cabinet. This chapter ignores some of the variation by focusing on ministers who are members of the cabinet and who also head a government department, but the reader should be aware that this is a simplification.

Finally, there also seems to be genuine doubt about the relevance of ministers as political actors, as testified by titles such as 'Do Ministers Matter?' (Chabal 2003), or 'Pouvoir et non-pouvoir du ministre' (Rigaud 1986). Headey went in search of a theory of executive political leadership to underpin his study of cabinet ministers, but even he seemed not entirely convinced that ministers are indeed leaders: 'by leaders we shall mean, simply, office-holders' (Headey 1974: 18). The question arises whether a handbook on political leadership should pay any attention to ministers at all. Are ministers leaders or followers? Or are they members of a collective leadership, the cabinet: are they team players?

2 MINISTERIAL LEADERSHIP: THE QUEST FOR COMPETENCE

'How will we know a ministrable politician if we see one? Ministrable politicians are not found underneath gooseberry bushes with the keys to a big black limousine around their necks' (Laver and Shepsle 2000: 114). No study has linked personal characteristics to ministerial success, however defined. Systematic studies of what relevant others (politicians, high-ranking civil servants) regard as the most desirable competences for ministerial leadership are rare (e.g. Cheong 2009; Lee, Moon, and Hahm 2010). In systems where ministers must also be MPs, we can infer the characteristics preferred by those making the appointments from a comparison of MPs who are appointed to the cabinet with their party colleagues who are left on the backbenches. For Canada, for example, Kerby (2009) found that being female, possessing legal training, having been a minister before, and having been a challenger to the party leadership all reduce the waiting time on the backbenches. In countries where ministerial recruitment is not restricted to parliamentarians, all we have is the empirical distribution of various competences among ministers.

With the exception of ministers without portfolio, *ministres delegués*, and so on, most ministers are the appointed heads of large and complex organizations. Yet, 'Ministers are not managers. It is not why they went into politics,' concludes Rhodes (2011: 292). Even if a definition of those elusive 'organizational skills' would be readily available, it is an aspect of the ministerial role that both ministers and political scientists have mostly ignored. Ministers seem happy to leave departmental management to their permanent secretaries, unless they enter departments with an explicit agenda of administrative reform. The discussion focuses on other competences. Ministers are the linchpins between the political world and the administrative world. To be influential in one, the minister should be a consummate politician with considerable experience in the corridors of power; to be effective in the other, the minister should be a technocrat, well versed in the intricacies of the relevant policy area. At the same time, it pays to be a generalist, in order to influence the direction of policy in cabinet meetings (Blondel 1985). In order to exercise their responsibility for the portfolio that has been assigned to them, however, ministers could benefit from specialized expertise. In practice, these two distinctions are thought to coincide: between 'all-rounders' with political skills, and specialist 'outsiders' (De Winter 1991: 61).

The literature on ministerial roles makes a similar distinction. In his pioneering study, Headey lists no less than twelve ministerial roles in four clusters: as head of department, as a member of the cabinet, as parliamentary and party leader, and in public relations. The distinction between departmental specialization and general politics can be seen in Headey's two cabinet membership roles: being either a 'Cabinet battle-axe' for departmental interests or being a 'Cabinet all-rounder' (Headey 1974: 58–65). In their update of Headey's study, Marsh, Richards, and Smith (2000) cluster the ministerial roles differently—for example, listing 'advocacy of department's position in Cabinet' as a 'political role', while I would see embracing that role more as a sign of departmental specialization.

The distinction between political all-rounders and departmental specialists as role conceptions is made most explicitly by Searing (1994: 321–6). Being a cabinet minister is such a constraining position, he argues, that there is little room for a personal interpretation of the role. The manifold demands made by the position on the incumbent produce a role overload, however, and ministers are forced to make choices. The most important choice they must make is between emphasizing Whitehall ('Administrators') or Westminster ('Politicians'). A minority of Searing's British ministers opted for the Administrator role, taking pride in developing departmental policies and getting them accepted, disliking parliamentary debate, being relatively insensitive to public opinion, and often leaving politics altogether when they lose office. The Politicians, on the other hand, are generalists, who enjoy the opportunity to be involved in the most pressing political issues, thriving on parliamentary debate and political conflict, keeping an ear to the ground for the mood of the electorate, and unable to see for themselves a life after politics. Although Searing saw ministers making a choice between the two roles, he found evidence for both roles in most of his interviews. The choice between them was a choice of emphasis. In a study of Dutch ministers, Andeweg suggests that this emphasis may be situational rather than dispositional:

> When these ex-ministers were asked whether they saw their role primarily as political or departmental, their answer was quite often that this depended on the issue that was at stake... All but a few ministers agreed that departmental interests guided their behaviour and structured conflicts in cabinet most of the time. Some issues, however, are from the outset politically charged. Then ministers and the cabinet as a whole change gears.
>
> (Andeweg 1988: 148)

However, the fact that Andeweg's Dutch ministers played a departmental role most of the time whereas only a minority of Searing's British ministers could be classified as departmental Administrators points to variation across countries as well.

The relative emphasis on these two clusters of roles and competences seems to be related to a number of factors. Some are constitutional. In Westminster democracies, ministers are required to be members of parliament by convention or constitutional provision. Ministerial recruitment relies heavily on political experience, and portfolio-specific expertise plays less of a role. As a consequence, the proportion of ministers who hold only one post in their cabinet career is considerably lower in, for example, Ireland and the UK (just over a third) than in other European countries where the combination of a seat in cabinet with a seat in parliament is not obligatory (well over half), and outsider specialists can be appointed (Bakema 1991: 90). At the other extreme, Neto and Strøm (2006) found semi-presidentialism and legislative powers of the head of state to be strong predictors of a relatively high proportion of ministers who are not even members of a political party (also Blondel 1985: 202–3). In such systems ministerial appointments may become a bone of contention between a prime minister and a head of state with different party preferences, resulting in agreement on non-partisan technocrats as a compromise. However, there is considerable variation in all this in countries with rather similar constitutional set-ups. Norway, the Netherlands, and Austria have many specialists (one-post ministers recruited from outside parliament), while Iceland, Italy, and Belgium have the most politicized ministers (recruited from parliament, with higher portfolio mobility). It is not entirely clear how we may account for such differences.

Interestingly, the differences between parties from different ideological families are marginal compared to the differences across government departments (Keman 1991). Outsiders/specialists are more often found in the Treasury, Economic Affairs, Justice, and Foreign Affairs than in the social welfare departments (De Winter 1991; Keman 1991).

Where the emphasis lies with political generalists, there is often concern about insufficient substantive expertise: 'the dilemma of policymaking by politicians is power without competence' (Aberbach, Putnam, and Rockman 1981: 255). In Australia, where ministers are drawn from a majority in a relatively small parliament (150 representatives and 75 senators), the recruitment pool is criticized as too shallow (Tiernan and Weller 2010: 51). In the UK, prime ministers can resort to awarding a life peerage when they want to appoint a minister from outside parliament. This practice rose under Blair, and particularly under Brown. 'However, it was, as most outsider ministers admitted, "horses for courses"...Outsider ministers worked best where their skills and experience matched their portfolios' (Yong and Hazell 2011: 43).

In Italy, where technocrat ministers used to be rare during the First Republic, and confined to portfolios such as Finance and Foreign Trade, there has been a noted increase in such ministers after the constitutional reforms of the 1990s (Verzichelli 2009: 86). At the same time, developments run in the opposite direction in countries with an emphasis on outsiders and/or specialists. In Germany, for example, this was the approach in the 1990s: 'the minister of agriculture...has to come from the farmers' lobby, whereas the job of employment minister goes to a union representative. A justice minister should be trained in law, while a minister responsible for the family and the young should not be a bachelor. As a rule defense ministers should have served in the armed forces' (Sturm 1994: 82). However, there has been a marked decline of specialist ministers in Germany in more recent decades: 'Only Justice is left as a domain where a professional background in law is seemingly a necessary condition for the minister' (Fischer and Kaiser 2009: 31).

The Dutch experience makes clear that political experience and portfolio expertise need not exclude each other: while the proportion of Dutch ministers with a political background went up from 57 per cent at the time of their first appointment in 1946–67 to 73 per cent in 1967–86, the proportion of ministers with specialized expertise did not decline as much: from 72 per cent to 65 per cent (Bakema and Secker 1988: 161). Apparently, many ministers possessed both specialized expertise and political experience. Looking at 182 appointments of ministers to economic portfolios in Swedish cabinets between 1917 and 2004, Beckman found that only 36 per cent of the appointees had educational or professional qualifications in that field. Eighty-eight per cent of them, however, had been politically active in that policy area prior to their appointment as minister—for example, by serving on the relevant parliamentary committee, or by having been responsible for the same portfolio in a previous government. If both political and non-political sources of portfolio expertise are taken into account, only 7 per cent of the appointments lacked any form of portfolio-related expertise (Beckman 2006). Such politically acquired specialized expertise is also found in the United Kingdom, where in new governments former Shadow ministers obtain those same portfolios (Berlinski et al. 2009: 61). In many countries, a growing proportion of ministers are 'hybrids': both politicians and specialists (Yong and Hazell 2011: 49).

3 Ministerial Leadership: The Quest for Discretion

Ministers matter most if they possess unfettered power to determine policy within their portfolio. This is the core assumption on which Laver and Shepsle build their portfolio allocation theory of coalition formation (Laver and Shepsle 1990, 1996). Because of the technical expertise needed to make policy, and because of the sheer volume of government activity, all governments are characterized by a division of labour—that is, by a departmentalized structure. Thus, with all their department's resources at their disposal, ministers effectively control policy in their portfolio. If government formation is relevant for the direction of public policy, it is through the appointment of particular politicians to particular portfolios. Once the appointments are made, cabinet meetings serve largely ritualistic purposes. Formally, that may be where the decisions are taken, but they are taken on the basis of a proposal that is made by the minister for that portfolio, and that is prepared by the department under the minister's control. Other ministers simply lack the time and the resources to develop an alternative proposal outside their jurisdiction, or even to judge the proposal on its merits. Moreover, most studies of cabinet decision-making in individual countries report the existence of a tacit rule of mutual non-intervention within the cabinet. Ministers forgo their right to interfere with other ministers' proposals to protect their own autonomy: if one criticizes the proposal of a colleague, one should expect that colleague to reciprocate likewise.

Laver and Shepsle's portfolio-allocation approach sparked vigorous debate about its relevance for coalition theory, but the focal point in that debate has been their assumption of ministerial autonomy (e.g. Warwick 1999; Dunleavy and Bastow 2001; Tsebelis 2002: 106–9). That assumption, it is argued, is subject to two considerable constraints: hierarchy and collective decision-making (Andeweg 2000; Blondel and Manning 2002).

Hierarchy

The prime minister, for example, is largely absent from Laver and Shepsle's analysis. He plays but a residual role: to adjudicate departmental boundary conflicts, or to initiate the discussion of the government's reaction to a policy problem that had not yet been foreseen when ministers were appointed to portfolios (but also see Weller, Chapter 32; Blick and Jones, Chapter 33, this volume, showing that most of the literature accords more power to the prime minister). Though Laver and Shepsle's theory is intended to improve our understanding of coalition government, the difference with prime ministers in single-party governments should not be overstated. Dowding and Dumont identify constitutional and party political constraints on the hiring and firing powers of prime ministers, and coalitions constitute only one of these constraints (Dowding and Dumont 2009a). Some parties (such as the Labor Party in Australia (at least until 2007) and New Zealand) have their MPs rather than the party leader/prime minister select the ministers. Sometimes a single-party government is divided into factions, such as Japanese Liberal Democratic Party governments or the Blair–Brown Labor governments in the UK, resembling a coalition government, and also constraining the prime minister's powers. Even where the prime minister is formally free to appoint, he often faces constraints in terms of achieving a gender balance, or regional representation, for example, or he feels forced to appoint his rivals for the party leadership. Kam et al. (2010) compared the political preferences of appointees to British cabinets from 1987 to 2005 with those of both the party leader and the parliamentary party as a whole, and actually found a better correspondence of ministers with the backbenchers than with the prime minister.

Dismissals can be a means to select the best ministers by trial and error, or to prevent the government's popularity from being contaminated by an individual minister's scandal or fiasco, but there is also evidence that dismissals and reshuffles help the prime minister to counteract agency loss (Indridason and Kam 2008). Surprisingly, given the greater information asymmetry between the prime minister and specialist ministers, prime ministers seem to be equally worried about ministerial drift among generalist and specialist ministers: the average length of tenure in a particular portfolio is not markedly higher for one-post ministers than it is for ministers holding several posts (Bakema 1991: 91). When it comes to firing or reshuffling ministers, prime ministers will also have to calculate the costs of removing a 'big beast of the jungle' to the backbenches (King and Allen 2010), but here the difference between single-party cabinets and coalition cabinets seems to be more pronounced than with regard to appointments. Analysing 2,477 dismissals from a particular portfolio of ministers in 19 parliamentary democracies from 1945 to 1999, Huber and Martinez-Gallardo report that the likelihood of being replaced is reduced by nearly 40 per cent for ministers in a coalition government compared to ministers in single-party governments, and that ministers from the prime minister's own party are 30 per cent more likely to be replaced than ministers from coalition partners (Huber and Martinez-Gallardo 2008: 176).

Even if ministers in coalition governments, and ministers from junior coalition parties in particular, still have less to fear from the prime minister, they cannot escape the shadow of hierarchy entirely. The prospective coalition parties increasingly negotiate a coalition agreement that outlines the policy programme of the new government (Müller and Strøm 2008; Strøm, Müller, and Smith 2010). To the extent that a coalition agreement dictates which policies are to be pursued in a particular department, it limits the autonomy of that department's minister (Moury 2011). The constraints imposed by the coalition agreement on individual ministers are particularly important where mechanisms are put in place to enforce the agreement. Coalition governments tend to have some form of collective leadership in which all governing parties are represented. Sometimes the coalition leadership is to be found within the cabinet ('inner cabinet'), sometimes it is composed of party leaders outside the cabinet ('party summit'), sometimes it brings together leaders both inside and outside the cabinet ('coalition committee'). Conflicts that do not threaten the government's survival, such as interde-partmental disputes, are dealt with by the coalition leadership within the cabinet, while potentially explosive conflicts between the coalition parties are referred to an external body (Andeweg and Timmermans 2008). In any case, the combination of the coalition agreement and the coalition leadership to some extent serves as the functional equiva-lent of the prime minister limiting ministerial autonomy in a single-party government.

Collective Decision-Making

However, when Laver and Shepsle put the assumption of ministerial autonomy under-lying their portfolio allocation theory to country experts from fourteen countries, the constraint on individual ministers that was emphasized most was not so much hierarchy, but collective decision-making in cabinets (Laver and Shepsle 1994). Individual minis-ters are still important as agenda-setters, but they are able to determine the outcome only to the extent that their colleagues let them. The rule of mutual non-intervention is not absolute.

First, it is rare for a policy to be confined entirely to a single departmental jurisdic-tion. Most cabinets have rules requiring the consent of other ministers whose portfo-lios are affected, or requiring preparatory deliberation in a cabinet committee bringing together the ministers in a particular policy field. A special case of overlapping juris-dictions involves the minister of finance. There are unlikely to be many proposals by departmental ministers that are entirely without budgetary consequences. Moreover, ministers of finance usually also have the resources to probe proposals by other min-isters in the form of a finance inspectorate or functional equivalent. Thus, departmen-tal ministers are constrained by their colleagues, even in a purely departmentalized government.

However, ministers may have more reasons to join cabinet discussions. In a study of the elaborate minutes of the Dutch cabinet, Andeweg (1990) found that 22 per cent of all ministerial contributions to cabinet discussions could not be traced to the speakers' departmental portfolio. One reason is that ministers may also feel responsible for an 'informal' portfolio that gives them the incentive and legitimacy to intervene outside their departmental portfolio (Andeweg 1997)—for example, female ministers on gen-der issues. In federal countries, ministers are expected to intervene when their region is affected by a policy proposal (e.g. Bakvis 1991). In coalition governments, ministers may speak out on behalf of their party as well as of their department. They themselves often lack information about a portfolio that is assigned to another party's minister, but they may be briefed by a junior minister in the relevant department from their own party. Seventy per cent of 192 governments had appointed at least one junior min-ister to a department headed by a cabinet minister from another party (Verzichelli 2008: 261). Such appointments occur more often in portfolios that are regarded as more important (Thies 2001). They strengthen collective decision-making against ministerial autonomy.

One survey of country experts included the question 'How much autonomy does a cabinet member have in making policy in her or his department?', with an answering scale ranging from 1 (great autonomy) to 9 (no autonomy) (Laver and Hunt 1992). The average of the country averages reported is 4.49, slightly to the autonomous side of the scale. The difference between the average for the twelve coalition countries in the study (4.15) and the twelve countries with single-party governments (4.82) is very small, with ministers in coalition countries enjoying only marginally greater autonomy. According to these country experts at least, the two mechanisms constraining ministers—hierarchy and collective decision-making—produce very similar results.

Department

Whatever one may prefer in terms of ministerial autonomy vis-à-vis the prime minister or party leader, and vis-à-vis the cabinet as a whole, there is little disagreement when it comes to the relationship between ministers and civil servants. In any 'public sector bargain' (Hood and Lodge 2006), departmental officials are expected to serve their minister loyally. This loyalty cannot be taken for granted, however. The combination of information asymmetry between ministers and civil servants and the huge span of control in modern-day government renders full ministerial control impossible. The debate focuses on the top-down process of departmental implementation of ministerial policies, and not on the bottom-up process of policy advice and formulation (Meier and O'Toole 2006). Yet, it is not implementation to which ministers refer when they occasionally complain about their departments in interviews or memoirs. In recent decades, in many countries, ministerial ex ante control over implementation has even been relaxed by agencification, privatization, and so on, as part of the New Public Management. Ministers seem to be worried more about the role of their department in shaping their own policies, or even their own preferences.

It would be neat if the roles of ministers and civil servants could be complementary, as when politicians bring values and direction to the policy-making process, and civil servants facts and professional standards (e.g. Svara 2001), but ministers are often recruited at least partly because of their specialized expertise in the relevant policy domain, and civil servants are increasingly required to be 'politically sensitive' in their advice to the minister. The greater the overlap, the greater the challenges to the minister's leadership in departmental policy-making. It is this side of the relationship between ministers and civil servants that has been immortalized in the television series *Yes, Minister* (see, e.g., Lynn and Jay 1982), based on a 'Whitehall model' of days gone by, in which politicians were unusually dependent on the career civil service, in particular for policy advice (Wilson and Barker 2003). In that model, ministers had little or no alternative advisory resources. They entered a 'total institution', with the predictable result that many ministers were 'captured', 'went native'. Much of Kaufman's famous *How to be a Minister* is devoted to the prevention of the dangerous disease of 'departmentalitis'

(Kaufman 1997: 15). Ministers 'going native' are found in many country's governments. An Australian minister complained:

> One of the problems with Cabinet government is that spending ministers tend to run the risk of seeing themselves as advocates for the interests in their area and they're not taking much interest in others and losing that sense of it being a whole-of-government and Cabinet government and losing a bit of objectivity about their own area. There is a real risk.
>
> (Quoted in Tiernan and Weller 2010: 172)

When interviewed by this author, a Dutch minister explained that bottles were uncorked at home after victory in an interdepartmental battle, but that she was met with long faces there after defeat in cabinet. 'Home', it transpired later in the interview, was not her family, but her department.

The occurrence of 'departmentalitis' in both British and Dutch governments is interesting, as the governments in these countries are at opposite extremes with regard to ministerial recruitment. Expert knowledge in the department's policy domain is often considered an asset for ministers in their efforts to lead the department; they are supposed to succumb to departmental 'capture' less easily. This may indeed be true, but the risk is that these appointees were already 'natives' before they became ministers, coming as they do from the very policy sector that they must now direct.

It is likely that the dependency and capture of ministers has declined, and not only in the UK: as Tiernan and Weller conclude for Australian government: 'If in the 1980s the public service could usually be sure that it would have the last word in policy advice, by 2009 it had to compete for its position at the table.' (Tiernan and Weller 2010: 122). With considerable variation across countries, ministers have gained more influence over the structure and staffing of their policy advice. In addition, more use is made of alternative advisers, such as outside consultants and think tanks. The occasional and isolated 'political adviser' has given way to substantial numbers of special advisers in the department, some of whom are experts in a particular policy field, but most of whom provide input from politics and public opinion. Marsh, Richards, and Smith found that, since the 1980s, in their relations with their departments, fewer ministers are content to be mere legitimators of departmental policy and more of them act as initiators of specific policy initiatives or even as overall agenda setters (Marsh, Richards, and Smith 2000: 321–3). Aberbach and Rockman concluded that 'over time, the views of politically appointed officials more and more closely resembled the politics (party and ideology) of the administration they were serving' (Aberbach and Rockman 2006: 988). This is likely to be the result of a changing political climate, in which a more volatile electorate forces ministers to take their party's election promises more seriously. The combination of lesser reliance on departmental advisers and a more proactive attitude of ministers may have created tensions in the relations between ministers and civil servants ('t Hart and Wille 2006), but it is likely to have strengthened ministers' position as leaders of their departments.

4 Conclusion

This review suggests that the leadership of ministers is constrained: the prime minister is not a residual head of government, cabinet serves more than ritual purposes, and the department is not just a responsive machine. The institutional variety is bewildering, but the resulting constraints on ministers rarely accumulate to the point where ministerial autonomy is too small to speak of leadership. Often the constraints are alternative rather than cumulative.

Many studies furthermore paint an over-institutionalized picture of cabinet ministers. The recent evolution towards more theoretically embedded research in this field is inspired primarily by rational choice institutionalism, which puts great stock in formal rules and structures: Laver and Shepsle's portfolio-allocation approach (Laver and Shepsle 1990, 1996), Tsebelis' veto player theory (Tsebelis 2002), and in particular the principal–agent framework (e.g. Strøm, Müller, and Bergman 2008) (see, further, Brennan and Brooks, Chapter 11, this volume). Other varieties of institutionalism are still less common in this field, but see Searing (1994) and Rhodes (2011). Such studies, inspired by sociological or normative institutionalism, are more open to informal rules and institutions, are more inductive, and may suffer more from the fact that the behaviour of cabinet ministers largely takes place behind closed doors, and that ministers with overloaded schedules are reluctant to agree to be interviewed. What are most conspicuously absent are psychological studies of cabinet ministers. Presidents and dictators attract psychobiographers, but ordinary ministers in parliamentary systems do not. Studies of group dynamics in political decision-making focus on informal groups of advisers, but not on cabinets (with notable exceptions, such as 't Hart 1994; Verbeek 2003; Kaarbo 2008, 2012). It is true that cabinet ministers live in a highly institutionalized world, but the constraints this imposes seem to vary across persons and situations. While some ministers play out their prescribed roles, others are able to ignore some of the constraints because of political weight or the force of personality. We still know very little of why and when some ministers are moulded by the institutions and others change them.

Recommended Reading

Elgie, R. (1997). 'Models of Executive Politics: A Framework for the Study of Executive Power Relations in Parliamentary and Semi-Presidential Regimes', *Political Studies*, 45/2: 217–31.

Kaarbo, J. (2012). *Coalition Politics and Cabinet Decision Making: A Comparative Analysis of Foreign Policy Choices*. Ann Arbor, MI: University of Michigan Press.

Rhodes, R. A.W. (2011). *Everyday Life in British Government*. Oxford: Oxford University Press.

REFERENCES

Aberbach, J. D., and Rockmann, B. A. (2006). 'The Past and Future of Political–Administrative Relations: Research from *Bureaucrats and Politicians* to *In the Web of Politics*—and Beyond', *International Journal of Public Administration*, 29/12: 977–95.

Aberbach, J. D., Putnam, R. D., and Rockman, B. A. (1981). *Bureaucrats and Politicians in Western Democracies*. Cambridge, MA: Harvard University Press.

Andeweg, R. B. (1988). 'Centrifugal Forces and Collective Decision-Making: The Case of the Dutch Cabinet', *European Journal of Political Research*, 16/2: 125–51.

Andeweg, R. B. (1990). 'Tweeërlei Ministerraad: Besluitvorming in Nederlandse Kabinetten', in R. B. Andeweg (ed.), *Ministers en Ministerraad*. Den Haag: SDU, 17–42.

Andeweg, R. B. (1997). 'Collegiality and Collectivity: Cabinets, Cabinet Committees and Cabinet Ministers', in P. Weller, H. Bakvis, and R. A. W. Rhodes (eds), *The Hollow Crown: Countervailing Trends in Core Executives*. London: Macmillan, 58–83.

Andeweg, R. B. (2000). 'Ministers as Double Agents? The Delegation Process between Cabinet and Ministers', *European Journal of Political Research*, 37/3: 377–95.

Andeweg, R. B., and Timmermans, A. (2008). 'Conflict Management in Coalition Government', in K. Strøm, W. C. Müller, and T. Bergman (eds), *Cabinets and Coalition Bargaining: The Democratic Life Cycle in Western Europe*. Oxford: Oxford University Press, 269–300.

Bagehot, W. (1963) [1867]. *The English Constitution*. London: Fontana.

Bakema, W. (1991). 'The Ministerial Career', in J. Blondel and J. L. Thiébault (eds), *The Profession of Government Minister in Western Europe*. London: Macmillan, 70–98.

Bakema, W., and Secker I. P. (1988). 'Ministerial Expertise and the Dutch Case', *European Journal of Political Research*, 16/2: 153–70.

Bakvis, H. (1991). *Regional Ministers: Power and Influence in the Canadian Cabinet*. Toronto: University of Toronto Press.

Beckman, L. (2006). 'The Competent Cabinet? Ministers in Sweden and the Problem of Competence and Democracy', *Scandinavian Political Studies*, 29/2: 111–29.

Berlinski, S., Dewan, T., Dowding, K., and Subrahmanyam, G. (2009). 'Choosing, Moving and Resigning at Westminster, UK', in K. Dowding and P. Dumont (eds), *The Selection of Ministers in Europe: Hiring and Firing*. London: Routledge, 58–78.

Blondel, J. (1985). *Government Ministers in the Contemporary World*. London: Sage.

Blondel, J., and Manning, N. (2002). 'Do Ministers Do what they Say? Ministerial Unreliability, Collegial and Hierarchical Governments', *Political Studies*, 50/3: 455–76.

Blondel, J., and Müller-Rommel, F. (1993) (eds). *Governing Together: The Extent and Limits of Joint Decision-making in Western European Cabinets*. London: Macmillan.

Blondel, J., and Thiébault, J. L. (1991) (eds). *The Profession of Government Minister in Western Europe*. London: Macmillan.

Blunkett, D. (2006). *The Blunkett Tapes: My Life in the Bear Pit*. London: Bloomsbury.

Chabal, P. M. (2003). 'Do Ministers Matter? The Individual Style of Ministers in Programmed Policy Change', *International Review of Administrative Sciences*, 69/1: 29–49.

Cheong, J. O. (2009). 'Suggested Capacities for Minister's Success: An Empirical Approach Based on Saaty's AHP', *International Journal of Public Administration*, 32/2: 136–51.

Crossman, R. (1975). *The Diaries of a Cabinet Minister*, i. *Minister of Housing 1964–66*. London: Hamish Hamilton and Jonathan Cape.

De Winter, L. (1991). 'Parliamentary and Party Pathways to the Cabinet', in J. Blondel and J. L. Thiébault (eds), *The Profession of Government Minister in Western Europe*. London: Macmillan, 44–69.

Dowding, K., and Dumont, P. (2009a). 'Structural and Strategic Factors Affecting the Hiring and Firing of Ministers', in K. Dowding and P. Dumont (eds), *The Selection of Ministers in Europe: Hiring and Firing*. London: Routledge, 1–20.

Dowding, K., and Dumont, P. (2009b) (eds). *The Selection of Ministers in Europe: Hiring and Firing*. London: Routledge.

Dunleavy, P., and Bastow, S. (2001). 'Modelling Coalitions that Cannot Coalesce: A Critique of the Laver–Shepsle Approach', *West European Politics*, 24/1: 1–26.

Fischer, J., and Kaiser, A. (2009). 'Germany: Hiring and Firing Ministers under Informal Constraints', in K. Dowding and P. Dumont (eds), *The Selection of Ministers in Europe: Hiring and Firing*. London: Routledge, 21–40.

Giroud, F. (1981). *La Comédie du pouvoir*. Paris: Fayard.

Headey, B. (1974). *British Cabinet Ministers: The Roles of Politicians in Executive Office*. London: George Allen and Unwin.

Hood, C., and Lodge, M. (2006). *The Politics of Public Sector Bargains: Reward, Competency, Loyalty—and Blame*. Oxford: Oxford University Press.

Huber, J. D., and Martinez-Gallardo, C. (2008). 'Replacing Cabinet Ministers: Patterns of Ministerial Stability in Parliamentary Democracies', *American Political Science Review*, 102/2: 169–80.

Indridason, I., and Kam, C. (2008). 'Cabinet Reshuffles and Ministerial Drift', *British Journal of Political Science*, 38/4: 621–56.

Kaarbo, J. (2008). 'Coalition Cabinet Decision Making: Institutional and Psychological Factors', *International Studies Review*, 10/1: 57–86.

Kaarbo, J. (2012). *Coalition Politics and Cabinet Decision Making: A Comparative Analysis of Foreign Policy Choices*. Ann Arbor, MI: University of Michigan Press.

Kam, C., Bianco, W. T., Sened, I., and Smyth, R. (2010). 'Ministerial Selection and Intraparty Organization in the Contemporary British Parliament', *American Political Science Review*, 104/2: 289–306.

Kaufman, G. (1997). *How to be a Minister*. London: Faber and Faber.

Keman, H. (1991). 'Ministers and Ministries', in J. Blondel and J. L. Thiébault (eds), *The Profession of Government Minister in Western Europe*. London: Macmillan, 99–118.

Kerby, M. (2009). 'Worth the Wait: Determinants of Ministerial Appointment in Canada, 1935–2008', *Canadian Journal of Political Science*, 42/3: 593–611.

King, A., and Allen, N. (2010). ' "Off with their Heads": British Prime Ministers and the Power to Dismiss', *British Journal of Political Science*, 40/2: 249–78.

Laver, M., and Hunt, W. B. (1992). *Policy and Party Competition*. New York: Routledge.

Laver, M., and Shepsle, K. A. (1990). 'Coalitions and Cabinet Government', *American Political Science Review*, 84/3: 873–90.

Laver, M., and Shepsle, K. A. (1994). 'Cabinet Government in Theoretical Perspective'. in M. Laver and K. A. Shepsle (eds), *Cabinet Ministers and Parliamentary Government*. Cambridge: Cambridge University Press, 285–309.

Laver, M., and Shepsle, K. A. (1996). *Making and Breaking Governments: Cabinets and Legislatures in Parliamentary Democracies*. Cambridge: Cambridge University Press.

Laver, M., and Shepsle, K. A. (2000). 'Ministrables and Government Formation: Munchkins, Players, and big Beasts of the Jungle', *Journal of Theoretical Politics*, 12/1: 113–24.

Lee, S. Y., Moon, M. J., and Hahm, S. D. (2010). 'Dual Faces of Ministerial Leadership in South Korea: Does Political Responsiveness or Administrative Responsibility Enhance Perceived Ministerial Performance?', *Administration and Society*, 42/1: 77–101.

Lynn, J., and Jay, A. (1982). *Yes, Minister: The Diaries of a Cabinet Minister by the Rt Hon. James Hacker MP. Volume One*. London: Crown Publications.

Mandelson, P. (2010). *The Third Man: Life at the Heart of New Labour*. London: Harper Press.

Marsh, D., Richards, D., and Smith, M. J. (2000). 'Re-Assessing the Role of Departmental Cabinet Ministers', *Public Administration*, 78/2: 305–26.

Meier, K. J., and O'Toole, L. J. (2006). *Bureaucracy in a Democratic State: A Governance Perspective*. Baltimore, MD: Johns Hopkins University Press.

Moury, C. (2011). 'Coalition Agreement and Party Mandate: How Coalition Agreements Constrain the Ministers', *Party Politics*, 17/3: 385–404.

Müller, W. C., and Strøm, K. (2008). 'Coalition Agreements and Cabinet Governance', in K. Strøm, W. C. Müller, and T. Bergman (eds), *Cabinets and Coalition Bargaining: The Democratic Life Cycle in Western Europe*. Oxford: Oxford University Press, 159–99.

Neto, O. A. and Strøm, K. (2006). 'Breaking the Parliamentary Chain of Delegation: Presidents and Non-Partisan Cabinet Members in European Democracies', *British Journal of Political Science*, 36/4: 619–43.

Rhodes, R. A. W. (2011). *Everyday Life in British Government*. Oxford: Oxford University Press.

Rhodes, R. A. W., Wanna, J., and Weller, P. (2009). *Comparing Westminster*. Oxford: Oxford University Press; especially chapter 4.

Rigaud, J. (1986). 'Pouvoir et non-pouvoir du ministre', *Pouvoirs*, 36: 5–14.

Searing, D. D. (1994). *Westminster's World: Understanding Political Roles*. Cambridge, MA: Harvard University Press.

Strøm, K., Müller, W. C., and Bergman, T. (2008) (eds). *Cabinets and Coalition Bargaining: The Democratic Life Cycle in Western Europe*. Oxford: Oxford University Press.

Strøm, K., Müller, W. C., and Smith, D. M. (2010). 'Parliamentary Control of Coalition Governments', *Annual Review of Political Science*, 13: 517–35.

Sturm, R. (1994). 'The Chancellor and the Executive', in S. Padgett (ed.), *Adenauer to Kohl: The Development of the German Chancellorship*. London: Hurst, 78–105.

Svara, J. H. (2001). 'The Myth of the Dichotomy: Complementarity of Politics and Administration in the Past and Future of Public Administration', *Public Administration Review*, 61/2: 176–83.

't Hart, P. (1994). *Groupthink in Government: A Study of Small Groups and Policy Failure*. Baltimore, MD: Johns Hopkins University Press.

't Hart, P., and Wille, A. (2006). 'Ministers and Top Officials in the Dutch Core Executive: Living Together, Growing Apart?', *Public Administration*, 84/1: 121–46.

Thies, M. F. (2001). 'Keeping Tabs on Partners: The Logic of Delegation in Coalition Governments', *American Journal of Political Science*, 45: 580–98.

Tiernan, A., and Weller, P. (2010). *Learning to be a Minister: Heroic Expectations, Practical Realities*. Melbourne: Melbourne University Press.

Tsebelis, G. (2002). *Veto Players: How Political Institutions Work*. Princeton: Princeton University Press.

Verbeek, B. (2003). *Decision-Making in Great Britain during the Suez Crisis: Small Groups and a Persistent Leader*. Aldershot: Ashgate.

Verzichelli, L. (2008). 'Portfolio Allocation', in K. Strøm, W. C. Müller, and T. Bergman (eds), *Cabinets and Coalition Bargaining: The Democratic Life Cycle in Western Europe*. Oxford: Oxford University Press, 237–67.

Verzichelli, L. (2009). 'Italy: The Difficult Road to a More Effective Process of Ministerial Selection', in K. Dowding and P. Dumont (eds), *The Selection of Ministers in Europe: Hiring and Firing*. London: Routledge, 79–100.

Warwick, P. V. (1999). 'Ministerial Autonomy or Ministerial Accommodation? Contested Bases of Government Survival in Parliamentary Democracies', *British Journal of Political Science*, 29/2: 369–94.

Wilson, G. K., and Barker, A. (2003). 'Bureaucrats and Politicians in Britain', *Governance*, 16/3: 349–72.

Yong, B., and Hazell, R. (2011). *Putting Goats amongst the Wolves: Appointing Ministers from Outside Parliament*. London: The Constitution Unit, University College London.

PART V

POLITICAL LEADERSHIP BELOW AND BEYOND THE NATIONAL LEVEL

CHAPTER 36

LOCAL POLITICAL LEADERS

COLIN COPUS AND STEVE LEACH

1 INTRODUCTION

THE study of local political leadership has been a long-established endeavour in the USA. Europe has more recently caught up in its desire to understand how locally elected leaders operate and their effectiveness in governing their localities.[1] The reason for the lag between US and European scholars reflects different expectations of the role and tasks of local government and councillors. Moreover, different constitutional settlements regarding local government are key influences in determining the role that it plays and the relationship it has with the centre and shape the way scholars study local political leadership (see Borraz and John 2004). Yet it would be wrong to draw an oversimplistic dichotomy between US and European scholarly approaches to local political leadership. Europe is not a cohesive whole when it comes to the position of local government or local leadership in constitutional settlements. In the USA there are different styles, structures, and approaches towards local government, both within and between states, which should be recognized. Constitutional arrangements, expectations, roles, functions, powers, and the raw politics of local government vary not only within and across continents, but over time.

In this chapter we begin by reviewing how academic study of local political leadership has changed and developed. Starting from the assumption that political leadership implies political action, we then examine the importance of the tasks of local political leaders, the context within which those tasks are carried out, and the influences that shape how political leaders act (Leach and Wilson 2000). In Section 3 we examine the

---

[1] That is not to say that studies of local politics and local government have not flourished outside the USA, as the existence of much in-depth case-study-based work, which spans the decades, has shown (Birch 1959; Bealey, Blondel, and McCann 1965; Jones 1969; Gerontas 1972; Newton 1976; Glassberg 1981; Green 1981; Borraz 1998; Spiggos 1998).

context within which local political leadership is conducted, highlighting the importance of understanding the constraints and opportunities that influence the use of political power by local leaders. Section 4 explores the tasks that local political leaders carry
out and the approaches they take towards dealing with those tasks within the contextual
setting of local political leadership. The fifth section examines the skills and capabilities
of local political leaders as a way of understanding how and why they do what they do.
The final section summarizes the conclusions of the chapter and outlines proposals for
rationalizing the study of local political leadership.

2 Developments in the Study of Local Political Leadership

Much of our understanding of local political leadership developed from studies conducted in the USA. Dahl's empirical study (1961) of political power in New Haven presented a pluralist perspective, where no one group dominated political space. Dahl
recognized the existence of inequalities in local political power and showed that the
mayor's office became a conduit through which inequalities could be attenuated and
new policy initiatives generated. Indeed, by access to political space created through
representative democracy, groups with varying resources could have some political
influence.

Dahl explored the politics of New Haven by examining three key areas—education,
development, and political office—to identify who dominated decisions and political
direction and what opposition they had to overcome. Observable political action and its
outcomes provide understanding of political leadership, and a pluralistic political system can be identified through the way in which politically active citizens forge access
to the mayor. The mayor responds by providing direction, shape, and focus to the wide
array of messages that would be received through the political system in which anyone,
albeit unequally, could participate.

Dahl's work was a response to earlier approaches developed by the school of elite theorist Hunter (1953). The work of this school was itself influenced by earlier elite theorists such as Pareto, Mosca, and Michels. Michel's 'iron law of oligarchy' (1915) holds
as inevitable that a small elite, often enhancing its status and position by the development of a bureaucratic structure, will dominate political systems and decision-making.
Political decision-making for Hunter (1953) was dominated by business elites, whose
privileged position and resources enabled them to protect and promote their own interests through the city's political system and its political leaders. Business elites, acting as
coherent groups, were able to control the political agenda, and the role of relatively weak
politicians is to respond positively to that agenda.

The problem for elite theorists is identifying the elite, particularly a business elite,
which is conducting most of its activities outside the public political space. Such elites

may not act as a cohesive group, but rather display different interests depending on the business concerned. Lukes's third dimension of power (1974) highlights the need to account for observable demonstrations of power, but also for hidden, unobservable, and even latent political power. The problem for elite theorists is to construct a convincing analysis of what cannot be seen without descending into conspiracy theories (see Pakulski and Korosenyi 2011). Yet we also know that, as the pluralists admit, power and access to it is unevenly distributed and, as a consequence, political leaders respond to some interests more than others, and that some interests will be ignored.

The case-study approach often used to explore political leadership focuses on the actions of particular political leaders in specific locations and provides a deep and rich picture of personalities, processes, and power. It can also explore the development of political leadership over time in given settings (see Jones and Norton 1978; Savitch and Thomas 1991). Studies of political leadership drawing on this wealth of empirical material are now able to construct an analytical framework that develops concepts of local political leadership to explain tasks, styles, context, and behaviour and that can account for the influence of structure across different local government systems (see Genieys, Ballart and Valarie 2004; Back 2005; Morrell and Hartley 2006).

The study of local political leadership has shifted over time from a deep case-based analysis of particular leaders, to a general concern with tasks and functions and an understanding of systemic constraints and enablers that have an impact on the effectiveness of political leaders. Studies are now able to draw out generalizable lessons that account for the formal and informal power available to local political leaders and their system-based resources and to do so in a way that crosses national boundaries.

3 Contextualizing Local Political Leadership

Local political leadership is multi-contextual, as a series of relationships and developments in structural frameworks and settings influence changes in the way political leadership operates. Borraz and John (2004) identify four European trends that provide a context within which political leadership is shaped and conducted: the development of new and complex governing networks; a new set of political values held by local political leaders (citing Clark and Hoffmann-Martinot 1998; see also Szucs and Stromberg 2009); the emergence of models of stronger, executive local leadership across Europe; and the mimicking of other forms and approaches to leadership from other governmental settings.

The interdependence of political actors, horizontally and vertically, and with local citizens, emphasizes the mutuality of leadership, working in conjunction with others, rather than leadership locally being the product solely of the strength of personality of the leader. Yet, John and Cole (1999) found, in Leeds, England, a stable, hierarchical, and deferential leadership arrangement where power rested with the council leader—a situation that did not change despite a change of leader and policy emphasis. It was the broader context of the 'political, cultural and institutional heritage' (John and Cole 1999: 106) of that city that was the powerful contextual setting that shaped the actions of two very different political leaders.

Goldsmith and Larsen (2004) argue that, even when acknowledging the contexts identified by Borraz and John (2004), the transformation of local political leadership, which they identify, is not assured. They demonstrate that local political leadership within Nordic countries, for historical, cultural, political, economic, social, and structural reasons, has undergone far less change than in other European nations. They argue that Nordic local government has been 'less exposed to the full impact of globalization' (Goldsmith and Larsen 2004: 121) and experienced less penetration of the ideas of New Public Management. As a consequence, Nordic local government has maintained a model of collective–consensus-style decision-making, within comparatively small and homogeneous municipalities, thus bucking a European trend towards stronger, individualized local political leadership—a trend also diluted in England with the reluctance of councils to introduce directly elected mayors (Copus 2006 and 2011).

Leach and Wilson (2002) support John and Cole's suggestion that there is no deterministic relationship between 'contextual pressure' (John and Cole 1999: 685) and leadership practice. Good access to central government, for example, is a structural and institutional context that provides local leaders with considerable influence, beyond their localities, which can also benefit those localities (Greamion 1976). Such access is effective only if the leader has the capabilities successfully to employ that resource: access does not determine success.

Lowndes and Leach linked the *capabilities* of political leaders (their skills and capacities), particularly those that enable leaders to 'interpret contextual variables and to mobilize political support' to 'institutional environments' or *contexts* (Lowndes and Leach 2004: 565). Key elements of the latter were the formal and informal rules, or *constitutions*, of a specific political setting, which could be protected from externally driven change. The contextual framework of local leaders consists of: the council constitution; local political and organizational traditions and culture; legislative structures; the wider, externally driven political agenda; and the socioeconomic/geographic profile of the locality (Lowndes and Leach 2004: 566). Context is not, however, deterministic; it demands a response from local leaders, and it sets the features and landscape that leaders must navigate if they are successfully to motivate and to shape political action. Indeed, leaders are both shaped by and in turn shape the context within which they are located and operate.

US studies by Svara (1990) and Morgan and Watson (1996) indicate that mayors can rise above system and structural constraints, even where those constraints have been designed to blunt political power, to extend their power and influence beyond formally recognized limits. The ability to do this brings us back to the individual capabilities of the leader. Systems constraints, however, may be about much more than blunting political power and involve changing the very nature of local political leadership.

Developments in US local politics and government exemplified a difference of ideology between politicians who recognized and used the powerful contextual resource of party politicization for their own ends and reformers who sought to change structures and powers to depoliticize local government. Indeed, for a time in the US machine politics had an easier ride at the municipal level than nationally.[2] Much of the municipal reformers' programme was aimed at diluting the party political context of local politics from which leaders drew strength and resources (see Ostrogorski 1902). Over time US local politics saw a contextual shift, with non-partisanship becoming widespread.

So far we have identified the local contexts within which local political leaders operate. These include the features, traditions, histories, and political cultures rooted in a specific locality bounded by the council, which influence, but do not fully determine, the dynamic of political leadership in a given locality. The meso-contextualization is created and structured by factors beyond the locality, such as the development of complex governing networks that operate at a supra-local and regional (or state) level.[3]

We now turn briefly to the macro-level. The constitutional status of local government marks out the freedom and independence it and local political leaders have from the centre and also whether the centre (or some other higher level of government) is able to re-engineer the structure, institutions, powers, functions, and responsibilities of political leadership.

In systems with written constitutions—either federal, such as Germany, or unitary, such as Sweden—a recognition of the rights of local self-government will be enshrined. The central state can further devolve responsibility for local government to the states within a federation, in which case the key relationship for local political leaders is with the state or region rather than at the federal level. Yet, even where a constitution provides local government with a recognized place in the governing framework, Egner and Heinelt (2006) have shown that local government is not free from centrally inspired reforms. Indeed, a pattern has emerged, across Europe, where relatively strong local government has been contextually altered through pressure by upper tiers of government (see Loughlin, Hendriks, and Lidstrom 2011).

The centre–local context may develop as a hybrid system where the focus of the local political leader on an upper tier of government may vary within a single state. The UK is currently an example of hybridization. The devolved Scottish Parliament, and Welsh and Northern Ireland Assemblies are democratic intermediary bodies between local government and UK central government. It is with those intermediary bodies that local political leaders interact in those countries. Such a body is lacking in England, which was excluded from the Celto-centric constitutional devolution arrangements. Local political leaders in England, with no such intermediary body with whom to interact or to act on their behalf, must face the UK central state.

---

[2] The Democratic Party's Tammany Hall machine, which held sway in New York for almost eighty years, provided political leaders—elected and un-elected—with a contextual setting in which they could wield considerable power over the daily lives and prospects of their fellow citizens (see Allen 1993; Finegold 1995; Burrows and Wallace 1999).

[3] Or, by distinctive economic, political, and socio-geographic factors that extend far beyond the boundaries of a council, but that are themselves constrained by wider national pressures, policy networks, and the nature of intergovernmental interactions and hierarchal relationships.

The context within which local political leadership operates is multi-level, developing from a set of local, specific features through to complex supra-local, regional (state) elements to national and constitutional settlements. The contextual levels provide a set of inter-related conditions that set the parameters within which political action can be taken. An appreciation of context is necessary to understand how and why local leadership varies and the way local leaders can effect action.

4 LOCAL POLITICAL LEADERSHIP IN ACTION

Political leadership is a dynamic process in which getting things done goes hand-in-hand with providing political direction (Mouritzen and Svara 2002: 52). In exploring how and why local leadership varies in effecting action, we need to examine their behaviour as well as tasks and functions. John and Cole (1999) identify four influences on leaders' styles and behaviour: psychological–personal; institutional factors; party organization and systems; and political culture. Leach and Wilson (2000) have stressed the link between political culture and leadership behaviour, which enables us to understand how a leader's ability to influence, inspire, or persuade others to follow ('soft' powers) (see Burns 1978; Elcock 2001) may compensate for a lack of formal 'hard' powers. To understand behaviour it becomes necessary to examine how local political leaders address their tasks or roles and then assess how the different attributes of political leaders influence their ability to effect action (Stone 1995).

Identifying and explaining leadership tasks has to be a key element in building an understanding of what political leaders do and why. In exploring how political leaders set about achieving their different tasks, Stone (1995) assessed differences that had occurred as a result of action taken by the leader. Leaders must overcome political resistance, relate to citizens and their input to political decision-making, and ensure that their values make a long-term and strategic difference (see Greasley and Stoker 2009). Should the leader be less than successful in carrying out the required tasks or in securing the achievement of his or her policy preferences, then the fault may lie with the inability of the leader fully to utilize the facilities (formal or informal) available him or her; alternatively, a leader skilled in building coalitions and engaging citizens can become effective in dealing with intransigent issues (Stone 1995).

Scholars commonly categorize types of local political leaders (Kotter and Lawrence 1974; Svara 1987; Stoker et al. 2003), and these categories often reflect the priority or preference political leaders give to one aspect or another of their tasks. Such choice is not unconstrained but is shaped by leadership preference, context and unexpected political, social, and economic events. Political leaders, however, will seek to shape, control, and lead events and to use them to pursue policy, and political and ideological goals. Indeed, task orientation is an indicator of the likely reactive or proactive approach to leadership that is taken—with the proactive leader displaying a clear 'personal agenda', as opposed to a 'reactive' leader being more likely to lack any clear agenda (see Leach and Wilson 2000: 32).

A leadership candidate not expecting to win an election can be propelled into office. Stuart Drummond, the directly elected mayor of Hartlepool in England, when he first stood, admitted to being a 'joke candidate'. Calling himself 'H'Angus the Monkey' after the mascot of the local football team, he donned a monkey costume while campaigning. The name H'Angus is a pun on a nickname for people from Hartlepool: 'monkey hangers'.[4] On becoming the surprise winner of the election, he quickly dropped the monkey suit and was re-elected twice. Although initially he showed the signs of a mayor who would lack a clear direction, Drummond's careful stewardship of the council, his 'independent' status, and his ability to work closely with officials have shown that political leadership need not require an ideological agenda, but does need a skilled operator to ensure task accomplishment.

It is possible that political leaders—working closely with council officials—are more 'responsive' than 'proactive' and are heavily influenced by the advice, support, and guidance received from officials (Leach 2010). The way local leaders carry out their tasks is shaped by their relationship with the local managerial elite. The division of labour and working relationship between political and managerial leaders will set the direction of the council and construct a set of positive or negative working conditions, pivotal for the success of either in their respective fields (Leach 2010).

Stone (1995: 96) emphasizes that 'leadership revolves around purpose and purpose is at the heart of the leader–follower relationship', but local, political, and managerial leaders have to work in tandem, otherwise the followers do not know whom to follow (Leach 2010). While political leaders can point to their election as a source of legitimacy, it will be insufficient to rely on this alone when constructing both 'purpose' and 'follower' relations; leaders who claim only office as a source of legitimacy and authority will sound hollow and unconvincing.

The skills leaders display in generating support for their vision and direction, and constructing public and media willingness to follow, are contingent on political acumen and circumstances. The mayor of London, Boris Johnson, capitalized on the London 2012 Olympic Games, through a careful mix of charisma, opportunism, and ambassadorial focus, to develop a stock of political capital valuable to securing future support.

5 The Power of Personal Factors in Politics

The example of the mayor of London, shows that a leader's personal qualities, characteristics, and public image need to be understood for what they contribute to local politics (see Elcock 2001: 62). Understanding personal qualities illuminates why some political

---

[4] The term comes from local folklore that during the Napoleonic Wars a monkey was washed ashore after a French shipwreck (allegedly wearing a French uniform, in which it may have been placed to amuse the crew). Local people, unable to understand its language, promptly hanged it as a French spy.

leaders act the way they do and why some are more successful than others at generating followers. Yet voters may know little of the skills of leadership candidates and rely on party label to make their choice; where leaders are chosen by a council majority group, the voters have no say, nor any knowledge of an individual candidate. Even so, potential and actual leaders must impress some constituency.

The skills political leaders display can be contradictory. Elcock (2001: 32–3) reminds us that great oratory and 'quiet competence' are two sides of the charisma coin. The leader's ability to communicate to mass audiences though large-scale public events of old, or today's mass media, contrasts with the need to work in small, complex networks. In local politics, opportunities to impress voters through an outpouring of rhetorical skill are limited. The grand speech may come in handy within a political party, and there is evidence that selectors—if not electors—are still impressed by passion and persuasion in swaying a party meeting (Copus 2004; Leach 2006). Local political leaders, however, require the skill to communicate, cajole, and convince a range of audiences: national and regional politicians, civil servants, local business, church and community leaders, and citizens; and to do so in small, discursive settings (Bjorna and Aarsaether 2009; Schaap, Daemen, and Ringeling 2009). Moreover, the challenge of convincing an expert manager or professional officer of a leader's desired course, or of spanning the political and managerial divide, is facilitated not only by structure and power but by personal skill (for a US example, see Lapuente 2010).

Determination in pursuit of simple decisions to long-term goals or vision, and an ability to garner political support inside and outside by developing community networks and deploying them as resources, add to the political leader's armoury (Boogers and van Ostaaijen 2009; Bochel and Bochel 2010). Flexibility and compromise are necessary in forging such networks, but these qualities are not always found in leaders determined to pursue an ideological agenda. English local government has been littered with ideologically driven local leaders who were not noted for their willingness to compromise. Most of these uncompromising leaders emerged during the 1980s in urban settings: Derek Hatton, Liverpool; Shirley Porter, Westminster; Ted Knight, Lambeth; and Ken Livingstone, Greater London Council. The achievement of their ideological agenda rested not on network-building outside the council, but on the existence of a group of like-minded individuals within a political party, sharing the leader's ideological goals and providing unified and reliable political support. As Mayor of London, however, Livingstone did recognize the need to operate outside the Mayor's office and to build wider coalitions, although these often reflected his left-wing politics (Livingstone 2011).

Given the trend towards the direct election of the mayor across Europe (Berg and Rao 2005; Denters and Rose 2005), we can see how personal factors or charisma increasingly becomes an issue. The term 'personality' is often used pejoratively in local politics to justify the view that a focus on policy is more important than individual qualities. As political leaders can wield considerable power and influence, some assessment of the characteristics of the potential leader, by the voter, makes sense; the voter will want to know if candidates at the very least possess qualities such as honesty and integrity. We now briefly review two different national settings—the Netherlands and France—to show how political and personal capability can be helped or hindered by constitutional arrangements and by the structure, power, and functions of the organizations that they lead.

In the Netherlands, the mayor is not an elected council member but is appointed by central government for a six-year period. Councils will make nominations to the government and can hold a consultative referendum on potential candidates. The Dutch minister, appointing the mayor, will take into account the political orientation of each council, and many mayors, although not members (or even residents) of the area, will be members of the governing political parties (see Hendriks and Schaap 2010). That mayors may have been nominated by a council means that there is some connection between mayor and council, but this is not as great as where the mayor is directly elected or an elected member of the council.

The mayor chairs the council and the College of Aldermen; the latter forms the council executive and consists of two to nine members with the mayor. The Aldermen are appointed by the council and on appointment cease to be a councillor (the next person on the party list takes the seat vacated by the new Alderman). Aldermen can be recalled by the council; the mayor cannot, but can lose the confidence of the council, and while he or she does not have to step down from office his or her authority will be undermined. Aldermen and the mayor may hold separate portfolios, but they act collectively in the day-to-day administration of the council and the implementation of its decisions. The Dutch mayor is more akin to a career civil servant than a politician, and, indeed, in some areas the mayor acts for the central state.

Political leadership in Dutch municipalities is of a collective and shared kind, resting on a division of political labour with blurred edges. Chairing the council and College of Aldermen provides influence but not hard political power to the mayor. As in any collective political process, the acumen and political skill of any individual and the ability to accrue resources and support may tip the balance of power; but a division of labour means that political players in Dutch municipalities can also provide leadership in their respective spheres.

By contrast, the French mayor holds considerable political power, being the elected head of the municipality and a representative of the central state within it. The mayor is appointed by the council, but is normally the individual heading the winning party list. In municipalities with a population of over 3,500, the mayor's power base is strengthened by the winning list, in either the first or second round of voting, being awarded half the council seats; the remaining seats are redistributed proportionally across all lists (lists are open, and so voters may vote across lists for individual candidates).

The French mayor is the executive head of the council and derives power from the structural setting within which the office is located, especially as it is the mayor who proposes and implements the council's budget. The mayor also implements decisions of the council, which, as a powerful local political leader, will be shaped by the mayor's own direction and desire to forge effective political action. Mayors are further able to enhance their position by appointing their own cabinet and delegating responsibilities to members, appointing support staff and other municipal posts.

Thoenig (2005) contends that councillors are politically dependent on the mayor and not the mayor on the very councillors who formally appoint him or her. Indeed, for councillors, simply securing election has not been seen as a sufficient source of political legitimacy; and proximity to a high-profile, publicly recognized and politically powerful mayor enhances the status and legitimacy of council members (see Thoenig 1995, cited in Mouritzen and Svara 2002). There is a local political centralization, with the mayor firmly placed at that centre.

The French mayor plays a pivotal role in linking the municipalities with the centre, often by working with locally based state agencies, thus increasing their political influence with the centre (Crozier and Thoenig 1976). The French tradition of mayors also holding higher political office, most notably at the centre, creates a flow of influence from the locality upwards through the mayor. Thus, the French mayor is granted formal organizational and political powers, which extend beyond the municipality itself and strengthen local political leadership while rooting it firmly in the locality.

6 Conclusion: Understanding Local Political Leadership

There is a pervasive assumption in much American literature and more recent UK studies that a reason for studying local political leadership is to change it. Its particular perspective (especially the perceived importance of limiting the power of local political leaders, and the associated opportunities for corruption) resulted, in many cases, in an instrumental approach to such studies that reduced the opportunities for a more balanced and productive evaluation.

Similarly, the UK literature since 2000 suggests that the desire to change local political systems may have provided a similar potential for distortion. The enthusiasm for directly elected mayors among academics and governments does not result in anything parallel to the 'city manager' movement in the USA. Enthusiasts for elected mayors have been eager to demonstrate the success of the new initiative, while those who have a more critical predisposition have tended to emphasize its drawbacks and limitations. Examples of perceived 'success' (Ray Mallon in Middleborough) and 'failure' (successive elected mayors in Doncaster) have been used selectively to strengthen the arguments that the proponents (or detractors) of the idea wish to make.

European literature has, by and large, managed to avoid the problems of distorted comparative evaluation experienced in the USA and the UK. Yet the uniqueness of national constitutional arrangements and political cultures has militated against fruitful comparisons. It is notable that, in many edited volumes seeking to make such comparisons, much space is committed to descriptions of particular constitutional arrangements, without it proving possible (for contributor or editor) to 'allow for' constitutional differences in their subsequent analysis. There are exceptions. The similarities of the constitutional arrangements and political cultures of the Scandinavian countries have resulted in some fruitful inter-nation comparisons (see, e.g., Goldsmith and Page 2010).

A further problem in synthesizing and comparing research findings, within and between countries, is inconsistency in the definition and application of the term 'leadership'. In the USA and the UK an unhelpful distinction has been made between 'strong' and 'weak' leadership (Judd 2000). Sometimes this distinction is applied to the range of powers enjoyed by the leader (for example, 'strong' and 'weak' mayors in the US literature). Sometimes it is applied to the behaviour of the leader concerned: in England, Ray Mallon is widely viewed as a 'strong' elected mayor, while his Hartlepool counterpart, Stuart Drummond, has been characterized as a relatively weak example, but has proved to be an 'effective' leader in task accomplishment, which has seen him twice re-elected.

The notion of 'effective' leadership is a more helpful aid to analysis than distinctions between 'strong' and 'weak' leadership. There are two ways in which effective leadership can be considered: the generic set of 'leadership tasks' (see Section 4); and effectiveness in achieving the leader's agenda, which would also include success in persuading the public to grant further terms of office. The Drummond example illustrates a further ambiguity in some leadership studies. There is a tendency to equate 'leadership' with what formally designated leaders do, or to assume that leadership is a process dominated by a single individual. Indeed, there are well-known examples of dominant leaders, including several who operated without the formal powers enjoyed currently by leaders in England (for example, Dame Shirley Porter, George Mudie, and T. Dan Smith). It may equally be the case that the formally designated leader is not the de facto leader (for example, John Hamilton in the Derek Hatton-dominated Liverpool City Council of the 1980s), or that leadership tasks are distributed among several individuals, or that leadership is operated on a 'collective' basis. Leadership should not too readily be 'individualized' if we are to understand the varied processes that operate in reality.

Despite these reservations and caveats, there are a number of concepts that are helpful in understanding (and comparing) local political leadership. The importance of constitutions, culture (political and organizational), and capabilities are highlighted time and time again in studies, although the terminology used to characterize them varies. The constitutional context in which political leaders operate, the legislation detailing powers and responsibilities, and the way this legislation is locally interpreted (there is often scope for choice) in the formal constitutions adopted by councils are a crucial influence on local political leadership. They constrain, provide opportunities, but do not determine the way leadership operates. Similarly, the local cultural context, embracing political and managerial traditions, expectations, values, and norms, is influential. In any nation, there will be a fair amount of common ground here (for example, in relation to the way party groups operate), but also a good deal of scope for local variation.

Whatever the powers enjoyed by a leader, capabilities will be crucial in influencing the extent to which he or she can take advantage of these opportunities, and provide 'effective leadership' (in terms of the criteria of 'effective leadership' identified earlier). Not least among these capabilities is the extent to which a leader works with a chief executive to ensure that the latter fully understands the leader's political priorities, and that a mutually acceptable division of labour in achieving them can be agreed (Leach 2010: 48).

There are three key research tasks for studies of local political leadership: first, to clarify what constitutes 'effective leadership' in the specific context studied (an identification of generic leadership tasks provides a basis for comparative work, within which the different agendas of individual leaders would need to be recognized). The second task is an assessment of the extent to which effective leadership is exercised (in relation both to generic tasks and to individual agendas). Finally, the third task is an examination of the part played by constitutions, culture, and capabilities in the extent to which these tasks/goals are achieved.

Although there is scope for international comparative analysis in these terms, the differences in constitutional arrangements and political culture will limit the extent to which generalizations can be made. Within nations, however, where constitutional arrangements will be similar, and there is likely to be a good deal of common ground in terms of political culture (for example, party group behaviour; national party expectations of local party groups), there is tremendous potential for fruitful comparative work, provided, of course, that the normative and instrumental predilections that have hampered studies of local political leadership in the past can be avoided or minimized.

RECOMMENDED READING

Borraz, O., and John, P. (2004). 'The Transformation of Urban Political Leadership in Western Europe', *International Journal of Urban and Regional Research*, 28/1: 107–20.
Leach, S., and Wilson, D. (2000). *Local Political Leadership*. Bristol: Policy Press.
Stone, C. (1995). 'Political Leadership in Urban Politics', in D. Judge, G. Stoker, and H. Wolman (eds), *Theories of Urban Politics*. London: Sage, 96–116.

REFERENCES

Allen, O. (1993). *The Tiger: The Rise and Fall of Tammany Hall*. Reading, MA: Addison-Wesley.
Back, H. (2005). 'The Institutional Setting of Local Political Leadership and Community Involvement', in M. Haus, H. Heinelt and M. Stewart (eds), *Urban Governance and Democracy: Leadership and Community Involvement*. London: Routledge, 65–101.
Bealey, F., Blondel, J., and McCann, W. P. (1965). *Constituency Politics: A Study of Newcastle-under-Lyme*. London: Faber and Faber.
Berg, R., and Rao, N. (2005) (eds). *Transforming Local Political Leadership*. Basingstoke: Palgrave Macmillan.
Birch, A. H. (1959). *Small Town Politics: A Study of Political Life in Glossop*. London: Oxford University Press.
Bjorna, H., and Aarsaether, N. (2009). 'Local Government Strategies and Entrepreneurship', *International Journal of Innovation and Regional Development*, 2/1: 50–65.

Bochel, H., and Bochel, C. (2010). 'Local Political Leadership and the Modernisation of Local Government', *Local Government Studies*, 36/6: 723–37.

Boogers, M., and van Ostaaijen, J. (2009). 'Who's the Boss in Sss? Power Structures in Local Governance Networks'. Unpublished conference paper. European Group for Public Administration conference, Malta.

Borraz, O. (1998). *Gouverner une ville: Besançon, 1959–1989*. Rennes: Presses Universitaires de Rennes.

Borraz, O., and John, P. (2004). 'The Transformation of Urban Political Leadership in Western Europe', *International Journal of Urban and Regional Research*, 28/1: 107–20.

Burns, J. (1978). *Leadership*. New York: Harper and Row.

Burrows, E., and Wallace, M. (1999). *Gotham: A History of New York City to 1898*. New York: Oxford University Press.

Clark, T. N., and Hoffmann-Martinot, V. (1998) (eds). *The New Political Culture*. Boulder, CO: Westview Press.

Copus, C. (2004). *Party Politics and Local Government*. Manchester: Manchester University Press.

Copus, C., (2006). *Leading the Localities: Executive Mayors in English Local Governance*. Manchester: Manchester University Press.

Copus, C., (2011). 'Elected Mayors in English Local Government: Mayoral Leadership and Creating a New Political Dynamic', *Lex Localis: The Journal of Local Self-Government*, 9/4: 335–51.

Crozier, M., and Thoenig, J. C. (1976). 'The Regulation Of Complex Organized Systems', *Administrative Science Quarterly*, 2/4: 547–70.

Dahl, R. A. (1961). *Who Governs?* New Haven, CT: Yale University Press.

Denters, B., and Rose, L. (2005). *Comparing Local Governance: Trends and Developments*. Basingstoke: Palgrave Macmillan.

Egner, B., and Heinelt, H. (2006). 'European Mayors and Administrative Reforms', in H. Back, H. Heinelt and A. Magnier (eds), *The European Mayor: Political Leaders in the Changing Context of Local Democracy*. Wiesbaden: Verlag für Sozialwissenschaften, 335–52.

Elcock, H. (2001). *Political Leadership*. Cheltenham: Edward Elgar.

Finegold, K. (1995). *Experts and Politicians: Reform Challenges to Machine Politics in New York, Cleveland, and Chicago*. Princeton: Princeton University Press.

Gerontas, D. (1972). *Historia tou Demou Athinaion (1835–1971)* (History of the Municipality of Athens (1835–1971)). Athens: Municipality of Athens.

Genieys, W., Ballart, X., and Valarie, P. (2004). 'From "Great" Leaders to Building Networks: The Emergence of a New Urban Leadership in Southern Europe?', *International Journal of Urban and Regional Research*, 28/1: 183–99.

Glassberg, A. (1981). *Representation and Urban Community*. Basingstoke: Macmillan.

Goldsmith, M., and Larsen, H. (2004). 'Local Political Leadership: Nordic Style', *International Journal of Urban and Regional Research*, 28/1: 121–33.

Goldsmith, M., and Page, E. (2010) (eds). *Changing Government Relations in Europe: From Localism to Intergovernmentalism*. London: Routledge/European Consortium for Political Research.

Greamion, P. (1976). *Le Pouvoir peariphearique*. Paris: Éditions du Seuil.

Greasley, S., and Stoker, G. (2009). 'Urban Political Leadership', in J. Davis and D. Imbroscio (eds), *Theories of Urban Politics*. London: Sage, 125–36.

Green, D. (1981). *Power and Party in an English City: An Account of Single-Party Rule*. London: Allen and Unwin.

Hendriks, F., and Schaap, L. (2010). 'The Netherlands: Reinventing Tradition in Local and Regional Democracy', in J. Loughlin, F. Hendriks, and A. Lidström (eds), *The Oxford Handbook of Local and Regional Democracy in Europe*. Oxford: Oxford University Press, 96–119.

Hunter, F. (1953). *Community Power Structure: A Study of Decision Makers*. Chapel Hill, NC: University of North Carolina Press.

John, P., and Cole, A. (1999). 'Political Leadership in the New Urban Governance: Britain and France Compared', *Local Government Studies*, 25/4: 98–115.

Jones, G. W. (1969). *Borough Politics: A Study of Wolverhampton Borough Council 1888–1964*. Basingstoke: Macmillan.

Jones, G. W., and Norton, A. (1978) (eds). *Political Leadership in Local Authorities*. Birmingham: Institute of Local Government Studies.

Judd, D. (2000). 'Strong Leadership', *Urban Studies*, 37/5: 951–61.

Kotter, J. P., and Lawrence, P. R. (1974). *Mayors in Action: 5 Approaches to Urban Governance*. New York: John Wiley and Sons.

Lapuente, V. (2010). 'A Tale of Two Cities: Bureaucratisation in Mayor-Council and Council-Manager Municipalities', *Local Government Studies*, 36/6: 739–57.

Leach, S. (2006). *The Changing Role of Local Politics in Britain*. Bristol: Policy Press.

Leach, S. (2010). *Managing in a Political World: The Life Cycle of Local Authority Chief Executives*. Basingstoke: Palgrave Macmillan.

Leach, S., and Wilson, D. (2000). *Local Political Leadership*. Bristol: Policy Press.

Leach, S., and Wilson, D. (2002). 'Rethinking Local Political Leadership', *Public Administration*, 80/4: 665–689.

Livingstone, K. (2011). *You can't Say That*. London: Faber and Faber.

Loughlin, J., Hendriks, F., and Lidstrom, A. (2011). *The Oxford Handbook of Local and Regional Democracy in Europe*. Oxford: Oxford University Press.

Lowndes, V., and Leach, S. (2004). 'Understanding Local Political Leadership: Constitutions, Contexts and Capabilities', *Local Government Studies*, 30/4: 557–75.

Lukes, S. (1974). *Power: A Radical View*. Basingstoke: Macmillan.

Michels, R. (1915). *Political Parties: A Sociological Study of the Oligarchical Tendencies of Modern Democracy*. Translated into English by Eden Paul and Cedar Paul. Glencoe, IL: Free Press. Originally published in German in 1911.

Morgan, D., and Watson, S. (1996). 'Mayors of American Cities: An Analysis of Powers and Responsibilities', *American Review of Public Administration*, 26/1: 113–25.

Morrell, K., and Hartley, J. (2006). 'A Model of Political Leadership', *Human Relations*, 59/4: 483–504.

Mouritzen, P., and Svara, J. (2002). *Leadership at the Apex: Politicians and Administrators in Western Local Governments*. Pittsburgh, PA: University of Pittsburgh Press.

Newton, K. (1976). *Second City Politics: Democratic Processes and Decision-Making in Birmingham*. Oxford: Clarendon Press.

Ostrogorski, M. (1902). *Democracy and the Organization of Political Parties*, Vols. I and II. New York: Macmillan.

Pakulski, J., and Korosenyi, A. (2011). *Toward Leader Democracy*. London: Athem Press.

Savitch, H., and Thomas, J. (1991) (eds). *Big City Politics in Transition*. London: SAGE.

Schaap, L., Daemen, H. H. F. M., and Ringeling, A. B. (2009). 'Mayors in Seven European Countries, Part II: Performance and Analysis', *Local Government Studies*, 35/2: 235–51.

Spiggos, G. N. 1998. *I Topiki Aftodiekisi stin Kerkyra 1864–1998*. Corfu: Apostrofos.

Stoker, G., Gains, F., John, P., Rao, N., and Harding, A. (2003). *Implementing the 2000 Act with Respect to New Council Constitutions and the Ethical Framework*. First Report of the Evaluating Local Governance Team, June. London: Office of the Deputy Prime Minister.

Stone, C. (1995). 'Political Leadership in Urban Politics', in D. Judge, G. Stoker, and H. Wolman (eds), *Theories of Urban Politics*. London: Sage, 96–116.

Svara, J. (1987). 'Mayoral Leadership in Council-Manager Cities: Preconditions versus Preconceptions', *Journal of Politics*, 49/1: 207–27.

Svara, J. (1990). *Official Leadership in the City: Patterns of Conflict and Cooperation*. Oxford: Oxford University Press.

Szucs, S., and Stromberg, L. (2009). 'The More Things Change, the More they Stay the Same: The Swedish Local Government Elite between 1985 and 2005', *Local Government Studies*, 35/2: 251–70.

Thoenig, J.-C. (1995). 'De l'incertitude en Gestion Territorial', *Politiques et management public*, 13/3: 1–27.

Thoenig, J.-C. (2005). 'Territorial Administration and Political Control: Decentralization in France', *Public Administration*, 83/3: 685–708.

CHAPTER 37

REGIONAL POLITICAL LEADERSHIP

JOHN WANNA

1 POLITICAL LEADERSHIP AT THE MESO-LEVEL: CHAMPIONS OF THE 'ELUSIVE SPACE'

REGIONAL political leaders occupy the 'second tier' meso-political domain, floating between the 'first tier' national (or international) government level and the community level including the 'third tier' municipal or local governments. Theirs is a form of constrained and territorially-bound political leadership that operates 'in-between' the standard categories of the jurisdictional matrix found within both federal and unitary nations. This meso-level can consist of fixed jurisdictional boundaries dictating the regional form (such as provinces or states within federations) where considerable regional autonomy is practised and constitutionally guaranteed (Sharpe 1993; Hueglin and Fenna 2006); or the notion of meso-politics can consist of subtler notions of geographic entity to which local residents subscribe a psychological or emotional attachment and which may constitute a sub-national administrative tier for certain policy or delivery functions (Hendriks, Raadshelders, and Toonen 1995). Furthermore, even within unitary states, distinct significant regions can express considerable autonomy due to historical legacies and prevailing regional attitudes (for example the Flemish region of Belgium). Some of these may even lack formal provincial status: for example, Greater Auckland in New Zealand (created 1963); or the Corsican or Bretagne regions of France which have no real provincial standing other than a district name; and we could include regions such as Friesland in the Netherlands or Il Mezzogiorno in Southern Italy which may have a 'provincial label' but enjoy limited regional autonomy while retaining a degree of distinct local identity. Hence, this meso-level is an 'elusive space' and has no precise political dimensions (unlike, say, nation states or even municipal government) and may exist *sui generis* in each polity in which it has historical expression and contemporary salience (Toonen 1993; Hooghe 1996; Keating 1998a, 2001b).

Regionalism is an expression of distinctiveness that provides identity to peripheries (Rokkan and Urwin 1983). The mix of forces that shape regional identity may vary considerably: it can consist of an ancient inherited identity or a process of identity-building; it can exist from reactions to centralization; or be founded on organic notions of self-reliance and local autonomy; it can be constituted by regional ethnic nationalism or even separatism; and even given salience through national disintegration (as in Yugoslavia). The characteristics and cogency of a 'region' usually define and shape the imperatives of its leadership principally according to its evolving governing traditions (shaped by political, economic, cultural, ethno-linguistic, and geographic factors), set against the prevailing patterns of national politics and vis-à-vis other regions with different traditions (Rokkan 1980). While regional identity was once considered to be declining in the face of centralized nationalism and increasing internationalization (especially in the immediate aftermath of the Second World War), it has not only retained its salience in many parts of the world but often been revived and become more robust than previously—so that scholars talk of 'new regionalism' and the 'growth of regional authority' (see Hooghe, Marks, and Schakel 2010). Detecting this trend in the 1970s–90s, writers such as Rokkan, Wright, Unwin, Keating, Crozier, Sharpe, Mughan, Almond, and Simeon all highlighted the salience of regionalism (or decentralism) as a political phenomenon, its irrepressibility despite national effort towards assimilation, and the fluctuating dynamics of centre–periphery relations across almost all continents (see Sharpe 1979; Meny and Wright 1985).[1]

As one author argued specifically in relation to European regions: 'the region has thus become a key level of political dialogue and action, where national, continental and global forces meet local demands and social systems, forcing mutual adaptations and concessions' (Keating 1995: 3). Regional institutions and regional political leadership mediate these dialogues, adaptations, and concessions.

Often centre-periphery politics (or even region-to-region politics) is a highly-contested and highly-politicized domain, but the basis of such contestation can vary, involving perhaps political, economic, religious, and ethnic differences; historical legacies; resourcing issues and relative administrative capacities; and iconic or

---

[1] Throughout much of the twentieth century scholars and commentators tended to assume nationalist and internationalist forces would be predominant and that the prognosis for regionalist politics would see regions decline as greater global integration occurred. Regions were regarded largely as anachronistic—pre-industrial hangovers or pre-modern phenomena, which would inevitably succumb to global pressures. In recent times and despite (or perhaps because of) globalization, however, there has been a widespread regeneration in 'new regionalism' and demands for self-government that are not confined to one part of the globe. These developments include: Scottish and Welsh devolution in the UK; the granting of 'special administrative region' status to regions such as Hong Kong and Macau in mainland China; regional independence within the Philippines post-1991; the re-establishment of regions in Argentina and Brazil after the 1980s; and in many post-communist Euro-Asian republics and Sahara African states (see Montero 2001b; Eaton 2004; Dickovick 2006).

symbolic disputes over cultural concerns and local languages. Some regions are routinely locked into fiercely-fought contests with political adversaries at the national level or from other regions (as is the case in, e.g., Spain, the Balkans, the UK, Italy, Canada, Turkey, China). Acrimonious relations may date back decades, even centuries, limiting the agendas and scope for joint collaboration or endeavours, implying that mutual non-antagonism may be a routine political default (for example, Quebec in Canada, the Basque and Catalonian regions in Spain, the Flemish and Walloon regions of Belgium, or the Serbian and Croatian regions of the former Yugoslavia—see Montero 2001a; Valcke et al. 2008). At their most extreme these tensions boil over into civil wars or separatist liberation campaigns (for example the violent campaigns waged by the Tamils in Sri Lanka or the Basque ETA organization in Spain), while other forms of regional politics can be quite benign and 'civilized' (the public deliberative practices followed by the Swiss cantons, the Dutch provinces, the German Lander, US and Australian states).

Political leadership at the meso-level exists to represent and defend regional or peripheral interests, and the voice of regional advocates gives particular expression to regional values and sentiments, reinforcing identity through historical traditions, myths and symbolic elements, and institutional separateness (Rokkan and Urwin 1983: chs 1 and 3; Keating, 1998). The *styles of regional leadership* and the *political complexion* or *the actors* may vary but the institutional imperatives of the positions they hold and the roles they are called on to perform remain relatively enduring. Regional leaders of discrete sub-national polities often have considerable jurisdictional or administrative authority and frequently juxtapose their political objectives or leadership styles in contrast to central or national leaders/governments. These actors enjoy proximate power and are closer to the community and to specific local interests; but at the same time they are circumscribed by national powers. They often occupy powerful positions yet are at best semi-sovereign and constrained by constitutions, national laws, even by international treaties/obligations. Hence, political leadership at the regional level is generally subordinate but not necessarily subservient to national governments, as well as being coexistent with other rival or competing regions at the same jurisdictional level, and in addition often overseeing local jurisdictions (municipalities) within their boundaries.

To many observers, the realm of sub-national leadership is a shadowy area largely in the backdrop of national and international politics/developments. How much influence regional leadership can achieve (or what they can prevent or rebuff) largely depends on context and circumstance. The context is shaped by institutional arrangements and the degree of structural autonomy, the availability of resources and capacities, the legitimacy and political capital of regional institutions and actors vis-à-vis national or federal ones; while the circumstance involves the type of issues addressed or confronted, the visibility and political skills of the local leaders, and their strategies and tactics. Yet, regional leaders retain an ability to influence not only regional dynamics, but also national policy orientations, through various political strategies, tactical positioning, and civic leadership (Putnam 1993). National governments often need to gain regional consent, cooperation, or compliance, and many nations have established formal and informal mechanisms to seek such rapprochements (such as regular consultations, inter-governmental fora, ministerial councils, or commissions and annual governors' conferences). Regional political leaders represent discrete sub-national constituencies (of interests and voting blocs) at the national realm; they have a component stake in national politics and policies, and transmit regional values into national politics, policy debates, and policy-making outcomes. Regions can rely on their latent power within the federal/unitary nation state or more actively seek to persuade, exert lobbying pressure or impose electoral sanctions on national governments to pursue certain agendas (perhaps using bloc voting, strategic party voting, and bet-hedging).

So how has regional political leadership been studied and what do we know about its expression? This chapter first introduces the main approaches used to explore regional leadership—beginning with actor-centred accounts (biographies, taxonomies of leadership qualities, and relational-contingent studies). This is followed by a discussion of theories of territorial differentiation and regional leadership. A small number of the 'must reads' in the field have been identified from both these principal approaches. The methodologies used to explain regional leadership are canvassed before a critical assessment of the field overall is provided. Finally the chapter offers some promising ways forward and possible future directions.

2 Competing Approaches

Explanations of regional leadership can either be derived from our conceptual and methodological approaches to the subject (where explanations are the dependent variables), or appear as a function of the factors or criteria to be explained (as independent variables). In the former, explanations are more genres of studies, while in the latter they tend to emphasize themes in political science or regional development. In this section we canvass the main approaches, beginning with various actor-centred accounts of political leaders themselves as key actors, followed by diverse theoretical approaches combining frameworks of analysis with thematic inquiry, before commenting on the different methodologies for gauging the dynamics of regional politics.

Actor-Centred Genres

Mostly, actor-centric studies of meso-level political leaders are personalized historical narratives that describe a leader in a specific context. Their leadership is usually captured (overtly or obliquely) in *leadership biographies* or *case studies*, and there are a great many rich and diverse veins within this genre. Most accounts discuss notable politicians who rise to occupy formal regional political roles (governors, premiers, regional heads, etc.); others focus on civic leaders largely without formal office but with moral or influential authority (for example Robert Moses in New York, Emiliano Zapata in Mexico, Ian Paisley and Gerry Adams in Northern Ireland, and even Eugene Terre Blanche in

South Africa); and there are rarer accounts of regional-based spiritual leaders, such as Martin Luther King in the southern USA or the Tibetan Dalai Lama. The rationales for focusing on the political lives of these leaders may be their longevity in office, a certain idiosyncratic or colourful style, sometimes their appearance as out-of-the-ordinary leaders, and their general popularity and attractiveness to biographers (see Pimlott 1994). Many of these studies are relatively hagiographic (the 'great man in history' genre), but not all: some are studious portraits of leaders in context, and finally others are highly critical if not acerbic accounts written to expose shortcomings or even discredit adversaries—a sub-genre dating back to Plutarch and Seutonius (see Caro 1974; Skidelsky 1975; Ryan and McEwen 1979). The combination of longevity and idiosyncrasy is often sufficient to warrant interest (as with studies of Ralph Klein in Alberta, Joey Smallwood in Newfoundland, Joh Bjelke-Petersen in Queensland, and Robert Moses of New York, who was one of the most influential non-elected regional leaders). These were among the successful long-stayers who survived in leadership sub-national posts long enough to make a mark or establish leadership 'reigns'—the local 'boss politicians' or 'tin gods'— (see Wanna and Williams 2005). By contrast, there are far fewer accounts of regional leaders who occupied office for shorter terms, or studies of a succession of short-term leaders (and one might wonder why, when explanations of volatility, high turn-over, and succession management might provide another useful window into regional leadership). Likewise, very few scholars have chosen to examine *failed* leaders as compared to the successful ones. The criteria for failure sometimes are less well explored than those of success (but see Reynolds 2002 who points to political vulnerabilities, personal hesitancy, an inability to engender loyalty among colleagues and rapid political change). Given the relatively small size of regional polities (that often possess fewer checks and balances or countervailing powerbases), there are ample studies of the abuse of power or of corrupt leaders. A good example might be the infamous Democrat Huey Long in Louisiana, who was described as 'Louisiana's Hitler': his style was more akin to fascism than socialism, linking populist authoritarianism with curtailing press freedoms and martial law (Hair 1991: 296). Both Hair and the fictionalized *All the King's Men* (1946 by Robert Penn Warren) trace the political shortcomings that led to Long's downfall and assassination.

Biographies of significant national leaders often devote sections to periods they spent in regional leadership prior to attaining higher office. Many national leaders began their political careers cutting their political teeth as regional leaders; signifying that regional politics constituted both a testing ground and a formative influence in their political apprenticeships and subsequent careers and styles of governing (many presidents and prime ministers demonstrate this, for example Harry Truman, Jimmy Carter, Ronald Reagan, Bill Clinton, and George W. Bush in the USA, the Canadian PM Jean Chretien, and Germany's Helmut Kohl). This phenomenon is more noticeable in presidential systems (especially federal ones) where successful regional political leaders can throw their hat in the national ring to be competitive as president. It is far less pronounced in parliamentary and unitary systems where national party seniority and standing may be far more important and regional leaders are deficient in this regard, even if they enjoy popular approval (the most popular Canadian or Australian premiers, for example, have never managed to scale the federal divide). There is also some popular and scholarly interest in noticeable regional leaders who may have been expected to become important national figures but did not quite make it (for example Dan Quayle and Sarah Palin in the USA, and Quebec leaders such as Rene Levesque or Lucien Bouchard in Canada).

If analytical themes are found in biographies and individual case studies, they often revolve around the personal style of leadership, how leaders managed their leadership responsibilities, how they worked with/through colleagues, their strategic capacities or pet agendas, their ruthlessness or intolerance of opposition, and even strokes of luck or misfortune.

A second actor-centric approach is taxonomy, with an interest in distinguishing and labelling various styles of regional leadership as observed by contemporaries or researchers. Classification and taxonomy involves identifying or stipulating various defining characteristics of leaders, especially the factors that characterize sub-national types. Classifications typically centre on the individual's styles and *modus operandi* or on their expression of inherent regional characteristics. Examples of the latter include the agrarian socialists and prairie leadership style found in Canada (often based on authoritarian boss politicians with social credit philosophies), Australia's bunyip aristocracy of notable families, tin-pot Napoleons who governed US states, and demagogic separatists in Quebec and Scotland. Individual leadership style tends to be categorized into two groups of qualities—attributes of a given style or the predominant roles skilfully undertaken. The attributes of leadership style can vary enormously and include the heroic, charismatic, idealist, populist, reclusive, decisive, consultative, routinizer, and so on. The distinctive roles taken by such leaders centre on their notable preoccupations or skills (such as reformers, communicators, crisis managers, brokers, boss politicians, dictators and 'party machine' warriors, loyal delegates, crusaders against national jurisdictions, local boosterists, transformational versus routine transactional roles (Lusztig, James, and Moon 1997). Too often these types of leadership styles are presented as 'ideal type' juxtapositions—seemingly forming mutually exclusive alternatives, possible to describe but difficult to validate empirically.

A third approach, and probably the most analytical within this genre, traces the patterns of relations leaders manage to conduct or negotiate with other significant actors. It investigates 'political leadership' through the prism of relationships, aiming to judge the performance of individuals in leadership positions. For regional leaders this involves dealing upwards with national governments and even with international actors (vertical relations), or it can also include relations downwards between provinces/states and local jurisdictions. Furthermore, regional leaders engage in a constellation of relationships with actors and institutions also located at the regional level (depending on the formalization of the region). They can concern relations with the legislature, with their political party colleagues and party structures, with the bureaucracy, with political opponents, with the media, and with local interest groups and constituents (de Clercy 2005). The crucial test applied is often how well a given regional leader is able to sustain his/her leadership through management skills, issue management, coalition-building, building local links, and how they negotiate proximate arenas of conflict. So when Canadians ask whether their premiers are 'scaled down prime ministers' the answer usually is that they perform *some* similar political head of government tasks but that the considerably smaller domain and set of responsibilities within which they operate changes remarkably the scale, timeframes, institutional complexity, and level of management involvement they are able to exert (White 1988: 160). Hence, regional leadership is a distinct domain separate and different to national leadership, with its own players, rules, tacit knowledge, instincts, and vocabularies (Pal and Taras 1988: xvi).

Among the actor-centric genre, Robert Caro's realpolitik studies of Robert Moses in New York (Caro 1974) and the early career of Lyndon Johnson in Texas (Caro 1982) stand out as important classics. They are inordinately rich in historical detail (much from official records and private papers), and informed by a deep understanding of American politics; and Caro manages to wrestle constantly with his subjects, fluctuating between admiration and admonishment in their use and abuse of power. The many studies of Louisiana's Huey Long also come close to seminal studies of regional leadership, locating him as a southern US leader within a tradition of authoritarian fascism, motivated by graft and corruption but somehow compelled to serve higher public interests. It is hard to find such sophisticated studies of sub-national leaders in other parts of the world that have received such international recognition.

Institutional Theories of Territorial Differentiation

The main analytical explanations of regional leadership almost invariably locate it within broader interpretations of inter-jurisdictional theories. Federalist theories explain divided powers and power-sharing arrangements/opportunities; inter-governmental theories talk of power dependency/interdependency, differentiated polities and network governance; the often normative devolution literature prizes the Jeffersonian or subsidiarity principle of locating political representation close to organic communities; political economy accounts provide accounts of regional development; and public choice theory attempts to model regional governmental behaviours vis-à-vis citizens' preferences especially at the competitive jurisdictional level (see Courchene 1986).

Theories of *federalism* derive from notions of divided or compartmentalized constitutionality (separate yet interlocking entities). Modernist federal explanations are predominantly structuralist accounts (from political institutionalist or economic reductionist genres) where actors largely from the first and second 'tiers' conform to almost predetermined patterns (and conflicts), or they focus on 'realist' power relations and realpolitik explanations centred on actors (not necessarily power-dependency or dispersed power theories, but organic/agency accounts of power are found here). Clearly sub-national regions as semi-sovereign 'second tier' jurisdictions feature prominently in this literature, but often more as rival and competing power blocs than as sites of distinct leadership. While the characteristics of federalism can be modelled in a great many ways (see Nice 1998 who identifies ten types), the standard explanation of power-sharing takes one of four forms—coordinate or dual federalism, coercive federalism, competitive federalism, and cooperative or shared-responsibilities federalism (Rosenthal and Hoefler 1989). Each has a different meaning and implication for regional leadership. Those writers sensing that federations will display centralizing tendencies tend to see internal provinces as anachronistic and parochial, and their leadership perennially problematic; those detecting reverse tendencies toward decentralization perceive provinces as vibrant and robust, and their leadership germane (see Hueglin and Fenna 2006; Galligan 2006). The main points to emerge from federalist theories is that federations tend to become jurisdictionally frozen at a particular point of time, and that their sub-national units enjoy constitutional protections and cannot be abolished or restructured by the centre (certainly without their agreement, see Courchene 1995). Often, national upper houses have entrenched regional representation which underscores the salience of regionalism (for example the USA, Canada, South Africa, Germany, Australia, and Brazil). These constitutional–institutional factors entrench regional leadership in federal systems, hardwiring its existence through separate jurisdictional structures. Much of the parliamentary-federalist literature depicts regional governments (executive leaders and legislatures) engaged in rear-guard activities to prevent the further erosion of their powers and prerogatives, against majoritarian-driven centripetal forces. There is also considerable interest in federal renewal and in revising federalist compacts, perhaps exchanging some powers or establishing new protocols of engagement.

Unitary state theory often obscures or disguises the significance of regionalism, air-brushing away often quite powerful political entities within nations. Since the 1970s, however, there has been a gradual and sustained interest in '*new regionalism*', explaining both its survival in a globalizing context and in many cases describing how it has actually gained strengths. The Scottish, Catalonian, and Quebec 'autonomist' stories are all strong illustrative cases here (see Edwards 1999; Keating 2001b, 2009; Roller and Sloat 2002; Giordano and Roller 2002; Colino 2009; Jeffrey 2009). Indeed, Keating has even promoted the idea of 'stateless nations in a post-sovereign era' leading to a 'plurinational democracy' (Keating 2001a); sometimes referred to by others as 'perforated sovereignty' (Duchacek, Latouche, and Stevenson 1998). This may exaggerate the influence of regionalism, but it makes the point, as does the federalist literature, that territorial identity and its political expression through ideas, institutions, and processes is constantly being renegotiated by a matrix of vertical and horizontal stakeholders (Breton and Fraschini 2003; Thoenig 2005). Unitary systems, however, may not wish to embrace federalism as a solution to territorial differentiation, because, as Keating (2001b: 51) has argued, federalism tends to adopt a 'uniform system in which all units of the federation enjoy the same powers and status and the federal government has the same relationship to all citizens. Yet [in unitary states] distinct territories and minorities may demand powers and arrangements which other constituent units do not wish to exercise themselves'. Paradoxically, therefore, unitary systems, if they relax central edicts, may allow greater diversity to sub-national units than federal systems.

Intergovernmental theory focuses on the inter-connecting sinews that operate in federations or in unitary systems, and draws heavily from network governance theory and differentiated power models. These theories investigate not only how power is dispersed, but importantly how power can be created and nurtured, how patterns of influence are assembled and organized, how actors build and interweave networks of governance. Accordingly, it stresses interdependencies, resource exchanges, bargaining, and incentives for cooperation and collaboration to achieve mutual goals. In federal and unitary nations it highlights multi-level policy fora, combined jurisdictional conferences, composite get-togethers, regional councils, co-governance and even inter-regional coordination (see Toonen 1990). Regional leaders are thus brokers with certain power resources but who need to work through other stakeholders to achieve desired outcomes. Some studies have explored sub-national intergovernmental conflict in unitary, federal, and quasi-federal contexts (Montero 2001a).

The literature on *devolution* practically springs from a defence of regionalism, and features to a greater or lesser degree in debates about the location of power in unitary and federalist systems (Breton 2000). It advocates normatively that decision making and often policy delivery is best located close to the community level (but usually unspecified—again indicating the elusiveness or shadowy nature of the 'region') rather than at national or supra-national levels. The principle of subsidiarity has been enshrined in European treaties as an aspired spatial counterweight to EU integration, and as an attempt to address the 'democratic deficit'. Critics may consider that devolution is more aspiration than reality, but many nations have devolved responsibilities (sometimes off-loading them) to lower jurisdictions or administrative units (for example Spain, Brazil, Argentina—see Montero 2001b) and/or granted limited degrees of devolution to special territorial entities (Scotland, Wales, Hong Kong, Kosovo).

Regionalist political economy (PE) theories explore the relations between state actors and local economic development, including growth machine models, local boosterism, different patterns of intervention, regional planning and urban governance, regulatory regimes, research incubation (Gottman 1980; Keating and Loughlin 1997). Empirical studies tend to focus on what best promotes regional economic growth, and which localist strategies best achieve growth outcomes. One of the factors often identified for particular mention is the importance of local champions (politicians, civil leaders, media or business leaders). Political economy case studies of regional growth, in most instances, present single cases and contrast growth outcomes temporally rather than comparatively (but see Castles 1999). Some PE writers have recently begun to extol the significance of sub-national entities ('re-scaling the state'), not because they have been successful in attracting economic development at the meso-level, but because they are rapidly becoming sites of advanced regulation of transnational firms and the global political economy (Paul 2002).

In *public choice theory* there is a distinct body of work on the limitations of collective decision making in Europe and North America. Some of this work highlights 'competitive federalism' involving vertical competition between federal and regional governments over diverse topics such as constraining governments with competition, taxation disciplines/profligacy (vertical fiscal imbalances), general policy dynamism versus spending controls, and relative economic management capacities (Migue 1997;

Breton and Fraschini 2003; Shughart and Tollison 2005). In terms of jurisdictional leadership this body focuses on the themes of responsiveness to local preferences and fiscal disciplines for policy responsibilities. Another branch of this literature, best described as 'competitive regionalism', focuses on region-to-region relations and on horizontal competition internal to a nation. It highlights (and often critiques) the jurisdictional competition in which provinces/states contest against each other for transitory opportunities (for example business investment, luring new firms or 'smokestack chasing', major events, construction activity). A third branch centres its analysis on citizen preferences and mobility, and using public choice modelling reduces regions essentially to maximizing entities competing for investment, resource inputs, and development while attempting to attract and hold mobile workforces/consumers (tax–benefit trade-offs) (Courchene 1986; Grossman 1989; Breton 2000). Such regional competition places a considerable onus on regional leaders, the local policies they propound and tax regimes they maintain, but such accounts tend to concentrate on the differentiation and appeal of policy mixes between regions rather than on the analysis of local leadership per se (but see Hepple 1989 on local leviathans and UK regional taxation regimes). Primarily, their focus is on modelling comparative citizen liberty; they have less interest in a fine-grained qualitative analysis of leadership options/behaviour.

Among regional scholars generally the works of Stein Rokkan and Michael Keating (including their many collections with others in the field) remain significant contributions. Their studies indicate their passionate advocacy of regional autonomy and forensic inquiry, while at the same time drawing on a range of political science theories and concepts to sustain their arguments (national identity, administrative devolution, local democracy, etc.).

3 METHODOLOGIES

By far the most utilized methodology adopted among regionalists is the single case study approach (either of a nation and its regions, or a specific region in itself—such as Scotland or Catalonia, see Edwards 1999; Keating 2001b, 2009; Colino 2009). The region is regarded as the unit of analysis. It typically describes the dynamics of the region as a political-cultural entity, tracing its relations with the national level (or even supra-national bodies such as the EU). Mostly these accounts derive from pro-regional scholars who attempt to outline the changing parameters of regional discretion over policy matters, administrative capacities, delivery responsibilities, and constituency representation (Jurewitz, Mazmanian, and Nelson 2008). There is often an emphasis on downward management such as regional planning, environmental protection and economic development, but occasionally regions performing as actors on the national stage and in international relations receive some attention (Michelmann and Soldatos 1990). Some of these regional case studies explore regions that have limited discernible political or administrative structures in place (hence, in the UK the north of England can be analysed as a region just as Scotland can, and the same with the Belgium or Dutch provinces and functional decentralized bodies even if they do not possess separate legislative and executive institutions—see Hendriks Raadshelders and Toonen 1995; Elcock and Keating 1998; Hulst 2005).

Comparative regional studies are rarer. Comparative analysis along thematic lines do exist, such as Keating's (2001a) analysis of emerging 'new nationalisms' and their accommodation within exiting national entities in Europe and Canada, but again the focus is largely on activities at the level of governments rather than regional leadership (Gomez 2003). A body of literature exists that attempts to score nations according to a decentralization index often according to crude criteria or subjective judgements (Lijphart 1999). Hooghe, Marks, and Schakel (2010) recently undertook a more systematic analysis of the dimensions of regional authority (institutional, fiscal, policy scope, etc.), producing a regional authority index. Others pursued comparative studies of sub-national governments in relation to specific areas of policy (such as Karapin's (1999) study of race-related immigration controls in the UK and Germany; Armstrong and Read (2003) on industry policies; Jonas and Ward's (2002) study of urban and regional planning; and Sharpe (1989) on decentralization trends and the dynamics of territorial fragmentation in Europe). There are a few comparative studies of regional leaders and those that exist often compare leadership styles or preferences (see Barton and van Onselen's (2003) comparative analysis of two Australian premiers).

4 A CRITICAL ASSESSMENT OF THE FIELD

An obvious point to make when considering regional political leadership is that it is often neglected as an important field of study. Regional scholars frequently highlight expressions of local autonomy rather than focus on political leadership in their accounts of regional entities (but see Gage 1993), and studies of individual regional leaders generally do not engage with wider political science theories. Regionalism is regarded as an unquestioned good, and something to be strengthened, while often leadership is a subliminal and implicit aspect of these studies.

There are groaning bookcases full of biographies and individual histories of regional leaders from practitioners, journalists, historians, and political scientists. There are also occasional autobiographical contributions from meso-politicians reflecting on themselves as subjects. Collectively, their strengths are usually the rich detail provided, the logic of chronology, trajectory and hindsight, and they provide context, 'feel' and colour, and a sense of local culture and political contest. They are almost inevitably descriptive and few of these authors engage with the professional literature or with various theoretical approaches before commencing their 'tales'. Their weaknesses are their insularity: they offer studies of 'their' subject alone, they invest in 'their' character—often succumbing to the great man/woman leader in history narrative, they are wise with hindsight and backwardly reflexive giving post hoc accounts, and there is a constant danger of hagiography or demonization. Furthermore, only the stand-out leaders seem to attract researchers and biographers; the boring ones, the lack-lustre or routine ones and short-term stayers all miss out entirely.

Within the literature on political leadership itself, the leadership shown at the regional or meso-level may be the perennial bridesmaid—close but never featured. Often not considered an important topic by regionalists, any focus on political leadership may be a relatively small component of regional studies (which often focuses on regional dynamics, broader political contours and the special characteristics of regions, such as economics, administration, ethnicity, and so on). Similarly, leadership scholars seem more interested in 'first tier' players at the national and international level, hence the regional levels attract far less interest from serious political leadership scholars. Few leadership scholars have probed the dynamics of sub-national leadership: its traditions, possibilities, and limitations, what analytical frameworks seem to apply, and how regional leaders compare, neither to one another or to leaders at local or national levels.

5 Future Directions

Accordingly, there is much research yet to be initiated. With regard to regional political leadership we have arguably only just begun to scratch the surface. Regionalism itself is typically a minor field of inquiry and within that governance and leadership seem more implicit rather than explicit foci. True, there is an increasing interest in sub-national politics and this may grow as the current fascination with globalization eventually wanes, or as regionalism challenges increased international integration. If regional governance achieves greater degrees of community consent or improved community well-being, then academic and practitioner interest will tend to gravitate more towards this tier of government.

Although more serious and systematic work needs to be undertaken on regional leadership, especially of a comparative nature, there is an extant foundation on which to build (see for instance Hooghe, Marks, and Schakel 2010). A more explicit focus is needed. Studies need to explore the limits and possibilities of regional leadership, on how such leaders construct their leadership in situ, their agendas and priorities, and how they manage to exert influence (but see Pal and Taras (1988) and Wanna and Williams (2005) who have undertaken such projects). Political leadership at the regional level can be important not only within their jurisdictions but also often on the larger national stage, and sometimes internationally. There is ample scope for scholars to apprehend the dimensions of regional leadership by using perhaps more creative approaches. For instance, we would benefit from more inductive and interpretativist accounts of leaders, examining their understandings of the roles they perform and how they deal with challenges and opportunities. There is also greater scope for more sophisticated evaluations and dispassionate assessments of the contributions regional leadership can make.

Studies that centred their analysis on the scope for sub-national authority and capacities would be a welcome development.

It is unlikely that the outpourings of the biographical genre will cease in the foreseeable future, featuring leaders who crafted their political and administrative skills at the meso-level, but many of the above-mentioned criticisms are likely to remain apposite. In political science, however, a greater commitment to programmatic research should be encouraged, aiming to provide a more ambitious and robust analysis of leadership at the regional level. It will necessarily need to focus on temporal and/or comparative assessments of regional leadership using various criteria to gauge the scope and potentiality of decentralized leadership. Case studies will continue to be written, and over time these may help create a meta-level literature drawing on the findings from many multiple cases. The value in such a broader programme of research will be in better understanding governance, relations between communities and state institutions, and the characteristics of regional identity. In the sub-field of regional leadership that task has commenced but much more needs to be done.

RECOMMENDED READING

Hooghe, L., Marks, G., and Schakel, A. (2010). *The Rise of Regional Authority*. Abingdon: Routledge.
Wanna, J. and Williams, P. (2005). *Yes, Premier: Labor Leadership in Australia's States and Territories*. Sydney: UNSW Press.
Pal, L. and Taras, D., eds. (1988). *Prime Ministers and Premiers: Political Leadership and Public Policy in Canada*. Ontario: Prentice Hall.

REFERENCES

Armstrong, H. and Read, R. (2003). 'Microstates and Subnational Regions: Mutual Industrial Policy Lessons', *International Regional Science Review*, 26/1: 117–41.
Barton, S. and P. van Onselen. (2003). 'Comparing Court and Kennett Leadership Styles', *Policy and Society*, 22/2: 119–43.
Breton, A. (2000). *Competition and Structure*. Cambridge: Cambridge University Press.
Breton, A. and Fraschini, A. (2003). 'Vertical Competition in Unitary States: The Case of Italy', *Public Choice*, 114: 57–77.
Caro, R. A. (1974). *The Power Broker*. New York: Vintage Books.
Caro, R. (1982). *The Years of Lyndon Johnson*, Vol. 1. New York: Knopf.
Castles, F. (1999). 'Decentralization and the Post-war Political Economy', *European Journal of Political Research*, 36/1: 27–53.
Colino, C. (2009). 'Constitutional Change without Constitutional Reform: Spanish Federalism and the Revision of Catalonia's Statute of Autonomy', *Publius: The Journal of Federalism*, 39/2: 262–88.
Courchene, T. (1986). *Economic Management and the Division of Powers*. Toronto: University of Toronto Press.

Courchene, T. (1995). *Celebrating Flexibility: An Interpretive Essay on the Evolution of Canadian Federalism*. Montreal: Howe Institute.

de Clercy, C. (2005). 'Leadership and Uncertainty in Fiscal Restructuring: Ralph Klein and Roy Romanow', *Canadian Journal of Political Science*, 38/1: 175–202.

Dickovick, T. J. (2006). 'Municipalization as Central Government Strategy: Central–Regional–Local Politics in Peru, Brazil, and South Africa', *Publius: The Journal of Federalism*, 37/1: 1–25.

Duchacek, I., Latouche, D., and Stevenson, G., eds. (1998). *Perforated Sovereignties and International Relations*. New York: Greenwood.

Eaton, K. (2004). *Politics Beyond the Capital: the Design of Subnational Institutions in South America*. Stanford, CA: Stanford University Press.

Edwards, S. (1999). 'Reconstructing the Nation: The Process of Establishing Catalan Autonomy', *Parliamentary Affairs*, 52/4: 666–76.

Elcock, H. and Keating, M. eds. (1998). *Remaking the Union*. London: Frank Cass.

Gage, R. (1993). 'Leadership and Regional Councils: A Mismatch between Leadership Styles Today and Future Roles', *State and Local Government Review*, 25/1: 9–18.

Galligan, B. (2006). 'Federalism', in R. A. W. Rhodes, S. Binder, and R. Rockman (eds), *Oxford Handbook of Political Institutions*. Oxford: Oxford University Press, 261–80.

Giordano, B. and Roller, E. (2002). 'Catalonia and the "Idea of Europe": Competing Strategies and Discourses within Catalan Party Politics', *European Urban and Regional Studies*, 9/2: 99–113.

Gomez, E. J. (2003). 'Decentralization and Municipal Governance: Suggested Approaches for Cross-regional Analysis', *Studies in Comparative International Development*, 38/3: 57–80.

Gottman, J., ed. (1980). *Centre and Periphery: Spatial Variations in Politics*. Beverly Hills, CA: Sage.

Grossman, P. (1989). *Fiscal Federalism: Constraining Governments with Competition*. Perth: Australian Institute for Public Policy.

Hair, W. I. (1991). *The Kingfish and his Realm: The Life and Times of Huey P. Long*. Baton Rouge, LA: Louisiana State University Press.

Hendriks, F., Raadshelders, J., and Toonen, T. (1995). 'European Regional Policy in the Netherlands', in B. Jones and M. Keating (eds), *The European Union and the Regions*. Oxford: Oxford University Press, 215–31.

Hepple, L. W. (1989). 'Destroying Local Leviathans and Designing Landscapes of Liberty—Public Choice Theory and the Poll Tax', *Transactions of the Institute for British Geographers*. 14/4: 387–99.

Hooghe, L., ed. (1996). *Cohesion Policy and European Integration*. Oxford: Oxford University Press.

Hooghe, L., Marks, G., and Schakel, A. (2010). *The Rise of Regional Authority*. Abingdon: Routledge.

Hueglin, T. and A. Fenna. (2006). *Comparative Federalism*. Quebec: Broadview Press.

Hulst, R. (2005). 'Regional Governance in Unitary States: Lessons from the Netherlands in Comparative Perspective', *Local Government Studies*, 31/1: 99–120.

Jeffrey, C. (2009). 'Devolution in the United Kingdom: Problems of a Piecemeal Approach to Constitutional Change', *Publius: the Journal of Federalism*, 39/2: 289–313.

Jonas, A. and Ward, K. (2002). 'A World of Regionalisms? Towards a US–UK Urban and Regional Policy Framework Comparison', *Journal of Urban Affairs*, 24/4: 377–401.

Jurewitz, J., Mazmanian, D., and Nelson, H. (2008). 'California's Climate Change Policy: The Case of a Subnational State Actor Tackling a Global Challenge', *The Journal of Environment Development*, 17/4: 401–23.

Karapin, R. (1999). 'The Politics of Immigration Control in Britain and Germany: Subnational Politicians and Social Movements', *Comparative Politics*, 31/4: 423–44.

Keating, M. (1988). *State and Regional Nationalism: Territorial Politics and the European State*. Brighton: Harvester.

Keating, M. (1995). *The European Union and the Regions*. Oxford: Oxford University Press.

Keating, M. (1998). *The New Regionalism in Western Europe: Territorial Restructuring and Political Change*. Cheltenham: Edward Elgar.

Keating, M. (2001a). *Plurinational Democracy: Stateless Nations in a Post-Sovereignty Era*. Oxford: Oxford University Press.

Keating, M. (2001b). *Nations Against the State: the New Politics of Nationalism in Quebec, Catalonia and Scotland*. 2nd edn. Houndmills: Palgrave.

Keating, M. (2009). *The Independence of Scotland: Self-Government and the Shifting Politics of Union*. Oxford: Oxford University Press.

Keating, M. and Loughlin, J., eds. (1997). *The Political Economy of Regionalism*. London: Frank Cass.

Lijphart, A. (1999). *Patterns of Democracy*. New Haven, CT: Yale University Press.

Lusztig, M., James, P., and Moon, J. (1997). 'Falling from Grace: Non-established Brokerage Parties and the Weight of Predominance in Canadian Provinces and Australian States', *Publius: The Journal of Federalism*, 27/1: 59–81.

Meny, Y. and Wright, V., eds. (1985). *Centre–Periphery Relations in Western Europe*. London: George Allen and Unwin.

Michelmann, H. and Soldatos, P., eds. (1990). *Federalism and International Relations: The Role Of Subnational Units*. Oxford: Clarendon.

Migue, J.-L. (1997). 'Public Choice in a Federal System', *Public Choice*, 90/2: 235–54.

Montero, A. P. (2001a). 'After Decentralization: Patterns of Intergovernmental Conflict in Argentina, Brazil, Spain, and Mexico', *Publius: the Journal of Federalism*, 31/4: 43–64.

Montero, A. P. (2001b). 'Decentralizing Democracy: Spain and Brazil in Comparative Perspective', *Comparative Politics*, 33/2: 149–69.

Nice, D. (1998). 'The Intergovernmental Setting of State–Local Relations', in R. L. Hanson (ed.), *Governing Partners*, Boulder, CO: Westview Press, 88–105.

Pal, L. and Taras, D., eds. (1988). *Prime Ministers and Premiers: Political Leadership and Public Policy in Canada*. Ontario: Prentice Hall.

Paul, D. E. (2002). 'Re-scaling IPE: Subnational States and the Regulation of the Global Political Economy', *Review of International Political Economy*, 9/3: 465–89.

Pimlott, B. (1994). *Frustrating their Knavish Tricks: Writings on Biography, History and Politics*. London: HarperCollins.

Putnam, R. (1993). *Making Democracy Work*. Princeton, NJ: Princeton University Press.

Reynolds, P. (2002). *Lock, Stock and Barrel: A Political Biography of Mike Ahern*. St Lucia, Queensland: University of Queensland Press.

Rokkan, S. (1980). 'Territories, Centers and Peripheries: Towards a Geoethnic–Geoeconomic–Geopolitical Model of Differentiation within Western Europe', in J. Gottman (ed.), *Center and Periphery: spatial variations in politics*. Beverly Hills, CA: Sage, 163–204.

Rokkan, S. and Urwin, D. (1983). *Economy, Territory and Identity: Politics of West-European Peripheries*. London: Sage.

Roller, E. and Sloat, A. (2002). 'The Impact of Europeanization on Regional Governance: A Study of Catalonia and Scotland', *Public Policy and Administration*, 17/2: 68–86.

Rosenthal, D. and Hoefler, J. (1989). 'Competing Approaches to the Study of American Federalism and Intergovernmental Relations', *Publius: the Journal of Federalism*, 19/1: 1–23.

Ryan, D. and McEwen, M. (1979). *It's Grossly Improper*. Adelaide: Wenan Books.

Sharpe, L. J., ed. (1979). *Decentralist Trends in Western Europe*. London: Sage.

Sharpe, L. J. (1989). 'Fragmentation and Territoriality in the European State System', *International Political Science Review*, 10/3: 223–38.

Sharpe, L. J., ed. (1993). *The Rise of Meso-government in Europe*. London: Sage.

Shughart, W. and Tollison, R. (2005). 'Public Choice in the New Century', *Public Choice*, 124/1: 1–18.

Skidelsky, R. (1975). *Oswald Mosley*. New York: Holt, Rinehart and Winston.

Thoenig, J.-C. (2005). 'Territorial Administration and Political Control; Decentralization in France', *Public Administration*, 83/3: 685–708.

Toonen, T. (1990). 'The Unitary State as a System of Co-governance: The Case of the Netherlands', *Public Administration*, 67/3: 281–96.

Toonen, T. A. J. (1993). 'Dutch Provinces and the Struggle for the Meso', in L. J. Sharpe (ed.), *The Rise of Meso Government in Europe*, London: Sage, 117–54.

Valcke, T., De Ceunink, K., Reynart, H., and Steyvers. K. (2008). 'Leadership, Governance and Legitimacy at an Intermediate Government Level: The Case of Belgian Governors', *Local Government Studies*, 34/2: 245–65.

Wanna, J. and Williams, P. (2005). *Yes, Premier: Labor Leadership in Australia's States and Territories*, Sydney: UNSW Press.

CHAPTER 38

LEADERSHIP AND INTERNATIONAL COOPERATION

CHARLES F. PARKER AND CHRISTER KARLSSON

1 THE IMPORTANCE OF LEADERSHIP

INTEREST in international cooperation, and the role leadership plays in overcoming the collective action problems that bedevil it, have flourished as states increasingly attempt to construct rule-based governance arrangements to guide behaviour and solve problems in a variety of issue areas, such as trade, security, human rights, and the environment. The scholarship focusing on how leadership dynamics have an impact on international cooperation has originated primarily from the international relations literature dealing with transnational cooperation, negotiations, regimes, and institutions.

A focus on leadership can offer important insights into our understanding of multilateral cooperation. Scholarship on international cooperation and negotiations has posited that leadership is a crucial determinant in overcoming the obstacles associated with reaching international agreements and establishing international institutions (Young 1991; Sjöstedt 1994; Underdal 1994; Hampson and Hart 1995).

There is today widespread agreement that many of the world's transnational problems, whether they are environmental, financial, or security based in nature, require the states of the world to close rank and forge cooperative arrangements and solutions to issues that no one state can manage alone. Despite the demand for global governance solutions, progress towards effective agreements and arrangements in a variety of issue areas—ranging from ozone protection to free trade to sustainable development among others—has been slow, and we could justifiably ask why so little has yet been achieved in solving many global problems. The answer, in part, is that the mere acknowledgement of a common challenge that urgently needs to be addressed is not sufficient for actors to join forces and forge a sustainable solution. Cooperation may still be difficult to establish, because reaching international agreement on appropriate action presents a number of vexing problems not easily overcome (see Sebenius 1983; Young 1991; Underdal 1994; Christoff 2010). When looking at international cooperation, we find a number of factors that have served as obstacles to success.

A first complication has to do with the sheer *complexity* of many transnational issues. Multilateral negotiations on issues such as climate change or arms control now often involve over 190 countries and touch on a wide range of issues in multiple policy areas. Another obstacle not easily overcome is the difficulty of agreeing on the content of a *negotiating agenda* (see Young 1991: 284). Even when most states agree that an issue is a major concern, they still often have different views on how the problem should be defined and what visions should guide efforts to reach solutions. A third problem relates to the fact that the bargainers (states) are 'complex collective entities' (Young 1991: 303), which sometimes arrive at international negotiations with *fixed preferences* and their hands tied as a result of domestic constraints (Christoff 2010: 643). The difficulties of cooperation are also compounded because actors may feel *uncertain* as to whether proposed solutions will work, or whether other states will actually honour the commitments they make. The fear of being placed at a competitive disadvantage, whether in the security sphere or in the global economy, means that states are often unwilling to act in the absence of international agreements that require similar commitments from other states (Hurrell and Kingsbury 1992: 5).

In situations like these, where commitments to act can so easily be blocked by collective action concerns and a number of complicating factors, leadership is crucial. Indeed, leadership can be considered a necessary, although not sufficient, condition for reaching agreement and forging global governance arrangements (Young 1991: 302). Given that leadership is considered crucial for succeeding in establishing global governance arrangements, it is important that we acquire a thorough understanding of the different forms that multilateral leadership takes and what role it plays in international negotiations and cooperative outcomes.

2 Leadership and Its Modes

In this section we will focus on key ideas, concepts, and questions, as well as looking at some significant debates present in this research field. More specifically, we will examine the key components of leadership, identify and discuss the main modes of leadership, and, finally, discuss the prerequisites for exercising effective leadership.

Defining Leadership: Four Key Components

While there are some controversies surrounding the meaning of leadership, it would be somewhat of a stretch to argue that leadership is an essentially contested concept. In fact, when looking at the bulk of scholarly work on leadership, one will soon find that most definitions of leadership share a number of key components. It is also striking that a vast majority of all the work done in the research field refers back to a handful of seminal contributions that can rightfully be labelled as classics. The works by Oran Young and Arild Underdal, in particular, stand out as key points of departure for most scholars who have attempted to come to grips with the concept of leadership and the role it plays in international cooperation.

What is meant by leadership is thus fairly well established in this subfield and is well represented by Underdal's definition of leadership (1994: 178) as an 'asymmetrical relationship of influence in which one actor guides or directs the behaviour of others toward a certain goal'. Other well-known definitions of leadership include Young's view of leadership as 'the actions of individuals who endeavor to solve or circumvent the collective action problems that plague efforts of parties seeking to reap joint gains' (Young 1991: 285), or Nye's definition of leadership as 'the power to orient and mobilize others for a purpose' (Nye 2008: 19), where a leader is seen as someone 'who guides or is in charge of others' (Nye 2008: 18).

On closer inspection we find a great deal of overlap between these definitions of leadership and if we combine them we find four key components: the *leader*, the *followers*, the form or *mode* of leadership, and the objective or *goal* of leadership. Let us now take a closer look at each of these elements.

The first key component is the leader. Underdal's definition states that a leader is an actor who guides or directs the behaviour of others towards a certain goal, but it does not specify what type of actor might qualify as a leader. In multilateral settings the key actors are no doubt states, but the role of leader is not reserved exclusively for states. International organizations such as the UN, the EU, or the World Bank can also take on the task of guiding or directing the behaviour of others. Even non-governmental organizations can be said to exercise a certain amount of leadership, even if they are less likely to do so effectively, since a leader may be called upon to mobilize power resources to induce others to act in a certain way.

When we speak of leadership in multilateral negotiations, we often refer to collective entities, such as states, as the leaders of interest to us. We may, for instance, seek to understand to what extent the EU has been an effective leader on climate change or through which means US leadership on world trade has been channelled. The focus on collective entities as the main unit of analysis does not, however, mean that individuals should be taken out of the equation. To the contrary, as Oran Young reminds us of, 'leaders are in the end individuals even if they act as representatives of collective entities such as states and international organizations' (Young 1991: 287). To what extent attempts at exercising leadership are successful or not will no doubt be largely dependent on characteristics possessed by the collective entity in question; however, the personal qualities of the individuals representing the state or international organization may also be important. The personal skills of the individual in charge of leading a negotiation team may, for instance, be crucial for determining to what extent a leader is successful in steering the process towards a desired outcome (see Malnes 1995; Andresen and Agrawala 2002).

Finally, the formal role occupied in a negotiation can matter a great deal, and it has been shown that the influence wielded by chairmen of multilateral negotiations can be decisive in shaping outcomes (Tallberg 2006).

A vast majority of past scholarship has focused on the leaders and the act of leadership. This preoccupation with what may be labelled the 'supply side' of the leadership equation (Underdal 1994) is as surprising as it is problematic. Most definitions of leadership treat leadership as a relational concept, which means that the 'demand side' of leadership and the followers are of equal importance. The obvious fact that the existence of a leader 'implies followers who move in the same direction' (Nye 2008: 18) indicates that this component of leadership deserves more attention than it has thus far received in leadership research. Followers are vital because they 'empower leaders' (Nye 2008: 35). If followers are required for a leader to be successful, it is axiomatic that the effectiveness of leadership efforts will be seriously undermined if an actor who aspires to be a leader fails to be recognized as such. Low levels of recognition for a particular leadership candidate, in turn, increase the likelihood that potential followers will not be willing to let their behaviour be guided in the direction suggested by the would-be leader.

In multilateral settings achieving universal leadership recognition can be difficult. Across the board leadership recognition requires an actor be acknowledged as a leader by prospective followers from different geographical regions holding diverging and even contradictory interests, rather than simply securing support from a small subset of close supporters (see Karlsson et al. 2011: 97–9). However difficult it may be for a leadership contender to please a diverse group of actors with diverging interests, it is nevertheless imperative that leaders do not 'fall short of meeting the minimum expectations of their followers', otherwise the likelihood, as Rosenau argues, is high 'that such leaders will lose favor' (Rosenau 2006). Therefore, attracting adherents requires 'the credible inclusion of the interests and/or ideas of potential followers into the leadership project' (Schirm 2010: 1).

The third component to the definition of leadership takes aim at the very act of exercising leadership—that is, the means through which a leader tries to guide or direct the behaviour of others. Leadership research has indeed responded to Oran Young's call to 'approach leadership in behavioral terms' by 'differentiating analytically among several forms of leadership' (Young 1991: 287). Clearly to define different forms of leadership and the specific instruments of influence that may be deployed as a group of actors search for solutions to joint problems has important methodological consequences. As Young points out, leadership studies have often resorted to post hoc reasoning by directing attention to successful outcomes and simply assuming the presence of leadership as an explanation for that outcome (Young 1991: 286). To avoid drawing flawed conclusions, the very act of exercising leadership needs to be analytically decoupled from outcomes. Scholars have now identified a number of different forms or modes of leadership through which a leader seeks to guide or direct the behaviour of others (Young 1991; Underdal 1994; Malnes 1995) and examined these in the context of specific issue areas such as climate change (Parker and Karlsson 2010; Saul and Seidel 2011), trade, forestry, and endangered species of animals and plants (Elgström 2007). The main modes of leadership will be examined in the section "Modes of leadership".

The fourth and final component has to do with the objectives or goals that a leader seeks to reach by directing or guiding the behaviour of others. Nye, for example, emphasizes that leadership is about mobilizing others for a *purpose* (Nye 2008: 19). However, to what extent does the nature of the goals matter? Must the goals be collective ones for the common good or can they be motivated by self-interest? There is some ambiguity and debate about this (Skodvin and Andresen 2006; Saul and Seidel 2011). Some scholars have an explicitly normative take on leadership and associate it with 'the collective pursuit of some common good or joint purpose' (Underdal 1994: 178–9; Malnes 1995: 92). According to Malnes, a 'leader is supposed to look beyond his or her own interests and concerns, to the interests of a wider group' (Malnes 1995: 93). However, a narrow conception of leadership (see Underdal 199: 178), concerned with the exercise of influence to set and achieve goals, does not require a would-be leader to push for particular or collectively beneficial goals for that behaviour to count as leadership. The goals may be common overarching ones (solving the climate change problem, protecting forests, eliminating dangerous weapons, and so on) or more concrete and limited ones (achieving targeted objectives during a negotiation round such as securing access to technology for developing countries in the context of an arms control regime). Finally, some scholars have downgraded the importance of a leader's true motivations: 'Whether a leader ultimately wants to solve a collective problem out of an altruistic concern or out of self-interest is irrelevant as long as he tries to solve it' (Saul and Seidel 2011: 904). Ideally, goals should be shared and for the common good, and, while an actor primarily motivated by self-interest can be a leader, leaders who act for the common good can be both effective and ethical (Nye 2008: 112).

Having acquainted ourselves with the key components of leadership in multilateral cooperation, we now turn our attention more specifically to the different forms or modes of leadership.

Modes of Leadership

There are a number of different, partly overlapping, classifications of the different modes, or forms, of leadership to be found in the literature. Furthermore, the terminology sometimes differs between scholars who are essentially talking about the same or very similar modes of leadership. All this has resulted in a certain amount of confusion surrounding the various modes of leadership. Young (1991: 287–8), for example, distinguishes between three modes of leadership: structural, intellectual, and entrepreneurial leadership. Underdal (1994: 183–91) also develops an analytical scheme that includes three modes of leadership, which he labels coercive, unilateral, and instrumental. Malnes (1995) produced yet another contending typology also with three modes: threats and offers, directional, and problem-solving leadership. However, what Underdal labels 'coercive' and what Malnes terms as 'threats and offers' leadership both correspond with Young's structural leadership, and all three are clearly resource-based forms of leadership. Young's entrepreneurial leadership is more or less the same as what Underdal refers to as instrumental leadership and what Malnes calls problem-solving leadership. However, there are substantive differences as well. For example, what Underdal refers to as 'leadership through unilateral action' (Underdal 1994: 183–6) and what Malnes identifies as 'directional leadership,' (Malnes 1995: 92–3), both of which are based on 'leading by example' (Parker and Karlsson 2010: 926–7), have no equivalent in Young's classification.

At first blush, all these differences may seem quite confusing. However, once one examines the various leadership modes on offer, it becomes manifest that there is actually much common ground to be found between the different contributions. So, although the terminology varies, we believe that it is possible to distinguish between four main modes of leadership: structural, directional, idea based, and instrumental.

Structural leadership (Young 1991: 288–93), also referred to as coercive leadership (Underdal 1994: 186–7), rests on the ability to take actions or deploy power resources that create incentives, costs, and benefits in a particular issue area. Structural leadership flows from an actor's aggregate power and can be pursued through coercion or constructive inducements. Structural leadership aims to alter the preferences and behaviour of other actors. By deploying sticks and carrots, the leader tries to change the pay-offs associated with different outcomes in an issue area to reach a solution to a collective problem.

Directional leadership (Malnes 1995: 92), or unilateral leadership (Underdal 1994: 183), rests on taking unilateral action and is accomplished by the demonstration effects of leading by example (Underdal 1994: 183–5; Gupta and Ringius 2001). By making the first move, it is possible to demonstrate the feasibility, value, and superiority of particular policy solutions. Demonstrating a commitment to act also removes uncertainty about whether the leader is actually devoted to the undertaking rather than just engaging in 'cheap talk' (Underdal 1994: 183–5).

Idea-based leadership, also referred to as intellectual (Young 1991: 298–302) leadership, is concerned with problem naming and framing and the promotion of particular policy solutions (Young 1991; Malnes 1995). This type of leadership includes discovering and proposing joint solutions to collective problems and is accomplished through 'consciousness-raising' (Malnes 1995: 101). To simplify, two dynamics are at work here: one involves efforts to change perceptions regarding the problem at hand; the other consists of making new proposals and suggesting innovative solutions. By bringing new knowledge to bear on a particular problem and illustrating the effects of inaction or failure to find a solution, a leader can try to change the positions of the other parties.

Finally, there is *instrumental* leadership (Underdal 1994: 187–91), sometimes referred to as entrepreneurial (Young 1991: 293–8) or problem-solving (Malnes 1995) leadership. This mode of leadership is closely related to idea-based leadership as it partly has to do with devising proposals to achieve common goals. The emphasis for an instrumental leader, however, has less to do with agenda setting or presenting new ideas intended to alter the fundamental preferences of the actors. Instead, an instrumental leader rather relies on 'negotiating skill' and seeks to 'put together deals that would otherwise elude participants' (Young 1991: 293). Another difference is that they operate on different time scales or phases in the negotiating process. An intellectual leader often can take a longer time perspective. The goal is to alter the opinions and goals of others over time—a process that may take many years. An instrumental leader on the other hand is more like a broker who is very much present during actual negotiations and seeks to make a difference in the short term by helping participants reach a deal and get to 'yes'.

While it is fruitful for analytical purposes to distinguish between various modes of leadership, we should recognize that in real life, we will usually find that leaders combine different modes of leadership. This is simply so because it will often take more than one form of leadership to effectively mobilize followers and guide their behaviour towards a certain goal. To be effective a leader often needs to combine different forms of leadership (Young 1991: 303). Providing good ideas or setting a good example which others may follow are important leadership tools, but they are unlikely to be sufficient in guaranteeing a positive outcome. Idea-based and directional leadership usually need to be accompanied by the bargaining leverage that stems from structural power. On the other hand, relying solely on structural leadership is rarely a recipe for success simply because it is difficult for any one actor to muster sufficient power-resources to make this a viable strategy.

Prerequisites for Effective Leadership

What then are the necessary prerequisites for the various modes of leadership to bear fruit? There is consensus among leadership scholars that effective leadership requires capabilities and credibility. Many studies examining the role of leadership have concluded that legitimacy and credibility are key for effective leadership (Young 1991, 304; Underdal 1994, 185; Elgström 2007, 455). However, we need to recognize that the various modes of leadership operate according to different logics and rely on different mechanisms whereby the leader attempts to guide or direct the behaviour of others. The various modes of leadership are therefore dependent on different types of credibility.

Structural leadership, for example, seeks to change the preferences and behaviour of other actors by using sticks and carrots. If an actor employs coercion, his or her threats must be sufficiently potent and credible so that other parties will acquiesce to the demands. Likewise, if an actor is trying to persuade others by making promises and offering positive inducements, the other parties must be convinced that the resources will exist to deliver the goods. If a would-be leader's threats or promises lack credibility, his or her bid for structural leadership will be seriously attenuated.

To be an effective directional leader is altogether another story. An important aspect of leading by example is to be able to demonstrate the feasibility of a proposed solution. This form of leadership is thus heavily dependent on the leader being perceived as someone who keeps his or her word and works to meet the goals set forth. Power resources are not especially important for directional leadership to be successful. Effective directional leadership instead makes strong demands on the leader's performance credibility: the realities of the leader's deeds must match his or her rhetoric.

A leader who seeks to guide the behaviour of others by a combination of structural and directional leadership is thus dependent on different types of credibility. The leader must be perceived as having the resources and political will necessary for structural leadership, but will also need to be able to deliver on his or her commitments and demonstrate the feasibility of his or her preferred solutions. This means that it will be a real challenge for any leader to be able to effectively exercise different forms of leadership. That said, even if credibility is compromised in one area, this does not necessarily mean that an actor's ambition to exercise leadership is undermined across the board. Performance and an actor's past track record are absolutely crucial for directional leadership, but it is far less relevant for structural leadership.

3 TAKING STOCK OF PREVIOUS AND CURRENT RESEARCH

In this section we take stock of previous research on leadership in multilateral cooperation. We first present some landmark contributions and then move on to discuss some of the main strands of research in the field.

Classics

If one reviews previous research on leadership and multilateral cooperation, it is striking that the works of two scholars are the point of departure for the vast majority of contributions made in this particular research field. We see it as fully understandable that Oran Young's path-breaking piece 'Political Leadership and Regime Formation: On the Development of Institutions in International Society' (1991) as well as Arild Underdal's milestone contribution 'Leadership Theory: Rediscovering the Arts of Management' (1994) are so widely cited. Both these contributions deserve to be labelled as classics.

Young's work on leadership is of crucial importance, as he provides a clear analytical framework that allows us to study leadership in action. By differentiating between different forms of leadership, Young has paved the way for future research efforts directed towards examining if and how leadership makes a difference in multilateral cooperation. Although the analytical scheme fleshed out by Young has not been accepted as the final word on how best to differentiate between various leadership forms and scholars continue to discuss and debate the various leadership modes, Young's work remains the starting point of this important subject.

Young's work also deserves to be seen as a major contribution to leadership research because he does more than provide an analytical framework that distinguishes between different forms of leadership. He also elaborates a number of testable hypotheses on 'the role of leadership as a determinant of success or failure in the process of institutional bargaining' (Young 1991: 302). In doing so, he focuses on the importance of the interplay of different leadership forms. In this respect, too, the work by Young stands out as truly innovative, and it is for this reason that it has served, and continues to serve, as a source of inspiration for leadership scholars.

Underdal's take on how work should proceed in the analysis of international leadership follows rather closely to the path staked out by Young. Hence, Underdal, too, emphasizes the importance of focusing on the different leadership modes when seeking to examine 'the leader/follower relationship more closely' (Underdal 1994: 183). As discussed above, Underdal presents an analytical scheme that differs somewhat from the one established by Young. However, Underdal's main contribution to leadership theory is not his refinement of the analytical scheme for examining the various leadership modes, but his insight that the strength of any leadership relationship is a 'function of the supply of and the demand for leadership services' (Underdal 1994: 181).

By underscoring that a match between the supply of and the demand for leadership is a prerequisite for the effective exercise of leadership, Underdal makes a strong case for why students of leadership need to take the study of followers seriously and not only focus their time and attention on the words and deeds of leaders. Underdal (1994: 182–3) then proceeds to elaborate testable hypotheses about what determines the demand for leadership. In doing so, much like Young's, Underdal's work facilitates future research in a very concrete way.

Main Strands of Research

Previous work on leadership may be conveniently grouped together and discussed under two main headings. The first strand of research has focused on the leaders and the supply side of leadership, whereas the other directs its attention to the followers and the demand side of the leadership equation.

If one looks at previous research on leadership, it becomes evident that the bulk of past scholarship has focused on the supply side of leadership and the strategies and actions of the leaders. Even if we do not necessarily agree with Underdal's claim that leaders are 'more fascinating objects of study than followers' (Underdal 1994: 181), we do believe that improving our understanding of leaders and aspiring leaders is an extremely important research task. For example, work in this area has been instrumental in increasing our knowledge of the motivations actors have for seeking leadership positions (Schreurs and Tiberghien 2007; Oberthür and Roche Kelly 2008).

The main thrust of the research on the supply side of leadership, however, has been directed towards increasing our knowledge on how the various modes of leadership have been deployed in various issue areas. These contributions (Gupta and Ringius 2001; Andresen and Agrawala 2002; Zito 2005; Parker and Karlsson 2010) have confirmed some of the results from the pioneering work done by Young and Underdal by showing that leaders actually do combine different leadership modes, rather than simply rely on one form of leadership to guide the behaviour of others. In the field of climate change, for example, the EU has been seeking to establish itself as a leader in the global struggle to combat climate change by combining idea-based leadership with unilateral measures intended to convince others of its ability to lead by example.

The research focusing on the supply side of leadership has also made important advances when it comes to understanding the prerequisites for effective leadership. Sjöstedt (1998) has emphasized the importance of domestic factors for explaining the successful deployment of leadership strategies at the international level. More recent contributions have helped to move the ball forward by showing how different modes of leadership are dependent on different types of credibility (Parker and Karlsson 2010), and by establishing that different leadership modes contribute in varying degrees to enhancing cooperation in multilateral settings (Saul and Seidel 2011).

In terms of the empirical ground covered by research on leadership and multilateral cooperation, it is striking that the recent contributions are dominated by a focus on environmental politics and especially climate change (e.g. Sjöstedt 1998; Gupta and van der Grijp 1999, 2000; Gupta and Ringius 2001; Andresen and Agrawala 2002; Zito 2005; Kilian and Elgström 2010; Parker and Karlsson 2010; Saul and Seidel 2011). However, important research has also been done in other policy areas, especially trade (Kindleberger 1988; Sjöstedt 1994; Elgström 2007; Tallberg 2010), but also in connection with international regimes dealing with fisheries (e.g. Underdal 1980), forestry and endangered species (e.g. Elgström 2007).

4 THE NEW WAVE OF INTERNATIONAL LEADERSHIP SCHOLARSHIP: LEADERSHIP RECOGNITION, SELECTION, AND IMPACT

A new wave of leadership research has attempted to build on previous work as well as fill in some of the voids in areas that have been comparatively neglected by past scholarship. Recent work has turned its attention to the demand side of leadership, leadership recognition, what factors influence leadership selection, how leadership dynamics have an impact on specific negotiation outcomes, and whether and how leadership affects cooperation.

Leadership Recognition and Selection

Traditionally studies on the supply of leadership have dominated this research field, but there are now a number of important studies that focus on the demand side of leadership and the follower side of the leader–follower relationship. Gupta and van der Grijp (1999, 2000) were among the first to examine followers' perceptions on leadership within the climate change regime. More recently, Elgström and Kilian have compared the EU's role perception of itself as a leader with the views held by potential followers concerning the EU's performance in different regime settings such as trade, forestry, endangered species, and climate change (Elgström 2007; Kilian and Elgström 2010).

In evaluating the EU's quest for a leadership role in various issues areas, these studies showed that EU interviewees and respondents from states outside the EU have different views on the EU's status as a leader. The latter tended to be more critical of the leadership provided by the EU. For example, Elgström (2007) found that within the World Trade Organization (WTO) EU respondents portrayed EU leadership as indisputable, while interviewees from non-EU states had a more mixed impression of the EU's leadership role.

Although these studies provide important insights into how followers perceive aspiring leaders and their leadership bids, the fact that they all build on interviews with a relatively limited number of respondents make them less useful for examining whether perceptions of leadership vary between subgroups of respondents in a manner predicted by leadership theory. Underdal (1994: 182), for example, argues that views on leadership may vary among different groups of individuals depending on their specific roles and how well informed they are. In a recent study (Karlsson et al. 2011) informed by responses from more than 200 climate change negotiation participants, it was shown that there is a strong geographical component to leadership recognition. Competing leadership contenders—in this case the USA, the EU, China, and G-77—'were more widely recognized as leaders in their "home constituencies" than among respondents in general' (Karlsson et al. 2011: 103).

The vast majority of the work on leadership has been devoid of any empirical evidence of actual leadership recognition or what factors motivate leadership selection. Some recent work, based on unique survey data collected at three consecutive Conference of Parties (COP) UN climate summits (Poznań 2008; Copenhagen 2009; Cancún 2010), has attempted to grapple with these issues by documenting which actors were actually perceived as leaders, charting how leadership perceptions evolved over time, and shedding light on which factors motivated the support of particular leadership candidates (Karlsson et al. 2011, 2012; Parker et al. 2012).

The results clearly showed that overall commitment to solving the climate change problem was the most important reported factor in motivating the support of a particular leader (Karlsson et al. 2012). Put differently, an actor aspiring to gather widespread support as a leader needs to work for, or at least be perceived as working for, the common good. At the other end of the spectrum, respondents reported that self-interest was the least important factor when selecting a leader. Conversely, the ability to engage in structural leadership by providing 'resources and inducements to address the problem' was rated as less important by respondents than idea-based or directional leadership.

Leadership Impact

What impact does leadership have on negotiation outcomes and how does it actually influence cooperation? Utilizing an analytical framework that incorporated the demand side of leadership, the supply side of leadership, the interplay of leadership visions and forms, and the fit between these elements, Parker, Karlsson, Hjerpe, and Linnér (2012) attempted to make sense of the outcome of the 2009 UN climate summit in Copenhagen. With the use of survey data, the study was able to show that the leadership landscape in this issue area was fragmented, with no one, clear-cut leader, that the main leadership contenders—the EU, the USA, and China—had conflicting visions of what should be achieved, and that none of them provided leadership that inspired overwhelming support. As a result of the mismatch between the supply and demand for leadership in Copenhagen and the fissures between the leading actors, instead of reaching an ambitious binding successor agreement to the Kyoto Protocol, all that could be achieved was an interim comprise agreement, the Copenhagen Accord.

Another recent study interested in the impact of leadership addressed the question of whether and how leadership affects cooperation in the realm of climate change mitigation policy by empirically testing various hypotheses of how leadership matters with the aid of a standardized quantitative framework, rather than relying on case study methodology, the approach that has dominated the field (Saul and Seidel 2011: 902). The findings from this study suggest that leadership does make a positive contribution to cooperation and that directional leadership appeared to be particularly important when it came to climate change mitigation cooperation (Saul and Seidel 2011: 917).

5 LOOKING BACK AND LOOKING FORWARD: AN AGENDA FOR FUTURE STUDIES

Although some have questioned the value of the leadership perspective (Skodvin and Andresen 2006), as this chapter has charted, important contributions have been made concerning the conceptualization of leadership, the motives actors have for engaging in leadership behaviour, the sources of leadership influence, the various modes of leadership, leadership recognition, what factors motivate the support of particular would-be leaders, and the impact of leadership on cooperation.

There are, of course, many open questions and unexplored research frontiers that demand future attention. For example, while there has been research that explicitly investigated leadership in the various stages of a regime's existence (Andresen and Agrawala 2002), the vast majority of scholarship on international leadership has focused on the agenda-setting, pre-negotiation phase and the negotiation phase—in other words, how leadership matters for institutional bargaining and for overcoming collective action impediments necessary to create regimes and cooperative arrangements in various issue areas. Much less work has been done concerning the role and importance leadership does or does not play concerning regime/agreement operationalization, implementation, compliance, and overall effectiveness. Leadership theory would also profit from being better able carefully to distinguish between leadership efforts directed towards broader overarching goals and leadership efforts directed towards narrower negotiation objectives. Research has also tended to concentrate disproportionately on particular issue areas, such as climate change, and on particular leadership candidates, such as the USA and the EU. This raises questions, such as, to what extent are outcomes agent specific and do the insights from one issue area apply to others? Clearly more comparative research is needed on multiple cases across issue areas. Finally, in an increasingly multipolar world, more research on distributed or shared leadership is essential.

The dense thicket of long-standing and emerging transnational problems that demand international solutions ensures that the subject of international cooperation and the debate over the importance and role of leadership in facilitating cooperative action will be of enduring relevance and interest to scholars and practitioners alike. Because we live in a complex global world with a vast array of vexing global challenges dealing with international economics, international security, and the environment, there is a strong need for global leadership and therefore a corresponding need for improved scholarly knowledge of the phenomena related to multilateral leadership in all its dimensions.

RECOMMENDED READING

Kindleberger, C. P. (1988). *The International Economic Order*. Cambridge, MA: Massachusetts Institute of Technology Press.

Underdal, A. (1994). 'Leadership Theory: Rediscovering the Arts of Management', in W. I. Zartman (ed.), *International Multilateral Negotiation: Approaches to the Management of Complexity*. San Francisco, CA: Jossey-Bass Publishers, 178–97.

Young, O. (1991). 'Political Leadership and Regime Formation: On the Development of Institutions in International Society', *International Organization*, 45/3: 281–309.

REFERENCES

Andresen, S., and Agrawala, S. (2002). 'Leaders, Pushers and Laggards in the Making of the Climate Regime', *Global Environmental Change*, 12/1: 41–51.

Christoff, P. (2010). 'Cold Climate in Copenhagen: China and the United States at COP-15', *Environmental Politics*, 19/4: 637–56.

Elgström, O. (2007). 'The European Union as a Leader in International Multilateral Negotiations: A Problematic Aspiration?', *International Relations*, 21/4: 445–58.

Gupta, J., and van der Grijp, N. (1999). 'Leadership in the Climate Change Regime: The European Union in the Looking Glass', *International Journal of Sustainable Development*, 2/2: 303–22.

Gupta, J., and van der Grijp, N. (2000). 'Perceptions of the EU's Role', in J. Gupta and M. Grubb (eds), *Climate Change and European Leadership: A Sustainable Role for Europe?* Dordrecht: Kluwer Academic Publishers, 67–82.

Gupta, J., and Ringius, L. (2001). 'The EU's Climate Leadership: Reconciling Ambition and Reality', *International Environmental Agreements: Politics, Law and Economics*, 1/2: 281–99.

Hampson, F. O., and Hart, M. (1995). *Multilateral Negotiations: Lessons from Arms Control, Trade, and the Environment.* Baltimore, MD: Johns Hopkins University Press.

Hurrell, A., and Kingsbury, B. (1992). *The International Politics of the Environment.* Oxford: Clarendon Press.

Karlsson, C., Parker, C., Hjerpe, M., and Linnér, B.-O. (2011). 'Looking for Leaders: Perceptions of Climate Change Leadership among Climate Change Negotiation Participants', *Global Environmental Politics*, 14/1: 89–107.

Karlsson, C., Hjerpe, M., Parker, C., and Linnér, B.-O. (2012). 'The Legitimacy of Leadership in International Climate Change Negotiations', *Ambio: A Journal of the Human Environment*, 41/1: 46–55.

Kilian, B., and Elgström, O. (2010). 'Still a Green Leader? The European Union's Role in International Climate Negotiations', *Cooperation and Conflict*, 45/3: 255–73.

Kindleberger, C. P. (1988). *The International Economic Order.* Cambridge, MA: Massachusetts Institute of Technology Press.

Malnes, R. (1995). ' "Leader" and "Entrepreneur" in International Negotiations: A Conceptual Analysis', *European Journal of International Relations*, 1/1: 87–112.

Nye, J. S. (2008). *The Powers to Lead.* Oxford: Oxford University Press.

Oberthür, S., and Roche Kelly, C. (2008). 'EU Leadership in International Climate Policy: Achievements and Challenges', *International Spectator*, 43/3: 35–50.

Parker, C., and Karlsson, C. (2010). 'Climate Change and the European Union's Leadership Moment: An Inconvenient Truth?', *Journal of Common Market Studies*, 48/4: 923–43.

Parker, C., Karlsson, C., Hjerpe, M., and Linnér, B.-O. (2012). 'Fragmented Climate Change Leadership: Making Sense of the Ambiguous Outcome of COP-15', *Environmental Politics*, 21/2: 268–86.

Rosenau, J. R. (2006). 'Followership and Discretion: Assessing the Dynamics of Modern Leadership', *Harvard International Review*, 26/3: 14–17.

Saul, U. and Seidel, C. (2011). Does Leadership Promote Cooperation in Climate Change Mitigation Policy?', *Climate Policy*, 11/2: 901–21.

Schirm, S. A. (2010). 'Leaders in Need of Followers: Emerging Powers in Global Governance', *European Journal of International Relations*, 16 (2): 197–221.

Schreurs, M., and Tiberghien, Y. (2007). 'Multi-Level Reinforcement: Explaining European Union Leadership in Climate Change Mitigation', *Global Environmental Politics*, 7/4: 19–46.

Sebenius, J. K. (1983). 'Negotiation Arithmetic: Adding and Subtracting Issues and Parties', *International Organization*, 37/2: 281–316.

Sjöstedt, G. (1994). 'Negotiating the Uruguay Round of the General Agreement on Tariffs and Trade', in W. I. Zartman (ed.), *International Multilateral Negotiation: Approaches to the Management of Complexity.* San Francisco: Jossey-Bass Publishers, 44–69.

Sjöstedt, G. (1998). 'The EU Negotiates Climate Change: External Performance And Internal Structural Change', *Cooperation and Conflict*, 33/3: 227–56.

Skodvin, T., and Andresen, S. (2006). 'Leadership Revisited', *Global Environmental Politics*, 6/3: 13–27.

Tallberg, J. (2006). *Leadership and Negotiation in the European Union.* Cambridge: Cambridge University Press.

Tallberg, J. (2010). 'The Power of the Chair: Formal Leadership in International Cooperation', *International Studies Quarterly*, 54/1: 241–65.

Underdal, A. (1980). *The Politics of International Fisheries Management: The Case of the North-East Atlantic.* Oslo: Scandinavian Press.

Underdal, A. (1994). 'Leadership Theory: Rediscovering the Arts of Management', in W. I. Zartman (ed.), *International Multilateral Negotiation: Approaches to the Management of Complexity*. San Francisco, CA: Jossey-Bass Publishers, 178–97.

Young, O. (1991). 'Political Leadership and Regime Formation: On the Development of Institutions in International Society', *International Organization*, 45/3: 281–309.

Zito, A. (2005). 'The European Union as an Environmental Leader in Global Environment', *Globalizations*, 2/3: 363–75.

CHAPTER 39

LEADERSHIP OF INTERNATIONAL ORGANIZATIONS

BOB REINALDA AND BERTJAN VERBEEK

1 INTRODUCTION

LEADERSHIP in the international realm is a classic theme, given the hero-in-history model based on the idea that a small group of leaders make world history. However, even if some well-known leaders of international organizations (IOs) may be considered world leaders—for instance, Dag Hammarskjöld or Kofi Annan—IO leadership is not a broadly researched theme, partly owing to the impact of the realist paradigm in international relations (IR) theory, which does not pay much attention to the room for manœuvre of IOs or their executives. Yet, various approaches applying organizational or sociological theories have discussed leadership of IOs more extensively.

This chapter provides an overview of leadership of IOs by discussing, first, the general context of IO leadership analyses in political science; second, the attempt to understand IO leadership from the 1950s to the 1970s, when a research programme was elaborated to see the internal dynamics of IOs, also paying attention to leadership; third, more recent analyses of leadership in the United Nations (UN) and European Union (EU) systems; and, finally, some promising ways of studying leadership of IOs by focusing on problem-solving and implementation.

2 THE CONTEXT OF IO LEADERSHIP ANALYSES

The hero-in-history model in the context of world politics focuses on the personality of leaders, their perceptions of what is going on, and their capacity to lead. Relevant factors are elements such as self-image (personal values, political preferences), personal characteristics, legitimacy, authority, and available information. When individual leaders of IOs are being discussed—for instance, in biographies of IO executives—one may recognize these elements. The limits of bureaucratic organization, as elaborated in the 1970s and 1980s through Graham Allison's bureaucratic politics model and Irving Janis's groupthink concept, have been discussed as a general theme in the field of foreign-policy analysis, but hardly in the context of IOs. Analyses of political executives and their officials as a subfield of political science, in particular political institutions, have focused on political institutions of the state (Campbell 1993). In the subfield of IR, IOs have met with scepticism, if not contempt, when being portrayed as the puppets of powerful member states, often accused of ineffectiveness and inefficiency or politicization. This has resulted in a limited amount of interest in analysing IOs and their leaders. However, when major trans-border upheavals and security or economic crises occur, IOs are looked towards for guidance, and it is obvious that in such emergency cases IOs need leadership in order to play their roles effectively.

These conflicting perspectives on what IOs can do raise the question of whether IOs possess 'agency': can they act in a purposeful way and with notable effect? We seek to determine the agency of IOs and to identify the conditions under which their executives are able to exercise leadership and to what effect. Our major claim is that (leaders of) IOs can indeed exercise leadership, but this leadership is contingent on various factors, in particular: (*a*) the room for manoeuvre allowed to IOs by their member states, whether formally or informally; (*b*) the extent to which the image of a neutral and impartial player can be maintained; (*c*) the specific phase in the policy cycle on which IOs seek to make an impact; and (*d*) the specific traits of individuals occupying consequential positions within IOs.

Although we speak of 'international organizations', it is more accurate to use the term intergovernmental organizations (IGOs). The latter term reminds of the fact that IOs are the creatures of nation states. IOs are founded by the conclusion of an inter-state treaty under international law. The treaty stipulates the official domain covered by the organization and its objectives, creates an assembly of some form in which the member states are represented, and establishes a secretariat that is entrusted with carrying out the decisions taken by the organization. With regard to agency of IOs, we can discern between two approaches. In the first, agency is made up of the member states, because the IO's policies and actions require the consent of the (most powerful) member states. This is true, for instance, for the UN Security Council and with regard to the EU for the consent of its two most powerful members, France and Germany. The second approach with regard to agency of IOs focuses on the international character of the secretariats. The idea that international civil servants have to serve their IO rather than their nation states was officially proclaimed in the League of Nations' Covenant (1919), with other IOs following the League in this respect. In principle, this point of departure allows the main executives of IOs to show agency by developing autonomous policies.

Rational choice theory has been helpful to clarify the relationship between states and (the bureaucracy of) an IO as one between principal and agent, in which the principal delegates, but does not surrender, authority to the agent. Although formally a principal can withdraw the delegated authority, this may be a costly measure and is complicated, because IOs have not one but many principals (which an agent can set against each other). An agent's freedom of manœuvre stems mainly from an asymmetrical distribution of information favouring the agent. This asymmetry then produces 'slippage': an agent pursuing interests of its own, with the principal's problem being how to control the agent and limit slippage. This can be done by oversight procedures, which, however, involve additional costs for principals. Darren Hawkins and others (2006: 8) argue that IOs are to be understood as bureaucracies that can be controlled to varying degrees by their 'masters'. They call independent action by an agent 'agency slack,' occurring in two forms: 'shirking' (when an agent minimizes the effort it exerts on its principal's behalf) and 'slippage' (when an agent shifts policy away from its principal's preferred outcome and towards its own preferences). 'Autonomy' is the extent of manœuvring available to agents after the principal has established control mechanisms. Hawkins et al. (2006: 342–3) found that some measure of agent autonomy is a prerequisite for enabling states to enhance their credibility, lock in favoured policies, overcome collective decision-making problems, or resolve disputes through delegation. They also found that IOs possess varying autonomy and potential for agency slack. When IOs become slack, member states periodically attempt to improve oversight of and performance by their agents. Unfortunately, rational choice theory has not been particularly helpful for identifying leadership in general (Rothstein 1996: 158), nor in IO, given its focus on action of the most powerful states, rather than on action by IOs.

In order to be successful in playing roles of their own, IOs must make sure that their policies are impartial or neutral in the sense of not favouring some member states over others and not provoking a specific state or group of states. IOs thus should be aware of the minefield of impartiality and neutrality. The extent to which they can use the room for manœuvre for autonomous or self-directed action depends on the tools of influence they have at their disposal (formal and informal tools) and on when they become involved in the various phases of the policy cycle (agenda-setting, decision-making, and implementation). During the agenda-setting phase IOs may raise awareness of an issue, raise an issue, or keep an issue on the agenda as a result of feedback processes to the IO. Although most IOs do not formally enjoy decision-making powers, they influence member-state decision-making by the technical expertise they have available as a result of regular reports on the implementation of their international policies and IOs' abilities in building coalitions with states and other actors, including experts and non-governmental organizations (NGOs). Finally, it should be taken into account that not all executives of IOs are leaders. Here the term leadership encompasses both positions at the head of large bureaucracies and the representation of the IO in its environment of states and other international actors, such as other IGOs, internationally active NGOs, and the media. The ability to combine internal and external leadership makes for the ideal leader of an IO.

3 OPENING UP THE BLACK BOX OF AN INTERNATIONAL ORGANIZATION

Various attempts to understand leadership of IOs have been made, in spite of the realist dominance in IR. Three will be discussed here: Inis Claude's 'leader-versus-clerk' image, the research programme of Ernst Haas, Robert Cox, and Harold Jacobson to 'open up the black box' of IOs, and Oran Young's leadership typology in the context of international regimes.

In his *Swords into Plowshares* of 1956 Claude discussed international organization as a historical process, in which the introduction of the secretariat is regarded as an innovation that transformed a series of multilateral conferences (part of the multilateralization and regularization of diplomacy in the nineteenth century) into an organization. While various actors may control an IO, the staff headed by a secretary or secretary-general *is* the organization and *is* the international component (Claude 1964: 174–5). Focusing on the still-young UN, Claude, a realist with an open mind, discerned three major problems presented by the need for an adequate secretariat: efficient administration, allegiance, and political initiative. The secretary-general (SG) needs to deal with these three interrelated problems in a state-dominated environment. The problem of political initiative refers to the ideal of political leadership by a SG in which he or she is also an 'international statesman' (for various reasons, a problematic term), rather than an 'anonymous, unobtrusive, administrative technician'. Claude (1964: 189) referred to significant limitations to the office, such as the absence of a coercive capacity and the question of the amount of 'international statesmanship' that is permitted by the realities of world politics. Notwithstanding his focus on these limitations, both as a manager (the first two problems) and as a political actor (the third problem), he also discussed the actual initiatives that specific SGs had taken as managers and politicians. He did so by comparing Albert Thomas, as the dynamic International Labour Organization (ILO) politician, with Sir Eric Drummond, as the sober civil servant of the League. This was referred to as 'leader versus clerk', later also termed active 'general' versus administrative 'secretary'. In his comparison of Hammarskjöld and Trygve Lie, Claude argued that Hammarskjöld's style of operation in combination with prevailing political circumstances allowed him to use the UN office as a political institution in a stronger way than his predecessor Lie. Claude concluded that serious limitations to the office do not rule out SGs taking initiative in managing the international secretariat or in showing political initiative and leadership, but that such 'international statesmanship' was exceptional.

In 1964 Haas published his book *Beyond the Nation State: Functionalism and International Organization*, in which he developed an analytical framework that combines 'dynamic functionalism' with organization theory, leaving plenty of room for realist factors. He called it rather 'eclectic' (Haas 1964: pp. vii, ix), but his framework revealed some interesting elements of IO autonomy resulting from an interaction of organizational dynamics and environmental inputs. This helped to map the ways in which an IO and its executive head may play a role of its own and make nation states comply with its rules. By applying Philip Selznick's theories of bureaucracy and organizational growth, notably Selznick (1957), Haas was able to explain how an IO (the ILO) acquires independence from its environment of states. He opened up the 'black box' to see what was going on inside. While neo-realist Kenneth Waltz argues that leaders of IOs are 'not masters of the matters their organizations deal with' and are concerned only 'to secure the continuity and health of the organization' (Waltz 1979: 111), Haas pointed out that leadership of the bureaucracy may produce instruments that enable the organization to be politically active in IR and take measures that effectively intrude into the national domains of the member states. Once leadership and motivated machinery have been built up internally, a process of choosing external clients and supporters and identifying competitors and enemies begins, followed by participation in the international game with regard to the matters of the IO. Hence, both internally directed management and externally oriented political pursuit are crucial for executive leadership. Applying organizational theory to IOs allowed Haas (1964: 111) to trace the possible patterns of outcomes: a minimum common denominator, splitting the difference and upgrading the common interests of the parties.

In his 1969 essay on leadership in international organization, Cox argued that an IO's executive head plays a key role in turning an IO into an international actor. He argued that Haas's framework of organizational ideology *plus* committed bureaucracy *plus* supporting coalition offered valid guidelines, but that the executive head had to be conscious of organizational constraints, such as bureaucratic immobilism, client control resulting from the institutionalization of client interests, and the pattern of conflicts and alignments that leaves either more or less room for the brokerage role an executive head may play. 'The personal idiosyncratic dimension enters both in the form of the executive head's ability to maintain himself as top man in bureaucratic politics and in the clarity of his perception of the significance for international organization of the prevailing pattern of conflicts and alignments' (Cox 1969: 229–30). Like Haas, Cox and Jacobson opened up the 'black box' in their *The Anatomy of Influence: Decision Making in International Organization* (1973) and attempted to overcome the constraints mentioned by Cox. Eight IOs were scrutinized in the book, based on the common framework developed by Cox and Jacobson. They discerned several types of decision and, following the ideas of David Easton (1965) on political systems, saw IOs as political systems with linkages to member states, rather than as independent islands of activity. The political system of an IO consists of two subsystems, a 'representative' one consisting of states and a 'participant' one consisting of all actors involved. While representative subsystems are 'oligarchic', participant subsystems can be either 'monarchic' (administered by the executive head and his or her confidants) or 'pluralistic–bargaining' (with many actors fighting for the microphone). The framework also takes environmental impacts into account, among them what Cox called the pattern of conflicts and alignments. The most important actors, according to their anatomic lesson, are the representatives of national governments, members of the bureaucracy, the executive heads, and also representatives of NGOs. Although Cox and Jacobson arrived at a realist conclusion (the more salient the decisions and areas of an organization under concern, the less autonomy it achieves), their analysis also showed that IOs can be fairly autonomous, depending on region, issue area, and type of decision. Hadewych Hazelzet (1998), who 'revisited' their *Anatomy* twenty-five years later, concluded that their analysis framework still holds true.

Although the resources available to SGs are limited, they have a few assets available that allow leadership. A first one is the ability of SGs to use the international bureaucracy, or elements of it, in ways they choose. SGs may initiate research to document arguments or to explore alternatives and they may maintain contacts or negotiate with states. Other assets are their strategic location in the communication networks of their IOs and the fact that their position affords them platforms from which they can make their views known. SGs can use these platforms to speak to larger and more limited groups, knowing that their position as executive head gives them a legitimate and sure means of stating views. Their key task here is to mobilize a consensus in support of organizational goals. The requirements for success with regard to an SG's qualities are an 'effective relationship between the personality and particular talents of the incumbent individual, the characteristics of the organization, and the opportunities presented by its world environment' (Cox and Jacobson 1973: 398). Among the minimum requirements for success are maintaining effective working relations with at least some of the key member states that control the resources for the organization's functioning, maintaining effective working relations with the voting majority in the organization's conference machinery, and ensuring that segments of the international bureaucracy do not work against the SG's policies.

Eighteen years later Michael Schechter (1987) criticized Cox's idea that effective leadership was the most critical single determinant of the growth in scope and authority of leadership of IOs. He believed that there was a bias towards the study of dynamic executive heads and argued that the skills of institutionalization may not be the most appropriate ones for effective leadership when there are limited resources available for multilateral, non-security activities. Effective leadership according to Schechter (1987: 197), who compared three different IOs in the 1970s and 1980s, is a product not only of systemic and organizational characteristics, but also of personal factors. Accordingly, 'the personal factors which are needed effectively to lead one organization may not be appropriate in another or in the same organization at different times'. Since there is still a gap in our understanding of the executive heads of IOs, both individually and collectively, in terms of who they are, where they come from, and how they affect the performance of IOs, the IO BIO Project was recently set up as a biographical dictionary of SGs of IOs, to provide short biographies of individual SGs as well as group analyses (see IO BIO 2012).

The promising research programme set up by Haas, Cox, and Jacobson was interrupted by a new group of scholars, who initiated a more general and soon dominant IR research programme in the 1970s in which the interest in formal IOs was restricted, because their focus was on theory and they first wanted to understand world politics. This approach resulted in the so-called regime theory. The term 'international institution' encompasses more than the classic 'IO', including IGOs, NGOs, and less formal regimes and conventions. Oran Young (1991: 285) tried to bring the individual back into the study of IR, without diminishing the role of collective entities. He defined leadership as the actions of individuals who endeavour to solve or circumvent the collective action problems that plague the efforts of parties seeking to reap joint gains in processes of institutional bargaining. With regard to the roles that leaders play in the formation of international institutions, he developed a tripartite typology of political leadership: structural, entrepreneurial, and intellectual. Entrepreneurial leaders are those who frame issues at stake, devise mutually acceptable formulas, and broker the interests of key players in building support for these formulas. Although Young did not focus directly on leadership of SGs of IOs, his typology can help to discern whether and when SGs exhibit structural, entrepreneurial, or intellectual leadership in institutional bargaining. Entrepreneurial leadership has played a central role in the constructivist 'transnational advocacy networks' approach, in which networks of activists coalesce and operate across national frontiers, targeting the policies of IOs and particular states (Keck and Sikkink 1998). A similar line of research consists in studies employing the concept of epistemic communities, which focused on the presence and collaborative efforts of like-minded actors (experts) across domestic and international organizations, both public and private (Haas 1992). Martha Finnemore and Kathryn Sikkink (1998) included the internal workings of IOs by generating a coherent set of propositions about the emergence of international norms, the mechanisms by which they exercise influence and the conditions under which norms will be influential in world politics. They argue that norms evolve in a patterned 'life cycle', with three stages: norm emergence, acceptance, and internalization. Persuasion by norm entrepreneurs who need to persuade a critical mass of states to become norm leaders and adopt new norms is the characteristic mechanism of the first stage. These entrepreneurs call attention to issues and 'frame' them by using language that names, interprets, and dramatizes the issues. In order to be effective, leadership is also relevant in the other two stages.

4 LEADERSHIP IN THE UNITED NATIONS AND THE EUROPEAN UNION

This section discusses the state of the art with regard to ideas about leadership in two large combinations of organizations, the UN and the EU.

The United Nations System

The literature on SG leadership has been dominated by a focus on the UN SGs, with a primary emphasis on their political role, in particular in peace and security, but the SGs of UN agencies and other IOs are being covered progressively (Kille 2013). A few recent books have focused on leadership aspects. In his book *From Manager to Visionary: The Secretary-General of the United Nations* (2006) Kent Kille discusses various leadership styles, which are made up of a set of interrelated personal characteristics that may char- acterize the behaviour of SGs, as opposed to national politicians, such as responsivity (which is a combination of self-confidence and conceptual complexity), 'beliefe that they can influence', 'need for recognition', 'need for relationships', 'supra-nationalism', and 'problem-solving emphasis'. Kille examines how a leadership style impacts on how SGs attempt to use their position in an influential manner, set out as available 'ave- nues of influence', with administrative duties as an avenue of influence with regard to bureaucracy, given the important capabilities that may be derived from administrative duties. Kille derives three key leadership styles (manager, strategist, and visionary), with Hammerskjöld representing the visionary style, Kurt Waldheim the manager style, and Annan the strategist style. SGs are thus viewed as individuals who bring a personal style to bear on their activities, be it within several contextual constraints. Kille does not con- sider personal traits and contextual variables as competing factors, but argues that the interaction of the two should provide the greatest explanatory value. The three styles are related to how SGs view constraints: as something to be challenged (Hammarskjöld, Boutros Boutros-Ghali), respected (Waldheim), or accommodated (Annan). In another, also comparative book Kille (2007: 348) has elaborated on SGs as moral leaders, who use their 'inner code' as a 'kind of spiritual filter' that helps to guide their interpreta- tion of the context in which they are operating.

The book *Secretary or General? The UN Secretary-General in World Politics*, edited by Simon Chesterman, does not discuss the administrative role of UN SGs but looks at their four political roles, as the UN SG's role 'has come to be seen as primarily politi- cal' (Chesterman 2007: p. xi). These roles cover the use of 'group of friends' (mobilizing governments through encouraging interested states to form supportive informal coali- tions), as well as being a 'bully pulpit' (acting as spokesman of universal values and for the interests of humanity as a whole), a norm entrepreneur (being embedded in the cre- ation of norms discussed before, not as a free agent but as one who has a privileged place in the organizational context), and a policy entrepreneurship (with a forward-looking vision, looking for new ideas and diverse policy solutions to complex global problems). Although not explicitly discussed in the book under leadership of IOs, the various polit- ical roles assume leadership, such as the ability to influence the resolution of conflicts (group of friends), to steer the course of the debate (bully pulpit) and to make proposals for action or long-term solutions for problems and adaption of the organization (both forms of entrepreneurship).

The European Union System

The literature on leadership in the EU has focused mainly on the role of supranational institutions—that is, the Commission and, to a lesser extent, the European Court of Justice (ECJ) and the European Central Bank (ECB). Most studies have focused on their relationship with the member states. Relatively little attention has been paid to specific characteristics of supranational leaders and the weight they may carry in accounting for this relationship.

The view of the Commission's role has changed with alterations in the EU's institutional make-up. When the European Coal and Steel Community and the European Economic Community were still highly intergovernmental in nature, based on unanimity between member states, the Commission was recognized as a potential 'honest broker' by promoting solutions that seemed to split the difference or upgrade the common interest (Haas 1958). In this era the ECJ also demonstrated leadership, although its accomplishments were not recognized until the 1980s. Its principal source of influence was the deliberate socialization of national judges towards the ECJ's perspective (Alter 2001: 182–208). By knowingly downplaying its own role, the Court managed to establish the revolutionary idea of 'direct rule' and to ensure the protection of individual rights vis-à-vis the member states and the European Community.

The Commission's leadership role expanded with the adoption of the Single European Act (SEA) in 1985. Its exclusive right of legislative initiative, its new task to ensure the implementation of a single market, and the introduction of the qualified majority decision rule in the Council increased its institutional resources, but above all invested new moral authority into the Commission. In fact, the SEA's adoption has been attributed to the exceptional leadership qualities of Commission President Jacques Delors. His shrewd strategy of framing the act as technical implementation of a decision that was already part of the 1958 Treaties of Rome made member states go along with a major deepening of European integration (see, e.g., Fligstein 1997). At the same time, Delors's leadership could be effective only because the policy preferences of the three largest member states at the time (France, Germany, the United Kingdom) happened to converge around the single market idea (Moravcsik 1991). Indeed, leadership in the EU is often contingent upon leadership of the most important states, currently France and Germany.

The SEA and later intergovernmental treaties (Maastricht 1992, Amsterdam 1997, Nice 1999, Lisbon 2009) both caused and resolved conflicts between member states and the Commission. The Commission developed from a 'broker' into a 'leader' in many areas, specifically when it could invoke its authority to ensure the completion of the internal market. It managed to initiate policies in areas that were often considered as off limits through 'creative legislation' and soft power techniques such as 'best practices' and 'technical advice' (Leibfried and Pierson 1995). The 1990s and 2000s thus witnessed a constant battle between the Commission and the member states over its exact mandate (for an overview, see Van Kersbergen and Verbeek 2007). A similar, though less pronounced, conflict characterized the relations with the ECJ (Burley and Mattli 1993). The 2012 conflict over solving the sovereign debt crisis of certain EU member states may spark a similar debate over the ECB's leadership. On the whole, then, even in a highly legalized international system like the EU, the organization's secretariat must be careful not persistently to antagonize its member states.

Interestingly, almost all studies of the EU's supranational institutions approach the players as unitary actors and attribute leadership qualities to these bodies. However, in reality the Commission, the ECJ, and the ECB each consists of a plurality of players. Little is known of the relevant personal characteristics or attitudes. Some research has been done into the leadership traits of Commission Presidents. An analysis of four presidents suggests that Delors's personality fits his dynamic leadership aimed at expansion of the Commission's role (Kille and Scully 2003). At the same time, next to nothing is known of his counterparts in Luxembourg and Frankfurt. The closest we come is information about the attitudes of top civil servants in the Commission. Most surveys focus on whether they are constrained by national loyalties or consider the Commission's position as autonomous (Page 1997; Hooghe 1999 and 2012; Hooghe and Marks 2012). A real lacuna remains the exercise of leadership within these collective decision-making bodies. Some studies suggest that policy-making is the result of negotiations between the Cabinets that head the Commission's Directorates-General to such an extent that the Commission itself can exert little leadership (Cini 1996: 154–160).

Although it is common to link EU leadership to the Commission, it is important to realize that it has always competed for leadership, particularly with the rotating President of the Council of Ministers (Tallberg 2006). This competition has increased with the creation of new institutions following the adoption of the Treaty of Lisbon. The Commission as such, and particularly its President, now faces competition from the permanent President of the European Council, currently taken by Herman Van Rompuy. Although he also faces competition from the member state that holds the Presidency for six months, Van Rompuy's modest, pragmatic leadership style as a broker between Commission and Council seems to strengthen the new function. At the same time, the Commission's potential leadership has been increased by the creation of the office of the High Representative of the Union for External Affairs and Security. Since 2010 national and European civil servants have merged into the European External Action Service. As a result, this position may prove an instrument of future EU leadership in foreign affairs (Vanhoonacker, Pomorska, and Maurer 2011).

5 PROMISING WAYS OF DEVELOPING IO
LEADERSHIP STUDIES (1): PROBLEM SOLVING

Although IO leadership is not a broadly or coherently researched theme in political science, the research programme to open up the black box of IOs, set up by Haas, Cox, and Jacobson and nuanced by Schechter, as well as Young's ideas about leadership in international regimes allow the understanding of both *internal* leadership qualities (as the head of an international bureaucracy) and *external* leadership (as a more or less autonomous player in international relations). The recent use of the sociology of organizations by constructivists Michael Barnett and Martha Finnemore in their influential book *Rules for the World* (2004) may help to understand faulty or failed leadership, but this approach's handicap is that it does not discuss leadership explicitly. It addresses the capability of IOs to exercise authority via their bureaucratic nature and focuses on the problems that arise when bureaucracies become obsessed with their own rules at the expense of their primary missions in ways that produce inefficient and self-defeating outcomes. Hence, IOs, just like other bureaucracies, are prone to dysfunctional behaviour or 'pathologies.'

Far more promising, also with regard to the practical implications of IO leadership, are Frank Biermann and Bernd Siebenhüner, who in their *Managers of Global Change* (2009) use a narrower definition of international bureaucracies than Barnett and Finnemore. They regard the secretariat rather than the entire organization as a bureaucracy and are less concerned with pathologies of bureaucracies than with their potential to contribute to problem-solving. While both principal–agent theory and sociological perspectives assume a self-centred interest of bureaucracies that leads to pathological behaviour, Biermann and Siebenhüner reject the assumption that international bureaucracies strive predominantly to maximize their mandate, funding, staff, and power. Instead, they found that international bureaucracies are more interested in resolving political problems than in increasing their power as such. Their nine case studies reveal that bureaucracies have a sizeable autonomous influence as actors in global environmental policy by acting as knowledge brokers, negotiation facilitators, and capacity builders. Drawing on organizational theory and its empirical notions of organizational cultures and internal procedures, they analyse international bureaucracies as social processes and collective entities constituted by their distinct organizational cultures, structures, and behaviours. They argue that much variation in the autonomous influence, and hence the leadership potential, of these bureaucracies can be traced back to differences in organizational cultures—that is, 'the "software" within bureaucracies that are otherwise similar in their legal mandate, resources, and general function' (Biermann and Siebenhüner 2009: 8).

Going into the internal factors (the people and procedures), Biermann and Siebenhüner discuss the role of leadership of an international bureaucracy through four organizational aspects: expertise (staff ability to generate and process knowledge), structure (formalized internal rules and procedures that assign tasks and positions in the hierarchy), culture (the set of commonly shared basic assumptions that result from previous organizational learning processes and include the staff's professional cultures and backgrounds), and leadership. They discern four styles of organizational leadership: hierarchical (where executives decide by themselves without involving their employees), consultative (in which executives ask for the opinion of their employees and decide by themselves), cooperative (in which directors together with employees search for new solutions but directors decide by themselves), and participatory (in which employees are granted far-reaching participation in decision-making). Leaders of bureaucracies can be popular, charismatic, and effective in this framework (or the opposite) and may exhibit structural, entrepreneurial, or intellectual leadership, as defined by Young. Other relevant aspects for leadership are the commitment and work ethics of the rank and file and the leader's flexibility and openness to change. Although Biermann and Siebenhüner do not refer to SGs, they have elaborated a clear idea of leadership of an IO. They define 'strong leadership' as the behaviour of a leader who follows a style of leadership that is charismatic, visionary, and popular as well as flexible and reflexive. It thus includes 'the ability to rapidly gain acceptance and acknowledgement by employees and externals, to develop, communicate, and implement visions, and to learn and change routines' (Biermann and Siebenhüner 2009: 58). Future research along this path will allow us to tackle a vital leadership issue that has so far been neglected: the extent to which (lack of) internal leadership affects an IO's external leadership.

Biermann and Siebenhüner's notion of problem-solving leadership can also be applied to the issue of IOs and crisis management. In times of crisis IOs are often called upon for help and need to show leadership in extremely difficult and complex situations. However, IR literature does not focus on the existing literature on crisis management and crisis decision-making (while crisis literature barely takes notice of IOs). The commonly held position among scholars examining crisis management has been that crises tend to centralize leadership at the highest organizational levels. This leads to the risk of creating bottlenecks in information flows and decision-making procedures through dysfunctional modes such as groupthink and bureau-political competition. A focus on the combination of internal and external IO leadership as well as 'strong' leadership styles may help to understand better the debate between centralized and decentralized crisis responses (with surprising events being better managed by those closer to the event than the IO leadership), but that assumes that the crisis management literature needs to be incorporated in studies of IO leadership, as argued by Olsson and Verbeek (2013).

6 Promising Ways of Developing IO Leadership Studies (2): Leadership During Implementation

So far, most attention has been paid to IO leadership in the agenda-setting phase of the international policy cycle. Formal competencies (for example, of the UN SG and the European Commission) and empowerment of specific actors (such as NGOs during international conferences) allow IOs to frame issues and thus affect decision-making (Joachim 2007). Future studies, however, should also investigate how IOs exercise leadership during the implementation phase of the policy cycle. Many IGOs have been entrusted with the oversight of national implementation of internationally agreed-upon policies or engage in implementing such policies themselves. Leadership is significant here, given the fact that IOs may employ three different strategies: (1) enforcement through dispute resolution mechanisms, or its softer approach of naming and shaming (which affects the reputation of governments), (2) a managerial approach by providing technical and other assistance for implementation (being helpful), and (3) a normative approach by putting forward substantive arguments favouring a certain international policy (also applied in crisis situations) (Joachim, Reinalda, and Verbeek 2008). In the oversight of national implementation, IOs are reluctant to apply hard power measures, such as sanctions, fearing to antagonize important member states. This is less the case in the EU, where the European Commission has a powerful deterrent of member-state non-compliance: (threatening to) start an infringement procedure (Tallberg 2002). However, when IOs are engaged in implementing structural policies or are flown in during emergency situations, they often operate in the sovereign territory of a host country. Even though they act upon internationally agreed policies, the principle of state sovereignty requires them to observe their impartiality meticulously and to walk a tightrope during implementation, careful not to give cause to be impeded or, at worst, expelled, and yet meeting the goals set out by the international community.

Studies of IO leadership should investigate how leaders choose between available implementation strategies and how their choices affect an IO's effectiveness. Another promising avenue for research is the choices IOs make in building coalitions with national and transnational actors, both governmental and non-governmental, in order to promote compliance with international policies. It is known that such coalitions are instrumental in enhancing IOs' effectiveness in implementation. Much less is known of the policy entrepreneurs at the IOs' offices whose leadership succeeds in forging such coalitions.

All in all, given the growth in the number of IOs over the past since the 1990s twenty and the escalating tasks delegated to them, IO leadership deserves to be a major subject of scholarly study. Its advancement depends not only on identifying the conditions of IO leadership in all phases of the policy cycle, but also on exploring the dynamics of how top bureaucrats lead their IOs. A precondition of this is the collection of data on such officials, as by the new IO BIO project. Only then will it be possible to assess the nexus between internal and external IO leadership. In the end, this also requires a change in the dominant methodology. Rather than zooming in on single instances of success or failure of leaders, scholars should employ a comparative design in order to establish and test the conditions of IO leadership.

RECOMMENDED READING

Cox, R. W., and Jacobson, H. K. (1973) (eds). *The Anatomy of Influence: Decision Making in International Organization*. New Haven, CT: Yale University Press.

Joachim, J., Reinalda, B., and Verbeek, B. (2008) (eds). *International Organizations and Policy Implementation: Enforcers, Managers, Leaders?* London: Routledge.

Tallberg, J. (2006). *Leadership and Negotiation in the European Union*. Cambridge: Cambridge University Press.

REFERENCES

Alter, K. J. (2001). *Establishing the Supremacy of European Law: The Making of an International Rule of Law in Europe*. Oxford: Oxford University Press.

Barnett, M., and Finnemore, M. (2004). *Rules for the World: International Organizations in Global Politics*. Ithaca, NY: Cornell University Press.

Biermann, F., and Siebenhüner, B. (2009) (eds). *Managers of Global Change: The Influence of International Environmental Bureaucracies*. Cambridge, MA: MIT Press.

Burley, A.-M., and Mattli, W. (1993). 'Europe before the Court: A Political Theory of Legal Integration', *International Organization*, 47/1: 41–76.

Campbell, S. J. (1993). 'Political Executives and their Officials', in A. W. Finifter (ed.), *Political Science: The State of the Discipline II*. Washington: American Political Science Association, 383–406.

Chesterman, S. (2007) (ed.). *Secretary or General? The UN Secretary-General in World Politics*. Cambridge: Cambridge University Press.

Cini, M. (1996). *The European Commission: Leadership, Organisation, and Culture in the EU Administration*. Manchester: Manchester University Press.

Claude, I. L., Jr (1964) [1956]. *Swords into Plowshares: The Problems and Progress of International Organization*. London: University of London Press.

Cox, R. W. (1969). 'The Executive Head: An Essay on Leadership in International Organization', *International Organization*, 23/2: 205–30.

Cox, R. W., and Jacobson, H. K. (1973) (eds). *The Anatomy of Influence: Decision Making in International Organization*. New Haven, CT: Yale University Press.

Easton, D. E. (1965). *A Systems Analysis of Political Life*. New York: Wiley.

Finnemore, M., and Sikkink, K. (1998). 'International Norm Dynamics and Political Change', *International Organization*, 52/4: 887–917.

Fligstein, N. (1997). 'Social Skill and Institutional Theory', *American Behavioral Scientist*, 40/4: 397–405.

Haas, E. B. (1958). *The Uniting of Europe*. Stanford, CA: Stanford University Press.

Haas, E. B. (1964). *Beyond the Nation State: Functionalism and International Organization* (Stanford, CA: Stanford University Press).

Haas, P. M. (1992). 'Epistemic Communities and International Policy Coordination', *International Organization*, 46/1: 1–35.

Hawkins, D. G., Lake, D. A., Nielson, D. L, Tierney, M. J. (2006) (eds). *Delegation and Agency in International Organizations*. Cambridge: Cambridge University Press.

Hazelzet, H. (1998). 'The Decision-Making Approach to International Organizations: Cox and Jacobson's Anatomic Lesson Revisited', in B. Reinalda and B. Verbeek (eds), *Autonomous Policy Making by International Organizations*. London: Routledge, 27–41.

Hooghe, L. (1999). 'Consociationalists or Weberians? Top Commission Officials on Nationalism', *Governance*, 12/4: 397–424.

Hooghe, L. (2012). 'Images of Europe: How Commission Officials Conceive their Institution's Role', *Journal of Common Market Studies*, 50/1: 87–111.

Hooghe, L., and Marks, G. (2012). 'The Authority of International Organizations'. Draft 3.0. Unpublished paper <http://www.unc.edu/~hooghe/research_wip.php>, accessed 15 December 2012.

IO BIO (2012). *Biographical Dictionary of Secretaries-General of International Organizations* <www.ru.nl/fm/iobio>, accessed 10 January 2013.

Joachim, J. (2007). *Agenda Setting, the UN, and NGOs: Gender Violence and Reproductive Rights*. Washington: Georgetown University Press.

Joachim, J., Reinalda, B., and Verbeek, B. (2008) (ed.). *International Organizations and Policy Implementation: Enforcers, Managers, Leaders?* London: Routledge.

Kille, K. J. (2006). *From Manager to Visionary: The Secretary-General of the United Nations* New York: Palgrave Macmillan.

Kille, K. J. (2007) (ed.). *The UN Secretary-General and Moral Authority: Ethics and Religion in International Leadership*. Washington: Georgetown University Press.

Kille, K. J. (2013). 'Secretaries-General of International Organizations: Leadership Capacity and Qualities', in B. Reinalda (ed.), *Routledge Handbook of International Organization*. Abingdon: Routledge, 218–30.

Kille, K. J., and Scully, R. M. (2003). 'Executive Heads and the Role Of Intergovernmental Organizations: Expansionist Leadership in the United Nations and the European Union', *Political Psychology*, 24/1: 175–98.

Keck, M. E., and Sikkink, K. (1998). *Activists beyond Borders: Advocacy Networks in International Politics*. Ithaca, NY: Cornell University Press.

Leibfried, S., and Pierson, P. (1995) (ed.). *European Social Policy: Between Fragmentation and Integration*. Washington: Brookings.

Moravcsik, A. (1991). 'Negotiating the Single European Act: National Interests and Conventional Statecraft in the European Community', *International Organization*, 45/1: 19–56.

Olsson, E.-K., and Verbeek, B. (2013). 'International Organizations and Crisis Management', in B. Reinalda (ed.), *Routledge Handbook of International Organization*. London: Routledge, 324–36.

Page, E. (1997). *People Who Run Europe*. Oxford: Oxford University Press.

Rothstein, B. (1996). 'Political Institutions: An Overview', in R. E. Goodin and H.-D. Klingemann (eds), *A New Handbook of Political Science*. Oxford: Oxford University Press, 133–66.

Schechter, M. G. (1987). 'Leadership in International Organizations: Systemic, Organizational and Personality Factors', *Review of International Studies*, 13/3: 197–220.

Selznick, P. (1957). *Leadership in Administration: A Sociological Interpretation*. Evanston, IL: Row, Petersen.

Tallberg, J. (2002). 'Paths to Compliance: Enforcement, Management, and the European Union', *International Organization*, 56/3: 609–43.

Tallberg, J. (2006). *Leadership and Negotiation in the European Union*. Cambridge: Cambridge University Press.

Vanhoonacker, S., Pomorska, K., and Maurer, H. (2011). 'The Presidency in EU External Relations: Who Is at the Helm?', *Politique européenne*, 35/3: 139–64.

Van Kersbergen, K., and Verbeek, B. (2007). 'The Politics of International Norms: Subsidiarity and the Imperfect Competence Regime of the European Union', *European Journal of International Relations*, 13/2: 217–38.

Waltz, K. N. (1979). *Theory of International Politics*. New York: McGraw-Hill.

Young, O. R. (1991). 'Political Leadership and Regime Formation: On the Development of Institutions in International Society', *International Organization*, 45/3: 281–308.

PART VI

POLITICAL LEADERSHIP BEYOND THE WEST

CHAPTER 40

....

POLITICAL LEADERSHIP
IN CHINA

....

BO ZHIYUE

1 INTRODUCTION

....

THIS chapter deals with the study of political leadership in China in terms of five aspects. First, it will look at China's political leadership from a historical perspective. Second, it will present ideologies, power struggles, and political succession during the eras of Mao Zedong and Deng Xiaoping. Third, it will present theoretical models of 'winner-takes-all' and 'power balancing' and introduce power structures in China. Fourth, it will provide a critical assessment of the state of the art in the subfield and reflect on its practical implications. Fifth, it will point to promising ways forward for future study.

2 CHINA'S POLITICAL LEADERSHIP IN
HISTORICAL PERSPECTIVE

....

It is not always obvious exactly what we mean by 'political leadership in China'. This is because historically there have been two 'Chinas'. The Republic of China (ROC) was established in 1912 after the 1911 Revolution, through which the imperial system of more than two millennia had been overthrown. The People's Republic of China (PRC) was established in 1949 after a three-year civil war between the armed forces of two of the most powerful political parties in China at the time—Guomindang (GMD) under Jiang Jieshi and the Chinese Communist Party (CCP) under Mao Zedong.

After his military defeat, Jiang fled, along with a million followers, to Taiwan, an island opposite the Fujian Province. According to the Constitution of the ROC, Jiang's government still retained its control over all the territories of China. In fact, though, the government of the ROC exercised actual authority over the island of Taiwan and a few adjacent islets. The ROC's membership on the Security Council and general assembly of the United Nations was also replaced by the PRC in 1971. Therefore, 'political leadership in China' here does not refer to political authorities in Taiwan.

Mao Zedong emerged as a victor of the civil war, and the CCP under his leadership established the People's Republic of China. 'Political leadership in China' in this chapter thus refers to political authorities in the PRC. During the cold war, the ROC was often referred to as 'free China' and the PRC was regarded as 'red China'. Nevertheless, 'free China' was not necessarily free from an authoritarian political leadership, and 'red China' experienced tremendous upheavals in its leadership.

Instead of a communist dictatorship as commonly perceived, the People's Republic of China was governed by a coalition of political elites of diverse backgrounds in its early years. The Chinese People's Political Consultative Conference, a political forum for all major political parties minus the Guomindang of Jiang Jieshi, served as the legislature, and the Common Programme, an agreement between the CCP and other political parties, was used as a temporary Constitution. In the newly elected central government, non-CCP elites took a large share of the political leadership. Within the CCP, Mao also practised a democratic leadership style in these years.

After the 1954 national elections, however, the CCP gradually dominated the central government. In contrast to the previous cabinet, where two out of four vice premiers were non-CCP personalities, for instance, ten vice premiers of the new cabinet were all CCP members. Mao Zedong also became more dictatorial. He turned against his non-CCP political collaborators in an anti-rightist campaign in 1957 and against his own colleagues within the CCP in the Cultural Revolution beginning in 1966 (MacFarquhar 1974, 1983, 1997).

3 IDEOLOGIES, POWER STRUGGLES, AND POLITICAL SUCCESSION

Mao Zedong's Era

Western scholars are often impressed by Mao Zedong's military genius and the PLA's prowess. They can all remember by heart Mao's famous statement, 'power comes from the barrels of a gun'. Their understanding of the role of ideology in power struggles within the CCP is less than adequate, however. In fact, Mao's fall from power in the early 1930s was due to his lack of ideological credentials as a Marxist. A seemingly innocent remark that 'mountain valleys cannot produce Marxism' was a fatal blow to Mao's authorities in Jiangxi revolutionary bases that he had created through military campaigns.

Mao regained his authority in the CCP only after he had successfully established himself as a genuine Marxist in China. Mao became the undisputable leader of the CCP at the Seventh National Party Congress in 1945 when his ideology—Mao Zedong Thought—was enshrined in the CCP's Constitution. Mao, however, suffered another major blow to his authority eleven years later at the Eighth National Party Congress in 1956, when Mao Zedong Thought was deleted from the CCP Constitution. In the name of preventing the repeat of the consequences of Stalinism in China, the CCP leadership decided to reign in the personality cult of Mao Zedong and replaced Mao Zedong Thought with collective leadership in the CCP Constitution in 1956. Mao Zedong decided to fight back and eventually launched a Cultural Revolution to regain his ideological authority. He purged those who dared to challenge his political power and reintroduced his ideology—Mao Zedong Thought—to the Constitution of the CCP at the Ninth National Party Congress in 1969.

In the early 1950s, Mao proposed a two-front arrangement partially as a scheme of political succession. According to the scheme, the CCP's top leadership was divided into two fronts. At the first front, party and government leaders such as Liu Shaoqi (President of the PRC), Zhou Enlai (Premier of the State Council), and Deng Xiaoping (General Secretary of the CCP) were given the assignment of managing day-to-day operations of the state affairs; and, at the second front, Mao Zedong (Chairman of the CCP) alone was supposed to ponder important theoretical issues. Mao intervened in the work of the first front leaders from time to time, however, and personally initiated at least three major political campaigns: the anti-rightist campaign, the Great Leap Forward, and the Cultural Revolution.

The two-front arrangement failed as a scheme of political succession. Two potential successors to Mao had a terrible end. Liu Shaoqi, who had been recognized as Mao's successor since 1945 and took over as President of the PRC in 1959, was tortured to death as a 'revisionist' in 1969. Marshal Lin Biao, one of Mao's favorite generals and 'comrade-in-arms', was designated Mao's successor in 1969 but later died in a plane crash in September 1971 after his alleged coup against Mao had failed. Before his death in 1976, Mao picked Hua Guofeng, former first party secretary of Hunan (Mao's hometown), as his successor.

Deng Xiaoping's Era

A short man of less than 5 feet tall, Deng Xiaoping was a political giant. In his political career of more than seventy years, Deng experienced three falls and three rises. In the early 1930s, Deng was removed from his positions within the CCP because he had followed Mao's political lines. After Mao had regained his authority subsequent to the famous Zunyi Conference in January 1935, Deng rose in politics as well. In 1956 Mao promoted him to be general secretary of the CCP as well as a member of the Politburo Standing Committee, a key decision-making body of the CCP. Ten years later, at the beginning of the Cultural Revolution, however, Deng was purged as the No. 2 capitalist roader in China. With Mao's protection, Deng avoided torture and escaped from the physical abuses of Red Guards and revolutionary rebels. Deng came back to the power centre in 1973 in the aftermath of the Marshal Lin Biao Affair, but was purged again in 1976 because of his revisionist tendencies. After Mao's death in 1976, Deng managed to come back to power for the third time in 1977. At the age of 73, Deng started introducing a series of reform and opening policies that eventually transformed China.

Deng's claim to power also has ideological bases. A revisionist to Maoist practices, Deng sought to reorient China's development from the politics-in-command mode to the economics-in-command mode. Through a nationwide debate on the criterion of truth, Deng Xiaoping and his close associates such as Hu Yaobang seriously undermined the ideological base of Hua Guofeng, Mao's successor in 1976. At the end of the debate, political leaders reached the consensus that practice is the sole criterion for testing truth and that whateverism ('Whatever policy Chairman Mao decided upon, we shall resolutely defend; whatever directives Chairman issued, we shall steadfastly obey') is not genuine Mao Zedong Thought. At the Third Plenum of the Eleventh Central Committee of the CCP in December 1978, Deng won the battle of political line. The CCP decided to switch its focus from politics to economics, ushering a new era of economic reform and opening to the outside world.

Deng also sought to undermine the power base of Hua Guofeng through a two-pronged strategy. On the one hand, he re-established the Secretariat of the CCP Central Committee as an alternative to the Politburo and installed Hu Yaobang as general secretary of the Secretariat. He later replaced Hua as chairman of the Party by Hu Yaobang. On the other hand, he had four close followers of Hua (known as the 'Little Gang of Four') dismissed from their official positions. Deng replaced Hua Guofeng as chairman of the Central Military Commission in June 1981 and further consolidated his power as the paramount leader of the Party.

Deng made efforts to put an end to the lifelong tenure. He established a Central Advisory Commission and persuaded veteran cadres of advanced ages to semi-retire into this institution. In form, this is similar to Mao's two-front arrangement. Instead of one person on the second front, however, a whole group of veteran leaders was placed on the second front as an institution. At the first front, there were political leaders such as General Secretary Hu Yaobang and Premier Zhao Ziyang.

While this institutionalized two-front arrangement as a scheme of succession, it was nevertheless a failure. Instead of staying at the second front, the Central Advisory Commission leaders intervened in the work of the leaders at the first front. They were responsible for the dismissal of two general secretaries of the CCP. On the excuse that Hu Yaobang was too sympathetic with student demonstrators, the veteran leaders removed him from the office as general secretary of the CCP at a party life meeting (an informal gathering of party members) in January 1987. The same group of veteran leaders again dismissed Zhao Ziyang as general secretary of the CCP in June 1989 because Zhao was considered too lenient towards student demonstrators.

In the aftermath of the Tiananmen Incident in which hundreds of student demonstrators were killed by the People's Liberation Army troops, Deng Xiaoping retired from the Central Military Commission. A few years later, however, Deng came back to the centre of Chinese politics at the age of 88 and started another round of reform and opening. In what is known as the 'southern tour' conducted in the spring of 1992, Deng sharply criticized the conservatives and pushed for bolder reform measures and more opening to the outside world.

In political terms, Deng introduced a theory of generational succession. He divided CCP leaders since 1935 into two generations. In his view, Mao Zedong, Zhu De, Liu Shaoqi, and Zhou Enlai belong to the first-generation leadership of the CCP with Mao at the core; the reform era leadership is the second-generation leadership, with Deng himself at the core. In 1989, he suggested that the new leadership would be the third-generation leadership and that Jiang Zemin, former party secretary of Shanghai, be at the core. In theory, there will be successive generations; and each generation will have a core. To ensure this core leader has real power in practice, Deng made sure that Jiang assumes all three most important positions in the Chinese political system: general secretary of the Party, chairman of the Central Military Commission, and president of the People's Republic of China. Jiang became general secretary of the CCP in June 1989, chairman of the Central Military Commission in November 1989, and president of the People's Republic of China in March 1993. At the Sixteenth National Party Congress in November 2002, the CCP witnessed an institutionalized power transfer from the third-generation leadership to the fourth-generation leadership.

4 'Winner-Takes-All', 'Power Balancing', and Power Structures

Students of China's political leadership, however, are divided on the nature of the power transfer at the Sixteenth National Party Congress. Joseph Fewsmith (2003) believes that the succession did not happen at the Party Congress. This is because Jiang was the one who read the political report to the National Party Congress; Jiang's ideology—'Three Represents'—was introduced to the CCP's Constitution as a guiding principle along with 'Deng Xiaoping Theory'; Jiang stayed on as chairman of the Central Military Commission; and Jiang's protégés dominated the Politburo Standing Committee of the CCP. In the meantime, Hu Jintao, the successor, did not inherit much power. He was reduced to applauding Jiang's achievements and became general secretary in name only.

Fewsmith's conclusion is based on a theory of elite politics in China, the 'winner-takes-all' model. Proposed by Tang Tsou (2002), the model sees power struggles among political elites as a zero-sum game. Since political power is indivisible, a political actor either gets all of it or none of it. There is nothing in between. The end result of power struggles, therefore, will produce a winner of all and a loser of all. Since Jiang Zemin was already a winner, he had to be the winner of all. Conversely, Hu Jintao had to be a loser, a loser of all.

Arguably, however, power transfer at the Sixteenth National Party Congress did take place (Bo 2005). This is because political power in China has been institutionalized. Office-holders have real power as soon as they obtain positions. In other words, those who have positions have power and those who are without a position do not have power. By having obtained the position of general secretary of the CCP, Hu Jintao became the top leader of the Party. Therefore, Hu Jintao was not a loser, let alone the loser of all. This is the 'authority of position'.

Moreover, owing to the division of labour among top political leaders, power is also divisible. The kind of power a political leader possesses is dependent on the kind of position he or she occupies. Jiang Zemin stayed on as chairman of the Central Military Commission, for instance, he thus had the power as commander-in-chief. This is the 'authority of expertise'. Jiang's case forms a clear contrast with that of Deng Xiaoping. After Deng had been retained as chairman of the Central Military Commission in 1987, he basically functioned as the top political leader of the Party. This is because the Chinese political system was not yet institutionalized at the time. After Jiang decided to stay on as chairman of the Central Military Commission, he would have to function as the top military leader of the Party. He was not supposed to interfere with party affairs any longer. Jiang Zemin was a winner, but he was not the winner of all. The net outcome of the power transfer at the Sixteenth National Party Congress was, therefore, power-balancing.

Although these perspectives are mutually exclusive, advocates of each perspective have generated complementary information about the dynamics of elite politics in China. Those who believe in the 'winner-takes-all' model tend to be more sensitive about differences/competitions/conflicts between different factions, and those who have more faith in the institutionalization theory are more successful in making predictions about leadership changes at both provincial and national levels.

In terms of power structures in China, there are four major formal institutions. They are the legislature, the State Council, provincial units, and the military. In the Chinese legislature, there are two parallel houses. One is the National Committee of the Chinese People's Political Consultative Conference (CPPCC), and the other is the National People's Congress (NPC). The CPPCC used to be the legislature of the People's Republic of China until 1954 and has since become an advisory council for the legislature. The NPC is the highest organ of state power in the PRC. The NPC has a standing committee, which is composed of a chairman, vice chairmen, and standing members. The State Council is the executive organ of state power, consisting of a premier, vice premiers, state councillors, and ministers.

There are thirty-three provincial units in the PRC: twenty-two provinces, four centrally administered municipalities, five autonomous regions, and two special administrative regions. Provincial leaders are powerful leaders in China, and China's provinces often serve as a training ground for national leaders (Bo 2003). The military in China is under the leadership of the Central Military Commission. At the centre there are four general departments: General Staff Department, General Political Department, General Logistics Department, and General Equipment Department. There are also three military services (navy, air force, and second artillery corps) as well as armed police. At the local level, there are seven military regions: the Beijing Military Region, the Shenyang Military Region, the Nanjing Military Region, the Chengdu Military Region, the Lanzhou Military Region, the Guangzhou Military Region, and the Jinan Military Region.

Political leaders in China are mostly Chinese Communist Party members, and they are ranked by their status within the Party. The President of the PRC, the chairman of the National People's Congress Standing Committee, and the premier of the State Council, for instance, are all members of the Politburo Standing Committee, the key decision-making organ of the Party.

5 Research Methods, Theoretical Gaps, and Practical Implications

Within the subfield of Chinese leadership studies, there are basically three major approaches. First, a large group of scholars have used case studies to analyse China's political leadership. Among them, some have dealt with individual leaders such as Mao Zedong (Jin 1996; Terrill 1999; Peng and Jin 2003; Chang and Halliday 2005), Zhou Enlai (Lee, C. 1994; Gao 2007), Liu Shaoqi (Dittmer 1974), Lin Biao (Jin 1999; Wen 2007), Chen Yun (Bachman 1985), and Deng Xiaoping (Evans 1993; Vogel 2011). Others have done research on individual events or political campaigns such as the Gao–Rao Affairs (Teiwes 1990), the Great Leap Forward (Bachman 1991; Yang 1996; Teiwes and Sun 1999), the Cultural Revolution (Lee, H. 1978), and the initiation of reform and opening policies (Baum 1994; Fewsmith 1994). Still others have tried to conduct comparative case studies to theorize about the nature of Chinese political leadership.

Second, a great number of scholars have made efforts to study groups of Chinese political leaders. Some have followed the evolution of the Central Committees of the Chinese Communist Party, especially since 1956, when the Eighth National Party Congress was held (Scalapino 1972; Li and White 1988; Shambaugh 1998; Bo 2004, 2007, 2010). They analyse the composition of the CCP Central Committee members in terms of demographic information such as age, gender, ethnicity, home province, political status, party standing, education, and family background. Others have made attempts to understand Chinese provincial leaders, military leaders, and central bureaucrats, trying to look at career patterns and political dynamics (Goodman 1984; Joffe 1987; Lieberthal and Oksenberg 1988; Bo 2002, 2003, 2006).

Third, a small but increasing number of scholars have used statistical methods to analyse groups of political leaders in China (Bo 2002; Landry 2008; Sheng 2010). They have tried to find correlations between demographic variables and performance indicators and political variables. Some have studied the relationship between economic performance and the political mobility of provincial leaders in China, and others have analysed the determinants of political mobility of central committee members.

Scholars of diverse research methods have generated a large body of knowledge on Chinese political leadership, yet there are still a number of significant theoretical gaps. Biographers of Chinese leaders have helped to bring to light the idiosyncratic personalities of these leaders as well as their contributions to China's development since 1949. There is, however, no clear consensus on how to assess these political leaders. In the eyes of their admirers, for instance, Mao Zedong was one of the most influential world leaders of the twentieth century. He was a philosopher, a brilliant military strategist, a powerful political leader, and a skilful statesman, who changed the fate of the most populous country in the world. As Dick Wilson put it, 'none... would deny that Mao has already influenced more human lives more profoundly than anyone else in our century, and is likely to remain persuasive beyond the grave' (Wilson 1977: p. vii). For his critics, Mao was a womanizer (Li, Z. 1994), a power-grabber, and an autocrat who was responsible for the death of millions of people. 'Mao Tse-tung, who for decades held absolute power over the lives of one-quarter of the world's population,' as Jung Chang and Jon Halliday exclaimed in the beginning of their book on Mao, 'was responsible for well over 70 million deaths in peacetime, more than any other twentieth century leader' (Chang and Halliday 2005: 3).

Using Max Weber's tripartite typology of legitimate authority, Frederick C. Teiwes tried to argue that Mao's legitimacy as the leader of the CCP had not only charismatic roots but also legal–rational and traditional elements (Teiwes 1984: 43–76). This is because, even though Mao's authority has rarely been defined in legal–rational terms, Mao did operate within the constraints of certain legal–rational rules such as Party norms. Moreover, the imperial tradition as well as party traditions did have some influence on authority relations in post-1949 China. Nevertheless, China is short on legal–rational authority and long on traditional authority. Others have extended the study of legitimacy from the authority of individuals to the regime survival. In his controversial book published in 2001, Gordon Chang predicted that China would collapse in 2006 (Chang 2001: p. xviii) because of various challenges that Beijing was ill prepared to deal with in the aftermath of China's accession to the World Trade Organization (WTO). Authors of a volume on holding China together, however, argued for China's resilience in spite of all these challenges (Naughton and Yang 2004).

Borrowing terms from international relations theories, Avery Goldstein (1991) introduced two theoretical models to analyse two periods of Mao's era through a systems approach instead of the common 'reductionist approach'. In his view, the major feature of the first period of Maoist era from 1949 to 1965 was 'bandwagon politics'. In the bandwagon polity, the system is hierarchically organized; there is very little functional differentiation; and capabilities are concentrated in the hands of superordinate actors (Goldstein 1991: 8). Therefore, bandwagoning becomes dominant behaviour in this structure (Goldstein 1991: 46). According to Goldstein, the Chinese political system during Mao's second period from 1966 to 1976 was a 'balance-of-power polity'. In this polity, authority of the CCP was shattered. The ideological message subverting authority in 1966, as Goldstein described it, was that the ultimate locus of authority was not the CCP as an institution but the 'Thought of Chairman Mao' (Goldstein 1991: 153). In this anarchical system, political communication became diversified and different actors have different political resources. Political actors form coalitions to ensure their political survival.

Goldstein's systems approach to Chinese politics is very helpful for clarifying basic characteristics of Mao's era, but it is difficult to understand the political dynamics of Mao's era fully without some understanding of Mao. In fact, Mao stood above everyone else and maintained a balance in his favour by using one group against another. There might be a balance of power among other politicians during the Cultural Revolution, but everyone else was bandwagoning with Mao. In a word, bandwagoning is the dominant feature of Chinese politics, though it has different manifestations in different political structures. This is because Mao was always the winner and everyone else had to get along with him. Moreover, Goldstein's approach was not very helpful for understanding political leadership under Deng.

Based on extensive studies of the Chinese Communist Party, Hong Yung Lee depicted a major transformation of Chinese political leadership from a group of revolutionary cadres to a group of party technocrats in the reform era under Deng Xiaoping (Lee, H. 1991). 'Selected from among the best-educated segment of the population,' as Lee described the new elites, 'the new Chinese leaders have their academic training mainly in engineering and production-related fields and their career backgrounds in specialist positions at functional organizations' (Lee, H. 1991: 388).

Scholars have generally followed Deng Xiaoping's advice and classified Chinese leaders into different generations. Because of two-term limits, each generation now lasts for about ten years. Following the third generation of Jiang Zemin and Zhu Rongji, there is the fourth generation of Hu Jintao and Wen Jiabao, which in turn is followed by the fifth generation of Xi Jinping and Li Keqiang.

In order to conceptualize political dimensions of different institutions in the Central Committee of the CCP, Bo Zhiyue (2004) has developed two indexes: power indexes and group cohesion indexes. Based on political weight within the Central Committee of the Chinese Communist Party, power indexes have been constructed for both formal institutions and factional groups. Bo has also created group cohesion indexes to measure the group cohesion of factional groups within the Central Committee. Using these indexes, he is able to map out the power balance of different institutions and factional groups as well as the rise and/or fall of these institutions and factional groups over time.

For those who are trying to study Chinese political leadership through quantitative methodology, preliminary results are encouraging, but there is still a long way to go. In a pioneering piece of research, Bo Zhiyue (2002) tried to find the correlation between economic performance of provinces and political mobility of provincial leaders. Based on a dataset of more than 2,000 provincial leaders since 1949, Bo used multinomial logit regression models to investigate causes of political mobility of powerful provincial leaders and proposed a performance model. As a result, positive correlations were seen between performance indicators, especially provincial revenue contributions to the central coffer, and promotion of provincial leaders. These research methods have been adopted by a number of other scholars for studying local leaders in China (Guo 2008;

Landry 2008; Lin 2008; Sheng 2010); however, it is more difficult to analyse elite politics with statistical methods.

Finally, the most significant theoretical debate is about factional politics in China. Andrew Nathan (1973) was probably the first scholar to undertake serious theoretical analyses of Chinese political leaders and their possible interactive dynamics. In an article published in the *China Quarterly* in 1973, Nathan proposed a factionalism model for understanding CCP politics. In this article, Nathan introduced the concepts of factions, illustrated characteristics of factional politics, and applied the factionalism model in analyzing the CCP elite politics.

Tang Tsou (1976), however, provided a critical review of the factionalism model in another article published in the *China Quarterly* in 1976. Tsou was not easy with the term of factions and not fully convinced of the utility of the model. He introduced an alternative concept of 'informal groups' and believed that the factionalism model, which suggested civility of factions towards each other, completely missed the target. China was in the midst of political turmoil of the Cultural Revolution, where former comrades were engaged in fierce power struggles and many veteran revolutionaries, including the President of the PRC, were tortured to death. As Tsou puts it bluntly, Nathan's theory 'does not fit CCP politics'. This is because, in Tsou's view, 'the basic assumption of CCP politics has been that a group or a coalition of groups can and does decisively defeat a major rival group or coalition, and eliminate it. Thus, any model of CCP politics must be built on an assumption diametrically opposite to Nathan's' (Tsou 1976: 102).

Partially inspired by Goldstein's 'bandwagon politics', Tang Tsou (2002) proposed a 'winner-takes-all' model for analysing Chinese elite politics. As mentioned above, he believes that power struggles at the top are zero-sum games because of indivisibility of power and that the net outcome of power struggles is a winner of all and a loser of all. Joseph Fewsmith applied this model to the study of the power transition at the Sixteenth National Party Congress in 2002.

Bo Zhiyue (2005) debated the merit and relevance of the 'winner-takes-all' model in twenty-first century Chinese politics and proposed a 'power-balancing' model. His basic assumption is that China's political system is institutionalized and that authority of position is very important. Those who take official positions acquire corresponding political powers. Political power is, therefore, divisible. The outcome of power competition is power-balancing.

The basic assumption, nevertheless, is that factions somehow exist. Some have identified four factions in Chinese politics in recent years—namely, the Shanghai Gang, the Qinghua Clique, the Princelings, and the CCYL Group. For some scholars, the latter groups are exclusive political factions with divergent policy orientations. Led by Xi Jinping, the Princelings tend to favour private sector and coastal areas. Led by Hu Jintao, Wen Jiabao, and Li Keqiang, the CCYL Group is more interested in the plight of underprivileged and inland regions (Li, C. 2009). For others, these groups are mostly categoric groups without political connotations. As children of the first generation of revolutionaries, princelings belong to the same category but not necessarily to the same political faction. Youth league cadres are people who have worked in the same institution in a broad sense, and they hardly constitute a coherent political faction. Moreover, there is a significant overlap between the Princelings and the CCYL Group at the top level (Bo 2007, 2010).

These theoretical debates have strong practical implications. First, the debate about Mao Zedong remains relevant to politics in China in the 2000s. The leftists believe that Deng Xiaoping's policy of 'allowing some people and regions to get rich first' has run out of steam and Mao's egalitarian ideology now provides an alternative. The liberals think that Mao was responsible for human disasters such as the Great Leap Forward and the Cultural Revolution and that any Maoist trappings may represent the danger of the return to those disastrous years. The two groups are sharply divided over the Chongqing Model, which employs some Maoist slogans and practices for the benefits of the local people. In the most serious political crisis since 1989, Bo Xilai, party secretary of Chongqing and a Politburo member as well as the son of Bo Yibo (one of the first generation revolutionaries), was dismissed from his post and suspended from his Politburo and Central Committee membership and subsequently expelled from the party. Although he was removed partly because of his wife's involvement in an alleged murder case, Bo's dismissal was a result of political struggles over the future of China.

Second, the debate about regime legitimacy has become a recurring topic on the sustainability of the communist regime in China. Naysayers have been making predictions about the collapse of the Chinese communist regime ever since 1989, and others have contended that the Chinese Communist Party is different from communist regimes in the former Soviet Union and other East European countries and is quite adaptive to the new realities (Shambaugh 2008).

Third, the debate on factional politics is closely related to leadership changes and generational transitions. Those who have strong faith in factional politics tend to see political factions in action and interpret leadership changes in these terms, but those who are suspicious of the very existence of political factions can find contradictions in these interpretations because of multiple identities of the same individuals.

6 FUTURE STUDIES OF CHINESE POLITICAL LEADERSHIP

In the foreseeable future, studies of Chinese political leadership would continue to benefit from the fact that political leadership is institutionalized and that political mobility follows certain rules. Future scholars would continue to observe similar patterns of political mobility with varying degrees of institutionalization at different levels of the government and over time, but they would have to conceptualize the nature of Chinese politics better and to come up with better indictors of factionalism.

In addition to studying central party leaders and provincial leaders, scholars of Chinese political leadership may want to pay attention to local leaders at the county level. There are more than 2,000 counties in China, and many counties are huge entities. There is abundant information on county leaders on the Internet, yet few have systematically studied this group of political leaders (Bo 2009). Another option would be to study business leaders, especially those of state-owned enterprises. In recent years, there have been frequent transfers between provincial/central leadership and business leadership. Yet few have studied patterns of transfers and followed career paths of business-cum-political leaders.

Because of internal changes and external pressures, however, political leadership in China will probably change dramatically in the long run. One possibility is the split of the Party elite into competing political factions. Similar to factions within the Liberal Democratic Party of Japan, CCP factions would openly compete for powers and advocate different policies. Another possibility is the emergence of multiple political parties in China as a result of democratization. In these drastically different political environments and cultures, political leaders would behave differently. Most importantly, scholars may want to analyse political cultural changes and how these changes increase the desirability of regime change.

Recommended Reading

Goldstein, A. (1991). *From Bandwagon to Balance-of-Power Politics*. Stanford, CA: Stanford University Press.

Bo, Z. (2002). *Chinese Provincial Leaders: Economic Performance and Political Mobility since 1949*. Armonk, NY: M. E. Sharpe.

Bo, Z. (2007). *China's Elite Politics: Political Transition and Power Balancing*. Singapore: World Scientific.

References

Bachman, D. (1985). *Chen Yun and the Chinese Political System*. Berkeley and Los Angeles: University of California Institute of East Asian Studies.

Bachman, D. (1991). *Bureaucracy, Economy, and Leadership in China: The Institutional Origins of the Great Leap Forward*. New York: Cambridge University Press.

Baum, R. (1994). *Burying Mao: Chinese Politics in the Age of Deng Xiaoping*. Princeton: Princeton University Press.

Bo, Z. (2002). *Chinese Provincial Leaders: Economic Performance and Political Mobility since 1949*. Armonk, NY: M.E. Sharpe.

Bo, Z. (2003). 'The Provinces: Training Ground for National Leaders or a Power in their Own Right?', in D. M. Finkelstein and M. Kivlehan (eds), *China's Leadership in the 21st Century*. Armonk, NY: M. E. Sharpe, 66–117.

Bo, Z. (2004). 'The 16th Central Committee of the Chinese Communist Party: Formal Institutions and Factional Groups', *Journal of Contemporary China*, 13/39: 223–56.

Bo, Z. (2005). 'Political Succession and Elite Politics in Twenty-First Century China: Towards a Power-Balancing Perspective', *Issues & Studies*, 41/1: 162–89.

Bo, Z. (2006). 'Princeling Generals in China: Breaking the Two Career Barriers?', *Issues & Studies*, 42/1: 195–232.

Bo, Z. (2007). *China's Elite Politics: Political Transition and Power Balancing*. Singapore: World Scientific.

Bo, Z. (2009). 'Political Mobility of County Leaders in China: The Case of Jiangsu', *Provincial China*, 1/2: 76–96.

Bo, Z. (2010). *China's Elite Politics: Governance and Democratization*. Singapore: World Scientific.

Chang, G. (2001). *The Coming Collapse of China*. New York: Random House.

Chang, R., and Halliday, J. (2005). *Mao: The Unknown Story*. London: Jonathan Cape.

Dittmer, L. (1974). *Liu Shiao-ch'I and the Chinese Cultural Revolution*. Berkeley and Los Angeles: University of California Press.

Evans, R. (1993). *Deng Xiaoping and the Making of Modern China*. London: Hamilton.

Fewsmith, J. (1994). *Dilemmas of Reform in China: Political Conflict and Economic Debate*. Armonk, NY: M. E. Sharpe.

Fewsmith, J. (2003). The Sixteenth National Party Congress: The Succession that Didn't Happen. *China Quarterly*, 173 (March), 1–16.

Gao, W. (2007). *Zhou Enlai: The Last Perfect Revolutionary*. Philadelphia, PA: Public Affairs.

Goldstein, A. (1991). *From Bandwagon to Balance-of-Power Politics*. Stanford, CA: Stanford University Press.

Goodman, D. S. G. (1984). 'Provincial Party First Secretaries in National Politics: A Categorical or a Political Group?', in D. S. G. Goodman (eds), *Groups and Politics in the People's Republic of China*. Armonk, NY: M. E. Sharpe, 68–82.

Guo, G. (2008). 'Vertical Imbalance and Local Fiscal Discipline in China', *Journal of East Asian Studies*, 8/1: 61–88.

Jin, C. (1996). *Mao Zedong Zhuan, 1893–1949*. Beijing: Zhonggong Zhongyang Wenxian Chubanshe.

Jin, Q. (1999). *The Culture of Power: The Lin Biao Incident in the Cultural Revolution*. Stanford, CA: Stanford University Press.

Joffe, E. (1987). *The Chinese Military after Mao*. Cambridge, MA: Harvard University Press.

Landry, P. (2008). *Decentralized Authoritarianism in China: The Communist Control of Local Elites in the Post-Mao Era*. New York: Cambridge University Press.

Lee, C. (1994). *Zhou Enlai: The Early Years*. Stanford, CA: Stanford University Press.

Lee, H. (1978). *Politics of the Chinese Cultural Revolution: A Case Study*. Berkeley and Los Angeles: University of California Press.

Lee, H. (1991). *From Revolutionary Cadres to Party Technocrats in Socialist China*. Berkeley and Los Angeles: University of California Press.

Li, C. (2009). 'China's Team of Rivals', *Foreign Policy*, 171 (March/April), 88–93.

Li, C., and White, L. (1988). 'The Thirteenth Central Committee of the Chinese Communist Party: From Mobilizers to Managers', *Asian Survey*, 28: 371–99.

Li, Z. (1994). *The Private Life of Chairman Mao*. New York: Random House.

Lieberthal, K., and Oksenberg, M. (1988). *Policy Making in China: Leaders Structures, and Processes*. Princeton: Princeton University Press.

Lin, T. (2008). 'Explaining the Intra-Provincial Inequality of Financing Compulsory Education in China: The Role of Finance Reform, Personnel Rules and Provincial Leaders, 1994–2001'. Ph.D. dissertation. Hong Kong: University of Hong Kong.

MacFarquhar, R. (1974). *The Origins of the Cultural Revolution I: Contradictions among the People 1956–1957*. New York: Columbia University Press.

MacFarquhar, R. (1983). *The Origins of the Cultural Revolution 2: The Great Leap Forward 1958–1960*. New York: Columbia University Press.

MacFarquhar, R. (1997). *The Origins of the Cultural Revolution 3: The Coming of the Cataclysm 1961–1966*. New York: Columbia University Press.

Nathan, A. (1973). 'A Factionalist Model of CCP Politics', *China Quarterly*, 53: 34–66.

Naughton, B. J., and Yang, D. L. (2004) (eds). *Holding China Together*. New York: Cambridge University Press.

Peng, X., and Jin, C. (2003). *Mao Zedong Zhuan, 1949–1976 (Biography of Mao Zedong, 1949–1976)*. Beijing: Zhonggong Zhongyang Wenxian Chubanshe.

Scalapino, R. (1972) (ed.). *Elites in the People's Republic of China*. Seattle: University of Washington Press.

Shambaugh, D. (1998). 'The CCP's 15th Congress: Technocrats in Command', *Issues and Studies*, 34/1: 1–37.

Shambaugh, D. (2008). *China's Communist Party: Atrophy and Adaptation*. Washington: Woodrow Wilson Center Press.

Sheng, Y. (2010). *Economic Openness and Territorial Politics in China*. New York: Cambridge University Press.

Teiwes, F. C. (1984). *Leadership, Legitimacy, and Conflict in China: From a Charismatic Mao to the Politics of Succession*. Armonk, NY: M. E. Sharpe.

Teiwes, F. C. (1990). *Politics at Mao's Court: Gao Gang and Party Factionalism in the Early 1950s*. Armonk, NY: M. E. Sharpe.

Teiwes, F. C., and Sun W. (1999). *China's Road to Disaster: Mao, Central Politicians, and Provincial Leaders in the Unfolding of the Great Leap Forward, 1955–1959*. Armonk, NY: M. E. Sharpe.

Terrill, R. (1999). *Mao: A Biography*. Stanford, CA: Stanford University Press.

Tang, Tsou,. (1976). 'Prolegomenon to the Study of Informal Groups in CCP Politics', *China Quarterly*, 65: 98–117.

Tang, Tsou (2002). 'Chinese Politics at the Top: Factionalism or Informal Politics? Balance-of-Power Politics or a Game to Win All?', in J. Unger (ed.), *The Nature of Chinese Politics: From Mao to Jiang*. Armonk, NY: M. E. Sharpe, 98–159.

Vogel, E. (2011). *Deng Xiaoping and the Transformation of China*. Cambridge, MA: Belknap Press of Harvard University Press.

Wen, X. (2007). *Wan Nian Lin Biao (Lin Biao in his Later Years)*. Hong Kong: East and West Culture Co. Ltd.

Wilson, Dick (1977). *Mao Tse-Tung in the Scales of History*. Cambridge: Cambridge University Press.

Yang, D. (1996). *Calamity and Reform in China: State, Rural Society, and Institutional Change since the Great Leap Forward*. Stanford, CA: Stanford University Press.

CHAPTER 41

LATIN AMERICAN LEADERSHIP

HARVEY F. KLINE

THE transition to democracy came with problems in many countries. The elected presidents of most countries are still constrained by the military with only Argentina, Costa Rica, Haiti, Mexico, Panama, and Uruguay enjoying full civilian control. Some other countries have changed to 'delegative democracy' in which the chief executive, while elected in periodic elections, has almost absolute power between them. This is especially the case in Venezuela, Bolivia, and Ecuador.

Historically Latin American countries have been characterized by strong leaders, with few or weak checks and balances. The countries began with a very centralized, elitist, and undemocratic tradition inherited from the colonizing countries. While there were various waves of democracy in the nineteenth and twentieth centuries, never did that political regime become as extensive as it did when in the 1990s nineteen of the twenty countries elected chief executives in what Samuel Huntington called the third wave of democratization. How to maintain the tradition of strong leadership with the current democratic regimes has been a problem in many of the countries. A new paradigm, combining elements of democracy with stronger leadership, has emerged. In all three paradigms, 'The Autocratic Model', 'Democracy', and 'Delegative Democracy', the question of leadership has been the central issue.

This chapter begins with a description of leadership in the model received from the colonizing powers and the variations during the period of autocracy that followed independence. The second part discusses the 'democratic wave' since the 1980s, emphasizing the difficulties of combining strong leadership with democracy. The third section analyses a particular regime called 'delegative democracy', under which the leader has immense powers between elections.

1   THE IBERIAN MODEL AND AUTOCRACY AFTER INDEPENDENCE

Traditionally the term 'Latin America' has been used to consider the twenty countries of Romance language background of the Western hemisphere. Eighteen were Spanish colonies while one was Portuguese (Brazil) and one was French (Haiti). While the commonality of philosophical heritage applies in general to all the countries, variations always existed. The Portuguese colonization of Brazil and the French colonization of Haiti were very different from that of the Spanish colonies. Within the Spanish colonies, variations included the strength of colonization, economic foundations, ethnic composition, and natural resources, and others.

Latin America was colonized by countries in which the king ruled by divine right, a doctrine that defended monarchical absolutism and asserted that kings derived their authority from God and could not therefore be held accountable for their actions by any earthly authority such as a parliament. The divine-right theory can be traced to the medieval conception of God's award of temporal power to the political ruler, paralleling the award of spiritual power to the Church. To extend this to the Spanish American colonies the Spanish king sent viceroys ('vice kings'), first to Mexico and Peru and later to Nueva Granada (Colombia) and Argentina. In theory, the king said what policies were and the viceroys carried them out. However, given communication difficulties, many times it was the viceroys who carried out policies as they saw fit. Nevertheless, whether the decisions were made in Europe or the Americas, a single person with a small group of advisors made them. There were no elective bodies in the colonies to operate as checks or balances.

After the central figures of this elitist system from the Old World were removed by the wars of independence, with the exception of Brazil, the countries searched for new power structures. While leaders were chosen by elections in some countries, with suffrage restricted in all cases and elections rigged in various cases, what really existed was a new elitist system that was dominated by three groups: the military, the Roman Catholic Church, and the large landholders. The armed forces were most important in nearly all countries, often exercising power directly. During the wars for independence, the Spanish American colonies developed armies led by a great variety of individuals, including well-born creoles, priests, and people of more humble background. The officers did not come from military academies but were self-selected or chosen by other leaders. Few of the officers had previous military training, and the armies were much less professional than the armies we know today.

2   THE RULE: AUTOCRATIC GOVERNMENTS

Before 1980 most Latin American countries had autocratic governments in which the chief executive was unchecked by democratically elected structures. Autocracies varied, Bolivian novelist Alcides Arguedas distinguishing between the 'caudillos bárbaros' and the 'caudillos letrados' while Dominican Juan Bosch called for a 'dictatorship with popular support,' and Venezuelan Laureano Vallenilla Lanz preferred 'democratic Caesarism'. The autocrats were constrained by the oligarchy of the Church, landowners, and the military. With social change, other relevant interest groups emerged. As Charles Anderson has argued, each new group had to prove that it had the power to be taken seriously. It also had to show that it would do nothing to eliminate or seriously harm groups that previously had entered the power structure. (Anderson 1967: ch. 4) To gain and maintain power the autocratic leader had to make sure that the power groups supported him, especially the military.

There were five kinds of autocracies in the period between independence and the late 1970s: military personalism; a person who had been in the military and was elected; the military after US intervention; the military as an institution; and a political party with a democratic facade.

Military Personalism

There were many varieties of military personalism. Perhaps the clearest case was that of José Gaspar Rodríguez de Francia in Paraguay, who called himself 'El Supremo'. Rodríguez ruled from 1814 until his death in 1840, succeeding almost single-handedly in building a strong, prosperous, secure, and independent nation at a time when Paraguay's continued existence as a distinct country seemed unlikely. While doing so, he trampled on human rights and imposed an authoritarian police state based on espionage and coercion. Under Rodríguez de Francia, Paraguay underwent a social upheaval that destroyed the old elites. In a similar fashion, in Venezuela at the beginning of the twentieth century Juan Vicente Gómez was a military general and de facto ruler from 1908 until his death in 1935. He was president on three occasions during this time, and ruled as an unelected military strongman for the rest of the era. Even later in the century, Alfredo Stroessner was a Paraguayan military officer and dictator from 1954 to 1989.

A similar example was that of Porfirio Díaz in Mexico. Although Díaz had a military background, he was first elected president in 1876 with the platform of 'effective suffrage and no reelection'. That notwithstanding, with the exception of four years, he then maintained power as elected president until 1911.

Military Officers Elected as Presidents

A second form of autocracy can be seen in the military officer who used that institution to construct his power base, resigned his commission, and was then elected president. Juan Domingo Perón in Argentina is the most notable case of that kind of autocracy. In 1943 a group of high-level officers conspired to implant a government modelled after Mussolini's fascist regime in Italy and took power. Among its members was Perón, a little known army colonel who asked for the management of the Secretariat of Labor and

Social Welfare. Previously he had served as Minister of War, a position he used to build a support base within the army.

As minister of labour, Perón began to settle disputes in the favour of labourers. He reversed longstanding anti-labour legislation and actively promoted legislation to improve workers' lives. The growing opposition to Perón led some officers to oust him from all government posts and put him under arrest. Faced with little alternative after labour marches and demonstrations, the military finally agreed to release Perón. On 17 October 1945, Perón appeared on the balcony of the presidential palace and saw the results of the hard work he had put into organizing the working classes.

The election of 1946 passed the mantle of power and legitimacy to Perón. Before the election, Perón had organized his own political party, the Labor Party, which mobilized his many supporters under his leadership. He had the solid support of the labour unions, many organized within the past three years; of factions of the military from whose ranks he came; and of the Catholic Church, as Perón had promised to retain its right to control education and to prevent divorce legislation. He was overthrown by the military in September 1955 after he had lost support from all three important power groups.

The Military after US Intervention

A third manifestation of autocracy took the form of a personalistic military regime that was the result of military intervention by the United States. In the early part of the twentieth century, US Marines were sent to various Caribbean countries, most notably the Dominican Republic and Nicaragua, to collect debts under the Roosevelt Corollary to the Monroe Doctrine. The USA established local National Guards to maintain order when the US troops left, soon dominated by Rafael Trujillo in the Dominican Republic and Anastasio Somoza García (and his sons) in Nicaragua. Trujillo ruled his country from 1930 until his assassination in 1961. He officially served as president from 1930 to 1938 and again from 1942 to 1952, otherwise ruling as an unelected military strongman. Somoza García was officially the president of Nicaragua from January 1937 to May 1947 and from May 1950 to September 1956, but ruled effectively as dictator from 1936 until his assassination in 1956. His sons Luis and Anastasio Somoza Debayle were de facto leaders from their father's death until July 1979, Luis officially serving as president from September 1956 to May 1963, and Anastasio from May 1967 to May 1972 and from December 1974 to July 1979.

Bureaucratic Authoritarianism

A fourth kind of autocracy appeared in Latin America in the 1960s. The success of guerrilla revolutions in China, Indochina, Algeria, and Cuba led to a new emphasis on the military's role in counterinsurgency and internal defence functions. In addition, Latin American militaries—encouraged by US military aid—began to assume responsibility for civic action programmes, which assisted civilians in the construction of roads, schools, and other public projects. This led to a broader responsibility for the military in nation-building.

The new professionalism, with its emphasis on counterinsurgency, was a product of the Cold War and was in keeping with the Latin American political tradition. Military skills—management, administration, nation-building—were no longer viewed as separate or different from civilian skills. The military was to acquire the ability to help solve those national problems that might lead to insurgency, which was, in its very essence, a political rather than an apolitical task. The implication of the new professionalism was that, besides combating active guerrilla factions, the military would take care that social and economic reforms necessary to prevent insurgency were adopted if the civilians proved incapable of doing so. Although the new professionalism was also seen in the developed Western world and in other parts of the Third World, it was particularly prevalent in Latin America. Professionalism in Latin America led to more military intervention in politics, not less.

The end result of this process was the rule of the military institution on a long-term basis, a period that lasted from the mid-1960s through to the mid-1980s, when the militaries in many countries were replaced by elected civilian governments. Seen especially in Argentina, Brazil, Chile, Peru, and Uruguay, this new form of military government was of the institution as a whole—not an individual general—and was based on the idea that the military could govern better than civilians. The military often governed repressively and violated human rights. The officer who was president, usually after consulting other officers, made the political decisions, including which officer would be the next president. In Brazil there were five presidents chosen in this manner. In Chile, however, Augusto Pinochet was the dictator for the entire period.

A Political Party with a Democratic Façade

A final kind of autocracy existed in Mexico from the 1920s until 2000, one in which a single political party won all the presidential elections. After the victory of the Mexican Revolution, top leaders met to choose the next president. The system evolved so that it was the incumbent president who selected the next one and all political power was monopolized by the Partido Revolucionario Institucional. The party was organized into peasant, labour, and 'popular' sectors, meaning that any interest group could join it. PRI won all the presidential elections between 1928 and 1994 and most of the seats of the national, provincial, and local legislative bodies. It seemed to be democratic yet no other party won much and in the case of an electoral dispute, the national congress judged who had won.

3   THE EXCEPTIONS: CHILE, COSTA RICA, URUGUAY, AND COLOMBIA

Many countries had brief periods of non-autocratic government, including Argentina (1916–30; 1946–53), Mexico (1855–67), Venezuela, (1945–8); Brazil (1950–64), and Cuba (1944–56). Yet even if a chief executive was elected, that did not mean that democratic rule existed. It was reported that the military told Guatemalan President Julio César Méndez Montenegro when he was elected in 1966 that he could do what he wanted, except anything that would damage the military or the landed elite. Méndez completed his four-year term, no doubt indicating that he accepted those terms.

Only four countries were characterized by having non-autocratic governments. Chile and Costa Rica came close to the democratic model and its constraints on leadership. Presidents in Uruguay and Colombia, because of numerous armed conflicts between its two major political parties, operated under the constraints of coalition government.

Between 1833 and 1973, Chile followed regular democratic procedures, with the exception of a period of civil war in 1891 and a period of military intervention between 1925 and 1932. The 1833 constitution created a strong role for the president, elected by property holders for a five-year term with the possibility of reelection for a second term, but it also gave the congress a role in approving the budget. A multiparty system developed and many times the president had difficulties in achieving a majority vote for his proposed laws. For example, Socialists and Conservatives formed a coalition against the proposals of Christian Democratic President Eduardo Frei (1964–70) while Christian Democrats and Conservatives opposed the laws recommended by Socialist Salvador Allende (1970–3).

Costa Rica was a similar case in Central America. Free and open elections were a hallmark of its politics. The national army was abolished in 1948 and the president was kept in check by both political parties and civilian interest groups.

Uruguay and Colombia maintained the trappings of free elections; however, each chief executive was constrained by coalition governments. José Batlle y Ordóñez articulated the political ideas that underlay Uruguayan democracy. Batlle was interim president in 1899 and president twice (1903–7 and 1911–15). At the end of his last presidency, fearing the power of a one-man executive, Batlle sought to reform the Uruguayan constitution by creating a collegiate executive. This effort aroused great opposition throughout the country and even divided his own political party. As a result, a new constitution promulgated in 1919 provided for a bifurcated executive—a president and national executive council. In 1951, an amendment to the constitution institutionalized a collegiate presidency of nine members elected for a four-year term. Six of those nine members represented the majority party and the remaining three were members of the opposition party. The four of the majority party acted as the chairpersons of this committee presidency, each serving for one year.

Colombian constitutions gave impressive powers to presidents but they were constrained by coalition governments made necessary because of violence between the Liberal and Conservative parties. In about 28 years between 1850 and 1930, such coalitions existed. Towards the end of the most violent period in the country's history, which lasted from 1946 to 1964, the two parties established the longest and most formal coalition between the two parties—the National Front (1958–74). Under the agreement first proposed by leaders of the Liberal and Conservative parties but later approved in a national referendum and as a constitutional amendment, the parties shared power equally. The presidency alternated between the two parties (no other was legal), while all legislative bodies were divided equally, as were executive cabinets at all levels, governors, mayors, and non-civil-service bureaucrats. The goal of the Front was to end violence based on party identification; in that goal, it was successful. It also brought near deadlock. Just as in the case of PRI in Mexico, the coalition of everyone made it very difficult for the president do anything.

4   THE THIRD DEMOCRATIC WAVE

It seemed that democracy had finally arrived in Latin America in the late 1950s when a number of Latin American dictators fell: Getulio Vargas in Brazil, Manuel Odría in Peru, Gustavo Rojas Pinilla in Colombia, and Marcos Pérez Jiménez in Venezuela. It was the 'Twilight of the Tyrants' and democracy seemed to have arrived. But in Brazil and Peru, new dictators soon appeared.

The Third Wave arrived in the late 1970s and the 1980s when military dictatorships ended in Brazil, Ecuador, Bolivia, Argentina, Uruguay, Chile, and several of the Central American countries. In Nicaragua, internationally monitored elections saw the defeat of the candidate of the ruling Sandinista party, which allowed the opposition candidate Violeta Barrios de Chamorro to take office. In Panama, albeit with the assistance of an armed intervention by the United States, strongman Manuel Antonio Noriega fell and the previously elected Guillermo Endara, whom Noriega had not allowed to take power, occupied the presidency. Finally, in Paraguay, Alfredo Stroessner—the longest power-holder of the Latin American caudillos—fell to a military coup that immediately called for elections. By the beginning of the twenty-first century, of the twenty Latin America countries, only Cuba did not have a democratically elected chief executive. At the same time, the Latin American militaries began transitions to constitutionalism, subservience to civilian control, and support of democratically elected presidents.

The transformation had its difficulties. Peruvian President Alberto Fujimori could not get his laws passed by the congress and faced opposition in the courts, leading him to disband congress and the courts in 1992. Fujimori could do this because the military backed him. The following year Guatemalan President Jorge Serrano tried to do the same thing. In this case, the president failed for lack of support from the armed forces and was removed from power by them. Both cases show that, even though excessive executive power detracts from democracy in Latin America, on occasion the chief executive has attempted to increase his already overwhelming power.

The power of the military was also seen in Ecuador in 1997 when opponents in congress looked for a way to remove President Abdalá Bucaram. Lacking the two-thirds majority necessary for impeachment, congressional deputies declared the president to be 'mentally incapacitated'. Since he had no support from the military, Bucaram had no choice but to flee the presidential palace and seek political asylum.

In less dramatic cases, it has always been difficult to compare the Latin American militaries cross-nationally. Trying to distinguish 'civilian' from 'military' regimes is similarly a meaningless task at times or at best a difficult one. Often military personnel temporarily resigned their commissions to take leadership positions in civilian bureaucracies or as government ministers. In almost all instances, coups d'état were not just simple military affairs but were supported by groups of civilians as well. It was not unheard of for civilians to take a significant part in the ensuing governments. Sometimes civilians actually drew the military into playing a larger political role. In short, Latin American governments were often coalitions made between certain factions of the militaries and certain factions of civilians in an attempt to control the pinnacles of power of the system.

Considering this very complicated question, Peter Smith, a leading expert on democracy in Latin America, in 2000 classified all Latin American countries into four types. In addition to complete 'military control', there are cases of 'military tutelage', where, in the case of a crisis of the civilian government, the armed forces supervise civilian authorities and play key roles in decision-making. Less intrusive is 'conditional military subordination', in which the armed forces keep careful watch over civilians to protect military prerogatives. Finally, there is 'civilian control'. While Smith judged that there were no cases of the first category in 2000, he believed the countries listed in Table 41.1 to fall as shown into the other categories in 2000. Since then Chile has moved from the second to the third category.

In addition, the formal authority of Latin American executives is extensive, deriving from a president's powers as chief executive, commander-in-chief, and head of state, and from the broad emergency powers to declare a state of siege or emergency, suspend constitutional guarantees, and rule by decree. The presidency has been a chief beneficiary of many twentieth-century changes, among them radio and television, concentrated war-making powers, and broad responsibility for the economy. In addition, some Latin American chief executives serve simultaneously as heads of state and presidents of their party machines. If the potential leader's route to power was the army, the president also has the enormous weight of armed might for use against foreign enemies and domestic foes.

In some countries (Chile, Colombia, Costa Rica) the congress has long enjoyed considerable independence and strength. A few congresses have gone so far as

Table 41.1 Latin American countries falling into Smith's categories of tutelage, conditional subordination, and civilian control in 2000

Tutelage	Conditional subordination	Civilian control
Ecuador, El Salvador, Guatemala, Venezuela	Bolivia, Brazil, Chile, Colombia, Dominican Republic, Honduras, Nicaragua, Paraguay, Peru	Argentina, Costa Rica, Haiti, Mexico, Panama, Uruguay

Source: Smith (2005: 103).

to defy the executive—and got away with it. In 1992–3, congresses in Brazil and Venezuela removed the president from office for fiscal improprieties. The congress may serve additionally as a forum that allows the opposition to embarrass or undermine the government, as a means of gauging who is rising and who is falling in official favour, or as a way of weighing the relative strength of the various factions within the regime.

One clear case is the considerable power of the Colombian president. Under the Constitution of 1991 the president is elected for a four-year term and was not eligible for reelection until a 2005 constitutional change made immediate reelection possible. The president is charged with maintaining national security, declaring war (with the permission of the senate, unless foreign aggression makes such impossible), and negotiating foreign treaties. He directs war operations, when necessary, as the commander of the armed forces. His formal powers in the day-to-day workings of the government are wide ranging, including those of conferring military degrees and directing the military; collecting taxes; regulating, directing, and inspecting national public education; negotiating contracts for public works; organizing public credit; exercising the inspection of banks and corporations; and preserving public order.

If the above powers were not impressive enough, the president—because of either international war or internal disturbances—in the Constitution of 1886 could declare a 'state of siege'. During the state of siege, congress continued to meet as it normally would, and all decrees promulgated had to be sent the following day to the Supreme Court, which could declare that they were unconstitutional.

The Constitution of 1991 recognized that the country in the past four decades had been under a state of siege more often than not, during which the president ruled by decree which had to be approved by all the ministers and could not overturn existing laws, but could suspend them. To be more democratic the new constitution gave more power to the congress and greatly limited the president's powers. He now can decree a 'state of internal commotion', but it can only last for 90 days in a calendar year. It can be extended for another 90 through a vote of the senate, but in no case can it go for more than 180 days in a year. In addition the Constitution now allows the president to declare a state of emergency in the case of economic problems and when there are ecological or social difficulties 'that constitute a grave public calamity'. The state of emergency can be declared for only 30 days at a time, and for only 90 days per calendar year. While these stipulations were far reaching, it is important to note that the Supreme Court and congress constrained them to a degree.

5 Delegative Democracy

In at least four cases Latin American presidents have found too many constraints on their leadership in liberal democracy. In all four cases, the presidents have used apparently constitutional means to increase their power, leading to a new kind of regime that

Guillermo O'Donnell (1992) has called 'delegative democracy'. This paradigm has five major characteristics:

1. The presidents are the embodiments of the nations and the main custodians of the national interest, which it is incumbent upon them to define.
2. What they do in government does not need to bear any resemblance to what they said or promised during the electoral campaign—they have been authorized to govern as they see fit.
3. Since these parental figures have to take care of whole nations, it is almost obvious that their support cannot come from parties; their political bases have to be movements, the supposedly vibrant overcoming of the factionalism and conflicts that parties bring about.
4. In this view, other institutions—such as congress and the judiciary—are nuisances that come attached to the domestic and international advantages of being democratically elected presidents.
5. Accountability to those institutions or to other private or semi-private organizations appears as an unnecessary impediment to the full authority that the presidents have been delegated to exercise.

(O'Donnell 1992)

O'Donnell's conclusions were based on happenings in Venezuela, Bolivia, and Ecuador. First, Hugo Chávez had participated in the 1992 coup attempt against the Venezuelan president and spent time in jail after that failure. In 1998, he had run for president, with few giving him much chance. He won on a platform that emphasized that the government and rich people must have been stealing profits from the Venezuelan petroleum industry. Delegative democracy is based on the lack of organization of poor people under the autocratic model; individuals who can mobilize them during the liberal democratic period can add power to the executive branch so that checks and balances are no longer relevant.

After he was inaugurated Hugo Chávez took rapid constitutional actions to change the Venezuelan regime: on 25 April 1999 a majority of the electorate voted in favor of a constituent assembly to write a new constitution; on 25 July 1999 they elected the assembly, giving a majority to Chávez supporters; and on 15 December 1999 they approved the new constitution. It created a stronger president, elected for a six-year term and eligible to be reelected once (later changed to twice). Powers of the legislative and judicial branches were curtailed. How this evolved was seen soon after Chávez was elected president under the new constitution in mid-2000. He passed by fiat a land reform measure that would confiscate private property and used military officers to carry out social projects. Victory in the regional and local elections of 31 October 2004 proved an important milestone in his drive to consolidate a 'different democracy'. His allies captured 21 of the 23 regional governorships (and the prestigious and powerful 'high mayor' of Greater Caracas) and 239 of the 335 mayoralties.

A similar case took place in Bolivia. Evo Morales, indigenous former head of the coca growers' union, became president in December 2005 and called for constitutional changes like those of Chávez in Venezuela. In the constituent assembly elections of July 2006, his Movimiento a Socialismo party (MAS) came close to accomplishing its objective. With 50.9 per cent of the vote, the MAS got 137 or 53.7 per cent of the assembly seats. It could also count upon the support of another dozen or so deputies, but it remained short of controlling a two-thirds majority in the assembly. In late January 2008, 61.43 per cent of the voters approved the 2009 Constitution. It expands the state's control over the economy and promotes the rights of indigenous peoples and social movements. In the hands of a well-disciplined party or tight coalition of interests, it promises to endow the executive with ability to marginalize the opposition. The constitution divides power not only between the three branches of government and an array of semi-autonomous institutions and oversight bodies, but also between the central, departmental, municipal, and autonomous indigenous communities.

Ecuador joined the delegative democracy ranks after Rafael Correa was sworn in as president on 15 January 2007. Like Chávez and Morales, Correa won the presidency with an ambitious agenda that offered sweeping change to voters weary of the traditional political establishment. Correa charged that Ecuador was a kidnapped country in the grip of an immoral mafia of politicians who acted in their own interests and colluded with the rich, foreign investors and the United States. He promised to render any sitting congress irrelevant by pushing forward with a plan to write an entirely new constitution.

To sweep away existing institutions and establish a new constitutional system, President Correa advanced his transformative agenda by using direct, unmediated appeals to the public in order to mobilize support. Doing so, he successfully set the country on a path of elections that consolidated his power. After winning more than 82 per cent of the vote in an April 2006 referendum on whether a constituent assembly should be held, the Correa administration scored a second stunning victory in the election for representatives to the assembly in September 2006. With a slate of candidates lead by leftist economist Alberto Acosta, Correa's Alianza PAIS ticket won 80 of the 130 seats in the new assembly.

The new constitution, written by the assembly after deliberating from November 2007 to July 2008, clearly established the legal basis for expanding the state's role in the economy. No longer designated as market-based, the economy is framed as 'social and [one of] solidarity'. In this new economy, the state is assigned rights to administer, regulate, control, and manage the strategic sector of the economy which includes energy, telecommunications, non-renewable natural resources, transportation, hydrocarbon refining, biodiversity, and water. Among the state's powers is the option to expropriate and redistribute land that is not being put to productive use (Conaghan 2011: 379).

Enhancing the powers of the presidency and trimming the powers of the unicameral national assembly figured prominently in the reforms. For the first time, a president is allowed to be re-elected in two successive terms of four years each. Moreover, if a president faces an uncooperative legislature, he or she has the power to dissolve the congress one time during the term and call for new elections. While the president would also have to run in a special election, the reform gives the president a powerful threat to wield in any executive–legislative conflict, making it near impossible for the congress to remove a president. In September 2008, 64 per cent of the public endorsed the new constitution in a referendum.

However, the 2005 case of Honduras makes it clear that delegative democracy is not the inevitable result of having liberal democracy in an area with a tradition of autocratic rule. Throughout most of its history, Honduras has been ruled by a succession of dictatorial political bosses and military strongmen. In spite of the end of formal military rule in the early 1980s, behind a democratic facade, the armed forces continued to exercise political control. in November 2005 Manuel Zelaya, a former bank director and congressman, defeated National Party candidate Porfirio Lobo Sosa in a hotly contested presidential election. Zelaya's Liberal Party, however, still remained the minority since the National Party shared an alliance with the Christian Democrats. Political opponents expressed their opposition to his foreign policy, particularly his alliance with Hugo Chávez, his friendship with Raúl Castro, as well as for his periodic criticism of the United States, and confrontations with the business sector. Zelaya had a somewhat adversarial relationship with his country's large media outlets.

In August 2008, President Zelaya announced his country's entry into the Venezuelan-sponsored Bolivarian Alternative for the Americas (ALBA), a 'fair trade' and social justice bloc being pushed by Hugo Chávez. After the surprising entry into ALBA, Zelaya became emboldened enough to call for a national referendum to replace the Honduran constitution. Zelaya first broached the topic on 11 November 2008 proposing that a fourth ballot box be installed at polling places on 29 November 2009.

Zelaya was seeking a changed constitution, which would allow him to run for reelection. On 24 March 2009 Zelaya announced, via executive decree, that this national referendum would take place no later than 28 June. The Honduran constitution, which contained 375 articles, could be amended by a two-thirds majority vote in congress. However, there are eight 'firm articles' which cannot be amended. These include presidential term limits, the system of government that is permitted and the process of presidential succession. Critics immediately labelled Zelaya's action as a blatant and cynical attempt to extend his term limits.

Zelaya did not precisely spell out what changes would be necessary in order to adapt the country's social contract to that new national reality but did announce that the new constitution would include direct democracy initiatives such as popular referendums and recall elections. Faced with mounting opposition, Zelaya announced on 3 April that the measure would not be carried out. In addition to other initiatives with questionable democratic content, Zelaya attempted to hamstring the other branches of government through legal technicalities and plenty of good old-fashioned red tape.

On 25 June, Hondurans awoke to discover that the previous night, President Zelaya had announced the firing of General Romeo Vásquez, head of the Honduran armed forces. General Vásquez had declined to lend logistical support to a referendum on constitutional reform that was scheduled to take place in the country on 28 June. The referendum had been declared illegal by congress and the Supreme Court, and Vasquez said that he would be violating the law by allowing the military to follow the president's directives.

On 28 June 2009 the military seized Zelaya and sent him to Costa Rica. The Honduran national congress announced that Zelaya was out, and its members named congressional leader Roberto Micheletti the new president. The Honduran Supreme Court also supported the removal of Zelaya, saying that the military was acting in defence of democracy. Democracy returned when Porfirio Lobo Sosa was elected president in November 2009.

6   CONCLUSION: THE STUDY OF LATIN AMERICAN LEADERSHIP

In this chapter, I have analysed the Latin American tradition of strong executive leadership. During the autocratic period (Independence–1980) there were distinctive recruitment structures; however, in almost all cases effective checks on the executive came from relevant power groups, especially the military, instead of democratically elected bodies. During the democratic period since 1980, constitutions have given more power to the president than in the United States. Nonetheless various presidents have been frustrated by the checks that do exist and have either have tried successfully (Peru, 1992) or unsuccessfully (Guatemala, 1993) to disband the legislative and judicial branches. The presidents of Venezuela, Bolivia, and Ecuador successfully mobilized lower income groups to devise what purports to be a hybrid system, not completely democratic or completely autocratic.

This 'delegative democracy' is not the inevitable conclusion from the combination of the Latin American tradition of strong leadership with democratic elections. The 2009 Honduran case shows that a president's ability to construct delegative democracy depends on the country's tradition, the size and nature of his popular support, and, most importantly, his relations with the military, as well as other factors. In addition, careful research needs to be done, with the goal of deciding if delegative democracy is just the latest way that Latin American leaders have learned to hide their true authoritarianism. Perhaps just as Anastasio Somoza Debayle reported data to the United Nations in such as way that his Nicaragua appeared to be very democratic, maybe Paul Sondrol is correct when he states 'Perhaps it is time to stop thinking in terms of the 'democratic transition' paradigm, and to start calling these semi-dictatorships what they really are' (Sondrol 2006: 2). Hugo Chávez died in 2013 and unstable government ensued.

Most studies of Latin American leadership are of individual countries and few are comparative studies, not surprising given the diversity of the twenty Latin American countries as well as the major systemic changes over their two centuries of history. There are major books, however, for each political period.

The most important books about the background and development of autocratic governments are James Malloy, *Authoritarianism and Corporatism in Latin America* (1977) and Howard J. Wiarda, *Corporatism and National Development in*

Latin America (1981, a must read). Another book on this topic is Claudio Véliz, *The Centrist Tradition in Latin America* (1980). While all present important ideas, none has led to empirical cross-national studies of leadership. Another must read is Charles Anderson, *Politics and Economic Change in Latin America* (1967), important because of its concern for the development of political rules after independence. Two books are most valuable in the study of the bureaucratic authoritarian period, David Collier, *The New Authoritarianism in Latin America* (1980, a must read) and Guillermo O'Donnell, *Modernization and Bureaucratic-Authoritarianism: Studies in South American Politics* (1973).

How leadership changed with the democratic transition is considered in general terms by Peter Smith in *Democracy in Latin America: Political Change in Comparative Perspective* (2005, a must read), Roderic Ai Camp, *Democracy in Latin America: Patterns and Cycles* (1996), Martin Needler, *The Problem of Democracy in Latin America* (1987) and Juan J. Linz and Alfred Stepan, *Problems of Democratic Transition and Consolidation: Southern Europe, South America, and Post-Communist Europe* (1996). Important books with greater specificity include J. Samuel Fitch, *The Armed Forces and Democracy in Latin America* (1998) and Scott Mainwaring and Matthew Soberg Shugart, *Presidentialism and Democracy in Latin America* (1997). The change to delegative democracy is most importantly studied by Guillermo O'Donnell in *Delegative Democracy?* (1992, a must read) while a serious questioning of the term can be found in Paul Sondrol, 'Semi-Authoritarianism in Latin America: Paraguay and Venezuela' (2006).

While not cross-national in focus, major books on individual countries include sections on leadership. The studies of the major countries are Barry Ames, *The Deadlock of Democracy in Brazil: Interests, Identities and Institutions in Comparative Politics* (2001); Emily Edmonds-Poli and David Al Shirk, *Contemporary Mexican Politics* (2009); Harvey F. Kline, *Colombia: Democracy Under Assault* (1995); Steven Levitsky and Maria V. Murillo, *Argentine Democracy: The Politics of Institutional Weakness* (2005); Lois Hecht Oppenheim, *Politics in Chile: Socialism, Authoritarianism, and Market Democracy* (2007); Jennifer L. McCoy and David J. Myers, *The Unraveling of Representative Democracy in Venezuela* (2005) and Juan M. Del Aguila, *Cuba: Dilemmas of a Revolution* (1994).

RECOMMENDED READING

Smith, P. H. (2005). *Democracy in Latin America: Political Change in Comparative Perspective.* New York: Oxford University Press.

O'Donnell, G. (1992). *Delegative Democracy?* Notre Dame, IN: Helen Kellogg Institute for International Studies.

Wiarda, H. J. (1981). *Corporatism and National Development in Latin America.* Boulder, CO: Westview Press.

REFERENCES

Ames, B. (2001). *The Deadlock of Democracy in Brazil: Interests, Identities and Institutions in Comparative Politics*. Ann Arbor, MI: University of Michigan Press.

Anderson, C. (1967). *Politics and Economic Change in Latin America*. New York: Van Nostrand.

Camp, R. A., ed. (1996). *Democracy in Latin America: Patterns and Cycles*. Wilmington, DE: Scholarly Resources.

Collier, D. (1980). *The New Authoritarianism in Latin America*. Princeton, NJ: Princeton University Press.

Conaghan, C. C. (2011). 'Ecuador: From Crisis to Left Turn', in H. J. Wiarda and H. F. Kline (eds), *Latin American Politics and Development* Boulder, CO: Westview Press, 363–82.

Del Aguila, J. M. (1994). *Cuba: Dilemmas of a Revolution*. Boulder, CO: Westview Press.

Edmonds-Poli, E. and Al Shirk, D. (2009). *Contemporary Mexican Politics*. Lanham, MD: Rowman and Littlefield.

Fitch, J. S. (1998). *The Armed Forces and Democracy in Latin America*. Baltimore, MD: Johns Hopkins University Press.

Kline, H. F. (1995). *Colombia: Democracy under Assault*. Boulder, CO: Westview Press.

Levitsky, S. and Murillo, M. V., eds. (2005). *Argentine Democracy: The Politics of Institutional Weakness*. University Park, PA: Penn State University Press.

Linz, J. J. and Stepan, A. (1996). *Problems of Democratic Transition and Consolidation: Southern Europe, South America, and Post-Communist Europe*. Baltimore, MD: Johns Hopkins University Press.

McCoy, J. L. and Myers, D. J. (2005). *The Unraveling of Representative Democracy in Venezuela*. Baltimore, MD: Johns Hopkins University Press.

Mainwaring, S. and Shugart, M. S., eds. (1997). *Presidentialism and Democracy in Latin America*. Cambridge: Cambridge University Press.

Malloy, J., ed. (1977). *Authoritarianism and Corporatism in Latin America*. Pittsburgh, PA: University of Pittsburgh Press.

Needler, M. (1987). *The Problem of Democracy in Latin America*. Lexington, MA: Lexington Books.

O'Donnell, G. (1973). *Modernization and Bureaucratic-Authoritarianism: Studies in South American Politics*. Berkeley, CA: Institute of Latin American Studies.

O'Donnell, G. (1992). *Delegative Democracy?* Notre Dame, IN: Helen Kellogg Institute for International Studies, available at <http://kellogg.nd.edu/publications/workingpapers/WPS/172.pdf>.

Oppenheim, L. H. (2007). *Politics in Chile: Socialism, Authoritarianism, and Market Democracy*. Boulder, CO: Westview Press.

Smith, P. H. (2005). *Democracy in Latin America: Political Change in Comparative Perspective*. New York: Oxford University Press.

Sondrol, P. (2006). Semi-authoritarianism in Latin America: Paraguay and Venezuela. Paper presented at the annual meeting of the International Studies Association, Town and Country Resort and Convention Center, San Diego, CA, USA, available at <http://citation.allacademic.com/meta/p_mla_apa_research_citation/0/9/8/8/8/pages98880/p98880-1.php>.

Veliz, C. (1980). *The Centrist Tradition in Latin America*. Princeton, NJ: Princeton University Press.

Wiarda, H. J. (1981). *Corporatism and National Development in Latin America*. Boulder, CO: Westview Press.

CHAPTER 42

POST-COMMUNIST LEADERSHIP

LESLIE HOLMES

1 INTRODUCTION

SOMETHING momentous and unexpected occurred in the late 1980s and early 1990s: very rapidly, the communist systems of Eastern Europe—and several in Asia and Africa—collapsed. Equally surprising was the total disintegration of the USSR in 1991. For decades, Communism had been seen as the principal competitor and threat to the West; suddenly it was gone—and with notable exceptions (such as Yugoslavia), it went quietly, with little resistance. By the mid-1990s, only five Communist states remained, and even these were showing signs of reform, albeit to varying degrees.

But what was to replace the Communist system? In particular, how were the countries emerging from Communist rule—post-communist states—to organize their political systems? Given the unprecedented nature of the collapse of Communist systems, there was no blueprint, and as the 1990s progressed, it became clear that, despite their similar pasts, different countries were adopting radically different approaches. Already by 1993, one leading scholar in the field argued that 'there are many ways to allocate the powers of president and assembly. The emerging democracies of East and Central Europe offer a more diverse range of configurations than any other region of the world' (Shugart 1993: 32).

Analysing the diverse ways in which post-communist states have structured their political systems would be too big a task here. Rather, the focus is on one key aspect of such systems, leadership arrangements. Although it was argued in the mid-1990s that leadership was the one major aspect of post-communist—or at least post-Soviet—politics to have been neglected by analysts (Colton 1995: 2), the situation has changed dramatically since. To keep the analysis within reasonable bounds, it is limited to the successor states in what was during the Communist era called Eastern Europe (minus the GDR, given its unique status), plus the Soviet successor states and Mongolia.

In line with the general template for this collection, the chapter begins by examining the significance and the uniqueness of post-communist leadership and studies of this. This is followed by an analysis of six key debates; a brief overview of landmark contributions; and conclusions that focus on the lessons learnt and the future research agenda.

2 Post-Communist Leadership Studies in Context

The post-communist states constitute the most significant group of transition states to have emerged in the past two decades, and have been the subject of considerable research by both area studies specialists and mainstream political scientists interested in transition studies and democratization. These countries had to undergo more radical transitions than the transition states of Latin America, Southern Europe and elsewhere (for example South Africa, Indonesia), since they had not only to transform their political systems, but also their economic, social (class), judicial, welfare, educational and ideological systems; many also had to settle territorial boundaries and reorient their foreign policies and international allegiances. To achieve these multiple objectives in the absence of precedents was always going to be difficult. The problems were compounded for Russia and Serbia (much less so Czechia), which had to contend with the identity and practical problems involved in losing control over larger political units. Some post-communist states (such as Estonia, Poland, Slovenia) have by now made a successful transition to democracy and have been fully integrated into 'the West', while others (for example Georgia, Moldova, Russia, Ukraine) appear to be in limbo, and a third group—all in the former USSR—have become consolidated post-communist dictatorships (such as Belarus, Turkmenistan). This chapter assesses the extent to which the type of leadership opted for, whether in constitutions or in informal politics, appears to explain these different trajectories.

3 Key Debates

The six significant debates on post-communist leadership explored here relate to:

- the nature of the system;
- the optimal leadership model;
- the optimal time for adopting a new constitution;
- the type of leaders that emerge and the impact this has on systems;
- 'second-stage' revolutions and their impact on leadership;
- the impact of external conditionality on post-communist leadership.

The first debate concerns the very nature of the political system. Some analysts (such as Protsyk 2011: 99) have argued that the dominant model in the region is the 'semi-presidential'. But such a claim is problematic. First, as most advocates—including Protsyk himself—of the term 'semi-presidentialism' acknowledge, the distinction drawn by Shugart and Carey (1992) between 'president-parliamentary' and 'premier-presidential' is still valid;[1] to call the latter semi-presidential is misleading, and it is more appropriate to call it 'semi-parliamentary'.[2] Second, it is important when classifying systems to be aware that formal constitutional descriptions may bear little resemblance to the actual exercise of power (see Hale 2011). Thus, while Protsyk (2011: 101) describes Belarus as a semi-presidential system of the 'president-parliamentary' type, few would describe the Belarusian as anything other than an authoritarian presidential system. Moreover, Protsyk also uses exactly the same label to describe Russia, Ukraine, and Armenia in the early 2000s, whereas others (for example Ishiyama and Kennedy 2001) have described these as 'super-presidential' systems; once Medvedev became president and Putin prime minister in 2008, Russia was described by some as a 'tandemocracy' (though it may be inappropriate to classify contemporary Russia as *any* form of democracy).

In this chapter, the term semi-presidential is used only for 'president-parliamentary' systems in which the president and the prime minister *de facto* share power, but in which the president is the more powerful partner; the term semi-parliamentary refers here to systems in which the balance of power between the president and parliament is reversed, but where the president is directly elected (that is, he or she enjoys a popular mandate). When a simple bifurcated approach is required for the purposes of discussion, semi-presidential will be included under presidential, and semi-parliamentary under parliamentary. Moreover, where there is widespread agreement among analysts that a *de jure* semi-presidential system is *de facto* presidential, that system is treated here as presidential. This approach is compatible with the view of the leading contemporary analyst of semi-presidential systems, Robert Elgie (2007: 61).

A final point to note is that some post-communist states have incorrectly been classified as semi-presidential even where the *de jure* (as well as the *de facto*) constitutional position is clearly presidential and/or the government formally declares the system to be presidential; Armenia and Kazakhstan are prime examples.

The second debate is the most significant, and is about whether or not it makes any difference to its democratization trajectory whether a transition state opts for a presidential, mixed (semi-presidential or semi-parliamentary) or parliamentary system. The seminal contributions on this issue from the 'pro-parliamentarism' camp are by Juan Linz (1985, 1990a, 1990b, with a 'more definitive' version in 1994, to cite Linz himself—Linz 1997: 1) and by Alfred Stepan and Cindy Skach (1993). Linz argued that democratic

---

[1] In a premier-presidential system, only the legislature—not the president—can dismiss the cabinet.
[2] Sartori (1994) also uses the term semi-parliamentary; but for him, it applies to a parliamentary system with a strong prime minister, as in the UK.

consolidation was considerably more difficult in presidentialist systems, and that only parliamentary systems would succeed long term, while Stepan and Skach argued along similar lines. In contrast, Scott Mainwaring and Matthew Shugart (1997) are among those who have argued that the parliamentarism-presidentialism division is too blunt, and that there are no *inherent* reasons why a presidentialist system cannot contribute to the consolidation of a transitional democracy. Their argument is basically that new democracies often have weak and unstable cabinets and party systems, so that a strong presidency can ensure effective decision-making that may in turn bed down a new system. Although Mainwaring and Shugart's argument is based mainly on their analysis of Latin American systems, it is offered as a general one, and Shugart himself (1993) has applied it to post-communist systems. As a third branch of this debate, Jean Blondel (1984) is one who has argued, albeit in a pre-post-communist context, that bicephalous (dual executive) leadership can help to stabilize new systems by providing a 'combination of authority and flexibility'; essentially similar conclusions have been drawn by, inter alia, Baylis (1996) and Sartori (1997).

Some two decades on, are we in a position to settle this debate? In order to answer this question, it is necessary first of all to determine the types of system adopted in the early post-communist era. Thomas Remington produced a useful overview of twenty-five post-communist systems in a 1994 analysis:

Parliamentary—Albania, Belarus, Bulgaria, Czecho-Slovakia, the GDR, Hungary, Latvia, Slovenia, Tajikistan ($N = 9$)

Semi-presidential—Armenia, Croatia, Estonia, Lithuania, Moldova, Poland, Romania, Ukraine, Rump Yugoslavia (Serbia and Montenegro) ($N = 9$)

Presidential—Azerbaijan, Georgia, Kazakhstan, Kyrgyzstan, Russia, Turkmenistan, Uzbekistan ($N = 7$)

One way of addressing this issue is to compare this classification with current perceived levels of democracy using the *Economist Democracy Index 2010*. The *Economist* Intelligence Unit has since 2006 been producing a score for each state it analyses based on sixty variables; it then classifies individual countries under one of four categories—full democracy, flawed democracy, hybrid, and authoritarian. The simplest way to present the results of this for twenty-nine of the thirty states analysed for this chapter—the *Economist* did not assess Kosovo in 2010—is in tabular form; as a cross-check, the *Freedom House* (FH) assessments for 2010 are presented in the final column, next to the *Economist*'s.

Despite some marginal differences of ranking and assessment between the *Economist* and *Freedom House* evaluations of individual countries, the overall pictures are remarkably similar and hence reassuring. Table 42.1 thus provides a clear answer to the question of the optimal leadership arrangements for transitional states wanting to become democracies: two decades or so after the collapse of Communist power, every one of the fully presidential post-communist states had an authoritarian system; most of the semi-presidential systems were slightly more

Table 42.1 Leadership arrangements and democracy level, 2010

Country	De facto system	Democracy level	Democracy score	FH status & score
Czechia	Parliamentary	Full	8.19	CD–6.89
Slovenia	Semi-parliamentary	Flawed	7.69	CD–7.24
Estonia	Parliamentary	Flawed	7.68	CD–7.24
Slovakia	Semi-parliamentary	Flawed	7.35	CD–6.37
Lithuania	Semi-parliamentary	Flawed	7.24	CD–6.79
Hungary	Parliamentary	Flawed	7.21	CD–6.27
Latvia	Parliamentary	Flawed	7.05	CD–6.94
Poland	Semi-parliamentary	Flawed	7.05	CD–6.84
Bulgaria	Semi-parliamentary	Flawed	6.84	SD–5.61
Croatia	Semi-Parliamentary	Flawed	6.81	SD–4.80
Romania	Semi-Parliamentary	Flawed	6.60	SD–5.10
Mongolia	Semi-Parliamentary	Flawed	6.36	n.a.
Moldova	Parliamentary	Flawed	6.33	Hybrid–2.91
Serbia	Semi-parliamentary	Flawed	6.33	SD–4.80
Ukraine	Semi-presidential	Flawed	6.30	Hybrid–3.41
Montenegro	Semi-parliamentary	Flawed	6.27	SD–4.54
Rep. Macedonia	Semi-parliamentary	Flawed	6.16	SD–4.54
Albania	Parliamentary	Hybrid	5.86	Hybrid–4.23
Bosnia & Herzegovina	Semi-parliamentary	Hybrid	5.32	Hybrid–3.83
Georgia	Semi-presidential*	Hybrid	4.59	Hybrid–3.06
Kosovo	Parliamentary	n.a.	n.a.	SA–2.60
Kyrgyzstan	Semi-presidential**	Hybrid	4.31	CA–1.27
Russia	Semi-presidential***	Hybrid	4.26	CA–1.17
Armenia	Presidential	Hybrid	4.09	SA–2.24
Belarus	Presidential	Authoritarian	3.34	CA–0.61
Kazakhstan	Presidential	Authoritarian	3.30	CA–0.81

(*Continued*)

Table 42.1 Continued

Country	De facto system	Democracy level	Democracy score	FH status & score
Azerbaijan	Presidential	Authoritarian	3.15	CA–0.77
Tajikistan	Presidential	Authoritarian	2.51	CA–1.22
Uzbekistan	Presidential	Authoritarian	1.74	CA–0.10
Turkmenistan	Presidential	Authoritarian	1.72	CA–0.10

Notes:

1. Scaling is 0–10–the higher the score, the more democratic. The *Freedom House* scores in the final column have been calculated by the author to render them more directly comparable with the *Economist* scores.

2. The classification of some states is disputed; many specialists on 'semi-presidential' systems include some of what others would describe as *de facto* parliamentary systems, such as Poland and Bulgaria.

3. In the final column, CD = Consolidated Democracy; SD = Semi-Consolidated Democracy; H = Transitional Governments or Hybrid Regimes; SA = Semi-Consolidated Authoritarian Regimes; CA = Consolidated Authoritarian Regimes.

* Under a 2010 constitutional amendment, Georgia is to become a semi-parliamentary system from late 2013.

** Following riots in 2010, a referendum was held, resulting in Kyrgyzstan formally committing itself to becoming a semi-parliamentary system. As of early 2012, it was too early to determine whether or not this would materialize and consolidate.

*** Russia is particularly difficult to categorize; as noted above, the constitutional arrangements have been described as 'super-presidential', while the actual arrangements 2008–12 were bicephalous, though many believed that *Prime Minister* Putin had more real power than *President* Medvedev.

Sources: Democracy level and score: Economist Intelligence Unit (2010: 3–8).
FH status and score: Walker et al. (2011: 21) (though if conflicting data, the individual country study has been used as the definitive source).

democratic than authoritarian systems (that is, they were mostly 'hybrids'); while most semi-parliamentary and parliamentary systems were classified as 'flawed democracies' by the *Economist.* Only one post-communist state—Czechia—was assessed by the *Economist* in 2010 as a 'full' democracy, and it was a parliamentary one. One case in isolation would not constitute strong evidence for the argument that democratic consolidation is better served by parliamentarism than by other arrangements; but it is noteworthy that the only full post-communist democracy as of 2010 was one of the few purely parliamentary systems. It is also worth noting that *Freedom House* classified eight post-communist states as consolidated democracies in 2010, and every one of them had either a parliamentary or semi-parliamentary system. A final way in which to convey the basic message of Table 42.1 is to note that there is a clear line in it, above which can be found almost exclusively parliamentary or semi-parliamentary systems, and below which are overwhelmingly semi-presidential or presidential systems; the sole exception to this rule is Kosovo, which is so new as an independent state that it is still finding its feet.

As a final check, we return to Remington's classification from the early 1990s. Of his nine parliamentary systems, there are currently nine sovereign states; the GDR is excluded here, while Czecho-Slovakia is now two separate states. Of these nine, one is classified by the *Economist* as a full democracy, five as flawed democracies, one as a hybrid, and two as authoritarian. But these last two changed their systems after Remington had produced his classification, and formally became presidential. Of the nine states he classified as semi-presidential—which became ten when rump Yugoslavia divided into Serbia and Montenegro in 2006—all of those here described as semi-parliamentary were categorized by the *Economist* as flawed democracies; the only state not so classified, Armenia, was the only one to be semi-presidential in the narrow sense used in this chapter. Finally, every one of the seven states Remington classified in the early 1990s as presidential was by 2010 either hybrid or authoritarian.

As noted, some states introduced significant changes to their systems after Remington had produced his classification. One of the most common has been to extend presidential terms following a referendum, which in most cases has been seen by outside observers as manipulated. This has been common in post-Soviet states, with the trend being set by Central Asian ones. In 2004, Lukashenka initiated a referendum, following which there are no longer limits on the number of terms the Belarusian president can serve. But such a move was largely unnecessary; the Belarusian assembly had already granted Lukashenka an indefinite term of office in December 1999, and the potentially legitimating role of a referendum is irrelevant if the latter has been stage-managed.

Having reduced the term of office of the Russian president from five to four years in 1996, the Russian parliament extended it in 2008 (effective 2012) to six years. While the Russian Constitution currently restricts the number of *consecutive* terms of office any one individual can serve as president, this does not prevent a given individual from running again for the presidency after someone else has occupied the office, as Putin demonstrated in 2012. Given that the musical chairs the current Russian president has demonstrated is constitutionally possible—with one individual moving every so often from the presidency to the prime ministership and back again—there is currently no limit on how long any one leader can *de facto* stay in power in Russia.

In sum, the jury is no longer out vis-à-vis the second debate; based on the post-communist transition experiences, presidential systems soon become either fully authoritarian or else clearly tending in that direction, while parliamentary systems (here including semi-parliamentary arrangements) gravitate towards democratic consolidation. The empirical findings thus support M. Steven Fish's argument (2006: 5) that 'The evidence shows that *the presence of a powerful legislature is an unmixed blessing for democratization*' (emphasis in original).

Before moving to our third debate, it is worth considering how our findings relate to the Schumpeter-inspired argument of Jan Pakulski and András Körösényi (2012) that many democracies (globally) have been moving away in recent decades from neo-classical, party-dominated democracy to what they call 'leader democracy' (see too

Körösényi 2005, where the term 'aggregative-pluralist democracy' is used rather than neoclassical). It might appear that the results of our analysis conflict with Pakulski and Körösényi's basic position. But this is not necessarily the case. Parliamentary and semi-parliamentary systems can still have strong leaders (see Sartori's point in note 2). Indeed, the type of inspirational but democratic leaders advocated by Pakulski and Körösényi are typically needed in transition states while party systems are bedding down, interests are still crystallizing, and the citizenry has only hazy ideas of the way forward (see too L. Holmes 1998).

A third debate has focused on constitutions: if consolidating democracy is a genuine objective, should they be produced and adopted quickly after the collapse of a previous dictatorship (as Bulgaria did)—or is it better to wait a few years and observe how political systems, including the leadership arrangements, emerge and stabilize (as was the case in Poland)? Stephen Holmes (1995: 81) is among those gradualists who have argued that post-communist states should postpone the adoption of constitutions until they have undergone a period of experimentation. In fact, however, few post-communist states waited long before adopting a new constitution. Moreover, if countries are listed by the date of their most recent constitution and then classified in terms of the *Economist*'s and *Freedom House* democracy assessments (see Table 42.2), no clear pattern emerges. While it might initially appear that flawed democracies tend to have adopted their constitutions earlier than hybrid or authoritarian systems—thus undermining Holmes' contention—the difference largely evaporates once the year of the collapse of the Communist system is recalled (so that Soviet successor states would be *expected* to adopt their constitutions a little later than most Central and East European states).

A fourth debate focuses on the type of person that becomes the top leader in a post-communist system. The main questions here are whether or not it makes any difference to the democratization process if post-communist leaders had been dissidents or *apparatchiks* during the communist era, and whether charisma matters. This was a topic of interest in the 1990s, when Czecho-Slovakia, Poland, and Lithuania all had charismatic heads of state—Havel, Wałęsa, and Landsbergis respectively—who had been leading dissidents during the Communist era (Baylis 1996). Hungary and Bulgaria also had former dissidents—Göncz and Zhelev respectively—as their presidents, though these were not generally seen as charismatic. Some have argued that even Russia had such a leader (Yeltsin), though his status was different from that of a Havel or Wałęsa (Strong 2009): Yeltsin had been part of the senior elite until the late-1980s, so that a more directly comparable situation to that in Czecho-Slovakia or Poland would have pertained had Alexander Solzhenitsyn, for instance, become Russia's first post-communist president.

This debate on the role of Communist-era dissidents in post-communist leadership positions has declined in significance. One reason is that few such leaders are still in power; Berisha in Albania is a rare exception. Another is that such leaders were typically presidents in either parliamentary or semi-parliamentary systems, so that their powers were limited. The clear exception to this was Yeltsin; but since his position as a dissident is ambiguous, the early interest in charismatic dissidents does not really apply. Moreover, the lustre—charismatic appeal—of many of these leaders dulled over time.

Table 42.2 Date of constitution*

Country	Date of most recent constitution	Significant amendments**	Economist democracy level	Freedom House democracy level***
Latvia	Feb 1922****	1997, 2004, 2009	Flawed democracy	CD
Croatia	Dec 1990	2000, 2001	Flawed democracy	SD
Bulgaria	Jul 1991		Flawed democracy	SD
Rep. Macedonia	Nov 1991	2001, 2009	Flawed democracy	SD
Romania	Dec 1991	2003	Flawed democracy	SD
Slovenia	Dec 1991		Flawed democracy	CD
Mongolia	Jan 1992	1999, 2001	Flawed democracy	n.a.
Turkmenistan	May 1992	1995, 1999, 2003, 2006, 2008*****	Authoritarian	CA
Estonia	Jun 1992		Flawed democracy	CD
Slovakia	Sep 1992	1999, 2001	Flawed democracy	CD
Lithuania	Oct 1992	2003	Flawed democracy	CD
Czechia	Dec 1992		Full democracy	CD
Uzbekistan	Dec 1992	2002, 2011	Authoritarian	CA******
Russia	Dec 1993	2008	Hybrid	CA
Belarus	Mar 1994	1996, 2004	Authoritarian	CA
Moldova	Jul 1994		Parliamentary*******	Hybrid
Tajikistan	Nov 1994	1999, 2003	Authoritarian	CA
Armenia	Jul 1995	2005	Hybrid	SD
Georgia	Aug 1995	2004, 2010	Hybrid	Hybrid
Kazakhstan	Aug 1995	1995, 1998, 2007	Authoritarian	CA
Azerbaijan	Nov 1995	2002, 2009	Authoritarian	CA
Bosnia & Herzegovina	Dec 1995		Hybrid	Hybrid
Ukraine	Jun 1996	2004	Flawed democracy	Hybrid
Poland	Apr 1997		Flawed democracy	CD
Albania	Nov 1998	2008	Hybrid	Hybrid
Serbia	Oct 2006		Flawed democracy	SD

(Continued)

Table 42.2   Continued

Country	Date of most recent constitution	Significant amendments**	Economist democracy level	Freedom House democracy level***
Montenegro	Oct 2007		Flawed democracy	SD
Kosovo	Apr 2008		n.a.	SD
Kyrgyzstan	Jun 2010		Hybrid	CA
Hungary	Apr 2011		Flawed democracy	CD

Notes:
* In most cases, the date given here is of adoption rather than effect.
** Given this chapter's focus, only amendments to the powers of the presidency, government, and parliament are noted.
*** See notes to Table 42.1 for explanation of abbreviations.
**** Latvia has not adopted a post-communist constitution; its 1922 constitution was re-adopted in 1993 and marginally amended in 1998.
***** Several commentators consider the 2008 amendments so substantial as to constitute a new Turkmen constitution.
****** In 2011, the powers of the Uzbek parliament were constitutionally increased at the expense of the president's, though it remains to be seen whether or not this has much impact.
******* The Moldovan authorities attempted to change the system to a semi-parliamentary one in 2010, but failed.

Finally, the declining interest among scholars is compatible with the fact that most adopted a basically Weberian approach to charisma (for an overview and broadening of this interpretation see Willner 1984: esp. 1–17), with a focus on the personal qualities of a leader especially in a revolutionary and immediate post-revolutionary era. But Michael Bernhard (1999) argues for an interpretation of Weber that sees charismatic leadership as compatible with democracy in the longer term *if* routinized in a legal-rational framework.

One other aspect of the 'type of person' variable is gender. As during the Communist era, very few women make it to the topmost leadership position in post-communist states. As of mid-December 2010, just three states—Croatia, Kyrgyzstan, and Slovakia— had female leaders.[3]

A fifth issue relates to 'second-stage' revolutions: why have some post-communist states, such as Georgia and Ukraine, overthrown elected leaders and installed new ones, and has this made any difference to their level of democracy? These related questions have led to lively debate and analysis (see McFaul 2005; Hale 2006; Fairbanks 2007).

---

[3] The reference to *mid*-December is because Croatian Prime Minister Jadranka Kosor lost office 23 December. On the problems facing women seeking high political office in the post-communist world, see Matland and Montgomery (2003); Rueschemeyer and Wolchik (2009).

But a recent study by Bunce and Wolchik (2011; see too, Bunce and Wolchik 2010) analysing six such successful changes (Slovakia 1998, Croatia 2000, Yugoslavia 2000, Georgia 2003–4, Ukraine 2004–5, and Kyrgyzstan 2005) and five failed cases (Armenia 2003, 2008; Azerbaijan 2003, 2005; Belarus 2006) provides the most comprehensive and authoritative analysis to date of what leads to a successful challenge to authoritarian leaders, and whether or not this makes much difference. Explaining why some challenges are successful and others fail, Bunce and Wolchik emphasize three factors. First, there was in the successful cases a determined *transnational* network. Second, this network was able to deploy a range of novel electoral strategies across state boundaries. Finally, elections can result in real democratic change, especially where civil society is strong, the transfer of power occurs through constitutional means, and opposition leaders come to power with small mandates.

Although it can be argued that the best known of these successful challenges—the Georgian 'Rose Revolution' and the Ukrainian 'Orange Revolution'—have in many ways been disappointing, closer analysis reveals real improvements in both countries. Georgia, for instance, has made significant progress in reducing corruption, at least at the 'petty' level; since this is in part a function of greater transparency, this could eventually result in deeper democratization. Moreover, the constitutional amendments referred to above mean that Georgia should become semi-parliamentary in 2013. And while Ukrainian President Yanukovych was long seen in the West as too Moscow-oriented, he has proven to be considerably more EU-friendly than anticipated since becoming president in February 2010.

Finally, and related to Bunce and Wolchik's argument, there is an extensive literature on the role of external conditionality on democratization and leadership arrangements (see Schimmelfennig and Sedelmeier 2004; Pridham 2005). Does the conditional promise of EU or NATO membership impact upon leadership arrangements and styles in post-communist systems? That the EU requires countries to be democratic before they can be permitted to join is undeniable. But two aspects of this condition are more blurred than is commonly realized. The first is that there is still no agreement on what constitutes a democracy. Within the literature, there are enormous differences between the democratic minimalists such as Schumpeter and Huntington, who focus primarily on elections, and those such as Habermas and Dryzek who argue that democracy is about far more than elections. Second, there is a causal directionality question here, in that those post-communist states that sought to become fully accepted as part of 'Europe' may have adopted political systems they knew were likely to develop into consolidated democracies.

4 Landmark Contributions

As emerges from the above analysis of the second debate, many of the landmark contributions in this area have been made by general comparativists—especially but not exclusively of transition states—applying their arguments to the post-communist states. But Thomas Baylis (1996, 2007), Ray Taras (1997), Robert Elgie and Sophia Moestrup (2008), and Valerie Bunce and Sharon Wolchik (2011) can be singled out for having made particularly insightful and trailblazing contributions to our understanding of political leadership specifically in the post-communist context. Since their analyses are considered elsewhere in this chapter, just one other contribution will be outlined here.

A heated debate on transition and the role leadership plays in this was conducted over three issues of *Slavic Review* in 1994–5 between Philippe Schmitter and Terry Lynn Karl (Schmitter and Karl 1994; Karl and Schmitter 1995) on one side, and Valerie Bunce (1995a, 1995b) on the other. This debate was about the appropriateness of general comparativists—especially those with primary expertise in areas such as Latin America, Southern Europe, or South Africa—making universalistic statements about democratization in transition states that included post-communist states as a sub-set. Schmitter and Karl argued that this was a legitimate exercise, while Bunce challenged this. For Bunce, the differences between the post-communist states and other transition states were so great that, for instance and of relevance to the present discussion, comparison of leadership arrangements in Latin America with those in the FSU were potentially misleading. For her, the transitions in Latin America and Southern Europe were primarily about *political* change (from authoritarianism to democracy), whereas those in the post-communist countries were far more complex—about economic, social, and other changes (what I have called the 'multiple and simultaneous revolution'—L. Holmes 1997: 15–21), so that comparison had to be circumspect.

5 Lessons Learnt and Future Research

The debates identified above demonstrate that there remain differences over terminology (definitions) and on the best way to measure political phenomena such as the level of democracy. There are also still debates on how best to determine whether or not a transitional system has consolidated. While, as noted by specialists such as Fish (2006), measurement techniques are both more sophisticated and more robust than they were in the 1990s—the *Economist*'s Democracy Index is a welcome addition to the toolkit— the cultural aspects of leadership arrangements remain contentious, and do not readily lend themselves to quantitative analysis; they are among the factors considered in this final section.

The debates on leadership in the post-communist world also have significant implications for other states either attempting to democratize or else likely to in coming years, including the still formally communist states (China, Cuba, Laos, North Korea, and Vietnam). While several factors pertaining to post-communist transition states are unique, some of the lessons to be drawn from their experiences have wider relevance for both developing and other types of transition states, and should make it easier for Western policy-makers to understand and even predict likely trajectories of post-authoritarian systems.

One lesson to be learnt from the post-communist experience is that the term 'semi-presidentialism' should no longer be used to refer to political systems in which the president is popularly elected but has limited powers in comparison with the prime minister; otherwise, the term can be misleading. Conversely, the term semi-parliamentarism deserves wider application.

The principal debate analysed in this chapter has been that on the optimal leadership arrangements for democracy. But we should also be asking supplementary questions in addressing this issue. For instance, what if many citizens prefer an effective authoritarian presidentialist system to a more democratic system that is less effective (in line with Mainwaring and Shugart's argument)? Determining the meaning of effective is not easy. But let us consider just three variables—economic growth rates, GDP per capita (PPP), and Gini coefficients.

Starting with the economic growth rates, the top five post-communist performers 2000–10 appear to be Azerbaijan (13.7 per cent average annual GDP growth rate), Turkmenistan (13.6 per cent), Armenia (8.0 per cent), Kazakhstan (8.0 per cent), and Tajikistan (7.7 per cent).[4] If the data are to be believed, the most obvious point is that many of the *least* democratic states were the best performers economically. In short, while it might be *normatively* preferable, especially to a Westerner, to have a higher level of democracy, citizens in many transition states might prefer other deliverables.

But is it appropriate or sufficient to consider only the average annual economic growth rates? If the states that perform well here were relatively underdeveloped as reflected in GDP per capita as of 2010, this would cast the first set of data in a different light. The following groupings are ranked in ascending order, so that Tajikistan has the lowest average per capita GDP, Slovenia the highest:

<US$10,000 (*N* = 14—**Tajikistan**; Kyrgyzstan; Kosovo; Moldova; Uzbekistan; Mongolia; Georgia; **Armenia**; **Turkmenistan**; Ukraine; Albania; Bosnia and Herzegovina; Rep. Macedonia; **Azerbaijan**)

>US$10,000 and <US$15,000 (*N* = 7—Montenegro; Serbia; Romania; Bulgaria; **Kazakhstan**; Belarus; Latvia)

>US$1,5000 (*N* = 9—Russia; Lithuania; Croatia; Estonia; Hungary; Poland; Slovakia; Czechia; Slovenia) (IMF statistics).

These data reveal that four of the five top performers (emboldened) in terms of GDP growth over the decade 2000–10 were still among the poorest of the post-communist states by the end of that period; even oil-rich Kazakhstan was only in the middle-income group. Hence, while many citizens *might* be willing to trade off democratic rights for

---

[4] *Global Finance* (using IMF data) website available at <www.gfmag.com/tools/global-database/economic-data/10304-countries-with-the-highest-gdp-growth-2000-2010.html#axzz1hF9mxFmj>.

improving living standards, the fact that most of the high-growth countries are still among the poorest post-communist states suggests that citizens may feel they are missing out on *both* political freedoms *and* economic well-being.

Another factor that can lead to popular resentment is perceived unfair distribution of wealth. Obtaining data on public attitudes towards income distribution is difficult, especially from authoritarian states. But distribution as reflected in Gini coefficients can be used as a proxy. The following groupings are ranked in ascending order, so that Azerbaijan has the lowest Gini coefficient (that is, the flattest income distribution), Russia the highest:

30 or less ($N = 9$—**Azerbaijan**; Czechia; Slovakia; Ukraine; Serbia; Belarus; Croatia; Bulgaria; Hungary)[5]

> 30 and < 35 ($N = 8$—**Armenia**; **Kazakhstan**; Slovenia; Romania; Albania; Kyrgyzstan; **Tajikistan**; Poland)

>35 ($N = 12$—Lithuania; Estonia; Bosnia and Herzegovina; Latvia; Uzbekistan; Mongolia; Montenegro; Moldova; Georgia; **Turkmenistan**; Rep. Macedonia; Russia) (based on Klugman et al. 2010: 152–5).

It transpires that in only one of our five countries—Azerbaijan—is the Gini coefficient in the least unequal category. Thus citizens in most of the economic 'star performers' in terms of GDP growth are not trading off political rights against what might be perceived as a fairer distribution of wealth.

A final point is that political culture must be included in any attempt to understand why some post-communist states now have democratic leadership arrangements, others dictatorships, while some remain in limbo. Political culture is notoriously difficult to define, and even more difficult to measure or operationalize for empirical analysis; here, just two observations will be made. First, most of the consolidated authoritarian regimes in the post-communist world are in predominantly Moslem societies; the only exceptions to this are Albania and Kosovo—both of which have been classified as the least democratic of the parliamentary systems. But the fact that these two are at least parliamentary, whereas all the others are presidential—using our simple bifurcated approach—may relate to a second observation. This is that historical factors have some bearing on the contemporary situation. Three such factors are considered here: pre-communist political traditions; how the Communists took power; and the situation pertaining in the final stages of Communist rule.

The only post-communist state to have had a consolidated democratic system prior to the Communist takeover was Czechoslovakia. It is therefore interesting—though hardly persuasive, given only one case—that Czechia was the only such state considered a fully-fledged democracy in the *Economist's* 2010 assessment. But another relevant aspect of the pre-communist political situation is that many of today's more

---

[5] No comparable data for Kosovo.

authoritarian states had not existed as sovereign states prior to the Communists coming to power. This point applies to the Central Asian states, so that we should allow for the possibility that nation-building has been more important than democratization in such states than in countries that already had a well-established identity.

Turning to the second factor, a clear pattern emerges whereby countries in which Communism was essentially imposed from outside are far more likely to be parliamentary or semi-parliamentary—and more democratic—than states in which indigenous Communists took power.

Third, and related to the first two points, former Soviet republics that had been independent states before being incorporated into the USSR during the Second World War (the Baltic states) were the first to exploit the political liberalization known as *glasnost* that occurred in the final years of Communist power, and have been among the most decisive in throwing off the Communist tradition of highly centralized leadership.

The research agenda on post-communist leadership includes ongoing analysis of democratic consolidation, how best to conceptualize and measure the impact of political culture, and, as further examples of mass unrest akin to the so-called coloured (that is, our second-stage) revolutions erupt, the factors leading to such mass discontent and its impact on political systems—above all, leadership arrangements. And if parliamentary systems appear from all the post-communist evidence to be much better suited to democratization than presidential ones, the kinds of issues raised by Thomas Baylis (2007) concerning the weakness of many post-communist prime ministers even in parliamentary systems will have to be analysed on an ongoing basis; the recent interest in 'leader democracy' is likely to grow. As—or perhaps if—more post-communist systems gradually tend towards parliamentarism, this issue might replace what has here been described as in many ways the most significant debate on post-communist leadership.

Recommended Reading

Baylis, T. (1996). 'Presidents versus Prime Ministers: Shaping Executive Authority in Eastern Europe', *World Politics*, 48/3: 297–323.
Bunce, V. and Wolchik, S. (2011). *Defeating Authoritarian Leaders in Post-Communist Countries*. New York: Cambridge University Press.
Elgie R. and Moestrup, S., eds. (2008). *Semi-Presidentialism in Central and Eastern Europe*. Manchester: Manchester University Press.

References

Baylis, T. (1996). 'Presidents versus Prime Ministers: Shaping Executive Authority in Eastern Europe', *World Politics*, 48/3: 297–323.
Baylis, T. (2007). 'Embattled Executives: Prime Ministerial Weakness in East Central Europe', *Communist and Post-Communist Studies*, 40/1: 81–106.

Bernhard, M. (1999). 'Charismatic Leadership and Democratization: A Weberian Perspective', in M. Kohn, K. Słomczynski and A. Jasinska-Kania (eds), *Power and Social Structure: Essays in Honor of Włodzimierz Wesołowski*. Warsaw: Warsaw University Press, 170–84.

Blondel, J. (1984). 'Dual Leadership in the Contemporary World: A Step towards Regime Stability?' in D. Kavanagh and G. Peele (eds), *Comparative Government and Politics: Essays in Honor of S.E. Finer*. Boulder, CO: Westview, 73–91.

Bunce, V. (1995a). 'Should Transitologists be Grounded?' *Slavic Review*, 54/1: 111–27.

Bunce, V. (1995b). 'Paper Curtains and Paper Tigers', *Slavic Review*, 54/4: 979–87.

Bunce, V. and Wolchik, S. (2010). 'Defeating Dictators: Electoral Change and Stability in Competitive Authoritarian Regimes', *World Politics*, 62/1: 43–86.

Bunce, V. and Wolchik, S. (2011). *Defeating Authoritarian Leaders in Post-Communist Countries*. New York: Cambridge University Press.

Colton, T. (1995). 'Introduction', in T. Colton and R. Tucker (eds), *Patterns in Post-Soviet Leadership*. Boulder, CO: Westview, 1–4.

Economist Intelligence Unit (EIU). (2010). *Democracy Index 2010: Democracy in Retreat*. London: EIU.

Elgie, R. (2007). 'Varieties of Semi-presidentialism and their Impact on Nascent Democracies', *Taiwan Journal of Democracy*, 3/2: 53–71.

Elgie, R. and Moestrup, S., eds. (2008). *Semi-Presidentialism in Central and Eastern Europe*. Manchester: Manchester University Press.

Fairbanks, C. (2007). 'Revolution Reconsidered', *Journal of Democracy*, 18/1: 42–57.

Fish, M. S. (2006). 'Stronger Legislatures, Stronger Democracies', *Journal of Democracy*, 17/1: 5–20.

Hale, H. (2006). 'Democracy or Autocracy on the March? The Colored Revolutions as Normal Dynamics of Patronal Presidentialism', *Communist and Post-Communist Studies*, 39/3: 305–29.

Hale, H. (2011). 'Formal Constitutions in Informal Politics: Institutions and Democratization in Post-Soviet Eurasia', *World Politics*, 63/4: 581–617.

Holmes, L. (1997). *Post-Communism*. Durham, NC: Duke University Press.

Holmes, L. (1998). 'The Democratic State or State Democracy? Problems of Post-communist Transition', Jean Monnet Chair Papers, No. 48. Florence: European University Institute.

Holmes, S. (1995). 'Conceptions of Democracy in the Draft Constitutions of Post-communist Countries', in B. Crawford (ed.), *Markets, States and Democracy: The Political Economy of Post-Communist Transformation*. Boulder CO: Westview, 71–81.

Ishiyama, J. and Kennedy, R. (2001). 'Superpresidentialism and Political Party Development in Russia, Ukraine, Armenia and Kyrgyzstan', *Europe-Asia Studies*, 53/8: 1177–91.

Karl, T. and Schmitter, P. (1995). 'From an Iron Curtain to a Paper Curtain: Grounding Transitologists or Students of Postcommunism?' *Slavic Review*, 54/4: 965–78.

Klugman, J. et al. (2010). *Human Development Report 2010—The Real Wealth of Nations: Pathways to Human Development*. Basingstoke: Palgrave Macmillan.

Körösényi, A. (2005). 'Political Representation in Leader Democracy', *Government and Opposition*, 40/3: 358–78.

Linz, J. (1985). 'Democracy: Presidential or Parliamentary—Does it Make a Difference?' Paper prepared for the project, 'The Role of Political Parties in the Return to Democracy in the Southern Cone', sponsored by the Latin American Program of the Woodrow Wilson International Center for Scholars, and the World Peace Foundation, available at <http://pdf.usaid.gov/pdf_docs/PNABJ524.pdf>.

Linz, J. (1990a). 'The Perils of Presidentialism', *Journal of Democracy*, 1/1: 51–69.

Linz, J. (1990b). 'The Virtues of Parliamentarism', *Journal of Democracy*, 1/4: 84–91.

Linz, J. (1994). 'Presidential or Parliamentary Democracy: Does it Make a Difference?' In Linz and Valenzuela 1994, Vol. 1: 3–87.

Linz, J. (1997). 'Introduction: Some Thoughts on Presidentialism in Postcommunist Europe', In Taras 1997: 1–14.

Linz, J. and Valenzuela, A., eds. (1994). *The Failure of Presidential Democracy: Comparative Perspectives*. Baltimore, MD: Johns Hopkins University Press; two volumes.

McFaul, M. (2005). 'Transitions from Postcommunism', *Journal of Democracy*, 16/3: 5–19.

Mainwaring, S. and Shugart, M., eds. (1997). *Presidentialism and Democracy in Latin America*. Cambridge: Cambridge University Press.

Matland, R. and Montgomery, K., eds. (2003). *Women's Access to Political Power in Post-Communist Europe*. Oxford: Oxford University Press.

Pakulski, J. and Körösényi, A. (2012). *Toward Leader Democracy*. London: Anthem.

Pridham, G. (2005). *Designing Democracy: EU Enlargement and Regime Change in Post-Communist Europe*. Basingstoke: Palgrave Macmillan.

Protsyk, O. (2011). 'Semi-presidentialism under Post-communism', in R. Elgie, S. Moestrup, and Y.-S. Wu (eds), *Semi-Presidentialism and Democracy*. Basingstoke: Palgrave Macmillan, 98–116.

Remington, T. (1994). 'Introduction: Parliamentary Elections and the Transition from Communism', in T. Remington (ed.), *Parliaments in Transition*. Boulder CO: Westview, 1–27.

Rueschemeyer, M. and Wolchik, S., eds. (2009). *Women in Power in Post-Communist Parliaments*. Bloomington, IN: Indiana University Press.

Sartori, G. (1994). Neither Presidentialism nor Parliamentarism', in J. Linz and A. Valenzuela, eds. (1994). *The Failure of Presidential Democracy: Comparative Perspectives*. Baltimore, MD: Johns Hopkins University Press 106–18.

Sartori, G. (1997). *Comparative Constitutional Engineering: An Inquiry into Structures, Incentives and Outcomes*, edn. 2nd New York: New York University Press.

Schmitter, P. and Karl, T. (1994). 'The Conceptual Travels of Transitologists and Consolidologists: How Far to the East should they Attempt to Go?' *Slavic Review*, 53/1: 173–85.

Schimmelfennig, F. and Sedelmeier, U. (2004). 'Governance by Conditionality: EU Rule Transfer to the Candidate Countries of Central and Eastern Europe', *Journal of European Public Policy*, 11/4: 669–87.

Shugart, M. (1993). 'Of Presidents and Parliaments', *East European Constitutional Review*, 2/1: 30–2.

Shugart, M. and Carey, J. (1992). *Presidents and Assemblies*. New York: Cambridge University Press.

Stepan A. and Skach, C. (1993). 'Constitutional Frameworks and Democratic Consolidation: Parliamentarianism versus Presidentialism', *World Politics*, 46/1: 1–22.

Strong, C. 2009. *The Role of Charismatic Leadership in Ending the Cold War: The Presidencies of Boris Yeltsin, Vaclav Havel, and Helmut Kohl*. Lewiston NY: Mellen.

Taras, R., ed. (1997). *Postcommunist Presidents*. Cambridge: Cambridge University Press.

Walker, C. with Habdank-Kolaczkowska, S., Roylance, T., Young, E., and Geber, N. (2011). *Nations in Transit 2011: The Authoritarian Dead End in the Former Soviet Union*, available at <http://www.freedomhouse.org/sites/default/files/inline_images/NIT-2011-Release_Booklet.pdf>.

Willner, A. R. (1984). *The Spellbinders: Charismatic Political Leadership*. New Haven: Yale University Press.

CHAPTER 43

AFRICAN POLITICAL LEADERSHIP

GERRIE SWART, JO-ANSIE VAN WYK, AND MARYKE BOTHA

Now is the time, I believe, for Africa to send its own tall ships across the waters, not to conquer, but to proclaim that Africa has found its will, that Africa has found its way and that Africa has earned its right to lead.

(Thabo Mbeki, 2006)

1 INTRODUCTION

A more holistic, in-depth, and incisive study of African political leadership has become an important part of scholarship in the study of political leadership.

This realization generates a number of critically important and related questions that the chapter will attempt to address: what is the state of the *study of* African political leadership? Which prominent scholars (internationally and on the African continent) have devoted significant time towards contributions in the field? Are there different approaches to the study of African political leadership that have been generated by scholars in the discipline? Has a sufficient amount of scholarship on African political leadership been generated to warrant speaking of different waves, schools, or traditions of scholarship in the study of African political leadership or is the study of African political leadership still in its infancy, consisting of only a few distinctive studies at present? It is essential to stress from the outset that this contribution will by no means represent an exhaustive account of the study of African political leadership. Instead a more modest objective which it will seek to achieve is to provide a primer on some salient and distinctive scholarship and studies already produced in various realms of African political leadership.

Most importantly, prior to commencing any further consideration of the aforementioned issues and questions, is the conceptualization of African political leadership: Is there a distinctively 'African' political leadership? Are there commonly held views and definitions of African political leadership? Are there particular traits, features and characteristics of African political leadership that significantly distinguishes it from any other leadership form?

2 POLITICAL LEADERSHIP: AN EMERGING 'AFRICAN' CONCEPTION AND CONNOTATION?

This section offers a brief perspective on the current understanding and meanings presently attached to the notion of 'African' political leadership (given that there appears to be no authoritative or singularly distinctive definition of the concept at present). What perhaps had set 'African' political leadership apart from the rest of perceived mainstream political leadership practice studied and frequently cited elsewhere by leadership scholars was its marginalized status.

For Cartwright (1983: 285–97), leadership is better defined as government by persuasion rather than force. The essence of leadership is the ability to persuade others to comply voluntarily with one's wishes and involves voluntary compliance by those over whom it is exercised. It is the ability to obtain non-coerced, voluntary compliance which enables followers to attain goals which they share with the leader (Cartwright 1983: 19, 21).

The majority of political science research into leadership looks at leadership stories in a biographical and narrative way, from a Western perspective, particularly British and American texts (Lyn de Ver 2008: 11). This could be one of perhaps several factors that initially contributed towards African political leadership's marginalized status in overall scholarship on political leadership. This begs the question whether a distinctive 'African' conception of political leadership has had the opportunity to emerge from the seeming dearth of literature that has been produced on the subject overall in the realm of political science?

Richard Bolden and Philip Kirk (2009) address African leadership from an indigenous perspective, looking at the meanings and connotations that the concept of 'African leadership' has for Africans in their research. Bolden and Kirk (2009) continued their research focus with an exploration of new understandings of 'African leadership'. The development of an Afro-centric perspective on leadership (in the words of Bolden and Kirk, 2009) and further research on leadership in Africa that steps outside dominant methodological and empirical paradigms is deemed to be an essential undertaking. Bolden and Kirk's research led to the gathering of a diverse array of research findings related to the emerging understandings of leadership in Africa. This included a number of connotations attached to African leadership. Bolden and Kirk (2009: 76) observe that, given the vastness of the continent and the immense national, tribal, ethnic, and religious diversity, it could be argued that the term 'African leadership' may be too broad in its ontological status to say anything much about 'leadership', let alone any sense of a distinctively 'African' leadership. The term did however evoke particularly strong reactions ranging from a sense of optimism to persistent negative connotations associated with the concept. For others the concept 'African leadership' evinced an overtly negative connotation with racist undertones and discrimination. Whatever the perspective, however, one salient issue that emerges is that the notion of 'African leadership' is frequently emotive. A distinctive 'African' conception and definition of political leadership therefore remains a work in progress, if it is to emerge at all.

3 Emerging Scholarship on African Political Leadership

What is the state of scholarship on African political leadership? Which prominent scholars (internationally and on the African continent) have devoted significant time towards contributions in the field? Are there different approaches to the study of African political leadership that have been generated by scholars in the discipline? Has a sufficient amount of scholarship on African political leadership been generated to warrant speaking of different waves, schools, or traditions of scholarship in the study of African political leadership, or is the study of African political leadership still in its infancy, consisting of only a few distinctive studies at present?

Studies on post-liberation African political leadership can be distinguished in several phases and schools. Scholarship on Africa's pre-liberation leaders was succeeded by several distinctive but overlapping phases. The first phase was approximately between 1958 (when Ghana became the first independent African state) and 1963 (when the Organization of African Unity (OAU) was established). This period focused on political leaders as the 'Great Men' and 'Heroes in History'. A second period focused on the leaders of coups d'état and military leadership which removed the generation of Africa liberation leaders. The third phase is distinguishable for the wave of democratization that swept through the continent. The fourth phases focused on failed and collapsed states. This scholarship focused on neo-patrimonialism and political corruption. The next phase focused on the 'new generation' of African leaders, whereas the final phases look at the post-new generation leadership in Africa.

Stella Nkomo (2006) succinctly probes what appears to represent the conundrum that is African leadership. Nkomo (2006: 10) from the outset observes the sobering reality that most leadership theory emanates from the United States, not even the 'West' and that approximately 98 per cent of existing research-based knowledge about leadership is based on US leaders and managers. It is US scholars who have dominated the development of leadership theory. Consequently Nkomo raises an important question: How has African leadership been portrayed in the literature and writings on leadership in the field of management and organization studies? (noting that the discipline of Political Science is not included by Nkomo). Nkomo observes that if one examines leadership textbooks used in courses about leadership, there appears to be scant reference to African leaders in the examples discussed.

Former South African President Nelson Mandela, however, frequently features as an example of charismatic and/or servant leadership. At least two leadership books have been written about Shaka Zulu. The renowned leadership scholar, Manfred Kets de Vries (2005), uses Shaka's reign as the King of the Zulus to illustrate despotic leadership. The number of books on African business leaders, too, pales in comparison to the number of books written on leadership by non-Africans. There also appears to be only fleeting reference to Africa in management textbooks. In another body of literature, scholars point to Africa's glorious past as evidence that a unique and effective form of leadership existed in Africa. As Nkomo (2006: 10) observes, if one examines the practice of leadership and management in terms of pre-colonial African history, there appears to be ample evidence of leadership practices reflecting democratic values and cultural norms respecting humanity. A number of writers in recent years—most notably prominent business leader Reuel Khoza (2006, 2011) in South Africa—have called for the practice of African leadership, notably 'attuned leadership'. The core of their approach is 'Ubuntu'—or African humanism, arguing that a unique African leadership can be developed by drawing upon the principles of Ubuntu.

Nkomo (2006) concludes her analysis by stressing that a number of challenges have to be soberly confronted if a theory of African leadership is to be successfully advanced and to overturn current practice where Africa still appears to be predominantly a net importer of leadership theory and practice. Particular obstacles to be overcome are whether an encompassing term such as 'African leadership' should be utilized and how to genuinely advance beyond Western notions of leadership in post-colonial Africa. As Mangu (2008: 7) observes, 'probably terrified by the brutal nature of political leadership in most African countries, African social scientists in general, and political scientists in particular, have shied away from the debate on leadership on their continent'.

4   Surveying the Field

It would appear that the scholarship already generated on African political leadership is limited at present, but certainly proliferating at a rapid pace. This section will therefore focus particularly on distinctive studies that have been generated on specific themes and issues of salience in African political leadership. This will include a focus on the study of African political leadership vis-à-vis the following salient themes (a thematic overview) that includes: the emerging scholarship on pre-colonial leadership and ethical leadership, the scholarship generated on the study of African leadership types, the study of visionary and transformative leadership, the study of leadership traits and characteristics, the scholarship generated on the legitimacy question vis-à-vis African political leadership, and charismatic leadership in Africa. As mentioned earlier, this list is not exhaustive and focuses on a few noteworthy studies. This section will therefore also identify some of the prominent scholars, both internationally and on the African continent that have devoted significant time towards contributions in this particular field, and whether they have developed distinctive approaches to the study of African political leadership.

Research on political leadership has been scattered. Some recent studies on political leadership in Africa focused on indigenous political leadership and institutions, traditional leadership, perspectives of leadership in African, Caribbean and Diaspora polities, warlords, former African presidents, neo-patrimonialism, African elites, recruitment, and succession (Van Wyk 2007: 5). These also include biographies and autobiographies of and by African leaders and make a significant contribution to the understanding of leadership and governance in Africa.

Scholarship focusing on *African leadership in pre-colonial times* is slowly emerging as a field of inquiry in its own right—one that is likely to elicit considerable research interest amongst African and international scholars alike. The focus on pre-colonial leadership studies has emerged in order to accord greater primacy to African leadership during this period in history, which appeared to have lacked dedicated scholarship in mainstream studies. Du Preez (2011) observes that Africans seem to be very slow or reluctant to seek leadership models in their own past, especially during the period just before and during the early phases of colonialism.

Another field of scholarly enquiry that has attracted particular attention and generated considerable interest within the overall scholarship that has been generated on African political leadership, is the focus on *leadership ethics in Africa*. Abiodun Salawu (2011) considers the leadership question in Africa and a possible panacea for it within the framework of the Paradigm of Ethical Development, which promotes an advanced and organized state of human social development brought about by the cultivation of mind for the higher ideals of the society. Salawu's contention is that African oral ethics is indispensable for inculcating in Africans, right from childhood, the values of good citizenry and leadership, necessary to create a Civilization (which is the essence of the Paradigm of Ethical Development). Osam Edim Temple (2011) focuses attention on what he terms the 'metaphysical' challenges of ethical leadership in Africa. Temple situates the challenges of ethical leadership within the province of metaphysics and argues that the challenges of ethical leadership in Africa are fundamentally metaphysical. Temple further explores at least three sources of metaphysical conflicts in Africa—the clan, the cults, and religion.

Kenyan scholar Ali A. Mazrui is considered to be one of the early pioneers of the study of *personal rule and leadership styles in Africa*. Most importantly Mazrui (2007) explores the typology of leadership in Africa in his essay, in particular the important influence of charismatic leadership at the time of independence. He further explores his typology with reference to the various categories of leaders—'mobilizational' leaders (such as Nkrumah, Nyerere, and Nasser), reconciliatory leaders (such as Nelson Mandela), a housekeeping style of political leadership (Kenya's political elite since the late 1980s), disciplinarian leadership (Nigeria's military leadership), a patriarchal form of leadership (such as Jomo Kenyatta of Kenya and Félix Houphouët-Boigny of the Côte d'Ivoire, who was also a patriarchal leader who presided over the destiny of independent Côte d'Ivoire from 1960 until his death in 1993) (Mazrui 2007). Mazrui also explores the ascendancy of technocratic political leadership in his analysis, and explores Africa's embrace of personalistic and monarchical political leadership, where Hastings Banda of Malawi epitomized personalistic rule, while monarchical political leadership was literally attempted by Jean-Bédel Bokassa who was crowned emperor of his self-proclaimed Central African Empire. Another aspect of the monarchical tendency discussed by Mazrui is the emerging dynastic trend in succession. In the Democratic Republic of the Congo (DRC), Laurent Kabila was succeeded by his son, Joseph Kabila, while Hosni Mubarak and Muammar Gaddafi were seemingly grooming their sons Gamal Mubarak and Seif al-Islam el-Gaddafi respectively to assume the political throne before their violent overthrow in 2011. Van Wyk (2007) also undertakes a similar study to come to grips with the multitude of leadership types and traits that can be distinguished on the continent.

Rotberg (2004, 2006, 2009, 2012) is another influential scholar engaged in the study of African political leadership, specifically *visionary and transformative leadership*. Rotberg's scholarship is specifically situated in the study of African political leadership in multiple spheres of interest. One aspect studied in earlier scholarship produced by Rotberg is a focus on strengthening African leadership. Rotberg (2004: 14) observes that 'Africa has long been saddled with poor, even malevolent, leadership: predatory kleptocrats, military-installed autocrats, economic illiterates, and puffed-up posturers'. Such leaders use power as an end in itself, rather than for the public good; they are indifferent to the progress of their citizens (although anxious to receive their adulation); they are unswayed by reason and employ poisonous social or racial ideologies; and they are hypocrites, always shifting blame for their countries' distress (Rotberg 2004: 15). Rotberg (2006: 2) states that 'one result, after almost five decades of African independence, is a paucity of good governance and an abundance of deficient leadership'.

He contrasts this by focusing on the few but striking examples of effective African political leadership in recent decades. These leaders stand out because of their strength of character, their adherence to the principles of participatory democracy, and their ability to overcome deep-rooted challenges. Rotberg's appraisal of effective African leadership places specific emphasis on Botswana as one of the best examples of good leadership in Africa. In explaining the origins of Botswana's leadership success, Rotberg delves into another facet of importance to his study and contribution towards an emerging scholarship on African political leadership—*visionary leadership* (given that vision, minimally, is what accomplished political leaders are meant to provide). He notes that it is Botswana's history of visionary leadership, especially in the years following independence that best explains its success. Rotberg's scholarship also extends into the realm of good governance in Africa. In this realm Rotberg (2009) studies the measurement of effective governance in Africa, including a specific focus on The Ibrahim Index of African Governance (of which Rotberg was a key architect).

Rotberg (2012) focuses on the role of good leadership, with a specific focus on imaginative and excellent political leadership. He further argues that accomplished leaders demonstrate a particular set of skills. Through illustrative case studies of leaders who have performed ably in the developing world—among them Nelson Mandela in South Africa, Seretse Khama in Botswana, Lee Kuan Yew in Singapore, and Kemal Ataturk in Turkey—Rotberg examines how these leaders transformed their respective countries.

Theron (2011) presents the study of African leadership from an alternative perspective in profiling the heads of state and government who have ruled sub-Saharan Africa since the advent of independence (approximately since 1960). The research reported in this paper sets out the initial findings of a project that aimed to capture the changing empirical characteristics of African political leaders (Heads of State) in the five decades from 1960 to 2010. The research draws on data contained in the database of the Developmental Leadership Program (DLP). The background details of African executive heads of states were entered into the DLP leadership database by collecting unexplored empirical data relating to the biographical details and characteristics of African Heads of State and Government. For the purpose of the study 158 presidents were selected. Theron's study provides statistical data on the types of rulers, their educational qualifications, their fields of tertiary study, the age at which they came to power, the number of years they spent in power, their career histories before becoming heads of state, their political backgrounds and how they gained and lost power (Theron 2011: 5). A number of equally insightful studies on South Africa, Botswana, Mauritius, and Zimbabwe have also been explored within the research currently being conducted by the DLP, which reinforces the widely-held argument that the study of leadership in Africa is growing in importance and significance.

A number of scholars have also delved more deeply into the *legitimacy of African political leadership*. The failure of African leaders to develop their own leadership style, different from that of their erstwhile colonial masters and their failure to genuinely improve their citizens' living conditions has prompted particular interest in the study of the legitimacy of African political leadership. One such study is undertaken by André Mbata B. Mangu (2008) who attributes the 'failure' of the 'first independence' and the development project to the state and leadership. His study in particular focuses on the state and leadership legitimacy, and their relationship with development in post-colonial Africa. Mangu's study in particular stresses the importance of the state and political leadership in achieving development on the continent and also provides reflection on the challenges to state reconstruction and leadership legitimacy as well as on their prospects under the African Union (AU), the New Partnership for Africa's Development (NEPAD), and the African Peer Review Mechanism (APRM). Africa's development crisis in this study is seen as primarily being one of state capacity and leadership legitimacy—two interrelated aspects. The study further probes the importance of state and leadership legitimacy grounded on the principles of constitutionalism and democracy. Mangu's study also emphasizes the important and critical role of individual leaders in promoting democracy or sustaining democratic political systems during periods when democracy was on the wane in a number of African countries. Another critical element probed in Mangu's study is the interplay between leadership legitimacy, constitutionalism and life after the Presidency, and the factors that often motivate incumbent African leaders in particular to cling to power beyond their constitutionally-mandated term in office.

Scholarship on *charismatic leadership in Africa* has also featured prominently amongst the scholarship generated on African political leadership. One such scholar, Eghosa E. Osaghae (2010) in particular explores the limits of charismatic authority and the challenges of leadership in Nigeria. As Osaghae observes, after independence the huge disappointments of the runaway gap between rising expectations and actual performance of governments reinforced the wherewithal of heroic leadership as opposition politicians, military adventurists, revolutionaries, strong men, and warlords capitalized on the frustrations of unfulfilled hopes and expectations to seize power and impose themselves on the people in the name of delivering 'strong' and redemptive leadership. The democratization or second independence struggles to liberate citizens and the state from the stranglehold of despots and authoritarian regimes marked another phase of the demands for exceptional and heroic leadership (Osaghae 2010: 408). Charismatic leaders emerge to champion popular causes, stabilize turbulent situations and restore the confidence of citizens. Osaghae further explores Nigeria's experience with charismatic leadership in particular and acknowledges the problems associated with charismatic authority, most notably the extent that charismatic authority has been conducive for the rise of strongmen and personality cults that equate the leader with the nation. Consequently, charismatic authority arguably constitutes an obstacle to the development and strengthening of rational-legal norms and institutions which are seen as the hallmarks of modern statehood. Osaghae's interest extends to addressing the reasons why the Nigerian elite has failed to provide the kind of leadership that matches the expectations elicited by charismatic legitimation (Osaghae 2010: 413).

5 RENAISSANCE, REVOLUTION, OR REVERSION? THE FUTURE STUDY OF AFRICAN POLITICAL LEADERSHIP

Mohiddin (2007: 28) correctly observes that, given the multifarious changes, challenges, and opportunities that have been witnessed in the world, there has never been a time in modern African history when the issue of leaders and quality of leadership have been so crucial. Mohiddin further argues that as the world is settling into the twenty-first century and globalization becomes inescapable, a new breed of leaders and leadership is needed in Africa. For scholars of African political leadership the task of coming to terms with the vast scholarship that is yet to be unearthed is equally challenging, and seemingly insurmountable given the vast expanse of the African continent. Yet simultaneously this reality holds even greater prospects for incredible growth, and the promise that the field will increase in prominence and importance in the near future. Consequently the research agenda should include some of the following key focal points.

First, Africa needs a new generation of democratic and corruption-free political leaders. Therefore, future studies on African political leadership should focus on democratizing Africa's political institutions to sustain democracy and remain intolerant to corruption, nepotism, and minimizing the role of the military. Future studies could also focus on the role of the AU in assisting leadership development on the continent and sanctioning corrupt leaders. Moreover, leadership studies should be anchored in Africans' conceptualization of leadership in order to contribute to an improvement of the continent's leadership.

Second, the growing ascendancy in the realm of political leadership of Africa's 'Altruists' and 'Activists' warrants greater scholarly attention, alongside the present study of Africa's 'Autocrats' and 'Absolutists'—a worthy endeavour currently beyond the ambit of this present chapter. This study should include a more in-depth exploration of new and emerging leadership typologies of African leaders.

Third, the election of South Africa's Dr Nkosazana-Dlamini Zuma as Chairperson of the African Union Commission in July 2012 (the first African woman to occupy this esteemed position) and the stellar rise of Malawian President Joyce Banda who appears deeply committed to the radical transformation and advancement of her nation, furthers the trend and trails blazed by other prominent African women. These trailblazers include Mozambique's Graça Machel, a prominent gender and children's rights advocate, first Education Minister of Mozambique and distinguished member of The Elders; Luisa Dias Diogo, elected Mozambique's first female Prime Minister in 2004; and President Ellen Johnson-Sirleaf of Liberia who was elected Africa's first female head of state in 2005 and who also was co-recipient of the Nobel Peace Prize 2011. These positive gains, advancing greater gender equality amongst African leaders also signal the advent of a distinctively different kind of African political leadership worthy of further study and scholarly inquiry especially from gender scholars.

Fourth, scholars should also shift attention and focus to the study of 'hybrid leadership' in Africa and the emergence of the 'benevolent dictator', of which Rwanda's President Paul Kagame appears to be a prominent example. Dambisa Moyo in her ground-breaking work, *Dead Aid* (2010) warns that 'the uncomfortable truth is that far from being a prerequisite for economic growth, democracy can hamper development as democratic regimes find it difficult to push through economically beneficial legislation amid rival parties and jockeying interests'. In a perfect world, Moyo observes that 'what poor countries at the lowest rungs of economic development need is not a multi-party democracy, but in fact a decisive benevolent dictator to push through the reforms required to get the economy moving (unfortunately, too often countries end up with more dictator and less benevolence)' (Moyo 2010: xi).

Fifth, the study of political leadership in Africa requires an approach consisting of both country and regional case studies as well. While other studies of political leadership focus on specific countries or one specific country, the tendency is to consider African political leadership from a continental perspective exclusively. While this is one approach, it often does not allow the consideration and in-depth investigation of developments in political leadership within a specific country or a specific region, which is likely to yield further significant insights into the state of political leadership in Africa. Equally, comparative studies could also prove useful and insightful in this regard.

Finally another salient leadership enigma and conundrum worthy of more in-depth scholarly attention is the resurgence and surprising popular support of military coups on the African continent, despite the AU's uncompromising and tough sanctioning of unconstitutional changes of government. Since the establishment of the continental body and Lomé Declaration on the Framework for an OAU Response to Unconstitutional Changes of Government adopted in 2000 there has been a dramatic increase in coups d'états. This includes coups carried out in Mauritania (2005, 2008), Guinea (2008), Niger (2010), Mali (2012), and Guinea-Bissau (2012). The coup executed in Niger in 2010 (following President Mamadou Tandja's unconstitutional attempts to cling to power) had the express aim of turning the country into an example of democracy and good governance and received considerable support from the population. Africa's coup leaders were at pains to stress that military rule was a temporary, but necessary measure to clear up the morass of corruption, mismanagement and other malpractices they claimed had prompted them to intervene and restore honest and efficient government and national integrity (Meredith 2011: 219). The seemingly popular legitimacy accorded to contemporary military takeovers (albeit of short duration) in the face of unconstitutional acts by incumbents that threaten the very fabric of democracy in Africa has proven interesting. Another important dimension to this is whether the AU should automatically impose sanctions against such instances of 'beneficial coups' (consequently setting a dangerous precedent of protecting would-be autocrats)—and this is likely to be one of the most important fields of research and vigorous debate for scholars of African political leadership in the immediate future.

There exists very little doubt that the African continent's leadership malaise is in a period of major flux, towards achieving stable, responsible and accountable leadership of which the continent is in dire need. The onus is therefore upon scholars of African political leadership to vigorously study, evaluate, understand, and capture this important point in the history of Africa.

RECOMMENDED READING

Khoza, R. J. (2011). *Attuned Leadership African Humanism as Compass*. South Africa: Penguin Books.

Maathai, W. (2009). *The Challenge for Africa: A New Vision*. London: William Heinemann.

Stengel, R. (2010). *Mandela's Way: Lessons on Life*. London: Virgin Books.

REFERENCES

Bolden, R. and Kirk, P. (2009). 'African Leadership: Surfacing New Understandings through Leadership Development', *International Journal of Cross Cultural Management*, 9/1: 69–86.

Cartwright, J. (1983). *Political Leadership in Africa*. London: St. Martin's Press.

Du Preez, M. (2011). 'The Socrates of Africa and his Student: A Case Study of Pre-colonial African Leadership', *Leadership*, 8/1: 7–15.

Kets de Vries, M. F. R. (2005). *Lessons on Leadership by Terror: Finding Shaka Zulu in the Attic*. Cheltenham: Edward Elgar Publishing.

Khoza, R. J. (2006). *Let Africa Lead: African Transformational Leadership for 21st Century Business*. Sunninghill: Vezubuntu.

Khoza, R. J. (2011). *Attuned Leadership African Humanism as Compass*. South Africa: Penguin Books.

Lyn de Ver, H. (2008). 'Leadership, Politics and Development: A Literature Survey', Leaders, Elites and Coalitions Research Programme, Background Paper No. 3, available at <www.dlprog.org>.

Mangu, A. M. B. (2008). 'State Reconstruction, Leadership Legitimacy and Democratic Governance in Africa', *Politeia*, 27/2: 1–24.

Mazrui, A. A. (2007). 'Pan-Africanism, Democracy and Leadership in Africa: The Continuing Legacy for the New Millennium', *Institute of Global Cultural Studies*, available at <http://igcs.binghamton.edu/igcs_site/dirton6.html#fn2>.

Mbeki, T. (2006). Address of the President of South Africa, at the Launch of the African Leadership Initiative, Sandton Convention Centre, Johannesburg, 13 July.

Meredith, M. (2011). *The State of Africa: A History of the Continent Since Independence*. Johannesburg and Cape Town: Jonathan Ball Publishers.

Mohiddin, A. (2007). 'African Leadership: The Succeeding Generation's Challenges and Opportunities', *Conflict Trends 'Leadership in Africa'*, 2/2007. Durban: ACCORD, available at <http://www.accord.org.za/publications/conflict-trends/downloads/420-conflict-trends-2007-2>.

Moyo, D. (2010). *Dead Aid: Why Aid is Not Working and How There is a Better Way for Africa*. New York: Farrar, Straus and Giroux.

Nkomo, S. (2006). 'In Search of African Leadership', *Management Today*, 22 (5, June).

Osaghae, E. E. (2010). 'The Limits of Charismatic Authority and the Challenges of Leadership in Nigeria', *Journal of Contemporary African Studies*, 28/4: 407–22.

Rotberg, R. I. (2004). 'Strengthening African Leadership', *Foreign Affairs*, 83/4: 14–18.

Rotberg, R. I. (2006). 'Renewing Good Leadership: Overcoming the Scourges of Africa', *Africa Policy Journal*, 1 (Spring).

Rotberg, R. I. (2009). 'Governance and Leadership in Africa: Measures, Methods and Results', *Journal of International Affairs*, 62/2: 113–26.

Rotberg, R. I. (2012). *Transformative Political Leadership: Making a Difference in the Developing World*. Chicago, IL: University of Chicago Press.

Salawu, A. (2011). 'The Paradigm of Ethical Development for *Civilized* Leadership in Africa', *Leadership*, 8/1: 17–27.

Temple, O. E. (2011). 'Metaphysical Challenges of Ethical Leadership in Africa', *Leadership*, 8/1: 47–65.

Theron, M. (2011). 'African Trends and Transformation: The Profiles of Sub-Saharan African Executive Heads of State since Independence', *Developmental Leadership Program, Research Paper 17*, November, available at <www.dlprog.org>.

Van Wyk, J. (2007). 'Political Leaders in Africa: Presidents, Patrons or Profiteers?' *ACCORD Occasional Paper Series*, 2:1. Durban: ACCORD.

PART VII

DEBATING
POLITICAL
LEADERSHIP

CHAPTER 44

CAN POLITICAL LEADERSHIP BE TAUGHT?

JEAN HARTLEY

1 INTRODUCTION

CAN training and development help political leaders to become more effective? If so, how and why? To examine these questions—and the subsidiary ones about what works, for whom, when, and why—the chapter will draw on insights from a range of disciplines and theoretical frameworks including organizational psychology, generic leadership theory and political science.

2 THE CONTEXT

Historically, in the classical ideal of the leader, the education, training, and development of rulers were central to the debates about politics and political theory. Plato proposed an ambitious plan for how wise and virtuous leaders might be selected and educated (see also Keohane, Chapter 2, this volume). He argued for a cadre of leaders to be selected (based on talent and potential), but selection was to be followed by education and training, with young children undergoing elaborate training that spanned decades and included a liberal education (philosophy, mathematics, drama), civil and military duties, and tasks to test their mettle as potential leaders and to weed out those not up to the task of ruling. Plato had a strong conviction that the capabilities of leadership can be nurtured.

Plato's emphasis on knowledge and character formation for leaders finds echoes in later work (Williamson 2008). The great man (and woman) theories of the early general leadership literature can be traced to these philosophical beginnings (Grint 2000), and this is a theme continued in the writings of Aristotle and Aquinas (Wren 2007). Plato's work also finds echoes in Machiavelli's interest in both selection and education to create statesmen of exceptional ability. He argued in *The Discourses* (trans. 2000) that 'education makes you know the world better' and was a necessary element of leader development.

Wren (2007) suggests that, around the time of the American Revolution, the focus shifted from 'leaders' to 'leadership', with the leader as a representative of the people, a more interactive view of leadership, and a consequent decline in elitist models of leadership. This may explain the overall fall-off in interest in training and development for political leaders. However, some lingering interest in educating leaders continued through the works of, for example, Madison and John Stuart Mill.

Since the 1990s, training and development for political leadership have made a bit of an academic come-back. This both recognizes certain continuities with Plato but also draws on new theory and evidence. There is less emphasis on finding exceptional individuals and more on developing capabilities, which is evident in three strands of research. First is a growing interest from organizational psychologists in questions of skills development, with insights from the field of managerial leadership development. Writers such as Bull (2012) and Hartley (2012) have examined the capabilities that distinguish accomplished politicians from those who are less so, and consider how such skills are acquired. Second, the recognition of the increasing complexity of both global and national challenges facing societies has led some researchers to argue for 'school for rulers' (Dror 2001), where politicians can engage in intensive periods of study, debate, and exploration of complex ideas. There are also systematic and professional approaches to induction and socialization for politicians to increase effectiveness rather than the sink-or-swim approach of the past (Coghill et al. 2008a; Rush and Giddings 2011). Third, there is a strand of interest in the career paths of politicians, reflecting the rise of the career politician (King 1981; Coghill et al. 2008a) and also the emergence of political leaders through experiences in social movements and emancipatory struggles.

In the policy and practice context, there is also evidence of increasing demand from politicians themselves for training and development opportunities (Hartley 2011; Inter-Parliamentary Union/United Nations Development Programme 2012). While some politicians are hostile to or suspicious of these developments (Lewis 2012; Steinack 2012), there has been an overall shift, from the idea of training and development as remedial action for poor performers towards continuing professional development.

Does it matter whether political leadership skills can be developed? The widespread assumption has been that politicians learn to be effective in the exercise of leadership solely or mainly by learning on the job. Many a politician has been catapulted into a leadership role after an election or a ministerial reshuffle and has then had to work out how to handle the job (Rosenblatt 2007; Hartley and Pinder 2010; Tiernan and Weller 2010; Rush and Giddings 2011). Do they really need any further support in honing their skills?

A further argument against training and development comes from democratic theory. A key strand in Western political thought has been sensitivity to the risk that a leadership elite might gain undue control over a republic or democracy (see Ruscio 2004; Keohane, Chapter 2, this volume). Enhancing skills and capabilities could distort democratic choices and processes, it is argued.

However, a number of theoretical and empirical arguments support the value and efficacy of training and development for political leaders. Recent evidence shows that professional development enables politicians to undertake their roles more effectively, becoming better informed and skilled (Coghill et al. 2008b; Coghill, Lewis, and Steinack 2012). Recent analysis of parliaments around the world revealed that the main problem, after resources, that prevented parliamentarians from being effective was 'lack of Parliamentary experience and technical knowledge', with 25 per cent of parliamentarians themselves saying this was a problem 'to a great extent' (Inter-Parliamentary Union/United Nations Development Programme 2012). The work of Rush and Giddings (2011) and others (Fox and Korris 2012) shows that early interventions to provide newly minted national politicians or reshuffled ministers with induction can enhance the politician's sense of their own effectiveness, and confidence in undertaking the role. Dror notes that even the best of rulers often fail to cope adequately and can make serious mistakes, so 'steps to improve the highest strata of policy makers are imperative' (Dror 2008: 80).

Furthermore, leadership development involves more than training in established knowledge and practices. Leadership can involve 'wicked problems' (Rittell and Webber 1973; Grint 2005), which require sophisticated approaches to sense-making (Weick 1995), where solutions are not known and even where the problem is not agreed and which call for adaptive leadership (Heifetz 1994).

The adoption of formal learning and development techniques by political leaders lags a long way behind comparable practices for managerial leaders. If, after analysing roles and contexts, leadership development can be devised for senior industrial leaders running large complex multinational corporations, then it ought to be possible to examine the skills and 'occupational' experiences of political leadership and devise some leadership development.

3 KEY CONCEPTS, QUESTIONS, AND DEBATES

Day and Sin note that the comparative lack of attention to leadership development theories in the academic literature is in part due to 'melding one fuzzy construct (leadership) with something that is equally complex and nebulous (development)' (Day and Sin 2011: 546). To this we add a further fuzzy construct—political leadership. So, in this section, some terms are defined and key concepts outlined. This section is therefore quite extended, as we tease out some key concepts before turning to examine key research studies.

Leadership: Nature or Nurture

How far are leadership capabilities inherent in individuals and how far are they acquired? If the former, then the focus of effort to identify effective leaders would lie in selection, while, if the latter, then training and development come to the fore.

Early research on leadership (up to and into the 1940s) focused on inherent qualities, such as personality, physique, intelligence, and cognitive style (House and Aditya 1997). Long lists were compiled of qualities thought to be associated with effective leadership (Stogdill 1974), but the approach often lacked a theoretical base, and many measures had limited validity and did not replicate across contexts. Another problem was that different leadership contexts and leadership challenges may require different behaviours and actions to be effective, so that a universalistic 'great-man' approach is now seen as unrealistic (e.g. Grint 2005; Yukl 2010).

More recent research, with better conceptualization and measurement, suggests a limited number of traits, such as motivation to be a leader (Day and Sin 2011) or leader flexibility (House and Aditya 1997). It is also accepted, however, that these qualities can be enhanced through experience (Day and Sin 2011). The leadership literature now tends to emphasize how leadership skills are acquired throughout life (e.g. Burgoyne 2010; Day, Harrison, and Halpin 2009), including in childhood (Murphy and Reichard 2011) and early adulthood (Altbach 1966).

Developmental Trajectories

Day, Harrison, and Halpin (2009) outline the concept of developmental trajectories, which occur over a life span. They assume that individuals initially have different levels of leadership motivation and effectiveness and that, therefore, how they grow as leaders will vary, and how they respond to development opportunities will also vary. Some experiences may build confidence, identity, and capability for a leader, while for others similar experiences may decrease these.

One concern in terms of development trajectories is the rise of the career politician, noted by Seligman (1950) and returned to in academic analysis since (King 1981). This is often treated with some disquiet, and a concern about socialization as a leader through a limited set of social experiences.

Adult experiences are important, with leaders across a range of contexts reporting that they become more effective over time (Day, Harrison, and Halpin 2009). Leader development is underpinned by theory about adult learning and adult development processes (Day, Harrison, and Halpin 2009; Kegan and Lahey 2010; Hartley 2011).

Research in the UK by Leach et al. (2005), also reported in Hartley (2011), examined the self-assessed leadership capabilities of 201 local politicians, based on a political leadership capability framework. In a comparison between senior compared with backbench roles (115 and 86 respectively), senior politicians rated themselves more highly than backbenchers on strategic direction and also political intelligence (understanding and working effectively with political currents and dynamics, both within and across groups). For the senior politicians, the longer they had held office, the more highly they rated themselves on these two dimensions, suggesting both length of service and seniority of role play a part.

Leadership Challenges

A starting point for leadership development analysis is or ought to be according to leadership development theory (James 2011), not the person but the purposes of leadership and the contexts in which leadership is exercised. For business organizations, this will include organizational strategy, though translating that into the political context might mean party political strategy or political group strategy. Leadership-needs analysis should occur prior to the provision of leadership development if development initiatives are to be appropriately targeted.

Many of the leadership challenges for politicians are 'wicked problems' (Rittell and Webber 1973) in that the problems being addressed are complex, interconnected with other problems and without shared views of the cause or the way to address them (on wicked problems, see also Grint 2005 and Hartley and Benington 2011). Dror (2008) calls these 'grand-policy' problems. This is particularly the case in democracies, where politicians have to exercise leadership as representatives of the people, taking into account a range of diverse interests, views, and opinions. They have to understand not only the issues and the stakeholders but the often dynamic and fluid context in which these problems are constructed and shaped. They have to exercise leadership in multiple arenas, and not only within formal political institutions (such as parliament or the council chamber) but in the context of polycentric governance, with multiple sources of power and legitimacy.

Capabilities and Forms of Knowledge

The range of knowledge, skills, expertise, and judgement required by leaders in the public eye is wide-ranging and diverse. In the leadership literature these are known generically as capabilities (Burgoyne 2010), sometimes called competencies (Boyatzis 2006), and often given the shorthand label of skills. Glatter (2009), discussing school leadership, notes that head teachers need both wisdom and a knowledge of bus schedules. That range, from detailed knowledge to an ability to engage with discernment in complex issues, is highly relevant to politicians (Hartley and Pinder 2010).

A number of leadership scholars have analysed the skills, capabilities, and judgement needed by leaders (e.g. Gardner 2004; Yukl 2010), including higher-order capabilities, such as wisdom, deliberation, and being able to 'read the context' and using intuition and political astuteness in complex situations. A focus on problem identification and not just problem-solving is increasingly considered to be a key skill for leaders (Hodgkinson and Sparrow 2002). Some scholars, including organizational psychologists, have examined capabilities for national or local politicians (e.g. Leach et al. 2005; Silvester and Dykes 2007; Bull 2012; Hartley 2012).

Increasingly, in the fields of leadership and leadership development, there is interest in wisdom as well as technical expertise. In the *Nichomean Ethics*, Aristotle (trans. 1999) sets out three forms of knowledge, or understanding: techne, episteme, and phronesis.

These are, I suggest, remain relevant to understanding political leadership. Techne, or know-how, is the knowledge of technical issues and their associated techniques. Leaders can improve their skills and knowledge base in this area. The knowledge of bus schedules for head teachers, or the understanding of the procedures of early day motions in Parliament are examples. Episteme, or conceptual knowledge, is about theory and frameworks. This is knowledge that helps to explain why things happen. It enables leaders to generalize from one situation to another and to transfer learning from one setting to another. Aristotle's third form of knowledge is phronesis, which is sometimes translated as 'practical wisdom'. Phronesis is the kind of knowledge, gained through lived experience and reflection on experience, that enables a person to act, with values, taking account of the particular context or circumstances.

The implications for leadership development are profound. If the aim is to achieve phronesis in order to grapple with complexity and wicked problems, rather than simply to master the procedures of political institutions, then leadership development requires more than techne gained in formal seminars, and more than learning on the job with little support or opportunities for reflection. In addition, a focus on developing phronesis means that leadership development implies creating exposure to *situations* (particular challenges, particular complex contexts, understanding other stakeholders' interests, engaging in understanding of international comparisons) and not just a focus on the personal qualities of individuals.

Training or Development?

Political scientists tend to use the concept of training in relation to political leadership, while organizational psychologists will use the concept of development. Is it possible to 'train' people to be leaders? Or, is leadership effectiveness developed through a process of enhancing existing abilities, skills, and judgement? It is important to be aware that in some circumstances the two concepts are used interchangeably. However, learning theorists would reserve the term 'training' for a type of learning that can be assessed against clear standards and is based on technical knowledge and/or detailed informational knowledge of institutional procedures and processes (Warr 2002). Politicians involved in induction and the acquisition of specialist and parliamentary and council knowledge may benefit from training (and the empirical evidence is that they do). On the other hand, leadership of wicked problems or leadership in the sense of mobilizing action towards framing or achieving a goal (Hartley and Benington 2011) is not something that is done to a standard. It is based not only on a range of practical skills but also on judgement and wisdom. In such contexts, development seems a more appropriate concept, one that is based on enhancing a leader's existing skills, taking a hard look at his or her strengths and weaknesses as a leader, and taking time to understand the context in which his or her leadership actions are undertaken in order to develop strategies as well as practices for addressing tough challenges. Development builds on the foundations of the experiences, abilities, and skills the person or group already has

(McCauley and van Elsor 2004; Pedler, Burgoyne, and Boydell 2006) and is focused on 'the more hazy and far-reaching goal of building individual and collective capacity to meet unforeseen challenges' (Day 2011: 41).

Leader Development or Leadership Development

A seminal article by Day (2001) made a valuable distinction between *leader* development and *leadership* development for managers, and this is also pertinent to considering political leadership:

> Leadership has been traditionally conceptualized as an individual-level skill...Within this tradition, development is thought to occur primarily through training individual, primarily intrapersonal, skills and abilities...These kinds of training approaches, however, ignore almost 50 years of research showing leadership to be a complex interaction between the designated leader and the social and organizational environment...a complementary perspective approaches leadership as a social process that engages everyone...Leadership is therefore an emergent property of effective systems design...[and]...consists of using social (i.e. relational systems) to help build commitments among members of a community of practice.
>
> (Day 2001: 583)

Having made this distinction, Day argues that both types of development are important and should be seen as complementary, a point confirmed by other writers (e.g. James 2011). This is relevant to politicians, who exercise leadership as a group or political party as well as individually. If leadership development is considered to be a collective not just an individual issue, then planned leadership development for politicians will consider strengthening the capabilities of the political leadership team or group not just of those in specific positions.

Development Interventions

Researchers concerned with managerial leadership development have noted that there are a variety of ways in which leadership effectiveness is enhanced (Gold, Thorpe and Mumford 2010; Yukl 2010), though not all interventions are equally effective, depending on the person or team, the leadership requirements, and the organizational culture and strategy (Day 2001; Hartley and Hinksman 2003).

The distinction between planned and emergent leadership development has been applied to politicians (Hartley 2011). Planned development is an intervention with the specific aim of enhancing learning by participants. Planned leadership development can include workshops and seminars, simulations, action learning sets, and formal coaching. Emergent leadership development occurs through activities that have not been undertaken with leadership development in mind, although the experiences (if reflected on appropriately) create learning that enhances development—for example, learning on the job or learning from making mistakes, which have been the hitherto dominant forms of leadership development for politicians.

Both action and reflection are needed, at different times, in development (McCall 2010). This is indicated in Kolb's learning cycle (1984) with four elements: concrete experience, reflective observation, abstract conceptualization, and active experimentation. Kolb's work is widely used in the design of leadership development to ensure that participants learn through all four elements, in order to consolidate learning. Glatter (2009) notes that experience-based learning needs to be complemented with reflection. McCall describes this as the experience conundrum—experience is said to be 'the best teacher', but experience does not equate with effectiveness without reflection. Exposure to a variety of experiences 'develop[s] leadership talent from an intuitive act into a systematic process' (McCall 2010: 681).

Day (2001) lists and evaluates the research evidence for the contribution of a wide range of development interventions used in managerial leadership, from 360-degree feedback interventions to action learning. He concludes that development interventions may be either beneficial or detrimental according to context and person and that the issue for development strategy may be less about particular interventions than about having consistent and intentional implementation, and with development linked to organizational purposes.

There is sometimes a view that there is a right or best (universal) approach to leadership development. Researchers conclude, however (Hartley and Hinksman 2003; Pedler, Burgoyne, and Boydell 2006), that there are a variety of ways in which leadership can be developed. It may vary by person, by position, by leadership challenge, and so on. Increasingly, leadership development is seen as something that is tailored for individuals and working groups, to reflect their needs.

Increasingly, large companies and large public-service organizations provide their managerial leaders with development opportunities that both include time out to reflect, take stock, and learn about themselves (for example, through psychometric analyses, or through coaching) and also provide stretching experiences in the workplace that draw on and extend their skills, accompanied by deep reflection on performance with coaches. Whatever the balance of planned and emergent leadership development, breadth of experiences is used as the basis for learning and is 'almost universally considered essential' (James and Burgoyne 2001: 10).

Frameworks and Studies

Leadership development for politicians is still a relatively new field of academic enquiry, and so the number and range of key or landmark studies are relatively scarce. Here, I present four frameworks that have been published, since 2000, three of which specifically pertain to politicians while one is drawn from wider theory about leadership development in general.

First, Dror (2008) makes a spirited argument for the need for the education and development of politicians. His work in this vein actually goes back a few years (Dror 1993) and has been widely cited (e.g. Dror 2001). He describes his approach as neoplatonic, in that it is focused on the ideal leader and his or her qualities, arguing that effective leaders in modern societies cannot afford to be amateur. He proposes that they need rigorous training and education to tackle difficult and complex policy problems—what he calls 'grand-policy' questions (or, in the language of this chapter, wicked problems). He states that he deliberately wishes to be provocative in his proposals for the improvement in the strategic use of evidence, wisdom, and decision-making by politicians. He argues, in part, by analogy with comprehensive education for senior public servants, which aims to provide high-level strategic thinking and decision-making, within a strong culture of democratic values. He suggests public policy colleges for politicians, as well as year-long study periods, and workshops and seminars to enhance capabilities. In his 2008 book chapter, Dror sets out a detailed curriculum for the 'training' of policy-makers, and most of the chapter concentrates on the topics on this proposed curriculum, including learning to separate policy from politics, value clarification and goal-setting, thinking in different time horizons simultaneously, cogitating, dreaming, and feeling, and integrating and absorbing evidence and values. It is an ambitious curriculum. He notes that not all rulers will be interested in this curriculum and therefore selection of participants will be important. It may be easier to recruit more junior politicians, on their way up, than existing senior politicians, owing to pressures on their time and attention.

The work on a school for rulers provides an analytical framework, but it has not been tested with research evidence, either for feasibility or for impact on leadership effectiveness. Interestingly, from a leadership development perspective, the focus is on the curriculum, and not on the politician. It is more about training than about development, despite the focus on wicked problems, and in this sense there is a mismatch between capability needs analysis and programme development.

Second, there are some studies that have examined how training and development take place at the induction stage of a parliamentary career (e.g. Coghill et al. 2008b; Rush and Giddings 2011), and these are valuable in collecting systematic data about the acquisition of knowledge and skills in parliaments, in the UK and Australia, as well as across a number of parliaments (Coghill et al. 2008a; Coghill, Lewis, and Steinack 2012). Coghill et al. (2008b) notes that it is harder to provide and to evaluate development at later stages in a parliamentary career. His study of senators' induction (with data collected both from senators but also from parliamentary officers) is based on a clear development framework of learning and feedback, with four stages. First, diagnosis, situational analysis, and needs assessment; second, programme design, curriculum design, and evaluation; third, programme implementation both on and off the job; and, fourth, impact and outcome evaluation. The Australian Senate induction programme Coghill et al studied occurred over four days, and the interviews indicated that senators were quite satisfied with the programme (though wanted more experiential learning), and also that they performed better in the chamber, were more confident in maiden speeches, and experienced more accelerated career progression than previous cohorts that had not been exposed to this induction programme. This is a small-scale study and therefore has limitations, but it exhibits some important features of research into training and development: a clear development framework, use of data from the focal person but also from observers, comparison across cohorts and the use of data about both satisfaction and performance. There is a need for a wider set of studies, including both local and national politicians and at all levels of their career.

The Inter-Parliamentary Union reports that induction programmes and documentary (written and video) materials are now common across many countries (Coghill et al. 2008a; Rush and Giddings 2011), though Coghill's analysis shows that much appears to be based on passive learning techniques ('chalk and talk') and to focus on what might be called technical matters—procedures and technical information. Reflective planned leadership development, however, also includes more tailored engagement with politicians. For example, the use of multi-source, multi-rater feedback (also called 360 feedback), which is widely used in senior managerial leadership development, has started to be adopted, particularly in local government (Hartley and Pinder 2010; Hartley 2012). Formal coaching has also become more prevalent amongst politicians (Hartley and Pinder 2010; Brill and Sloan 2011), as well as formal peer-mentoring schemes, particularly in local government.

Third, Hartley (2011) examines why, there has been little interest from politicians in continuing professional development, and proposes an analytical framework for leadership development for politicians. This framework is based on leadership development theory drawn from studies of managerial leaders, but applies and modifies those ideas to reflect the context and purposes of political leadership. The basis of the framework is therefore from a synthesis of ideas from another field, combined with the literature on political leadership.

Hartley's framework proposes two dimensions for conceptualizing leadership development for politicians. One dimension is concerned with whether development is planned or emergent and the other is whether the development activity consists primarily of action or reflection (see Section "Development interventions"). The combination of dimensions provides the framework shown in Figure 44.1.

Each quadrant is characterized by a particular set of activities that can support but also frustrate learning and development. 'Daily political life' is learning on the job, which for politicians tends to be frenetic, occurring in multiple arenas, and generally in the public eye. 'Mulling things over' is the area of informal reflection on past performance. These are the opportunities when politicians can reflect on their leadership goals and their capabilities. 'Structured learning' is the formal training or development activities. The 'deliberate practice of new skills' takes place when a new idea or approach is tried out in practice and feedback obtained.

Hartley's framework is analytical rather than primarily theoretical. It draws on adult learning theory to provide an understanding of why and how particular development interventions could be beneficial to leadership development for politicians. The fact that 'daily political life' and 'structured learning and reflection' are diametrically opposed on the two dimensions suggests why many politicians find it difficult to engage in formal

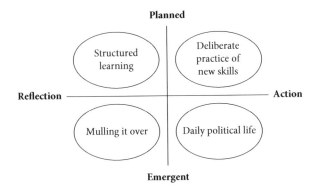

Planned

Structured learning

Deliberate practice of new skills

Reflection ———————————————— **Action**

Mulling it over

Daily political life

Emergent

FIGURE 44.1 A framework for leadership development for politicians

Source: Hartley (2011).

development programmes. It helps to show how some ideas developed in the managerial sphere may need to be adapted to the political sphere. However, it has not been tested empirically, as a means either to enhance leadership effectiveness or to examine whether the proposed barriers to leadership development operate in practice.

The final framework explored in this section is the work of Day and colleagues, in particular the contributions by Day (2001), Day, Harrison, and Halpin (2009), and Day and Sin (2011). This research has been undertaken by reviewing leadership development interventions used in business for managerial leaders and with some empirical work with young leaders. It is, therefore, the framework that is the most distant ontologically from training and development for political leaders, but is also a framework that, with careful attention to context, could be of value to understanding the training and development of politicians.

Day, Harrison, and Halpin (2009) proposed that observable leadership capabilities, evident in behaviours and skills, are underpinned by deeper-level processes. At the meso-level, leadership skills acquisition is enhanced by leader identity and self-regulation, which creates the motivation to exercise leadership and which motivates the acquiring of capabilities and the seeking-out of opportunities to practise leadership for developmental reasons. At a deeper level yet, they argued that leader development takes place in the context of ongoing adult development, not all of which is under conscious control or awareness. This is shown in Figure 44.2.

Day and Sin (2011) tested, longitudinally but only over thirteen weeks, certain hypotheses using a large sample of first-year students. While the sample and task are a far cry from mature elected politicians, this is a potentially useful framework for leadership development for politicians, because it focuses not only on capabilities but also on underlying processes of leader identity and motivation, and adult development, and is suggestive of a spiral of leadership development, with those holding a strong leader identity more likely to seek out leader development opportunities, which in turn enhances their leader identity.

FIGURE **44.2** A general heuristic depicting the levels of supporting processes in leader development

Source: Adapted from Day and Sin (2011).

4 THE STATE OF ACADEMIC KNOWLEDGE

Is it possible to train and develop political leaders? While the field remains small at present, it is growing, and there is at least some limited evidence to suggest that training and development are feasible and can achieve positive outcomes for the leadership behaviours and outcomes of politicians, as judged by both themselves and knowledgeable others. However, these are tiny signs in a wide landscape, and there is a need for many further studies, so that it is possible to build up a much more theoretically informed and empirically justified picture about what works in the way of training and development, for what kinds of leaders, at what stage in their careers, or facing what kinds of leadership challenges, and why. Also, there are more studies on induction than on later careers, and this deserves rectification.

All the frameworks in the previous section are more concerned with leader development than with leadership development, in the sense of the whole team or group. Furthermore, few studies are based on empirical data with political leaders rather than arguing by analogy from managerial or other types of leader. Given the paucity of studies and of evidence, however, these frameworks have started to provide a foundation for further theory-building and research.

Theoretically, there is a need for a clearer linking of leadership development theory (adult learning; developmental trajectories; capability needs analysis; programme design and development techniques sensitive to context and role) with empirical research, so that studies are used to test processes of learning and development and to understand the contexts in which they are effective. There is also the question, also found in the managerial literature, as to whether it is the development technique or the willingness of the participant to engage with the technique that is most effective (Hartley and Hinksman 2003). It may be that certain personalities, or those in particular roles or with particular leader identities, or with particular champions, find development interventions most valuable. Rather than expecting universal benefits from particular types of development activity, there is a pressing case in leadership development theory to take a critical realist approach—what works, for whom, in what circumstances, and why (Pawson and Tilley 1997; Hartley and Tranfield 2011).

There are particular barriers and cultural factors for training and development for political leaders (Hartley 2011; Lewis 2012), which makes generalization from the world of managerial leadership to the world of politics tentative. The roles and requirements of political compared with managerial leaders are different, as are the sources of their authority and legitimacy; their career paths are different, and the complex processes of election and representation create different opportunities and constraints (Morrell and Hartley 2006). Nevertheless, it is still valuable to learn from other academic fields and professions and to adapt (or abandon) ideas with careful consideration of context and cultural, social and institutional processes.

5 FUTURE ISSUES: TRAINING AND DEVELOPMENT IN A DEMOCRACY

Not all political leadership is exercised in democratic societies, but democracy does present particular challenges for leadership and therefore for leadership development. Leadership is about exercising influence as a representative.

Day (2001) argues that leadership development requires conceptualizing the whole system of which leadership is a part, which goes beyond honing the capabilities of individuals. For politicians, this includes the capabilities of connection with the public and about shaping and guiding public purposes. There are tensions between elitist and participationist approaches to political leadership (Wren 2007) and therefore with how training and development can be used to support democratic goals.

Heifetz (1994) describes leadership (in general) as the mobilizing of attention to tackle tough problems. His purpose-driven view of leadership identifies a set of practices that could be valuable for political leadership in democratic settings (Wren 2007; Hartley and Pinder 2010; Hartley and Benington 2011), where leadership needs to be sensitive to, and shaping of, the concerns of the electorate. Leadership development, therefore, is not just about improving the capability of individual politicians, but is about fostering wisdom, expertise, and leadership qualities in citizens. In the managerial world, fostering leadership in others is increasingly seen as a critical contribution of leaders (Tichy and Cohen 1997; Burke 2006).

Theorizing and researching both leader development and leadership development are important (Day 2001). In each approach, there is a need for theoretically informed empirical studies of training and development for and with politicians to build on existing foundations. This needs to cover both planned and emergent development, and to theorize why particular activities and techniques work for some politicians and not for others, and perhaps at certain stages in their political career. Studies could be qualitative or quantitative, with each providing answers to certain questions, and overall providing some degree of triangulation over time and types of politician. Evaluation of leadership development can be systematic, recognizing that the complexity of the subject and the problems of interpretation of effectiveness (of development, of leadership, of effectiveness) mean that research designs are more likely to be at the narrative than the controlled experiment end of a continuum of evaluation designs (Hartley and Tranfield 2011). There is also a need for longitudinal designs to help tease out context, intervention, effect, and impact. There is enough evidence from the generic leadership development field to know that universal approaches are a chimera and that it is better to reflect on the realist evaluation set of questions: what works, for whom, in what circumstances, and why (Pawson and Tilley 1997; Hartley and Tranfield 2011).

Can training and development help politicians to become more effective? This review of the field suggests, from the limited research so far, that the answer is probably yes. However, there is not yet enough evidence about how and why training and development (where they occur) creates greater effectiveness. There are many concepts and theories that can be deployed from the generic leadership field and from organizational psychology to start exploring these issues in more detail. This is a field that is growing in academic interest and in practical interest.

RECOMMENDED READING

Coghill, K., Lewis, C., and Steinack, K. (2012). 'How should Elected Members Learn Parliamentary Skills: An Overview', *Parliamentary Affairs*, 65/3: 509–19.

Day, D. (2001). 'Leadership Development: A Review in Context', *Leadership Quarterly*, 11/4: 581–613.

Day, D., Harrison, M. and Halpin, S. 2009. *An Integrative Approach to Leader Development*. Abingdon, Oxon: Routledge.

Hartley, J. (2011). 'Learning in the Whirlwind: Politicians and Leadership Development', *Public Money and Management*, 31/5: 331–38.

REFERENCES

Altbach, P. (1966). 'Students and Politics', *Comparative Education Review*, 10/2: 175–87.

Aristotle (trans. 1999). *Nichomean Ethics*. Indianapolis, IN: Hackett.

Boyatzis, R. (2006). 'Leadership Competencies, in R. Burke (ed.), *Inspiring Leadership*. London: Routledge, 119–31.

Brill, P., and Sloan, K. (2011). 'Peak Performance for the Political Leader', *Journal of Leadership Studies*, 5/1: 76–83.

Bull, P. (2012). 'What Makes a Successful Politician? The Social Skills of Politics', in A. Weinberg (ed.), in *The Psychology of Politicians*. Cambridge: Cambridge University Press, 61–75.

Burgoyne, J. (2010). 'Crafting a Leadership and Management Development Strategy', in J. Gold, R. Thorpe, and A. Mumford (eds), *Gower Handbook of Leadership and Management Development*. Aldershot: Gower, 41–55.

Burke, R. (2006). 'Inspiring Leaders: An Introduction', in R. Burke and C. Cooper (eds.), *Inspiring Leaders*. London: Routledge, 1–30.

Coghill, K., Lewis, C., and Steinack, K. (2012). 'How should Elected Members Learn Parliamentary Skills: An Overview', *Parliamentary Affairs*, 65/3: 509–19.

Coghill, K., Holland, P., Donahue, R., Richardson, A., and Neesham, C. (2008a). 'Capacity Building for New Parliamentarians: Survey of Orientation and Induction Programmes'. Working paper. Melbourne: Monash University.

Coghill, K., Holland, P., Donohue, R., Rozzoli, K., and Grant, G. (2008b). 'Professional Development Programmes for Members of Parliament', *Parliamentary Affairs*, 61/1: 73–98.

Day, D. (2001). 'Leadership Development: A Review in Context', *Leadership Quarterly*, 11/4: 581–613.

Day, D. (2011). 'Leadership Development', in A. Bryman, D. Collinson, K. Grint, B. Jackson, and M. Uhl-Bien (eds), *Sage Handbook of Leadership*. London: Sage, 37–50.

Day, D., and Sin, H. (2011). 'Longitudinal Tests of an Integrative Model of Leadership Development: Charting and Understanding Developmental Trajectories', *Leadership Quarterly*, 22/3: 545–60.

Day, D., Harrison, M., and Halpin, S. (2009). *An Integrative Approach to Leadership Development*. Abingdon, Oxon: Routledge.

Dror, Y. (1993). 'School for Rulers', in K. Green (ed.), *A Systems-Based Approach to Policymaking*. Boston, MA: Kluwer, 139–74.

Dror, Y. (2001). *Capacity to Govern: A Report to the Club of Rome*. London: Frank Cass.

Dror, Y. (2008). 'Training for Policy Makers', in M. Moran, M. Rein, and R. Goodin (eds), *The Oxford Handbook of Public Policy*. Oxford: Oxford University Press, 80–106.

Fox, R., and Korris, M. (2012). 'A Fresh Start? The Orientation and Induction of New MPs at Westminster Following the 2010 General Election', *Parliamentary Affairs*, 65/3: 559–75.

Gardner, H. (2004). *Changing Minds*. Boston: Harvard Business School Press.

Glatter, R. (2009). 'Wisdom and Bus Schedules: Developing School Leadership', *School Leadership and Management*, 29/3: 225–37.

Gold, J., Thorpe, R., and Mumford, A. (2010). *Gower Handbook of Leadership and Management Development*. Aldershot: Gower.

Grint, K. (2000). *The Arts of Leadership*. Oxford: Oxford University Press.

Grint, K. (2005). 'Problems, Problems, Problems: The Social Construction of "Leadership"', *Human Relations*, 58/11: 1467–94.

Hartley, J. (2011). 'Learning in the Whirlwind: Politicians and Leadership Development', *Public Money and Management*, 31/5: 331–8.

Hartley, J. (2012). 'Political Leadership and its Development', in A. Weinberg (ed.), *The Psychology of Politicians*. Cambridge: Cambridge University Press, 97–119.

Hartley, J., and Benington, J. (2011). 'Political Leadership', in A. Bryman, B. Jackson, K. Grint, and M. Uhl-Bien (eds), *Sage Handbook of Leadership*. London: Sage, 201–12.

Hartley, J., and Hinksman, B. (2003). *Leadership Development: A Systematic Review of the Literature. Report*. London: NHS Leadership Centre.

Hartley, J., and Pinder, K. (2010). 'Coaching Political Leaders', in J. Passmore (ed.), *Leadership in Coaching*. London: Kogan Page, 159–75.

Hartley, J., and Tranfield, D. (2011). *Leadership Learning in Changing Times: Evaluating Leadership Development in the Civil Service*. London: National School of Government.

Heifetz, R. (1994). *Leadership without Easy Answers*. Cambridge, MA: Harvard University Press.

Hodgkinson, G., and Sparrow, P. (2002). *The Competent Organization: A Psychological Analysis of the Strategic Management Process*. Buckingham: Open University Press.

House, R., and Aditya, R. (1997). 'The Social Scientific Study of Leadership: Quo Vadis?', *Journal of Management*, 23/3: 409–73.

Inter-Parliamentary Union/United Nations Development Programme (2012). *Global Parliamentary Report*. Geneva: Inter-Parliamentary Union.

James, K. T. (2011). *Leadership in Context: Lessons from the New Leadership Theory and Current Leadership Development Practice*. London: King's Fund.

James, K. T. and Burgoyne, J. (2001). *Leadership Development: Best Practice Guide for Organizations*. London: Council for Excellence in Management and Leadership.

Kegan, R., and Lahey, L. (2010). 'Adult development and organizational leadership', in N. Nohria and R. Khurana (eds), *Handbook of Leadership Theory and Practice*. Boston: Harvard Business School Press, 769–87.

King, A. (1981). 'The Rise of the Career Politician—and its Consequences', *British Journal of Political Science*, 11/3: 249–85.

Kolb, D. (1984). *Experiential Learning: Experience as a Source of Learning and Development*. Upper Saddle River, NJ: Prentice Hall.

Leach, S., Hartley, J., Lowndes, V., Wilson, D., and Downe, J. (2005). *Local Political Leadership in England and Wales*. York: Joseph Rowntree Foundation.

Lewis, C. (2012). 'Barriers to Prioritising Education and Training for Parliamentarians: Role Complexity and the Media', *Parliamentary Affairs*, 65/3: 699–714.

McCall, M. (2010). 'The Experience Conundrum', in N. Nohria and R. Khurana (eds), *Handbook of Leadership Theory and Practice*. Boston: Harvard Business School Press, 679–707,

McCauley, C., and van Elsor, E. (2004). *Handbook of Leadership Development*. The Center for Creative Leadership. San Francisco, CA: Jossey Bass.

Machiavelli, N. (trans. 2000). *The Discourses*. London: Penguin.

Morrell, K., and Hartley, J. (2006). 'A Model of Political Leadership', *Human Relations*, 59/4: 483–504.

Murphy, S., and Reichard, R. (2011) (eds). *Early Development and Leadership: Building the Next Generation of Leaders*. New York: Psychology Press/Routledge.

Pawson, R., and Tilley, N. (1997). *Realistic Evaluation*. London: Sage.

Pedler, M., Burgoyne, J., and Boydell, T. (2006). *A Manager's Guide to Self-Development*. Maidenhead: McGraw-Hill.

Rittell, H., and Webber, M. (1973). 'Dilemmas in a General Theory of Planning', *Policy Sciences*, 4/2: 155–69.

Rosenblatt, G. (2007). 'A Year in the Life: From Member of Public to Member of Parliament', *Parliamentary Affairs*, 60/3: 510–17.

Ruscio, K. (2004). *The Leadership Dilemma in Modern Democracy*. Cheltenham: Edward Elgar.

Rush, M., and Giddings, P. (2011). *Parliamentary Socialisation*. New York: Palgrave Macmillan.

Seligman, L. (1950). 'The Study of Political Leadership', *American Political Science Review*, 44/4: 904–15.

Silvester, J., and Dykes, C. (2007). 'Selecting Political Candidates: A Longitudinal Study of Assessment Centre Performance and Political Success in the 2005 UK General Election', *Journal of Occupational and Organizational Psychology*, 80/1: 11–25.

Steinack, K. (2012). 'Between Apathy and Enthusiasm: An International Comparison of MPs' Attitudes towards Parliamentary Training', *Parliamentary Affairs*, 65/3: 541–58.

Stogdill, R. (1974). *Handbook of Leadership*. New York: Free Press.

Tichy, N., and Cohen, E. (1997). *The Leadership Engine: How Winning Companies Build Leaders at Every Level*. New York: HarperCollins.

Tiernan, A., and Weller, P. (2010). *Learning to be a Minister*. Carlton, Victoria: Melbourne University Press.

Warr, P. B. (2002). 'Learning and Training', in P. B. Warr (ed.), *Psychology at Work*. 5th revised edition. Harmondsworth: Penguin, 153–77.

Weick, K. (1995). *Sense-Making in Organizations*. Thousand Oaks, CA: Sage.

Williamson, T. (2008). 'The Good Society and the Good Soul: Plato's *Republic* on Leadership', *Leadership Quarterly*, 19/4: 397–408.

Wren, T. (2007). *Inventing Leadership*. Cheltenham: Edward Elgar.

Yukl, G. (2010). *Leadership in Organizations*. Upper Saddle River, NJ: Pearson Prentice Hall.

CHAPTER 45

....

DOES GENDER MATTER?

....

PATRICIA LEE SYKES

1 INTRODUCTION

GENDER matters to political leaders and the study of leadership in a couple of ways. Because of gender, women and others who fail to fit conventional sex roles have historically been excluded from positions of political leadership, and the number of female leaders has begun to increase significantly only since the late twentieth century. Further, gender as a concept or conceptual lens is a relatively recent development: although it has seldom been used to examine political leaders, it provides an analytic tool that can give fresh insights on the leadership of both men and women and facilitate theory-building in the field of leadership studies. This chapter looks through a gender lens at the empirical data on, and evolving knowledge of, female leaders and then considers how the concept of gender might be used to enhance our understanding of leadership and its context. Exploring how gender matters can provide a different perspective on leaders and suggest an alternative approach to questioning political leadership.

2 SCHOLARSHIP ON WOMEN AS POLITICAL LEADERS

The study of female leaders presents several challenges. To some extent, those challenges resemble the difficulties associated with the study of political leadership in general, which several chapters in this handbook identify. The circumstances surrounding particular leaders and their individual traits often make leadership seem highly individualistic and unique, thereby thwarting generalizations and instead fuelling biographical work and case studies. Moreover, the subject invites an interdisciplinary approach, as the multiple dimensions of leadership tap numerous traditions and diverse disciplines. That might boost the volume of work on leadership, but it also impedes the development of coherent schools of thought and diffuses discussion of scholarly debate. In the case of female leaders, an interdisciplinary approach to leadership (political and otherwise) has produced an abundance of empirical evidence, which has been successfully compiled as a useful reference book (O'Connor 2010). Nevertheless, within disciplines such as the social sciences, too often gender studies and scholarship on political leadership remain relatively distinct fields that rarely overlap empirically or theoretically.

For social scientists, the paucity of female leaders limits quantitative analysis, and quantitative methodology usually drives major developments in their disciplines. Quantitative social scientists might argue that the small number of cases makes the study of women as political leaders subjective and susceptible to bias, but of course the alternative creates a bias against women by leaving them out of leadership studies. Those seeking scientific conclusions might find in the field of female leadership propositions that can be tested by applying them to men now and more women in the future. Although the small 'N' helps to explain why social scientists tend to marginalize or dismiss women, it fails to excuse the oversight or justify the omission.

It is even easier to understand why women's and gender studies have neglected to focus on female leaders, particularly in positions of formal power. As Laura Sjoberg, explains in her chapter, conventional studies of leadership usually assume a relatively autonomous concept of human decision-making, and feminists endorse a relational approach to understanding leadership and power. Even more fundamentally, women's and gender studies originally developed to redress the scholarly emphasis on formal leadership positions where women had been excluded. For this reason, paths to participation as well as power are discovered more often at the grassroots than in the corridors of parliament (Singerman 1996). Where women have been banned from public office, as in much of the Arab world, feminists find examples of leadership in sometimes surprising places—such as the harem (Shaarawi 1998). Scholars in women's and gender studies generally question the centrality of formal leadership; as a result, unwittingly they have tended to downplay the significance of women as political leaders.

Along with the challenges of studying female leaders comes opportunity. While it proves difficult to give a definitive overview of the subject and identify irrefutable landmarks in the evolution of scholarship, accumulated knowledge of female leaders can be teased out of the countless case studies and edited collections organized by topic or regions of the world. This chapter sums up those findings as well as some of the refinements that follow in four categories: selection and election, legislative and party leadership, executive leadership, and, as this handbook classifies it, leadership 'below and beyond the national level'.

Within each of these categories, many of the same factors affect both men and women, but looking at female leaders reveals an aspect of leadership that the study of men alone tends to conceal: leaders often wield power in a gender-specific environment moulded by 'masculinist' norms and expectations. Gender studies have generated the term 'masculinism' to denote the privileged status of conventional masculine attributes. Applied to political leadership, masculinism prefers characteristics such as conviction, confrontation, and combativeness. The roots of this preference can be traced to an idealized concept of the individual as independent and acquisitive in modern political theory (DiStefano 1998), and ample empirical evidence from some of the earliest studies of women demonstrates how masculinism erects obstacles to female political leaders (Duerst-Lahti and Kelly 1995: 21–6). By contrast, 'feminalism' favours traditional qualities associated with women such as conciliation, cooperation, and consensus-building. The degree of masculinism and feminalism varies, but, in most political systems most of the time, masculinism prevails and permeates the context of leadership. Though masculinism and feminalism can be distinguished from their socially constructed counterparts, for the sake of simplicity this chapter employs the adjectives masculine and feminine.

3 The Selection and Election of Female Leaders

Gender matters in the selection and election of female leaders, as their careers follow a distinctly gender-specific path to power. Whether selected by their peers, partisans, or the public, women struggle to satisfy the masculine expectations of leadership inherent in the combative environment of adversarial systems. Among Anglo nations, only New Zealand has ever managed to rank high on the worldwide list of the representation of women. As of 30 November 2011, New Zealand was ranked twenty-first, while Australia and Canada tied for thirty-ninth place, the United Kingdom was forty-ninth, and the United States was seventy-first. Scandinavian systems provide a striking contrast: Sweden ranked third, Finland eighth, Norway tenth, and Denmark thirteenth. To explain policy outcomes and access to labour markets, scholars who emphasize cultural and historical factors have categorized countries as constituting a 'family of nations' (Esping-Andersen 1990; Castles 1993). Applied to women's representation and their access to leadership positions, the Scandinavian family proves to be the most feminine: with multi-party systems, a high degree of consensus, and a large public sector devoted to domestic policy, it values and rewards feminine features of leadership.

Several early cross-national studies indicated that certain electoral factors enhance the prospect of women's representation, including some forms of proportional representation (PR) and the use of quotas (Lijphart 1991; Rule and Zimmerman 1994). Initial research on the importance of PR alone might have overestimated its impact (Salmond 2006). Subsequent studies highlight the significance of cultural, socioeconomic, and political variables (Tremblay 2008: 7–11), especially the nature of political parties and the degree of their commitment to the selection of female candidates (Galligan and Tremblay 2005: 4).

While PR played some role in further promoting women to leadership in New Zealand, for example, that country achieved relatively high levels of women's representation even before it adopted PR. Since the 1990s, New Zealand has had at least 30 per cent women in parliament and two women prime ministers (Jenny Shipley in 1997–9 and Helen Clark in 1999–2008), though the number of women declined slightly after the formation of the conservative Fifth National Government in 2008 (from forty-one to thirty-nine members). The success of women might be better attributed to New Zealand's small size and secondary status in global affairs, its relatively early enfranchisement of women (1893), and its vibrant women's movement. Most significant, the women's movement influenced New Zealand's Labour Party, which recruited and advanced women without the need for quotas (Sawer, Tremblay, and Trimble 2006: 13). In this respect, New Zealand illustrates another aspect that affects the advancement of women: left-of-centre parties prove more likely to select female candidates than right-of-centre parties (Reynolds 1999).

In some countries, the scarcity of female candidates helps explain the absence or under-representation of women in leadership positions. Where neither PR nor quotas exist, as in the USA, women prove more reluctant than men to run for public office (Elder 2004; Lawless and Fox 2010). In the UK, the Labour Party used quotas for the first time selecting candidates for the 1997 general election, and consequently substantial numbers of women stood for parliament and won seats (although it took legislation following the 2001 election to make quotas legal). Documentation of any 'ambition gap' between men and women should take care to avoid blaming the victims by suggesting that women lack ambition. Wherever daunting obstacles to selection and election exist (and in the absence of PR or quotas), women's reluctance to run constitutes a rational response to masculine electoral politics and governing structures.

In much of the developing world—particularly Asia and Latin America—family ties have tended to pave the path to power for women (Genovese 1993: 211–18). The daughter of Zulfikar Bhutto, the civilian prime minister in 1971–7, Prime Minister Benazir Bhutto (1988–90, 1993–6), led Pakistan, a country where military and conservative Muslim governments generally dominate. As prime minister of India (1966–77, 1980–4), Indira Gandhi followed in the footsteps of her grandfather, Indian Nationalist Leader Motilal Nehru, and her father, Jawaharlal Nehru, leader of the independence movement and the first prime minister of an independent India. For several other female leaders, marriage established the pathway to a political career. Consider the cases of Argentine presidents Isabel Perón (1974–6) and Cristina Fernandez de Kirchner (2007–), as well as President Corazon Aquino (the Philippines, 1986–92) and President Violeta Chamorro (Nicaragua, 1990–7). In recent years, women in Latin America have become national leaders in their own right: for example, Michelle Bachelet (Chile, 2006–10) and Dilma Rousseff (Brazil, 2010–). Yet historically family connections enabled women to overcome the privileged status of masculinity that pervades many Asian and Latin cultures, while they also escaped the masculine individualism that often limits women in Western, industrialized countries.

In sub-Saharan Africa, few women have benefited from their connection with power-ful men, but civil conflicts in the 1990s created other opportunities for change. By 2010, eight African nations ranked among the top thirty, with 30 per cent or more women in ministerial positions, and eight made the top thirty-five, with 26–56 per cent repre-sentation of women in the legislature (Bauer 2011: 85–90). Though the specific paths to power might differ regionally, cross-national studies on the representation of women find few firm connections between a nation's stage of development, the status of women, and their rise to top leadership positions (Bauer and Tremblay 2011: 3–4).

4 LEGISLATIVE AND PARTY LEADERSHIP

Less scholarship exists on female legislative and party leadership than on the selection and election of female leaders, but several scholars who investigate the role of women in politics have increased our knowledge about women legislators and the (under-) repre-sentation of women in party leadership positions. General texts on women in politics within specific countries include data on women's representation in legislative bod-ies (Galligan 1998; Trimble and Arscott 2003; Dolan, Deckman, and Swers 2006), and edited volumes track the increased number of women by the start of the twenty-first century (Sawer, Tremblay, and Trimble 2006). As of November 2011, women comprised 19.8 per cent of national assemblies worldwide.

The legislative arena provides both opportunities and obstacles for female leaders. In adversarial systems that concentrate power in the leadership of two major parties and rely on combat between them, women must satisfy highly masculine standards, but when they do become leaders, they often gain considerable power. From 2007 until 2010, Nancy Pelosi (Democrat from California) served as the Speaker of the US House of Representatives. The daughter of a US Representative, Pelosi nevertheless worked her way up the ranks of the congressional party. She demonstrated her 'tough-ness' both in dealing with the opposition and in holding together her own party, as indi-cated by her success in safeguarding significant domestic programmes when President George W. Bush and his Republican Party attempted to abolish them. Other influen-tial women in Congress like Stephanie Tubbs Jones (Democrat from Ohio), the first African-American woman elected to Congress from Ohio, have also made a differ-ence. At a time when scandals plagued the lower house, as Chair of the House Ethics Committee, she appeared to fulfil the feminine role of ethical or moral leadership that the mass public and the political elite expect from women.

Indeed, what one early volume documented remains a valid observation—namely, that the public looks to female leaders in times of turmoil or after major scan-dals (Genovese 1993: 214; Jalalzai 2008: 208). While it is not strictly speaking a posi-tion of political leadership, the directorship of the International Monetary Fund went to a woman, Christine Lagarde, after a sex scandal involving her male predeces-sor. Following the financial crisis in the Republic of Ireland, in 2011 the Dail voted for legislation adopting quotas to elect more women to parliament. Similarly the Icelandic government that came to power in 2009 as a result of the financial crisis approved the use of gender quotas on company boards, following the example of Norway. In these cases, gender stereotypes seem to serve the interests of women as the public turns to female leaders to 'clean house' and trusts them to be more honest.

Though limited, some empirical evidence supports the stereotype. One study finds women less likely to be involved in bribery or to condone bribe-taking, and corruption is less severe in situations where women hold a larger share of parliamentary seats and a higher percentage of senior positions in the bureaucracy (Swamy et al. 2001). Another report documents public perceptions about the greater honesty of female politicians and their ability to 'keep government honest' (Pew Research Center 2008). Of course, there exist many individual cases of women who behave 'just like men' as leaders, abusing their power and betraying the public trust, but those examples have not yet shattered the stereotype of women as morally superior.

Furthermore, when a major political party plummets in the polls and faces defeat, the party elite sometimes look for a female leader and hope that the novelty—and increased support among female voters—will revive party fortunes. Canada's first and only female prime minister, Kim Campbell, led for a meagre few months before her Progressive Conservative Party failed to win the general election in 1993. In the USA the only two women to run as vice presidential candidates from major parties proved similarly situated: Geraldine Ferraro (US Representative, Democrat from New York) lost in the 1984 landslide, while Sarah Palin, Governor of Alaska (2006–9), joined the ill-fated Republican ticket in 2008. All these women encountered harsh criticism for failing to live up to masculine expectations, as they were generally perceived as inexperienced and ill-equipped to lead. Women are much more likely to lead minor political parties, though it remains unclear whether they are attracted to the ideological purity that often characterizes minor parties or benefit from the absence of masculine rules and norms that obstruct women in older, traditional parties—or both. Leaders of minor parties generally wield less influence, especially in first-past-the-post electoral systems, but they can help set the agenda or voice opposition, when the major parties fail to address significant issues, collude to cut critical programmes, or adopt a controversial course of action.

In general, substantive representation proves more difficult to assess than symbolic or descriptive representation, but some studies have indicated that women as legislators behave differently from men and that difference matters to the interests of women as a group (Swers 2002; Chen 2010). On issues ranging from social policy to peace, female legislators have influenced the agenda (Tremblay 1998; Cowell-Meyers 2003). Of course, power is more dispersed and shared in the legislative arena than in the executive, even in adversarial systems. Generally, the more concentrated the power, the less likely women will wield it. As a result, more women make it into the legislature than the executive, and women are more likely to become executive leaders where power is shared (Reynolds 1999; Jalalzai 2008). Because of their small numbers, it is even more difficult to generalize about female national executives and their impact.

5 Executive Leadership

As with the study of female leaders in general, research on women as executives has tended to produce collections of case studies or in one instance a compilation of interviews (Liswood 1995). Even where no woman has occupied the top spot, country-specific research has examined the relationship between executive leadership and women's interests (Martin 2003). Only one comprehensive edited volume has scanned the full scope of women in the executive—as cabinet ministers as well as at the pinnacle of power as prime ministers or presidents—by regions and from a global perspective (Bauer and Tremblay 2011).

In addition, some ambitious efforts have been made to move beyond single-nation studies and edited books. One creative attempt to assess how personality affects the leadership styles of executives focused on Indian Prime Minister Indira Gandhi, Israeli Prime Minister Golda Meir, and British Prime Minister Margaret Thatcher, and identified the 'dominant pattern' of their personalities as rigid, dogmatic, and firm (Steinberg 2008). As the three subjects were chosen because they represent strong, influential leaders, that finding is not surprising—and factors other than early life experience or innate attributes might explain the success of such personality types, particularly among female executives in masculine systems. Nevertheless, psychological analysis provides one avenue for fruitful comparative research based on qualitative as well as quantitative data. As the number of female executives increases worldwide, more genuine cross-national studies using quantitative methods are likely to appear (Jalalzai 2008).

Between 1960 and 2011, eight-two women became national executives. Twelve led in Sub-Saharan Africa, fourteen in Asia, five in the Caribbean, twenty one in Western Europe, thirteen in Eastern Europe, eleven in Latin America, two in the Middle East (Israel), three in Oceania, and only one in North America (Canada) (Inter-Parliamentary Union 2011). Women governed in geographically diverse locations and encountered a range of obstacles and opportunities. In the USA, for example, the president's institutional role of Commander in Chief and the nation's superpower status magnify the masculine requirements for leadership. During the 2008 presidential primaries, Senator Hillary Clinton struggled to convince voters that she could perform such a commanding role. While the USA might raise the highest bar for women to meet, some measure of masculine attributes characterizes executive leadership in most systems, and female executives usually need to develop styles and strategies to show they are capable of being strong, determined, and decisive.

British Prime Minister Thatcher (1979–90)—the best-known and most influential female leader in the Anglo world—adopted exactly that approach. Thatcher insisted that she alone had a remedy for the problems that plagued the United Kingdom, and she described her neo-liberal public philosophy in highly masculine terms by extolling the virtues of rugged individualism and fierce anti-communism. Moreover, she developed a distinctly masculine style, which she described as 'conviction politics', an approach that shunned conciliation and consensus-building and embraced conflict and conquest. Her style evoked the image of Boadicea—the ancient Roman warrior queen—and earned her the appellation Iron Lady.

Women often get tagged with the label Iron Lady. Before Thatcher, the title went to Israeli Prime Minister Golda Meir (1969–74) whose firm leadership during the Yom Kippur War of 1973 solidified her reputation for decisiveness and determination. Later Liberian President Ellen Johnson Sirleaf (2006–) acquired the nickname Iron Lady for her 'take-no-prisoners style' of leading her wartorn nation (Cooper 2010: 44). German Chancellor Angela Merkel (2005–) was known as the Iron Frau in the early days of her first coalition government before she proved willing to compromise, and she later lived up to the label when she emerged as the 'strong leader' during the European Union's financial crisis. The label has also landed on less successful, short-term executives, such as Edith Cresson, prime minister of France (1991–2), although her critics used it to disparage her and depict her as insensitive to the concerns of ordinary people. Whether the label Iron Lady conveys admiration or approbation, it indicates the masculine expectations of leadership, often magnified by the demands of wartime leadership, a nation's global status, or the degree of concentrated power in its executive.

Presidential systems place women at a greater disadvantage because they concentrate power in the hands of a single person rather than in the collective leadership of a cabinet with a prime minister as 'first among equals'. Across systems, the political elite as well as the mass public appear to have reservations about a woman wielding power with a high degree of independent authority and discretion. If that prejudice continues, then the presidentialization of parliamentary systems could make it even more difficult for women to become executives in parliamentary systems in the future.

Where and when presidentialization occurs, it can also diminish the authority of cabinet ministers, at a time when more women are moving into those positions of executive leadership (16.9 per cent in 2010). In the UK under the leadership of Prime Minister Tony Blair (1997–2007), the Labour Party reserved seats in cabinet for women, but Blair often bypassed the cabinet and relied on his own advisers at Number 10 Downing Street. Furthermore, in his first government, he placed a woman in charge of feminine domestic policies such as health and education at a time when neo-liberal fiscal constraints required cuts in expenditures. Margaret Beckett, who endorsed Blair's views, later became foreign secretary for a brief period (2006–7), although she garnered criticism as being too soft and subservient to the prime minister. Women were not limited to 'pink-collar' portfolios, but Blair's leadership style tended to diminish the overall influence and integrity of cabinet. In many countries, women have moved into cabinet posts just as institutional and ideological developments restricted their opportunities to influence the direction of public policy (Sykes 2009).

In the relatively brief history of female cabinet ministers, the most masculine posts that pertain to national defence have largely remained reserved for men and for the few women who live up to the label Iron Lady, but that might be starting to change. Looking below the ministerial level to the permanent government, where merit matters more, women are advancing at a greater rate: by 2012, 50 per cent of the permanent secretaries in the UK were women, with one of them in the very masculine position of Permanent Secretary of Defence. One study of cabinets in eighteen Latin American countries observed the gendered pattern of ministerial appointments but also found that, as the number of women increase, they tend to move into more powerful ministries (Escobar-Lemmon and Taylor-Robinson 2009). Subsequent research documents the same phenomenon in other regions and questions the traditional distinction between hard and soft portfolios as their significance varies by time and place (Bauer and Tremblay 2011: 179).

Finally, gender seems to matter more in cases of female cabinet ministers than female heads of government. The impact of female prime ministers and presidents remains idiosyncratic: President Sirleaf immediately gave six top cabinet posts (of twenty-two) to women, while Prime Minister Thatcher appointed only one woman to a minor ministry in eleven years. But evidence indicates that female cabinet ministers more consistently work to advance the interests of women as a group, and they can have a greater impact on public policy and practices, including gender mainstreaming, than women in the legislature (Bauer and Tremblay 2011: 5).

6 Below and Beyond the National Level

When it comes to advancing the interests of women, federalism presents a long, complex list of pros and cons (Sawer, Tremblay, and Trimble 2006: 6), but federal systems such as Canada, Australia, and the USA can provide additional opportunities for female political leadership. Where public service in the national capital requires substantial travel and women continue to bear the brunt of child-rearing responsibilities, state and provincial governments allow women to lead and remain close to home. While national ideological trends that have been rolling back the state can also limit local and regional leaders, states and provinces often provide laboratories for innovative leaders to test new policies. In the cases of large diverse nations, they can also prove more representative than the federal government. Francophone women in Quebec, for example, are more inclined to trust their provincial government to deliver essential social services. Where devolution has recently occurred as in the UK, women have achieved greater representation in the assemblies in Scotland and Wales (Stirbu 2011). Finally, for women, the state or province can provide a platform to launch a national career, and particularly in the USA many women move from their positions as governors to the national cabinet or other key positions in the administration of the federal government.

Various case studies document why and how female leaders at the subnational level have influenced such policies as childcare, women's safety, parental leave, reproductive rights, and social policy (Thomas 1991; Carroll 2001; Haussman, Vickers, and Sawer 2010).

Women's leadership has also been increasing at the international level. Female membership in the European Parliament (more than 30 per cent) far exceeds their representation in national legislatures (on average 22 per cent), though it is not clear why women fare better on the international level than within individual member countries (Stockemer 2008). The number of women on the European Commission has been steadily rising—with mixed results for the representation and reputation of female leaders. (During the Santer Commission from 1995 to 1999, France's Commissioner, former prime minister Cresson, became embroiled in a serious scandal concerning the fraudulent use of funds and favouritism, producing one of those examples that calls into question the superior integrity of women.) In the United Nations General Assembly, there have been 3 female presidents—Vijaya Lakshmi Pandit (India 1953), Angie E. Brooks (Liberia 1969), and Sheikha Haya Rashed Al Khalifa (Bahrain 2006)—and 107 female permanent representatives and ambassadors to the UN, though no woman has yet reached the top spot of General Secretary.

Some female leaders have shown how gender can matter when women move from the national stage to the international arena—in both formal and informal roles. A former prime minister of Norway (1981, 1986–9, 1990–6), Gro Harlem Brundtland became the Director-General of the World Health Organization (1998–2003), and Irish President Mary Robinson (1990–7) became the United Nations High Commissioner for Human Rights (1997–2002). As members of the international group known as 'the elders' (former national leaders who work to resolve global conflicts), Brundtland and Robinson demonstrate some of the ways women can advance international peace and enhance awareness of global challenges. In addition, three women won the Nobel Peace Prize in 2011: President Sirleaf, Liberian peace activist Leamah Gbowee, and Tawakkul Karman—known as the 'mother of the revolution' in Yemen. All three have fought to protect the rights of women and girls as they promote peace within their own countries and regionally. One of several avenues for future research might consider why and how female leaders fulfil feminine expectations of women as peacemakers and explore the ways they can engender change on a global scale.

7 UNDERSTANDING HOW GENDER MATTERS: SUGGESTIONS FOR FUTURE RESEARCH

To understand how gender matters, the comparative study of similar systems suggests one promising approach that can help reveal the gender-specific character of critical contextual factors. Research on (male) leadership has traditionally grouped together nations such as 'Westminster systems', for example, and some research on women has examined their presence in Westminster-style parliaments while also making comparisons with their cousin country the USA, usually on a case-by-case basis (Sawer, Tremblay, and Trimble 2006; Curtin 2011). Anglo nations have enough in common to invite reasonable comparisons—such as shared legal and philosophical foundations. At the same time, sufficient differences exist to help explain variations among nations within the Anglo 'family' and within any particular country. Genuine cross-national comparisons rather than single-nation case studies might foster theory-building about gender and leadership; at the very least, such research indicates how Anglo institutions and their development are distinctly gendered in ways that matter to political leadership.

The masculine bias of Anglo systems becomes most apparent in the adversarial institutional arrangements that traditionally characterize such countries. To facilitate programmatic change, adversarial systems concentrate power in the executive, and, to ensure accountability, they rely on combat between two major parties. The more adversarial the system, the more masculine its norms and expectations of leadership tend to be. The institutional preference for masculine leadership provides at least one explanation for the success of a decisive, determined prime minister such as Thatcher and helps account for the general preference for strong leadership in most Anglo nations. By contrast, when New Zealand adopted PR, it altered leadership expectations and norms in ways that made them more feminine—and conducive to the conciliatory, consensus-building leadership of Prime Minister Clark. Institutional departures from the 'Westminster model' are likely to alter the gendered requirements for leadership.

Furthermore, institutional context changes within nations throughout political development, and two types of time—linear historical and cyclical political—matter to leaders. Despite the dominance of masculinity, Anglo institutions also include feminine aspects. Even in adversarial systems, institutions tend to operate with a high degree of consensus and debate generally occurs within the context of mutually agreed-upon principles. In addition, within a system some leadership roles prove more masculine than others: leading a party in parliament generally requires an aggressive, masculine approach, but guiding cabinet (or Congress in the USA) usually calls for more feminine, conciliatory leadership. For this reason, it is possible for Anglo leaders to be considered simultaneously too weak and too strong, as happened to US President Barack Obama (2009–) and Australian Prime Minister Julia Gillard (2010–2013). If Anglo institutions contain both masculine and feminine elements, then the gendered nature of governance and leadership can also shift at different junctures in development. As a result, time itself becomes gendered. While linear, historical time has tended to concentrate power in the executive and magnify masculinity, cyclical political time fluctuates between stages of construction, maintenance, and degeneration (Skowronek 2006), and the gendered character of those stages varies.

Contrast the opportunities of regime-builder Thatcher to those of most female prime ministers, who led at the latest stage of the regime cycle when leadership proves severely circumscribed. At those moments, the historical institutional preference for strong, masculine leadership conflicts with the political need to adopt a softer approach in order to salvage what remains of a regime in the dire state of degeneration, a dilemma that engulfed both Shipley and Campbell. Men as well as women struggle at such junctures in political development, though at least initially men get greater room to manoeuvre when they adopt a feminine approach, as they bring masculinity to leadership positions simply by being men.

In addition to comparing similar systems, this chapter suggests several other avenues for future research. Where and when globalization matters and international organizations prove significant, more research is needed about the presence and role of female leaders (Meyer and Prugl 1999). At the same time, in federal systems more attention should focus on women at the subnational levels of government, where the substantial number of female executives would overcome the methodological problem of the limited 'N' for national leaders. Just as significant, scholarly interest in the intersectionality of gender with race and class should grow (Parker 2005; Duerst-Lahti 2008), and gender studies should continue to consider not only women but also sexual preference and gender identity (Fassinger, Shullman, and Stevenson 2010). Perhaps most important, the gender lens should be employed to examine all leaders: men have gender too, and gender matters even (sometimes especially) where and when women are absent.

8 CONCLUSION

Using a gender lens might alter the way scholars assess and predict leadership success. Gender-based norms become embedded in institutions and ideas, subject to change at different junctures in development, and gender provides a lens that filters leadership traits and determines their value. Depending on the context, the gendered nature of leadership styles helps shape perceptions of leaders as weak or strong, empathetic and compassionate, or unresponsive and out of touch.

By drawing attention to gender, the study of women can reveal the requirements of leadership that all leaders must seek to meet. Scholarship that builds on the lessons of leadership acquired since the 1960s would do well to consider the more recent experience of women and ask: how does gender matter? Feminist theory and gender studies also echo the age-old lesson of leadership research—namely, that the most significant relationship exists between leaders and their followers (Burns 1978). As a result, so long as gender matters to the state and society at large, it will matter to political leadership.

RECOMMENDED READING

Bauer, G. and Tremblay, M., eds. 2011. *Women in Executive Power: A Global Overview*. New York: Routledge.
Galligan, Y. and Tremblay, M., eds. 2005. *Sharing Power: Women, Parliament, Democracy*. Aldershot: Ashgate.
Haussman, M., Vickers, J. and Sawer, M., eds. 2010. *Federalism, Feminism, and Multilevel Governance*. Aldershot: Ashgate.

REFERENCES

Bauer, G. (2011). 'Sub-Saharan Africa', in G. Bauer and M. Tremblay (eds), *Women in Executive Power: A Global Overview*. New York: Routledge, 85–104.

Bauer, G., and Tremblay M. (2011) (eds). *Women in Executive Power: A Global Overview.* New York: Routledge.

Burns, J. M. (1978). *Leadership.* New York: Harper and Row.

Carroll, S. (2001). 'Representing Women: Women State Legislators as Agents of Policy-Related Change', in S. Carroll (ed.), *The Impact of Women in Public Office.* Bloomington, IN: Indiana University Press, 3–21.

Castles, F. G. (1993). *Families of Nations: Patterns of Public Policy in Western Democracies.* Aldershot: Dartmouth Publishing.

Chen, L. (2010). 'Do Gender Quotas Influence Women's Representation and Policies?' *European Journal of Comparative Economics,* 7/1: 13–60.

Cooper, H. (2010). 'Iron Lady: The Promise of Liberia's Ellen Johnson Sirleaf', *World Affairs,* 173/4: 43–50.

Cowell-Meyers, K. (2003). 'Women Legislators in Northern Ireland: Gender and Politics in the New Legislative Assembly'. Centre for the Advancement of Women in Politics, Occasional Paper No. 3. Belfast: Queen's University Belfast.

Curtin, J. (2011). '(Re) Gendering Political Institutions: Westminster Women and Executive Leadership', *Social Alternatives,* 30/3: 20–25.

DiStefano, C. (1998). *Configurations of Masculinity: A Feminist Perspective on Modern Political Theory.* Ithaca, NY: Cornell University.

Dolan J., Deckman, M., and Swers, M. (2006). *Women and Politics: Paths to Power and Political Influence.* Upper Saddle River, NJ: Prentice Hall.

Duerst-Lahti, G. (2008). 'Seeing what has Always Been: Opening Study of the Presidency', *PS: Political Science and Politics,* 41/4: 733–737.

Duerst-Lahti, G., and Kelly, R. M. (1995) (eds). *Gender Power, Leadership, and Governance.* Ann Arbor, MI: University of Michigan.

Elder, L. (2004). 'Why Women don't Run: Explaining Women's Underrepresentation in America's Political Institutions', *Women and Politics,* 26/2: 27–56.

Escobar-Lemmon, M., and Taylor-Robinson, M. M. (2009). 'Getting to the Top: Career Paths of Women in Latin American Cabinets', *Political Research Quarterly,* 62/4: 685–99.

Esping-Andersen, G. (1990). *The Three Worlds of Welfare Capitalism.* Princeton: Princeton University Press.

Fassinger, R. E., Shullman, S. L., and Stevenson, M. R. (2010). 'Toward an Affirmative Lesbian, Gay, Bisexual, and Transgender Leadership Paradigm', *American Psychologist,* 65/3: 201–15.

Galligan, Y. (1998). *Women and Politics in Contemporary Ireland: From the Margins to the Mainstream.* London: Pinter.

Galligan, Y., and Tremblay, M. (2005) (eds). *Sharing Power: Women, Parliament, Democracy.* Aldershot: Ashgate Press.

Genovese, M. A. (1993) (ed.). *Women as National Leaders.* Newbury Park, CA: SAGE.

Haussman, M., Vickers, J., and Sawer, M. (2010) (eds). *Federalism, Feminism, and Multilevel Governance.* Aldershot: Ashgate Press.

Inter-Parliamentary Union (2011). 'Women in National Parliaments' <www.ipu.org/wmn-e/classif.htm>, accessed 11 January 2013

Jalalzai, F. (2008). 'Women Rule: Shattering the Executive Glass Ceiling', *Politics & Gender,* 4/2: 205–31.

Lawless, J., and Fox, R. (2010). *It Still Takes a Candidate: Why Women don't Run for Office.* Cambridge: Cambridge University Press.

Lijphart, A. (1991). 'Debate: Proportional Representation: III. Double Checking the Evidence', *Journal of Democracy*, 2/3: 41–8.

Liswood, L. A. (1995). *Women World Leaders: Fifteen Great Politicians Tell their Stories*. San Francisco, CA: Pandora.

Martin, J. M. (2003). *The Presidency and Women: Promise, Performance, and Illusion*. College Station, TX: Texas A&M University Press.

Meyer, M. K., and Prugl, E. (1999) (eds). *Gender Politics in Global Governance*. Lanham, MD: Rowman & Littlefield.

O'Connor, K. (2010). *Gender and Women's Leadership: A Reference Handbook*. 2 vols. Thousand Oaks, CA: Sage.

Parker, P. S. (2005). *Race, Gender, and Leadership: Re-Envisioning Organizational Leadership from the Perspectives of African American Women Executives*. Mahwah, NJ: LEA Publishers.

Pew Research Center (2008). 'A Paradox in Public Attitudes—Men or Women: Who's the Better Leader?' Report released 25 August.

Reynolds, A. (1999). 'Women in the legislatures And Executives Of The World: Knocking at the Highest Glass Ceiling'. *World Politics*, 51 (4): 547–72.

Rule, W., and Zimmerman, J. (1994) (eds). *Electoral Systems in Comparative Perspective: Their Impact on Women and Minorities*. Westport, CT: Greenwood.

Salmond, R. O. B. (2006). 'Proportional Representation and Female Parliamentarians', *Legislative Studies Quarterly*, 31/2: 175–204.

Sawer, M., Tremblay, M., and Trimble, L. (2006) (eds). *Representing Women in Parliament: A Comparative Study*. New York: Routledge.

Shaarawi, H. (1998). *Harem Years: The Memoirs of an Egyptian Feminist*. Cairo: American University in Cairo Press.

Singerman, D. (1996). *Avenues of Participation: Family, Politics, and Networks in Urban Quarters of Cairo*. Princeton: Princeton University Press.

Skowronek, S. (2006). 'Presidential Leadership in Political Time', in M. Nelson (ed.), *The Presidency and the Political System*. 8th edn. Washington: Congressional Quarterly Press, 111–56.

Steinberg, B. S. (2008). *Women in Power: The Personalities and Leadership Styles of Indira Gandhi, Golda Meir, and Margaret Thatcher*. Montreal: McGill-Queen's University Press.

Stirbu, D. S. (2011). 'Female Representation beyond Westminster: Lessons from Scotland and Wales', *Political Insight*, 2/3: 32–3.

Stockemer, D. (2008). 'Women's Representation in Europe: A Comparison between the National Parliaments and the European Parliament', *Comparative European Politics*, 6/4: 463–85.

Swamy, A., Knack, S., Lee, Y., and Azfar, O. (2001). 'Gender and Corruption', *Journal of Development Economics*, 64: 25–55.

Swers, M. (2002). *The Difference Women Make: The Policy Impact of Women in Congress*. Chicago: University of Chicago Press.

Sykes, P. L. (2009). 'Incomplete Empowerment: Female Cabinet Ministers in Anglo-American Systems', in J. Kane, H. Patapan, and P. 't Hart (eds), *Dispersed Leadership in Democracy: Foundations, Opportunities, Realities*. Oxford: Oxford University Press, 37–58.

Thomas, S. (1991). 'The impact of women on state legislative policies', *Journal of Politics*, 53/4: 958–76.

Trimble, L., and Arscott, J. (2003). *Still Counting: Women in Politics across Canada*. Ontario: Broadview Press.

Tremblay, M. (1998). 'Do Female MPs Substantively Represent Women? A Study of Legislative Behaviour in Canada's 35th Parliament', *Canadian Journal of Political Science/Revue canadienne de science politique*, 31/3: 435–65.

Tremblay, M. (2008) (ed.). *Women and Legislative Representation: Electoral Systems, Political Parties, and Sex Quotas.* New York: Palgrave Macmillan.

···

CHAPTER 46

WHAT HAVE WE LEARNED?

···

JEAN BLONDEL

> Political biography as a field of political science has long been relied upon
> to furnish a vivid corrective to the overemphasis laid upon the study of
> institutional 'mechanisms', 'structures' and 'systems'.
>
> (Lasswell 1966: 1)

1 POLITICAL LEADERSHIP: CONTESTED, CHANGING, AND SEEMINGLY INESCAPABLE

···

POLITICAL leadership measures the extent to which political life in a polity can be attributed to the top ruler or rulers of that polity. It is a subcategory of leadership in general—for instance, in business and in other organizations. Political leadership has wide credentials in the history of political thought, from Plato and Aristotle to Machiavelli: the notion that there is a leader or perhaps a very small group of leaders at the 'helm' (the image of the 'ship of state' is a recurrent theme in political analysis) is one that has had considerable support in both historical analysis and current political discourse.

Yet political leadership has been a particularly contested concept—apparently appreciably more contested than leadership in business has been, for instance. Political leadership is indeed contested on both empirical and normative grounds. The empirical objections stem from the fact that some have doubted, as we shall have occasion to see, whether leaders are truly influential in shaping the life of their countries: the evidence is indeed difficult to collect in an entirely convincing manner. Others, possibly many more, have contested the concept on the normative ground that what has occurred in the history of humankind suggests that political leadership has been typically bad, indeed sometimes appallingly bad, as in the twentieth century: not only has political leadership ostensibly led to horrible developments in countries hitherto described as 'civilized', in Europe in particular, but the emergence of new countries after the Second World War has been associated with atrocities and graft on a huge scale seemingly stemming from actions of leaders. It is thus difficult to know, at any rate at first sight, whether the impact of political leadership is exaggerated in view of the role of other forces in society.

Meanwhile, political leadership is also altering its character, partly as a result of changing values in many polities. The twentieth century, despite its horrors, has also been associated with the surge of democratic ideals, in many societies—not just in the West, but gradually across the 'developing countries'. The spread of democratic ideals has affected the very notion of political leadership: if we assume for a moment that political leadership has indeed some impact, it could be argued that much political leadership, even if benign, means little democracy: if the democratic ideal is to spread, this must be to an extent at least at the expense of 'strong political leadership'. The balance is difficult to maintain between the two ideals, but it is not surprising that some should have reflected about bringing about changes in the way in which political leadership should be exercised: the notion of 'soft' power, in contrast to 'hard' power, has thus been suggested as a means of introducing more democracy in the leadership context.

This is not the only way in which change is or might be taking place with respect to leadership: it results also from the transformations that are occurring in societies in particular as a result of globalization: much of it has been more ostensibly on the economic plane, but the consequences of economic and indeed technical changes are increasingly affecting political life. Whether polities are reacting to these pressures as quickly as they should is a moot question, but one of the main questions that arises in this context is whether the state can be regarded any longer as important enough to be able to confront realistically the problems that are arising.

Thus, however contested it may be, the concept of political leadership continues to be on the agenda: it seems prima facie inescapable; it is therefore more rational to operate on the hypothesis that it is likely to remain an important element in the structure of political life. The aim of this chapter is to explore the extent to which leadership has thus played a part in the political life of the countries of the world: while doing so we shall discover that there have indeed been marked variations across the world in the way in which political leadership has been received, so to speak, by the members of these polities. This will enable us to describe, in the first part of the chapter, the panorama of political leadership in the world in the early decades of the twenty-first century. We will then examine the directions in which political leadership would need to move in the future if it were to play a significant part in helping to improve the conditions of human beings.

2   PATTERNS OF POLITICAL LEADERSHIP IN THE CONTEMPORARY WORLD

Three Distinct Sets of Reactions to Political Leadership in the World

Attitudes to political leadership across the world can be said to fall broadly into three groups. The United States has always been the country that showed the most positive approach towards political leadership, possibly in part because the presidential system worked well in that country and has done so without interruption for over 200 years. The record of the United States can be regarded as doubly positive, both in terms of what leaders can achieve and in terms of the desire of leaders to achieve as much as they can for their country. This doubly positive attitude may also explain in part (although the fact that political science developed much more quickly in the USA than elsewhere in the world may have helped) why studies of political leadership have been more numerous and often technically more advanced than elsewhere.

In Europe, more specifically in Western Europe, on the other hand, attitudes on the subject have been more mixed, to say the least. The widespread tradition of authoritarian monarchical governments resulted in normative ambivalence about political leadership; but to that ambivalence was added the view, from the middle of the nineteenth century onwards, that political leadership was perhaps not as important as it had been felt to be. Sociological studies and in particular Marxist analyses have stressed the point that the socio-economic context was what counted most. To this must further be added the fact that, as West European countries democratized, the governmental system did tend to be based, at least formally, on collective cabinets and not on presidencies: only in the late 1950s did France adopt a 'semi-presidential' system, while Finland had done so since independence in 1918 and Portugal for a relatively short period in the 1970s and the 1980s. There were thus in Europe a combination of reasons leading to doubts about the worth of leadership, as came out in influential studies of parties of the late nineteenth and early twentieth centuries, such as those of Ostrogorski (1902), Michels (1949), and Mosca (1939), as well as some scepticism about the importance to be attributed to leadership.

In the Third World, although the independence of Latin America had shown for over a century that there were serious problems associated with leadership in the subcontinent, these feelings were amplified as a result of the decolonization process, following the short period of optimism resulting from the maintenance of democratic practices in India after independence. From the 1960s, political leadership came to be viewed profoundly negatively across the developing countries: in Africa, for instance, rulers were widely described as neo-patrimonial and highly clientelistic; they were shown to have used their position to enrich themselves and their families often to a massive extent, while being also in many cases markedly repressive. Yet these normative negative views appear to have been combined with the sentiment that, if political leaders had acted differently, they would have had a positive impact on the polities that they ruled: had leaders not been considered to be able to have such an impact, there would have been little reason, apart from a purely 'moral' standpoint, for criticizing them for their neo-patrimonial or clientelistic practices. It has indeed been remarked that these polities typically lacked strong institutions and, therefore, that personalization of leadership could be expected to be overwhelming or at least very high (Jackson and Rosberg 1982).

Two points need to be made about these conclusions, however, First, there have, of course, been exceptions to the negative role of rulers in developing countries. Second, negative views about the behaviour of rulers may be receding somewhat, as the incidence of military coups declined appreciably in the last decades of the twentieth century, the number of explicit military fell markedly, and pluralistic political systems, on the other hand, increased appreciably (Hyden 2008).

Given the differences that exist among the United States, Western Europe, and at least many countries of the 'new' developing world about both the worth and the importance of leadership, it is understandable that it should have been in the United States that a major emphasis was placed on the study of the personal characteristics of leaders. It is also understandable that greater emphasis was placed on the context in West European countries, and that the examination of the misdeeds of leaders, together with the weakness of the institutions in which these leaders operated, should have widely taken place in developing countries. These contrasts raise the question as to whether there is any unity in the analysis of political leadership: the matter needs therefore to be examined as the future directions that need to be adopted for the analysis of political leadership are considered.

3 The Development of Leadership Studies in the Twentieth and Early Twenty-First Centuries

It is probably fair to say that the first real boost given to the analysis of political leadership was due to Max Weber (1968): while two of the three forms of authority that he described were the result of the organization of society (tradition and legalism), the third had to do with personal ('charismatic') characteristics of the leaders, admittedly only if the structure of the society had broken down. The fact that Max Weber was a sociologist may have played some part in this relative weighting. Quite independently, however, early in the 1930s, an attempt was made in the United States, under the label of 'psychopathology', to categorize types of political leaders according to what they aimed at achieving: Lasswell was to be the most famous exponent of that approach in his *Psychopathology and Politics*, published in 1930, the source of the approach being, not Weber, but a number of psychiatrists and Freud in particular. Curiously enough, this kind of approach seemed possibly to anticipate the worst episodes of appalling leadership that were to occur from the 1930s; however, after the Second World War, the subject of the 'authoritarian personality' gave rise to a number of studies in Western Europe and in particular those of T. Adorno et al., published in 1969, precisely on *The Authoritarian Personality*.

Meanwhile, while charismatic leadership was to become a key topic in leadership studies from the 1980s, three waves of other approaches had become prominent, in the United States: in his work on *The Powers to Lead*, J. S. Nye (2008: 22) suggests that the 1940s and 1950s were when the 'trait-centred' approach dominated; that period was followed by the 'style' approach in the 1960s, and by the 'contingency' approach up to the

1980s. These developments were following those that occurred in relation to business in a number of countries, also principally in the United States. A large compendium about leadership edited by R. M. Stogdill (1974), and published for the first time in 1948, described in detail the traits that were regarded as characteristic of leaders: despite all the criticisms attached to the approach, it led eventually to the elaboration of the 'Big Five' traits of the personality—neuroticism, extraversion, openness, agreeableness, and conscientiousness. A subsequent general textbook on business leadership by P. G. Northouse (2007), which underwent a variety of editions after being published for the first time in 1997, traces systematically the variety of theories or principles on the basis of which leadership is conducted in the business context. Indeed, it was almost exclusively in the business world that the study of leadership first developed, the examination of leadership in other types of social bodies and in particular in associations having remained originally less developed. Analyses of business leadership led in particular to the recognition of the importance of the context: this suggested that leadership was 'contingent' on the environment, a view developed by F. E. Fiedler in his 1967 study *A Theory of Leadership Effectiveness*, in which he distinguished between two fundamental types of leaders, those concerned with 'men' and those concerned with 'things'.

Studies on business leadership, in which the importance of that concept for business organizations was not questioned at all, probably had an effect on the development of analyses of *political* leadership, at least in America, where the main spur was at first the study of the presidency. At first, detailed 'psychological' case studies were published, the most famous early volume based on that approach having appeared in 1956 and being by A. L. and J. L. George on Woodrow Wilson. Attempts were then made to compare findings among presidents, an assessment that was undertaken in particular by J. D. Barber (1977) in *The Presidential Character*), as a result of which presidents were divided into a number of psychological types. A move from case studies to analyses of general characteristics of presidential leadership was then made by J. McGregor Burns: having devoted his attention essentially to F. D. Roosevelt, in *Roosevelt: The Lion and the Fox*, published in 1963, Burns went on to publish in 1978 what was to be a classic, *Leadership*, in which the author put forward the distinction between its 'transformational' and its 'transactional' forms, a distinction that came to be adopted in the study of business as well. In the 1990s, Burns went further and launched a major undertaking, by means of a variety of workshops bringing together specialists from the humanities and the social sciences: the aim was to elaborate a 'general theory of leadership'. It did not prove possible to come to a commonly held conclusion, but the enquiry, which took place over a substantial period up to the early years of the twenty-first century, contributed markedly to a deepening of the understanding of the characteristics of political leadership in the contemporary world (Goethals and Sorenson 2006).

Meanwhile, from the 1960s, F. I. Greenstein was exercising a major influence by opening the field well beyond the (American) presidency towards all aspects of problems raised by leadership in his volume on *Personality and Politics*, published in 1969. Greenstein eventually turned to a presidential case study published in 2004 on Eisenhower as president, *The Presidential Difference*, in which he showed that Eisenhower had played a markedly greater personal part than was commonly believed: he was to state that six qualities helped to determine the extent to which there was a 'presidential difference', these qualities being emotional intelligence, cognitive style, policy vision, political skills, organization skills, and communication skills. Burns and Greenstein were thus the two key members of the profession who led what had come to be by the 1980s the lively subdiscipline of political leadership analysis in America.

Developments that took place in Europe were more low key. The reticence about political leadership in both academic circles and the public at large was apparent, although the media did increasingly extol the role of leadership. The notion of presidential leadership also began to play a part (Poguntke and Webb 2005), but the reluctance to recognize the part played by leaders at elections was far from being overcome (King 2002), although some efforts began to be made to measure what that impact could be (Sanders 2001).

What was increasingly taking place, both in Europe and in America, possibly partly as a result of the emphasis placed by the media on the role of leaders, were compromises between those who strongly believed in the key role of political leadership and those who displayed scepticism in the matter. The context was increasingly viewed as a critical element of the leadership 'equation'. Some radicals went appreciably further, admittedly, perhaps not surprisingly among West European scholars: thus K. Grint, in particular in *Leadership: Limits and Possibilities* (2005), denied that leadership could be regarded as existing objectively. Rather, it was the result of subjective appreciations by outsiders. Yet the main emphasis, perhaps principally in America, was on the general institutional and behavioural arrangements to which leadership had to belong if it was to have a role. Thus leadership had to be analysed in conjunction with other elements of the society and not as a separate characteristic over and above that society.

The concept of agency has come to play a part in what could be regarded as endeavours to 'redimension' leadership, undertaken by those who felt that too large a space was given to leaders. If individuals were to exercise influence alongside or perhaps more correctly above the socio-economic substructure of society, it was unrealistic to believe that leaders could be the only agents: leaders may occupy a special position; but they could not do so and play a part at all unless there were other agents around or below the leaders, with whom these were in an often close rapport. That idea was rendered more rigorous by reflections undertaken about the concept of followership, to which B. Kellerman devoted a volume, indeed entitled *Followership*, published in 2008. Followers were viewed as shaping in many ways the characteristics of leaders: thus the characteristics of followers needed to be examined perhaps as much as the characteristics of leaders. These followers were indeed found to fall into a number of types in terms of the extent to which they were close to leaders. Thus the concept of agency contributed to a reduction of the individual influence of leaders by comparison with the prestige that had been classically accorded to national leaders.

There is a further problem in the context of followership, however—namely, whether the bulk of the supporters of leaders, for instance at elections, form part of that followership. Given the fact that the nature of the support that is provided in this way is likely to be not just passive but fleeting, the concept of followership scarcely applies among at least many of those belonging to the category of 'supporters': it can at most be said that these electors provide the leaders with a stock of legitimacy that the leaders require. Moreover, the nature of the link between political leaders and these supporters may be different from the kind of links that exist between leaders and those who are truly followers. The link between leaders and followers is typically regarded as being a form of power, in that leaders may induce these followers to do what they might otherwise not have done: whether this is so in the case of the relationship between leaders and the bulk of their supporters is at least questionable.

There is a general tendency in political science to refer to 'power' so often that it is difficult to know whether power is not then somewhat devalued, so to speak, and becomes merely synonymous with 'relationship'. Perhaps it can be argued that the relationship that leaders may have with ordinary supporters is a form of power if it has a 'charismatic' character, especially in the sense that was given to charisma in the form that Weber gave it originally; but Weber himself devalued the concept of charisma by referring to its 'routinization', at which point it becomes less clear that power is genuinely at stake. Together with other mechanisms adopted by leaders to obtain support, the question of the relationship between leaders and the various strata of the population needs, therefore, to be examined more closely: this is one of the three outstanding important problems posed by the future of political leadership.

4 THE FUTURE OF POLITICAL LEADERSHIP STUDIES

Three major problems need to be fully investigated in the context of political leadership. The first is the 'unity' of the field. Understandably, the study of political leadership has been undertaken at a higher level of sophistication in the United States; moreover, political leadership may have developed markedly more satisfactorily in that country than, at the other extreme, in many of the 'new' countries that had limited experience of government, democratic or even otherwise. It is perhaps also understandable that Western Europeans should be somewhat sceptical about the true importance of political leadership, given that they had often had a long experience of highly authoritarian governments before liberalization and democratization processes were introduced gradually in the nineteenth century. Yet, the very existence of a concept of political leadership entails that there be more commonality than there is currently among the various strands of analysis in the subject.

The second problem with which the analysis of political leadership needs to be more concerned relates, as we just saw, to the nature of the relationship between the leaders and the led, whether in relation to followers in the narrower sense of the word or more generally in relation to supporters within the population at large. Such an analysis is particularly important, since, with the spread of democratic modes of behaviour, the methods used by leaders with respect to 'others' have tended to change and to (have to) become, so to speak, milder.

The third question, as indicated earlier in this chapter, is concerned with the major changes that are taking place in the relationships among nations in the twenty-first century. These changes have led to a view, perhaps still somewhat unclear, that the state is no longer the adequate level at which many key decisions need to be taken. Yet the state remains the formal repository of 'sovereignty' as well as the framework within which the legitimacy of leaders does emerge and develop: this poses a serious problem for political decision-making in the global age, a problem that needs to be analysed with care to see whether multi-state organizations can constitute satisfactory substitutes.

5 Treating Political Leadership as a Single Problem

Political leadership must be treated as a single problem in order to make it possible to assess what that leadership can achieve. Currently, as we saw, it is segmented geographically into three approaches, each with their different preoccupations. Yet, while the analysis of political leadership is ostensibly segmented geographically, that segmentation is in reality based on two wholly general dimensions, one of which is about what leaders *can* achieve in the polity and the other about what leaders *want to* achieve.

In the United States, the answer is prima facie positive on both dimensions: the basic assumptions are, first, that leaders want to achieve what is 'best for America', at least according to their own values, and, second, that, on the whole, it is believed that they can achieve much: the idea of 'transformational' leadership is based on such an assumption, although it has gradually become accepted by those who study the subject that the context does also have to play a part.

In the 'newer' countries, for example, some of the African countries, the assumptions are that leaders could achieve much, but, instead of doing what is best for their country, they do what is best for themselves and those closest to them: hence the emphasis in the literature on the 'neo-patrimonial' or 'clientelistic' character of the rule of many leaders. However, as was indicated earlier, such a view could scarcely be held on a rational basis if it was felt that in any case these leaders could not be expected to achieve much for their polity.

In Western Europe, the prevailing notion is that leaders, by and large, attempt to achieve what they can for the polity, but cannot do much. The impact of the socio-economic environment is felt to be such that it seems to be believed that leaders can act only at the margin, whatever they might themselves say about what they do and whatever the media may say about the role of leaders in general. In such a perspective, the overall viewpoint is relatively optimistic, as leaders are so constrained that they cannot have too negative an impact, but, conversely, the weight of socio-economic conditions is felt to be such that the role of leadership is in effect reduced.

These three 'ideal-type' presentations vary of course to an extent depending on those who write on the subject and depending on the country concerned, especially with respect to the 'developing' countries; but the traditions and techniques of rule on which specialists of the countries base their assessment tend to constitute the framework for categorization.

This geographically based compartmentalization of the approaches is detrimental to the development of the study of political leadership; it is no longer justified in view of the much greater exchange of experiences and practices across the political systems. On the contrary, identical instruments should be used to conduct analyses across the countries of the world. Specifically, there is no reason why typologies of leadership that have been developed and that proved to be useful in the United States should not be used to study the characteristics of leadership in new countries. Indeed, the fact that in Latin America, Africa, and the ex-Soviet Union presidential systems (of whatever form) came to be widely in force means that the instruments adopted to assess leadership in the United States can be directly adopted in these regions. Admittedly, the situation is not identical in the European context, where, in most countries, despite what is said about the growth of 'presidentialization' in the area, leadership at the top does not have the same 'exalted' position, by and large, as in the United States. Yet efforts at building typologies of prime ministers should be undertaken. Moreover, systematic analyses at the level of public opinion, especially in the context of voting studies, should help to assess systematically the extent to which the decisions made by European electors in this respect are affected by their attitudes to the leaders as well as by other factors.

There is every reason to develop a much greater level of interchange among studies of political leadership across the world at a time when increased globalization is almost universally recognized on so many fronts. While 'area studies' of a traditional character are likely to remain essential to determine many aspects of political behaviour at the grass roots, political leadership as an overall phenomenon at the top is regarded as being so widespread and has such an impact over the borders of states that it must be treated as a universal phenomenon, even if different emphases prevail, in particular from time to time, from one state to another. There is no doubt that the cross-fertilization that will take place as a result will lead to a better understanding of the two crucial questions that have to be raised about national political leadership at the top—namely what it can achieve and what the leaders want to achieve.

6 THE INSTRUMENTS USED BY POLITICAL LEADERS, AND IS 'SOFT' POWER THE ANSWER?

The second area on which reflection is needed about the future of political leadership concerns the instruments that leaders are more likely to use in the future. A distinction was made by J. S. Nye in the 1990s between 'soft' and 'hard' power: the question naturally arises as to the circumstances within which one or the other of these two forms is to be used; one can even wonder whether soft power might not gradually replace hard power altogether. J. S. Nye did not suggest such a replacement: indeed, he coined the expression 'smart' power as a combination of the two forms of power (Nye 2008: p. x). Yet the question arises as to whether leaders might not use soft power increasingly instead of hard power in the future. This could be because leaders have to do so if they are to exercise power at all and be able to maintain their support among the broad mass of the population, especially assuming that a general move towards 'more democracy' takes place in the countries that are being ruled. It can even be argued that such a move has already been taking place to a substantial extent: democratic practices could be said to have been, overall, softer than non-democratic practices: for instance, if it is the case, as has been claimed with considerable empirical support, that democracies do not go to war against each other, such a development could be argued to be the consequence of the fact that democracies are, as a general category, softer than non-democracies.

Assuming that leaders are to use soft rather than hard power, the conditions under which this substitution is likely to take place need, therefore, to become an issue in political leadership analysis in the future. J. S. Nye offers no guidance in this respect. He seems content to say that soft power is more in use than in the past; he is unquestionably satisfied that this should be the case, but he does not make any proposals as to how far and when any changes might take place. Perhaps one should indeed leave it to the practitioners to decide when to use soft or hard power; but, given the fact that this runs against the many efforts that are made to render social interrelationships more 'civilized' than they were, it would seem more appropriate to try and limit the use of hard power and, therefore, perhaps even to reject the notion of 'smart' power coined by J. S. Nye, as such an expression suggests that there is something intrinsically valuable in combining hard with soft power. Thus one could specify that soft power should be the norm and hard power be used only in extreme cases when the use of soft power has proved inoperative.

Nor is it even sufficient to leave vague, indeed indeterminate, the distinction between these two concepts. The definition given by J. S. Nye is even somewhat frightening: 'Soft power rests on the ability to shape the preferences of others to want what you want' (Nye 2008: 29). He adds: 'Smart executives know that leadership is not just a matter of issuing commands, but also involves leading by example and attracting others to do what you want them to do' (Nye 2008: 29). Such a presentation suggests a degree of cynicism, which may well be justified to achieve one's immediate aims but is far from bringing about a relationship of 'understanding'. As the idea of soft power becomes gradually analysed more closely and its characteristics are more precisely defined, a distinction has to be made between at least two types of 'soft power'—that which is truly, as the relationship between war and politics, hard power by other means, and that which is concerned to examine the views of others and is prepared to rethink and reassess what is being proposed as a result of objections raised by others.

Thus the types of power that are used, hard or soft, have to be studied and analysed systematically; they have also to be studied in relation to what may be other ways in which influence is exercised. Leadership, political or otherwise, does not axiomatically entail that the person who holds the relevant position has to make those who do not hold that position entirely rally to the views of the leader. What needs to be ascertained—and this is surely important for the future of political leadership in general—is the extent to which leadership can be exercised also by way of compromises, a point that leads directly to the matter of the way in which leadership can be exercised 'above' the state and in 'multi-state' organizations in general.

7 Political Leadership in 'Multi-State' Organizations

Much political decision-making has come to take place—and is increasingly likely to take place—above the level of the state in organizations that include many states, if not all the states, such as the United Nations. Yet, even if these situations are multiplying, they are highly peculiar from the point of view of political leadership. They are peculiar, because they do not give rise to a development of political leadership in the way political leadership develops in a state. Political leadership is based on the premiss that there is a 'people' from within which the political leaders emerge and to whom the leader can and indeed may have to refer for support. Leadership in a 'multi-state' situation, let alone in the whole world, cannot have these characteristics: there is no 'whole people' to whom the leader can appeal: the example of the most developed of the regional multi-state organizations, the European Union, is a case in point. The repeated difficulties experienced by that body in taking key decisions stem from the fact that there is not one 'people', but a number of 'peoples', belonging to the organization.

Yet, as globalization is indeed taking place, political leadership cannot just be concerned with state decision-making. Multi-state action has to be taken: such action requires, therefore, the development of political leadership at that multi-state level—that is to say, the development of some kind of process of decision-making that can take place in a single but overall reference frame. Since very difficult decisions have to be taken globally, as the history of the European Union and also of the United Nations has shown repeatedly, a reflection has to take place about how global political leadership can be fostered in the absence of a single people. One suggestion has been to do so by means of 'networking' (Masciulli and Knight 2009). Soft power is obviously one of the key means by which such networking can develop.

There are instances of leaders who appear to have succeeded, at least from time to time, in such situations, an example being that of Kofi Annan as Secretary General of the United Nations (Masciulli and Knight 2009: 113–16). If the United Nations is seen as the example *par excellence* of such a 'new' type of leadership, the person who embodies that leadership is the Secretary General; but that leadership is highly peculiar, as it does in no way originate from a legitimacy emanating, even indirectly, from one people.

Analogous situations are likely to emerge in the case of agencies of the United Nations, the IMF, the World Bank, and the World Trade Organization. Perhaps the most likely development in the future will be as a result of the build-up of 'regional organizations', although (except in the case of the European Union and even then with severe limitations) these have, so far, rarely tended to develop positions in which the holders of these positions are able to exercise political leadership over decisions affecting the whole 'region'. This has been noticeable, for instance in the case of the Latin American Mercosur or of Asean in East and South-East Asia.

The development of a kind of multi-state leadership—the expression 'supranational' leadership scarcely applies in these situations—corresponds to the move towards globalization that is taking place at both political as well as economic levels. As the process is increasing, it is essential for political science to look carefully at the conditions that must be fulfilled for political leadership to develop adequately, even in circumstances in which there is no direct relationship (as there is at the state level) between the positions that are held and the character of the legitimacy framework within which multi-state political leaders can operate. There are no obvious instruments on the basis of which these developments can occur; thus, more than in relation to the other two fields in which political leadership must develop in the future, political science must exercise considerable imagination with respect to the problems posed by political leadership in 'multi-state' organizations, since these are likely to be set up more and more to deal with the problems arising in the 'globalized' world.

The study of political leadership advanced markedly in the course of the twentieth century, especially after the Second World War. During that period, for the first time, progress was made in order to discover precisely the psychological characteristics of leaders, to assess the nature of the context that can and does affect the role and behaviour of leaders and to take stock of the highly unpleasant and at times appalling conditions under which political leadership emerges and even thrives. This is especially true in new countries: these are the states in which institutions tend to be very weak and where there is little or no previous experience of truly satisfactory governmental action.

The analysis of political leadership needs to go further, however. It must face the fact that nations are now operating in one world. It must be based simultaneously on personalities and on context, on both established and new institutions and on both established and new practices. The development of modes of democratic behaviour and the fact that there are ever closer interconnections among the countries of the world mean that political leadership has to adjust to new modes of action: mechanisms have therefore to be found for such an adjustment. Both realism and imagination are thus required to ensure that political leadership becomes universally a spur for positive action and can no longer be, as it has been and is indeed viewed to be in many cases, a handicap for the development of human societies.

Recommended Reading

Burns, J. M. (1978). *Leadership*. New York: Harper and Row.

Goethals, G. R., and Sorensen, G. L. J. (2006). *The Quest for a General Theory of Leadership*. Cheltenham: Edward Elgar.

Masciulli, J., Molchanov, M., and Knight, W. A. (2009). *The Ashgate Research Companion to Political Leadership*. Farnham: Ashgate.

Nye, J. (2008). *The Power to Lead*. Oxford: Oxford University Press.

References

Adorno, T. W., Frenkel-Brunswik, E., Levinson, D. J., and Sanford, N. (1969). *The Authoritarian Personality*. New York: Norton.

Barber, J. D. (1977). *The Presidential Character*. Englewood Cliffs, NJ: Prentice-Hall.

Burns, J. M. (1963). *Roosevelt: The Lion and the Fox*. Cambridge, MA: Harvard University Press.

Burns, J. M. (1978). *Leadership*. New York: Harper and Row.

Fiedler, F. E. (1967). *A Theory of Leadership Effectiveness*. Maidenhead: McGraw Hill.

George, A. L., and George, J. L. (1998) [1956]. *Presidential Personality and Performance*. Boulder, CO: Westview.

Goethals, G. R., and Sorensen, G. L. J. (2006). *The Quest for a General Theory of Leadership*. Cheltenham: Edward Elgar.

Greenstein, F. I. (1969). *Personality and Politics*. Chicago: Markham.

Greenstein, F. I. (2004). *The Presidential Difference: Leadership Style from FDR to G. W. Bush*. Princeton: Princeton University Press.

Grint, K. (2005). *Leadership: Limits and Possibilities*. Basingstoke: Palgrave Macmillan.

Hyden, G. (2008). *African Politics in Comparative Perspective*. New York: Cambridge University Press.

Jackson, R. H., and Rosberg, C. G. (1982). *Personal Rule in Black Africa: Prince, Autocrat, Prophet, Tyrant*. Berkeley and Los Angeles: University of California Press.

Kellerman, B. (2008). *Followership*. Boston, MA: Harvard Business School.

King, A. (2002) (ed.). *Leaders' Personalities and the Outcome of Democratic Elections*. New York: Oxford University Press.

Lasswell, H. D. (1966). *Psychology and Politics*. New York: Viking.

Lasswell, H. D. (1930). *Psychopathology and Politics*. Chicago: Chicago University Press.

Llanos, M., and Marsteintredet, L. (2010) (eds). *Presidential Breakdowns in Latin America: Causes and Outcomes of Executive Instability in Developing Democracies*. New York: Palgrave Macmillan.

Masciulli, J., and Knight, W. A. (2009). 'Conceptions of Global Leadership for Contextually Intelligent, Innovative Political Leaders', in J. Masciulli, M. A. Molchanov, and W. A. Knight (eds), *The Ashgate Research Companion to Political Leadership*. Farnham: Ashgate, 102–3.

Masciulli, J., Molchanov, M. A., and Knight, W. A. (2009). *The Ashgate Research Companion to Political Leadership*. Farnham: Ashgate.

Michels, R. (1949). *Political Parties*. New York: Free Press.

Mosca, G. (1939). *The Ruling Class*. New York: McGrawHill.

Northouse, P. G. (2007). *Leadership: Theory and Practice*. 4th edn. London: Sage.

Nye, J. S. (2008). *The Powers to Lead*. Oxford: Oxford University Press.

Ostrogorski, M. (1902). *Democracy and the Organization of Political Parties*. New York: Macmillan.

Poguntke, T., and Webb, P. (2005) (eds). *The Presidentialization of Politics*. Oxford: Oxford University Press.

Sanders, D. (2001). 'The Economy and Voting', in P. Norris (ed.), *Britain Votes*. Oxford: Oxford University Press, 125–38.

Stogdill, R. M. (1974) [1948] (ed.). *Handbook of Leadership*. New York: Free Press.

Weber, M. (1968) (ed.). *Economy and Society*. 3 vols. New York: Bedminster Press.

Name Index

Note: Includes all referenced authors.

SUBJECT INDEX

Made in the USA
San Bernardino, CA
23 August 2017